UK Accounting Practice

UK Accounting Practice

Glynis Morris BA, FCA

LexisNexis®
Butterworths

Members of the LexisNexis Group worldwide

United Kingdom	LexisNexis Butterworths, a Division of Reed Elsevier (UK) Ltd, Halsbury House, 35 Chancery Lane, LONDON, WC2A 1EL, and RSH, 1–3 Baxter's Place, Leith Walk EDINBURGH EH1 3AF
Argentina	LexisNexis Argentina, BUENOS AIRES
Australia	LexisNexis Butterworths, CHATSWOOD, New South Wales
Austria	LexisNexis Verlag ARD Orac GmbH & Co KG, VIENNA
Canada	LexisNexis Butterworths, MARKHAM, Ontario
Chile	LexisNexis Chile Ltda, SANTIAGO DE CHILE
Czech Republic	Nakladatelství Orac sro, PRAGUE
France	Editions du Juris-Classeur SA, PARIS
Germany	LexisNexis Deutschland GmbH, FRANKFURT and MUNSTER
Hong Kong	LexisNexis Butterworths, HONG KONG
Hungary	HVG-Orac, BUDAPEST
India	LexisNexis Butterworths, NEW DELHI
Italy	Giuffrè Editore, MILAN
Malaysia	Malayan Law Journal Sdn Bhd, KUALA LUMPUR
New Zealand	LexisNexis Butterworths, WELLINGTON
Poland	Wydawnictwo Prawnicze LexisNexis, WARSAW
Singapore	LexisNexis Butterworths, SINGAPORE
South Africa	LexisNexis Butterworths, Durban
Switzerland	Stämpfli Verlag AG, BERNE
USA	LexisNexis, DAYTON, Ohio

© Reed Elsevier (UK) Ltd 2005

Published by LexisNexis Butterworths

A CIP Catalogue record for this book is available from the British Library.

ISBN 0 7545 2801 4

Typeset by Letterpart Ltd, Reigate, Surrey

Printed and bound in Great Britain by William Clowes Limited, Beccles, Suffolk

Visit LexisNexis Butterworths at www.lexisnexis.co.uk

Contents

CHAPTER 2 THE ASB 'STATEMENT OF PRINCIPLES FOR FINANCIAL REPORTING'

CHAPTER 3 THE TRUE AND FAIR VIEW 67–74

CHAPTER 4 SUBSTANCE OVER FORM 75–94

CHAPTER 6 COMPARATIVE FIGURES AND PRIOR PERIOD ADJUSTMENTS 105–120

CHAPTER 7 FOREIGN CURRENCY TRANSLATION 121–142

CHAPTER 9 PROFIT AND LOSS ACCOUNT FORMATS

CHAPTER 11 STAFF COSTS AND EMPLOYEE NUMBERS 261–284

CHAPTER 16 DIVIDENDS AND OTHER APPROPRIATIONS 365–384

CHAPTER 17 DIRECTORS' REMUNERATION AND BENEFITS 385–428

CHAPTER 18 OTHER PROFIT AND LOSS ACCOUNT DISCLOSURES

CHAPTER 19 BALANCE SHEET FORMATS 453–464

CHAPTER 20 INTANGIBLE FIXED ASSETS 465–490

CHAPTER 21 TANGIBLE FIXED ASSETS.....................491–548

CHAPTER 23 STOCKS 569–588

CHAPTER 27 BANK LOANS AND OVERDRAFTS 659–668

CHAPTER 28 LEASING AND HIRE PURCHASE LIABILITIES 669–676

CHAPTER 29 OTHER CREDITORS, ACCRUALS AND DEFERRED INCOME

CHAPTER 30 PROVISIONS FOR LIABILITIES 693–714

CHAPTER 31 DEFERRED TAXATION 715–728

CHAPTER 32 SHARE CAPITAL AND RESERVES 729–754

CHAPTER 36 OTHER STATEMENTS 803–818

CHAPTER 37 DIRECTORS' LOANS AND OTHER TRANSACTIONS 819–848

CHAPTER 39 OPERATING AND FINANCIAL REVIEW 879–890

CHAPTER 40 CORPORATE GOVERNANCE DISCLOSURES 891–924

CHAPTER 44 REQUIREMENT FOR GROUP ACCOUNTS

CHAPTER 45 SUBSIDIARIES 987–998

CHAPTER 48 CONSOLIDATION GOODWILL 1041–1058

CHAPTER 49 ACQUISITIONS, DISPOSALS AND MERGERS

CHAPTER 50 ACCOUNTING FOR FOREIGN OPERATIONS

Chapter 1   Accounting Standards, Accounting Principles and Accounting Rules

ACCOUNTING STANDARDS

The present regime

1.1   Accounting standards are currently developed in the UK by the Accounting Standards Board (ASB) under the auspices of the Financial Reporting Council (FRC). Both bodies were established in 1990, together with the Financial Reporting Review Panel (FRRP) and the Urgent Issues Task Force (UITF). The structure of these bodies can be summarised as follows:

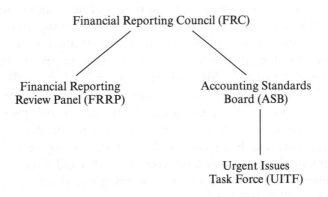

The FRC's original remit has now been widened to give it a more active role in relation to corporate governance and new responsibilities in relation to auditing standards and the oversight of the regulation of the professional accountancy bodies. As a result, the Auditing Practices Board, the Professional Oversight Board for Accountancy and the Accountancy Investigation and Discipline Board also come under the umbrella of the FRC in the same way as the ASB and FRRP.

Prior to 1990, standards were developed by the Accounting Standards Committee (ASC). At its first meeting, the ASB formally adopted all existing accounting standards (22 at the time) developed by the ASC, but many of these have now been revised or superseded by new standards issued by the ASB. Standards issued by the ASC were described as Statements of Standard Accounting Practice (SSAPs) and those issued by the ASB are described as Financial Reporting Standards (FRSs). Some of the present accounting standards are therefore in the form of SSAPs whilst others are FRSs, but all have the same status for practical purposes.

Potential topics for accounting standards are identified by the ASB from its own research and also from external sources, and ASB staff then undertake a programme of consultation and research, considering conceptual issues, existing practice in the UK, any existing pronouncements (both in the UK and abroad), and the practical implications of introducing new requirements in the UK. A Discussion Paper is usually prepared setting out the main issues and inviting comments on the ASB's initial proposals. Following this initial consultation, a Financial Reporting Exposure Draft (FRED) is published to give those who are interested a chance to comment on the proposals and to enable the ASB to assess the likely level of acceptance. The draft document may be amended in the light of the comments received, but the final decision on the content of an FRS rests with the ASB.

Changes to the role of the ASB

1.2   In March 2005, the ASB published an Exposure Draft of a Policy Statement setting out the Board's views on its future role. With the introduction of the requirement for listed groups to adopt international accounting standards (IASs) and the ASB's published plans to converge UK accounting practice with international requirements (see 1.6 below), much of the detailed work on the development of accounting standards will in future be undertaken by the International Accounting Standards Board (IASB) and the future role of the ASB therefore needs to be reassessed. The Exposure Draft 'Accounting Standard-Setting in a Changing Environment: The Role of the Accounting Standards Board' promotes the view that the ASB will continue to have a significant role in the development of IASs through participation in debates on the key issues and by responding to IASB consultations. It will also act as a link between the IASB and interested parties in the UK by maintaining a two-way dialogue and ensuring that the views and concerns of UK parties are relayed to the IASB.

The other main activities of the ASB in the future are expected to include:

(i)   implementation of the UK convergence project (see 1.6 below);

(ii)   improving communication between companies and their investors, particularly through the development of OFR reporting; and

(iii)   influencing European policy on accounting standards.

The role of the Urgent Issues Task Force (see 1.11 below) is also expected to change, as any necessary interpretation of international standards will generally be dealt with by the International Financial Reporting Interpretations Committee (IFRIC). However, where it seems that IFRIC will be unable to issue guidance in time to meet UK needs, the UITF may consider issuing non-mandatory guidance.

The UK IAS framework

1.3   Listed companies are required to prepare group accounts in accordance with international accounting standards (IASs) rather the UK accounting standards for accounting periods beginning on or after 1 January 2005. All companies other than charitable companies have the option of preparing both individual and group accounts in accordance with IASs from the same date. Those most likely to take advantage of the IAS option are stand-alone listed companies, to make them more comparable with listed groups, and subsidiaries of listed companies, to avoid having to prepare two sets of figures each year (one based on IASs for consolidation purposes and another using UK standards for statutory accounts purposes). However, it is expected that many companies will continue to prepare their accounts in accordance with UK accounting standards, in the immediate future at least.

The *Companies Act 1985 (International Accounting Standards and Other Accounting Amendments) Regulations 2004* (SI 2004/2947) were laid before Parliament in November 2004 and come into effect for accounting periods beginning on or after 1 January 2005. The main purpose of these Regulations is to introduce into UK company law a framework to give companies the option of preparing their annual accounts in accordance with IASs, although they are much more wide-ranging than their title might imply and introduce a number of other changes that could have a significant impact on the preparation of company accounts.

The Regulations amend the existing provisions of CA 1985 to allow most companies to choose whether to prepare Companies Act accounts or IAS accounts. However, the option to prepare IAS accounts will not be available to charitable companies, on the basis that IASs have been drafted with profit-making entities in mind and are therefore not considered appropriate for the charity sector at present. A decision to adopt IASs will generally not be reversible, although a company will be permitted to revert to the adoption of UK standards where:

(i)   the company ceases to be listed;

(ii)   the company's parent ceases to be listed; or

(iii)   the company becomes a subsidiary of a parent that does not prepare IAS accounts.

Where appropriate, the fact that the accounts have been prepared in accordance with IASs must be disclosed in the notes to the accounts.

Continuing requirements

1.4   When a company opts to prepare IAS accounts, the provisions of CA 1985 on the form and content of statutory accounts no longer apply. However, this does not mean that all accounting provisions in the legislation can be ignored. In particular, the provisions that will continue to apply even where IAS accounts are prepared include:

(i)   the requirement to prepare and file annual accounts;

(ii)   where relevant, the requirement to prepare group accounts;

(iii)   the disclosure requirements in respect of directors' remuneration and employee numbers and costs; and

(iv)   the disclosure requirements in respect of subsidiaries and other related undertakings.

In June 2005, the FRRP published an opinion by Freshfields Bruckhaus Deringer on the effect of the IAS Regulation on the requirement in CA 1985 for accounts to show a true and fair view. The key points highlighted in this opinion are:

(i)   the true and fair override no longer applies to companies who prepare their accounts in accordance with IASs;

(ii)   for companies preparing IAS accounts, references to the 'true and fair view' in the legislation are references to the requirement under IASs for accounts to achieve a fair presentation;

(iii)   the application of IASs, together with additional disclosure where necessary, is presumed to result in financial statements that achieve a fair presentation;

(iv)   IAS 1 'Presentation of Financial Statements' acknowledges that it may be necessary to depart from strict compliance with a requirement of a standard or related interpretation in order to achieve a fair presentation, but only in very rare circumstances, and where such a departure is required, certain additional disclosures must be given, including that nature of the departure and the reasons for it.

Companies that continue to prepare accounts in accordance with UK accounting standards remain subject to the overriding requirement that the accounts must give a true and fair view and this will require compliance with UK accounting standards, other than in exceptional circumstances. The legal opinion can be obtained from the FRRP website at http://www.frc.org.uk/frrp/press/pub0826.html

Impact for groups

1.5   The option of adopting IASs will operate independently for group and individual accounts. There is consequently nothing to prevent a parent company from preparing group accounts on the basis of IASs and individual accounts on the basis of UK standards (or vice versa), although it seems likely that few will choose to do so because of the additional work that this would inevitably involve. Directors of parent companies are expected to ensure consistency in the adoption of IASs within the group, unless there are good reasons against this, and subsidiaries will generally be expected to prepare their accounts on the basis used by the parent for its own individual accounts, although there is a specific exception where the parent prepares both IAS group and IAS individual accounts.

UK convergence with IASs

1.6   In March 2004, the ASB issued a Discussion Paper – *UK Accounting Standards: A Strategy for Convergence with IFRS* – setting out its detailed plans for achieving the convergence of UK accounting standards with IASs. The Discussion Paper outlines the ASB's overall strategy and also sets out specific proposals on the development or revision of individual accounting standards in the next few years. It is still not clear how many unlisted companies will take up the option to adopt IASs from January 2005, but it seems likely that most will continue with UK accounting standards for the immediate future at least. However, the ASB is clear in its own mind that, in the medium to long term, there can be no case for maintaining two wholly different sets of accounting standards in the UK. This would create additional burdens for those preparing accounts, undermine the credibility of financial reporting in the UK and hamper comparability. The Board also takes the view that convergence in the form of broadly equivalent requirements will generally not be sufficient – the only way to prevent different interpretations arising in similar circumstances is for UK standards and international standards to be expressed in the same words. To try and minimise the burdens of this change, the ASB plans to adopt a phased approach to convergence. A number of new UK standards were issued towards the end of 2004 to deal with emerging issues and these come into effect in 2005 and 2006. From 2007 onwards, in a series of 'step changes', the ASB plans to replace existing UK standards with new ones based on the international standards.

The EU has already specified that, for listed companies, national authorities such as the ASB should not impose requirements that are additional to those set out in international accounting standards. The ASB does not plan to introduce new UK standards that are more demanding or restrictive than the equivalent international standards, but where current UK requirements are already more demanding, these will generally be retained if it seems that the relevant international standard will eventually be improved. On the other hand, the ASB acknowledges that there may well be cases where UK requirements could be less onerous than the equivalent international standards, particularly in the area of disclosure, given that they will apply mainly to unlisted companies. Alongside the convergence project, the ASB confirms that it will continue to maintain the FRSSE and to oversee the development of SORPs where appropriate.

Scope and application of accounting standards

1.7   Accounting standards apply to all accounts that are required to show a true and fair view of the profit or loss for the financial period and of the state of affairs of an entity at its balance sheet date. Consequently they apply not only to companies and groups, but also to unincorporated entities if these are required to prepare accounts that show a true and fair view. However, the requirements of accounting standards need not be applied to items that are considered immaterial in the context of the accounts as a whole. They also do not override any exemption from disclosure that is available by law. In its guidance, the ASB emphasises that, when applying accounting standards, preparers of accounts should follow the spirit and reasoning behind the requirements as explained in the standards themselves and in the ASB's *Statement of Principles for Financial Reporting*.

Effective date of accounting standards

1.8   Each accounting standard is effective from a specific date set out in the standard. The date chosen by the ASB will take into account the fact that companies may need time to put detailed procedures into place in order to comply with the new accounting requirements. However, the effective date set by the ASB is the latest date by which compliance must be achieved, and early adoption of new accounting standards is usually encouraged unless there are legal reasons why this is not possible. The question sometimes arises as to whether new requirements apply to all transactions or only to those arising after the effective date of the standard. The ASB's general view is that the requirements of accounting standards should be regarded as applying to all transactions, regardless of when they took place, unless a particular accounting standard specifies a different approach. Care is also required over the early adoption of accounting treatments proposed in Discussion Papers and FREDs. If the subject matter of a Discussion Paper or FRED is not covered by an existing accounting standard, the exposure document may be regarded as indicative of best practice and it may therefore be acceptable to adopt the accounting treatment proposed, bearing in mind that the final FRS may impose slightly different requirements. If the subject matter of the Discussion Paper or FRED is already covered in an accounting standard, the existing standard remains in force until it is replaced and accounts must therefore be prepared in accordance with the existing standard, even if it is expected that the standard will be superseded by new requirements. In these circumstances, it may be appropriate to explain the effect of the new proposals in a note to the accounts.

Disclosure of compliance with accounting standards

1.9   CA 1985 Sch 4 para 36(a) requires the directors to state whether the company's accounts have been prepared in accordance with applicable accounting standards. There is an exemption from the disclosure requirement (but not from the requirement to follow applicable standards) for companies that qualify as small or medium-sized under the legislation. If there has been a departure from applicable accounting standards, particulars must be given, together with the reasons for the departure. The *Foreword to Accounting Standards* and FRS 18 'Accounting Policies' also require disclosure of the financial effect of a material departure from accounting standards.

Applicable accounting standards

1.10   CA 1985 s 256 defines accounting standards as 'statements of standard accounting practice issued by such body or bodies as may be prescribed by regulations'. Applicable accounting standards are those that are relevant to the company's circumstances and to the accounts. For the purposes of UK company law, FRSs and SSAPs constitute 'accounting standards' for accounting periods beginning before 1 January 2005. For accounting periods beginning on or after 1 January 2005, UK accounting standards will continue to be the applicable accounting standards when Companies Act accounts are prepared, but IASs will be the applicable accounting standards when IAS accounts are prepared.

Role of the UITF

1.11   The role of the Urgent Issues Task Force (UITF) is to help the ASB to fulfil its aim of responding promptly on urgent matters as they arise. The UITF considers issues that are covered by an existing accounting standard or a provision in company law but where conflicting or unacceptable interpretations have developed, or seem likely to develop. Having considered the issue and reached a conclusion, the UITF issues its consensus in the form of an Abstract, which usually becomes effective shortly after publication. Once it is in force, a UITF Abstract has the same authority, scope and application as an accounting standard and therefore forms part of standard accounting practice.

Role of the FRRP

1.12   The Financial Reporting Review Panel (FRRP) enquires into accounts that appear to depart from the requirements of company law, accounting standards and UITF Abstracts, including the requirement to show a true and fair view. To date, reviews have concentrated on the accounts of public companies and larger private companies, but technically all companies come within the remit of the FRRP unless they qualify as small or medium-sized under CA 1985. Historically, the FRRP has not reviewed accounts on a routine basis but has acted on matters drawn to its attention, either directly or indirectly. Qualified audit reports, press comment and referrals by individuals or companies could all result in an enquiry. Where revision of the accounts is considered necessary, the FRRP usually tries to reach voluntary arrangement with the directors, but it can seek a court order for revision of the accounts under CA 1985 s 245B if it is unable to reach a satisfactory agreement with the directors.

The various post-Enron reviews undertaken in the UK resulted in recommendations that the FRRP should develop a more proactive element to its work, that the Financial Services Authority should have a greater role in the enforcement process and that the Government should explore the scope for opening legal gateways to enable relevant information to be passed between the Inland Revenue and the FSA, FRRP and DTI to help in the identification of high-risk accounts. The *Companies Act (Audit, Investigations and Community Enterprise) Act 2004* includes provisions reflecting these recommendations. In particular, a new provision allows the Secretary of State to appoint a body or bodies to keep the periodic accounts and reports of listed companies under review and, where relevant, inform the Financial Services Authority of any conclusions reached. This provision is effective from 1 January 2005 and the FRRP has already begun to adopt a process of risk-based selection of accounts for review and to cover all published information issued by listed companies, including interim reports and preliminary announcements. The Panel announced in December 2004 that, on the basis of a recent risk assessment, its monitoring activity in 2005 would focus on the following industry sectors:

(i)   automobile;

(ii)   pharmaceutical;

(iii) retail;

(iv)   transport; and

(v)   utilities.

It also plans to carry out targeted reviews on interim reports, especially for companies whose accounts will be subject to significant change in 2005 as a result of the adoption of international accounting standards.

Other provisions in the *Companies Act (Audit, Investigations and Community Enterprise) Act 2004* allow the Inland Revenue to disclose relevant information to facilitate the investigation of company accounts by the FRRP, enable the FRRP to require a company and any officer, employee or auditor to provide information relevant to an investigation of the company's accounts for compliance with the requirements of CA 1985 and establish gateways to enable the FRRP to disclose certain information to bodies such as the DTI, Treasury, Bank of England, FSA and Inland Revenue to assist them in carrying out their legal functions. These provisions come into effect on 6 April 2005. The statutory Operating and Financial Review prepared by quoted companies will also come within the remit of the FRRP, but not until accounting periods beginning on or after 1 April 2006.

In conjunction with these changes, the FRRP published a revised version of its Operating Procedures in April 2005. This confirms the Panel's intention to encourage directors to make additional information available on a voluntary basis as far as possible and only to use its new powers to require the provision of information as a last resort.

Financial Reporting Standard for Smaller Entities (FRSSE)

1.13   *A Financial Reporting Standard for Smaller Entities* (FRSSE) was first published in November 1997 and came into immediate effect. A number of revised versions have been published, the latest one becoming effective in January 2005. The FRSSE may be adopted in financial statements that are intended to give a true and fair view of the financial performance and financial position of companies that qualify as small under CA 1985 and of other entities that would qualify if they were incorporated under CA 1985. If the FRSSE is adopted, this fact must be stated in the accounts. The contents of the FRSSE are based on other accounting standards, but definitions and accounting requirements are set out in a more straightforward manner, and more complex issues that are not expected to arise in smaller entities are excluded. The document is reviewed on an annual basis so that its requirements are kept up to date with developments in accounting practice. An appendix to the FRSSE links its requirements with those in accounting standards, and where issues arise that are not specifically covered in the FRSSE, those preparing the accounts are required to have regard to other standards and UITF Abstracts as a means of establishing current practice. The FRSSE includes a specific additional requirement for the accounts to disclose any personal guarantees given by the directors in respect of company borrowings.

SORPs

1.14   Statements of Recommended Practice (SORPs) set out recommended accounting practice for specialised sectors or industries. They are developed by bodies representing the appropriate sector or industry and are supplementary to accounting standards, legislation and other regulations affecting the business. Bodies wishing to develop a SORP are expected to meet criteria laid down by the ASB and to develop the SORP in accordance with the ASB's Code of Practice. The ASB will review the proposed SORP and, where appropriate, issue a 'negative assurance' statement for publication in the document, confirming that:

— the SORP does not appear to contain any fundamental points of principle that are unacceptable in the context of current accounting practice; and

— the SORP does not conflict with an accounting standard or with the ASB's plans for future accounting standards.

The contents of a SORP do not override the requirements of accounting standards, UITF Abstracts or relevant legislation. The ASB Code of Practice specifically notes that the fact that a SORP has not been updated does not exempt relevant entities from complying with more recent accounting standards and UITF Abstracts. If new standards and Abstracts conflict with the provisions of a SORP, those provisions cease to have effect. FRS 18 'Accounting Policies' requires specific disclosures to be given in the accounts when an entity comes with the scope of a SORP.

ACCOUNTING PRINCIPLES

CA 1985 requirements

1.15   CA 1985 Sch 4 requires the preparation of Companies Act accounts to be based on the principles of:

— going concern;

— consistency;

— accruals;

— prudence, and

— substance over form (for accounting periods beginning on or after 1 January 2005).

The Act also requires the individual components of assets and liabilities to be considered separately when calculating the aggregate value of the asset or liability.

ASB Statement of Principles and FRS 18 'Accounting Policies'

1.16   SSAP 2 'Disclosure of Accounting Policies' was published in November 1971. At that time, there was no formal framework of accounting principles in the UK and SSAP 2 therefore set out and defined four fundamental accounting concepts – going concern, accruals, consistency and prudence – which were considered to underlie the periodic financial statements of a business enterprise and which were subsequently incorporated into company law. However, the standard made clear that these concepts represented a practical approach based on generally accepted assumptions at the time that the standard was issued, and it was envisaged that more theoretical ideals would evolve over the years as accounting thought and practice developed.

A lengthy ASB project on the development of a conceptual framework culminated in the publication of the 'Statement of Principles for Financial Reporting' in December 1999. This Statement took into account the developments in accounting practice in the long period since the publication of SSAP 2 and the impact of those developments on the fundamental accounting concepts identified in the standard. Going concern, accruals, consistency and prudence all feature in the Statement of Principles but they are no longer referred to as fundamental accounting concepts and the roles attributed to them in the Statement differ from those set out in SSAP 2. In particular, the relative importance attached to each of the concepts varies in the Statement, whereas under SSAP 2 they were accorded similar weight, albeit with the proviso that in any conflict between the accruals concept and the prudence concept, the prudence concept should always prevail.

During the exposure period of the draft 'Statement of Principles for Financial Reporting', it was clear that the requirements of SSAP 2 would need to be updated to remove conflicts between the Statement and the accounting standard and a new accounting standard, FRS 18 'Accounting Policies' was issued in December 2000 and superseded SSAP 2 for accounting periods ending on or after 22 June 2001.

Going concern

1.17   CA 1985 specifies that, for accounts purposes, a company is presumed to be carrying on business as a going concern [*CA 1985, Sch 4 para 10*] but does not provide any further guidance on this issue. Under FRS 18, financial statements should be prepared on a going concern basis unless the entity is being liquidated or has ceased trading, or the directors intend to liquidate the company or to cease trading, or have no realistic alternative but to do so. The standard originally noted that a different basis of preparation may be appropriate in these circumstances, but for accounting periods beginning on or after 1 January 2005 it has been updated to state categorically that the accounts should be prepared on a basis other than going concern. Under FRS 21 'Events After the Balance Sheet Date', management decisions in the period between the balance sheet date and the date on which the financial statements are authorised for issue must be taken into account in making the assessment. FRS 18 defines the going concern assumption as 'the hypothesis that the entity is to continue in operational existence for the foreseeable future' and notes that financial information will usually be most relevant if it is prepared on this hypothesis.

Significance of the going concern assumption

1.18   The use of the going concern basis for the preparation of accounts is of particular significance in assessing the appropriateness of the accounting policies to be adopted. Some items in the accounts would be unchanged if the entity was not considered to be a going concern, but other items might be significantly affected by this. For instance, fixed assets are usually included in the balance sheet at cost or valuation, depreciated to reflect the proportion of the life of the asset that has been used up in the business to date. The balance sheet value of the fixed assets essentially represents the value of those assets to the business as a going concern. It will not necessarily represent the amount that would be realised if the individual assets had to be sold. If an entity is being liquidated or has ceased trading, a different accounting treatment may be needed for fixed assets (e.g. they may need to be valued on a break-up basis). Other costs and liabilities may also need to be included in the accounts – for instance, redundancy payments and penalties for the breach or early termination of contracts such as leases and other rental agreements.

Directors' assessment

1.19   FRS 18 requires the directors to assess, at the time that the accounts are prepared, whether there are any significant doubts about the entity's ability to continue as a going concern. In making this assessment, the directors must take into account all available information about the foreseeable future. The guidance in the standard emphasises that the degree of consideration needed to make this assessment will vary depending on the circumstances of the entity. If there is a history of profitable operations with ready access to financial resources, and this situation is expected to continue, detailed consideration of the going concern issue may not be necessary. In other situations the directors may need to consider factors such as expected profitability, debt repayment schedules and alternative sources of finance.

Additional guidance

1.20   Additional detailed guidance on the consideration of going concern issues can be found in International Standard on Auditing 570 (ISA 570) 'Going Concern' and the document 'Going Concern and Financial Reporting' published in November 1994 under the auspices of the Cadbury Committee. Although the latter was developed to provide guidance for directors of UK listed companies reporting under the Cadbury Code (and now the Combined Code), many of the points included in the document are equally relevant to other entities. The key points raised in these two documents are summarised in Appendices 3A and 3B.

Foreseeable future

1.21   FRS 18 does not define the foreseeable future in the context of going concern, nor does it specify the period that should be considered by the directors in their assessment of whether there are any significant doubts over the entity's ability to continue as a going concern. The guidance emphasises that this will once again depend on the circumstances of each case. However, the minimum period for the assessment is usually considered to be a period of twelve months from the date on which the financial statements are approved by the directors. This is reinforced by the fact that, where the directors' assessment has been limited to a shorter period, FRS 18 requires this fact to be disclosed in the notes to the accounts.

Material uncertainties

1.22   Where the directors are aware of material uncertainties that may cast significant doubt on the entity's ability to continue as a going concern, FRS 18 requires those uncertainties to be disclosed in the accounts. Such a situation might arise where loan covenants have been breached so that the loan has technically become repayable on demand, and the loan facility is in the course of being renegotiated but the outcome is still unknown at the time that the financial statements are approved by the directors.

Example 1.1 – Breached covenants: Explaining the use of the going concern basis

At the balance sheet date, the company has breached certain covenants relating to the bank loan of £100,000 and the lender is therefore entitled to recall the loan. The directors are in the process of renegotiating this facility and as yet repayment of the loan has not been requested. The directors are optimistic about the outcome of the negotiations, but these are still at an early stage and it is not possible to predict with any certainty what the outcome will be.

Having considered all the information available to them up to the date on which the financial statements were approved, the directors consider that it is appropriate to prepare the financial statements on a going concern basis. Consequently the financial statements do not include any adjustments that may be necessary if the loan facility is not successfully renegotiated.

Note, however, that in this situation, the loan will usually need to be shown as a current rather than a long-term liability, on the basis that it has become repayable on demand and the renegotiated facility is not in place at the balance sheet date. This is not a going concern adjustment, but a reflection of the entity's financial position at the balance sheet date. For accounting periods beginning on or after 1 January 2005, FRS 25 'Financial Instruments: Disclosure and Presentation' deals specifically with the accounting treatment and disclosures that are required in these circumstances (see Chapter 26).

Other situations that may need explanation

1.23   It is not usually considered necessary to disclose the fact that the going concern basis has been adopted and users are entitled to presume that this is the case in the absence of any disclosure to the contrary. However, where it is not apparent from the financial statements themselves that the entity is a going concern (e.g. where the entity has made a loss during the year and the balance sheet shows net liabilities) it is good practice to confirm that the going concern basis has been used and to explain why the directors consider this to be appropriate. For instance, it may be that a parent undertaking has formally guaranteed ongoing financial support to the reporting entity and that the directors have taken this into account in making their going concern assessment.

Example 1.2 – Going concern disclosure: Subordination of balance due to parent undertaking

The company's parent undertaking has confirmed that it will not seek repayment of the amount owed to it until the company's other liabilities have been met in full. Having considered this and all other information available to them up to the date on which the financial statements were approved, the directors consider that it is appropriate to prepare the financial statements on a going concern basis.

Example 1.3 – Going concern disclosure: Ongoing financial support from parent undertaking

The company's parent company has confirmed that it will continue to make available such financial support as is required to enable the company to continue to trade for the foreseeable future. Having considered this and all other information available to them up to the date on which the financial statements were approved, the directors consider that it is appropriate to prepare the financial statements on a going concern basis.

Directors' statement of responsibilities

1.24   Because the use of the going concern basis is so fundamental to the accounts, the directors are specifically required to refer to it in the formal statement of their responsibilities in respect of the accounts. This statement is considered in more detail in Chapter 38.

Where the going concern basis is not appropriate

1.25   Where an entity is being liquidated or has ceased trading, or the directors have no realistic alternative but to liquidate the entity or to cease trading, the financial statements must be prepared on a different basis. In this case, the financial statements must disclose:

—   the fact that they are not prepared on a going concern basis;

—   the basis on which they have been prepared; and

—   the reason why the entity is not considered to be a going concern.

Accruals

1.26   CA 1985 requires all income and charges in respect of the financial year to which the accounts relate to be taken into account, regardless of the date of receipt or payment, [*CA 1985, Sch 4 para 13*]. As with the going concern concept, no further guidance on this is provided in the legislation. FRS 18 specifically requires financial statements (other than cash flow information) to be prepared on the accruals basis of accounting. It defines this as requiring the non-cash effects of transactions and events to be reflected, as far as is possible, in the financial statements for the accounting period in which they occur, and not in the period in which any related cash is received or paid. The standard makes a clear link with the definitions of assets and liabilities set out in FRS 5 'Reporting the Substance of Transactions' (and also in the Statement of Principles) and notes that the use of those definitions to determine which items should be recognised as assets and liabilities in the balance sheet is consistent with the accruals concept.

Practical effect

1.27   The practical effect of FRS 18 is that accruals must be made for expenses and losses that relate to the reporting period, and for income and profits relating to that period, subject to the *Companies Act 1985* requirement that only profits realised at the balance sheet date should be included in the profit and loss account. For instance, overhead expenses such as electricity and telephone charges which have been incurred during the year must be included in the accounts, even if they are not paid for until after the balance sheet date. Similarly, expenses that have been paid in advance (e.g. rental costs, insurance, service and maintenance contracts covering an extended period) must be apportioned over the period to which they relate and a prepayment included in the accounts where necessary. However, the 'matching' of income and expenditure that was required under SSAP 2 has now been superseded in FRS 18 by the need to consider which items need to be reflected as assets and liabilities in the balance sheet at the end of the financial reporting period as a result of past transactions and events.

Realisation issues

1.28 FRS 18 also includes a reference to the CA 1985 requirement that only profits realised at the balance sheet date should be included in the profit and loss account and the following definition of realised profits and losses set out in the legislation:

> 'such profits and losses as fall to be treated as realised in accordance with principles generally accepted, at the time when the accounts are prepared, with respect to the determination for accounting purposes of realised profits and losses.' [*CA 1985, s 262(3)*]

The guidance in FRS 18 notes that profits are to be treated as realised, for these purposes, only when they have been realised in the form of cash or of other assets the ultimate cash realisation of which can be assessed with reasonable certainty. These requirements are to apply unless there are special reasons for departing from them, in which case two additional rules come into effect:

— such 'special reasons' will not exist unless, as a minimum, it is possible to be reasonably certain that an unrealised gain exists and can be measured with sufficient reliability; and

— due consideration must be given to whether a departure from the requirements would result in the use of valuation bases or accounting treatments not permitted by companies' legislation and which could therefore only be used if the true and fair override was justified.

Consistency and comparability

1.29 CA 1985 requires accounting policies to be applied consistently within the same set of accounts and from one financial year to the next. [*CA 1985, Sch 4 para 11*]. There is also a separate requirement for the corresponding figures for the previous financial period to be comparable for those with the current year. This is considered in more detail in Chapter 5. FRS 18 does not specifically discuss consistency, but concentrates instead on comparability as one of the four objectives against which the appropriateness of accounting policies should be judged. Comparability is important to enable users to identify and evaluate similarities in, and differences between, the nature and effects of transactions and events taking place over time and in different reporting entities. The usefulness of financial information is therefore enhanced if it can be compared with similar information about the entity for another period or point in time, or with similar information about other entities. Comparability is usually achieved through a combination of consistency and disclosure, but the guidance in the standard emphasises that consistency is not an end in itself, and there will inevitably be circumstances in which it needs to be sacrificed. In particular, consistency should not be used to prevent improvements in accounting, and where the introduction of a new accounting policy would be of overall benefit to users, the need for consistency should not be used to justify not making the change.

Changes in accounting policy

1.30   Situations will inevitably arise from time to time which make it appropriate for an entity to change one of its accounting policies. For instance, a new accounting standard may have been introduced which requires a different accounting treatment to the one adopted by the entity in previous years. Similarly, the nature or scale of an entity's activities or transactions may change, so that an accounting policy previously adopted is no longer acceptable (i.e. because items that were previously immaterial have now become material). Examples of this might include:

—   an entity which had previously only entered into minor finance leases entering into a finance lease agreement in respect of a substantial asset or assets;

—   an entity that had previously only carried out an insignificant level of research and development expanding its activities in this field by becoming involved in a major product development project.

Where it is necessary to implement a new accounting policy, or to change an existing policy, the guidance in FRS 18 notes that the entity should ensure wherever possible that the new policy adopted is in accordance with recently issued accounting standards.

Regular review of accounting policies

1.31   FRS 18 requires accounting policies to be regularly reviewed to ensure that they remain the most appropriate in the particular circumstances of the entity, but also notes that in considering whether a new policy is more appropriate, due weight should be given to the potential impact on comparability. The guidance in the standard explains that frequent changes to accounting policies could be detrimental to comparability over the longer term, and the impact of past and expected future changes should therefore be taken into account when assessing whether a change in accounting policy is appropriate. Accounting policies should generally only be changed when the benefits to users will outweigh the disadvantages. Unless other accounting standards or UITF Abstracts require a different treatment, FRS 18 notes that a material adjustment to earlier years as a result of a change in accounting policy should be accounted for as a prior period adjustment in accordance with FRS 3 'Reporting Financial Performance'.

Estimation techniques

1.32   FRS 18 makes a clear distinction between changes in accounting policy and changes in estimation techniques. A change in an estimation technique should not be accounted for as a prior period adjustment unless it:

—   represents the correction of a fundamental error; or

—   is required by another accounting standard, UITF Abstract or companies' legislation to be accounted for as a prior period adjustment.

Prudence

1.33   CA 1985 includes the following requirements [*CA 1985, Sch 4 para 12*]:

—   the amount of any item must be determined on a prudent basis;

—   only profits realised at the balance sheet date should be included in the profit and loss account; and

—   all liabilities which have arisen in respect of the current financial year or any previous financial year must be taken into account – this should include any liabilities that only become apparent between the balance sheet date and the date on which the accounts are approved and signed by the directors.

SSAP 2 defined the prudence concept in the context of the realisation of profits, on the basis that, at the time that the standard was developed, the main concern was to prevent profits from being overstated. Subsequently, concern began to centre around the need to prevent the smoothing of profits through the deliberate understatement of assets or the deliberate overstatement of liabilities. In particular, the ASB frequently expressed concern at the nature and extent of provisions that were sometimes included in accounts, usually on the grounds that it was prudent to do so, since these could both distort trends in the profit and loss account and also result in substantial amounts of expenditure being 'hidden', in that costs were subsequently charged against the provision rather than as expenses in the profit and loss account. Specific rules were therefore set out in FRS 3 'Reporting Financial Performance' on the timing and content of provisions relating to the sale or termination of an operation, and these were developed further in FRS 12 'Provisions, Contingent Liabilities and Contingent Assets'. Broadly, a provision can now only be recognised when an entity has a legal or constructive obligation at the balance sheet date, and it is probable that this will result in the transfer of economic benefits. The guidance in FRS 12 states unequivocally that:

—   uncertainty should not be used to justify excessive provisions or a deliberate overstatement of liabilities; and

—   a board or management decision before the balance sheet date will not usually result in a constructive obligation at that date, unless the decision has already been put into effect or has been communicated to those affected in a way that raises a valid expectation that it will be carried out.

Current definition of prudence

1.34   Prudence is defined in the ASB's 'Statement of Principles for Financial Reporting' as:

> 'the inclusion of a degree of caution in the exercise of the judgements needed in making the estimates required under conditions of uncertainty, such that gains or assets are not overstated and losses or liabilities are not understated. In particular, under such conditions it requires more confirmatory evidence about the existence of, and a greater reliability of measurement for, assets and gains than is required for liabilities and losses.'

FRS 18 discusses prudence in the context of the reliability of financial information – reliability being one of the objectives against which the appropriateness of accounting policies should be measured. The standard notes that there will often be uncertainty about the existence of assets, liabilities, gains, losses and changes to shareholders' funds, or about the amount at which they should be measured. Prudence therefore requires that the accounting policies adopted should take account of such uncertainty in recognising and measuring items in the financial statements. The standard also emphasises that more confirmatory evidence is required about the existence of an asset or gain than for a liability or loss, and that greater reliability of measurement is needed for assets and gains than for liabilities and losses.

Inappropriate use of prudence

1.35   The standard makes two specific additional points in respect of prudence, both of which are also included in the 'Statement of Principles':

—   it is not necessary to exercise prudence when there is no uncertainty; and

—   it is not appropriate to use prudence as a reason for creating hidden reserves or excessive provisions, deliberately understating assets or gains, or deliberately overstating liabilities or losses – to do this would impair the reliability of the financial statements as they would no longer be free from bias.

Substance over form

1.36   For accounting periods beginning on or after 1 January 2005, the *Companies Act 1985 (International Accounting Standards and Other Accounting Amendments) Regulations 2004* (SI 2004/2947) insert a new paragraph 5A into Schedule 4 to CA 1985, which requires the directors to have regard to the substance of the reported transaction or arrangement, in accordance with generally accepted accounting principles, when determining how items are presented in the profit and loss account and balance sheet. Prior to this, the principle that the economic or commercial substance of a transaction should take precedence over its legal form was not referred to in company law, although it has been an accepted element of UK accounting practice since the publication of FRS 5 'Reporting the substance of transactions'. Similar amendments are made to Schedule 8, Schedule 9 and Schedule 9A so that the new provision also applies to small companies preparing shorter form accounts and to banks and insurance companies. The concept of substance over form, and its practical implications, are considered in more detail in Chapter 4.

Relevance, reliability and understandability

1.37   FRS 18 identifies four objectives against which the appropriateness of accounting policies should be assessed – relevance, reliability, comparability and understandability. The objective of financial statements is to provide information about an entity's financial performance and financial position that is useful to users in assessing the stewardship of management and making economic decisions. The guidance in FRS 18 notes that financial information is relevant if it has the ability to influence the economic decisions of users and is provided in time to influence those decisions. Financial information is considered to be reliable if:

—   it can be depended upon to represent faithfully what it purports to represent or could reasonably be expected to represent – in other words, if the way in which transactions and events are recognised, measured and presented in the financial statements corresponds closely to their substance and practical effect;

—   it is free from deliberate or systematic bias;

—   it is free from material error;

—   it is complete within the bounds of materiality; and

—   under conditions of uncertainty, a degree of caution has been applied in making the necessary judgements and estimates – in other words, it has been prudently prepared.

Under FRS 18, financial information is understandable if it can be understood by users who have a reasonable knowledge of business and economic activities and who are willing to study the information provided with reasonable diligence. The adoption of appropriate accounting policies should result in the presentation of financial information that is relevant, reliable and understandable to users of the accounts.

Off-setting

1.38   The off-setting of assets and liabilities and income and expenditure in annual accounts is prohibited by CA 1985 Sch 4 para 5. Paragraph 14 of Sch 4 also requires individual assets and liabilities to be considered separately when calculating aggregate amounts. Paragraph 29 of FRS 5 'Reporting the Substance of Transactions' reinforces the requirements of CA 1985 by stating that:

—   assets and liabilities should not be off-set; and

— debit and credit balances should only be aggregated into a single net item where they do not constitute separate assets and liabilities.

For accounting periods beginning on or after 1 January 2005, the offset of financial assets and financial liabilities is covered by FRS 25 'Financial Instruments: Disclosure and Presentation' and FRS 5 is amended to emphasise this. Under FRS 25, a financial asset and a financial liability should be offset so that the net amounted is presented in the balance sheet when, and only when, the entity:

— currently has a legally enforceable right to set off the recognised amounts; and

— intends either to settle on a net basis, or to realise the asset and settle the liability simultaneously.

In all other cases, financial assets and liabilities should continue to be presented separately in the accounts.

Similarly, the ASB's 'Statement of Principles for Financial Reporting' notes that:

— gains and losses should not normally be offset in the financial performance statement, except where they relate to the same event or circumstance and disclosing the gross components is not likely to provide useful information for the assessment of either future results or the effects of past transactions and events; and

— assets should not be offset against liabilities when reporting an entity's financial position.

Departure from accounting principles set out in CA 1985

1.39   CA 1985 permits the directors to depart from the accounting principles set out in the Act where there are special reasons for doing so, provided that the accounts disclose:

— particulars of the departure;

— the reasons for the departure; and

— the effect of the departure.

FRS 18 states unequivocally that, where companies' legislation frames the disclosure of a departure from a specific statutory requirement in these terms, the details given must include:

— a clear and unambiguous statement that there has been a departure from the requirements of an accounting standard, a UITF Abstract or companies' legislation (as appropriate) and that the departure is necessary to give a true and fair view;

— a statement of the treatment that accounting standards, UITF Abstracts or companies' legislation would normally require and a description of the treatment actually adopted;

— a statement of why the usual treatment would not give a true and fair view; and

— a description of how the position shown in the financial statements is different as a result of the departure – this should include quantification of the effect except where:

— this is already evident in the financial statements themselves; or

— the effect cannot be quantified, in which case the circumstances should be explained.

This information must be given in the note on compliance with applicable accounting standards (see 1.9 above) or cross-referenced to that note. If the departure continues in subsequent years, the disclosures must be given in each year, with comparatives. Where only the comparatives are affected, the disclosures must still be given in respect of those figures. The disclosure requirements are considered in more detail in Chapter 3.

Examples of departures from the CA 1985 accounting principles

1.40 The following examples illustrate some of the situations where departure from the accounting principles set out in the *Companies Act 1985* will usually be required:

— where an entity is not considered to be a going concern – in this case the accounts will need to be prepared on a different basis;

— the inclusion of certain unrealised exchange gains and losses in the profit and loss account in accordance with the accounting requirements of SSAP 20 'Foreign Currency Translation' – this is considered in more detail in Chapter 7 and also referred to in Chapter 3;

— a change of accounting policy as discussed in 1.30 above – this is considered in more detail in Chapter 5 along with the related accounts disclosures.

ACCOUNTING RULES

Alternative sets of accounting rules

1.41 CA 1985 sets out two alternative sets of accounting rules:

(i) the historical cost accounting rules [*CA 1985, Sch 4 para 16–28*];

(ii) the alternative accounting rules [*CA 1985, Sch 4 para 29–34*].

The two sets of rules are given equal status in the Act and companies are free to choose which they adopt in their accounts. The alternative accounting rules can be applied to all aspects of the accounts to achieve full current cost accounting, or only to selected items. The most common practice in the UK is to adopt the historical cost accounting rules, but often with selective adoption of the alternative accounting rules, most commonly to allow land and buildings to be shown at valuation rather than original cost. The notes to the accounts should state which accounting convention has been adopted.

Example 1.3 – Accounting convention adopted

Basis of preparation

The financial statements have been prepared under the historical cost accounting convention.

or

Basis of preparation

The financial statements have been prepared under the historical cost accounting convention, modified to include the revaluation of land and buildings.

Chapter 6 of the ASB 'Statement of Principles' deals with measurement in financial statements. Under the principles set out in the Statement, the most appropriate measurement basis (either historical cost or current value) should be selected for each category of assets and liabilities – this should be the basis that best meets the objective of financial statements and the demands of the qualitative characteristics of financial information, taking into account the nature of the items concerned and the circumstances involved. At present, this approach might conflict with companies' legislation in the case of certain current assets. FRS 18 'Accounting Policies' defines measurement bases, accounting policies and estimation techniques and sets out requirements on the selection of appropriate accounting policies and estimation techniques.

Determining amounts under the historical cost accounting rules

1.42   *Paragraphs 16–28* of *Sch 4* to the Act set out detailed rules on determining the amount to be shown in the accounts under the historical cost accounting rules for:

—   tangible fixed assets;

—   development costs;

—   goodwill;

—   current assets;

—   an excess of money owed over value received.

The rules on tangible fixed assets, development costs and goodwill are discussed in detail in the relevant chapters. The general rules on the other items are discussed in 1.43 and 1.44 below. The Act also includes detailed guidance on determining the purchase price or production cost of an asset and this is considered at 1.45–1.48 below.

Current assets

1.43   Current assets are defined in CA 1985 s 262(1) as assets that are not intended for use on a continuing basis in the company's activities. They normally include stocks, debtors, cash and short-term investments. Current assets must be stated at the lower of net realisable value and purchase price or production cost (see below). Where a provision has been made to write down a current asset to its net realisable value and the reasons for the write-down have ceased to apply, either fully or in part, the provision should be written back accordingly. For example, under these rules, the value of debtors should be reduced by appropriate provisions for bad and doubtful debts. However, if circumstances change and a debt previously provided for becomes fully or partially recoverable, the provision should be written back to the extent necessary to state the debt at its expected recoverable amount.

Excess of money owed over value received

1.44   The legislation considers a situation where the amount owed by a company exceeds the value of the consideration received in the transaction giving rise to the liability. For instance, this will arise where debentures issued by the company are issued at a discount, or are redeemable at a premium at a future date. In these circumstances the Act permits (but does not require) the difference in value to be treated as an asset, provided that:

—   it is written off by annual instalments of a 'reasonable' amount;

—   it is completely written off before the amount owed by the company is repaid;

—   the unamortised amount is shown separately in the accounts, either on the balance sheet or in a note to the accounts.

The provisions of the Act are considered in detail in Chapter 13, in conjunction with the related requirements of accounting standards.

Determining purchase price or production cost

1.45   There is also detailed guidance on determining the purchase price or production cost of an asset. The rules cover both fixed and current assets. The purchase price of an asset is the actual price paid, plus any expenses incidental to its acquisition. Such expenses would include the cost of getting the asset to its present location and into its present condition. The purchase price of an asset also includes any attributable VAT where this is not recoverable by the purchaser. Any VAT that is recoverable should be excluded from the cost of the asset. The production cost of an asset is to be calculated by adding together the purchase price of the raw materials and consumables used and the direct costs of production. In addition, the following may be included in production cost under CA 1985:

—   a reasonable proportion of indirect production costs, but only to the extent that they relate to the period of production;

—   interest on capital borrowed to finance the production of the asset, but again
      only to the extent that it relates to the period of production.

In the case of current assets, the Act specifically prohibits the inclusion of
distribution costs in 'production cost'. The interaction of these provisions with the
requirements of SSAP 9 'Stocks and Long Term Contracts' is considered in
Chapter 23. The inclusion of relevant indirect costs in production cost will often
involve the use of estimation techniques and the requirements of FRS 18 'Accounting Policies' on the selection of appropriate estimation techniques are covered in
Chapter 5. Where interest is included in the production cost of an asset, the notes to
the accounts must disclose:

—   the fact that interest has been included in the production cost of the asset;

—   the amount of interest included.

The inclusion of interest in asset values is considered further in Chapters 21 and 23.

Unknown purchase price or production cost

1.46   Where there is no record of the purchase price or production cost of an
asset, or any of the amounts needed to calculate purchase price or production cost
as set out in CA 1985, or where these details cannot be obtained without
unreasonable expense or delay, the value given to the asset in the earliest available
record on or after its acquisition or production by the company is to be treated as
the purchase price or production cost. Where a company takes advantage of this
provision, the first accounts to include the asset on the basis of its earliest recorded
value must include a note explaining this.

Stocks and fungible assets

1.47   The Act allows a company to apply special rules in the case of stocks and
fungible assets, including investments. Fungible assets are assets of any description
that are substantially indistinguishable one from another. For instance, many small
consumables (e.g. screws, nuts and bolts, pens and pencils etc.) which are generally
interchangeable, would come within this definition. FRS 18 'Accounting Policies'
notes that specific accounting requirements for fungible assets may be set out in
accounting standards, UITF Abstracts and companies' legislation. Where fungible
assets are recorded at historical cost, the accounting policy may require cost to be
determined on an asset-by-asset basis or may consider the assets in aggregate by
using a measurement basis such as weighted average historical cost, or historical cost
measured on a first in, first out (FIFO) basis. The guidance in FRS 18 notes that an
accounting policy that considers fungible assets in aggregate will be more consistent
with the underlying objective of comparability.

The Act allows stocks and fungible assets to be valued for accounts purposes by one
of the following methods, rather than requiring them to be included at actual
purchase price or production cost:

— first in, first out (FIFO);

— last in, first out (LIFO);

— a weighted average price;

— any other method similar to the above methods.

Not all of these methods are generally acceptable under SSAP 9 'Stocks and Long Term Contracts' – this is considered further in Chapter 23. The method chosen must be one which the directors consider appropriate to the circumstances of the company. This is reinforced by FRS 18 'Accounting Policies' which requires an entity to adopt accounting policies (and, where appropriate, estimation techniques) that enable its financial statements to give a true and fair view and that are consistent with the requirements of accounting standards, UITF Abstracts and companies' legislation. Where more than one policy or technique satisfies these conditions, and it is therefore necessary to choose between them, the standard requires the entity to select whichever policy or technique is considered most appropriate to its particular circumstances for the purpose of giving a true and fair view. The requirements of FRS 18 are considered in detail in Chapter 5.

If the value included in the accounts for stocks and fungible assets differs materially from the replacement cost of the assets at the balance sheet date, the difference must be disclosed in a note to the accounts. The comparison can be with the most recent actual purchase price or production cost before the balance sheet date where the directors consider this to be more appropriate. The disclosure requirement is considered further in Chapter 23.

Raw materials and consumables

1.48   CA 1985 permits raw materials and consumables to be included in the accounts at a fixed quantity and value provided that:

— the assets are constantly being replaced;

— their overall value is not material to an assessment of the company's state of affairs;

— their quantity, value and composition do not vary materially.

The interaction of this provision with SSAP 9 'Stocks and Long Term Contracts' is considered in Chapter 23.

Determining amounts under the alternative accounting rules

1.49   The alternative accounting rules set out in *paras 29–34* of *Sch 4* to the Act cover the following assets:

— intangible assets, other than goodwill;

— tangible fixed assets;

— investments shown as fixed assets;

—   investments shown as current assets;

—   stocks.

Each of these is considered briefly below. More detailed consideration of the practical implications of applying the alternative accounting rules to these assets can be found in the chapters dealing with the relevant assets.

Accounting for asset valuations

1.50   The subject of valuations in financial reporting has been considered in various ASB documents, culminating in the publication of FRS 15 'Tangible Fixed Assets' in February 1999. One of the objectives of this standard is to ensure that, where an entity chooses to revalue tangible fixed assets, the valuation is performed on a consistent basis and kept up to date, and that gains and losses on revaluation are recognised in the accounts on a consistent basis. The requirements of FRS 15 on valuation are considered in detail in Chapter 21.

Current cost

1.51   The alternative accounting rules allow certain assets to be shown at current cost. The term 'current cost' is not defined in the Act and there is not yet any formal guidance on 'current cost' within accounting standards. In the absence of formal guidance, valuation on the basis of current cost usually follows the guidelines set out in *Accounting for the Effects of Changing Prices: a Handbook* published by the Accounting Standards Committee in 1986. This defines current cost as the lower of:

—   the asset's net current replacement cost; and

—   its recoverable amount.

An asset's recoverable amount is defined as the higher of:

—   its net realisable value; and

—   the amount recoverable from its future use.

This is developed further in FRS 11 'Impairment of Fixed Assets and Goodwill', which is considered in more detail in Chapter 21. Chapter 6 of the ASB 'Statement of Principles' also considers how the current value of assets might be determined.

Intangible fixed assets

1.52   Intangible fixed assets, other than goodwill, may be included in the accounts at their current cost. Goodwill can never be carried at more than its historical cost, less any amounts by which it has already been amortised. The accounting treatment of goodwill is considered further in Chapter 20.

Tangible fixed assets

1.53   Tangible fixed assets may be included in the accounts at either:

— market value as at the date of their last valuation; or

— current cost.

There is no requirement under the Act for market values to be kept up to date. However, FRS 15 'Tangible Fixed Assets' now sets out stringent requirements to ensure that, once assets have been included in the accounts at valuation, their value is kept up to date, and also that all items within an individual class of assets are treated consistently. These requirements are considered in detail in Chapter 21. Where an asset is included in the accounts under one of the valuation bases permitted by the alternative accounting rules, this value becomes the basis for the depreciation charge. This point is considered in more detail in Chapter 13.

Investments

1.54   Investments shown as fixed assets may be included in the accounts at:

— market value as at the date of their last valuation; or

— at a value determined on any basis which the directors consider to be appropriate in the company's circumstances.

For example, the second approach could be used to establish a value for unlisted investments, for accounts purposes, using either an earnings basis or a net asset basis. Where the second approach is adopted, a note to the accounts must disclose details of the method of valuation adopted and the reasons for choosing this method. It is not sufficient simply to state that the investments have been valued by the directors. Investments shown in the accounts as current assets may be included at their current cost.

Stocks

1.55   Under CA 1985, stocks may be included in the accounts at their current cost. However, this is generally not an acceptable accounting treatment under SSAP 9 'Stocks and Long Term Contracts'.

Disclosure of use of the alternative accounting rules

1.56   Whenever a company adopts the alternative accounting rules, the notes to the accounts must include:

— a note of each item accounted for under the alternative accounting rules; and

— the basis of valuation used for each of those items.

For each balance sheet item, other than stocks, which has been accounted for under the alternative accounting rules, the accounts must show, either separately on the balance sheet or in a note to the accounts:

— the amount at which the item would have been included in the accounts under the historical cost accounting rules, or the difference between this and the amount actually shown in the accounts; and

—   the cumulative figures for depreciation or diminutions in value that would
      have been included in the accounts under the historical cost accounting rules.

The first disclosure must also be given for each of the main balance sheet headings
affected (i.e. items given a letter or Roman numeral in the balance sheet formats set
out in the Act) as well as for the individual items concerned. Where any assets are
included in the accounts at valuation and this affects the profit and loss account (for
instance, in terms of the amount of depreciation charged), FRS 3 'Reporting
Financial Performance' requires disclosure of what the profit or loss for the year
would have been under the historical cost accounting rules. This additional disclosure is considered in Chapter 36.

Revaluation reserve

1.57   Where any asset is revalued under the alternative accounting rules, the
difference between the previous accounts value and the revalued amount must be
credited or debited to a revaluation reserve. Each asset that is revalued must be
considered individually. The revaluation reserve must be shown:

—   separately in the balance sheet;
—   in the prescribed place for the revaluation reserve within the standard balance
      sheet format.

However, the reserve need not be called a revaluation reserve in the accounts. The
treatment for taxation purposes of any amount credited or debited to the revaluation reserve must also be disclosed in a note to the accounts. If any amount
transferred to the revaluation reserve is no longer necessary for the purpose of the
valuation method used, the amount must be removed from the revaluation reserve.
For instance, if a company sells an asset that has previously been revalued, any
amount in the revaluation reserve in respect of that asset must be removed as it is
no longer needed under the alternative accounting rules. It will normally be
transferred to the profit and loss account reserve as a reserves movement during the
year in which the asset is sold. The rules relating to the revaluation reserve are
considered in more detail in Chapter 32.

Fair value accounting

1.58   The 4th and 7th EC Company Law Directives, which form the basis of the
CA 1985 requirements on individual and consolidated accounts, have been amended
by the EU Fair Value Directive to allow certain financial instruments to be included
in the balance sheet at fair value, and changes in that fair value to be reflected in the
profit and loss account. In effect, the new provisions allow certain investments to be
marked to market and also facilitate the use of hedge accounting in specific
circumstances. Prior to the legal changes, financial instruments were usually
accounted for at cost, which in the case of derivatives is often nil. Even if advantage

was taken of the alternative accounting rules, any changes in value had to be dealt with through the revaluation reserve rather than the profit and loss account.

The UK Government decided to make fair value accounting optional rather than mandatory, and to apply it to both individual and consolidated accounts. The *Companies Act 1985 (International Accounting Standards and Other Accounting Amendments) Regulations 2004* (SI 2004/2947) insert the following new paragraphs into Schedule 4 to CA 1985:

(i)   paragraphs 34A to 34 F which set out detailed provisions on the adoption of fair value accounting; and

(ii)   paragraphs 45A to 45D which deal with the additional disclosures that must be given in the accounts when fair value accounting has been adopted.

Similar amendments have been made to Schedule 8, Schedule 9 and Schedule 9A to the Companies Act 1985, so that fair value accounting is available to all companies, including small companies preparing shorter form accounts and banks and insurance companies.

Application to financial instruments

1.59   Under the new legislation, most financial instruments (including derivatives) may be included in the accounts at fair value provided that this can be determined reliably on the following basis:

(i)   if a reliable market for the instrument can be readily identified, fair value should be determined by reference to its market value;

(ii)   if no such market can be readily identified for the financial instrument as a whole, but can be identified for its components or for similar instruments, fair value should be determined by reference to the market value of the components or of a similar instrument; and

(iii)   if neither (i) nor (ii) applies, fair value can be determined by using generally accepted valuation models and techniques, provided that these ensure a reasonable approximation of the market value of the financial instrument.

However, fair value accounting cannot be applied in the case of financial liabilities unless they are derivatives or are held as part of a trading portfolio.

FRS 25 'Financial instruments: Disclosure and Presentation' and FRS 26 'Financial Instruments: Measurement' set out the detailed UK framework for the adoption of fair value accounting, together with FRS 23 'The Effects of Changes in Foreign Exchange Rates' and FRS 24 'Financial Reporting in Hyperinflationary Economies' where relevant. The presentation requirements of FRS 25 apply for accounting periods beginning on or after 1 January 2005 and the disclosure requirements apply no later than the accounting period in which FRS 26 is adopted. FRS 26 applies for accounting periods beginning on or after 1 January 2005 for listed companies and for accounting periods beginning on or after 1 January 2006 for any other entity which adopts fair value accounting (voluntary adoption from 1 January 2005 is also acceptable in this case). The requirements of FRS 25 and FRS 26 are considered in more detail in Chapters 22 and 26.

Application to other assets

1.60   The legislation also permits fair value accounting to be applied to investment property and to living animals and plants, where such treatment is permitted under international accounting standards. In each case, the same accounting treatment must be applied to all investment property, and/or to all living animals and plants, for which a fair value can be determined reliably. In the UK, investment property must currently be accounted for in accordance with SSAP 19 'Accounting for Investment Properties'. There are no UK accounting standards dealing specifically with living animals and plants at present, but the ASB plans to issue an exposure draft based on IAS 41 'Agriculture' towards the end of 2005. Where investment properties and living animals and plants have been included at fair value, CA 1985 requires disclosure of:

(i)   the balance sheet items affected and the basis of valuation adopted in each case; and

(ii)   in the case of investment property, comparable amounts (including depreciation) under the historical cost accounting rules or the differences between those amounts and the amounts shown in the balance sheet.

Accounting for changes in fair value

1.61   A change in the fair value of a financial instrument or other asset accounted for under the fair value accounting rules should normally be included in the profit and loss account. However, in the following two cases, the change should be debited or credited to a separate fair value reserve:

(i)   where a financial instrument is a hedging instrument accounted for under a hedge accounting system that allows some or all of the change in value not to be shown in the profit and loss account; and

(ii)   where the change in value relates to an exchange difference arising on a monetary item that forms part of a company's net investment in a foreign entity.

A change in value may also be debited or credited to the fair value reserve where the financial instrument in question is an available for sale financial asset and is not a derivative. The fair value reserve should be adjusted where any of the amounts included in it are no longer required for the purposes of fair value accounting (for instance, where the related item has been disposed of).

Accounts disclosures

1.62   Where fair value accounting is adopted, CA 1985 requires detailed disclosures to be given in the accounts, including:

(i)　where financial instruments have been included under the fair value accounting rules:

- the significant assumptions underlying any valuation models and techniques that have been used to establish fair value;

- for each category of financial instrument, the fair value of the instruments in that category, the changes in value included in the profit and loss account, and any changes in value debited or credited to the fair value reserve;

- for each class of derivative, the extent and nature of the instruments, including any significant terms and conditions that may affect the amount, timing or certainty of future cash flows;

(ii)　a table of movements on the fair value reserve; and

(iii)　the treatment for tax purposes of any amounts debited or credited to the fair value reserve.

Disclosures where accounting is not at fair value

1.63　Companies not applying the fair value accounting rules may nevertheless be required to give additional disclosures in the accounts. Where the company has financial fixed assets that could be accounted for at fair value but which are included in the accounts at an amount in excess of fair value, without any provision for diminution in value, the accounts must disclose:

(i)　the amount at which those assets are included (either individually or in appropriate groupings):

(ii)　the fair value of the assets (or the relevant groupings); and

(iii)　the reason for not making a provision for diminution in value, including the nature of any evidence which supports the expectation of a recovery in value.

Where the company has derivatives which have not been included in the accounts at fair value, the accounts must disclose for each class of derivatives:

(i)　the fair value of the derivatives in that class, if this can be calculated in accordance with paragraph 34B of Schedule 4; and

(ii)　the extent and nature of the derivatives.

A small company preparing shorter form accounts under Schedule 8 to CA 1985 is not required to give the disclosures in respect of derivatives.

APPENDIX 1

Summary of the key points on the appropriateness of the going concern basis raised in International Standard on Auditing 570 (ISA 570) ' Going Concern'

Foreseeable future

In its definition of the going concern assumption, FRS 18 'Accounting Policies' refers to the ability of the entity to continue in operational existence for the foreseeable future. It does not specify any minimum period that should be covered in the going concern review but does require the directors to disclose the fact that the period reviewed is less than twelve months from the balance sheet date where relevant. Under ISA 570 the auditors must also ask the directors to extend the period of their review to twelve months from the balance sheet date if their review has covered a shorter period.

ISA 570 emphasises that the directors will need to look forward for a period of time, but the exact period covered may vary, depending on the particular circumstances of the entity. To attempt to specify a minimum period would necessarily be artificial and arbitrary. Factors to take into account in assessing the adequacy of the period of the review include:

(i)   the nature, size and complexity of the entity;

(ii)   the entity's reporting and budgeting systems;

(iii) the extent to which information relates to future events and, if so, how far into the future those events lie.

It is usually accepted that the review should cover a period of at least one year from the date of approval of the accounts.

Financial indicators of potential going concern difficulties

The following list illustrates some of the financial issues that may give rise to concern over an entity's ability to continue as a going concern:

—   an excess of liabilities over assets;

—   a net liability or net current liability position;

—   necessary borrowing facilities not yet agreed;

—   fixed-term borrowings approaching maturity without realistic prospects of renewal or repayment;

—   excessive reliance on short-term borrowings to finance long-term assets;

—   major debt repayment falling due where refinancing is necessary to entity's continued existence;

—   major restructuring of debt;

— indications of withdrawal of support by lenders and other creditors;

— negative operating cash flows indicated by historical or prospective financial statements;

— adverse key financial ratios;

— substantial operating losses or significant deterioration in the value of assets used to generate cash flows;

— major losses or cash flow problems that have arisen since the balance sheet date;

— arrears or discontinuance of dividends;

— inability to pay creditors on due dates;

— inability to comply with the terms of loan agreements;

— reduction in normal terms of trade credit by suppliers;

— change from credit to cash-on-delivery transactions with suppliers;

— inability to obtain financing for essential new product development or other essential investments;

Operational and other indicators of potential going concern difficulties

The following list illustrates some of the operational issues that may give rise to concern over the entity's ability to continue as a going concern:

— loss of key management and/or staff without replacement;

— loss of a major market, franchise, licence or principal supplier;

— labour difficulties;

— shortage of important supplies;

— fundamental changes in the market, or in technology, to which the entity is unable to adapt adequately;

— excessive dependence on a few product lines where the market is depressed;

— technical developments which render a key product obsolete.

Other indicators of potential going concern difficulties

Other potential indicators of going concern difficulties include:

— non-compliance with capital or other statutory requirements;

— pending legal or regulatory proceedings against the entity that may, if successful, result in claims that are unlikely to be satisfied;

— changes in legislation or government policy expected to adversely affect the entity;

— issues which involve a range of possible outcomes so wide that an unfavourable result could affect the entity's ability to continue as a going concern.

For each of the above, consideration should also be given to any mitigating factors –
for instance, management's plans to raise finance from other sources, or to seek
alternative sources of supply, and the extent to which these are likely to be
successful.

APPENDIX 2

Summary of the key points on the appropriateness of the going concern basis raised in the Joint Working Group Guidance (JWG) 'Going Concern and Financial Reporting'

Contents of the document

The Cadbury Code of Best Practice (now the Combined Code) recommends that the directors state in the accounts that the business is a going concern (with supporting assumptions or qualifications where necessary) primarily to ensure that directors take appropriate steps to satisfy themselves that it is reasonable to prepare the accounts on a going concern basis. The Joint Working Group Guidance was developed to help directors comply with the recommendation.

The document comprises the following sections.

— Introduction – which sets out the scope of the document and the background to the going concern concept.

— Procedures – which indicates the procedures that the directors should follow in assessing the appropriateness of the going concern basis. Additional detail is given in an Appendix to the document.

— Disclosure – which considers the accounts disclosures that should be given in different situations.

— Other – which includes consideration of the issue of going concern in the context of a group.

Guidance on procedures

The guidance on procedures includes the following points.

— As a minimum, budgets and forecasts should be prepared for the period to the next balance sheet date; further periods will normally be covered by medium or long-term plans which will give a general indication of how the directors expect the business to fare.

— Borrowing facilities should be reviewed and compared to detailed cash flow forecasts for the period to the next balance sheet date (as a minimum) to confirm that there are no expected:

— shortfalls in facilities against requirements,

— arrears of interest,

— breaches of covenants.

Any potential difficulties should be discussed with the company's bankers, as this may prevent potential problems crystallising.

— Sensitivity analyses should be used on all critical assumptions and care should be taken to include all known cash outflows (e.g. loan repayments, payment of tax liabilities).

— The directors should consider the company's exposure to contingent liabilities such as:

   — legal proceedings,

   — guarantees and warranties,

   — product liability not covered by insurance,

   — environmental clean-up costs.

— The directors should assess the major aspects of the economic market in which the company operates and in particular assess for each main product:

   — the size and strength of the market,

   — the company's market share,

   — any economic, political or other factors that may cause the market to change.

— The directors should assess the company's exposure to financial risks such as fixed price contracts and movements in exchange rates.

— The directors should also assess the company's financial adaptability (i.e. its ability to alter the amount or timing of cash flows to respond to unexpected needs or opportunities) – this may help to mitigate some of the other factors referred to above.

Chapter 2   The ASB 'Statement of Principles for Financial Reporting'

INTRODUCTION AND OVERVIEW

Background

2.1   The publication in December 1999 of the final version of the ASB's 'Statement of Principles for Financial Reporting' represented the culmination of a lengthy project. The ASB began work on the development of a conceptual framework for financial reporting in the early 1990s and initially published drafts of individual chapters of the proposed Statement. Following this initial exposure period, revised versions of the chapters were combined into an Exposure Draft of the entire 'Statement of Principles', published in November 1995. This document attracted a considerable response, including a number of criticisms and misgivings about the proposed Statement. The ASB responded by publishing a revised Exposure Draft in March 1999 to clarify issues that it felt had not been well understood and to respond to the criticisms made. The revision also enabled the Board to take into account its practical experience of working with the draft principles in the development of recent accounting standards and the revision of existing standards.

Purpose of the Statement

2.2   The purpose of the 'Statement of Principles' is to set out the principles that the ASB believes should underlie the preparation and presentation of general purpose financial statements. The Statement is intended to provide a coherent frame of reference to be used by the Board in the development and review of accounting standards. The aim is to ensure that accounting standards are developed on a consistent basis (which has not always been the case in the past) and to reduce the need for fundamental issues to be debated in detail during the development process. It is also hoped that publication of the Statement will allow preparers, users and auditors of financial statements to gain a better understanding of the Board's approach to formulating accounting standards and that the document will help them in analysing new or emerging issues for which accounting standards have not yet been developed. At the time of publication, the ASB noted that the Statement may be reviewed from time to time in the light of experience and in response to developments in accounting thought. However, the increasing convergence of UK accounting standards with international accounting requirements means that much of the development work in respect of accounting standards is now undertaken by the International Accounting Standards Board (IASB) rather than the ASB (see 1.2 above) and the IASB's 'Framework for the Preparation and Presentation of Financial Statements' on which the ASB Statement was based is therefore likely to be of greater relevance in the future.

Status and scope

2.3   The document states unequivocally that it is not an accounting standard, does not have a status equivalent to that of an accounting standard and does not set out requirements on how financial statements should be prepared or presented. The Statement is intended to be relevant to the financial statements of profit-orientated reporting entities of all sizes, including relevant entities in the public sector. It is also expected to be broadly relevant to the financial statements of not-for-profit entities, although some of the principles may need to be re-expressed, or the emphasis changed, in order to be applicable to that sector (see 2.8 below). For the purposes of the Statement, financial information is categorised as follows:

(i)   special purpose financial reports: these are reports prepared by the entity at the behest of, and in the form specified by, persons with the authority to obtain information required to meet their needs (e.g. regulatory returns, tax returns, financial reports prepared for bankers);

(ii)   general purpose financial reports: these are reports prepared by the entity, but not in the form of a special report. They include:

●   general purpose financial statements, such as annual financial statements and the financial sections of interim reports, preliminary announcements and summary financial statements; and

●   other types of general purpose financial report, such as directors' reports, statements by the chairman, operating and financial reviews, historical summaries and letters to shareholders;

(iii)   other financial information: this is information that has not been prepared by the entity itself (e.g. analysts' reports, news articles).

The primary focus of the Statement is on general purpose financial statements intended to give a true and fair view of financial performance and financial position (or to be consistent with financial statements that give such a view). The scope of the Statement therefore includes preliminary announcements, interim reports and summary financial statements, although it notes that additional considerations may be relevant in the context of these statements.

True and fair view

2.4 The Statement emphasises that the concept of the true and fair view lies at the heart of financial reporting in the UK. Financial statements will not be true and fair unless the information that they provide is sufficient in quality and quantity to satisfy the reasonable expectations of users to whom they are addressed. Expectations inevitably change over time, and the ASB seeks to respond to, and to influence, these expectations through the development of accounting standards. The Statement does not define the meaning of true and fair, but it has the concept of the true and fair view at its foundation.

The standard-setting process

2.5 The ASB emphasises that the principles set out in the Statement are only one of the factors that are considered when setting or reviewing accounting standards. Other factors that are taken into account include:

(i)   legal requirements;

(ii) cost/benefit considerations;

(iii) industry-specific issues;

(iv) the desirability of evolutionary changes; and

(v)   implementation issues.

The relative importance of each will vary between accounting standards. As a result, accounting standards may occasionally adopt an approach that differs from that suggested by the principles. For instance, where there is an inconsistency between the principles and the law, an accounting standard will usually need to adopt an approach that is consistent with the law. However, the Board believes that as legal requirements, accounting techniques and markets evolve, it will be possible to reduce potential conflicts.

Relationship with existing accounting standards and company law

2.6 On a number of issues, the Statement goes beyond current accounting practice and, in some cases, may conflict with existing accounting standards. In this situation, the principles do not override the requirements of an accounting standard and compliance with the standard is still required. In some cases, the concepts set out in the Statement also go beyond the requirements of present companies' legislation. At the time that the Statement was published, this applied particularly in respect of the:

(i)   presentation of dividends in the accounts;

(ii)   treatment of realised and unrealised profits;

(iii)   measurement of current assets;

(iv)   identification of subsidiaries for consolidation purposes.

The principles set out in the Statement are intended to apply to the financial statements of all profit-orientated entities, rather than just to companies, and the ASB therefore felt that it was inappropriate for the Statement to be constrained by the current requirements of company law. The inconsistencies that do exist are not expected to cause significant difficulties in the setting of new accounting standards. In cases where the Statement requires a different approach to that set out in companies' legislation, the requirements of the law must prevail unless departure from these requirements is necessary for the accounts to give a true and fair view. Recent changes to company law have already resolved some of the original conflicts (see 2.65 to 2.69 below).

Structure of the Statement

2.7   The Statement considers the following issues in detail:

  (i)   the objective of financial statements;

 (ii)   the reporting entity;

(iii)   the qualitative characteristics of financial information;

(iv)   the elements of financial statements;

  (v)   recognition in financial statements;

(vi)   measurement in financial statements;

(vii)   presentation of financial information; and

(viii)   accounting for interests in other entities.

Each section sets out a summary of the relevant principles and then provides a more detailed explanation of the underlying issues.

Application to Public Benefit Entities

2.8   In May 2003, the ASB published a new Discussion Paper 'Statement of Principles for Financial Reporting: Proposed Interpretation for Public Benefit Entities'. The 'Statement of Principles for Financial Reporting' was written primarily with profit-oriented entities in mind, and some public benefit entities (which are defined as including charities and other not-for-profit organisations) have encountered difficulty in applying the principles and related accounting standards in certain areas. In many cases, the fundamentals of accounting are considered to be the same as for profit-oriented entities but the ASB acknowledges that re-expression of the principles is required in certain areas. Particular issues considered in the Discussion Paper include:

(i)   the definition of public benefit entities;

(ii) the defining class of user of the financial statements of public benefit entities;

(iii) the boundary of the reporting entity and in particular whether this can and should be based on control as in the case of profit-oriented entities;

(iv) the definition of assets where goods and services are provided free of charge, or on a substantially subsidised basis;

(v)   the recognition of commitments to provide public benefits;

(vi) whether controlling parties have a similar interest in a public benefit entity to that of owners in a profit-oriented entity;

(vii) at which point revenue should be recognised; and

(viii) accounting for combinations of public benefit entities.

The June 2005 edition of the ASB's Technical Plan for 2005 indicates that it intends to publish a revised 'Statement of Principles for Financial Reporting: Proposed Interpretation for Public Benefit Entities' as an Exposure Draft in the third quarter of 2005.

THE OBJECTIVE OF FINANCIAL STATEMENTS

Principles

2.9   The Statement sets out three principles on the objective of financial statements:

(i)   the objective of financial statements is to provide information about the reporting entity's financial performance and financial position that is useful to a wide range of users for assessing the stewardship of management and for making economic decisions;

(ii) that objective can usually be met by focusing exclusively on the information needs of present and potential investors, the defining class of user;

(iii) present and potential investors need information about the reporting entity's financial performance and financial position that is useful to them in evaluating the entity's ability to generate cash (including the timing and certainty of its generation) and in assessing the entity's financial adaptability.

Users of the accounts

2.10   Many different people are potentially interested in an entity's financial statements and for a variety of purposes. The Statement identifies the following and summarises the nature of their interest:

   (i)   present and potential investors;

  (ii)   lenders;

 (iii)   suppliers and other trade creditors;

 (iv)   employees;

  (v)   customers;

 (vi)   governments and their agencies;

(vii)   the public.

Although financial information about an entity may be needed for a variety of purposes, most of these purposes involve taking informed economic decisions (e.g. whether to hold or sell an investment, whether to lend to, or trade with, an entity) and there will be some overlap in the information required. The objective of general financial purpose reports is to focus on this common interest of users and to provide information about the financial performance and financial position of the entity as a whole that is useful to a wide range of users.

Limitations of financial statements

2.11   Financial statements do not seek to meet all information needs and users will usually need to supplement the details provided with information obtained from other sources. Also, there are a number of inherent limitations to financial statements, for example:

  (i)   they involve a substantial degree of classification and aggregation, and the allocation of the effects of continuous operations to discrete reporting periods;

 (ii)   they focus on the financial effects of transactions and events;

(iii)   they provide information that is largely historical.

As a result certain information needs to be provided in other general purpose financial reports (e.g. an operating and financial review) to put the numerical information into context. Notwithstanding these limitations, financial statements are the principal means of communicating accounting information to interested parties and are a central feature of general purpose financial reporting.

Financial performance

2.12   The financial performance of an entity is described as comprising the return it obtains on the resources it controls, the components of that return and the characteristics of those components. Information on financial performance is useful in assessing:

(i)   the stewardship of management and the past and anticipated performance of the entity;

(ii)   the entity's capacity to generate cash flows from its existing resource base; and

(iii) the effectiveness with which the entity has employed its resources and might employ additional resources.

It also provides feedback on previous assessments of financial performance and can therefore assist in developing expectations about future periods.

Financial position

2.13   An entity's financial position is defined as:

(i)   the economic resources that it controls;

(ii)   its financial structure;

(iii) its liquidity and solvency;

(iv) its risk profile and risk management approach; and

(v)   its capacity to adapt to changes in the environment in which it operates.

Information on financial position helps in the assessment of:

(i)   the stewardship of management and the entity's ability to generate cash flows in the future;

(ii)   how future cash flows will be distributed among those with an interest in or claims on the entity;

(iii) how successfully the entity has managed its resources;

(iv) the entity's requirements for future finance and its ability to raise that finance;

(v)   the entity's ability to meet its financial commitments as they fall due; and

(vi) the extent to which the entity is at risk, or able to benefit, from unexpected changes.

Generation and use of cash

2.14   Information on the ways in which an entity generates and uses cash in its operations, investment activities and financial activities (e.g. in the form of a cash flow statement) provides an additional perspective on financial performance. This information is largely free from allocation and valuation issues and is useful in assessing:

(i)   liquidity and solvency;

(ii)   the relationship between profits and cash flows;

(iii) the implications that financial performance has for future cash flows; and

(iv) other aspects of financial adaptability.

Financial adaptability

2.15   Financial adaptability is defined as the ability of the entity to take effective action to alter the amount and timing of cash flows so that it can respond to unexpected needs or opportunities. It includes the ability to:

(i)   raise new capital at short notice;

(ii)   repay capital or debt at short notice;

(iii)   obtain cash by selling assets without disrupting continuing operations; and

(iv)   achieve a rapid improvement in the net cash inflows generated by operations.

Financial adaptability can help an entity to mitigate risks, to survive in times of low or negative cash flows from operations and to take advantage of unexpected investment opportunities.

THE REPORTING ENTITY

Principles

2.16   Two principles are identified in this chapter of the Statement:

(i)   an entity should prepare and publish financial statements if there is a legitimate demand for the information that its financial statements would provide and it is a cohesive economic unit;

(ii)   the boundary of the reporting entity is determined by the scope of its control. For this purpose, first direct control and then direct plus indirect control are taken into account.

Control

2.17   Control is defined as the ability to deploy the economic resources involved and the ability to benefit (or suffer) from their deployment. An entity must have both of these abilities in order to have control. An entity has direct control of an asset if it has the ability in its own right to obtain the future economic benefits embodied in the asset and to restrict the access of others to those benefits. An entity has indirect control of an asset if it has control of an entity that directly controls the asset (e.g. a parent company has indirect control of the assets of its subsidiary). The Statement uses direct control to determine the boundary of a reporting entity preparing single entity financial statements, and direct plus indirect control to determine the boundary of a reporting entity preparing consolidated financial statements.

When does one entity control another?

2.18   An entity will have control of a second entity if it has the ability to direct the operating and financial policies of that entity, with a view to gaining economic benefit from its activities. Traditionally, control has involved share ownership and voting rights, but it can also be evidenced in a variety of other ways. Some forms of control do not involve investment. It is the relationship in practice that should be considered, rather than the theoretical level of influence. Factors to be taken into account might include:

(i)   powers of veto and reserve powers;

(ii)   predetermined operating and financial policies; and

(iii)   latent control.

The Statement notes that control needs to be distinguished from management. In particular, if an entity manages a second entity on behalf of another party, it is not exposed to the inherent benefits and risks of the second entity and therefore does not have control.

THE QUALITATIVE CHARACTERISTICS OF FINANCIAL INFORMATION

Principles

2.19   Nine principles are identified in this section of the Statement:

(i)   information provided by financial statements needs to be relevant and reliable and, if a choice exists between approaches that are both relevant and reliable but which are mutually exclusive, the approach chosen needs to be the one that results in the relevance of the information provided being maximised;

(ii)   information is relevant if it has the ability to influence the economic decisions of users and is provided in time to influence those decisions;

(iii)   information is reliable if:

- it can be depended upon by users to represent faithfully what it either purports to represent or could reasonably be expected to represent, and therefore reflects the substance of transactions and other events that have taken place;

- it is free from deliberate or systematic bias and material error, and is complete; and

- in its preparation under conditions of uncertainty a degree of caution has been applied in exercising the necessary judgements;

(iv)   information provided by financial statements needs to be comparable;

(v)   to aid comparability, information in financial statements should be prepared and presented in a way that enables users to discern and evaluate similarities in, and differences between, the nature and effects of transactions and other events over time and across different reporting entities;

(vi)   information needs to be understandable, although information should not be excluded from financial statements simply because it would not be understood by some users;

(vii)   information is understandable if its significance can be perceived by users with a reasonable knowledge of business and economic activities and accounting and a willingness to study the information provided with reasonable diligence;

(viii)   information that is material needs to be given in the financial statements, but information that is not material need not be provided;

(ix)   information is material to the financial statements if its misstatement or omission might reasonably be expected to influence the economic decisions of users.

Relevance

2.20   For information to be relevant, it must have the ability to influence the economic decisions of users of the accounts and must be provided in time to do so. It will have either:

(i)   predictive value, in that it helps a user to evaluate or assess past, present or future events and therefore predict future outcomes on the basis of this; or

(ii)   confirmatory value, in that it helps a user of the accounts to confirm or correct an evaluation or assessment that they made at some point in the past.

Some information will have both predictive and confirmatory value. The way in which financial information is presented can enhance its usefulness for making evaluations or assessments (e.g. the separate disclosure of unusual or infrequent gains and losses). The Statement notes that there are many perspectives from which an entity's financial performance and financial position could be viewed, but the most relevant perspective will usually be the one based on the assumption that the entity will continue in operational existence for the foreseeable future (i.e. the going concern basis).

Reliability

2.21   The section on reliability of financial information considers:

(i)   faithful representation;

(ii)   neutrality;

(iii)   completeness and accuracy; and

(iv)   prudence.

Faithful representation

2.22   It will often be possible to portray a transaction or event in the financial statements in a number of ways depending on:

(i)   how rights and obligations arise and the weight attached to each;

(ii)   how the rights and obligations to which most weight is attached are characterised; and

(iii)   which measurement bases and presentation techniques are used to depict the rights and obligations.

(iv)   the way in which elements arising from the transaction or event are presented in the financial statements.

A transaction or event is represented faithfully in the financial statements if it is recognised, measured and presented in a way that closely corresponds to its commercial effect. The substance of a transaction may differ from its legal form, and faithful representation of a transaction or event therefore involves:

(i)   identifying all rights and obligations;

(ii)   attaching greater weight to those most likely to have practical commercial effect; and

(iii)   accounting for the transaction or event in a way that reflects that commercial effect.

The transaction or event should be considered as a whole and the effect of any related transactions should also be taken into account. Similarly, a group or series of transactions will usually need to be considered as a whole in order to assess the overall effect and to account for its substance.

Neutrality, completeness and accuracy

2.23   Information provided by financial statements should be neutral in the sense that it should be free from deliberate or systematic bias. It will not be neutral if it has been selected or presented in a way that is designed to influence the making of a decision or judgement. Information should also be complete and free from error within the bounds of materiality. Information containing a material error or omitted from financial statements other than on the grounds of materiality might cause the financial statements to be false or misleading.

Prudence

2.24   Prudence is defined as 'the inclusion of a degree of caution in the exercise of the judgments needed in making the estimates required under conditions of uncertainty, such that gains or assets are not overstated and losses or liabilities are not understated.' The Statement goes on to emphasise that it is not appropriate to use the need for prudence as a reason for creating hidden reserves or excessive provisions, or for deliberately understating assets and gains, or overstating liabilities and losses. Similarly, it is not necessary to exercise prudence when there is no uncertainty. The uncertainty that inevitably surrounds many events or circumstances reported in financial statements should be dealt with by disclosing the nature and extent of the uncertainty as well as by exercising an appropriate degree of prudence.

Comparability

2.25   Comparability is essential to enable users to identify trends over a period of time and to relate the financial performance and position of an entity to those of other entities. Comparability can usually be achieved through a combination of:

(i)   consistency – information should be consistent within each accounting period, between accounting periods and between entities; and

(ii)   disclosure of the accounting policies adopted, any changes in those policies and the effect of any such changes.

However, consistency is not an end in itself and the need for consistency should not prevent the introduction of improved accounting practices (e.g. a change to a more appropriate accounting policy).

Understandability

2.26   Whether financial information is understandable will usually depend on:

(i)   the way in which the details are aggregated, classified and reported;

(ii)   the way in which information is presented; and

(iii)   the capabilities of users.

Preparers of accounts are entitled to assume that users have a reasonable knowledge of business and economic activities and of accounting, and that they are willing to study the information provided with reasonable diligence.

Materiality

2.27   Materiality is described as a threshold quality that is demanded of all information given in financial statements and the final judgement of what information should be provided. Information is material if its misstatement or omission might reasonably be expected to influence the economic decisions of users, including their assessments of management's stewardship. Information that is immaterial should not be presented in financial statements as its inclusion could obscure and impair understanding of other material information. The materiality of a particular item of information will usually depend on its size and nature. The principal factors to be taken into account will usually include:

(i)   its size in the context of the financial statements as a whole and of the other information available to users (e.g. how the item might affect the evaluation of trends);

(ii)   the transaction or event giving rise to it;

(iii) the legality, sensitivity, normality and potential consequences of the transaction or event;

(iv)   the identity of the parties involved; and

(v)   the individual headings and disclosures affected.

The materiality of two or more similar items should be assessed in aggregate as well as individually.

Conflicts between qualitative characteristics

2.28   Conflicts may occasionally arise between the characteristics of relevance, reliability, comparability and understandability. For instance, when measuring an asset the most relevant information may not be the most reliable. The Statement notes that in these circumstances it will usually be appropriate to identify reliable information and then use the most relevant of the reliable options identified. Timeliness of information may also be an issue, in that delays to achieve reliability may result in the information being less relevant, and reporting before uncertainties are resolved may result in the information being unreliable. The guidance notes that although information should generally be made available as soon as possible, it should not be provided until it is reliable.

THE ELEMENTS OF FINANCIAL STATEMENTS

Principles

2.29   Eight principles are identified in this chapter of the Statement:

(i)   the elements of financial statements are:

- assets;
- liabilities;
- ownership interest;
- gains;
- losses;
- contributions from owners; and
- distributions to owners;

(ii)   assets are rights or other access to future economic benefits controlled by the entity as a result of past transactions or events;

(iii) liabilities are obligations of the entity to transfer economic benefits as a result of past transactions or events;

(iv) ownership interest is the residual amount after deducting all of the entity's liabilities from all of its assets;

(v) gains are increases in ownership interest not resulting from contributions from owners;

(vi) losses are decreases in ownership interest not resulting from distributions to owners;

(vii) contributions from owners are increases in ownership interest resulting from transfers from owners in their capacity as owners; and

(viii) distributions to owners are decreases in ownership interest resulting from transfers to owners in their capacity as owners (e.g. payment of a dividend, return of capital).

The preparation of financial statements inevitably involves a high degree of classification and aggregation of the effects of transactions and events. This must be carried out in an orderly manner and with a consistent approach. The Statement notes that an orderly process is created by specifying and defining the elements of financial statements that encapsulate the key aspects of the effects of transactions and events.

Assets

2.30 Assets are defined in the Statement as 'rights or other access to future economic benefits controlled by an entity as a result of past transactions or events'. An asset, therefore, is not an item of property but control of the rights and economic benefits that derive from it. An asset may be acquired in a variety of ways, including:

 (i) legal ownership of the underlying item of property;

 (ii) by leasing the underlying item of property; or

(iii) through a patent or trade mark.

An asset can also exist without any legal rights, as in the case of an unpatented invention. An entity may also derive economic benefits from factors such as its market share, management ability or good labour relations. However, these are not recognised as assets because the entity cannot choose if and when to realise these economic benefits and it therefore does not have control of the items as defined in the Statement.

Future economic benefits

2.31 The Statement identifies the capacity to obtain future economic benefits as the essence of an asset and the element that is common to all assets, whatever their form. There will often be some uncertainty over the extent to which the expected future economic benefits will be obtained, and in some cases this may result in the asset not being recognised. Future economic benefits will eventually result in net cash inflows to the entity, and assets include any rights and other benefits that can be used to generate future cash flows. They also include items that represent the right to exchange property on terms that will or may be favourable (e.g. an option to acquire an asset).

Control

2.32   The definition of an asset requires the rights or other access to future economic benefits to be controlled by the reporting entity. Control does not need to be legally enforceable and is defined in the Statement as 'the ability both to obtain for itself any economic benefits that will arise and to prevent or limit the access of others to those benefits'. This definition means that no item should be treated as an asset of more than one entity, although a single item may give rise to assets of more than one entity. Where two entities control rights to different future economic benefits from the same item of property, each will have an asset but they will not be the same asset (e.g. a leased property may be recognised as an asset in the accounts of both the lessee and the lessor, but each will represent different future economic benefits).

Past transactions or events

2.33   An asset arises where an entity derives control over future economic benefits from a past transaction or event. The Statement notes that where an entity has access to future economic benefits at the balance sheet date, but is not able to restrict the access of others to those benefits until after that date, the entity does not have control, and consequently does not have an asset, at the balance sheet date.

Liabilities

2.34   Liabilities are defined in the Statement as 'obligations of an entity to transfer economic benefits as a result of past transactions or events'. An obligation may be either legal or constructive and implies that the entity is not free to avoid the outflow of resources. A decision to transfer economic benefits will not necessarily create an obligation because the transfer of benefits can be avoided by changing the decision. However, such a decision will create a constructive obligation if it is coupled with an event that creates a valid expectation that the decision will be implemented and means that the entity cannot realistically withdraw from it. A constructive obligation can also be created by an established pattern of past practice. It is not necessary for the amount of the transfer of economic benefits to be known with certainty, or for it to be certain that the obligation will result in a transfer of future economic benefits (e.g. a guarantee creates a liability, even though this may not be recognised in the financial statements). In some cases, it may be necessary for a series of events to take place before an obligation to transfer economic benefits arises – whether a liability exists in these circumstances will depend on whether any of the events yet to take place are under the entity's control (i.e. whether the entity is in a position to avoid the transfer of future economic benefits). In October 2002, the ASB published a document entitled 'Liabilities and how to account for them: An exploratory essay'. This paper is intended as a contribution to conceptual thinking on accounting issues, particularly as there are currently differences in the definitions of liabilities used by different standard-setters. It includes the following sections:

(i)   contractual obligations and the value to the business model;

(ii)   a selection of liabilities;

(iii) the definition of liabilities and its implications for measurement;

(iv)   the objective of financial statements and users' needs; and

(v)   concluding comments

The paper can be downloaded from the ASB website at http://www.frc.org.uk/asb/publications/other.cfm.

Offset of rights and obligations

2.35   A transaction or event will sometimes give rise to a number of rights and obligations and this may raise the following issues on offsetting:

(i)   whether the rights and obligations represent separate assets and liabilities, or whether some or all of them should be aggregated or offset;

(ii)   whether the rights and obligations should be combined and recognised as a single asset or liability – the Statement does not envisage any circumstances when this treatment will be appropriate;

(iii) whether it is appropriate to present assets offset against liabilities (or vice versa) in the balance sheet.

The Statement concludes that where an entity has both a right to receive future economic benefits and an obligation to transfer future economic benefits, and has an assured ability to insist on net settlement of the balances, the right and the obligation together form a single asset or liability, regardless of how the balance will be settled in practice. The Statement also considers in more detail the position in the case of unperformed contracts and partially performed executory contracts.

Ownership interest

2.36   The distinction between liabilities and ownership interest is very significant: owners have a residual interest in the entity but do not have the ability to insist on a transfer of economic benefits (e.g. the payment of a dividend or the return of capital).

RECOGNITION IN FINANCIAL STATEMENTS

Principles

2.37   Three principles are identified in this chapter of the Statement:

(i)   if a transaction or event has created a new asset or liability or added to an existing asset or liability, the effect should be recognised if:

- there is sufficient evidence that the new asset or liability has been created, or that there has been an addition to an existing asset or liability; and

- the new asset or liability, or addition to an existing asset or liability, can be measured at a monetary amount with sufficient reliability;

(ii)   where the transaction involves the provision of services or goods for a net gain, the above recognition criteria will be met on the occurrence of the critical event in the operating cycle involved; and

(iii)   an asset or liability should be wholly or partly derecognised if:

- there is sufficient evidence that the transaction or other past event has eliminated all or part of a previously recognised asset or liability; or

- although the item continues to be an asset or liability, the recognition criteria are no longer met.

Recognition process

2.38   The Statement identifies the following stages in the recognition process:

(i)   initial recognition – where an item is depicted in the financial statements for the first time;

(ii)   subsequent remeasurement – where the amount of an existing asset or liability is changed in the financial statements; and

(iii)   derecognition – where an existing item ceases to be recognised.

All events that may have an effect on elements of the financial statements should be identified and reflected in an appropriate manner in the financial statements. Most changes will result from transactions, but changes may also arise from other events such as discovery, innovation, an event that causes damage to an asset (e.g. fire) and the elapse of time.

Effect of transactions and other events

2.39   Transactions and other events may have one of several effects on the assets and liabilities of a reporting entity:

(i)   the creation of a new asset or liability (which may or may not be recognised);

(ii) an addition to an existing asset or liability (which may or may not be recognised);

(iii) new or additional evidence about an existing asset or liability that might result in a previously unrecognised item being recognised;

(iv) a change in the nature of the item which may require a change in the description or classification of the item in the financial statements, and possibly a change in the amount at which it is stated (e.g. raw material converted to finished goods, convertible debt converted into equity shares);

(v) a change to the flow of benefits associated with a recognised asset or liability which may require a change in the amount at which it is stated (e.g. a change in the market value of a property, doubts over the recoverability of a debtor);

(vi) transferring, using up or consuming an asset, or part of an asset, which may require derecognition of the asset, in whole or in part;

(vii) settling, extinguishing or transferring a liability or part of a liability, which may require derecognition of the liability, in whole or in part.

The guidance notes that the definitions of assets and liabilities should ensure that transactions and other events are reflected in the financial statements in the period in which they occur, and not in the period in which any related cash is paid or received. In other words, transactions and events will be accounted for under the accruals concept.

Uncertainty

2.40   The Statement emphasises that entities operate in an uncertain environment and this uncertainty may sometimes result in a delay in the recognition process. Financial statements should seek to achieve a balance between reliability and relevance by:

(i) providing information that has no more than an acceptable degree of uncertainty; and

(ii) not trying to provide information that is totally free from uncertainty.

Where it is not possible to reduce uncertainty to an acceptable level, the recognition process will be deferred until the uncertainty reaches such a level. Disclosure of the transaction or event may still be needed in the notes to the financial statements, even though no asset or liability is recognised.

Initial recognition of assets and liabilities

2.41   The Statement identifies two broad categories of uncertainty that may arise in the initial recognition process:

(i) element uncertainty – uncertainty over whether an item exists and meets the definitions of the elements of the financial statements; and

(ii)   measurement uncertainty – uncertainty over the monetary amount at which the item should be recognised.

In order to recognise an item, it is necessary to have sufficient evidence (in both amount and quality) that the item exists and is an asset or liability of the reporting entity. This will be a matter of judgement in each case. The guidance notes that the evidence should be adequate but need not (and often cannot) be conclusive, and that it might include:

(i)   evidence provided by the event giving rise to the possible asset or liability;

(ii)   past experience with similar items;

(iii) current information relating to the possible asset or liability; and

(iv)   evidence provided by transactions of other entities in similar assets and liabilities.

Attributing a monetary amount to an item involves selecting a suitable measurement basis and then determining an appropriate monetary amount under that basis.

Prudence in the context of recognition

2.42   In the context of the recognition principles, the guidance notes that prudence requires more confirmatory evidence of the existence of an asset or gain than of a liability or loss, and greater reliability of measurement for assets and gains than for liabilities and losses. However, the application of prudence does not justify:

(i)   the omission of assets or gains when there is sufficient evidence that they exist and can be measured reliably;

(ii)   the inclusion of liabilities and losses when there is insufficient evidence that they exist and can be measured reliably; or

(iii) any other deliberate and systematic understatement of assets or gains, or overstatement of liabilities and losses.

Derecognition of assets and liabilities

2.43   The guidance notes that it is usually relatively straightforward to determine when a previously recognised asset or liability needs to be derecognised. Difficulties are most likely to arise where transactions leave intact certain of the rights to future economic benefits that are inherent in an asset, or certain of the obligations inherent in a liability, but eliminate others. This may result in partial derecognition of the asset or liability, or the derecognition of the existing asset or liability and recognition of a new asset or liability.

Matching

2.44   The guidance identifies two elements to matching:

(i)   time matching – where expenditure directly associated with the passage of
        time is recognised as a loss on a systematic basis over the period involved; and

(ii)   revenue/expenditure matching – where expenditure directly associated with
        the generation of specific gains is recognised as a loss in the same period as
        the gains are recognised, rather than in the period in which the expenditure is
        incurred.

The Statement does not treat matching as the main driver of the recognition
process, noting that an unrestricted use of matching would make it possible to delay
the recognition of most expenditure in the performance statement, on the basis that
it was undertaken to achieve future benefits. Instead, it allows matching to provide a
framework for determining how the cost of an asset should be allocated across
accounting periods in the performance statement. This approach should ensure that:

(i)   expenditure that cannot justifiably be shown to be associated with the control
        of rights or access to future economic benefits will be recognised as a loss in
        the performance statement in the period in which it is incurred; and

(ii)   expenditure incurred in the hope of achieving future economic benefits, but
        where the relationship with the benefits is too uncertain to permit recognition
        of an asset, will be recognised immediately as a loss.

Critical events in the operating cycle

2.45   The second recognition principle requires gains arising from the provision
of goods and services to be recognised on the occurrence of the critical event in the
operating cycle. At this point there will usually be sufficient evidence that the gain
exists, and it will be possible to measure the gain with sufficient reliability. The
guidance notes that, in many cases, the critical event will be synonymous with full
performance, but this will not always be the case, and in some instances there may
be more than one critical event in the operating cycle. It gives the following
examples:

(i)   if the entity has carried out all its obligations other than a few minor acts of
        performance, the critical event will have occurred;

(ii)   if a sale is contingent on acceptance by the buyer, the critical event will not
        have occurred if the likelihood of non-acceptance is significant; and

(iii)   where the operating cycle involves a series of significant acts of performance
        over a period of time (e.g. a large building contract), these should be viewed
        as a series of critical events, with the gain expected on the contract as a whole
        allocated among the critical events.

MEASUREMENT IN FINANCIAL STATEMENTS

Principles

2.46   Four principles are set out in this chapter of the Statement:

(i)   when preparing financial statements, a measurement basis (either historical cost or current value) needs to be selected for each category of assets and liabilities – this should be the basis that best meets the objective of financial statements and the demands of the qualitative characteristics of financial information, taking into account the nature of the items concerned and the circumstances involved;

(ii)   an asset or liability being measured on the historical cost basis should be recognised initially at transaction cost, and an asset or liability being measured using the current value basis should be recognised initially at its current value at the time that it was acquired or assumed;

(iii)   subsequent remeasurement may be necessary to ensure that:

- assets measured at historical cost are carried at the lower of cost and recoverable amount;

- monetary items denominated in a foreign currency are carried at amounts based on up-to-date exchange rates; and

- assets and liabilities measured on the current value basis are carried at up-to-date values;

(iv)   such remeasurements should only be recognised if:

- there is sufficient evidence that the monetary amount of the asset or liability has changed; and

- the new amount of the asset or liability can be measured with sufficient reliability.

Measurement bases

2.47   The guidance notes that measurement bases can be used in several ways:

(i)   all assets and liabilities can be measured using historical cost;

(ii)   all assets and liabilities can be measured using current value; or

(iii)   some categories of assets and liabilities can be measured using historical cost and some using current value – this is described as a mixed measurement system.

A further possibility, that assets or liabilities are measured at current value and then retained at that amount for a long period of time, is rejected on the grounds that it fails to achieve comparability and consistency. The Statement envisages that a mixed measurement system will usually be adopted. The guidance notes that, if only one measurement basis is reliable, that basis should be used provided that it is also relevant. If both the historical cost and current value measures are reliable, the choice will depend on which is the most relevant. A measure derived from a generally accepted valuation methodology and supported by a reasonable amount of confirmatory evidence will usually constitute a sufficiently reliable measure.

Determining current value – assets

2.48   The guidance notes that the current value of an asset might be determined by reference to:

(i)   replacement cost;

(ii)   net realisable value; or

(iii)   value in use.

For some assets (e.g. listed investments), these three measures will usually produce similar amounts, but for other assets they may be significantly different. The most relevant measure should be selected using the value to the business (or deprival value) rule – that the current value of an asset is the loss that the entity would suffer if it were deprived of it. The following examples are given:

(i)   where an asset is being put to profitable use, its recoverable amount will exceed its replacement cost – if deprived of the asset, the entity would replace it and current value will therefore be replacement cost;

(ii)   an entity will not replace an asset if the cost of replacing it exceeds its value in its most profitable use – in this case the asset's current value is its recoverable amount measured as follows:

- when the most profitable use of the asset is to sell it, recoverable amount will be net realisable value;

- when the most profitable use of the asset is to consume it (i.e. by continuing to use it), recoverable amount will be value in use.

Determining current value – liabilities

2.49   In the case of a liability, current value is usually taken to be the lowest amount at which the entity could divest itself of the obligation involved (i.e. the lowest amount at which the entity could hypothetically settle the obligation).

Measurement on initial recognition

2.50   Regardless of the measurement basis being used, assets and liabilities arising from transactions carried out at fair value will be measured on initial recognition at transaction cost, because the fair value of the consideration paid or received will be equal to both the fair value of the asset or liability acquired and its current value at the time of acquisition. The guidance notes that, in the absence of any evidence to the contrary, it can usually be assumed that a transaction has been carried out at fair value. Where an asset or liability arises as a result of a transaction that is not carried out at fair value, it will usually be more appropriate to measure the asset or liability at current value.

Subsequent remeasurement

2.51 Remeasurements should only be recognised if there is sufficient evidence that the amount of the asset or liability has changed and the new amount can be measured with sufficient reliability. The guidance notes that what constitutes sufficient evidence will be a matter of judgement, taking into account the persuasiveness of the evidence and whether the change implies that a gain or loss has occurred. It emphasises that evidence should be adequate but need not (and usually cannot) be conclusive. A primary source of evidence will be past or present experience with the individual item or similar items, including:

(i)   current information relating directly to the asset or liability;

(ii) other entities' transactions in similar assets and liabilities – the persuasiveness of this evidence will usually depend on the frequency of transactions and the similarity of the items;

(iii) past experience with similar assets and liabilities.

Discounting

2.52 The guidance notes that historical cost and replacement cost are market prices and will therefore reflect factors such as the time value of money and the risk associated with future expected cash flows. To be consistent, these factors should also be reflected in other measures used to determine the carrying amounts of assets and liabilities when these are calculated by reference to expected future cash flows. In other words, the future cash flows should be discounted. The discount rate should reflect the risks associated with the future cash flows (unless they have already been risk-adjusted) and the time value of money – in other words, it should reflect the risks specific to the item being measured rather than the more general risks of the entity as a whole.

Dealing with uncertainty

2.53 There will often be some degree of uncertainty about the appropriate monetary amount of an asset or liability. In these circumstances, the only way to determine the appropriate amount is through the use of estimates. This is acceptable provided that:

(i)   a generally accepted estimation method is used; and

(ii) the measure is supported by a reasonable amount of confirmatory evidence.

Where the monetary amount of an asset or liability is subject to significant uncertainty, the degree of uncertainty should usually be disclosed to avoid the impression that the outcome is certain. Disclosure might include:

(i)   the significant assumptions and measurement basis used;

(ii)   the range of possible outcomes; and

(iii)   the principal factors affecting the outcome.

Capital maintenance and changing prices

2.54   Under the approach described in the Statement, the surplus of gains over losses in a period represents the return on capital for that period. There is no actual return of capital and therefore no adjustment is needed to ensure that capital is being maintained. The Statement notes that this approach may not be satisfactory when general or specific price changes are significant, and gives the following guidance:

(i)   general price changes can affect the significance of reported profits and ownership interest – it may be necessary to adopt an approach that involves recognising profit only after adjustments have been made to maintain the purchasing power of the entity's financial capital;

(ii)   specific price increases can affect the significance of reported profits and financial position – it may be necessary to adopt a system of accounting that informs the user of the significance of specific price changes for the entity's financial performance and financial position.

PRESENTATION OF FINANCIAL INFORMATION

Principles

2.55   The Statement summarises the objective of presentation as being 'to communicate clearly and effectively and in as simple and straightforward a manner as possible, without loss of relevance or reliability and without unnecessarily increasing the length of the financial statements'. Five principles are identified in relation to the presentation of financial information:

(i)   financial statements comprise primary financial statements and supporting notes that amplify and explain the primary statements – the primary statements comprise:

- the statement of financial performance;

- the statement of financial position (or balance sheet); and

- the cash flow statement;

(ii)   the presentation of information on financial performance focuses on the components of financial performance and their characteristics;

(iii)   the presentation of information on financial position focuses on the types and functions of the assets and liabilities held and the relationship between them;

(iv) the presentation of cash flow information shows the extent to which the entity's various activities generate and use cash, distinguishing in particular between cash flows resulting from operations and those resulting from other activities;

(v) disclosure of information in the notes to the financial statements is not a substitute for recognition and does not correct or justify any misrepresentation or omission in the primary financial statements.

Structure of financial statements

2.56 The presentation of financial information inevitably involves a high degree of interpretation, simplification, abstraction and aggregation. If this process is carried out in an orderly manner, it can result in a presentation which:

(i) conveys information that might otherwise have been obscured;

(ii) highlights items, and relationships between items, that are of most significance;

(iii) facilitates comparison with other entities; and

(iv) is more understandable to users.

The primary financial statements and the notes to those statements should form an integrated whole. The notes should amplify and explain the primary statements by:

(i) providing more detailed information on items recognised in the primary statements – setting this information out in the notes avoids obscuring the message of the primary statements;

(ii) giving an alternative view of items recognised in the primary statements – for instance, by providing details of the range of outcomes for a disputed item; and

(iii) setting out relevant information that it is not practical to incorporate into the primary statements.

The notes to the financial statements are also used to provide segmental information, whilst the primary statements usually focus on the entity as a whole.

Classification

2.57 The guidance notes that similar items should be presented together and distinguished from dissimilar items to facilitate analysis of the information and consideration of the relationships between different items. For instance, different types of current asset are usually shown next to each other and current liabilities are usually presented in a way that highlights their relationship to current assets.

Statement of financial performance

2.58   The guidance notes that the various components of financial performance have different characteristics in terms of nature, cause, function, continuity or recurrence, stability, risk, predictability and reliability. Good presentation enables attention to be focused on these components and their characteristics and typically includes:

(i)   recognising only gains and losses in the financial performance statement;

(ii)   classifying components according to a combination of function (e.g. production, selling, administration) and nature (e.g. employment costs, interest payable);

(iii)   distinguishing any amounts that are affected in different ways by changes in economic conditions or business activities (e.g. the separate disclosure of income from continuing, and discontinued operations); and

(iv)   showing separately:

●   any items that are unusual in amount or incidence;

●   items with special characteristics (e.g. financing costs, taxation); and

●   items related primarily to the profits of future accounting periods (e.g. research and development expenditure).

Gains and losses should not normally be offset in the financial performance statement. The only exception to this is where they relate to the same event or circumstance and disclosing the gross components is not likely to provide useful information for the assessment of either future results or the effects of past transactions and events.

Statement of financial position

2.59   Good balance sheet presentation typically involves:

(i)   recognising only assets, liabilities and ownership interest in the balance sheet;

(ii)   highlighting the entity's resource structure (major classes and amounts of assets) and financial structure (major classes and amounts of liabilities and ownership interest) – the result should help users to assess:

●   the nature, amounts and liquidity of available resources; and

●   the nature, amounts and timing of obligations that require, or may require, liquid resources for settlement;

(iii)   distinguishing assets by function – for instance, by separating assets held for sale from those held for use in the business on a continuing basis.

Assets and liabilities should not be offset when reporting on an entity's financial position.

Accompanying information

2.60   Financial statements are often accompanied, and complemented, by additional information, for instance five-year historical summaries, operating and financial reviews, directors' reports and statements by the chairman. The Statement notes that this type of accompanying information will usually provide:

(i)   narrative disclosures describing and explaining the entity's activities;

(ii)   historical summaries and information on trends;

(iii)   non-accounting or non-financial information; and

(iv)   evolutionary or experimental disclosures.

Accompanying information should always be consistent with the financial statements. The inclusion of an objective and comprehensive analysis of the main features underlying financial performance and financial position becomes particularly important in the case of more complex entities. The guidance notes that disclosures will usually be most useful if they discuss:

(i)   the principal risks, uncertainties and trends in each of the main business areas and how the entity is responding to them;

(ii)   its strategies on capital structure and treasury policy; and

(iii)   activities and expenditure during the period that is regarded as a form of investment for the future.

Highlights and summary indicators

2.61   Amounts, ratios and other computations are sometimes included in financial statements and accompanying information in an attempt to distil key information about financial performance and financial position. The guidance emphasises that these indicators, on their own, cannot adequately describe financial performance or financial position and do not provide a basis for meaningful analysis or prudent decision-making. Where such information is presented, care is needed to ensure that its importance is not exaggerated. However, the guidance acknowledges that the inclusion of summary indicators may be helpful:

(i)   for users who require only very basic information; and

(ii)   to highlight features that users may wish to analyse in more detail.

ACCOUNTING FOR INTERESTS IN OTHER ENTITIES

Principles

2.62   Six principles are identified in this chapter of the Statement:

(i)   single entity financial statements and consolidated financial statements present from different perspectives the interests that the reporting entity may have in other entities;

(ii)   in single entity financial statements, interests in other entities are dealt with by focusing on the income and (depending on the measurement basis adopted) the capital growth arising in the interest;

(iii) in consolidated financial statements, the way in which interests in other entities are dealt with depends on the degree of influence involved:

- an interest that involves control of another entity's operating and financial policies is dealt with by incorporating the controlled entity as part of the reporting entity:

- an interest that involves joint control of, or significant influence over, another entity's operating and financial policies is dealt with by recognising the reporting entity's share of the other entity's results and resources in a way that does not involve showing them as if they were controlled by the reporting entity;

- other interests in other entities are dealt with in the same way as other assets;

(iv)   consolidated financial statements are prepared from the perspective of the shareholders of the parent entity;

(v)   consolidated financial statements reflect the whole of the parent's investment in its subsidiaries, including purchased goodwill;

(vi)   a transaction involving the amalgamation of two or more reporting entities is reflected in the consolidated financial statements in accordance with its character:

- an acquisition is reflected as if the acquirer purchased the acquiree's assets and liabilities as a bundle of assets and liabilities on the open market;

- a merger is reflected as if a new reporting entity has been formed, comprising all the parties to the transaction.

Degree of influence

2.63   The Statement notes that the highest degree of influence that an investor can have over an investee is control. Control has two aspects:

(i)   the ability to deploy the economic resources involved; and

(ii)   the ability to benefit (or to suffer) as a result of their deployment.

Ownership of shares and voting rights is usually the main basis of influence. However, level of ownership is not by itself sufficient to define the relationship or degree of influence of the investor over the investee, because this may be affected by other agreements, arrangements or working practices Any mixture of share ownership, voting rights or agreements (either formal or informal) can provide a means of influencing or controlling another entity. The Statement defines the following categories of control:

(i)   control – the investor controls the investee;

(ii)   joint control – the investor shares control of the investee jointly with others through some form of arrangement;

(iii)   significant influence – the investor has neither control nor joint control, but exerts a degree of influence over the investee's operating and financial policies that is at least significant and at most just short of joint control;

(iv)   lesser or no influence – any control that the investor has over the operating and financial policies of the investee is less than significant.

Reflecting interests involving control

2.64   Consolidated financial statements are prepared by aggregating the assets, liabilities, gains, losses and cash flows of the parent and its subsidiaries. These items are included in full in the consolidated financial statements, even if the subsidiary is not wholly-owned. This reflects the parent's ability, through its control, to deploy both its own economic resources and those of its subsidiaries. The effect of any outside equity interest (the minority interest) on benefit flows must be separately identified in the consolidated financial statements.

POTENTIAL CONFLICTS WITH COMPANY LAW

Presentation of dividends

2.65   Under the principles set out in the Statement, dividends are distributions to owners and should therefore be reported in the reconciliation of movements in shareholders' funds and not in the financial performance statement. This represented a conflict with company law when the ASB Statement was published, because the Companies Act 1985 required dividends to be reported in the profit and loss account. However, for accounting periods beginning on or after 1 January 2005, the law has been amended by the *Companies Act 1985* (*International Accounting Standards and Other Accounting Amendments*) *Regulations 2004* (SI 2004/2947) to remove this requirement. This allows dividends to be accounted for as transactions with shareholders rather than as profit and loss account items and will enable companies to comply with the presentation requirements of FRS 25 'Financial Instruments: Disclosure and Presentation' which also come into effect for accounting periods beginning on or after 1 January 2005.

Accounting for proposed dividends

2.66   A proposed dividend does not meet the definition of a liability set out in the Statement as it does not represent an obligation at the balance sheet date to transfer economic benefits. The company is not obliged to pay the dividend until it has been formally approved by the shareholders. This also represented a conflict with company law when the ASB Statement was published, because the Companies Act 1985 effectively required proposed dividends to be recognised as liabilities in the accounts. However, for accounting periods beginning on or after 1 January 2005, this conflict has also been removed by the *Companies Act 1985 (International Accounting Standards and Other Accounting Amendments) Regulations 2004* (SI 2004/2947). From this date, the legislation simply requires any proposed dividends which do not represent a genuine liability at the balance sheet date to be disclosed in the notes to the accounts.

Unrealised gains and losses

2.67   Under the *Companies Act 1985*, only those profits that have been realised at the balance sheet date can be included in the profit and loss account. The Statement makes no reference to realised or unrealised gains. Instead, it adopts the approach of restricting the recognition of gains to those that exist and can be measured with sufficient reliability. Appendix 1 to the Statement notes that, although there is clearly a difference in approach, the exact effect of this difference is not clear, particularly as the definition of realised profits in the Act allows the precise meaning of the term to develop over time.

Measurement of current assets

2.68   Although the *Companies Act 1985* allows certain assets to be included in the accounts at current cost or market value under the alternative accounting rules, or fair value under the fair value accounting rules, it requires most current assets to be included in the accounts at the lower of cost and net realisable value. The Statement suggests that, if current value is considered to be the most appropriate measurement basis for a category of assets, all assets in that category should be recognised at current value. This would not be permitted under the Act for certain current assets. Also, as the Act refers only to current cost and market value, some of the current value measures set out in the Statement would not be permitted under present legislation.

Identification of subsidiaries for consolidation purposes

2.69   Both the *Companies Act 1985* and the Statement provide for the inclusion of subsidiaries in consolidated financial statements on the basis of the control that the parent is able to exercise. However, the definition of control in the Statement is not wholly consistent with that currently set out in the legislation. Consequently, the entities that are identified as subsidiaries under the Act may not always correspond to those identified as subsidiaries under the Statement.

Chapter 3   The True and Fair View

COMPANY LAW

Company law requirements

3.1   Where Companies Act accounts are prepared, CA 1985 requires the balance sheet to give a true and fair view of the state of affairs of the company at the end of the financial period and the profit and loss account to give a true and fair view of the profit or loss of the company for the financial period. There can be no precise definition of what constitutes a true and fair view. This is essentially a question of judgement and, as a legal concept, it can only be interpreted by the court, although such an interpretation will usually be governed by generally accepted accounting practice and the requirements of accounting standards in particular. The true and fair view is a dynamic concept and the interpretation of it will vary over time, as a result of developments in accounting practice and the introduction of new accounting standards, many of which come about as a result of changes in business practice and general economic development. An accounting treatment that was accepted as achieving a true and fair view ten years ago will not necessarily be acceptable today. The ASB 'Statement of Principles for Financial Reporting' emphasises that the true and fair view lies at the heart of financial reporting in the UK and that, in order to give a true and fair view, financial statements must present information that is sufficient in both quantity and quality to satisfy the reasonable expectations of users.

Small companies

3.2   The requirement for the accounts to give a true and fair view of the state of affairs of the company and of its profit or loss for the period, applies to all companies, irrespective of their size. The true and fair requirement therefore continues to apply in the case of shorter form accounts prepared by a small company. Shorter form and abbreviated accounts for small companies are considered in more detail in Chapter 8. Small companies can choose to adopt the *Financial Reporting Standard for Smaller Entities* (FRSSE) in which case they need not follow the requirements of other accounting standards. The detailed requirements of the FRSSE in respect of the true and fair view and disclosure of the use of the true and fair override are also considered in Chapter 8. If the FRSSE is not adopted, the requirements of all other accounting standards apply to the accounts of a small company.

Overriding requirement for accounts to give a true and fair view

3.3   Under CA 1985, the requirement for accounts to give a true and fair view is of paramount importance and *s 226* (ie now s 226A) therefore provides for those situations where following the detailed requirements set out in the Act does not achieve this:

(i)   if the requirements of the Act are not sufficient for the accounts to show a true and fair view of the company's results or financial position, the additional information necessary to achieve this should be given in the accounts, or in a note to the accounts;

(ii)   if compliance with the requirements of CA 1985 is inconsistent with the overriding requirement for the accounts to show a true and fair view, the directors must depart from the provisions of the Act and the following must be given in a note to the accounts:

— particulars of the departure;

— the reasons for the departure; and

— the effect of the departure.

Departure from the requirements of the Act

3.4   A departure from the requirements of the Act can arise in two ways:

— some accounting standards require departure from certain provisions of the Act for the accounts to show a true and fair view – examples include:

— the non-depreciation of investment property under SSAP 19 'Accounting for Investment Properties';

— the treatment of certain exchange gains and losses under SSAP 20 'Foreign Currency Translation';

— in rare circumstances, a departure from accounting standards may be required for the accounts to show a true and fair view – as the Act normally requires accounts to be prepared in accordance with applicable accounting standards, such a departure may in effect also require use of the true and fair override.

Departure from the requirements of the Act in order to achieve compliance with individual accounting standards will arise from time to time in practice. Departure from accounting standards should only arise in very exceptional circumstances (see 3.6 below).

The relationship between accounting standards and the true and fair requirement

3.5   The 'Foreword to Accounting Standards' considers the status of accounting standards within UK companies' legislation and includes as an appendix an opinion by Miss Mary Arden QC (now Dame Mary Arden) entitled 'The True and Fair Requirement'. This considers in detail the relationship between accounting standards and the requirement of the Act for accounts to give a true and fair view and makes the following points:

— Although the true and fair requirement is a question of law and the interpretation of the requirement must therefore be dealt with by the court, this cannot be carried out without evidence of the practice and views of accountants. The more authoritative the practices and views, the more ready the court will be to follow them.

— Amendments to the Act through the *Companies Act 1989* have given statutory recognition to accounting standards.

— As the Act requires disclosure of non-compliance with accounting standards, rather than compliance with them, the court is likely to infer that accounts will usually follow accounting standards in meeting the true and fair requirement and that any departure from an accounting standard needs therefore to be explained and justified.

— Once an accounting standard has been issued, the court is likely to hold that compliance with the standard will be necessary for accounts to show a true and fair view. This is likely to be strengthened by the extent to which the standard is subsequently accepted in practice.

— However, the converse will not necessarily apply. A lack of support for a standard will not automatically lead the court to conclude that compliance with the standard is not necessary for the accounts to show a true and fair view.

— The fact that a departure from an accounting standard is disclosed in accordance with the Act does not mean that the departure is necessarily permitted under the Act.

The full Opinion should be read in any cases where it is intended to depart from the requirements of an accounting standard on the basis that the departure is required in order for the accounts to give a true and fair view. Legal advice may also need to be taken.

Departure from accounting standards

3.6   FRS 18 'Accounting Policies' requires an entity to adopt accounting policies that will enable its financial statements to give a true and fair view, and requires those policies to be consistent with the requirements of accounting standards, UITF Abstracts and companies' legislation. Departures from the requirements of accounting standards and UITF Abstracts should be rare in practice as they are only permissible to the extent that compliance with a standard or Abstract would be inconsistent with the overriding requirement for the accounts to give a true and fair view. In particular, the requirements of accounting standards and UITF Abstracts will not be inconsistent with the true and fair view requirement if such a view can be achieved through additional disclosure in the accounts. It is therefore not acceptable to depart from accounting standards and UITF Abstracts in these circumstances.

Use of the true and fair override

3.7   The most common use of the true and fair override in practice is in order to comply with those accounting standards which require a departure from the requirements of the Act (e.g. SSAP 19 'Accounting for Investment Properties' and SSAP 20 'Foreign Currency translation'). Where the true and fair override is invoked, *CA 1985* requires disclosure of the following in a note to the accounts:

(i)   particulars of the departure;

(ii)   the reasons for the departure; and

(iii)   the effect of the departure.

However, the Act does not provide any further guidance on the details that should be included in these disclosures.

Disclosure requirements under FRS 18

3.8   FRS 18 'Accounting Policies' now specifies that the following details should be given whenever CA 1985 requires disclosure of the particulars of a departure from a specific statutory requirement, the reasons for it and the effect:

—   a clear and unambiguous statement that there has been a departure from the requirements of an accounting standard, a UITF Abstract or companies' legislation (as appropriate) and that the departure is necessary to give a true and fair view;

—   a statement of the treatment that accounting standards, UITF Abstracts or companies' legislation would normally require and a description of the treatment actually adopted;

—   a statement of why the usual treatment would not give a true and fair view; and

— a description of how the position shown in the financial statements is different as a result of the departure – this should include quantification of the effect except where:

— this is already evident in the financial statements themselves; or

— the effect cannot be quantified, in which case the circumstances should be explained.

Examples of how these requirements might be met in the case of the more common departures from the requirements of the Act are set out in the appendix to this chapter. If the departure from *CA 1985* continues in subsequent years, the full disclosures required by FRS 18 must continue to be given each year. If there is no departure in the current year but there was a departure in the previous accounting period (e.g. the company previously held an investment property but this has been disposed of) details must continue to be shown for the comparative figures. FRS 18 also requires the disclosures to be given:

— as part of the note on compliance with applicable accounting standards required by *Sch 4 para 36A* (see 1.9 above); or

— elsewhere in the notes to the accounts, but cross-referenced to the note on compliance with applicable accounting standards.

This should help to ensure that the departure receives the appropriate degree of prominence in the accounts.

APPENDIX

Example wordings for the use of the true and fair override

1. Non-depreciation of investment properties under SSAP 19 – 'Accounting for Investment Properties'

As the Act does not distinguish between investment properties and other properties, and thus requires an investment property to be included in the accounts at either cost or valuation and to be depreciated over its useful life in the same way as any other tangible fixed asset, compliance with the requirements of SSAP 19 in respect of investment properties will usually constitute a departure from the requirements of the Act. Compliance with SSAP 19 will therefore usually require the use of the true and fair override, unless:

—   the estimated residual value of the property (calculated in accordance with FRS 15) is at least equal to its carrying value; or

—   the estimated residual value of the property is so close to its carrying value that any depreciation would be immaterial.

Further consideration of both of these issues is set out in Chapter 13.

The following is an example of wording that might be appropriate to explain the use of the true and fair override where investment properties are accounted for under SSAP 19.

Example 3.1 – Non-depreciation of investment properties: true and fair override

In accordance with SSAP 19:

—   investment properties are revalued annually and the aggregate surplus or deficit is transferred to a revaluation reserve, and

—   no depreciation or amortisation is provided in respect of freehold investment properties and leasehold investment properties with over 20 years to run.

The *Companies Act 1985* requires tangible fixed assets to be depreciated systematically over their estimated useful economic lives. However, investment properties are held for investment rather than consumption. The directors therefore consider that depreciation on a systematic basis would not be appropriate in this case and that the accounting policy adopted is necessary for the accounts to give a true and fair view. Depreciation or amortisation is only one of the many factors reflected in the annual valuation and the amount which might otherwise have been shown cannot be separately identified or quantified.

In this case, it is usually accepted that the effect of not depreciating the properties does not require disclosure. This is considered in more detail in Chapter 21.

2. Inclusion of unrealised exchange gains and losses in the profit and loss account under SSAP 20 — 'Foreign Currency Translation'

The accounting treatment required by SSAP 20 in respect of unsettled long-term monetary transactions means that unrealised exchange gains and losses will usually be included in the profit and loss account when a company has long-term assets and liabilities denominated in a foreign currency. Under the Act, only profits realised at the balance sheet date may be included in the profit and loss account. [*CA 1985, Sch 4 para 12(a)*]. Compliance with SSAP 20 in these circumstances may therefore constitute a departure from the accounting requirements of the Act under the true and fair override.

The following is an example of wording that might be appropriate to explain the use of the true and fair override where exchange gains relating to long-term monetary transactions are accounted for in accordance with SSAP 20.

Example 3.2 – Inclusion of unrealised exchange gains and losses in the profit and loss account: true and fair override

In accordance with SSAP 20, exchange gains and losses on the translation of monetary items are taken to the profit and loss account for the year. In the case of unrealised exchange gains arising on the translation of unsettled long-term monetary transactions, this treatment represents a departure from the requirement under the *Companies Act 1985* that only profits realised at the balance sheet date should be included in the profit and loss account. However, as explained in paragraph 10 of SSAP 20, exchange gains on unsettled transactions can be determined at the balance sheet date no less objectively than exchange losses; deferring the gains whilst recognising the losses would in effect deny that any favourable movement in exchange rates had occurred and would also inhibit fair measurement of the performance of the company in the year. The directors therefore consider that recognition of such unrealised exchange gains is necessary in order for the accounts to show a true and fair view. The effect of this departure is to increase the profit before taxation by £ ... (200X: £ ...) and to increase the value of ... (asset/liability) ... by £ ... (200X: £ ...).

Further details of the requirements of SSAP 20 are given in Chapter 7.

Chapter 4   Substance Over Form

BACKGROUND TO FRS 5 'REPORTING THE SUBSTANCE OF TRANSACTIONS'

Off balance sheet financing

4.1   The publication of FRS 5 'Reporting the Substance of Transactions' in April 1994 marked the end of a long process of developing an accounting standard to deal with the problem of off balance sheet financing. The first step in tackling this issue was the introduction of SSAP 21 'Accounting for Leases and Hire Purchase Contracts', which attempted to ensure that assets held under finance leases were brought onto the balance sheet, together with the related financing liabilities. However, companies were still able to find ways of structuring lease agreements so that they did not meet the SSAP 21 definition of a finance lease and thus avoided disclosure on the balance sheet. Similarly, increasingly complex financing arrangements have been developed over the years, many with the aim of keeping the financing off the borrower's balance sheet.

Conceptual nature of FRS 5

4.2   FRS 5 is deliberately conceptual rather than factual in nature, on the basis that there is little point in laying down stringent rules (as was done in SSAP 21) if subsequent transactions are simply structured to avoid those rules. As FRS 5 sets out the underlying concepts, and then illustrates their application to specific types of transaction, it is inevitably wide in scope and companies are required to apply its spirit rather than being required to follow a prescriptive set of rules.

Transactions covered by the standard

4.3   FRS 5 applies to all transactions, irrespective of when they took place. When FRS 5 was first introduced, companies were therefore required to review the accounting treatment that they had adopted for transactions that took place in earlier years and consider whether this was still appropriate under the requirements of FRS 5. However, the vast majority of commercial transactions will not be affected by the detailed requirements of FRS 5. The main aim of FRS 5 is to ensure that appropriate accounting treatments are adopted for more complex transactions and arrangements, where the commercial substance of the transaction is not always easily identifiable. This will often be the case where:

— the principal benefits of an item are separated in some way from its legal ownership;

— the overall commercial effect of a series of transactions differs from the apparent effect of the individual transactions;

— the transaction includes options or conditions which are not commercially realistic (e.g. the terms of an option mean that it will almost certainly be exercised).

Excluded transactions

4.4   The following transactions are specifically excluded from the requirements of FRS 5 'Reporting the Substance of Transactions', unless they form part of a transaction that does fall within the scope of the standard:

— forward contracts;

— futures;

— contracts for differences;

— purchase commitments and orders (i.e. before payment or delivery has taken place);

— employment contracts.

Application of FRS 5 in practice

4.5   As FRS 5 requires the application of concepts rather than detailed rules, it can be a difficult standard to apply in practice. This is exacerbated by the fact that it is particularly designed to cover transactions whose commercial substance is not readily apparent, and in some cases it may be genuinely difficult to agree on what the true substance of the transaction really is.

Impact of FRS 18 'Accounting Policies'

4.6   FRS 18 'Accounting Policies' sets out four objectives – relevance, reliability, comparability and understandability – against which an entity should judge the appropriateness of its accounting policies and the constraints that should be taken into account in making such an assessment. The guidance on the reliability of financial information emphasises that one of the key factors is that the information can be depended upon by users to represent faithfully what it purports to represent or could reasonably be expected to represent – in other words, that the way in which a transaction or event is recognised, measured and presented in the financial statements corresponds closely to its substance and practical effect.

Company law requirement

4.7 For accounting periods beginning on or after 1 January 2005, the *Companies Act 1985 (International Accounting Standards and Other Accounting Amendments) Regulations 2004* (SI 2004/2947) insert a new paragraph 5A into Schedule 4 to CA 1985, which requires directors to have regard to the substance of the reported transaction or arrangement, in accordance with generally accepted accounting principles, when determining how items are presented in the profit and loss account and balance sheet. Prior to this, the principle that the economic or commercial substance of a transaction should take precedence over its legal form was not referred to in company law. Similar amendments are made to Schedule 8, Schedule 9 and Schedule 9A so that the new provision also applies to small companies preparing shorter form accounts and to banks and insurance companies. In particular, the change enables companies to comply more easily with the requirements of FRS 25 'Financial Instruments: Disclosure and Presentation' on the disclosure and accounting treatment of preference shares and their related dividends.

DETAILED REQUIREMENTS OF FRS 5

Assessing commercial substance

4.8 Under FRS 5, financial statements should report the commercial substance of the transactions entered into by an entity. In assessing the substance of a transaction, greater emphasis should be given to those aspects that are likely to have a practical commercial effect. Where an overall commercial effect is achieved by a series of transactions, the series should be considered as a whole rather than as individual transactions.

Relationship with other accounting standards and with company law

4.9 Where the treatment of a transaction, asset or liability is covered more specifically in another accounting standard or in company (or other) law, the more specific provisions should be followed. However, the requirements of FRS 5 will still have an impact, as the explanatory notes to FRS 5 emphasise that the provisions of other standards or law should be applied to the substance of a transaction rather than to its legal form. Where the requirements of FRS 5 are more specific than those in another accounting standard or in company (or other) law, the requirements of FRS 5 should be followed.

Identifying and recognising assets and liabilities

4.10   Assessing the substance of a transaction involves identifying whether it has given rise to new assets and liabilities for the reporting entity, or has changed the entity's existing assets and liabilities.

Assets are defined as rights or access to future economic benefits, and liabilities are defined as obligations to transfer economic benefits. These definitions are consistent with those set out in the ASB 'Statement of Principles'. An asset or liability should be recognised in the financial statements if there is sufficient evidence of its existence and the monetary amount can be measured with sufficient reliability. The recognition of assets and liabilities is considered in more detail at 4.18-4.21 below.

Options and guarantees

4.11   Where a transaction includes an option, guarantee or conditional provision, the assessment of the commercial effect of the transaction should take into account the likely practical effect of the option, guarantee or condition.

Subsequent transactions in respect of recognised assets

4.12   Depending on the circumstances, a subsequent transaction in respect of a recognised asset may result in:

—   the entire asset continuing to be recognised in the accounts;

—   the entire asset ceasing to be recognised in the accounts;

—   a change to the description or monetary amount of the asset and the recognition of a liability for any obligation to transfer economic benefits.

Non-recourse finance arrangements

4.12   Under certain circumstances, a linked presentation is required in respect of non-recourse finance. In this case, the gross amount of the asset and the deduction for the related finance must both be shown on the face of the balance sheet. This treatment can only be adopted where all of the conditions laid down in FRS 5 are satisfied. This aspect of FRS 5 is considered in detail in the context of factored debts in Chapter 25 which includes an example of linked presentation under the standard.

Additional disclosures

4.14   The disclosure of a transaction in the accounts should be sufficient to enable a user of the accounts to understand its commercial effect. Where assets and liabilities are recognised which are different in nature from those usually included under the relevant balance sheet heading, the differences should be explained in the accounts. Transactions which do not result in assets and liabilities being recognised in the accounts may nevertheless require disclosure in the notes to the accounts if they give rise to guarantees, commitments, rights or obligations.

Off-setting

4.15   For accounting periods beginning before 1 January 2005, detailed guidance on the offset of debit and credit balances is set out in FRS 5. The standard requires credit and debit balances to be aggregated into a single net item where all of the following conditions are met:

(i)   the amounts owed to and by the reporting entity are determinable monetary amounts, which are denominated in the same currency or in freely convertible currencies (i.e. currencies for which quoted market rates are available and for which there is an active market);

(ii)   the reporting entity can insist on a net settlement of the outstanding balances – in particular, there must be no possibility that the reporting entity could be required to make payment of the creditor balance in its accounting records without first being able to recover payment of the debtor balance; and

(iii)   the reporting entity's ability to insist on a net settlement of the balances must be assured beyond all doubt and in particular must be capable of surviving the insolvency of the other party.

Legal advice may need to be taken to confirm some of these points. If all of the conditions are met, the balances are not regarded as separate assets and liabilities under the standard, and they are therefore required to be off-set for accounting purposes. For accounting periods beginning on or after 1 January 2005, the offset of financial assets and financial liabilities is covered by FRS 25 'Financial Instruments: Disclosure and Presentation' and FRS 5 is amended to emphasise this. The requirements of FRS 5 remain in force for other assets and liabilities, although the detailed guidance referred to above has been deleted from the standard, so that it now simply states that:

(i)   assets and liabilities should not be offset; and

(ii)   debit and credit balances should be aggregated into a single net item where, and only where, they do not constitute separate assets and liabilities.

Offsetting is considered in more detail at 4.31 to 4.39 below.

Quasi-subsidiaries

4.16   Where the reporting entity controls another entity that is in substance no different from a subsidiary (i.e. it is a quasi-subsidiary), the assets, liabilities, profits, losses and cash flows of the quasi-subsidiary should normally be included in the group accounts of the reporting entity. If the reporting entity does not have subsidiaries, consolidated accounts for the reporting entity and the quasi-subsidiary should be prepared in accordance with FRS 2 'Accounting for Subsidiary Undertakings' and should be presented as part of the reporting entity's financial statements, with equal prominence to its own individual accounts. The inclusion of quasi-subsidiaries in group accounts is considered in more detail in Chapter 45.

Application Notes

4.17   FRS 5 includes six detailed Application Notes which explain how its requirements should be applied to the following transactions.
—   Consignment stock (A1–A12).
—   Sale and repurchase agreements (B1–B21).
—   Factoring of debts (C1–C20).
—   Securitised assets (D1–D26).
—   Loan transfers (E1–E24).
—   Private Finance Initiative and similar contracts (F1–F60).
—   Revenue Recognition (G1 – G72)

The Application Notes 'Consignment stocks' and 'Sale and repurchase agreements' are considered in Chapter 23 and the Application Note 'Factoring of debts' is considered in Chapter 25. The Application Note 'Revenue Recognition', which was added to the FRS in November 2003, is considered in Chapter 10. The other Application Notes relate to more specialised transactions and have therefore not been covered in detail here.

THE RECOGNITION OF ASSETS AND LIABILITIES

Identification of assets and liabilities

4.18   The first step in evaluating the substance of a transaction is to identify the new assets and liabilities that arise as a result of the transaction, or the effect that the transaction has on the entity's existing assets and liabilities. Assets are defined in FRS 5 as 'Rights or other access to future economic benefits controlled by an entity as a result of past transactions or events'. Access to benefits will often, but not always, be associated with legal rights. Control is defined as 'The ability to obtain the future economic benefits relating to an asset and to restrict the access of others to those benefits'. Therefore, the ability to prevent others gaining access to the benefits must also be taken into account.

Impact of risk

4.19 The impact of risk is seen as a key element in identifying an asset under FRS 5. The inherent future economic benefits of an asset are rarely certain. For instance:

— the actual benefits may be greater than expected;

— the actual benefits may be lower than expected;

— the benefits may arise sooner than expected;

— the benefits may arise later than expected.

For example, an amount due from an overseas debtor may:

— result in an exchange gain;

— result in an exchange loss;

— be paid in advance of the due date;

— be paid after the due date.

These aspects are identified in FRS 5 as the risks involved in holding the asset. It can therefore be seen that, in this context, risk encompasses both the potential to gain as a result of holding the asset (i.e. realising an exchange gain or achieving early payment in the above example) and the possible exposure to loss (i.e. realising an exchange loss or suffering poor cash flow, or even a bad debt, in the above example). The entity that has access to the benefits of an asset will in most cases also gain or lose if the actual benefits are different to the expected benefits. Identifying who gains or loses in these circumstances therefore helps to identify who controls access to the benefits of an asset.

Definition of liabilities

4.20 Liabilities are defined in FRS 5 as 'an entity's obligations to transfer economic benefits as a result of past transactions or events'. In many cases, a liability will represent a legal obligation, but this need not necessarily be the case. FRS 5 quotes the example of an entity being commercially obliged to adopt a particular course of action because, in the long term, it is in its best interest to do so. The key issue in identifying a liability is that the entity is not free to avoid an outflow of resources at some point in the future. However, the standard emphasises that it will not always be necessary to recognise a liability in the accounts even though it is possible that a future outflow of resources may not be avoided. For instance, in the case of a contingent liability, an accounting treatment in accordance with FRS 12 'Provisions, Contingent Liabilities and Contingent Assets' will be sufficient.

Recognising assets and liabilities

4.21 The general criteria for recognising assets and liabilities are consistent with those set out in the ASB 'Statement of Principles'. Recognition should only take place where:

— there is sufficient evidence that the asset or liability exists; and

— the monetary amount can be measured with sufficient reliability.

However, the application of prudence will usually mean that the interpretation of 'sufficient reliability' will vary depending on whether the item in question is an asset or a liability (i.e. a lower degree of reliability will usually be acceptable when recognising a liability than when recognising an asset).

THE COMMERCIAL EFFECT OF TRANSACTIONS

Linked transactions

4.22   In considering the commercial effect of a transaction, it is important to take into account any associated transactions, as consideration of the arrangement as a whole may indicate a different commercial effect. For instance, if an entity sells an asset, but is committed to repurchasing the item after a number of years, the overall effect may be that the 'seller' retains the main benefits and risks associated with the asset (depending on the detailed terms of the arrangement). In this case, the 'seller' has not in fact sold the asset and should not record the transaction as a sale. The asset should be retained on the balance sheet, along with the corresponding liability to the other party (i.e. in respect of the 'repurchase' commitment).

Options

4.23   The assessment of the commercial effect of options included in an agreement can be a particularly difficult issue. For instance, a transaction such as that described in 4.22 above, may include an option for the 'seller' to repurchase the asset, rather than a commitment for him to do so. This may seem to indicate that the 'seller' does not have an unavoidable obligation to repurchase the asset and that the transaction can therefore be recorded as a sale. However, the terms of the option will usually need to be carefully reviewed to ensure that it is a genuine option. For instance, there may be a substantial penalty if the option is not exercised, which will have the effect of ensuring that the 'seller' will always choose to exercise the option. There may also be commercial reasons why the 'seller' will inevitably choose to exercise the option to repurchase. For instance, the asset may be essential to the future operation of the business. Particular caution is needed where the arrangement includes both an option for the 'seller' to repurchase and an option for the 'purchaser' to resell. In this situation it will be virtually certain that one of the parties will exercise the option. FRS 5 emphasises that all aspects and implications of a transaction must be identified but that greater weight should be given to those that will have a practical commercial effect. It should also be assumed that all parties to the transaction will act in their own best interest.

Importance of commercial logic

4.24 It is particularly important that the commercial logic of each party in entering into a transaction should be fully understood. If there appears to be no commercial logic to the transaction for one of the parties, this may suggest that there are other aspects to the arrangement that have not yet been identified and which may be important in establishing the substance of the transactions and hence the appropriate accounting treatment. The position of all parties must therefore be considered, not just the position of the reporting entity.

The lender's return

4.25 Where one party to a transaction receives no more than a lender's return, the substance of the transaction will usually be that of a financing arrangement (e.g. a loan that is in effect secured on the asset that is supposedly 'sold' as part of the arrangement). This aspect of FRS 5 will often be particularly relevant in assessing the substance of sale and repurchase arrangements or leasing transactions. A lender's return is described in FRS 5 as interest on the investment (i.e. the 'loan'), and perhaps a relatively small fee, but no more than this. The implication of an arrangement being made on this basis is that:

— if the 'lender' is satisfied with a lender's return, he must be satisfied that he is not taking on any significant risk of loss by entering into the arrangement (other than the normal commercial risk of the 'borrower' failing to repay the amount of the 'loan'); and

— if the 'borrower' is satisfied with the arrangement, he must be satisfied that he is not relinquishing any substantial benefits attached to the asset that has supposedly been 'sold'.

For instance, if A Ltd sells an asset to B Ltd with an option to repurchase it in ten years' time at original cost, plus an amount that in effect represents interest on 'cost' for a period of ten years, B Ltd will not receive more than a lender's return. The transaction should therefore be accounted for as a loan repayable in ten years' time, and the interest cost should be accrued over the period of the loan. The asset will remain on A Ltd's balance sheet throughout the ten-year period.

Subsequent transactions in assets previously recognised

4.26 Depending on the circumstances, a subsequent transaction in respect of an asset that has already been recognised in the accounts may result in:

— the entire asset continuing to be recognised in the accounts;

— the entire asset ceasing to be recognised in the accounts;

— a change to the description or monetary amount of the asset and the recognition of a liability for any obligation to transfer economic benefits.

Continued recognition

4.27   Where the transaction does not result in any significant change in the entity's:

— rights to the benefits relating to the asset; or

— risks in relation to the asset (i.e. both the potential for gain and the exposure to loss);

there will be no change to the recognition of the asset in the accounts. For instance, if a company sells its debtors to another party but:

— the other party has recourse to the company for all bad debts; and

— the level of the finance charges paid varies depending on the speed of payment by the debtors;

there is no change to the company's rights or risks in respect of the debts and they should continue to be shown in the accounts. Depending on the terms of the arrangement (e.g. whether legal title is transferred or not), additional details of the arrangements may need to be disclosed.

Derecognition

4.28   Derecognition of the asset will be required where a transaction transfers all the significant rights to benefits, and all the significant risks relating to the asset to another party. For instance, if a company sells its debtors for a single, non-refundable cash payment and there is no recourse to the company in respect of bad debts or slow payment, the debtors should be removed from the company's balance sheet.

Special cases

4.29   Most transactions will result in either continued recognition or derecognition of an asset. In certain circumstances, a transaction may result in significant changes to the benefits and risks associated with a previously recognised asset, but not transfer them completely to another party. In these cases, it may be necessary to:

— change the description of the asset;

— change the monetary amount of the asset; or

— recognise a new liability for any obligations assumed or risks retained.

These special circumstances will arise where:

— only part of the asset is transferred;

— the whole of the asset is transferred, but for only part of its life (e.g. under a sale and repurchase agreement); or

— the whole of the asset is transferred for all of its life, but the entity retains some right to significant benefits, or some exposure to significant risk, in respect of the asset.

A common example of the transfer of an asset with the retention of some risk by the seller is the sale of an item of equipment with either a related warranty in respect of the standard of the equipment, usually for a specified period of time, or with a guaranteed residual value. The buyer therefore acquires the rights to the benefits relating to the equipment and assumes most of the risks associated with it, but the seller retains an element of risk in the form of liability to bear the cost of any repair work necessary if the equipment does not meet the standard specified, or to make good any deficit in the residual value of the asset. The seller may need to recognise these liabilities in the accounts, depending on the likelihood of a liability crystallising.

Significant benefits and risks

4.30 FRS 5 considers the interpretation of significant in relation to benefits and risks and once again places the emphasis on the likely commercial effect in practice. For instance, a company has debtors totalling £50,000 and expects bad debts to amount to no more than £1,000. If it sells the debtors for £45,000 but the purchaser has recourse to the company for bad debts up to £3,000, the company has in effect retained all the risk relating to the debtors (i.e. in practice, the company has all the risk in respect of the expected bad debts of £1,000). The debtors would therefore normally remain on the balance sheet, with the payment of £45,000 being recognised as a financing liability.

Off-setting

Accounting periods beginning before 1 January 2005

4.31 For accounting periods beginning before 1 January 2005, detailed guidance on the offset of debit and credit balances is set out in FRS 5 'Reporting the substance of transactions'. Under this standard, credit and debit balances should be aggregated into a single net item where, and only where, all of the following conditions are met:

(i) the amounts owed to and by the reporting entity are determinable monetary amounts, which are denominated either in the same currency or in freely convertible currencies (a freely convertible currency is defined as one for which quoted market rates are available and for which there is an active market, so that the amount to be off-set could be exchanged without a significant effect on the exchange rate);

(ii) the reporting entity has the ability to insist on a net settlement of the outstanding balances; and

(iii)   the reporting entity's ability to insist on a net settlement of the balances is assured beyond all doubt.

If all of these conditions are met, the balances are not regarded as separate assets and liabilities they should therefore be off-set for accounting purposes.

Net settlement assured beyond all doubt

4.32   In order to meet this condition, FRS 5 emphasises that there must be no possibility that the reporting entity could be required to transfer economic benefits to another party without being able to enforce its own access to economic benefits. In other words, there must be no possibility that the company will have to make payment of the creditor balance in its accounting records without first being able to recover payment of the debtor balance. Confirmation on this point should include consideration of the maturity dates of both the debit and the credit balance, and also the potential impact of the insolvency of the other party. The maturity date of the debit balance must be no later than the maturity date of the credit balance, so that the company is entitled to receive payment in respect of the debtor before, or at the same time as, it must pay the amount that it owes to the other party. If the company has the ability to accelerate maturity of the debt or to defer maturity of the liability, and thus achieve the same result, this condition can usually be regarded as satisfied. The company's ability to insist on a net settlement of the amounts due must be assured beyond any doubt and in particular must be capable of surviving the insolvency of the other party. Legal advice will usually need to be taken to confirm this point.

Where the company's right to insist on a net settlement of the amounts due is contingent on any other matter or event, it should only be taken into account if the company would be able to enforce net settlement in all situations where the other party defaults on payment.

Members of a group

4.33   The same principles apply in the case of a group of companies, where different companies within the group may have amounts due to or from a particular third party. If all the conditions are met, off-set of the relevant credit and debit balances in the group accounts is required under the standard. However, where different legal entities are involved in the various transactions (and both the group and the third party could have more than one legal entity involved) it is less likely that all of the conditions set out in FRS 5 will be properly satisfied.

Changes in respect of financial instruments

4.34   Although the basic requirement of paragraph 29 of FRS 5 remains in force, the detailed guidance in that standard on the offset of financial assets and liabilities is superseded by FRS 25 'Financial Instruments: Disclosure and Presentation' for accounting periods beginning on or after 1 January 2005. Under this standard, offset is required when, and only when:

(i)   the entity has a legally enforceable right to set off the asset and the liability; and

(ii) the entity intends either to settle on a net basis or to realise the asset and settle the liability simultaneously.

A net presentation should therefore only be adopted in the accounts if this reflects the future cash flows that are expected to arise from the settlement of the separate financial instruments. In all other cases, the instruments should be recognised separately.

Legally enforceable right of set-off

4.35   A legal right of set-off can arise by contract or other agreement and will usually be a direct arrangement between a debtor and a creditor. However, the guidance in the standard notes that, in exceptional circumstances, a debtor may have a legal right to apply an amount due from a third party against the amount due to a creditor, and this may create an enforceable right of set-off it there is a clear agreement between all the parties involved. The legal jurisdiction in which any arrangement is made, and the laws applicable to the various parties, will need to be carefully reviewed to establish whether a legally enforceable right of set-off has been created.

Settlement intention

4.36   The existence of a legally enforceable right of set-off is not sufficient to justify the adoption of a net presentation in the accounts, because that right will not affect the future cash flows of the entity unless it is actually exercised. Equally, an intention by one party, or by both parties, to settle on a net basis without a legally enforceable right to do so cannot justify a net presentation. In this situation, the rights and obligations associated with the underlying financial instruments would remain unaltered and adopting a net presentation would therefore not give an true reflection of the arrangement. Where an entity has a right of set-off but does not intend to enforce this, or to realise the asset and settle the liability simultaneously, and this affects the entity's exposure to credit risk and liquidity risk, additional disclosures may need to be given in the accounts. The detailed disclosure requirements of the standard apply for accounting periods beginning on or after 1 January 2005 in the case of listed companies, and from the period in which FRS 26 'Financial Instruments: Measurement' is applied in other cases. For practical purposes, this will generally be if and when the entity chooses to adopt fair value accounting.

Simultaneous settlement

4.37 Simultaneous settlement of the asset and the liability may occur through the operation of a clearing house in an organised financial market or a face-to-face exchange. The critical point is that there should be no exposure to credit or liquidity risk as a result of the transactions. If the entity is exposed to such risks, even relatively briefly, settlement is not regarded as simultaneous. For instance, where two instruments are to be settled by the receipt and payment of separate amounts, the entity will usually be exposed (however briefly) either to credit risk in respect of the full amount of the asset, or liquidity risk for the full amount of the liability. The standard consequently requires this to be reflected in the separate presentation of the financial asset and the financial liability. The exposure to risk can only be avoided if the transactions occur at the same moment.

Situations where offsetting is inappropriate

4.38 The standard notes specifically that offsetting will not usually be appropriate in the following situations:

(i) where several different financial instruments are used to emulate the features of a single financial instrument;

(ii) where financial assets and liabilities arise from financial instruments with the same primary risk exposure but involve different counterparts;

(iii) where financial or other assets are pledged as collateral for non-recourse financial liabilities;

(iv) where financial assets are set aside in trust by a debtor for the purpose of discharging an obligation without the creditor actually accepting those assets in settlement;

(v) where obligations are expected to be recovered from a third party under an insurance claim.

This is on the basis that the two conditions required for offsetting will not generally be met in the above circumstances.

Master netting arrangements

4.39 A master netting arrangement is described in the standard as one where an entity undertakes a number of financial instrument transactions with a single counterparty and enters into an agreement that provides for a single net settlement of all the instruments covered by the agreement in the event of a default on, or termination of, any one contract. A key point is that such an agreement only creates a legally enforceable right of set-off in the event of a default or other circumstances not expected to arise in the normal course of business. The guidance therefore concludes that such an arrangement does not provide the basis for offsetting in the accounts, unless both of the criteria specified in 4.19 are also satisfied. However, the effect of the arrangement on the entity's exposure to credit risk will usually need to be disclosed.

LEASING TRANSACTIONS

The interaction of FRS 5 with SSAP 21

4.40   FRS 5 is clear that it does not supersede the requirements of other accounting standards or company law, and that transactions, assets and liabilities that are dealt with in more detail elsewhere should continue to be accounted for in accordance with those requirements. The only proviso is that the requirements of other accounting standards and company law should always be applied to the substance of transactions, rather than to their legal form, if this is different.

Where the requirements of FRS 5 may be relevant

4.41   There is inevitably a close relationship between FRS 5 and SSAP 21 'Accounting for Leases and Hire Purchase Contracts', as both standards are attempting to deal with a similar accounting issue. In the case of leasing arrangements, the provisions of SSAP 21 are generally more detailed than those set out in FRS 5. However, the requirements of FRS 5 will be relevant for the following:

— the classification of individual leases as finance leases or operating leases – a lease which fails to meet the value criteria (such as the '90% test') set out in SSAP 21 for classification as a finance lease may nevertheless need to be accounted for as a finance lease under the requirements of FRS 5; and

— leasing arrangements that form part of a larger transaction, or a series of transactions, which must be considered together under the requirements of FRS 5.

The requirements of SSAP 21 are considered in more detail in Chapters 21 and Chapter 28.

Guidance in Application Note B to FRS 5

4.42   The guidance in Application Note B to FRS 5 ('Sale and repurchase agreements') will also often be relevant in evaluating a sale and leaseback arrangement, and is generally more detailed than the guidance provided in SSAP 21. It should also be noted that Application Note B specifically states that it covers any arrangement where one party holds an asset on behalf of another. Any leased asset will generally fall within this definition, and consequently the guidance in Application Note B will generally be relevant in assessing the substance of any leasing arrangement.

ACCOUNTING FOR ESOP TRUSTS

Usual features of ESOPs

4.43   Employee Share Ownership Plans operate in a variety of ways but often include the following features:

—   a trust provides a means of purchasing and holding shares to be transferred to employees;

—   share purchases are often funded by interest-free finance from the sponsoring company or by bank loans guaranteed by the company – the company may also assume responsibility for funding interest payments in respect of a bank loan;

—   shares are distributed to employees through some form of employee share scheme – there are many different arrangements that can be put in place;

—   although the trustees must act in the interests of the beneficiaries, in practice the company will often have *de facto* control of the shares held by the trust.

Accounting treatment

4.44   The consensus reached in UITF 38 'Accounting for ESOP Trusts' is that certain assets and liabilities of such a trust should be recognised on the balance sheet of the sponsoring company where it has *de facto* control of the shares held by the trust, and therefore bears the benefits and risks relating to those shares. In this case:

(i)   the consideration paid for any shares in the company that are held by the ESOP trust should be deducted in arriving at shareholders' funds, until those shares vest unconditionally in employees;

(ii)   other assets and liabilities of the ESOP trust should be treated as assets and liabilities of the sponsoring company;

(iii)   consideration paid and received for the purchase or sale of the company's own shares held by the ESOP trust should be shown as separate items in the reconciliation of movements in shareholders' funds;

(iv)   no gain or loss should be recognised in the profit and loss account or statement of total recognised gains and losses on the purchase, sale, issue or cancellation of own shares;

(v)   finance costs and administration expenses should be charged as they accrue and not as funding payments are made to the ESOP trust; and

(vi)   any dividend income arising on own shares held by the ESOP trust should be excluded in arriving at profit before tax and deducted from the aggregate of dividends paid and proposed.

The Abstract applies for accounting periods ending on or after 22 June 2004, although earlier adoption is encouraged. The previous UITF Abstract on this subject required own shares held by an ESOP trust to be included in the sponsoring company's fixed assets or current assets as appropriate. However, this treatment was not consistent with international accounting standards or with the ASB Statement of Principles and the UITF therefore decided to amend its requirements when the issue was considered again in the context of treasury shares.

Disclosure

4.45 UITF 38 also requires disclosure of sufficient information for a user of the company's accounts to be able to understand the significance of the ESOP trust. This should include:

(i)   a description of the main features of the trust, including the arrangements for distributing shares to employees;

(ii)   the amount deducted from shareholders' funds in respect of own shares held by the trust;

(iii) the number of own shares held by the trust which have not yet vested unconditionally in employees and, if the company's shares are listed or publicly traded, the market value of those shares; and

(iv)   the extent to which own shares held by the trust are under option to employees or have been conditionally gifted to them.

EMPLOYEE BENEFIT TRUSTS AND OTHER INTERMEDIATE PAYMENT ARRANGEMENTS

UITF Abstract 32

4.46 The requirements of UITF Abstract 32 'Employee benefit trusts and other intermediate payment arrangements' apply for accounting periods ending on or after 23 December 2001. The Abstract applies where an entity sets up and provides funds to an employee benefit trust or other intermediary and the trust's or intermediary's accumulated assets are used to remunerate the entity's employees or other service providers. The Abstract is drafted in the context of payments to employees through an intermediary, but emphasises that the requirements apply equally to intermediate payment arrangements used to compensate other suppliers of goods and services. Employee share ownership plans (ESOPs) and pension funds are specifically excluded from the scope of the Abstract as they are already dealt with in UITF Abstract 13 'Accounting for ESOP trusts' and FRS 17 'Retirement Benefits' respectively.

Structure of the intermediary

4.47 The Abstract notes that the relationship between the intermediary and the sponsoring entity may take a variety of forms. In many cases the intermediary will be structured as a trust and the sponsoring entity will not have a right to direct its activities. However, the sponsoring entity may still give advice to the intermediary, or the intermediary may rely on the sponsoring entity to provide the information that it needs to carry out its activities. Also, the sponsoring entity will often have the right to appoint, or veto the appointment of, the trustees (or equivalent) of the intermediary. Payments to the intermediary will usually be in cash, but may take the form of the transfer of other assets.

Employee benefit trusts

4.48   The usual arrangement in an employee benefit trust is that the sponsoring employer makes payments to the trust and the trust uses assets accumulated from those payments to pay the employees, as beneficiaries of the trust, for some or all of their services to the sponsoring employer. The intermediary is usually constituted as a trust but may take a different form and the employees may not be the only beneficiaries – for instance, past employees and their dependants may also benefit from the arrangements, or the intermediary may be authorised to make charitable donations. The precise identity of those who will receive payments from the trust, and the amounts that they will receive, will not usually be known at the outset.

Whether a payment represents an immediate expense

4.49   The main issue considered in the Abstract is whether a payment from the sponsoring employer to the intermediary represents an immediate expense. The Abstract notes that most expenses are incurred when a liability arises rather than at the time of payment. For instance, an entity's liability for services provided to it is incurred as those services are received, not when they are paid for. The same principle applies when the services are paid for through an intermediary – in other words, the liability for employee costs arises when the employee services are provided. The payment to the intermediary will often be made either in advance of the liability arising or in order to settle a liability that has already arisen – only rarely will it be made as the services are actually received.

Creation of an asset

4.50   An asset is defined in the ASB's 'Statement of Principles for Financial Reporting' as a right or other access to future economic benefits that is controlled by the entity as a result of a past transaction or event. UITF Abstract 32 concludes that, in the case of intermediate payment arrangements, the benefit to the sponsoring entity takes the form of meeting some or all of the cost of goods or services provided to the entity. Such a benefit can constitute an asset even though it is not capable of being turned into cash or of being distributed in a liquidation. Control is defined as the ability to direct and the ability to benefit from that direction, and the Abstract notes that control can be exercised by means other than intervention and instruction on an ongoing day-to-day basis. A sponsoring employer may therefore have *de facto* control of an intermediate's assets and liabilities as explained in UITF Abstract 38 'Accounting for ESOP Trusts'.

Impact of FRS 5

4.51 The Abstract also considers the requirements of FRS 5 'Reporting the Substance of Transactions' and, in particular, the need to consider the underlying practical commercial effect of each transaction. The UITF concludes that it would be highly unusual for an entity to pay a significant amount to a third party without receiving something in return, and therefore takes the view that, where an entity transfers funds to an intermediary, there should be a rebuttable presumption that the entity will receive future economic benefits from the amount transferred and that it has the control of the rights or other access to those benefits. This presumption can only be rebutted where:

— the sponsoring entity will not obtain future economic benefit from the amounts transferred (e.g. the only beneficiaries are registered charities or a benevolent fund that is in no way linked to amounts otherwise due from the entity); or

— the sponsoring entity does not have control of the rights or other access to the future economic benefits it is expected to receive (i.e. there is evidence that payments by the intermediary are not habitually made in a way that is in accordance with the wishes of the sponsoring entity).

The Abstract notes that the presumption would not be rebutted where payments by the intermediary relieve the sponsoring entity from paying for items such as retirement benefit increases or benefits in kind, such as medical insurance cover. The presumption of control is rebutted if, at the time that payment is made to the intermediary, the amount transferred vests unconditionally in identified beneficiaries.

Accounting for the asset

4.52 Where the presumption cannot be rebutted, the payment involves the exchange of one asset for another and no immediate expense is incurred. This applies regardless of whether the intermediary changes some or all of the amount transferred for other assets. The UITF therefore takes the view that the sponsoring entity has *de facto* control of the intermediary's assets and liabilities and should account for the intermediary as an extension of its own business. The intermediary's assets and liabilities should therefore be recognised as assets and liabilities of the sponsoring entity. Once recognised, the accounting treatment of those assets and liabilities should follow normal accounting rules. An asset held by the intermediary will therefore usually cease to recognised as an asset of the sponsoring entity once it vests unconditionally in identified beneficiaries.

Disclosure

4.43   Where the assets and liabilities of an intermediary are recognised in the accounts of the sponsoring entity in accordance with UITF Abstract 32, sufficient information should be disclosed in the notes to the accounts to enable readers to understand any restrictions relating to those assets and liabilities.

Chapter 5   Accounting Policies

BACKGROUND TO ACCOUNTING POLICIES

Definition of accounting policy

5.1   Accounting policies are defined in FRS 18 'Accounting Policies' as:

'Those principles, bases, conventions, rules and practices applied by an entity that specify how the effects of transactions and other events are to be reflected in its financial statements through:

(i)   recognising;

(ii)   selecting measurement bases for; and

(iii)   presenting;

assets, liabilities, gains, losses and changes to shareholders' funds.'

In other words, accounting policies provide the framework within which the elements of financial statements are measured. The standard goes on to note that accounting policies do not include estimation techniques.

Measurement bases

5.2   Measurement bases are defined in FRS 18 as the monetary attributes of the elements of financial statements (i.e. assets, liabilities, gains, losses and shareholders' funds) that are reflected in financial statements. The qualities of an individual asset might be expressed in a number of different 'values' (for instance, original cost, current net realisable value and current replacement cost) and these values are all examples of the asset's monetary attributes. Monetary attributes may also be combined into a formula – for instance, the lower of cost and net realisable value. They fall into two broad categories: attributes reflecting historical values and attributes reflecting current values. Not all monetary attributes will be suitable for use in financial statements and the term 'measurement basis' is restricted to those monetary attributes that are suitable for such use.

Purpose of accounting policies

5.3   It is impossible for financial statements to present all of the available information about the monetary attributes of the underlying assets, liabilities, gains, losses and changes in shareholders' funds. For instance, although an asset may have both a historical cost and a current value, it is not possible to reflect both of these in the entity's balance sheet. Accounting policies are therefore used to determine which attribute of the asset is to be measured and how it is to be presented.

Change of measurement basis

5.4   The measurement bases to be used in financial statements will often be prescribed by accounting standards or companies' legislation. However, measurement bases are always a matter of accounting policy, irrespective of whether they are selected or prescribed. Therefore, if an entity has previously reported an asset on a historical cost basis but changes to a current value basis, this will constitute a change of accounting policy and must be accounted for as such.

Fungible assets

5.5   Fungible assets are assets that are substantially indistinguishable from one another in economic terms. Specific accounting requirements for fungible assets may be set out in accounting standards, UITF Abstracts and companies' legislation. Where fungible assets are recorded at historical cost, the accounting policy may require cost to be determined on an asset-by-asset basis or may consider such assets in aggregate by using a measurement basis such as weighted average historical cost, or historical cost measured on a first in, first out (FIFO) basis. The guidance in FRS 18 notes that an accounting policy that considers fungible assets in aggregate will be more consistent with the objective of comparability.

Alternative treatments

5.6   Occasionally, accounting standards allow a choice of what can be recognised in financial statements in respect of a particular transaction. For instance, FRS 15 'Tangible Fixed Assets' allows interest costs that are directly attributable to the construction of a tangible fixed asset to be accounted for as part of the cost of the asset or as an expense. In these circumstances, the choice of which treatment to adopt is a matter of accounting policy.

Presentational changes

5.7   A change in the way in which a particular item is presented in the financial statements is a change of accounting policy. Therefore, if certain overheads have previously been shown as part of cost of sales, but it is in future considered more appropriate to include them within administrative expenses, this change in presentation will constitute a change of accounting policy. However, the guidance in FRS 18 makes clear that the presentation of additional information does not constitute a change of accounting policy, although any corresponding figures should be reanalysed so that they are presented in the same amount of detail. Particular care is needed when an accounting change involves both a change in presentation and a change in estimation techniques – the former is a change of accounting policy but the latter is not, and the two elements of the change must therefore be accounted for separately.

SELECTION OF ACCOUNTING POLICIES

Requirement for a true and fair view

5.8   FRS 18 requires the adoption of accounting policies that enable financial statements to give a true and fair view and that are consistent with the requirements of accounting standards, UITF Abstracts and companies' legislation. In exceptional circumstances, it may be necessary to depart from the requirements of accounting standards and UITF Abstracts. This will only be appropriate when compliance with standards or Abstracts would be inconsistent with the overriding requirement for the financial statements to give a true and fair view. The guidance in FRS 18 emphasises that departure will not be appropriate when a true and fair view can be achieved by additional disclosure in the accounts. These issues are considered in more detail in Chapter 3. FRS 18 also identifies two concepts that are considered to play a pervasive role in financial statements and therefore in the selection of appropriate accounting policies – the going concern concept and the accruals concept. These two concepts are considered in more detail in Chapter 1.

Choice of accounting policies

5.9   Where more than one accounting policy would satisfy the requirements set out in 5.8, the entity should select whichever of those policies is judged the most appropriate to its particular circumstances for the purpose of giving a true and fair view. The appropriateness of a policy should be judged against the objectives of relevance, reliability, comparability and understandability and taking into account:

— the need to balance these objectives; and

— the need to balance the cost of providing information against its likely benefit to users of the financial statements (although cost/benefit considerations will never justify the adoption of an accounting policy that is inconsistent with the requirements of accounting standards, UITF Abstracts and companies' legislation).

Balancing objectives

5.10   Tensions will sometimes arise between the four objectives identified in the standard. For instance, the accounting policy that is most relevant might not be the most reliable, and vice versa. In this situation, the entity should select the most relevant of the accounting policies that are reliable. The guidance also discusses the potential conflict between neutrality (i.e. freedom from bias) and prudence, which by definition includes a degree of judgement and is therefore potentially biased. A balance that prevents the deliberate and systematic understatement of assets and gains, and the overstatement of liabilities and losses, should resolve any potential conflict between neutrality and prudence.

Use of additional disclosures

5.11   The guidance in FRS 18 emphasises that the disclosure of additional information in the financial statements will not justify or remedy the adoption of an accounting policy that is not judged to be the most appropriate to the circumstances of the entity.

Industry practices

5.12   In selecting accounting policies, due consideration should be given to industry practices and whether these are appropriate to the particular circumstances of the entity. The guidance in FRS 18 notes that industry practices will be particularly persuasive if they are set out in a SORP that has been generally accepted by the industry or sector.

REVIEW OF ACCOUNTING POLICIES

The need for regular review

5.13   FRS 18 requires accounting policies to be regularly reviewed to ensure that they remain the most appropriate in the circumstances of the entity for the purpose of giving a true and fair view. Accounting policies may need to be changed to take account of changes and developments in the business or to implement the requirements of a new accounting standard. The guidance in FRS 18 emphasises that such a review of accounting policies does not require the early adoption of new accounting standards (although this is usually encouraged in each standard) – the effective date for each new standard is set to allow sufficient time for entities to consider the issues surrounding implementation, and make any necessary changes to the underlying management and reporting processes. However, where it is considered necessary to implement a new accounting policy, or to change an existing policy, the entity should ensure wherever possible that the new policy is in accordance with any recently issued accounting standards.

Accounting for a change in accounting policy

5.14   Unless accounting standards, UITF Abstracts or companies' legislation require otherwise, a material adjustment to prior periods as a result of a change in accounting policy should be accounted for as a prior period adjustment in accordance with the requirements of FRS 3 'Reporting Financial Performance'. Accounting for prior period adjustments is considered in more detail in Chapter 6.

Impact on comparability

5.15   Frequent changes to accounting policies may be detrimental to comparability – one of the objectives against which the appropriateness of accounting policies should be judged. The impact of past and expected future changes should therefore be taken into account when assessing whether a change in accounting policy is appropriate and accounting policies should generally only be changed when the benefits to users will outweigh the disadvantages. However, the standard emphasises that consistency is not an end in itself, and it should not be used to prevent improvements in accounting. Where the introduction of a new accounting policy would be of overall benefit to users, the need for consistency should not be used to justify not making the change.

DISCLOSURE OF ACCOUNTING POLICIES

Requirements under the Companies Act 1985

5.16   CA 1985 Sch 4 requires disclosure of the accounting policies adopted by the company in determining amounts to be included in the balance sheet and the profit or loss for the year. The Act specifically requires disclosure of the policies in respect of the depreciation and diminution in value of assets and the translation of amounts denominated in foreign currencies.

Requirements under FRS 18

5.17   FRS 18 requires the following disclosures to be given in respect of accounting policies:

— a description of each of the accounting policies that is material in the context of the entity's financial statements – where a policy is prescribed in detail in an accounting standard, UITF Abstract or companies' legislation, a brief description will suffice but where there is no such prescription, or where there are optional treatments, fuller details should be provided;

— details of any changes to the accounting policies followed in the previous financial period, including:

— a brief explanation of why each new policy is considered more appropriate;

— where practicable, the effect of a prior period adjustment on the results of the preceding financial period, in accordance with the requirements of FRS 3 'Reporting Financial Performance' – if this is not practicable, this fact must be stated and the reasons explained;

— where practicable, an indication of the effect of the change in accounting policy on the results for the current period – if this is not practicable, this fact must be stated and the reasons explained.

The objective is that users with a reasonable knowledge of business and economic activities who are willing to study the information provided with reasonable diligence should understand the accounting policies adopted. The standard also requires specific disclosures in relation to going concern and departures from accounting standards, UITF Abstracts or companies legislation – these are considered in Chapters 1 and 3 respectively. The disclosure requirements in respect of estimation techniques and SORPs are considered below.

Disclosure requirements under other accounting standards

5.18   A number of other accounting standards require disclosure of the accounting policy adopted in respect of the subject covered in the standard. The following standards specifically require disclosure of an accounting policy:

— SSAP 4 'Accounting for government grants'

— SSAP 9 'Stocks and Long Term Contracts'

— SSAP 13 'Accounting for Research and Development'

— SSAP 20 'Foreign Currency Translation'

— SSAP 21 'Accounting for Leases and Hire Purchase Contracts'

— FRS 10 'Goodwill and Intangible Assets'

— FRS 15 'Tangible Fixed Assets'.

Location of disclosures

5.19   It is normal practice to disclose all accounting policies in a single statement, usually as the first note to the financial statements. This helps to ensure that presentation of the detailed policies is clear and receives the appropriate level of prominence in the accounts. However, neither the Act nor accounting standards specify the form of the disclosure, requiring only that the details are given in the notes to the accounts. Some companies therefore choose to give each accounting policy as part of a relevant note to the accounts (e.g. by explaining the depreciation policy as part of the note on fixed assets). This may be acceptable where the accounts are basic and therefore straightforward to follow, but where more complex transactions arise, it can be difficult to decide where to give the disclosures (e.g. in the accounts of a lessee, leasing transactions may involve disclosures in notes to the profit and loss account, fixed assets and creditors). This approach can also result in the accounting policies becoming obscured by the other details that are required to be given in the notes to the accounts. A separate statement of the accounting policies adopted is therefore the preferred form of presentation.

Accounting convention adopted

5.20   The accounts will also usually need to state the accounting convention that has been followed, as this will have a material effect on the measurement bases used for items included in the profit and loss account and balance sheet. Accounting conventions are considered in more detail in Chapter 1.

ESTIMATION TECHNIQUES

Definition of estimation techniques

5.21   Estimation techniques are defined in FRS 18 as 'the methods adopted by an entity to arrive at estimated monetary amounts, corresponding to the measurement bases selected for assets, liabilities, gains, losses and changes to shareholders' funds'. An accounting policy will therefore specify the basis on which an item is to be measured, and an estimation technique may be needed to arrive at the amount at which the item is to be reflected in the financial statements. Examples of estimation techniques include:

—   depreciation methods (e.g. straight line, reducing balance) used to estimate the proportion of the economic benefits of asset that have been consumed during an accounting period;

—   methods used to estimate the proportion of trade debts that will not be recovered, where these are based on the population as a whole rather than individual balances;

—   methods used to calculate the proportion of indirect costs attributable to production.

Selection of estimation techniques

5.22   Where estimation techniques need to be used to enable the chosen accounting policies to be applied, FRS 18 requires the entity to select estimation techniques that:

—   enable the financial statements to give a true and fair view; and

—   are consistent with the requirements of accounting standards, UITF Abstracts and companies' legislation.

Where more than one estimation technique would satisfy these conditions, the entity should choose the technique that is most appropriate to its particular circumstances for the purpose of giving a true and fair view.

Factors to be taken into account

5.23   It is important for any estimation technique used in the preparation of financial information to be reliable and the technique chosen should usually be the one that gives the best approximation to the monetary amount of the asset, liability, gain, loss or change in shareholders' funds. There will always be a degree of uncertainty, as estimation techniques only need to be used when the actual amount is unknown. Materiality and cost/benefit considerations may come into play as well – there will often be situations where the time and cost involved in calculating a more accurate estimate will outweigh the benefits to be achieved by doing so. Once the improvement in the accuracy of the estimates ceases to be material, the cost of achieving the higher degrcc of accuracy will no longer be justified. Where disclosure of an estimation technique is required by FRS 18, the guidance also suggests that the understandability of each technique to users, and the extent to which it will facilitate comparison with other entities, should also be taken into account when deciding which technique is most appropriate.

Disclosure of techniques adopted

5.24   The standard requires the financial statements to include a description of any estimation techniques adopted that are considered significant. An estimation technique will be significant only if the range of reasonable monetary amounts is so large that the use of a different amount from within that range could materially affect the view shown by the financial statements. Consideration of whether or not an estimation technique is significant will usually involve assessing the impact of the various assumptions underlying the technique. Most estimation techniques will result in monetary amounts that fall within a relatively narrow range, and disclosure under FRS 18 is therefore expected to be rare in practice. Where disclosure is required, the description should include details of the underlying assumptions to which the monetary amount is particularly sensitive.

Changes in estimation techniques

5.25   A change in estimation techniques should not be accounted for as a change in accounting policy, unless accounting standards, UITF Abstracts or companies' legislation specifically require this treatment. A change in estimation techniques will therefore not usually result in a prior period adjustment unless it results from the correction of a fundamental error in previous years. The distinction between a change in estimation techniques and a change in accounting policy is considered in more detail in Chapter 6. Where the effect of a change in an estimation technique is material, FRS 18 requires the financial statements to include a description of the change and, where practicable, the effect on the results for the current period. There is no requirement to disclose the effect on the results for the previous year.

STATEMENTS OF RECOMMENDED PRACTICE (SORPS)

Definition of SORP

5.26   FRS 18 defines a Statement of Recommended Practice (SORP) as an existing SORP developed either:

—   in accordance with the ASB statement 'SORPs: Policy and Code of Practice' and including a statement by the Board in accordance with that Statement; or

—   franked by the former Accounting Standards Committee under its process for the approval of SORPs.

Further details on SORPs and the ASB's Code of Practice are given in Chapter 1.

Disclosure of adoption

5.27   Where an entity's financial statements come within the scope of a SORP, FRS 18 'Accounting Policies' requires the accounts to disclose:

—   the title of the SORP;

—   whether the accounts have been prepared in accordance with the current provisions of the SORP;

—   in the event of a departure from the SORP, a description of the departure including:

    —   the reasons why the treatment adopted is considered more appropriate to the entity's particular circumstances; and

    —   details of any disclosures recommended by the SORP which have not been given, together with the reasons for non-disclosure.

The ASB believes that these disclosures will enhance comparability between the financial statements of entities in the specific industries and sectors for which SORPs have been developed. Quantification of the effect of the departure is not required unless this is necessary for the financial statements to give a true and fair view (this is expected to arise only rarely in practice).

Entities who voluntarily comply with a SORP

5.28   Entities whose accounts do not fall within the scope of a SORP but who nevertheless choose to comply with its recommendations are encouraged to disclose the fact that the accounts have been prepared in accordance with the relevant SORP.

Chapter 6 Comparative Figures and Prior Period Adjustments

COMPARATIVE FIGURES

Company law requirements

6.1   CA 1985 Sch 4 para 4(1) requires corresponding amounts for the previous financial period to be given for each item in the profit and loss account and balance sheet. In general, corresponding amounts must also be given for each item that has to be disclosed in the notes to the accounts, although CA 1985 Sch 4 para 58(3) specifically exempts the following disclosures from this requirement:

— detailed opening and closing balances and movements during the year in respect of fixed assets;

— movements on provisions for liabilities;

— movements on reserves;

— detailed information on loans and other transactions involving directors;

— detailed information on shareholdings in other undertakings;

— detailed information on acquisitions.

CA 1985 Sch 4 para 57(1) also requires separate disclosure of any amount relating to the preceding year which is included in any item in the profit and loss account for the current year.

Comparative figures where there is no current year item

6.2   CA 1985 generally allows a company to exclude a heading or sub-heading normally required by the standard profit or loss account and balance sheet formats if there is no amount to be shown for that heading. However, if an amount was shown under that heading in the accounts for the previous financial period, the heading must be repeated in the current year's accounts so that the comparative figure can be correctly shown, with a nil figure for the current year.

Adjustment of comparative figures

6.3 If the corresponding figure previously reported for any item is not comparable with the figure disclosed in the current year, the corresponding figure must be adjusted and a note to the accounts must disclose:

— particulars of the adjustment – this will usually require both the original and the adjusted figures to be stated; and

— the reasons for making the adjustment.

This allows prior period adjustments to be made in accordance with FRS 3 'Reporting Financial Performance'. Where comparative figures have been adjusted for any reason, it is good practice to include the word 'restated' under the previous year heading on each of the primary statements and any relevant notes to the accounts. This helps to draw the attention of the reader to the fact that the figures have been adjusted. The reason for the restatement should be explained in the notes to the accounts.

Requirements of accounting standards

6.4 FRS 3 'Reporting Financial Performance' requires comparative figures to be given for all items included in the primary statements (i.e. the profit and loss account, balance sheet, cash flow statement and statement of total recognised gains and losses) and all related notes. Comparative figures should also be given for the reconciliation of movements in shareholders' funds and the note of historical cost profits and losses. Where there are both continuing and discontinued activities, FRS 3 requires the comparative figures in the profit and loss account to be adjusted so that the 'continuing' category includes only the results of operations that are classified as continuing in the current year. The detailed requirements of FRS 3 on the disclosure of continuing, acquired and discontinued activities are considered in Chapter 9.

Proposals for change

6.5 The DTI document 'A Consultation on Extending the Use of Summary Financial Statements and Other Minor Changes' published in March 2005 includes a proposal to amend the statutory requirement for comparative figures to be adjusted so that this becomes discretionary rather than mandatory. The ASB published FRED 35 'Corresponding Amounts' at the same time as the DTI consultation document. This proposed standard would generally maintain the position currently set out in company law, but enable individual accounting standards to specify a different approach where appropriate (for instance, as a transitional measure on the implementation of a new accounting standard). The DTI plans to lay the proposed regulations before Parliament in the summer or early autumn of 2005 and expects them to come into force on 1 October 2005. The June 2005 version of the ASB's Technical Plan indicates that it plans to issue a new standard based on FRED 35 in the final quarter of 2005.

PRIOR PERIOD ADJUSTMENTS

Definition of prior period adjustment

6.6   FRS 3 'Reporting Financial Performance' defines prior period adjustments as material adjustments relating to previous accounting periods as a result of changes in accounting policy or the correction of fundamental errors. They do not include normal recurring adjustments or corrections of accounting estimates made in prior periods.

Changes in accounting estimates

6.7   Many items in a set of accounts will require a degree of estimation and it is natural that some correction and adjustment to these estimates will be required as time passes and more accurate details become available. For instance, it is often necessary to estimate amounts to be included in accruals in respect of expenses relating to the year (e.g. electricity and telephone costs) but which have not yet been charged to the company. When the actual charges become known, some adjustment to the original estimates may be necessary. These adjustments should be dealt with in the profit and loss account for the period in which they are identified. In most cases, separate disclosure will not be required. The adjustments should not be considered exceptional or extraordinary simply because they relate to an earlier year. Where the effect of any under or over-estimation in earlier years is material, the effect should be separately disclosed in the notes to the accounts.

Reassessment of provisions

6.8   In some cases, changes may need to be made to original estimates as more experience is acquired or additional information is obtained. Examples of this are provisions for claims relating to faulty products and provisions for future claims against warranties given by a company in respect of its products. As time progresses the company will be able to maintain records of the claims actually received and should therefore be able to predict more accurately what the overall level of claims is likely to be. The provisions can then be reassessed each year in the light of the information received during that year. Any changes made to the provisions will arise from new information received during the year and should therefore be reflected in the profit and loss account for that year. If the provision made at the end of the previous period was the best estimate that could be made at the time, based on the information then available, there is not a fundamental error in the calculations simply because more recent information has resulted in the estimate being revised.

Use of estimation techniques

6.9   FRS 18 'Accounting Policies' considers the use of estimation techniques, which are defined as 'the methods adopted by an entity to arrive at estimated monetary amounts, corresponding to the measurement bases selected for assets, liabilities, gains, losses and changes to shareholders' funds'. An accounting policy will therefore specify the basis on which an item is to be measured, and an estimation technique may be needed to arrive at the amount at which the item is to be reflected in the financial statements. Examples of estimation techniques include:

—   depreciation methods (e.g. straight line, reducing balance) used to estimate the proportion of the economic benefits of asset that have been consumed during an accounting period;

—   methods used to estimate the proportion of trade debts that will not be recovered, where these are based on the population as a whole rather than individual balances;

—   methods used to calculate the proportion of indirect costs attributable to production.

The requirements of the standard on the selection of appropriate estimation techniques, the need for regular review of the techniques adopted and the disclosure of estimation techniques are covered in Chapter 5.

Distinction between estimation techniques and accounting policies

6.10   FRS 18 includes detailed discussion on the distinction between estimation techniques and accounting policies. Whilst accounting policies will usually prescribe the measurement bases to be used for particular assets and liabilities, they do not usually specify the method to be used to arrive at the required monetary amount. In some cases this amount will be known and there will be no uncertainty over its measurement. In other cases some form of estimate may need to be made. For example, an accounting policy may involve the current disposal value of a particular asset. This value may be estimated by reference to recent disposals of similar assets or by reference to prices quoted in advertisements for similar assets. Either method should arrive at a reasonable estimate of the monetary amount required. A change from one method of estimation to the other would be a change in estimation techniques, not a change in accounting policy. An appendix to FRS 18 gives practical examples of the distinction between changes in estimation techniques and changes in accounting policies. These include:

— interest relating to the construction of fixed assets has previously been charged to the profit and loss account but is now to be capitalised – this is a change of accounting policy;

— an entity reassesses the proportion of indirect costs attributable to production – this is a change of estimation technique;

— overheads previously classified as cost of sales are now to be shown within administrative expenses – this is a change of accounting policy;

— an asset previously depreciated using the reducing balance method is now to be depreciated using the straight line method – this is a change of estimation technique (i.e. the accounting policy is still to depreciate the asset over its useful economic life – the change is in the estimation technique used to measure the unexpired portion of the asset's economic benefits);

— deferred tax is to be reported on a discounted basis for the first time – this is a change in measurement basis and is therefore a change of accounting policy (i.e. FRS 19 allows an option of reporting deferred tax on a discounted or undiscounted basis);

— a provision has previously been measured on an undiscounted basis because the effect of discounting was not material, but the estimates of future cash flows have now changed with the result that the effect of discounting is material and the provision must therefore be reported at a discounted amount under the requirements of FRS 12 – this is a change of estimation technique (i.e. the policy is still to report the provision at the best estimate of the expenditure required to settle the obligation, but the method of arriving at that 'best estimate' has changed).

As can be seen from the above, the circumstances of each case must be considered very carefully to establish whether the change affects the measurement basis, and therefore the accounting policy, or simply the technique used to arrive at the amount required by the accounting policy. Particular care is needed when an accounting change involves both a change in presentation and a change in estimation techniques – the former is a change of accounting policy but the latter is not, and the two elements of the change must therefore be accounted for separately.

Changes in estimation techniques

6.11 A change in estimation techniques should not be accounted for as a change in accounting policy, unless accounting standards, UITF Abstracts or companies' legislation specifically require this treatment. A change in estimation techniques will therefore not usually result in a prior period adjustment unless it results from the correction of a fundamental error in previous years. Where the effect of a change in an estimation technique is material, FRS 18 requires the financial statements to include:

(i)   a description of the change; and

(ii)   where practicable, the effect on the results for the current period.

There is no requirement to disclose the effect on results for the previous year.

Change of accounting policy

6.12   Consistency of accounting treatment is one of the accounting principles identified in CA 1985. FRS 18 'Accounting Policies' also considers consistency but in the context of the need for comparability in the presentation of financial information. The standard notes that consistency is not an end in itself and should not be allowed to impede improvements in accounting. FRS 18 requires accounting policies to be regularly reviewed to ensure that they remain the most appropriate in the particular circumstances of the entity for the purpose of giving a true and fair view. They should generally only be changed when the benefits to users will outweigh the disadvantages.

Reasons for changing an accounting policy

6.13   Situations will inevitably arise from time to time which make it appropriate for an entity to change one of its accounting policies. For instance, a new accounting standard may have been introduced which requires a different accounting treatment to the one adopted by the entity in previous years – as an example, the introduction of FRS 12 'Provisions, Contingent Liabilities and Contingent Assets' required many companies to reassess whether provisions already included in their accounts were still justified under the new rules. Similarly, the nature or scale of an entity's activities or transactions may change, so that an accounting policy previously adopted is no longer acceptable (i.e. because items that were previously immaterial have now become material). Examples of this might include:

—   an entity which had previously only entered into minor finance leases entering into a finance lease agreement in respect of a substantial asset or assets;

—   an entity that had previously only carried out an insignificant level of research and development expanding its activities in this field by becoming involved in a major product development project.

Where it is necessary to implement a new accounting policy, or to change an existing policy, the guidance in FRS 18 notes that the entity should ensure wherever possible that the new policy adopted is in accordance with recently issued accounting standards.

Change in the method of applying an accounting policy

6.14   It is important to distinguish a change in the way an accounting policy is applied from a change in the accounting policy itself. For instance, in the case of depreciation, the underlying policy is to depreciate assets over their useful economic lives. If a company reassesses the economic lives of its assets and this results in the rate of depreciation being changed, this is simply a change in the way that the accounting policy is applied, rather than a change in the policy itself. Alternatively, where a company has a policy of not depreciating land and buildings and decides that, in future, buildings will be depreciated, this may constitute a change in accounting policy. However, the findings of the Financial Reporting Review Panel, published in September 2001 following a review of the accounts of Groupe Chez Gerard plc for the period ended 25 June 2000, emphasised that this will depend on the reasons for non-depreciation in previous years. For instance, if the assets were not previously depreciated on the grounds of immateriality but revisions to useful economic lives and residual values result in a depreciation charge being introduced, this would not constitute a change in accounting policy. The carrying amounts of the relevant assets would therefore be depreciated prospectively over their remaining useful economic lives in accordance with the normal requirements of FRS 15.

Accounting treatment on change of accounting policy

6.15   Where an accounting policy is changed, the figures for the current and the previous financial period should be stated on the basis of the new policy. This will result in a prior period adjustment which, under FRS 3, should be accounted for by:

— restating the relevant corresponding amounts in each of the primary statements;

— restating the relevant corresponding amounts in the notes to the accounts, including the note of historical cost profits and losses;

— adjusting the opening balance on reserves by the cumulative effect of all the necessary adjustments to the figures for previous periods;

— noting the cumulative effect of the adjustments at the foot of the statement of total recognised gains and losses for the current period – this is because the adjustment represents a gain or loss that has been recognised in the period, even though it actually relates to previous periods;

— adjusting the opening balance on the reconciliation of shareholders' funds for the previous year for the cumulative effect of adjustments to that date.

A worked example showing the presentation of a prior period adjustment in the accounts is given in the Appendix to this chapter.

Disclosure of change in accounting policy

6.16   On a change of accounting policy, the notes to the accounts should explain:

— the new accounting policy;

— the previous accounting policy;

— the reasons for the change; and

— the effect of the change in accounting policy on the results for the current financial period and the previous financial period.

In setting out the reasons for the change in accounting policy it is not sufficient simply to state that the new accounting policy is more appropriate. The notes must explain briefly why this is the case. If it is not practicable to disclose the effect of the change on the results for the current or preceding financial period, this fact must be stated and the reasons why disclosure is not practicable must also be given.

Correction of fundamental error

6.17   In certain circumstances, it is possible that the accounts for earlier years included errors that were so significant that they destroyed the true and fair view and thus the validity of those accounts. However, such errors should be very rare in practice. Where they do arise, they should be accounted for by restating the results for earlier years and adjusting the opening balance on the profit and loss reserve. In effect, this results in a prior period adjustment as discussed in 6.15 above. In practice, it may sometimes be difficult to make the distinction between the normal revision of an accounting estimate and a fundamental error. The emphasis in FRS 3 on the 'exceptional circumstances' of a fundamental error suggests that most items should be classified as normal revisions to accounting estimates, with separate disclosure where the effect is material. Where the accounts include a prior period adjustment to correct a fundamental error, the notes to the accounts should explain the reason for the adjustment and the amounts involved.

APPENDIX

Worked example of a prior period adjustment

The draft accounts of X Ltd for the year ended 31 December 20X5 and the comparatives from the statutory accounts for 20X4 are as follows.

Profit and loss account

	20X5	20X4
	£	£
	(Draft)	(Actual)
Turnover	541,960	487,732
Cost of sales	(375,998)	(331,750)
	165,962	155,982
Distribution costs	(85,670)	(74,669)
Administrative expenses	(50,443)	(43,771)
Operating profit	29,849	37,542
Interest receivable and similar income	10,976	8,751
Interest payable and similar charges	(8,779)	(11,772)
Profit on ordinary activities before taxation	32,046	34,521
Taxation	(9,550)	(8,750)
Profit on ordinary activities after taxation and for the financial year	22,496	25,771

Statement of total recognised gains and losses

	20X5	20X4
	£	£
Profit for the financial year	22,496	25,771
Unrealised surplus on revaluation of leasehold property	15,650	—
	38,146	25,771

Balance sheet

	20X5 £ (Draft)	20X4 £ (Actual)
Fixed assets:		
Tangible assets	175,690	145,788
Current assets:		
Stocks	195,678	185,743
Debtors	90,665	85,721
Cash at bank and in hand	10,250	7,564
	296,593	279,028
Creditors: amounts falling due within one year	(175,673)	(160,309)
Net current assets	120,920	118,719
Total assets less current liabilities	296,610	264,507
Creditors: amounts falling due after more than one year	(145,575)	(130,875)
Provisions for liabilities	(51,784)	(57,527)
	99,251	76,105
Called up share capital	30,000	30,000
Revaluation reserve	15,650	—
Profit and loss account	53,601	46,105
	99,251	76,105

Reconciliation of movements in shareholders' funds

	20X5 £	20X4 £
Profit for the financial year	22,496	25,771
Dividends paid	(15,000)	(15,000)
	7,496	10,771
Other gains and losses relating to the year	15,650	—
Net addition to shareholders funds	23,146	10,771
Opening shareholders funds	76,105	65,334
Closing shareholders funds	99,251	76,105

Movements on reserves

	Profit and loss account	Revaluation reserve
At 1 January 20X5	46,105	—
Retained profit for the year	7,496	—
Surplus on revaluation of leasehold property	—	15,650
At 31 December 20X5	53,601	15,650

In previous years, X Ltd has not depreciated its freehold property. Following a review of the accounting policies, the directors have decided that the freehold building should be depreciated over its expected useful economic life. The building was acquired on 1 January 20X0 at a cost of £75,000 and its estimated useful life is 50 years from the date of acquisition. The freehold building is used only for administration purposes. All manufacturing is carried out in the leasehold property. The building is currently included in the draft accounts for 1996 and the accounts for 1995 at its original cost of £75,000. If it had been depreciated since acquisition, its value would be:

	£
Cost 1 January 20X0	75,000
Depreciation 20X0 75,000 x 2%	(1,500)
NBV at 31 December 20X0	73,500
Depreciation 20X1 75,000 x 2%	(1,500)
NBV at 31 December 20X1	72,000
Depreciation 20X2 75,000 x 2%	(1,500)
NBV at 31 December 20X2	70,500
Depreciation 20X3 75,000 x 2%	(1,500)
NBV at 31 December 20X3	69,000
Depreciation 20X4 75,000 x 2%	(1,500)
NBV at 31 December 20X4	67,500
Depreciation 20X5 75,000 x 2%	(1,500)
NBV at 31 December 20X5	66,000

Fixed assets at 31 December 20X4 therefore need to be reduced by £7,500 (i.e. £75,000 – £67,500) and fixed assets in the draft accounts at 31 December 20X5 need to be reduced by £9,000 (i.e. £75,000 – £66,000).

The profit and loss account for both years needs to include a depreciation charge of £1,500, and opening reserves at 1 January 20X4 need to be reduced by £6,000 to reflect the depreciation that should have been charged in 20X0 to 20X3 inclusive (i.e. four years at £1,500 each year). The depreciation charge is treated as an additional administrative expense, as the freehold building is only used for administration. After the prior period adjustment, the accounts will be presented as follows.

Profit and loss account for the year ended 31 December 20X5

	20X5	20X4
	£	£
		Restated
Turnover	541,960	487,732
Cost of sales	(375,998)	(331,750)
	165,962	155,982
Distribution costs	(85,670)	(74,669)
Administrative expenses*	(51,943)	(45,271)
Operating profit	28,349	36,042
Interest receivable and similar income	10,976	8,751
Interest payable and similar charges	(8,779)	(11,772)
Profit on ordinary activities before taxation	30,546	33,021
Taxation	(9,550)	(8,750)
Profit on ordinary activities after taxation and for the financial year	20,996	24,271

* £50,443 + £1,500 = £51,943 in 20X5
£43,771 + £1,500 = £45,271 in 20X4

Statement of total recognised gains and losses

	20X5	20X4
	£	£
		Restated
Profit for the financial year	20,996	24,271
Unrealised surplus on revaluation of leasehold property	15,650	—
Total gains and losses recognised relating to the year	36,646	24,271
Prior year adjustment (as explained in note)*	(7,500)	
Total gains and losses recognised since the last annual report	29,146	

*£1,500 relating to 20X4 + £6,000 relating to 20X0 – 20X3

The figure disclosed as the total gains and losses recognised since the last report can be reconciled as follows:

	£
Total gains and losses recognised in the year	29,146
Dividends paid	(15,000)
	14,146
Shareholders funds at 31 December 20X4 as reported in 20X4 statutory accounts	76,105
Shareholders funds at 31 December 20X5 as reported in final accounts for 20X5	90,251
	14,146

Balance sheet as at 31 December 20X5

	20X5	20X4
	£	£
		Restated
Fixed assets:		
Tangible assets*	166,690	138,288
Current assets:		
Stocks	195,678	185,743
Debtors	90,665	85,721
Cash at bank and in hand	10,250	7,564
	296,593	279,028
Creditors: amounts falling due within one year	(175,673)	(160,309)
Net current assets	120,920	118,719
Total assets less current liabilities	287,610	257,007
Creditors: amounts falling due after more than one year	(145,575)	(130,875)
Provisions for liabilities	(51,784)	(57,527)
	90,251	68,605
Called up share capital	30,000	30,000
Revaluation reserve	15,650	—
Profit and loss account	44,601	38,605
	90,251	68,605
* Reduced by £9,000 in 20X5 and £7,500 in 20X4 to reflect the depreciation charged to date under the new accounting policy		

Reconciliation of movements in shareholders' funds

		20X5		*20X4*
		£		*£*
				Restated
Profit for the financial year		20,996		24,271
Dividends paid		(15,000)		(15,000)
		5,996		9,271
Other gains and losses relating to the year		15,650		
Net addition to shareholders funds		21,646		9,271
Opening shareholders funds:				—
As previously reported	76,105		65,334	
Prior period adjustment	(7,500)		(6,000)	
		68,605		59,334
Closing shareholders funds		90,251		68,605

Movements on reserves

	Profit and loss account	*Revaluation reserve*
	£	*£*
At 1 January 20X5 as previously reported	46,105	—
Prior period adjustment	(7,500)	—
At 1 January 20X5 as restated	38,605	—
Retained profit for the year	5,996	—
Surplus on revaluation of leasehold property	—	15,650
At 31 December 20X5	44,601	15,650

Change of accounting policy

Freehold buildings were not depreciated in previous years as their estimated future residual value was considered to be at least equal to their book value. In the light of current best practice, the directors now consider it more appropriate to provide for the depreciation of freehold buildings on a straight-line basis over the expected useful economic life of the building. The effect of this change in accounting policy has been to increase the depreciation charge within administrative expenses by £1,500 in both 20X5 and 20X4, and to reduce reserves at 1 January 20X4 by £6,000 in respect of the depreciation that would have been charged in earlier years. In the balance sheet, the value of tangible fixed assets has been reduced by £9,000 at 31 December 20X5 and by £7,500 at 31 December 20X4.

Chapter 7   Foreign Currency Translation

GENERAL BACKGROUND TO FOREIGN CURRENCY TRANSLATION

Relevant accounting standards

7.1   At present, SSAP 20 'Foreign Currency Translation' continues to be the relevant accounting standard for most UK entities. However, in December 2004, the ASB published a package of new UK accounting standards (based on equivalent international accounting standards) that apply to listed companies for accounting periods beginning on or after 1 January 2005, and to other entities for accounting periods beginning on or after 1 January 2006 but only if they choose to adopt fair value accounting (see Chapter 1). The package of new standards comprises:

(i)   FRS 23 'The Effects of Changes in Foreign Prices';

(ii)   FRS 24 'Financial Reporting in Hyperinflationary Economies';

(iii)   the disclosure requirements of FRS 25 'Financial Instruments: Disclosure and Presentation' (note that the presentation requirements of this standard apply to all entities for accounting periods beginning on or after 1 January 2005); and

(iv)   FRS 26 'Financial Instruments: Measurement'.

In April 2005, the ASB published an Exposure Draft 'Amendment to FRS 26: Extension of Scope and Recognition and Derecognition'. This proposes extending the scope of FRS 26 so that it applies to all UK entities (other than those adopting the FRSSE). Entities brought within the scope of FRS 26 as a result of this change would also have to comply with FRS 23, FRS 24 and the disclosure requirements of FRS 25. The Exposure Draft proposes that this change should apply for accounting periods beginning on or after 1 January 2007, although the ASB notes that the effective date may be deferred to 2008 if responses to the proposals indicate that entities need more time to prepare for the change.The new standards cannot be adopted early because many of their requirements hinge on company law changes that also come into effect on 1 January 2005. Entities who are required to adopt the package from 1 January 2006 can voluntarily apply the new standards from 1 January 2005 if they wish, provided that they apply all of the standards in the package – it is not acceptable to adopt some of the standards but not the others. Entities that have not adopted FRS 26 are not permitted to adopt FRS 23 or FRS 24. For entities that are required to adopt the package, FRS 23 supersedes SSAP 20 and FRS 24 supersedes UITF Abstract 9 'Accounting for Operations in Hyperinflationary Economies'. The requirements of SSAP 20 (and UITF Abstract 9, where relevant) remain in force in all other cases.

The sections below deal primarily with the accounting issues that arise from SSAP 20, on the basis that most UK entities are likely to continue to apply this standard for the immediate future at least, but significant changes under the new standards are also highlighted where relevant.

Objectives of foreign currency translation

7.2   In the case of individual transactions denominated in other currencies, the explanatory note to SSAP 20 defines the objectives of foreign currency translation as follows:

—   to produce results which are generally compatible with the effect of rate changes on a company's cash flows and its equity; and

—   to ensure that the accounts present a true and fair view of the results of management actions.

Although SSAP 20 has been in issue since 1983, foreign currency translation remains a problematic area, although most of the difficulties arise from translation for consolidation purposes rather than the translation of transactions for inclusion in an individual company's accounts.

FRS 23 notes that the objective of the standard is to prescribe how to include foreign currency transactions and foreign operations in the financial statements of an entity. FRS 23 also deals with the translation of the financial statements as a whole into a different currency for presentation purposes, an issue that is not common practice in the UK and is not covered in SSAP 20.

Both SSAP 20 and FRS 23 deal with two separate aspects of dealing with foreign currency items in the context of annual accounts:

(i)   the translation of business transactions in other currencies entered into by an individual company;

(ii)   the translation of the results and net assets of foreign operations conducted through entities which maintain their accounting records in another currency.

This chapter deals only with the first aspect of the standards The translation of the accounts of foreign operations for consolidation purposes is considered in Chapter 50.

Need for consistency

7.3   A particular concern is the fact that, in some cases, differing treatments are equally acceptable under SSAP 20, so that two sets of accounts reflecting similar foreign currency transactions may show substantially different results. This makes understanding the figures and comparison between companies more difficult and is one reason why a clear description of the accounting policy adopted in respect of foreign currency translation is so important.

The other important point is the need for consistency from year to year within an individual company. Although different treatments may be acceptable under SSAP 20, this does not mean that a company is free to choose which treatment to adopt each year. Where a choice is available, the decision on which treatment to adopt must be taken when foreign currency translation first affects the accounts, and the treatment chosen should be adopted each year from then on unless there are good reasons for making a change.

To help ensure consistency between years, companies may find it helpful to document the detailed policies adopted in respect of foreign currency translation. Although the basic policy requires disclosure in the annual accounts, additional detail will usually be necessary to ensure that there is complete consistency year by year. Formal documentation of the detail behind the policy can be particularly useful where there are changes in the personnel responsible for preparing the company's accounts.

FRS 23 does not offer the same degree of flexibility as SSAP 20, so that lack of comparability between entities should not be a such significant issue where this standard is applied.

Basis of invoicing

7.4   The need for foreign currency translation in respect of trading items only arises if the company invoices customers in a foreign currency and/or commits itself to making payments in another currency for goods and services that it has received. For instance, if the company reaches agreement with its customers that all sales invoices will be raised in sterling, it is the sterling values that will be recorded in the accounting records and there will be no need for translation. In this case, the customer will bear any potential exchange loss and benefit from any potential exchange gain. Similarly, if the company is able to agree with its overseas suppliers that all invoices will be raised in sterling, there is no need to record any foreign currency amounts in the accounting records and hence no requirement for translation. Here the supplier will bear any potential exchange loss and benefit from any potential exchange gain. The following guidance, therefore, relates only to situations where a company is either receiving or making payment in a foreign currency.

Translation

7.5   Translation is defined in SSAP 20 as 'the process whereby financial data denominated in one currency are expressed in terms of another currency'. The definition emphasises that translation applies both to individual transactions and also to a full set of accounts.

Local currency

7.6   Local currency is defined in SSAP 20 'the currency of the primary economic environment in which [the company] operates and generates net cash flow'. For most UK accounting purposes, therefore, foreign currency translation refers to the conversion of amounts denominated in other currencies into sterling.

FRS 23 takes a different approach and includes separate definitions of foreign currency, functional currency and presentation currency. Functional currency is defined as the currency of the primary economic environment in which the entity operates and foreign currency is defined as any currency other than the entity's functional currency. The standard includes detailed guidance on the factors that should be taken into account in determining functional currency – for instance, these might include:

(i)   the main influences on sales prices;

(ii)   the main influences on labour, materials and other costs;

(iii)   the currency in which funds from financing activities are generated;

(iv)   the currency in which receipts from operating activities are usually retained

Of these, (i) and (ii) are considered to be the primary indicators of functional currency. Once established, the functional currency should not be changed unless there is a change in the underlying transactions, events and conditions (see 7.36 below). Special requirements also apply under FRS 23 where the functional currency is that of a hyperinflationary economy (see 7.39 to 7.41 below)

Presentation currency is defined as the currency in which the financial statements are presented. Under FRS 23, there is no requirement for this to be the functional currency, but specific translation requirements apply where the presentation currency differs from the functional currency (see 7.37 below).

Exchange rate and closing rate

7.7 An exchange rate is defined in SSAP 20 as 'a rate at which two currencies may be exchanged for each other at a particular point in time'. The closing rate is defined as 'the exchange rate for spot transactions ruling at the balance sheet date'. The closing rate is also defined in more detail as the average of buying and selling rates at the close of business on the day for which the rate is to be ascertained. Therefore, if the balance sheet date is 31 March, the closing rate will be the average of the buying and selling rate at the close of business on 31 March. If there is no trading on the balance sheet date, the equivalent rate on the last previous trading day is usually used as the best approximation.

FRS 23 defines an exchange rate as the ratio of exchange for two currencies and the closing rate as the spot exchange rate at the balance sheet date. The standard also defines the spot exchange rate as the exchange rate for immediate delivery.

Forward contract

7.8 A forward contract is defined in SSAP 20 as 'an agreement to exchange different currencies at a specified future date and at a specified rate'. Forward contracts are a useful way of hedging against exposure to potentially significant exchange losses. For instance, if a company is due to receive a payment in a foreign currency, by taking out a forward contract it can guarantee that it will be able to exchange the currency for a specific sterling value. However, by removing the potential risk attached to the foreign currency receipt, the company will usually also lose the potential benefit of realising an exchange gain.

FRS 23 does not include an equivalent definition as hedge accounting is dealt with in FRS 26 'Financial Instruments: Measurement' rather than in FRS 23.

Monetary items

7.9 Monetary items are defined in SSAP 20 as 'money held and amounts to be received or paid in money'. Monetary items will usually comprise cash, bank balances, loans, debtors and creditors. SSAP 20 also requires each monetary item to be classified as short-term or long-term, as different accounting treatments may be necessary in the case of some long-term items. A short-term item is defined as one which falls due within one year of the balance sheet date.

FRS 23 defines monetary items as units of currency held, and assets and liabilities to be received or paid in a fixed or determinable number of units of currency. The guidance notes the following examples of monetary items:

(i)   pensions and other employee benefits to be paid in cash;

(ii)   provisions to be settled in cash;

(iii)   cash dividends recognised as a liability; and

(iv)   a contract to receive or deliver a variable number of the entity's own equity instruments, or a variable amount of assets, in which the fair value to be received or delivered equals a fixed or determinable number of units of currency.

Examples of non-monetary items include goodwill, intangible assets, property, plant and equipment, stocks, prepayments for goods and services, and provisions to be settled by the delivery of a non-monetary asset.

TRANSLATION OF FOREIGN CURRENCY TRANSACTIONS

Basic requirement

7.10   The basic accounting treatment under SSAP 20 is that each individual foreign currency transaction should be translated into local currency (which in most cases will be sterling) at the exchange rate ruling when the transaction occurred. If a company has only one or two foreign currency transactions a year, translation on this basis should be relatively straightforward. However, where a company regularly enters into such transactions (e.g. it makes significant purchases from overseas suppliers or sells regularly to overseas customers), this approach is clearly impractical. The standard therefore permits the use of an average rate for a period, as an approximation to the actual rate, provided that rates do not fluctuate widely.

The same basic requirement continues to apply under FRS 23, in that the standard requires a foreign currency transaction to be recorded on initial recognition in the functional currency by applying the spot exchange rate between the two currencies at the date of the transaction. The guidance also notes that, for practical purposes, a rate approximating the actual rate is often used and that an average rate for a week/month might be used provided that exchange rates do not fluctuate significantly during that period.

Date when the transaction occurs

7.11   SSAP 20 requires translation to be at the rate ruling when the transaction occurred but does not provide any guidance on how this date should be established. For instance it might be the date when:

—   a contract was signed;

—   a formal order was placed; or

—   the goods or services were delivered.

If exchange rates are fluctuating, the amount of exchange gain or loss recorded on the transaction could be substantially different, depending on which date is used. The most straightforward approach, and the most common approach in practice, is to use the date when the transaction is first recorded in the accounting records (assuming that the accounting records are properly prepared and kept up to date). This will often be the date of delivery as this is when:

— in the case of purchases, the receipt of the goods or services, and the company's liability to pay for them, will first be recorded in the accounting records in some way;

— in the case of sales, the company will record the sale and the fact that the customer has a liability to pay for the goods or services that he has received.

At the time of invoicing the company needs to record either a creditor or a debtor in its accounting records, based on the actual exchange rate on the delivery date or the average rate that the company is using for that period.

The guidance in FRS 23 is more slightly specific that the date of a transaction is the date on which it first qualifies for recognition in accordance with accounting standards.

Contracted rate

7.12   Under SSAP 20, if the terms of the transaction specify that it is to be settled at a contracted rate, this rate should be used to translate the transaction when it is recorded in the company's accounting records. This situation is almost equivalent to the company buying or selling in sterling as the company knows how much it must pay, or how much it will receive, and as a result it does not bear any exchange risk in relation to the transaction.

FRS 23 does not make any exception to the use of the spot rate on the date of the transaction and so does not permit the use of a contracted rate for the initial recording of a foreign currency transaction.

Calculation of exchange gains and losses

7.13   The exchange gain or loss in respect of each transaction will be the difference between the amount recorded in the accounting records (i.e. based on the translation procedure outlined above) and the exchange rate ruling on the date that payment is actually received or made.

Example 7.1 – Calculation of exchange gains and losses

On 1 April 200X, A Ltd delivered goods to a German company, the value of the sale being 7,500 Euros. The customer paid for the goods on 15 May 200X.

The relevant £ : Euro exchange rates were:

1 April 200X	£1:	1.64 Euros
15 May 200X	£1:	1.57 Euros

Therefore:

— at the time the goods were delivered, A Ltd should have recorded a sale (and an equivalent debtor) of £4,573.17 (i.e. 7,500 Euros at an exchange rate of £1: 1.64 Euros);

— when payment is made, the company will in effect receive £4,777.07 (i.e. 7,500 Euros at an exchange rate of £1: 1.57 Euros).

The company will therefore record an exchange gain of £203.90 on this transaction.

Use of a forward contract

7.14   Under SSAP 20, where a company takes out a matching or related forward contract to hedge against any exposure to exchange risk, the exchange rate specified in the forward contract may be used to translate the transaction. This is expressed in the standard as an option rather than a requirement. Using the contract rate means that the transaction is recorded from the outset at the value that it will eventually realise and that no exchange gain or loss will be recorded. If a company wishes to adopt this treatment, it must adopt it for all foreign currency transactions which have related or matching forward contracts. UITF Abstract 21 clarifies that the introduction of the euro should not have any impact on the accounting treatment used by entities that adopt this policy.

As noted at 7.12 above, FRS 23 does not permit the use of anything other than the spot rate on the date of the transaction (or a close approximation to it) for the initial recording of a foreign currency transaction. However, the standard notes specifically that it does not apply to hedge accounting in respect of foreign currency items. Where a foreign currency transaction qualifies as a hedged item under FRS 26 'Financial Instruments: Measurement', and the entity comes within the scope of FRS 26 (see 7.1 above), the requirements of that standard should be applied .

Options

7.15   A company may also hedge against the potential exposure to exchange losses by taking out an option to buy or sell currency at a specified rate (as opposed to a forward contract, where the company is committed to buy or sell at the specified rate). Where the company takes out an option rather than a forward contract, the option can be exercised to prevent an exchange loss arising (i.e. if exchange rates at the time of payment are unfavourable). If exchange rates at the time of payment are favourable, the company can ignore the option and buy or sell at the prevailing rate to realise an exchange gain. In other words, taking out an option enables a company to hedge against a potential risk of an exchange loss without forfeiting the potential benefit of an exchange gain. Although options are not specifically discussed in SSAP 20, there seems to be no reason why they should not be treated in the same way as forward contracts, because the company has taken the decision to guarantee a minimum level of income in each case. If the transaction is recorded at the rate specified in the option and the option is exercised, there will be no exchange gain or loss to record. If the option is not exercised (i.e. because prevailing exchange rates at the time of payment are more favourable), the company will record an exchange gain representing the effect of the difference between the exchange rate in the option and the prevailing rate at the time of payment.

Example 7.2 – Using options

On 1 April 200X A Ltd delivered goods to a German company, the value of the sale being 7,500 Euros.

The relevant £ : Euro exchange rates were:

1 April 200X £1: 1.64 Euros

15 May 200X £1: 1.70 Euros

16 June 200X £1: 1.50 Euros

A Ltd had also taken out a related option at £1: 1.60 Euros.

(i) The customer pays on 15 May 200X.
   — A Ltd can record the sale at the exchange rate at the date of delivery as in Example 7.1 (i.e. £4,573.17). As a result of taking out the related option, A Ltd will eventually receive £4,687.50 (i.e. 7,500 Euros at an exchange rate of £1: 1.60 Euros) in respect of the transaction, and will therefore record an exchange gain of £150.33.
   — Alternatively, A Ltd can use the exchange rate in the related option to record the sale at the date of delivery, as this is the minimum amount that it is guaranteed to receive in respect of the sale; in this case the sale would be recorded at £4,687.50 and no exchange gain or loss will arise when payment is received.

(ii) The customer pays on 16 June 200X.
   — A Ltd can record the sale at the exchange rate at the date of delivery as in Example 7.1 (i.e. £4,573.17). As the exchange rate at the date of payment is £1: 1.50 Euros, A Ltd will choose not to exercise the option that it holds. It will therefore receive £5,000.00 at the date of payment and record an exchange gain of £426.83.
   — Alternatively, A Ltd can use the exchange rate in the related option to record the sale at the date of delivery as this is the minimum amount that it is guaranteed to receive in respect of the sale; in this case the sale would be recorded at £4,687.50 (i.e. 7,500 Euros at an exchange rate of £1: 1.60 Euros). As the exchange rate at the date of payment is £1: 1.50 Euros, A Ltd will choose not to exercise the option that it holds. It will therefore receive £5,000.00 at the date of payment and record an exchange gain of £312.50.

FRS 23 does not permit the use of anything other than the spot rate on the date of the transaction (or a close approximation to it) for the initial recording of a foreign currency transaction. However, where a foreign currency transaction qualifies as a hedged item under FRS 26 'Financial Instruments: Measurement', and the entity comes within the scope of FRS 26 (see 7.1 above), the requirements of that standard should be applied.

Impact on the profit and loss account

7.16   The above examples illustrate how the amounts shown as turnover and exchange gains or losses in the accounts can vary SSAP 20 depending on which approach is adopted. The same applies to items of expenditure denominated in a foreign currency. This reinforces the need for a consistent approach to be taken year by year. However, it should be noted that the net profit or loss in respect of an individual transaction reflected in the profit and loss account will be the same, regardless of which approach is used – it is just the analysis between individual profit and loss account headings that will differ. The treatment of exchange gains and losses in the profit and loss account is considered below (see 7.20–7.28).

TRANSLATION OF ASSETS AND LIABILITIES

Non-monetary assets

7.17   Non-monetary assets comprise assets such as:

—   property;

—   plant and machinery;

—   investments;

—   intangible fixed assets;

—   stocks.

These assets should be translated on the basis described above, at the date when they are acquired and no further exchange adjustment should generally be necessary.

Example 7.3 – Non-monetary assets

A Ltd buys a machine costing DM 100,000 from a supplier in Germany. The machine is delivered on 1 September 199X and A Ltd pays for the machine on 15 October 199X.

The exchange rates are:

1 September 199X £1: DM 2.20

15 October 199X £1: DM 2.23

When the machine is delivered A Ltd should record it in fixed assets at £45,455 (i.e. DM 100,000 at an exchange rate of £1 : DM 2.20). This will be the cost of the asset for depreciation purposes and no further currency adjustments will need to be made to the value of the plant.

When A Ltd pays for the machine on 15 October it will actually pay £44,843 (i.e. DM 100,000 at an exchange rate of £1 : DM 2.23). It should therefore record an exchange gain of £612 in the profit and loss account for the year.

An alternative to the above treatment for non-monetary assets may be adopted in the case of foreign equity investments (see 7.30).

Under FRS 23, non-monetary items measured at historical cost in a foreign currency should be translated using the exchange rate at the date of the transaction, and non-monetary items measured at fair value in a foreign currency should be translated using the exchange rate at the date when fair value was determined. Where the carrying amount of an item is determined by comparing two or more amounts (e.g. the lower of cost and net realisable value), the guidance in FRS 23 notes that the carrying amount should be determined by comparing the cost (or other carrying amount) translated at the date when that amount was determined with the net realisable value (or other recoverable amount) translated at the date when that value was determined (e.g. the closing rate at the balance sheet date). This may result in an impairment loss being recognised in the functional currency but not in the foreign currency (or vice versa).

Monetary assets and liabilities

7.18   At the balance sheet date, a company may hold monetary assets and liabilities denominated in a foreign currency, for instance foreign currency loans, foreign currency bank balances or overdrafts, overseas debtors and/or overseas creditors. For accounts purposes, these assets and liabilities should be translated at the closing rate of exchange unless they are due to be settled at a contracted rate, in which case this rate should be used. If the company has taken out matching or related forward contracts, the rates in these contracts may be used instead.

Under FRS 23, monetary assets and liabilities denominated in a foreign currency must be translated at the closing rate at the balance sheet date. There is no option to use a contracted rate as under SSAP 20.

Overseas debtors and creditors

7.19   Sales and purchases will usually have been translated at the exchange rate prevailing at the date of the transaction and the related debtor or creditor will have been recorded at the same amount. At the balance sheet date, therefore, any outstanding overseas debtors or creditors will be stated in the accounting records at a sterling value, but if exchange rates have varied, this will not be the same as the original currency value translated at the closing exchange rate. The balances in the accounting records will therefore need to be adjusted and an exchange gain or loss recorded. If the company has taken out a matching or related forward contract to limit the potential exposure to an exchange loss, SSAP 20 allows the rate specified in the contract to be used to translate the year-end balance for accounts purposes. However, for consistency, this should only be done if the company has used the contract rate to translate the original transaction.

RECORDING EXCHANGE GAINS AND LOSSES

Settled transactions

7.20   Exchange gains and losses on transactions that have been settled during the year should be included in the profit and loss account for the year. Where exchange gains and losses arise on transactions between members of a group, the gains and losses should be included in the profit and loss account of each individual company in exactly the same way as those arising on transactions with third parties.

Unsettled short-term monetary transactions

7.21   Exchange gains and losses on short-term monetary transactions that are still outstanding at the balance sheet date should also be included in the profit and loss account for the year. This is on the basis that it is reasonably certain that the gains or losses in respect of these transactions will be reflected in the company's cash flows in the near future, even though they are not actually realised at the balance sheet date (e.g. balances appearing in trade debtors and creditors will usually be paid within a few weeks of the balance sheet date).

Unsettled long-term monetary transactions

7.22   In most cases, exchange gains and losses on unsettled long-term monetary transactions (i.e. those that are due more than one year after the balance sheet date) should also be recognised in the profit and loss account for the year. Paragraph 10 of SSAP 20 discusses the rationale behind this requirement. However, in exceptional circumstances, it may be necessary, on the grounds of prudence, to restrict the amount of the exchange gain that is recognised in the profit and loss account, or the amount by which an exchange gain exceeds exchange losses recorded in previous years in respect of the same asset or liability. Such restrictions are rare in practice and should arise only where there are concerns over whether the currency in question is convertible or marketable.

FRS 23 requires all exchange gains and losses on monetary items to be recognised in the profit and loss account in the period in which they arise.

Impact on distributable reserves

7.23   The accounting treatment generally required by SSAP 20 (and FRS 23) in respect of long-term monetary assets and liabilities means that unrealised gains and losses may be included in the profit and loss account. Where a company has such long-term assets and liabilities it is helpful to maintain a separate record of the unrealised gains and losses credited or charged to the profit and loss account in respect of each item. If a company with unsettled foreign currency long-term monetary transactions wishes to make a distribution, particular care will be needed in establishing the amount of reserves that are available for distribution, and legal advice may need to be taken.

True and fair override

7.24   The accounting treatment required by SSAP 20 (and FRS 23) in respect of unsettled long-term monetary transactions means that unrealised exchange gains and losses will usually be included in the profit and loss account whenever a company has long-term assets and liabilities denominated in a foreign currency. Under CA 1985, only profits realised at the balance sheet date may be included in the profit and loss account. Compliance with SSAP 20 (or FRS 23) in these circumstances therefore constitutes a departure from the accounting requirements of the Act under the true and fair override and requires disclosure in the accounts. A suggested disclosure is given in the appendix to Chapter 3.

Post balance sheet events

7.25   SSAP 20 (and FRS 23) requires monetary assets to be translated at the closing rate for inclusion in the company's balance sheet. If significant fluctuations take place between the balance sheet date and the date of settlement of the transaction, and this gives rise to a material exchange difference in the subsequent accounting period, this may require disclosure in the notes to the accounts as a non-adjusting post balance sheet event (see Chapter 34).

PROFIT AND LOSS ACCOUNT DISCLOSURE

Gains and losses on ordinary activities

7.26   Exchange gains and losses will arise in respect of the translation of:

— foreign currency transactions during the year; and

— monetary assets and liabilities at the balance sheet date.

Gains and losses on exchange recognised during the year should normally be included as part of the profit or loss for the year on ordinary activities. The only exception to this is where an exchange gain or loss relates to an item that is itself classified as extraordinary. In this case the exchange gain or loss should be included as part of the extraordinary item. Extraordinary items are extremely rare under the requirements of FRS 3 and it is therefore unlikely that this situation will arise in practice.

FRS 23 also requires gains and losses arising on monetary and non-monetary items items to be recognised in the profit and loss account in the period in which they arise. However, where a gain or loss on a non-monetary item is recognised directly in the statement of total recognised gains and losses under the requirements of other accounting standards, FRS 23 requires any exchange gain or loss relating to that item to be similarly recognised through the statement of total recognised gains and losses.

Inclusion under statutory headings

7.27   The appropriate statutory heading in the profit and loss account for each exchange gain or loss will depend on the nature of the underlying transaction. The usual practice is:

— exchange gains and losses relating to trading transactions are included in other operating income or other operating expenses; this would include, for instance, gains and losses arising on:

— sales to overseas customers,

— purchases from overseas suppliers,

— purchases of plant and equipment from overseas suppliers;

— exchange gains and losses relating to financing transactions are included in 'interest receivable and similar income', or 'interest payable and similar charges' as appropriate.

In each case, the amount included in respect of exchange gains and losses should be separately disclosed. SSAP 20 includes specific disclosure requirements in respect of exchange gains and losses on foreign currency borrowings and deposits (see 7.33 below).

Exceptional items

7.28   Exceptional items are required by FRS 3 'Reporting Financial Performance' to be included under the relevant statutory heading or, in specific cases, shown under one of the additional headings introduced by FRS 3. Where appropriate, exchange gains and losses relating to exceptional items should be separately disclosed as part of the exceptional item.

Cash flow statement

7.29   The cash flow impact of movements in exchange rates must also be reflected in the cash flow statement. Chapter 35 includes guidance on dealing with foreign currency items in the cash flow statement.

FOREIGN EQUITY INVESTMENTS

Alternative accounting treatment

7.30   The usual method of accounting for foreign currency non-monetary assets under SSAP 20 is considered in 7.17 above. The standard recognises one situation where this treatment may not be appropriate and where an alternative accounting treatment is offered. Where a company has taken out foreign currency borrowings to finance or hedge against a foreign equity investment, it may adopt the following accounting treatment, but only where the conditions set out in 7.31 apply:

— carry the equity investments at their foreign currency value and translate this value at the closing rate at each balance sheet date;

— take any exchange differences arising on this translation directly to reserves (i.e. in this case, the exchange gain or loss is not credited or charged to the profit and loss account);

— off-set exchange gains and losses arising on the translation of the related foreign currency borrowings against the gains or losses on the investment, also as a reserves movement.

There is no specific requirement for the investments and the borrowings to be in the same currency. In cases where the gain or loss on retranslation of the borrowings is taxable (e.g. where a matching election is not made for tax purposes), UITF Abstract 19 'Tax on gains and losses on foreign currency borrowings that hedge an investment in a foreign enterprise' requires any tax charges or credits that are directly and solely attributable to the exchange differences to be similarly taken to reserves and reported in the statement of total recognised gains and losses.

This accounting treatment cannot be adopted in individual accounts under FRS 23.

Conditions to be satisfied

7.31 The following conditions must be satisfied for the above treatment to be adopted:

— in any accounting period, exchange gains and losses arising on the borrowings may only be off-set to the extent of the exchange gains and losses arising on the equity investments (i.e. any gain or loss on the borrowings in excess of that on the investments will have to be charged or credited to the profit and loss account);

— the foreign currency borrowings in respect of which gains and losses are off-set should not exceed, in aggregate, the total amount of cash that the investments are expected to be able to generate, from profits or otherwise;

— if a company chooses to adopt this treatment, it must be applied consistently from year to year; where relevant, this would include the year in which the investment is sold.

Under UITF Abstract 19, the first restriction must be applied after taking into account any tax charges or credits that are directly and solely attributable to the borrowings, and the comparison in the second restriction should also be considered in after-tax terms. If both the investment and the loan show a gain for the year, the gain on the loan must be credited in full to the profit and loss account. Similarly, if both show a loss for the year, the loss on the loan must be charged in full to the profit and loss account. The gain or loss on the investment will always be taken directly to reserves.

Disclosure of adoption

7.32   The fact that this treatment has been adopted should be disclosed in the accounting policy on foreign currency translation (see 7.33) below). UITF Abstract 19 specifically requires disclosure of the amount of tax charges or credits taken directly to reserves and reported in the statement of total recognised gains and losses, in addition to the gross amount of the exchange differences.

ACCOUNTS DISCLOSURE REQUIREMENTS

General disclosure requirement

7.33   The following information must be given in the notes to the accounts under SSAP 20:

—   the methods used for translating foreign currency transactions;

—   the treatment adopted for exchange differences arising on the translation of foreign currency transactions;

—   the net amount of exchange gains and losses on foreign currency borrowings less foreign currency deposits, showing separately:

—   the amount off-set in reserves, with separate disclosure of any tax charges or credits;

—   the amount credited or charged to the profit and loss account; and

—   the net movement on reserves relating to exchange differences.

Compliance with the requirements of SSAP 20 will usually satisfy the CA 1985 disclosure requirement in respect of foreign currency translation.

FRS 23 requires disclosure of:

(i)   the amount of exchange differences recognised in the profit and loss account (except for those arising on financial instruments measured at fair value through profit and loss under FRS 26); and

(ii)   the net exchange differences recognised in the statement of total recognised gains and losses, together with a reconciliation of the amount of such differences at the beginning and end of the year.

Additional disclosure requirements apply when the presentation currency differs from the functional currency and when there is a change in the functional currency (see 7.36 and 7.37 below). The basis used for translating amounts denominated in foreign currencies will also need to be disclosed in order to meet the disclosure requirements of CA 1985.

FRS 23 deals separately with the display or presentation of financial information in a currency other than the entity's functional currency or presentation currency (see 7.38 below).

Accounting policy

7.34   The first two disclosure requirements will usually be met by a detailed note on the accounting policy adopted in respect of foreign currency translation. The wording of the policy will clearly depend on the company's circumstances, but the following might be suitable in a straightforward case.

Example 7.4 — Accounting policy disclosure

Transactions in foreign currencies are translated into sterling at the rate of exchange ruling on the date when the transaction occurred.

Monetary assets and liabilities are translated into sterling at the rate ruling at the balance sheet date, except where:

(i) they are to be settled at a contracted rate, in which case the contracted rate is used,

(ii) they are covered by a matching forward contract, in which case the rate specified in the contract is used.

Gains and losses arising on translation are included in the profit and loss account.

Where a company chooses to adopt the alternative treatment in respect of foreign equity investments, this will also need to be explained in the accounting policy note.

Example 7.5 — Alternative treatment for foreign equity investments

Where foreign equity investments are financed or hedged by foreign currency borrowings, the investments are denominated in the appropriate foreign currency and translated into sterling at the closing rate at each balance sheet date. Gains and losses arising on this translation are taken directly to reserves and are off-set by gains and losses on translation of the related borrowings. Any gains and losses on translation of the borrowings which are in excess of the gains or losses on the investments are included in the profit and loss account.

Other disclosure requirements

7.35   The remaining disclosure requirements will usually be dealt with in:

—   the reserves note; and

—   the notes to the profit and loss account detailing:

  —   specific amounts charged against or credited to operating profit,

  —   other interest receivable and similar income, and

  —   interest payable and similar charges.

Gains and losses taken directly to reserves will also be included in the statement of total recognised gains and losses.

OTHER CHANGES UNDER FRS 23 AND FRS 24

Change in functional currency

7.36   An entity's functional currency is defined as the currency of the primary economic environment in which the entity operates (see 7.6 above). Once established, the functional currency should not be changed unless there is a change in the underlying transactions, events and conditions. Where there is a change in the functional currency of the reporting entity, the translation procedures applicable to the new functional currency must be applied prospectively from the date of the change. All items must therefore be translated into the new currency at the date of change, and the resulting translated amounts of non-monetary items are treated as their historical cost. The fact that the functional currency has changed must be disclosed in the accounts, together with the reasons for the change.

Using a different presentational currency

7.37   FRS 23 permits an entity to present its results in a currency other than its functional currency. In this situation, the standard requires the results and financial position of the entity to be translated as follows, provided that its functional currency is not one of a hyperinflationary economy:

(i)   assets and liabilities should be translated at the closing rate at the balance sheet date;

(ii)   income and expenses should be translated at the exchange rates at the date of the transactions – for practical purposes, it is acceptable to use an average exchange rate for the period, unless exchange rates have fluctuated significantly; and

(iii)   all resulting exchange differences should be recognised in the statement of total recognised gains and losses.

The results and financial position of any entity within the reporting entity (e.g. a subsidiary, associate, joint venture or branch) which has a different functional currency must also be translated into the presentation currency in accordance with the standard.

Where the functional currency of the reporting entity is the currency of a hyperinflationary economy and a different presentation currency is to be used, the standard requires the following approach:

(i)   the financial statements should be restated in accordance with FRS 24 'Financial Reporting in Hyperinflationary Economies' (see 7.39 below); and

(ii)   all amounts (including comparatives) should then be translated at the closing rate at the date of the most recent balance sheet, except that where amounts are translated into the currency of a non-hyperinflationary economy, comparative amounts should be those that were presented in the previous financial year without adjustment for subsequent in price levels or exchange rates.

If the economy ceases to be hyperinflationary and the entity no longer needs to translate its financial statements in accordance with FRS 24, the amounts restated to the price level at the date that the entity ceased restating its financial statements are to be treated as the historical costs for the purposes of translation into the presentation currency.

Where the presentation currency is different from the entity's functional currency, the notes to the accounts must disclose:

(i)   the fact that a different presentation currency has been used;

(ii)   the functional currency; and

(iii)   the reason for using a different presentation currency;

Disclosure of financial information in a different currency

7.38   If an entity displays its financial statements or other financial information in a currency other than its functional currency or its presentation currency without complying with all of the requirements of applicable FRSs and interpretations, it must:

(i)   clearly identify the information as supplementary, to distinguish it from information that complies with FRSs;

(ii)   disclose the currency in which the information is presented; and

(iii)   disclose the functional currency and the translation method used to determine the supplementary information.

Dealing with hyperinflationary economies

7.39   Under FRS 24, the financial statements of an entity whose functional currency is the currency of a hyperinflationary economy must be stated in terms of the measuring unit current at the balance sheet date. Corresponding figures for the previous period and any information in respect of earlier periods must also be stated in terms of the measuring unit current at the end of the reporting period. The gain or loss on the net monetary position should be included in the profit and loss account. The standard sets out detailed guidance on the procedures that should be adopted to achieve this restatement. The key issues covered include:

(i)   monetary assets and liabilities are not restated as they are already expressed in terms of the monetary unit current at the balance sheet date;

(ii)   assets and liabilities linked by agreement to changes in prices (e.g. index linked bonds and loans) should be adjusted according to the agreement to establish the amount outstanding at the balance sheet date;

(iii) non-monetary assets carried at amounts current at the balance sheet date (e.g. net realisable value or market value) are not restated;

(iv)   other non-monetary balance sheet amounts should be restated by applying a general price index;

(v)   where necessary, the restated amounts of non-monetary items should be reduced in accordance with other accounting standards (e.g. to recoverable amount or market value);

(vi)   at the beginning of the first period in which FRS 24 is applied, owners' equity (excluding any retained earnings and any revaluation surplus) should be restated by applying a general price index from the date the components were contributed or arose – in subsequent periods, owners' equity is restated by applying a general price index from the beginning of the period or from the date of contribution if later;

(vii) any revaluation surplus is eliminated and restated earnings are derived from all other restated figures in the balance sheet;

(viii) differences between the carrying amount of individual assets and liabilities and their tax bases arising as a result of the restatement should be accounted for in accordance with FRS 19 'Deferred Tax';

(ix)   all items in the income statement should be restated by applying the change in the general price index from the dates when the individual items of income and expense were initially recorded in the financial statements; and

(x)   all items in the cash flow statement should be expressed in terms of the measuring unit current at the balance sheet date.

Accounts disclosure

7.40   The standard requires the following disclosures to be given in the accounts:

(i)   the fact that the financial statements and the corresponding figures for previous periods have been restated for changes in the general purchasing power of the functional currency and, as a result, are stated in terms of the measuring unit current at the balance sheet date;

(ii)   whether the financial statements are based on a historical cost approach or a current cost approach; and

(iii) the identity and level of the price index at the balance sheet date, and the movement in the index during the current and previous reporting period.

Economies ceasing to be hyperinflationary

7.41   When an economy ceases to be hyperinflationary and the reporting entity therefore ceases to prepare financial statements in accordance with FRS 24, the amounts expressed in the measuring unit current at the end of the previous reporting period are treated as the basis for the carrying amounts in subsequent financial statements.

Chapter 8 Small and Medium-sized Companies

QUALIFICATION AS A SMALL COMPANY

Company qualifying as small

8.1   The general rule is that a company qualifies as small in relation to a specific financial year if it meets the criteria set out in CA 1985 in:

—   the financial year under consideration, and

—   the previous financial year.

If a company meets the criteria in its first financial year, it qualifies as a small company for that year. However, a parent company cannot qualify as a small company unless the group which it heads qualifies as a small group (see 8.6–8.8 below).

Company treated as qualifying as small

8.2   A company is also treated as qualifying as small in relation to a specific financial year if:

(i)   it qualified as small in the previous financial year or was treated as qualifying as small in the previous year under (ii) below; or

(ii)   it qualifies as small in the current financial year and was treated as qualifying as small in the previous year.

Practical effect

8.3   This sounds extremely complicated, but the purpose is to enable a company to continue to qualify as small even if it exceeds the qualifying criteria in one year. If it exceeds the criteria in two consecutive years, then it can no longer be treated as a small company. The effect is illustrated below.

Example 8.1 – Meeting the criteria as a small company

The position of Company A is as follows:

2000	Meets the criteria for a small company
2001	Exceeds the criteria for a small company
2002	Meets the criteria for a small company
2003	Exceeds the criteria for a small company
2004	Exceeds the criteria for a small company

In 2000, it meets the criteria in its first year and therefore qualifies as a small company.

In 2001, it is treated as qualifying as a small company because it qualified as small in the previous year.

In 2002 it is treated as qualifying as small because it meets the criteria in the current year and was treated as qualifying as small in the previous year.

In 2003 it is treated as qualifying as small because it met the criteria in the previous year and was treated as qualifying as small in that year.

In 2004 it does not qualify as small because it fails to meet the criteria in the current year and was only treated as qualifying as small in the previous year (i.e. it did not actually meet the criteria in that year).

Qualifying conditions

8.4   The criteria that must be met are termed 'qualifying conditions' and are set out in CA 1985 s 247(3). The financial limits that form part of these conditions have been updated on a number of occasions since the small company provisions were first introduced. The present criteria are:

—   turnover of not more than £5.6 million (if the accounting period is less than or more than a year, this limit must be adjusted proportionately);

—   balance sheet total of not more than £2.8 million;

—   number of employees not more than 50.

The above thresholds were introduced by the *Companies Act 1985 (Accounts of Small and Medium-Sized Enterprises and Audit Exemption)(Amendment) Regulations 2004* (SI 2004/16) and represent the maximum thresholds currently permitted by EC Directives. They are effective for accounting periods ending on or after 30 January 2004, although the previous lower thresholds continue to apply to an accounting reference period that only ends on or after this date because a notice of extension was given to the registrar on or after 9 January 2004 (the date on which the Regulations were laid before Parliament). For accounting periods beginning on or after 1 January 2005, eligibility as a small company can be assessed on the basis of either Companies Act or IAS accounts.

Definitions

8.5 The term 'balance sheet total' is defined as the aggregate of the amounts shown as assets in the balance sheet, i.e. *before* making any deductions for liabilities. The term 'number of employees' is defined as the average number of persons employed by the company in the year, determined on a monthly basis. The figure should therefore be calculated by adding together the number of persons employed under contracts of service each month (regardless of whether they were employed for the full month) and dividing this by the number of months in the financial year.

Qualification as a small group

8.6 The rules under which a parent company and its subsidiaries qualify as a small group are similar to those for qualification as a small company. A group, which in this instance means a parent company and its subsidiary undertakings, qualifies as small if it meets the criteria set out in the Act in:

— the financial year under consideration; and

— the previous financial year.

If a group meets the criteria in the parent company's first financial year, it qualifies as a small group for that year. A group is also treated as qualifying as small in relation to a specific financial year if:

(i) it qualified as small in the previous financial year or was treated as qualifying as small in the previous year under (ii) below; or

(ii) it qualifies as small in the current financial year and was treated as qualifying as small in the previous year.

These rules apply in exactly the same way as for an individual company as described in 8.3 above and have the same effect (i.e. that a group may continue to qualify as small if it exceeds the qualifying criteria in one year, but if it exceeds them in two consecutive years, it will no longer qualify as a small group).

Qualifying conditions

8.7 The present criteria for a small group are:

— aggregate turnover of not more than £5.6 million net or not more than £6.72 million gross (if the accounting period is less or more than a year, these limits must be adjusted proportionately);

— aggregate balance sheet total of not more than £2.8 million net or not more than £3.36 million gross;

— aggregate number of employees not more than 50.

The same definitions apply as in the case of an individual company (see 8.5 above). A group must meet two or more of the conditions in order to qualify as small. As with the small company criteria (see 8.4 above), the above thresholds represent the maximum currently permitted by EC Directives and are generally effective for accounting periods ending on or after 30 January 2004 (see 8.4 above). For accounting periods beginning on or after 1 January 2005, eligibility as a small group can be assessed on the basis of either Companies Act or IAS accounts.

'Gross' and 'net'

8.8   'Gross' figures within the criteria are those before the adjustments required by CA 1985 Sch 4A (i.e. the set-offs and other adjustments normally made in preparing consolidated accounts) and 'net' figures are after those adjustments have been made. Being able to use 'gross' figures means that a group does not have to go through the mechanics of consolidation in order to demonstrate that it is not required to prepare group accounts. There is no requirement in the Act for the turnover and balance sheet criteria to be considered on the same basis. It is therefore possible to look at (say) net figures when considering turnover and gross figures when considering the balance sheet total, and vice versa. The figures to be used for each subsidiary in the aggregation are those shown in the subsidiary's accounts for:

—   the financial year that ends with that of the parent company, if it makes up its accounts to the same date as the parent company; or

—   the last financial year ending before the financial year end of the parent company.

The latest available figures may be used if the above details cannot be obtained without undue delay or disproportionate expense.

ACCOUNTS EXEMPTIONS AVAILABLE TO SMALL COMPANIES AND GROUPS

Accounts exemptions for small companies

8.9   Two main accounts exemptions are available to most companies that qualify as small under the Act:

—   a small company can prepare its annual accounts in accordance with the requirements set out in CA 1985 Sch 8 (which are less detailed than those in Sch 4) and can file these accounts with the registrar;

—   a small company can file abbreviated accounts with the registrar – however, full or shorter form accounts must still be prepared for presentation to the members of the company.

A small company does not have to take advantage of either exemption and can prepare and file full accounts if it wishes. For accounting periods beginning on or after 1 January 2005, the option to prepare shorter form accounts only applies where the company prepares Companies Act accounts. Also, whilst certain filing and disclosure exemptions will continue to apply to small companies that prepare IAS accounts, the full small company abbreviated accounts regime is only available to those preparing Companies Act accounts.

Ineligible companies

8.10   The above exemptions are not available to the following companies, even if they meet the qualifying conditions:

— a public company;

— a person who has permission under Part 4 of the Financial Services and Markets Act 2000 (FSMA 2000) to carry on one or more regulated activities;

— a person who carries on an insurance market activity; or

— a member of an ineligible group.

An ineligible group is defined as a group where any of the members is:

— a public company;

— a body corporate that has the power to issue shares or debentures to the public;

— a person who has permission under Part 4 of FSMA 2000 to carry on one or more regulated activities; or

— a person who carries on an insurance market activity.

In the case of an intermediate parent company, it is necessary to consider the wider group and not just the one headed by the intermediate parent. The second category here does not need to be a British institution, so the UK subsidiary of a foreign undertaking will not be entitled to the exemptions if the parent has the power to issue shares or debentures to the public. It should also be noted that it is the power to issue shares and debentures, rather than their actual issue, that is the deciding factor.

However, as explained at 8.13 below, for accounting periods beginning on or after 1 April 2005, the exemptions in respect of the directors' report continue to apply to a company that is a member of an ineligible group provided that it would otherwise satisfy the criteria for exemption.

Shorter form accounts

8.11   Under CA 1985 s 246(2), a small company is permitted to prepare shorter form accounts, provided that there is a statement in a prominent position on the balance sheet, above the director's signature, that the accounts are prepared in accordance with the special provisions of Part VII of CA 1985 relating to small companies (see 8.14 below). Small companies can also adopt the requirements of the Financial Reporting Standard for Smaller Entities (FRSSE) (see 8.26 below). If a small company decides not to adopt the FRSSE, all of the measurement and disclosure requirements set out in other accounting standards must be followed, except where specific exemption is granted. Schedule 8 to CA 1985 does not require a small company to disclose the fact that its accounts have been prepared in accordance with applicable accounting standards (although this does not alter its obligation to apply appropriate standards). The position of small companies in relation to accounting standards generally is considered in 8.21 below.

Additional disclosure exemptions

8.12   A small number of additional exemptions are set out in CA 1985 s 246(3). Under these provisions, the accounts of a small company need not give:

(i)   financial years of subsidiary undertakings (normally required by Sch 5 para 4);

(ii)   the number of directors exercising share options or receiving shares under long term incentive schemes (normally required by Sch 6 para 1(2)(b);

(iii)   the emoluments of the highest paid director (normally required by Sch 6 para 2); or

(iv)   details of any excess retirement benefits to directors and past directors (normally required by Sch 6 para 7).

In addition, only the total of the aggregates for directors' emoluments and other benefits needs to be given in the accounts of a small company, rather than the aggregate for each individual item. However, any compensation for loss of office must continue to be shown separately. For accounting periods beginning on or after 1 January 2005, these disclosure exemptions continue to apply to both Companies Act and IAS accounts.

Modified directors' report

8.13   A small company need not give all the disclosures that are normally required to be given in the directors' report. Under CA 1985 s 246(4), the directors' report of a small company need not include:

(i)   a fair review of the business (normally required by s 234(1)(a) or, for accounting periods beginning on or after 1 April 2005, by section 234ZZB);

(ii)   the amount recommended to be paid as dividend (normally required by s 234(1)(b) or, for accounting periods beginning on or after 1 April 2005, by section 234ZZA(1)(c));

(iii)   a statement of the market values of certain fixed assets where these are substantially different from the amounts included in the balance sheet (normally required by Sch 7 para 1(2));

(iv)   important events since the balance sheet date (normally required by Sch 7 para 6(a));

(v) an indication of likely future developments in the business (normally required by Sch 7 para 6(b));

(vi) details of research and development activities (normally required by Sch 7 para 6(c));

(vii) an indication of the existence of branches outside the UK (normally required by Sch 7 para 6(d));

(viii) details of employee involvement (normally required by Sch 7 para 11); and

(ix) for accounting periods beginning on or after 1 January 2005, disclosures in respect of the use of financial instruments (otherwise required by paragraph 5A of Schedule 7, which was inserted by the *Companies Act 1985 (International Accounting Standards and Other Accounting Amendments) Regulations 2004*).

For accounting periods beginning on or after 1 January 2005, these disclosure exemptions continue to apply irrespective of whether the company prepares Companies Act or IAS accounts.

The disclosure requirements of Sch 7 relating to payment of creditors only apply to public companies and members of a group headed by a public company – they therefore do not apply to a company that qualifies as small. If advantage is taken of any of the exemptions listed above, the report must include a statement in a prominent position, above the signature of the director or secretary, that it is prepared in accordance with the special provisions of Part VII of CA 1985 relating to small companies (see 8.14 below). The exemptions in respect of the accounts and directors' report operate entirely independently.

For accounting periods beginning on or after 1 April 2005, companies that meet the size criteria for a small company but do not generally qualify for SME exemptions because they are part of an ineligible group (see 8.10 above) are granted the same exemptions as other small companies in respect of the directors' report, although they continue to be ineligible for the other accounts exemptions.

Directors' statement

8.14 The directors' statement in respect of shorter form accounts must be given in a prominent position on the face of the balance sheet, immediately above the signature of the director. Where a modified directors' report is prepared, a statement must also be given in the report, immediately above the signature of the director or secretary.

Example 8.2 – Directors' statement – shorter form accounts

Balance sheet

These accounts are prepared in accordance with the special provisions of Part VII of the Companies Act 1985 relating to small companies.

Approved by the board of directors on [date] and signed on its behalf by:

....

[Typed name] Director

Directors' report

This report is prepared in accordance with the special provisions of Part VII of the Companies Act 1985 relating to small companies.

Approved by the board of directors on [date] and signed on its behalf by:

....

[Typed name] Secretary/Director

In the case of a dormant company, neither statement is required if the directors take advantage of the audit exemption conferred by CA 1985 (see 8.122–8.127).

True and fair view

8.15   Shorter form accounts prepared by a small company are still required to show a true and fair view, even though they are not required by CA 1985 to give all of the detailed disclosures set out for other companies, and the auditors are required to express their opinion on whether the accounts show a true and fair view (unless the company qualifies for audit exemption). In certain circumstances, additional disclosure may need to be given in the shorter form accounts to achieve a true and fair view. For instance, although CA 1985 may permit certain items of income or expenditure to be grouped together for disclosure purposes, separate disclosure may be considered necessary for the accounts to show a true and fair view. Also, the exemptions granted under CA 1985 relate only to disclosure requirements imposed by that Act, and so shorter form accounts must still give any additional disclosures required by applicable accounting standards or the FRSSE.

Abbreviated accounts

8.16   CA 1985 s 246(5) permits a small company to file abbreviated accounts with the registrar. Abbreviated accounts can only be used for filing purposes and full accounts, or shorter form accounts, must still be prepared each year for presentation to the members. Filing abbreviated accounts enables a small company to preserve some degree of confidentiality about its activities, but against this must be weighed the disadvantage of having to prepare two sets of accounts each year. The Company Law Review recommended that the abbreviated accounts regime should be abolished and the Government White Paper 'Modernising Company Law issued in July 2002 confirmed the intention to proceed with this. However, a subsequent White Paper Company Law Reform, published in March 2005, notes that the Government has now decided to retain the abbreviated accounts regime but intends to require all small and medium-sized companies to disclose their turnover for the year in their published accounts.The provisions in respect of abbreviated accounts are set out in s 246(5) and Sch 8A and the following exemptions apply for small companies:

— there is no requirement for the directors' report to be filed;

— there is no requirement for the profit and loss account to be filed;

— the balance sheet only needs to show those items that are assigned a letter or a Roman number in the standard balance sheet formats – therefore only total figures need to be given for the main asset and liability headings, rather than the detailed analyses required in full accounts, except that the following details must still be given, either on the balance sheet or in a note to the accounts:

— the aggregate of debtors due after more than one year;

— the aggregate of creditors due within one year; and

— the aggregate of creditors due after more than one year;

— the notes to the accounts only need to cover the following disclosures [CA 1985, Sch 8A references given in brackets]:

— the accounting policies adopted [para 4],

— details of share capital [para 5],

— details of share allotments during the year [para 6],

— movements in fixed assets, including depreciation, but only for main headings (i.e. those assigned a letter or Roman number) [para 7],

— for accounting periods beginning on or after 1 January 2005, details of certain financial fixed assets that are included at an amount in excess of their fair value (para 7A – inserted by the *Companies Act 1985 (International Accounting Standards and Other Accounting Amendments) Regulations 2004*);

— details of borrowings [para 8],

— the basis of foreign currency conversion [para 9(1)],

— corresponding amounts [para 9(2)];

— in the case of a dormant company which has acted as an agent for another party, a statement of that fact (para 9A).

— CA 1985 s 246(6) gives specific exemption from the following disclosures:

— financial years of subsidiary undertakings and details of shares in the company held by subsidiary undertakings (normally required by Sch 5 paras 4 and 6);

— directors' emoluments, pensions and compensation for loss of office (normally required by Part I of Sch 6);

— auditors' remuneration (normally required by s 390A(3)).

If the directors of a small company wish to take advantage of the option to prepare abbreviated accounts for filing purposes, the balance sheet must include a statement that the accounts are prepared in accordance with the special provisions of Part VII of CA 1985 relating to small companies (see 8.14 above).

For accounting periods beginning on or after 1 January 2005, the exemption from filing the profit and loss account and directors' report and the disclosure exemptions set out in s 246(6) apply to all small companies, irrespective of whether they prepare Companies Act or IAS accounts, but the exemptions in respect of the balance sheet and related notes apply only where Companies Act accounts are prepared.

Special auditors' report

8.17   Where abbreviated accounts are delivered to the registrar, they must be accompanied by a special report from the auditors stating whether, in their opinion:

— the company is entitled to deliver abbreviated accounts prepared in accordance with section 246(5) and (6) of CA 1985 ss 246(5) and (6); and

— the abbreviated accounts have been properly prepared in accordance with those sections.

The complete text of the auditors' report on the company's full or shorter form accounts must also be included where that report:

— was qualified, in which case additional details may also need to be given to enable the qualification to be understood; or

— included a statement under CA 1985 s 237(2) (inadequate accounts, records or returns, or accounts not in agreement with the records and returns); or

— included a statement under CA 1985 s 237(3) (failure to obtain all the information and explanations that the auditors considered necessary).

However, if the company is eligible for total audit exemption, and the directors have taken advantage of this, there is no requirement for any report to be attached to the abbreviated accounts. If the company is a charity and meets the report conditions for audit exemption, a copy of the special accountant's report on the full accounts must be filed with the abbreviated accounts. In this situation, the Auditing Practices Board recommends that an explanatory statement is added to the report to clarify the fact that it relates to the full accounts rather than the abbreviated accounts. Further details are given at 8.121 below.

Accounts exemptions for small groups

8.18   Two main exemptions are available to most small groups:

— a group that qualifies as small may be exempt from the requirement to prepare group accounts;

— a small company that prepares shorter form individual accounts under the special provisions of CA 1985 and is preparing group accounts for the same financial year may prepare the group accounts in accordance with Sch 8.

However, there is no provision in CA 1985 enabling a small group to file abbreviated group accounts. For accounting periods beginning on or after 1 January 2005, the second exemption applies only where the company prepares Companies Act group accounts.

Exemption from preparing group accounts

8.19   A parent company is not required to prepare group accounts for a financial year in which the group which it heads qualifies as a small group and is not an ineligible group. An ineligible group is defined in CA 1985 s 248(2) as a group where any of the members is:

—   a public company;

—   a body corporate that has the power to issue shares or debentures to the public;

—   a person who has permission under Part 4 of FSMA 2000 to carry on one or more regulated activities; or

—   a person who carries on an insurance market activity.

There was previously a requirement for the auditors to provide the directors with a special report confirming that, in their opinion, the company was entitled to the exemption. This is no longer required. However, if the directors take advantage of the exemption and, in the opinion of the auditors, they are not entitled to do so, the auditors are required to state this in their report on the accounts. FRS 2 'Accounting for Subsidiary Undertakings' repeats the exemption set out in the Act for small groups, but requires disclosure of:

—   the fact that the accounts present information about the parent as an individual undertaking and not about the group; and

—   the grounds on which the parent is exempt from preparing consolidated accounts for the group.

Shorter form group accounts

8.20   A small company that prepares shorter form individual accounts under the Act and is preparing group accounts for the same financial year can prepare the group accounts in accordance with Schedule 8, except that under the balance sheet heading 'Investments' it must show separately:

—   shares in group undertakings;

—   shares in associated undertakings; and

—   other participating interests.

This is in addition to the analysis required by Sch 8. The exemptions set out in s 246(3) and the requirement to include a directors' statement also continue to apply to shorter form group accounts (see 8.12 and 8.14 above). For accounting periods beginning on or after 1 January 2005, the option to prepare shorter form group accounts only applies where the company prepares Companies Act group accounts. However, the disclosure exemptions in s 246(3) continue to apply where IAS group accounts are prepared, as does the requirement for a directors' statement where advantage is taken of any of the exemptions.

ACCOUNTING STANDARDS AND THE SMALL COMPANY

Compliance with accounting standards

8.21   In general, the requirements of accounting standards apply to all accounts that are required to show a true and fair view, irrespective of the size of the entity. In preparing their annual accounts, small companies must therefore comply either with the FRSSE (see 8.25 below) or with all other applicable accounting standards and UITF Abstracts, except in the few cases where an individual standard specifically exempts smaller entities from compliance with some or all of the detailed requirements. At present, these exceptions comprise:

— SSAP 13 'Accounting for research and development' – small companies need not disclose the amount charged to the profit and loss account in respect of research and development, although the other requirements of SSAP 13 (both measurement and disclosure) continue to apply.

– SSAP 25 'Segmental reporting' – small companies need not comply with the additional disclosure requirements set out in this accounting standard.

— FRS 1 'Cash Flow Statements' – small companies are exempt from the requirement to include a cash flow statement in their accounts (see 8.32 below).

— FRS 13 'Derivatives and other financial instruments: Disclosures' – this standard applies only to listed companies, banks and other financial institutions, and is generally superseded by FRS 25 'Financial Instruments: Disclosure and Presentation' for accounting periods beginning on or after 1 January 2005.

— FRS 14 'Earnings per share' (or, for accounting periods beginning on or after 1 January 2005, FRS 22 'Earnings per share') – this standard applies only to companies whose shares are publicly traded and any others who opt voluntarily to disclose earnings per share (which is rare in practice).

Compliance with UITF Abstracts

8.22   At present, UITF Abstract 17 and all subsequent Abstracts grant exemption from their requirements to entities adopting the Financial Reporting Standard for Smaller Entities (FRSSE). The only exception is UITF Abstract 37 'Purchases and Sales of Own Shares', which does not include the usual exemption statement for smaller entities adopting the FRSSE, but companies that qualify as small are generally unlikely to be able to purchase, hold or sell their own shares. (The Abstract is also superseded by FRS 25 'Financial Instruments: Disclosure and Presentation' for accounting periods beginning on or after 1 January 2005.) However, in its Information Sheet No 43, published in November 2000, the UITF issued a clarification of the position of smaller entities in relation to UITF Abstracts. The exemption note in each UITF Abstract reflects the ASB's policy of including all the requirements applying to smaller entities in a single document. The FRSSE is regularly reviewed and updated, and at each review the ASB considers whether the requirements of recent UITF Abstracts should be incorporated into the document. The exemption note should therefore not be read as implying that the requirements of the Abstract are not appropriate to a smaller entity. When accounting for transactions and events not dealt with in the FRSSE, smaller entities are expected to have regard to other accounting standards and UITF Abstracts, not as mandatory documents in this case, but as a means of establishing current practice. This point is also emphasised in the current version of the FRSSE (published in April 2005).

Disclosure of compliance with accounting standards

8.23 Small companies are specifically exempt from the requirement to state whether the accounts have been prepared in accordance with applicable accounting standards. This exemption relates only to the disclosure requirement. It does not grant any exemption from compliance with the requirements of accounting standards or the FRSSE.

Abbreviated accounts and accounting standards

8.24 Abbreviated accounts (see 8.16 above) are essentially an extract of the full accounts or shorter form accounts that the company is required to prepare for the members. They are not required to show a true and fair view and, in practice, will not do so because of the reduced disclosures. As explained above, both full accounts and shorter form accounts must comply with the requirements of accounting standards and UITF Abstracts or with the FRSSE. In the case of abbreviated accounts, a distinction is effectively made between the measurement requirements of accounting standards (or the FRSSE) and the additional disclosure requirements:

— Measurement requirements – the abbreviated accounts are extracts of the full or shorter form accounts and they must therefore follow all of the measurement requirements set out in applicable accounting standards or in the FRSSE (e.g. assets held under finance leases must be accounted for in accordance with the FRSSE or with SSAP 21 *Accounting for leases and hire purchase contracts*).

— Disclosure requirements – abbreviated accounts are not required to show a true and fair view and the additional disclosures required by accounting standards or the FRSSE need not be given (e.g. the additional disclosures in respect of leased assets required by the FRSSE or by SSAP 21 need not be given in abbreviated accounts but must be given in full or shorter form accounts in order to show a true and fair view).

FINANCIAL REPORTING STANDARD FOR SMALLER ENTITIES (FRSSE): AN OVERVIEW

Background to the FRSSE

8.25   As accounting standards became increasingly complex, and in many cases required more detailed disclosures in the accounts, concern was expressed over the merit of applying these standards to smaller companies. The Consultative Committee of Accountancy Bodies (CCAB), in conjunction with the Accounting Standards Board (ASB), therefore set up a working party to examine the issue of how smaller entities might be granted exemption from compliance with accounting standards, and their work resulted in the publication of the Financial Reporting Standard for Smaller Entities (FRSSE). This was first issued in November 1997 and came into immediate effect. Four revised versions have been issued. The latest version was issued in April 2005 and is effective for accounting periods beginning on or after 1 January 2005, although the new requirements in respect of defined benefit retirement schemes are only fully effective for accounting periods ending on or after 22 June 2006. Early adoption of the revised FRSSE is not permitted. Regular revision of the FRSSE is necessary to ensure that it is kept up to date with current accounting practice, and the document is therefore reviewed at not less than yearly intervals. An overview of the FRSSE is set out in this section and the detailed requirements of the latest version (excluding those arising from company law) are explained in 8.39–8.107 below.

'One-stop shop' document

8.26   The version of the FRSSE published in April 2005 takes the form of a 'one-stop shop' document, encompassing all of the accounting requirements that apply to small companies. Company law requirements are distinguished from other aspects of the FRSSE by being set out in small capitals in the text, and reflect the provisions that apply for accounting periods beginning on or after 1 January 2005. Only the most common balance sheet format (Format 1, Sch 8, CA 1985) is included in the document but companies applying the FRSSE continue to have the option of adopting the alternative balance sheet format if they wish. However, in the case of the profit and loss account, only Formats 1 and 2 from CA 1985 will be available in future to companies applying the FRSSE. The ASB emphasises that smaller unincorporated entities adopting the FRSSE are not bound by the company law requirements set out in the document, but notes that they should have regard to the accounting principles, presentation and disclosure requirements set out in company law (or other equivalent legislation) that are necessary for the presentation of a true and fair view.

Scope and objective of the FRSSE

8.27   The FRSSE may be applied to financial statements that are intended to give a true and fair view of the results and financial position of small companies or groups (as defined in CA 1985) and entities that would qualify as small if they were incorporated under the Act. As eligibility rests on the CA 1985 criteria, the FRSSE cannot be adopted in the accounts of:

—   public companies, or any member of a group which includes a public company; or

—   entities that are regulated under Part 4 of the FSMA 2000, or which carry on an insurance market activity; or

—   any entity that does not meet the relevant size criteria (see 8.4 and 8.7 above).

The objective of the FRSSE is to ensure that entities falling within its scope provide financial information that is useful in assessing the stewardship of management and for making economic decisions. For accounting periods beginning on or after 1 January 2005, the FRSSE is only relevant to small companies if they prepare Companies Act accounts.

Disclosure of adoption

8.28   Adoption of the FRSSE is optional for reporting entities that come within its scope. If it is not adopted, the requirements of all other accounting standards and UITF Abstracts must be followed. If the FRSSE is adopted, this fact must be stated in the accounts. The disclosure can be combined with the directors' statement required under CA 1985 where the small company provisions of the Act have been applied (see 8.14 above) or can be given separately in the notes to the accounts. Early adoption of the latest version of FRSSE is usually encouraged, but the version published in April 2005 cannot be adopted for accounting periods beginning before 1 January 2005 as some of the requirements hinge on company law changes that also come into effect from that date.

Relationship with SORPs

8.29   The FRSSE notes that Statements of Recommended Practice (SORPs) that were already in issue when the FRSSE was first published were prepared on the basis that the financial statements would comply with the requirements of SSAPs, FRSs and UITF Abstracts. Accounts that refer to compliance with such a SORP should therefore observe the requirements of those standards, even though the reporting entity may technically come within the scope of the FRSSE. However,

SORPs and other equivalent guidance published since November 1997 may specify when the FRSSE can be adopted. For instance, the revised SORP 'Accounting and Reporting by Charities', which applies for accounting periods beginning on or after 1 January 2001, specifically states that a charity which qualifies as small may prepare its accounts in accordance with the FRSSE, as does the updated version published in March 2005, which is effective for periods beginning on or after 1 April 2005.

Definitions

8.30   The FRSSE includes a separate definitions section. All definitions are the same as those in other accounting standards, or a simplified version of them, and items included in the definitions section are identified by bold text in the FRSSE.

Items not specifically covered in the FRSSE

8.31   The issues covered in the FRSSE are restricted to those expected to arise most frequently in smaller entities. The more complex issues covered in many accounting standards are therefore excluded from the FRSSE on the basis that they will not usually be relevant to a smaller entity. Where transactions or events arise that are not specifically covered in the FRSSE, preparers of accounts are required to have regard to other accounting standards and UITF Abstracts, not as mandatory documents in this case, but as a means of establishing current practice.

Voluntary presentation of cash flow statement

8.32   Under FRS 1 *Cash flow statements* companies which meet the CA 1985 criteria for a small company are exempt from the requirement to include a cash flow statement in their accounts. In a separate 'Voluntary disclosure' section, the FRSSE encourages the inclusion of a cash flow statement in the accounts of a smaller entity on the grounds that management of cash is fundamental to the success of a small business, and a cash flow statement can provide a useful focus for discussion and a reference point for more detailed analysis. However, the FRSSE does not require such a statement to be presented as part of the accounts. If a cash flow statement is prepared, the FRSSE sets out the following guidance:

—   the statement should be presented using the indirect method (i.e. starting with operating profit and adjusting for non-cash items to arrive at the figure for cash generated from operations);

—   cash should be cash at bank and in hand, less overdrafts repayable on demand, and these figures should be reconciled to those shown in the balance sheet;

—   cash flows should be net of any attributable VAT (or other sales tax) except where the reporting entity cannot recover the tax;

— material transactions not resulting in cash movements should be disclosed in the notes if this is necessary for the underlying transactions to be properly understood.

An illustrative example of a cash flow statement prepared on this basis is set out in Appendix III to the FRSSE.

Statement of total recognised gains and losses

8.33   Appendix III to the FRSSE also sets out an example of a statement of total recognised gains and losses, but emphasises that the individual circumstances of each entity will indicate the best approach to this disclosure. The example uses the following form of presentation:

Example 8.3 – Statement of total recognised gains and losses

	2004 £	2003 £ (*restated*)
Profit for the financial year	25,000	13,000
Unrealised surplus on revaluation of property in the year	7,000	4,500
Total recognised gains and losses relating to the year	32,000	17,500
Prior year adjustment (see note x)	(13,000)	
Total gains and losses recognised since the last annual report	19,000	

Link with accounting standards

8.34   Appendix V to the FRSSE provides details of the source of each requirement set out in the FRSSE and shows whether the source requirement has been adopted in full, with minor amendment or with major changes.

Principal relaxations in requirements

8.35   Generally, the measurement requirements of accounting standards are retained in the FRSSE (sometimes in simplified form) but many of the more detailed disclosure requirements are excluded, especially those that relate to events and circumstances that generally do not arise in smaller entities. The principle relaxations can be summarised as follows:

Profit and loss account

— the profit and loss account section makes no reference to continuing and discontinued operations;

— where all the recognised gains and losses are included in the profit and loss account, no separate statement to this effect is required;

— there is no requirement for a reconciliation of movements in shareholders' funds;

— there is no requirement to disclose special circumstances affecting tax on exceptional items;

— there is no requirement for a note of historical cost profits and losses;

Intangible assets and goodwill

— the FRSSE does not allow the useful economic lives of goodwill and intangible assets to exceed 20 years;

— internally generated intangible assets cannot be capitalised, even if they have a readily ascertainable market value;

— intangible assets cannot be revalued;

— the FRSSE does not require the fair values of intangible assets purchased with a business to be restricted to an amount that does not create or increase negative goodwill;

— the FRSSE does not specify how negative goodwill should be disclosed on the balance sheet – FRS 10 requires it to be shown immediately below positive goodwill, with a sub-total of the two amounts;

— none of the detailed disclosure requirements on goodwill are included;

Tangible fixed assets

— there is no reference to:

    — the start up or commissioning period of a tangible fixed asset;

    — when capitalisation of finance costs should begin;

    — the construction of a fixed asset in parts;

    — accounting for a major inspection or overhaul of a tangible fixed asset;

    — renewals accounting;

— the bases for revaluation of tangible fixed assets are simplified:

— the treatment of revaluation losses is simplified;

— there is no specific requirement for an annual impairment review where depreciation is omitted as immaterial or where the remaining useful economic life of a tangible fixed asset exceeds 50 years;

— residual values and useful economic lives are required to be reviewed regularly (rather than annually) and revised when necessary;

— disclosure requirements for tangible fixed assets are limited to the following for (i) land and buildings and (ii) other assets in aggregate:

    — depreciation methods;

    — useful economic lives or depreciation rates;

— where material, the financial effects of changes in useful economic lives and residual values;

(NB: certain additional disclosures are required by company law, particularly in the case of revalued assets);

— the FRSSE allows more flexibility in the calculation of value in use;

— the sum recorded as an asset and liability at the inception of a finance lease should normally be the fair value (rather than the present value of the minimum lease payments);

— the FRSSE emphasises that the straight-line method of allocating finance charges to accounting periods may provide a reasonable approximation to a constant periodic rate of charge;

— operating lease commitments do not need to be analysed by type of lease;

Taxation

— the detailed disclosure requirements of FRS 16 and FRS 19 are omitted from the FRSSE and replaced with a more flexible requirement to disclose:

  — material components of the current and deferred tax charges or credits;

  — material components of the deferred tax balance; and

  — material components of the movement in the deferred tax balance;

Provisions, contingent liabilities and contingent assets

— there is no reference to:

  — financial instruments, executory contracts, future operating losses, onerous contracts, restructuring, or the sale of an operation;

  — cases where it is not clear whether there is a present obligation;

  — the need to take account of risks, uncertainties and future events when measuring a provision;

  — capitalisation of related assets;

— the detailed rules on discounting are omitted (although discounting is still required where the effect is material);

— there is no restriction on the amount that may be recognised as reimbursements;

— disclosure requirements are limited to the nature and effect of contingent liabilities (unless remote) and probable contingent assets (although additional disclosures may be required by company law);

Other

— only related party transactions that are considered material to the reporting entity need to be disclosed (i.e. there is no need to consider the materiality of the transaction to the related party);

— there is an overall requirement to disclose the accounting policies followed for items judged material or critical in determining the profit or loss for the period and in stating the entity's financial position – the FRSSE emphasises that this disclosure should be clear, fair and as brief as possible;

— there is no requirement to disclose the power of owners or others to amend the financial statements after issue, or to update disclosures relating to conditions that existed at the balance sheet date in the light of new information received after that date.

The specific requirements of the FRSSE are considered in more detail at 8.39 below.

Disclosure of directors' personal guarantees

8.36 The FRSSE includes a specific additional requirement for the accounts of a smaller entity to disclose any personal guarantees given by the directors in respect of company borrowings.

Group accounts

8.37 Small groups that come within the scope of the FRSSE are not required to prepare group accounts under UK company law. However, the ASB recognises that where a small group prepares group accounts voluntarily, it is appropriate to allow it to take advantage of the FRSSE. To avoid making the FRSSE over-complicated, small groups are simply required to follow those accounting standards and UITF Abstracts that deal with consolidated financial statements, in addition to the FRSSE, if they choose to prepare group accounts.

Possible changes to small entity reporting

8.38 In June 2004, the International Accounting Standards Board (IASB) published a discussion paper 'Preliminary Views on Accounting Standards for Small and Medium-sized Entities' outlining its initial thoughts on this issue and inviting comments before the next stage in the development process. Given the ASB's programme to converge UK accounting standards with international requirements (see 1.6 above), this could eventually impact on smaller entities in the UK. However, what the IASB currently has in mind is significantly different from the small company financial reporting regime that that has developed here in recent years. The IASB proposes that its SME pronouncements would apply to entities that do not have public accountability rather than to entities that meet a certain size criteria. The discussion paper suggests that an entity would be regarded as having public accountability if there is a high degree of outside interest from non-management investors or other stakeholders, or if the entity has an essential public service responsibility because of the nature of its operations. Furthermore, every entity will be regarded as having public accountability until it has informed each of its owners (including any not otherwise entitled to vote) of the intention to adopt SME standards and none of them objects to this. Adoption of the SME standards would have to be disclosed in the accounts and also in any auditors' report.

The IASB considers that International Financial Reporting Standards (IFRSs) should be regarded as suitable for all entities, regardless of size or other factors. It does acknowledge, though, that there may be advantages in developing separate SME standards, hence this consultation. However, it is planning a complete series of SME standards rather than a stand-alone document like the FRSSE, and the discussion paper proposes that these should follow the existing IFRS numbering system. This differs significantly from the current UK approach which has always focused on making the relevant material more easily accessible to users by publishing it in a single reference document.

The suggested objectives of the SME standards include a focus on the needs of users of SME accounts and reducing the financial reporting burden for relevant businesses, whilst still allowing an easy transition to IFRSs as and when necessary. The discussion paper suggests that any modifications would be most likely to relate to disclosure and presentation issues, and that there should be a rebuttable presumption that no changes would be made to recognition and measurement principles. Whilst the approach appears to be broadly similar to that adopted in developing the FRSSE, the UK simplifications for small companies do currently encompass certain recognition and measurement issues as well as disclosure and presentation points – for instance, by excluding from the FRSSE detailed recognition and measurement requirements relating to transactions that arise only rarely in SMEs.

However, in the light of responses to the discussion paper, the IASB has made some changes to its original plans. In particular, it has agreed that measurement and recognition simplifications should be considered as well as disclosure and presentation issues and that SME standards should be arranged topically (for instance, in balance sheet and income statement order) rather than following the IFRS numbering system. Further progress on the project is expected during the course of 2005.

THE FINANCIAL REPORTING STANDARD FOR SMALLER ENTITIES (FRSSE): DETAILED REQUIREMENTS

True and fair view

8.39 The financial statements of a smaller entity should show a true and fair view of the results of the period and the state of affairs at the period end. In achieving this, the substance of any arrangement or transaction, or series of arrangements or transactions, entered into by the entity during the period should be taken into account. This will involve determining whether the transaction has given rise to any new assets or liabilities, or has changed any of the entity's existing assets and liabilities.

True and fair override disclosures

8.40   Where the true and fair override is applied, the following disclosures should be given:

— a clear and unambiguous statement that the override has been applied;

— a statement of the treatment normally required and a description of the treatment actually adopted;

— an explanation of why the normal treatment would not give a true and fair view; and

— quantification of the effect, unless this is already evident from the financial statements – if the effect cannot be quantified, the circumstances should be explained.

If the override is applied for more than one year, these disclosures should be given each year, with comparatives for the previous year.

Transactions and arrangements, and the accounting treatment adopted, should be explained in the notes to the accounts if there is doubt over whether applying provisions of the FRSSE would be sufficient to give a true and fair view.

Disclosure of adoption

8.41   The financial statements should state that they have been prepared in accordance with the Financial Reporting Standard for Smaller Entities (effective January 2005).

Accounting policies and estimation techniques

8.42   The following requirements apply in respect of accounting policies and estimation techniques:

— accounting policies and estimation techniques should be consistent with the requirements of the FRSSE and of company law (or the equivalent);

— where a choice of policy or technique is permitted, the entity should select the policies and techniques that are most appropriate to its particular circumstances for the purpose of giving a true and fair view, taking into account the objectives of relevance, reliability, comparability and understandability;

—   accounting policies should be regularly reviewed to ensure they remain the most appropriate – however, in judging whether to adopt a new policy, due consideration should be given to the impact on comparability;

—   where an accounting policy is changed, the amounts for the current and corresponding periods should be restated on the basis of the new policy;

—   the accounts should be prepared on the going concern basis unless the directors determine after the balance sheet date that they intend to liquidate the entity or to cease trading, or that they have no realistic alternative but to do so;

—   when preparing financial statements, directors should assess whether there are significant doubts about the entity's ability to continue as a going concern – any material uncertainties of which the directors are aware should be disclosed;

—   where the period considered by the directors is less than one year from the date of approval of the financial statements, this fact should be stated;

—   the amount of any item should be determined on a prudent basis, but it is not necessary to exercise prudence where there is no uncertainty, nor is it appropriate to use prudence to deliberately understate assets or overstate liabilities;

—   financial statements (other than cash flow information) should be prepared on an accruals basis of accounting;

—   the financial statements should include:

—   a description of each material accounting policy followed;

—   details of any changes to the accounting policies followed in the preceding period, a brief explanation of why each new policy is considered to be more appropriate and, where practicable, an indication of the effect of the change on the results for the current period (NB this is in addition to the normal prior period adjustment disclosures); and

—   where the effect of a change in estimation techniques is material, a description of the change and, where practicable, the effect on the results for the current period.

Prior period adjustments

8.43   Prior period adjustments should be accounted for by:

—   restating comparative figures for the previous year in the primary statements and the notes to the accounts;

—   adjusting opening reserves for the cumulative effect;

— noting the cumulative effect at the foot of the statement of total recognised gains and losses; and

— disclosing the effect on the results of the previous period where this is material.

Gains and losses

8.44 All gains and losses recognised during the year must be included in the profit and loss account or in the statement of total recognised gains and losses. Individual gains and losses may only be excluded from the profit and loss account where this is permitted or required by CA 1985.

Exceptional items

8.45 The following items (including provisions) should be shown separately on the face of the profit and loss account after operating profit and before interest:

— profits and losses on the sale or termination of an operation;

— costs of a fundamental reorganisation or restructuring that has a material effect on the nature and focus of the entity's operations;

— profits and losses on the disposal of fixed assets.

Other exceptional items should be included under the relevant statutory format heading and disclosed on the face of the profit and loss account (if sufficiently material) or in the notes to the accounts. Sufficient detail should be given to enable a user of the accounts to understand the nature of the item.

Profit or loss on disposal

8.46 The profit or loss on disposal of an asset should be calculated as the difference between the net sales proceeds and the net carrying value of the asset. Where a previously acquired business is disposed of, any attributable purchased goodwill that has not already been charged in the profit and loss account should be included in the profit or loss on disposal.

Extraordinary items

8.47 Extraordinary items should be extremely rare, but where they do arise they should be shown separately on the face of the profit and loss account, after the profit or loss on ordinary activities after taxation.

Revenue recognition

8.48 A seller should recognise revenue under an exchange transaction with a customer when, and to the extent that, it obtains the right to consideration in exchange for its performance. A new asset (eg a debtor) is usually recognised at the same time. Where a seller receives payment in advance of performance, it should recognise a liability representing its obligation under the contract. This liability is reduced as the seller obtains the right to consideration through performance, and the amount of the reduction is recognised in revenue. A seller may obtain a right to consideration when some, but not all, of its contractual obligations have been fulfilled. Where contractual obligations have been partially performed, revenue should therefore be recognised to the extent that the seller has obtained a right to consideration as a result of its performance.

Revenue should be measured at the fair value of the right to consideration, which will normally be the price specified in the contract, net of discounts, VAT and other sales taxes. However, the following additional requirements also apply:

(i)   where the effect of the time value of money is material to reported revenue, the amount recognised as revenue should be the present value of the expected cash inflows, and the unwinding of the discount should be credited to finance income on the basis that it represents a gain from a financing transaction; and

(ii) where, at the time of recognition, there is a significant risk of a default on the amount of consideration due and the effect is material to reported revenue, an appropriate adjustment should be made to the amount of revenue recognised.

Subsequent adjustments to a debtor (ie after initial recognition) as a result of changes in the time value of money or credit risk should not be included in revenue.

Other exchange transactions, such as the sale of fixed assets, do not give rise to turnover as they do not normally relate to supply of the goods and services that the entity is in business to provide.

Appendix III to the FRSSE sets out additional guidance on:

(i)   revenue recognition and service contracts;
(ii)   bill and hold arrangements;
(iii) sales with a right of return; and
(iv)   presentation of turnover as principal or agent.

Statement of total recognised gains and losses

8.49   A statement of total recognised gains and losses should be presented as a primary statement, with the same degree of prominence as the profit and loss account. Transactions with shareholders should be excluded from this statement. An example of a statement of total recognised gains and losses is given in Appendix III to the FRSSE and is also illustrated in 8.33 above. If all the recognised gains and losses are included in the profit and loss account, no separate statement to this effect needs to be given.

Expenditure on research and development

8.50   The cost of fixed assets acquired or constructed for use in research and development activities over a number of years should be capitalised and written off through the profit and loss account over their useful lives. The costs of pure and applied research should be written off in the profit and loss account as they are incurred. Development expenditure should be written off in the profit and loss account as it is incurred, except that it may be deferred to future periods where all of the following apply:

—   there is a clearly defined project; and

—   the related expenditure is clearly identifiable; and

—   the outcome of the project has been assessed with reasonable certainty as regards both its technical feasibility and its ultimate commercial viability (taking into account likely market conditions, public opinion, consumer and environmental legislation etc); and

—   the aggregate of:

   —   deferred development costs; and

   —   any further development costs; and

   —   any related production, selling and administration costs

is reasonably expected to be exceeded by related future sales and other revenues; and

—   adequate resources exist, or are reasonably expected to be available, to complete the project and to provide any necessary increases in working capital.

Where an entity adopts a policy of deferring development expenditure, the policy should be applied to all projects that meet the above criteria. Deferred development costs should be amortised, commencing on the commercial production or application of the product or service, by allocating the costs on a systematic basis to each accounting period by reference to either the sale or use of the product or service, or the period over which it is expected to be used or sold. The deferred expenditure for each project should be reviewed at the end of each accounting period and written off immediately where the circumstances that justified deferral no longer apply. The amount of development expenditure carried forward at the beginning and end of each year should be disclosed on the face of the balance sheet or in the notes to the accounts.

Goodwill and intangible assets

8.51 Positive purchased goodwill and purchased intangible assets should be capitalised. Internally generated goodwill and intangible assets should not be capitalised. An intangible asset purchased with a business should be recognised separately from the purchased goodwill if its value can be measured reliably. It is important to note that purchased goodwill in this context means goodwill arising in the accounts of an individual entity. If an entity adopting the FRSSE also prepares group accounts, any goodwill arising on consolidation must be accounted for in accordance with FRS 10 'Goodwill and Intangible Assets'. Once capitalised, goodwill and intangible assets should not be revalued.

Depreciation of goodwill and intangible assets

8.52 Capitalised goodwill and intangible assets should be depreciated on a straight-line (or more appropriate) basis over their useful economic lives, which must not exceed 20 years. A residual value may be assigned to an intangible asset if this value can be established reliably (e.g. where it has been agreed contractually). No residual value can be assigned to goodwill. The useful economic lives of goodwill and intangible assets should be reviewed at the end of each reporting period and should be revised where necessary. However, the revised life should not exceed 20 years from the date of acquisition. The carrying amount of the asset at the date of the revision should be depreciated over the revised estimate of the remaining useful economic life.

Negative goodwill

8.53 Where an acquisition appears to give rise to negative goodwill, fair values should be checked to ensure that the assets acquired have not been overstated and that the liabilities acquired have not been understated. Negative goodwill up to the fair values of the non-monetary assets acquired should be released to the profit and loss account over the lives of those assets. Any additional negative goodwill should be recognised in the profit and loss account over the period expected to benefit from it. The accounts should disclose the amount of the negative goodwill and the period(s) over which it is being recognised.

Transitional arrangements

8.54 All goodwill that was eliminated against reserves in accordance with an accounting policy permitted until 23 March 1999 may remain eliminated against reserves. Alternatively, an entity may reinstate all such goodwill by prior period adjustment in its first accounting period beginning on or after 31 March 1999.

Tangible fixed assets

8.55   The requirements of this section of the FRSSE apply to all tangible fixed assets except investment properties (see 8.67 below). A tangible fixed asset should initially be measured at cost, and then written down to recoverable amount if necessary. In the case of an asset received by a charity as a gift or donation, the initial carrying amount should be the asset's current value on the date of receipt (i.e. the lower of replacement cost and recoverable amount). Only costs that are directly attributable to bringing the asset into working condition for its intended use should be included in its measurement. Where an entity adopts an accounting policy of capitalising finance costs, finance costs directly attributable to the construction of the asset should be capitalised as part of the cost of the asset. The total finance costs capitalised during an accounting period should not exceed the total finance costs incurred during that period. Capitalisation of costs (including finance costs) should be suspended during extended periods when active development is interrupted. Capitalisation should cease when substantially all the activities necessary to get the asset ready for use have been completed, even if the asset has not yet been brought into use.

Subsequent expenditure on tangible fixed assets

8.56   Subsequent expenditure on a tangible fixed asset should only be capitalised if it enhances the economic benefits of the asset beyond those previously assessed (i.e. it represents an improvement), or if it replaces or restores a component that has been separately depreciated. Other expenditure should be recognised in the profit and loss account as it is incurred.

Revaluation of tangible fixed assets

8.57   Where an entity adopts an accounting policy of revaluing tangible fixed assets, all assets of the same class (i.e. having a similar nature, function or use in the business) should be revalued, but it is not necessary to apply a policy of revaluation to all classes of asset. The carrying amount of a revalued asset should be its market value (or the best estimate thereof) at the balance sheet date. Where the directors consider that market value is not an appropriate basis for valuation, current value (i.e. the lower of replacement cost and recoverable amount) may be used instead. It may be possible to establish values for certain tangible fixed assets by reference to active second-hand markets or appropriate indices where these are publicly available. Properties and other assets should be valued by an experienced valuer (i.e. one with recognised and relevant recent professional experience, and sufficient knowledge of the market and location) at least every five years. The valuation should be updated by an experienced valuer in the intervening years where it is likely that there has been a material change in value. Where relevant, alternative approaches set out in sector-specific guidance and SORPs may be followed instead.

Revaluation gains and losses

8.58　　Revaluation losses caused only by changing prices should be recognised in the statement of total recognised gains and losses until the carrying amount of the asset reaches its depreciated historical cost. Other revaluation losses should be recognised in the profit and loss account. Revaluation gains should be recognised in the statement of total recognised gains and losses except to the extent that, after adjusting for subsequent depreciation, they reverse revaluation losses on the same asset that were previously recognised in the profit and loss account. Such gains should be recognised in the profit and loss account. The adjustment for subsequent depreciation achieves the same result as if the downward revaluation had not taken place.

The FRSSE also requires a similar treatment to be applied in the recognition of revaluation gains and losses on fixed asset investments included in the financial statements at market value or another appropriate valuation and to any gains and losses recognised on current asset investments.

Transitional arrangements

8.59　　Where an entity does not adopt an accounting policy of revaluing tangible fixed assets for its first accounting period ending on or after 23 March 2000, but the carrying amount of tangible fixed assets reflects previous revaluations, it may:

— 　retain the book amounts of the assets and disclose:

　— 　the fact that the transitional provisions of the FRSSE are being followed;

　— 　the date of the last revaluation; and

　— 　the fact that the valuation has not been updated; or

— 　as a change in accounting policy, restate the carrying amount of the assets to historical cost less restated accumulated depreciation.

Depreciation of tangible fixed assets

8.60　　The cost (or revalued amount) of a tangible fixed asset, less its estimated residual value, should be depreciated on a systematic basis over the useful economic life of the asset. The depreciation method used should reflect as fairly as possible the pattern in which the asset's economic benefits are consumed by the entity. The depreciation charged should be recognised as an expense in the profit and loss account unless it is permitted to be included in the carrying amount of another asset. With certain exceptions (e.g. land used for extractive purposes), land has an unlimited life and is not depreciated. Where an asset comprises two or more major components with substantially different useful economic lives, each component should be accounted for separately for depreciation purposes and depreciated over its useful economic life. Where, for its first accounting period ending on or after

23 March 2000, an entity separates tangible fixed assets into separate components in this way for the first time, the changes should be dealt with as a change in accounting policy.

Review of useful economic lives and residual values

8.61   The useful economic lives and residual values of tangible fixed assets should be regularly reviewed and revised where necessary. The carrying amount of the asset at the date of revision, less its revised residual value, should be depreciated over its revised remaining useful economic life.

Change in depreciation method

8.62   A change in the method of depreciation is only permissible on the grounds that the new method will give a fairer presentation of the entity's financial position and results. A change in method does not constitute a change in accounting policy. The carrying amount of the asset should be depreciated using the revised method over its remaining useful economic life, beginning in the accounting period in which the change is made. The reasons for the change and the effect (where material) should be disclosed in the financial statements.

Depreciation disclosures

8.63   The following should be disclosed for (i) land and buildings and (ii) other tangible fixed assets in aggregate:

—   depreciation methods used;

—   useful economic lives or depreciation rates used;

—   where material, the financial effect of a change during the period in the estimate of useful economic lives or residual values.

Additional disclosures are required where the method of depreciation is changed (see 8.61 above).

Write-downs to recoverable amount

8.64   The requirements of the FRSSE on write-downs to recoverable amount apply to capitalised goodwill and all categories of fixed assets except investment properties (see 8.66 below) and financial instruments. Investments in subsidiaries, associates and joint ventures are specifically covered by the requirements. Fixed assets and goodwill should be carried in the balance sheet at no more than recoverable amount, which is defined as the higher of the amounts that can be obtained from selling the asset (i.e. net realisable value) or continuing to use the asset in the business (i.e. value in use). Value in use is calculated as the present value of the future cash flows obtainable as a result of the asset's continued use (and ultimate disposal), or a reasonable estimate thereof. If the net book amount of a fixed asset or of goodwill is considered not to be fully recoverable at the balance sheet date, it should be written down to the estimated recoverable amount, and this should then be written off over the remaining useful economic life of the asset or goodwill.

Reversal of write-down

8.65   In the case of tangible fixed assets and investments, if the recoverable amount subsequently increases as a result of a change in economic conditions or in the expected use of the asset, the net book amount should be written back to the lower of recoverable amount and the amount at which the asset would have been recorded if the original write-down had not been made. In the case of intangible assets and goodwill, the net book amount should only be written back if an external event caused the original write-down and subsequent external events clearly and demonstrably reverse the effects of the first event in a way that was not foreseen when the original write-down was calculated.

Recognition of write-downs and reversals

8.66   Write-downs should normally be charged (and any reversals credited) to the profit and loss account for the period. However, write-downs of revalued assets that reverse previous revaluation gains simply as a result of changing market prices should be recognised in the statement of total recognised gains and losses to the extent that the carrying amount of the asset is greater than its depreciated historical cost.

Investment properties

8.67   Leased investment properties should be depreciated, at least over the period when the unexpired term of the lease is 20 years or less. Other investment properties should be included in the balance sheet at open market value, with their carrying value displayed prominently on the face of the balance sheet or in the notes to the accounts, and the following disclosures should be given:

—   names of those carrying out the valuation, or details of their qualifications – if the valuer is an employee or officer of the company or group, this fact must be disclosed;

—   the bases of valuation used.

Changes in market value should be taken to the statement of total recognised gains and losses except where a deficit on an individual investment property is expected to be permanent, in which case it should be charged to the profit and loss account of the period. Where such a deficit reverses in a future period, the reversal should be credited to the profit and loss account of that period.

Government grants

8.68   Government grants should be recognised in the profit and loss account so that they are matched with the expenditure towards which they are expected to contribute. Where a grant is given towards the cost of a fixed asset, UK companies legislation does not permit the cost of the asset to be reduced and the grant should therefore be accounted for as deferred income. A grant should not be recognised in the profit and loss account until all conditions relating to its receipt have been met and receipt of the grant is reasonably assured. Potential liabilities to repay grants should be provided for only to the extent that repayment is probable. The repayment of a grant should be set against any unamortised deferred income relating to the grant and any excess should be charged immediately to the profit and loss account. The following details should be disclosed in the accounts:

— the effects of government grants on the results of the period and/or the financial position of the entity; and

— where the results of the period are materially affected by the receipt of government assistance other than grants, the nature of the assistance and, where practicable, an estimate of the effect.

Hire purchase contracts

8.69   Hire purchase contracts of a financing nature should be accounted for on the same basis as finance leases and the asset should be depreciated over its useful economic life. Other hire purchase contracts should be accounted for on the same basis as operating leases.

Lessees: Accounting for finance leases

8.70   A finance lease should be recorded in the lessee's balance sheet as an asset and as an obligation to pay future rentals. The amount recorded as an asset and a liability at the inception of the lease should normally be the fair value of the asset. If this does not give a realistic estimate of the cost to the lessee (for instance, where the lessee is able to benefit from grants and capital allowances that reduce the minimum lease payments to a total that is less than the fair value of the asset) a better estimate should be used, based on an approximation of the present value of the minimum lease payments (e.g. by discounting them at the interest rate implicit in the lease). The total finance charge under a finance lease should be allocated to accounting periods during the lease term in a way that produces a constant periodic rate of charge on the outstanding obligation, or a reasonable approximation to this. The straight-line method may provide such an approximation. The lease term is the period for which the lessee has contracted to lease the asset, plus any further terms where the lessee has an option to lease, with or without payment, and it is reasonably certain at the inception of the lease that the option will be exercised. An asset leased under a finance lease should be depreciated over the shorter of the lease term or the useful life of the asset.

Lessees: Accounting for operating leases

8.71   Operating lease rentals should be charged to the profit and loss account on a straight-line basis over the lease term, even if payments are made on a different basis. Another systematic and rational basis may be used if this is more appropriate. The lease term is as defined in 8.69 above.

Lessees: Accounting for lease incentives

8.72   Incentives to sign a lease, whatever their form, should be allocated on a straight-line basis over the shorter of:

—   the lease term; or

—   the period to the review date when the rental is first expected to be adjusted to prevailing market rates.

Lessors: Accounting for finance leases

8.73   The amount due from the lessee under a finance lease should be recorded as a debtor in the lessor's balance sheet at the amount of the net investment in the lease, after making provision for bad and doubtful items where necessary. The net investment in a lease is the gross investment in the lease less gross earnings allocated to future periods. Total gross earnings under a finance lease should be recognised on a systematic and rational basis. This will usually give a constant periodic rate of return on the net investment in the lease. Where the lessor is a manufacturer or dealer, the selling profit should be restricted to the excess of the fair value of the asset over the manufacturer's or dealer's cost, less any grants receivable.

Lessors: Accounting for operating leases

8.74   An asset held for use in an operating lease should be recorded as a fixed asset and depreciated over its useful life. Rental income under an operating lease should be recognised on a straight-line basis over the period of the lease, even if payments are made on a different basis. Another systematic and rational basis may be used if this is more representative of the time pattern in which the benefit from the lease is received. A manufacturer or dealer lessor should not recognise a selling profit in respect of an operating lease.

Sale and leaseback transactions

8.75   Where a sale and leaseback transaction results in a finance lease, any apparent profit or loss should be deferred by the seller/lessee and amortised over the shorter of the lease term or the useful life of the asset. Where the transaction results in an operating lease, any profit or loss should be recognised immediately, except where:

—   the selling price is below fair value and the apparent loss is compensated for by future rentals below market value — the loss should be deferred to that extent and amortised over the shorter of the lease term and the period during which reduced rentals are charged;

—   the selling price is above fair value — the excess over fair value should be deferred and amortised over the shorter of the lease term and the period to the next rent review (if any).

A buyer/lessor should account for sale and leaseback transactions in the same way as other leases (i.e. as described in 8.73–8.74 above).

Disclosure by lessees

8.76   A lessee should include the following disclosures in the accounts:

—   the gross amount of assets held under finance leases and the related accumulated depreciation, analysed into the following categories:

  —   land and buildings; and

  —   other fixed assets (in aggregate).

As an alternative, details for leased assets may be aggregated with those for owned assets provided that there is separate disclosure (in the two categories described above) of:

  —   the net amount of assets held under finance leases; and

  —   depreciation in the period in respect of those assets;

—   obligations relating to finance leases, net of finance charges allocated to future periods (i.e. separately from other liabilities) — this may be given on the face of the balance sheet or in the notes to the accounts;

—   the amount of any commitments under finance leases entered into at the balance sheet date but where inception occurs after the year-end; and

—   the commitments in the next twelve months under operating leases, analysed into amounts relating to leases which expire:

  —   in the next year;

  —   in 2 to 5 years inclusive; and

  —   more than 5 years from the balance sheet date.

Disclosure by lessors

8.77 A lessor should include the following disclosures in the accounts:

— the gross amount of assets held for use in operating leases and the related accumulated depreciation;

— the cost of assets acquired (by purchase or under finance leases) for letting under finance leases;

— the net investment in (i) finance leases and (ii) hire purchase contracts at each balance sheet date.

Stocks

8.78 Stocks should be included in the financial statements at the lower of the cost and net realisable value of the separate items or groups of similar items. Appendix III to the FRSSE provides additional guidance on the allocation of overheads, methods of costing, determining net realisable value and the application of net realisable value. The key points included in this guidance are as follows:

— any abnormal conversion costs (e.g. exceptional spoilage, idle capacity) should be excluded in calculating the cost of stock and long-term contracts;

— where firm sales contracts are in place, overheads relating to design, and to marketing and selling costs incurred before manufacture, may be included in arriving at cost;

— the costs of general management, as distinct from functional management, should be excluded from the cost of stock and long-term contracts – however in a smaller business where management may be involved in more than one function it will usually be appropriate to allocate management costs to the various functions (e.g. production, marketing, selling and administration) on a suitable basis;

— the costs of central service departments (e.g. the accounts department) should be allocated to the functions that the department serves on a suitable basis;

— the allocation of overheads to stocks and long-term contracts should be based on the entity's normal level of activity, taking one year with another, and giving due consideration to:

  — the volume of production that the facilities are designed to achieve under the working conditions prevailing during the year (e.g. single shift, double shift etc);

  — the budgeted level of activity for the current year and the following year; and

  — the level of activity achieved in the current year and in previous years.

— where management accounts are prepared on a marginal cost basis, any production overheads not included in marginal cost will need to be added in for valuation purposes;

— the accounting principle of prudence should not be used to justify the exclusion of certain overheads from the valuation – it should instead be taken into account when determining net realisable value;

— the method of costing chosen should provide the fairest possible approximation to cost;

— where standard costs are used, they should be regularly reviewed and updated where necessary;

— methods such as 'base stock' and 'LIFO' will not usually be appropriate as they result in stock valuations that bear little relationship to recent cost levels;

— in certain circumstances it may be appropriate to arrive at cost by valuing stock at selling price less an estimated margin, but only if it can be shown that this gives a reasonable approximation to actual cost;

— where the cost of minor by-products cannot be separated from the cost of the principal products, it may be appropriate to include stocks of the by-products at net realisable value – in this case, the costs of the main products should be calculated after deducting the net realisable value of the by-products;

— initial provisions to reduce cost to net realisable value will often be based on the use of formulae (for instance, to take account of age, past movements, expected future movements etc) but the results should always be reviewed in the light of other available information (e.g. the current order book);

— where provision needs to be made to reduce the value of finished goods below cost, the stock of parts and assemblies held for the production of those goods should also be reviewed to establish whether additional provision is required against these items;

— where stocks of spares are held for sale, the determination of net realisable value should take into account:

   — the number of units sold to which they relate;

   — the estimated frequency with which a spare part is required; and

   — the expected useful life of the unit to which they relate.

— events between the balance sheet date and completion of the financial statements need to be taken into account in assessing net realisable value (e.g. changes in prices) – however it will not usually be necessary to write down the purchase price of raw materials provided that the goods into which they will be incorporated can still be sold at a profit (i.e. after taking account of the materials at actual cost);

— net realisable value is most likely to be less than cost where there have been:

— increases in costs or reductions in selling prices;

— physical deterioration of the items in stock;

— obsolescence of the products (e.g. due to technological change);

— a strategic decision to sell certain products at a loss;

— errors in purchasing or production.

Long-term contracts

8.79 Long-term contracts should be assessed on an individual basis and should be reflected in the profit and loss account by recording turnover and the related costs as the contract progresses. The calculation of turnover should be appropriate to the stage of completion of the contract and to the type of business undertaken. Where the outcome of a long-term contract can be assessed with reasonable certainty before its conclusion, the attributable profit, calculated on a prudent basis, should be recognised in the profit and loss account as the difference between turnover and related costs for that contract. Appendix III to the FRSSE sets out additional guidance on long-term contracts, including:

— it is not usually appropriate to include interest on borrowings in the costs of a long-term contract – however, this may be acceptable where specific borrowings can be identified as financing specific contracts, in which case the accounts should disclose both the fact that interest is included and the amount involved;

— where contract prices are determined and invoiced as separate parts of a contract, it will usually be appropriate to match revenue and costs for each separable part and to reflect the profit accordingly – however future revenues and costs should also be reviewed to establish whether any provision is required for expected future losses;

— only profit that prudently reflects the amount of work performed to date should be recognised in the accounts, and the method used for taking up such profit should be consistently applied;

— in calculating total estimated profit on a contract, the total sales value of the contract should be compared with:

— total costs to date;

— total estimated future costs to completion;

— the estimated future costs of rectification and guarantee work; and

— the estimated future costs of any further work to be undertaken under the terms of the contract;

— in considering future costs, the following should be taken into account to the extent that they are not recoverable from the customer:

— likely increases in wages and salaries;

— likely increases in raw material prices; and

— likely increases in general overheads;

— where approved variations have been made to a contract but the amount to be received has not yet been settled and is likely to be a material factor in the outcome of the contract, the total sales value should include a conservative estimate of the amount likely to be received – allowance should also be made for expected claims or penalties arising from delays or other factors;

— the settlement of claims is generally subject to a high degree of uncertainty and it is generally prudent to recognise receipts in respect of claims only when negotiations have reached an advanced stage and there is sufficient evidence both that the claim has been accepted and that adequate resources are available to meet it.

Disclosure of long-term contracts

8.80   Long-term contracts should be disclosed in the balance sheet as follows:

— an excess of turnover over payments on account should be shown separately within debtors as 'amounts recoverable on contracts';

— an excess of payments on account over the amount matched with turnover and the amount offset against long-term contract balances should be shown separately within creditors as 'payments on account';

— the amount of long-term contracts at cost, less amounts transferred to cost of sales and after deducting foreseeable losses and payments on account not matched with turnover, should be shown separately within the balance sheet heading 'stocks' and classified as 'long-term contract balances' – the notes to the accounts should show separately:

— net cost less foreseeable losses; and

— related payments on account;

— where the accrual or provision for foreseeable losses exceeds cost (after transfers to cost of sales), the excess should be shown within 'creditors' or 'provisions for liabilities and charges' as appropriate.

Consignment stocks

8.81   Where consignment stock is in substance an asset of the dealer, both the stock and the corresponding liability to the manufacturer should be shown on the dealer's balance sheet. Any deposit paid by the dealer should be deducted from the liability and the remaining balance should be classified as a trade creditor. Where the consignment stock is not an asset of the dealer it should be excluded from the dealer's balance sheet until title has transferred. Any deposit paid by the dealer should be shown under 'other debtors'. Appendix III to the FRSSE sets out a table to help identify whether the substance of the agreement is that the stock is an asset of the dealer (i.e. whether the dealer has access to the benefits of the stock and is exposed to the inherent risks).

Debt factoring

8.82 Where all significant benefits (i.e. future cash flows) and all significant risks (i.e. slow payment and non-payment) relating to the factored debts have been transferred to the factor, and the entity has no obligation to repay the factor, the debts should be removed from the reporting entity's balance sheet. A profit or loss should be recognised, calculated as the difference between the carrying value of the debts and the proceeds received. A linked presentation should be adopted where significant benefits and risks relating to the debts have been retained by the reporting entity and all of the following conditions are met:

— there is no doubt whatsoever that the entity's exposure to loss is limited to a fixed monetary amount;

— amounts received from the factor are secured only on the debts factored;

— the debts factored can be separately identified;

— the factor has no recourse to other debts or assets;

— the entity has no right to reacquire the debts at some point in the future; and

— the factor has no right to return the debts, even if the factoring agreement ceases.

The linked presentation involves separate disclosure on the face of the balance sheet of the gross amount of the factored debts (after providing for bad debts, credit protection charges and accrued interest where relevant) and amounts received from the factor:

Example 8.4 – Linked presentation of factored debts

	£	£
Stocks		233
Debtors:		
Gross debtors factored without recourse	100	
Less: Non-returnable proceeds	(75)	
	25	
Other debtors	124	
		149
Cash at bank and in hand		50
Current assets		432

A note to the accounts should disclose the fact that the entity is not required to support bad debts in respect of factored debts and that the factor has given a written undertaking not to seek recourse other than out of factored debts. Interest charged by the factor should be recognised as it accrues and should be included with other interest in the profit and loss account. In all other cases where significant benefits and risks relating to the debts have been retained by the reporting entity, the following accounting treatment (separate presentation) should be adopted:

—   the gross amount of the debts should be shown as an asset on the balance sheet;

—   a corresponding liability in respect of the proceeds received from the factor should be shown within liabilities; and

—   interest charged by the factor should be recognised as it accrues and should be included with other interest in the profit and loss account.

Appendix III to the FRSSE sets out a table of terms commonly included in factoring agreements with guidance on whether these indicate that derecognition, a linked presentation or separate presentation is appropriate.

Start-up costs and pre-contract costs

8.83   Start-up costs should be accounted for on a basis consistent with the accounting treatment of similar costs incurred as part of the entity's ongoing activities. Where there are no similar costs, start-up costs that do not meet the criteria for recognition as an asset under other specific requirements of the FRSSE should be recognised as an expense when they are incurred.

Pre-contract costs should generally be expensed as incurred. However, costs that relate directly to securing a specific contract should be recognised as an asset if:

(i)   they are incurred after both of the following asset recognition criteria for pre-contract costs have been met:

●   it is virtually certain that the contract will be obtained; and

●   the contract is expected to result in future net cash inflows with a present value no less than all amounts recognised as an asset; and

(ii)   they are separately identifiable and can be measured reliably.

Costs incurred before the asset recognition criteria are met should not be recognised as an asset.

Taxation

8.84   Current and deferred tax should be recognised in the profit and loss account, except to the extent that it is attributable to a gain or loss recognised directly in the statement of total recognised gains and losses, in which case the tax should also be recognised in that statement. The material components of the current and deferred tax charge or credit for the period should be disclosed separately. Any special circumstances affecting the overall tax charge or credit for the period, or which may affect those of future periods, should be disclosed in the notes to the accounts, with quantification of their individual effects. The effects of a fundamental change in the basis of taxation should be included in the tax charge for the year and should be disclosed separately on the face of the profit and loss account.

Recognition of deferred tax

8.85 Deferred tax should be recognised in respect of all timing differences that have originated but not reversed by the balance sheet date, except that it should not be recognised on:

— revaluation gains and losses unless, at the balance sheet date, the entity has entered into a binding agreement to sell the asset and has revalued it to selling price; or

— taxable gains arising on revaluation or sale, if it is more likely than not that the gain will be rolled over into a replacement asset.

Deferred tax should not be recognised on permanent differences. Deferred tax should be recognised when tax allowances for the cost of a fixed asset are received before or after the recognition of the related depreciation in the profit and loss account. However, once any conditions for retaining the tax allowances have been met, the deferred tax should be reversed. Unrelieved tax losses and other deferred tax assets should be recognised only to the extent that it is more likely than not that they will be recovered against the reversal of deferred tax liabilities or against future taxable profits. The FRSSE warns that the very existence of unrelieved tax losses is strong evidence that there may not be any future taxable profits available for such recovery.

Measurement of deferred tax

8.86 Deferred tax should be measured at the average tax rates that are expected to apply when the timing differences reverse, based on tax rates and laws enacted by the balance sheet date. Deferred tax assets and liabilities do not need to be discounted. If an entity adopts a policy of discounting, it should discount all deferred tax balances that have been measured by reference to undiscounted cash flows and for which the impact of discounting is material. The unwinding of the discount should be disclosed separately as part of the tax charge.

Disclosure of deferred tax

8.87 The following items should be disclosed:

— the deferred tax balance and its material components;

— the movement between the opening and closing deferred tax balances, and the material components of that movement; and

— if assets have been revalued, or if their market values are disclosed, the amount of tax that would be payable or recoverable if the assets were sold at those values.

Tax on dividends

8.88   Outgoing dividends and similar amounts payable, and incoming dividends and similar income, should be recognised at an amount that includes any withholding tax but excludes other taxes, such as attributable tax credits. Any withholding tax suffered should be shown as part of the tax charge.

VAT

8.89   Turnover should exclude output VAT or VAT inputed under the flat rate VAT scheme. Any irrecoverable input VAT should be included in the cost of the relevant item where practicable and material.

Defined contribution retirement schemes

8.90   The cost of a defined contribution scheme is equivalent to the amount of the contributions payable to the scheme for the accounting period. This cost should be recognised within operating profit in the profit and loss account. The following should be disclosed:

— the nature of the scheme (i.e. defined contribution);

— the cost for the period; and

— any outstanding or prepaid contributions at the balance sheet date.

Defined benefit retirement schemes

8.91   As few smaller entities participate in defined benefit schemes, the requirements on accounting for such schemes are set out in Appendix II to the FRSSE rather than in the main document. The Appendix sets out requirements based on those in FRS 17 *Retirement Benefits* and applies these for accounting periods ending on or after 22 June 2006, although earlier adoption is encouraged. Separate requirements are set out for accounting periods ending before 22 June 2006 where the new requirements are not adopted early.

Accounting periods ending before 22 June 2006

8.92   Where the requirements for accounting periods ending on or after 22 June 2006 are not adopted early, the following accounting treatment should be applied:

— the employer should recognise the expected cost of providing pensions and other post-retirement benefits on a systematic and rational basis over the period during which it derives benefit from the employees' services;

— the pension cost should be calculated using actuarial valuation methods – the actuarial assumptions and method should be compatible and should result in the actuary's best estimate of the cost of providing the promised pension benefits;

— the method of providing for pension costs over the service lives of the employees should result in the regular pension cost being a substantially level percentage of the current and expected future pensionable payroll, in the light of the current actuarial assumptions;

— variations from regular cost should be allocated over the expected remaining service lives of the current employees in the scheme (a period representing average service lives may be used);

— to the extent that the capital cost of ex gratia pensions is not covered by a surplus, it should be recognised in the profit and loss account in the accounting period in which they are granted;

— where the actuarial assumptions do not allow for discretionary or ex gratia increases in pensions, the capital cost of such increases should be recognised in the profit and loss account for the period in which they are initially granted, to the extent that they are not covered by a surplus;

— where the cumulative pension cost recognised in the profit and loss account has not been completely discharged by the payment of contributions or directly paid pensions, the excess should be shown as a net pension provision, and any excess of contributions or directly paid pensions over the cumulative pension cost should be shown as a prepayment;

— the following disclosures should be given:

  — the nature of the scheme (i.e. defined benefit);

  — whether it is funded or unfunded;

  — whether the pension cost and pension provision are assessed with the advice of a professionally qualified actuary and, if so, the date of the last formal valuation (or later formal review);

  — the pension cost charge for the period;

  — any provision or prepayment in the accounts resulting from a difference between the amount recognised as the cumulative pension cost and the amount funded or paid directly;

  — the amount of any deficiency on a current funding level basis and an indication of the action being taken to deal with this;

  — an outline of the result of the latest formal actuarial valuation (or later formal review) of the scheme on an ongoing basis;

— any commitment to make additional payments over a limited number of years;

— details of the expected effect on future costs of any material changes in the company's (or group's) pension arrangements;

— the fair value of scheme assets, the present value of scheme liabilities and the resulting surplus or deficit determined in accordance with the requirements on accounting for defined benefit schemes for accounting periods ending on or after 22 June 2006;

— where the surplus or deficit in the scheme differs from the amount that would be recognised under those requirements, an explanation of the difference;

— for accounting periods ending on or after 22 June 2003, comparative figures must be given for the two previous disclosures, together with an analysis of the movements in the surplus or deficit in the scheme during the current period ;

— for accounting periods ending on or after 22 June 2004, comparative figures must also be given for the analysis of the movement in the surplus or deficit.

A subsidiary that is a member of a group scheme should disclose this fact and the nature of the group scheme, indicating where appropriate that contributions are based on pension costs for the group as a whole. Such a company is exempt from the detailed disclosures on funding levels and the results of the most recent actuarial valuation (or later review), provided that:

— the notes to the accounts give the name of the holding company in whose financial statements this information can be found; and

— that holding company is registered in the UK or Republic of Ireland.

Accounting periods ending on or after 22 June 2006

8.93   The following requirements apply to defined benefit schemes for accounting periods ending on or after 22 June 2006:

— scheme assets should be measured at fair value at the balance sheet date;

— scheme liabilities (which comprise benefits promised under the scheme and any constructive obligations for further benefits) should be measured on an actuarial basis using the projected unit method;

— the assumptions underlying the valuation should be mutually compatible and should result in the best estimate of the future cash flows that will arise – the directors have ultimate responsibility for the assumptions but should seek appropriate advice from an actuary;

— any assumptions that are affected by economic conditions should reflect market expectations at the balance sheet date;

— scheme liabilities should be discounted at the current rate of return on a high quality corporate bond of equivalent currency and term;

— full actuarial valuations by a professionally qualified actuary should be obtained at least every three years and the actuary should review and update the latest valuation at each intervening balance sheet date;

— the excess or shortfall of the value of scheme assets over the present value of scheme liabilities represents the surplus or deficit in the scheme – the employer should:

    — recognise an asset to the extent that it can recover a surplus through reduced contributions or a refund from the scheme; and

    — recognise a liability to the extent that it reflects a legal or constructive obligation;

— any unpaid contributions to the scheme should be shown as creditors due within one year;

— the defined benefit asset or liability should be shown separately on the face of the balance sheet as follows:

    — in a balance sheet prepared under Format 1 under CA 1985 Sch 8, after item J (Accruals) but before item K (Capital and reserves); and

    — in a balance sheet prepared under Format 2 under CA 1985 Sch 8, an asset should be shown after Assets item D (Prepayments and accrued income) and a liability should be shown after Liabilities item D (Accruals and deferred income);

— any deferred tax relating to the defined benefit asset or liability should be offset against that asset or liability (i.e. it should not be included with other deferred tax assets or liabilities);

— the individual components of the change in the defined benefit asset or liability (other than contributions to the scheme) should be shown as follows:

    — the current service cost should be included in operating profit in the profit and loss account;

    — the net of interest cost and the expected return on assets should be shown as other finance costs (or income) adjacent to interest;

    — actuarial gains and losses should be recognised in the statement of total recognised gains and losses;

    — past service costs should be recognised in the profit and loss account in the period in which the increased benefits vest;

    — losses arising on a settlement or curtailment should be recognised in the profit and loss account when the employer becomes demonstrably committed to the transaction – gains should be recognised only when all parties whose consent is required are irrevocably committed;

— the following disclosures should be given:

   — the nature of the scheme (i.e. defined benefit);

   — the date of the latest full actuarial valuation on which amounts included in the accounts are based – if the actuary is an employee or officer of the reporting entity (or of another member of the group), this fact should be disclosed;

   — the contributions made in respect of the accounting period and any agreed contribution rates for future years;

   — for closed schemes and those in which the age profile of the active membership is rising significantly, the fact that, under the projected unit method, the current service cost will increase as members approach retirement;

   — the fair value of scheme assets, the present value of scheme liabilities and the resulting surplus or deficit in the scheme;

   — where the defined benefit asset or liability in the balance sheet differs from the surplus or deficit in the scheme, an explanation of the difference; and

   — an analysis of movements in the surplus or deficit during the period.

Provisions

8.94   The section of the FRSSE on provisions, contingent liabilities and contingent assets does not apply to retirement benefits, deferred tax or leases, as these are dealt with in separate, more specific sections. A provision should be recognised only when it is probable (i.e. more likely than not) that a present obligation exists as a result of a past event and that a transfer of economic benefits will be required to settle the obligation, and when the amount of the transfer can be estimated reliably. The amount recognised as a provision should be the best estimate of the expenditure required to settle the obligation at the balance sheet date. Where the effect of the time value of money is material, the amount of a provision should be the present value of the expenditures required to settle the obligation. There are a number of acceptable discounting methods, and the appropriate discount rate will depend on the method used. If cash flows have already been adjusted for risk, it will usually be appropriate to use a risk-free discount rate. Where discounting is used, the unwinding of the discount should be shown as other finance costs adjacent to interest. An illustrative example of discounting a provision is given in Appendix III to the FRSSE. Where some or all of the expenditure needed to settle the obligation may be reimbursed by a third party (e.g. an insurer), the reimbursement should be recognised (as a separate asset) only when it is virtually certain to be received if the entity settles the obligation. A net presentation of the provision and the reimbursement may be given in the profit and loss account. Gains from the expected disposal of assets should be excluded from the measurement of a provision. Provisions should be reviewed at each balance sheet date and adjusted to reflect the current best estimate of the amount required to settle the obligation at that date and a provision should only be used for the purpose for which it was originally recognised.

Contingent liabilities and contingent assets

8.95 Contingent liabilities and contingent assets should not be recognised. The following details should be disclosed for contingent liabilities (except where they are remote), and for probable contingent assets:

— brief description of the nature of the contingent item; and

— where practicable, an estimate of its financial effect.

Financial instruments

8.96 A financial instrument, or its component parts, should be classified as a financial asset, a financial liability or an equity instrument, according to the commercial substance of the contractual agreement rather than its legal form. For instance, a preference share that provides for mandatory redemption by the issuer for a fixed or determinable amount at a fixed or determinable future date, or which gives the holder the right to require redemption by the issuer on or after a particular date, is a financial liability rather than an equity instrument. Borrowings (i.e. financial instruments that are classified as liabilities) should be stated initially at the fair value of the consideration given and should then be:

(i) increased by the finance costs charged in respect of the period; and

(ii) reduced by any payments made in respect of the borrowings during the period.

Finance costs in respect of borrowings should be allocated to accounting periods over the term of the borrowings at a constant rate on the carrying amount and should be charged in the profit and loss account. Finance costs are the difference between the net proceeds of the instrument and the total payments (or other transfer of economic benefits) that the issuer may be required to make in respect of the instrument (other than arrangement fees). If an arrangement fee represents a significant additional cost of finance (e.g. when compared with the total interest charge over the life of the instrument), it should be accounted for in the same way as finance costs. In other cases the arrangement fee should be charged in the profit and loss account when it is incurred.

Note that, whilst the above is similar to the treatment required by the previous version of the FRSSE in respect of capital instruments, the classification of certain shares as financial liabilities on the balance sheet is only permitted for accounting periods beginning on or after 1 January 2005 as a result of company law changes that come into effect from the same date (see 4.7 above).

Dividends

8.97   A dividend in respect of a financial instrument that is a financial liability (or the component of a financial instrument that is a financial liability) should be recognised as an expense in the profit and loss account. Distributions to holders of an equity instrument should be debited directly to equity, net of any related income tax benefit. Dividends declared after the balance sheet date should not be recognised as liabilities at that date. (Note that this treatment of dividends cannot be adopted for accounting periods beginning on or before 1 January 2005 as it hinges on company law changes coming into effect from that date – see 9.10 below).

Translation of foreign currency transactions, assets and liabilities

8.98   Assets, liabilities, revenues and costs relating to transactions denominated in a foreign currency should be translated into local currency at the exchange rate ruling on the date of the transaction. An average rate over a period may be used as an approximation of the actual rate, provided that rates do not fluctuate significantly. There are two exceptions to this general rule:

—   where the transaction is to be settled at a contracted rate, that rate should be used for the conversion; and

—   where a trading transaction is covered by a matching or related forward contract, the rate specified in that contract may be used.

Once non-monetary assets have been translated and recorded, no subsequent translations should normally be made, except in the case of foreign equity investments financed by foreign currency borrowings (see 8.99 below). At the balance sheet date, monetary assets and liabilities denominated in a foreign currency should be translated into local currency using the closing rate, except in the following circumstances:

—   where the transaction is to be settled at a contracted rate, that rate should be used for the conversion; and

—   where a trading transaction is covered by a matching or related forward contract, the rate specified in that contract may be used.

Exchange gains and losses on settled transactions and unsettled monetary items should be reported in the profit and loss account as part of the profit or loss on ordinary activities for the year.

Foreign equity investments financed by foreign currency borrowings

8.99   Where foreign equity investments are financed or hedged by foreign currency borrowings the following accounting treatment may be adopted:

— the equity investments may be denominated in the relevant foreign currency and translated at the closing rate of exchange at each balance sheet date for inclusion in the reporting entity's financial statements;

— any exchange differences arising should be taken to reserves; and

— exchange gains or losses arising on translation of the related foreign currency borrowings should be offset, as a reserves movement, against those exchange differences, subject to the following rules:

— in any accounting period, exchange gains and losses on foreign currency borrowings can only be offset to the extent of exchange differences arising on the related investments;

— those foreign currency borrowings should not exceed, in aggregate, the total amount of cash that the investments are expected to generate, from profits or otherwise.

Where this accounting treatment is adopted, it must be applied consistently from year to year.

Incorporating the accounts of foreign entities

8.100   The accounts of foreign entities (including associated companies and branches) should normally be incorporated into the accounts of the reporting entity using the closing rate/net investment method of translation. Exchange differences arising on translation should be recorded as a movement on reserves. The profit and loss account of a foreign entity should be translated at the closing rate, or at an average rate for the period, calculated in the most appropriate way taking into account the circumstances of the entity. If an average rate is used, the difference between the translation of the profit and loss account at the closing rate and at the average rate should be treated as a movement on reserves. Where the trade of the foreign entity depends more on the economic environment of the investing entity's currency than on that of its own currency, transactions recorded by the foreign entity should be translated as if they were undertaken by the investing entity (i.e. as set out in 8.98). The method of translation adopted for the accounts of a foreign entity should be applied consistently from year to year, unless there is a change in the financial and other operational relationships with the investing entity.

Investments in foreign entities financed by foreign currency borrowings

8.101   Where investments in foreign entities have been financed or hedged by foreign currency borrowings, exchange gains and losses on the borrowings may be offset as a reserves movement against exchange differences arising on retranslation of the investments, subject to the following rules:

— the relationship between the foreign entity and investor must justify the use of the closing rate method for consolidation purposes;

— in any accounting period, exchange gains and losses on foreign currency borrowings can only be offset to the extent of exchange differences arising on the net investments in foreign entities;

— those foreign currency borrowings should not exceed, in aggregate, the total amount of cash that the net investments are expected to generate, from profits or otherwise.

Where this accounting treatment is adopted, it must be applied consistently from year to year. Where an investor prepares group accounts and in its individual accounts has applied the accounting treatment set out in 8.99 to investments in foreign entities that are not subsidiaries or associates, it may adopt the same treatment in its consolidated financial statements.

Post balance sheet events

8.102 The amounts recognised in the financial statements should be amended to reflect adjusting events after the balance sheet date, but should not be amended to reflect non-adjusting events arising after that date. Events after balance sheet date are events (both favourable and unfavourable) between the balance sheet date and the date on which the financial statements are authorised for issue. An adjusting event is one that provides evidence of conditions that existed at the balance sheet date. A non-adjusting event indicates conditions that arose after that date.

The financial statements should disclose the following for each material category of non-adjusting event after the balance sheet date:

(i)   the nature of the event; and

(ii) an estimate of the financial effect, or a statement that such an estimate cannot be made.

Date of approval of financial statements

8.103 The financial statements should disclose the date on which they were approved for issue and who gave that approval.

Related party disclosures

8.104 Where the reporting entity enters into a transaction with or on behalf of a related party, irrespective of whether a price is charged, and the transaction is material to the reporting entity, the following details should be disclosed in the financial statements:

— the names of the related parties entering into the transaction;

— a description of the relationship between them;

— a description of the transaction;

— the amounts involved;

— any other elements of the transaction that are necessary for a proper understanding of the financial statements;

— the amounts due to or from related parties at the balance sheet date;

— any provisions for doubtful debts due from related parties at the balance sheet date; and

— amounts written off during the period in respect of debts due to or from related parties.

Purchases, sales, transfers of goods or other assets or liabilities, services rendered or received, and the provision or receipt of finance or financial support are all covered by the disclosure requirements. However, the following items do not require disclosure as related party transactions:

— pension contributions paid to a pension fund;

— emoluments in respect of services as an employee of the reporting entity;

— transactions with the following parties simply as a result of their role:

    — providers of finance (in the course of that business);

    — utility companies;

    — government departments and sponsored bodies;

    — a customer, supplier, franchis or, distributor or general agent.

Transactions may be disclosed in aggregate (i.e. the aggregation of similar transactions by type of related party) unless disclosure of individual transactions (or connected transactions) is necessary for a proper understanding of the impact of the transactions on the financial statements or is required by law. Also, where the reporting entity is part of a group that prepares publicly available consolidated financial statements, it is entitled to the exemption in paragraph 3(a)–(c) of FRS 8 *Related Party Disclosures*.

Personal guarantees given by directors

8.105   The financial statements should disclose any personal guarantees given by the directors in respect of the reporting entity's borrowings.

Disclosure of controlling party

8.106   Where the reporting entity is controlled by another party, the following disclosures should be given, regardless of whether there have been any transactions between the parties:

— the related party relationship and the name of that party; and

— the name of the ultimate controlling party, if different.

If the controlling party or ultimate controlling party is not known, this fact should be explained in the financial statements.

Consolidated financial statements

8.107   Where the reporting entity prepares consolidated financial statements, the detailed requirements (including disclosure requirements) set out in the following accounting standards should be applied:

— FRS 2 – 'Accounting for Subsidiary Undertakings'

— FRS 6 – 'Acquisitions and Mergers'

— FRS 7 – 'Fair Values in Acquisition Accounting'

The FRSSE also requires compliance with the relevant sections of the following:

— FRS 5 'Reporting the Substance of Transactions';

— FRS 9 'Associates and Joint Ventures';

— FRS 10 'Goodwill and Intangible Assets'; and

— FRS 11 'Impairment of Fixed Assets and Goodwill'.

However, the requirements of FRS 10 and FRS 11 apply only in respect of any goodwill arising on consolidation.

MEDIUM-SIZED COMPANIES AND GROUPS

Qualification as a medium-sized company

8.108   The rules on qualification as a medium-sized company and their practical effect are identical to those described in 8.1 to 8.8 above in relation to small companies, except that the qualifying conditions are increased to:

— turnover of not more than £22.8 million (if the accounting period is less than or more than a year, this limit must be adjusted proportionately);

— balance sheet total of not more than £11.4 million;

— number of employees not more than 250.

A parent company cannot qualify as a medium-sized company unless the group which it heads qualifies as a medium-sized group. The rules on qualifying as a medium-sized group are as described in 8.6 to 8.8 above, and the qualifying conditions are as follows:

— aggregate turnover of not more than £22.8 million net or not more than £27.36 million gross (if the accounting period is less than or more than a year, these limits must be adjusted proportionately);

— aggregate balance sheet total of not more than £11.4 million net or not more than £13.68 million gross;

— aggregate number of employees of not more than 250.

The above thresholds for both companies and groups were introduced by the *Companies Act 1985 (Accounts of Small and Medium-Sized Enterprises and Audit Exemption)(Amendment) Regulations 2004* (SI 2004/16) and represent the maximum thresholds currently permitted by EC Directives. They are effective for accounting periods ending on or after 30 January 2004, although the previous lower thresholds continue to apply to an accounting reference period that only ends on or after this date because a notice of extension was given to the registrar on or after 9 January 2004 (the date on which the Regulations were laid before Parliament). For accounting periods beginning on or after 1 January 2005, eligibility as a medium-sized company or group can be assessed on the basis of either Companies Act or IAS accounts.

Accounts exemptions available to medium sized companies

8.109   Most companies that qualify as medium-sized can file abbreviated accounts with the registrar but the permitted abbreviations are very limited compared with those available to small companies. The exemption relates only to the filing requirement and full accounts must still be prepared each year for presentation to the members. A medium-sized company does not have to take advantage of the exemption and can therefore file a copy of the full accounts if it wishes. Medium-sized companies are also exempt from the requirement to state whether the accounts have been prepared in accordance with applicable accounting standards. This exemption relates only to the disclosure requirement and does not grant any exemption from compliance with the requirements of accounting standards.

For accounting periods beginning on or after 1 January 2005, the option for a medium-sized company to file abbreviated accounts is only available where the company prepares Companies Act accounts (see 1.3 above).

There are no exemptions in respect of the directors' report of a medium-sized company for accounting periods beginning before 1 April 2005 but, for accounting periods beginning on or after this date, medium-sized companies are granted exemption from some of the detailed disclosures that would otherwise need to be given in the directors' report under changes introduced by the *Companies Act 1985 (Operating and Financial Review and Directors' Report etc.) Regulations 2005* (SI 2005/1011). As a result, the business review prepared by a medium-sized company need not include analysis using key performance indicators (KPIs) in respect of non-financial information (for instance, employee matters and environmental issues), although financial KPIs must still be given. Companies that meet the size criteria for a medium-sized company but do not generally qualify for SME exemptions because they are part of an ineligible group (see 8.110 below) are also granted the same exemptions as other medium-sized companies in respect of the directors' report, although the position remains unchanged in respect of other accounts exemptions.

Ineligible companies

8.110   As with small companies, the exemptions are not available to the following companies, even if they meet the qualifying conditions for a medium-sized company:

— a public company;

— a person who has permission under Part 4 of the Financial Services and Markets Act 2000 (FSMA 2000) to carry on one or more regulated activities;

— a person who carries on an insurance market activity; or

— a member of an ineligible group.

An ineligible group is defined as a group where any of the members is:

— a public company;

— a body corporate that has the power to issue shares or debentures to the public;

— a person who has permission under Part 4 of FSMA 2000 to carry on one or more regulated activities; or

— a person who carries on an insurance market activity.

However, as noted at 8.109 above, the new exemption in respect of the directors' report continues to apply to a company that is a member of an ineligible group provided that it would otherwise satisfy the criteria for exemption.

In the case of an intermediate parent company, it is necessary to consider the wider group and not just the one headed by the intermediate parent. The second category here does not need to be a British institution, so the UK subsidiary of a foreign undertaking will not be entitled to the exemptions if the parent has the power to issue shares or debentures to the public. It should also be noted that it is the power to issue shares and debentures, rather than their actual issue, that is the deciding factor.

Abbreviated accounts for medium-sized companies

8.111   Under CA 1985 s 246(3), the following exemptions apply for medium-sized companies preparing Companies Act accounts:

— the company may file a profit and loss account that begins with 'gross profit or loss' where this figure combines the figures for:

— turnover, cost of sales, and other operating income; or

— turnover, change in stocks of finished goods and work in progress, own work capitalised, other operating income, raw materials and consumables, and other operating charges

depending on which standard format is used for the profit and loss account;

— the notes to the accounts need not give the analysis of turnover by class of business and by geographical market normally required by CA 1985 Sch 4 para 55.

There are no exemptions in respect of disclosures in the balance sheet and directors' report. The recent company law review concluded that the abbreviated accounts regime should be abolished and the Government White Paper *Modernising Company Law* issued in July 2002 confirmed the intention to proceed with this. However, a subsequent White Paper *Company Law Reform*, published in March 2005, notes that the Government has now decided to retain the abbreviated accounts regime but intends to require all small and medium-sized companies to disclose their turnover for the year in their published accounts.

Directors' statement

8.112   If the directors of a medium-sized company wish to take advantage of the option to prepare abbreviated accounts for filing purposes, the balance sheet in the abbreviated accounts must include a statement that the accounts are prepared in accordance with the special provisions of Part VII of CA 1985 relating to medium-sized companies. This statement must be given in a prominent position immediately above the director's signature.

Special auditors' report

8.113   Where abbreviated accounts are delivered to the registrar, they must be accompanied by a special report from the auditors stating whether, in their opinion:

— the company is entitled to deliver abbreviated accounts prepared in accordance with CA 1985 s 246(3); and

— the abbreviated accounts have been properly prepared in accordance with that sections.

The complete text of the auditors' report on the company's full accounts must also be included where that report:

— was qualified, in which case additional details may also need to be given to enable the qualification to be understood; or

— included a statement under CA 1985 s 237(2) (inadequate accounts, records or returns, or accounts not in agreement with the records and returns); or

— included a statement under CA 1985 s 237(3) (failure to obtain all the information and explanations that the auditors considered necessary).

Exemption from preparing group accounts

8.114   A parent company is not required to prepare group accounts for a financial year in which the group which it heads qualifies as a medium-sized group and is not an ineligible group. An ineligible group is defined in CA 1985 s 248(2) as a group where any of the members is:

—   a public company;

—   a body corporate that has the power to issue shares or debentures to the public;

—   a person who has permission under Part 4 of FSMA 2000 to carry on one or more regulated activities; or

–   a person who carries on an insurance market activity.

There was previously a requirement for the auditors to provide the directors with a special report confirming that, in their opinion, the company was entitled to the exemption. This is no longer required. However, if the directors take advantage of the exemption and, in the opinion of the auditors, they are not entitled to do so, the auditors are required to state this in their report on the accounts. FRS 2 'Accounting for Subsidiary Undertakings' repeats the exemption set out in the Act for medium sized groups, but requires disclosure of:

—   the fact that the accounts present information about the parent as an individual undertaking and not about the group; and

—   the grounds on which the parent is exempt from preparing consolidated accounts for the group.

AUDIT EXEMPTION

Categories of audit exemption

8.115   CA 1985 s 249A identifies two categories of conditions for audit exemption: total exemption conditions and report conditions. A company that meets the total exemption conditions in respect of a financial year is not required to have an audit for that year. A company that meets the report conditions in respect of a financial year is exempt from an audit for that year, provided that the directors arrange for a special report on the company's accounts to be made to the members by a reporting accountant. Regulations that came into force on 15 April 1997 mean that the report conditions now only apply in the case of a company that is a charity. Separate audit exemption arrangements also apply in the case of a dormant company (see 8.123 below).

Total exemption conditions

8.116   A company will usually meet the total exemption conditions for a financial year if:

—   it qualifies as a small company for that year under CA 1985 s 246 (see 8.1–8.8 above);

—   if it is a charity, its gross income for the year is not more than £90,000 or, if it is not a charity, its turnover for the year is not more than £5.6 million; and

—   its balance sheet total for the year is not more than £2.8 million.

The above thresholds generally apply for accounting periods ending on or after 30 March 2004 and, with the exception of the gross income threshold for charitable companies (which has been in force for some time), were introduced by the *Companies Act 1985 (Accounts of Small and Medium-Sized Enterprises and Audit Exemption)(Amendment) Regulations 2004* (SI 2004/16). It should be noted that the Regulations increased the balance sheet threshold for total audit exemption to £2.8 million for all companies, including those with charitable status, although the DTI had originally indicated that there was no intention to alter this threshold in the case of charities. However, the equivalent threshold in respect of the report conditions set out in section 249A(4) of the Act (see 8.117 below) has not been increased by SI 2004/16 and so remains at £1.4 million. Further changes to the thresholds for charities are expected to be introduced in conjunction with the proposed new Charities Bill.

All three conditions must be met for the company to qualify for the exemption. In the case of a charity, gross income is defined as income from all sources, as shown in the company's income and expenditure account. If the accounting period is more than a year or less than a year, the turnover (or gross income) limit is adjusted proportionately but there is no change to the other criteria. Balance sheet total has the same definition as for the small company qualification criteria (see 8.5 above).

Where the directors take advantage of total audit exemption, there is no requirement to make the statement on disclosure of information to the auditors that must otherwise be given in a directors' report for accounting periods beginning on or after 1 April 2005.

Report conditions

8.117   The report conditions are now only relevant for a company that is a charity. A charitable company will usually meet the report conditions for a financial year if:

—   it qualifies as a small company for that year under CA 1985 s 246;

—   its gross income for the year is more than £90,000 but not more than £250,000; and

—   its balance sheet total for the year is not more than £1.4 million.

All three conditions must be met to qualify for the exemption. Gross income is as defined in 8.116 above. If the accounting period is more than a year or less than a year, the gross income limit is adjusted proportionately but there is no change to the other criteria. It should be noted that, although the balance sheet threshold for total audit exemption has been increased to £2.8 million for all companies by the *Companies Act 1985 (Accounts of Small and Medium-Sized Enterprises and Audit Exemption)(Amendment) Regulations 2004* (SI 2004/16), these regulations have not introduced a similar increase to the balance sheet threshold in section 249A(4).

Ineligible companies

8.118   The exemptions are not available to the following companies, even if they meet the specified conditions:

— a public company;

— a parent company or a subsidiary undertaking (except in the specific circumstances described in 8.119 below);

— a person with permission under Part 4 of FSMA 2000 to carry on one or more regulated activities;

— a person who carries on an insurance market activity;

— an appointed representative, within the meaning of s 39 of FSMA 2000; or

— a special registered body as defined in the Trade Union and Labour Relations (Consolidation) Act 1992 s 117(1) or an employers' association as defined in s 122 of that Act.

Special provisions for dormant subsidiaries and small groups

8.119   The exemptions are not generally available to parent and subsidiary undertakings, but the legislation includes specific provisions to cater for the following:

— a subsidiary that has been dormant under CA 1985 s 249AA throughout the financial year is specifically granted the exemption by s 249B(1A); and

— a parent or subsidiary undertaking will not be regarded as ineligible if, throughout the period that it was a parent or subsidiary, it was a member of a group that:

— qualifies as a small group (see 8.6 above) for the financial year covering that period (or would so qualify if all bodies corporate in the group were companies) and was not at any time within that year an ineligible group (see 8.10 above);

— in the case of a company that is not a charity, has an aggregate turnover in that year of not more than £5.6 million net or £6.72 million gross;

— in the case of a company that is a charity, has an aggregate turnover in that year of not more than £350,000 net or £420,000 gross; and

— has an aggregate balance sheet total for that year of not more than £2.8 million net or £3.36 million gross.

The definition of 'balance sheet total' and the use of 'gross' and 'net' figures apply in the same way as for qualification as a small group (see 8.7 and 8.8 above).

The above thresholds for a company that is not a charity were introduced by the *Companies Act 1985 (Accounts of Small and Medium-Sized Enterprises and Audit Exemption) (Amendment) Regulations 2004* (SI 2004/16) and generally apply for accounting periods ending on or after 30 March 2004.

Members requiring an audit to be carried out

8.120 Any member or members of a company who hold not less than 10% (in nominal value) of the issued share capital or any class of share capital may require an audit for any year by depositing a written notice at the company's registered office no later than one month before the end of that financial year. If the company does not have a share capital, the minimum becomes not less than 10% of the members of the company in number terms.

Directors' statement

8.121 The exemptions are only available if the balance sheet includes a statement by the directors to the effect that:

— for the year in question, the company is entitled to the exemption in CA 1985 s 249A(1) or (2);

— no notice has been deposited under CA 1985 s 249B(2) requiring an audit for that year; and

— the directors acknowledge their responsibilities for:

— ensuring that the company maintains accounting records which comply with CA 1985 s 221; and

— preparing accounts which give a true and fair view of the state of affairs of the company at the end of the financial year and of the profit or loss for that year in accordance with CA 1985 s 226, and which comply with the relevant accounting requirements of the Act.

This statement must be positioned above the director's signature on the balance sheet. Where the company also prepares shorter form accounts, the statement is usually combined with the directors' statement on the shorter form accounts (see 8.14 above). A suitable wording to meet these requirements might be:

Example 8.5 – Directors' statement – audit exemption

(a) In the case of total exemption:

The company is entitled to exemption under Companies Act 1985 s 249A(1) from the requirement to have its accounts for the financial year ended [date] audited.

No notice has been deposited under s 249B(2) of that Act requiring the accounts of the company for that financial year to be audited.

The directors acknowledge their responsibilities for:

(i) ensuring that the company keeps accounting records which comply with Companies Act 1985 s 221; and

(ii) preparing accounts which give a true and fair view of the state of affairs of the company at the end of the financial year and of its profit or loss for that year in accordance with the requirements of s 226 of that Act, and which otherwise comply with the requirements of that Act relating to accounts, so far as these are applicable to the company.

(b) In the case of report exemption:

The company is entitled to exemption under Companies Act 1985 s 249A(2) from the requirement to have its accounts for the financial year ended [date] audited, provided that the accounts are subject to a limited review by a reporting accountant.

No notice has been deposited under s 249B(2) of that Act requiring the accounts of the company for that financial year to be audited.

The directors acknowledge their responsibilities for:

(i) ensuring that the company keeps accounting records which comply with Companies Act 1985 s 221; and

(ii) preparing accounts which give a true and fair view of the state of affairs of the company at the end of the financial year and of its profit or loss for that year in accordance with the requirements of s 226 of that Act, and which otherwise comply with the requirements of that Act relating to accounts, so far as these are applicable to the company.

Special report by reporting accountants

8.122   A charitable company that meets the report conditions in respect of a financial year is exempt from an audit for that year, provided that the directors arrange for a special report on the company's accounts to be made to the members by a reporting accountant. CA 1985 s 249D specifies who is eligible to act as a reporting accountant. The requirements are similar to those applying to the appointment of auditors. The reporting accountant must be:

— a member of one of the recognised bodies specified in s 249D(3) (i.e. one of the principal UK accountancy bodies); and

— entitled to engage in public practice.

For accounting periods ending on or after 30 January 2004, the *Companies Act 1985 (Accounts of Small and Medium-Sized Enterprises and Audit Exemption)(Amendment) Regulations 2004* (SI 2004/16) amend section 249D(3) so that members of the Institute of Chartered Secretaries and Administrators (ICSA) are also allowed to act as a reporting accountant to eligible charitable companies.

The same rules on independence apply as in the case of auditors. The reporting accountant must express an opinion on whether:

— the accounts are in agreement with the company's accounting records;

— the accounts are drawn up in a manner consistent with the relevant provisions of the Act;

— the company satisfied the report conditions set out in s 249A;

— the company did not at any time during the year fall within any categories not entitled to the exemption.

The Act clarifies that the last three opinions above are to be given on the basis of the information in the accounting records. Detailed guidance on the work required to support this report and example wordings for the report are given in 'Audit Exemption Reports', a Statement of Standards for Reporting Accountants issued by the Auditing Practices Board in October 1994. If the directors wish to take advantage of the option to file abbreviated accounts, there is no requirement for a separate report by the reporting accountant on the abbreviated accounts. However, the reporting accountant's report on the full accounts must be delivered to the registrar with the abbreviated accounts. To avoid any confusion, the APB Statement recommends that some explanatory wording is attached, along the following lines.

Example 8.6 – Explanatory note to report filed with abbreviated accounts

The following reproduces the text of the report prepared for the purposes of Companies Act 1985 s 249A(2) in respect of the company's annual accounts, from which the abbreviated accounts (set out on pages .... to ....) have been prepared.

Dormant companies

8.123 A company that is dormant, as defined in CA 1985, is usually entitled to exemption from an annual audit under s 249AA of the Act. The exemption is automatically available to companies that meet the conditions set out in the legislation. A company is classed as dormant for any accounting period during which it does not have a 'significant accounting transaction'. This is defined in the legislation as any transaction which requires an entry to be made in the accounting records, other than:

— the taking up of shares by a subscriber in pursuance of an undertaking given by him in the Memorandum of Association;

— a fee payable to the registrar on a change of the company's name;

— a fee payable to the registrar on the re-registration of the company (i.e. on a change in status from private to public, or vice versa);

— a penalty under CA 1985 s 242A for failure to deliver accounts; and

— a fee payable to the registrar for the registration of the company's annual return.

Entries such as transfers between inter-company accounts will count as significant accounting transactions and will prevent a company from being classified as dormant. A company that is dormant ceases to be so as soon as a significant accounting transaction takes place.

Where the directors take advantage of this exemption, there is no requirement to make the statement on disclosure of information to the auditors that must otherwise be given in a directors' report for accounting periods beginning on or after 1 April 2005.

Conditions for dormant company audit exemption

8.124   A company is eligible to take advantage of the exemption from audit granted by CA 1985 s 249AA for a financial year if it has been:

— dormant since its formation; or

— dormant since the end of the previous financial year, and is:

   — entitled to prepare its individual accounts in accordance with CA 1985 s 246 (see 8.9 above) or would have been so entitled if it had not been a member of an ineligible group; and

   — not required to prepare group accounts for that year.

The directors are also required to make a formal statement in the accounts that the company is entitled to the exemption (see 8.127 below) and the members can require an audit to be carried out in the same way as for other small companies (see 8.120 above).

Ineligible companies

8.125   A company is not entitled to audit exemption as a dormant company if it is:

— a person who has permission under Part 4 of FSMA 2000 to carry on one or more regulated activities; or

— a person who carries on an insurance market activity.

Accounts requirements for dormant companies

8.126   The exemption relates only to the audit requirements of CA 1985 and a dormant company must therefore continue to prepare and file annual accounts in the normal manner. The Act requires all companies to prepare a profit and loss account and this applies equally to dormant companies. In the year following the year in which a company becomes dormant, a full profit and loss account will need to be prepared in order to show the detailed comparative figures. Where a company has been dormant for two consecutive years, there will be no detailed figures to disclose in the profit and loss account. In this case it will usually be appropriate to present a narrative profit and loss account.

Example 8.7 — Narrative profit and loss account for dormant company

Profit and loss account for the year ended 31 December 20X2

During the financial year and the preceding financial year, the company did not trade, received no income and incurred no expenditure. Consequently the company made neither a profit nor a loss in either year.

This is usually given immediately before the detailed notes to the accounts.

Directors' statement

8.127 —The exemption from audit is only available if the balance sheet in the company's accounts includes a statement by the directors to the effect that:

—   for the year in question, the company is entitled to the exemption in CA 1985 s 249AA (1);

—   no notice has been deposited under CA 1985 s 249B(2) requiring an audit for that year;

—   the directors acknowledge their responsibilities for:

—   ensuring that the company maintains accounting records which comply with CA 1985 s 221; and

—   preparing accounts which give a true and fair view of the state of affairs of the company at the end of the financial year and of the profit or loss for that year in accordance with CA 1985 s 226, and which comply with the relevant accounting requirements of the Act.

The statement must be given on the balance sheet, immediately above the directors' signature required by CA 1985 s 233. A suitable wording to meet the requirements of the Act might be:

Example 8.8 – Directors' statement – dormant company audit exemption

The company is entitled to exemption under Companies Act 1985 s 249AA(1) from the requirement to have its accounts for the year ended [date] audited.

No notice has been deposited under s 249B(2) of that Act requiring the accounts of the company for that financial year to be audited.

The directors acknowledge their responsibilities for:

(i) ensuring that the company maintains accounting records which comply with Companies Act 1985 s 221; and

(ii) preparing accounts which give a true and fair view of the state of affairs of the company at the end of the financial year and of the profit or loss for that year in accordance with s 226 of the Act, and which otherwise comply with the requirements of that Act relating to accounts, so far as these are applicable to the company.

Dormant companies acting as agents

8.128   Where the directors take advantage of the exemption from audit conferred by CA 1985 s 249AA and the company has acted as agent for another party during the year, the accounts are required to disclose this fact. CA 1985 Sch 4, Sch 8 and

Sch 8A all incorporate this disclosure requirement and the information must therefore also be given in abbreviated accounts where the company chooses to prepare these for filing purposes.

Chapter 9
Profit and Loss Account Formats

COMPANY LAW REQUIREMENTS

CA 1985 Prescribed formats

9.1   CA 1985 prescribes standard formats for the profit and loss account and the balance sheet which must be followed by both individual companies and by groups when preparing their annual accounts. The Act provides a choice of four formats for the profit and loss account – these are set out in the Appendix to this chapter. The directors are free to decide which format to use, but once a particular format has been chosen it must be used consistently year by year unless there are good reasons for changing (see 9.4 below). The major differences between the formats relate to the presentation of operating costs. Other items in the profit and loss account (e.g. turnover, income from fixed asset investments, interest payable) are generally presented in the same way, although the order of presentation varies between formats.

For accounting periods beginning on or after 1 January 2005, the standard formats and other detailed requirements of Schedule 4 are only relevant where the company opts to prepare Companies Act accounts (as opposed to IAS accounts). Also, the latest 'one-stop shop' version of the Financial Reporting Standard for Smaller Entities (FRSSE), which incorporates company law requirements on the form and content of accounts as well as requirements that stem from UK accounting practice, only permits the use of the two more common profit and loss account formats (Format 1 or Format 2). Companies adopting the FRSSE will therefore be restricted to one of these formats for accounting periods beginning on or after 1 January 2005.

Presentation of operating costs

9.2   The formats follow two basic approaches to presenting operating costs. Formats 1 and 3 are centred around the nature or purpose of the various items of expenditure (eg costs of sales, distribution costs, administrative costs). Formats 2 and 4 are centred around the categories or type of expenditure (e.g. raw materials and consumables, staff costs). Formats 1 and 2 present the information vertically and combine income and expenditure, whilst Formats 3 and 4 present it horizontally, grouping together the various types of income and the various charges. In practice, companies usually choose to adopt Format 1 or Format 2 (ie the vertical form of presentation). The nature of the company's activities may indicate which of the formats is more appropriate. For instance, a sales and distribution company is more likely to choose Format 1 because this includes separate headings for cost of sales, distribution and administrative expenses, which will be key features of the business. A construction company is more likely to use Format 2 because this highlights changes in stocks and work in progress, any of the company's own work that has been capitalised, and the charges for raw materials and consumables and staff costs, all of which may be important features in understanding a construction company's results.

Potential sensitivity of information

9.3   In choosing the format for the profit and loss account, companies may also wish to bear in mind the potential sensitivity of some of the information in a commercial context. For instance, Format 1 requires the disclosure of the gross profit or loss for the period and this figure can also be calculated from the details given in Format 3. The gross profit or loss for the period is not evident from the information required under Formats 2 and 4. If a company wishes to avoid disclosing its gross profit or loss, it can therefore do so by choosing Format 2 (or Format 4) rather than Format 1 (or Format 3). Similarly some of the details that are required to be disclosed under Formats 2 and 4 are not disclosed under Formats 1 and 3.

Change of format

9.4   The directors may only change the format of the profit and loss account if, in their opinion, there are special reasons for doing so (for instance, if the nature of the company's activities changes significantly, and as a result a different profit and loss account format would provide a more appropriate way of presenting the company's results). If the format of the profit and loss account is changed, the accounts must disclose:

—   the fact that a different format has been used;

—   the reasons for changing to a different format.

In practice, changing the format of the profit and loss account can lead to a considerable amount of work as the previous year's figures need to be restated and presented under the new format so that the details are comparable with those for the current year.

Order of headings and sub-headings

9.5   The profit and loss account formats are set out using a hierarchy of letters and Arabic numerals to prescribe the order in which the individual headings and sub-headings must appear. The letters and numerals do not have to be reproduced in the accounts but are provided so that other sections of the Act can refer to the headings by category. Although the headings and sub-headings should normally follow the order prescribed in the formats, the Act requires the directors to adapt or rearrange the items identified by Arabic numerals if the special nature of the company's business requires this. Items may be shown in greater detail than required by the formats and additional items may be shown, provided that they are not already covered elsewhere in the standard format. Items identified by Arabic numerals may be combined if:

— the individual amounts are not material; or

— combining them facilitates assessment of the profit or loss for the year. although in this case the individual components must be disclosed in the notes to the accounts.

If there is no amount to be shown for a particular heading or sub-heading in either the current or the previous financial year, that heading or sub-heading should not appear in the profit and loss account.

Analysis between headings

9.6   CA 1985 provides definitions of turnover and staff costs but does not provide any guidance on the items that should be included under the other headings in the statutory formats. The headings are broad in nature and this has led to different interpretations being applied in practice. It is not practical to provide definitive guidance on what should be included under each heading, although some indications are given in the following chapters where relevant. The most important point is that the approach decided on by each individual company is applied consistently from year to year. Under FRS 18 'Accounting Policies' a change in the way in which a particular item is presented in the financial statements is a change of accounting policy and must be accounted for as such in the year in which the change takes place. In a group of companies it is important that clear decisions are taken on how expenses are to be categorised and that these are conveyed to those responsible for preparing accounts for each company within the group. This should ensure that a consistent approach is adopted throughout the group in each year, as well as from year to year.

Condensed presentation

9.7   Each item in the profit and loss account formats is given an Arabic number. The presentation on the face of the profit and loss account can therefore be condensed to key figures, with the detail required by the Act being given in the notes to the accounts, if this will help in understanding the results for the period. However, the profit or loss on ordinary activities before taxation must always be shown on the face of the profit and loss account, as must dividends paid and proposed and transfers, or proposed transfers, to and from reserves.

Potential duplication of headings and sub-totals

9.8   Where one or more of the standard headings are not required, because there are no items to be disclosed in either the current or previous year, this may give rise to a potential problem over the heading given to sub-totalled items. For instance, if there is no taxation charge, the sub-total for the profit or loss for the year before taxation will be the same as that for the profit or loss for the year after taxation, and the question arises whether there is any need to disclose both headings. In most cases it is usually simplest to combine the headings.

Example 9.1 – Combining headings

	20X4	20X3
	£'000	£'000
Operating profit	675	581
Interest payable	(14)	(10)
Profit on ordinary activities before and after taxation	661	571

Similarly, where there are no extraordinary items (and these are now very rare under the requirements of FRS 3 'Reporting Financial Performance') the profit and loss on ordinary activities after taxation will usually be the same as the profit or loss for the financial year and it is usually simplest to combine the headings.

	20X4	20X3
	£'000	£'000
Profit on ordinary activities before taxation	844	975
Tax on profit on ordinary activities	(250)	(311)
Profit on ordinary activities after taxation and for the financial year	594	664

Comparative figures

9.9   Comparative figures must be given for each item in the profit and loss account. If any item appeared in the previous year but does not appear in the current year, the heading and comparative amount must still be shown in the profit and loss account. Comparative amounts are considered in more detail in Chapter 6.

Additional disclosures

9.10   In addition to the items set out in the standard formats, for accounting periods beginning before 1 January 2005, the legislation requires every profit and loss account to show:

(i)   the profit or loss on ordinary activities before taxation;

(ii)   the aggregate amount of any dividends paid and proposed;

(iii)   the aggregate amount of any proposed dividends, if this is not disclosed in the notes to the accounts;

(iv)   any amount transferred, or proposed to be transferred, from the profit and loss account to reserves;

(v)   any amount transferred, or proposed to be transferred, from reserves to the profit and loss account.

For accounting periods beginning on or after 1 January 2005, para 3(7) of Schedule 4, which requires the disclosures set out in (ii) to (v) above, is removed by the *Companies Act 1985 (International Accounting Standards and Other Accounting Amendments) Regulations 2004* (SI 2004/2947) and is replaced by a new paragraph 35A of Schedule 4 which requires the notes to the accounts to show:

(i)   amounts set aside or withdrawn from reserves;

(ii)   the aggregate of dividends paid in the year, other than those for which a liability existed at the previous balance sheet date;

(iii)   the aggregate amount of dividends that the company is liable to pay at the balance sheet date; and

(iv)   the aggregate amount of dividends proposed before the date of approval of the accounts and not included in the above disclosures.

This change enables companies to comply with FRS 21 'Events after the balance sheet date' which also comes into effect on 1 January 2005. FRS 21 does not permit a proposed dividend which is still subject to shareholder approval to be included in the balance sheet, on the basis that it does not meet the accounting definition of a liability at the balance sheet date. The change also removes the requirement for dividends paid during the year to be reported in the profit and loss account, and so allows them to be accounted for as transactions with shareholders rather than as profit and loss account items. This enables companies to comply with the presentation requirements of FRS 25 'Financial Instruments: Disclosure and Presentation' which also come into effect for accounting periods beginning on or after 1 January 2005.

The profit and loss account formats also include notes which require additional information or analyses to be given for certain items. These details are usually given in the notes to the accounts, although they may be given on the face of the profit and loss account if this is considered necessary or helpful. Where appropriate these are discussed in the following chapters.

CONTINUING, DISCONTINUED AND ACQUIRED OPERATIONS

Operating profit

9.11   FRS 3 'Reporting Financial Performance' requires each item from turnover through to operating profit to be analysed into amounts relating to continuing, discontinued and newly-acquired operations. The heading 'operating profit' does not appear in the standard formats and is not a term that is used or defined in CA 1985. The standard states that for most companies, operating profit (or loss) will usually be the profit or loss before income from shares in group companies. In the case of Formats 1 and 2 therefore (the most common formats for the profit and loss account), operating profit will usually appear in the following place:

— in Format 1, between 'Other operating income' and 'Income from shares in group undertakings'; and

— in Format 2, between 'Other operating charges' and 'Income from shares in group undertakings'.

As a result of the introduction of this new heading, the reported operating profit or loss has become a key feature of accounts. Before FRS 3, many of the presentation debates centred around whether an individual charge or credit was extraordinary or not. FRS 3 has virtually removed extraordinary items from accounts but to some extent the debate has now transferred to the operating profit heading, the main issue usually being whether a particular charge or credit should be reflected within or below operating profit in the profit and loss account. It is also important to recognise that executive bonus schemes may be related to the operating profit shown in the accounts and the decision on whether a particular charge or credit is taken before or after operating profit may consequently increase or reduce the base figure for bonus payments.

Classification of discontinued operations

9.12   FRS 3 sets out a lengthy definition of discontinued operations. All of the following conditions must be met if an operation is to be classified and disclosed as a discontinued operation under the standard:

— the sale or termination must be completed in the accounting period or before the earlier of:

— three months after the beginning of the next accounting period, and

— the date on which the accounts are approved by the directors;

—   if the discontinuation is a termination, the former activities must have ceased permanently;

—   the sale or termination must have:

        —   a material effect on the nature and focus of the reporting entity's operations, and

        —   represent a material reduction in its operating facilities, resulting either from withdrawal from a particular market or from a material reduction in turnover in the continuing markets;

—   the assets, liabilities, results of operations and activities must be clearly distinguishable – physically, operationally and for financial reporting purposes.

Any operation that is sold or terminated during the year but which does not meet all of these conditions must be classified under continuing operations for financial reporting purposes. The definition of discontinued operations under FRS 3 is therefore quite restrictive and it is clearly intended that only sales and terminations of very significant activities should be reported separately. It is unlikely that many companies will need to disclose information on discontinued operations on a regular basis.

Completion of sale

9.13   No guidance is given in the standard on what constitutes 'completion' in the case of a sale. FRS 2 'Accounting for Subsidiary Undertakings' provides some guidance in the context of changes in group membership and states that: 'The date for accounting for an undertaking ceasing to be a subsidiary undertaking is the date on which its former parent undertaking relinquishes control over that undertaking'. Control is defined as 'the ability of an undertaking to direct the financial and operating policies of another undertaking with a view to gaining economic benefit from its activities'. These sections of FRS 2 can be used as a benchmark for assessing when the sale of an operation has been completed. In straightforward cases, completion will usually be identified with a binding, unconditional contract or the date when consideration actually passes between the parties. However, the terms of a particular contract can be complex and the circumstances of each case must therefore be assessed individually.

Completion of termination

9.14   Where former activities are terminated rather than sold, FRS 3 does provide some guidance on what constitutes completion, by stating that the former activities must have ceased permanently. However, this can also give rise to problems – for instance:

— what is the position if the company is still completing contracts already in progress but is not taking on new work?

— what is the position if the company has completed all contracts and therefore has no ongoing work in this field, but is still committed to warranty or maintenance work under previous contracts?

Once again, each case must be assessed individually and the materiality of any ongoing activities should be taken into account. For instance, in the first example quoted above, it will usually be difficult to argue that operations have ceased permanently if there is a substantial level of activity on the remaining contracts, even though new work is not being accepted. In the second example, the decision may rest on the level of work normally required under warranties or maintenance agreements. If experience has shown that this is minimal, it may be acceptable to say that the operations have to all intents and purposes ceased permanently.

Deadline for completion of sale or termination

9.15 In order to be treated as a discontinued operation in the current year's accounts, the sale or termination must either:

— be completed during the accounting period; or

— be completed by the earlier of:

— three months from the beginning of the next accounting period, and

— the date of approval of the accounts.

Example 9.2 – Where date of approval is used

A Ltd prepares its accounts to 31 December each year. The accounts for the year to 31 December 20X4 are approved by the board of directors on 27 February 20X5. Therefore, if any operations are to be classified as discontinued operations, the sale or termination must have been completed by 27 February 20X5 at the latest (i.e. the date of approval of the accounts).

Example 9.3 – Where three months from the beginning of the next accounting period is used

A Ltd prepares its accounts to 31 December each year. The accounts for the year to 31 December 20X4 are approved by the board of directors on 24 April 20X5. Therefore, if any operations are to be classified as discontinued operations, the sale or termination must have been completed by 31 March 20X5 at the latest (i.e. within three months of the start of the next financial year).

Operational effect of a discontinuation

9.16 In order to meet the conditions for a discontinued operation, a sale or termination must:

— have a material effect on the nature and focus of the entity's operations; and

— represent a material reduction in its operating facilities, resulting from:

—   withdrawal from a particular market, or

—   a material reduction in turnover in the continuing markets.

Paragraph 42 of FRS 3 explains that the nature and focus of an entity's operations refers to the positioning of the entity's products or services in the market place and that this includes both quality and location. The standard quotes various examples within the hotel industry to illustrate this.

—   If a hotel company operating in the lower end of the general hotel market sells its existing hotels and replaces them with a number of luxury hotels, it will change the nature and focus of its business, even though it will still be operating in the hotel business.

—   The same would apply if the company was initially operating hotels in America and decided to sell these and replace them with a chain of hotels in Europe. The nature and focus of the company's operations would change as a result of the completely new geographical location.

—   However, the regular sale of individual hotels and their replacement with other hotels in similar markets and locations (i.e. routine changes to a portfolio of properties) would not constitute a change in the nature and focus of the operations.

Material effect on turnover

9.17   The sale or termination must also have a material effect on the company's operating facilities and overall turnover in order to meet the definition of a discontinued operation. It must therefore result in either:

—   withdrawal from a particular market – this can be either a class of business or a geographical market; or

—   a material reduction of turnover in a market in which the company is continuing to operate.

The explanatory material in FRS 3 goes further than this and emphasises that the reduction in turnover must be the result of a strategic decision by the company either to withdraw from a particular market or to significantly reduce its presence in a continuing market. Therefore, where a strategic decision to improve productivity or reduce costs in one part of the business results, in turn, in the withdrawal from a different market or a reduction in turnover, the latter will not usually meet the conditions set out in the standard for a discontinuation of operations. Any costs resulting from these decisions would therefore be included in the results of continuing operations. The following examples illustrate how this part of the standard might apply in practice.

—   A company manufactures the same products in two factories, one in England and one in Wales. Management decide to close the site in England and transfer all production to the newer factory in Wales. By working additional shifts and improving efficiency, they expect to be able to match the present output levels from both factories. The closure of the factory in England will not be classified as a discontinued operation because there has not been any termination of activities. Production levels (and therefore, presumably, turnover) will be unaffected and the company will continue to produce and sell the same number of items to the same customers.

— A company manufactures two completely separate products in two factories, one in England and one in Wales. Demand for the product made in England is falling and management decide to sell the factory. By introducing new plant, working additional shifts and improving efficiency at the factory in Wales, they expect to be able to increase both output and profitability at this site. Products from the factory in England previously represented approximately 25% of the company's turnover. Provided that the other conditions in FRS 3 are also met, the closure of the factory in England will be classified as a discontinued operation, on the basis that:

— the company has taken a strategic decision to withdraw from a particular market (i.e. the remaining factory has a different product and a different market);

— products from the factory in England previously contributed 25% of the company's turnover; and

— the focus of the business will in future be concentrated on one product and one operational unit.

However, decisions on these issues will always be subjective to some degree, and there will be many cases where there is no obviously right or wrong answer.

Separate identification of operation

9.18 The final condition for a discontinued operation is that all of the following must be separately identifiable:

— assets;

— liabilities;

— results of operations;

— activities.

In addition, the clear distinction must apply physically, operationally and for financial reporting purposes. The explanatory material in the standard emphasises that if the assets, liabilities or results of an operation can only be identified by making allocations of material items of income and expenditure in the accounting records, the condition will not be met. Therefore if significant expenses are incurred by the company as a whole and have to be apportioned in some way between the company's various activities in order to establish the individual results of each operation, the operations are not considered to be clearly distinguishable for financial reporting purposes under FRS 3.

Consideration individually or in aggregate?

9.19   One aspect of FRS 3 that is not clear is whether sales and terminations that might potentially be classified as discontinued operations should be considered individually or in aggregate. Individual consideration appears to be more in keeping with the spirit of the standard, unless the sales and terminations effectively form part of one overall transaction. An individual approach may result in a company being involved in a number of smaller sales and terminations, none of which qualify as discontinued operations, but which taken together are significant to the company as a whole. In this situation, it may be necessary to disclose details of these sales and terminations in a note to the accounts, even though they must be included under continuing operations for financial reporting purposes.

Disclosure of continuing, discontinued and acquired activities

9.20   FRS 3 requires each of the standard profit and loss account headings from turnover to operating profit to be analysed into:

—   amounts relating to discontinued operations;

—   amounts relating to continuing operations, which must be further analysed to show amounts relating to:

  —   acquired operations,

  —   other continuing operations.

As a minimum, turnover and operating profit for the current year must be analysed in this way on the face of the profit and loss account. The analysis of the other figures and of the comparatives may be given in the notes to the accounts. The purpose of a detailed analysis of results is to enable a user of the accounts to assess the financial performance of various aspects of entity's activities and to provide a more realistic basis for an assessment of future income and results. It also enables a user of the accounts to distinguish organic growth from acquisitive growth. Where an acquisition, sale or termination has a material impact on a major segment of the business, FRS 3 requires this fact to be disclosed and explained in the accounts.

Columnar format

9.21   Companies are free to choose any disclosure format that meets the requirements of the standard, but whatever format is chosen should be used consistently. The appendix to FRS 3 includes illustrative examples setting out how the disclosure requirements might be met and most companies have followed these. The most straightforward presentation is a columnar format across the page with headings for the required categories.

Example 9.4 – Columnar disclosure

	Continuing operations	Acquisitions	Discontinued operations	Total 200X	Total 200Y
	£'000	£'000	£'000	£'000	£'000
Turnover	5,672	784	591	7,047	6,434
Cost of sales	(3,982)	(660)	(503)	(5,145)	(4,876)
	1,690	124	88	1,902	1,558
Distribution costs	(978)	(58)	(61)	(1,097)	(994)
Administrative expenses	(531)	(21)	(29)	(581)	(476)
	181	45	(2)	224	88
Other operating income	53	20		73	42
Operating profit	234	65	(2)	297	130

Where this format is used, the analysis of the comparative figures is usually given in the notes to the accounts.

Alternative presentation

9.22   Although the layout used in 9.21 above is perhaps the clearest presentation from the reader's point of view, it can be difficult to present all the necessary columns on one page and the concentration of figures can sometimes mask the key features. An alternative presentation adopted by a number of companies is to give a sub-analysis under the statutory heading, with only the total being shown in the profit and loss account itself. This can be a useful format where only the minimum disclosure is given on the face of the profit (i.e. the analysis of current year turnover and operating profit).

Example 9.5 – Disclosure under statutory headings

	20X4 £'000	20X4 £'000	20X3 £'000
Turnover:			
Continuing operations	5,672		6,434
Acquisitions	784		____
	6,456		
Discontinued operations	591		—
		7,047	6,434
Cost of sales		(5,145)	(4,876)
		1,902	1,558
Distribution costs		(1,097)	(994)
Administrative expenses		(581)	(476)
		224	88
Other operating income		73	42
Operating profit:			
Continuing operations	234		
Acquisitions	65		
	299		
Discontinued operations	(2)		
		297	130

The analysis of other headings and the comparatives must be given in the notes to the accounts. Where acquisitions are comparatively small, a further possibility is to include headings for continuing and discontinued operations only, and to disclose the details for acquisitions as part of the heading for continuing operations.

Example 9.6 – Acquisitions disclosed under continuing operations

	20X4 £'000	20X4 £'000	20X3 £'000
Turnover:			
Continuing operations (acquisitions £784,000)	6,456		
Discontinued operations	591		
		7,047	6,434
Cost of sales		(5,145)	(4,876)
		1,902	1,558
Distribution costs		(1,097)	(994)
Administrative expenses		(581)	(476)
		224	88
Other operating income		73	42
Operating profit:			
Continuing operations (acquisitions £65,000)	234		
Discontinued operations	(2)		
		297	130

No discontinued operations or acquisitions during the year

9.23 If a company has no material acquisitions and no discontinued operations during the year, there is no formal requirement to state that all the turnover and results relate to continuing operations. However, it is helpful to include a footnote to the profit and loss account or a note to the accounts to clarify this point.

Disclosures in respect of acquisitions

9.24 The standard recognises that it may not always be possible to identify the relevant figures in respect of acquisitions. For instance, an operation may be acquired with the intention that it should be fully integrated with an existing part of the company. Where the post-acquisition results cannot be separately identified, the standard requires the accounts to give an indication of the amount that the acquisition has contributed to turnover and operating profit. If such an indication cannot be given, the accounts must state this fact and explain the reason why the information cannot be provided. Where operations are acquired towards the end of the accounting period, the full impact will not be apparent until the following accounting period. FRS 3 therefore notes that in some circumstances it may be helpful to give separate disclosure of the results of acquired operations for their first full year as part of the reporting entity as well as in the year of acquisition.

Disclosures in respect of discontinued operations

9.25 The column or heading for discontinued operations should only include income and costs relating directly to the operation that has been discontinued. Where, as a result of the sale or termination of an operation, other parts of the business are reorganised or restructured, the costs relating to this must be included under the heading of continuing operations. Where the discontinued operation is sold or terminated in the early part of the following accounting period (as permitted under the standard), the discontinued column or heading in the accounts for the current year must only include the results of the discontinued operation up to the balance sheet date. The results of any trading in the early part of the following accounting period (i.e. up to the date of sale or termination) must be included in the accounts for that year, and may need to be shown separately as discontinued operations if the figures are material.

Sale or termination not yet completed

9.26 Where a sale or termination is in progress but has not been completed within the financial year or the early part of the following accounting period (as defined in the standard), the results of the operation must be included under continuing operations. However, the standard recognises that in some cases, it may be appropriate to provide additional information in the notes to the accounts on operations that are in the process of being discontinued. In these circumstances, it is likely that the sale or termination will meet the conditions for a discontinued operation in the following year, in which case it will be disclosed as such in the accounts for that year under the requirements of FRS 3.

Additional analysis of interest and tax

9.27 The standard only requires analysis of profit and loss account headings from turnover to operating profit. Analysis of the other headings is not encouraged in view of the fact that this will usually involve a high degree of subjectivity, which might cast doubt on the reliability of the figures. If a company chooses to provide additional analyses of the figures for interest and tax, the standard requires the method of allocation and the underlying assumptions to be disclosed in the accounts.

Comparative figures

9.28 Comparative figures must be given for all the disclosures required under FRS 3. However, in the case of the profit and loss account, the comparative figures for continuing operations must reflect only the results of the operations that are still classified as continuing in the current year. The comparative figures will therefore not necessarily be the same as those disclosed in the previous year's accounts. Where discontinued operations are disclosed in the accounts for the current year, the comparative figures will need to be restated to move the results of those activities from continuing to discontinued operations in the previous year. The comparative figures for discontinued operations will therefore comprise:

— the previous year's results of any operations classified as discontinued operations in the previous year; and

— the previous year's results for any operations classified as discontinued activities in the current year.

Example 9.7 – Comparatives for continuing and discontinued operations

A Ltd's accounts for 20X4 showed the following analysis for turnover.

		£
Turnover:	Continuing operations	506,100
	Discontinued operations	124,732
		630,832

During 20X5 it has discontinued a further operation, which contributed £98,750 to turnover in 20X4. In the 20X5accounts, the comparative figure for turnover will therefore need to be restated as follows.

		£
Turnover:	Continuing operations (a)	407,350
	Discontinued operations (b)	223,482
		630,832

(a) £506,100 – £98,750

(b) £124,732 + £98,750

Where this is done the headings to the profit and loss account and the relevant notes to the accounts should indicate that the figures have been restated. There is no requirement to analyse the comparative figures for discontinued activities into those discontinued in the previous year and those discontinued in the current year, although in some circumstances this may be helpful.

Potential changes in requirements

9.29   The ASB published FRED 32 'Disposal of non-current assets and presentation of discontinued operations' in July 2003 as part of its project to achieve convergence between UK and international accounting standards. These proposals will:

(i)   change the definition of discontinued operations currently included in FRS 3;

(ii)   alter the timing of the recognition of the loss on disposal of certain assets;

(iii)   require separate disclosure on the balance sheet of non-current assets (and, in the case of disposal groups, liabilities) held for sale;

(iv) remove the requirement to depreciate non-current assets held for sale;

(v) require newly acquired assets that meet the criteria for assets held for sale (eg surplus assets acquired as part of a business combination) to be recognised at fair value less disposal costs rather than at fair value; and

(vi) remove the exemption from consolidation for subsidiaries acquired and held exclusively with a view to resale.

Paragraph 23 of FRED 32 defines a discontinued operation as:

'a component of an entity that has either been disposed of or is classified as held for sale, and:

i. the operations and cash flows of which have been (or will be) eliminated from the ongoing operations of the entity as a result of the disposal transaction; and

ii. in which the entity will have no significant continuing involvement after the disposal transaction.'

A component of an entity comprises an operation and cash flows that can be distinguished clearly from the rest of the entity, both operationally and for financial reporting purposes. This definition does not include the current requirement under FRS 3 that the effect of the sale or termination should be material. The ASB expresses concern that discontinued operations would be reported more frequently under these proposals and questions the usefulness of this in the case of relatively small components of an entity. It also highlights the additional costs involved in restating comparatives when smaller components are reported as discontinued operations. However, the joint ASB/IASB project on reporting financial performance includes consideration of the reporting of discontinued operations and could result in this aspect of the Exposure Draft being superseded in due course.

FRED 32 also proposes a new classification of assets held for sale, which are required to be shown separately on the balance sheet. The criteria for classifying such assets are specified in an Appendix to the proposed standard and are generally based on management's plans for the asset, although they do require it to be highly probable that the asset will be sold within one year. FRED 32 proposes that such assets should be carried at the lower of carrying value and fair value less disposal costs, the latter being essentially the same as net realisable value under FRS 11 'Impairment of Tangible Fixed Assets and Goodwill'. The proposals conflict to some extent with current accounting practice in the UK, in that where the value in use of an asset is higher than its net realisable value but the entity nevertheless decides to sell it, FRED 32 requires it to be written down to net realisable value, with any loss recognised in the period in which the decision to sell is taken. In the preface to the Exposure Draft, the ASB expresses the view that the loss should be recognised when the sale occurs (as under FRS 3) and not when the entity classifies the asset as held for sale.

The current version of the ASB's Technical Plan, published in June 2005, indicates that new UK standards on presentation in financial statements, including the treatment of discontinued operations and non-current assets held for sale, are planned to be effective for accounting periods beginning on or after 1 January 2007.

ADDITIONAL FORMAT HEADINGS

Requirements of FRS 3 'Reporting Financial Performance'

9.30 FRS 3 introduced three additional headings, to be shown in the profit and loss account after operating profit and before interest:

— profits and losses on the sale or termination of an operation;

— costs of a fundamental reorganisation or restructuring that has a material effect on the nature and focus of the entity's operations;

— profits and losses on the disposal of fixed assets (other than marginal adjustments to depreciation previously charged).

These headings must be used whenever any of the items arise in the current year or in the previous year. There was initially some confusion over whether the headings were only intended to be used for items that met the definition of exceptional items (caused mainly by the fact that the introduction of the headings is covered in the section of FRS 3 headed 'Exceptional items'). However, it is now clear that the headings should be used whenever there are material items to be disclosed in these categories, regardless of whether the items would be classified as exceptional under the definition in FRS 3 (see 9.36 below). The disclosures should cover both actual income and costs during the year, and any provisions in respect of these categories (see Chapter 30). Although the headings come below operating profit in the profit and loss account, FRS 3 specifically requires any items disclosed under these headings to be classified as relating to continuing or discontinued operations (see 9.11–9.28 above).

Profits or losses on the sale or termination of an operation

9.31 This disclosure covers all sales and terminations during the year, not just those that are classified as discontinued operations for accounting purposes. It is therefore quite possible for the total figure in this category to be analysed partly to continuing operations and partly to discontinued operations. FRS 3 also sets out specific rules on the timing and content of provisions in respect of a decision to sell or terminate an operation. These rules are considered in Chapter 30.

Costs of a fundamental reorganisation or restructuring

9.32 A fundamental reorganisation or restructuring is defined as one which has a material effect on the nature and focus of the entity's operations, but this is not considered further in either the standard or the explanation. However, the phrase 'nature and focus of the entity's operation' is considered in the context of discontinued operations. In practice it is unlikely that many reorganisations will meet this definition and most reorganisation and restructuring costs should therefore be included in arriving at the operating profit or loss for the year. They should be disclosed as exceptional items if they meet the necessary criteria.

Profits and losses on the disposal of fixed assets

9.33   Significant profits and losses on the sale or other disposal of fixed assets should normally be disclosed under this heading. The standard specifies that marginal adjustments to depreciation charged in previous years should not be reported under this heading. Such adjustments should be included as part of the depreciation charge in arriving at the operating profit or loss for the year. The calculation of profits and losses on the disposal of fixed assets under FRS 3 is covered in Chapter 13.

Additional disclosure requirements

9.34   The standard also requires disclosure of the tax effect of the items appearing under these additional profit and loss account headings. Further details are given in Chapter 15. Where the net profit or loss on the sale or termination of operations or the disposal of fixed assets is small, but the gross profits and losses making up that figure are material, the standard requires the heading to appear on the face of the profit and loss account with a cross reference to a note to the accounts analysing the relevant profits and losses.

FRS 17 'Retirement Benefits'

9.35   FRS 17 'Retirement Benefits' was published in November 2000 and is fully effective for accounting periods beginning on or after 1 January 2005, although earlier adoption is encouraged. In the case of defined benefit retirement schemes, the standard requires interest cost and the expected return on assets to be presented as a separate item (other finance costs) adjacent to interest in the standard profit and loss account formats. The standard also amends FRS 12 'Provisions, Contingent Liabilities and Contingent Assets' to require the unwinding of any discount in respect of provisions to be included under the same heading.

DISCLOSURE OF EXCEPTIONAL ITEMS

Definition of exceptional

9.36   The tightening of the definitions of ordinary activities and extraordinary items under FRS 3 reduced significantly the number of items disclosed as extraordinary in annual accounts. The converse effect is that many of the items that might once have been classified as extraordinary are now disclosable as exceptional items. FRS 3 includes the following definition of exceptional items.

'Material items which derive from events or transactions that fall within the ordinary activities of the reporting entity and which individually or, if of a similar type, in aggregate, need to be disclosed by virtue of their size or incidence if the financial statements are to give a true and fair view.'

Exceptional items are a normal part of business activities and most companies will need to disclose an exceptional charge or credit to the profit and loss account at some point. Depending on the circumstances, exceptional items might include:

— a large bad debt;

— a significant charge to the profit and loss account for redundancy costs;

— the write-down of a fixed asset by a significant amount to recognise a permanent diminution in its value;

— reorganisation costs that do not meet the FRS 3 definition of a fundamental reorganisation.

Presentation of exceptional items

9.37   FRS 3 introduced a significant change to the way in which exceptional items are reported in the accounts. Previously it had become common practice to disclose exceptional items as a separate line within the profit and loss account. Under FRS 3, exceptional items must be included under the statutory profit and loss account heading to which they relate. In most cases, additional detail should then be given in the notes to the accounts, either:

— individually for each exceptional item; or

— where there are a number of items of a similar type, in aggregate by type of exceptional item.

Where it is considered necessary for a true and fair view, exceptional items may be disclosed separately on the face of the profit and loss account but this must still be within the appropriate statutory heading.

Use of columnar format

9.38   Where an individual transaction gives rise to a number of exceptional charges or credits under different statutory headings, some companies have found it useful to present the detail in a columnar format.

Example 9.8 – Columnar disclosure of exceptional items

	Before exceptional items	Exceptional items (Note xx)	Total
	£'000	£'000	£'000
Turnover	6,705		6,705
Cost of sales	(3,916)	(785)	(4,701)
	2,789	(785)	2,004
Distribution costs	(564)		(564)
Administrative expenses	(344)	(213)	(557)
	1,881	(998)	883
Interest receivable	124		124
Profit/(loss) on ordinary activities before taxation	2,005	(998)	1,007
Taxation	(346)	145	(201)
Profit on ordinary activities after taxation	1,659	(853)	806

This presentation has the advantage of highlighting the overall effect of the exceptional items. However, the disadvantage is that it can become very complex where there are also details of discontinued and acquired operations to report. It will usually be most suitable where the materiality of the exceptional items requires them to be given the prominence of appearing on the face of the profit and loss account. However there may be situations where a columnar layout in the notes to the accounts could also be useful to indicate the overall impact of an exceptional item on the accounts.

Continuing and discontinued operations

9.39 FRS 3 requires exceptional items to be allocated between continuing and discontinued operations in the same way as any other charge or credit to the profit and loss account. Two items of a similar type should therefore not be combined for disclosure purposes if individually they relate to continuing and to discontinued operations.

DISCLOSURE OF EXTRAORDINARY ITEMS

CA 1985 requirements

9.40 Each of the four standard Formats for the profit and loss account requires separate disclosure of:

— extraordinary income;

—   extraordinary charges; and

—   tax on extraordinary profit or loss.

In addition, Formats 1 and 2 require disclosure of the extraordinary profit or loss for the year. CA 1985 Sch 4 para 57(2) requires particulars to be given of any extraordinary income or of charges arising in the year. The details can be disclosed on the face of the profit and loss account or in the notes to the accounts. It is normal practice for companies to show the net effect in the profit and loss account under the heading 'Extraordinary items' and disclose the detailed analysis in the notes to the accounts.

Classification of income or expenditure as extraordinary

9.41   Whether a particular item of income or expenditure is extraordinary to an individual company will be a matter of judgement and will depend to a large extent on the nature of the company's activities. CA 1985 does not provide any guidance on what constitutes extraordinary income or expenditure. Extraordinary items are defined in FRS 3 as:

'Material items possessing a high degree of abnormality which arise from events or transactions that fall outside the ordinary activities of the reporting entity and which are not expected to recur. They do not include exceptional items nor do they include prior period items merely because they relate to a prior period.'

To appreciate the full impact of this, the FRS 3 definition of ordinary activities must also be considered.

'Any activities which are undertaken by a reporting entity as part of its business and such related activities in which the reporting entity engages in furtherance of, incidental to, or arising from, these activities. Ordinary activities include the effects on the reporting entity of any event in the various environments in which it operates, including the political, regulatory, economic and geographical environments, irrespective of the frequency or unusual nature of the event.'

The definition of ordinary activities given in FRS 3 is therefore very broad, and items that were previously classified as extraordinary under its predecessor standard (SSAP 6) are unlikely to meet the definition in the present standard. Extraordinary items now appear only rarely, if at all. In view of the expected rarity of extraordinary items under these requirements, FRS 3 does not give any examples of items that might fall within the definition.

Suggested disclosure

9.42   FRS 3 requires any extraordinary profit or loss to be shown separately on the face of the profit and loss account, below the profit or loss on ordinary activities after taxation and before any appropriation for dividends. In effect, this is the same as the disclosure required by CA 1985. The standard also requires each extraordinary item to be shown separately, either on the face of the profit and loss account or in the notes to the accounts, with a description that enables its nature to be understood. The tax on any extraordinary profit or loss must be shown separately as part of the extraordinary item, either on the face of the profit and loss account or in the notes to the accounts. If the tax on extraordinary items requires adjustment in subsequent years, the adjustment must be disclosed as an extraordinary item in the year in which it is reflected in the accounts. If, in rare circumstances, it is considered necessary to disclose one or more items of income or expenditure as extraordinary, the following layout would meet the requirements of FRS 3:

Example 9.9 – Disclosure of extraordinary items

	20X4 £	20X4 £	20X3 £
Extraordinary income:			
Full description of item a		x	—
Full description of item b		x	—
		x	
Extraordinary expenditure:			
Full description of item c	x		
Full description of item d	x		
		(x)	—
Extraordinary profit before taxation		x	—
Tax on extraordinary profit		(x)	—
Extraordinary profit after taxation		x	—

LIKELY FUTURE DEVELOPMENTS

FRED 22 'Review of FRS 3: Reporting Financial Performance'

9.43 The ASB published FRED 22 'Revision of FRS 3: Reporting Financial Performance' in December 2000. The exposure draft puts forward some significant changes to current reporting and disclosure requirements and is based on the ASB Discussion Paper 'Reporting Financial Performance: Proposals for Change' published in June 1999. The proposals reflect an agreed international approach to reporting financial performance and the ASB considers them to be a natural progression from the requirements of the present FRS 3, which was a groundbreaking standard when it was introduced in 1992. Under the proposals, the profit and loss account and statement of total recognised gains and losses would be replaced with a single performance statement showing all gains and losses recognised during the reporting period and relating to that period. The format of the proposed performance statement mirrors more closely that of the cash flow statement, and the ASB hopes that this will help users of the accounts to understand the cashflow effects of items shown in the performance statement. In its White Paper 'Modernising Company Law' issued in July 2002, the Government supports the view that the profit and loss account should become a wider performance statement reporting all gains and losses, and notes that current moves to modernise EC Directives include similar proposals. The proposals are now being taken forward as a joint ASB/IASB project.

Structure of financial performance statement

9.44   The performance statement proposed in FRED 22 is divided into three sections:

— operating;

— financing and treasury; and

— other gains and losses.

An Appendix to the FRED sets out an illustrative example, together with some of the suggested supporting notes. Most gains and losses will be shown in the operating section and this at least will continue to be analysed between acquisitions, continuing operations and discontinuing operations. Only items specified in the revised FRS 3, or in other accounting standards and UITF Abstracts, will be reported in the other two sections of the statement. Where a choice of section is permitted, any plans to change the section in which particular gains and losses are reported should be considered in accordance with the requirements of FRS 18 'Accounting Policies' relating to a change in accounting policy. However, the project to develop a single statement of financial performance is now being influenced by the need for increased convergence with international accounting standards. In the April 2002 edition of its 'Inside Track' newsletter, the ASB reported that a number of possible formats for the performance statement, including that proposed in FRED 22, were currently under consideration. Pensions accounting, and in particular the treatment of actuarial gains and losses in the performance statement, is proving a particularly difficult issue and problems are also being encountered as a result of the varied accounting treatments adopted for fixed assets (especially revalued assets) and depreciation in national accounting regimes.

Financing and treasury section

9.45   The following gains and losses would be recognised in the financing and treasury section of the performance statement:

— interest payable and receivable;

— the unwinding of the discount on long-term items;

— income from investments held as part of treasury activities;

— gains and losses arising on the repurchase or early settlement of debt; and

— any other gains and losses identified for inclusion by other accounting standards or UITF Abstracts.

The total for each of the above headings should be disclosed in the notes to the accounts if the details are not shown separately on the face of the performance statement.

Other gains and losses section

9.46 The following gains and losses would be recognised in the other gains and losses section of the performance statement:

— revaluation gains and losses on fixed assets;

— gains and losses on the disposal of properties in continuing operations;

— actuarial gains and losses arising on defined benefit schemes;

— profits and losses on disposal of discontinuing operations;

— exchange translation differences on foreign currency net investments;

— revaluation gains and losses on investment properties;

— amounts previously recognised in respect of warrants that have lapsed unexercised; and

— any other gains and losses identified for inclusion by other accounting standards or UITF Abstracts.

The total for each of the above headings should be disclosed in the notes to the accounts if the details are not shown separately on the face of the performance statement.

Continuing operations, discontinuing operations and acquisitions

9.47 The aggregate results for each of continuing operations, acquisitions and discontinuing operations should be shown separately for the results of the operating section of the performance statement. The same information should be shown for the other two sections of the statement unless it is impracticable to do so or the resulting information would be misleading. As a minimum, turnover and operating profit must be analysed in this way on the face of the performance statement. The analysis of other items may be given in the notes to the accounts. In the case of financing and treasury items, and other gains and losses, the underlying assumptions used in making any allocations between the categories should be disclosed. The post-acquisition results for the period in which an acquisition occurs should also be disclosed. Where this is impracticable, the financial statements should give an indication of the contribution to turnover and operating profit. If this information cannot be given, that fact and the reasons should be explained.

A subsequent Exposure Draft, FRED 32 'Disposal of non-current assets and presentation of discontinued operations' – once again based on international proposals – puts forward certain changes to the definition and accounting treatment of discontinued operations and non-current assets held for sale. These are considered briefly at 9.29 above.

Discontinuing operations

9.48   The following details should be disclosed for a discontinuing operation in the financial statements in which the initial disclosure event occurs (both discontinuing operation and initial disclosure event are defined in the FRED):

— description of the discontinuing operation;

— business or geographical segment in which it is reported;

— date and nature of the initial disclosure event;

— date or period in which discontinuance is expected to be completed (if known or determinable);

— carrying amounts at the balance sheet date of the total assets and liabilities to be disposed of;

— results of the discontinuing operations for the period;

— amounts of net cash flows attributable to the operating activities of the discontinuing operation in the current reporting period.

If an initial disclosure event occurs after the balance sheet date but before the date of approval of the financial statements, the above disclosures should be given for the period covered by the financial statements. Additional disclosures are required in respect of the disposal of assets and liabilities relating to a discontinuing operation. All disclosures should continue to be given for periods up to and including the period in which the discontinuance is completed.

Prohibition on recycling

9.49   The recycling of gains and losses between the different sections will be prohibited – in other words, once a gain or loss has been shown in one section of the statement, it cannot be shown again in a different section in a future period.

Offsetting

9.50   No change is proposed to the present requirement that gains and losses should generally not be offset when presenting information on financial performance unless:

— they relate to the same event or circumstance; or

— disclosing the gross components is unlikely to be useful in assessing either future results or the effects of past transactions and events.

Taxation

9.51   Two figures will be given for taxation on the face of the performance statement – one for tax attributable to the operating and financing sections (to be shown after the statutory heading 'Profit on ordinary activities before taxation') and one for tax attributable to other gains and losses (to be shown within that section of the performance statement). Any special circumstances that affect the overall tax charge or credit for the reporting period, or that will affect those of future periods, should be disclosed. An optional note is also suggested to show the unusual tax implications of certain gains and losses.

Dividends

9.52   Dividends will not be reported in the performance statement as they represent transactions with owners rather than elements of financial performance. However, the FRED proposes they should be shown as a memorandum item at the foot of the statement. There was a potential conflict with company law when these proposals were first issued, in that CA 1985 required dividends to be reported in the profit and loss account. However, for accounting periods beginning on or after 1 January 2005, the law has been amended by the *Companies Act 1985 (International Accounting Standards and Other Accounting Amendments) Regulations 2004* (SI 2004/2947) to remove this requirement and so allow dividends to be accounted for as transactions with shareholders rather than as profit and loss account items (see 9.10 above).

Earnings per share

9.53   The FRED also proposes that earnings per share is shown as a memorandum item at the foot of the performance statement and reinforces the requirements of FRS 14 'Earnings per Share' on consistency of disclosure where alternative versions are given in addition to the basic earnings per share calculated in accordance with the standard. For accounting periods beginning on or after 1 January 2005, FRS 14 is superseded by FRS 22 'Earnings per share' as part of the project to converge UK accounting standards with international requirements (see 1.6 above). FRS 14 and FRS 22 are considered in more detail in Chapter 18.

Prior period adjustments

9.54   Prior period adjustments will continue to be accounted for by restating the comparative figures for the preceding period in the primary statements and the supporting notes, and adjusting the opening balance of reserves for the cumulative effect. The FRED also proposes that the cumulative gain or loss arising from a prior period adjustment should be shown as a memorandum item at the foot of the performance statement. The correction of fundamental errors will continue to be accounted for by means of a prior period adjustment.

Notes to the accounts

9.55   The proposals specify comprehensive notes to accompany the performance statement, including a reserves note and a table of exceptional items reported over the last five years. The note of historical cost profits and losses (currently required by FRS 3) becomes an optional disclosure.

Ownership interests

9.56   A reconciliation of ownership interests must be given as a primary statement. This brings together the performance for the period and all other changes in ownership interests, including dividends paid and new capital contributed. It is very similar to the reconciliation of shareholders' funds currently required by FRS 3.

Investment properties

9.57   SSAP 19 'Accounting for Investment Properties' requires changes in the market value of investment properties to be taken to the statement of total recognised gains and losses. FRED 22 follows this approach by requiring them to be reported in the 'Other gains and losses' section of the performance statement, but notes that it may be more logical for such gains and losses to be shown as operating items. As a result of the convergence project, it is now likely that SSAP 19 will be replaced with a new standard based on IAS 40 'Investment Property' although the June 2005 version of the ASB's Technical Plan indicates that this is not expected to come into effect until 1 January 2008.

Specialised sectors

9.58   The FRED considers separately how the single performance statement might be adapted for specialised entities such as banking, insurance and investment companies' and notes that the ASB expects these and other sectors to develop the basic format where necessary through relevant Statements of Recommended Practice (SORPs). There are also specific requirements in the FRED for banking companies and groups, insurance companies and groups and investment companies.

Comparatives

9.59   Comparative figures should be given for all items in the primary statements and the notes required by the draft standard. The comparative figures for the continuing category should include only the results of operations that are included in the current period's continuing operations. Where financial statements show a discontinuing operation, the comparatives for preceding periods should be restated to segregate continuing and discontinuing assets, liabilities, income, expenses and cash flows. If a new accounting standard is issued on the basis of the exposure draft, comparative figures in the financial statements for the period in which the new standard is implemented will need to be restated to comply with the new formats and presentational requirements.

Impact on other standards

9.60 The exposure draft includes a substantial number of proposed amendments to other accounting standards and UITF Abstracts to bring these into line with the new requirements. The main changes are:

— references to the profit and loss account are to be read as references to the statement of financial performance;

— where an accounting standard or UITF Abstract requires a gain, loss, revenue or expense to be recognised in the profit and loss account, it should generally be reported in the operating section of the performance statement;

— where an accounting standard or UITF Abstract requires a gain, loss, revenue or expense to be recognised in the statement of total recognised gains and losses, it should generally be reported in the other gains and losses section of the performance statement;

— references to the reconciliation of shareholders' funds are generally to be replaced by reference to the reconciliation of ownership interests.

APPENDIX

Profit and loss account: Format 1

1.   Turnover.
2.   Cost of sales.
3.   Gross profit or loss.
4.   Distribution costs.
5.   Administrative expenses.
6.   Other operating income.
7.   Income from shares in group undertakings.
8.   Income from participating interests.
9.   Income from other fixed asset investments.
10. Other interest receivable and similar income.
11. Amounts written off investments.
12. Interest payable and similar charges.
13. Tax on profit or loss on ordinary activities.
14. Profit or loss on ordinary activities after taxation.
15. Extraordinary income.
16. Extraordinary charges.
17. Extraordinary profit or loss.
18. Tax on extraordinary profit or loss.
19. Other taxes not shown under the above items.
20. Profit or loss for the financial year.

Profit and loss account: Format 2

1.   Turnover.
2.   Change in stocks of finished goods and work in progress.
3.   Own work capitalised.
4.   Other operating income.
5.   (a)   Raw materials and consumables.
     (b)   Other external charges.
6.   Staff costs:
     (a)   wages and salaries,
     (b)   social security costs,
     (c)   other pension costs.

7. (a) Depreciation and other amounts written off tangible and intangible fixed assets.

    (b) Exceptional amounts written off current assets.

8. Other operating charges.

9. Income from shares in group undertakings.

10. Income from participating interests.

11. Income from other fixed asset investments.

12. Other interest receivable and similar income.

13. Amounts written off investments.

14. Interest payable and similar charges.

15. Tax on profit or loss on ordinary activities.

16. Profit or loss on ordinary activities after taxation.

17. Extraordinary income.

18. Extraordinary charges.

19. Extraordinary profit or loss.

20. Tax on extraordinary profit or loss.

21. Other taxes not shown under the above items.

22. Profit or loss for the financial year.

Profit and loss account: Format 3

A. Charges

1. Cost of sales.

2. Distribution costs.

3. Administrative expenses.

4. Amounts written off investments.

5. Interest payable and similar charges.

6. Tax on profit or loss on ordinary activities.

7. Profit or loss on ordinary activities after taxation.

8. Extraordinary charges.

9. Tax on extraordinary profit or loss.

10. Other taxes not shown under the above items.

11. Profit or loss for the financial year.

B. Income

1. Turnover.

2. Other operating income.

3. Income from shares in group undertakings.

4. Income from participating interests.

5. Income from other fixed asset investments.

6. Other interest receivable and similar income.

7. Profit or loss on ordinary activities after taxation.

8. Extraordinary income.

9. Profit or loss for the financial year.

Profit and loss account: Format 4

A. Charges

1. Reduction in stocks of finished goods and work in progress.

2. (a) Raw materials and consumables.

 (b) Other external charges.

3. Staff costs:

 (a) wages and salaries,

 (b) social security costs,

 (c) other pension costs.

4. (a) Depreciation and other amounts written off tangible and intangible fixed assets.

 (b) Exceptional amounts written off current assets.

5. Other operating charges.

6. Amounts written off investments.

7. Interest payable and similar charges.

8. Tax on profit or loss on ordinary activities.

9. Profit or loss on ordinary activities after taxation.

10. Extraordinary charges.

11. Tax on extraordinary profit or loss.

12. Other taxes not shown under the above items.

13. Profit or loss for the financial year.

B. Income

1. Turnover.

2. Increase in stocks of finished goods and work in progress.

3. Own work capitalised.

4. Other operating income.
5. Income from shares in group undertakings.
6. Income from participating interests.
7. Income from other fixed asset investments.
8. Other interest receivable and similar income.
9. Profit or loss on ordinary activities after taxation.
10. Extraordinary income.
11. Profit or loss for the financial year.

Chapter 10 Turnover

SEGMENTAL ANALYSIS OF TURNOVER

CA 1985 requirements

10.1   If a company has carried on two or more classes of business during the year and, in the opinion of the directors, these classes of business differ substantially from one another, the accounts must include:

— a description of each class of business;

— the amount of turnover attributable to each class of business.

If a company has supplied different geographical markets during the year and, in the opinion of the directors, these markets differ substantially from each other, turnover must also be analysed by geographical market supplied. These requirements only apply in the case of material items. Therefore, where the amounts attributable to a particular class of business or geographical market are not material, they may be combined with the amounts relating to another class or market.

Requirements of SSAP 25 'Segmental reporting'

10.2   SSAP 25 reinforces the segmental disclosure requirements of CA 1985 and also contains additional disclosure requirements which apply to any entity that:

— is a public limited company or has a public limited company as a subsidiary;

— is a banking or insurance company or group (as defined in CA 1985); or;

— exceeds the criteria, multiplied in each case by ten, for defining a medium-sized company under CA 1985 s 247, as amended from time to time by statutory instrument (see 8.108).

Subsidiary companies that are not public companies or banking or insurance companies are not required to comply with the additional disclosure requirements of SSAP 25 provided that the parent company gives appropriate segmental information in its own accounts, although the CA 1985 disclosure requirements continue to apply. SSAP 25 also requires disclosure of inter-segment sales and transfers where these are material.

Identification of classes of business and geographical markets

10.3 It is for the directors to decide whether the company has carried on different classes of business or supplied differing geographical markets during the year. CA 1985 does not provide any definitions or detailed guidance to assist directors in deciding when classes of business or geographical markets 'differ substantially', although it does require the directors to take account of the way in which the company's activities are organised. For instance, if the company operates through separate divisions, this might provide a suitable basis for the analysis by class of business. The explanatory notes to SSAP 25 do provide some useful guidance on these issues. They explain that the directors should bear in mind the overall purpose of providing segmental information. For instance, a reader or user of the accounts may need to know that the company is operating in business areas or geographical markets that are subject to different degrees of risk, have experienced different growth rates or have different future potential. SSAP 25 suggests that any business or geographical segment that represents 10% or more of total turnover should be regarded as significant and should therefore be treated as a 'reportable segment'.

Separate classes of business

10.4 SSAP 25 defines a separate class of business as a distinguishable part of an entity that provides:

— a separate product or service; or

— a separate group of related products or services.

As well as taking account of the manner in which the company's activities are organised, the directors should consider:

— the nature of the products or services;

— the nature of the production processes;

— the markets in which the products or services are sold;

— the distribution channels for the products;

— any separate legislative framework relating to part of the business.

Geographical segments

10.5 A geographical segment may be an individual country or a group of countries. SSAP 25 suggests that the following factors may be relevant in deciding on suitable reporting segments:

— differing economic climates;

— stable or unstable political regimes;

— exchange control regulations;

— exchange rate fluctuations.

CA 1985 requires turnover to be analysed by geographical market supplied. SSAP 25 also requires analysis by geographical origin (i.e. the area from which goods or services are supplied). If there is no material difference between the two, this can simply be stated in the accounts. A suitable geographical analysis for a company with major activities in the UK and Germany and a smaller level of activity elsewhere might be as follows:

Example 10.1 – Geographical analysis

	Turnover by origin 20X4	*Turnover by origin 20X3*	*Turnover by destination 20X4*	*Turnover by destination 20X3*
United Kingdom				
Germany				
Rest of Europe				
Asia				
Rest of the world				

Redefining reporting segments

10.6 The general requirement for accounting information to be presented on a consistent basis year by year applies equally to segmental disclosure. SSAP 25 requires the directors to redefine the reporting segments where appropriate. This might be necessary where the company diversifies into new activities, acquires a new business or ceases part of its previous activities. If the definitions of segments are changed, the nature of the change should be disclosed in the accounts, with details of the reason for and the effect of the change, and comparative figures should be restated accordingly.

Exemption from segmental disclosure

10.7 If the directors are of the opinion that making the required segmental disclosures would be seriously prejudicial to the interests of the company, the information need not be given, but the fact that disclosure has not been made must be stated in the accounts. The reasons for non-disclosure do not have to be given.

Neither the Act nor the standard provides further guidance on this point, but it is usually accepted that the exemption cannot be used simply to avoid disclosing information that competitors may find useful. It is only available when the segmental disclosure could potentially cause serious damage to the company's operations. This is likely to be rare in practice. One example might be the supply of substantial amounts of goods or services to two countries that have significantly different political ideologies. If the future success of the business is heavily dependent on continued trading with both countries, and disclosure of the level of trading with one country might lead to loss of business with the other, disclosure may be considered seriously prejudicial to the company's interests. If the directors believe that it is appropriate to take advantage of this exemption, it would be advisable for them to formally document their reasons for doing so.

Subsidiary companies that meet the SSAP 25 criteria are not required to comply with the additional disclosure requirements of SSAP 25 if the parent company provides appropriate segmental information in its own accounts. This exemption does not apply to subsidiary companies that are public companies or banking or insurance companies. However, the CA 1985 disclosure requirements on segmental information continue to apply to all subsidiary companies.

Maintaining appropriate records

10.8   It is clear that companies need to maintain detailed records as the year progresses to provide the information for these disclosure requirements. Obtaining information by class of business is usually relatively straightforward, especially as it will often form part of regular management information reports during the year. However, the collation of details by geographical market may require more thought and planning.

Likely future changes

10.9   As part of its project to converge UK accounting standards with international accounting requirements, the ASB plans to replace SSAP 25 with IAS 14 'Segment Reporting' in due course. IAS 14 is currently under review and an exposure draft of an updated standard is expected to be published later in 2005. The latest version of the ASB's Technical Plan, published in June 2005, indicates that the effective date of the new UK standard will be determined after taking into account various factors, including the entities that might apply the standard and the effective date of the new IAS 14.

Turnover relating to continuing, discontinued and acquired activities

10.10   FRS 3 'Reporting Financial Performance' requires separate disclosure of the results of continuing, acquired and discontinued operations. This analysis must be given for all statutory headings in the profit and loss account from turnover through to operating profit. The requirements are considered in more detail in Chapter 9.

ACCOUNTING POLICIES AND REVENUE RECOGNITION

Profit and loss account formats

10.11   Where a company prepares Companies Act accounts, CA 1985 requires a company's profit and loss account to be presented in one of four standard formats prescribed in the Act. More detail on these formats is given in Chapter 9. Turnover is one of the separate items that must be shown, regardless of which format is chosen. Turnover is defined in CA 1985 as the amount derived from the provision of goods and services falling within the company's ordinary activities, after deduction of:

—   trade discounts;

—   value added tax; and

—   any other taxes based on the amounts so derived.

SSAP 5 'Accounting for Value Added Tax' also requires turnover to exclude VAT.

Requirements of FRS 18

10.12   Revenue recognition concerns when revenue is recorded as such in an entity's profit and loss account. FRS 18 'Accounting Policies' requires an entity to adopt accounting policies that enable its financial statements to give a true and fair view and that are consistent with the requirements of accounting standards, UITF Abstracts and companies' legislation. Where more than one accounting policy would satisfy these requirements, the entity should select whichever of those policies is judged the most appropriate to its particular circumstances for the purpose of giving a true and fair view. The standard also requires financial statements (other than cashflow information) to be prepared on the accruals basis of accounting, which it defines as requiring the non-cash effects of transactions and events to be reflected, as far as is possible, in the financial statements for the accounting period in which they occur and not in the period in which any related cash is received or paid. The standard refers to the CA 1985 requirement that only profits realised at the balance sheet date should be included in the profit and loss account, and notes that profits are to be treated as realised for these purposes only when they have been realised in the form of cash or of other assets the ultimate cash realisation of which can be assessed with reasonable certainty. These requirements are to apply unless there are special reasons for departing from them, in which case two additional rules come into effect:

— such 'special reasons' will not exist unless, as a minimum, it is possible to be reasonably certain that an unrealised gain exists and can be measured with sufficient reliability;

— due consideration must be given to whether a departure from the requirements would result in the use of valuation bases or accounting treatments not permitted by companies' legislation and which could therefore only be used if the true and fair override was justified.

Further guidance on the requirements of FRS 18 can be found in Chapter 1 and Chapter 5. The ASB *Statement of Principles for Financial Reporting* also provides guidance on the recognition of transactions and events in financial statements. This is considered in Chapter 2.

Revenue recognition under FRS 5

10.13   In November 2003, the Accounting Standards Board published an additional Application Note to FRS 5 'Reporting the Substance of Transactions' on the subject of 'Revenue Recognition'. This deals with the recognition of revenue from the supply of goods and services to customers and sets out the basic principles that should be applied, together with more specific guidance on applying these principles to five types of transaction which have been subject to differing interpretations in practice. The objective is to ensure that entities report turnover in accordance with the substance of their contractual arrangements with customers, and at the point at which their performance entitles them to recognise either an increase in assets or a decrease in liabilities. The Application Note applies for accounting periods ending on or after 23 December 2003, although earlier adoption is encouraged.

Convergence with international requirements

10.14   The addition of Application Note G to FRS 5 is seen as an interim measure, pending the introduction in the UK of a new accounting standard based on IAS 18 'Revenue'. When the Application Note was published, the ASB expressed the view that its requirements would generally ensure compliance with IAS 18, although the UK document may sometimes result in turnover being recognised later than is implied by certain examples in the current version of IAS 18. The Application Note also provides more detail than the current international standard on the principles that should be applied in the recognition of turnover. The latest version of the ASB's Technical Plan, published in June 2005, indicates that a UK exposure draft based on IAS 18 will be published in the second final of 2005 and that implementation of the new standard is planned for accounting periods beginning on or after 1 January 2006 or 1 January 2007.

What is turnover?

10.15   Turnover is defined in the Application Note as the revenue resulting from exchange transactions under which a seller supplies to customers the goods or services that it is in business to provide. A business may enter into other exchange transactions (eg the sale of fixed assets) but these will not usually be classed as turnover because they will not meet the above definition.

Recognising turnover

10.16   The basic principles note that turnover arises as follows:

(i)   a seller should recognise revenue under an exchange contract when, and to the extent that, it obtains the right to consideration in exchange for its performance under the contract – at the same time, the seller will usually recognise a new asset (eg a debtor), reflecting its right to be paid;

(ii)   where a customer pays in advance of performance by the seller, the seller will recognise a liability equal to the consideration received, representing its obligation to provide goods or services under the contract – when performance takes place, and the seller obtains the right to the consideration as a result, the liability is reduced and the amount of that reduction is reported simultaneously as turnover; and

(iii)   where a seller has performed some, but not all, of its contractual obligations, it should recognise revenue to the extent that it has obtained a right to consideration as a result of its performance under the contract.

Measuring revenue

10.17   Revenue should be measured at the fair value of the right to consideration. This will normally be the amount specified in the contract, net of discounts, value added tax and other sales taxes. However, where the effect of the time value of money is material to reported revenue, the amount recognised should be the present value of the cash flows expected to be received from the customer in settlement, and the unwinding of the related discount should be credited to finance income on the basis that it represents a gain from a financing transaction. Also, if there is a significant risk that there will be a default on the consideration due and the effect is material, the amount of revenue recognised should be adjusted accordingly. This applies only where the expected default is apparent at the time that the revenue is originally recognised. Any subsequent adjustments to a debtor as a result of changes in the time value of money or credit risk should be not be reflected within revenue.

Long-term contractual performance

10.18   The Application Note refers to the guidance in SSAP 9 'Stocks and long term contracts' on accounting for long-term contracts and emphasises that there is no change to the requirements of that standard. However, FRS 5 now offers the following additional guidance in respect of accounting for long-term contracts:

(i)   changes in assets and liabilities, and related turnover, should be recognised over the course of the contract, reflecting the accrual of the seller's right to consideration;

(ii)   the amounts recognised should be derived from an assessment of the fair value of the goods or services provided as a proportion of the total fair value of the contract; and

(iii)   the fair values used should be those applicable at the inception of the contract, unless the contract terms provide for price increases to be passed on to the customer.

In some contracts, the proportion in (ii) above will correspond with the proportion of expenditure incurred compared with total expenditure, but this will not always be the case. It is also important to recognise that the relative profitability of the different stages of a contract may vary. The recognition of turnover should not generally follow the pattern of costs incurred, unless this provides evidence of the extent to which the seller has completed its contractual obligations. The guidance emphasises that the application of SSAP 9 should result in long term contractual performance being recognised as contract activity progresses, to the extent that the outcome of the contract can be assessed with reasonable certainty, and that the turnover recognised should reflect the extent of the seller's right to consideration.

Revenue recognition and services contracts

10.19   Following the publication of Application Note G, a number of concerns were raised over the interaction between this pronouncement and the requirements of SSAP 9 'Stocks and Long Term Contracts' in the context of contracts for professional services. The Urgent Issues Task Force was asked to consider this and published its consensus as Abstract 40 'Revenue recognition and service contracts' in March 2005. Although the concerns were raised mainly in the context of professional services contracts, the UITF concluded that the same principles should be applied to all contracts for services, so the impact of the Abstract may be wider than was initially expected. The Abstract applies for accounting periods ending on or after 22 June 2005, although earlier adoption is encouraged.

The key issue is whether revenue should be recognised as contract activity progresses, or only on completion of the contract. The Abstract notes that it is impractical to provide definitive guidance for every situation, as the detailed terms and commercial substance of services contracts vary considerably. Each reporting entity must therefore apply the underlying principles to its own circumstances – in some cases a single approach will be appropriate for all contracts that the entity undertakes, but in others different approaches may be needed to cater for different types of contract. The Abstract also notes that where a single contract has distinguishable phases, it may be appropriate to account for the contract as two or more separate transactions, provided that the value of each phase can be estimated reliably. As with all accounting issues, a consistent approach should be applied from year to year for all similar contracts.

Provision of services on an ongoing basis

10.20   The guidance notes that contracts dealing with the provision of services on an ongoing basis rather than the provision of a single service, or the provision of a number of services that constitute a single project, do not fall within the SSAP 9 definition of a long-term contract. Consequently, revenue resulting from such contracts should be accounted for as it arises.

Contract for a single service or project

10.21   By contrast, a contract for a single service, or a single project, which either lasts for more than one year or spans more than one accounting period, will need to be accounted for as a long-term contract if failure to do so would result in a material distortion of turnover and results. The Abstract emphasises that materiality should be assessed in relation to assets and liabilities as well as turnover and profits, and that the aggregate effect of all such contracts on the accounts as a whole should also be considered. Where the service provider's contractual obligations under such a contract are performed gradually over a period of time, revenue should be recognised as contract activity progresses. This applies even though the services may culminate in an end product (such as the preparation of a report) and reflects the fact that the service provider has accrued some right to consideration as a result of the work performed to date. The Abstract recognises only one exception to this accounting treatment – where the service provider's right to consideration is conditional or contingent on a specific future event or outcome which is outside the control of the service provider. In this case, the revenue should not be recognised until the critical event actually occurs.

Where terms and substance of the contract require revenue to be recognised as contract activity progresses, the amount recognised should be based on an appropriate proportion of the fair value of the contract, but should also take into account the amount that the customer is likely to accept and their ability to pay. For instance, if fees are based on the time spent on the work but there are doubts over whether the customer will accept the actual time incurred as reasonable, appropriate adjustments will need to be made to the amount recognised as revenue in the accounts.

Separation and linking of contractual arrangements

10.22   This section of the Application Note considers specific issues that may arise in the following situations:

(i)   a contractual arrangement which requires the seller to provide a number of different goods and services to customers and these are either:

  ● unrelated and capable of being sold separately; or

  ● so closely related that separate sale is not commercially feasible (for either the seller or the customer); and

(ii)   a contractual arrangement whereby a seller provides a package of goods and services to a customer and the amount payable is less than the price at which the items would be sold individually.

Where the commercial substance of a transaction is that the individual components operate independently (ie each element represents a separable good or service that the seller can provide on a stand alone basis or as an optional extra, or one or more components could be provided by another supplier), it should be accounted for as two or more separate transactions. Where components of a contract need to be unbundled in this way, the seller should be able to attribute a reliable fair value to each component by reference to individual transactions. Where the fair value of the package is less than the fair values of the individual components, the reduction should be allocated to the components pro rata to their fair values. If fair values cannot be attributed to the individual components, unbundling of the contract will only be appropriate if fair values can be obtained for either the completed or the uncompleted components of the contract. If reliable fair values cannot be established for the uncompleted components, particular care should be taken to ensure that turnover for the completed components is not overstated. Where reliable fair values cannot be attributed to either the completed or the uncompleted components, the seller should recognise turnover and changes in assets and liabilities on the basis of a single unbundled contractual arrangement. The requirements of SSAP 9 in respect of long term contracts may also need to be taken into account. The Application Note illustrates these principles with examples relating to:

(i)   the sale of software and related maintenance services;

(ii)   non-refundable fees charged at the inception of a contract; and

(iii) a contractual arrangement involving vouchers that are redeemable against future purchases of good or services.

Bill and hold arrangements

10.23   A bill and hold arrangement arises where a contractual arrangement relates to the supply of goods and there is a transfer of title, but physical delivery is deferred to a later date. The general principles of FRS 5 require the seller to have transferred the principal risks and benefits of the goods to the customer in order to recognise changes in its assets and/or liabilities. For the customer, the principal benefits will include:

(i)   the right to obtain the goods as and when required;

(ii)   the sole right to the goods for sale to a third party and to the future cash flows from such a sale; and

(iii)   protection from price increases charged by the seller.

The principal risks for the customer will include increased financing costs arising from slow movement of the goods, potential obsolescence and being compelled to take delivery of goods that are not readily saleable or saleable only at a reduced price.

For the seller to be in a position to recognise turnover in respect of a bill and hold arrangement, the transaction should include all of the following characteristics:

(i)   the goods should be complete and ready for delivery

(ii)   the seller should not retain any performance obligations other than the safe-keeping of the goods and their shipment on request;

(iii)   subject to normal rights of return (ie those that apply for sales not made on a bill and hold basis), the seller should have the right to consideration regardless of whether the goods are shipped, at the customer's request, to its delivery address;

(iv)   the goods should be identified separately from the seller's stock and should not be capable of being used to meet other orders received between the date of the bill and hold sale and the date of shipment; and

(v)   the terms of the arrangement should meet the commercial objectives of the customer rather than the seller – for instance, the delay in delivery is due to the customer's need for flexibility over the timing or place of delivery.

Where the substance of the transaction is that the goods represent an asset of the customer, and the seller therefore has a right to consideration, the seller should recognise the relevant change in assets and/or liabilities and the related turnover. Where the substance of the transaction is that the goods remain an asset of the seller, they should be retained in the seller's balance sheet and any amounts paid by the customer should be included within creditors.

Sales with a right of return

10.24   Rights of return may be explicit or implicit in a contractual agreement, or may arise as a matter of law. Where a contractual arrangement includes a right of return, this may affect either the quantification of the seller's right to consideration and/or the point at which that right should be recognised for accounting purposes, depending on the extent to which the risks associated with the related goods are retained by the seller. The seller will usually be able to make a reliable estimate of the sales value of returns, based on historic experience, and this expected loss should be excluded from turnover. Estimates should be reviewed at each reporting date to take account of changes in expectations and any expiry of contractual rights of return, and any adjustments to the original estimate should be included in revenue. If the seller is unable to make a reliable estimate of the sales value of returns, the maximum potential value of returns should be calculated, based on the terms of the contractual arrangement, and this value should be excluded from turnover. Where substantially all of the risks relating to the goods remain with the seller and consequently the seller has no right to consideration, the seller should not recognised any turnover or changes in assets/liabilities in respect of the transaction. In these circumstances, any amounts paid by the customer should be included within creditors, and the related turnover and changes in assets/liabilities should be recognised on the earlier of:

(i)   the date when a reliable estimate of the level of returns can be made; and

(ii)   the date when the right of return expires or is surrendered.

Acting as principal and agent

10.25   A seller may act as a principal in a transaction, or as an intermediary earning a fee or commission for arranging the provision of goods or services. The guidance notes that, in order for a seller to account for an exchange transaction as a principal, it should normally have exposure to all the significant benefits and risks associated with at least one of the following:

(i)   the ability to establish the selling price with the customer either directly or indirectly (eg by providing additional goods or services or adjusting the terms of a linked transaction); or

(ii)   exposure to the risk of damage, slow movement or obsolescence of the goods and to changes in the suppliers' prices.

There is a rebuttable presumption that a seller who has not disclosed that it is acting as agent is acting as principal. A number of other factors may indicate that a seller is acting as principal, including performance of part of the services supplied, modification to the goods supplied, the assumption of credit risk and discretion in selecting the supplier. A seller who acts as principal should report turnover based on the gross amount received or receivable for performing its obligations under the contract. By contrast, a seller who acts as agent will not usually be exposed to the substantial risks and rewards associated with the transaction. Situations indicating that the seller is acting as an agent include:

(i)   the seller has disclosed the fact that it is acting as agent;

(ii)   the seller has no further involvement in the performance of the obligations once the customer's order has been confirmed with the third party;

(iii)   the seller earns a predetermined amount (eg a fixed fee or a stated percentage of the amount billed to the customer);

(iv)   the seller bears no stock or credit risk (other than risk that it has agreed to assume on the payment of additional consideration by the ultimate supplier).

A seller acting as agent should report as turnover the fee or commission received or receivable for its performance under the contractual arrangement (ie the amount billed to the customer, less the amount paid to the principal). The guidance illustrates the above points with examples relating to a construction contract, sales made through a retail website and the rental of department store space to concessionaires. A seller acting as agent is encouraged, where practicable, to disclose the gross value of sales throughput and to give a brief explanation of the relationship between recognised turnover and the disclosed gross sales value.

Leasing income in the accounts of a lessor

10.26 SSAP 21 'Accounting for Leases and Hire Purchase Contracts' sets out separate requirements on accounting for rental income from operating leases and finance leases, and requires the aggregate rentals from each type of lease to be shown separately in the accounts.

Income from operating leases

10.27 In the case of an operating lease, SSAP 21 requires a lessor to account for rental income on a leased asset on a straight-line basis over the period of the lease, regardless of the actual timing of the rental payments. Another systematic and rational basis may be used to allocate the income if this is more representative of the way in which the benefit from the leased asset is receivable. Any charges for services such as insurance and maintenance of the asset should be treated separately from rental income in the accounts of the lessee. Direct costs incurred in arranging a lease (e.g. commissions, legal fees) may be charged to the profit and loss account as they are incurred, or may be apportioned over the period of the lease on a systematic and rational basis. SSAP 21 requires disclosure of the accounting policy adopted and the following wording may be suitable (although this will depend on the precise treatment adopted):

10.2 – Income from operating leases

Gross earnings from operating leases are recognised in the profit and loss account on a straight-line basis over the period of each lease. The initial direct costs incurred in negotiating and arranging operating leases are charged to the profit and loss account in the period in which they are incurred.

Operating lease incentives

10.28 Incentives offered to encourage a lessee to enter into a lease agreement will usually be structured to give the lessor the market return that he requires, but in a way that meets the cash flow requirements of the lessee. Thus, where a lease agreement includes an incentive (e.g. a cash payment or rent-free period), the level of rental payments will usually be higher than prevailing market rates, even though they may be described in the agreement as being at market rates. A payment or other transfer of value from the lessor to, or for the benefit of, the lessee should be regarded as a lease incentive when that fairly reflects its substance. Under UITF Abstract 28 'Operating Lease Incentives', all incentives for the agreement of a new or renewed operating lease should be recognised as an integral part of the net payment agreed for the use of the leased asset, irrespective of the nature or form of the incentive or the timing of the payments. A lessor should therefore recognise the aggregate cost of incentives as a reduction of rental income and should allocate this cost over the lease term or a shorter period ending on the date from which the prevailing market rental is expected to be payable. The allocation should be on a straight line basis unless another systematic basis is more representative of the time pattern in which the benefit from the leased asset is receivable by the lessee.

Income from finance leases

10.29   In the case of a finance lease, the total gross earnings under the lease should normally be allocated to accounting periods so that each period shows a constant periodic rate of return on the lessor's net cash investment in the lease. The net cash investment in the lease at any one point in time is defined as the amount of funds invested in the lease by the lessor, comprising the cost of the asset, plus or minus the following payments and receipts where relevant:

—   grants receivable towards the purchase or use of the asset;

—   rentals received;

—   tax payments and receipts, including the effect of capital allowances;

—   any residual value at the end of the lease term;

—   any interest payments;

—   any interest received on any cash surplus; and

—   any profit taken out of the lease.

The net cash investment in the lease should not be confused with the net investment in the lease which forms the basis for recording the amount due from the lessee in the balance sheet of the lessor (see Chapter 25). Rentals received from the lessee represent partly gross income for the lessor and partly a repayment of capital. The rental receipts must therefore be apportioned between these two elements. The guidance in SSAP 21 illustrates in detail two methods of allocating gross earnings to accounting periods in a way that meets the requirements of the standard:

—   the actuarial method after tax; and

—   the investment period method.

These are the two most commonly used methods, but others may be equally appropriate. Direct costs incurred in arranging a lease (eg commissions, legal fees) may be charged to the profit and loss account as they are incurred, or may be apportioned over the period of the lease on a systematic and rational basis. SSAP 21 requires disclosure of the accounting policy adopted and the following wording may be suitable (although this will depend on the precise treatment adopted):

10.3 – Income from finance leases

Rental payments under finance leases are apportioned between interest, which is credited to the profit and loss account as gross earnings, and repayment of capital which reduces the amount due from the lessees. Gross earnings from finance leases are allocated to accounting periods to give a constant periodic rate of return on the net cash investment in the lease, using the investment period method of allocation. The initial direct costs incurred in negotiating and arranging finance leases are charged to the profit and loss account in the period in which they are incurred.

Where the lessor is eligible for a tax free grant in respect of a leased asset, the grant should be spread over the period of the lease and accounted for as non-taxable income. Where a manufacturer or dealer offers a customer a choice between buying an asset or leasing it under a finance lease and the leasing option is taken up, the transaction will generate two elements of income for the manufacturer or dealer:

(i)   the initial profit or loss at the outset of the lease – this will be equivalent to the profit or loss that would have been accounted for if the asset had been sold outright; and

(ii)   the gross earnings over the period of the lease.

However, the pricing of the agreement will not necessarily be based on the selling price that would have been achieved in an outright sale. The standard therefore requires the recognition of any initial profit to be restricted to an amount that will enable the gross earnings on the leasing element of the transaction to be based on the rate of interest that would normally be charged to a lessee.

Disclosure of accounting policy

10.30   Because there are different methods of recognising revenue, and because turnover is usually both material and critical to the calculation of the profit or loss for the year, the accounting policy for turnover and/or revenue recognition will usually need to be explained in the notes to the accounts. For many companies a simple statement on turnover will suffice but other businesses, and in particular those with the type of contractual arrangements discussed in 10.18 to 10.29 above, may need to give additional details to explain the basis on which revenue has been recognised in the accounts.

Issues to consider when drafting accounting policy notes on turnover and revenue recognition include the following.

—   Does the company have more than one income stream? If so, do these income streams need to be considered and explained separately?

—   Is the timing of the recognition of income critical? If so, the treatment adopted will need to be explained in the note.

LONG-TERM CONTRACTS

Definition of long-term contract

10.31   SSAP 9 'Stocks and Long-term Contracts' considers the accounting treatment of turnover in respect of long-term contracts. A long-term contract is defined in the standard as one which relates to:

(i)   the design, manufacture or construction of a single substantial asset, or a combination of assets which together constitute a single project, or

(ii)   the provision of a service or a combination of services that together constitute a single project,

where the time taken to complete the work is such that the contract activity falls into more than one accounting period. In other words, it will usually be a contract that runs for more than one year. However, the fact that a contract runs for less than a year does not necessarily mean that it should not be accounted for as a long-term contract. If the contract is material and spans two accounting periods, it will usually be appropriate to account for it as a long-term contract. The identification of long-term contracts is considered in more detail in Chapter 24.

Guidance issued by the UITF on recognising revenue under services contracts that meet the definition of a long-term contract is considered in more detail at 10.19 to 10.21 above.

Accounting treatment

10.32   If long-term contracts were not accounted for until they were complete, the accounts would not reflect the results of contract activity during the year. Instead they would show the results of contracts completed during the year, which could give a very different picture. It is therefore considered more appropriate to take account of turnover, and the profit or loss earned, as the work proceeds. Calculation of the profit or loss earned to date is considered further in Chapter 24.

Calculating turnover

10.33   Each long-term contract should be considered separately. The calculation of the amount of turnover to be included for each contract should take into account:

—   the nature of the contract;

—   the stage of completion of the work;

—   the contractual relationship with the customer.

For instance, in the case of a construction contract, the amount to be included in turnover may be based on a formal valuation of the work completed to date. In the case of other types of contract, the specification may require the work to be analysed into specific stages and these can be used to assess the value of work completed to date.

Variations to original specification

10.34   A common feature of long-term contracts is variations to the original specification, which are often approved as the contract progresses. Where these have been agreed but not yet fully settled, it will usually be appropriate to estimate the amount likely to be received and include this in turnover as the relevant work is completed. However, a prudent approach should be taken in all cases where the final outcome is not known. The final negotiation of claims can often be a protracted exercise and income in respect of claims is usually only included as turnover when negotiations have reached an advanced stage and there is sufficient evidence that eventual receipt is reasonably certain. The accounting treatment of variations and claims is considered in more detail in Chapter 24.

Disclosure of method of calculating turnover

10.35   As there are many different ways of calculating turnover for long-term contracts, SSAP 9 is not prescriptive on the method that should be used. It therefore requires disclosure of the method adopted. An example of the type of explanation that should be given in accounting policy notes on long-term contracts is given in Chapter 24.

BARTER TRANSACTIONS FOR ADVERTISING

Scope of UITF Abstract 26

10.36   UITF Abstract 26 'Barter transactions for advertising' was issued in November 2000 and considers the accounting treatment that should be adopted when an entity agrees to provide advertising in exchange for advertising services provided by its customer rather than for cash consideration. At the moment, this situation is most likely to arise in the context of commercial websites that display advertising in exchange for advertising their own services on another website. However, the Abstract applies to barter transactions in all media and not just to website transactions. Barter transactions for services other than advertising are not covered, although the UITF notes that the principles in the Abstract may be relevant to such transactions.

Presentational issue

10.37   The accounting treatment of barter transactions for advertising will have no overall effect on the profit or loss for the period, but could affect the amount of turnover and costs recognised in the profit and loss account. Turnover is often regarded as a critical figure, and this is particularly the case with internet companies.

Recognition criteria

10.38   The Abstract refers to the recognition criteria set out in the ASB 'Statement of Principles for Financial Reporting', and notes that a barter transaction provides little or no evidence of the value of the services provided. It therefore concludes that it would not be appropriate to recognise turnover and costs in respect of such transactions unless there is persuasive evidence of the value at which the advertising would have been sold for cash, in a similar transaction, if it had not been the subject of an exchange.

Substance of the transaction

10.39   The Abstract also refers to the requirements of FRS 5 'Reporting the Substance of Transactions' and in particular the requirement that:

— all aspects and implications of a transaction should be identified; and

— greater weight should be given to those aspects that are more likely to have commercial effect in practice.

On this basis, an arrangement should be regarded as a barter transaction where this fairly reflects the substance of the transaction. Consequently, a contract to provide advertising for cash consideration may nevertheless be a barter transaction if it is made on the understanding that a reciprocal arrangement will also be entered into. Arrangements involving a third party may also constitute a barter transaction – for instance, where the purchaser of the advertising agrees to procure advertising services from another party in exchange, rather than providing these services itself.

Accounting treatment

10.40   Turnover and costs in respect of barter transactions for advertising should not be recognised unless there is persuasive evidence of the value at which the advertising, if not exchanged, would have been sold for cash in a similar transaction. This will only be the case where:

— the entity has a history of selling similar advertising for cash; and

— substantially all of the turnover from advertising within the accounting period is represented by cash sales.

Persuasive evidence

10.41   In order to provide persuasive evidence of the value of exchanged advertising, cash sales of advertising must be similar in all material respects – in other words:

— they must relate to advertising space in the same vehicle (e.g. the same website or magazine);
— they must have taken place within a reasonably short period of the exchange transaction (in no case more than six months before or after it); and
— there must be no other factors that would be expected to make the value of the advertising sold for cash significantly different from that exchanged – specific issues to consider here include:
   — circulation, exposure or saturation within an intended market;
   — timing (e.g. time of day, day of week, regularity, season of the year etc)
   — prominence;
   — demographics of readers, viewers or customers;
   — duration (i.e. length of time advertising will be displayed).

Even where similar advertising has been sold for cash, the Abstract notes that due consideration should still be given to whether, in the light of all the available information, there is persuasive evidence of the value at which the exchanged advertising would have been sold. Specific factors to consider here include:

— the entity's practice in setting prices for advertising and the circumstances in which discounts are offered;
— the probability that a cash sale would have taken place if the advertising had not been exchanged; and
— the value to the entity of the advertising received in exchange and whether there is evidence that the entity would have been willing to buy that advertising for cash if it had not obtained it through the exchange transaction.

Disclosure

10.42 Where the stringent conditions set out in the Abstract are met, and both turnover and costs are therefore recognised in the profit and loss account, the notes to the financial statements should disclose the total amount that is included in turnover in respect of barter transactions for advertising. The Abstract also encourages the disclosure of additional information on the volume and type of these transactions, and other forms of barter transactions, irrespective of whether they are included in turnover, but does not specifically require this.

CONTRACTS FOR SALES OF CAPACITY

Sale of the right to use capacity

10.43 UITF Abstract 36 'Contracts for sales of capacity' was published in March 2003 and is effective for accounting periods ending on or after 22 June 2003. Entities in some industries (such as telecommunications and electricity) sell rights to use capacity on their networks, sometimes entering into exchange or reciprocal transactions ('capacity swaps') and the Abstract sets out the limited circumstances under which transactions in capacity should be reported as sales.

The guidance in the Abstract notes that contracts conveying right of use are similar to leases and that SSAP 21 'Accounting for Leases and Hire Purchase Contracts' prohibits a lessor from accounting for a lease as a sale unless the lease is a finance lease (ie one under which substantially all the risks and rewards of ownership of the asset are transferred to the lessee). Consequently, the seller of a right to use capacity should not report the transaction as a sale unless:

(i)   the purchaser's right of use is exclusive and irrevocable;

(ii)   the asset component is specific and separable, so that the purchaser's exclusivity is guaranteed and the seller has no right to substitute other assets;

(iii)   the term of the contract is for a major part of the asset's useful economic life;

(iv)   the attributable cost or carrying value of the asset can be measured reliably; and

(v)   no significant operational risks in respect of the asset are retained by the seller.

Even if all of these conditions are met, the proceeds from the sale should only be reported as turnover if the assets were designated as held for resale, and classified as stock, when first acquired or when construction was completed. In all other cases, the transaction should be recorded as a fixed asset disposal. Where sales of capacity are reported within operating results, the accounts should disclose:

(i)   any amounts included in turnover; and

(ii)   the profits recorded on the transactions.

Capacity swaps

10.44   Where an entity sells capacity on a network in exchange for receiving capacity on another entity's network, revenue or gains should only be recognised if the assets or services provided or received have a readily ascertainable market value as defined in FRS 10 'Goodwill and Intangible Assets' (see Chapter 20). This applies irrespective of whether any cash is exchanged in respect of the transaction.

Artificial transactions

10.45   No accounting recognition should be given to transactions that are artificial or lacking in substance – for instance, where exchange transactions are entered into for capacity for which the transacting parties have no current need and which would otherwise be unlikely to be saleable.

Chapter 11   Staff Costs and Employee Numbers

DISCLOSURE OF STAFF COSTS

CA 1985 disclosure requirements

11.1   Section 231A of CA 1985 requires details of staff costs to be disclosed each year (with comparatives), analysed into the following aggregate amounts:

(i)   wages and salaries paid or payable in respect of the year to the company's employees;

(ii)   social security costs incurred by the company on behalf of its employees;

(iii)   other pension costs incurred by the company on behalf of its employees.

For accounting periods beginning before 1 January 2005, this disclosure requirement was set out in paragraph 56 of Schedule 4 to CA 1985, but it was moved to a new section 231A by the *Companies Act 1985 (International Accounting Standards and Other Accounting Amendments) Regulations 2004* (SI 2004/2947) to ensure that all companies continue to be required to give information, irrespective of whether they prepare Companies Act accounts or IAS accounts. However, there is no requirement to repeat the information in the notes if it is already given elsewhere in the accounts (for instance, as part of the standard profit and loss account format).

Where Companies Act accounts are prepared:

(i)   a company that has chosen Format 2 or Format 4 for its profit and loss account must disclose staff costs as part of the profit and loss account, but the information may be given either on the face of the profit and loss account or in the notes to the accounts;

(ii)   a company that has chosen Format 1 or Format 3 must give details of staff costs in the notes to the accounts.

Paragraph 56 was not repeated in Schedule 8 to CA 1985, and a small company preparing shorter form accounts (see Chapter 8) for accounting periods beginning before 1 January 2005 and using either Format 1 or 3 for the profit and loss account is therefore not required to disclose details of staff costs. However, staff costs continue to be disclosable as part of the profit and loss account where Format 2 or Format 4 is adopted in shorter form accounts. Section 231A does not include any similar exemption for small companies and so, for accounting periods beginning on or after 1 January 2005, all small companies are currently required to give details of staff costs in their accounts. The DTI has subsequently indicated that it intends to reinstate this exemption for small companies, although the relevant regulations for this are not expected to come into force until 1 October 2005.

Requirements of FRS 3 'Reporting Financial Performance'

11.2 FRS 3 requires all figures from turnover to operating profit or loss to be analysed between continuing, discontinued and newly-acquired activities (see Chapter 9). A company using Format 2 or Format 4 for its profit and loss account must therefore give this analysis for staff costs where appropriate. The disclosure may be given on the face of the profit and loss account or in the notes to the accounts. A company using Format 1 or Format 3 for its profit and loss account is not required to analyse staff costs in this way, as the detailed disclosure of staff costs is supplementary to the profit and loss account rather than an integral part of it.

Wages and salaries

11.3 Wages and salaries are defined in CA 1985 Sch 4 para 94(3) as payments made or costs incurred in respect of persons employed by the company (as defined for the purposes of calculating the average number of employees – see 11.8 below) but there is no further guidance on which items should be included. The amount disclosed is usually the gross amount paid in respect of wages and salaries, including amounts such as overtime and bonus payments.

Benefits in kind

11.4 In particular there is no specific reference to the benefits in kind that may be made available to employees (e.g. use of a company car, private health insurance). In the case of directors, the Act states that the estimated money value of benefits in kind must be included as remuneration. The term 'costs incurred' in para 94(3) could be interpreted as including benefits in kind, but it is normal practice at present to exclude benefits from staff costs.

Social security costs

11.5 Social security costs are defined in CA 1985 Sch 4 para 94(1) as contributions by the company to any state social security or pension scheme, fund or arrangement. The amount disclosed under this heading will usually represent the total of employers' national insurance contributions paid or payable by the company during the year. For share options granted after 5 April 1999 under unapproved schemes, this will include employers' national insurance contributions payable on gains made by directors and employees on the exercise of the options.

Pension costs

11.6   Pension costs are defined in to CA 1985 Sch 4 94(2) as including:

— any costs incurred by the company in respect of any pension scheme established for the purpose of providing pensions for current or former employees;

— any sums set aside for the future payment of pensions directly by the company to current or former employees;

— any pensions paid directly to current or former employees without having first been set aside.

The accounting treatment of pension costs is considered in more detail in Chapter 12.

CALCULATION OF AVERAGE NUMBER OF EMPLOYEES

CA 1985 disclosure requirements

11.7   All companies are required to disclose the average number of employees during the year, in total and analysed by category. The categories used are to be decided by the directors, taking into account the way in which the company's activities are organised.

For accounting periods beginning before 1 January 2005, this disclosure requirement was included in paragraph 56 of Schedule 4 to CA 1985 but, like the disclosure requirement in respect of staff costs, it has been moved to a new section 231A by the *Companies Act 1985 (International Accounting Standards and Other Accounting Amendments) Regulations 2004* (SI 2004/2947) to a ensure that all companies continue to be required to give this information, irrespective of whether they prepare Companies Act accounts or IAS accounts.

The same issues in respect of the exemption for small companies arise as in the case of the disclosure of staff costs (see 11.1 above).

Basic rules

11.8   The Act is very specific on how the average number of employees should be calculated. The figure must be calculated by:

(i)   ascertaining the number of people employed by the company under contracts of service in each month of the financial year, regardless of whether they were employed for the full month or only for part of it;

(ii)   adding up the numbers ascertained in this way for each month of the financial year;

(iii) dividing the resultant total by the number of months in the financial year.

A contract of service (or a contract of employment) is a formal agreement between the employer and employee under which the employee agrees to work for the employer and the employer agrees to pay the employee a wage or salary in respect of that work. All employees should have a formal contract of service or employment.

Contracts for services

11.9   Certain individuals may carry out work for a company under a contract for services, as opposed to a contract of service. In this case, the individual will usually be self-employed (e.g. a consultant, or a contractor) and will be engaged to carry out specific duties. They will not usually be required to work full-time for the company. Individuals who carry out work for the company under a contract for services will not normally be included in the calculation of the average number of employees. Similarly, amounts paid to them should not be included as staff costs. They will usually be disclosed instead as 'other external charges' or 'other operating costs'.

Directors

11.10   Executive directors will often have a contract of service with the company and they should therefore be included in the calculation of the average number of employees, even though separate details of their remuneration must also be given in the accounts (see Chapter 17). It is usually helpful to explain that executive directors are included in the figure for the average number of employees, although there is no specific requirement to do so. Non-executive directors will usually have contracts for services and should therefore be excluded from the calculations.

Employees working overseas

11.11   The Act makes no separate mention of employees working wholly or mainly overseas in the context of these disclosures. Overseas employees should therefore be included in the calculation of the average number of employees during the year.

Arrangements which may give rise to problems

11.12   In some situations a strict interpretation of the requirements of the Act could result in misleading details being disclosed. It may therefore be necessary to depart from the strict requirements in order for the accounts to show a true and fair view. In these circumstances, details of the departure, the reasons for it and the effect should be disclosed. Some of the more common situations are considered below.

Temporary or casual employees

11.13   Temporary or casual employees are normally excluded from the calculations on the basis that they do not usually have formal contracts of employment with the company and they will often be used only to cover for existing staff (e.g. to cover absence through illness). In these circumstances, the numbers involved are likely to be relatively low. However, in situations where temporary or casual staff are employed in larger numbers and on a more regular basis (e.g. in the hotel and catering industry, where business is often seasonal and wide use is made of temporary staff as a result) it may be necessary to treat them as employees for the accounts to show a true and fair view.

Staff employed by a different company

11.14   This problem is most likely to arise in a group situation, where staff may have service contracts with one company but carry out work for one or more other companies within the group. They may also be paid by the company employing them rather than by the company or companies for which they actually work. In some cases, the companies for which they work may be recharged with their salary cost, but this is not always done. Examples of these arrangements and suggested disclosures in each case are set out below.

Disclosure in subsidiary company's accounts

11.15   The following treatment and disclosures will usually be appropriate in a situation where staff are employed by the holding company A, but work for its subsidiary company B.

Example 11.1 – Where staff are employed by holding company A but work for subsidiary B

The staff work full-time for B, and B effectively pays the relevant staff salaries and related costs (either directly or by means of a recharge).

— Treat the payments as staff costs in B's accounts.

— Include the staff in the average number of employees in B's accounts.

— Explain in the notes to the accounts that staff are under contracts of employment with A but work full-time for B and that they have therefore been included in the average number of employees and in staff costs.

— Explain that this constitutes a departure from the requirements of the Act but is necessary for the accounts to show a true and fair view.

Example 11.2 – Where staff work for B and B bears a management charge

The staff work full-time for B, and B bears a group management charge, which effectively includes the relevant salary cost but does not separately identify this amount.

The notes to B's accounts should explain that:

— staff are under contracts of employment with A but work full-time for B;

— B is recharged for the cost of these employees by means of a group management charge, but it is not possible to identify separately the element relating to staff costs;

— details of the total number of A's employees and their staff costs are given in the accounts of A.

It may be helpful to give details of the number of staff working for B, but this is not strictly a requirement in this situation.

Example 11.3 – Where staff work for B, but B does not pay their salaries in any way

The staff work full-time for B, but B does not pay their salaries, either directly or indirectly.

The notes to B's accounts should explain that:

— staff are under contracts of employment with A but work full-time for B;

— B is not recharged for the cost of these employees;

— details of the total number of A's employees and their staff costs are given in the accounts of A.

It may be helpful to give details of the number of staff working for B, but this is not strictly a requirement in this situation.

Example 11.4 – Where staff split work between B and another company and B bears relevant costs

The staff work partly for B and partly for other group companies, and B bears an appropriate level of the relevant staff costs.

B's accounts should explain the situation and follow the disclosures in Example 11.1.

Example 11.5 – Where staff split work between B and another company but B bears no cost

The staff work partly for B and partly for other group companies, but B does not bear any of the relevant staff costs.

B's accounts should explain the situation and follow the disclosures in Example 11.3.

Disclosure in holding company accounts

11.16   In the above examples, if A prepares group accounts, no additional disclosures will usually be required as the staff costs and employee details will cover the group as a whole. However, if A is exempt from preparing group accounts, an explanation of the arrangements and the treatment adopted may also need to be given in A's accounts in order for them to show a true and fair view.

Arrangements involving another group company

11.17 Where arrangements similar to those described above operate through a different structure (e.g. staff employed by another subsidiary within the group rather than by the holding company) the arrangements will usually need to be explained in the accounts of both companies.

Disclosure of number of employees by category

11.18 The Act requires the average number of employees during the year to be disclosed in total and by category. The directors are free to choose how to categorise employees, although they must take account of the way in which the company's activities are organised. Most companies give the analysis of employee numbers by function, for example:

— production;

— sales and distribution;

— management;

— administration.

However, others have chosen categories such as:

— full-time and part-time;

— hourly-paid, weekly-paid and salaried;

— by division (e.g. manufacturing, retail, construction);

— by geographical area.

The analysis can be given in more than one way if this is considered helpful. The number of employees by category should be calculated in the same way as the average number of employees in total.

Link between staff costs and employee numbers

11.19 CA 1985 Sch 4 para 94(3) defines the amount to be shown as wages and salaries and social security costs, within staff costs, as payments made or costs incurred in respect of all persons employed by the company during the year who are taken into account in calculating the average number of employees. There is consequently a direct link between the staff costs and employee numbers disclosures, and the two should therefore be shown on a consistent basis (i.e. if it is appropriate to exclude certain individuals from employee numbers because they do not meet the criteria specified in the Act, payments to those individuals should not be treated as staff costs in the accounts).

EMPLOYEE SHARE SCHEMES UNDER UITF ABSTRACT 17

Requirements of UITF Abstract 17

11.20   UITF Abstract 17 'Employee Share Schemes' considers the accounting treatment of shares awarded to employees through annual bonuses or long-term incentive schemes. The requirements apply to all share schemes including:

— those that clearly involve employee remuneration, such as approved profit-sharing schemes under the *Income and Corporation Taxes Act 1988*;

— new types of scheme, such as the all-employee share plan introduced in 2000; and

— where, on the initial listing of a company, employees are given the opportunity to subscribe for shares or rights to shares at a discount to the float price payable by public investors.

The only exception is that the Abstract need not be applied to Inland Revenue approved SAYE schemes and equivalent overseas schemes. Where an entity chooses to take advantage of this exemption, it must disclose in the notes to the accounts that it has done so.

The Abstract is superseded by FRS 20 'Share-based Payment' which applies as follows:

(i)   for accounting periods beginning on or after 1 January 2005 in the case of listed companies; and

(ii)   for accounting periods beginning on or after 1 January 2006 for all other entities.

Consequently, the following paragraphs are relevant only to the accounts of unlisted companies for accounting periods beginning before 1 January 2006.

The requirements of FRS 20 are considered at 11.38 to 11.46 below.

Recognition of the cost of share awards

11.21   The consensus reached by the UITF on accounting for the award of shares, or rights to shares, to employees is that:

— the cost should be recognised over the period to which the employee's performance relates;

— the amount charged to the profit and loss account should be based on the fair value of the shares at the date they are awarded to the employee;

— the minimum amount to be recognised should be the difference between:

— the fair value of the shares at the date the award is made to participants in the scheme; and

— the amount of any consideration that participants may be required to pay for the shares.

The wording of the Abstract originally required book values (rather than fair values) to be used in calculating the minimum amount to be recognised in the case of shares purchased by an ESOP trust, but this was amended by UITF Abstract 38 'Accounting for ESOP Trusts', which is effective for accounting periods ending on or after 22 June 2004.

The fair value of the shares at the date they are awarded to the employee reflects the amount that the employer would receive if the shares were issued for cash, and also the value of the award to the employee. The guidance explains that fair value will usually be equivalent to the market value of the shares at the date of issue. UITF Abstract 30 'Date of Award to Employees of Shares and Rights to Shares' clarifies what constitutes the date of the award when:

— the award is subject to approval by the shareholders (see 11.22 below); or

— the award is conditional on the company's shares becoming publicly traded or on a trade sale taking place (see 11.23 below).

Need for shareholder approval

11.22   Under CA 1985 s 80, a company will often need authorisation from its shareholders in order to allot shares or rights to shares. In practice, many companies seek advance authorisation from their shareholders at each Annual General Meeting to cover planned share awards during the coming year, but this will not happen in every case. The UITF therefore considered the situation where shares or share options are promised to employees, but the arrangements are subject to shareholder approval. It concluded that the company does not have the power to make the award, or grant the options, until the shareholders have approved the arrangements. In these circumstances, therefore, the date of the award of the shares, or the granting of the options, is the date on which formal shareholder approval is given. Any charge to the profit and loss account will therefore be based on the fair value of the shares at that time rather than at the date when the promise was originally made.

Creation of an obligation

11.23   Where an award of shares or options is subject to shareholder approval, the employer may nevertheless create an obligation to the employee, either explicitly or implicitly. For instance, an explicit obligation will be created if the company agrees to pay a cash bonus to the employee in the event that the share award is not approved by the shareholders. An implicit obligation may arise through the employee having redress against the company for failure to carry out the promise made. The UITF consensus is that, where the company creates an obligation that may involve a future transfer of economic benefits, a charge should be made to the profit and loss account on the date that the arrangement is entered into. The amount charged should be calculated in accordance with UITF Abstract 17 and should take account of any performance criteria relating to the award. Changes in the share price between the date of the arrangement and the date of approval will therefore affect the total amount charged to the profit and loss account. If the shareholders subsequently approve the share award, any charge required by Abstract 17 at the date of the award will be based on the fair value of the shares at the date of approval and should be adjusted for the amount already charged to the profit and loss account in making provision for the obligation. The provision made should be treated as part of the consideration for the share award and should be transferred to shareholders' funds.

Shares becoming publicly traded

11.24   Shares and options may sometimes be awarded to employees in anticipation of the company's shares becoming publicly traded on a stock exchange, or of a trade sale taking place, and the award may be made conditional on such arrangements being put into place. The UITF consensus is that this constitutes a performance condition of the award. The date of the award will therefore be the date on which the condition is satisfied (e.g. the date on which the shares become listed). This ensures that the amount charged to the profit and loss account under Abstract 17 is based on the fair value of the shares after listing and not on a value applying before the shares are publicly traded.

Consideration paid by employee

11.25   Where the employee is required to make some contribution to the cost of the shares awarded under the scheme, this should be deducted from the amount to be charged to the profit and loss account.

Shares purchased by ESOP trust

11.26   UITF Abstract 17 originally included separate requirements on the calculation of the profit and loss account charge where shares were purchased through an Employee Share Ownership Plan (ESOP) trust. These were based on the requirements of UITF Abstract 13, which provided the initial guidance on accounting for ESOP trusts, but the treatment set out in this Abstract has now been superseded by that in UITF Abstract 38 'Accounting for ESOP Trusts'. UITF Abstract 17 has consequently been amended to remove the separate references to shares purchased through an ESOP trust. The illustrative examples in the Appendix to revised UITF Abstract 17 have also been updated to make clear that the cost of shares purchased through an ESOP trust no longer has any effect on the calculation of the amount charged to the profit and loss account in respect of shares awarded to employees. The requirements of Abstract 38 are considered in Chapter 4.

Uncertainty over achievement of performance criteria

11.27   In some cases, particularly where the award relates to a long-term incentive scheme, there may be a degree of uncertainty over whether the performance criteria underlying the award will actually be met. Some schemes may also allow for employees to receive a proportion of the award where the performance criteria are partially achieved. UITF Abstract 17 requires the effect of uncertainty to be dealt with by making a reasonable estimation of the number of shares that may be required to be issued under the scheme, based on the extent to which the performance criteria are expected to be met. Therefore, in the case of awards under a long-term incentive scheme:

—   the amount initially recognised should be based on a reasonable expectation of the extent to which the relevant performance criteria will be met;

—   this amount should be charged to the profit and loss account over the period to which the performance criteria relate, either on a straight line basis or on another basis that more fairly reflects the services received from the employee; and

—   subsequent adjustments should be made as necessary to deal with changes in the probability of the performance criteria being met, lapses in conditional awards or purchases of shares at different prices.

Schemes requiring employees to retain shares awarded

11.28   Some schemes may incorporate a requirement, or an encouragement, for employees to retain shares awarded under the scheme for a minimum period. The UITF concluded that the amount charged to the profit and loss account in respect of the share award should not be adjusted in any way to reflect conditions of this nature.

Revision of charge in subsequent years

11.29   Under UITF Abstract 17, the fair value of the shares expected to be awarded should be determined at the time that a conditional award is made. This initial estimate may need to be revised in subsequent years, for instance to reflect:

—   changes in the probability of the performance criteria being met, which may change the estimate of the number of shares expected to be issued; or

—   expected awards which lapse due to the employee leaving the company.

However, no adjustment should be made to reflect increases or decreases in the value of the shares to which employees will become entitled in due course.

When should the award be recognised in the accounts?

11.30   The Abstract requires the cost of employee share awards to be recognised over the period to which the employee's performance criteria relates. Where the share award relates to an annual bonus scheme, the award should be recognised in the year to which the bonus relates. In the case of a long-term incentive scheme, the total amount to be recognised should be spread over the period covered by the performance criteria. The amount to be charged to the profit and loss account each year should reflect the service provided by the employee during that period. In most cases, a straight line charge will be appropriate, but an alternative basis should be used if this results in a more appropriate allocation of the costs over the total performance period. The annual charge will also include the effect of any adjustments required to reflect changes in estimates and expectations as explained in 11.29 above. Where no performance criteria are included in the scheme, and it is clear that the share award is not related to past performance, the cost of the award should be spread over the period from the date the award is made to the date when the employee becomes unconditionally entitled to the shares.

Requirement for further period of employment

11.31   Some schemes may include a requirement for an employee to complete an additional period of continued employment before the share award becomes unconditional. This additional period should not normally be included in the period over which the costs are spread. However, if it is clear that the effect of the scheme is to reward services during the additional period as well as the original period, the cost of the award should be spread over the full period (i.e. the original period plus the additional period of continued employment).

Share options

11.32   Where the scheme involves the award of share options, the total amount to be charged to the profit and loss account should be based on the difference between the exercise price of the option and market value at the date of the grant. This cost should be spread over the relevant performance period in the same way as any other share award.

Accounting for share awards in the company's balance sheet

11.33   The amount accrued in the accounts in respect of employee share awards should be included within shareholders' funds in the balance sheet. When the shares are eventually issued, the total amount accrued should be allocated between share capital and reserves. As shares cannot be issued at a discount, the amount allocated to share capital will usually be equal to the par value of the shares. No amount should be allocated to the share premium account, as the UITF has received legal advice that the share premium account is normally only required to reflect cash subscribed for shares. In most cases, the balance will be allocated to the profit and loss account reserve, which should mean that distributable reserves are not affected by the profit and loss account charge in respect of the share award.

Shares held by ESOP trust

11.34   If the shares are held in an ESOP trust before being transferred to participants in the scheme, the shares should be accounted for under UITF Abstract 38 (i.e. any consideration in respect of them should be deducted in arriving at shareholders' funds and should not be treated as an asset). The requirements of Abstract 38 are considered in Chapter 4.

Inclusion in reconciliation of movements in shareholders' funds

11.35   The credit entry for the amount charged to the profit and loss account each year should be reported in the reconciliation of movements in shareholders' funds. This reflects the fact that the amount charged is in effect the proceeds of an issue of shares. It would therefore be inappropriate for the credit entry to be reported in the statement of total recognised gains and losses.

Worked example

11.36   The following example illustrates how the requirements of Abstract 17 might be applied in practice:

Example 11.6 – Accounting for share award to employees

Company A operates a long-term incentive scheme for senior staff. Participants in the scheme are granted a conditional award of up to 1,000 shares on 1 January 2001. The nominal value of each share is £1 and the market price is £8. The shares will be transferred to the participants after a period of 3 years, provided that specific performance targets have been achieved. The scheme provides for a proportion of the shares to be transferred if the targets are only partially met. Participants in the scheme are not required to contribute towards the shares.

The company makes up its accounts to 31 December each year. The expected share transfers to employees at the end of the 3 years, based on the information available at the end of each accounting period, are as follows:

31 December 2001	60% of the maximum award
31 December 2002	80% of the maximum award
31 December 2003	75% of the maximum award (actual award)

750 new shares of £1 were issued on 1 January 2004 and transferred to the scheme participants. The price of the shares on 1 January 2004 was £11.

The accounting treatment over the 3-year period would be:

(i)   At 31 December 2001 the company would accrue costs of £1,600 calculated as follows:

Maximum award	1,000 shares x £8 =	£8,000
Expected award of 60%	60% x £8,000 =	£4,800
First year of 3-year period	£4,800 x 1/3 =	£1,600

£1,600 would be charged to the profit and loss account for the year and shown in the reconciliation of movements in shareholders' funds, and £1,600 would be shown within shareholders' funds in the balance sheet.

(ii)   At 31 December 2002 the company would accrue a total of £4,267 calculated as follows:

Maximum award	1,000 shares x £8 =	£8,000
Expected award of 80%	80% x £8,000 =	£6,400
Second year of 3-year period	£6,400 x 2/3 =	£4,267

£2,667 would be charged in the profit and loss account for the year (£4,267 – £1,600) and shown in the reconciliation of movements in shareholders' funds and £4,267 would be shown within shareholders' funds in the balance sheet.

(iii)   At 31 December 2003 the actual award is known to be £6,000, calculated as follows:

Maximum award	1,000 shares x £8 =	£8,000
Actual award of 75%	75% x £8,000 =	£6,000

£1,733 would be charged in the profit and loss account for the year (£6,000 – £4,267) and shown in the reconciliation of movements in shareholders' funds and £6,000 would be shown within shareholders' funds in the balance sheet.

When the new shares are issued on 1 January 2004, the nominal value of the shares (750 x £1 = £750) will be allocated to share capital and £5,250 (£6,000 – £750) will be allocated to reserves. [NB The price of the shares at the date of issue is not relevant for accounting purposes.]

Other examples

11.37   UITF Abstract 17 also includes a number of illustrative examples, some of which cover situations where shares are acquired at the start of the scheme, or during the scheme, and are then held by an ESOP trust until the date of transfer to participants.

SHARE-BASED PAYMENT UNDER FRS 20

FRS 20 – 'Share-based Payment'

11.38   The ASB published FRS 20 'Share-based Payment' in April 2004. The standard incorporates into UK accounting the requirements of International Financial Reporting Standard 2 (IFRS 2) which is effective for accounting periods beginning on or after 1 January 2005. For companies preparing accounts in accordance with UK accounting standards, FRS 20 is effective as follows:

(i)   for accounting periods beginning on or after 1 January 2005 in the case of listed entities; and

(ii)   for accounting periods beginning on or after 1 January 2006 for all other entities.

Earlier adoption is encouraged, although the fact that the standard has been adopted in advance of its effective date should be disclosed where relevant. The standard applies to all share-based payment transactions, including employee share option schemes, Save-As-You-Earn (SAYE) plans and similar arrangements, and all share-based payment transactions involving the receipt of goods and non-employee services. UITF Abstract 17 'Employee Share Schemes' and UITF Abstract 30 'Date of Award to Employees of Shares or Rights to Shares' are withdrawn from the relevant effective date of the new standard (see 11.20 to 11.37 above), and UITF Abstract 38 'Accounting for ESOP Trusts' is amended from the same date (see Chapter 4).

Underlying principles

11.39   FRS 20 is based on the following principles:

(i)   when an entity receives goods or services under a share-based payment transaction, it should recognise an expense (or, where appropriate, an asset);

(ii)   the expense or asset should be recognised over the period in which the services are rendered or when the goods are received; and

(iii)   the goods or services received under a share-based payment transaction should be measured at fair value.

The standard identifies two main types of share-based payment:

(i)equity-settled share-based payments – where payment under the transaction is made in the form of equity instruments; and

(ii)cash-settled share-based payments – where payment is made in cash or other assets, but the amount paid is based on the value of an equity instrument of the reporting entity.

Recognition of share-based payments

11.40   When an entity receives or acquires goods or services in a share-based payment transaction, those goods or services should be recognised as they are received. In the case of a cash-settled share-based payment, the entity should recognise a liability. In the case of an equity-settled share-based payment, the entity should recognise a corresponding increase in equity. The goods or services should be recognised as expenses unless they qualify for recognition as assets.

Cash-settled share-based payment transactions

11.41   A cash-settled share-based payment transaction is one where:

(i)   the settlement amount is calculated by reference to the price of an equity instrument of the payee; and

(ii) settlement is made by means of a payment in cash or other assets rather then by the issue of equity instruments.

Goods and services received by means of a cash-settled share-based payment transaction should be measured at the fair value of the liability. Fair value should be remeasured at each reporting date, with any changes recognised in the profit and loss account, until the liability is settled.

Equity-settled share-based transactions

11.42   An equity-settled share-based payment transaction is one where:

(i) the settlement amount is calculated by reference to the price of an equity instrument of the payee; and

(ii) settlement is made by issuing equity instruments rather than by means of a payment in cash or other assets.

Most employee share option plans and all Inland Revenue approved SAYE plans are equity-settled share-based payment transactions. Where a reporting entity acquires goods or services through such a transaction, both the goods and services and the corresponding increase in equity should be measured directly at the fair value of the goods or services received at the date of receipt. If this cannot be estimated reliably, fair value should be measured indirectly by reference to the fair value of the equity instrument granted.

For transactions with parties other than employees, there is a rebuttable presumption that the fair value of the goods or services received is the more readily determinable fair value. Transactions with employees should be measured by reference to the fair value of the equity instrument granted, on the grounds that it is not usually possible to measure the services received for individual components of an employee's remuneration package, particularly where bonus or incentive arrangements are involved. If the equity instruments vest immediately and unconditionally, the entity should recognise the services received in full, with a corresponding increase in equity. If the instruments do not vest until a specified period of service has been completed, the services should be recognised as they are rendered during the vesting period, with a corresponding increase in equity. The standard includes additional guidance on:

(i) measuring the services received in each period;

(ii) establishing the fair value of the equity instruments granted; and

(iii) dealing with any modifications to the terms and conditions on which equity instruments were granted.

Share-based payment transactions with cash alternatives

11.43   Where either the reporting entity or the other party can choose whether the transaction is settled in cash or by the issue of equity instruments, the entity should account for the transaction (or any relevant components of the transaction) as a cash-settled share-based payment transaction if a liability has been incurred, and as an equity-settled share-based payment transaction if no such liability has been incurred. The draft standard sets out detailed guidance and accounting treatments in each case (ie depending on whether the option rests with the reporting entity or with the other party).

Accounts disclosures

11.44   The following minimum disclosures are required:

(i)   a description of each type of share-based payment arrangement that has existed during the reporting period, including the general terms and conditions of each arrangement, such as:

- vesting rights;
- the maximum term of options granted; and
- the method of settlement (ie cash or equity)

(the information may be aggregated unless separate disclosure is necessary to enable users to understand the nature and extent of the share-based payment arrangements that existed during the year);

(ii)   the number and weighted average exercise prices of options for options:

- outstanding at the beginning of the period;
- granted during the period;
- forfeited during the period;
- exercised during the period;
- outstanding at the end of the period; and
- exercisable at the end of the period;

(iii)   for options exercised during the period, the weighted average share price at the date of exercise (if options were exercised on a regular basis throughout the period, the weighted average share price during the period may be given instead);

(iv)   for options outstanding at the end of the period, the range of exercise prices and weighted average remaining expected life and contractual life (if the range of exercise prices is wide, the options should be divided into ranges that allow a meaningful assessment of the number and timing of future share issues and the cash that may be received on exercise of the options);

(v)   if the entity has measured the fair value of goods and services received by reference to the fair value of equity instruments granted:

- the weighted average fair value of options granted during the period and details of how fair value was measured (the standard specifies the information that should be included);

- the number and weighted average fair value of any shares or other equity instruments granted during the year, and information on how fair value was measured (the standard specifies the information that should be included);

- the weighted average fair value of any rights to cash, or rights to either cash or equity instruments, granted during the year (analysed into debt and equity components where appropriate) and details of how fair values were measured;

- where share-based payment arrangements have been modified during the period, an explanation of the modifications, the incremental fair value granted as a result and details on how this was measured;

- for options, shares and other equity instruments that vested during the period (or would have done so if vesting conditions had been satisfied), a comparison of the percentage or number of equity instruments that vested and the grant date estimate of the percentage or number expected to vest;

- for options exercised during the period, a comparison of actual option life and the grant date estimate of expected life;

(vi) where the fair value of goods and services received during the period has been measured directly, how that fair value was determined;

(vii) where appropriate, an explanation of why the presumption in 11.42 above has been rebutted;

(viii) the total expenses recognised for the period arising from share-based payment transactions;

(ix) for liabilities arising from share-based payment transactions:

- the total carrying amount at the end of the period; and

- the total intrinsic value at the end of the period for which the counterparty's right to cash or other assets had vested by the end of the period.

Additional information must be given where this is necessary to enable users to understand the extent and nature of share-based payment arrangements in the period, how fair values have been determined for share-based payment transactions, and the effect of such transactions on the profit and loss account.

Transitional provisions: Equity-settled transactions

11.45   In the case of equity-settled share-based payment transactions, the standard should be applied to grants of shares, share options or other equity instruments that were granted after 7 November 2002 and had not vested at the relevant effective date of the standard (ie 1 January 2005 for listed companies and 1 January 2006 for other entities).

Entities are encouraged to apply the standard to other grants of equity instruments if the fair value of the instruments as at the measurement date has been publicly disclosed. For all grants of equity instruments where the standard is applied, comparative figures should be restated and a prior period adjustment recognised. For grants of equity instruments where the standard has not been applied, the detailed disclosures referred to in 11.44 above should still be given, and any modifications to the terms and conditions of the grant made after the effective date of the standard should be accounted for in accordance with FRS 20.

Transitional provisions: Cash-settled transactions

11.46   For cash-settled transactions, the standard should be applied retrospectively and comparatives should be restated to reflect any liabilities existing at the effective date of the standard, except that no restatement is required in respect of of information relating to a period or date earlier than 7 November 2002. Entities are encouraged, but are not required, to apply the standard retrospectively to other liabilities arising from cash-settled share-based payment transactions (eg liabilities that were settled in a period for which comparative figures are presented in the accounts).

NATIONAL INSURANCE CONTRIBUTIONS ON SHARE OPTION GAINS

Charge to NI

11.47   A charge to national insurance (NI) has been introduced in respect of share options granted to directors and employees after 5 April 1999 under unapproved share option schemes (i.e. schemes that have not been approved by the Inland Revenue). The employer is required to pay NI contributions on any gains on the options made by directors and employees, calculated by reference to the exercise price paid and the market value of the shares at the date of the exercise.

When the liability arises

11.48   UITF Abstract 25 'National Insurance contributions on share option gains' notes that the granting of a share option is an event that gives rise to a present obligation on the employer to pay NI contributions when the option is subsequently exercised. The amount that will be payable is uncertain as it will depend on the share price at the date on which the option is exercised, but it is possible to make a reliable estimate of the liability at each intervening balance sheet date on the basis of the outstanding options that are expected to be exercised and the market price of the shares at that date. Where it is probable that a cash outflow will occur, a provision for the liability should therefore be made in accordance with the requirements of FRS 12 'Provisions, Contingent Liabilities and Contingent Assets'. The provision should be calculated using the latest enacted NI rate applied to the difference between the market value of the underlying shares at the balance sheet date and the option exercise price.

Impact of employee performance criteria

11.49   If the granting of the option is not linked to a performance period, full provision for the NI liability should be made at the time that the option is granted. The liability should then be adjusted at each balance sheet date to take account of any changes in the market value of the shares. A different approach is required if the granting of the option is linked to the performance of services by the employees over a specified period. For instance, the grant may be conditional on the employee meeting certain performance criteria over a specified period or remaining in the reporting entity's employment for an agreed period (or a combination of the two). The employee will therefore not become unconditionally entitled to the option until the performance period has been completed. Where the option is linked to a performance period, the Abstract requires the liability to be accrued systematically over the period from the date of the grant of the option to the end of the performance period. From that date to the date of actual exercise of the option, the calculations should be updated at each balance sheet date to reflect any changes in the market value of the shares and any other changes affecting the expected liability. For instance, assumptions on whether the full entitlement will in fact be exercised may change as a result of employees leaving before the end of the agreed service period or failing to meet some or all of the performance criteria. The charge in each period will therefore represent a combination of:

—   the charge for that year; and

—   adjustments to the opening accrual in respect of previous years in the performance period to reflect changes in the market price of the shares and any changes in the assumptions on the extent to which the options will be exercised.

Date of grant of the option

11.50   UITF Abstract 30 'Date of Award to Employees of Shares and Rights to Shares' clarifies what constitutes the date of the grant of the option. Where the grant is subject to shareholders' approval, the date of the award is the date on which that approval is given, and the provision for related NI should therefore be accrued from that date.

Worked example

11.51   The following example illustrates the accounting requirements of UITF Abstract 25 in the case of a performance-related option scheme.

Example 11.7 – Calculating and accruing the NI provision on share option gains in a performance-related scheme

A Ltd grants 20,000 share options to its employees on 1 July 2000 at an exercise price of £1 (equivalent to the market value at that date). The options are conditional on the employees meeting agreed performance criteria in the period from 1 July 2000 to 30 June 2002 and remaining in the company's employment for a further year until 30 June 2003. The options are exercisable from 1 July 2003 to 1 July 2004.

The current rate for employer's NI contributions is 12.2%.

The company's accounting date is 31 December.

Year to 31 December 2000

The market price of the shares at 31 December 2000 is £1.50.

The company estimates that the full amount of the options will be exercised.

Market value at 31 December 2000	£1.50
Exercise price	£1.00
Expected gain per share option	£0.50
Total expected gain: 20,000 x £0.50	£10,000
Employers NI: £10,000 x 12.2%	£1,220
Total performance period:	
1 July 2000–30 June 2003	36 months
Provision required at 31 December 2000:	
6/36 x £1,220	£203
Charge for the year	£203

Year to 31 December 2001

The market price of the shares at 31 December 2001 is £2.20.

The company still expects the full amount of the options to be exercised.

Market value at 31 December 2001	£2.20
Exercise price	£1.00
Expected gain per share option	£1.20
Total expected gain: 20,000 x £1.20	£24,000
Employers NI: £24,000 x 12.2%	£2,928
Total performance period:	
1 July 2000–30 June 2003	36 months
Provision required at 31 December 2001:	
18/36 x £2,928	£1,464
Charge for the year: £1,464–£203	£1,261

Year to 31 December 2002

The market price of the shares at 31 December 2002 is £2.70.

The company now expects only 18,000 of the options to be exercised.

Market value at 31 December 2002	£2.70
Exercise price	£1.00
Expected gain per share option	£1.70
Total expected gain: 18,000 x £1.70	£30,600
Employers NI: £30,600 x 12.2%	£3,733
Total performance period:	
1 July 2000–30 June 2003	36 months
Provision required at 31 December 2002:	
30/36 x £3,733	£3,111
Charge for the year: £3,111–£1,464	£1,647

Year to 31 December 2003

17,500 options vested during the year, but none were exercised.

The market price of the shares at 31 December 2003 was £3.00.

Market value at 31 December 2003	£3.00
Exercise price	£1.00
Expected gain per share option	£2.00
Total expected gain: 17,500 x £2.00	£35,000
Employers NI: £35,000 x 12.2%	£4,270
Charge for the year: £4,270–£3,111	£1,159

Year to 31 December 2004

All 17,500 options are exercised on 31 March 2004 when the market value of the shares was £3.20.

Market value at 31 March 2004	£3.20
Exercise price	£1.00
Gain per share option	£2.20
Total gain: 17,500 x £2.20	£38,500
Employers NI: £38,500 x 12.2%	£4,697
Charge for the year: £4,697–£4,270	£427

Recognition in the accounts

11.52   All amounts provided for NI on share option gains should be charged to the profit and loss account as part of staff costs, except where they form part of staff costs capitalised under companies' legislation and accounting standards (e.g. own labour used in the construction of tangible fixed assets).

Reimbursement by employee

11.53   Legislation before Parliament when the Abstract was issued (and which has since been enacted) permits some or all of the NI liability in respect of gains on share options to be transferred from the employer to the employee, where the employee agrees to this. Where there is a formal agreement between the employer and employee, under which the employee agrees to reimburse all or part of the NI, the expected reimbursement should be accounted for by the employer as a separate asset if it is virtually certain to be received. This is in line with the requirements of FRS 12 'Provisions, Contingent Liabilities and Contingent Assets' in respect of any reimbursement expected in relation to a provision. A net presentation is permitted in the profit and loss account.

Transfer of liability to employee

11.54   Where there is a joint election by the employer and the employee under which the NI liability is formally transferred to the employee, the Abstract notes that no provision will be necessary in the accounts of the employer. However, it will be important to determine that the liability has been genuinely transferred in full to the employee before such an accounting treatment can be adopted.

Disclosure

11.55   FRS 12 requires detailed disclosures for each class of provision recognised in the accounts, including an indication of the uncertainties over the timing or amount of the transfer of economic benefits and the main assumptions made concerning future events. UITF Abstract 25 notes that it may be necessary to disclose the share price used in calculating the NI provision, together with the effect of a significant movement in that price.

Other situations

11.56   The Abstract is drafted specifically in the context of NI contributions on share option gains, but the UITF has taken the opportunity to emphasise that the principles apply equally to other analogous situations that give rise to employer NI liabilities.

Chapter 12   Retirement Benefits

TYPES OF RETIREMENT SCHEME

What are retirement benefits?

12.1 Many employers include the provision of a pension, and possibly other retirement benefits, in the remuneration package that they offer to employees, and retirement benefits can often form a significant element of total staff costs for the year, hence the requirement for separate disclosure of pension costs under CA 1985 (see Chapter 11). FRS 17 'Retirement Benefits' defines retirement benefits as:

> 'All forms of consideration given by an employer in exchange for services rendered by employees that are payable after the completion of employment.'

The guidance in the standard emphasises that retirement benefits do not include termination benefits payable on termination of employment before the employee's normal retirement date or where an employee accepts voluntary redundancy in exchange for the benefits. This is on the basis that such benefits are not given in exchange for employee services. The objective of FRS 17 is to ensure that:

— financial statements reflect at fair value the assets and liabilities arising from an employer's retirement benefit obligations and any related funding;

— the operating costs of providing retirement benefits are recognised in the accounting period(s) in which the benefits are earned by the employees, and the related financing costs and other changes in the value of the assets and liabilities are recognised in the accounting periods in which they arise; and

— there is adequate disclosure of the cost of providing retirement benefits and the related assets, liabilities, gains and losses.

Employer commitments

12.2   FRS 17 covers all retirement benefits that an employer is committed to making, regardless of whether the commitment is statutory, contractual or implicit. Each of the following would therefore come within the scope of the standard:

—   a commitment to provide pension and other retirement benefits (e.g. medical care) set out in the employee's contract of employment;

—   a commitment arising from custom and practice over a period of time (i.e. where the employer has traditionally made retirement arrangements for employees, even though it has no contractual obligation to do so); or

—   a commitment arising when an employer makes *ex gratia* or discretionary payments on a case by case basis.

Commitments arising outside the UK are also covered.

Unfunded schemes

12.3   Where an employer operates an unfunded scheme (i.e. benefits are simply paid as they fall due and no payments are made to fund benefits earned during the period), FRS 17 still requires a liability to be recognised in the financial statements as the benefits are earned by the employees, rather than as the actual payments become due.

Defined contribution schemes

12.4   A defined contribution scheme is defined in FRS 17 as:

> 'A pension or other retirement benefit scheme into which an employer pays regular contributions fixed as an amount or as a percentage of pay and will have no legal or constructive obligation to pay further contributions if the scheme does not have sufficient assets to pay all employee benefits relating to employee service in the current and prior periods.'

The definition goes on to explain that the benefits of an individual member are determined by reference to the contributions paid into the scheme in respect of that member, usually increased by an amount based on the investment return on the contributions. Defined contribution schemes may also provide death-in-service benefits, but these are not deemed to relate to employee service in the current and prior reporting periods.

Defined benefit schemes

12.5   A defined benefit scheme is defined in FRS 17 as 'a pension or retirement benefit scheme other than a defined contribution scheme'. The definition goes on to explain that the scheme rules will usually define the benefits independently of the contributions payable, and the benefits will not usually be directly related to the scheme investments. A defined benefit scheme may be funded or unfunded.

Difficulties in accounting for defined benefit schemes

12.6   Under a defined benefit scheme, the benefits paid to an employee on retirement will usually be based in some way on the length of service provided and his/her salary during the period of employment. Benefits may be based on an average salary for the period, but are more commonly based on final salary or an average salary over (say) the last three years of employment. The benefits are therefore not specifically linked to the contributions paid into the scheme and the employer will usually have a commitment to ensure that there are sufficient funds in the scheme to pay the appropriate benefits, and may be required to make good any potential deficit in the funding of the scheme. In the case of a defined benefit scheme, therefore, the full extent of the employer's commitment is more difficult to quantify and to account for. Actuarial calculations must be carried out on a regular basis to establish the overall funding level of the scheme and to assess the level of contributions required to maintain adequate funding of the scheme. One of the particular problems is the very long-term nature of such schemes and the fact that a number of assumptions about future events will need to be made in order to carry out the calculations. Most of the detailed requirements of FRS 17 therefore deal with accounting for defined benefit retirement schemes.

ACCOUNTING FOR DEFINED CONTRIBUTION SCHEMES

Profit and loss account

12.7   FRS 17 notes that the cost of a defined contribution scheme is equal to the contributions payable to the scheme for the accounting period. Where an employer operates a defined contribution scheme, the charge to the profit and loss account each year will therefore represent the contributions payable by the employer in respect of that accounting period. This figure must be calculated on an accruals basis and the amount charged may therefore not be the same as the amount actually paid over to the scheme during the period. As the contributions payable represent the full extent of the employer's commitments under the scheme, this accounting treatment meets the objective of FRS 17. The standard specifies that the cost must be recognised in arriving at operating profit in the profit and loss account.

Disclosure

12.8   The accounts must include the following disclosures:

—   the nature of the scheme (i.e. the fact that it is a defined contribution scheme);

—   the cost for the period; and

— any outstanding or prepaid contributions at the balance sheet date.

These disclosure requirements might be met as follows:

Example 12.1 – FRS 17 disclosure requirement

The company operates a defined contribution pension scheme which is open to all employees. The assets of the pension scheme are held separately from those of the company in an independently administered fund. The amount payable to the pension scheme during the year in respect of the company's contributions amounted to £35,700 (20XX: £35,400). At the end of the year contributions of £2,540 (20XX: £2,150) had not been paid over to the scheme. These are included in creditors due within one year.

Any unpaid contributions at the end of the accounting period should be shown within creditors due within one year, and any prepaid contributions should be shown within debtors.

Accounting policy

12.9 It will usually also be appropriate to disclose the accounting policy adopted for a defined contribution scheme. Wording along the following lines might be suitable:

Example 12.2 – Accounting policy disclosure (defined contribution scheme)

Retirement benefits

The company operates a defined contribution pension scheme which is open to all employees. In accordance with FRS 17 'Retirement Benefits', the company's contributions to this scheme are charged in arriving at operating profit in the profit and loss account in the year to which they relate. No other retirement benefits are provided.

MULTI-EMPLOYER SCHEMES

Group retirement schemes

12.10 In some cases, more than one employer may participate in the same retirement scheme. This situation is relatively common in groups of companies, where a single retirement scheme is operated for the whole group and each subsidiary participates in the scheme in respect of its own employees.

Defined contribution schemes

12.11 If the scheme is a defined contribution scheme, the multi-employer aspect does not give rise to any particular accounting issues. Each employer's commitment is limited to the contributions that it is expected to make in respect of its own employees, and the cost in each reporting period will be the contributions due for that period.

Defined benefit schemes

12.12   Where more than one employer participates in a defined benefit scheme, the general requirement under FRS 17 is that each employer should account for the scheme as a defined benefit scheme. However, the standard recognises that this may not be appropriate or practical in every case and two specific exceptions to this general rule are therefore permitted:

—   where the employer's contributions are set in relation to the current service period only (i.e. they are not affected by any surplus or deficit in the scheme relating to the past service of its own employees or any other members of the scheme), the scheme should be accounted for as a defined contribution scheme – this treatment should only be adopted where there is clear evidence that the employer cannot be required to pay additional contributions relating to past service, including the existence of a third party which accepts the obligation to fund the pension payments if the scheme's assets should prove to be insufficient;

—   where the employer's contributions are affected by a surplus or deficit in the scheme but the employer is unable to identify its share of the underlying assets and liabilities in the scheme on a consistent and reasonable basis, the employer should account for the scheme as a defined contribution scheme but should disclose:

   —   the fact that the scheme is a defined benefit scheme but that the employer is unable to identify its share of the underlying assets and liabilities; and

   —   any available information on the surplus or deficit in the scheme and the implications for the employer.

In the case of a group scheme, the second exception only enables the individual subsidiaries (and, where appropriate, the parent company in its own individual accounts) to account for the scheme as a defined contribution scheme. However, the scheme must still be accounted for as a defined benefit scheme in the group accounts, as it does not constitute a multi-employer scheme at this level and the impracticality of identifying individual shares of the underlying assets and liabilities is no longer relevant.

ACCOUNTING FOR DEFINED BENEFIT SCHEMES

FRS 17 'Retirement benefits'

12.13   FRS 17 'Retirement Benefits' is fully effective for accounting periods beginning on or after 1 January 2005. The standard makes some very significant changes to the previous accounting practice on accounting for pension and similar costs, bringing UK requirements more into line with international developments, and the ASB therefore set a long implementation period, although early adoption has always been encouraged. If the new standard is not adopted for an accounting period beginning before 1 January 2005, the entity should:

(i)   follow the accounting requirements of SSAP 24 'Accounting for Pension Costs' in the profit and loss account and balance sheet;

(ii)   give the detailed disclosures required by SSAP 24 ; and

(iii) in addition, disclose in the notes to the accounts detailed information on the charges (or credits), assets and liabilities that would have been reflected in the accounts if FRS 17 had been applied.

The accounting requirements of FRS 17 must be adopted for accounting periods beginning on or after 1 January 2005. Gains and losses arising on the initial recognition of items in the primary statements under FRS 17 should be dealt with as prior period adjustments in accordance with FRS 3 'Reporting Financial Performance'.

Actuarial valuations

12.14   Actuarial valuations provide the actuary's best estimate of the cost to the employer of providing the promised retirement benefits to employees. In carrying out a valuation, a number of assumptions about future events will need to be made and the decisions taken here can have a very significant effect on the level of contributions required from the employer (and, where relevant, the employees). The main assumptions will cover issues such as:

—   future pay increases;

—   future rates of inflation;

—   increases in pension payments;

—   changes to the number of employees in the scheme;

—   the age profile of employees; and

—   expected earnings from scheme investments.

Once decisions have been reached on these factors, the actuary will assess how the scheme should be funded to ensure that adequate resources are available to meet the pension commitments as they fall due. The aim is to ensure that present and future contributions to the scheme will be sufficient to secure payment of the agreed benefits to former employees.

Valuation methods

12.15   Various actuarial methods can be used to determine the liabilities of a defined benefit scheme and thus the level of contributions needed to achieve and maintain adequate funding. The two principal categories of actuarial valuation methods are:

— accrued benefits methods – these are based on the principle that the obligation to provide retirement benefits to an employee will be greater as that employee gets closer to retirement; and

— prospective benefits methods – these are based on the principle that the obligation to provide retirement benefits to an employee accumulates evenly throughout the period of that individual's employment.

FRS 17 requires scheme liabilities to be measured using the projected unit method. This is an accrued benefits valuation method under which allowance is made for projected earnings. Further guidance on this method is given in Guidance Note 26 (GN26) issued by the Faculty and Institute of Actuaries.

Measurement of scheme assets

12.16   Under FRS 17, scheme assets should be measured at their fair value at the balance sheet date. Scheme assets include current assets as well as investments, and any liabilities (such as accrued expenses) should be deducted. The standard includes the following specific guidance on establishing fair value for each category of asset:

— for quoted securities, the mid-market value is to be taken as fair value;

— in the case of unquoted securities, an estimate of fair value should be used;

— for unitised securities, the average of the bid and offer prices should be taken;

— property should be valued at open market value or on another appropriate basis in accordance with the Appraisal and Valuation Manual published by the Royal Institution of Chartered Surveyors (RICS);

— insurance policies that exactly match the amount and timing of some or all of the benefits payable should be measured at the same amount as the related obligations;

— for other insurance policies, the entity should choose the valuation method that gives the best approximation to fair value, given the circumstances of the scheme.

The guidance also notes that notional funding of a pension scheme does not give rise to assets in a scheme for the purpose of the standard.

Measurement of scheme liabilities

12.17   Scheme liabilities are liabilities for outgoings due after the valuation date, reflecting the benefits that the employer is committed to providing for employee services provided up to that date. They should be measured on an actuarial basis using the projected unit method. Scheme liabilities comprise:

— benefits promised under the formal terms of the scheme; and

—   any constructive obligations for further benefits where a public statement or
     past practice by the employer has created a valid expectation in the employees
     that these benefits will be granted.

Benefits should be attributed to periods of service according to the scheme's benefit
formula, except where this attributes a disproportionate share of the benefits to
later years of service. In this case, the benefit should be attributed on a straight line
basis over the period during which it is earned. Where the scheme rules require a
surplus in the scheme to be shared between the employer and the scheme members,
or where past practice has established a valid expectation that this will be done, the
amount that will be passed to the members should be treated as increasing the
scheme liabilities.

Actuarial assumptions

12.18   Actuarial assumptions underlying the valuation of scheme liabilities should
be mutually compatible (i.e. they must reflect the underlying economic factors on a
consistent basis), and they should lead to the best estimate of the future cash flows
that will arise. The directors (or equivalent) have ultimate responsibility for the
assumptions, but they should be set on advice given by an actuary. Any assumptions
that are affected by economic conditions should reflect market expectations at the
balance sheet date. The assumptions should also reflect expected future events that
will affect the cost of the benefits to which the employer is committed (either legally
or constructively) at the balance sheet date. Depending on the nature of the scheme
these will usually include:

—   expected cost of living increases – these may be provided for in the scheme
     rules or may have been established by the past practice of the employer, so
     that employees have developed a valid expectation of receiving them;

—   salary increases (where the pension is to be based on final salary);

—   expected early retirement (where the scheme gives this right to employees);

—   expected future changes in the cost of retirement health care – the guidance
     notes that these costs are particularly difficult to estimate and suggests a
     number of factors that may need to be taken into account, including:

     —   advances in medical skills and technologies, which may result in higher
          treatment costs;

     —   a rise in the expectations of prospective patients; and

     —   in the light of the above, the possibility of employers and other benefit
          providers reducing benefits and making the patient pay a proportion of
          the costs.

Expected future redundancies should not be reflected in the assumptions as the
employer is not committed to making them. When the employer does become
committed to making redundancies, the impact on the scheme should be treated as a

settlement or curtailment. Also, it should not be assumed that benefits will be reduced below those currently promised (e.g. on the grounds that the employer will curtail the scheme at some point in the future).

Discounting of scheme liabilities

12.19 Scheme liabilities should be discounted at a rate reflecting the time value of money and the characteristics of the liability. This should be assumed to be the current rate of return on a high quality (AA) corporate bond of equivalent currency and term to the scheme liabilities. The guidance notes that, if no suitable corporate bond can be identified, the rate of return on appropriate government bonds, together with a margin for assumed credit risk spreads (from the global bond markets), may provide an acceptable alternative.

Frequency of valuations

12.20 Full actuarial valuations by a professionally qualified actuary should be obtained for a defined benefit scheme at intervals not exceeding three years. The actuary should review the valuation at each balance sheet date and update it to reflect current conditions – for instance, the fair values of scheme assets and financial assumptions such as the discount rate may need to be adjusted each year.

Balance sheet recognition of surplus or deficit

12.21 The surplus or deficit in a defined benefit scheme is the excess or shortfall of the value of the scheme assets over or below the present value of the scheme liabilities. The employer should recognise a liability to the extent that it reflects a legal or constructive obligation to make good the deficit. The employer should recognise an asset to the extent that it is able to recover this through reduced contributions or through refunds from the scheme.

Determination of employer's liability

12.22 A legal obligation to make good a deficit in the scheme may arise under the terms of the trust deed. A constructive obligation may arise if the employer has in the past acted to make good such deficits. Where the employees also contribute to the scheme, any deficit should be assumed to be borne by the employer unless the scheme rules specifically require employee contributions to be increased to help fund the deficit. In these circumstances, the present value of the additional employee contributions should be treated as reducing the deficit to be borne by the employer.

Determination of employer's asset

12.23   A scheme surplus will give rise to an asset for the employer to the extent that:

— the employer has control over its use – for instance, the employer can use the surplus to generate future economic benefits, in the form of reduced contributions or a refund from the scheme; and

— that control arises as a result of past events.

Under most schemes, an employer's obligation will be to pay contributions at the level recommended by the actuary to keep the scheme fully funded. There will not usually be any requirement to generate a surplus in the scheme. Where a surplus does arise, it is therefore unlikely that the employer could be required to continue to make contributions to maintain the surplus. Also, the decision on whether the surplus should be used to improve scheme benefits will usually rest with the employer. In most cases, therefore, control over the use of a surplus will rest with the employer.

Asset resulting from reduced contributions

12.24   When determining an asset to be recognised in the balance sheet, the amount that can be recovered through reduced future contributions is the present value of the liability expected to arise from future service by current and future scheme members, less the present value of future employee contributions. No growth in the number of active scheme members should be assumed, but a decline in membership should be reflected if appropriate. The amount that can be recovered should be based on the assumptions used under the accounting standard, rather than on funding assumptions, and the present value of the reduction in future contributions should be determined using the discount rate applied to measure the defined benefit liability.

Refunds from the scheme

12.25   The amount to be recovered from refunds should reflect only refunds agreed by the pension scheme trustees at the balance sheet date.

Improvement in benefits

12.26   Where some or all of the surplus is used to improve members' benefits under the scheme, this should be accounted for as a past service cost at the time that it occurs. It should not be anticipated by reducing the amount recognised as an asset in the balance sheet of the employer.

Balance sheet presentation

12.27 Any unpaid pension contributions at the balance sheet date should be shown within creditors due within one year. The defined benefit asset or liability, net of any related deferred tax balance, should be shown separately on the face of the balance sheet as follows:

— in a balance sheet prepared under Format 1, Companies Act 1985 Sch 4, after item J (Accruals and deferred income) but before item K (Capital and reserves);

— in a balance sheet prepared under Format 2, Companies Act 1985 Sch 4, an asset should be shown after item D (Prepayments and accrued income) in the 'Assets' section and a liability should be shown after item D (Accruals and deferred income) in the 'Liabilities' section.

Appendix I to FRS 17 suggests the following layout for this disclosure:

Example 12.3 – Balance sheet disclosure of pension asset

	20X2	20X1
	£	£
Net assets excluding pension asset	70,400	65,200
Pension asset	3,500	1,450
Net assets including pension asset	73,900	66,650

Where an employer has more than one scheme, the total of any defined benefit assets and the total of any defined benefit liabilities should be shown separately on the face of the balance sheet.

Deferred tax

12.28 The deferred tax relating to the defined benefit asset or liability should be offset against the defined benefit asset or liability and not included with other deferred tax assets or liabilities.

Recognition in performance statements

12.29 The change in the net defined benefit asset or liability (other than changes arising from contributions to the scheme) should be analysed into:

— periodic costs:

  — current service cost;

  — interest cost;

  — expected return on assets;

  — actuarial gains or losses;

— non-periodic costs:

—   past service costs; and

—   gains and losses on settlements and curtailments.

Current service cost

12.30   Current service cost is the increase in the present value of the scheme liabilities expected to arise from employee service in the current period. The current service cost should be based on the most recent actuarial valuation at the beginning of the period, with the financial assumptions updated to reflect conditions at that date. It should be included within operating profit in the profit and loss account, except to the extent that employee remuneration is capitalised in accordance with another accounting standard. Any contributions from employees should be set against the current service cost.

Interest cost

12.31   Interest cost is the expected increase during the period in the present value of scheme liabilities because the benefits are one period closer to settlement. The interest cost should be based on the discount rate and the present value of the scheme liabilities at the beginning of the period. In addition, it should reflect changes in the scheme liabilities during the period. The net of the interest cost and the expected return on assets should be included as other finance costs (or income) adjacent to interest.

Expected return on assets

12.32   The expected rate of return on assets is the average rate of return (both income and changes in fair value), net of scheme expenses, expected over the remaining life of the related obligation on the actual assets held by the scheme. The expected return on assets should be based on long-term expectations at the beginning of the period and is expected to be reasonably stable. For quoted corporate or government bonds, the expected return should be calculated by applying the current redemption yield at the beginning of the period to the market value of the bonds at that date. For other assets, such as equities, the expected return should be calculated by applying the expected long-term rate of return at the beginning of the period to the fair value of the assets held by the scheme at that date. The expected return on assets should also reflect changes in the assets during the period as a result of contributions paid into and benefits paid out of the scheme. The expected rate of return should be set by the directors (or equivalent), based on advice given by an actuary. The net of the expected return on assets and the interest cost should be included as other finance costs (or income) adjacent to interest.

Actuarial gains and losses

12.33   These are changes in actuarial deficits or surpluses that arise because events have not coincided with the actuarial assumptions made at the time of the last valuation (i.e. experience gains and losses), or because the actuarial assumptions have changed. They may arise in relation to both scheme assets and scheme liabilities and comprise:

—   differences between the expected and actual returns on scheme assets;

—   differences between the actuarial assumptions underlying scheme liabilities and actual experience during the period;

—   the effect of changes in the actuarial assumptions underlying the scheme liabilities; and

—   any adjustments resulting from the limit on the recognition of a defined benefit asset in the employer's balance sheet.

Actuarial gains and losses arising from a new valuation or from an update of the latest valuation should be recognised in the statement of total recognised gains and losses for the period. Once recognised in this way, the gains and losses should not be recognised again in the profit and loss account in subsequent accounting periods.

Past service costs

12.34   Past service costs are the increase in the present value of the scheme liabilities related to employee service in prior periods arising in the current period as a result of the introduction of new or improved retired benefits. They arise when an employer makes a commitment to provide a higher level of benefit than previously promised (e.g. a new pension benefit for a spouse). This includes improvements made as a result of the scheme being in surplus – this still represents a cost to the employer, because using the surplus to improve benefits means that the employer cannot benefit from it in other ways. However, past service costs do not include increases in the expected costs of benefits that the employer is already committed to provide (e.g. cost of living increases) – these are covered by the actuarial assumptions and differences between the assumptions and actual experience, and the effect of any changes in the assumptions, are actuarial gains and losses and should be accounted for as such. Past service costs should be recognised in the profit and loss account on a straight-line basis over the period in which the increases in benefit vest. Where benefits vest immediately, the past service cost should be recognised immediately. Any unrecognised past service costs should be deducted from the scheme liabilities, and the balance sheet asset or liability should be adjusted accordingly.

Settlements and curtailments

12.35   A settlement is an irrevocable action that relieves the employer (or the defined benefit scheme) of the primary responsibility for a pension obligation and eliminates significant risks relating to the obligation and the assets used to effect the settlement. Settlements include:

—   a lump-sum cash payment to scheme members in exchange for their rights to receive specified pension benefits;

—   the purchase of an irrevocable annuity contract sufficient to cover vested benefits; and

—   the transfer of scheme assets and liabilities relating to a group of employees leaving the scheme.

A curtailment is an event that reduces the expected years of future service of present employees or reduces for a number of employees the accrual of defined benefits for some or all of their future service. Curtailments include:

—   early termination of employees' services (e.g. through closure of a factory or discontinuation of a business segment); and

—   termination of, or amendment to, the terms of a defined benefit scheme so that some or all future service by current employees will no longer qualify for benefits or will only qualify for reduced benefits.

Where the scheme rules permit employees to retire early or transfer out of the scheme, the related settlements and curtailments will be reflected in the actuarial assumptions – any gains or losses are actuarial gains and losses and should be accounted for as such. However, gains and losses may also arise on a settlement or curtailment that has not been allowed for in the actuarial assumptions – for instance, a reduction in the number of employees as a result of the sale or termination of an operation, or a decision to transfer the accrued benefits of some members into a defined contribution scheme. Losses should be measured at the date on which the employer becomes demonstrably committed to the transaction and should be recognised in the profit and loss account covering that date. Gains should be measured at the date on which all parties whose consent is required are irrevocably committed to the transaction and should be recognised in the profit and loss account in the period covering that date. These gains and losses should be recognised within operating profit unless they relate to an item that is required to be shown separately after operating profit.

Impact of limit on balance sheet asset

12.36   The limit on the amount that can be recognised as a defined benefit asset may result in some part of a defined benefit scheme surplus not being recognised in the balance sheet. In this case, the amounts recognised in the profit and loss account and statement of total recognised gains and losses should be adjusted as follows:

—   if any refund is agreed and is covered by the unrecognised surplus, it should be recognised as other finance income adjacent to interest, with separate disclosure in the notes – refunds from schemes where the whole of the surplus is already regarded as recoverable do not give rise to gains, as the cash received (together with any related tax effect) simply reduces the asset shown in the employer's balance sheet;

—   next, the unrecognised surplus should be applied to extinguish past service costs or losses on settlements or curtailments that would otherwise be charged in the profit and loss account for the period, and the notes to the accounts should disclose the items and amounts extinguished;

—   next, the expected return on assets should be restricted so that it does not exceed the total of the current service cost, interest cost (and any past service costs and losses on settlements and curtailments not covered by the unrecognised surplus) and any increase in the recoverable surplus;

—   any further adjustment necessary should be treated as an actuarial gain or loss.

An increase in the recoverable amount of a surplus as a result of an increase in the active membership of the scheme (for instance, due to increased recruitment or the acquisition of another business) should be recognised as an operating gain. In the case of an acquisition, the gain should be accounted for as a post-acquisition operating gain and not as an adjustment to the purchase consideration and related goodwill. A decrease in the recoverable amount of a surplus arising from a fall in the active membership of the scheme should be treated as an actuarial loss unless it arises from an event not covered by the assumptions underlying the amount originally regarded as recoverable (e.g. a settlement or curtailment). In this case, it should be treated as part of the loss arising on that event.

Tax

12.37   Where current tax relief arises on contributions made to the scheme, it should be allocated to the profit and loss account or statement of total recognised gains and losses on the basis that the contribution covers firstly items reported in the profit and loss account and then any actuarial losses recognised in the statement of total recognised gains and losses, unless it is clear that another method of allocation is more appropriate (e.g. tax relief on a special contribution to fund a deficit arising from an actuarial loss should be allocated to the statement of total recognised gains and losses as this is where the actuarial loss itself is recognised). To the extent that the contribution exceeds these items, the current tax relief attributable to the excess should be allocated to the profit and loss account, unless it is clearly more appropriate to allocate it to the statement of recognised gains and losses. FRS 16 'Current Tax' requires disclosure of any current tax recognised in the profit and loss account and statement of total recognised gains and losses.

Death-in-service and incapacity benefits

12.38 A charge should be made to operating profit to reflect the expected cost of providing any death-in-service or incapacity benefits for the period. Any difference between that expected cost and the amounts actually incurred should be treated as an actuarial gain or loss. Where the costs of death-in service or incapacity benefits are insured by the scheme, the expected cost for the accounting period will be the insurance premium payable for that period. If the costs are not insured, the expected cost should take into account the probability of employee deaths or incapacity during service and the benefits that would be payable in these circumstances. UITF Abstract 35 'Death-in-service and incapacity benefits' now clarifies that uninsured benefits should be measured using the projected unit method of valuation in the same way as other scheme liabilities.

Disclosure

12.39 The following disclosures should be given for a defined benefit scheme:

— nature of the scheme;

— date of the most recent full actuarial valuation on which amounts in the financial statements are based;

— if the actuary is an employee or officer of the reporting entity, this fact must be disclosed;

— contributions made in respect of the accounting period and any agreed contribution rates for future years;

— for closed schemes and those in which the age profile of the active membership is rising significantly, the fact that under the projected unit method the current service cost will increase as the members of the scheme approach retirement;

— each of the main financial assumptions used at the beginning of the period and at the balance sheet date, including:

    — inflation assumption;

    — rate of increase in salaries;

    — rate of increase for pensions in payment and deferred pensions; and

    — rate used to discount scheme liabilities.

These details should be disclosed as separate figures and should not be combined or netted;

— the fair value of the assets held by the scheme at the beginning and end of the period, analysed into the following classes, together with the expected rate of return assumed for each class for the period and the subsequent period:

    — equities;

    — bonds;

— other (sub analysed if material);

— the following amounts included within operating profit (or capitalised as part of employee remuneration where relevant) should be disclosed in the notes to the financial statements:

    — current service cost;

    — any past service costs;

    — any previously unrecognised surplus deducted from past service costs;

    — gains and losses on any settlements and curtailments; and

    — any previously unrecognised surplus deducted from settlement or curtailment losses;

— any gains and losses on settlements and curtailments (and any previously unrecognised surplus deducted from the losses) included within a separate item after operating profit;

— the following amounts included as other finance costs (or income) should be disclosed separately in the notes to the financial statements:

    — interest cost; and

    — expected return on assets in the scheme;

— the following amounts included within the statement of total recognised gains and losses should be disclosed separately in the notes to the financial statements:

    — difference between the expected and actual return on assets;

    — experience gains and losses arising on scheme liabilities;

    — effects of changes in the demographic and financial assumptions underlying the present value of scheme liabilities.

Reconciliation to the balance sheet

12.40 Where an entity operates a defined benefit scheme, the following amounts should be disclosed in a note to the balance sheet:

— fair value of scheme assets;

— present value of scheme liabilities (based on the accounting assumptions);

— the resulting surplus or deficit; and

— an analysis of the movement in the surplus or deficit during the period.

Where the defined benefit asset or liability in the balance sheet differs from the scheme surplus or deficit shown in the note, an explanation of the difference should be given. Differences will usually arise because of the need to account for deferred tax on the asset or liability, or the need to restrict the amount recognised as an asset.

Five-year summary

12.41 In addition, where an entity operates a defined benefit scheme, the financial statements must include a five-year summary of the following:

— the difference between expected and actual returns on assets, expressed as (a) an amount and (b) a percentage of the scheme assets at the balance sheet date;

— experience gains and losses arising on scheme liabilities expressed as (a) an amount and (b) a percentage of the present value of scheme liabilities at the balance sheet date; and

— the total actuarial gain or loss expressed as (a) an amount and (b) a percentage of the present value of the scheme liabilities at the balance sheet date.

This disclosure is to highlight trends, which will generally be more relevant than gains or losses in one period. For instance, a consistent trend of experience losses may indicate that actuarial assumptions have been over-optimistic and could cast doubt on the reliability of amounts included in the profit and loss account. However, the standard does not require retrospective creation of five-year summaries of amounts recognised in the statement of total recognised gains and losses.

Analysis of reserves

12.42 Where an entity operates a defined benefit scheme, the analysis of reserves in the notes to the financial statements should distinguish the amount relating to the defined benefit asset or liability, net of related deferred tax. Appendix I to FRS 17 suggests the following layout:

Example 12.4 – Analysis of reserves note

	20X2 £	20X1 £
Profit and loss reserve, excluding pension asset	20,500	19,250
Pension reserve	3,500	1,450
Profit and loss reserve	24,000	20,700

Entities with more than one defined benefit scheme

12.43 Where an employer has more than one defined benefit scheme, the required disclosures may be given in total, separately or in such groupings as are felt to be most useful (e.g. by geographical location, or where schemes are subject to significantly different risks). Where the disclosures are given in total, the assumptions should be given in the form of weighted averages or relatively narrow ranges, with separate disclosure of any items outside the range.

Accounting policy

12.44 It will usually also be appropriate to disclose the accounting policy adopted for a defined benefit scheme. Wording along the following lines might be suitable:

Example 12.5 – Accounting policy disclosure (defined benefit scheme)

Retirement benefits

The company operates a defined benefit pension scheme which is open to all employees. The assets of the scheme are held separately from those of the company in an independently administered fund, and pensions payable under the scheme are based on final pensionable salary. In accordance with FRS 17 'Retirement Benefits', the operating costs of providing these benefits are recognised in the profit and loss account in the accounting period in which the benefits are earned by the employees, and related financing and other costs are recognised in the period in which they arise. No other retirement benefits are provided.

Chapter 13   Depreciation

NATURE AND METHODS OF DEPRECIATION

Definition of depreciation

13.1 Depreciation is defined in FRS 15 as 'the measure of the cost or revalued amount of the economic benefits of the tangible fixed asset that have been consumed during the period. Consumption includes the wearing out, using up or other reduction in the useful economic life of a tangible fixed asset whether arising from use, effluxion of time or obsolescence through either changes in technology or demand for the goods and services produced by the asset.' Depreciation reflects the fact that most fixed assets have a finite useful economic life within the organisation that has acquired them. Fixed assets are defined in CA 1985 as assets intended for use on a continuing basis in the company's activities. FRS 15 defines tangible fixed assets as 'assets that have physical substance and are held for use in the production or supply of goods or services, for rental to others, or for administrative purposes on a continuing basis in the reporting entities' activities'. FRS 10 'Goodwill and Intangible Assets' sets out detailed requirements on the amortisation of intangible assets and goodwill, determining useful economic lives for these assets and the need to carry out impairment reviews. These requirements and their practical application are considered in more detail in Chapter 19.

Fair allocation of cost

13.2 Where an asset is purchased for continuing use in the business over a number of years, it would be inappropriate to charge the full amount of the expenditure on the asset to the profit and loss account in the year of purchase. There should instead be a charge against income for the use of the asset during its useful life and this is done by means of the annual depreciation charge. Depreciation is therefore intended to provide a fair allocation of the cost of the asset to each accounting period during which the company benefits from the use of the asset. FRS 15 emphasises that a charge to operating profit should continue to be made, even if the asset has risen in value or has been revalued. The depreciation charge for each period should be recognised in the profit and loss account unless it is permitted to be included in the carrying amount of another asset.

Key factors

13.3   The assessment of the total amount to be charged over the life of the asset and the allocation of that charge to individual years involves consideration of the following key factors:

—   the amount at which the asset is recorded in the accounting records – this will be its original cost, or its value if it has been revalued;

—   the expected useful economic life of the asset within the organisation;

—   the estimated residual value of the asset once it has reached the end of its useful economic life within the business.

Purchase price or production cost

13.4   CA 1985 sets out specific rules for determining the purchase price or production cost of both fixed and current assets (see Chapter 1). Where fixed assets are shown in the accounts at historical cost, the purchase price or production cost will form the basis for the annual depreciation charge in respect of those assets.

Residual value

13.5   Under both CA 1985 and FRS 15, the depreciable amount of an asset is its cost (or revalued amount) less its estimated residual value. This recognises the fact that some assets will still have a value, even though they no longer have a useful life in the company.

Example 13.1 – Calculating the depreciable amount

A Ltd purchases a new car at a cost of £11,350. It intends to keep the car for use in the business for four years, after which a replacement will be purchased. When the replacement is purchased, A Ltd estimates that it will be able to part-exchange the existing car for £2,500.

	£
Purchase price	11,350
Estimated residual value	(2,500)
Depreciable amount	8,850

The depreciable amount of £8,850 should be charged to the profit and loss account on a systematic basis over four years.

The Act provides no guidance on establishing the residual value of an asset, but residual value is defined in FRS 15 as:

> 'the net realisable value of an asset at the end of its useful economic life. Residual values are based on prices prevailing at the date of acquisition (or revaluation) of the asset and do not take account of expected future price changes'.

One of the difficulties in estimating residual value, therefore, is that the assessment must be based on present prices and the potential effect of inflation over the expected life of the asset must be ignored.

Regular review of residual value

13.6   FRS 15 requires residual values to be reviewed at the end of each reporting period and revised where necessary. As far as is practicable, the revised residual value should be stated in terms of the price level that existed when the asset was acquired (or revalued). If this is not possible, the residual value should only be revised to current values where the current residual value is lower than the original estimate of residual value. In other words, residual value should not be increased in these circumstances. The standard also emphasises that events or changes in circumstances that cause residual value to fall may also be indicators that the asset has become impaired, in which case it should be reviewed for impairment in accordance with FRS 11 'Impairment of Fixed Assets and Goodwill'.

Impact of revision of residual value

13.7   Where it is necessary to revise residual values, the change should be accounted for prospectively over the remaining useful economic life of the asset. No adjustment should be made to the depreciation charged in previous years. If the asset is impaired, the impairment will need to be accounted for in accordance with FRS 11. The report published by the Financial Reporting Review Panel in September 2001, following its review of the accounts of Groupe Chez Gerard plc for the period ended 25 June 2000, emphasised that revisions to residual values may result in the depreciation of assets that were previously not depreciated on the grounds of immateriality. In these circumstances, the commencement of depreciation does not represent a change in accounting policy and the carrying amounts of the assets should be depreciated prospectively over their remaining useful economic lives, as in any other case where residual values are revised.

Useful economic life

13.8   CA 1985 also fails to provide any guidance on assessing the useful economic life of an asset. FRS 15 defines the useful economic life of an asset as 'the period over which the entity expects to derive economic benefit from that asset'. The key factor, therefore, is the length of time for which the company expects to use the asset. This will not necessarily be the same as the asset's expected total useful life, although in some cases it may be. For instance, many companies choose to replace motor vehicles on a fairly regular basis (e.g. every three or four years) on the grounds that repair costs may become excessive and the vehicle may not run efficiently if it is retained for a longer period. However, the company will usually be able to sell a three- or four-year old car and it will continue to be used by the new owner (i.e. the car will not have reached the end of its entire useful life when it is sold by the company). For depreciation purposes, the expected useful economic life of the car from the company's point of view will be three or four years (i.e. the period for which it expects to use the car). In the case of items of plant and equipment and furniture and fittings, the company is more likely to retain the asset for the whole of its useful life, or at least a substantial proportion of it. The expected residual value of these assets will usually be much lower. In some cases, the only amount to be recognised, if any, might be the underlying scrap value.

Other factors to take into account

13.9   FRS 15 emphasises that, although the economic benefits embodied in a tangible fixed asset are consumed mainly through use of the asset, other factors may also diminish the benefits that would otherwise have been available. The assessment of the useful economic life and residual value of an asset should therefore also take into account:

— the expected usage of the asset, assessed by reference to expected capacity or physical output;

— the expected physical deterioration of the asset through use or the effluxion of time – this may depend on the repair and maintenance programme for the asset;

— economic or technological obsolescence (e.g. resulting from changes or improvements in production, or changes in market demand for a product or service); and

— legal or similar restrictions on the use of the asset (e.g. the expiry date of a related lease).

These issues may also affect the choice of depreciation method.

Review of asset lives

13.10   FRS 15 requires the useful economic lives of assets to be reviewed at the end of each reporting period. Where necessary, as a result of this review, asset lives should be revised. This should help to ensure that companies do not carry significant amounts of fully depreciated assets in their accounts. The FRRP report on the accounts of Groupe Chez Gerard plc (referred to in 13.7 above) also emphasised that revisions to useful economic lives may result in the depreciation of assets that were previously not depreciated on the grounds of immateriality. Where asset lives need to be revised, the remaining net book values of the relevant assets should be written off over their revised remaining useful economic lives. Changes to asset lives are most likely to be due to changes in circumstances (e.g. technological changes, changes to product lines, changes in the general economic climate) or to the fact that, with the benefit of experience and hindsight, more informed decisions can be made about the expected lives of individual assets. In the case of revalued assets, and in particular those valued at depreciated replacement cost, a reassessment of useful economic life may indicate that a further revaluation of the asset is necessary.

Disclosure of revision of asset lives

13.11   Asset lives (or depreciation rates) are required to be disclosed under FRS 15. Any change to those lives should therefore be disclosed in the accounts in the year of the change. The financial effect of the change in asset lives should also be shown if it is material. However, this situation should arise only rarely if asset lives are reviewed regularly. It is important to recognise that a change in asset lives does not constitute a change in accounting policy. The underlying accounting policy is to depreciate fixed assets over their expected useful economic lives and this has not changed in any way. The assessment of asset lives will always be a matter of judgement and it is right that this assessment should be refined in the light of actual experience to allow the accounting policy to be properly implemented.

Assets purchased under finance lease or hire purchase contract

13.12   In the accounts of a lessee, SSAP 21 'Accounting for Leases and Hire Purchase Contracts' requires an asset purchased under a finance lease to be depreciated over the shorter of the lease term and the useful economic life of the asset. The lease term is defined as the period for which the lessee has contracted to lease the asset and any further term for which he has the option to continue to lease the asset, where it is reasonably certain at the start of the lease that the option will be exercised. An asset purchased under a hire purchase contract should be depreciated over its useful economic life.

Impairment reviews

13.13   FRS 15 requires a tangible fixed asset, other than non-depreciable land, to be reviewed for impairment at the end of any reporting period where its estimated remaining useful economic life is more than 50 years.

Methods of depreciating assets

13.14   Both CA 1985 and FRS 15 require the depreciable amount of an asset to be written off in a fair and systematic way over its useful economic life. There are various ways of achieving a fair and systematic charge for depreciation and a company is free to choose whichever method is considered most appropriate. FRS 15 emphasises that the method chosen should result in a depreciation charge throughout the asset's useful economic life and not just towards the end of that life or when the asset is falling in value. The Financial Reporting Review Panel report following its review of the accounts of Wyevale Garden Centres plc for the year ended 31 December 2000 also emphasised the need for depreciation to be charged from the date of acquisition of the asset rather than from another date (e.g. the start of the next full accounting period). The most common depreciation methods are:

—   straight-line;

—   reducing balance.

Others are possible (e.g. sum of the digits) but these are used so rarely in practice that they are not covered here.

Straight-line method

13.15   This is probably the easiest and most straightforward method of calculating depreciation and is consequently in common use. It assumes that equal amounts of the asset's economic benefits are consumed in each year of its life and results in a consistent charge for depreciation throughout the life of the individual asset.

Example 13.2 – Using the straight-line method

Using the details of the car in Example 13.1.

	£
Purchase price	11,350
Estimated residual value	2,500
Depreciable amount	8,850

The car has an expected useful life in the company of four years and the annual depreciation charge will therefore be the depreciable amount (£8,850) divided by four, giving an annual depreciation charge of £2,212.50.

FRS 15 notes that, when the pattern of the consumption of economic benefits is unclear, the straight-line method of depreciation should usually be adopted. The only potential disadvantage to the straight-line method of depreciation is that the profit and loss account receives the same annual charge when the asset is a few years old as when it was new. In some cases, this may not properly reflect the benefit to the company of using the asset, but in most instances the effect of any such distortion will not be significant.

Reducing balance method

13.16   The alternative method of calculating depreciation, also in common use, is the reducing balance method. This is slightly more complicated and may involve keeping more detailed records to enable the calculations to be carried out. The depreciation charge is based on a constant percentage of the asset's carrying value. Under this method, therefore, the depreciation charge is higher in the early years than towards the end of the asset's life. In some cases, this may give a better reflection of the consumption of benefits. For instance, an asset may provide greater benefits when it is new than when it is older and possibly more prone to breakdown, or less capable of providing a high quality output.

Example 13.3 – Using the reducing balance method

Using the details from Example 13.1.

	£
Purchase price	11,350
Estimated residual value	2,500
Depreciable amount	8,850

Using a depreciation rate of 50% the depreciation in years one to four will be calculated as follows.

Year 1	Depreciable amount	8,850.00
	Depreciation at 50%	4,425.00
Year 2	Carrying value	4,425.00
	Depreciation at 50%	2,212.50
Year 3	Carrying value	2,212.50
	Depreciation at 50%	1,106.25
Year 4	Carrying value	1,106.25
	Depreciation at 50%	553.13
		553.12

The potential disadvantages to the reducing balance method of depreciation are:

—   the depreciable amount is never fully written off;

—   the depreciation charge in the early years is very high;

—   it is more complicated to calculate an appropriate rate to ensure the asset is written down, as far as possible, to its residual value by the end of its useful economic life.

Comparison of straight-line and reducing balance methods

13.17   Examples 13.2 and 13.3 illustrate that the annual depreciation charge and carrying values of the asset are very different over the four years, depending on which depreciation method is used.

Example 13.4 – Comparing the methods

	Straight line £	Reducing balance £
Annual depreciation charge:		
Year 1	2,212.50	4,425.00
Year 2	2,212.50	2,212.50
Year 3	2,212.50	1,106.25
Year 4	2,212.50	553.13
Carrying value of asset:	£	£
Year 1	6,637.50	4,425.00
Year 2	4,425.00	2,212.50
Year 3	2,212.50	1,106.25
Year 4	0.00	553.12

This highlights the importance of disclosing the depreciation method used.

Change in method of depreciating assets

13.18   A change in the method of providing depreciation is only permitted under FRS 15 where the new method is considered to give a fairer presentation of the company's results and financial position. Where the method is changed, the net book value of the assets should be written off under the new method over their remaining useful economic lives. The following disclosures should be given in the accounts:

—   a statement that the method of calculating depreciation has been changed;

—   an explanation of why the new method is considered to give a fairer presentation of the company's results and financial position;

—   the financial effect of the change on the depreciation charge for the year, if the effect is material.

However, a change in the method of calculating depreciation does not constitute a change in accounting policy.

Assets with two or more major components

13.19   Where a tangible fixed asset has two or more major components with substantially different useful economic lives, FRS 15 requires each component to be treated separately for depreciation purposes. Each component should therefore be depreciated over its individual useful economic life. The standard gives as examples land and buildings, which comprise separable components for accounting purposes (even though they may be purchased together), and the structure of a building and the items within the structure, such as general fittings. The standard notes, however, that it is not appropriate to treat the trading potential associated with a property such as a hotel or public house as a separate component of the asset, if the value and life of the trading potential is inherently inseparable from that of the property.

RENEWALS ACCOUNTING

Conditions

13.20   FRS 15 permits renewals accounting to be used to estimate the depreciation charge on certain assets within an infrastructure system or network. Definable major assets or components within the system or network must always be separately identified and depreciated over their individual useful economic lives. The remaining assets may be treated as one asset and the depreciation estimated using the renewals method where all of the following conditions are met:

— the infrastructure is a system or network that, as a whole, is intended to be maintained at a specified level of service potential by the continuing replacement and refurbishment of its components; and

— the level of annual expenditure required to maintain the operating capacity or service potential of the infrastructure asset is calculated from an asset management plan certified by a person who is both appropriately qualified and independent of the reporting entity; and

— the system or network is in a mature or steady state.

The guidance in the standard suggests that a system or network is in a mature or steady state when the annual cost of maintaining it is relatively constant.

Accounting treatment

13.21   Where renewals accounting is adopted, the accounting treatment is as follows:

— the annual expenditure required to maintain the infrastructure asset (as described in 13.20 above) should be treated as the depreciation charge for the period and deducted from the carrying value of the asset as part of accumulated depreciation;

— the actual expenditure should be capitalised as part of the cost of the asset in the period in which it is incurred; and

— the carrying amount of the parts of the system or network that are replaced or restored by subsequent expenditure should be removed from the carrying value of the asset.

Renewals accounting is an optional accounting treatment where the conditions are met. If it is not adopted, maintenance costs should be charged to the profit and loss account as they are incurred, and depreciation on the remaining infrastructure assets should be calculated in the usual way.

NON-DEPRECIATION OF ASSETS

The general rule

13.22   FRS 15 states categorically that subsequent expenditure on an asset to maintain or enhance its standard of performance does not in itself negate the need to charge depreciation on the asset. The assessment of the useful economic life of the asset will usually take account of the fact that routine expenditure will be incurred to maintain the expected performance standard of the asset (e.g. the routine servicing and overhauling of equipment). If this expenditure was not incurred, the expected useful economic life of the asset would be reduced and the depreciation charge would be higher. Routine maintenance expenditure of this nature should be charged to the profit and loss account as it is incurred.

These principles were highlighted by the Financial Reporting Review Panel (FRRP) in May 2004 when it published its findings following a review of the accounts of Thorns Group Plc for the year ended 30 April 2002. The group had not depreciated hire stock on the grounds that its value was maintained through the regular replacement of broken or obsolete items. The FRRP drew attention to the fact that under FRS 15:

(i)   the only grounds for not charging depreciation are that the depreciation charge and accumulated depreciation are immaterial;

(ii)   the estimate of a tangible fixed assets' useful economic life cannot be extended limitlessly through maintenance, refurbishment, overhaul or replacement; and

(iii)   expenditure that maintains or enhances the previously assessed performance standard of an asset does not negate the need to depreciate the asset.

The Panel therefore concluded that non-depreciation of the hire stock did not comply with FRS 15. The directors accepted the FRRP's view and agreed to introduce a depreciation policy for the relevant assets.

Enhancement of the asset

13.23   In some cases, subsequent expenditure may:

— enhance the economic benefits of the asset beyond the previously assessed standard of performance;

— restore or replace a component that has been separately depreciated; or

— restore the economic benefits of the asset.

This expenditure may extend the expected useful economic life of the asset but cannot increase it indefinitely and does not negate the need for depreciation to be charged. In these cases, the subsequent expenditure should be capitalised as it is incurred and depreciated over the useful economic life of the asset (or component), or over the period to the next major overhaul.

Where depreciation is immaterial

13.24   Under FRS 15, the only grounds for not charging depreciation on a tangible fixed asset (other than non-depreciable land) are that the depreciation charge and accumulated depreciation are immaterial. FRS 15 acknowledges that the depreciation charge may be immaterial in two situations:

— where the estimated remaining useful economic life of the asset is long; or

— where the estimated residual value of the asset is not materially different from its carrying value.

It is important to remember that the materiality of the depreciation charge must be assessed in terms of both the charge for the year and the accumulated depreciation. The materiality of any uncharged depreciation must also be assessed in aggregate as well as for the individual assets. Where depreciation is omitted from the accounts on the grounds that it is immaterial, the potential depreciation charge will still need to be calculated (and accumulated) to support this view. FRS 15 notes that the depreciation charge for the year and accumulated depreciation are immaterial if they would not reasonably influence the decisions of a user of the accounts. The report published by the Financial Reporting Review Panel in September 2001, following its review of the accounts of Groupe Chez Gerard plc for the year ended 25 June 2000, emphasised that revisions to useful economic lives and residual values may result in the depreciation of assets that were previously not depreciated on the grounds of immateriality. This does not constitute a change in accounting policy and the carrying amounts of the relevant assets should therefore be depreciated prospectively over their remaining useful economic lives in accordance with the normal requirements of FRS 15.

High residual values

13.25   FRS 15 notes that high residual values may occur when:

— an entity has a policy and practice of regular maintenance and repair (the costs of which are charged to the profit and loss account) so that the asset is kept at its previously assessed standard of performance;

— the asset is unlikely to suffer from economic or technological obsolescence; and

— where residual values are material:

— the entity has a policy and practice of disposing of similar assets well before the end of their economic lives; and

— the disposal proceeds of similar assets (after excluding the effect of price changes since the date of acquisition or last revaluation) have not been materially lower than their carrying amounts.

It should also be noted that the standard requires residual values to be reviewed at the end of each reporting period.

Annual impairment review

13.26   FRS 15 requires a tangible fixed asset to be reviewed for impairment at the end of each reporting period when either:

— no depreciation has been charged, on the grounds that it is immaterial; or

— the estimated remaining useful economic life of the asset exceeds 50 years.

This does not apply in the case of non-depreciable land. Where an impairment review is required, it should be carried out in accordance with FRS 11 'Impairment of Fixed Assets and Goodwill'. If it is not practicable to carry out an impairment review of an individual asset, the review should be completed for groups of assets as part of income-generating units. Once the first impairment review has been carried out, it can simply be updated in subsequent accounting periods. If expected cash flows and discount rates have not changed significantly, such updates should be relatively straightforward to perform.

Freehold land

13.27   Freehold land does not usually require any regular provision for depreciation. The only exception is where the land is depleted in some way (e.g. a working quarry or mine), in which case depreciation will usually need to be charged. This does not mean that the value of freehold land will not change. The value of land is as susceptible as other assets to external changes and economic factors. Environmental issues in particular can have a significant effect on the value of land. Where the value of freehold land has become impaired, it should be written down in the same way as any other fixed asset.

DEPRECIATION OF REVALUED ASSETS

Alternative accounting rules

13.28   Under the alternative accounting rules, CA 1985 permits certain assets to be included in the accounts at valuation rather than historical cost. These are:

— intangible fixed assets (other than goodwill) which may be included at their current cost; and

— tangible fixed assets which may be included at either market value (as at the date of their last valuation) or current cost.

Further guidance on the operation of the alternative accounting rules is given in Chapter 1. CA 1985 makes no reference to the frequency of valuation where the alternative accounting rules are used, but FRS 15 now includes a specific requirement for valuations to be kept up to date once they have been incorporated into the accounts. This requirement is considered in more detail in Chapter 21.

Basis of depreciation charge

13.29 Where assets have been revalued, both the Act and FRS 15 require the depreciation in respect of those assets to be based on the valuation figure rather than on original cost. The full amount of this depreciation must be charged to the profit and loss account. If a revaluation has a material effect on the depreciation charge for the year, details should be disclosed in the accounts for the year in which the revaluation takes place. FRS 15 notes that ideally the depreciation charge should be based on the average value of the asset for the period, but in practice either the opening or closing value may be used as the basis for the charge, provided that a consistent approach is adopted in each accounting period and between accounting periods.

Amount charged to the profit and loss account

13.30 CA 1985 permits depreciation on the revalued element of the asset to be disclosed separately, either on the face of the profit and loss account or in the notes to the accounts. The wording of this part of the Act is not particularly clear and it has been suggested in the past that it might permit the depreciation charge in the profit and loss account to be restricted to the depreciation based on historical cost. Even if the Act can be interpreted in this way, FRS 15 ensures that the full amount of depreciation is charged to the profit and loss account.

Transfers between reserves

13.31 There is, however, no reason why the additional depreciation charge relating to the revaluation of an asset should not be debited to the revaluation reserve and credited to the profit and loss account reserve as a reserves movement. Many companies choose to do this. Such a transfer reflects the fact that, under CA 1985, only depreciation charged on the original cost of an asset is regarded as a realised loss for distribution purposes.

Example 13.5 – Reserves transfers in respect of depreciation

B Ltd has freehold land and buildings with an original cost of £70,000. The buildings, which have an original cost of £50,000, are being depreciated over 50 years. B Ltd's accounting date is 31 December.

The land and buildings are professionally valued at £95,000 at 31 December 20X4 (£22,000 for the land and £73,000 for the buildings) and this valuation is incorporated in the accounts. The expected useful economic life of the buildings is unchanged and they have a remaining life of 43 years. Depreciation is charged on a straight line basis.

In the 20X5 accounts, the depreciation charge will be £1,698 (i.e. the valuation of £73,000 depreciated over the remaining useful life of 43 years). This amount must be charged to the profit and loss account.

B Ltd can then transfer £698 (i.e. the additional depreciation over and above the £1,000 that would be charged on the original cost of £50,000) from the revaluation reserve to the profit and loss account reserve as a reserves movement.

Such a transfer is specifically permitted under the alternative accounting rules by CA 1985 Sch 4 para 34(3), because the additional depreciation has been charged to the profit and loss account.

Historical cost profits and losses

13.32   FRS 3 'Reporting Financial Performance' requires most accounts to include a separate note of historical cost profits and losses. This also highlights the difference between depreciation based on the historical cost of assets and the actual depreciation charge in the accounts. The note of historical cost profits and losses is considered in detail in Chapter 36.

Depreciation in the year of revaluation

13.33   Depreciation should continue to be charged on the original cost of the asset up to the date of the first valuation. There may be a temptation to disregard this depreciation charge in the year of revaluation, but to do so would not comply with the requirements of FRS 15. The effect would be to understate the depreciation charge in the profit and loss account and understate the credit to the revaluation reserve by the same amount. If an asset is revalued part way through the financial year, rather than at the year-end, depreciation should strictly be based on the original cost of the asset up to the date of valuation and on the new valuation for the remainder of the year. When further revaluations take place, the standard permits the charge for the year to be based on either the opening or the closing balance, provided that a consistent approach is taken between accounting periods.

PROFIT OR LOSS ON DISPOSAL OF ASSETS

Measurement rules

13.34   FRS 3 'Reporting Financial Performance' paragraph 21 requires profits and losses on the disposal of assets to be accounted for:

—   in the period in which the disposal occurs; and

—   as the difference between net sales proceeds and the carrying value of the asset.

This means that, where an asset has been revalued for accounts purposes, any profit or loss on disposal must be based on the revalued figure rather than on historical cost.

Example 13.6 – A loss on disposal

Using the details from Example 13.5:

The land and buildings are sold for £90,000 on 2 January, two years after the valuation was incorporated in the accounts. There have been no additions to the building during this time.

Valuation at 31 December 2001	95,000
Depreciation for two subsequent years at £1,698 each year (see Example 13.5)	(3,396)
Carrying value at date of disposal	91,604
Sales proceeds	90,000
Loss on disposal	1,604

The standard also requires profits and losses on the disposal of fixed assets to be disclosed separately on the face of the profit and loss account, unless they are in effect no more than marginal adjustments to depreciation previously charged (see Chapter 9).

Revaluation reserve

13.35   Prior to FRS 3, some companies chose to calculate the profit or loss on disposal as the difference between sales proceeds and historical cost (rather than the valuation figure) by crediting any remaining balance on the revaluation reserve to the profit and loss account. Any remaining balance on the revaluation reserve, relating to the asset that has been disposed of, should now be transferred to the profit and loss account reserve as a reserves movement.

Example 13.7– Remaining balances on revaluation reserve

Using the details from Examples 13.5 and 13.6:

	£	£
Revaluation reserve at 1 January 20X4 (assumed)		34,500
Surplus on revaluation:		
Original cost	70,000	
Depreciation to 31 December 20X4:		
£50,000 x 2% x 7 years	(7,000)	
Carrying value	63,000	
Valuation	95,000	
		32,000
Revaluation reserve at 31 December 20X4		66,500
Transfers to profit and loss account reserve in respect of freehold buildings		
2 years at £698 (see Example 13.5)		(1,396)
Transfers to profit and loss account in respect of other revalued assets (assumed)		(1,475)
Balance on revaluation reserve immediately prior to disposal of freehold land and buildings		63,629
Transfer to profit and loss account reserve in respect of buildings disposed of (£32,000–£1,396)		(30,604)
Balance remaining on revaluation reserve in respect of other revalued assets		33,025

The transfer to the profit and loss account reserve reflects the fact that the surplus recognised at the time of revaluation has now been realised as a result of the disposal of the freehold land and buildings.

Note of historical cost profits and losses

13.36   The amount transferred between reserves in this way also appears within the note of historical cost profits and losses as it is an item that arises from the use of valuation rather than historical cost in accounting for fixed assets. In historical cost terms, this amount represents an additional gain on disposal of the asset. This gain has been recognised in the accounts in previous years (by including the asset at valuation) but is only realised when the asset is disposed of.

ACCOUNTING FOR IMPAIRMENT

Permanent and temporary diminutions in value

13.37   Where a fixed asset suffers a permanent diminution in value, CA 1985 requires a provision to be made for this. The provision must be charged to the profit and loss account and must be shown separately, either on the face of the profit and loss account or in the notes to the accounts. The Act makes no reference to temporary diminutions in value, other than in the case of fixed asset investments, where provision may be made but is not required.

Impact of FRS 11 'Impairment of Fixed Assets and Goodwill'

13.38   The distinction effectively made in CA 1985 between permanent and temporary diminutions in value was the cause of considerable difficulty for many years. Following the publication of FRS 11 'Impairment of Fixed Assets and Goodwill', the requirement to make provision for a permanent diminution in value is encompassed in the requirement under that standard for fixed assets and goodwill to be written down to their recoverable amount when there are indications that impairment has occurred. Appendix II to FRS 11 notes that the distinction between permanent and temporary diminutions in value is recognised inherently in the standard, in that it requires all impairments that are clearly due to the consumption of economic benefits (and which are therefore clearly permanent) to be charged to the profit and loss account.

The need to carry out an impairment review

13.39   Impairment is defined in FRS 11 as a reduction in the recoverable amount of a fixed asset or goodwill below its carrying amount. Under this standard, an impairment review should be carried out when events or changes in circumstances indicate that the carrying value of a fixed asset (including goodwill) may not be recoverable. A review will therefore not necessarily be required every year – it will usually only need to be carried out when something has happened to the asset or to the economic environment in which the asset is used. The systematic charging of depreciation will usually ensure that the carrying amount of a fixed asset is reduced throughout its useful life to reflect the reduction in the asset's recoverable amount arising from the consumption of economic benefits. FRS 11 therefore notes that, for most assets, impairments should be a relatively infrequent addition to normal depreciation.

Events and changes that might prompt a review

13.40   FRS 11 gives examples of events and changes that may indicate impairment of an asset has occurred. These include:

—   a current operating loss or net cash outflow, combined with either similar losses or outflows in the past, or the expected continuation of losses or outflows in the future;

—   a significant decline in the market value of an asset;

—   physical damage or obsolescence;

— a significant adverse change in the business or market in which the asset is used (e.g. a major new competitor);

— a significant adverse change in the statutory or other regulatory environment in which the business operates;

— a significant adverse change in any indicator (such as turnover) used to measure the fair value of the asset at the time of acquisition;

— a commitment by management to undertake a major reorganisation.

The standard emphasises that the useful economic lives and residual values of the assets affected may also need to be reviewed in these circumstances. Even if the assets are not actually impaired, their expected useful lives and residual values may have changed.

Separate requirements for intangible assets and goodwill

13.41   It is important to note that FRS 10 'Goodwill and Intangible Assets' imposes more specific requirements for impairment reviews in the case of goodwill and intangible assets. Separate requirements apply depending on the period over which the intangible asset or goodwill is being amortised. Goodwill and intangible assets amortised over a finite period of 20 years or less from the date of acquisition should be reviewed for impairment at the end of the first full financial year following acquisition (and the standard permits a less extensive review process to be used for this) and in other periods if events or changes in circumstances indicate that the carrying value of the asset or goodwill may not be recoverable. Goodwill and intangible assets amortised over a period of more than 20 years from the date of acquisition, and any that are not amortised, must be reviewed for impairment at the end of each reporting period. Further details are given in Chapter 20.

Recognition of impairment losses

13.42   The general rule is that an impairment loss (i.e. the difference between the carrying amount of a fixed asset or goodwill and its recoverable amount) should be recognised in the profit and loss account of the period. However, a different approach is required in the case of fixed assets that have previously been revalued. If an impairment loss relating to a revalued fixed asset is caused by a clear consumption of economic benefits (for example, physical damage or a deterioration in the quality of service provided by the asset), it should be recognised in the profit and loss account. Other impairments of revalued assets (for instance, those arising from a general fall in prices) should be recognised in the statement of total recognised gains and losses until the carrying amount of the asset reaches its depreciated historical cost. Any further reduction below this amount should be recognised in the profit and loss account. It is important to keep detailed records of where impairment losses are recognised, in case reversals of the losses should need to be recognised in subsequent years.

Presentation of impairment losses

13.43 Impairment losses recognised in the profit and loss account should be included within operating profit under the appropriate statutory heading, which will usually be that for depreciation and diminutions in value. Impairment losses recognised in the profit and loss account should be disclosed as exceptional items where they are material. Impairment losses recognised in the statement of total recognised gains and losses should be disclosed separately on the face of that statement. In the notes to the financial statements for accounting periods after the impairment, the impairment loss should be treated as follows:

— for assets held on a historical cost basis, the impairment loss should be included within cumulative depreciation – the cost of the asset should not be reduced;

— for revalued assets held at market value (e.g. existing use or open market value), the impairment loss should be included within the revalued carrying amount; and

— for revalued assets held at depreciated replacement cost:

   — an impairment loss charged to the profit and loss account should be included within cumulative depreciation (i.e. the carrying amount of the asset should not be reduced); and

   — an impairment loss charged to the statement of total recognised gains and losses should be deducted from the carrying amount of the asset.

Reversal of an impairment loss

13.44 The standard sets out different rules on the recognition of a reversal of an impairment loss for tangible fixed assets and investments, and for intangible assets and goodwill:

— in the case of tangible fixed assets and investments for which an impairment loss has been recognised, if the recoverable amount increases as a result of a change in economic conditions or in the expected use of the asset, the reversal should be recognised to the extent that it increases the carrying amount of the asset up to the amount that it would have been if the original impairment had not occurred;

— in the case of intangible assets and goodwill, the reversal of an impairment loss should only be recognised if:

   — an external event caused the recognition of the impairment loss in previous periods and subsequent external events clearly and demonstrably reverse the effects of that event in a way that was not foreseen in the original impairment calculations; or

—   the impairment loss arose on an intangible asset with a readily ascertainable market value and the net realisable value based on that market value has increased to above the asset's carrying amount.

Recognition of a reversal of an impairment loss

13.45   The reversal of an impairment loss should be recognised in the profit and loss account of the current period, unless it relates to a revalued asset, in which case it should be recognised in the profit and loss account to the extent that the original impairment loss (adjusted for subsequent depreciation) was recognised in the profit and loss account and any additional amount should be recognised in the statement of total recognised gains and losses. It is therefore important to keep detailed records of where impairment losses are recognised, in case reversals of the losses should need to be recognised in subsequent years. In the year in which it is recognised, the accounts should disclose the reason for the reversal of the original impairment loss, including any changes in assumptions upon which the calculation of recoverable amount is based.

Further detail

13.46   The requirements of FRS 11 on the measurement of impairment losses, the recognition of impairment losses in the accounts, the allocation of impairment losses and the recognition of the reversal of an impairment loss are considered in more detail in Chapter 20.

Depreciation of impaired assets

13.47   Where an impairment loss is recognised, the remaining useful economic life and residual value of the fixed asset or goodwill should be reviewed and revised where necessary. The revised carrying amount should be depreciated over the revised estimate of the remaining useful economic life. This is consistent with the requirements of FRS 15 on the depreciation of assets following a revision of useful economic life.

TRANSFERS FROM CURRENT TO FIXED ASSETS

Requirements of UITF Abstract 5

13.48   UITF 5 'Transfers from Current Assets to Fixed Assets' tackles the issue of how to account for an asset that was not initially intended for continuing use in the business, but which subsequently becomes a fixed asset. An example might be the case of a property construction company that builds a property initially for sale in the ordinary course of its business, but then decides to use the building as its own office. The Abstract requires the following approach to be adopted:

— assess the net realisable value of the asset at the date of transfer;

— if net realisable value is below cost, the asset must be written down to net realisable value before it is transferred;

— any provision needed to reduce cost to net realisable value must be charged to the profit and loss account, recognising the loss suffered by the company during the time that the asset was held as a current asset;

— the asset is then subject to the normal rules for fixed assets (i.e. those set out in CA 1985 and FRS 15) from the date of transfer, and should be treated as an asset recorded at valuation under the alternative accounting rules of the Act.

Example 13.8 – A transfer from current to fixed assets

C Ltd has constructed a property at a cost of £46,000. It initially intended to sell the property but has decided to use it as the company's head office from 1 January 20X1. The net realisable value of the property at 1 January 20X1 is £39,000. It has an expected useful economic life of 45 years and an expected residual value of £10,000. The company uses the straight-line method of depreciation.

C Ltd must charge the diminution in the value of the property of £7,000 (i.e. £46,000 – £39,000) to the profit and loss account and then record the new office as a fixed asset, shown at a valuation of £39,000. Depreciation of £644 must be charged each year in respect of the property (i.e. £39,000 – £10,000 over 45 years).

DEPRECIATION DISCLOSURES

Disclosure of accounting policy on depreciation

13.49 FRS 18 'Accounting Policies' requires financial statements to include a description of each of the accounting policies that is material in the context of the entity's financial statements and CA 1985 specifically requires disclosure of the policy on depreciation and the diminution of assets. FRS 15 specifies that the disclosure must include:

— the depreciation methods used; and

— the useful economic lives or depreciation rates used.

FRS 15 requires these disclosure to be given for each class of tangible fixed assets. A class of tangible fixed assets is defined in the standard as 'a category of tangible fixed asset having a similar nature, function or use in the business of the entity'. This is considered further in the context of the valuation of assets in Chapter 20. The disclosures on economic lives or depreciation rates should normally correspond with the categories of asset shown in the detailed movements table for fixed assets in the notes to the accounts. Some companies choose to disclose asset lives (or depreciation rates) in the fixed asset note rather than as part of the accounting policy on depreciation and this is quite acceptable. The following wordings might be appropriate for the accounting policy note.

Example 13.9 – Depreciation policy note (I)

Depreciation is provided on the straight-line method to write off the cost or valuation of tangible fixed assets, less any estimated residual value, over their expected useful economic lives.

The following asset lives are used:

Freehold buildings	45 years
Leasehold property	The life of the lease; current leases range from 10 to 20 years
Plant and machinery	7 to 10 years
Fixtures and fittings	10 years

No depreciation is provided on freehold land.

Example 13.10 – Depreciation policy note (II)

Depreciation is provided on the reducing balance method to write off the cost or valuation of tangible fixed assets, less any estimated residual value, over their expected useful economic lives.

The following depreciation rates are used:

Plant and machinery	40%
Motor vehicles	50%
Computer equipment	70%

Reasons for non-depreciation of assets

13.50   If certain categories of asset are not depreciated, the accounting policy note should explain why this is considered appropriate. For instance, in a case where depreciation is considered to be immaterial, the following wording might be appropriate.

Example 13.11 – Immaterial depreciation

The estimated residual value of the company's freehold property is approximately equal to its net book value. It is the company's policy to maintain this property to a high standard, so that the estimated residual value will not be impaired over time. The costs of this maintenance are charged to the profit and loss account as they are incurred. The directors are of the opinion that any depreciation in respect of the company's freehold property would be immaterial and consequently no provision is made in the accounts for such depreciation.

As discussed in 13.22–13.27 above, careful consideration must be given to a number of factors before adopting an accounting policy along these lines.

Disclosure when depreciation method is changed

13.51   The effect of any change in the method of providing depreciation must be disclosed in the year of the change, if it is material. This information may be given in the accounting policy note or in the detailed note on fixed assets. The accounting policy note will need to include details of both the previous and the new depreciation method, as the comparative figures will have been calculated under the previous method. The reasoning behind the change of method should also be explained.

Other accounts disclosures

13.52   Other required disclosures are:

— The total depreciation charge for the period – this is usually given as part of the profit and loss account if Format 2 or Format 4 is used and in a note to the accounts if Format 1 or Format 3 is used. A company that has chosen Format 1 or Format 3 for its profit and loss account must include any relevant provisions for depreciation or diminution of assets values in the figures for:

—   cost of sales;

—   distribution costs;

—   administrative expenses.

FRS 15 also requires the charge for the year to be analysed by class of asset – this is usually covered in the detailed fixed assets movements table in the notes to the accounts.

— Separate disclosure of the depreciation charged in the year in respect of leased assets, as required by SSAP 21 – this is usually given as part of the detailed note to the accounts on fixed assets or within the note that sets out the total depreciation charge for the period;

— The cumulative amount of provisions for depreciation and impairment at the beginning and end of the period (also by class of asset) – this is usually given as part of the detailed note to the accounts on fixed assets;

— The effect on the depreciation charge of any revaluation during the year, if the effect is material – this information is usually given as part of the detailed note on fixed assets or within the note that sets out the total depreciation charge for the period.

LIKELY FUTURE DEVELOPMENTS

FRED 29 'Property, plant and equipment; Borrowing costs'

13.53   The ASB issued FRED 29 'Property, plant and equipment; Borrowing costs' in May 2002 as part of its project to achieve convergence between UK accounting standards and international accounting standards (see 1.6 above). The Exposure Draft proposes replacing FRS 15 'Tangible fixed assets' with two new standards based on a revised IAS 16 and the existing IAS 23. Much of the content of these two international standards is consistent with current UK requirements. The main differences are in relation to the accounting treatment of revalued assets, in particular the use of a 'fair value' model rather than the UK's present 'value to the business' approach. A separate international group is currently considering the issue of revaluation and whether changes should be made to the present IAS requirements. The ASB is participating in this project and is continuing to press for IAS 16 to incorporate the revaluation principles currently set out in FRS 15. The main changes affecting depreciation (under FRED 29) would be:

— where residual values need to be revised, the revision should be based on current prices rather than those at the date of acquisition or revaluation;

— there is no guidance on when uncharged depreciation may be regarded as immaterial;

— there is no specific requirement for annual impairment reviews on assets that are not depreciated; and

— there is no reference to renewals accounting, and thus no alternative to the principle that depreciation is determined by reference to the depreciable amount of an asset.

However, the current version of the ASB's Technical Plan, published in June 2005, indicates that new UK accounting standards in respect of tangible fixed assets are not planned to come into effect until accounting periods beginning on or after 1 January 2008 and that no further Exposure Drafts on this subject are expected to be issued in the near future.

FRED 32 'Disposal of non-current assets and presentation of discontinued operations'

13.54   The ASB published FRED 32 'Disposal of non-current assets and presentation of discontinued operations' in July 2003, once again as part of its project to achieve convergence between UK and international accounting standards (see 1.6 above). If implemented, the proposals in FRED 32 will alter the timing of the recognition of the loss on disposal of certain assets and remove the requirement for certain assets to be depreciated. The Exposure Draft introduces a new classification of assets held for sale, which are required to be shown separately on the balance sheet. The criteria for classifying such assets are specified in an Appendix to the proposed standard and are generally based on management's plans for the asset, although they do require it to be highly probable that the asset will be sold within one year. FRED 32 proposes that such assets should be carried at the lower of carrying value and fair value less disposal costs, the latter being essentially the same as net realisable value under FRS 11. The proposals conflict to some extent with current accounting practice in the UK, in that where the value in use of an asset is higher than its net realisable value but the entity nevertheless decides to sell it, the Exposure Draft requires it to be written down to net realisable value, with any loss recognised in the period in which the decision to sell is taken. In the preface to the Exposure Draft, the ASB expresses the view that the loss should be recognised when the sale occurs (as under FRS 3) and not when the entity classifies the asset as held for sale.

Chapter 14   Other Expenses

FINANCE COSTS OF DEBT UNDER FRS 4

Accounting for debt instruments

14.1 Under the requirements of FRS 4 'Capital Instruments', a debt instrument should be recorded at the time of issue at the amount of the net issue proceeds. The carrying value of the debt will subsequently be:

— increased each year by the finance costs charged to the profit and lost account in respect of the debt; and

— reduced by the payments made by the issuer in respect of the debt.

The classification of capital instruments is considered in Chapter 26 and accounting for finance costs in respect of non-equity shares is covered in Chapter 16.

For accounting periods beginning on or after 1 January 2005, the paragraphs of FRS 4 relating to the presentation and disclosure of dividends in respect of equity and non-equity shares and finance costs in respect of non-equity shares are superseded by FRS 25 'Financial Instruments: Disclosure and Presentation' (see 14.19 below). Other aspects of the standard, including those on the presentation and disclosure of finance costs in respect of debt, continue in force for entities that are not required to adopt FRS 26 'Financial Instruments: Measurement' (see Chapter 46). Consequently, these requirements continue to apply to unlisted entities that have not chosen to adopt fair value accounting.

Finance costs

14.2 The total finance costs of a debt instrument are defined as the difference between:

— the net issue proceeds, after deduction of any direct issue costs; and

— the total amount of the payments or other transfers of economic benefits that the issuer may be required to make in respect of the instrument.

However, payments that are contingent on an uncertain future event (for instance, changes in an index) should only be included in finance costs once the event that gives rise to the payment has actually occurred.

Issue costs

14.3   Issue costs are defined in FRS 4 as the costs that are incurred directly in connection with the issue of a capital instrument – that is, those costs that would not have been incurred had the specific instrument in question not been issued. The Explanatory Notes to the standard set out more detail on the type of costs that should be treated as issue costs. In particular, the definition does not allow the following costs to be treated as issue costs:

— the costs of researching and negotiating finance;

— the costs of ascertaining the suitability or feasibility of particular capital instruments;

— allocations of internal costs which would still have been incurred regardless of whether the instrument was issued (e.g. the remuneration of the individuals involved in the negotiation process);

— costs relating to a financial restructuring or renegotiation.

These costs must be charged to the profit and loss account as they are incurred. A tightly drawn definition of issue costs is necessary, as these costs effectively become part of the finance costs of the instrument and are charged to the profit and loss account over the term of the debt. A wide definition of issue costs would therefore result in the finance cost of the debt being overstated.

Calculation of net issue proceeds

14.4   The net issue proceeds are calculated by deducting the eligible issue costs from the fair value of the consideration received.

Example 14.1 – Net issue proceeds calculation

A Ltd issues a debt instrument on 1 January 20X2 for cash of £5,000.

The direct issue costs amount to £250.

The net issue proceeds are therefore £4,750 (i.e. £5,000 – £250).

Calculation of finance costs

14.5   The finance costs are calculated by comparing the net issue proceeds with the total payments (or other transfers of benefits) that the issuer may be required to make in respect of the debt. Payments that the issuer may be required to make will usually include interest and any amounts payable on redemption of the debt.

Example 14.2 – Finance costs calculation

In 20X2, B Ltd issues a 5% bond at its nominal value of £8,000. The bond is redeemable in 10 years later in 20Y2 at a premium of 10%. The direct issue costs in respect of the bond amount to £750.

The net issue proceeds are £7,250 (i.e. £8,000 – £750).

The total payments required from B Ltd in respect of the bond are:

	£
Interest on £8,000 at 5% = £400 p.a. x ten years	4,000
Repayment of the bond on redemption	8,000
Premium payable on redemption £8,000 at 10%	800
	12,800

The finance costs in respect of the bond are therefore:

Total payments in respect of the bond	12,800
Less: Net issue proceeds	7,250
Finance costs	5,550

Allocation of finance costs over the term of the debt

14.6   The total finance costs of a debt instrument must be allocated over the term of the debt, at a constant rate on its carrying value.

Example 14.3 – Allocation of finance costs

Using the details in Example 14.2, the total finance cost of £5,550 should be allocated over ten years at a constant rate on the carrying amount of the debt. The effective rate will therefore be approximately 7.06% and the accounting entries will be as follows.

Date	Opening carrying amount £	Finance costs (P&L account) £	Amounts actually paid £	Closing carrying amount £
Year 1	7,250	512	(400)	7,362
Year 2	7,362	520	(400)	7,482
Year 3	7,482	528	(400)	7,610
Year 4	7,610	537	(400)	7,747
Year 5	7,747	547	(400)	7,894
Year 6	7,894	557	(400)	8,051
Year 7	8,051	569	(400)	8,220
Year 8	8,220	580	(400)	8,400
Year 9	8,400	593	(400)	8,593
Year 10	8,593	607	*(9,200)	—

*	Interest	400
	Redemption premium	800
	Repayment of bond	8,000
		9,200

Convertible debt

14.7   For accounting periods beginning before 1 January 2005, where the debt is convertible into shares at the option of the investor, it should be accounted for on the basis that it will not be converted, until conversion actually takes place. Therefore, where convertible debt includes a redemption premium that is payable only if conversion does not take place, the premium should be treated as a payment that the issuer may be required to make (i.e. it should be treated as part of the finance costs of the instrument).

Example 14.4 – Finance costs of convertible debt

In 20X2, B Ltd issues a 5% convertible bond at its nominal value of £8,000. The bond is convertible to shares between 20Y0 and 20Y2 (ie after 8–10 years) but if it is not converted, it will be redeemed in 2006 at a premium of 10%. The direct issue costs in respect of the bond amount to £750.

The net issue proceeds are £7,250 (i.e. £8,000 – £750).

Assuming that conversion does not take place, the total payments required from B Ltd in respect of the bond will be:

	£
Interest on £8,000 at 5% = £400 pa x 10 years	4,000
Repayment of the bond on redemption	8,000
Premium payable on redemption £8,000 at 10%	800
	12,800
The finance costs in respect of the bond are therefore:	
Total payments in respect of the bond	12,800
Less: Net issue proceeds	7,250
Finance costs	5,550

This will give the same allocation of finance costs as is shown in Example 14.3 above.

However, for accounting periods beginning on or after 1 January 2005, paragraph 25 of FRS 4, which requires the above treatment, is withdrawn by FRS 25 'Financial Instruments: Disclosure and Presentation'. FRS 25 requires the component parts of a compound financial instrument to be accounted for separately. So, where a financial instrument includes both a financial liability component and an equity component, these elements must be classified and accounted for separately. Income, expenses, gains and losses relating to the financial liability will therefore be dealt with in the profit and loss account, and those relating to the equity element should be accounted for within shareholders' funds. The classification of financial instruments, and the accounting treatment to be applied to compound financial instruments are considered in more detail in Chapter 26.

Accounting treatment on subsequent conversion

14.8   If the debt is subsequently converted into shares, the amount recognised as shareholders' funds at the time of conversion will be the amount shown as the liability in respect of the debt at the date of conversion. No gain or loss should be recognised at the time of conversion.

Example 14.5 – Conversion occurs

The details are as in Example 14.4 above.

If the bond is converted to shares at the end of 2005 (i.e. at the end of Year 9), the carrying value of the bond of £8,593 at that date (see Example 14.3) will be recognised as shareholders' funds at the time of conversion.

For accounting periods beginning on or after 1 January 2005, this requirement of FRS 4 is also withdrawn by FRS 25 'Financial Instruments: Disclosure and Presentation'.

Gains and losses on repurchase of debt

14.9   Gains and losses on the repurchase or early settlement of debt should be recognised in the profit and loss account in the period in which the repurchase or early settlement takes place. Such gains and losses must be disclosed separately within or adjacent to 'interest payable and similar charges' in the profit and loss account.

Options

14.10   The term of a debt instrument is usually clearly stated, but in some cases either the issuer or the investor may have the option of redeeming the instrument early. The explanatory notes to FRS 4 emphasise that options should be carefully evaluated. Where both parties have the option to redeem the instrument early, the term of the debt should normally be assumed to end on the earliest date on which redemption can take place. The finance costs of the instrument will therefore be spread over the period from the date of issue to the earliest date of redemption. However, this treatment should not be adopted if there is no genuine commercial possibility that the option will be exercised (i.e. the option is artificial). When evaluating options, it should be assumed that each party to the debt instrument will act in their own economic and commercial interest.

Option to extend the term of the debt

14.11   Similarly, if the term of a debt instrument can be extended, the extended period should not be taken into account unless it is virtually certain that extension will take place. The finance costs should therefore normally be allocated over the original term of the debt (i.e. excluding any extension that may, or might not, take place). Once again, it will be necessary to consider whether the extension is a genuine option at the end of the original term of the debt, or whether the arrangement will only make commercial sense if extension actually takes place (i.e. the option for extension is in effect artificial because it will always be exercised).

Options held by the issuer only

14.12   UITF Abstract 11 'Capital Instruments: Issuer Call Options' was issued to clarify the accounting treatment that should be adopted where the issuer of a debt instrument holds an option to redeem the instrument early, but the investor does not hold a similar option. In these circumstances, any additional premium payable by the issuer on exercise of the option should not be treated as part of the finance costs of the instrument but should be charged to the profit and loss account as part of the gain or loss arising on early settlement or repurchase of the debt. However, the term of the debt will continue to end on the earliest date on which redemption can take place (in accordance with FRS 4 – see 14.10 above).

Example 14.6 – Treatment in line with UITF 11

In 20X2, B Ltd issues a 5% bond at its nominal value of £8,000. The bond is redeemable in 20Y5. The direct issue costs in respect of the bond amount to £750. B Ltd has the option of redeeming the bond in 20Y2 (ie after 10 years) on payment of a premium of £800.

The option is held by the issuer only and the premium payable on early redemption should therefore be ignored when calculating the finance costs.

The finance costs are therefore:

	£
Interest on £8,000 at 5% = £400 p.a. x 10 years	4,000
Repayment of the bond on redemption	8,000
	12,000
Less: Net issue proceeds	7,250
Finance costs	4,750

The finance costs of £4,750 must be allocated over the ten-year term (i.e. to the earliest date of redemption) at a constant rate on the carrying amount of the debt. A rate of approximately 6.29% will achieve this as follows:

Date	Opening carrying amount £	Finance costs (P&L account) £	Amounts actually paid £	Closing carrying amount £
Year 1	7,250	456	(400)	7,306
Year 2	7,306	460	(400)	7,366
Year 3	7,366	463	(400)	7,429
Year 4	7,429	467	(400)	7,496
Year 5	7,496	472	(400)	7,568
Year 6	7,568	476	(400)	7,644
Year 7	7,644	481	(400)	7,725
Year 8	7,725	486	(400)	7,811
Year 9	7,811	491	(400)	7,902
Year 10	7,902	498	(400)	8,000

If B Ltd exercises its option to redeem the bond early in 20Y2 the premium of £800 payable on exercise of the option will be charged to the profit and loss account in that year, as part of the loss on early redemption of the debt.

	£
Amount to be repaid	8,000
Carrying value of the debt (end of year 10)	8,000
	—
Premium payable on early redemption	800
Loss on early redemption	800

If B Ltd decides not to exercise the option, interest of £400 p.a. will continue to be paid (and will be charged to the profit and loss account each year) for the remaining five years of the original term of the debt (i.e. until it is redeemed in 20Y5).

Premiums payable on redemption of debt

14.13　　The above treatment only applies in the case of a redemption premium that is payable by the issuer on exercise of the option that he holds. Any premium that is payable on redemption of the debt is unaffected.

Example 14.7 – Premium payable on redemption of debt

In 20X2, B Ltd issues a 5% bond at its nominal value of £8,000. The bond is redeemable in 20Y5 on payment of a premium of £800. The direct issue costs in respect of the bond amount to £750. B Ltd has the option of redeeming the bond in 20Y2 (ie after 10 years) on payment of an additional premium of £600.

The total payments required from B Ltd in respect of the bond are:

	£
Interest on £8,000 at 5% = £400 p.a. x 10 years	4,000
Repayment of the bond on redemption	8,000
Premium payable on redemption £8,000 at 10%	800
	12,800

The finance costs in respect of the bond are therefore:

	£
Total payments in respect of the bond	12,800
Less: Net issue proceeds	7,250
Finance costs	5,550

The total finance costs of £5,550 should be allocated over ten years (i.e. to the earliest date of redemption) at a constant rate on the carrying amount of the debt. The effective rate will therefore be approximately 7.06% and the accounting entries will be as follows.

Date	Opening carrying amount	Finance costs (P&L account)	Amounts actually paid	Closing carrying amount
	£	£	£	£
Year 1	7,250	512	(400)	7,362
Year 2	7,362	520	(400)	7,482
Year 3	7,482	528	(400)	7,610
Year 4	7,610	537	(400)	7,747
Year 5	7,747	547	(400)	7,894
Year 6	7,894	557	(400)	8,051
Year 7	8,051	569	(400)	8,220
Year 8	8,220	580	(400)	8,400
Year 9	8,400	593	(400)	8,593
Year 10	8,593	607	(400)	8,800

If B Ltd exercises its option to redeem the bond early in 20Y2 (i.e. at the end of year 10) the premium of £600 payable on exercise of the option will be charged to the profit and loss account in that year, as part of the loss on early redemption of the debt.

	£
Amount to be repaid	8,800
Carrying value of the debt (end of year 10)	8,800
	—
Premium payable on early redemption	600
Loss on early redemption	600

If B Ltd decides not to exercise the option, interest of £400 p.a. will continue to be paid (and will be charged to the profit and loss account each year) for the remaining five years of the original term of the debt (i.e. until it is redeemed in 20Y5).

Situations where UITF 11 does not apply

14.14 The accounting treatment set out in UITF Abstract 11 does not apply where:

— the option held by the issuer is not a genuine option – for instance, where it is clear from the terms of the agreement that the issuer will always gain a commercial benefit by exercising the option and there is therefore no question that he will take advantage of the option on the exercise date; or

— the effective rate of interest in respect of the debt increases after the date on which the option is exercisable – in this case, the exercise premium is deemed to compensate the investor for forgoing the additional interest that would have been payable.

In these cases the exercise premium should be treated as a cost that the issuer may be required to pay and should therefore be included as part of the finance costs charged to the profit and loss account in respect of the debt.

Charging of issue expenses to the share premium account

14.15   CA 1985 s 130 permits the share premium account to be used to:

— write-off issue expense relating to shares and debentures;

— provide for a premium payable on the redemption of debentures.

Paragraph 97 of FRS 4 emphasises that the requirements of the standard are not intended to prohibit the subsequent charging of issue costs to the share premium account. However, the costs must first be charged to the profit and loss account (as required by the standard) and then transferred to the share premium account by means of a reserves transfer.

More complex debt instruments

14.16   FRS 4 includes a separate section of Application Notes which consider how the requirements of the standard should be applied to specific types of capital instrument. The items covered in this guidance include:

— capital contribution;

— convertible capital bonds;

— convertible debt with a premium put option;

— convertible debt with enhanced interest;

— debt issued with warrants;

— deep discount bonds;

— index linked loans;

— limited recourse debt;

— perpetual debt;

— repackaged perpetual debt;

— stepped interest bonds;

— subordinated debt.

The guidance includes worked examples to illustrate how the requirements of FRS 4 should be applied in practice to these more complex instruments. They are also useful as a point of reference on how to deal with individual features that may be attached to other debt instruments.

For accounting periods beginning on or after 1 January 2005, both the Application Notes and the worked examples are withdrawn by FRS 25 'Financial Instruments: Disclosure and Presentation' as they are no longer relevant under the presentation requirements of the new standard.

ACCOUNTING FOR INCOME, EXPENSES, GAINS AND LOSSES UNDER FRS 25

Scope and effective date of FRS 25

14.17   FRS 25 'Financial Instruments: Disclosure and Presentation was issued by the ASB in December 2004. The presentation requirements of the standard apply to all entities (other than those adopting the FRSSE) for accounting periods beginning on or after 1 January 2005. They cannot be adopted early because some aspects hinge on company law changes that also come into effect on 1 January 2005.

The disclosure requirements of FRS 25, together with the requirements of FRS 23 'The Effects of Changes in Foreign Exchange Rates', FRS 24 ' Financial Reporting in Hyperinflationary Economies' and FRS 26 'Financial Instruments: Measurement', form a package of new UK accounting standards that apply to listed companies for accounting periods beginning on or after 1 January 2005, and to other entities for accounting periods beginning on or after 1 January 2006 if they choose to adopt fair value accounting. These entities can voluntarily apply the new standards from 1 January 2005 if they wish, provided that they apply all of the standards in the package – in other words, it is not acceptable to adopt some of the standards but not the others. Entities who are not required to adopt FRS 26 are nevertheless encouraged to comply with the disclosure requirements of FRS 25.

However, the ASB published an Exposure Draft 'Amendment to FRS 26 – Financial Instruments: Measurement' in April 2005 and this proposes extending the scope of the standard and also introducing into UK accounting the recognition and derecognition requirements of the underlying international accounting standard. Further details are given in Chapter 26.

Accounting for interest, dividends, gains and losses

14.18   The presentation requirements of FRS 25 apply to all types of financial instruments, apart from certain items that are specifically excluded (eg interests in group undertakings, employers' rights and obligations under employee benefit plans). The standard requires each financial instrument, or its component parts, to be classified on initial recognition as a financial asset, a financial liability or an equity instrument based on the substance of the contractual arrangements and the definitions set out in FRS 25. Further details on the classification of financial instruments are given in Chapter 26. The classification of the instrument also determines the accounting treatment of any related interest, dividends, gains and losses. This will mean that certain payments that are legally classified as dividends will need to be accounted for as interest in the profit and loss account. This is considered in more detail in Chapter 16.

Under FRS 25 income, expenses, gains and losses relating to financial assets and financial liabilities should be recognised in the profit and loss account, and material items should be separately disclosed. As a minimum, the accounts should disclose the total interest income and total interest expense for financial assets and financial liabilities that are not accounted for at fair value.

Where dividends need to be presented in the accounts as if they were interest, they can either be combined with actual interest charges or shown as a separate item. The guidance in FRS 25 notes that issues such as the different treatment of interest and dividends for tax purposes might make separate disclosure advisable.

Other disclosure requirements

14.19   The detailed disclosure requirements set out in FRS 25 are intended to provide information to help users of the accounts understand the significance of financial instruments to the entity's financial position, performance and cash flows, and also the amount, timing and certainty of future cash flows relating to the instruments. The disclosures therefore focus on market risk, credit risk, liquidity risk and cash flow interest rate risk. The standard does not prescribe the format, location or level of detail of the required disclosures, although guidance is provided on the issues to be taken into account in making judgements on these. As explained at 14.17 above, the disclosure requirements of the standard only apply when FRS 26 has been adopted, although disclosure on a voluntary basis by other entities is encouraged.

The disclosure requirements of FRS 25 are considered in more detail in Chapter 26.

Requirements of FRS 26

14.20   The requirements of FRS 26 on accounting for gains and losses on financial instruments are considered in more detail in Chapter 26. There are separate rules depending on whether or not the instrument forms part of a hedging relationship.

Transitional arrangements

14.21 FRS 25 includes special transitional arrangements in respect of the restatement of comparative information. Where an entity adopts:

(i) the presentation requirements of the standard for an accounting period beginning before 1 January 2006; or

(ii) the disclosure requirements of the standard for an accounting periods beginning before 1 January 2007,

it need not restate comparative information to comply with those requirements. Instead, the preceding year's figures can continue to be presented on the basis of the entity's previous accounting policies for financial instruments and the accounts should disclose:

(i) the fact that this approach has been taken;

(ii) the accounting policies adopted for the comparative information; and

(iii) the nature of the adjustments that would be needed to make the comparative information comply with FRS 25 – the standard does not require the adjustments to be quantified, but it does require any adjustment between the closing balance sheet for the comparative period (ie prepared on the basis of the previous accounting policies) and the opening balance for the current period (ie prepared on the basis of the FRS 25 requirements) to be treated as arising from a change in accounting policy, with the disclosures required by FRS 18 'Accounting policies'.

FINANCE CHARGES IN RESPECT OF FINANCE LEASES

Initial recording of asset and liability

14.22 Under SSAP 21 'Accounting for Leases and Hire Purchase Contracts', leases that are classified as finance leases should be recorded in the lessee's balance sheet as an asset and as an obligation to pay future rentals to the lessor. The classification of leases is considered in more detail in Chapter 21. At the inception of the lease (which is defined in the standard as the earlier of the date when the asset is brought into use or the date from which rental payments accrue), the amount recorded as an asset and the obligation recorded to the lessor will be the same. Strictly this should be the present value of the minimum lease payments. The minimum lease payments are defined in the standard as the minimum payments over the remaining part of the lease term (excluding charges for services and taxes to be paid by the lessor) and, in the case of the lessee, any residual amounts guaranteed by him or by a party related to him. However, SSAP 21 emphasises that, for practical purposes, the fair value of the leased asset will usually be a sufficiently close approximation to the present value of the minimum lease payments to make the fair value an acceptable figure to use when initially recording the asset and the related obligation to the lessor. Fair value is defined as the price at which an asset could be exchanged in an arm's length transaction less, where applicable, any grants receivable towards the purchase or use of the asset.

Calculating the present value of lease payments

14.23   If the fair value of the asset is not known, or is not considered a suitable figure to use, the present value of the lease payments should be calculated by discounting the minimum payments to be made under the lease at the interest rate implicit in the lease.

Example 14.8 – Present value calculation

F Ltd enters a finance lease in respect of an item of plant. The rental payments under the lease are £2,000 p.a., payable in advance, and the lease is for a term of four years. F Ltd establishes that the implicit rate of interest for such a lease is 8%. The payments are therefore discounted as follows.

Year	Discount factor (at 8%)	Payment	Present value
0	1.000	2,000	2,000
1	0.926 (a)	2,000	1,852
2	0.857 (b)	2,000	1,714
3	0.794 (c)	2,000	1,588
		8,000	7,154

(a) = 1.00/1.08

(b) = 0.926/1.08

(c) = 0.857/1.08

The asset and liability should therefore be recorded at the present value of £7,154.

Depreciation of asset

14.24   The leased asset must be depreciated over its expected useful economic life in the same way as any other fixed asset, but the life used should not exceed the lease term. The lease term is defined as:

— the period for which the lessee has contracted to lease the asset; and

— any further terms for which the lessee has the option to continue to lease the asset, with or without further payment, when it is reasonably certain at the inception of the lease that the lessee will exercise this option.

The depreciation of fixed assets is considered in Chapter 13.

Analysis of rental payments

14.25   The rental payments made by a lessee under a finance lease will consist of two elements:

— partial repayment of the amount due to the lessor; and

— finance charges in respect of the amount effectively 'borrowed' from the lessor to finance the purchase of the asset.

The rental payments must be analysed between these two elements for accounting purposes. The finance charges will be charged to the profit and loss account, as part of 'interest payable and similar charges' and the amount representing the repayment of 'borrowings' will reduce the balance due to the lessor.

Calculation of total finance charge

14.26   The total finance charge represents the difference between the fair value of the asset at the inception of the lease (or the present value of the minimum lease payments) and the total payments to be made by the lessee under the agreement.

Example 14.9 – Total finance charge

Using the details given in Example 14.8 above, the total finance charge is £846 (i.e. the difference between the total payments of £8,000 and the present value of those payments of £7,154).

Allocation of finance charge

14.27   SSAP 21 requires the total finance charge to be allocated to accounting periods over the term of the lease in a way that produces a constant periodic rate of charge on the balance outstanding in respect of the lessee's obligation to the lessor (or a reasonable approximation of this). There are three common methods of allocating the finance charge:

— the straight-line method;

— the sum of the digits (or rule of 78) method; and

— the actuarial method.

Each of these gives a different degree of accuracy, and the suitability of each method will depend on the materiality of the lease to the reporting entity.

The straight-line method

14.28   This is the least accurate method of allocating the finance charge, but is easy to apply and may be suitable where the amounts involved are small.

Example 14.10 – Allocating the finance charge (straight-line method)

G Ltd leases an asset under a finance lease with a primary term of four years, with the option to continue to lease for as long thereafter as the company wishes on payment of a nominal rental. The rental payments during the primary term of the lease are £3,000 pa, payable in arrears. The cash purchase price of the asset at the inception of the lease was £9,500.

The asset (and the related liability) will therefore be recorded at £9,500. Actual payments during the primary term of the lease will amount to £12,000 (i.e. £3,000 p.a. for four years).

The total finance charge is therefore £2,500 (i.e. £12,000 – £9,500).

If the finance charge is allocated on the straight line method, the annual charge will be £2,500/4 = £625.

The rental payments for each year will therefore be analysed as:

	£
Finance charge	625
Capital repayment	2,375
	3,000

The sum of the digits method

14.29   The sum of the digits (or rule of 78) method provides a reasonable approximation to the actuarial method (which gives the most accurate allocation of the finance charge) provided that:

— the lease term is not too long (e.g. up to five years);

— the interest rate is not very high.

To apply this method, it is necessary to calculate the number of periods over which the finance is to be allocated and assign a weighting to each period. The allocation can be done on a monthly, quarterly or an annual basis. Again this will give differing degrees of accuracy, and the most suitable method will depend on the materiality of the amounts involved.

Example 14.11 – Allocating the finance charge (sum of the digits method)

Using the same details as for Example 14.10.

The total finance charge is £2,500

Allocation on an annual basis using sum of the digits:

Year	Weighting	Fraction	Finance charge
			£
1	4	4/10	1,000
2	3	3/10	750
3	2	2/10	500
4	1	1/10	250
	10		2,500

The analysis of rental payments between capital repayments and finance charges will therefore be:

Year	Capital repayment	Finance charge	Total rental
	£	£	£
1	2,000	1,000	3,000
2	2,250	750	3,000
3	2,500	500	3,000
4	2,750	250	3,000
	9,500	2,500	12,000

The actuarial method

14.30 This method is the most complicated method to apply but gives the most accurate result and should always be used where the level and value of finance leases is significant in the context of the company. The appropriate rate of finance charge can be calculated by:

— using a calculator or computer program;

— using a mathematical formula;

— using present value tables;

— trial and error.

Once again, the calculation can be done on a monthly, quarterly or annual basis and the degree of accuracy will vary accordingly.

Example 14.12 – Allocating the finance charge (actuarial method)

Using the same details as for Example 14.10.

The total finance charge is £2,500.

Allocation on an annual basis using the actuarial method, with a rate of charge of 10.05%.

Year	Opening capital sum	Rental payment	Finance charge (10.05%)	Closing capital sum
	£	£	£	£
1	9,500	(3,000)	955	7,455
2	7,455	(3,000)	749	5,204
3	5,204	(3,000)	523	2,727
4	2,727	(3,000)	273	—
		12,000	2,500	

The analysis of rental payments between capital repayments and finance charges will therefore be:

Year	Capital repayment £	Finance charge £	Total rental £
1	2,045	955	3,000
2	2,251	749	3,000
3	2,477	523	3,000
4	2,727	273	3,000
	9,500	2,500	12,000

Comparison of results

14.31   The results of the three methods can be compared by considering the finance charge for each year in Examples 14.10 to 14.12.

Year	Straight-line £	Sum of the digits £	Actuarial £
1	625	1,000	955
2	625	750	749
3	625	500	523
4	625	250	273
Total	2,500	2,500	2,500

As the lease is short, the amounts are comparatively low and all of the calculations were carried out on an annual basis, the sum of the digits method gives a similar result to the actuarial method. However, this will not always be the case. Where finance leases are material, it will usually be necessary to use the actuarial method to achieve an accurate result and to use a monthly or quarterly basis (depending on the payment schedule) for the calculations. Where leases are less significant, the sum of the digits method may provide an acceptable alternative as the basis for allocating the finance charge. The straight line method will usually only be acceptable where finance leases are not significant to the company.

Lease payments in advance

14.32   The above examples are calculated on the basis that the rental payments are paid annually in arrears (i.e. at the end of the relevant year). Where payments are made in advance (i.e. at the beginning of the year, quarter or month), the number of periods over which the finance charge is allocated will alter.

Example 14.13 – Allocation of finance charge (payments in advance)

G Ltd leases an asset under a finance lease with a primary term of four years, with the option to continue to lease for as long thereafter as the company wishes on payment of a nominal rental. The rental payments during the primary term of the lease are £3,000 p.a.

(i) If the rental payments are made annually in arrears (i.e. at the end of Years 1 to 4), the finance charge will be allocated over four years.

(ii) If the rental payments are made annually in advance (i.e. at the beginning of Years 1 to 4), the full amount of 'finance' will be repaid at the beginning of Year 4 and it would therefore be inappropriate to allocate a finance charge to Year 4. The finance charge will therefore be allocated over Years 1, 2 and 3 only.

Lease variation clauses

14.33   Lease agreements sometimes include variation clauses which adjust the rental payments:

—   by reference to interest rate indicators (e.g. base rate);

—   to protect the parties to the lease from the effects of any tax changes that may take place during the term of the lease.

Where the level of rental payments changes as a result of a variation clause in the lease taking effect, the increase or decrease in payments should normally be accounted for as an increase or decrease in the finance charges in the period in which the variation takes place. It will not usually be necessary to rework the finance charge calculations carried out at the start of the lease.

Accounts disclosure

14.34   SSAP 21 also requires the following profit and loss account disclosures in respect of finance leases in the accounts of a lessee:

—   the accounting policy for leases (see Chapter 21); and

–   the aggregate finance charge in respect of finance leases — this is usually given in the note to the accounts dealing with interest payable and similar charges.

OPERATING LEASE CHARGES IN THE ACCOUNTS OF THE LESSEE

Accounting for rental payments

14.35   In the accounts of a lessee, rental payments under an operating lease should normally be accounted for on a straight line basis over the term of the lease, regardless of the actual timing of the payments. However, another systematic and rational basis of allocating the rental charges may be used if this is more appropriate. For instance, an alternative allocation might be appropriate if the rental charges are related to the amount of use that the lessee makes of the asset. Most operating lease agreements will be relatively straightforward, in that rental charges will usually be paid on a regular basis over the term of the lease. The charge to the profit and loss account for the year will therefore often be equivalent to the amount paid in the year, although some adjustment may be needed to reflect accruals and/or prepayments at the end of each accounting period (e.g. where rental is paid quarterly in advance).

Irregular payments

14.36   In some cases, the rental charges may not be paid systematically over the term of the lease. For instance, there may be a substantial initial payment followed by a number of small monthly, quarterly or annual payments. SSAP 21 'Accounting for Leases and Hire Purchase Contracts' is clear that the timing of the rental payments should not affect the accounting treatment. In this situation, therefore, the total payments over the term of the lease must be calculated and then allocated over the lease term on a straight-line basis.

Example 14.14 Accounting for irregular rental charges

A Ltd takes out a four-year operating lease on an item of equipment. The rental charges are as follows:

Year 1 – initial charge	£10,000
Year 1 – annual charge	£750
Year 2 – annual charge	£750
Year 3 – annual charge	£750
Year 4 – annual charge	£750
	£13,000

A Ltd must account for the rental payments by charging £3,250 to the profit and loss account each year for Years 1 to 4. The accounts will therefore show a prepayment at the end of Years 1 to 3, as a substantial element of the total rental has been paid in the form of the initial charge in Year 1.

Accounting for incentives

14.37   It has become relatively common in recent years for lessors to include various lease incentives in the arrangements to encourage a lessee to enter into a leasing agreement, particularly in the case of property leases. Such incentives include:

—   up-front cash payments by the lessor to the lessee (known as reverse premiums);

—   contributions to some of the costs to be incurred by the lessee (for instance, in fitting out the property to meet its own specific needs or in relocating from another site);

—   a rent-free period;

—   the assumption by the lessor of the lessee's rental commitments under an existing lease.

Incentives of this type were not as common when SSAP 21 was issued and so the accounting treatment is not covered in the standard. The latest guidance is contained in UITF Abstract 28 'Operating Lease Incentives'. This Abstract concludes that most lease agreements that include incentives will have been structured by the lessor to provide the overall market return required, but in a way that meets the cash flow requirements of the lessee. Therefore, where an operating lease agreement includes an incentive such as a cash payment or rent-free period, the level of the rental payments under the lease will usually be higher than would normally be expected under prevailing market rates (even though the rentals may be described in the agreement as being at market rates). Without this, the lessor would not be able to achieve the required rate of return. In these circumstances, application of the accruals concept requires the benefit of the incentive to be matched with the additional costs to the lessee in subsequent years in the form of higher rental payments. The effect of any incentive should therefore be spread over the term of the lease, except where there is provision for the rental payments to be adjusted to market rates during the term of the lease, in which case it will usually be appropriate to spread the incentive over a shorter period.

Review of rental payments

14.38 Where the lease agreement provides for the rental payments to be reviewed during the term of the lease and adjusted to prevailing market rates, it will usually be appropriate to spread the benefit of the incentive over the period to the first review, if it is reasonably expected that the rental payments will be adjusted to genuine market rates at that point.

Method of spreading the incentive

14.39 The benefits of the incentive should usually be spread over the term of the lease (or the period to the first review date) on a straight-line basis. However, the Abstract does permit another systematic allocation method to be used if this will give a more accurate reflection of the time pattern of the benefit that the lessee receives from the use of the asset.

Accounts disclosure

14.40 SSAP 21 requires disclosure of the total operating lease rentals charged to the profit and loss account, analysed between:

— hire of plant and machinery; and

— other operating leases.

The disclosure of commitments under operating leases in Chapter 33.

Chapter 15   Taxation

TAX ON THE PROFIT OR LOSS ON ORDINARY ACTIVITIES

Requirement of CA 1985

15.1   Each of the standard formats for the profit and loss account requires separate disclosure of tax on the profit or loss from ordinary activities and tax on any extraordinary profit or loss. The formats also have a further heading for 'other taxes not shown under the above items'. This heading is not generally used in the UK at present. In addition, CA 1985 requires the following details to be disclosed:

— details of any special circumstances which affect the tax liability in respect of profits, income or capital gains for the current year or any future year;

— the amount charged in respect of UK corporation tax;

— the amount that would have been charged for UK corporation tax but for the availability of double tax relief;

— the amount charged in respect of UK income tax;

— the amount of any taxation imposed outside the UK in respect of profits, income and capital gains (so far as these are charged to revenue).

The last four disclosures must be given separately in respect of tax on the profit or loss on ordinary activities and tax on any extraordinary profit or loss. Compliance with the disclosure requirements of FRS 3 'Reporting Financial Performance', FRS 16 'Current tax' and FRS 19 'Deferred tax' will usually be sufficient to ensure compliance with CA 1985.

For accounting periods beginning on or after 1 January 2005, the detailed requirements of Schedule 4 are only relevant where the company prepares Companies Act accounts (as opposed to IAS accounts).

Current tax

15.2 FRS 16 defines current tax as: 'the amount of tax estimated to be payable or recoverable in respect of the taxable profit or loss for a period, together with adjustments to estimates in respect of previous periods'. The current tax charge or credit on the profit or loss on ordinary activities will usually comprise some or all of the following items:

— a charge or credit in respect of UK corporation tax;

— a charge or credit in respect of foreign tax;

— a charge or credit in respect of group relief payable or receivable;

— adjustments to tax provided in previous years.

Recognition of current tax

15.3 FRS 16 requires all current tax to be recognised in the profit and loss account, except where the gain or loss to which it relates is (or has been) dealt with directly in the statement of total recognised gains and losses. In this case, the attributable tax should also be recognised directly in the statement of total recognised gains and losses. The guidance in the standard notes that where it is difficult to determine the amount of current tax relating to items recognised in the statements of total recognised gains and losses (and this is only expected to happen in exceptional circumstances), tax should be allocated on a pro-rata basis, or using another allocation method that is more appropriate in the circumstances.

Taxable profit or loss

15.4 FRS 16 defines a taxable profit or loss as: 'the profit or loss for the period, determined in accordance with the rules established by the tax authorities, upon which taxes are assessed'. The charge or credit for UK corporation tax will be the estimated tax payable or recoverable as a result of trading profits or losses, capital gains or losses and other income and charges arising during the year, as shown by the draft corporation tax computation.

Tax rate

15.5 FRS 16 requires current tax to be measured at the amounts expected to be paid or recovered, using tax rates and laws that have been enacted, or substantively enacted, by the balance sheet date. Substantively enacted is defined as included in either:

— a Bill that has been passed by the House of Commons and is awaiting only passage through the House of Lords and Royal Assent; or

— a resolution having statutory effect that has been passed under the Provisional Collection of Taxes Act 1968 (this is rarely used in practice).

There is no formal requirement to disclose the tax rate used, but it has become normal practice to do so.

Effect of double tax relief

15.6   In some cases, the charge in respect of corporation tax may be reduced by the availability of double tax relief. In this situation, FRS 16 requires UK tax disclosures to be given both before and after the double tax relief. Appendix 1 to the standard gives the following method of disclosure as an example:

Example 15.1 – Disclosure of double tax relief

	£	£
UK corporation tax:		
Current tax on income for the period	10,500	
Adjustments in respect of prior periods	(345)	
	10,155	
Double tax relief	(625)	
		9,530

Charge or credit for deferred taxation

15.7   FRS 19 'Deferred Tax' requires the deferred tax charge or credit for the accounting period to be recognised in the profit and loss account, except to the extent that it is attributable to a gain or loss that is, or has been, recognised directly in the statement of total recognised gains and losses. In this case, the attributable deferred tax should also be recognised directly in the statement of total recognised gains and losses. The guidance notes that, in exceptional circumstances, it may be difficult to determine the amount of deferred tax relating to gains and losses recognised in the statement of total gains and losses, in which case a reasonable pro-rata or other more appropriate allocation may be used. All deferred tax that is recognised in the profit and loss account must be included in tax on profit or loss on ordinary activities. The recognition and measurement requirements of FRS 19 are considered in Chapter 31.

Separate disclosure of deferred tax

15.8   The accounts must show separately:

—   the amount of deferred tax charged or credited within tax on profit or loss on ordinary activities; and

—   the amount of deferred tax charged or credited in the statement of total recognised gains and losses for the period.

In each case, the deferred tax charge or credit must be analysed into the following components, if the amounts involved are material:

— the origination and reversal of timing differences;

— changes in tax rates and laws;

— adjustments to deferred tax assets arising in previous periods; and

— where relevant, changes in the amount of discount deducted in arriving at the deferred tax balance.

Example 15.2 – Disclosure and analysis of deferred tax

	20X2 £		20X1 £
UK corporation tax:			
Current tax on income for the period	7,450		6,321
Adjustments in respect of prior periods	40		(131)
	7,490		6,190
Deferred tax:			
Origination and reversal of timing differences	390	275	
Effect of decrease in tax rate on opening liability	(70)	—	
	320		275
Tax on profit on ordinary activities	7,810		6,465

Reconciliation of tax charge

15.9   As part of the requirement to disclose the circumstances that affect the current and total tax charges and credits for the current period, or might affect those of future periods, FRS 19 requires the notes to the accounts to include a reconciliation of the current tax charge or credit on ordinary activities for the period (i.e. the tax charge or credit before taking into account any deferred tax) to the current tax charge that would result from applying a relevant standard rate of tax to the profit or loss on ordinary activities before tax. Either the monetary amounts or the tax rates can be reconciled – it is anticipated that most companies will choose to use monetary amounts in the reconciliation. The note should also explain the basis on which the standard tax rate has been determined.

Example 15.3 – Reconciliation of current tax charge

Factors affecting the current tax charge for the period:

	20X2 £	20X1 £
Profit on ordinary activities before tax	41,350	32,300
Multiplied by standard rate of UK corporation tax for small companies – 20% (20X1: 20%)	8,270	6,460
Effects of:		
Expenses not deductible for tax purposes (primarily goodwill amortisation)	3,155	1,634
Capital allowances for period in excess of depreciation	(4,480)	(1,246)
Utilisation of tax losses	—	(527)
Higher tax rates on overseas earnings	505	—
Adjustments to tax charge in respect of prior periods	40	(131)
Current tax charge for period	7,490	6,190

Foreign tax

15.10 If the company has overseas interests and part of the profit or loss for the year is therefore subject to foreign tax, the amount of this tax must be separately disclosed.

Example 15.4 – Separate disclosure of foreign tax

	20X2 £		20X1 £	
UK corporation tax:				
Current tax on income for the period	7,450		6,321	
Adjustments in respect of prior periods	40		(131)	
		7,490		6,190
Foreign tax:				
Current tax on income for the period	80		20	
Adjustments in respect of prior periods	(5)		—	
		75		20
		7,565		6,210
Deferred tax:				
Origination and reversal of timing differences	390		275	
Effect of decrease in tax rate on opening liability	(70)		—	
		320		275
Tax on profit on ordinary activities		7,885		6,485

Tax recognised in the statement of total recognised gains and losses must be similarly analysed.

Withholding tax

15.11   Withholding tax is defined in FRS 16 as: 'tax on dividends or other income that is deducted by the payer of the income and paid to the tax authorities wholly on behalf of the recipient'. Where an entity receives (or is due to receive) dividends, interest or other similar income, the amount shown as income in the profit and loss account should include any amount deducted for withholding tax but should exclude any other taxes and any notional tax. Income received after the deduction of withholding tax should therefore be grossed up for the amount of tax deducted, and this tax should be shown as part of the entity's tax charge for the year.

Example 15.5 – Accounting for income subject to withholding tax

A Ltd has received income of £17,000 from which withholding tax of £3,000 has been deducted. The profit and loss account will therefore show the gross income of £20,000 and £3,000 will be deducted from profit before tax as part of the current tax charge for the year.

Similarly, any outgoing dividends paid by the entity, or any interest or similar payments made, should include the amount of any withholding tax but should exclude any other taxes (e.g. the attributable tax credit on UK dividends). All other income and expenses should be included in pre-tax results on the basis of the amount receivable or payable. No adjustment should be made to reflect a notional amount of tax that would have been paid or relieved in respect of the transaction if it had been taxable or allowable for tax on a different basis.

Dividend income

15.12   The tax credit attributable to UK dividends is not the same as withholding tax. In effect, the tax credit is a notional amount, reflecting the fact that the dividend has been paid out of income that has been taxed, rather than an actual amount of tax deducted from the dividend. UK dividend income should not be grossed up to reflect this notional tax and the amount included in income will therefore be the actual sum received or receivable. Under certain circumstances, companies with overseas interests and activities may be able to pay a dividend under the foreign income dividend (FID) scheme. A dividend paid under this scheme does not carry a tax credit. Where a company receives a dividend which has been paid under the FID scheme, the amount to be recorded as income will be the amount actually received (i.e. with no adjustment for tax).

Transitional arrangements for charities

15.13   Certain non-taxpaying entities (e.g. charities) are entitled to transitional relief following the removal of their right to reclaim tax credits on UK dividends. FRS 16 permits these entities to continue to gross up dividend income for this transitional relief, provided that the nature and amount of the relief is disclosed separately in the accounts.

Group relief

15.14 Where potential tax liabilities are covered by group relief, the company receiving the relief may pay the surrendering company for the relief given. Payment may be made at any amount up to the gross amount of the group relief received, but in most cases the amount paid will be based on the equivalent rate of corporation tax. Particular care should be taken if it is proposed to make payments at a higher or lower rate, or to make no payment for group relief, as this could be considered to be a transaction at undervalue or overvalue between the companies and could give rise to legal difficulties if one of the companies becomes insolvent.

Disclosure of payments for group relief

15.15 Where the payment for group relief is based on the equivalent rate of corporation, the charge (or credit) should be included in the current tax charge or credit on the profit or loss on ordinary activities for the year and should be disclosed separately.

Example 15.6 – Separate disclosure of payment for group relief

	20X2 £		20X1 £
UK corporation tax:			
Current tax on income for the period	3,250	6,321	
Payment to a fellow subsidiary for group relief (at 30%)	4,200	—	
Current tax for the period	7,450	6,321	
Adjustments in respect of prior periods	40	(131)	
		7,490	6,190
Deferred tax:			
Origination and reversal of timing differences	390	275	
Effect of decrease in tax rate on opening liability	(70)	—	
		320	275
Tax on profit on ordinary activities		7,810	6,465

If, in certain circumstances, it is considered appropriate to make payments at other rates, or to make no payment in respect of group relief, full details should be disclosed in the accounts. Where amounts are paid in excess of or below the rate of corporation tax, the payments are usually disclosed as separate items on the face of the profit and loss account, immediately above the profit or loss before taxation, rather than as part of the tax charge or credit for the year. Additional information will usually need to be given in the notes to explain the transaction.

Adjustments in respect of prior periods

15.16   Tax figures are usually included in the accounts on the basis of draft computations, and adjustments are often needed in the subsequent year (or years) to reflect the final figures. Charges and credits relating to previous years should be shown separately as part of the appropriate element (i.e. current tax, foreign tax, deferred tax) of the tax charge or credit on the profit or loss on ordinary activities. If the adjustments relate to an item that was recognised in the statement of total recognised gains and losses, the tax adjustments should also be recognised in that statement and should be analysed into the various components in the same way as the tax charge or credit in the profit or loss account. If they relate to an item that was classified as extraordinary for accounting purposes, the tax adjustment should also be recognised as an extraordinary item.

Tax on extraordinary items

15.17   Where the accounts include an extraordinary profit or loss, any tax relating to this profit or loss must be shown separately as part of the extraordinary item. The tax element must be analysed into its component parts (e.g. current tax, foreign tax, deferred tax) where relevant. As explained in Chapter 9, the stringent requirements of FRS 3 'Reporting Financial Performance' mean that extraordinary items will now appear in accounts only rarely, if at all. FRS 3 sets out rules for calculating the tax effect of an extraordinary item. This is to be done by:

—   determining the tax on the profit or loss on ordinary activities as if the extraordinary item did not exist;

—   comparing this with the tax charge on the profit or loss for the period, including the extraordinary item.

Any difference in the tax charge or credit (including deferred tax) is the tax to be attributed to the extraordinary item. If there is no difference, then the extraordinary item has no tax effect. It is helpful if this fact is stated in the note to the accounts setting out details of the extraordinary item.

Tax on additional FRS 3 Format headings

15.18   FRS 3 'Reporting Financial Performance' identifies three specific items which it requires to be shown separately on the face of the profit and loss account, after operating profit and before interest:

—   profits or losses on the sale or termination of an operation;

—   costs of a fundamental reorganisation or restructuring having a material effect on the nature and focus of the reporting entity's operations;

—   profits and losses on the disposal of fixed assets (other than marginal adjustments to depreciation previously charged).

The requirements of FRS 3 are considered in more detail in Chapter 9. Where any of these specific items are disclosed in the accounts, FRS 3 also requires information on the tax effect to be given in the notes to the accounts. The tax effect is to be calculated in the same way as for an extraordinary item (see 15.17 above). As a minimum, the tax effect should be disclosed for these items in aggregate, but if the tax effect of individual items is different, further detail should be given to clarify the impact on the accounts. If there is no tax effect, it is helpful to state this in the notes to the accounts.

Special circumstances affecting the tax charge

15.19   FRS 3 'Reporting Financial Performance' requires the accounts to include disclosure of any special circumstances affecting:

—   the tax charge or credit for the year;

—   the expected tax charge or credit for future years.

This requirement is very broad and the disclosures will inevitably depend on individual circumstances, but the following are examples of some of the issues that might be covered:

—   the effect of significant levels of losses brought forward, utilised in the year or carried forward to future years;

—   the effect on the tax charge for the year of significant amounts of disallowable expenditure;

—   the inclusion in the profit and loss account for the year of other items that do not have a tax effect (e.g. the receipt of a significant tax free grant).

In each case, the individual effects should be quantified. FRS 19 'Deferred Tax' amplifies the disclosure requirement of FRS 3 by requiring the notes to the accounts to include a reconciliation of the current tax charge or credit on ordinary activities for the period to the current tax charge that would result from applying a relevant standard rate of tax to the profit or loss on ordinary activities before tax (see 15.9 above).

Change in the basis of taxation

15.20   If there is a fundamental change in the basis of taxation, the effect of the change should be treated as part of the tax charge or credit for the year on the profit or loss on ordinary activities but should be shown separately on the face of the profit and loss account. Such fundamental changes are likely to be rare in practice. It is important to recognise that a change in the basis of taxation does not constitute a change in accounting policy. The underlying accounting policy is to provide for the amount of taxation that is expected to become payable. The fact that the basis of the taxation charge has altered does not change the underlying accounting policy.

The effect is therefore reflected in the accounts in the year that the change takes place, but is separately disclosed because of its significance.

Changes in tax rates and allowances

15.21 Changes in the rates of taxation or in tax allowances will usually affect the provision for deferred taxation. The effect of such changes should be included in the tax charge or credit on the profit or loss on ordinary activities but should be shown separately. Disclosure in the notes to the accounts will usually be sufficient. Once again, there is no change in accounting policy when the underlying rate of taxation changes or when tax allowances are altered. The underlying accounting policy for deferred taxation is to provide for the liability that is expected to crystallise, and provision will be made at the existing rate of tax and on the basis of the existing system of tax allowances if there is no indication that these are expected to change. If changes do subsequently take place, they do not alter the fact that the previous provision was the best estimate on the basis of the information available at the time that the provision was made. Therefore the effect of any change must be reflected in the accounts for the year when the change occurs and should not be treated as a prior year adjustment.

ACCOUNTING FOR RECOVERABLE ADVANCE CORPORATION TAX

Background

15.22 Prior to April 1999, companies paying a dividend to their shareholders were required to pay advance corporation tax (ACT) in respect of the dividend. ACT paid in this way was normally recoverable by being offset against the corporation tax liability on the profits of the year in which the dividend was paid or against the profits of future years, although there were also provisions which allowed ACT to be carried back or surrendered to other group companies. A shadow ACT system continues to operate, allowing companies with unrecovered ACT carried forward after April 1999 to continue to recover this in the same way as if the previous ACT system still existed. Appendix II to FRS 16 sets out transitional arrangements on accounting for ACT that becomes recoverable after April 1999. These arrangements are based on the accounting treatment adopted in SSAP 8 'The Treatment of Taxation under the Imputation System in the Accounts of Companies' which was superseded by FRS 16.

Recoverable ACT

15.23 ACT can be carried forward indefinitely for tax purposes, although the shadow ACT system imposes a restriction on the set-off of ACT so that it is only recoverable to the same extent as under the previous tax system. For accounting purposes, an assessment must be made of the likely recoverability of any ACT that is unrecovered at the balance sheet date. In most cases, its recoverability will be dependent on the level of corporation tax in future years, which in turn will depend on the company's profitability in those years, along with various other factors, such as the level of capital expenditure and any disallowable expenditure in those years. Under the guidance in FRS 16, an amount of ACT previously paid on outgoing dividends is regarded as recoverable when it can be:

—   offset against a corporation tax liability on the profits of the current accounting period or of previous accounting periods;

—   properly offset against a credit balance on the deferred tax account; or

—   expected to be recoverable, taking into account expected profits and dividends – normally those of the next accounting period only.

Offset against deferred tax balance

15.24   If the accounts include a provision for deferred tax, unrecovered ACT can be deducted from the amount provided on the basis that this represents future corporation tax against which the ACT can be recovered. However, the amount offset in this way should not exceed the amount that can actually be recovered against that liability, taking into account the restrictions on recoverability imposed by the tax system.

Future period considered

15.25   Where there is no deferred tax provision, or where the total unrecovered ACT exceeds the amount that can be offset against the deferred tax provision, the recoverability of the remaining ACT needs to be carefully assessed. In considering the recoverability of ACT for accounting purposes, only the immediate and foreseeable future should be taken into account. The guidance in Appendix II to FRS 16 does not impose a formal limit on the future period considered, noting that this will depend on the circumstances of each case, but it suggests that the future period should not extend beyond the next accounting period.

Recognition of recoverable ACT

15.26   Any ACT that is regarded as recoverable under the stringent requirements of the standard should be recognised in the accounts and either:

—   deducted from the deferred tax provision, if there is one; or

—   shown as a deferred tax asset.

Change in assessment of recoverability

15.27   If ACT that was previously regarded as recoverable becomes irrecoverable, it should be charged in the profit and loss account as a separately disclosed component of the tax charge for the period. Similarly, if ACT that was not previously recognised in the accounts is recovered under the tax system applying after April 1999, it should be credited to the profit and loss account as a separately disclosed component of the tax charge (or credit) for the period.

Chapter 16   Dividends And Other Appropriations

ACCOUNTING AND DISCLOSURE BEFORE 1 JANUARY 2005

CA 1985 requirements

16.1 For accounting periods beginning before 1 January 2005, CA 1985 requires every company profit and loss account to show the aggregate amount of any dividends paid or proposed, with the aggregate amount of any proposed dividends shown separately. The total of dividends paid and proposed must be shown on the face of the profit and loss account, but the additional details may be given in the notes to the accounts (and this is the usual practice).

A small company which prepares shorter form accounts under Schedule 8 to CA 1985 must continue to disclose the aggregate of dividends paid and proposed on the face of the profit and loss account, but there is no requirement in this case to show proposed dividends separately. A small company which files abbreviated accounts need not file its profit and loss account and so details of dividends paid and proposed will not be published.

Additional disclosure under FRS 4

16.2 For accounting periods beginning before 1 January 2005, FRS 4 'Capital Instruments' also requires:

(i) separate disclosure of equity and non-equity dividends; and

(ii) separate disclosure of the aggregate dividend for each class of shares, including the totals for:

- equity dividends;
- participating dividends; and

- non-equity dividends.

A participating dividend is defined in FRS 4 as a dividend (or part of a dividend) on a non-equity share that, in accordance with a company's memorandum and articles of association, is always equivalent to a fixed multiple of the dividend payable on an equity share. The most common example of a dividend that would meet this definition, and the one referred to in the Application Notes to the standard, is the dividend on participating preference shares, where the shares carry an entitlement both to a fixed dividend for each accounting period and also to an additional amount based on a proportion of the dividend paid to the holders of equity shares.

The required disclosures can be given on the face of the profit and loss account or in the notes to the accounts. They are usually given in the notes on the basis that the level of detail required will make disclosure on the face of the profit and loss account inappropriate. Where the analysis of dividends between equity and non-equity is not given on the face of the profit and loss account, FRS 4 requires the heading to make clear that amounts relating to non-equity shares are included. The distinction between equity and non-equity shares under FRS 4 is considered in detail in Chapter 31. Examples of two possible disclosures are set out below:

Example 16.1 – Equity and non-equity shares (I)

		20X2		20X1
	£	£	£	£
Profit or loss for the financial year		362		247
Dividends paid and proposed:				
Equity shares	(90)		(80)	
Non-equity shares	(40)		(40)	
		(130)		(120)
Retained profit for the year transferred to reserves		232		127

The dividends figure should be cross-referenced to a note showing the amounts of any proposed dividends.

Example 16.2 – Equity and non-equity shares (II)

	20X2	20X1
	£	£
Profit or loss for the financial year	362	247
Dividends paid and proposed on equity and non-equity shares	(130)	(120)
Retained profit for the year transferred to reserves	232	127

In this case, the dividends figure should be cross-referenced to a note to the accounts giving the required analysis between equity and non-equity dividends, as well as separate details of any proposed dividends.

The following example takes the details given in Examples 16.1 and 16.2 and shows a suggested note disclosure that would meet the basic requirements of both CA 1985 and of FRS 4.

Example 16.3 – Disclosure to meet basic requirements of FRS 4 and the Act

Dividends paid and proposed

	20X2	20X1
	£	£
Equity shares:		
Interim dividend paid during the year		20
Proposed final dividend	60	60
	90	80
Non-equity shares:		
Dividend paid during the year	40	40
	130	120

ESOP trusts

16.4   Under the requirements of UITF Abstract 38 'Accounting for ESOP Trusts', where the assets and liabilities of an ESOP trust are included in the accounts of the sponsoring company because it has de facto control over them, any dividend income arising on own shares held by the trust should be excluded in arriving at profit before tax and deducted from the aggregate of dividends paid and proposed. Accounting for ESOP trusts is considered in more detail in Chapter 4.

Finance costs of non-equity shares

16.5   FRS 4 also requires all finance costs in respect of non-equity shares to be treated as appropriations of profit. Finance costs are to be calculated in the same way as for debt and specifically include:

(i)   dividends payable in respect of the shares;

(ii)   any direct issue costs in respect of the shares;

(iii)   any other payments made in respect of the shares (e.g. an additional amount payable on redemption of the shares).

The total finance costs of non-equity shares are defined as the difference between the net issue proceeds of the shares (i.e. after deduction of any direct issue costs) and the total amount payable in respect of the shares (e.g. dividends and any amounts payable on redemption). The detailed requirements of FRS 4 on the calculation and accounting treatment of finance costs are considered in more detail in Chapter 14.

Treatment of share issue costs

16.6   The definition of issue costs under FRS 4 is considered in more detail in Chapter 14. In the case of non-equity shares, costs that meet the definition must be accounted for initially as a reduction in the proceeds of issue of the shares. Any issue costs that do not meet the definition must be charged to the profit and loss account as they are incurred. The usual accounting treatment is to debit the direct issue costs to the share premium account. The accounting entries at the time of issue of the shares would therefore be as follows.

Example 16.4 – Treatment of issue costs

Issue of 500 4% preference shares of £1 with direct issue costs of £60.

Dr	Cash received	£440	
Dr	Share premium account	£60	
Cr	Share capital account		£500

If there is no balance on the share premium account, or the balance is insufficient to absorb the issue costs, the costs should be debited directly to the profit and loss account reserve.

Distinction between redeemable and non-redeemable shares

16.7   If the non-equity shares are not redeemable at a specified future date, there is no obligation for the issuer to make a repayment in respect of the shares. In this case, the finance costs of the shares will simply be the amount of dividend payable each year. Any direct issue costs relating to the shares will remain within shareholders' funds (usually as a reduction of the share premium account) until the shares are redeemed or cancelled, when the issue costs will be taken to the profit and loss account.

The definition of finance costs explained in 16.4 above means that any direct issue costs in respect of redeemable non-equity shares are effectively appropriated in the profit and loss account over the life of the shares as part of the annual finance cost. The total finance costs must therefore be allocated over the life of the shares, at a constant rate on the carrying value of the shares.

Example 16.5 – Issue costs of redeemable shares

Issue of 500 4% preference shares of £1 at the beginning of the year with direct issue costs £60. Shares are redeemable at par at the end of five years.

The initial accounting entries would be:

Dr	Cash received	£440	
Dr	Share premium account	£60	
Cr	Share capital account		£500

The total finance costs of the shares are calculated as:

	£
Dividends payable 4% on 500 for five years	100
Repayment at par at the end of ten years	500
Total amount payable in respect of the shares	600
Less: Net issue proceeds	(440)
Total finance cost	160

The total finance cost of £160 should be appropriated in the profit and loss account over five years at a constant rate on the carrying amount of the shares. The effective rate will therefore be approximately 6.9% and the accounting entries will be:

Date	Opening carrying amount	Finance costs (P&L account)	Amounts actually paid	Closing carrying amount
	£	£	£	£
Year 1	440	30	(20)	450
Year 2	450	31	(20)	461
Year 3	461	32	(20)	473
Year 4	473	33	(20)	486
Year 5	486	34	(520)	—

The profit and loss account disclosure in Year 1 might be as follows (assuming dividends of £35 on equity shares):

	£	£
Profit for the financial year (assumed)		110
Dividends paid and proposed on equity and non-equity shares	(55)	
Other finance costs in respect of non-equity shares	(10)	
		(65)
Retained profit for the year transferred to reserves		45

With a note to the accounts showing the following detail:

Dividends and other appropriations

Equity shares:

Interim dividend paid during the year	15		
Proposed final dividend	20		
		35	

Non-equity shares:

Dividend paid during the year	20		
Other finance costs	10		
		30	
		65	

Share issue expenses charged to share premium account

16.8   Section 130 of CA 1985 permits the expenses of an issue of shares to be charged to the share premium account. FRS 4 emphasises that the requirements of the standard are not intended to prohibit the subsequent charging of share issue costs to the share premium account. This must be done by means of a reserves transfer. As the share issue costs may well have been debited to the share premium account at the time of the share issue, this means that the issue costs appropriated in the profit and loss account in any one year will effectively be credited to the share premium account at the time of appropriation and then debited again as a reserves transfer.

Example 16.6 – Share issue expenses charged to share premium account

Using the details from Example 16.5:

	Profit and loss reserve	Share premium	Non-equity share capital
	£	£	£
Opening balance (assumed)	400	100	100
Issue of non-equity shares	–	(60)	500
Year 1 finance costs (appropriated in P&L account)	–	10	–
Retained profit transferred from P&L account	45	–	–
Transfer of issue costs to share premium	10	(10)	–
Closing balance	455	40	600

Insufficient distributable reserves

16.9   FRS 4 requires the full amount of the finance costs of non-equity shares to be appropriated from the profit and loss account each year. This includes the amount of any dividend payable and applies even if the company does not have sufficient reserves to pay the relevant dividend. However, in these circumstances it would generally be unacceptable to describe the amount appropriated as a dividend. It will usually be more appropriate to describe such an amount as other finance costs in respect of non-equity shares.

Example 16.7 – Insufficient distributable reserves

Dividend payable on non-equity shares of £40 p.a.

Dividend actually paid in 20X2 restricted to £20 due to unavailability of distributable profits.

Dividends and other appropriations

	20X2	20X1
	£	£
Non-equity shares:		
Dividend paid	20	40
Other finance costs	20	–
	40	40

The notes to the accounts should explain how the additional finance costs arise in the current year.

Accruals basis for dividends

16.10   FRS 4 emphasises that dividends should normally be accounted for on an accruals basis, except in circumstances where ultimate payment is remote. An example of the latter situation given in the standard is where profits are insufficient to support the declaration and payment of a dividend and the dividend rights are non-cumulative. In practice many non-equity shares will carry cumulative dividend rights. Where dividend rights are cumulative, shareholders retain their right to the dividend, even if distributable reserves are insufficient to pay the dividend. FRS 4's requirements mean that the dividends on cumulative non-equity shares must always be appropriated in the profit and loss account as part of the overall finance costs of the shares, regardless of whether they can be legally declared and paid.

Difficulty often arises over where the credit entry for this appropriation should be made. If the dividend cannot be legally declared and paid, it is not appropriate to include it as an amount payable within current liabilities. The credit should usually be taken to the profit and loss account reserve and the arrears of the dividend should be disclosed in the notes on reserves. In the year in which the dividend arrears are paid, the notes to the accounts should disclose the total amount paid in respect of non-equity dividends and the fact that part of this amount was appropriated in the accounts of previous years. The amount shown as dividends paid and proposed in the profit and loss account will be the dividend relating to the current year only, as the amount paid in respect of the previous years will have already been shown as an appropriation in the profit and loss account for those years. The following disclosure might be appropriate.

Example 16.8 – Payment of dividend arrears

Using the details from Example 16.7 and assuming the dividend arrears are paid in the following year.

Extract from profit and loss account:

	£	20X3 £	£	20X2 £
Profit for the financial year		90		20
Dividends paid and proposed on non-equity shares	(40)		(20)	
Other finance costs in respect of non-equity shares	–		(20)	
		(40)		(40)
Retained profit/(loss) transferred to reserves		50		(20)

Extract from the notes to the accounts:

Dividends and other appropriations

	£	20X3 £	£	20X2 £
Non-equity shares:				
Dividends paid during the year		60		20
Dividends appropriated in previous year	(20)		–	
Additional finance costs	–		20	
		(20)		20
		40		40

Scrip dividends

16.11   Shareholders may sometimes be offered additional shares as an alternative to cash dividends. These are known as scrip dividends. FRS 4 includes specific guidance on accounting for scrip dividends in the accounts of the issuer and requires the value of any shares issued in this way to be taken as the amount that would have been receivable if the shareholder had chosen the cash dividend alternative. The amount appropriated in the profit and loss account should be the value of the shares taken up by shareholders, plus the amount actually paid in cash dividends. The amount appropriated in the profit and loss account will therefore always be the same, irrespective of whether the dividend is payable in cash or in the form of shares.

Bonus issue of shares

16.12   A scrip dividend often takes the legal form of a bonus issue of shares and shareholders who opt to take the share alternative will usually do so before they become entitled to the cash dividend. In this case, the amount appropriated in the profit and loss account in respect of the scrip dividend should be written back as a movement on the profit and loss account reserve and an appropriate amount should be transferred between reserves and share capital to record the capitalisation of reserves. The amount transferred will usually be the nominal value of the shares issued.

Issue of shares for cash

16.13   If the shareholder has not elected to take the share alternative before becoming entitled to the dividend, the legal form of the share issue is slightly different. In this case, the shareholder who takes up additional shares has effectively invested the cash received in the form of a dividend in the additional shares taken up. The amount of the cash dividend therefore represents the issue proceeds of the shares, and if these are greater than the nominal value of the shares, a share premium will need to be recorded in the accounts.

Uncertainty over take-up

16.14   Where there is uncertainty over how many shareholders will elect to take the share alternative, FRS 4 requires the accounts to reflect the dividend on the basis that the full amount will be payable in cash. The full amount will therefore be appropriated as a proposed dividend in the profit and loss account and the liability to pay the dividend in cash will be shown as a creditor in the balance sheet. In the following year, adjustments will have to be made to reserves and share capital to reflect the actual take-up of the share alternative. No adjustment should be required in the profit and loss account, as FRS 4's requirement means that the appropriation will always be based on the full amount of the cash alternative.

ACCOUNTING AND DISCLOSURE AFTER 1 JANUARY 2005

CA 1985 requirements

16.15   For accounting periods beginning on or after 1 January 2005, paragraph 3(7) of Schedule 4 is removed by the *Companies Act 1985* (*International Accounting Standards and Other Accounting Amendments*) *Regulations 2004* (SI 2004/2947) and is replaced by a new paragraph 35A of Schedule 4 which requires the notes to the accounts to show:

(i)   amounts set aside or withdrawn from reserves;

(ii)   the aggregate amount of dividends paid in the year, other than those for which a liability existed at the previous balance sheet date;

(iii)   the aggregate amount of dividends that the company is liable to pay at the balance sheet date; and

(iv)   the aggregate amount of dividends proposed before the date of approval of the accounts and not included in the above disclosures.

In other words, company law no longer requires proposed dividends to be recognised in the accounts, or dividends to be shown in the profit and loss account.

These changes enable companies to comply with FRS 21 'Events after the balance sheet date' which also comes into effect on 1 January 2005. FRS 21 does not permit a proposed dividend which is still subject to shareholder approval to be included in the balance sheet, on the basis that it does not meet the accounting definition of a liability at the balance sheet date. The change also removes the requirement for dividends paid during the year to be reported in the profit and loss account, and so allows them to be accounted for as transactions with shareholders, as required by FRS 25 'Financial Instruments: Disclosure and Presentation'.

Schedule 8 to CA 1985 is amended in the same way as Schedule 4 and so the new disclosures must also be given in shorter form accounts, but they do not need to be given in abbreviated Companies Act accounts where these are prepared for filing purposes.

Classification of financial instruments

16.16   FRS 25 'Financial Instruments: Disclosure and Presentation' introduces a new requirement for each financial instrument to be classified as a financial asset, a financial liability or an equity instrument, and for dividends, interest and other gains and losses to be recognised in the accounts on the basis of this classification. The classification must be based on the substance of the contractual arrangements rather than their legal form. This could result in certain instruments being classified as financial liabilities, even though they may be called shares for legal purposes, and in any related dividends payable being accounted for as an interest charge in the profit and loss account rather than as a distribution to shareholders. Gains and losses on instruments classified as financial liabilities should also be recognised in the profit and loss account.

For instance, a preference share that is redeemable by the issuer for a fixed or determinable amount at a fixed or determinable future date will constitute a financial liability. Similarly, if the holder of a preference share has the right to require the issuer to redeem it on or after a particular date for a fixed or determinable amount, the instrument will be a financial liability. In these situations, any preference dividends payable will be accounted for as interest charges rather than distributions to shareholders. The classification of financial instruments is considered in more detail in Chapter 26.

Compound financial instruments

16.17   In some cases, a financial instrument may include both a liability and an equity component – for instance, where the holder of a bond has the right to convert it into a fixed number of ordinary shares. FRS 25 requires the two components of the financial instrument to be accounted for separately. This is also considered in more detail in Chapter 26. Income and expenses, and where appropriate gains and losses, in respect of any component that is classified as a financial liability should therefore be recognised in the profit and loss account in the same way as those relating to other financial liabilities.

Presentation of equity dividends

16.18   Dividends on any shares that are classified as equity instruments under FRS 25 should be accounted for directly in the reconciliation of shareholders' funds (see Chapter 36). Any transaction costs relating to the issue of an equity instrument, or to the equity component of a compound instrument, should also be accounted for as a deduction from equity, net of any related income tax benefit. This does not include transaction costs that are directly attributable to the acquisition of a business, which should be accounted for in accordance with FRS 6 'Acquisitions and Mergers'. The standard also requires any transaction costs accounted for as deduction from equity to be disclosed separately. This disclosure forms part of the presentation requirements of the standard and so applies in all cases for accounting periods beginning on or after 1 January 2005.

Presentation of dividends as an interest expense

16.19   Where dividends need to be presented in the accounts as if they were interest, they can either be combined with actual interest charges or shown as a separate item. The guidance in FRS 25 notes that issues such as the different treatment of interest and dividends for tax purposes might make separate disclosure advisable. Any dividends accounted for as an interest expense will also still need to be included in the aggregate amount of dividends paid in the year shown in the notes to the accounts in order to satisfy the disclosure requirements of company law.

DISTRIBUTABLE RESERVES

Significance of distributable reserves

16.20   CA 1985 does not often use the term 'dividend' but refers instead to a 'distribution'. Under the Act, a distribution can only be made if the individual company has sufficient distributable reserves available. This is a highly complex area and only a brief outline of the issues is given here. Legal advice should always be sought in cases where there is any doubt over the potential availability of reserves for distribution. Sections 270 to 274 of CA 1985 set out detailed rules on the accounts that must be used as the basis for establishing whether a company has profits available for a distribution.

Definition of distribution

16.21   Section 263(2) of CA 1985 defines a distribution as any distribution of a company's assets to its members, in cash or in any other form, except distributions by way of:

(i)   an issue of fully-paid or partly-paid bonus shares;

(ii)   the redemption or purchase of the company's own shares out of:

- capital;
- the proceeds of a fresh issue of shares; or
- unrealised profits;

in accordance with Chapter VII of Part V of the Act;

(iii)   the reduction of share capital by:

- extinguishing the liability of any members in respect of share capital not paid up;
- reducing the liability of any members in respect of share capital not paid up; or
- paying off paid up share capital; or

(iv)   a distribution of assets to members on the winding up of the company.

Profits available for distribution

16.22   A company may only make a distribution out of profits that are available for that purpose. Profits available for distribution are defined in section 263(3) of CA 1985 as:

(i)   accumulated, realised profits, to the extent that these have not been previously distributed or capitalised, less

(ii)   accumulated, realised losses to the extent that these have not previously been written off in a reduction or reorganisation of capital.

Separate rules apply in the case of investment companies. These are set out in sections 265 and 266 but are not considered here. Reference should also be made to the company's memorandum and articles of association, as these may contain additional, more restrictive rules on the distribution of the company's profits.

Additional rules for public companies

16.23   Additional rules apply in the case of public companies. A public company may only make a distribution if:

(i)   at the time of the distribution, the amount of its net assets is not less than the aggregate of its called up share capital and undistributable reserves; and

(ii)   the distribution does not reduce the amount of its net assets to less than that aggregate.

Again, separate rules apply to investment companies.

In this context, net assets is defined as the aggregate of the company's assets less the aggregate of its liabilities. Uncalled share capital cannot be treated as an asset for this purpose and liabilities specifically include any provisions for liabilities. The effect of this section is that a public company must take account of any unrealised losses when establishing profits available for distribution. A private company needs only to consider realised profits and realised losses.

Undistributable reserves

16.24   A company, whether public or private, may not distribute any of the following reserves:

(i)   the share premium account;

(ii)   the capital redemption reserve;

(iii)   the excess of accumulated, unrealised profits over accumulated, unrealised losses (to the extent that profits have not been previously capitalised and losses have not been previously written off in a reconstruction or reorganisation – in this context, a transfer to the company's capital redemption reserve made on or after 22 December 1980 is not regarded as a capitalisation of reserves); or

(iv)   any other reserve which the company is prohibited from distributing by its memorandum or articles of association or by any other enactment.

Definition of realised profit and losses

16.25   The interpretation of realised profits and losses is covered by sections 262(3) and 742(2) of CA 1985. Realised profits and losses are the profits and losses that fall to be treated as realised, in accordance with the principles generally accepted for determining realised profits and losses for accounting purposes, at the time the accounts are prepared.

ICAEW guidance

16.26   Additional guidance can be found in 'Guidance on the determination of realised profits and losses in the context of distributions under the Companies Act 1985' published by the Institute of Chartered Accountants in England and Wales (ICAEW) in June 2003. This supersedes the guidance previously set out in two technical releases (TR 481 and TR 482) issued by the ICAEW in 1982 and can be found on the ICAEW website at http://www.icaew.co.uk. The latest guidance reflects the law at 31 December 2002 and accounting standards in issue at that date. It should not be used to question the lawfulness of earlier distributions, but directors may need to re-examine reserves balances in the light of the new guidance before making or recommending future distributions. All losses should be regarded as realised, except to the extent that the law, accounting standards or the ICAEW guidance provide otherwise. A profit is to be regarded as realised when it arises from:

(i)   a transaction or event where the consideration received is qualifying consideration;

(ii)   an event which results in the company receiving qualifying consideration without giving any consideration;

(iii) proper use of the marking to market method of accounting;

(iv)   the translation of a monetary asset comprising qualifying consideration, or of a liability, denominated in a foreign currency;

(v)   the reversal of a loss previously regarded as realised;

(vi)   an appropriate proportion of a profit previously regarded as unrealised becoming realised as a result of:

- consideration previously received becoming qualifying consideration;

- the disposal of the related asset for qualifying consideration;

- recognition of a realised loss on the disposal or scrapping of the asset;

- recognition of a realised loss on the write-down of the asset for depreciation, amortisation, diminution in value or impairment; or

- the distribution in specie of the related asset;

(vii) a court-sanctioned reduction or cancellation of capital, unless the court directs, or the company undertakes, that the amount credited to reserves is not to be treated as a realised profit; or

(viii) in the case of an unlimited company, a reduction or cancellation of capital which results in a credit to reserves, to the extent that the consideration received meets the criteria set out in the guidance.

The guidance provides practical examples of transactions and events that will normally give rise to realised profits and realised losses. A separate section of the guidance deals with marking to market in the context of banking companies and their subsidiaries and other market makers and investment dealers.

Qualifying consideration

16.27   Qualifying consideration is defined in the ICAEW guidance as:

(i)   cash;

(ii)   an asset for which there is a liquid market (as defined in the guidance);

(iii)   the total or partial release, settlement or assumption by another party of a liability of the company, unless:

- the liability arose from the purchase of an asset that does not meet the definition of qualifying consideration and has not been disposed of for qualifying consideration; and

- the purchase and release are part of a group or series of transactions or arrangements that are artificial, linked or circular;

(iv)   an amount receivable in any of the above forms, where:

- the debtor is capable of settling the amount within a reasonable period of time;

- it is reasonably certain that the debtor will be capable of settling when called upon to do so; and

- there is an expectation that the amount will be settled.

Linked transactions

16.28   The ICAEW guidance emphasises that a series of artificial, linked or circular transactions and arrangements, designed to achieve an overall commercial effect, should be viewed as whole when assessing whether a profit has been realised. A realised profit will only arise where the end result for the company meets the criteria set out in the guidance. Appendix A to the guidance considers the application of this principle to certain intra-group transactions, including:

(i)   group treasury functions and cash pooling arrangements;

(ii)   dividends received or receivable from subsidiaries;

(iii)   asset sales between a parent and its subsidiaries, and between fellow subsidiaries;

(iv)   dividends in specie; and

(v)   returning a capital contribution to the donor.

Changes in circumstances

16.29   The classification of a profit or loss as realised or unrealised is not fixed and may change as a result of a change in the realisation principles, a change in the law, accounting standards or UITF Abstracts, or some other change in circumstances (eg where an amount receivable no longer meets the definition of qualifying consideration). The guidance explains in detail how to establish which profits should be treated as previously distributed when a profit initially regarded as realised is reclassified as unrealised. When considering the payment of an interim dividend, directors should assess the effect of any known or likely changes on the expected level of profits available for distribution at the year end – for instance, the potential impact of a new accounting standard that requires the recognition of additional liabilities or provisions in the accounts.

Deferred tax, exchange gains and goodwill

16.30   The ICAEW guidance includes specific consideration of issues relating to deferred tax, goodwill, asset exchanges, hedging transactions and foreign exchange profits and losses. A provision for deferred tax should generally be regarded as a realised loss, except that deferred tax relating to an unrealised gain on a revalued asset should be treated as a reduction of that gain. Unless there are doubts about the convertibility or marketability of the currency in question, foreign exchange profits arising on the translation of monetary items should be regarded as realised, irrespective of the maturity date of the asset or liability. Goodwill becomes a realised loss over its useful economic life. Where it was eliminated against reserves under SSAP 22 'Accounting for Goodwill' and remains eliminated under the transitional provisions of FRS 10 'Goodwill and Intangible Assets', the write-off does not constitute an immediate realised loss, but becomes a realised loss over time.

This is considered in more detail in Chapter 38. Negative goodwill credited directly to reserves under SSAP 22 similarly becomes a realised profit on the same basis as if it had been accounted for under FRS 10.

Development costs

16.31 Under section 269 of CA 1985, any development costs shown as an asset in a company's accounts are to be treated as a realised loss, with the following exceptions:

(i)   if the costs have been revalued, any element that represents an unrealised profit need not be treated as a realised loss;

(ii) if there are special circumstances which justify the directors' decision not to treat the costs as a realised loss, and the note to the accounts on development costs:

- states that the costs are not to be treated as a realised loss, and

- explains the circumstances relied on by the directors to justify their decision.

There is no further guidance on these special circumstances in the Act, but it is generally acknowledged that the carry forward of development costs in accordance with SSAP 13 'Accounting for Research and Development' will usually justify a decision by the directors not to treat the costs as a realised loss for distribution purposes.

Revaluation of fixed assets

16.32 Under section 275(1) of CA 1985, a provision mentioned in paragraphs 88 and 89 of Schedule 4 to the Act is to be treated as a realised loss. These paragraphs relate respectively to:

(i)   provisions for depreciation or diminution in value of assets and amounts written off assets; and

(ii) provisions for liabilities and charges.

However, a specific exception is made in the case of a diminution in value of a fixed asset which arises on a revaluation of all of the company's fixed assets (or all of its fixed assets except goodwill). A formal revaluation of all the assets is not necessarily required. Section 275(4) of CA 1985 states that any consideration by the directors of the value at any particular time of a fixed asset is treated as a revaluation of the asset in determining whether a revaluation of the company's assets has taken place for the purposes of section 275(1). In considering the value of fixed assets in this way, the directors must be satisfied that the aggregate value is not less than the aggregate amount at which the assets are stated in the accounts. In other words, there must not be an overall deficit which has not been recognised in the accounts. Specific disclosures must be given in the notes to the accounts if the directors wish to take advantage of this exception.

Depreciation charged on revalued assets

16.33   As noted in 16.32, provisions for depreciation are to be regarded as realised losses. However, if an asset has been revalued and depreciation is charged on the revalued amount (in accordance with present accounting requirements), section 275(2) of CA 1985 requires the depreciation on the revaluation surplus to be treated as a realised profit. The effect of this is that only depreciation based on the original cost of the asset is treated as a realised loss for distribution purposes. If the original cost of an asset is not readily available, its cost is taken to be the value shown in the earliest available record since acquisition by the company.

Pension liabilities

16.34   FRS 17 'Retirement Benefits' was published in November 2000 and is fully effective for accounting periods beginning on or after 1 January 2005. Under this standard, a deficit arising in a defined benefit pension scheme will usually need to be included as a liability in the accounts of an employer. This might inhibit the ability of the company to pay a dividend – for instance, where the defined benefit liability is so large that it reduces distributable reserves below the level needed to cover a proposed distribution. Appendix IV to the standard notes that this situation is not expected to arise very often in practice. It was therefore not considered appropriate to deal with it in the standard, and companies who do encounter the problem are advised to discuss the matter with their legal advisors.

ESOP trusts

16.35   UITF Abstract 38 'Accounting for ESOP trusts' requires the sponsoring company of an ESOP trust to recognise in its own accounts the assets and liabilities of the trust over which it has de facto control. Under the Abstract, the consideration paid for any shares in the company that are held by the ESOP trust should be deducted in arriving at shareholders' funds, until those shares vest unconditionally in employees. The previous Abstract on this issue required such shares to be shown within fixed assets or current assets as appropriate. The Abstract includes consideration of the legal aspects of its accounting requirements and notes that deducting the consideration from shareholders' funds does not imply that the shares have been purchased by the company as a matter of law or that they are required to be cancelled. The UITF has also received legal advice that the acquisition of shares in the company by an ESOP trust does not of itself affect the amount of the company's realised profits or realised losses, although other related transactions (eg a loan to the ESOP trust to fund the acquisition of the shares) may do so.

However, the accounting treatment required by UITF Abstract 38 will reduce the aggregate value of the company's net assets (because own shares held will be deducted from shareholders' funds rather than shown as assets) and this may have implications for a public company as a result of the additional rules on the maintenance of share capital and reserves (see 16.23 above).

Chapter 17 Directors' Remuneration And Benefits

DISCLOSURE BY QUOTED COMPANIES

The Directors' Remuneration Report Regulations 2002

17.1   A company's annual accounts must include detailed information on remuneration paid to, or receivable by, anyone who was a director during the year. The legislation requires basic disclosures to be given by all companies, and then makes a clear distinction between quoted and unquoted companies in requiring more detailed information to be given. The requirements were broadly similar for accounting periods ending before 31 December 2002, although greater detail was required in the case of quoted companies, but the *Directors' Remuneration Report Regulations 2002* (SI 2002/1986) introduced significant changes to the disclosure requirements for quoted companies for accounting periods ending on or after 31 December 2002. For these purposes, a quoted company is defined as a company whose equity share capital is:

(i)   included in the Official List of the London Stock Exchange;

(ii)   officially listed in an EEA State; or

(iii)   admitted to dealing on the New York Stock Exchange or the NASDAQ exchange.

The Regulations require the directors of a quoted company to prepare a directors' remuneration report containing the detailed information specified in Schedule 7A to CA 1985. This is in addition to the aggregate information on directors' remuneration already required to be disclosed in the notes to the accounts under CA 1985, Sch 6, para 1. The report must be formally approved by the directors and must be signed on behalf of the board by a director or by the company secretary. A signed copy must be delivered to the registrar as part of the company's annual reports and accounts.

The Regulations also require the general meeting at which the annual reports and accounts are laid to include a resolution enabling the shareholders to approve the directors' remuneration report, and details of the resolution must be set out in the notice of the meeting. However, the legislation notes that this requirement does not mean that the entitlement of any individual to the remuneration shown in the report is conditional on the resolution being passed.

Aggregate disclosures by quoted companies

17.2　　The basic requirement under paragraph 1 of Schedule 6 to CA 1985 is that every quoted company must disclose in the notes to the accounts:

(i)　the aggregate of the emoluments paid to, or receivable by, the directors in respect of their qualifying services (see 17.21 to 17.37 below);

(ii)　the aggregate gains made by directors on the exercise of share options (see 17.38 to 17.44 below);

(iii)　the aggregate of the amounts paid to, or receivable by, directors under long-term incentive schemes in respect of qualifying services and the net value of any assets (other than cash or share options) receivable by directors under such schemes (see 17.45 to 17.52 below);

(iv)　the aggregate value of any contributions paid by the company in respect of directors into a pension scheme where the benefits depend on the level of contributions paid;

(v)　the number of directors who are accruing retirement benefits under money purchase schemes; and

(vi)　the number of directors who are accruing retirement benefits under defined benefit schemes.

These basic disclosure requirements are not affected by the *Directors' Remuneration Report Regulations 2002* (SI 2002/1986). However, paragraph 1(6) of Schedule 6 to CA 1985 specifically provides for a situation where more detail is given in a separate report (e.g. a directors' remuneration report) and generally means that the aggregate figures, total numbers and other required disclosures do not have to be given in the notes to the accounts if they are readily ascertainable from other information included in the annual reports and accounts. The one exception is the aggregate gains made by directors on the exercise of share options which must always be shown separately in the notes to the accounts. If the aggregate disclosures required by the legislation are not given in the notes to the accounts, it is good practice to include a cross-reference showing where the detailed information can be found.

It should be noted that pension contributions relating to defined benefit schemes for directors are not included in these disclosures. Separate disclosure requirements apply in respect of pension benefits receivable by directors under such schemes (see 17.53 to 17.62 below).

Directors' remuneration report

17.3   For accounting periods ending on or after 31 December 2002, the directors of a quoted company are required to prepare a directors' remuneration report containing the detailed information specified in Schedule 7A to CA 1985. Current directors and those who have served as director in the preceding five years are given a specific duty to disclose relevant information to the company to enable the report to be prepared.

The legislation generally requires detailed information to be given in tabular form and in a way that links the information to each director by name. The requirements on the detailed contents of the directors' remuneration report are divided into two elements – those that are subject to audit and those that are not. The auditors are required to report on the auditable aspects of the report (see 17.4 to 17.5 below) and to include any missing information in their audit report, so far as they are reasonably able to do so.

In effect, the new legislation encompasses detailed disclosure requirements and recommendations previously set out in the UK Listing Rules, the Combined Code and UITF Abstract 10 'Disclosure of Directors' Share Options' as well as introducing a number of new disclosures. As a result, the original recommendations on the preparation of a directors' remuneration report were removed from the Combined Code during its 2003 revision and UITF Abstract 10 has been withdrawn.

Contents subject to audit

17.4   The following information must be disclosed and is also subject to audit:

(i)   for each director who served during the financial year, the total amount of:

- salary and/or fees,
- bonuses,
- expense allowances that are chargeable to UK income tax,
- any compensation for loss of office and similar payments,
- the estimated money value of any benefits in kind, and
- the sum total of all these amounts, and the equivalent total for the previous financial year;

(ii)   the nature of any element of a remuneration package which is not cash;

(iii)   for each director who served during the financial year, the number of shares subject to a share option (distinguishing between those with different terms and conditions) at:

- the beginning of the year, or the date of appointment if later,
- the end of the year, or the date of ceasing to be a director if earlier;

(iv)   information on share options awarded, exercised and lapsed during the year, and any variations to terms and conditions;

(v)   for each share option that was unexpired at any time during the year:

- the price (if any) paid for its award,
- the exercise prices,
- the date from which the option can be exercised, and
- the date on which the option expires;

(vi)   a summary of any performance criteria upon which the award or exercise of a share option is conditional, and any changes made in the year;

(vii)   for any share option exercised during the year, the market price at the time of exercise;

(viii)   for each share option that was unexpired at the end of the financial year:

- the market price at the year-end date, and
- the highest and lowest market price during the year;

(ix)   for each director who served during the financial year, details of interests in long-term incentive schemes, showing:

- interests at the beginning of the year, or the date of appointment if later,
- awards during the year, and
- interests at the end of the year, or on ceasing to be a director if earlier;

(x)   for each disclosed interest in long-term incentive schemes, the date by which the qualifying conditions have to be fulfilled and details of any variations in the terms and conditions made during the year;

(xi)   for each scheme interest that has vested during the year, details of any shares, the amount of any money and the value of any other assets that have become receivable as a result;

(xii)   for each director who served during the financial year and has rights under a defined benefit retirement scheme:

- details of any changes during the year in their accrued benefits under the scheme;
- the accrued benefits at the end of the year;
- the transfer value of the accrued benefits, calculated as recommended by the Institute of Actuaries and Faculty of Actuaries; and

- the equivalent transfer value at the end of the previous year and the difference between this and the current transfer value, after deducting any contributions made by the director in the current year;

(xiii) for each director who served during the financial year and has rights under a money purchase retirement scheme, details of the contributions paid or payable by the company during the year;

(xiv) details of certain excess retirement benefits paid to directors or former directors;

(xv) details of any significant awards to former directors (e.g. compensation for loss of office, pensions); and

(xvi) for each director who served during the financial year, the aggregate amount of any consideration (including any benefits in kind) paid to, or receivable by, a third party for making available the services of the individual as a director.

The legislation allows a limited degree of aggregation of the information on share options where the required details would otherwise result in a disclosure of excessive length.

Compensation payments to directors may also require shareholder approval under CA 1985, although this is not usually necessary for genuine payments in respect of damages for breach of contract or for pensions in respect of past services. If significant non-cash items are included, the compensation payments may also require approval under the provisions on substantial property transactions in section 320 of CA 1985.

Payments to third parties for the services of a director arise most commonly where a substantial investor (e.g. a bank or venture capital company) has the right to appoint a director to the board of the investee company and payment for the services of this director is made to the investor rather than to the director himself.

Audit requirements

17.5   If the accounts do not include all of the required disclosures in respect of directors' emoluments and other benefits, or transactions between the company and its directors or other officers, section 237(4) of CA 1985 imposes a duty on the auditors to include a statement of the missing details in their audit report, so far as they are reasonably able to do so. In the case of quoted companies, this responsibility extends to certain of the disclosures required under the *Directors' Remuneration Report Regulations 2002* (SI 2002/1986) and the UK Listing Rules.

Bulletin 2002/2 'The United Kingdom Directors' Remuneration Report Regulations 2002', issued by the Auditing Practices Board (APB) in October 2002, sets out guidance for auditors on this reporting responsibility and includes an example of an auditors' report on the accounts of a quoted company updated to reflect the current reporting requirements.

In May 2005, the APB published a draft Bulletin 2005/4 setting out revised illustrative examples of auditors' reports on the accounts of companies incorporated in Great Britain and Northern Ireland, reflecting the following recent developments:

(i)   the requirement for EU listed companies to prepare group accounts in accordance with international financial reporting standards (IFRSs) for accounting periods beginning on or after 1 January 2005;

(ii) the option for most other companies to adopt IFRSs from the same date;

(iii) recent changes to the requirements of the *Companies Act 1985*; and

(iv) the adoption in the UK of International Standards on Auditing (ISAs) for accounting periods beginning on or after 15 December 2004.

At this stage, the Bulletin has been issued in draft form in order to provide interim guidance on the various complex issues that arise from these changes. The updated examples cover both quoted and unquoted companies.

Contents not subject to audit

17.6   The following information must also be given in the directors' remuneration report, but is not subject to audit:

(i)   the names of the members of any committee that considered directors' remuneration during the year and the names of any other individuals (whether directors or not) who provided advice or services to that committee, together with details of the nature of the advice or services;

(ii) a statement of the company's policy on directors' remuneration for the forthcoming year and for subsequent financial years – this must include for each individual who has served as a director between the end of the financial year under review and the date on which the annual reports and accounts are laid before the members:

- a detailed summary of any performance conditions in respect of awards under share option or long-term incentive schemes,

- an explanation of why these performance conditions were chosen,

- a summary of the methods used in assessing whether the performance conditions are met, and why those methods were chosen, and

- if any performance condition involves comparison with external factors, a summary of the factors to be used and the identify of any companies or index used for comparison purposes;

(iii) a description of, and explanation for, any significant changes to the terms and conditions of entitlement under share option or long-term incentive schemes;

(iv) an explanation of why any entitlements under share option or long-term incentive schemes are not subject to performance conditions;

(v) the relative importance of elements of remuneration that are related to performance and those that are not;

(vi) a summary of the company's policy on the duration of directors' service contracts and on notice periods and termination payments under those contracts;

(vii) the following information on the contract of service, or contract for services, of each person who served as a director during the financial year:

- the date of the contract, the unexpired term and any notice period,

- any provision for compensation on early termination, and

- sufficient information on any other provisions to enable a member to estimate the company's liability in the event of early termination of the contract;

(viii) an explanation for any significant awards during the year to former directors (eg compensation for loss of office, pensions); and

(ix) a line graph showing the total shareholder return for the last five years on:

- a holding of the class of equity shares whose public trading has resulted in the company meeting the definition of a quoted company, and

- a hypothetical holding of shares, based on a broad equity market index, together with the name of index and why it was chosen.

In the case of the share performance graph, there is no requirement to disclose information for periods before the new regulations came into effect – in the early years, therefore, information will be given for one to four years as appropriate. The legislation includes detailed guidance on calculating total shareholder return for this purpose.

Additional disclosures under the UK Listing Rules

17.7 Most of the disclosure recommendations set out in the original Combined Code were also incorporated into Chapter 12.43A(c) of the UK Listing Rules. These now generally overlap with the disclosures required under the *Directors' Remuneration Report Regulations 2002*. However, the following additional disclosures are required under the UK Listing Rules but not specifically by company law, although they may be considered to be encompassed by some of the more general disclosure requirements:

(i) a statement of the company's policy on the granting of options or awards under employee share schemes and other long term incentive schemes and an explanation and justification of any departure from, or change in, that policy during the year;

(ii)   the unexpired term of of any directors' service contract of a director proposed for election or re-election at the forthcoming AGM, or if any such director does not have a service contract, a statement of that fact;

(iii)   details of any service contracts which provide for, or imply, notice periods in excess of one year, or which include provisions for pre-determined compensation which exceeds one year's salary and benefits, together with an explanation of the reasons; and

(iv)   an explanation of, and justification for, any elements of remuneration other than basic salary that are pensionable.

DISCLOSURE BY UNQUOTED COMPANIES

Aggregate disclosures by unquoted companies

17.8   The basic requirement under paragraph 1 of Schedule 6 to CA 1985 is that every company that is not a quoted company, and does not qualify as a small company, must disclose in the notes to the accounts:

(i)   the aggregate of the emoluments paid to, or receivable by, the directors in respect of their qualifying services (see 17.21 to 17.37 below);

(ii)   the number of directors who exercised share options during the year (see 17.38 to 17.44 below);

(iii) the number of directors who received shares during the year under long-term incentive schemes in respect of qualifying services (see 17.45 to 17.52 below);

(iv)   the aggregate of the amounts paid to, or receivable by, directors under long-term incentive schemes in respect of qualifying services and the net value of any assets (other than cash, share options or shares) receivable by directors under such schemes (see 17.45 to 17.52 below);

(v)   the aggregate value of any contributions paid by the company in respect of directors into a pension scheme where the benefits depend on the level of contributions paid;

(vi)   the number of directors who are accruing retirement benefits under money purchase schemes;

(vii) the number of directors who are accruing retirement benefits under defined benefit schemes.

The distinction made between quoted and unquoted companies avoids the need for unquoted companies to value shares granted to directors under long-term incentive schemes and to calculate gains made by directors on the exercise of share options. Special provisions apply in the case of companies that qualify as small under CA 1985 (see 17.10 below)

It should also be noted that pension contributions relating to defined benefit schemes for directors are not included in the above disclosures. Separate disclosure requirements apply in respect of pension benefits receivable by directors under such schemes (see 17.53 to 17.62 below).

Highest paid director

17.9   Where the aggregate of emoluments and amounts receivable by directors under long term incentive schemes (other than shares and share options) exceeds £200,000, an unquoted company must give the following additional details in the notes to the accounts:

(i)   the amount, in total, that relates to the highest paid director;

(ii)   whether the highest paid director exercised any share options during the year;

(iii)   whether the highest paid director received any shares during the year in respect of qualifying services under a long-term incentive scheme;

(iv)   the amount of any company pension contributions to money purchase schemes for that director; and

(v)   if retirement benefits may be payable to this director under a defined benefit scheme, his accrued pension at the end of the year and, where applicable, the amount of any accrued lump sum under the scheme.

The legislation includes specific provisions on how accrued pensions and accrued lump sum entitlements should be calculated (see 17.57 below). A company that qualifies as small under CA 1985 is not required to give these additional disclosures.

Small companies

17.10   Under section 246(3) of CA 1985, a company that qualifies as small is only required to give the following details in respect of directors' emoluments and other benefits in its accounts:

(i)   the aggregate of the amounts that would otherwise be disclosable individually – i.e:

●   emoluments paid to or receivable by the directors;

●   money or assets received or receivable by the directors under long-term incentive schemes (other than shares and share options); and

●   company contributions to money purchase pension schemes for the benefit of directors;

(ii)   the number of directors accruing retirement benefits under money purchase schemes; and

(iii)   the number of directors accruing retirement benefits under defined benefit pension schemes.

There is, therefore, no requirement for a small company to disclose:

(i)   the emoluments of the highest paid director, even if total emoluments are more than £200,000;

(ii) the number of directors exercising share options;

(iii) the number of directors receiving shares under long-term incentive schemes; or

(iv) details of excess retirement benefits paid to directors and former directors (see 17.14 below).

The exemption relates only to the emoluments and benefits disclosures. Other disclosure requirements (e.g. compensation for loss of office) continue to apply. Qualification as a small company under CA 1985 is explained in Chapter 8. A small company which chooses to file abbreviated accounts need not give any of the information on directors' remuneration, pensions or compensation for loss of office normally required by Part 1 of Schedule 6 to CA 1985 in those accounts, but the disclosures outlined above will still need to be given in the full or shorter form accounts that have to be prepared for the members. There are no exemptions from the disclosures for medium-sized companies in either full or abbreviated accounts.

Compensation for loss of office

17.11   The aggregate compensation for loss of office paid to, or receivable by, directors and former directors must also be disclosed by all unquoted companies, regardless of size. Compensation for loss of office constitutes a separate category of payment to directors and should not be included in the figure for directors' emoluments for the period. Where compensation payments include non-cash benefits, these should be included in the disclosures at their estimated money value and the nature of the benefit must be disclosed.

The disclosure of compensation payments to directors is considered in more detail at 17.63 to 17.69 below.

Pension arrangements

17.12   For the purposes of the CA 1985 disclosures referred to in 17.8 above, all pension schemes must be classified as either defined contribution or defined benefit schemes. Any death in service benefits are to be disregarded when classifying a pension scheme for disclosure purposes. A pension scheme under which a director will be entitled to receive both money purchase benefits and defined benefits is classified as a defined benefit scheme for disclosure purposes. Where a scheme provides for the director to receive money purchase benefits or defined benefits, whichever is the greater, the company is allowed to assume for disclosure purposes that the benefits will be whichever appears more likely at the end of the financial year in question.

The detailed disclosure requirements in respect of pension arrangements are considered in more detail at 17.53 to 17.62 below.

Payments to third parties

17.13 The accounts of all unquoted companies must also disclose the aggregate amount paid to, or receivable by, third parties for making available the services of any person as a director of the company or otherwise in connection with the management of the affairs of the company or group. The most common example of this is an arrangement whereby a substantial investor in a company (e.g. a bank or venture capital company) has the right to appoint a director to the board of the investee company and payment for the services of this director is made to the investor rather than to the director himself.

Excess retirement benefits

17.14 Under paragraph 7 of Schedule 7 to CA 1985, an unquoted company must disclose in its annual accounts the aggregate amount of any retirement benefits paid to, or receivable by, directors or former directors that are in excess of the retirement benefits to which they were entitled on 31 March 1997, or the date when benefits first became payable, if later. However, this disclosure is not required where the funding of the scheme allowed the amounts to be paid without recourse to additional contributions and the amounts were paid to, or receivable by, all pensioner members of the scheme on the same basis.

Duties of directors and auditors

17.15 All directors have a duty to make information on their remuneration available to the company so that the necessary details can be disclosed in the accounts. Failure to do so is an offence and could result in a fine. If the relevant information is not disclosed, section 237(4) of CA 1985 requires the auditors to include it in their audit report, as far as they are reasonably able to do so.

Voluntary disclosure

17.16 CA 1985 provides for a situation where an unquoted company voluntarily discloses detailed information for each director. In this case, aggregate totals need not be given and the highest paid director need not be identified. Similarly, if the aggregate figures or total numbers required by the regulations are readily identifiable from other information in the accounts, they generally do not have to be disclosed again.

Amounts to be included

17.17 The amounts to be disclosed each year are:

(i)   amounts receivable in respect of that year, regardless of when payment is actually made

(ii)   for amounts not receivable in respect of a specific period, the amount paid.

If any amounts are not disclosed on the grounds that the director is liable to account to the company or any of its subsidiary undertakings for the amount received, or that they are expense allowances which are not chargeable to UK income tax and subsequently the director's liability to account for the amounts received is partly or wholly released, or the expense allowance is charged to UK income tax, the amounts must be disclosed separately in the first set of accounts in which it is practicable to show them. Where a single amount is paid to a director to cover more than one element of emoluments and similar benefits, and the amount relating to each element is not specified, CA 1985 allows the directors to make an appropriate apportionment of the amount received in order to comply with the disclosure requirements.

Comparative figures

17.18   Comparative figures must be given for all amounts requiring disclosure under Schedule 6 to CA 1985.

Positioning of disclosures

17.19   The disclosures on directors' emoluments are extensive and should be dealt with in a separate note within the section of the notes to the accounts relating to profit and loss account items. Emoluments may include amounts paid by other companies and persons as well as amounts paid by the company itself, and may include estimated values to reflect benefits received in kind. For this reason it is not appropriate to include details of directors' remuneration in the note to the accounts which sets out details of individual items charged or credited in arriving at the operating profit or loss for the year.

Example disclosures

17.20   Examples of the disclosures for an unquoted company and a small company are given in the appendix to this Chapter.

EMOLUMENTS

Amounts to be included

17.21   Emoluments are defined in paragraph 1(3)(a) of Schedule 6 to CA 1985. As well as salary and bonus payments, emoluments include fees, benefits-in-kind, expense allowances (if these are chargeable to UK income tax) and amounts paid on acceptance of office as director ('golden hellos'). The use of the word 'include' in this paragraph suggests that the list is not intended to be exhaustive and that any other similar amounts paid to, or receivable by, directors will therefore be disclosable. However, share options, pension contributions and amounts payable to directors under long-term incentive schemes are specifically excluded from the definition of emoluments as they are subject to separate disclosure requirements. These items should, therefore, not be included in the figures for emoluments.

Details to be disclosed

17.22 All companies must disclose the aggregate amount of emoluments paid to, or receivable by, the directors in respect of qualifying services, although special provisions apply in the case of companies that qualify as small under CA 1985 (see 17.10 above). Qualifying services are defined as follows in paragraph 1(5) of Schedule 6 to CA 1985:

(i) services as a director of the company;

(ii) whilst a director of the company, services as a director of any of its subsidiary undertakings; and

(iii) services otherwise in connection with the management of the affairs of the company or any of its subsidiary undertakings.

Payments on acceptance of office as director

17.23 Payments to a person in respect of acceptance of office as director of a company are also specifically included in the CA 1985 definition of emoluments. This was introduced by the *Companies Act 1989* in order to bring 'golden hellos' within the disclosure requirements. Prior to this, companies sometimes sought to avoid disclosure of these payments on the grounds that 'golden hellos' were not payments in respect of services as a director of the company.

Calculating the figures

17.24 The amounts to be disclosed as emoluments each year are the amounts receivable in respect of that year, regardless of when payment is actually made. Where amounts are not receivable in respect of a specific period, the total paid in the year should be treated as emoluments for that year. In the case of salary and bonus payments, the amounts to be disclosed are the gross figures before any deductions in respect of taxation, employee national insurance contributions or contributions by the director into a pension scheme. The treatment of bonus payments is considered in more detail below. Emoluments do not include employer's national insurance contributions paid by the company in respect of the directors.

Emoluments in the year of appointment or retirement

17.25   If a director holds office for only part of the year, the disclosures should cover only the period during which he actually held office. For instance, if an existing company employee was appointed as director half-way through the financial year, any remuneration that he received for his services as director during the last six months of the year would be disclosable as directors' emoluments. The salary he received as an employee for the earlier part of the year would not be disclosable as directors' remuneration.

Accounting periods of more or less than one year

17.26   Where the accounting period is more or less than one year, the disclosures should cover the amounts actually paid or receivable in respect of that period. In this situation, some companies choose to make additional disclosure of the equivalent annual sums. This can be helpful in explaining apparently large movements between the current and previous years which arise only as a result of the differing lengths of the accounting periods. However, the statutory information must always be given – the twelve month details are simply additional information given voluntarily by the company.

Bonus payments

17.27   Bonus payments to directors are generally disclosable as emoluments. However, it may be difficult to establish when they should be included in the disclosures. The difficulties usually arise where the payment is dependent or conditional on some other event, such as approval by the shareholders or the completion of a specified contract term by the director. Where the payment depends on company performance over a longer period than one year, it will normally constitute a payment under a long-term incentive scheme rather than a bonus, and will be subject to separate disclosure requirements (see 17.45 to 17.52 below)

Timing of recognition as emoluments

17.28   In accounting terms, provision for bonus payments should be made in each period in which the director performs the services that are to be paid for or rewarded through the bonus payment. Appropriate accruals should, therefore, be made in the accounts each year to reflect the amount of bonus 'earned' in respect of that year. However, under Schedule 6 to CA 1985, emoluments are only disclosable when they are paid to, or receivable by, the director. The director must, therefore, have the right to receive a sum before it becomes disclosable as emoluments.

Bonus payments should normally be disclosed as emoluments in the year in which the director becomes entitled to receive payment. This will not always match the timing of the actual payment. A bonus payment will often be based on the profits of a particular financial year but will not be payable until the following financial year. Once the results of the current year are known, the director will become entitled to receive a bonus (assuming that the appropriate level of profitability has been achieved), even though it may not actually be payable until some time later. In this case, the conditions attaching to the bonus will usually have been satisfied by the date that the accounts are approved and signed. The accounts should, therefore, include provision for the bonus that is expected to be paid and this should be disclosed within emoluments for the period.

Shareholder approval

17.29 A bonus payment to directors may require approval by the shareholders before the directors are entitled to receive it. In these circumstances, it is usual to treat the bonus as being receivable by the directors (and therefore disclosable within directors' emoluments) in the year in which shareholder approval is given.

Bonus contingent on future events

17.30 The payment of a bonus to the directors may be contingent on future events, such as achievement of profit targets over a specified period or completion of a defined period of service. In this situation, the director will not usually be entitled to receive the bonus until the conditions have been met and, even though it will usually be necessary to accrue for the bonus payments in each year for accounting purposes, the bonus will not become disclosable as emoluments until all of the conditions have been met and the director becomes entitled to receive the bonus. A scheme where payments are based on performance over a period of more than one year will usually meet the definition of a long-term incentive scheme and the payments will be subject to separate disclosure requirements (see 17.45 below). Therefore, they should not be treated as bonus payments included within emoluments.

Benefits-in-kind

17.31 Under CA 1985, emoluments specifically include 'the estimated money value of benefits-in-kind received by a director otherwise than in cash'. This can be one of the most difficult aspects of directors' remuneration to deal with. The most common benefits-in-kind are:

(i)   the provision of a company car;

(ii)   the provision of free or subsidised accommodation;

(iii) the provision of insurance for the benefit of the director (e.g. private health cover, indemnity insurance, personal accident cover);

(iv)   loans at preferential interest rates; and

(v)   relocation costs (in some circumstances).

Some of these may also be disclosable in the annual accounts as loans or transactions with directors under the provisions of CA 1985 (see Chapter 37). Share options are subject to separate disclosure requirements and are, therefore, specifically excluded from the definition of emoluments for disclosure purposes.

Estimated money value

17.32   The main difficulty with benefits-in-kind is establishing an appropriate and realistic monetary value for the benefit. CA 1985 does not provide any detailed guidance on this. There are two possible interpretations of 'value' in this context, either:

(i)   the value of the benefit to the director (or the saving achieved by him/her as a result of being given the benefit); or

(ii)   the cost to the company.

In some cases, it has become common practice to use taxable amounts as an indication of the value of the benefit. For instance, the taxable amount in respect of a company car is often used as the estimated money value of the benefit for disclosure purposes, although this will not always be a realistic assessment of the true value of the benefit.

Wherever possible, market value should be used as the basis for valuing the benefit-in-kind. In some cases, this will be relatively easy to assess. For instance, where the company provides free or subsidised accommodation, it will usually be relatively straightforward to establish the normal rental value. In the case of insurance cover, the premium actually paid by the company is usually used as the value of the benefit. In the case of preferential loans, the value of the benefit is usually established by taking the difference between the interest actually paid and the interest that would be payable on the loan at normal commercial rates.

If a director makes any contributions to the company in respect of benefits-in-kind received by him, these should be deducted from the value of the benefit included in emoluments.

Relocation expenses

17.33   The reimbursement of relocation expenses may constitute a benefit but will not always do so. The key factor is usually whether the director chooses to move of his own accord, or whether he moves at the company's request or insistence. Where a director moves of his own volition, any relocation expenses borne by the company will usually be disclosable as a benefit-in-kind. If the company instigates the move, the reimbursement of relocation expenses will not usually constitute a benefit. However, if the expenses are paid in the form of an allowance rather than the reimbursement of actual expenses incurred, and the allowance is chargeable to UK income tax, it will fall within the definition of emoluments and must be included in emoluments for disclosure purposes.

Payments to connected parties

17.34   CA 1985 specifically includes amounts paid to, or receivable by, a person connected with a director, or a body corporate controlled by him, within the disclosure requirements. Therefore, disclosure of emoluments and other benefits cannot be avoided simply by arranging for the payment to be made to another person. However, amounts should not be counted twice. Thus, payments to a director's wife would not be treated as emoluments of the director if his wife was also a director of the company and received the emoluments in her own right.

In the case of payments to a company owned by the director, the emoluments note to the accounts usually includes an explanation that some or all of the payments have been made through the company owned or controlled by the director:

Example 17.1 – Payment to company owned by director

Included within emoluments is £... which was paid to ABC Limited, a company owned by Mr J T Smith, in respect of his services as a director of the company.

Such arrangements may also require disclosure as a transaction in which a director had a material interest (see Chapter 37).

Payments by third parties

17.35   The amounts to be included as emoluments for disclosure purposes are all relevant amounts in respect of a directors' services paid by, or receivable from:

(i)   the company;

(ii)   the company's subsidiary undertakings; and

(iii)   any other person.

Payments from a parent undertaking are therefore disclosable, but only if they relate to the director's services to the company. However, if a director must in turn account to the company or any of its subsidiary undertakings for the amounts that he has received, those amounts are not disclosable as emoluments.

Example 17.2 – Amounts paid over to another group company

Mr Andrews is a director of ABC Limited and also of its subsidiary companies, CDE Limited and EFG Limited. He receives emoluments of £20,000 from ABC Limited in respect of his services as director of that company. He also receives emoluments of £5,000 from CDE Limited, but is required to pay these over to ABC Limited. He also receives emoluments of £4,000 from EFG Limited.

In the accounts of CDE Limited, Mr Andrews' emoluments will be shown as £5,000.

In the accounts of EFG Limited, Mr Andrews' emoluments will be shown as £4,000.

In the accounts of ABC Limited, Mr Andrews' emoluments will be shown as £24,000.

(That is the £20,000 he receives from ABC Limited plus the £4,000 he receives from EFG Limited. The £5,000 from CDE Limited is excluded as the director is required to pay this over to ABC Limited).

Subsequent adjustments

17.36   CA 1985 deals with two situations where changes in circumstances may affect the amount disclosable as emoluments. If any amounts are not disclosed as emoluments, on the grounds that:

(i)   the director is liable to account to the company or any of its subsidiary undertakings for the amount received; or

(ii)   they are expense allowances which are not chargeable to UK income tax,

and subsequently the director's liability to account for the amounts received is partly or wholly released, or the expense allowance is charged to UK income tax, the amounts paid to the director must be disclosed as emoluments in the first set of accounts in which it is practicable to show them, and they must also be shown separately in those accounts.

Apportionment of amounts received

17.37   Where a single amount is paid to a director to cover more than one element of emoluments and similar benefits, and the amount relating to each element is not specified, CA 1985 allows the directors to make an appropriate apportionment of the amount received, in order to comply with the disclosure requirements.

EXECUTIVE SHARE OPTIONS

Difficulties with share option disclosure

17.38   Share options granted to directors have been a particularly difficult area in terms of assessing the estimated money value of the benefit. It is usually acknowledged that the benefit arises when the option is granted rather than when it is exercised. However, the value of the option is often negligible at the time that it is granted – the true value to the director only arises when the option is exercised. As share option schemes often operate as an incentive to encourage directors and employees to achieve good company performance, it is appropriate that the value of the option increases with the passage of time.

Disclosure requirements

17.39   For accounting periods ending on or after 31 December 2002, the *Directors' Remuneration Report Regulations 2002* (SI 2002/1986) require a quoted company to give detailed disclosures on share options exercised and granted, and on the company's policy on the use of share options to remunerate directors, in the annual directors' remuneration report (see 17.1 to 17.6 above). In the case of an unquoted company, CA 1985 only requires the notes to the accounts to show the number of directors who exercised share options during the year. The disclosures in respect of the highest paid director must also state whether he/she exercised any share options during the year, but there is no requirement to attribute any value to the transaction(s). In effect, the special provisions for unquoted companies avoid the need for them to calculate gains made by directors on the exercise of share options.

Disclosure of options granted or exercised during the year

17.40   Paragraph 2B of Schedule 7 to CA 1985 also requires the directors' report (or the notes to the accounts) to state individually for each person who was a director at the end of the financial year whether, according to the register of directors' interests, any right to subscribe for shares in, or debentures of, the company (or another body corporate in the same group) was granted to or exercised by that director or a member of his/her immediate family during the year. For each director who had disclosable interests in options at the end of the year, the following details must be given:

(i)   the name of the company (or companies) in which he/she was granted, or exercised, a right to subscribe;

(ii)   the number of shares in each company in respect of which he/she was granted, or exercised, a right to subscribe; and

(iii) the amount of debentures of each company in respect of which he/she was granted, or exercised, a right to subscribe.

A negative statement must also be given for any directors who do not hold any rights to subscribe for shares or debentures at the end of the financial year .

In each case, rights granted to, or exercised by, a member of the director's immediate family are to be included in the disclosures. In this context a director's immediate family means his/her spouse and infant children or step-children. However, options should not be counted twice. Thus, options held by a director's wife should not be treated as granted to, or exercised by, him if his wife is also a director of the company – they will instead be disclosable as options granted to, or exercised by her as a director of the company.

Where a director of a wholly-owned subsidiary is also a director of the holding company, options held by him/her will be disclosed in the directors' report of the holding company. In such circumstances, the information need not be given in the directors' report of the subsidiary. In this case it is usual to explain in the directors' report of the subsidiary why the information has not been disclosed and where it can be found.

Charge to National Insurance

17.41   For share options granted after 5 April 1999, employers' National Insurance (NI) contributions are payable on the gains made by directors and employees on the exercise of options issued under unapproved share option schemes (i.e. those not approved by the Inland Revenue). The charge is based on the difference between the exercise price paid by the director or employee and the market value of the shares at the date of exercise. By granting such share options, the company takes on an obligation to pay the NI contributions, and provision for the cost should therefore be made in the accounts during the period that the share options are outstanding, even though payment will not actually be made until the options are exercised.

However, it is important to recognise that this NI will not affect the accounts disclosure requirements in respect of directors' remuneration, because employers' NI contributions are not disclosable as emoluments. The NI costs will, however, be included as part of the staff costs disclosures in the annual accounts in the year in which the relevant provision is made. The ASB's Urgent Issues Task Force (UITF) Abstract 25 'National Insurance contributions on share option gains' sets out guidance on how the provision should be calculated and when it should be recognised in the accounts (see Chapter 11).

Combined Code recommendations

17.42   The best practice provisions of the Combined Code include the following recommendations in respect of the use of share options to reward executives:

(i)   executive share options should not be offered at a discount, except as permitted by Chapter 13.30 and Chapter 13.31 of the UK Listing Rules;

(ii) traditional share option schemes should be weighed against other types of long-term incentive scheme;

(iii) in normal circumstances, shares granted should not vest, and options should not be exercisable, in under three years;

(iv) directors should be encouraged to hold their shares for a further period after vesting or exercise, subject to the need to finance any costs of acquisition and associated tax liability;

(v)   payouts or grants under incentive schemes, including new grants under existing share option schemes, should be subject to challenging criteria reflecting the company's objectives; and

(vi) grants under executive share option and other long-term incentive schemes should normally be phased over a period of time rather than awarded in one large block (to reduce the possibility of significant share price fluctuations arising).

Shareholder approval of new share option schemes

17.43   Chapter 13.13 of the UK Listing Rules requires certain incentive schemes to be approved by an ordinary resolution of the shareholders in general meeting before adoption. The following schemes must be approved in this way:

(i)   an employee share scheme which involves, or may involve, the issue of new shares; and

(ii)   a long-term incentive scheme in which one or more of the directors is eligible to participate.

However, under UK Listing Rule 13.13A, approval is not required in respect of a long-term incentive scheme involving:

(i)   an arrangement under which participation is offered on similar terms to all or substantially all employees of the issuer or any of its subsidiary undertakings whose employees are eligible to participate (provided that all, or substantially all, of the employees are not directors of the issuer); or

(ii)   an arrangement in which the only participant is a director of the issuer (or a prospective director) and the arrangement is established specifically to facilitate, in unusual circumstances, the retention or recruitment of that individual – in this case, the first annual report after the date on which the individual becomes eligible to participate in the arrangement must include:

- an explanation of why the circumstances were unusual;

- the conditions to be satisfied under the terms of the arrangement; and

- the maximum award(s) under the terms of the arrangement, or if there is no maximum, the basis on which awards will be determined.

Apart from these specific exceptions, the approval requirement applies to any scheme operated by a listed company incorporated in the UK, or by any of its subsidiary undertakings regardless of where they are incorporated.

Provision B.2.4 of the revised Combined Code (see Chapter 40) also recommends that any new long-term incentive schemes and significant changes to existing schemes should be approved by the shareholders, subject to the provisions of Chapter 13.3A to the UK Listing Rules.

Disclosure of policy on granting of options and awards to employees

17.44   Chapter 12.43A (c)(viii) of the UK Listing Rules requires the annual report to shareholders on remuneration issues to include a statement on the company's policy on the granting of options and awards under employee share schemes and other long-term incentive schemes. Any change in the policy from the preceding year, and any departure from the stated policy in the period under review, should be explained and justified. This disclosure should include share options granted to directors as well as those granted to other employees.

The *Directors' Remuneration Report Regulations 2002* (SI 2002/1986), which apply to all quoted companies, require similar disclosures to be given in the directors' remuneration report (see 17.1 to 17.7 above).

LONG-TERM INCENTIVE PLANS

Disclosure requirements

17.45

In the case of quoted companies, the *Directors' Remuneration Report Regulations 2002* (SI 2002/1986) amend CA 1985 to require detailed disclosures on awards under long-term incentive schemes, and on the company's policy on the use of such schemes to remunerate directors, to be given in the directors' remuneration report (see 17.1 to 17.7 above). Unquoted companies are required to disclose:

(i)   the number of directors who received shares under long-term incentive schemes in respect of qualifying services; and

(ii)   the aggregate of amounts paid to, or receivable by, directors under long-term incentive schemes in respect of qualifying services and the net value of any assets (other than cash, shares and share options) received or receivable by the directors under such schemes.

A key difference, therefore, is that unquoted companies are not required to place a value on any shares received by the directors under long-term incentive schemes, but simply have to disclose the number of directors who received such shares. Quoted companies have to value the shares and include this value in the total amount paid to, or receivable by, the directors.

Where payment is made in the form of assets rather than cash, the amount to be included for disclosure purposes is the net value of that asset, which is defined as the value after deducting any money paid or any other value given by the director in respect of that asset. Where payment is in the form of shares, these should be valued at market price on the day that they are received (or become receivable) by the director. Shares are defined as shares in the company or in any other undertaking within the group, and the term specifically includes share warrants.

Definition of long-term incentive scheme

17.46   A long-term incentive scheme is defined in CA 1985 as any agreement or arrangement under which money or other assets become receivable by a director and where one or more of the qualifying conditions relating to service or performance cannot be fulfilled within a single financial year. Bonuses relating to an individual year (which will normally come within 'emoluments'), termination payments and retirement benefits are specifically excluded from the disclosure requirements in respect of long-term incentive schemes.

Provisions for payments under long-term incentive schemes

17.47   In accounting terms, provision for payments under long-term incentive schemes should be made in each period in which the director performs the services that are to be paid for under, or rewarded through, the scheme. Appropriate accruals should, therefore, be made in the accounts each year to reflect the amount 'earned' in respect of that year. In complex schemes, where the director has to meet targets over a number of years, this will usually require overall estimates to be made in order to spread the total expected 'cost' of the scheme over the period in question.

When do payments become disclosable?

17.48   Under CA 1985, amounts payable under long-term incentive schemes are disclosable when they are paid to, or receivable by, the director. Therefore the director must have the right to receive a sum before it becomes disclosable. As a result, amounts should normally be disclosed in the year in which the director becomes entitled to receive payment. In the case of a long-term incentive scheme, the director will not usually be entitled to receive payment until all the specified conditions have been met. Even though it will usually be necessary to accrue for the payments in each accounting year, these sums will not become disclosable until all the relevant conditions have been met and the director becomes entitled to receive payment. As with annual bonuses, this will not always match the actual timing of the payment.

Guaranteed Minimum Payment

17.49   Complex incentive schemes which extend over a number of years will sometimes include the provision of a guaranteed minimum payment to the directors, once a specified target has been achieved. In this case, the guaranteed minimum payment will become disclosable in the year in which the target is achieved, as this is when the directors become entitled to the minimum payment.

Combined Code recommendations

17.50   As the main purpose of long-term incentive schemes is to improve company performance over an extended period, the Combined Code recommends that performance criteria for such schemes should be challenging, should reflect the company's objectives and should relate the company's performance to that of a group of comparator companies. The Code also recommends that remuneration committees should consider whether directors should be eligible for benefits under long-term incentive schemes and that grants under executive share option and other long-term incentive schemes should generally be phased rather than awarded in one large block.

Shareholder approval of long-term incentive schemes

17.51   Chapter 13.13 to the UK Listing Rules requires certain incentive schemes to be approved by an ordinary resolution of the shareholders in general meeting before adoption (see 17.43 above). Apart from the specific exceptions noted in the Listing Rules, the approval requirement applies to any scheme operated by a listed company incorporated in the UK, or by any of its subsidiary undertakings regardless of where they are incorporated.

Paragraph B.2.4 of the revised Combined Code specifically recommends that shareholders should be invited to approve all new long-term incentive schemes (including share option schemes) and significant changes to existing schemes except in the circumstances set out in Chapter 13.13A to the Listing Rules.

Disclosure of policy on granting of options and awards to employees

17.52   Chapter 12.43A(c)(viii) to the UK Listing Rules requires the report to shareholders on remuneration issues to include a statement on the company's policy on the granting of options and awards under employee share schemes and other long-term incentive schemes. Any change in the policy from the preceding year, and any departure from the stated policy in the period under review, should be explained and justified. The *Directors' Remuneration Report Regulations 2002* (SI 2002/1986) require similar disclosures to be given by all quoted companies (see 17.1 to 17.7 above).

PENSION ARRANGEMENTS

Pension contributions and arrangements

17.53   CA 1985 sets out various definitions in respect of pensions and pension schemes, and also requires separate disclosure of certain pension contributions for the benefit of directors, basic details of pension arrangements for directors, and certain pension scheme retirement benefits paid to directors and former directors. As a minimum, all companies must disclose in their accounts:

(i)   the aggregate amount of company contributions to pension schemes in respect of qualifying services where the benefits payable to the directors will be calculated on the basis of the contributions paid;

(ii)   the number of directors accruing retirement benefits under money purchase schemes; and

(iii)   the number of directors accruing retirement benefits under defined benefit schemes.

Contributions to money purchase (defined contribution) schemes are considered to provide a reasonable measure of the benefit to the director and are, therefore, disclosable. This is not necessarily the case with defined benefit schemes – therefore, the level of contributions to such schemes for directors is not required to be disclosed. The number of directors accruing benefits under each type of pension scheme must be disclosed in all cases.

Qualifying services are defined as in 17.22 above. Company contributions are defined as any payment (including insurance premiums) made, or treated as made, to a pension scheme in respect of a director by any person other than the director.

Hybrid pension schemes

17.54 For disclosure purposes, all pension schemes must be classified as either money purchase schemes (in which case contributions in respect of directors are disclosable) or defined benefit schemes (in which case contributions during the year in respect of directors do not need to be disclosed). CA 1985 defines a money purchase scheme as one where all the benefits that may become payable to the director are money purchase benefits (i.e. they are calculated by reference to the contributions made and are not average salary benefits). A defined benefit scheme is defined as a pension scheme that is not a money purchase scheme. A hybrid pension scheme under which a director will be entitled to receive both money purchase benefits and defined benefits will therefore be classified as a defined benefit scheme for disclosure purposes. The legislation states specifically that any death in service benefits should be disregarded when classifying a pension scheme for disclosure purposes.

Pension scheme with an underpin

17.55 CA 1985 also provides specifically for a pension scheme where the benefits payable to, or receivable by, a director will be money purchase benefits or defined benefits, whichever is the greater. In this case, the company is allowed to assume for disclosure purposes that the benefits will be either money purchase benefits or defined benefits, whichever appears more likely at the end of the financial year in question.

Additional disclosures for defined benefit schemes

17.56 Where a company makes contributions to a defined benefit retirement scheme in respect of a director, certain additional disclosure requirements apply:

(i) where the aggregate of emoluments and amounts receivable by directors under long-term incentive schemes (other than shares and share options) exceeds £200,000, an unquoted company must generally disclose the accrued pension benefit of the highest paid director and, where applicable, the amount of any accrued lump sum receivable by him/her under the scheme (see 17.9 above); and

(ii)   under the *Directors' Remuneration Report Regulations 2002* (SI 2002/1986), a quoted company must disclose the following information for each director who served during the financial year and has rights under a defined benefit retirement scheme:

- details of any changes during the year in their accrued benefits under the scheme;

- the accrued benefits at the end of the year;

- the transfer value of the accrued benefits, calculated as recommended by the Institute of Actuaries and Faculty of Actuaries; and

- the equivalent transfer value at the end of the previous year and the difference between this and the current transfer value, after deducting any contributions made by the director in the current year.

Accrued pension benefits

17.57   The accrued pension and accrued lump sum entitlement of a director at the end of the financial year are defined in CA 1985 as the annual pension and lump sum that would be payable under the scheme on the director attaining normal retirement age:

(i)   if he/she had left the company at the end of the year;

(ii)   if there were no inflationary increases between the end of the year and the date he/she reached normal retirement age;

(iii)   if there were no commutation of the pension or inverse commutation of the lump sum; and

(iv)   disregarding any amounts attributable to voluntary contributions or to money purchase benefits under the scheme.

The following example illustrates how the accrued pension and accrued lump sum might be calculated for disclosure purposes:

Example 17.3 – Accrued Pension Benefits

The director was 55 at the start of the financial year and 56 at the end. He joined the company pension scheme at the age of 25 and will retire at the age of 60. His maximum pension entitlement is 35/80 of final salary, after 35 years in the scheme. The maximum lump sum payable to him after 35 years in the scheme is 105/80 of final salary. His salary in the previous financial year was £105,000 and in the current year is £110,000.

The following calculations can be made for disclosure purposes:

Accrued pension at beginning of year	30/80 x £105,000 = £39,375
Accrued pension at end of year	31/80 x £110,000 = £42,625
Accrued lump sum at beginning of year	90/80 x £105,000 = £118,125
Accrued lump sum at end of year	93/80 x £110,000 = £127,875

Transfer values

17.58 Defined benefit schemes usually link pension entitlement to final salary or average salary over a fixed period (say the last three years). The Greenbury Report (see Chapter 40) suggested that, in these circumstance, the best measure of the pension entitlement earned by an individual director during the year was the present value of the additional entitlement earned as a result of the additional length of service, any increase in salary and any changes in the scheme, less any pension contributions made by the director during the period. It also recommended that any major changes compared with the previous year should be explained. However, these recommendations did not completely solve the problem, as there are two possible methods of calculating pension entitlement: the accrued benefit method and the transfer value method.

A consultation exercise did not produce any clear consensus on which approach should be used for disclosure purposes – directors and companies were generally in favour of the accrued benefit method, whilst investors and their representatives generally preferred the transfer value method. Therefore, the Institute of Actuaries and Faculty of Actuaries put forward recommendations proposing two separate disclosures for each director. These were:

(i)   the increase in his/her accrued pension entitlement, excluding any annual inflation adjustment made to all deferred pensions; and

(ii)   the transfer value of the increased benefit, disclosed either as a figure calculated on the basis of actuarial advice, or by disclosing sufficient information for shareholders to make a reasonable assessment of the value.

These disclosure recommendations were initially incorporated into UK Listing Rules, together with disclosure of the total accrued pension entitlement of each director at the end of the financial year, and were subsequently included in the *Directors' Remuneration Report Regulations 2002*.

Where a transfer value is disclosed, it should be calculated in accordance with Actuarial Guidance Note 11 (GN11) but should not include any deduction for underfunding. Where the company adopts the approach of providing additional information, this should normally include:

(i)   the current age of the director;

(ii)   the normal retirement age of the director;

(iii)   any contributions paid or payable by the director during the year under the terms of the scheme;

(iv)   details of spouse and dependants' benefits;

(v)   details of early retirement rights and options, and expectations of pension increases after retirement (whether guaranteed or not);

(vi)   discretionary benefits for which allowance is made in transfer values on leaving, and

(vii)   any other relevant information which will significantly affect the value of benefits.

Voluntary contributions and benefits should not be included in any of these disclosures.

Pensionable remuneration

17.59   Chapter 12.43(c)(v) of the UK Listing Rules currently requires companies to explain and justify any elements of directors' remuneration other than basic salary that are treated as pensionable. This reflects the view, broadly accepted to date, that performance-related elements of pay and benefits received in kind should generally not be pensionable. However, as more emphasis is placed on performance-related pay rather than basic salary, for instance under the recommendations set out in the Combined Code, it is possible that there will be a greater need for some elements of performance-related remuneration (eg annual bonuses) to become pensionable.

Disclosure of excess retirement benefits

17.60   CA 1985 requires disclosure of any pension scheme retirement benefits paid to, or receivable by, directors or past directors that are in excess of the retirement benefits to which they were entitled at the date the benefits first became payable, or on 31 March 1997 if earlier. However, excess amounts need not be included in this disclosure if:

(i)   the funding of the scheme was sufficient to enable the payments to be made without recourse to additional contributions; and

(ii)   the additional amounts were paid to, or receivable by, all pensioner members of the scheme.

For instance, regular inflationary increases that are paid to all pensioners in the scheme will not usually be disclosable. However, any other discretionary increases to the pensions of directors and former directors will normally have to be disclosed.

Benefits other than in cash

17.61   Where pension benefits include non-cash items, these should be included in the disclosures at their estimated money value and the nature of the benefit must be disclosed. The most common example is where a director continues to be given the use of a company car after he has retired.

Additional pensions

17.62   Care is needed over the treatment of any additional or 'top hat' pensions paid by the company to directors or former directors. These will often require disclosure as they will not be provided through the standard pension scheme.

COMPENSATION FOR LOSS OF OFFICE

Separate category of payment

17.63   The directors' remuneration report of a quoted company should include details of any compensation for loss of office awarded to directors and former directors. In the case of an unquoted company, CA 1985 requires disclosure of the aggregate amount of compensation for loss of office paid to, or receivable by, directors and former directors. This constitutes a separate category of payment to directors and should not be included in the figure for directors' emoluments for the period. Under paragraph 8(4)(a) of Schedule 6 to CA 1985, compensation for loss of office specifically includes payments connected with a director's retirement from office. However, this does not include normal pension payments, as these are covered by separate disclosure requirements (see 17.52 to 17.62 above).

Examples of compensation payments

17.64   The most common examples of compensation payments are:

(i)   ex gratia payments made by the company when a director resigns; and

(ii)   payments in respect of breach of contract if a director is dismissed by the company before his service contract expires.

Both the nature and the circumstances of such payments need to be considered when deciding whether or not they are disclosable under CA 1985. In particular, payments that are described as ex gratia will often have a degree of compensation attached to them and will therefore be disclosable. The legislation makes it clear that payments for damages as a result of breach of contract and payments to settle a claim for breach of contract are to be treated as compensation for loss of office for disclosure purposes.

Shareholder approval

17.65   Many compensation payments to directors will also require shareholder approval under sections 312 or 313 of CA 1985, although this is not usually required for genuine payments in respect of damages for breach of contract or for pensions in respect of past services. If significant non-cash items are included, the compensation payments may also require approval under the provisions on substantial property transactions in section 320 of CA 1985.

Pension top-ups

17.66   Compensation might also include pension top-up payments made when a director ceases to hold office. However, if these payments are made simply to make good a deficiency in the pension fund rather than to increase the director's pension, it will usually be more appropriate to treat them as normal pension contributions.

This is because the company will usually be liable for making good the deficiency in the pension fund regardless of whether the director ceases to hold office and in these circumstances the top-up should not be treated as relating to the director's loss of office.

Benefits other than in cash

17.67   Where compensation payments include non-cash benefits, these should be included in the disclosures at their estimated money value and the nature of the benefit must be disclosed. The most common example is where a director is given his company car as part of the compensation arrangements.

Continuing involvement

17.68   In some cases directors who have officially retired may continue to have an involvement with the company in a part-time or consultancy capacity, or may even continue to receive a normal salary, even though they carry out only minimal duties. Where payments to former directors are in excess of normal market rates for the work that they perform, there may well be an element of compensation for loss of office, in which case the details should be disclosed under the requirements of CA 1985.

Example disclosure

17.69   The disclosure on compensation for loss of office is usually given in narrative form, although a table may be used if this gives a clearer presentation:

Example 17.4 – Compensation for loss of office

Payments of £... (20X1 £...) were made to directors during the year in connection with the termination of their service contracts. One director retained his company car and the payments shown above include the estimated market value of the car at the date on which his service contract was terminated.

In the case of a quoted company, details will need to be given individually for each director concerned.

POTENTIAL PROBLEMS IN GROUPS OF COMPANIES

Payments for services to holding company and fellow subsidiaries

17.70   The directors' remuneration disclosures cover all amounts paid to, or receivable by, a director in respect of his services as a director of the company (and any of its subsidiaries) or in an executive or managerial capacity for any of those companies. However, they do not cover any payments relating to services by the same director to a holding company or to a fellow subsidiary company:

Example 17.5 – Disclosure of emoluments within a group

RST Limited has 2 subsidiary undertakings, JKL Limited and MNO Limited. JKL Limited has 1 subsidiary undertaking, PQR Limited.

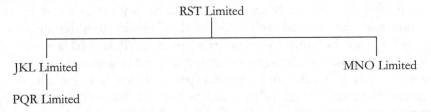

Mr Green is a director of JKL Limited, MNO Limited and PQR Limited. He is not a director of the overall holding company, RST Limited, but he is a manager in that company. In 20X4 he received the following remuneration.

(i)   As director of JKL Limited – £20,000 from JKL Limited.

(ii) As director of MNO Limited – £22,000 from MNO Limited.

(iii) As director of PQR Limited – £10,000 from JKL Limited.

(iv) As a manager of ABC Limited – £40,000 from RST Limited.

The following amounts are disclosable.

(i)   In the accounts of JKL Limited – £30,000 (i.e. his remuneration in respect of his services to the company and its subsidiary PQR Limited).

(ii) In the accounts of MNO Limited – £22,000 (his remuneration in respect of his services to that company only).

(iii) In the accounts of PQR Limited – £10,000 (his remuneration in respect of services to that company only).

(iv) In the accounts of RST Limited – no disclosure as he is not a director of RST Limited.

Remuneration paid by the holding company

17.71   In some groups, all directors' remuneration is paid by the holding company. Recharges may be made to subsidiary undertakings to reflect the cost of the services of their directors, but this will not always be done. This can cause difficulties over the disclosure of directors' remuneration in the accounts of the holding company and the subsidiaries.

Directors' remuneration in the accounts of the holding company will comprise:

(i)   remuneration paid to directors of the holding company in respect of their services to the company and management of the company and group; and

(ii)   if any holding company directors are also directors of one or more of the subsidiaries, remuneration paid to them for their services in relation to these companies.

Remuneration paid to those who are directors of subsidiaries, but who are not directors of the holding company, is not disclosable in the accounts of the holding company. The same disclosure requirements apply in the holding company's accounts, regardless of whether some or all of the remuneration costs are recharged to the subsidiaries.

Where the holding company recharges the subsidiaries with the cost of remunerating their directors, each subsidiary should disclose as directors' remuneration the amount paid to the holding company in respect of directors' services to the company. In some cases, the holding company may make a global recharge to the subsidiaries to cover general management costs, which will include directors' remuneration, but may include other costs as well. If the element for directors' remuneration cannot be separately identified, an appropriate apportionment should be made for disclosure purposes.

Where the holding company does not recharge the subsidiaries with the cost of remunerating their directors, the amounts paid by the holding company for the services of the subsidiary directors are still disclosable as directors' remuneration in the accounts of the subsidiary. It is usually helpful to explain that this cost has been borne by the holding company and has not been recharged to the subsidiary, although this is not a disclosure requirement under CA 1985. It is not sufficient to simply disclose the fact that the directors have been remunerated by the holding company and not quantify the amount that they have received.

No remuneration in respect of services to subsidiary

17.72   Where directors of a subsidiary are also directors or employees of the holding company, it is sometimes argued that the holding company remunerates them only for their services to the holding company, and that they receive no remuneration in respect of their services as directors of the subsidiary. The validity of this argument will usually depend on the amount of time that the director or employee devotes to the subsidiary company. If the time is relatively small (e.g. the role is in effect that of a non-executive director) it may be acceptable that he/she does not receive remuneration for services as a director of the subsidiary. In this case, an explanation should be included in the subsidiary's accounts:

Example 17.6 – No remuneration as director of subsidiary

Mr L Brown and Ms T Smith are also employees of ABC Limited, the company's ultimate holding company. They do not receive any remuneration specifically in respect of their services as directors of the company.

DIRECTORS' SERVICE CONTRACTS

The need for service contracts for directors

17.73   An executive director is in effect an employee of the company and it is appropriate that the terms and conditions of his/her appointment should be set out in a written contract of service between the director and the company. A comprehensive service contract can help to prevent misunderstandings and provides a useful point of reference if problems arise. Non-executive directors have a very different role to executive directors and the terms and conditions of their appointment will usually be set out in a contract for services.

Contents of a contract of service

17.74   A contract of service for an executive director should normally include:

  (i)   specific duties of the director, including the proportion of time to be spent on company activities (this may be particularly important where the individual also holds other posts, such as non-executive directorships in other businesses);

 (ii)   remuneration, including details of any arrangements involving:

- benefits-in-kind (e.g. private health cover, accommodation, company car);

- bonus schemes;

- long-term incentive plans; and

- share options;

(iii)   holiday entitlement;

(iv)   arrangements in the case of prolonged absence through illness;

 (v)   pension arrangements;

(vi)   required notice period, and procedures in the case of dismissal (including any compensation arrangements); and

(vii)   confidentiality arrangements.

Other issues may need to be covered, depending on the circumstances. The Institute of Directors publishes a specimen form of a contract of service for executive directors.

In June 2003 the DTI issued a consultation document 'Rewards for Failure: Directors' Remuneration – Contracts, Performance and Severance' which focused on directors' performance, contract and notice periods, and compensation payments, particularly in the case of individuals who are considered to have underperformed. The issues set out for consideration included:

  (i)   whether directors' contracts should be limited to one year or less;

 (ii)   the present failure to distinguish clearly between contract periods and notice periods;

(iii)   the use of liquidated damages clauses and whether a cap should be set on the level of compensation payable;

(iv)   whether compensation should be paid in instalments and cease on the director taking up a new employment; and

(v)   the implications of 'rolling contracts'.

Comments on the points raised in the document were requested by 30 September 2003 but no firm proposals for change have been put forward as yet.

Contents of a contract for services

17.75   The main role of non-executive directors is to make a positive contribution to the development of company strategy, and on matters such as company performance, standards of conduct and corporate governance issues. They should generally be independent of the company. Provision A.7.2 of the revised Combined Code recommends that non-executive directors are appointed for a specified term and that their reappointment should not be automatic. Non-executive directors will usually be paid either a fixed fee, or a fixed retainer plus fees for attendance at specific meetings. It is helpful to all parties for the terms of their appointment to be set out in a written contract for services. This will usually specify:

(i)   the expected commitment, in terms of attendance at meetings of the board and its sub-committees; and

(ii)   fee arrangements.

The Cadbury Report (see Chapter 40) emphasised the importance of striking an effective balance between recognition of the value of non-executive directors and their contribution to the company, and the need to ensure that any payments that they receive do not in effect undermine their independence. It recommends that the fee arrangements should reflect the time commitment expected from the non-executive directors, and it notes that it can be helpful for them to take into account specific additional responsibilities, such as Chairmanship of one or more of the sub-committees of the main board. These issues have been reflected in provision B.1.3 of the revised Combined Code. It is not usually considered appropriate for non-executive directors to participate in company share option schemes, or to be provided with pension arrangements, as these could hamper their independence.

Requirement to keep copies of contracts

17.76   Where a director has a written contract of service with the company, section 318 of CA 1985 requires the company to retain a copy of the contract at one of the following locations:

(i)   the company's registered office;

(ii)   the place where the register of members is kept (if this is not the registered office); or

(iii)   its principal place of business (provided that this is in the part of Great Britain where the company is registered).

If a director does not have a written contract of service, the company must keep a written memorandum of the terms of his/her appointment. The same rules apply to a variation of a director's contract and to contracts with shadow directors. A parent company is also required to keep copies of service contracts between its subsidiaries and their directors, or a written memorandum of the terms if these contracts are not in writing. All copies of contracts or memoranda of terms must be kept in the same place.

Each company must notify the Registrar of Companies of the place where copies of the contracts and memoranda are held, unless they are at the company's registered office, and notify any changes in location.

However, where a director of the company, or of one of its subsidiaries, is required under his/her contract to work wholly or mainly outside the UK, the company is not required to keep a copy of the contract but it must keep a memorandum giving the director's name and the provisions of the contract relating to its duration. In the case of a contract for a director of a subsidiary, the name and place of incorporation of the subsidiary must also be recorded in the memorandum. These memoranda must be kept in the same place as the contracts and memoranda relating to the other directors.

Also, there is no formal requirement for a company to retain a copy of a contract, variation or memorandum when the unexpired term is less than twelve months, or where the contract can be terminated by the company within the next twelve months without the payment of compensation.

Any member of the company is entitled to inspect the copies of the directors' contracts of service (or the memoranda where there is no written service contract) without charge. If the company refuses to allow a member to inspect a contract or memorandum, the court can require immediate inspection.

Shareholder approval for contracts for more than five years

17.77   Under section 319 of CA 1985, a director cannot be given the right of employment with the company (or, where relevant, with the group) for a period of more than five years under an agreement which does not allow the company to give unconditional notice at any time, unless this term of the contract has been first approved by the company in general meeting (or, in the case of a private company, by written resolution). However, prior approval by the shareholders is not required in the case of a company which is a wholly-owned subsidiary. Employment is defined as including employment under a contract for services (for instance, a consultancy agreement). Where the director is also a director of the company's holding company, prior approval to the arrangement must normally be given by both the subsidiary and the holding company (unless the subsidiary is wholly-owned, in which case prior approval of the arrangement by the subsidiary is not required). By implication, a company is permitted to enter into an agreement giving a director employment for more than five years without prior shareholder approval, provided that the company is free to give unconditional notice at any time.

A written memorandum setting out the proposed agreement must be available for inspection by the members at the company's registered office for a period of at least 15 days before the meeting at which approval is to be sought and at the meeting itself. In the case of a private company where agreement is to be by written resolution, a copy of the memorandum must be sent to each member before, or at the same time as, the resolution is provided for signature. A term included in a director's contract in contravention of section 319 of CA 1985 is void, and the agreement is deemed to include a term entitling the company to terminate the agreement at any time by the giving of reasonable notice.

The final consultation document in the company law review 'Modern Company Law for a Competitive Economy: Completing the Structure', published by the DTI in November 2000, proposed that the maximum permitted term for a director's initial employment contract with the company should be three years, and that this should reduce to one year for subsequent contracts. In both cases, the members of the company in general meeting would have the power to authorise a longer term. The document also proposed that any contractual arrangement entitling a director to an amount in excess of one year's remuneration on loss of office should be unlawful unless it had been approved in advance by the members of the company in general meeting. All of these recommendations were reinforced in the DTI document 'Modern Company Law for a Competitive Economy: Final Report', published in July 2001.

Extension of contract

17.78   Where a director is, or is to be, employed under an agreement which the company is not free to terminate by unconditional notice, and an additional agreement is entered into more than six months before the expiry of the earlier agreement, the unexpired period of the original agreement must be added to the period of the additional agreement in order to establish whether prior shareholder approval is required. This is intended to prevent a company avoiding the approval requirements by entering into a series of agreements with the same director. However, it seems that this can still be done provided that the unexpired period of the original agreement and the period of the additional agreement do not amount to more than five years.

Combined Code recommendations

17.79   The Combined Code recommends that:

(i)   notice or contract periods should be set at one year or less;

(ii)   if it is necessary to offer longer notice or contract periods to new directors recruited from outside the company, such periods should reduce to one year or less after the initial period; and

(iii)   the remuneration committee should consider carefully what compensation commitments (including pensions) would be entailed in the event of early termination of the contract – the aim should be to avoid rewarding poor performance and to take a robust line on reducing compensation to reflect a departing director's obligation to mitigate loss.

In June 2003 the DTI issued a consultation document 'Rewards for Failure: Directors' Remuneration – Contracts, Performance and Severance' which focuses on directors' performance, contract and notice periods, and compensation payments, particularly in the case of individuals who are considered to have underperformed (see 17.67 above).

Additional requirements for listed companies

17.80   Listed companies are required under Chapter 12.43A(c)(vi) and (vii) of the UK Listing Rules to include in the report to shareholders on directors' remuneration:

(i)   details of any director's service contract with a notice period in excess of one year or with provisions for pre-determined compensation on termination which exceeds one year's salary and benefits in kind, giving the reasons for such notice period;

(ii)   the unexpired term of any service contract for a director proposed for election or re-election at the forthcoming general meeting; and

(iii)   where a director proposed for election or re-election does not have a service contract, a statement to that effect.

For accounting periods ending on or after 31 December 2002, the details in (i) above are in effect also required to be given by all quoted companies under *Directors' Remuneration Report Regulations 2002* (SI 2002/1986) (see 17.1 to 17.6 above).

REMUNERATION COMMITTEES

Need for a remuneration committee

17.81   The Combined Code recommends that:

(i)   the board should establish a remuneration committee of at least three non-executive directors to determine, within agreed terms of reference, the

company's policy on executive remuneration and specific remuneration packages for each individual executive director, and the chairman, including
pension rights and any compensation payments;

(ii) the remuneration committee should consist exclusively of non-executive
directors who:

- are independent of management;

- have no personal financial interest in the matters to be decided (other
than as shareholders);

- have no potential conflicts of interest arising from cross-directorships;
and

- have no day-to-day involvement in running the business;

(iii) the membership of the remuneration committee should be disclosed in the
committee's annual report to shareholders;

(iv) the remuneration committee should consult the Chairman and/or Chief
Executive about their proposals and should have access to professional advice
(both inside and outside the company) where necessary;

(v) the remuneration committee should be responsible for appointing any consultant on executive remuneration; and

(vi) the Chairman of the remuneration committee should attend the annual
general meeting to answer shareholders' questions about directors' remuneration, and the Chairman of the board should ensure that the company keeps in
contact with the principal shareholders on remuneration issues.

(vii) the remuneration committee should make publicly available its terms of
reference, and to explain its role and the authority delegated to it by the
board; and

(viii) if executive directors or senior management are involved in advising or
supporting the remuneration committee, care should be taken to recognise
and avoid any conflicts of interest.

Research carried out as part of the Higgs Review indicated that most listed
companies already have a separate remuneration committee. It is important that
such a committee is properly constituted and has a clear remit and designated
authority.

Terms of reference

17.82   The terms of reference of the remuneration committee should set out the
committee's delegated responsibilities, should be subject to annual review and
should be made publicly available. Annex E to the Higgs Report summarised the
main duties of the remuneration committee as follows:

(i) **Remuneration policy**: The remuneration committee should determine and agree with the board the framework or broad policy for the remuneration of the chairman and of other executives, as designated by the board. The guidance notes that the remuneration committee may be asked to consider the remuneration packages of all executives at or above a specified management level, or to deal with all packages above a certain figure. In particular, the Higgs Report emphasises that:

- as a minimum, the remuneration committee should have delegated responsibility for setting the remuneration for all executive directors, the chairman and the company secretary;

- the remuneration of the non-executive directors should be considered by the chairman and the executive directors; and

- no director or manager should be involved in setting his/her own remuneration.

(ii) **Performance-related pay**: The remuneration committee should determine the targets for any performance-related pay schemes operated by the company.

(iii) **Pension arrangements**: The remuneration committee should determine the policy for, and scope of, the pension arrangements for each executive director.

(iv) **Termination payments**: The remuneration committee should ensure that contractual terms in respect of termination payments, and any payments actually made, are fair to both the individual and the company. In particular, the committee has a responsibility to ensure that failure is not rewarded and that the duty to mitigate loss is fully recognised. The guidance recommends that the committee considers agreeing a standard form of contract for the executive directors and then ensures that new appointees are offered and accept terms within the agreed level. Close co-operation will be required between the nomination and remuneration committees in order to achieve this.

(v) **Individual remuneration packages**: The remuneration committee should determine the remuneration of each executive director, within the terms of the agreed policy, including where appropriate the award of bonuses, incentive payments and share options. In doing so, the committee should give due regard to the recommendations in the Combined Code and related guidance and, where appropriate, any requirements of the UK Listing Authority.

(vi) **Expenses**: The remuneration committee should agree the policy for authorising claims for expenses by the chairman and the chief executive.

(vii) **Employee benefits**: The remuneration committee should be aware of, and advise on, any major changes in employee benefit structures within the company or group.

(viii) **External advice**: Where remuneration consultants are to be appointed in an advisory capacity, the remuneration committee should have exclusive responsibility for establishing the selection criteria and for selecting, appointing and setting their terms of reference.

(ix) **Disclosure**: The remuneration committee is responsible for ensuring that:

- the company complies with the disclosure requirements of the *Directors' Remuneration Report Regulations 2002* and the Combined Code;

- the frequency of, and attendance levels at, meetings of the remuneration committee are disclosed in the company's annual report; and

- the committee's terms of reference are made publicly available.

The Institute of Chartered Secretaries and Administrators (ICSA) produces a useful specimen terms of reference for a remuneration committee, which has recently been updated to take account of the recommendations in the Higgs Report.

Remuneration policy

17.83   Recommendations on remuneration policy are set out in section B.1.1 of, and Schedule A to, the Combined Code. These include:

(i) a remuneration committee must develop the remuneration packages needed to attract, retain and motivate directors of the appropriate quality, but should avoid paying more than is necessary for this;

(ii) the committee should judge where to position the company in relation to other companies – they should therefore be aware of other companies' remuneration policies and also their relative performance but should use such comparisons with care in view of the risk of raising remuneration levels without a corresponding improvement in performance;

(iii) the committee should also be sensitive to the wider scene, including employee pay and conditions within the company, especially when considering annual salary increases;

(iv) any performance-related elements of remuneration should be designed to align the interests of the directors and of the shareholders, and should give directors keen incentives to perform at the highest levels;

(v) the committee should consider whether directors should be eligible for annual bonuses and, if so, should ensure that performance conditions are relevant, stretching and designed to enhance the business and that upper limits are always considered; and

(vi)   the committee should consider the pension consequences and associated costs to the company of increases in basic salary and other changes in remuneration, especially as directors get close to retirement – generally neither annual bonuses nor benefits-in-kind should be pensionable.

There are also various recommendations in respect of share option and other long-term incentive schemes, which are considered in more detail at 17.38 to 17.52 above.

APPENDIX

Example emoluments and benefits disclosures for a small company and an unquoted company

Example 1 – Small company with no long-term incentive schemes

	20X2 £	20X1 £
Directors' emoluments and company contributions to money purchase schemes in relation to directors' pensions	108,950	99,760

Two directors are accruing pension benefits under money purchase schemes and two directors are accruing pension benefits under a defined benefit scheme.

Example 2 – Unquoted company with no share options or long-term incentive schemes

	20X2 £	20X1 £
Directors' emoluments	304,900	289,950
Company contributions to money purchase schemes in relation to directors' pensions	11,800	7,500

Two directors are accruing pension benefits under money purchase schemes and one director is accruing pension benefits under a defined benefit scheme.

The above details include the following amounts in respect of the highest paid director:

	20X2 £	20X1 £
Emoluments	103,854	95,677
Company contributions to money purchase pension scheme	5,750	4,250

Example 3 – Unquoted company with share options and long-term incentive schemes

	20X2 £	20X1 £
Company contributions to money purchase schemes in relation to directors' pensions	11,800	7,500
Aggregate amounts receivable by directors in respect of long-term incentive schemes (other than shares and share options)	6,250	10,800

In addition to the above, one director received shares during the year under a long-term incentive scheme.

One director exercised share options during the year.

Two directors are accruing pension benefits under money purchase schemes and one director is accruing pension benefits under a defined benefit scheme.

The above details include the following amounts in respect of the highest paid director:

	20X2 £	20X1 £
Emoluments and amounts receivable under long-term incentive schemes (other than shares and share options)	103,854	95,677
Company contributions to money purchase pension scheme	5,750	4,250

During the year, this director also received shares under a long-term incentive scheme.

Chapter 18   Other Profit and Loss Account Disclosures

REMUNERATION OF THE AUDITORS AND THEIR ASSOCIATES

CA 1985 disclosure requirements

18.1   CA 1985 currently requires separate disclosure of the following amounts:

— the remuneration paid to the auditors in respect of their work as auditors, including any amounts in respect of expenses and any benefits in kind; and

— the remuneration paid to the auditors or their associates in respect of non-audit work.

The disclosures should be given in the notes to the accounts. Small and medium-sized companies are not required to disclose details of remuneration for non-audit work, but remuneration for audit services must be disclosed.

Changes are being made to the present requirements and are likely to come into effect for accounting periods beginning on or after 1 October 2005. Brief details are given at 18.7 to 18.9 below.

Remuneration for services as auditors

18.2   The amount to be disclosed in respect of their work as auditors includes:

— the audit fee;

— any expenses incurred by the auditors which have been reimbursed by the company; and

— the estimated money value of any benefits in kind received by the auditors in respect of their services as auditors and the nature of any such benefit.

In practice, professional and ethical guidelines will usually prevent auditors from accepting benefits in kind from the company. The amount to be disclosed is the audit fee in respect of the current year. This will usually be an estimate of the amount to be charged in respect of the audit and will often be the figure included in accruals. The legislation does not consider a situation where the actual fee in respect of any year is different to the amount provided and disclosed in the accounts for that year. Minor adjustments to the figure are not usually disclosed, but if the audit fee for a particular year has effectively been under or overstated by a material amount, it will usually be appropriate to disclose the adjustment separately in the following year's accounts.

Example 18.1 – Where disclosed audit fee is materially different to actual one

Auditors' remuneration, including expenses:

	20X2	20X1
	£	£
Current year	3,100	2,950
Additional fee in respect of previous year	400	—

Remuneration for other services

18.3   Remuneration receivable by the auditors and their associates in respect of other services provided to the company might include fees and expenses in respect of:

—   accountancy assistance;

—   payroll services;

—   tax compliance work;

—   tax advisory work; and

—   consultancy work.

The detailed requirements in respect of these disclosures are set out in the *Companies Act 1985 (Disclosure of Remuneration for Non-Audit Work) Regulations 1991* (SI 1991/2128), as amended by SI 1995/1520. The figure to be disclosed is the aggregate amount of remuneration in respect of work carried out during the financial year, regardless of whether it has been billed to the company. Comparative information must also be given. Once again, remuneration specifically includes the estimated money value of benefits in kind, although these are likely to be rare in practice, and both the nature and the estimated money value of any such benefits must be disclosed. Where the auditors (or their associates) are also the auditors of any UK subsidiary undertaking of the company (as defined in CA 1985), any amounts in respect of services to the subsidiary must be included in the aggregate remuneration. The auditors have a duty under the Regulations to provide the company with such information as it needs to be able to comply with the disclosure requirements. Where more than one auditor has held office during the year, separate disclosure is required in respect of each auditor and their associates.

Associates of auditors

18.4 The definition of associates is very complex but it broadly includes:

— any partnership in which the auditors are a partner or with which the auditors have a partner in common;

— any body corporate in the same group as the auditors;

— any directors of the auditors; and

— any body corporate in which the auditor, a partner of the auditors or a director of the auditors controls the exercise of 20% or more of the voting rights, or any other body corporate in the same group as such a body corporate.

If such a relationship exists at any time during the financial year, the entity is regarded as an associate of the auditors for that year. Reference should be made to the detail in the Regulations if there is any doubt over whether an entity should be treated as an associate of the auditors. Amendments to the Regulations introduced in 1995 specifically exclude entities that might otherwise have been treated as associates of the auditors as a result of insolvency and receivership appointments.

ICAEW recommendations on additional disclosure

18.5 Guidance on more extensive disclosure of the nature and value of non-audit services provided by auditors was published by the ICAEW in July 2003. The document is aimed at companies whose securities are quoted on a regulated market, but the introduction notes that it may also be helpful to the management of other entities disclosing non-audit fees. The guidance is based on EC recommendations and recommends that full and transparent disclosure should be made of all fees due to the principal audit firm and its network firms in relation to work performed during the period for the audit client and all entities controlled by that client alone. In the case of joint audits, the same disclosures should be given for each audit firm. The disclosures should cover both the nature and extent of the services provided and the review and approval process followed, and should provide sufficient information to enable a user of the accounts to judge whether the potential for conflicts of interest has been satisfactorily addressed. The guidance recommends that fees are analysed into the following categories:

(i) Audit services:

- statutory audit;

- audit-related regulatory reporting.

(ii) Further assurance services

(iii) Tax services:

- compliance services;
- advisory services.

(iv) Other services:

- financial information technology;
- internal audit;
- valuation;
- litigation;
- recruitment;
- other services giving rise to a self interest threat (listed separately);
- other services.

There is detailed guidance on which items should be included under each heading. For instance, regulatory reports required to be given by the company's auditors should be included under 'audit-related regulatory reporting', as should the review of interim financial information. Services that are not specifically related to the audit should be disclosed under 'further assurance services' (eg advice on accounting matters, non-regulatory reporting on internal controls, due diligence work on acquisitions). Fees should be calculated on an accruals basis and should include fees for all services where the substance of the arrangement is that the service has been rendered to the client, even if the fee itself has been paid by another party (eg the client's solicitor in the case of litigation support). Further analysis should be given where the amounts in individual categories are material and differ substantially from one another, and narrative explanations should be given where this would be helpful

Presentational issues

18.6   The recommended disclosures are broader than the present CA 1985 disclosure requirements. In particular, they cover overseas as well as UK entities and define the network of the principal auditor more widely. However, they are restricted to disclosures relating to the principal auditor, whereas company law requires the inclusion of amounts paid to any secondary auditors. Clear presentation of the information will therefore require some careful thought in order to achieve compliance with current legal requirements as well as the ICAEW recommendations, and additional analyses may need to given to enable users to reconcile the different figures provided.

Changes from 1 October 2005

18.7   The *Companies (Audit, Investigations and Community Enterprise) Act 2004*, which received Royal Assent in October 2004, includes new provisions on the disclosure of services provided by auditors and the related remuneration received by them. The provisions amend section 390A of CA 1985 and replace section 390B. The legislation as amended will specify that the Secretary of State may make provision for disclosure of the nature of the services provided, and require the details to be given by a particular class or description, and may require the disclosure of the separate amounts received by the auditors and their associates, or the disclosure of aggregate amounts. Future regulations will also be able to specify that disclosure should be given in the notes to the accounts, the directors' report or the auditors' report. All of these new provisions come into force on 1 October 2005.

DTI consultation on proposed regulations

18.8   Initial indications suggested that the DTI would monitor the impact of the voluntary disclosure recommendations issued by ICAEW in July 2003 (see 18.5 above) before making any further changes. However, a consultation document on proposed new regulations was issued in February 2005. The Foreword to this document emphasises that the proposals are part of a package of interlinking measures, both legislative and non-legislative, developed as a result of the various post-Enron reviews carried out in the UK. The major concern is that the provision of non-audit services to an audit client could undermine the auditors' independence and that shareholders and others need to be given sufficient and appropriate information to be able to assess this potential threat and to make relevant comparisons between companies. Many companies are now giving more than the statutory minimum disclosures, but there is still concern that the voluntary disclosure approach is resulting in a lack of comparability.

The consultation document covers the following issues:

(i)   the definition of an auditors' associates – in particular, the proposed definition includes overseas associates and entities associated with the auditors through the intentional use of a common or similar name or the sharing of significant professional resources;

(ii)   the definition of a company's associates – in particular, the proposed definition here includes pension schemes, overseas subsidiaries, and certain joint ventures and similar entities that need to be fully consolidated into the accounts;

(iii) a proposed requirement for companies to give separate disclosure of each type of service specified in the draft regulations and the amount paid to the auditors and their associates for that service, with no de minimis exemptions – the separate categories proposed for disclosure include:

- auditing under CA 1985;
- other services provided under legislation;
- tax compliance services;
- tax advisory services;

- other assurance services;
- IT services in respect of financial systems;
- internal audit;
- valuation services;
- litigation services; and
- recruitment services.

The DTI proposes that these detailed disclosures should be given in the notes to the accounts.

Proposed exemptions

18.9 It is proposed that, as at present, companies that qualify as small or medium-sized will be exempt from the disclosures in respect of fees for non-audit services, although the audit fee will continue to be disclosable in all cases. There is also a proposal to exempt the individual accounts of a parent company, and of its subsidiaries, when group accounts are prepared under CA 1985, on the basis that detailed disclosure at group level will suffice in these circumstances.

RELATED PARTY DISCLOSURES

Requirements of FRS 8 'Related Party Disclosures'

18.10 FRS 8 'Related Party Disclosures' requires disclosure of material transactions undertaken by the reporting entity with a related party, irrespective of whether a price is charged. The disclosures must include:

— the names of the parties involved;

— a description of the relationship between them;

— a description of the transaction (or transactions);

— any additional details of the transaction necessary for an understanding of the financial statements;

— the amounts due to or from related parties at the balance sheet date;

— any provisions for doubtful debts due from related parties; and

— any amounts written off during the year in respect of debts due to or from related parties.

The standard applies to all accounts that are required to give a true and fair view. The disclosure requirements therefore apply to all companies, regardless of their size, and also to non-corporate entities, such as charities, if their accounts are required to show a true and fair view. However, exemptions are granted in a small number of cases as explained in 18.23 below.

Objective of FRS 8

18.11 The primary objective of FRS 8 is 'to draw attention to the possibility that the reported financial position and results may have been affected by the existence of related parties and by material transactions with them'. This recognises that, where a related party relationship exists, transactions between the entities may not be carried out at arm's length – for instance:

— prices may not be freely negotiable between the parties;

— prices may not be based on commercial or market rates;

— the parties may be prepared to enter into transactions with each other that they would not be willing to undertake with an independent third-party; or

— the parties may be prepared to agree terms with each other (eg on payment dates) that they would not accept from an independent third-party.

This should not be taken to imply that all transactions between related parties will be on artificial or uncommercial terms. The aim of the standard is to highlight the possibility that this might be the case so that the potential impact can be borne in mind when considering the results and financial position of the company.

Definition of related party

18.12 Two or more parties are related when:

— one has direct or indirect control of the other;

— both are subject to common control from the same source;

— one has influence over the financial and operating policies of the other to such an extent that the latter may be inhibited from pursuing its own interests; or

— in respect of a particular transaction, both parties are subject to influence from the same source to such an extent that one party subordinates its own interests.

Example 18.2 – Common control and direct control

A Ltd controls both B Ltd and C Ltd

Therefore:
— A Ltd is related to B Ltd.
— A Ltd is related to C Ltd.
— B Ltd is related to C Ltd.

Example 18.3 – Influence

D Ltd controls E Ltd and is able to influence F Ltd.

Therefore:

— D Ltd is related to E Ltd.

— D Ltd is related to F Ltd.

E Ltd and F Ltd are not related parties simply as a result of their relationship with D Ltd, but they might become related in respect of a particular transaction as a result of the influence exercised by D Ltd (eg if D Ltd requires E Ltd to sell goods to F Ltd at cost rather than market price).

Where a related party relationship exists, the disclosure requirements apply to both parties. In the case of the fourth definition above, all transactions between the parties during the year become disclosable, even though the relationship arises as a result of one specific transaction.

Parties that will always be related to the reporting entity

18.13   To avoid doubt, the standard specifies that the following should always be treated as a related party of the reporting entity:

— its ultimate parent, immediate parent, subsidiary undertakings and fellow subsidiary undertakings;

— associates and joint ventures;

— an investor or venturer in respect of which the reporting entity is an associate or joint venture;

— directors of the reporting entity and of any parent (ultimate or intermediate);

— pension funds for the benefit of employees of:

— the reporting entity,

— a related party of the reporting entity.

Directors include shadow directors as defined in CA 1985.

Parties that are presumed to be related to the reporting entity

18.14   The following should be presumed to be related parties of the reporting entity unless it can be demonstrated that neither has influenced the financial and operating policies of the other so as to prohibit the pursuit of own interests:

— key management of the reporting entity;

— key management of any parent undertaking;

— a person owning, or able to exercise control over, 20% or more of the voting rights of the reporting entity, whether directly or indirectly;

— each person able to exercise control or influence over the reporting entity by acting in concert;

— an entity managing or managed by the reporting entity under a management contract.

Example 18.4 – Acting in concert

G Ltd, H Ltd and K Ltd, by acting together, are able to control D Ltd.

Therefore:

— G Ltd and D Ltd are related.

— H Ltd and D Ltd are related.

— K Ltd and D Ltd are related.

However, G Ltd, H Ltd and K Ltd will not be related parties simply by virtue of their relationship with D Ltd (although they may be related by some other means).

In addition, the following are also to be presumed to be related parties of the reporting entity, unless it can be demonstrated otherwise:

— members of the close family of any related party referred to in 18.12–18.14 above;

— partnerships, trusts or other entities in which any individual mentioned in 18.12–18.14 above (or any member of their close family) has a controlling interest.

Other related parties

18.15   The standard emphasises that none of these lists is intended to be exhaustive. Parties which do not specifically appear in the lists may, therefore, still be related for the purposes of the standard and, if so, transactions between them will require disclosure.

Definition of control and influence

18.16   Control is defined in the standard as 'the ability to direct the financial and operating policies of an entity with a view to gaining economic benefits from its activities'. Influence is not included in the definitions in the standard but is to be interpreted as the ability to inhibit a party from pursuing, at all times, its own separate interests. Two parties are subject to common control when they are controlled by the same entity. They are also deemed to be subject to common control when they are subject to control from boards which have a controlling nucleus of directors in common.

Close family members

18.17   Close family members are defined as 'family members, or members of the same household, who may be expected to influence, or be influenced by, that person in their dealings with the reporting entity'. This definition is much wider than a director's 'immediate family' under CA 1985 in the context of transactions between the company and its directors.

Disclosure of control

18.18   Where the reporting entity is controlled by another party, FRS 8 requires disclosure of:

—   the related party relationship;

—   the name of the controlling party; and

—   the name of the ultimate controlling party (if different).

These disclosures must be given even if there have been no disclosable transactions between the parties during the year. If details of the controlling party or ultimate controlling party are not known, this fact must be stated in the accounts.

Disclosure of related party transaction

18.19   The disclosure requirement covers all transactions between related parties, not just those that might be considered to be abnormal. The standard defines a related party transaction as 'the transfer of assets or liabilities or the performance of services by, to or for a related party irrespective of whether a price is charged'. Where material transactions with a related party (or parties) have taken place during the year, irrespective of whether a charge has been made or not, the following details must be disclosed:

—   the names of the parties involved;

—   a description of the relationship between them;

—   a description of the transaction (or transactions);

—   any additional details of the transaction necessary for an understanding of the financial statements;

—   the amounts due to or from related parties at the balance sheet date;

—   any provisions for doubtful debts due from related parties; and

—   any amounts written off during the year in respect of debts due to or from related parties.

Additional details may need to be given in some cases, depending on the nature of the transaction. For instance, the fact that the sale of a significant asset took place at a value substantially below the normal commercial rate might need to be disclosed. Comparative information should be given for all related party disclosures.

Aggregation of transactions

18.20   In order to avoid excessive detail, the disclosures may be aggregated (ie similar transactions by type of related party) unless individual disclosure of a particular transaction, or a series of connected transactions, is necessary to enable the reader to understand the impact on the financial statements. However, different categories of transaction should not be aggregated. For instance, where a company buys both raw materials and fixed assets from the same related party, these transactions should not be aggregated for disclosure purposes. In the case of transactions involving directors, individual disclosure will usually be required by the provisions of CA 1985.

Examples of related party transactions

18.21   The following are examples of transactions which will require disclosure where they involve related parties:

— the purchase or sale of goods, property or other fixed assets;

— the rendering or receiving of services;

— agency agreements;

— leasing agreements;

— the provision of finance; and

— the provision of guarantees or security.

The Explanatory Notes to the standard include further examples.

Materiality

18.22   In the context of FRS 8, transactions are to be considered material if 'their disclosure might reasonably be expected to influence decisions made by users of general purpose financial statements'. Where a related party transaction involves:

— a director, key manager or other individual in a position to influence, or accountable for stewardship of, the reporting entity; or

— a member of the close family of any individual mentioned above; or

— an entity controlled by any of these individuals,

the materiality of the transaction should be judged in relation to that individual (or party) as well as in terms of its significance to the reporting entity.

Exemptions from disclosure

18.23   The standard allows the following exemptions from the normal disclosure requirements:

— transactions and balances between group companies which have been eliminated on consolidation do not have to be disclosed in the consolidated accounts;

— disclosure of related party transactions is not required in the individual accounts of a parent company, if group accounts are also presented;

— transactions with members of the group or investees of the group do not require disclosure in the accounts of a subsidiary undertaking where 90% or more of the voting rights are controlled within the group, provided that:

— consolidated accounts, which include the subsidiary, are publicly available, and

— the subsidiary's accounts state that advantage has been taken of this exemption;

— pension contributions paid to a pension fund do not require disclosure as related party transactions (although they still require disclosure under FRS 17 'Retirement benefits' – see Chapter 12);

— emoluments in respect of services as an employee of the reporting entity do not require disclosure as related party transactions.

Confidentiality

18.24   The disclosure requirements do not override any duty of confidentiality that arises through the operation of law. For instance, banks will not be expected to disclose confidential information in respect of customers. However, disclosure of a particular transaction cannot be avoided simply by including a confidentiality clause in a contract.

Identification of disclosable transactions

18.25   One of the main practical difficulties in complying with the standard is establishing systems and procedures to identify related parties and collate details of disclosable transactions as they arise during the year. Identification will usually be particularly difficult where no price is actually charged in respect of the transaction. Statement of Auditing Standards 460 (SAS 460) 'Related Parties', which was issued shortly after FRS 8, includes some useful guidance on the issues to be considered by both management and auditors when considering the identification and disclosure of related party transactions.

For accounting periods beginning on or after 15 December 2004, SAS 460 is replaced by the UK and Ireland version of ISA 550 'Related Parties' which sets out similar guidance.

Potentially illegal transactions

18.26   Where significant transactions take place between any entities at an undervalue or overvalue, this could give rise to serious legal difficulties. Companies should always take appropriate legal advice before entering into such a transaction.

Likely future developments

18.27   The ASB issued FRED 25 'Related party disclosures' in May 2002 as part of its project to achieve convergence between UK accounting standards and international accounting standards. The Exposure Draft proposes replacing FRS 8 'Related party disclosures' with requirements based on the revised IAS 24, although retaining the present UK requirement for an entity's controlling party to be named. The June 2005 version of the ASB's Technical Plan indicates that a new standard is expected to be published in the final quarter of 2005 and to be effective for accounting periods beginning on or after 1 January 2006.

Changes to exemptions

18.28   A number of changes to the current exemptions are proposed. In particular, the exemption for subsidiaries will in future only be available to wholly-owned subsidiaries, whereas entities that are 90% owned are currently exempt from the disclosure requirements of FRS 8. FRED 25 also gives no exemption for pension contributions paid to a pension fund. FRS 8 currently exempts these amounts from its disclosure requirements, although, in practice, the details have to be given under the requirements of FRS 17 'Retirement Benefits'. FRS 8 also notes that its disclosure requirements do not override a duty of confidentiality arising by law. There is no equivalent exemption in FRED 25, although there will no longer be a requirement to name the transacting parties.

Definition of related party

18.29   The new proposals will change the definitions of related parties. In particular, whilst FRS 8 identifies separately parties that are related parties and those that are presumed to be related parties, all those listed in FRED 25 are considered to be related parties. Otherwise, the lists are broadly equivalent, except that:

—   FRED 25 identifies a related party relationship where one party has an interest that gives it significant influence over the other – FRS 8 currently defines in more detail the level of influence that triggers such a relationship;

—   there is no reference in FRED 25 to the situation where transacting parties are subject to influence from the same source to such an extent that one subordinates its own separate interests; and

—   FRED 25 makes no specific reference to shadow directors, to persons acting in concert to exercise control or influence, or to management of an entity through a management contract.

Disclosure

18.30   When developing FRS 8, the ASB took the view that disclosure of the identity of a controlling party is relevant information for users and it has, therefore, retained this disclosure requirement in FRED 25 even though it is not included in IAS 24. The other disclosure requirements are broadly in line with those currently required, except that under FRED 25:

— there is no requirement to disclose the names of the transacting parties; and

— where amounts are due to or from related parties, the Exposure Draft specifically requires disclosure of the terms and conditions, the nature of the consideration and details of any related guarantees.

Also, under FRED 25, the required disclosures must be given separately for each of the following categories: parent, entities with joint control or significant influence, subsidiaries, associates, joint ventures, key management personnel of the entity or its parent, and other related parties.

GEOGRAPHICAL ANALYSIS OF RESULTS

Scope of SSAP 25 'Segmental Reporting'

18.31   SSAP 25 'Segmental Reporting' repeats some of the segmental disclosure requirements of CA 1985 and also requires certain additional disclosures. These additional disclosure requirements apply to any entity that:

— is a public limited company or has a public limited company as a subsidiary;

— is a banking or insurance company or group; or

— exceeds the CA 1985 criteria, multiplied in each case by ten, for defining a medium-sized company (see Chapter 8).

Subsidiary companies that are not public companies or banking or insurance companies are not required to comply with the additional disclosures, provided that the parent company gives appropriate segmental information in its own accounts. All other entities are encouraged to apply the provisions of the standard in accounts that are required to show a true and fair view.

Disclosure requirements

18.32   SSAP 25 requires the following items in the accounts to be analysed by class of business and by geographical segment:

— turnover (see Chapter 10);

— the profit or loss before taxation; and

— net assets (see Chapter 34).

Comparative information should be provided for all segmental disclosures. The standard sets out detailed guidance on determining classes of business and geographical segments for reporting purposes. This guidance is considered in more detail in Chapter 10. If, in the opinion of the directors, the disclosures required by the standard would be seriously prejudicial to the interests of the reporting entity, the information need not be disclosed, but the fact that the disclosures have not been given must be stated in the accounts. This aspect of the standard is also considered in more detail in Chapter 10.

Consistency

18.33   The general requirement for accounting information to be presented on a consistent basis year by year applies equally to segmental disclosure. However, SSAP 25 requires the directors to redefine the reporting segments where appropriate. This might be necessary where the company diversifies into new activities, acquires a new business or ceases part of its previous activities. If the definitions of segments are changed, the nature of the change should be disclosed in the accounts, with details of the reason for and the effect of the change, and comparative figures must be restated to reflect the change.

Apportionment of costs

18.34   The geographical analysis of results should normally be based on the areas from which goods or services are supplied. Costs that relate directly to a segment should be allocated to that segment for reporting purposes. Where costs cover a number of segments, rather than relating to one individual segment, the directors should establish an appropriate method of apportioning the costs in order to arrive at the segmental analysis of results. If it would be misleading to apportion the costs in this way, they may be treated as a deduction from the total of the segmental results.

Treatment of interest

18.35   Where the accounts include a segmental analysis of the results for the year, the figure to be analysed should normally be the profit or loss for the year before interest and taxation. This reflects the fact that any interest charged or received will usually result from the overall financial policy of the entity rather than from the activities of an individual segment. However, where all or part of the entity's business is to earn interest, or interest paid or received is central to the business, the segmental analysis should be provided for the profit or loss after interest but before taxation. In this case, interest bearing assets and liabilities should be also included in the net assets analysis to ensure that the analyses of results and net assets are given on a consistent basis (see Chapter 33).

Link with profit and loss account

18.36   The total of the amounts disclosed in the segmental analysis should agree with the net result shown in the profit and loss account. If it does not, a reconciliation of the two amounts should also be provided.

EXPENDITURE ON RESEARCH AND DEVELOPMENT

Requirements of SSAP 13 'Accounting for Research and Development'

18.37   SSAP 13 'Accounting for Research and Development' requires disclosure of the amount of research and development expenditure charged in the profit and loss account, analysed between:

— current year expenditure; and

— amounts amortised from deferred expenditure.

However, this disclosure requirement only applies to a company that:

— is a public limited company or has a public limited company as a subsidiary;

— is a banking or insurance company or group; or

— exceeds the CA 1985 criteria, multiplied in each case by ten, for defining a medium-sized company (see Chapter 8).

EARNINGS PER SHARE

Requirements of accounting standards

18.38   For accounting periods beginning before 1 January 2005, disclosure requirements in respect of earnings per share are set out in FRS 14 'Earnings per share'. For accounting periods beginning on or after 1 January 2005, FRS 14 is superseded by FRS 22 'Earnings per share', which is based on the equivalent international standard (IAS 33). Early adoption of FRS 22 is not permitted. The scope and detailed requirements of FRS 14 and FRS 22 are broadly similar, although there are certain differences which are highlighted in the following paragraphs. There are no company law requirements on the disclosure of earnings per share, other than the overriding requirement for companies to apply appropriate accounting standards.

Scope and objective

18.39   The stated objective of both standards is to set out principles for the calculation and disclosure of earnings per share in order to facilitate comparison of the performance of an entity with its own performance in other accounting periods, and with the performance of other entities in the same accounting period. In addition, FRS 22 notes that, although data on earnings per share will always have limitations because the accounting policies that determine earnings may vary between entities, the use of a consistently determined denominator enhances financial reporting.

Both standards apply to entities whose ordinary shares or potential ordinary shares are publicly traded, and to entities who are in the process of issuing ordinary shares or potential ordinary shares in public securities markets. The requirements also apply to any other entity that voluntarily discloses earnings per share in the annual accounts (although this is rare in practice). An ordinary share is defined in FRS 22 as an equity instrument that is subordinate to all other classes of equity instrument and a potential ordinary share is defined as a financial instrument or other contract that may entitle the holder to ordinary shares. FRS 14 includes the following examples of potential ordinary shares:

(i)   debt or equity instruments (including preference shares) that are convertible into ordinary shares;

(ii)   share warrants and options that give the holder the right to purchase or subscribe for ordinary shares;

(iii)   rights granted under employee share plans that may entitle employees to receive ordinary shares as part of their remuneration; and

(iv)   contingent rights to shares resulting from contractual arrangements such as the purchase of a business.

Measuring basic earnings per share

18.40   Basic earnings per share should be calculated by dividing the net profit or loss for the period attributable to the ordinary equity shareholders of the entity (or, in the case of a group, of the parent entity) by the weighted average number of ordinary shares outstanding during the period. FRS 22 requires the calculations to be carried out separately for both the profit or loss for the period and, where relevant, the profit or loss from continuing operations.

Under FRS 22, the earnings figure used in the calculation should be the relevant profit or loss figure for the period, adjusted for the after tax amounts of any preference dividends, differences arising on the settlement of preference shares and any other similar effects of preference shares that are classified as equity under FRS 25 'Financial Instruments: Disclosure and Presentation' (see Chapter 26). For accounting periods to which FRS 14 applies, similar requirements apply but in this case adjustments should be made in respect of dividends and other appropriations relating to shares classified and accounted for as non-equity shares under FRS 4 'Capital Instruments'.

In the case of cumulative preference shares, the amounts deducted from profit should:

(i)   include the full after-tax amount of the dividend for the period, regardless of whether this has actually been declared; and

(ii)   exclude any dividends paid or declared during the current accounting period in respect of previous accounting periods.

FRS 22 also includes additional guidance on dealing with more complex preference share transactions, such as increasing-rate preference shares (i.e. those that provide either for a low initial dividend or for an above-market dividend in later periods), a repurchase of preference shares by the entity, and the early conversion of preference shares as a result of inducements such as favourable changes to the conversion terms or the payment of additional consideration.

FRS 14 specifies that, if the entity has more than one class of ordinary shares, earnings should be apportioned between the different classes in accordance with their dividend rights or other rights to share in profits.

Weighted average number of ordinary shares

18.41   Under both FRS 14 and FRS 22, the weighted average number of ordinary shares is the number of ordinary shares outstanding at the beginning of the period, adjusted for any shares issued or bought back during the period multiplied by a time-weighting factor. Both standards give examples of these calculations. A reasonable approximation of the weighted average will be acceptable in most circumstances.

Shares should be included in the calculations from the date consideration is receivable, which will usually be the date of issue. Both standards give specific guidance on the appropriate date to use in the case of shares issued on the conversion of debt instruments, in place of the interest or principal on other financial instruments, to settle a liability or in connection with an acquisition or merger, and in the case of contingently issuable shares. FRS 22 also covers ordinary shares issued on the voluntary reinvestment of dividends, ordinary shares issued for the rendering of services to the entity, and ordinary shares that are contingently returnable. The new standard also emphasises that due consideration should always be given to the substance of any contract associated with the share issue. The guidance in FRS 14 notes that ordinary shares issued in partly paid form should be treated as a fraction of an ordinary share to the extent that they are entitled to participate in dividends relative to a fully paid up ordinary share.

Adjustments should also be made for events other than the conversion of potential ordinary shares that have changed the number of ordinary shares outstanding, without a corresponding change in resources (e.g. bonus or capitalisation issues, a bonus element in a rights issue, share splits, share consolidations). Again, both standards give examples of the necessary calculations.

FRS 14 includes additional requirements on dealing with shares held by a member of the group and not cancelled, and shares held by an ESOP trust and reflected as assets in the balance sheet. In calculating earnings per share, the standard requires such shares to be treated as cancelled (i.e. they should be excluded from the calculations). Under UITF Abstract 37 'Purchase and sale of own shares' and UITF Abstract 38 'Accounting for ESOP trusts' the consideration paid for such shares should be treated as a deduction from shareholders' funds rather than as an asset for accounting periods ending on or after 22 June 2004, and a similar approach is required by FRS 25 'Financial Instruments: Disclosure and Presentation' for accounting periods beginning on or after 1 January 2005 (see Chapter 32).

Measuring diluted earnings per share

18.42 Dilution is defined in FRS 22 as a reduction in earnings per share (or an increase in loss per share) resulting from the assumption that convertible instruments are converted, options or warrants are exercised or that ordinary shares are issued following the satisfaction of certain special conditions. Potential dilutive ordinary shares therefore include debt or equity instruments that are convertible into ordinary shares, share warrants and options, rights granted under employee share plans and other share purchase plans, and rights to ordinary equity shares that are contingent on certain conditions being satisfied.

When measuring diluted earnings per share, both the net profit or loss attributable to ordinary shareholders and the weighted average number of shares outstanding should be adjusted for the effects of all dilutive potential ordinary shares. However, potential ordinary shares are only treated as dilutive if their conversion would decrease the net profit or increase the net loss per share from continuing operations (see 18.43 below). The effects of any anti-dilutive potential ordinary shares are ignored in the calculations.

Diluted earnings per share should be based on the net profit or loss for the period attributable to ordinary shareholders, adjusted for the post-tax effect of:

(i)   any dividends or other items relating to dilutive potential ordinary shares that have been deducted in arriving at the net profit or loss;

(ii)   any interest recognised in respect of dilutive potential ordinary shares; and

(iii) any other changes in income or expenses that would result from the conversion of those shares.

These adjustments reflect the fact that, once the dilutive potential ordinary shares are converted into ordinary shares, charges for dividends, interest and other expenses associated with the existing financial instruments or rights will no longer be incurred by the reporting entity.

FRS 22 requires diluted earnings per share to be calculated for both the profit and loss for the year and the profit or loss attributable to continuing operations

Dilutive or not?

18.43 Potential ordinary shares should only be treated as dilutive if their conversion into ordinary shares would decrease earnings per share (or increase loss per share). This should be assessed by using the profit or loss from continuing operations, adjusted as explained in 18.40 above, as the control figure. FRS 3

'Reporting Financial Performance' only requires amounts to be analysed into continuing operations, acquisitions and discontinued operations to the level of profit before interest. FRS 14 therefore includes additional guidance on allocating interest and tax between these categories in order to arrive at a reasonable estimate of the net profit or loss from continuing operations. This guidance is retained as non-mandatory guidance in an Appendix to FRS 22. Each issue or series of potential ordinary shares should be considered separately and should be considered in sequence, from the most dilutive to the least dilutive. This is illustrated by the examples in both FRS 14 and FRS 22. Similarly, the calculation of diluted earnings per share should not assume conversion, exercise or issue if the resulting shares would have an antidilutive effect on earnings per share.

Assumptions on timing

18.44 The calculation of diluted earnings per share should assume that all dilutive potential ordinary shares are converted into shares at the beginning of the reporting period or on the date that they were actually issued, if later. FRS 22 specifies that the calculations must be carried out independently for each period for which earnings per share information is presented. Potential ordinary shares that are cancelled or allowed to lapse during the period should be included in the calculations only for the period during which they were outstanding. Those that are converted during the course of the reporting period should be treated as dilutive shares from the beginning of the year to the date of conversion. After that, the resulting ordinary shares will included in the calculation of both basic and diluted earnings per share.

Share warrants and options

18.45 In calculating diluted earnings per share, the entity should assume that dilutive options, warrants and similar instruments are exercised. These instruments will be dilutive if they would result in the issue of shares for less than the average market price, and the amount of the dilution will be the difference between the average market price and the issue price. The assumed proceeds should be treated as receipts from the issue of ordinary shares at the average market price of ordinary shares during the period, and the difference between the number of shares assumed to be issued and the number of shares that would have been issued at the average market price should be treated as ordinary shares issued for no consideration. In effect, the shares that are assumed to be issued at average market price are treated as neither dilutive nor antidilutive and so are ignored in the calculation of diluted earnings per share. By contrast, the shares that are assumed to be issued for no consideration are dilutive and so should be included in the number of ordinary shares outstanding.

There is additional guidance in FRS 22 on dealing with share options and other share based payment arrangements accounted for under FRS 20 'Share-based Payment' and with employee share options in general.

Convertible instruments

18.46   Convertible preference shares will be antidilutive if the dividend declared or accumulated for the current year is more than basic earnings per share, and convertible debt will be antidilutive if the related interest (net of tax and other related charges or expenses) is more than basic earnings per share. In each case, the dividend or interest for the year needs to be assessed on the basis of a converted ordinary share. Additional requirements apply where early redemption or conversion is induced for a portion of convertible preference shares.

Contingently issuable shares

18.47   In the case of contingently issuable shares, the calculation is based on the number of shares that would be issuable if the end of the reporting period was the end of the contingency period. A condition expressed as an average over a period has the same effect as if it was expressed as a cumulative amount over that period, and the performance achieved to date is deemed to be the performance for the whole of the contingency period. For instance, if the issue of shares depends on whether annual profits average £100,000 over a three-year period, the cumulative target is £300,000 over the three-year period. If profits at the end of the first year are £150,000, the target has not been reached at that date and no additional shares should be brought into the calculation of diluted earnings per share. If the earnings target has already been achieved by the end of the reporting period, the additional ordinary shares are treated as outstanding and should be included in the diluted earnings per share calculations, even if there is an additional requirement for the earnings target to be maintained for a further period.

Where the number of shares that may be issued in the future depends on the market price of the issuer's shares, the diluted earnings per share calculations should include the number of shares that would be issued on the basis of the market price at the end of the current reporting period or the average market price over a specified period, depending on the terms of the underlying contract.

FRS 22 includes additional guidance on situations where the number of shares to be issued depends on future earnings and future share prices, or on conditions that are independent of earnings or market price.

Contracts with a settlement option

18.48   There are certain differences between the requirements of FRS 14 and FRS 22 in respect of contracts that may be settled in either ordinary shares or cash. Under FRS 14, the treatment to be adopted depends on the facts available in each reporting period and, unless past experience or a stated policy provides a basis for concluding on how the contract will be settled, it is presumed that settlement will be by the more dilutive method. Under FRS 22, the treatment depends on whether the option rests with the holder or the issuer:

(i)   if the holder of instrument can choose the settlement method, the more dilutive option should be assumed;

(ii)   if the option rests with the issuer, there is a non-rebuttable presumption that the contract will be settled in shares.

FRS 22 also includes specific requirements in respect of written put options, which require the issuer to repurchase its own shares and which should be included in the calculations if the effect is dilutive.

Restatement for comparative purposes

18.49   Both standards also deal with the restatement of earnings per share disclosures for comparative purposes. If the number of ordinary or potential ordinary shares outstanding changes as a result of events other than the conversion of potential ordinary shares, without a corresponding change in resources (eg bonus issues, share splits, share consolidations), the calculation of basic and diluted earnings per share for all periods presented should be adjusted retrospectively. Also, if the changes occur after the balance sheet date but before the date on which the financial statements are authorised for issue, all per share calculations should be based on the new number of shares and this fact should be disclosed.

Where other transactions in ordinary shares or potential ordinary shares take place after the balance sheet date (eg issue of shares for cash, redemption of ordinary shares, issue of potential ordinary shares, conversion of potential ordinary shares into ordinary shares, achievement of conditions which result in the issue of contingently issuable shares), earnings per share should not be adjusted, but the accounts should include a description of the transaction if:

(i)   under FRS 22, the number of shares included in the earnings per share calculations would have changed significantly; or

(ii)   under FRS 14, non-disclosure would affect the ability of users to make proper evaluation and decisions.

In addition, FRS 22 states specifically that basic and diluted earnings per share figures for all periods presented should be adjusted for the effects of any errors and adjustments resulting from changes in accounting policies that are applied retrospectively.

FRS 14 includes the following additional points which are not included in FRS 22:

(i)   the disclosures for basic and diluted earnings per share for all periods presented should also be adjusted for the effects of a business combination that is accounted for as a merger; and

(ii)   any record of equity dividends set out in historical summaries in the form of pence per share should be adjusted in the same way as the main disclosures and the fact that the figures have been restated should be disclosed.

Both standards specify that diluted earnings per share should not be restated for changes in the assumptions used or for the conversion of potential ordinary shares into ordinary shares.

Presentation requirements

18.50   There are a number of differences in the presentation requirements of the two standards. For accounting periods beginning on or after 1 January 2005, FRS 22 requires both basic and diluted earnings per share to be presented on the face of the profit and loss account for:

(i)   the profit or loss from continuing operations attributable to the ordinary equity holders of the parent entity; and

(ii)   the profit or loss for the period attributable to the ordinary equity holders of the parent entity.

The details must be given for each class of ordinary shares that has a different right to share in the profit or loss for the period and the presentation of basic and diluted earnings per share must be given equal prominence for all periods presented. Dual presentation is permitted if basic and diluted earnings per share are the same. The standard also requires an entity reporting discontinued operations to disclose the basic and diluted earnings per share for these either on the face of the profit and loss account or in the notes to the accounts. If any of the required 'per share' amounts are negative (i.e. a loss per share) they must still be disclosed.

For earlier accounting periods, FRS 14 requires both basic and diluted earnings per share to be disclosed on the face of the profit and loss account for each class of ordinary share that has a different right to share in the net profit for the period. The required disclosures must be given with equal prominence for all periods presented. Under this standard, therefore, there is no requirement to give disclosures in respect of the profit or loss on continuing operations.

Under both standards, if the entity chooses to present additional amounts per share, these disclosures should be no more prominent than those required under the standard, and where additional disclosures are given for both basic and diluted amounts per share, they should be presented with equal prominence. The weighted average number of ordinary shares should be determined in accordance with the standard for each additional disclosure that is given. FRS 14 requires additional amounts per share to be presented on a consistent basis over time, but there is no specific reference to this in FRS 22. FRS 14 also requires the additional amounts per share to be reconciled with those required under the standard and the reasons for disclosing the additional figures to be explained. These reconciliations and explanations should be presented alongside the additional per share figures, or there should be a clear cross-reference to where these details can be found. FRS 22 requires the notes to the accounts to include:

(i)   an explanation of the basis on which each numerator is determined;

(ii)   whether the additional 'per share' amounts are before or after tax; and

(iii)   if the additional 'per share' amounts are based on a component that is not separately reported in the profit and loss account, a reconciliation between that figure and a line item that is reported in the profit and loss account.

Other disclosures

18.51   Both standards require disclosure of:

(i)   the amounts used as numerators in calculating basic and diluted earnings per share, and a reconciliation of those amounts to the profit or loss for the period; and

(ii)   the weighted average number of ordinary shares used as the denominator in calculating both basic and diluted earnings per share and a reconciliation of these denominators to each other, including the individual effect of each class of instruments that affects earnings per share.

In addition, FRS 22 also requires the notes to the accounts to give details of any instruments that could potentially dilute basic earnings per share in the future but which have not been included in the calculation of diluted earnings per share because they are antidilutive for the periods presented.

Chapter 19   Balance Sheet Formats

COMPANY LAW REQUIREMENTS

CA 1985 prescribed formats

19.1   CA 1985 prescribes standard formats for the profit and loss account and the balance sheet which must be followed by both individual companies and by groups when preparing their annual accounts. The Act provides a choice of two formats for the balance sheet – these are set out in the Appendix to this Chapter. The directors are free to decide which format to use, but once a particular format has been chosen it must be used consistently year by year unless there are good reasons for changing. If a format is changed, details must be given in the accounts and the reason for the change must be explained. A small company which chooses to prepare shorter form accounts can reduce some of the detailed balance sheet disclosures (see Chapter 8)

For accounting periods beginning on or after 1 January 2005, the detailed requirements of Schedule 4 are only relevant where the company prepares Companies Act accounts (as opposed to IAS accounts).

Vertical or horizontal structure

19.2   Format 1 for the balance sheet presents assets and liabilities in a continuous vertical format and separates creditors into those falling due within one year and those falling due after more than one year. There is no indication where the balance sheet totals should be drawn. The most common practice is to draw the main balance sheet total after item J (Accruals and deferred income) and thus match net assets (or liabilities) with the total of capital and reserves. However, it is also possible to draw the total after item G (Total assets less current liabilities) and match this with the aggregate of creditors falling due after more than one year, provisions for liabilities and charges, accruals and deferred income (where these are shown separately) and capital and reserves. Format 2 discloses similar details but groups together all of the company's assets, followed by all of its liabilities (including capital and reserves). Although the headings are set out vertically in the Act, this format can be used to present a horizontal balance sheet. The two sub-totals for net current assets (or liabilities) and total assets less current liabilities set out in Format 1 are not required (or indeed possible) under Format 2. The other main difference is that creditors are presented in total under Format 2, although for each item within creditors, the following information must be given in the notes to the accounts:

— the amount falling due within one year;

— the amount falling due after more than one year.

The aggregate amounts due within one year and after more than one year must also be shown. In practice, most companies prepare their balance sheet in line with Format 1 and Format 2 is rarely seen.

Change of format

19.3   The directors may only change the format of the balance sheet if, in their opinion, there are special reasons for doing so. It is possible to imagine how changes in a company's activities might justify a change of format for the profit and loss account, but it is more difficult to envisage a situation which might justify a change in the format of the balance sheet, particularly as the two formats present the required information under broadly the same headings. If the format of the balance sheet is changed, the accounts must disclose:

— the fact that a different format has been used;

— the reasons for changing to a different format.

Order of headings and sub-headings

19.4   The balance sheet formats are set out using a hierarchy of letters, Roman numerals and Arabic numerals to prescribe the order in which the individual headings and sub-headings must appear. The letters and numerals do not have to be reproduced in the accounts but are provided so that other sections of the Act can refer to the headings by category. Although the headings and sub-headings should normally follow the order prescribed in the formats, the Act requires the directors to adapt or rearrange the items identified by Arabic numerals if the special nature of the company's business requires this. Items may also be shown in greater detail than required by the formats and additional items may be shown, provided that they are not already covered elsewhere in the standard format. Items identified by Arabic numerals may be combined if:

— the individual amounts are not material; or

— combining them facilitates assessment of the state of the company's affairs (in this case the individual components must be disclosed in the notes to the accounts).

If there is no amount to be shown for a particular heading or sub-heading in either the current or the previous financial year, that heading or sub-heading should not appear in the balance sheet.

Condensed presentation

19.5   The main headings on the balance sheet are prefixed with letters and Roman numerals and must therefore always be disclosed on the face of the balance sheet. However, the more detailed items are given Arabic numerals and disclosure of these items may therefore be given in the notes to the accounts if this results in a clearer presentation of the company's state of affairs. Most companies adopt this approach in practice. Items designated by Arabic numerals may also be combined if the individual amounts that would otherwise be disclosed are not material.

Alternative positions

19.6   The formats allow alternative positions for three items in the balance sheet:
— pre-payments and accrued income may be disclosed as a sub-heading within debtors or may appear as a separate heading on the balance sheet after current assets;
— accruals and deferred income may be disclosed as a sub-heading within creditors (in which case items may need to appear in both amounts falling due within one year and amounts falling due after more than one year) or all accruals and deferred income may be shown under a separate heading on the balance sheet after provisions for liabilities and charges;
— called up share capital not paid may be included as a separate item on the balance sheet, or may be included as a sub-heading within debtors.

The notes to the formats emphasise that these are alternative positions and it is therefore clear that each company should decide which position to use and group together all the relevant items in that position (i.e. the headings should not appear in both positions in the same set of accounts). In the case of pre-payments and accrued income and accruals and deferred income, both forms of presentation are in common usage, although it is probably more usual for pre-payments and accrued income to be included within debtors, and for accruals and deferred income to be included within creditors, than for separate headings for these items to be shown on the balance sheet. By its very nature, called up share capital not paid does not arise frequently in annual accounts. Where it does arise, it is probably more common for the balance to be included within debtors than for it to be treated as a separate heading on the balance sheet.

Changes in presentation

19.7 FRS 18 'Accounting Policies' emphasises that any change in the way in which a particular item is presented in the balance sheet or profit and loss account is a change of accounting policy. However, the presentation of additional information (e.g. analysing a particular heading in more detail than previously) does not constitute a change of accounting policy, although any corresponding figures should be reanalysed so that they are presented in the same amount of detail.

Comparative figures

19.8 Comparative figures must be given for each item in the balance sheet. If any item appeared in the previous year but does not appear in the current year, the heading and comparative amount must still be shown in the balance sheet. Comparative amounts are considered in more detail in Chapter 6.

Additional disclosures

19.9 The balance sheet formats include notes which require additional information or analyses to be given for certain items. These details are usually given in the notes to the accounts, although they may be given on the balance sheet if this is considered necessary or helpful. CA 1985 Sch 4 paras 37–51 also set out requirements on the disclosure of information to supplement the balance sheet items or to assist generally in the assessment of the company's state of affairs. Where appropriate these are discussed in the following chapters.

Items which must not be treated as assets

19.10 CA 1985 does not permit the following items to be treated as assets in a company's balance sheet:

(i)   preliminary expenses;

(ii)   expenses of, and commission on, any issue of shares and debentures;

(iii)   costs of research.

The accounting treatment of issue costs in respect of shares and debentures is considered in more detail in Chapters 14 and 32. Although research costs cannot be treated as assets, the Act does permit development costs to be treated as an asset in special circumstances. This is considered in conjunction with the requirements of SSAP 13 'Accounting for Research and Development' in Chapter 20.

DEFINED BENEFIT ASSETS AND LIABILITIES

Requirements of FRS 17

19.11 FRS 17 'Retirement Benefits' was published in November 2000 and supersedes SSAP 24 'Accounting for Pension Costs' for accounting periods beginning on or after 1 January 2005, although earlier adoption is encouraged. The standard requires the defined benefit asset or liability in respect of retirement benefits, net of any related deferred tax balance, to be shown separately on the face of the balance sheet as follows:

— in a balance sheet prepared under Format 1, after item J (Accruals and deferred income) but before item K (Capital and reserves);

— in a balance sheet prepared under Format 2, an asset should be shown after item D (Prepayments and accrued income) in the 'Assets' section and a liability should be shown after item D (Accruals and deferred income) in the 'Liabilities' section.

Where an employer has more than one scheme, the total of any defined benefit assets and the total of any defined benefit liabilities should be shown separately on the face of the balance sheet. The requirements of FRS 17 are considered in detail in Chapter 12.

APPENDIX 1

Balance sheet: Format 1

A.   Called up share capital not paid.

B.   Fixed assets.

    1   Intangible assets.

          1   Development costs.

          2   Concessions, patents, licences, trade marks and similar rights and assets.

          3   Goodwill.

          4   Payments on account.

    II   Tangible assets.

          1   Land and buildings.

          2   Plant and machinery.

          3   Fixtures, fittings, tools and equipment.

          4   Payments on account and assets in course of construction.

    III   Investments.

          1   Shares in group undertakings.

          2   Loans to group undertakings.

          3   Participating interests.

          4   Loans to undertakings in which the company has a participating interest.

          5   Other investments other than loans.

          6   Other loans.

          7   Own shares.

C.   Current assets.

    I   Stocks.

          1   Raw materials and consumables.

          2   Work in progress.

          3   Finished goods and goods for resale.

          4   Payments on account.

    II   Debtors.

          1   Trade debtors.

          2   Amounts owed by group undertakings.

          3   Amounts owed by undertakings in which the company has a participating interest.

      4   Other debtors.

      5   Called up share capital not paid.

      6   Pre-payments and accrued income.

  III   Investments.

      1   Shares in group undertakings.

      2   Own shares.

      3   Other investments.

  IV   Cash at bank and in hand.

D.   Pre-payments and accrued income.

E.   Creditors: amounts falling due within one year.

     1   Debenture loans.

     2   Bank loans and overdrafts.

     3   Payments received on account.

     4   Trade creditors.

     5   Bills of exchange payable.

     6   Amounts owed to group undertakings.

     7   Amounts owed to undertakings in which the company has a participating interest.

     8   Other creditors including taxation and social security.

     9   Accruals and deferred income.

F.   Net current assets (liabilities).

G.   Total assets less current liabilities.

H.   Creditors: amounts falling due after more than one year.

     1   Debenture loans.

     2   Bank loans and overdrafts.

     3   Payments received on account.

     4   Trade creditors.

     5   Bills of exchange payable.

     6   Amounts owed to group undertakings.

     7   Amounts owed to undertakings in which the company has a participating interest.

     8   Other creditors including taxation and social security.

     9   Accruals and deferred income.

I   Provisions for liabilities.

     1   Pensions and similar obligations.

2   Taxation, including deferred taxation.

3   Other provisions.

J.   Accruals and deferred income.

K.   Capital and reserves.

    I   Called up share capital.

    II   Share premium account.

    III   Revaluation reserve.

    IV   Other reserves.

        1   Capital redemption reserve.

        2   Reserve for own shares.

        3   Reserves provided for by the articles of association.

        4   Other reserves.

    V   Profit and loss account

APPENDIX 2

Balance sheet: Format 2

Assets

A.   Called up share capital not paid.

B.   Fixed assets.

    I   Intangible assets.

        1   Development costs.

        2   Concessions, patents, licences, trade marks and similar rights and assets.

        3   Goodwill.

        4   Payments on account.

    II   Tangible assets.

        1   Land and buildings.

        2   Plant and machinery.

        3   Fixtures, fittings, tools and equipment.

        4   Payments on account and assets in course of construction.

    III   Investments.

        1   Shares in group undertakings.

        2   Loans to group undertakings.

        3   Participating interests.

        4   Loans to undertakings in which the company has a participating interest.

        5   Other investments other than loans.

        6   Other loans.

        7   Own shares.

C.   Current assets.

    I   Stocks.

        1   Raw materials and consumables.

        2   Work in progress.

        3   Finished goods and goods for resale.

        4   Payments on account.

    II   Debtors.

        1   Trade debtors.

        2   Amounts owed by group undertakings.

3   Amounts owed by undertakings in which the company has a participating interest.

4   Other debtors.

5   Called up share capital not paid.

6   Pre-payments and accrued income.

III   Investments.

1   Shares in group undertakings.

2   Own shares.

3   Other investments.

IV   Cash at bank and in hand.

D.   Pre-payments and accrued income.

Liabilities

A.   Capital and reserves.

I   Called up share capital.

II   Share premium account.

III   Revaluation reserve.

IV   Other reserves.

1   Capital redemption reserve.

2   Reserve for own shares.

3   Reserves provided for by the articles of association.

4   Other reserves.

V   Profit and loss account.

B.   Provisions for liabilities.

1   Pensions and similar obligations.

2   Taxation, including deferred taxation.

3   Other provisions.

C.   Creditors.

1   Debenture loans.

2   Bank loans and overdrafts.

3   Payments received on account.

4   Trade creditors.

5   Bills of exchange payable.

6   Amounts owed to group undertakings.

7   Amounts owed to undertakings in which the company has a participating interest.

8   Other creditors including taxation and social security.

9   Accruals and deferred income.

D.   Accruals and deferred income.

Chapter 20   Intangible Fixed Assets

COSTS OF RESEARCH AND DEVELOPMENT

CA 1985 requirements

20.1   CA 1985 sets out separate requirements in respect of research costs and development costs but does not define either of these. The costs of research must not be treated as an asset in a company's balance sheet. Development costs may only be treated as an asset in special circumstances. Where development costs are included in the balance sheet, the accounts must disclose:

— the reasons for capitalising these costs;

— the period over which the costs are being, or are to be, written off.

The carry forward of development costs in accordance with SSAP 13 'Accounting for Research and Development' is usually accepted as complying with the requirements of the Act. The CA 1985 balance sheet formats require disclosure of the total amount of intangible fixed assets, together with the following analysis.

— Development costs.

— Concessions, patents, licences, trade marks and similar rights and assets.

— Goodwill.

— Payments on account (i.e. in respect of the purchase of intangible fixed assets).

The total must be disclosed on the face of the balance sheet but the detailed analysis may be given in the notes to the accounts. The legislation also requires a detailed analysis of movements in the year to be given for each category of intangible fixed asset identified in the balance sheet format. Comparative figures are not required for these disclosures.

Categories of research and development

20.2   SSAP 13 'Accounting for Research and Development' identifies three broad categories of research and development:

— *pure (or basic) research* – this is defined as 'experimental or theoretical work undertaken primarily to acquire new scientific or technical knowledge for its own sake rather than directed towards any specific aim or application';

— *applied research* – this is defined as 'original or critical investigation undertaken in order to gain new scientific or technical knowledge and directed towards a specific practical aim or objective'; and

— *development* – this is defined as the 'use of scientific or technical knowledge in order to produce new or substantially improved materials, devices, products or services, to install new processes or systems prior to the commencement of commercial production or commercial applications, or to improving substantially those already produced or installed'.

The standard sets out some examples of the type of activity that should normally be classed as research and development. These include:

— work aimed at the discovery of new knowledge or the advancement of existing knowledge;

— formulation and design of possible applications for such work;

— testing or evaluation of alternative products, services or processes;

— design, construction and testing of prototypes, models and development batches; and

— design of products, services or processes involving new technology.

The requirement for a substantial element of scientific or technical knowledge was emphasised in an FRRP report, issued in January 2003, following its review of the report and accounts of Finelot Plc for the year ended 31 July 2001. During the year, the company paid a third party £966,000 to carry out pre-production work for a new life-style magazine and capitalised this amount as development costs. The work included concept design and establishing distribution and marketing networks, and in the opinion of the Panel it did not include a substantial element of scientific or technical knowledge in the sense that was intended by SSAP 13. In the Panel's view, therefore, the costs incurred were not for 'development' as defined within SSAP 13, nor did they satisfy the criteria for recognition as an asset under any other relevant accounting standard. Therefore, the costs should have been written off as incurred, as required by UITF Abstract 24, 'Accounting for start-up costs'.

Activities that do not constitute research and development

20.3   Activities that should not usually be classified as research and development include:

— testing for the purposes of quality or quantity control;

— periodic alterations to products, services or processes, even though these may involve some improvement;

— general operational research;

— legal and administrative work connected with patents, licences or litigation; and

— market research.

Research costs

20.4 Both CA 1985 and SSAP 13 require costs relating to research to be written off as they are incurred, irrespective of whether the research is pure or applied. SSAP 13 specifies that these costs should be charged to the profit and loss account. The only exception to this is in the case of fixed assets acquired for use in research work. These assets should be capitalised in the same way as any other fixed asset, and depreciated over their expected useful liives in accordance with the requirements of FRS 15 'Tangible Fixed Assets'.

Development costs

20.5 The main distinction between development and research is that development is an evident precursor to commercial production or application. Development work will not usually be undertaken unless there is a reasonable prospect of commercial success at the end of the development phase. This success may take the form of either increased revenue or reduced costs. FRS 18 'Accounting Policies' requires financial statements (other than cash flow information) to be prepared on the accruals basis of accounting, which it defines as requiring the non-cash effects of transactions and events to be reflected, as far as is possible, in the financial statements for the accounting period in which they occur and not in the period in which any related cash is received or paid. The standard makes a clear link with the definitions of assets and liabilities set out in FRS 5 'Reporting the Substance of Transactions' (and also in the ASB Statement of Principles) and notes that the use of those definitions to determine which items should be recognised as assets and liabilities in the balance sheet is consistent with the accruals concept. Development costs which meet the definition of assets (i.e. rights or other access to future economic benefits controlled by the entity as a result of past transactions or events) can therefore be recognised as such in the balance sheet. However, SSAP 13 does not require development costs to be recognised in this way, even where the conditions set out in the standard appear to be met, and many companies continue to write off such costs as they are incurred, usually because of the high degree of uncertainty over the expected future benefits to which the costs provide access. It should be noted that SSAP 13 was developed before publication of the ASB 'Statement of

Principles for Financial Reporting' and of FRS 18 'Accounting Policies' – it therefore does not present the issues in quite the same way as the later documents, although the end result is broadly the same.

Prudent approach

20.6   The conditions set out in SSAP 13 are stringent and many of the related issues will be highly judgmental and surrounded by uncertainties. The standard emphasises the importance of involving a wide spectrum of individuals in assessing the various aspects of the project (i.e. technical, commercial and financial viability) and the expected future benefits, and the need for a prudent view to be taken on all issues. If adequate evidence is not available to support the assumptions, the development costs should not be deferred but should be charged to the profit and loss account as they are incurred.

Conditions for deferral of development costs

20.7   SSAP 13 sets out a number of conditions, all of which must be met if development costs are to be deferred. The costs of any development work which does not meet these conditions must be charged to the profit and loss account as they are incurred. The detailed conditions are as follows:

— there must be a clearly defined project;

— the related expenditure must be separately identifiable;

— the outcome must have been assessed with reasonable certainty and this assessment must cover both:

— technical feasibility, and

— ultimate commercial viability;

— there must be a reasonable expectation that future sales or other revenues will exceed the aggregate of:

— the costs that are being deferred,

— any further development costs to be incurred on the same project, and

— the related production, selling and administration costs;

— adequate resources must already exist, or there must be a reasonable expectation that they will be available, to allow the project to be completed and to provide any additional working capital that may be required as a result.

Amortisation of development costs

20.8   Development costs should only be deferred until commercial production or application of the product or service begins. At this point, the costs should start to be amortised on a systematic basis. The standard sets out two methods of allocating the costs to match them with the related revenue:

— by reference to the actual sale or use of the product or service;

— by reference to the period over which the product or service is expected to be used or sold.

The nature of the product or service will usually decide which of these is the most appropriate method of allocation. Whichever allocation method is used, the period over which the costs are to be charged to the profit and loss account should be finite and should be both prudent and realistic. In many cases the period will be relatively short (e.g. three or four years).

Annual review

20.9   At the end of each year, every project in respect of which development costs are carried forward in the accounts must be reviewed so that the expected recoverability of the costs can be reassessed. If circumstances have changed, or if there is any doubt over the assumptions previously made, the related costs should be charged to the profit and loss account to the extent that they are no longer considered recoverable. In carrying out this review, and any related write-off, each project must be considered individually (i.e. potential under-recoveries on one project should not be ignored on the basis that there are significant over-recoveries on other projects).

Consistency of accounting

20.10   Although the standard does not require development costs to be carried forward, even where the conditions are met, it does require a consistent approach to be taken within an individual organisation. Therefore, where a company adopts a policy of deferring development costs, this accounting treatment should be followed for all projects that meet the criteria set out in SSAP 13.

Exceptions to the normal rules

20.11   SSAP 13 does not apply to the following:

— the location and exploitation of oil, gas and mineral deposits (however, the development of new surveying methods and techniques will usually qualify as research and development);

— development work carried out under a contract with a third party, where the expenditure is to be fully reimbursed by the third party;

— work carried out under a contract to develop and manufacture at an agreed price, which is calculated to reimburse the development costs as well as the costs of production.

In the last two cases, any costs that have not been reimbursed at the balance sheet date should be accounted for as contract work in progress (see Chapter 24).

Accounts disclosure

20.12   SSAP 13 requires disclosure of the accounting policy on research and development. Where development costs are capitalised, the Act specifically requires disclosure of the reason for this treatment and the period over which they are to be amortised. The following wordings might be suitable to meet both requirements.

Example 20.1 – Disclosure of accounting policy on research and development (I)

Expenditure on research and development is charged to the profit and loss account in the year in which it is incurred.

Example 20.2 – Disclosure of accounting policy on research and development (II)

Expenditure on research is charged to the profit and loss account in the year in which it is incurred. Expenditure on development is charged to the profit and loss account as it is incurred, except where it relates to individual projects. Where the recoverability of expenditure on individual projects is reasonably assured, the expenditure is deferred until the commencement of commercial production and then amortised by reference to sales of the relevant products over a period of four years.

Both CA 1985 and SSAP 13 require disclosure of opening and closing balances in respect of deferred development costs and details of any movements during the year. The following layout will usually be suitable.

Example 20.3 – Layout for disclosing movements

	£
Development costs	
Cost:	
Balance at 1 January 20X2	49,786
Additions during the year	45,670
Balance at 31 December 20X2	95,456
Amortisation:	
Balance at 1 January 20X2	14,561
Amortisation during the year	32,345
Balance at 31 December 20X2	46,906
Net book value at 31 December 20X2	48,550
Net book value at 31 December 20X1	35,225

Amount charged to the profit and loss account

20.13   For larger companies only (see 18.37), SSAP 13 requires disclosure of the total charged to the profit and loss account in the year in respect of research and development expenditure; this must be analysed between:

— expenditure incurred in the current year;

— amounts amortised from deferred development expenditure.

This disclosure is normally given in the notes to the accounts, usually as part of a note disclosing specific amounts charged or credited in arriving at the operating profit or loss for the year. The amount disclosed as expenditure incurred during the year should include any depreciation charged on fixed assets acquired for use in general research and development work. This amount will also need to be disclosed as depreciation of fixed assets in accordance with FRS 15 'Tangible Fixed Assets'.

Treatment as unrealised loss

20.14   Under CA 1985 s 269, any development costs shown as an asset are to be treated as a realised loss for distribution purposes, unless:

— there are special circumstances which justify the directors' decision not to treat the costs as a realised loss;

— the note to the accounts on development costs states that they are not to be treated as a realised loss and explains the circumstances relied on by the directors to justify their decision.

The Act does not provide any further guidance on these points, but it is usually acknowledged that the carry forward of development costs in accordance with SSAP 13 'Accounting for Research and Development' will usually justify a decision by the directors not to treat the costs as a realised loss for distribution purposes. The following wording might be suitable as a footnote to the note on development costs.

Example 20.4 – Footnote to note on development costs

Development costs represent expenditure on individual development projects. Where the recoverability of such expenditure is reasonably assured, the expenditure is deferred until the commencement of commercial production and then amortised by reference to sales of the relevant products over a period of four years. The directors consider that the development costs deferred on this basis should not be treated as a realised loss.

Directors' report

20.15   The directors' report must give an indication of any activities in the field of research and development. The contents of the directors' report, and the need for consistency between the accounts and the directors' report, are considered in Chapter 38.

CONCESSIONS, PATENTS, LICENCES, TRADE MARKS AND SIMILAR INTANGIBLE ASSETS

Capitalisation under company law

20.16   Under CA 1985, a company's balance sheet may only include amounts in respect of concessions, patents, licences, trade marks and similar rights if:

— the assets were acquired for valuable consideration and are not required to be shown under goodwill; or

— the assets were created by the company itself.

Requirements of FRS 10

20.17   Definitive guidance on accounting for intangible assets is set out in FRS 10 'Goodwill and intangible assets'. The standard defines intangible assets as 'non-financial fixed assets that do not have physical substance but are identifiable and are controlled by the entity through custody or legal rights'. Additional guidance is provided on applying this definition in practice:

— an identifiable asset is one that can be disposed of separately without disposing of the business of the entity (UITF Information Sheet No 34 has subsequently clarified that where the terms of a licence make it non-transferable and thus incapable of separate disposal, this does not imply that the licence is no longer an intangible asset – the issue is whether in principle the item could be disposed of separately from the business and any particular circumstances that make a disposal uneconomic or illegal are not relevant);

— an asset that can only be disposed of as part of the revenue-earning activity to which it contributes is regarded as being indistinguishable from the goodwill relating to that activity and is therefore accounted for as part of that goodwill;

— control of an intangible asset is usually secured by legal rights, which either grant access to economic benefits (e.g. through a franchise or licence) or restrict the access of others (e.g. through a patent or trade mark);

— control is more difficult to demonstrate in the absence of legal rights, but may be obtained through custody – however, in the case of assets such as confidential technical or intellectual knowledge, an expectation that the present situation will continue will not usually give the entity sufficient control over the expected future benefits to justify recognition of the item as an asset in the accounts (e.g. a team of skilled staff will not be recognised as an intangible asset because the entity will not usually have custody of, or a legal right to retain, those skills);

— software development costs that are directly attributable to bringing a computer system or other computer-related equipment into working order should be treated as part of the cost of the related hardware.

Certain intangible assets (such as research and development costs and oil and gas exploration and development costs) are excluded from FRS 10 on the basis that they are covered by more specific accounting requirements.

Initial recognition

20.18   FRS 10 sets out separate requirements on initial recognition for intangible assets that are purchased externally and those that are developed internally. Purchased intangible assets are classified further into those acquired as part of a business and those purchased separately. The following requirements apply:

—   an internally-developed intangible asset should only be capitalised if it has a readily ascertainable market value;

—   an intangible asset purchased separately from a business should be capitalised at cost; and

—   an intangible asset acquired as part of a business should be capitalised separately from goodwill if its value can be measured reliably at the time of initial recognition – in other cases the value of the intangible asset should be subsumed within the amount attributed to goodwill.

Readily ascertainable market value

20.19   Readily ascertainable value is defined in FRS 10 as a value established by reference to a market where:

—   the asset belongs to a homogeneous population of assets that are equivalent in all material respects; and

—   an active market, evidenced by frequent transactions, exists for that population of assets.

The guidance suggests that certain operating licences, franchises and quotas might meet these conditions, but a brand, publishing title or patent would not usually do so as each of these is inevitably unique, even though other similar assets may exist and may be traded from time to time. This point was emphasised in the FRRP report, published in July 2002, on the results of its enquiry into the report and accounts of Equator Group Plc for the year ended 31 December 1999. The matter at issue was the accounting treatment adopted for the purchase of Equator Films Limited in June 1999 and the subsequent accounting for the film libraries acquired. The Panel took the view that:

—   although the rights attaching to each film were similar, the films themselves were unique and could not, therefore, belong to a homogenous population of assets that was equivalent in all respects; and

—   the market in which film libraries are bought and sold is not an 'active market'.

The Panel therefore concluded that the films did not have a readily ascertainable market value, as defined in FRS 10.

Valuing an intangible asset acquired as part of a business

20.20   An intangible asset acquired as part of a business should initially be recorded at fair value, but where the asset does not have a readily ascertainable market value, the fair value should be restricted to an amount that does not create or increase any negative goodwill arising on the acquisition. This point was also emphasised in the FRRP case referred to in 20.19 above. Fair value should be established in accordance with FRS 7 'Fair Values in Acquisition Accounting'. This requires fair value to be based on replacement cost, which in most cases will be the estimated market value of the asset. The standard also considers fair value in the context of unique intangible assets for which replacement cost or market values may be difficult to determine. In some cases techniques have been developed for estimating the value of such assets (e.g. brands, publishing titles) for the purpose of sale and purchase agreements, and the guidance in the standard notes that these may also be used to establish fair value for initial recognition purposes.

Amortisation

20.21   CA 1985 requires any items capitalised as intangible fixed assets to be amortised over their expected useful economic lives in the same way as any other fixed assets. Under FRS 10, an intangible asset that is regarded as having a limited useful economic life must be amortised on a systematic basis over that life, but an intangible asset that is regarded as having an indefinite useful economic life should not be amortised. Amortisation charged in the year will need to be disclosed as required by the standard profit and loss account formats.

Determining useful economic life

20.22   FRS 10 defines the useful economic life of an intangible asset as 'the period over which the entity expects to derive economic benefit from that asset'. There is a rebuttable presumption that the useful economic life of an intangible asset should be no more than 20 years, and this presumption can only be rebutted if:

—   the durability of the intangible asset can be demonstrated and justifies a life of more than 20 years; and

—   the intangible asset is capable of continued measurement so that annual impairment reviews can be carried out.

FRS 10 notes that the useful economic lives of intangible assets will often be uncertain, but this does not justify an assumption that the life of a particular intangible asset is 20 years, or that its life is indefinite. Conversely, uncertainty should not be used to justify the adoption of an unrealistically short life. A prudent but realistic estimate of the useful economic life must be made for each intangible asset. The standard also notes that an asset will not be capable of continued measurement where the cost of carrying out the measurement is unjustifiably high – for instance, where the amounts involved are not sufficiently material to justify the detailed procedures needed to carry out an annual impairment review.

Legal rights granted for a finite period

20.23   Legal factors may also influence the useful economic life of an intangible asset, in that they may restrict the period during which the reporting entity has access to the economic benefits associated with the asset. The guidance notes that the useful economic life of an intangible asset is the shorter of:

— the period over which the future benefits are expected to arise; and

— the period over which the reporting entity is expected to have control of those benefits.

Where access to the benefits is granted for a finite period, the useful economic life of the asset will usually be limited to that period. The life of the asset should only be extended beyond this period if, and to the extent that, the legal rights over the asset are renewable and renewal is assured. Any costs that are expected to recur each time the legal rights are renewed should be excluded from the amount treated as having a longer life. The standard gives the following additional guidance on when the renewal of rights may be regarded as being assured:

— if the value of the intangible asset does not reduce as the initial expiry date approaches, or where the value reduces only by an amount reflecting the cost of renewal of the rights;

— where there is evidence that the rights will be renewed, for instance on the basis of past experience; and

— where there is no evidence that the entity has breached any conditions under the terms of the original rights which might otherwise prevent the rights being renewed.

Residual value

20.24   A residual value should only be assigned to an intangible asset if it can be measured reliably. The guidance in the standard notes that the residual value of an intangible asset will usually be insignificant. Residual value is defined as 'the net realisable value of an asset at the end of its useful economic life' and should be based on prices prevailing at the date of acquisition (or revaluation) without taking account of any expected future price changes. The residual value of an intangible asset will generally only be significant and capable of reliable measurement where the entity has a legal or contractual right to receive a certain sum at the end of the period during which it has use of the asset, or where there is a readily ascertainable market value for the residual asset. This point was also emphasised in the FRRP case referred to in 20.19 above.

Method of amortisation

20.25   FRS 10 requires amortisation to be charged on a systematic basis over the useful economic life of the asset, using a method that reflects the expected pattern of depletion of the asset. A straight-line method should be used unless another method can be shown to be more appropriate. For instance, where a licence covers production of a finite quantity of a particular product rather than unlimited production over a period of time, it may be more appropriate to base amortisation on the quantity produced rather than the period of the licence. The ASB has proposed an amendment to FRS 10 to clarify that:

—   it is unlikely that there will be circumstances that would support a method of amortisation that is less conservative than straight-line;

—   interest rate methods, such as the 'reverse sum of digits' or the annuity method, are not appropriate methods of amortising intangible assets.

Review and revision of economic lives

20.25   The useful economic lives of intangible assets should be reviewed at the end of each accounting period and revised where necessary. Where the useful economic life of an intangible asset is adjusted, the carrying value of the asset should be amortised over its revised remaining useful economic life. UITF Abstract 27 'Revision to estimates of the useful economic life of goodwill and intangible assets' clarifies that this applies equally where the presumption of a 20-year life has previously been rebutted, on the basis that a decision not to rebut the presumption is not a change of accounting policy, but a change in the way in which useful economic life is estimated. If the revision extends the life of the asset to a period of more than 20 years from the date of its acquisition, the additional requirements of FRS 10 on annual impairment reviews automatically come into effect.

Requirement for impairment reviews

20.27   Intangible assets that are amortised over a period of 20 years or less should be reviewed for impairment at the end of the first full financial year following acquisition and in other periods if events or changes in circumstances indicate that the carrying value of an asset may not be fully recoverable. Intangible assets that are amortised over a period of more than 20 years, or are not amortised, should be reviewed for impairment at the end of each accounting period. Impairment is defined in FRS 10 as 'a reduction in the recoverable amount of a fixed asset or goodwill below its carrying value.' Recoverable amount is defined as the higher of:

— net realisable value – which is the amount at which an asset could be disposed of, less any direct selling costs; and

— value in use – which is the present value of the future cash flows obtainable as a result of an asset's continued use, including those resulting from its ultimate disposal.

Impairment reviews should generally be carried out in accordance with the requirements of FRS 11 'Impairment of Fixed Assets and Goodwill'. However, the first year impairment review for intangible assets amortised over 20 years or less may be carried out by comparing post-acquisition performance in the first year with pre-acquisition forecasts used to support the purchase price, and only carrying out a full impairment review if this exercise indicates that post-acquisition performance has failed to meet expectations, or if other factors indicate that the carrying value of the asset may not be fully recoverable.

Accounting for impairment losses

20.28   Impairment losses should be accounted for in accordance with FRS 11. If an impairment loss needs to be recognised, the revised carrying value of the intangible asset should be amortised over the current estimate of the remaining useful economic life of the asset. The reversal of an impairment loss in respect of an intangible asset can only be recognised when:

— the original impairment loss was caused by an external event; and

— subsequent external events clearly and demonstrably reverse the effects of that event in a way that was not foreseen when the original impairment calculations were carried out.

The guidance in the standard emphasises that most reversals will be the result of the internal generation of intangible asset value and should therefore not be recognised in the accounts. Where a reversal is recognised, it should be treated as arising in the current year.

Revaluation of intangible assets

20.29   CA 1985 permits intangible fixed assets (other than goodwill) to be included in the accounts at their current cost, subject to specific disclosure requirements (see Chapter 1). Under FRS 10, where an intangible asset has a readily ascertainable market value, as defined in the standard, it may be revalued to market value, provided that all other capitalised intangible assets of the same class are revalued at the same time. The standard defines a class of intangible assets as 'a category of intangible assets having a similar nature, function or use in the business of the entity' and suggests that licences, quotas, patents, copyrights, franchises and trade marks are examples of such classes. The guidance also notes that further subdivision may be appropriate in certain cases, for instance where an entity holds licences with different functions within the business. Intangible assets used in different segments of the business may also be treated as separate classes of intangible assets. The standard does not specify a frequency of revaluation, but states that, once an intangible asset has been revalued, the valuation should be updated sufficiently often to ensure that the carrying value of the asset does not differ materially from its market value at the balance sheet date.

Amortisation of revalued assets

20.30   Where an intangible asset has been revalued, the amortisation charge should be based on the revalued amount and the remaining useful economic life of the asset. Amortisation charged before the revaluation took place should not be written back in the profit and loss account.

Accounts disclosure

20.31   CA 1985 requires disclosure of opening and closing balances in respect of each category of intangible asset identified in the Act, details of any movements during the year and additional details where assets have been included in the accounts at valuation. FRS 10 requires the following detailed disclosures, which effectively encompass those set out in the Act.

—   the method used to value intangible assets;

—   for each class of intangible asset capitalised on the balance sheet:

    —   the cost or revalued amount at the beginning and end of the period;

    —   the cumulative provision for amortisation or impairment at the beginning and end of the period;

    —   a reconciliation of movements, showing additions, disposals, revaluations, transfers, amortisation, impairment losses, reversals of past impairment losses and negative goodwill written back; and

    —   the net carrying amount at the balance sheet date;

—   the methods and periods of amortisation of intangible assets and the reasons for choosing those periods;

—   where an amortisation period is shortened or extended after a review of remaining useful economic lives, the reasons and the effect if material (i.e. in the year of change only);

—   where the amortisation method has been changed, the reasons and the effect if material (i.e. in the year of change only);

—   where the amortisation period is more than 20 years from the date of acquisition, or where no amortisation is charged, the grounds for rebutting the 20 year presumption, including specific factors contributing to the durability of the intangible asset (in a press release issued in May 2004, the

FRRP referred to a number of cases investigated by the Panel where directors had argued that the factors supporting the durability of intangible assets (and of brands in particular) were already well known and understood and that further comment in the accounts was considered unnecessary – the FRRP did not accept these arguments and concluded that there were no grounds for failing to give the detailed disclosures required by FRS 10);

— where a class of intangible assets has been revalued:

— the year of valuation, the values and the bases of valuation,

— the original cost (or fair value) of the assets and the amortisation that would have been recognised if they had continued to be valued at this amount;

— where an asset has been revalued during the year, the name and qualifications of the valuer.

Details of opening and closing balances and movements in the year are usually presented in one note as follows:

Example 20.5 – Disclosure of opening and closing balances and movements in the year

Intangible fixed assets

	Development costs £	Patents £	Total £
Cost:			
Balance at 1 January 20X2	49,786	6,500	56,286
Additions during the year	45,670	–	45,670
Disposals during the year	–	(3,000)	(3,000)
Balance at 31 December 20X2	95,456	3,500	98,956
Amortisation:			
Balance at 1 January 20X2	14,561	1,250	15,811
Amortisation during the year	32,345	750 ·	33,095
Eliminated in respect of disposals		(900)	(900)
Balance at 31 December 20X2	46,906	1,100	48,006
Net book value at 31 December 20X2	48,550	2,400	50,950
Net book value at 31 December 20X1	35,225	5,250	40,475

The other disclosures required by FRS 10 will usually be given as narrative notes below this table, or included within the accounting policy note where appropriate.

Accounting policy

20.32   Depending on the circumstances, wording along the following lines will usually be suitable for the accounting policy note:

Example 20.6 – Accounting policy for intangible assets

Licences are capitalised at their historical cost and amortised on a straight-line basis over the period of the licence, being the period during which the company expects to have control of the benefits associated with the asset. The licences currently held are being amortised over periods of 4 to 6 years.

GOODWILL

Nature of goodwill

20.33   This section considers the accounting treatment of purchased goodwill in the accounts of an individual company (for instance, on the acquisition of an unincorporated business). FRS 10 'Goodwill and intangible assets' defines purchased goodwill as 'the difference between the cost of an acquired entity and the aggregate of the fair values of that entity's identifiable assets and liabilities'. Identifiable assets and liabilities are defined as 'the assets and liabilities of an entity that are capable of being disposed of or settled separately, without disposing of a business of the entity'. Positive goodwill arises where the cost of acquisition exceeds the aggregate fair values of the identifiable assets and liabilities of the business acquired – in other words, where the value of the business as a whole is considered to be more than the aggregate of the values of its component parts and the purchaser is therefore prepared to pay more than the value of individual assets and liabilities that make up the business. Negative goodwill arises in the converse situation – where the value of the business is considered to be less than the value of the component parts and the aggregate fair values of the identifiable assets and liabilities are therefore more than the cost of acquisition. Negative goodwill is expected to arise only rarely.

Recognition of goodwill

20.34   Neither CA 1985 nor FRS 10 permit internally generated goodwill to be recognised on the balance sheet. Goodwill is therefore only recognised for accounting purposes when the business to which it relates is purchased by another party. Under FRS 10:

—   positive purchased goodwill should be capitalised and classified as an asset on the balance sheet;

—   any negative goodwill that arises on an acquisition should be recognised in the accounts and shown separately on the face of the balance sheet immediately below the goodwill heading. A sub-total of the net amount of positive and negative goodwill should also be given.

Purchased goodwill arising on a single transaction should not be divided into positive and negative components.

Value of purchased goodwill

20.35   When a business is acquired, the value of the purchased goodwill is established by comparing the fair values of the various assets and liabilities at the time of acquisition with the fair value of the consideration given by the purchaser. Any excess of the consideration over the fair values of the net assets represents the value of the purchased goodwill. Where an intangible asset is acquired as part of the transaction, it should normally be capitalised separately. However, if its value cannot be measured reliably, it should be subsumed within the amount of the purchase price attributed to goodwill.

Value of negative goodwill

20.36   The standard emphasises that, where an acquisition appears to give rise to negative goodwill, the fair values of the assets acquired should be tested for impairment and the fair values of the liabilities acquired should be reviewed carefully to confirm that they have not been understated and that no items have been overlooked. The requirements of FRS 10 in respect of intangible assets require the fair values of certain intangibles to be limited to an amount that does not create or increase any negative goodwill arising on the acquisition (see 20.20 above).

Fair values

20.37   FRS 7 'Fair Values in Acquisition Accounting' provides detailed guidance on establishing the fair values of individual assets and liabilities at the time of acquisition and the fair value of the purchase consideration (which will not necessarily be in the form of cash).

Amortisation

20.38   Under FRS 10:

—   where purchased goodwill is regarded as having a limited useful economic life, it should be amortised on a systematic basis over that life;

—   where purchased goodwill is considered to have an indefinite useful economic life, it should not be amortised.

CA 1985 requires goodwill to be amortised systematically over a finite period, and an entity following the requirements of FRS 10 in respect of goodwill that is considered to have indefinite life will therefore need to adopt the true and fair override and make appropriate disclosures in the accounts (see Chapter 3). No residual value should be attributed to purchased goodwill. The standard requires amortisation to be charged on a systematic basis over the useful economic life of the goodwill, using a method that reflects the expected pattern of depletion. A straight-line method should be used unless another method can be shown to be more appropriate. The guidance notes that, in the case of goodwill, an amortisation method that is less conservative than the straight-line method is unlikely to be justifiable. In particular, interest rate methods, such as the 'reverse sum of digits' or the annuity method, are not appropriate methods of amortising goodwill. Amortisation charged in the year should be disclosed as required by the standard profit and loss account formats.

Determining the useful economic life of goodwill

20.39 FRS 10 defines the useful economic life of purchased goodwill as 'the period over which the value of the underlying business acquired is expected to exceed the values of its identifiable net assets'. The standard also notes that, if purchased goodwill includes intangible assets that have not been recognised separately because their values cannot be measured reliably, the useful economic lives of the intangible assets will need to be taken into account when assessing the useful economic life of the goodwill. There is a rebuttable presumption that the useful economic life of goodwill should be no more than 20 years, and this presumption can only be rebutted if:

— the durability of the acquired business can be demonstrated and justifies a life of more than 20 years; and

— the goodwill is capable of continued measurement so that annual impairment reviews can be carried out.

The guidance in the standard emphasises that it is inappropriate to assume that the premium of an acquired business over its net asset value can be maintained indefinitely. In practice, purchased goodwill will usually be replaced by internally generated goodwill over time and, because internally generated goodwill should not be recognised for accounting purposes, it is important that the write-off period for the purchased goodwill is sufficiently short to allow it to be eliminated from the accounts before it is fully replaced with internally generated goodwill. The standard notes that the useful economic life of goodwill will often be uncertain, but this does not justify an assumption that it has a life of 20 years, or that its life is indefinite. Conversely, uncertainty should not be used to justify the adoption of an unrealistically short life. A prudent but realistic estimate of the useful economic life must be made in each case where goodwill arises.

Durability and continued measurement

20.40 The guidance in the standard emphasises that the durability of a business will vary depending on various factors, including:

— the nature of the business;

— the stability of the industry in which it operates;

— the typical lifespan of the products to which the goodwill relates;

— the extent to which the acquisition overcomes market entry barriers that will continue to exist; and

— the expected impact of competition in future years.

In practice, these are factors that will also need to be considered when determining the useful economic life of goodwill. The standard also notes that the goodwill will not be capable of continued measurement where the cost of carrying out the measurement is unjustifiably high — for instance, where the acquired business is merged with an existing business to such an extent that the acquired goodwill cannot be separately identified and reviewed in future years.

Review and revision of economic life

20.41 The useful economic life of purchased goodwill should be reviewed at the end of each accounting period and revised where necessary. Where the useful economic life is adjusted, the carrying value of the goodwill should be amortised over its revised remaining useful economic life. UITF Abstract 27 'Revision to estimates of the useful economic life of goodwill and intangible assets' clarifies that this applies equally where the presumption of a 20-year life has previously been rebutted, on the basis that a decision not to rebut the presumption is not a change of accounting policy, but a change in the way in which useful economic life is estimated. If the revision extends the life of the goodwill to a period of more than 20 years from the date of its acquisition, the additional requirements of FRS 10 on annual impairment reviews automatically come into effect.

Requirement for impairment reviews

20.42 Goodwill that is amortised over a period of 20 years or less should be reviewed for impairment at the end of the first full financial year following acquisition and in other periods if events or changes in circumstances indicate that its carrying value may not be fully recoverable. Goodwill that is amortised over a period of more than 20 years, or is not amortised, should be reviewed for impairment at the end of each accounting period. Impairment is defined in FRS 10 as 'a reduction in the recoverable amount of a fixed asset or goodwill below its carrying value'. Recoverable amount is defined as the higher of:

— net realisable value – which is the amount at which an asset could be disposed of, less any direct selling costs; and

— value in use – which is the present value of the future cash flows obtainable as a result of an asset's continued use, including those resulting from its ultimate disposal.

Impairment reviews should generally be carried out in accordance with the requirements of FRS 11 'Impairment of Fixed Assets and Goodwill'. However, the first year impairment review for goodwill amortised over 20 years or less may be carried out by comparing post-acquisition performance in the first year with pre-acquisition forecasts used to support the purchase price, and only carrying out a full impairment review if this exercise indicates that post-acquisition performance has failed to meet expectations, or if other factors indicate that the carrying value of the goodwill may not be fully recoverable.

Accounting for impairment losses

20.43 Impairment losses should be accounted for in accordance with FRS 11. If an impairment loss needs to be recognised, the revised carrying value of the goodwill should be amortised over the current estimate of its remaining useful economic life. The guidance in FRS 10 emphasises that:

— the recognition of an impairment loss must be justified by reference to expected future cash flows, in the same way as the absence of an impairment loss;

— the fact that the value of the goodwill may not be capable of continued measurement in future does not necessarily justify writing off the entire balance at the time of the first year impairment review.

The reversal of an impairment loss in respect of goodwill can only be recognised when:

— the original impairment loss was caused by an external event; and

— subsequent external events clearly and demonstrably reverse the effects of that event in a way that was not foreseen when the original impairment calculations were carried out.

The guidance in the standard emphasises that most reversals will be the result of the internal generation of goodwill and should therefore not be recognised in the accounts. Where a reversal is recognised, it should be treated as arising in the current year.

Accounting for negative goodwill

20.44 Negative goodwill up to the fair values of the non-monetary assets acquired should be recognised in the profit and loss account in the period in which those assets are recovered (i.e. through depreciation or on sale of the assets). Any negative goodwill in excess of the fair values of the non-monetary assets acquired should be recognised in the profit and loss account in the periods expected to benefit.

Accounts disclosure

20.45 CA 1985 requires disclosure of opening and closing balances in respect of goodwill, details of any movements during the year, the period of write-off and the reasons for choosing that period. FRS 10 requires the following detailed disclosures, which effectively encompass those set out in the Act:

— separately for positive goodwill and negative goodwill:

— the cost at the beginning and end of the period;

— the cumulative provision for amortisation or impairment at the beginning and end of the period;

— a reconciliation of movements, showing additions, disposals, transfers, amortisation, impairment losses, reversals of past impairment losses and negative goodwill written back in the period; and

— the net carrying amount at the balance sheet date;

— the profit or loss on each material disposal of a previously acquired business or business segment;

— the methods and periods of amortisation and the reasons for choosing those periods;

— where an amortisation period is shortened or extended after a review of remaining useful economic lives, the reasons and the effect if material (i.e. in the year of change only);

— where the amortisation method has been changed, the reasons and the effect if material (i.e. in the year of change only);

— where the amortisation period is more than 20 years from the date of acquisition, or where no amortisation is charged, the grounds for rebutting the 20 year presumption, including specific factors contributing to the durability of the acquired business (in a press release issued in May 2004, the FRRP referred to a number of cases investigated by the Panel where directors had argued that the factors supporting the durability of intangible assets and goodwill were already well known and understood and that further comment in the accounts was considered unnecessary – the FRRP did not accept these arguments and concluded that there were no grounds for failing to give the detailed disclosures required by FRS 10);

— where goodwill is not amortised, the true and fair override disclosures (which should incorporate the explanation of the specific factors contributing to the durability of the acquired business);

— the period(s) in which any negative goodwill is being written back in the profit and loss account; and

— where negative goodwill exceeds the fair values of the non-monetary assets acquired, an explanation of the amount and source of the excess and of the period(s) in which it is being written back.

Movements on the goodwill account should be disclosed within the note giving details of all intangible fixed assets. The other disclosures are usually covered in a footnote to the movements table:

Example 20.7 – Goodwill disclosure within intangible assets

Intangible fixed assets:

	Development costs £	Patents £	Purchased goodwill £	Total £
Cost:				
Balance at 1 January 20X2	49,786	6,500	25,000	81,286
Additions during the year	45,670	–	12,000	57,670
Disposals during the year	–	(3,000)	–	(3,000)
Balance at 31 December 20X2	95,456	3,500	37,000	135,956
Amortisation:				
Balance at 1 January 20X2	14,561	1,250	10,000	25,811
Amortisation during the year	32,345	750	8,000	41,095
Eliminated in respect of disposals	–	(900)	–	(900)
Balance at 31 December 20X2	46,906	1,100	18,000	66,006
Net book value at 31 December 20X2	48,550	2,400	19,000	69,950
Net book value at 31 December 20X1	35,225	5,250	15,000	55,475

The company acquired an unincorporated business on 1 January 20X2 for consideration of £45,000, which gave rise to purchased goodwill of £12,000. This is being amortised on a straight line basis over its expected useful economic life of 4 years. Goodwill in respect of a business acquired in previous years is being amortised over its expected useful economic life of 5 years. In the opinion of the directors, these periods represents a reasonable and prudent estimate of the time during which the company will derive economic benefit from the goodwill acquired.

Accounting policy

20.46   In a straightforward case of positive goodwill, the following wording will usually be suitable:

Example 20.8 – Accounting policy for purchased goodwill

Purchased goodwill represents the difference between the cost of an acquired business and the aggregate of the fair values of its identifiable assets and liabilities. Purchased goodwill is capitalised and amortised through the profit and loss account on a straight-line basis over its useful economic life.

Transitional arrangements

20.47   The predecessor accounting standard to FRS 10 was SSAP 22 'Accounting for Goodwill' and this allowed two alternative accounting treatments for purchased goodwill: capitalisation and amortisation, or immediate write-off against reserves. FRS 10 notes that any changes in accounting policy necessary to implement its requirements should be applied retrospectively. The preferred treatment, therefore, is for goodwill that has previously been eliminated against reserves to be reinstated to the extent that it would not have been fully written down under the requirements of the new standard. However, the ASB accepted that this would not always be practicable and included certain transitional arrangements in FRS 10.

Reinstatement of goodwill previously eliminated

20.48   Where goodwill previously eliminated against reserves is reinstated on implementing FRS 10:

— any impairment attributed to prior periods must be determined on the basis of reviews performed in accordance with FRS 11;

— the notes to the accounts should disclose:

— the original cost of the goodwill,

— the amount attributed to prior period amortisation, and

— the amount attributed to prior period impairment;

— intangible assets subsumed within the goodwill need not be identified separately.

The reinstatement of the goodwill will therefore give rise to a prior period adjustment (see Chapter 6).

Goodwill not reinstated

20.49   Where goodwill that was previously eliminated against reserves is not reinstated on the implementation of FRS 10, the following treatment should be adopted:

— the accounting policy followed in respect of that goodwill should be disclosed;

— the cumulative amounts of positive goodwill eliminated against reserves and negative goodwill added to reserves (net of any goodwill attributable to businesses disposed of before the balance sheet date) should be shown, except that:

— amounts relating to overseas business need not be given if it would be prejudicial to the business and official agreement has been obtained; and

—　disclosure need not be made for acquisitions before 23 December 1989 if the information is unavailable or cannot be obtained without unreasonable expense or undue delay;

(the exclusion of these amounts, and the reasons for it, should be explained);

—　the eliminated goodwill should be offset against the profit and loss account or another suitable reserve – it should not be shown as a debit balance on a goodwill write-off reserve, nor should the amount by which the profit and loss account or other reserve has been reduced be shown separately on the face of the balance sheet;

—　in the reporting period in which the related business is disposed of or closed, the profit or loss on disposal or closure should include any attributable goodwill not already written off in the profit and loss account, and this should be separately disclosed as a component of the profit or loss (if it is not practicable to ascertain the goodwill attributable to a business acquired before 1 January 1989 this fact, and the reasons, should be disclosed).

Impact of goodwill on distributable reserves

20.50　　The issue of distributable reserves and realised profits and losses is considered briefly in Chapter 16. This is a highly complex area and only an outline of the main issues is given in this book. The potential impact of goodwill on distributable reserves is not an issue where goodwill is accounted for in accordance with FRS 10 'Goodwill and Intangible Assets'. However, where a company follows the transitional arrangements in FRS 10 and does not reinstate goodwill previously eliminated directly against reserves, the impact of this write-off on distributable reserves may still need to be considered. The write-off of purchased goodwill must eventually give rise to a realised loss, and under the requirements of FRS 10 this loss will be recognised as the goodwill is amortised through the profit and loss account. Where a company adopted the policy of writing off purchased goodwill against reserves immediately on acquisition under SSAP 22 'Accounting for Goodwill' and does not reinstate any of this goodwill on implementing FRS 10, the question arises whether the full amount written off should be treated as a realised loss, and thus as a reduction of distributable reserves. This issue was considered in an appendix to SSAP 22 'Accounting for Goodwill', which is reproduced as Appendix V to FRS 10. The guidance concluded that the write-off of goodwill against reserves did not constitute an immediate reduction in the company's realised reserves, unless the goodwill had suffered a permanent diminution in value. This was on the basis that the write-off was usually a matter of accounting policy rather than the recognition of a diminution in value. It was therefore suggested that the company could deem the amount written off not to be an immediate realised loss, and recognise it as being realised on a systematic basis over the useful economic life of the goodwill, giving the same effect on reserves as when goodwill is capitalised and amortised through the profit and loss account over its useful economic life. Where the goodwill was initially written off against an unrealised reserve, it should be transferred to realised reserves on a systematic basis over its useful economic life.

Public companies

20.51   Additional rules apply in the case of public companies. In particular, a public company must take account of unrealised losses when establishing the profits available for distribution. Therefore the immediate write-off of goodwill, even against an unrealised reserve, may have a significant effect on the ability of a public company to pay a dividend.

Negative goodwill

20.52   Although SSAP 22 required negative goodwill to be credited to reserves at the time of acquisition, it should not have been treated immediately as a realised reserve. It should instead have been credited to an unrealised reserve, and should be transferred to realised reserves in line with the depreciation or realisation of the assets acquired.

Need for legal advice

20.53   If a company proposes to pay a dividend at any time when there is any doubt over the availability of sufficient distributable reserves, legal advice should always be taken before proposing and paying the dividend.

Chapter 21 Tangible Fixed Assets

CLASSIFICATION OF ASSETS

Definition of fixed asset

21.1   Under CA 1985, all assets must be categorised as either fixed assets or current assets. There is no flexibility for presenting items outside these two categories. The legislation defines a fixed asset as one which the company intends to use on a continuing basis in its activities. FRS 11 'Impairment of Fixed Assets and Goodwill' and FRS 15 'Tangible Fixed Assets' define tangible fixed assets as: 'Assets that have physical substance and are held for use in the production or supply of goods or services, for rental to others, or for administrative purposes on a continuing basis in the reporting entity's activities.' A current asset is any asset that does not meet the fixed asset definition. The wording of the Act and of the standards suggests that it is the intended use of the asset at the balance sheet date that decides whether a particular asset is fixed or current. This can give rise to difficulties in accounting for fixed assets which the company proposes to sell and for current assets which the company decides to retain.

Proposed sale of fixed asset

21.2   If a company has decided to sell an asset but is still using it at the balance sheet date, and plans to continue to use it until it is actually sold, there seems to be little difficulty in continuing to show the asset as a fixed asset in the account until it is physically disposed of.

Example 21.1 – When a fixed asset is to be sold but is still being used at balance sheet date

A Ltd operates two factories but decides to transfer all production to the newer of the two sites in due course. The older site is, therefore, put on the market but A Ltd proposes to continue to operate from that site until a buyer is found.

Both factories should, therefore, continue to be shown as fixed assets in the accounts.

However, in this situation the carrying value of the asset in the accounts may need further consideration to ensure that it is not overstated in light of the planned disposal. If the company has stopped using the asset that is to be sold, it would seem that the asset ceases to meet the definition of a fixed asset set out in CA 1985.

Example 21.2 – When a fixed asset is to be sold and is not being used

A Ltd operates two factories but decides to transfer all production to the newer of the two sites on 1 June 20X2. The older site is put on the market but is still unsold at 30 September 20X2, the end of the company's financial year.

The older site has, therefore, ceased to meet the definition of a fixed asset set out in CA 1985.

The accounting treatment in this situation is more difficult. It may seem appropriate to transfer the asset from fixed assets to current assets but this is likely to give rise to problems if, for instance:

—   the fixed asset is included in the accounts at valuation – a company is permitted to include fixed assets in the accounts at cost or valuation, but current assets must usually be included in the accounts at the lower of cost and net realisable value;

—   the asset is significant and disposal may take more than 12 months (eg a major property which is put up for sale when the market is depressed) – the inclusion of such an item in current assets could significantly distort the accounts.

In the light of these difficulties, it has become normal practice to continue to include assets in the course of disposal within fixed assets and to show them separately as 'assets awaiting disposal' or 'assets held for sale', rather than to transfer them to current assets. FRS 15 acknowledges this by setting out a specific valuation basis for properties surplus to requirements where the entity adopts a policy of revaluation. Any profit or loss on the eventual disposal will usually be separately disclosable under the requirements of FRS 3 'Reporting Financial Performance'. New proposals on accounting for assets held for sale have been put forward in FRED 32 'Disposal of non-current assets and presentation of discontinued operations' (see 21.121 below) but are not expected to come into effect until 1 January 2007.

Transfers from current assets to fixed assets

21.3   UITF 5 'Transfers from Current Assets to Fixed Assets' tackles the issue of how to account for an asset that was not initially intended for continuing use in the business, but which subsequently becomes a fixed asset. An example might be where a property construction company builds a property initially for sale in the ordinary course of its business, but then decides to use the building as its own office. The Abstract requires the following approach:

—   assess the net realisable value of the asset at the date of transfer;

—   if net realisable value is below cost, the asset must be written down to net realisable value before it is transferred;

—   any provision needed to reduce cost to net realisable value must be charged to the profit and loss account (this recognises the loss suffered by the company during the time that the asset was held as a current asset);

—   the asset is then subject to the normal rules for fixed assets (i.e. those set out in the Act and FRS 15) from the date of transfer, and should be treated as an asset recorded at valuation under the alternative accounting rules of the Act (see Chapter 1).

Analysis of tangible fixed assets

21.4   CA 1985 requires tangible fixed assets to be analysed into the following categories.

—   Land and buildings.

—   Plant and machinery.

—   Fixtures, fittings, tools and equipment.

—   Payments on account and assets in the course of construction.

This detail is usually given in the notes to the accounts, although it may be given on the face of the balance sheet. Depending on the nature of the company's business, categorising fixed assets into these headings may not always be straightforward.

Class of tangible fixed assets

21.5   FRS 15 defines a class of tangible fixed assets as 'a category of tangible fixed assets having a similar nature, function or use within the business of the entity'. This definition is particularly relevant where the reporting entity adopts a policy of revaluation, because all tangible fixed assets in the same class must be revalued at the same time. The guidance in the standard notes that the categories set out in CA 1985 are broad categories and, for the purposes of valuation, entities may adopt other, narrower categories within the main headings. For instance, land and buildings may be analysed into specialised properties, non-specialised properties and short lease-hold properties. However, where narrower classifications are adopted, it should be remembered that the disclosures required under the standard must be given by class of asset, rather than simply by the main categories identified in CA 1985.

Land and buildings

21.6   Land and buildings is probably the most straightforward of the three main categories and will normally comprise freehold, long leasehold and short leasehold properties. A long lease is defined in CA 1985 as a lease that has not less than 50 years remaining at the balance sheet date. All other leases are short leases. The Act requires separate details for each of these headings and this information is usually disclosed in a note to the accounts. The Act is not totally specific as to what is required and refers only to an analysis of 'amounts' relating to freehold and leasehold tenure. The minimum disclosure would, therefore, be an analysis of the net book value of land and buildings.

Example 21.3 – Analysis of land and buildings

The net book value of land and buildings comprises:

	20X2	20X1
	£	£
Freehold	239,750	245,600
Long leasehold	35,671	37,849
Short leasehold	25,600	29,780
	301,021	313,229

However, many companies give full details of the movements during the year in respect of each category.

Example 21.4 – Fuller analysis of land and buildings

	Freehold	Leasehold Long	Leasehold Short	Total
	£	£	£	£
Cost:				
Balance at 1 January 20X2	287,733	47,477	34,230	369,440
Additions	—	5,400	—	5,400
Disposals	—	—	(3,250)	(3,250)
Balance at 31 December 20X2	287,733	52,877	30,980	371,590

Depreciation:			
Balance at 1 January 20X2	42,133	9,628	4,450	56,211
Charge for the year	5,850	7,578	3,430	16,858
Eliminated on disposals	—	—	(2,500)	(2,500)
Balance at 31 December 20X2	47,983	17,206	5,380	70,569
Net book value 31 December 20X2	239,750	35,671	25,600	301,021
Net book value 31 December 20X1	245,600	37,849	29,780	313,229

Other asset categories

21.7   In a production company, plant and machinery will usually comprise assets relating to the company's main production activities. Fixtures, fittings, loose tools and equipment will then cover the remaining assets such as small tools and office furniture and equipment, including computers. Non-production companies will often not hold assets in the plant and machinery category and will therefore classify all of their assets, other than property, under fixtures, fittings, tools and equipment. One common problem in practice is that the headings in CA 1985 do not cater specifically for motor vehicles. The Act permits information to be given in greater detail than is required by the formats and allows additional headings to be included, provided that the items in question are not dealt with elsewhere in the formats. If the value of motor vehicles is significant, it is therefore acceptable:

—   to show motor vehicles as a separate category within plant and machinery or within fixtures, fittings, loose tools and equipment as appropriate; or

—   to include a separate heading for motor vehicles in the table of fixed assets.

Similar arguments might apply to computer equipment if this is particularly significant in the context of the company's assets. A further point to remember is that FRS 15 also requires disclosure of the asset lives or depreciation rates used (see Chapter 13). The categories used for this disclosure should be consistent, as far as possible, with the analysis of fixed assets given in the accounts (eg if motor vehicles are sufficiently material to be shown as a separate category within fixed assets, the depreciation rate for motor vehicles should also be disclosed).

Payments on account and assets in the course of construction

21.8   This category represents payments the company has made in respect of assets that are in the process of construction or installation but which are incomplete at the balance sheet date. It is normal practice to charge depreciation from the date that an asset comes into use. It could, therefore, be misleading to include in the main asset categories significant amounts relating to assets still in the course of construction or development. The payments are, therefore, required to be disclosed separately within fixed assets until the asset is brought into use, at which point the cost should be transferred to the appropriate asset categories.

Example 21.5 – Disclosure of assets in the course of construction

	Plant and machinery £	Assets in the course of construction £
Cost:		
Balance at 1 January 20X2	546,780	26,700
Additions during the year	35,660	9,850
Disposals during the year	(14,677)	—
Transfer on completion of asset	36,550	(36,550)
Balance at 31 December 20X2	604,313	—

INITIAL MEASUREMENT OF TANGIBLE FIXED ASSETS

Measurement at cost

21.9   Where the historical cost accounting rules are adopted, both CA 1985 and FRS 15 require a tangible fixed asset to be measured initially at cost. In the case of assets that are purchased, the Act defines purchase price as the actual price paid, plus any expenses incidental to the acquisition, and also notes that this includes any consideration given in respect of the asset, regardless of whether it is in cash or some other form. The guidance in FRS 15 explains that any related trade discounts and rebates should be deducted from the cost of the asset.

Cost of production

21.10   The production cost of an asset is calculated by adding together the purchase price of the raw materials and consumables used, and the direct costs of production. In addition, the Act permits the inclusion of a reasonable proportion of indirect production costs and interest on capital borrowed to finance the production of the asset, but in each case only to the extent that the costs relate to the period of production. FRS 15 is more specific than the Act and only allows the inclusion of costs that are directly attributable to bringing the asset into working condition for its intended use. Directly attributable costs are defined as:

—   the labour costs of own employees arising from the construction or acquisition of the specific tangible fixed asset (but not more general employee costs); and

—   the incremental costs that would have been avoided only if the tangible fixed asset had not been acquired.

Under the standard, therefore, it is not permissible to include an element of general overhead or administration costs in the cost of a fixed asset as these are, by their very nature, costs that would have been incurred regardless of whether the asset was constructed (or acquired) or not.

Examples of directly attributable costs

21.11   The standard sets out examples of directly attributable costs, which include:

—   acquisition costs such as stamp duty, import duties and non-refundable purchase taxes (eg irrecoverable VAT);

—   costs of site preparation and clearance;

—   initial delivery and handling costs;

—   installation costs;

—   professional fees (eg architects, engineers);

—   the estimated cost of dismantling and removing the asset and restoring the site, to the extent that this is recognised as a provision under FRS 12 'Provisions, Contingent Liabilities and Contingent Assets' – these costs can still be capitalised even if they do not become apparent until some time after the asset was acquired (eg where a liability arises as a result of changes in legislation).

Exclusion of abnormal costs

21.12   Abnormal costs, such as those arising from design errors, industrial disputes, idle capacity, wastage and production delays must not be included in the cost of the asset. Similarly, costs such as operating losses resulting from the suspension of a revenue activity whilst a tangible fixed asset is constructed, are not directly attributable costs and should not be included in the cost of the asset.

Cessation of capitalisation of costs

21.13   FRS 15 requires the capitalisation of directly attributable costs to cease as soon as substantially all of the activities necessary to get the asset ready for use have been completed. This applies even though the asset may not actually have been brought into use at that time. The standard notes that an asset is ready for use when its physical construction is complete.

Start-up or commissioning period

21.14   Certain assets require a start-up or commissioning period, during which it is not possible for the asset to operate at normal levels. For instance, machinery may need to be run in, specific equipment may need to be tested, or checks may need to be made to confirm that the plant is functioning properly before actual production begins. Under FRS 15, where an asset is available for use, but not capable of operating at normal levels without such a start-up or commissioning period, the costs associated with that period should be included in the cost of the asset. UITF Abstract 24 'Accounting for Start-up Costs' sets out the accounting treatment that should be applied to start-up costs that do not meet the specific conditions for recognition in FRS 15:

—   where similar costs are incurred by the entity as part of its ongoing activities, the start-up costs should be accounted for on a consistent basis with those similar costs;

—   where no similar costs are incurred, start-up costs that do not meet the specific conditions for recognition as assets under FRS10 'Goodwill and Intangible Assets', FRS 15 'Tangible Fixed Assets' or SSAP 13 'Accounting for Research and Development', should be recognised as an expense when they are incurred.

Start-up costs that meet the definition of an exceptional item set out in FRS 3 'Reporting Financial Performance' should be disclosed separately in accordance with the requirements of that standard (see Chapter 9).

Initial operating period

21.15   FRS 15 makes a clear distinction between a genuine start-up or commissioning period (as described above) and an initial operating period, where the plant or asset is available for use and capable of running at normal levels, but it is operated at a lower level because demand has not yet built up. The standard gives, as examples, a new hotel or retail shop, where reputation and customer demand will only build up over a period of time. The guidance in the standard emphasises that there is no justification for including the costs of such a period in the cost of the asset.

Gifts and donations

21.16   The issue of donated assets arises most frequently in the charity sector. FRS 15 requires assets received by way of gift or donation to be included in the accounts initially at their current value at the date they are received. Current value is defined in the standard as the lower of replacement cost and recoverable amount. However, the guidance acknowledges that there may be circumstances where a conventional approach to valuation is not appropriate (for instance, where the asset cannot be disposed of, or is of particular historical or artistic significance), and also that the significant costs associated with a valuation may make this approach inappropriate. In these situations, the standard permits a different approach to valuation and refers entities to sector-specific guidance and relevant Statements of Recommended Practice (SORPs).

Capitalisation of finance costs

21.17 CA 1985 permits the capitalisation of interest on capital borrowed to finance the production of an asset, but only to the extent that it relates to the period of production. Once again, FRS 15 is more specific on this issue. There is no requirement to capitalise finance costs but, where an entity adopts such a policy, it should be applied consistently to all tangible fixed assets where finance costs fall to be capitalised. Finance costs are defined as the difference between the net proceeds of an instrument and the total amount of payments or other transfers of economic benefits that the issuer may be required to make in respect of the instrument. They include interest on bank overdrafts and loans, the amortisation of discounts or premiums relating to debt and the amortisation of ancillary costs incurred in connection with the arrangement of debt. In the case of leased assets, finance costs should be accounted for in accordance with SSAP 21 'Accounting for Leases and Hire Purchase Contracts'.

Directly attributable finance costs

21.18 Where an entity opts to capitalise finance costs, the finance costs that are directly attributable to the construction of the tangible fixed asset should be capitalised as part of the cost of the asset. However, the total amount of finance costs capitalised during a period should not exceed the total amount of finance costs incurred in that period. Directly attributable finance costs are defined as those that would have been avoided if there had been no expenditure on the asset. For instance, finance costs might have been avoided by not taking out additional borrowings or by using funds expended on the asset to repay existing borrowings. Finance costs should be capitalised gross (i.e. without the deduction of any tax relief arising from them).

Specific and non-specific borrowings

21.19 Where an entity borrows funds specifically to finance the construction of a tangible fixed asset, the relevant finance costs are easily identified. The amount that can be capitalised is limited to the actual costs incurred on the borrowings during the period in which expenditure on the asset has been incurred to date. In some cases, the funds used to finance the construction of a tangible fixed asset may be part of the entity's general borrowings. In this situation, the amount capitalised should be calculated by applying a capitalisation rate to the expenditure incurred on the asset, as follows:

— the capitalisation rate for the accounting period should be based on the weighted average of rates applicable to the general borrowings outstanding during the period; and

— the expenditure on the asset is the weighted average carrying amount of the asset during the period, including any finance costs already capitalised in previous periods.

The objective of this exercise is to make a reasonable estimate of the finance costs that are directly attributable to the construction of the tangible fixed asset. Borrowings should, therefore, exclude any borrowings taken out for specific purposes such as financing other tangible fixed assets or hedging foreign investments. Other adjustments may also need to be made in order to select the borrowings most likely to achieve the objective of the calculation.

Commencement of capitalisation of finance costs

21.20   Where finance costs are capitalised, capitalisation should begin when:

— finance costs are being incurred;

— expenditures for the asset are being incurred; and

— activities that are necessary to get the asset ready for use are in progress.

The activities that are necessary to get an asset ready for use may encompass more than its physical construction. The guidance in the standard gives, as an example, preparatory technical work, such as obtaining necessary permits. However, finance costs should not be capitalised when an asset is simply held for future development (ie when no changes are being made to the condition of the asset). For example, finance costs should not be capitalised on land held for future development, although capitalisation can commence once activities on the site are under way.

Suspension of capitalisation of finance costs

21.21   Capitalisation should be suspended during extended periods in which active development of the tangible fixed asset is interrupted.

Cessation of capitalisation of finance costs

21.22   Capitalisation should cease when substantially all the activities needed to get the tangible fixed asset ready for use are complete. When the construction of a tangible fixed asset is completed in parts, and each part is capable of being used while construction continues on other parts, capitalisation of finance costs relating to a part should cease when substantially all the activities needed to get that part ready for use are complete. The guidance in the standard gives, as an example, the construction of a business park, where each building can be brought into use as soon as it has been completed, even though construction work may still be continuing on other buildings forming part of the site. On the other hand, a major industrial plant such as a steel mill, which involves a number of processes carried out in sequence, cannot be operated until all the relevant parts have been constructed.

Finance costs disclosures

21.23   Where an entity adopts a policy of capitalising finance costs, the financial statements should show:

— the accounting policy adopted;

— the aggregate amount of finance costs included in the cost of tangible fixed assets;

— the amount of finance costs capitalised during the period;

— the amount of finance costs recognised in the profit and loss account in the period; and

— the capitalisation rate used to determine the amount of finance costs capitalised during the period.

These details will usually be given in a narrative note below the fixed assets table.

Write-down to recoverable amount

21.24   The amount recognised under these requirements as the initial purchase or construction cost of a tangible fixed asset may exceed the recoverable amount of the asset. In this case, it should be written down to recoverable amount in accordance with the requirements of FRS 11 'Impairment of Fixed Assets and Goodwill'. However, there is no requirement to carry out an impairment review of a new fixed asset unless there is some indication that impairment has occurred. Further guidance on this is given in FRS 11 (see 21.54).

Subsequent expenditure on fixed assets

21.25   The accounting treatment adopted for subsequent expenditure on a tangible fixed asset should reflect the circumstances taken into account on initial recognition and in determining useful economic life and residual value for depreciation purposes. Subsequent expenditure to ensure that the asset maintains its previously assessed standard of performance should normally be recognised in the profit and loss account as it is incurred. Routine repair and maintenance expenditure on the asset will usually have been assumed when assessing the useful economic life of the asset for depreciation purposes.

Capitalisation of subsequent expenditure

21.26   There are three circumstances in which subsequent expenditure on an asset should be capitalised:

—   where it enhances the economic benefits of the asset beyond the previously assessed standard of performance (for instance, where the asset is modified or upgraded to increase capacity or improve the quality of output);

—   where a component of the asset that has been treated separately for depreciation purposes is replaced or restored;

—   where it relates to a major inspection or overhaul of the asset that restores the economic benefits that have already been consumed by the entity and have been reflected in depreciation (ie where an amount equivalent to the cost of the inspection or overhaul has been depreciated over the period up to the date of the inspection or overhaul).

Where tangible fixed assets have not been separated into individual components for depreciation purposes (for instance, because the expected lives of the major components are not substantially different from those of the remaining parts of the asset), or no part of the asset has been depreciated over a different time scale to reflect the cost of a major inspection or overhaul, the costs of replacing, restoring, inspecting or overhauling the asset should be charged to the profit and loss account as they are incurred.

VALUATION OF TANGIBLE FIXED ASSETS

Alternative accounting rules and fair value accounting rules

21.27   Under the alternative accounting rules, tangible fixed assets may be included in the accounts at their market value at the date of the last valuation, or at current cost. Further guidance on the operation of the alternative accounting rules is given in Chapter 1. In practice, the only widespread use of the alternative accounting rules is the inclusion of freehold and leasehold properties in the accounts at valuation. CA 1985, FRS 15 and the Royal Institute of Chartered Surveyors 'Appraisal and Valuation Manual' all require additional disclosures to be given in the accounts when assets have been included at valuation. These are considered in more detail at 21.51–21.54 below.

The 4th and 7th EC Company Law Directives, which form the basis of the *Companies Act 1985* requirements on individual and consolidated accounts, have been amended by the EU Fair Value Directive to allow certain assets to be included in the balance sheet at fair value, and changes in that fair value to be reflected in the profit and loss account. Fair value accounting has been introduced in the UK as an option rather than as a mandatory requirement, and it can be adopted in both individual and consolidated accounts, including those prepared by small or specialised companies, for accounting periods beginning on or after 1 January 2005. The fair value accounting rules operate independently of both the historical cost accounting rules and the alternative accounting rules.

Under the legislation, and subject to specific conditions, the fair value accounting rules can be applied to:

(i)   certain financial instruments:

(ii) investment property; and

(iii) living plants and animals.

In the case of (ii) and (iii) in particular, the legislation specifies that fair value accounting can only be applied where it is permitted under international accounting standards. In the UK, investment property must currently be accounted for in accordance with SSAP 19 'Accounting for Investment Properties' and there are no UK accounting standards at present dealing specifically with living animals and plants. However, the latest version of the ASB's Technical Plan, published in June 2005 includes proposals to:

(i)   introduce a new accounting standard on 'Agriculture' as part of the ASB's project to converge UK accounting with international standards (see 1.6 above) – an exposure draft is expected to be published in the final quarter of 2005, based on the equivalent IAS (IAS 41);

(ii) replace SSAP 19 with a new standard based on the equivalent international standard (IAS 40), although this is not expected to come into effect until 1 January 2008.

The fair value accounting rules are considered in more detail in Chapter 1.

Adopting a policy of valuation under FRS 15

21.28   FRS 15 also permits assets to be revalued, but only where the entity adopts a policy of revaluation. Where such a policy is adopted, it must be applied consistently within a class of tangible fixed assets, and all tangible fixed assets in the same class must be revalued at the same time. However, the revaluation policy need not be applied to all classes of tangible fixed assets. Prior to FRS 15, there was no formal guidance on how frequently tangible fixed assets should be revalued once they had been included in the accounts at a valuation. FRS 15 now clarifies the position by stating that, where a tangible fixed asset is subject to a policy of revaluation, its carrying amount in the accounts should be its current value at the balance sheet date. Current value is defined as the lower of replacement cost and recoverable amount. The guidance in FRS 15 outlines the procedures that should be adopted to achieve this, although formal valuations can be carried out more frequently where appropriate. The guidance also notes that the suggested approach may be inappropriate for charities and other not-for-profit organisations because of the cost implications, and refers these bodies to relevant sector-specific guidance and Statements of Recommended Practice (SORPs).

Keeping property valuations up to date

21.29   In the case of properties, there are two acceptable ways of meeting the requirement to show revalued assets at their current value at the balance sheet date without undertaking a full revaluation each year:

— a full valuation should be carried out at least every five years, with an interim valuation:

— at the end of year three; and

— at the end of years one, two and four if it is likely that there has been material change in value in those years; or

— for portfolios of non-specialised properties, a full valuation may be performed on a rolling basis designed to cover all the properties over a five-year cycle, with an interim valuation on the remaining four-fifths of the portfolio where it is likely that there has been a material change in value.

The second approach can only be adopted where the portfolio consists of a number of broadly similar properties that are likely to be affected by the same market factors, and the properties in the portfolio can be divided on a continuing basis into five groups of a broadly similar spread. A material change in value is described in the standard as a change in value that would reasonably influence the decisions of a user of the accounts. This assessment should take into account the combined impact of all relevant factors (eg physical deterioration, general market price movements).

Full valuation

21.30   A full valuation will usually involve:

— detailed inspection of the interior and exterior of the property;

— inspection of the locality;

— enquiries of local planning and similar authorities; and

— research into market transactions in similar properties, identification of market trends, and application of these to determine the value of the property.

A full valuation must either be carried out by a qualified external valuer, or carried out by a qualified internal valuer and subject to review by a qualified external valuer. Such a review should involve:

(i)   the independent valuation of a sample of properties, representing a genuine cross-section of the entity's property portfolio;

(ii)   the comparison of these valuations with those prepared by the qualified internal valuer; and

(iii)   the expression of a formal opinion on the overall accuracy of the internal valuation on the basis of the results in (i) and (ii) above.

Qualified valuer

21.31   FRS 15 defines a qualified valuer as a person who:

— holds a recognised and relevant professional qualification; and

— has recent post-qualification experience and sufficient knowledge of the state of the market in the location and category of tangible fixed asset being valued.

An internal valuer is a director, officer or employee of the reporting entity. An external valuer is someone who is not a director, officer or employee of the entity, and who has no significant financial interest in the entity.

Interim valuation

21.32   An interim valuation may be carried out by either a qualified external valuer or a qualified internal valuer and includes:

— research into market transactions in similar properties, identification of market trends and the application of these to determine the value of the property under consideration;

— confirmation that there have been no changes of significance to the physical buildings, legal rights or local planning considerations; and

— inspection of the property or locality by the valuer, to the extent considered professionally necessary after taking into account, for instance, recent changes to the property or locality and the date of the last inspection.

Keeping other asset valuations up to date

21.33   In practice, it is comparatively rare for assets other than property to be included in the accounts at valuation. However, FRS 15 caters for this to be done and suggests that, for certain assets (eg cars), there may be a sufficiently active secondhand market, or appropriate indices, which will enable the directors to establish the asset's value with reasonable reliability. In this case the valuation may be updated annually by the directors. Where indices are used, they must:

— be appropriate to the class of asset being valued and to its location and condition, and take account of technological change;

— have a proven record of publication and use; and

— be expected to continue to be available for the foreseeable future.

For other assets, a valuation should be carried out by a qualified valuer at least every five years, with an update (also by a qualified valuer) in year three. Updates should also be carried out in the intervening years if it is likely that there has been a material change in value. If a qualified internal valuer carries out the five-yearly valuation, it should be reviewed by a qualified external valuer.

Valuation basis – properties

21.34   Where a policy of revaluation is adopted, the following valuation bases should be used for properties that are not impaired:

—   non-specialised properties should be valued on the basis of existing use value, with the addition of notional directly attributable acquisition costs where these are material. Where open market value is materially different from existing use value, the open market value and the reasons for the difference should be disclosed in the notes to the accounts;

—   specialised properties should be valued on the basis of depreciated replacement cost;

—   properties that are surplus to the entity's requirements should be valued on the basis of open market value, after deducting expected directly attributable selling costs where these are material.

The terms 'specialised' and 'non-specialised' have the meaning set out in the RICS 'Appraisal and Valuation Manual'. Broadly, specialised properties are those which, due to their specialised nature, are rarely sold on the open market for single occupation for a continuation of their existing use, other than through sale of the business in occupation. They include:

—   oil refineries and chemical works;

—   power stations and dock installations;

—   schools, colleges and universities;

—   hospitals and other specialised health care premises;

—   museums and libraries; and

—   properties whose construction, arrangement, size, specification or location is such that there is no market for them.

The non-specialised category essentially covers all other properties and would normally include shops, offices, standard industrial buildings and warehouses, public houses, garages and residential property.

Impaired properties

21.35   Where there is an indication that the value of a property is impaired, an impairment review should be carried out in accordance with FRS 11 'Impairment of Fixed Assets and Goodwill' and the property should be written down to the lower of its revalued amount and its recoverable amount.

Notional acquisition costs

21.36   Notional acquisition costs directly attributable to the property are costs such as professional fees, duties and non-recoverable taxes. The guidance in the standard notes that the costs of obtaining planning consent, preparing and clearing sites and making site improvements are not included as they will already be reflected in the existing use value. For practical purposes, notional acquisition costs may be ignored if they are not material.

Non-specialised properties valued as businesses

21.37   Certain non-specialised properties are bought and sold as businesses and, therefore, need to be valued as an operational entity. In this case the existing use value of the property should take into account the trading potential of the property but should exclude any personal goodwill created by the present owner and management, as this may not remain with the business if it is sold.

Adaptation works

21.38   Structural changes or special fittings made to meet the needs of individual businesses usually have a low or nil market value because of their specialised nature. If only the shell of the property (ie excluding the adaptation works) is valued using the existing use value, the adaptation works should be included at depreciated replacement cost or depreciated historical cost.

Specialised properties

21.39   As explained at 21.34, specialised properties are not usually sold on the open market and consequently do not have a market value. They are, therefore, valued at depreciated replacement cost. This is defined by the RICS as 'the aggregate amount of the value of the land for the existing use or a notional replacement site in the same locality, and the gross replacement cost of the buildings and other site works, from which appropriate deductions may then be made to allow for the age, condition, economic or functional obsolescence, environmental and other factors; all of these might result in the existing property being worth less to the undertaking in occupation than would a new replacement'. The objective of using depreciated replacement cost is to make a reasonable estimate of the current cost of constructing an asset with the same service potential as the existing property.

Valuation basis – other assets

21.40   Tangible fixed assets other than property should be valued using market value, with the addition of notional directly attributable acquisition costs where these are material. Where assets are surplus to requirements, the expected selling costs should be deducted from market value if material. Where market value is not obtainable, the assets should be valued on the basis of depreciated replacement cost. In this case, depreciated replacement cost is defined as 'the cost of replacing an existing tangible fixed asset with an identical or substantially similar new asset having a similar production or service capacity, from which appropriate deductions are made to reflect the value attributable to the remaining portion of the total useful economic life of the asset and the residual value at the end of the asset's useful economic life.' Costs that are directly attributable to bringing the asset into working condition for its intended use (transportation, installation and commissioning costs, irrecoverable taxes etc) should be included in the value, and the deductions should take account of the age, condition and economic and functional obsolescence of the asset, together with any environmental or other relevant factors. Professional assistance from a qualified valuer will usually be needed in valuing assets at depreciated replacement cost.

Consistency within a class of assets

21.41   Where a tangible fixed asset is revalued, all assets in the same class should be revalued. The only exception permitted by the standard is where it is impossible to obtain a reliable valuation of an asset held outside the UK and the Republic of Ireland, but this situation is expected to be rare in practice. If an asset is excluded from the valuation on these grounds, the accounts must disclose the carrying value of the asset and the fact that it has not been revalued.

Accounting entries on revaluation of assets

21.42   Where a tangible fixed asset is to be included in the accounts at valuation rather than historical cost, the following steps should usually be taken:

—   compare the valuation figure for the asset in question with its net book value at the date of the valuation to calculate the uplift required;

—   adjust both the original cost of the fixed asset and cumulative depreciation to date, so that the cost of the asset becomes the valuation figure and cumulative depreciation to the date of valuation is eliminated; and

—   credit the net adjustment to the revaluation reserve.

The important point to note is that the cumulative depreciation to date is not written back to the profit and loss account but forms part of the credit to the revaluation reserve.

Example 21.6 – Incorporating a revaluation of fixed assets

B Ltd has freehold land and buildings with an original cost of £70,000. The buildings, which have an original cost of £50,000 are being depreciated over a life of 50 years.

B Ltd's accounting date is 31 December.

The land and buildings are professionally valued at £95,000 at 31 December 20X2 and this valuation is to be incorporated in the accounts at 31 December 20X2.

The net book value of the land and buildings at 1 January 20X2 was as follows.

	£
Cost:	
Land	20,000
Buildings	50,000
	70,000
Depreciation:	
Buildings	(6,000)
Net book value at 1 January 20X2	64,000

There have been no movements in land and buildings during the year.

As the valuation is at 31 December 20X2, a full year's depreciation charge must be incorporated for 20X2 (ie £1,000). This will reduce the net book value at 31 December 20X2 to £63,000. The uplift required to incorporate the valuation is therefore £32,000 (ie £95,000 – £63,000). This should be accounted for as follows.

Land and buildings at cost at 1 January 20X2	70,000
Surplus on revaluation	25,000
Land and buildings at valuation at 31 December 20X2	95,000
Depreciation at 1 January 20X2	6,000
Depreciation for 2002	1,000
Adjustment on revaluation	(7,000)
Depreciation at 31 December 20X2	0

The entries in the revaluation reserve will be as follows:

Dr Fixed assets – land and buildings cost	25,000	
Cr Revaluation reserve		25,000
Dr Fixed assets – depreciation	7,000	
Cr Revaluation reserve		7,000

Resulting in a credit balance of £32,000 on the revaluation reserve.

Alternative approach where depreciated replacement cost is used

21.43 FRS 15 allows an alternative approach to be adopted where the valuation is calculated on the basis of depreciated replacement cost. In this case, both the cost (or revalued amount) and the accumulated depreciation at the date of revaluation can be adjusted, so that the net carrying amount of the asset after revaluation equals the revalued amount.

Example 21.7 – Alternative approach

C Ltd has a specialised property with an original cost of £70,000 on which depreciation of £5,000 has been charged to date. The property is revalued at depreciated replacement cost as follows:

	£
Gross replacement cost	120,000
Adjustments	(25,000)
Depreciated replacement cost	95,000

Under the alternative approach this could be incorporated into the accounts as:

	£
Original cost	70,000
Gain on revaluation	50,000
	120,000
Depreciation to date	5,000
Adjustment on revaluation	20,000
	25,000
Net book value	95,000

The net credit to the revaluation reserve is still £30,000 (ie £50,000 less £20,000).

Depreciation in the year of valuation

21.44   Depreciation should continue to be charged in the year in which the valuation takes place, even though it may subsequently be eliminated when the valuation is incorporated into the accounts. This is considered in more detail in Chapter 12.

Recognition of revaluation gains

21.45   A revaluation gain should only be recognised in the profit and loss account to the extent that it reverses a revaluation loss already recognised in the profit and loss account. The gain that is recognised in the profit and loss account should be reduced by the amount of depreciation that would have been charged on the asset if the original revaluation loss had not been recognised. All other revaluation gains must be recognised in the statement of total recognised gains and losses.

Example 21.8 – Recognition of revaluation gains

D Ltd has a property with an original cost of £70,000. This was revalued in 20X0 at £65,000. Depreciation is charged at 2% pa. In 20X2 the property is revalued again at £75,000.

The surplus on the second revaluation is accounted for as follows:

	£
Original cost	70,000
Loss on first revaluation	(5,000)
Revalued amount	65,000
Less: 2 years' depreciation at 2% on 65,000	(2,600)
Carrying amount in accounts	62,400
Gain on second revaluation	12,600
	75,000

The amount of the gain recognised in the profit and loss account is:

Loss previously recognised in profit and loss account	5,000
Less: additional depreciation that would have been charged if loss had not been recognised:	
5,000 × 2% for 2 years	(200)
Gain to be recognised in profit and loss account	4,800

The remaining gain of £7,800 (ie £12,600 – £4,800) should be recognised in the statement of total recognised gains and losses.

The amount actually charged to the profit and loss account for the two years is:

Original loss on revaluation	5,000
Actual depreciation for the two years	2,600
Gain subsequently recognised	(4,800)
	2,800

This is equivalent to two years' depreciation on the original cost of £70,000 (ie £70,000 × 2% × 2 years) – the amount that would have been charged if the first revaluation had not taken place.

Recognition of revaluation losses

21.46   All revaluation losses that are caused by a clear consumption of economic benefits (eg physical damage or a deterioration in the quality of service provided by the asset) must be recognised in the profit and loss account. Other revaluation losses (eg those resulting from a general decline in the market) should be recognised in the statement of total recognised gains and losses until the carrying amount of the asset reaches depreciated historical cost. Any further loss should be recognised in the profit and loss account. The only exception permitted by the standard is where the recoverable amount of the asset is demonstrably greater than its revalued amount. In this case, the difference between recoverable amount and revalued amount should be recognised in the statement of total recognised gains and losses, with any further loss recognised in the profit and loss account.

No aggregation of gains and losses

21.47   Material gains and losses on individual assets within a class of assets must not be aggregated when determining the performance statement in which gains and losses should be recognised.

Transitional arrangements under FRS 15

21.48   There may be entities who do not wish to adopt a policy of revaluation of tangible fixed assets under the requirements of FRS 15, but who have revalued certain assets in previous years when the requirements were not as stringent. FRS 15 provides two options to cater for this situation:

— the entity can retain the book amounts (ie the previously revalued amounts) of these assets, subject to the requirement to test for impairment under FRS 11 'Impairment of Fixed Assets and Goodwill', provided that the accounts disclose:

— the fact that the transitional provisions of FRS 15 are being followed;

— the fact that the valuation has not been updated; and

— the date of the last valuation; or

— the entity can restate the carrying amounts of the previously revalued assets to historical cost, less any equivalent accumulated depreciation, as a prior period adjustment arising on a change in accounting policy.

The first of these transitional arrangements can only be used when FRS 15 is first implemented (ie it cannot be used to justify a failure to keep subsequent valuations up to date as required by the standard).

PRINCIPAL ACCOUNTS DISCLOSURES

Movements in the year

21.49   CA 1985 and FRS 15 require considerable detail to be disclosed on the movements in both cost and depreciation during the year. This is usually presented in the form of a table in the notes to the accounts. The Act requires the disclosures to be given separately for the categories of asset identified in the legislation. FRS 15 requires the details to be given for each class of asset, as defined in the standard (see 21.4 and 21.5 above). The specific disclosures required are:

— cost or valuation at the beginning of the year and at the balance sheet date;

— the effect of any revaluation during the year;

— any additions during the year;

— any disposals during the year;

— any transfers during the year;

— the cumulative amount of depreciation at the beginning of the year and at the balance sheet date;

— the amount provided for depreciation during the year;

— any adjustments to depreciation in respect of disposals during the year;

— any other adjustments to depreciation during the year.

Example 21.9 – Movements in cost and depreciation

	Land and buildings	Plant and machinery	Fixtures, fittings, tools and equipment	Assets in the course of construction	Total
	£'000	£'000	£'000	£'000	£'000
Cost:					
Balance at 1.1.X2	369	547	57	27	1,000
Additions	5	36	9	10	60
Disposals	(3)	(15)	—	—	(18)
Transfers	—	37	—	(37)	—
Revaluation	79	—	—	—	79
Balance at 31.12.X2	450	605	66	—	1,121
Depreciation:					
Balance at 1.1.X2	56	321	27	—	404
Charge for the year	17	82	4	—	103
Eliminated on disposal	(3)	(12)	—	—	(15)
Revaluation	(70)	—	—	–	(70)
Balance at 31.12.X2	—	391	31	—	422
Net book value:					
At 31.12.X2	450	214	35	—	699
At 31.12.X1	313	226	30	27	596

Additional disclosures are required where interest has been capitalised as part of the cost of certain assets (see 21.23 above)

Disclosures in respect of revalued assets

21.50   Where certain assets are included in the accounts at valuation rather than historical cost, the following details must be given by class of revalued asset in each reporting period:

— the name and qualifications of the valuer(s) or the valuer's organisation and a description of its nature;

— the basis (or bases) of valuation, including whether notional directly attributable acquisition costs have been included, or expected selling costs deducted;

— the dates and amounts of the valuations;

— where historical cost records are available, the carrying amount that would have been included in the financial statements if the tangible fixed assets had been included at historical cost less depreciation, and the cumulative figures for depreciation or diminutions in value that would have been included in the accounts under the historical cost accounting rules;

— whether the person (or persons) carrying out the valuation is internal or external to the entity;

— where the directors are not aware of any material change in value and the valuation has therefore not been updated, a statement to that effect;

— where the valuation has not been updated, or is not a full valuation, the date of the last full valuation.

The following details must also be given for revalued properties:

— where properties have been valued as fully-equipped operational entities, having regard to their trading potential, a statement to that effect and the carrying amount of those properties; and

— where material, the total amount of notional directly attributable acquisition costs included in the carrying amount, or the total amount of expected selling costs deducted.

All of this information will usually be set out in a note below the fixed assets table.

Disclosures required by the RICS

21.51   Practice Statement 7 in the RICS 'Appraisal and Valuation Manual' also requires specific disclosures to be given in the accounts. Some of these overlap with the requirements of the Act and FRS 15, but some are additional to those requirements:

— the name and qualification of the valuer or the valuer's organisation and a description of its nature;

— whether the valuer is internal, external or independent;

— the date and basis of the valuation;

— confirmation that the valuation has been made in accordance with the RICS 'Appraisal and Valuation Manual' (or a named alternative where relevant), or the extent of, and reasons for, any departure;

— where valuation figures are given, the valuation basis and full details of any special assumptions adopted;

— where a definition is included, the whole of the definition;

— where the publication includes statements attributed to the valuer on the prospect of future growth in rent and/or capital values, a statement that such growth may not occur and that values can fall as well as rise; and

— where relevant, a statement that the property has been valued as a fully-equipped operational entity and with regard to its trading potential.

Written consent

21.52 The company should obtain written consent from the valuer before including his name in the accounts and the valuer will usually be responsible for ensuring that the disclosures are accurate and adequate and that there is no risk of the reader being misled. The precise wording must, therefore, be discussed and agreed with the valuer in each case.

Example disclosure

21.53 The details disclosed will inevitably vary depending on the circumstances of each case, but wording along the following lines will usually be appropriate:

Example 21.10 – Disclosures for revalued assets

Accounts for the year ended 31 December 20X2

The company's freehold property was professionally valued at £250,000 at 31 December 20X1. The valuation was carried out externally by Messrs ...., Chartered Surveyors, on the basis of open market value for existing use and in accordance with the RICS 'Appraisal and Valuation Manual'. No notional directly attributable acquisition costs were included in the valuation on the grounds that these would not be material.

If the freehold property had been included in the accounts at historical cost, it would have been included at the following amount:

	£
Cost	120,000
Accumulated depreciation	(9,000)
	£111,000

The directors are not aware of any material change in the value of the property since 31 December 20X1 and the valuation has, therefore, not been updated in the current year.

IMPAIRMENT REVIEWS

The need to carry out an impairment review

21.54 Impairment is defined in FRS 11 'Impairment of Fixed Assets and Goodwill' as a reduction in the recoverable amount of a fixed asset or goodwill below its carrying amount. Under this standard, an impairment review should be carried out when events or changes in circumstances indicate that the carrying value of a fixed asset (including goodwill) may not be recoverable. A review will, therefore, not necessarily be required every year – it will usually only need to be carried out when something has happened to the asset or to the economic environment in which the asset is used. The systematic charging of depreciation will usually ensure that the carrying amount of a fixed asset is reduced throughout its useful life to reflect the reduction in the asset's recoverable amount arising from the consumption of economic benefits. FRS 11, therefore, notes that, for most assets, impairments should be a relatively infrequent addition to normal depreciation. However, FRS 15 requires an annual impairment review to be carried out when an asset is not depreciated or when its remaining useful economic life exceeds 50 years.

Events and changes that might prompt a review

21.55   FRS 11 gives examples of events and changes that may indicate impairment of an asset has occurred. These include:

— a current operating loss or net cash outflow, combined with either similar losses or outflows in the past, or the expected continuation of losses or outflows in the future;

— a significant decline in the market value of an asset;

— physical damage or obsolescence;

— a significant adverse change in the business or market in which the asset is used (eg a major new competitor);

— a significant adverse change in the statutory or other regulatory environment in which the business operates;

— a significant adverse change in any indicator (such as turnover) used to measure the fair value of the asset at the time of acquisition;

— a commitment by management to undertake a major reorganisation.

The standard emphasises that the useful economic lives and residual values of the assets affected may also need to be reviewed in these circumstances (see Chapter 12). Even if the assets are not actually impaired, their expected useful lives and residual values may have changed.

Separate requirements for intangible assets and goodwill

21.56   FRS 10 'Goodwill and Intangible Assets' imposes more specific requirements for impairment reviews in the case of goodwill and intangible assets. Separate requirements apply depending on the period over which the intangible asset or goodwill is being amortised. Goodwill and intangible assets, amortised over a finite period of 20 years or less from the date of acquisition, should be reviewed for impairment at the end of the first full financial year following acquisition (and the standard permits a less extensive review process to be used for this) and in other periods if events or changes in circumstances indicate that the carrying value of the asset or goodwill may not be recoverable. Goodwill and intangible assets amortised over a period of more than 20 years from the date of acquisition, and any that are not amortised, must be reviewed for impairment at the end of each reporting period. Further details are given in Chapter 20.

Fixed assets not held to generate cash flows

21.57   The guidance in FRS 11 notes that, where fixed assets are not held for the purpose of generating cash flows, either individually or in conjunction with other assets (for instance, certain fixed assets held for charitable purposes), it may not be appropriate to write down the asset to recoverable amount on the basis of expected future cash flows. In this case, an alternative measure of service potential may be more appropriate.

Measuring impairment losses

21.58   When an impairment review is required, it should be carried out by comparing the carrying amount of the fixed asset with its recoverable amount. Recoverable amount is defined as the higher of net realisable value and value in use. Net realisable value is the amount at which the asset could be disposed of, less any direct selling costs. Value in use is the present value of the future cash flows obtainable as a result of the asset's continued use, including those resulting from its ultimate disposal. If the carrying value of the asset exceeds its recoverable amount, it is impaired and should be written down to the recoverable amount.

Using net realisable value

21.59   The first stage in an impairment review will usually be to estimate the net realisable value of the asset. If this is higher than the carrying amount, the asset is not impaired and no further work is required. If net realisable value is lower than the carrying amount of the asset, value in use will need to be established to see whether this is higher or lower than net realisable value. Even in this case, detailed value in use calculations will not always be required – a simple estimate will often be sufficient to indicate whether or not value in use is more than the carrying value of the asset (in which case there is no impairment) or less than net realisable value (in which case net realisable value will form the basis for recoverable amount). If value in use is lower than carrying value but higher than net realisable value, the impairment write-down will be based on value in use rather than on net realisable value, and more detailed calculations of value in use will be needed. If it is not possible to make a reliable estimate of net realisable value, the comparison of carrying amount with recoverable amount will need to be based on detailed calculations of value in use.

Impact of taxation

21.60   The guidance in FRS 11 emphasises that, in establishing whether recoverable amounts should be based on net realisable value or value in use, the deferred tax balances that would arise in each case must be taken into account. For example:

Example 21.11 – Impact of tax on recoverable amount

	Net realisable value £	Value in use £
Asset value	100	110
Tax effect	(30)	(45)
	70	65

Although value in use may appear to be higher than net realisable value, after taking account of the tax effects in this case, it is clear that recoverable amount should be based on net realisable value and not on value in use.

Calculating net realisable value

21.61   Where an asset is traded on an active market, net realisable value should be based on market value. In other cases, it will be necessary to estimate the amount at which the asset could be disposed of. Any direct selling costs relating to the disposal of the asset, such as legal costs and stamp duty, should be deducted in arriving at net realisable value. The guidance in the standard also notes that costs relating to the removal of a sitting tenant are direct costs of selling the relevant building. However, costs that relate to a reduction or reorganisation of the business rather than the sale of the fixed asset are not direct selling costs and should not be taken into account.

Calculating value in use

21.62   The value in use of an asset is the present value of the future cash flows obtainable from the continued use of the asset and from its ultimate disposal. The standard requires value in use to be calculated for individual fixed assets wherever possible. In practice, it will often not be possible to calculate cash flows for an individual fixed asset. Cash flows normally result from the use of a group of assets and liabilities rather than from individual assets. In these circumstances, value in use can only be calculated for each group of assets and liabilities. The standard describes such a group of assets and liabilities as an income-generating unit. However, the guidance does note that only material impairments need to be identified and it may, therefore, be acceptable in certain circumstances to consider a group of income-generating units together rather than individually.

Identifying income-generating units

21.63 An income-generating unit is defined as:

'A group of assets, liabilities and associated goodwill that generates income that is largely independent of the reporting entity's other income streams. The assets and liabilities include those directly involved in generating the income and an appropriate proportion of those used to generate more than one income stream.'

Income-generating units should be identified by dividing the total income of the entity into as many largely independent income streams as is reasonably practicable. The individual income streams identified should be capable of being monitored separately and the units should be as small as is reasonably practicable. This approach is consistent with the normal prohibition on portfolio accounting. In practice, the income streams identified will usually reflect the way in which management monitors the business and takes decisions on the continuation or discontinuation of different lines of business. Income-generating units might be identified by reference to major products or services, or by reference to individual intangible assets, such as brands. The standard includes a number of examples showing how income-generating units might be identified in particular circumstances:

— a transport company running a network of trunk routes fed by a number of supporting routes, where decisions on continuing or closing the supporting routes are based on the contribution made to returns generated by the trunk routes – an income-generating unit comprises a trunk route plus the supporting routes associated with it;

— a manufacturer producing a product at a number of sites, not all of which are operating at full capacity so that the manufacturer can choose how much to make at each site, but with insufficient surplus capacity to enable any one site to be closed – the income-generating unit comprises all the sites at which the product can be made;

— a restaurant chain with a large number of restaurants throughout the country, for which cash flows can be individually monitored and to which costs can be allocated sensibly – each restaurant is an income-generating unit, although it may be acceptable to group together restaurants affected by the same economic factors;

— an entity with three stages of production:

   — growing and felling trees, some of the timber being transferred to the second production stage and some being sold externally;

   — creating parts of wooden furniture, all of which are transferred to the final production stage; and

   — assembling the parts into finished goods.

The first production stage forms an income-generating unit, and stages two and three together form a separate income-generating unit. The guidance notes that the cash flows for the two units should be based on market prices for the timber and not on any internal transfer pricing arrangements that may be in place.

Allocation of assets and liabilities

21.64   All of the assets and liabilities of the entity other than taxation, interest-bearing debt, dividends payable and other items relating wholly to financing, should be allocated to, or apportioned between, the income-generating units. The guidance notes that the income stream of a fixed asset that is awaiting disposal will be largely independent of the income streams of other assets and the asset should, therefore, be treated as a separate income-generating unit. Also, if there is any working capital in the balance sheet that will generate cash flows equal to its carrying amount, the guidance allows the carrying amount to be excluded from the value of the income-generating units and the cash flows to be excluded from the value in use calculations.

Allocation of central assets

21.65   In some cases it will be clear that individual assets and liabilities are directly related to the activities of one income-generating unit. In other cases, central assets may need to be apportioned across all the income-generating units on a logical and systematic basis. Central assets might include group and regional head offices and working capital. The total of the carrying amounts of the income-generating units should equal the carrying amount of the net assets (other than financing and taxation) of the entity as a whole. FRS 11 para 30 illustrates how this might work in practice:

Example 21.12 – Allocation of central assets

An entity has three independent income streams with the following directly involved net assets:

A   Net assets of 100 million
B   Net assets of 150 million
C   Net assets of 200 million

In addition, there are head office net assets of £18 million, which are used by the three income streams in the proportion 2:3:4.

The income-generating units are defined as follows:

	A	*B*	*C*	*Total*
	£m	£m	£m	£m
Net assets directly attributable	100	150	200	450
Head office net assets	4	6	8	18
Total	104	156	208	468

If a fixed asset in income-generating unit B was thought to be impaired, the recoverable amount of B should be compared with its carrying value of £156 million and the cash flows of B should include the relevant proportion of any cash outflows resulting from the central overheads.

Central assets that cannot sensibly be allocated

21.66   The standard acknowledges that, in some cases, it will not be possible to allocate certain central assets across the income-generating units in a sensible or logical manner. In this case, it requires the impairment review to be completed in two stages:

—   the carrying amount of assets allocated directly to each individual income-generating unit should be compared with the value in use of the unit;

—   the central assets should be tested for impairment by comparing the carrying value of all the income-generating units to which the central assets contribute, with the combined value in use of those units.

Example 21.13 – Testing central assets for impairment

Using the details in Example 21.12, but assuming that the central net assets cannot be sensibly allocated between the income-generating units, the first stage would be to compare the recoverable amount of B with its carrying value of £150 million in this case, and the second stage would be to compare the recoverable amount of the entity as a whole with its overall carrying value of £468 million.

Capitalised goodwill

21.67   Goodwill should be allocated to income-generating units in the same way as other assets and liabilities. However, where a number of income-generating units are acquired together as one investment, the units may be combined in order to assess the recoverability of the goodwill. This will also require the impairment review to be carried out in two stages:

—   the income-generating units should be reviewed individually to assess the recoverability of tangible fixed assets and any intangible assets that have been capitalised;

—   the combined units should then be reviewed to assess the recoverability of the goodwill.

FRS 11 para 35 illustrates this as follows:

Example 21.14 – Combining units to review goodwill

An entity acquires a business with three income-generating units. After five years, the carrying amount of the net assets in the units and the purchased goodwill compares with value in use as follows:

	A	*B*	*C*	*Goodwill*	*Total*
	£m	£m	£m	£m	£m
Carrying amount	80	120	140	50	390
Value in use	100	140	120		360

An impairment loss of £20 million should be recognised in respect of unit C to reduce its carrying amount to £120 million. This will reduce the total carrying amount of the entity to £370 million. A further impairment loss of £10 million will need to be recognised in respect of the goodwill to reduce the overall carrying amount of the entity to its value in use of £360 million.

Cash flows

21.68   The value in use of the individual income-generating units is the present value of the future cash flows obtainable as a result of their continued use and ultimate disposal. The standard requires the expected future cash flows, which should include those relating to any central overheads allocated to the units, to be:

— based on reasonable and supportable assumptions; and

— consistent with the most up-to-date budgets and plans already approved by management.

Cash flows for future periods not covered by formal plans and budgets should assume a steady or declining growth rate not exceeding the long-term average growth rate for the country or countries in which the business operates. The guidance notes that higher growth rates may be assumed in exceptional circumstances, for example, where the long-term growth rate for the industry is expected to be significantly higher than the average growth rate for the relevant country, and the business is expected to grow as rapidly as the industry as a whole, after allowing for the likelihood of new competitors. Specific additional disclosures are required in the accounts in any case where:

— the period before a steady or declining long-term growth rate has been assumed extends to more than five years; or

— the long-term growth rate used exceeds the long-term average growth rate for the country or countries in which the business operates.

Newly acquired units

21.69   The general rule is that future cash flows should be estimated for individual assets or income-generating units in their current condition. In particular they should not include:

— future cash outflows or related cost savings (eg reduced staff costs) or benefits expected to arise from a future reorganisation for which provision has not yet been made; or

— future capital expenditure that will improve or enhance the asset or income-generating unit in excess of the originally assessed standard of performance, or the related future benefits of this future expenditure.

However, in the case of a newly acquired income-generating unit (eg a new subsidiary), the standard acknowledges that the purchase price will often reflect the expected opportunities for making more effective use of the assets as a result of the acquisition. In some cases, the purchaser will undertake related capital expenditure, and possibly a reorganisation of the business, in order to maximise the benefits from its investment. In this situation, the standard allows the impairment review to take into account the costs and benefits of capital expenditure and reorganisations anticipated in the period up to the end of the first full year after acquisition, provided that they are consistent with management's budgets and plans at that time. If the capital expenditure or reorganisation does not take place as planned, the costs and benefits should be excluded from the cash flow projections prepared for subsequent impairment reviews. Failure to carry out the planned investment or reorganisation may be an indication that assets have become impaired and thus necessitate an impairment review.

Discount rates

21.70 The standard requires the expected future cash flows of an income-generating unit to be discounted at an estimate of the rate that the market would expect on an equally risky investment. The guidance notes that discount rates may be estimated by reference to:

— the rate implicit in market transactions of similar assets;

— the current weighted average cost of capital of a listed company whose cash flows have similar risk profiles to those of the income-generating unit;

— the weighted average cost of capital for the entity, provided that this is adjusted for the specific risks associated with the income-generating unit under review – the guidance emphasises that, if discount rates were calculated for each individual income-generating unit, the weighted average discount rate should equal the entity's overall weighted average cost of capital.

The standard requires the discount rate to be a pre-tax rate, and guidance is given in Appendix I to the standard on making appropriate adjustments to the weighted average cost of capital (which will be a post-tax rate). If cash flows are expressed in current prices, a real discount rate should be used, but if cash flows use expected future prices, a nominal discount rate will be used. In all cases, the discount rate used should be disclosed in the accounts.

Reflecting risk

21.71   As noted above, the standard requires the discount rate to reflect the risks associated with the cash flows by requiring the discount rate to be equivalent to the rate that the market would expect on an equally risky investment. The guidance explains that, as an alternative, it may be acceptable for the cash flows to be adjusted for risk and then discounted at a risk-free rate. The important point is to ensure that risk is not double-counted, for instance, by adjusting the cash flows for risk and then reflecting risk again in the discount rate that is applied to the adjusted cash flows. Where a risk-free discount rate is used, the accounts should include an indication of the risk adjustments that have been made to the cash flows.

Subsequent monitoring of cash flows

21.72   The standard includes specific measures to prevent abuse of the somewhat subjective and judgmental issues inevitably involved in basing impairment reviews on assessments of value in use. In each case, where an impairment review has involved the calculation of value in use, the actual cash flows must be compared with the projected cash flows for the five years following the review. Where the actual cash flows are significantly different from those forecast, such that a more accurate projection of the cash flows might have required the recognition of an impairment loss, the standard requires the original calculations to be reworked on the basis of the actual cash flows, but without altering other assumptions. Any impairment identified in the exercise must be recognised in the current period. The only exception is where the impairment has subsequently reversed and the recognition of the reversal would have been permitted under the strict requirements set out in the standard. In this case, the original impairment and its subsequent reversal must be disclosed in the accounts.

ACCOUNTING FOR IMPAIRMENT LOSSES

General rule

21.73   The general rule is that an impairment loss (ie the difference between the carrying amount of a fixed asset or goodwill and its recoverable amount) should be recognised in the profit and loss account of the period. However, a different approach is required in the case of fixed assets that have previously been revalued, as explained in 21.74 below.

Revalued fixed assets

21.74   If an impairment loss relating to a revalued fixed asset is caused by a clear consumption of economic benefits (for example, physical damage or a deterioration in the quality of service provided by the asset), it should be recognised in the profit and loss account. Other impairments of revalued assets (for instance, those arising from a general fall in prices) should be recognised in the statement of total recognised gains and losses until the carrying amount of the asset reaches its depreciated historical cost. Any further reduction below this amount should be recognised in the profit and loss account. It is important to keep detailed records of where impairment losses are recognised, in case reversals of the losses should need to be recognised in subsequent years.

Reversal of an impairment loss

21.75   The standard sets out different rules on the recognition of a reversal of an impairment loss for tangible fixed assets and investments, and for intangible assets and goodwill:

— in the case of tangible fixed assets and investments for which an impairment loss has been recognised, if the recoverable amount increases as a result of a change in economic conditions or in the expected use of the asset, the reversal should be recognised to the extent that it increases the carrying amount of the asset up to the amount that it would have been if the original impairment had not occurred;

— in the case of intangible assets and goodwill, the reversal of an impairment loss should only be recognised if:

— an external event caused the recognition of the impairment loss in previous periods and subsequent external events clearly and demonstrably reverse the effects of that event in a way that was not foreseen in the original impairment calculations; or

— the impairment loss arose on an intangible asset with a readily ascertainable market value and the net realisable value based on that market value has increased to above the asset's carrying amount.

Tangible fixed assets and investments

21.76   Events and circumstances that indicate an increase in the recoverable amount of an impaired asset are likely to be the reverse of those used in the standard to illustrate when impairment may have occurred. The guidance notes that they might include situations where capital investment or a reorganisation of the business, the benefits of which were excluded from the original calculations, have increased the recoverable amount of existing assets. However, increases in value that arise simply from the passage of time (eg increases in the discounted value of future cash inflows as they become closer) should not be recognised in the accounts. Any reversal recognised should only increase the asset to the value at which it would have been shown in the accounts if the original impairment loss had not been recognised. The recognition of any further increase in value would constitute a revaluation of the asset.

Intangible assets and goodwill

21.77 More stringent requirements apply in the case of intangible assets and goodwill and the approach in FRS 11 is consistent with that in FRS 10 'Goodwill and Intangible Assets'. Once again, where the recognition of a reversal is permitted by the standard, it should only increase the carrying amount of the goodwill or intangible asset to the amount at which it would have been shown if the original impairment loss had not been recognised. The recognition of any further increase in value would constitute a revaluation. FRS 10 specifically prohibits the revaluation of goodwill but permits the revaluation of intangible assets in certain circumstances as described in Chapter 19.

Recognition of a reversal of an impairment loss

21.78 The reversal of an impairment loss should be recognised in the profit and loss account of the current period unless it relates to a revalued asset, in which case it should be recognised in the profit and loss account to the extent that the original impairment loss (adjusted for subsequent depreciation) was recognised in the profit and loss account, and any additional amount should be recognised in the statement of total recognised gains and losses. It is, therefore, important to keep detailed records of where impairment losses are recognised, in case reversals of the losses should need to be recognised in subsequent years. In the year in which it is recognised, the accounts should disclose the reason for the reversal of the original impairment loss, including any changes in assumptions upon which the calculation of recoverable amount is based.

Allocation of impairment losses

21.79 The carrying amounts of the income-generating units under review should be calculated as the net of the carrying amounts of the assets, liabilities and goodwill allocated to the unit. To the extent that the carrying amount of the unit exceeds its recoverable amount, the unit is impaired. In the absence of an obvious impairment of specific assets within the unit, the impairment should be allocated in the following order:

— first, to any goodwill in the unit;

— then, to any capitalised intangible asset in the unit (subject to the proviso set out below); and

— finally, to the tangible assets in the unit, on a pro-rata or more appropriate basis (subject to the proviso below).

This allocation aims to write down the assets with the most subjective valuation first. However, no intangible asset with a readily ascertainable market value should be written down below its net realisable value. Similarly, no tangible asset with a net realisable value that can be measured reliably should be written down below its net realisable value. The standard gives the following example of the allocation and reversal of impairment losses:

Example 21.15 – Allocation and reversal of impairment losses

The recoverable amount of an income-generating unit falls to £60 million compared with a carrying amount of £140 million as a result of the product it makes being overtaken by a technologically advanced model produced by a competitor. The impairment loss is allocated as follows:

	Carrying amount	Impairment	Revised amount
	£m	£m	£m
Goodwill	40	(40)	
Patent (with no market value)	20	(20)	
Tangible fixed assets	80	(20)	60
	140	(80)	60

After three years, the company makes a technological breakthrough of its own and the recoverable amount of the income-generating unit increases to £90 million. If the impairment had not occurred, the carrying value of the tangible fixed assets would have been £70 million.

The reversal of the impairment loss is recognised to the extent that it increases the carrying amount of the fixed assets to what it would have been if the original impairment had not been recognised – ie £10 million of the impairment loss is reversed to increase the carrying value of tangible fixed assets to £70 million.

No reversal is recognised in respect of the impairment of the goodwill and intangible asset, because the effect of the external event that caused the impairment has not reversed (ie the original product has still been overtaken by a more advanced model).

Goodwill in a merged business

21.80   Where an acquired business is merged with an existing business it will result in an income-generating unit that contains both purchased and internally-generated goodwill (ie goodwill that is not allowed to be recognised for accounts purposes). In this case, a notional adjustment should be made to the carrying amount of the income-generating unit to take account of the goodwill of the existing business at the date of the acquisition so that any future impairment can be apportioned between the two elements of the merged business. The process will, therefore, be as follows:

—   the notional carrying amount of the internally-generated goodwill should be estimated by deducting the fair values of the net assets and purchased goodwill within the existing income-generating unit from its estimated value in use before the combination with the acquired business – the notional goodwill should be assumed to be subject to the same pattern of amortisation as the purchased goodwill;

— the notional value of the internally-generated goodwill of the existing business should be added to the carrying amount of the income generating unit for the purposes of performing impairment reviews;

— any impairment of the existing business will have been recognised in the comparison of fair values with value in use in the first stage above – any impairment arising on merging the businesses should, therefore, be allocated solely to the purchased goodwill within the newly-acquired business;

— subsequent impairments should be allocated between the goodwill of the acquired business and that of the existing business, pro rata to their carrying values;

— the impairment allocated to the existing business should be allocated first to the notional internally-generated goodwill; and

— only the impairments allocated to purchased goodwill (and, if necessary, to any recognised intangible or tangible assets) should be recognised in the financial statements.

Paragraph 53 of the standard includes an example of this process. The calculations will need to be carried out whenever an acquisition that gives rise to goodwill is merged with an existing business.

Presentation of impairment losses

21.81   Impairment losses recognised in the profit and loss account should be included within operating profit under the appropriate statutory heading and disclosed as an exceptional item if appropriate. Impairment losses recognised in the statement of total recognised gains and losses should be disclosed separately on the face of that statement. In the notes to the financial statements for accounting periods after the impairment, the impairment loss should be treated as follows:

— for assets held on a historical cost basis, the impairment loss should be included within cumulative depreciation – the cost of the asset should not be reduced;

— for revalued assets held at market value (eg existing use or open market value), the impairment loss should be included within the revalued carrying amount; and

— for revalued assets held at depreciated replacement cost:

    — an impairment loss charged to the profit and loss account should be included within cumulative depreciation (ie the carrying amount of the asset should not be reduced); and

    — an impairment loss charged to the statement of total recognised gains and losses should be deducted from the carrying amount of the asset.

Additional disclosures

21.82   The standard requires the following additional disclosures in the notes to the financial statements:

— if the impairment loss is measured by reference to the value in use of a fixed asset or income-generating unit, the discount rate applied to the cash flows should be disclosed – if a risk-free discount rate is used, some indication of the risk adjustment made to the cash flows should be given;

— where an impairment loss previously recognised is reversed in the current period, the financial statements should disclose the reason for the reversal, including any changes in the assumptions upon which the calculation of recoverable amount is based;

— where an impairment loss would have been recognised in an earlier period if the forecasts of future cash flows had been more accurate, but the impairment has reversed and recognition of the reversal is permitted, the impairment now identified, and its subsequent reversal, should be disclosed;

— where, in measuring value in use, the period before a steady or declining long-term growth rate has been assumed to extend to more than five years, the length of the longer period and the circumstances justifying it should be disclosed;

— where, in measuring value in use, the long-term growth rate used has exceeded the long-term average growth rate for the country or countries in which the business operates, the growth rate assumed and the circumstances justifying it should be disclosed.

INVESTMENT PROPERTIES

Treatment under accounting standards

21.83   For accounting periods beginning before 1 January 2005, the expression 'investment property' is not used in CA 1985 and no distinction is made in the legislation between accounting for investment properties and accounting for other properties shown as tangible fixed assets in the accounts. In contrast, accounting standards require totally different accounting treatments for investment properties and other properties included in tangible fixed assets. FRS 15 'Tangible Fixed Assets' covers all other tangible fixed assets but does not apply to investment properties. SSAP 19 'Accounting for Investment Properties' sets out the accounting treatment to be adopted for this particular category of property. As is usual with accounting standards, the requirements of SSAP 19 need not be applied to immaterial items. The materiality of an investment property should, therefore, be considered in the context of the company's other assets. For instance, if a large manufacturing company with several freehold production sites also holds one relatively small investment property, it will not usually be necessary to apply SSAP 19 to the investment property.

For accounting periods beginning on or after 1 January 2005, Schedule 4 to CA 1985 is amended to allow fair value accounting to be applied to investment properties, but only where this treatment is permitted by international accounting standards. In the UK, the accounting treatment adopted must continue to comply with SSAP 19 at present. As part of its project to converge UK accounting requirements with international accounting standards (see 1.6 above), the ASB plans to replace SSAP 19 with the equivalent international standard (IAS 40) in due course, but this new standard is not expected to come into effect until 1 January 2008. Further details on the fair value accounting rules can be found at 21.27 above and in Chapter 1.

Definition of investment property

21.84   An investment property is defined in SSAP 19 as an interest in land and buildings:

—   in respect of which construction work and development have been completed; and

—   which is held for its investment potential, any rental income being negotiated at arm's length.

Investment properties may be held by a company specialising in investments, such as an investment trust or a property investment company, or may be held by a company which has a different business as its main activity. However, a property owned and occupied by a company for its own purpose, or let to and occupied by another group company, is specifically excluded from the definition of an investment property.

Need for different treatment

21.85   The introductory note to SSAP 19 explains that a different accounting treatment is considered necessary for such properties because:

—   the properties are held for investment rather than consumption, and disposal would not materially affect the trading operations of the entity;

—   the current value of the investment, and changes in that value, are of more importance than systematic depreciation.

The only exception to this is in the case of leasehold property with a relatively short term remaining, where annual depreciation should continue to be charged. In practice this is usually taken to be a remaining term of 20 years or less.

Requirements of SSAP 19

21.86 SSAP 19 requires an investment property to be accounted for as follows:

— the property should be included in the balance sheet at its open market value;

— changes in the market value should normally be taken to an investment revaluation reserve, and reflected in the statement of total recognised gains and losses, unless a deficit is considered to be permanent, in which case it should be charged to the profit and loss account;

— the property should not be subject to periodic charges for depreciation.

Separate rules apply in the case of investment companies, property unit trusts, insurance companies and pension funds. These are not dealt with in this manual. Property valuations will sometimes include an element that reflects rent on a lease agreed with a tenant. UITF Abstract 28 'Operating Lease Incentives' emphasises that the value at which an investment property is stated in the balance sheet should not include any amount that is already reported as a separate asset in the same balance sheet. For instance, SSAP 21 'Accounting for Leases and Hire Purchase Contracts' and UITF Abstract 28 require both the rent receivable under a lease and any related incentive to be recognised over the term of the lease (or the period to the first rent review if shorter), usually on a straight-line basis. Where a lease includes an incentive such as an initial rent-free period, the timing of the recognition of the rent receivable will differ from the actual cash flows, and the lessor's balance sheet will, therefore, include a debtor for accrued rent receivable. If the open market value of the investment property includes an element to reflect rent receivable under the lease, the amount already included as a debtor should be deducted from the valuation to prevent any double-counting of this element of the asset.

Departure from the requirements of CA 1985

21.87 Since CA 1985 does not distinguish between investment properties and other properties and, therefore, requires an investment property to be included in the accounts at either cost or valuation and to be depreciated over its useful life in the same way as any other tangible fixed asset, compliance with the requirements of SSAP 19 in respect of investment properties will usually constitute a departure from the requirements of the Act. Compliance with SSAP 19 will, therefore, usually require the use of the true and fair override, unless:

— the estimated residual value of the property (calculated in accordance with FRS 15) is at least equal to its carrying value; or

— the estimated residual value of the property is so close to its carrying value that any depreciation would be immaterial.

Further consideration of both of these issues is set out in Chapter 13.

Disclosure of true and fair override

21.88   The use of the true and fair override is considered in more detail in Chapter 3, along with the specific disclosures required under FRS 18 'Accounting Policies'. The disclosures normally require the effect of the departure from the Act to be quantified. In the case of investment properties, this would require disclosure of the effect of not depreciating the investment property. However, the calculation of depreciation in respect of an investment property may not always be possible. In 1981 the Department of Trade and Industry recognised this by indicating to the accountancy bodies at the time that inclusion of the following wording in respect of depreciation would meet the disclosure requirements of the Act in this case: 'Depreciation or amortisation is only one of the many factors reflected in the annual valuation and the amount which might otherwise have been shown cannot be separately identified or quantified'. The following is an example of wording that might be appropriate to explain the use of the true and fair override where investment properties are accounted for under SSAP 19.

Example 21.16 – Disclosure to reflect the true and fair view override

In accordance with SSAP 19:

— investment properties are revalued annually and the aggregate surplus or deficit is transferred to a revaluation reserve; and

— no depreciation or amortisation is provided in respect of freehold investment properties and leasehold investment properties with over 20 years to run.

The Companies Act 1985 requires tangible fixed assets to be depreciated systematically over their estimated useful economic lives. However, investment properties are held for investment rather than consumption; the directors therefore consider that depreciation on a systematic basis would not be appropriate in this case and that the accounting policy adopted is necessary for the accounts to give a true and fair view. Depreciation or amortisation is only one of the many factors reflected in the annual valuation and the amount which might otherwise have been shown cannot be separately identified or quantified.

Valuation of investment properties

21.89   SSAP 19 does not require the annual valuation to be carried out independently of the company or by professional or qualified valuers. However, where investment properties represent a substantial proportion of total assets, and the company is a major enterprise, the notes suggest that:

— the annual valuation should normally be carried out by persons holding a recognised professional qualification and with appropriate recent experience of the relevant locality and the type of property being valued;

— the valuation should be carried out by an external valuer at least every five years.

Accounts disclosures

21.90   SSAP 19 requires the following details to be given in the accounts:

— the names of the valuers, or details of their qualifications;

— the bases of valuation used;

— if the valuer is an employee or officer of the company, this fact must also be disclosed.

The standard also requires the carrying value of investment properties and the investment revaluation reserve to be displayed prominently in the annual accounts. Additional disclosures may be needed under RICS requirements (see 21.51 above).

Historical cost of investment properties

21.91   The historical cost of investment properties will continue to require disclosure under CA 1985 (because investment properties are fixed assets included in the accounts at valuation under the alternative accounting rules – see Chapter 1), but there will be no related cumulative depreciation to disclose.

Accounting policy

21.92   SSAP 19 does not specifically require disclosure of the accounting policy adopted in respect of investment properties, but where they are sufficiently material to be accounted for in accordance with the standard, disclosure will normally be necessary under the requirements of FRS 18 'Accounting Policies'. Normal practice would be to include the explanation of the accounting policy and the use of the true and fair override in the section of the accounts setting out the detailed accounting policies (see 21.87 above).

Tangible fixed asset or investment?

21.93   Neither the Act, nor SSAP 19, provides any guidance on whether investment properties should be included in the balance sheet under tangible fixed assets or under investments. Arguments can be put forward for disclosure in either category and the main issue, therefore, is for each individual company to be consistent in its approach.

ACCOUNTING FOR LEASED ASSETS

Distinction between leases and hire purchase agreements

21.94   Under a lease agreement, a company usually obtains the right to use an asset, but title to the leased asset does not usually pass to the lessee under the agreement. Hire purchase contracts are similar to leases, but in this case legal title will usually pass at the end of the agreement, sometimes on the exercise of an option by the purchaser. Hire purchase contracts which are similar in characteristics to finance leases should be accounted for in the same way as finance leases.

Definition of a finance lease

21.95   Under SSAP 21 'Accounting for Leases and Hire Purchase Contracts', both lessees and lessors must classify all leasing agreements as finance leases or operating leases and apply different accounting treatments, depending on the nature of the lease. A finance lease is defined in SSAP 21 as a lease that transfers substantially all the risks and rewards of ownership of an asset to the lessee. Under a finance lease, the lessee will usually pay the full cost of the asset, together with a return to the lessor in respect of the finance that has effectively been provided. A lease should normally be presumed to be a finance lease when, at the inception of the lease, the present value of the minimum lease payments, including any initial payment, amounts to substantially all of the fair value of the leased asset. 'Substantially all' is defined as normally 90% or more. However, this presumption will not apply if it is clear that the lease does not transfer substantially all the risks and rewards to the lessee, even if the 90% condition is met. Any lease that does not qualify as a finance lease is an operating lease.

Asset value at end of lease term

21.96   The expected value of the asset at the end of the lease term, and who benefits from this, can also help to establish whether the lease is a finance lease. If the value of the asset is likely to be insignificant, the lease will usually be a finance lease. If the value of the asset is significant and the benefit will rest with the lessee, this will also usually indicate that the lease is a finance lease. For instance, a lease agreement will often include a clause preventing the lessee from purchasing the asset at the end of the agreement but, if the lessee has the right to any sales proceeds relating to the asset, or has a right to a guaranteed residual value at the end of the agreement, the benefit to the lessee will be similar to that of having title to the asset at the end of the agreement.

Impact of FRS 5 'Accounting for the Substance of Transactions'

21.97   The classification of leases can be a highly complex issue, especially as agreements sometimes include clauses which are intended to ensure that the lease fails the 90% test in SSAP 21, or which appear to leave most of the risks with the lessor (although, in some cases, the actual risk retained by the lessor through these clauses may be minimal). Such clauses are intended to enable the lessee to justify not bringing the lease and the related obligation onto the balance sheet. Although the detailed requirements of SSAP 21 still stand, the more general requirements of FRS

5 'Accounting for the Substance of Transactions' apply equally to leasing transactions (see Chapter 4). Where the substance of a lease agreement is that of a finance lease, it will have to be accounted for as such, even though the specific tests in SSAP 21 may not be met.

Guidance notes on SSAP 21

21.98   The guidance notes on SSAP 21 set out in considerable detail the practical issues relating to both lessee and lessor accounting, and as well as considering some of the general problem areas associated with lease accounting, provide guidance on accounting for some of the particularly complex leasing transactions such as:

— sale and leaseback arrangements;

— sub-leases and back-to-back leases;

— leasing by manufacturers and dealers.

Initial recording of asset and liability by lessee

21.99   Under SSAP 21, leases that are classified as finance leases should be recorded in the lessee's balance sheet as an asset and as an obligation to pay future rentals to the lessor. At the inception of the lease (which is defined in the standard as the earlier of the date when the asset is brought into use or the date from which rental payments accrue), the amount recorded as an asset and the obligation recorded to the lessor will be the same. Strictly this should be the present value of the minimum lease payments. The minimum lease payments are defined in the standard as:

'the minimum payments over the remaining part of the lease term (excluding charges for services and taxes to be paid by the lessor) and, in the case of the lessee, any residual amounts guaranteed by him or by a party related to him.'

This should include any initial payment made by the lessee under the agreement. However, the standard emphasises that, for practical purposes, the fair value of the leased asset will usually be a sufficiently close approximation to the present value of the minimum lease payments to make the fair value an acceptable figure to use when initially recording the asset and the related obligation to the lessor. Fair value is defined as 'the price at which an asset could be exchanged in an arm's length transaction less, where applicable, any grants receivable towards the purchase or use of the asset'. An example of the calculation of the present value of the minimum lease payments is given in Chapter 14, along with examples of accounting for finance charges in respect of leased assets.

Depreciation of asset by lessee

21.100   The leased asset must be depreciated over its expected useful economic life in the same way as any other fixed asset, but the life used should not exceed the lease term. The lease term is defined in SSAP 21 as:

—   the period for which the lessee has contracted to lease the asset; and

—   any further terms for which the lessee has the option to continue to lease the asset, with or without further payment, when it is reasonably certain at the inception of the lease that the lessee will exercise this option.

Consideration of whether an option is likely to be exercised will usually include:

—   how the lessee has dealt with similar lease options in the past;

—   whether there are any penalties for not extending the lease, which might, therefore, encourage the lessee to exercise the option;

—   whether the terms of the option are commercially realistic (ie is the option genuine, or will the agreement only make commercial sense if the lessee exercises the option?).

The depreciation of fixed assets is considered in more detail in Chapter 13.

Accounts disclosures by lessee

21.101   The policies adopted for accounting for operating leases and finance leases must be disclosed in the accounts of the lessee. Wording along with following lines will usually be appropriate:

Example 21.17 – Disclosure of accounting policies

Finance leases

Where the company enters into a lease which transfers substantially all the risks and rewards of ownership of the asset to the company, the lease is accounted for as a finance lease. The leased asset is included in tangible fixed assets at its fair value at the inception of the lease and the company's obligation to the lessor is recorded at the same amount. The asset is depreciated on the straight-line basis over the shorter of the lease term and the expected useful economic life of the asset. Rental payments are apportioned between the finance charge, which is charged to the profit and loss account, and the capital repayment element, which reduces the outstanding obligation, so that the finance charge for each accounting period represents a constant percentage of the capital sum outstanding.

Operating leases

Other leases are accounted for as operating leases, and the rental payments are charged to the profit and loss account on a straight-line basis over the term of the lease.

Where assets under finance leases (or hire purchase contracts similar to finance leases) are included in fixed assets, SSAP 21 also requires the following disclosures in the accounts:

— the gross amounts of assets held under finance leases and the related accumulated depreciation by each major class of asset; or

— where leased assets are integrated with other fixed assets, the net amount of assets held under finance leases, together with the depreciation for the period in respect of leased assets.

There are two alternative methods of meeting the disclosure requirements in respect of assets under finance leases within tangible fixed assets, both of which are in common use:

— a separate column (or columns, if the assets fall into more than one main category) can be included in the fixed assets table, headed 'Assets under finance leases' – in this case, all movements during the year in respect of the leased assets will be disclosed; or

— the net book value of leased assets can be included as a footnote to the table and the depreciation charge in respect of leased assets can be disclosed as part of this note or as part of the profit and loss account disclosures on depreciation for the year.

Example 21.18 – Footnote disclosures for leased assets

The above net book values include the following amounts in respect of assets held under finance leases.

	20X2	20X1
	£	£
Plant and machinery	125,460	89,670
Fixtures, fittings, tools and equipment	85,673	56,799
	211,133	146,469

Depreciation of £40,561 (20X1: £23,557) was charged in the year in respect of these assets.

Assets held by lessor for use in operating leases

21.102 In the accounts of a lessor, assets held for use in operating leases must be recorded as fixed assets and depreciated over their expected useful economic lives. The assets should, therefore, be capitalised in accordance with the normal requirements of CA 1985 (ie usually at purchase price or production cost) and depreciated in accordance with the requirements of FRS 15 'Tangible Fixed Assets'. Within fixed assets, the gross amount of assets held for use in operating leases must be disclosed, along with the related accumulated depreciation. This disclosure requirement is usually met by including these assets in a separate column in the fixed assets table, and thus disclosing all movements during the year, including depreciation. The policies adopted for accounting for operating leases and finance leases must also be disclosed in the accounts of the lessor including, in detail, the policy for accounting for finance lease income. The following wording may be suitable, but this will, of course, depend on the exact policies followed.

Example 21.19 – Disclosures of policies for operating leases and finance leases

Assets held for use in operating leases are included in tangible fixed assets at cost and are depreciated on the straight-line method over their expected useful economic lives. The following asset lives are used:

…………..	…	years	
…………..	…	years	

Gross earnings from operating leases are recognised in the profit and loss account on a straight-line basis over the period of each lease. The initial direct costs incurred in negotiating and arranging operating leases are charged to the profit and loss account in the period in which they are incurred.

Amounts due from lessees in respect of assets held under finance leases are included in debtors at the amount of the net investment in the lease.

Rental payments under finance leases are apportioned between interest, which is credited to the profit and loss account as gross earnings, and repayment of capital, which reduces the amount due from the lessee. Gross earnings from finance leases are allocated to accounting periods to give a constant periodic rate of return on the net cash investment in the lease, using the investment period method of allocation. The initial direct costs incurred in negotiating and arranging finance leases are charged to the profit and loss account in the period in which they are incurred.

Classification of property leases

21.103   SSAP 21's requirements apply to property leases in the same way as to leases involving other assets. Both lessees and lessors must, therefore, classify each property lease as either a finance lease or an operating lease and the normal accounting and disclosure requirements will apply. Short-term leases will generally be operating leases, as the lessor will usually retain the long-term benefits of ownership of the property, although the position may be different if the property is very specialised. In general, long-term leases are more likely to be finance leases, although the specific terms of the lease agreement, and the length of the agreement, may mean that the lease qualifies as an operating lease.

Sale and leaseback arrangements

21.104   Particular care is required in accounting for sale and leaseback transactions involving property. Many of these will be financing arrangements rather than genuine sales and, if so, should be accounted for as finance leases under the requirements of both SSAP 21 and FRS 5. Sale and leaseback arrangements are considered in detail in the guidance notes attached to SSAP 21 and, in effect, are also covered by Application Note B of FRS 5. Where a sale and leaseback arrangement results in a finance lease, SSAP 21 requires any difference between the selling price and the previous carrying value to be deferred and amortised in the accounts of the seller/lessee over the shorter of the lease term or the useful life of the asset. Where a sale and leaseback arrangement results in an operating lease, SSAP 21 requires the following treatment of any profit or loss on the sale:

— if it is clear that the transaction is at fair value, the profit or loss should be recognised immediately;

— if the selling price is below fair value, any profit or loss should be recognised immediately, except where the apparent loss is compensated for by future rentals that are below market price – in this case, the loss should be deferred and amortised over the remainder of the lease term (or the period during which the reduced rentals apply, if this is shorter);

— if the selling price is above fair value, the excess over fair value should be deferred and amortised over the remainder of the lease term (or the period to the next rent review, if this is shorter).

ACCOUNTING FOR COSTS RELATING TO THE INTRODUCTION OF THE EURO

The basic issues

21.105 UITF Abstract 21 'Accounting Issues Arising from the Proposed Introduction of the Euro' notes that entities may incur a variety of costs associated with the introduction of the euro. Depending on individual circumstances, these might include:

— administrative and planning costs;

— staff training;

— the provision of relevant information to customers;

— software modification costs; and

— the adaptation of relevant hardware (vending machines, cash registers etc).

There may also be implications for accounting for foreign currency translation. The issues considered by the UITF included:

— whether costs incurred in connection with the introduction of the euro should be charged as an expense or capitalised as an asset, and what disclosure should be given in the accounts;

— the impact that the irrevocable locking of the national currencies of participating Member States will have on cumulative foreign exchange differences recognised in periods before the introduction of the euro; and

— the impact that the irrevocable locking of the national currencies of participating Member States will have on anticipatory hedging instruments existing at the date of introduction of the euro in respect of future transactions.

Accounting for modification of assets

21.106 The consensus on accounting for costs arising from the introduction of the euro is that the costs of modifying or adapting assets to deal with the introduction of the euro should generally be written off to the profit and loss account. The only exception is where the entity already has an accounting policy for capitalising assets of the relevant type and the expenditure clearly results in an enhancement of economic benefits by extending the service potential of an asset beyond that originally assessed, rather than merely maintaining its current service potential. Costs that do not give rise to assets should be charged to the profit and loss account as they are incurred.

When provision should be made

21.107 Under the requirements of FRS 12 'Provisions, Contingent Liabilities and Contingent Assets', a mere intention or even the necessity to undertake future expenditure will not necessarily give rise to a liability. Costs associated with the introduction of the euro should, therefore, be recognised in the accounting period in which the work is actually carried out and no provision should be made in earlier accounting periods for estimated future costs.

Disclosure

21.108 In some cases, costs associated with the introduction of the euro may require disclosure as exceptional items under the requirements of FRS 3 'Reporting Financial Performance' and significant commitments in respect of modification costs may need to be disclosed under the requirements of CA 1985. The Abstract also recommends that additional information is given where the potential impact for the reporting entity is likely to be significant. The additional disclosures should include an indication of the total costs likely to be incurred and can be given in the directors' report, an operating and financial review or any other statement published as part of the annual report.

ACCOUNTING FOR WEBSITE DEVELOPMENT COSTS

Categories of development cost

21.109 Websites are now used for a wide range of business purposes and companies frequently incur significant costs in developing their websites. UITF Abstract 29 'Website Development Costs' was issued in February 2001 and is effective for accounting periods ending on or after 23 March 2001, although earlier adoption is encouraged. The Abstract analyses website development costs into four principle categories:

— planning costs;

— application and infrastructure costs;
— design costs; and
— content costs.

Planning costs

21.110   Planning costs include the costs of undertaking a feasibility study, determining the objectives of the website, exploring ways of achieving those objectives, identifying appropriate hardware and software and choosing suitable suppliers and consultants. The Abstract notes that planning costs do not in themselves give rise to future economic benefits controlled by the entity and should, therefore, not be recognised as assets in the financial statements. All website planning costs should be charged to the profit and loss account as they are incurred.

Application and infrastructure costs

21.111   Application and infrastructure costs include the costs of obtaining and registering a domain name, and buying or developing appropriate hardware and operating software. These costs will usually give rise to an asset and should therefore be capitalised. The UITF specifically considered whether such costs should be capitalised as tangible or intangible assets and concluded that, although websites do not fit either classification perfectly, it is most appropriate for the costs to be capitalised as tangible fixed assets. This is mainly on the basis of FRS 10 'Goodwill and Intangible Assets' para 2 which states that:

> 'Software development costs that are directly attributable to bringing a computer system or other computer-operated machinery into working condition for its intended use within the business are treated as part of the cost of the related hardware rather than as a separate intangible asset.'

The guidance in the Abstract notes that this treatment should be adopted irrespective of whether the reporting entity owns the related hardware.

Design and content costs

21.112   Website design and content costs are considered together in the Abstract. They include costs to develop the design and appearance of individual website pages and preparing and posting the website content. As there is often uncertainty over the viability, value and useful economic life of a website, the UITF took the view that website design and content costs should be capitalised only to the extent that they lead to the creation of an enduring asset that delivers benefits at least as great as the amount capitalised. This will only apply where:

— the expenditure is separately identifiable;

— the technical feasibility and commercial viability of the website have been assessed with reasonable certainty;

— the website will generate sales or other revenues directly (eg orders placed via the website, amounts paid by subscribers for access to information on the website, revenues from selling advertising space on the website), and the expenditure makes an enduring contribution to the development of the revenue-generating capabilities of the website – where the website is used only for advertising or promotion, it will not usually be possible to demonstrate that sales or revenue are generated directly from the website;

— there is a reasonable expectation that the present value of future cash flows to be generated by the website will be no less than the amounts capitalised in respect of the revenue-generating activity; and

— adequate resources exist, or are reasonably expected to be available, to enable the website project to be completed and to provide any consequential increases in working capital.

If there is insufficient evidence on which to base reasonable estimates of the economic benefits to be generated, website design and content costs should be charged to the profit and loss account as they are incurred.

Capitalisation of costs

21.113   The UITF concluded that it would be difficult to separate website development costs into tangible and intangible assets, and that to do so would serve no practical purpose. Therefore, where capitalisation of website design and content costs is justified:

— they should be capitalised as tangible fixed assets, together with the related application and infrastructure costs, in accordance with the requirements of FRS 15 'Tangible Fixed Assets';

— the asset should be amortised over its estimated useful economic life which, given the rapid rate of technological development, is likely to be short – the useful life should be reviewed at the end of each accounting period and revised where necessary;

— where the design or content of a website requires more frequent replacement than the website as a whole, it may be appropriate to select a shorter depreciation period for the design and content costs than for the remaining elements of the asset;

— the asset should be reviewed for impairment if events or changes in circumstances indicate that the carrying amount may not be recoverable.

Accounting for subsequent costs

21.114   Expenditure to maintain or operate a website once it has been developed should be charged to the profit and loss account as incurred, in accordance with the requirements of FRS 15 'Tangible Fixed Assets'.

LIKELY FUTURE DEVELOPMENTS

Convergence with international standards

2.115   In March 2004, the ASB issued a Discussion Paper 'UK Accounting Standards: A Strategy for Convergence with IFRS' setting out its detailed plans for achieving the convergence of UK accounting standards with international accounting standards (see 1.6 above). FRED 29 was published in May 2002 (see 21.116 to 21.120 below) and proposes replacing FRS 15 with new standards based on IAS 16 'Property, plant and equipment' and IAS 23 'Borrowing costs'. Further exposure drafts are expected to be issued in due course, based on IAS 17 'Leases' and IAS 40 'Investment property'. The latest version of the ASB's Technical Plan, published in June 2005, indicates that all of these new standards are expected to come into effect for accounting periods beginning on or after 1 January 2008.

The ASB also published FRED 32 'Disposal of non-current assets and presentation of discontinued operations' in July 2003 as part of the convergence project, and the June 2005 version of the Board's Technical Plan suggests that this is expected to come into effect for accounting periods beginning on or after 1 January 2007. Further details are given at 21.121 to 21.125 below.

FRED 29 'Property, plant and equipment; Borrowing costs'

21.116   The ASB issued FRED 29 'Property, plant and equipment; Borrowing costs' in May 2002 as part of its project to achieve convergence between UK accounting standards and international accounting standards. The Exposure Draft proposes replacing FRS 15 'Tangible fixed assets' with two new standards based on IAS 16 and IAS 23. Much of the content of these two international standards is consistent with current UK requirements. The main differences are in relation to the accounting treatment of revalued assets, in particular the use of a 'fair value' model rather than the UK's present 'value to the business' approach. A separate international group is currently considering the issue of revaluation and whether changes should be made to the present IAS requirements. The ASB is participating in this project and is continuing to press for IAS 16 to incorporate the revaluation principles currently set out in FRS 15.

Proposed changes in respect of revaluations

21.117   If the proposals in FRED 29 are implemented, the main changes in respect of revalued assets will be:

— FRED 29 requires revaluation to fair value, whereas FRS 15 requires revaluation to current value – in particular, FRED 29 states that the fair value of property, plant and equipment is usually its market value, whilst FRS 15 requires valuation on the basis of existing use value for non-specialised properties, depreciated replacement cost for specialised properties and open market value for properties that are surplus to the entity's requirements;

— FRED 29 requires valuations to be kept up to date but does not specify a maximum period between valuations, although it indicates that annual revaluation may be needed for assets that experience significant and volatile changes in value and that revaluation every three to five years will usually be sufficient for other assets – FRS 15 requires a full valuation at least every five years with interim updates in the intervening period;

— the basis of valuations is covered in less detail in FRED 29 – for instance:

    — there is no requirement to use an external valuer at least every five years (although FRED 29 does note that property valuations should normally be undertaken by qualified valuers);

    — the detailed guidance in FRS 15 on full and interim valuations is not repeated in FRED 29;

    — there is no guidance on the use of appropriate indices to value plant and machinery;

    — there is no reference to notional directly attributable acquisition or selling costs;

— FRED 29 proposes that any revaluation loss that exceeds an existing revaluation surplus, in respect of the same asset, should be recognised as an expense in the profit and loss account – FRS 15 requires recognition in the profit and loss account only to the extent that the asset is impaired;

— FRED 29 requires a revaluation loss to be recognised in the statement of total recognised gains and losses to the extent that there is a revaluation surplus in respect of the same asset – FRS 15 requires any element that is caused by impairment to be recognised in the profit and loss account.

The ASB notes that it proposes to retain, as a transitional measure, the special treatment given in FRS 15 to gains and losses on the revaluation of assets held by insurance companies and groups as part of their insurance operations, even though this is not included in IAS 16.

Other changes proposed

21.118   The other main changes to current UK accounting practice proposed in FRED 29 are:

— there is a new requirement for an item of property, plant or equipment acquired in exchange for another item of property, plant or equipment to be measured at fair value, based on the fair value of the asset given up or, if more clearly evident, the fair value of the asset received – however, if fair value cannot be determined reliably, the acquired asset should be measured at the carrying value of the asset given up;

— there is no reference to accounting for donated assets received by charities;

— where residual values need to be revised, the revision should be based on current prices rather than those at the date of acquisition or revaluation;

— there is no guidance on when uncharged depreciation may be regarded as immaterial;

— there is no specific requirement for annual impairment reviews on assets that are not depreciated; and

— there is no reference to renewals accounting and, thus, no alternative to the principle that depreciation is determined by reference to the depreciable amount of an asset.

Borrowing costs

21.119   The capitalisation of borrowing costs would continue to be optional under the proposals in FRED 29. The definition of borrowing costs in IAS 23 allows certain exchange differences to be capitalised as borrowing costs, but the ASB does not intend to incorporate this element into UK accounting standards. The main differences from present UK accounting requirements are:

— the scope of the international standard is wider than that of FRS 15 and, its requirements consequently apply to certain inventories as well as to tangible fixed assets;

— under the proposals in FRED 29, if specific borrowings are taken out to fund a qualifying asset, the borrowing costs eligible for capitalisation are the actual costs less any investment income received from the temporary reinvestment of unused borrowings – under FRS 15 only interest on borrowings actually spent on the asset to date can be capitalised (any investment income on surplus borrowings must be recognised in the profit and loss account);

— two disclosures required under FRS 15 are not repeated in FRED 29:

— the aggregate amount of finance costs included in the cost of tangible fixed assets – this disclosure is also required by CA 1985; and

— the amount of finance costs recognised in the profit and loss account for the period.

Transitional arrangements

21.120   FRS 15 includes special transitional arrangements for entities who had previously revalued tangible fixed assets but did not wish to adopt a policy of revaluation when implementing FRS 15 for the first time. IAS 16 does not include such a provision, but the ASB states in FRED 29 that it proposes to include in any new UK standard a transitional arrangement equivalent to that in FRS 15 to enable entities who have taken advantage of the existing provision to continue their present accounting treatment.

FRED 32 'Disposal of non-current assets and presentation of discontinued operations'

21.121   The ASB published FRED 32 'Disposal of non-current assets and presentation of discontinued operations' in July 2003 as part of its project to achieve convergence between UK and international accounting standards. The proposals in FRED 32 are based on an equivalent exposure draft issued by the IASB, and require separate disclosure on the balance sheet of non-current assets (and, in the case of disposal groups, liabilities) held for sale and remove the requirement to depreciate non-current assets that are held for sale. A new standard based on FRED 32 is expected to come into effect for accounting periods beginning on or after 1 January 2007.

Assets held for sale

21.122   The Exposure Draft introduces a new classification of assets held for sale, which applies to individual non-current assets and also to a disposal group, which is defined as:

(i)   a group of assets to be disposed of by sale or otherwise, as a group, in a single transaction; and

(ii)   the liabilities directly associated with the assets that form part of the transaction.

The proposals require such assets (and, where appropriate, liabilities) to be shown separately on the face of the balance sheet. The criteria for classifying assets as held for sale (all of which must be met) are specified in an Appendix to the proposed standard and include:

(i)   management with appropriate authority committing to a plan to sell the asset or disposal group;

(ii)   the asset or disposal group being available for immediate sale in its present condition, subject only to terms that are usual and customary for such assets;

(iii)   an active programme to find a buyer and other actions necessary to complete the plan to sell;

(iv)   the asset or disposal group being actively marketed for sale at a price that is reasonable in relation to its fair value; and

(v)   no indications that the plan to sell will be significantly changed or withdrawn.

It should also be highly probable that the sale will be completed within one year from the date on which the asset or disposal group is classified as being held for sale, although the Exposure Draft does cater for exceptions to this where a delay is caused by certain events or circumstances that are beyond the entity's control.

Depreciation of assets held for sale

21.123   FRED 32 also proposes that assets held for sale should not be depreci- ated, regardless of whether they are still in use in the business. In the preface to the Exposure Draft, the ASB notes that FRS 15 does not grant any exemption from depreciation for assets held for disposal. The IASB was unable to achieve a consensus on this point and the alternative views of two Board members are published in an Appendix to the Exposure Draft. The ASB expresses the view that it is inappropriate to suspend depreciation on assets that are continuing to be used simply because they have been identified as being held for sale within a period of twelve months.

Recognition of profit or loss on disposal

21.124   FRED 32 proposes that assets held for sale should be carried at the lower of carrying value and fair value less disposal costs, the latter being essentially the same as net realisable value under FRS 11. The proposals conflict to some extent with current accounting practice in the UK, in that where the value in use of an asset is higher than its net realisable value but the entity nevertheless decides to sell it, the Exposure Draft requires it to be written down to net realisable value, with any loss recognised in the period in which the decision to sell is taken. In the preface to the Exposure Draft, the ASB expresses the view that the loss should be recognised when the sale occurs (as under FRS 3) and not when the entity classifies the asset as held for sale.

Balance sheet presentation

21.125   The proposed international accounting standard requires these items to be disaggregated into major classes of asset or liability and shown separately on the face of the balance sheet or in the notes to the accounts. In the preface to FRED 32, the ASB notes that companies that are not required, or have not chosen, to adopt international accounting standards will still have to comply with the disclosure requirements and balance sheet formats of CA 1985. The ASB has therefore amended the IASB proposals to require the major classes of assets and liabilities held for sale to be separately disclosed on the face of the balance sheet under the appropriate statutory format heading.

Chapter 22   Investments

CLASSIFICATION AS FIXED OR CURRENT ASSETS

Balance sheet disclosure

22.1   Depending on their nature, investments may be classified in the balance sheet as fixed assets or current assets. In both cases, the heading is given a Roman numeral in the formats and the totals for fixed asset investments and current asset investments must therefore be shown on the face of the balance sheet. The balance sheet formats require the following analysis of investments:

— investments classified as fixed assets:
  — shares in group undertakings;
  — loans to group undertakings;
  — participating interests;
  — loans to undertakings in which the company has a participating interest;
  — other investments other than loans;
  — other loans; and
  — own shares;
— investments classified as current assets:
  — shares in group undertakings; and
  — own shares;
  — other investments.

These sub-headings are given Arabic numerals in the formats. The details may therefore be given in the notes to the accounts and the figures may be combined if the individual amounts are not material.

Definition of fixed asset investment

22.2 The usual CA 1985 definitions of fixed asset and current asset apply equally to investments. A fixed asset investment is therefore an investment which the company intends to retain and use on a continuing basis in its activities. All other investments should be classified as current assets. Although the balance sheet formats allow for the inclusion of shares in group undertakings under current assets, most group shareholdings will meet the definition of fixed assets and should therefore be accounted for under this heading.

Loans to group undertakings

22.3 Particular care is needed over the treatment of loans to group undertakings. In this case, the classification will normally depend on whether the loan is seen as providing long-term financing to another group undertaking (in which case it will usually be a fixed asset investment) or whether it is more in the nature of an inter-company account, in which case it may be more appropriate to disclose the balance in debtors. The treatment and disclosure of group loans should be consistent between companies within the group. For instance, it will not usually be appropriate for the lender to treat a group loan as a fixed asset investment and for the borrower to treat the same loan as being payable within one year. Proper documentation of the terms of the loan should help to establish the appropriate treatment in the accounts of both companies.

Disclosure of movements in the year

22.4 The general disclosure requirements of CA 1985 in respect of fixed assets apply equally to any investments shown as fixed assets. The accounts must therefore show for each category of fixed asset investment set out above:

— cost or valuation at the beginning of the year and at the balance sheet date;
— the effect of any revaluation during the year;
— any additions during the year;
— any disposals during the year;
— any transfers during the year;
— the cumulative amount provided for any diminution in value at the beginning of the year and at the balance sheet date;
— the amount provided for any diminution in value during the year;
— any adjustments to such provisions in respect of disposals during the year;

—   any other adjustments to such provisions during the year.

Comparative figures are not required for these disclosures.

Current asset investments

22.5   Although the balance sheet formats allow for three categories of current asset investments, in practice, investments which are held as current assets will usually comprise items such as:

—   listed investments;

—   unlisted investments;

—   certain bank and building society deposit accounts (although this will depend very much on the nature and purpose of the account).

All of these would come under the category of 'other investments'.

GROUP INVESTMENTS

Definition of group undertaking

22.6   Under CA 1985, the following are defined as group undertakings:

—   a parent undertaking or a subsidiary undertaking; and

—   a subsidiary undertaking of any parent undertaking of that undertaking.

An undertaking is defined as a body corporate or partnership, or an unincorporated association carrying on a trade or business, with or without a view to profit. Entities other than companies are therefore encompassed although, in practice, most group undertakings will be other companies. The disclosure for shares in and loans to group undertakings will therefore cover:

—   any parent undertaking of the company (i.e. not just the company's immediate parent, but also any intermediate or ultimate parent);

—   any subsidiary of the company;

—   any fellow subsidiary – this might be another subsidiary of the company's immediate parent, or a subsidiary of another parent undertaking in a wider group.

In practice, any shareholdings will usually relate only to a company's own subsidiaries. However, loans may involve a wider range of group companies.

Straightforward presentation of information

22.7   The most appropriate way of presenting the required information will depend on the complexity of the investments, the level of detail disclosed on the face of the balance sheet and whether there have been any (or many) movements during the year. If there are no (or few) movements to report, the following format is usually the most straightforward:

Example 22.1 – Shares in and loans to group undertakings

Fixed asset investments

Investments in group undertakings

	20X2	20X1
	£	£
Shares in group undertakings	452,000	452,000
Loans to group undertakings	66,500	88,500
Total investments in group undertakings	518,500	540,500

Movements during the year on loans to group undertakings were as follows:

At 1 January 20X2	88,500
Loans advanced	10,000
Loans repaid	(32,000)
At 31 December 20X2	66,500

Where movements during the year are more complicated, a full movements table may be required, as shown for other investments in Example 22.4 (see 22.36 below). CA 1985 Sch 5 also requires the disclosure of detailed information in respect of a company's subsidiary undertakings.

Definition of participating interest

22.8   A participating interest is defined in CA 1985 as an interest held by an undertaking in the shares of another undertaking which it holds on a long-term basis for the purpose of securing a contribution to its activities by the exercise of control or influence arising from, or related to, that interest. The expression 'shares' includes an interest which is convertible into shares and an option to acquire shares or to acquire an interest in shares, regardless of whether the shares are issued or unissued at the time. A holding of 20% or more of the shares of another undertaking is presumed to be a participating interest, unless it can be demonstrated that this is not the case. In this case, interests which are convertible into shares and options to acquire shares or interests do not have to be taken into account. No minimum holding is laid down in CA 1985, and it is therefore possible that a holding of less than 20% could still qualify as a participating interest if the other conditions are fulfilled. The legislation notes specifically that, in the case of the balance sheet and profit and loss account formats, a participating interest does not include an interest in a group undertaking. Any interests in group undertakings must therefore be shown under that heading in the accounts and not as participating interests.

Associated undertakings

22.9   An associated undertaking is defined in CA 1985, in the context of group accounts, as an undertaking in which an undertaking included in the consolidation has a participating interest and over whose operating and financial policy it exercises a significant influence, and which is not a subsidiary undertaking of the parent company, or a joint venture included in the accounts by proportional consolidation. FRS 9 'Associates and Joint Ventures' defines:

— an associate as an entity (other than a subsidiary) in which another entity (the investor) has a participating interest and over whose operating and financial policies the investor exercises a significant influence; and

— a joint venture as an entity in which the reporting entity holds an interest on a long-term basis and which is jointly controlled by the reporting entity and one or more other venturers under a contractual arrangement.

It follows from these definitions that an associated undertaking (or an associate) will invariably qualify as a participating interest under CA 1985, but a participating interest will not necessarily meet the definition of an associated undertaking or of an associate under FRS 9. Accounting for associates is considered in more detail in 22.12 below.

Holding of own shares

22.10   The formats allow for the inclusion of 'own shares' under fixed asset investments or current asset investments, but these headings are rarely used in practice. The purchase by a company of its own shares is strictly controlled by CA 1985 and, where purchase or acquisition is possible, the company is usually required to cancel the shares at the time of purchase.

A company may be able to hold its own shares for a period of time where the shares are acquired for forfeiture, or where the shares are surrendered in lieu of forfeiture, for failure to pay any sums due in respect of the shares. From 1 December 2003, certain companies are also permitted to purchase their own shares and hold them in treasury (see Chapter 32). UITF Abstract 37 'Purchases and Sales of Own Shares' requires any consideration paid for own shares to be deducted in arriving at shareholders' funds and does not allow it to be shown in the balance sheet as an asset. Although the Abstract was developed with treasury shares in mind, its requirements have been applied to all purchases and sales of own shares. For accounting periods beginning on or after 1 January 2005, UITF Abstract 37 is superseded by an equivalent accounting requirement in FRS 25 'Financial Instruments: Disclosure and Presentation'. A similar treatment is also required by UITF

Abstract 38 'Accounting for ESOP Trusts' where the assets and liabilities of an ESOP trust are required to be included in the accounts of the sponsoring company and the assets include shares in the company.

The number and nominal value of any own shares held should always be disclosed.

ACCOUNTING FOR ASSOCIATES, JOINT VENTURES AND JOINT ARRANGEMENTS

Identification of associates, joint ventures and joint arrangements

22.11 The requirements of CA 1985 and FRS 9 'Associates and Joint Ventures' on the separate identification of associates, joint ventures and joint arrangements that are not entities are considered in detail in Chapter 46.

FRS 9 'Associates and Joint Ventures'

22.12 FRS 9 'Associates and Joint Ventures' deals mainly with the accounting treatment of an associate or joint venture in the context of group accounts, but there are also separate requirements on the treatment to be adopted in the investing company's individual accounts. Additional disclosures are required where the investor does not prepare group accounts, unless it is exempt from preparing group accounts, or would be exempt if it had subsidiaries. Exemption from the preparation of group accounts is considered in more detail in Chapter 44.

Accounting treatment in the individual accounts of the investor

22.13 In the individual accounts of the investor, FRS 9 requires an interest in an associate or joint venture to be accounted for as a fixed asset investment and shown at either cost, less amounts written off, or at valuation. Income from the associate or joint venture should be brought into the accounts on the basis of the amounts received or receivable during the year. The basic treatment of an associate or joint venture in the investor's individual accounts is therefore the same as for any other fixed asset investment. In consolidated accounts, an associate should be accounted for using the equity method of accounting and a joint venture should be accounted for using the gross equity method of accounting (see Chapter 46).

Joint venture with little commonality of interest

22.14 It is possible to set up a structure that appears to be a joint venture, but where the participants are simply using the structure as a means of carrying out their own business and there is little commonality of interest between them. In these circumstances, FRS 9 requires each participant to account for its own share of the assets, liabilities and cash flows within the structure rather than treating it as a joint venture.

Non-corporate associate or joint ventures

22.15   Where an investor holds an interest in a non-corporate associate or joint venture it is particularly important to ensure that all of the investor's liabilities in relation to the investment are properly reflected in the accounts. For instance, in a case of joint and several liability, a liability could arise in excess of the investor's share of the entity's net assets. This may need to be reported as a contingent liability or, where necessary, provided for in the accounts.

Joint arrangements that are not entities

22.16   In the course of their activities, businesses enter into a variety of agreements with other entities, but these agreements do not always result in formation of another wholly separate entity. In practice, joint activities that are not entities are likely to involve some element of cost-sharing or risk-sharing in carrying out a process that forms part of the business activities of the participants. The standard gives as examples a joint marketing or distribution network, or a shared production facility. Also, where a joint arrangement is set up to carry out one specific project, there is no continuing activity and the arrangement therefore will not usually constitute a separate trade or business. The guidance in FRS 9 on these issues is considered in more detail in Chapter 46.

The standard sets out separate requirements on accounting for joint arrangements that are not entities. The participants should account for their own share of the assets, liabilities and cash flows of the joint arrangement, measured according to the terms of the overall agreement. The same treatment applies in both individual and consolidated accounts. However, the standard notes that the nature of a joint arrangement may change over time, so that it becomes a joint venture and in this case the accounting treatment should be amended in the year of the change to reflect the new nature of the joint activities.

Additional accounts disclosures

22.17   Unless it is exempt from preparing group accounts, or would be exempt if it had subsidiaries, an investor that does not prepare consolidated financial statements must present the relevant amounts for associates and joint ventures in its own accounts. Two alternative forms of presentation are offered:

—   the investor can prepare a separate set of financial statements to include the associate or joint venture; or

—   the investor can show the relevant amounts, together with the effects of including them, as additional information to its own financial statements.

The use of a pro forma profit and loss account and balance sheet will usually be the clearest way of presenting the required information. If the alternative approach is used (ie supplementary details are included in the company's statutory profit and loss account and balance sheet), particular care will be required to ensure that the results of the associate or joint venture do not appear to be reported as realised profits of the investor. The standard also requires the following disclosures in respect of each principal associate or joint venture:

— its name;

— the proportion of the issued shares in each class held by the investing company or group, together with an indication of any special rights or constraints attaching to them;

— the accounting period or date of the financial statements used, if these differ from those of the investing company or group; and

— an indication of the nature of its business.

Accounting period and date of associates and joint ventures

22.18 Wherever possible, the information included in the investor's accounts should be based on financial statements for the associate or joint venture made up to the accounting date of the investor. Where this is not practicable, the associate or joint venture may be included on the basis of accounts prepared for a period ending not more than three months before the accounting date of the investor. If this would result in the release of restricted, price-sensitive information, accounts for a period ending not more than six months before the accounting date of the investor may be used. Where different accounting dates are used, changes between the accounting date of the associate or joint venture and the accounting date of the investor should be adjusted for if they materially affect the view given by the investor's accounts.

Becoming or ceasing to be an associate

22.19 An investment becomes an associate on the date on which the investor begins to fulfil the two essential elements of the definition of an associate:

— the holding of a participating interest; and

— the exercise of significant influence.

An investment ceases to be an associate on the date on which the investor ceases to fulfil either of these two essential elements. If an investment in an associate is acquired or disposed of in stages, a similar process to that required for subsidiaries under FRS 2 'Accounting for Subsidiary Undertakings' should be followed (see Chapter 49).

Becoming or ceasing to be a joint venture

22.20 An investment becomes a joint venture on the date on which the investor begins to control the entity jointly with the other venturers, provided that its interest is long-term. An investment ceases to be a joint venture on the date on which the investor ceases to have joint control with the other venturers. If an investment in a joint venture is acquired or disposed of in stages, a similar process to that required for subsidiaries under FRS 2 'Accounting for Subsidiary Undertakings' should be followed (see Chapter 49).

Disclosure of decision not to treat as an associate

22.21   Where an investor holds 20% or more of the shares in another entity but is deemed not to have a participating interest in the entity, the reasons must be explained in a note to the accounts. Similarly, where the investor holds 20% or more of the voting rights but is deemed not to exercise significant influence over the entity, the reasons should be explained.

Notes on contingent liabilities and commitments

22.22   Where the notes to the associate's or joint venture's accounts include matters that are material to understanding the effect of the investment on the investor, or if the notes would have included such matters if the investor's accounting policies had been followed, details should also be disclosed in the investor's accounts. These disclosures should include in particular:

—   the investor's share in contingent liabilities incurred jointly with other investors; and

—   the investor's share of the capital commitments of associates and joint ventures.

Significant restrictions on ability to distribute reserves

22.23   Where the ability of an associate or joint venture to distribute its reserves is significantly restricted as a result of statutory, contractual or exchange control requirements, the extent of the restriction should be indicated in the accounts of the investor. This does not apply to reserves that are shown as non-distributable in the accounts of the associate or joint venture.

Amounts owed to or by associates and joint venture

22.24   Any amounts owed to or by associates or joint ventures should be analysed into:

—   amounts relating to loans; and

—   amounts relating to trading balances.

This disclosure may be combined with the disclosures required under FRS 8 'Related Party Disclosures' (see Chapter 18).

Significant associates and joint ventures

22.25   Additional disclosures are required when certain thresholds in respect of:

—   gross assets;

—   gross liabilities;

—   turnover; and

—   operating results (on a three-year average),

are exceeded. The thresholds are applied by comparing the relevant figures for the investor (excluding any amounts included for associates and joint ventures under the equity method of accounting) with the investor's share of the equivalent figures for associates in aggregate, joint ventures in aggregate and for individual associates and joint ventures. These disclosure requirements are explained in more detail in Chapter 46.

ACCOUNTING POLICIES

Historical cost accounting rules

22.26   Under the historical cost accounting rules, fixed assets investments should be included in the accounts at their purchase price. Under CA 1985, provision must be made for any permanent diminution in value and may be made for any temporary diminution in value. Such provisions should be charged to the profit and loss account and shown separately, either on the face of the profit and loss account or in the notes to the accounts. Provisions should be written back in the same way to the extent that they are no longer necessary. Current asset investments should be included in the accounts at the lower of purchase price and net realisable value. Once again, any provision to write down a current asset investment to its net realisable value should be written back to the extent that it is no longer necessary. There is no specific requirement for the accounting policy in respect of investments to be disclosed in the accounts, but where investments are significant it is usual to give a brief description of the accounting treatment.

Example 22.2 – Disclosure of accounting policy on investments

Investments held as fixed assets are included in the accounts at cost, less any provisions for impairment. Investments held as current assets are included in the accounts at the lower of cost and net realisable value.

Alternative accounting rules

22.27   Under the alternative accounting rules, fixed asset investments may be included in the accounts at:

—   market value as at the date of their last valuation; or

—   at a value determined on any basis which the directors consider to be appropriate in the company's circumstances.

Current asset investments may be included at their current cost.

Example 22.3 – Alternative accounting rules (disclosure of policy for accounting for investments)

Listed investments held as fixed assets are included in the accounts at their market value at the balance sheet date. Investments held as current assets are included in the accounts at their current cost at the balance sheet date.

The option to value fixed asset investments on a basis considered appropriate by the directors could be used to value an unlisted investment on an earnings basis or a net asset basis. Whenever this approach is used, the notes to the accounts must disclose details of the valuation method adopted and the reasons for choosing this method. It is not sufficient simply to state that the investments have been valued by the directors. The use of the alternative accounting rules, and the disclosures that are required when they are adopted, are considered in more detail in Chapter 1. In the case of fixed asset investments other than listed investments, the following details must also be given:

—   the years and amounts of the valuations; and

—   for assets revalued during the year, the names or qualifications of the valuer(s) and the valuation bases used.

Impairment of investments

22.28   Investments in subsidiary undertakings, associates and joint ventures are specifically included within the scope of FRS 11 'Impairment of Fixed Assets and Goodwill'. The standard requires fixed assets and goodwill to be reviewed for impairment if events or changes in circumstances indicate that the carrying amount of the asset or goodwill may not be recoverable. To the extent that the carrying amount exceeds the recoverable amount, the fixed asset or goodwill is impaired and should be written down. The requirements of FRS 11 are considered in more detail in Chapter 21.

Fair value accounting

22.29   For accounting periods beginning on or after 1 January 2005, CA 1985 has been amended to allow certain assets to be included in the balance sheet at fair value, and changes in that fair value to be reflected in the profit and loss account. Fair value accounting has been introduced in the UK as option rather than as a mandatory requirement, and it can be adopted in both individual and consolidated accounts, including those prepared by small or specialised companies, for accounting periods beginning on or after 1 January 2005. The fair value accounting rules are considered in more detail in Chapter 1.

Under the new legislation, certain financial instruments (including derivatives) may be included in the accounts at fair value provided that this can be determined reliably on the following basis:

(i) if a reliable market for the instrument can be readily identified, fair value should be determined by reference to its market value;

(ii) if no such market can be readily identified for the financial instrument as a whole, but can be identified for its components or for similar instruments, fair value should be determined by reference to the market value of the components or of a similar instrument; and

(ii) if neither (i) nor (ii) applies, fair value can be determined by using generally accepted valuation models and techniques, provided that these ensure a reasonable approximation of the market value of the financial instrument.

Financial instruments (other than derivatives) held to maturity, investments in group undertakings and joint ventures, loans and receivables not held for trading purposes and certain other investments are specifically excluded from the scope of the fair value accounting rules. FRS 25 'Financial instruments: Disclosure and Presentation' and FRS 26 'Financial Instruments: Measurement' set out the detailed UK framework for the adoption of fair value accounting.

Measurement of financial assets

22.30 FRS 26 'Financial Instruments: Measurement' applies to listed companies for accounting periods beginning on or after 1 January 2005, and to other entities for accounting periods beginning on or after 1 January 2006 but only if they choose to adopt fair value accounting (and adoption from 1 January 2005 is also acceptable in this case). However, the scope of the standard is expected to be extended in due course (see 22.35 below). The standard includes detailed requirements on:

(i) initial measurement of financial assets and financial liabilities;

(ii) subsequent measurement of financial assets and financial liabilities;

(iii) recognising gains and losses on financial assets and liabilities;

(iv) accounting for impairment and uncollectibility in respect of financial assets; and

(v) hedge accounting.

The requirements apply to all types of financial instruments, apart from certain items that are specifically excluded in the standard – these include interests in group undertakings that are included in the consolidated accounts of the entity – however, an interest in a group undertaking that is accounted for at fair value or as held for resale, and derivatives on interests in group undertakings do come within the scope of the standard.

The standard requires a financial asset to be measured at fair value on initial recognition. In the case of a financial asset not at fair value through the profit and loss account, this value should be increased by any transaction costs directly attributable to the acquisition or issue of the financial asset. After initial recognition, financial assets should be measured at fair value without any deduction for transaction costs that may be incurred on sale or disposal, except that:

(i) loans and receivables and held-to-maturity investments should be measured at amortised cost using the effective interest method;

(ii) investments in equity instruments that do not have a quoted market price in an active market, and whose fair value cannot be measured reliably, should be measured at cost, as should any derivatives that are linked to, and must be settled by, delivery of such investments; and

(iii) financial assets designated as hedged items should be measured under the hedge accounting requirements of the standard.

All financial assets except those measured at fair value through profit and loss are subject to review for impairment under the requirements of standard.

Accounting for gains and losses

22.31   Gains and losses on financial assets that are not part of a hedging relationship should be recognised as follows:

(i) those on financial assets classified as at fair value through profit and loss should be recognised in the profit and loss account;

(ii) those on available-for-sale financial assets should be recognised through the statement of total recognised gains and losses until the asset is derecognised, at which time the cumulative gains and losses recognised in that statement should be recognised in the profit and loss account – however, the following exceptions apply:

● where the asset is impaired, the cumulative loss should be immediately recognised in the profit and loss account, even though the asset has not been derecognised; and

● foreign exchange gains and losses on financial assets that are monetary items should be accounted for in accordance with FRS 23 'The Effects of Changes in Foreign Exchange Rates' (see Chapter 7); and

(iii) those on financial assets carried at amortised cost should be recognised in the profit and loss account when the asset is derecognised or impaired, or through the amortisation process.

Impairment and uncollectibility

22.32   An assessment must be made at each balance sheet date of whether there is any objective evidence that a financial asset or group of financial assets is impaired. The standard sets out detailed requirements on:

(i)   measuring impairment losses for each type of financial asset;

(ii)   where such impairment losses should be recognised in the accounts; and

(iii)   accounting for the reversal of such impairment losses in subsequent periods.

Hedging

22.33   The standard sets out detailed requirements on the designation of hedging instruments and the accounting treatment to be applied to gains and losses arising on a hedged item and the hedging instrument where a designated hedging relationship exists between the two. The detailed coverage includes:

(i)   which financial instruments qualify as hedging instruments;

(ii)   which items qualify as hedged items;

(iii)   the designation of hedging instruments and hedged items;

(iv)   types of hedging relationships (ie fair value hedge, cash flow hedge and hedge of a net investment in a foreign operation);

(v)   the conditions that must be met for hedge accounting to be applied; and

(vi)   the hedge accounting treatment to be applied to each type of hedge.

The hedging requirements of the standard are considered in Chapter 26.

Transitional arrangements

22.34   The standard generally requires retrospective application of its requirements, unless the restating of the information for earlier periods would be impracticable, in which case that fact and the extent to which restatement has taken place must be disclosed. Also, an entity that first adopts FRS 26 for an accounting period beginning before 1 January 2007 need not restate comparative information to comply with the new requirements. Instead, the preceding year's figures can continue to be presented on the basis of the entity's previous accounting policies for financial instruments and the accounts should disclose:

(i)   the fact that this approach has been taken;

(ii)   the accounting policies adopted for the comparative information; and

(iii)   the nature of the adjustments that would be needed to make the comparative information comply with FRS 25 – the standard does not require the adjustments to be quantified, but it does require any adjustment between the closing balance sheet for the comparative period (ie prepared on the basis of the previous accounting policies) and the opening balance for the current period (ie prepared on the basis of the FRS 25 requirements) to be treated as arising from a change in accounting policy, with the disclosures required by FRS 18 'Accounting policies'.

Also, on first application of the standard, an entity is permitted to designate a previously recognised financial asset or financial liability as a financial asset or financial liability at fair value through profit or loss or available for sale, even though the standard normally requires such a designation to be made on initial recognition. The standard specifies how the cumulative changes in fair value should be accounted for in these circumstances. There is also detailed transitional guidance on accounting for hedges on first application of the standard, particularly where transactions previously been designated as hedges or hedged items no longer qualify under the new requirements.

Likely future developments

22.35   In April 2005, the ASB issued an Exposure Draft 'Amendment to FRS 26 – Financial Instruments: Measurement' which proposes extending the scope of the standard and introducing into UK accounting the recognition and derecognition requirements of the underlying international accounting standard. The ASB is currently proposing that the extension in scope should apply for accounting periods beginning on or after 1 January 2007, or possibly 1 January 2008 if more preparation time is needed. However, the Board is aware of the considerable practical difficulties that listed entities are facing at present in applying FRS 26 or the underlying international accounting standard, IAS 39, which is itself in the process of revision by the International Accounting Standards Board (IASB).

The proposed derecognition requirements would supersede the derecognition principles in FRS 5 'Reporting the Substance of Transactions' for financial assets, but the FRS 5 requirements would remain in force for non-financial assets. The related IAS disclosure requirements in respect of recognition and derecognition would also be added to FRS 25. The ASB proposes that the recognition and derecognition requirements should apply for accounting periods beginning on or after 1 January 2007, with earlier adoption permitted. However, if the measurement aspects of FRS 26 are deferred to a later date for entities not currently within the scope of the standard, the recognition and derecognition requirements would be similarly deferred. Certain transitional provisions will be included to prevent entities having to restate all earlier transactions on the new basis.

OTHER ACCOUNTS DISCLOSURE

Fixed asset investments

22.36   In the case of fixed asset investments, CA 1985 requires considerable detail to be given in respect of opening and closing balances and movements during the year. This is usually presented in the form of a table, but other forms of presentation may be more appropriate depending on how many categories of investment need to be included and the complexity of the movements during the year.

Example 22.4 – Table detailing fixed asset movements

	Participating interests		Other Investments	Total
	Shares	*Loans*		
Cost	£	£	£	£
At 1 January 20X2	556	150	75	781
Additions	—	—	10	10
Disposals	—	—	(20)	(20)
At 31 December 20X2	556	150	65	771
Provisions				
At 1 January 20X2	—	50	—	50
Charged in the year	—		7	7
Written back in the year	—	(30)	—	(30)
At 31 December 20X2	—	20	7	27
Net book value				
At 31 December 20X2	556	130	58	744
At 31 December 20X1	556	100	75	731

Current asset investments

22.37 In the case of current asset investments, movements during the year do not have to be disclosed. The only disclosure will therefore be the analysis by category for each year and the information on listed investments discussed in 22.52 to 22.55 below.

Listed investments

22.38 For any item shown in the accounts as investments (in either fixed assets or current assets), CA 1985 requires separate disclosure of:

— the amount relating to listed investments;

— the aggregate market value of the listed investments, if this is different to the amount included in the accounts; and

— both the market value and the stock exchange value of the listed investments, where the market value is taken as being higher than the stock exchange value for accounts purposes.

Most listed investments will be disclosed as 'other' investments within fixed assets or current assets. However, it is possible that shares in group undertakings or in participating interests will include listed investments, in which case the analysis will need to be given for these categories as well.

Definition of listed investment

22.39 CA 1985 defines a listed investment as 'an investment as respects which there has been granted a listing on a recognised investment exchange (other than an overseas investment exchange) or on any stock exchange of repute outside Great Britain'.[1] The terms 'recognised investment exchange' and 'overseas investment exchange' are as defined in the Financial Services and Markets Act 2000. Investments in companies traded on other markets (such as the Alternative Investment Market) should be classified as unlisted investments. In the case of companies listed on overseas stock exchanges, what constitutes a stock exchange of repute will to some extent be a matter of judgement, but investments listed on well recognised foreign exchanges should be treated as listed investments for disclosure purposes.

Example disclosures

22.40 The disclosure requirements might therefore be met by the following presentation in the case of fixed asset investments.

Example 22.5 – Analysis of other fixed asset investments to show details of listed investments

	Listed in the UK	Unlisted	Total
	£	£	£
Cost			
At 1 January 20X2	61	14	75
Additions	10	—	10
Disposals	(18)	(2)	(20)
At 31 December 20X2	53	12	65
Provisions			
At 1 January 20X2	—	—	—
Charged in the year	—	7	7
At 31 December 20X2	—	7	7
Net book value			
At 31 December 20X2	53	5	58
At 31 December 20X1	61	14	75

The aggregate market value of the listed investments at 31 December 20X2 was £89,000 (20X1: £97,000).

In the case of current asset investments, the disclosure is less detailed, as movements during the year do not have to be disclosed. The following will therefore usually be sufficient.

Example 22.6 – Disclosure of listed investments within current assets

	20X2	*20X1*
	£	£
Listed investments	76	59
Unlisted investments	13	12
	89	71

The aggregate market value of the listed investments at 31 December 20X2 was £93,000 (20X1: £67,000).

Separate disclosure of stock exchange value

22.41 The requirement to disclose both the market value and the stock exchange value of the listed investments (where the market value is taken as being higher than the stock exchange value for accounts purposes) will not often arise in practice. It might be necessary where, for instance, the shareholding represents a controlling interest. Where disclosure is required, wording along the following lines will usually satisfy the requirement.

Example 22.7 – Where market value is higher than stock exchange value

The aggregate market value of the listed investments at 31 December 20X2 was £89,000 (20X1: £97,000). This market value includes certain investments for which market value is considered to be higher than their stock exchange value. The market value of these investments at 31 December 20X2 was £47,000 and their stock exchange value at that date was £41,000.

Details of significant shareholdings

22.42 CA 1985 requires additional details in respect of any investment where:

— the company's shareholding amounts to 20% or more of the nominal value of any class of shares in that undertaking; or

— the amount of the investment (as shown in the company's accounts) represents more than one-fifth of the company's net assets.

A shareholding of this level will usually mean that the undertaking is an associate, and the accounting requirements of FRS 9 will therefore also apply (see 22.12 to 22.25 above). An investment in a subsidiary undertaking is not covered by these disclosure requirements, as separate disclosures in respect of subsidiaries are set out in CA 1985 Sch 5. The following details must be given for significant shareholdings other than subsidiaries:

— the name of the undertaking;

— its country of incorporation, if this is outside Great Britain;

— if it is unincorporated, the address of its principal place of business;

— the identity of each class of shares held by the company; and

—   the proportion of the nominal value of shares in that class held by the company.

The information is usually given in narrative form, as part of the notes on investments. The disclosures apply to both fixed asset and current asset investments.

Example 22.8 – Narrative disclosure of significant share holdings

The total for investments listed in the UK includes an interest of 21.4% in the preference shares of ....plc and the total for unlisted investments includes a 24% interest in the ordinary shares of B Limited.

Where the company needs to disclose information in respect of a number of other entities, presentation in a table might be more appropriate.

Example 22.9 – Where information on a number of entities is needed

Name	*Country of incorporation*	*Class of shares held*	*Percentage held*
Listed investments:			
A plc		Preference	21.4%
Unlisted investments:			
B Limited		Ordinary	24.0%
C Limited	Ireland	Ordinary	32.2%

Financial information in respect of significant investments

22.43   Where the company has one or more significant shareholdings (as defined in 22.42 above), the following details must also be disclosed:

—   the aggregate amount of the capital and reserves of the undertaking at the end of its relevant financial year; and

—   its profit or loss for that year.

This additional information does not have to be given if:

—   the information is immaterial;

—   the company is exempt from preparing group accounts under CA 1985 s 228 (ie it is part of a larger group) and the company's investment in all such undertakings is shown in aggregate in the notes to the accounts by way of the equity method of valuation (ie the company's share of the net assets of the undertakings); or

—   the investment is in an undertaking that is not required by CA 1985 to deliver a copy of its balance sheet to the registrar and does not otherwise publish its balance sheet in Great Britain, and the company's shareholding is less than 50% of the nominal value of the shares in the undertaking.

Also, the information normally required in relation to significant shareholdings need not be given in respect of an undertaking which is established under the law of a country outside the UK or carries on business outside the UK if:

— in the opinion of the directors, the disclosure would be seriously prejudicial to the business of that undertaking, or to the company or any of its subsidiaries; and

— the Secretary of State agrees that the information need not be disclosed.

In this case, the fact that the company has taken advantage of the exemption must be stated in the notes to the accounts.

Avoiding a disclosure of excessive length

22.44 CA 1985 s 231(5)allows some restriction of the detailed information where the disclosures in respect of subsidiaries and other significant investments would otherwise be of excessive length because of the number of entities involved. The accounts must state that information is only given in respect of the undertakings specified in CA 1985 s 231(5) and that full information will be attached to the next annual return. The information included with the annual return must cover the undertakings that were disclosed in the accounts as well as those that were not.

Financial fixed assets not at fair value

22.45 Where a company has financial fixed assets that could be accounted for at fair value but which are included in the accounts at an amount in excess of fair value, without any provision for diminution in value, the accounts must disclose:

(i) the amount at which those assets are included (either individually or in appropriate groupings);

(ii) the fair value of the assets (or the relevant groupings); and

(iii) the reason for not making a provision for diminution in value, including the nature of any evidence which supports the expectation of a recovery in value.

Derivatives not at fair value

22.46 Where the company has derivatives which have not been included in the accounts at fair value, the accounts must disclose for each class of derivatives:

(i) the fair value of the derivatives in that class, if this can be calculated in accordance with paragraph 34B of Schedule 4 (see 22.29 above); and

(ii) the extent and nature of the derivatives.

However, a small company preparing shorter form accounts under Schedule 8 to CA 1985 is not required to give these disclosures.

Chapter 23 Stocks

GENERAL PRINCIPLES OF STOCK VALUATION

Accruals concept under FRS 18

23.1 FRS 18 specifically requires financial statements (other than cash flow information) to be prepared on the accruals basis of accounting, which it defines as requiring the non-cash effects of transactions and events to be reflected, as far as is possible, in the financial statements for the accounting period in which they occur and not in the period in which any related cash is received or paid. The standard makes a clear link with the definitions of assets and liabilities set out in FRS 5 'Reporting the Substance of Transactions' (and also in the Statement of Principles), and notes that the use of those definitions to determine which items should be recognised as assets and liabilities in the balance sheet is consistent with the accruals concept. Where an entity has unused or unsold stocks at the end of an accounting period, it will usually expect to use or sell those items in the following accounting period or, in some cases, in a future accounting period (eg where stocks require time to mature before they can be sold). The company will therefore have incurred costs in buying or producing the stock items in anticipation of earning revenues from them at some time in the future. Consequently, the stock items meet the definition of assets (rights or other access to future economic benefits owned by an entity as a result of past transactions or events) and it is therefore appropriate to carry them forward in the balance sheet.

'Cost' of stocks

23.2 The value carried forward for stocks should represent the expenditure incurred in the normal course of business in purchasing the goods or producing the goods (ie bringing them to their present location and condition). However, in most cases it will not be possible to identify the precise purchase price or production cost for each item held in stock at the end of the year, and in practice an element of averaging, costing and allocation of overheads will usually be required in order to calculate the 'cost' of the stock.

Sensitivity of stock valuation

23.3   The value of closing stocks will be adjusted for when calculating the charge to the profit and loss account in respect of cost of sales (or, where Format 2 is used for the profit and loss account, the charge in respect of raw materials and consumables and the adjustment for the change in stocks of finished goods and work in progress). Consequently, if the value carried forward for stocks at the end of an accounting period is overstated or understated, this will have a direct impact on the operating profit or loss that is reported for the period. The value of stocks is therefore a highly sensitive figure in the accounts, but also one of the most difficult figures to calculate in view of the degree of judgment that will usually be required in the valuation process.

Historical cost accounting rules

23.4   Stocks are classified as current assets in the balance sheet formats and, under the historical cost accounting rules, should therefore be shown at the lower of:

—   purchase price or production cost; and

—   net realisable value.

The historical cost accounting rules and the rules on determining purchase price and production cost are covered in Chapter 1. However, CA 1985 allows a company to apply special rules in the case of stocks and fungible assets. Fungible assets are defined as assets of any description that are substantially indistinguishable from one another. CA 1985 allows stocks and fungible assets to be valued for accounts purposes by one of the following methods, rather than requiring them to be included at actual purchase price or production cost:

—   first in, first out (FIFO);

—   last in, first out (LIFO);

—   a weighted average price; and

—   any other method similar to the above methods.

However, not all of these methods are generally acceptable for the purpose of valuing stocks under SSAP 9 'Stocks and Long-term Contracts'. Where stocks are included in the accounts on the basis of one of these methods any material difference between the amount shown in the accounts and the replacement cost of the stocks must be disclosed in the accounts.

Alternative accounting rules

23.5 Under the alternative accounting rules (see Chapter 1), stocks may be included in the accounts at their current cost. However, this treatment is rarely adopted in practice as it does not generally comply with the accounting requirements of SSAP 9 'Stocks and Long-term Contracts'.

CA 1985 rules on purchase price and production cost

23.6 CA 1985 sets out specific rules on the calculation of purchase price or production cost. These apply to all assets and are considered here in the context of stocks. The more general application of these rules is covered in Chapter 1. The purchase price of an asset is the actual price paid plus any expenses incidental to its acquisition. Incidental expenses include the cost of getting the asset to its present location and into its present condition. The production cost of an asset is to be calculated by adding together:

— the purchase price of the raw materials and consumables used; and

— the direct costs of production.

In addition, CA 1985 permits the following items to be included in production cost:

— a reasonable proportion of indirect production costs, but only to the extent that they relate to the period of production; and

— interest on capital borrowed to finance the production of the asset, but again only to the extent that it relates to the period of production.

Where interest is included in production cost, the notes to the accounts must disclose the fact that interest has been included and the amount of interest involved. In the case of stocks (and other current assets), CA 1985 specifically prohibits the inclusion of distribution costs in production cost.

Requirements of SSAP 9 'Stocks and Long-term Contracts'

23.7 SSAP 9 'Stocks and Long-term Contracts' recognises that it will not usually be possible to identify the exact purchase price or production cost of each item held in stock at the end of the period, particularly where stocks consist of a large number of comparatively small items. There will often be a variety of methods that could potentially be used to allocate costs to stocks and the standard therefore states that the methods used should be 'selected with a view to providing the fairest possible approximation to the expenditure actually incurred in bringing the product to its present location and condition'. The guidance notes set out some of the practical considerations relating to the allocation of costs.

Definition of 'cost'

23.8   SSAP 9 defines 'cost' as 'that expenditure which has been incurred in the normal course of business in bringing the product or service to its present location and condition'. It identifies two elements to cost – cost of purchase and cost of conversion. Cost of purchase is defined as 'purchase price, including import duties, transport and handling costs and any other directly attributable costs, less trade discounts, rebates and subsidies'. Therefore, any costs relating directly to the purchase and transport of items held in stocks should be included in the stock valuation. However, where trade discounts and rebates are reflected in the accounts in relation to these purchases, they must also be adjusted for when valuing the stock, in order to arrive at the closest approximation to the price actually paid for the goods. Costs of conversion are defined as:

— costs which are specifically attributable to units of production, e.g. direct labour, direct expenses and sub-contracted work;

— production overheads (which are separately defined); and

— other overheads, if any, attributable in the particular circumstances of the business to bringing the product or service to its present location and condition.

This is consistent with the requirements set out in CA 1985 on the inclusion of overheads in production cost.

Production overheads

23.9   Production overheads are defined as 'overheads incurred in respect of materials, labour or services for production, based on the normal level of activity, taking one year with another'. A crucial point here is that the allocation of production overheads must be based on a normal level of activity, so that the costs of any inefficiency, excessive wastage or idle time is written off in the year in which it is incurred and is not carried forward to future years within the stock valuation. This is considered further in 23.17. to 23.19.

Net realisable value

23.10   Net realisable value is defined in SSAP 9 as the actual or estimated selling price (net of trade but before settlement discounts) less:

— all further costs to completion; and

— all costs to be incurred in marketing, selling and distributing.

Therefore, although selling and distribution costs must not be included in production cost, they should be taken into account when assessing the net realisable value of stocks and the need for any provisions to reduce the cost of stocks to net realisable value. SSAP 9 also reinforces the requirement under CA 1985 that stocks should be stated at the lower of cost and net realisable value, and specifies that the comparison of cost and net realisable value should be made for each individual stock item, or by groups or categories of similar items where individual consideration is not possible. If this comparison was only carried out on a total basis, it might result in unacceptable offsetting of potential losses against potential profits. The SSAP 9 requirement is therefore consistent with the requirement in CA 1985 that individual components of assets and liabilities should be considered separately when calculating the aggregate value of an asset or liability.

ACCEPTABLE COSTING METHODS

Principal types of costing system

23.11   Most companies will need to make use of some form of costing system to gather together the direct costs of purchasing or producing goods or of providing services. At a basic level, they will need this information to enable them to price their products and services effectively (ie by taking account of all raw material costs, time spent on producing goods or performing services, an allowance for related overheads and the margin of profit that they expect to achieve). The more usual types of costing system are:

—   job costing;

—   batch costing;

—   process costing; and

—   standard costing.

The most appropriate system will depend on the nature of the company's product or services and the volume of goods produced. A job costing system or process costing system might be appropriate for a production activity that results in a small number of large products, such as the manufacture of machines. A batch costing system may well be more appropriate if the production activity involves producing a large quantity of small items in each production run, for instance the manufacture of items such as bearings or nuts and bolts. Under a standard costing system, management estimates the expected cost of producing each item, usually based on experience to date, and accounts for production on the basis of these standard costs. To be effective the system requires actual cost to be compared with standard cost on a regular basis, with a detailed analysis and review of any variances.

Costing in the services sector

23.12   In the services sector, the major cost will be the time of the staff involved on each project or assignment, and costs will usually be accumulated by recording the time spent by each individual and costing this at standard rates, usually depending on the degree of experience or knowledge required and calculated to recover salary costs and other overheads.

Valuation of stocks

23.13   Any of these methods will usually provide an appropriate basis for valuing items included in stocks at the end of the accounting period. In a manufacturing company the costs to be included will often vary depending on the stage of completion of the product. Raw materials for use in the process will be valued at purchase price; finished goods will include all the costs of raw materials, labour and other production overheads; work-in-progress will include some raw materials, labour and overhead costs, but not all, the amount included being dependent on the stage of production that has been reached for each item. However, in all cases care must be taken to exclude any inappropriate overheads or any profit margin that may be built into the costing system.

Purchase or production cost of identical items

23.14   Another factor that needs to be taken into account where large volumes of similar goods are purchased or produced, and the purchase price or production cost varies, is a method for deciding how to establish the cost of the items remaining in stock at the end of the accounting period. A common approach is to use the FIFO (first in, first out) method of allocating costs. This assumes that the goods that were purchased or produced first will have been used first, and that those remaining in stock at the end of the period will therefore have come from the latest purchases or production run.

Example 23.1 – Remaining stock calculated using FIFO

A Ltd has made the following purchases of the same raw material for use in production:

Date	Quantity	Price per tonne
16 January	50 tonnes	£23.45
5 February	65 tonnes	£25.60
29 March	44 tonnes	£23.78
23 April	52 tonnes	£27.45
18 May	60 tonnes	£22.95

At the end of the accounting period on 31 May, A Ltd has 127 tonnes of this raw material in stock. Using a FIFO basis, the year-end stocks will be assumed to relate to the last three purchases and stock will therefore be valued as follows:

60	tonnes at £22.95	£1,377
52	tonnes at £27.45	£1,427
15	tonnes at £23.78	£356
127		£3,160

Another method in fairly common usage is to calculate an average cost over a suitable period of time and apply this to the quantity in stock at the end of the period.

Example 23.2 – Remaining stock calculated using average cost

The details are as for Example 23.1.

Date	Quantity	Price per tonne	Total cost
16 January	50 tonnes	£23.45	£1,173
5 February	65 tonnes	£25.60	£1,664
29 March	44 tonnes	£23.78	£1,046
23 April	52 tonnes	£27.45	£1,427
18 May	60 tonnes	£22.95	£1,377

Based on normal stock-holding and usage patterns, the company uses an average cost over a three-month period to value stocks. The average cost for year-end purposes will therefore be based on:

44	tonnes at 23.78	£1,046
52	tonnes at 27.45	£1,427
60	tonnes at 22.95	£1,377
156		£3,850

The average cost is therefore £3,850/156 = £24.68 per tonne and the year-end stocks will be valued at £3,134 (ie 127 tonnes at £24.68).

A further averaging method permitted under the CA 1985 is LIFO. This takes the opposite approach to FIFO, and assumes that the latest purchases or production are used first and that the oldest items therefore remain in stock. Base stock is a method that applies a fixed unit value to a specified stock quantity. Any stocks in excess of this quantity are valued on a different basis. Neither LIFO nor base stock will usually be an acceptable method of valuing stocks under SSAP 9, because these methods give little weight to the recent cost of acquiring or producing the goods that are held in stock at the end of the accounting period. They will therefore not meet the SSAP 9 requirement that the valuation gives the fairest approximation to actual cost, and they can give rise to serious distortions in the accounts, particularly when prices are increasing.

Use of estimation techniques

23.15   Under FRS 18 'Accounting Policies', where estimation techniques are needed to enable the adopted accounting policies to be applied, the techniques chosen should enable the financial statements to give a true and fair view and should be consistent with the requirements of accounting standards, UITF Abstracts and companies' legislation. Where it is necessary to choose between estimation techniques that satisfy these conditions, the entity should select the technique that is judged to be the most appropriate to its particular circumstances for the purpose of giving a true and fair view. Estimation techniques are considered in more detail in Chapter 5. The guidance in FRS 18 also notes that specific accounting requirements for fungible assets (which the standard defines as assets that are substantially indistinguishable from one another in economic terms) may be set out in accounting standards, UITF Abstracts and companies' legislation. Where fungible assets are recorded at historical cost, the accounting policy may require cost to be determined on an asset-by-asset basis or may consider such assets in aggregate by using a measurement basis such as weighted average historical cost, or historical cost measured on a first in, first out (FIFO basis). The guidance notes that an accounting policy that considers fungible assets in aggregate will be more consistent with the objective of comparability.

Inclusion of raw materials and consumables at a fixed amount

23.16   CA 1985 permits raw materials and consumables to be included at a fixed quantity and value, provided that:

—   they are assets of a kind that are constantly being replaced;

—   their overall value is not material; and

—   their quantity, value and composition do not vary materially.

As with all accounting standards, SSAP 9 need not be applied to immaterial items, and there is consequently nothing in the standard to prohibit this approach being used for items that are not material. It can be a useful and convenient means of accounting for minor consumable items such as screws, nuts, bolts, etc.

ALLOCATION OF OVERHEADS

Overheads to be included

23.17   The allocation of overheads cannot be a precise exercise and will inevitably involve a degree of subjectivity and judgment. There are two key aspects to the allocation:

—   only production-related overheads should be included; and

—   the allocation should be based on the company's normal level of activity.

In order to carry out the appropriate allocation, all of the company's overheads must be analysed by function, the normal analysis being:

—   production;

—   marketing, selling and distribution; and

—   general administration.

Certain overheads will fall clearly into one category, and will either be included in or excluded from the stock valuation accordingly. The main difficulty relates to those overheads that cover more than one function. In this case, the proportion of the overhead relating to production needs to be established, so that this can be included in the stock valuation. For instance, the apportionment may be based on space (eg to establish the proportion of rent and rates relating to the factory) or on time (eg to allocate the salary cost of an individual who carries out work for more than one function). SSAP 9 makes the point that overheads should not be excluded from the stock valuation on the grounds of prudence. Whilst it is right that a prudent approach should be taken to the valuation of stock, this should be dealt with by the review of net realisable values and not by excluding certain costs from the valuation of stock items.

Management costs

23.18   Where members of management have functional responsibility (eg a production director), their salary and related costs can be charged to that function, and in smaller businesses, where individuals might have more than one responsibility, an appropriate apportionment may be made. However, the principle in SSAP 9 is that other general management costs should not be carried forward within the stock valuation.

Normal level of activity

23.19   SSAP 9 requires overheads to be allocated to production units on the basis of the company's normal level of activity, taking one year with another. The main purpose of this is to ensure that avoidable costs, such as those arising from inefficiencies, excessive wastage (eg due to problems or faults with production plant) and idle time are charged to the profit and loss account in the year in which they are incurred and are not carried forward to future periods in the stock valuation. The factors to be considered when assessing the company's normal level of activity will usually include:

—   the volume of production that the facilities should normally achieve – among other things, this will depend on the working conditions that management set for the year under review (eg whether the factory operates for one shift, two shifts or 24 hours a day etc);

—   the budgeted level of activity for the current year and for the next year;

—   the level of activity actually achieved during the current year and during the previous year.

A normal level of activity will usually be established for a period of more than a year, and certain temporary variations may be acceptable without amendment to the overall calculations, but the level of activity should nevertheless be reviewed each year and, if it is clear that variances are recurring each year and are expected to continue, the normal level of activity for overhead allocation purposes will usually need to be revised.

ASSESSING NET REALISABLE VALUE

Situations where provision may be needed

23.20   Having valued stock at purchase price or production cost, including any relevant overheads, an assessment needs to be made of whether the stocks will realise at least this value when sold. The assessment must be made by individual item or, where individual consideration is not practical, by groups or categories of similar items. Any stock items that are not expected to realise the value attributed to them must be written down to their net realisable value. Many companies need to make provision against stock values in this way, some of the more common reasons being:

— general obsolescence of the product (eg as a result of advances in technology or changes in the market);

— a slow-moving market for individual products;

— physical deterioration in the goods – particular attention is required where goods have a limited shelf life (eg certain chemical or medical products);

— management decisions to sell certain products at a loss (eg as part of a marketing strategy);

— increases in costs; and

— reductions in selling prices (eg as a result competitive pricing).

Provisions on a formula basis

23.21   In some companies, initial provision is made on the basis of an agreed formula, developed on the basis of actual experience in previous years. This can be a useful method of calculating a provision in order to recognise the fact that certain goods are moving slowly.

Example 23.3 – Formula for calculating a provision for slow-moving goods

On the basis of experience in recent years B Ltd calculates that the following provision is required in respect of slow-moving goods:

Last recorded movement	*Provision*
Goods that have moved in the last 6 months	Nil
Goods that last moved 6–12 months ago	35%
Goods that last moved 12–18 months ago	70%
Goods that last moved over 18 months ago	100%

Depending on the nature of the goods and the company's activity, formula provisions can also be based on:

— the age of the products;

— firm orders over the coming months;

— expected future sales.

However, this type of provision alone is unlikely to be adequate to cover all cases where net realisable value may be lower than cost and more detailed reviews of individual items will be required as well to cover the other factors outlined in 23.19 above.

Calculating net realisable value

23.22   Net realisable value is the expected selling price of the goods, less:

—   any trade discounts likely to be given (but not settlement discounts);

—   any further costs to complete the product; and

—   all costs to be incurred in marketing, selling and distributing the product.

Overheads relating to marketing, selling and distribution will need to be identified on a similar basis to production overheads, to enable the comparison of net realisable value and cost to be carried out. It is important to recognise that a straight comparison of cost with expected selling price (net of trade discounts) will not necessarily be sufficient to meet the requirements of SSAP 9, although it may be adequate as a first step. If this initial comparison indicates that there is a substantial margin between cost and selling price, further work will not usually be necessary. However, if selling price is above cost, but only marginally so, further investigation will usually be required, as the impact of any costs to complete, and marketing, selling and distribution expenses, may well erode and reverse a small margin.

Provisions against raw material stocks

23.23   Where net realisable value provisions need to be made against finished goods, this may cast doubt on the stock value of any raw materials or other parts that are used in the production of these items and additional provisions may therefore be needed against the value of raw material stocks or even work-in-progress. When assessing the value of raw material stocks, it is usually necessary to look at the expected realisable value of the end product, not just the realisable value of the raw materials. For instance, if the price of a raw material has fallen, but calculations show that the product in which the raw material is to be used will still be sold at a profit (ie with the raw material included in the calculation at cost rather than realisable value), no provision against the stock value of raw material will usually be required. The situations when provision may be required against raw material stocks are:

—   if the end product has a net realisable value below cost;

—   if the raw material stocks are likely to be sold rather than used in production (eg because the end product is no longer viable).

ACCOUNTS DISCLOSURES

Analysis of stocks

23.24   The balance sheet formats set out in CA 1985 require separate disclosure of stocks, analysed into the following categories:

— raw materials and consumables;

— work in progress;

— finished goods and goods for resale; and

— payments on accounts.

The heading for stocks is given a Roman numeral and must therefore be shown on the face of the balance sheet. The sub-headings are given Arabic numerals and the detailed analysis of stocks may therefore be given in the notes to the accounts. The figures may also be combined if the individual amounts are not material. The 'payments on account' sub-heading is intended to be used to disclose payments made by the company on account of stock items, but is rarely seen in practice. The accounting treatment of payments on account received from customers in respect of contract work is considered in Chapter 24. SSAP 9 requires a similar analysis of stocks by category.

For accounting periods beginning on or after 1 January 2005, the detailed requirements of CA 1985 on the form and content of accounts are only relevant where the company prepares Companies Act accounts (as opposed to IAS accounts).

Disclosure of accounting policy

23.25   SSAP 9 requires disclosure of the accounting policy adopted in respect of stocks. The level of detail required will depend on the nature of the stocks and the variety of stock categories held. The following wording may be suitable in a straightforward case.

Example 23.4 – Disclosure of accounting policy on stock

Stocks are included at the lower of cost and net realisable value. In the case of raw materials, consumables and goods purchased for resale, stocks are valued at purchase price using the first in, first out method. In the case of work in progress and manufactured goods, stocks are valued at production cost to the relevant stage of manufacture; production cost consists of direct material and labour costs, together with an appropriate proportion of production overheads.

Replacement cost of stocks

23.26   Where stocks have been valued on the basis of one of the averaging methods permitted by CA 1985, any material difference between this value and the replacement cost of the stocks must be disclosed in the accounts. Where the actual purchase price or production cost of stock items has been calculated on an individual basis (ie without the need for one of the methods set out in CA 1985), this disclosure need not be given. Replacement cost will usually be the amount that would need to be paid to replace the stocks at their current cost. However, CA 1985 permits the disclosure to be based on the most recent purchase price or production cost, but only if this will give a more appropriate standard of comparison for the class of items in question. The disclosure is usually given in a narrative footnote to the analysis of stocks.

Example 23.5 – Disclosure on replacement cost

Stocks	20X2	20X1
	£	£
Raw materials and consumables	546	481
Work in progress	143	128
Finished goods	322	279
	1,011	888

The current replacement cost of stocks is £1,250,000 (20X1: £925,000).

There is no specific requirement in CA 1985 for a statement where the difference is not considered material, but it is good practice to include this where appropriate.

Example 23.6 – Where difference is not material

There is no material difference between the replacement cost of stocks and the value included in the balance sheet.

CONSIGNMENT STOCKS

Nature of consignment stocks

23.27 The requirements of FRS 5 'Reporting the Substance of Transactions' are considered in Chapter 4. Consignment stocks are one of the items potentially affected by this accounting standard and accounting for consignment stocks is specifically considered in the Application Notes to FRS 5. Consignment stocks are particularly common in the motor dealership trade, but may arise in a number of businesses. Essentially consignment stock is held for sale by one party but legally owned by another party. In the case of motor dealerships, the stock is usually held by the dealer but is legally owned by the manufacturer. The dealer is given the right to sell the stock in the normal course of business, with the option of returning unsold stock to the manufacturer, usually within a specified time limit. In most cases, the stock will be physically held at the dealer's business premises. The discussion below uses a motor dealership as an example, but the principles apply equally to other types of consignment stocks.

Transfer of legal title

23.28   Under most consignment stock arrangements for motor dealerships, legal title remains with the manufacturer until:

—   the dealer sells the car to a third party;

—   the dealer elects to take the car as a demonstration model; or

—   a specified time period elapses, after which the dealer must formally acquire the goods (unless he has previously exercised the option to return them to the manufacturer).

Legal title passes to the dealer when one of these events takes place and at that point he is required to pay the manufacturer for the goods.

Deposit arrangements

23.29   Under some agreements the dealer is required to pay a deposit to the manufacturer. This may be a fixed amount or may vary over a period of time and may or may not be interest free. In some cases, the deposit may be arranged through a financing institution (sometimes linked to the manufacturer) which makes the payment direct to the manufacturer but charges interest to the dealer.

On or off balance sheet?

23.30   The issue here is: does the dealer have an asset (usually vehicle stocks) and a liability (the equivalent finance effectively provided by the manufacturer) which should be recorded on his balance sheet? This must be assessed by considering the access that the dealer has to the benefits of the stock and the exposure that he has to any inherent risks associated with the benefit. The solution will depend on the precise terms of the agreement between the dealer and the manufacturer and the impact of the following issues will often be relevant:

—   whether the dealer is protected against increases in the manufacturer's price for the cars;

—   whether the dealer bears the risk of holding slow-moving or obsolete stock and having to sell this at reduced prices; and

—   the potential financing arrangements, including any deposit and any interest charges which the dealer may be required to pay.

An assessment of each factor will not necessarily lead to the same conclusion, and it may therefore be necessary to weigh up which are the most important factors for each particular situation.

Dealer's protection against price increases

23.31   As explained in 23.28 above, legal title will usually pass to the dealer on the occurrence of a particular event (eg the sale of the car to a third party) and at this point the dealer will be required to pay the manufacturer for the car. The key issue here will usually be the basis of the payment, which may be:

—   a price fixed at the date that the dealer took delivery of the car; or

—   the manufacturer's list price at the date that legal title passes.

The first situation indicates that the car became an asset of the dealer at the date of delivery (ie because the price was fixed at that date and the manufacturer is unable to pass on any subsequent price increases). The second situation indicates that the car is an asset of the manufacturer until the date when legal title passes, because the dealer has no protection against price increases between the date of delivery and the date that title passes.

Right to return the car to the manufacturer

23.32   Under some agreements the dealer will have the right to return the car to the manufacturer (usually within a specified time limit) without any penalty. In this case, the dealer does not bear any risk of the stock being slow-moving or becoming obsolete. This suggests that the stock is an asset of the manufacturer rather than the dealer (ie because the manufacturer bears the risk). If the dealer does not have the right to return the car without payment of a penalty this suggests that the car is an asset of the dealer, because he bears the risk of having to sell at a reduced price if the car proves to be slow-moving or becomes obsolete. In some situations it will be necessary to look at the actual practice in respect of the return of cars to the manufacturer, as well as the rights of each party under the agreement. If the dealer has the right to return cars within a specified time but rarely does so, this indicates that the cars are his stock because he is accepting the potential commercial risk of holding them. Conversely, if the manufacturer introduces incentives to encourage the dealer not to return the cars (eg by extending the consignment period at no financial detriment to the dealer), the fact that the dealer retains the cars will not necessarily indicate that they are his stock, because he may not be taking any additional risk by not returning them to the manufacturer.

Right of manufacturer to require return of the car

23.33   The manufacturer may retain the right to require the dealer to return the car, or to transfer the car to another dealer. Where the dealer receives no compensation, and cars are frequently removed in this way in practice, this would indicate that the stock belongs to the manufacturer rather than the dealer. If the dealer receives compensation from the manufacturer for such returns, or transfers are not actually requested in practice, the stock is more likely to be considered to belong to the dealer.

Accounting treatment – asset of the dealer

23.34   Where the substance of the arrangement is that the consignment stock is effectively an asset of the dealer, the stock should be brought onto the balance sheet, along with the corresponding liability to pay the manufacturer. Where the dealer has paid a deposit to the manufacturer, this should normally be deducted from the liability. The notes to the accounts will need to include:

—   an explanation of the arrangement;

—   the principal terms; and

—   the amount of consignment stock included in the balance sheet.

Accounting treatment – asset of the manufacturer

23.35   Where the substance of the arrangement is that the consignment stock remains an asset of the manufacturer, stock items will only be included in the dealer's balance sheet when legal title has effectively passed (eg the consignment period has expired and the dealer has not elected to return the car). Where the dealer has paid a deposit to the manufacturer, this should normally be included in debtors, as no liability to the manufacturer will be recorded in the balance sheet. The notes to the accounts will need to include:

—   an explanation of the arrangement;

—   the principal terms; and

—   the amount of consignment stock held at the year-end.

SALE AND REPURCHASE AGREEMENTS

Nature of a sale and repurchase agreement

23.36   Sale and repurchase agreements are another type of transaction potentially affected by FRS 5 'Reporting the Substance of Transactions' and the Application Notes to the standard specifically cover the accounting treatment of such agreements. The requirements of FRS 5 are considered in detail in Chapter 4. The paragraphs below only consider sale and repurchase agreements which might have an impact on stocks. A sale and repurchase agreement is an agreement under which one party agrees to sell an asset to a second party but where the terms of the agreement provide for the first party to repurchase the asset at some point in the future. The issue is whether the original sale should be recorded as such, or whether the terms of the agreement effectively mean that the asset was not sold, but rather that finance was provided by the second party, effectively secured on the asset. This type of agreement has been particularly common in situations where stock is required to be held for a considerable period of time before it can be sold to customers.

Example 23.7 – Sale and repurchase in practice

An often quoted example is that of a whisky distiller, who 'sells' whisky stock to a bank, with the option to repurchase at a higher price in (say) ten years (ie when the stock has matured). In most cases such an agreement will effectively be a loan from the bank to the distiller, secured on the whisky stock, with the difference between the original selling price and the higher repurchase price representing the interest charge on the loan.

Benefits and risks

23.37   In order to assess the commercial reality of the transaction, it is necessary to consider:

—   which party benefits from the use, development or ultimate sale of the asset; and

—   which party bears the potential risks of decreases in value of the asset.

In the case of a sale and repurchase agreement, the key features which will decide the commercial effect of the transaction, and thus how it should be accounted for, will usually be:

—   the original selling price;

—   the repurchase price; and

—   the nature of the repurchase part of the agreement, which may take the form of:

    —   an option for the seller to repurchase,

    —   an option for the buyer to resell,

    —   a combination of these options, or

    —   an unconditional commitment for both parties.

Original selling price

23.38   Where the selling price is not equivalent to market value at the date of the transaction, there is a strong indication that the seller is in effect retaining some of the benefits and risks relating to the asset. He will therefore still retain an asset (which may or may not be the original asset) and a potential liability to the buyer.

Unconditional commitment to repurchase

23.39   Where the seller has an unconditional commitment to repurchase the asset, there is no question that he has both a liability to the buyer and an asset (ie continued access to the benefits of the original asset), both of which should be recorded on the seller's balance sheet. It is important to recognise that a commercial commitment may exist even if a legal commitment does not, for instance where the asset is essential to the seller's future business or there is an unwritten agreement that repurchase will take place. Returning to the example of the whisky stocks above (Example 23.7 above), the distiller will undoubtedly repurchase the stocks because he will need them to continue in business. Equally, the transaction would make little commercial sense for the bank if it was not on the understanding that the distiller would repurchase the stocks.

Options to repurchase and resell

23.40   Options must also be viewed from the point of view of commercial sense. If it is inevitable that the option will be exercised (ie because the transaction would not make sense for one, or both, parties if this did not happen), the option is effectively artificial and the situation is not really any different to an unconditional commitment. The terms of an option may make it inevitable that one party will exercise it. However, if there is a genuine commercial possibility that an option will not be exercised, this may strengthen the argument that the seller does not have an asset and liability that should be reflected on his balance sheet. In this case the other terms of the agreement may well be the deciding factors.

Accounting treatment

23.41   Where the substance of the sale and repurchase agreement is that the transaction is a secured loan, the asset should remain on the seller's balance sheet and the proceeds should be shown as a liability. The liability should be treated in the same way as any other loan, and if interest is effectively chargeable, it should be accrued over the period of the loan. If the value of the asset decreases, an appropriate provision should be made in the accounts. The notes to the accounts should include an explanation of:

—   the main features of the agreement;

—   the status of the asset; and

—   the relationship between the asset and the liability.

Where the substance of the agreement is that the original asset has been sold, but the seller has an option to repurchase the asset, the new asset (eg the option to repurchase) and the contingent liability should be accounted for prudently and in the same way as any other contingencies (ie in accordance with FRS 12 'Provisions, Contingent Liabilities and Contingent Assets'). Therefore:

—   any unconditional commitment should be included on the balance sheet;

—   provision should be made for any expected loss; and

—   contingent assets and gains should only be recognised when realised.

In this case, the notes to the accounts should include:

— an explanation of the main features of the agreement;
— an explanation of the status of the asset;
— an explanation of the relationship between the asset and the liability;
— the terms of any provision for repurchase; and
— details of any guarantees under the arrangement.

Chapter 24   Long-term Contracts

IDENTIFICATION OF LONG-TERM CONTRACTS

Definition of long-term contract

24.1   Long-term contracts are considered separately within SSAP 9 'Stocks and Long-Term Contracts'. The standard defines a long-term contract as:

> 'A contract entered into for the design, manufacture or construction of a single substantial asset or the provision of a service (or of a combination of assets or services which together constitute a single project) where the time taken substantially to complete the contract is such that the contract activity falls into different accounting periods.'

The key factors therefore are that the contract relates to a single project and that the time taken to complete the work spans at least two accounting periods. Long-term contracts arise mainly within activities such as construction or engineering (e.g. the construction of an office block, the construction of a road, the installation of major plant and equipment, the installation of a public address system in a large complex) but they can easily occur in other businesses as well.

Accounting treatment to avoid distortion

24.2   Under normal accounting requirements, sales are usually recognised as turnover when delivery or completion has taken place. However, if this approach is adopted in the case of long-term contracts, the accounts might not give a fair view of the activity that has taken place during the year (i.e. the accounts would show the results of contracts completed during the year rather than work undertaken during the year). SSAP 9 therefore requires turnover and profits (or losses) in respect of long-term contracts to be recognised as the work proceeds, subject to the following stringent conditions:

— the amount of turnover recognised must be appropriate to the stage of completion of the contract;

— attributable profit should be recognised only where the outcome of the contract can be assessed with reasonable certainty;

— attributable profit must be calculated on a prudent basis;

— expected losses must be provided for in full as soon as they are foreseen.

Contracts lasting more or less than one year

24.3   SSAP 9 explains that a long-term contract will usually extend for a period of more than one year, but this is not an essential feature of a long-term contract. Contracts lasting less than 12 months may therefore meet the definition of a long-term contract if:

— they satisfy the criteria set out in the standard; and

— they are sufficiently material that failure to account for them as long-term contracts could distort the turnover and profits disclosed in the accounts.

Need for consistency

24.4   The definition of a long-term contract in SSAP 9 allows companies a degree of flexibility in establishing which transactions should be accounted for as long-term contracts and it specifically requires the assessment to take account of the company's business and the industry within which it operates. It is quite possible under SSAP 9 for one company to classify a contract as short-term whilst a second company classifies a very similar contract as long-term. One of the most important points, therefore, is that each company should adopt a consistent approach year by year. To achieve this, a company potentially involved in long-term contracts should:

— develop its own precise definition for a long-term contract, following the guidance set out in SSAP 9 and the related notes;

— apply this definition consistently year by year to the contracts in which it is involved;

— explain clearly in the accounting policy note how it defines a long-term contract for accounting purposes.

Contracts with separable parts

24.5   In some long-term contracts, the overall project is broken down into clearly defined parts, for which sales values are agreed and invoiced. SSAP 9 requires these contracts to be accounted for by matching costs and revenues for each separate part of the contract (i.e. by effectively treating each separate part of the contract as a contract in its own right). However, an overall assessment of the project will still be required (i.e. expected future revenues compared with expected future costs for the project as a whole) to establish whether any provision is required in respect of foreseeable losses.

Changing circumstances

24.6   Where a contract extends over several accounting periods, the estimated outcome of the contract may vary quite substantially over the period of the contract. This may be as a result of unforeseen difficulties over the work, variations to the contract whilst the work is in progress, or the incidence of claims and counter-claims relating to the contract. At the end of each accounting period, the profit and loss account and balance sheet should reflect the best estimate of the expected outcome of the contract at that point in time. The results shown in the profit and loss account for each year will therefore reflect the profit or loss in respect of work completed during the year, and also the impact of any changes in circumstances that have arisen during that year, which result in changes to the estimated outcome of the contract as a whole.

RECOGNITION OF TURNOVER

Individual consideration of contracts

24.7   In assessing and recognising turnover and attributable profit for accounts purposes, the standard requires each long-term contract to be considered individually. Carrying out the assessment on a total basis might result in unacceptable off-setting of potential losses against potential profits. SSAP 9's requirement is consistent with the requirement in CA 1985 that individual components of assets and liabilities should be considered separately when calculating the aggregate value of an asset or liability.

Ascertaining turnover

24.8   The turnover recognised in the profit and loss account for each contract should reflect the value of work carried out and SSAP 9 requires the assessment of turnover to take account of:

— the stage of completion of the work;

— the company's business; and

— the industry in which it operates.

For example, in the case of long-term construction work, turnover will often be based on internal, or in some cases independent, valuations of work completed by the balance sheet date. In other contracts, there may be specific points during the work where sales values can be established with reasonable accuracy (e.g. where the customer has taken delivery), so that only work completed since that point needs to be assessed and valued. Application Note G to FRS 5 'Reporting the Substance of Transactions' provides additional guidance on the recognition and measurement of turnover. This Application Note was added to FRS 5 in November 2003 and is effective for accounting periods ending on or after 23 December 2003. It includes a separate section on long-term contracts and this sets out the following requirements:

(i)   changes in assets and liabilities, and related turnover, should be recognised over the course of the contract, reflecting the accrual of the seller's right to consideration;

(ii)   the amounts recognised should be derived from an assessment of the fair value of the goods or services provided as a proportion of the total fair value of the contract; and

(iii) the fair values used should be those applicable at the inception of the contract, unless the contract terms provide for price increases to be passed on to the customer.

In some contracts, the proportion in (ii) above will correspond with the proportion of expenditure incurred compared with total expenditure, but this will not always be the case. It is also important to recognise that the relative profitability of the different stages of a contract may vary. The recognition of turnover should not generally follow the pattern of costs incurred, unless this provides evidence of the extent to which the seller has completed its contractual obligations.

The guidance emphasises that the application of SSAP 9 should result in long term contractual performance being recognised as contract activity progresses, to the extent that the outcome of the contract can be assessed with reasonable certainty, and that the turnover recognised should reflect the extent of the seller's right to consideration. The Application Note also provides guidance on the separation and linking of contracts (including when a contract should be 'unbundled' into its constituent parts) which might also be relevant to the assessment of long-term contracts. These issues are considered in more detail in Chapter 10.

Services contracts

24.9   Following the publication of Application Note G to FRS 5, a number of concerns were raised over the interaction between this pronouncement and the requirements of SSAP 9 in the context of contracts for professional services. The Urgent Issues Task Force was asked to consider this and published its consensus as Abstract 40 'Revenue recognition and service contracts' in March 2005. Although the concerns were raised mainly in the context of professional services contracts, the UITF has concluded that the same principles should be applied to all contracts for services. The Abstract applies for accounting periods ending on or after 22 June 2005, although earlier adoption is encouraged.

The key issue is whether revenue under such contracts should be recognised as contract activity progresses, or only on completion of the contract. The Abstract notes that it is impractical to provide definitive guidance for every situation, as the detailed terms and commercial substance of services contracts vary considerably. Each reporting entity should therefore apply the underlying principles to its own circumstances. As with all accounting issues, a consistent approach should be applied from year to year for all similar contracts. The main points from the UITF consensus are that:

(i) contracts dealing with the provision of services on an ongoing basis rather than the provision of a single service (or the provision of a number of services that constitute a single project) do not fall within the SSAP 9 definition of a long-term contract – revenue under such contracts should therefore be accounted for as it arises;

(ii) by contrast, a contract for a single service (or a single project) which either lasts for more than one year or spans more than one accounting period, will need to be accounted for as a long-term contract if failure to do so would result in a material distortion of turnover and results – revenue should therefore be recognised as contract activity progresses.

The only exception to (ii) above is where the service provider's right to consideration is conditional or contingent on a specific future event or outcome which is outside the control of the service provider. In this case, the revenue should not be recognised until the critical event actually occurs.

The requirements of UITF Abstract 40 are considered in more detail in Chapter 19.

Disclosure of method used

24.10 SSAP 9 recognises that there are different ways of establishing turnover, any of which might meet its requirements, and therefore does not prescribe how turnover should be calculated. As a result, the accounting policy note is required to explain the method used to ascertain turnover in respect of long-term contracts for inclusion in the accounts.

CALCULATION OF ATTRIBUTABLE PROFIT

Definition of attributable profit

24.11 SSAP 9 defines attributable profit as:

'That part of the total profit currently estimated to arise over the duration of the contract, after allowing for estimated remedial and maintenance costs and increases in costs so far as not recoverable under the terms of the contract, that fairly reflects the profit attributable to that part of the work performed at the accounting date. (There can be no attributable profit until the profitable outcome of the contract can be assessed with reasonable certainty)'.

The amount of attributable profit must be calculated on a prudent basis.

Contract outcome assessed with reasonable certainty

24.12   The first stage, before any profit is recognised in the accounts, is that the company must be able to assess the likely outcome of the contract and be reasonably certain of the level of profit that will be achieved. SSAP 9 does not provide any further guidance on this point, although the notes to the standard state that, for each contract, the company should define the point before which no profit will be recognised. In the early stages of a contract it will usually be difficult to assess the end result with the appropriate degree of certainty. In practice, many companies take the view that profit should not be recognised until the contract is at least 50% complete. History and experience will usually indicate the appropriate percentage to use. Although it will not usually be acceptable to recognise profit in the early stages of a contract, it may nevertheless be appropriate to recognise as turnover the value of the work completed up to the balance sheet date and to include costs up to this level in the profit and loss account (unless an overall loss is anticipated, in which case full provision for this will need to be made – see 24.16 below).

Costs to be included

24.13   The overall profitability of each contract is assessed by comparing expected future revenues with projected costs, including:

— costs actually incurred to date;

— estimated costs to be incurred in completing the work;

— the estimated costs of any rectification work, or any work that might be required under guarantees given in respect of the contract – these can be difficult to assess and some companies provide for them on the basis of a percentage of total contract costs, the percentage being based on past experience on similar contracts; and

— the costs of any other future work to be undertaken under the terms of the contract.

The estimates for future costs should take into account:

— likely increases in wages and salaries;

— increases in the price of raw materials; and

— the effect of inflation on general overheads,

unless it is clear that the contract provides for these increases to be passed on to the customer.

Profit earned to date

24.14   Where the comparison of expected revenues and projected costs for the contract as a whole indicates that a profit is likely to be achieved, and the contract is sufficiently far advanced for this assessment to be reasonably certain, the total profit on the contract must be apportioned between the element earned to date (which will be recognised in the accounts) and the element to be earned in the remaining part of the contract. The notes to SSAP 9 require the recognition of profits in the accounts to be:

— on a prudent basis, and

— based on a method that is applied consistently from year to year.

For instance, profit may be apportioned on the basis of the stage of completion of the contract as at the balance sheet date, the proportion of total costs incurred to that date or on the basis of the work that has been valued and accepted by the customer at the balance sheet date (on major contracts, inspection and valuation by the customer is usually carried out at specific stages during the contract). In the same way that the method of ascertaining turnover must be disclosed, SSAP 9 requires the accounting policy note to explain the method of ascertaining attributable profit.

Accounting entries

24.15   Once attributable profit has been calculated for each contract, the appropriate element of costs to date should be transferred from total costs incurred on the contract to cost of sales in the profit and loss account (or to the appropriate profit and loss account headings where Format 2 is used):

Example 24.1 – Calculating attributable profit

Contract 1	£
Value of work done to date	245,000
Total costs incurred to date	267,000
Total contract value	320,000
Expected total costs	307,000
Expected profit	13,000
Attributable profit to be recognised in accounts: 245/320 x 13,000	9,950
Turnover recognised in accounts	245,000
Attributable profit	(9,950)
Cost of sales to be recognised	235,050
Total costs incurred to date	267,000
Transferred to cost of sales	(235,050)
Costs carried forward	31,950

ESTIMATION OF FORESEEABLE LOSSES

Provision for projected loss

24.16   Where, on the basis of the costs set out in 24.13 above, a contract is projected to result in an overall loss, SSAP 9 requires full provision to be made in the accounts as soon as the loss is foreseen. This should be done irrespective of:

—   whether or not work has yet commenced on the contract;

—   the proportion of work carried out by the balance sheet date;

—   the amount of profits expected to arise on other contracts.

Example 24.2 – Recognising an estimated loss

Contract 2	£
Value of work done to date	245,000
Total costs incurred to date	267,000
Total contract value	320,000
Expected total costs	327,900
Expected loss	(7,900)
Turnover recognised to date	245,000
Projected loss recognised in full	7,900
Costs of sales to be recognised	252,900
Total costs to date	267,000
Transferred to cost of sales	252,900
Costs carried forward	14,100

The provision for the loss should normally be treated as part of the overall charge to the profit and loss account in respect of costs relating to the turnover recognised in the accounts.

Cost of sales greater than costs incurred to date

24.17   Where the provision for the loss results in a cost of sales charge that is greater than the amount of costs incurred to date, the excess should be shown in the accounts as a provision or accrual for a future loss.

Example 24.3 – Cost of sales greater than costs incurred to date

Contract 3

	£
Value of work done to date	245,000
Total costs incurred to date	247,000
Total contract value	320,000
Expected total costs	327,900
Expected loss	(7,900)
Turnover recognised to date	245,000
Projected loss recognised in full	7,900
Cost of sales to be recognised	252,900
Total costs to date	247,000
Transferred to cost of sales	(252,900)
Provision/accrual for expected loss	(5,900)

Treatment of loss as provision or accrual

24.18   SSAP 9 requires a provision or accrual for a foreseeable loss to be included within provisions for liabilities or within creditors, as appropriate. However, it is singularly unhelpful in explaining the distinction between a provision and an accrual in these circumstances. CA 1985 defines a provision as:

> 'any amount retained as reasonably necessary for the purpose of providing for any liability or loss which is either likely to be incurred, or certain to be incurred but uncertain as to the amount or as to the date on which it will arise.'

It would therefore seem that a provision for a foreseeable loss on a long-term contract should be included under provisions for liabilities if there is a degree of uncertainty over the eventual amount or expected timing of the loss. If the loss can be established with certainty, it should be treated as an accrual and included with creditors (or under the separate heading for accruals and deferred income where this is used).

ACCOUNTING FOR CONTRACT VARIATIONS AND CLAIMS

Impact of variations and claims

24.19   Two of the most complex aspects of long-term contracts are the agreement of variations which arise whilst the contract is in progress and the settlement of claims relating to the contract (e.g. where the customer claims penalties for delays or late completion of the work). The situation can become even more complicated where the contractor issues counter-claims against the customer or where sub-contractors are involved and the main contractor issues equivalent claims for penalties against the sub-contractors.

Contract variations

24.20   If significant variations to the contract have been approved during the course of the work, but the additional sums to be paid for these variations have not been agreed, a reasonable but prudent estimate of the likely value of the additional work should be made and should be included as part of the total sales value of the contract (i.e. when carrying out assessments of overall revenue, costs and profitability).

Claims

24.21   In the case of claims, or unapproved variations, the situation will usually be much more uncertain, even if negotiations are in progress. On larger contracts, negotiations can be very protracted and can themselves extend over more than a year. Claims and unapproved variations should generally only be recognised in the accounts when negotiations have reached an advanced stage. In particular there should be:

— evidence that the customer is prepared to accept the claim (or unapproved variation) in principle; and

— a clear indication of the amount that is likely to be paid.

ACCOUNTS DISCLOSURES

Location of disclosures

24.22   Depending on the individual circumstances of each contract, disclosures may be required on the balance sheet within:

— stocks;

— debtors;

— creditors; or

— provisions for liabilities.

The following paragraphs consider the detailed disclosure requirements and the related accounting entries.

Inclusion of long-term contracts in stocks

24.23   The value of long-term contracts in progress should be shown as a separate item (long-term contract balances) within stocks. Each individual contract should be shown at total costs incurred to date, less:

— amounts transferred to cost of sales;

— provisions for foreseeable losses;

— payments on account not matched with turnover.

Separate disclosure should be made of:

— net costs, less foreseeable losses; and

— payments on account.

Example 24.4 – Long-term contracts included in stocks

Contract 1	£
Value of work done to date	245,000
Total costs incurred to date	267,000
Payments received on account	215,000
Total contract value	320,000
Expected total costs	307,000
Expected profit	13,000
Attributable profit to be recognised in accounts: 245/320 x 13,000	9,950
Turnover recognised in accounts	245,000
Attributable profit	(9,950)
Cost of sales to be recognised	235,050

The amount included in stocks in respect of this contract will be:

	£
Total costs incurred to date	267,000
Transferred to cost of sales	(235,050)
Included in long-term contract balances	31,950

Contract 2	£
Value of work done to date	245,000
Total costs incurred to date	267,000
Total contract value	320,000
Expected total costs	327,900
Expected loss	(7,900)
Turnover recognised to date	245,000
Projected loss recognised in full	7,900
Cost of sales to be recognised	252,900

The amount to be included in stocks in respect of this contract will be:

	£
Total costs incurred to date	267,000
Transferred to cost of sales (including loss provision)	(252,900)
Included in long-term contract balances	14,100

Inclusion of amounts recoverable on contracts within debtors

24.24   Where the amount recognised as turnover exceeds payments received on account, the excess should be shown separately within debtors as 'amounts recoverable on contracts'.

Example 24.5 – Excess turnover shown within debtors

Contract 1	£
Value of work done to date	245,000
Total costs incurred to date	267,000
Payments received on account	215,000
Amount recognised as turnover	245,000
Payments on accounts	215,000
Amounts recoverable on contracts	30,000

(included as a separate heading in debtors)

This treatment reflects the fact that once the value of work done has been recognised in the profit and loss account as turnover, it is not appropriate to continue to show it under stocks in the balance sheet. It is therefore disclosed as an amount recoverable from the customer even though it may not have been invoiced at the balance sheet date.

Inclusion of payments on account in creditors

24.25   Where payments on account received from the customer exceed:

—   the amounts matched with turnover; and

—   the amounts off-set against long-term contract balances,

the excess should be shown separately under creditors as payments on account.

Example 24.6

Contract 4	£
Value of work done	105,000
Total costs incurred to date	118,000
Payments on account	118,000
Total expected revenue	130,000
Total expected costs	144,000
Foreseeable loss	(14,000)
Amount recognised as turnover	105,000
Amount recognised as cost of sales	(119,000)
Loss recognised in the accounts	(14,000)

The amount to be recognised in the balance sheet is therefore:

Turnover	105,000
Payments on account received	(118,000)
Excess payments on account	(13,000)

The amount recognised as long-term contract balances is:

Total costs incurred to date	124,000
Transferred to cost of sales	(119,000)
	5,000

Therefore, £5,000 of the excess payments on account should be off-set against this balance; the remaining £8,000 should be included in creditors as payments on account.

The note to the accounts on long-term contracts should show separately:

	£
Net costs, less foreseeable losses	5,000
Payments on account	(5,000)
	—

Excess provision for foreseeable losses

24.26   If the provision or accrual for foreseeable losses exceeds the costs incurred (after adjusting for transfers to cost of sales), the excess should be included under provisions for liabilities or under accruals. This is illustrated in Example 24.3 above.

Summary of disclosures

24.27   The appendix to this chapter draws together the details from Examples 24.3 to 24.6 to illustrate the overall disclosures that should be given in the accounts if these four contracts were in progress within one company.

Accounting policy

24.28   SSAP 9 requires disclosure of the accounting policy that has been applied in respect of long-term contracts, and in particular the method of calculating turnover and attributable profit. The wording of the policy in each individual company will vary, depending on the exact policies adopted, but Example 24.7 illustrates the type of explanation that should be given.

Example 24.7 – Disclosure of accounting policy for long-term contracts

The company classifies as long-term those contracts which relate to the construction of a single asset, where the contract activity extends over more than one accounting period. The length of these contracts usually exceeds 12 months.

The amount recognised as turnover represents the value of work carried out during the period. Where the outcome of a contract can be assessed with reasonable certainty, attributable profit is recognised in proportion to the amount of turnover recognised in the accounts. No profit is recognised in respect of contracts that are less than 50% complete at the balance sheet date. Full provision is made for any foreseeable losses.

Long-term contract balances are included in the balance sheet at net cost, less foreseeable losses, and after deduction of any related payments on account. Where the amount recognised as turnover exceeds the payments on account in respect of that contract, the balance is included in debtors under amounts recoverable on contracts.

Inclusion of interest in the cost of long-term contracts

24.29   CA 1985 allows the production cost of an asset (including stock) to include interest on capital borrowed to finance production, but only to the extent that it relates to the period of production. The notes to SSAP 9 emphasise that it will not usually be appropriate to include interest payable on borrowings as part of the cost of long-term contracts (or, indeed, of other stock items). If, in exceptional circumstances, it is considered appropriate to include interest (i.e. where specific borrowings can be identified as financing individual long-term contracts) the notes to the accounts should disclose the fact that interest has been included and the amount involved. This is consistent with the disclosure requirements of the Act.

LIKELY FUTURE DEVELOPMENTS

FRED 28 – 'Inventories; Construction and service contracts'

24.30   The ASB issued FRED 28 'Inventories; Construction and service contracts' in May 2002 as part of its project to achieve convergence between UK accounting standards and international accounting standards. The Exposure Draft sets out the proposed text of two new accounting standards intended to replace SSAP 9 'Stocks and long-term contracts' with requirements based on a proposed revision of IAS 2 and the existing IAS 11. The aspects of IAS 18 'Revenue' that deal with service contracts are also incorporated into FRED 28. No major changes to UK requirements are proposed, but the following differences in respect of the accounting treatment to be applied to contract costs and revenue will have some effect:

—   FRED 28 proposes that contract revenue and related costs should be recognised when the outcome of a contract can be 'estimated reliably' – this is more consistent with FRS 18 'Accounting policies' and the ASB Statement of Principles than the SSAP 9 references to prudence and outcomes that can be assessed with 'reasonable certainty';

—   FRED 28 proposes that any amounts received from a customer before work is performed should be recognised as a separate liability, but that any remaining balance sheet amount should be presented as a single asset or liability – SSAP 9 currently requires a more detailed analysis, potentially involving debtors, creditors, stock and provisions; and

— FRED 28 notes that its requirements may be applied to separately identifiable components of a single contract or to a group of contracts together, if this reflects the substance of the transaction – the ASB considers that the practical effect of this will be no different to applying the present SSAP 9 within the context of FRS 5 'Reporting the substance of transactions'.

The current version of the ASB's Technical Plan, published in June 2005, indicates that new UK accounting standards in respect of inventories and construction contracts will be published in the final quarter of 2005 and are planned to come into effect for accounting periods beginning on or after 1 January 2006. A further Exposure Draft based on IAS 'Revenue' is also expected to be published in the last quarter of 2005.

APPENDIX

Summary of disclosures

Profit and loss account	*Contract 1* (Example 24.4) (Example 24.5)	*Contract 2* (Example 24.4)	*Contract 3* (Example 24.3)	*Contract 4* (Example 24.6)	*Total*
Turnover – value of work done	245,000	245,000	245,000	105,000	840,000
Cost of sales	(235,050)	(252,900)	(252,900)	(119,000)	(859,850)
Recorded profit/(loss)	9,950	(7,900)	(7,900)	(14,000)	(19,850)
Balance sheet					
Long-term contract balances:					
Net costs, less foreseeable losses	31,950	14,100	—	5,000	51,050
Payments on account	—	—	—	(5,000)	(5,000)
	31,950	14,100	—	—	46,050
Debtors – amounts recoverable on contracts	30,000	—	—	—	30,000
Creditors/provisions – provisions for expected losses	—	—	(5,900)	—	(5,900)
Creditors – payments on account	—	—	—	(8,000)	(8,000)
Cash: Paid (i.e. costs incurred to date)	(267,000)	(267,000)	(247,000)	(124,000)	(905,000)
Received (i.e. payments on accounts)*	215,000	245,000	245,000	118,000	823,000
	9,950	(7,900)	(7,900)	(14,000)	(19,850)

*In contracts 2 and 3, payments on account are assumed to equal turnover (i.e. the value of work done).

Chapter 25   Debtors, Prepayments and Accrued Income

TRADE DEBTORS

Sales ledger balances

25.1   Trade debtors will normally comprise the aggregate of the outstanding balances shown on the company's sales ledger at the end of the accounting period. As debtors are shown within current assets, they must be stated at the lower of purchase price and net realisable value. The definition of purchase price in the Act effectively allows debtors to be stated at an amount that includes the profit element to be earned by the company, but if the net realisable value of debtors is lower than the amount recorded in the company's books, appropriate provision must be made. Provisions made against the balances recorded in the sales ledger will normally comprise provisions:

— for bad and doubtful debts;

— for credit notes due to be issued;

— in respect of settlement discount to be allowed.

Bad and doubtful debts

25.2   All debts shown on the ledger at the end of the accounts period should be reviewed for expected recoverability, with particular attention being paid to amounts that are outstanding for more than the credit period normally granted by the company. Where payment seems unlikely to be received, or may not be received in full, provision should be made. A bad debt provision may be totally specific (i.e. relating entirely to known problem debtors) or may be partly general. General provisions can be particularly useful where there are a large number of relatively small balances on the ledger. The general provision reflects the fact that a proportion of these balances may not be paid, even though it may not be possible to identify individual bad debts at the balance sheet date. General provisions are usually calculated as a set percentage of the total amount outstanding in respect of unprovided debts. Where possible, this percentage should be based on past experience of bad debts. Although a prudent approach should be taken when assessing the recoverability of debts, provisions should nevertheless be reasonable (i.e. the best estimate of the likely outcome) rather than excessively pessimistic.

Credit notes

25.3 Provision should also be made where credit notes have been issued after the year-end in respect of invoices included in the year-end balances, or where it is known that such credit notes will be issued (e.g. because a price amendment has recently been agreed with the customer). Once again, this recognises that, in these cases, the full amount of the debt shown at the end of the year will not actually be paid by the customer.

Settlement discounts

25.4 Where a company gives discounts for early settlement of invoices, the full amount of the sales value is usually invoiced to the customer. The appropriate discount is then deducted by the customer when making payment. The availability of settlement discounts will therefore mean that the full amount of the balances shown on the sales ledger may not be paid in cash. Settlement discounts are normally only given for prompt payment (e.g. within 7 or 14 days of the invoice date) and in most cases, there will be little difficulty in establishing the amount of discount actually taken in respect of balances which were outstanding at the end of the accounting period. For accounts purposes, year-end trade debtors should be reduced by the amount of discount actually granted by the company in respect of those balances (i.e. the discount should be treated as a cost in the year in which the sale was recorded). In exceptional circumstances (e.g. where the accounts need to be finalised very quickly after the end of the accounting period) it may be necessary to estimate the amount of settlement discount that will be taken by customers. It will usually be possible to calculate the proportion of customers who take advantage of the discount, based on past experience and apply this to those balances that are still within the discount period, to arrive at an appropriate provision for accounts purposes (e.g. where discount is allowed for payment within 21 days, invoices outstanding for more than 21 days should not be included in the calculations, as customers will not be entitled to settlement discount in respect of these items).

Credit balances

25.5 Small credit balances arising on the sales ledger can usually be ignored on the grounds that they are immaterial, but if a material credit balance arises on a debtor account (e.g. as a result of the customer paying an invoice twice by mistake), the credit balance should normally be transferred from debtors to creditors. This is particularly relevant if the company is likely to make a cash payment to the customer to clear the balance.

Uninvoiced sales

25.6   There is no guidance on how to classify any uninvoiced sales arising around the year-end date. In many cases, the sales ledger will be held open for a day or two after the year-end to allow invoices in respect of sales made on the last day (or days) to be processed. In this case, they will form part of the year-end sales ledger and will automatically be included in trade debtors for accounts purposes. Where this does not happen, an adjustment will need to be made to incorporate the sales values of any items delivered in the accounting period but not invoiced at the balance sheet date. Such items should normally be shown as part of trade debtors as they relate to turnover. However, if the amounts involved are not material, they are sometimes included under one of the other headings (e.g. other debtors or accrued income).

LESSOR'S NET INVESTMENT IN FINANCE LEASES

Nature of a finance lease

25.7   When a lessor enters into a finance lease with a lessee, the lessor retains legal title to the asset, but transfers substantially all the risks and rewards of ownership of the asset to the lessee. In return for this, the lessor receives an income stream in the form of lease rentals. The underlying substance of the transaction, therefore, is that the lessor provides finance to the lessee to enable the latter to have access to, and use of, the asset, and that the lessor expects a return from the lessee on the finance provided. SSAP 21 'Accounting for Leases and Hire Purchase Contracts' requires a finance lease to be recorded in the accounts of a lessor based on the underlying substance of the agreement. As a finance lease is similar in character to a loan from the lessor to the lessee, SSAP 21 requires it to be:

—   shown within debtors in the lessor's balance sheet;

—   included at the amount of the lessor's net investment in the lease.

Net investment in the lease

25.8   At the beginning of the lease agreement, the lessor's net investment in the lease will be the cost of the asset to the lessor, less any grants receivable by him in respect of the asset. In other words, it will be the fair value of the asset at the beginning of the lease agreement.

Payments during the period of the lease

25.9   The lease rentals received from the lessee during the period of the lease must be apportioned between repayment of the 'capital' element of the lease and interest charges on the amount outstanding. During the course of the lease agreement, therefore, the original value of the lessor's net investment in the lease will be reduced by those elements of the lease rentals that are identified as being repayment of the 'capital' effectively advanced to the lessee. The apportionment of lease rentals in the accounts of the lessor is considered in more detail in Chapter 14.

Balance sheet disclosure

25.10   The net investment in respect of finance leases must be shown separately within debtors as 'amounts receivable under finance leases'. Where the lessor has also entered into hire purchase agreements with customers, the amount receivable under these agreements must also be disclosed as a separate sub-heading. In effect, the amount disclosed each year will represent:

—   the total of the remaining payments due from lessees under the agreements *plus*

—   any residual values in respect of the assets (net of any rental rebates that are payable to the lessee in respect of residual value) *less*

—   the earnings to be allocated to future accounting periods.

Finance leases and hire purchase agreements will usually extend for more than 12 months, and the amounts receivable in respect of these agreements must therefore be analysed between amounts due within one year of the balance sheet date and those due more than one year after this date.

Provision for bad and doubtful debts

25.11   As with any other debtor, the amount recorded in the balance sheet must be the amount that is expected to be recovered. At the end of the accounting period, the lessor must therefore review the expected recoverability of the amount receivable under each agreement and make appropriate provisions for bad and doubtful debts where necessary.

OTHER DEBTORS

Items normally included

25.12   CA 1985 provides no guidance on how individual items should be classified within the main heading of debtors, but 'other debtors' will usually comprise non-trading amounts receivable, such as sundry loans (e.g. loans advanced to employees), sales proceeds in respect of fixed assets, and other similar items that meet the criteria for recognition as assets.

Tax balances

25.13 Other debtors might also include items such as:

— corporation tax recoverable;

— advance corporation tax recoverable;

— VAT repayment due from Customs and Excise.

There is no requirement under CA 1985 to show tax balances separately when they appear within debtors, although tax creditors do require separate disclosure. If the amounts involved are material, it will usually be advisable to show them separately in the analysis, especially where this will help a reader of the accounts to understand the cash flows relating to tax shown in the cash flow statement.

PREPAYMENTS AND ACCRUED INCOME

Prepayments

25.14 Prepayments will generally comprise pre-paid elements of general overhead expenses, such as rent and rates, insurance, maintenance agreements and vehicle licences. In most cases the amounts involved will not be significant. One significant item that might be included is a prepayment in respect of pension contributions under SSAP 24 'Accounting for pension costs'. SSAP 24 requires an employer to recognise the cost of providing pension benefits on a systematic and rational basis over the period during which the company benefits from the services of the relevant employees. As a result, the accounting treatment of pension costs in respect of defined benefit schemes can be very different to the related cash payments, giving rise to either a prepayment or a liability in the employer's accounts. For accounting periods beginning on or after 1 January 2005, SSAP 24 is superseded by FRS 17 'Retirement Benefits' which requires a different balance sheet presentation in respect of the defined benefit asset or liability (see Chapter 12). However, any prepaid contributions at the end of the accounting period should continue to be shown within debtors or prepayments.

Accrued income

25.15 The amounts included as accrued income will vary depending on the nature of the company's activities. Items which might be shown under this heading include:

— amounts receivable in respect of insurance claims

— grants receivable;

— rents receivable; and

— sundry sales income (i.e. sales not relating to the main trading activity).

Rent receivable under an operating lease

25.16   Where an asset, including property, is rented out under an operating lease, SSAP 21 and UITF Abstract 28 'Operating Lease Incentives' require both the rent receivable under the lease and any related incentive offered to the lessee to be recognised over the term of the lease (or the period to the first rent review if shorter), usually on a straight-line basis. The timing of the recognition of the rent receivable may therefore differ from the actual cash flows, and the lessor's balance sheet will include a debtor for accrued rent receivable For instance where an operating lease includes an incentive such as an initial rent free period, no rental will be received during this period but rental income will need to be reflected in the profit and loss account.

Example 25.1 – Accrued rent receivable

A property is rented out for five years under an operating lease. The first year is rent-free. Rent is payable at £5,000 pa for the remaining four years. Total rental income is therefore £20,000 which should be recognised in the lessor's profit and loss account at £4,000 per year for the five years of the lease.

Year 1	Income per accounts	4,000
	Cash received	—
	Debtor	4,000
Year 2	Income per accounts	4,000
	Cash received	5,000
		(1,000)
	Debtor b/fwd	4,000
	Debtor c/fwd	3,000
Year 3	Income per accounts	4,000
	Cash received	5,000
		(1,000)
	Debtor b/fwd	3,000
	Debtor c/fwd	2,000
Year 4	Income per accounts	4,000
	Cash received	5,000
		(1,000)
	Debtor b/fwd	2,000
	Debtor c/fwd	1,000
Year 5	Income per accounts	4,000
	Cash received	5,000
		(1,000)
	Debtor b/fwd	1,000
	Debtor c/fwd	—

UITF Abstract 28 makes two points in relation to the accrued rent receivable carried forward each year:

— where a building is accounted for as an investment property, the value at which it is stated in the balance sheet should exclude any amount that is reported as a separate asset, such as accrued rent receivable; and

— in accordance with normal accounting practice, an amount recognised as a debtor in respect of an operating lease incentive should be written down to the extent that it is not expected to be recoverable.

ACCOUNTING FOR FACTORED DEBTS

Main reasons for factoring debts

25.17   The factoring of debts has become increasingly common as a means of:

— raising finance, by converting debts into cash more quickly than might otherwise be the case;

— providing a degree of protection against the risks of slow payment and bad debts (depending on the nature of the agreement).

In some cases, the factor may also manage the company's sales ledger, but this is usually a completely separate arrangement and will not normally have any impact on the accounting treatment of the debts.

Impact of FRS 5

25.18   The treatment of factored debts is considered in the Application Notes to FRS 5 'Reporting the Substance of Transactions'. The following sections consider only the issues relating specifically to factored debts. The wider impact of FRS 5 is considered in more detail in Chapter 4. The principles set out in FRS 5 and the Application Notes apply equally to other arrangements similar to factoring, such as invoice discounting and export financing arrangements.

Importance of reviewing precise terms and conditions

25.19   Factoring agreements take many different forms, and different accounting treatments will be required, depending on the precise terms of each agreement. A thorough understanding of the terms and conditions is therefore necessary in order to establish which of the three possible accounting treatments is appropriate. This should include an understanding and assessment of the commercial and practical effect of the terms and conditions, as well as the theoretical detail.

Usual features of factoring agreements

25.20   Some of the more common features of factoring agreements are as follows:

— The company sells or assigns specific debts to the factor.

— The factor will provide finance to the company usually based on a fixed percentage of the face value of the debts transferred. This may be a non-returnable amount (in which case it will usually be based on a lower percentage of total debts), but in many cases it will be repayable by the company from the amounts actually collected from the relevant debtors.

— The factor will make a charge for the factoring services. This may be a fixed amount, or may vary depending on the amounts actually collected from debtors. The timing of payment may also vary.

— The factor may offer credit protection or insurance cover in respect of unpaid debts, subject to a separate charge usually based on the gross value of factored debts. This will limit the company's potential exposure in respect of slow payment and bad debts.

— The factor may administer the company's sales ledger and thus assume responsibility for the collection of debts and following up non-payment. This is usually subject to a separate arm's length agreement and will not normally affect the accounting treatment of the factored debts.

Possible accounting treatments

25.21 Depending on the precise circumstances of the arrangements, there are three possible accounting treatments in respect of factored debts:

— derecognition;

— separate presentation;

— linked presentation.

The main features of these treatments are considered in the following paragraphs.

Derecognition

25.22 In this case the debts are completely removed from the balance sheet and no liability to the factor is recorded. This treatment is only available where the company does not retain any benefits or risks in connection with the factored debts. This will usually require:

— an outright sale of the debts to the factor at an arm's length price;

— receipt by the company of a fixed, non-returnable payment from the factor in respect of the debts sold;

— no recourse whatsoever to the company in respect of slow payment or non-payment of the debts; and

— no benefit to the company if the debtors pay more promptly than had been anticipated.

Very few factoring agreements will meet all of these requirements. If the conditions are fulfilled, the company will need to record a profit or loss (invariably a loss) on disposal of the debts, representing the difference between the face value of the debts and the fixed payment received from the factor.

Separate presentation

25.23   Under this accounting treatment, the company must continue to show the value of the factored debts on the balance sheet (as part of debtors) and record a liability to the factor (within creditors), representing the finance effectively provided by him in respect of the debts. This approach should be followed where the company has retained significant benefits and risks in relation to the factored debts. The factor's charges should be accrued, and the interest element should be included as part of the interest charge for the year in the profit and loss account. The value of factored debts outstanding at the balance sheet date should be disclosed in the notes to the accounts.

Linked presentation

25.24   Under the linked presentation, the factored debts continue to be shown within debtors but the amount included is reduced by the value of the non-returnable proceeds received by the company from the factor; both amounts must be disclosed separately on the face of the balance sheet. This form of presentation should only be used where the company has retained significant benefits and risks in respect of the factored debts, but the level of its exposure is limited to a specific amount. The interest element of the factor's charges should be included as part of the interest charge for the year in the profit and loss account. The following details should be disclosed in the notes to the accounts:

— the principal terms of the factoring arrangement;

— the gross amount of factored debts outstanding at the balance sheet date;

— the factoring charges recognised in the period, analysed between interest and other charges;

— a statement by the directors that the company is not obliged to support any losses in respect of the debts, nor does it intend to do so;

— a statement that the factor has agreed in writing that it will not require repayment of the amount paid and will not seek recourse from the company in any other form.

Assessment of benefits and risks

25.25   In order to decide which of these three presentations should be used, the benefits and risks retained by the company under the agreement must be assessed. The benefits will usually comprise the future cash flows arising from payments by the debtors. The risks will usually be the risk of slow payment and non-payment (i.e. bad debts). Of these two elements, the risks retained by the company will usually be more critical in the assessment of the transaction for accounting purposes.

Benefits retained by the company

25.26   Under many factoring agreements, the benefits of future cash flows in respect of the debts will appear to rest with the factor (e.g. cash collected in respect of the factored debts will usually be paid into a separate bank account or direct to the factor). However, this may not be the true effect in practice. For instance, where the company is committed to repaying the sums advanced by the factor on or before a specified date (regardless of the level of payment received from the debtors during the period), it will usually be the company that benefits from the cash received from the debtors (i.e. this cash will form a source of funds from which the company can repay the factor). Equally, the company bears the risks of the debtors not making payment before the date when it is committed to repaying the factor. In this case the company will have to use other funds to make the repayment.

Benefits resting with the factor

25.27   However, if the company receives a non-returnable payment from the factor and is then responsible for passing on all sums received from the debtors, as and when payments are made, the benefit of receiving payment from the debtors will usually rest with the factor, as will the risks relating to the slow payment and non-payment of the debts.

The risk of slow payment

25.28   The basis of the factoring charges will often be a key factor in the assessment of who bears the risk of slow payment. Where charges are raised for a fixed sum, agreed at the time that the debts are transferred, the factor will usually bear the risk of slow payment. Where the factoring charges are variable, depending on the level of payment received from debtors, the risk will usually remain with the company (i.e. if the debtors are slow in paying, the company will bear higher factoring costs). In assessing the risks, it is important to consider the commercial implications of all clauses in the factoring agreement. For instance, the inclusion of bonus payments for early settlement, or retrospective changes to the amounts paid in respect of the debts may alter the overall assessment of risk.

The risk of bad debts

25.29   In some cases the factor may retain all the risk in respect of bad debts. Other agreements may provide for debts that remain uncollected after a specified period (e.g. 90 days) to be transferred back to the company. In this case, the company will retain all the risk of bad debts arising. This may also indicate that the company bears some risk in respect of slow payment, in that a bad debt may be the end result of slow payment.

Practical application

25.30   The application of these requirements may be illustrated by the following basic examples, which consider only the main features of a factoring agreement (in practice, the detailed terms of most factoring agreements will be much more complex).

Example 25.2 – Debt factoring: three scenarios

X Ltd factors debts of £100,000 for:

(A) an initial non-returnable payment from the factor of £75,000, plus further deferred sums, based on the amounts actually collected from the debtors,

(B) a fixed sum of £80,000, with no further amount payable by the factor, and no recourse to the company in respect of bad debts,

(C) a sum of £85,000, which is repayable to the factor in three months' time, at which point any unpaid debts will be transferred back to X Ltd.

Situation A

In this case, X Ltd retains:

— some of the benefits of future payments from debtors, because further sums will be receivable from the factor, depending on the level of payment by the debtors;

— some of the risks of non-payment by the debtors (e.g. if payments do not reach a specified level, no further sums will be paid by the factor). However, X Ltd has limited its potential exposure to the risk of slow payment or bad debts to £25,000 (i.e. proceeds of £75,000 are guaranteed as this sum is non-returnable).

The company should therefore adopt a linked presentation on its balance sheet:

	£	£
Current assets:		
Stocks		233
Debtors:		
Gross debtors factored without recourse	100	
Less: Non-returnable proceeds	(75)	
	25	
Other debtors	124	
		149
Cash at bank and in hand		50
		432

The disclosures outlined in paragraph 25.24 above will also need to be given.

Situation B

In this case, X Ltd has sold the debts outright for a fixed sum and therefore does not retain any benefits from the actual payments made by the debtors. Equally the company does not bear any further risk in relation to the debts.

The company should therefore adopt the derecognition treatment in respect of these debts and will record an overall loss of £20,000 in respect of the factored debts.

Situation C

In this case, X Ltd has retained all the benefits and risks in relation to the debts:

— if the debtors are slow in paying, the company will have to find other funds to repay the factor in three months' time – conversely, if the debtors pay promptly, the company will have the benefit of this;

— all potential bad debts revert to the company after three months – conversely if all the debtors pay in full, the company retains the benefit of this.

In effect, the factor has lent X Ltd £85,000 for a period of three months. The company should therefore adopt separate presentation in its balance sheet. It will record:

— debtors of £100,000;

— a liability to the factor of £85,000.

The value of factored debts will need to be disclosed in the accounts.

In both (A) and (C), the recoverability of the amount included in debtors would need to be considered and provision made where necessary.

ACCOUNTING FOR PRE-CONTRACT COSTS

UITF Abstract 34

25.31   Early in 2002, the UITF considered the accounting treatment to be adopted for pre-contract costs. Some entities incur significant costs in bidding for and securing contracts and the issue had therefore arisen whether pre-contract costs should be recognised as an asset and charged as expenses during the period of the contract and, if so, how such an asset should be measured. The Abstract applies to costs incurred by a supplier in respect of tendering for or securing contracts for:

— the design, construction, manufacture or operation of assets;

— the provision of services; or

— the provision of a combination of assets and services.

It does not apply to costs that are subject to more specific requirements set out in accounting standards (such as FRS 10 'Goodwill and intangible assets', FRS 15 'Tangible fixed assets' or SSAP 13 'Accounting for research and development') or to costs incurred by insurers in acquiring insurance policies.

Whether pre-contract costs are an asset

25.32   An asset is defined in the ASB's 'Statement of Principles' as 'rights or other access to future economic benefits controlled by an entity as a result of past transactions or events'. The Abstract notes that the right to bid for a contract, and the bidding process itself, do not necessarily give rise to rights or access to future economic benefits that are controlled by the entity – if it is possible that a contract will be awarded there may well be an expectation that benefits will accrue to the supplier, but the supplier has no control over the benefits at that stage. The supplier is therefore not in a position to recognise an asset in respect of the potential contract. Expenditure that is invested in tendering for a contract before the supplier obtains control over the future benefits should therefore be charged as an expense as it is incurred.

When an asset is created

25.33   The UITF took the view that, in the context of bidding for contracts, control over the future economic benefits does not arise until it is virtually certain that the contract will be awarded to the supplier – prior to that point there will not be sufficient evidence that an asset has been created. The point at which the awarding of the contract becomes virtually certain will depend on the particular circumstances of each case. Only one bidder can recognise an asset reflecting access to the future benefits from a particular contract – an asset can therefore only be created if there are no other bidders in competition. However, whilst it is essential that there are no other bidders in order for the award of a contract to be virtually certain, this situation will not in itself mean that the supplier is in a position to recognise an asset (for instance, the customer may not accept the sole bidder's proposals and may decide to re-tender). The Abstract also emphasises that:

— the actual award of the contract should be expected within a reasonable timescale;

— the proposed contractual arrangements should have been specified in sufficient detail to provide evidence that any pre-contract costs to be recognised as an asset will be recovered from the contract's net cash inflows (ie future revenues less attributable costs); and

— virtually certainty will not have been achieved if the award of the contract is subject to uncertainties that are not wholly within the control of the supplier – the Abstract quotes the example of the need for regulatory approval, or the likelihood of legal challenge.

Measuring the asset

25.34   The UITF considered various options for measuring the asset that arises when the recognition criteria are met. It concluded that only directly attributable pre-contract costs incurred from the date on which the recognition criteria are met should be recognised as an asset. Any pre-contract costs incurred before this point (for instance, during the competitive tendering stage) should be recognised as expenses as they are incurred and should not be reinstated at the time that the asset recognition criteria are met. Directly attributable costs are defined in the Abstract as costs that relate directly to securing the specific contract after the asset recognition criteria are met, provided that they can be separately identified and measured reliably.

Consortium members

25.35   The Abstract notes that a consortium of bidders will sometimes establish a special-purpose entity (for instance, an associate or joint venture) to undertake the contract and that the consortium members may transfer pre-contract costs to that entity once the contract has been awarded. The amount recovered by a consortium member in this way may exceed the amount of pre-contract costs recognised as an asset under the requirements of the Abstract. The UITF emphasises that the accounting treatment adopted by consortium members for the recovery of pre-contract costs from the special-purpose entity should reflect the principles set out in the Abstract and, in particular, that costs written off as an expense before the recognition criteria are met should not subsequently be reinstated as an asset. The UITF also notes that, where the special-purpose entity is an associate or joint venture, the recovery of an amount in excess of the pre-contract costs recognised as an asset does not result in an immediate gain in the consolidated accounts of a consortium member to the extent that the transaction is in substance a financing arrangement.

ACCOUNTS DISCLOSURES

Analysis of debtors

25.36   When the requirements of accounting standards are taken into accounts, the analysis of debtors set out in the CA 1985 balance sheet formats is expanded as follows:
—   Trade debtors (see 25.1–25.6 above).
—   Amounts recoverable on contracts (see Chapter 23).
—   Amounts owed by group undertakings.
—   Amounts owed by undertakings in which the group has a participating interest.
—   Amounts receivable in respect of finance leases (see 25.7–25.11 above).
—   Amounts receivable in respect of hire purchase contracts.
—   Other debtors (see 25.12–25.13 above).
—   Called up share capital not paid.
—   Pre-payments and accrued income (see 25.14–25.16 above).

Each sub-heading need only be used where there are material items to be disclosed in that category. The heading for debtors is given a Roman numeral and must therefore be shown on the face of the balance sheet. The sub-headings are given Arabic numerals and the detailed analysis of debtors may therefore be given in the notes to the accounts. The figures may also be combined if the individual amounts are not material. Called up share capital not paid can be shown as a separate heading before fixed assets, and pre-payments and accrued income can be shown as a separate heading after current assets. These are alternative positions (i.e. in each case, amounts should only be shown in one of the positions). Each company should therefore choose which position to use and then adopt this presentation consistently from year to year. Whichever presentation method is used, prepayments and accrued income must always be taken into account in calculating net current assets or liabilities.

For accounting periods beginning on or after 1 January 2005, the detailed disclosure requirements of CA 1985 are only relevant where the company prepares Companies Act accounts (as opposed to IAS accounts).

Separate disclosures of amounts due after more than one year

25.37   For each item included within debtors, CA 1985 requires separate disclosure of the amount falling due after more than one year. In most cases this detail will be given in the notes to the accounts. Where called up share capital not paid and pre-payments and accrued income are shown as sub-headings within debtors, any amounts due after more than one year must therefore be shown separately, although there is no specific requirement in the Act for the analysis to be given where these items are shown as main headings on the balance sheet. In assessing whether an amount is due within, or after more than, one year, it is normal practice to take the earliest date on which payment is expected to be made. Various forms of presentation are possible, and the most appropriate one will usually depend on the level of detail requiring disclosure.

Example 25.3 – Amounts due after more than one year disclosed as a narrative footnote

Debtors	20X2	20X1
	£	£
Trade debtors	344	298
Amounts recoverable on contracts	199	143
Other debtors	24	36
Pre-payments and accrued income	56	44
	623	521

Amounts recoverable on contracts includes £54,000 (20X1: £37,000) in respect of retentions, which are due after more than one year.

Example 25.4 – Columnar disclosure

Debtors	20X2 Due within 1 year	20X2 Due after more than 1 year	20X1 Due within 1 year	20X1 Due after more than 1 year
	£	£	£	£
Trade debtors	344	—	298	—
Amounts recoverable on contracts	145	54	106	37
Amounts due from group undertakings	211	100	254	100
Other debtors	20	4	30	6
Pre-payments	56	—	44	—
	776	158	732	143

Example 25.5 – Disclosure as a footnote giving details by category of debtor

Debtors	20X2 £	20X1 £
Trade debtors	344	298
Amounts recoverable on contracts	199	143
Amounts due from group undertakings	311	354
Other debtors	24	36
Pre-payments and accrued income	56	44
	934	875

These figures include the following amounts which are due after more than one year:

	20X2 £	20X1 £
Amounts recoverable on contracts	54	37
Amounts due from group undertakings	100	100
Other debtors	4	6
	158	143

Where all the amounts included within debtors are due within one year, there is no requirement to state this fact in the accounts, but it is good practice to do so.

Disclosure as current assets

25.38   Even where amounts included in debtors are due after more than one year, they must still be shown as current assets on the balance sheet to comply with the requirements of CA 1985. Under the Act, all assets must be classified as either fixed assets or current assets. A fixed asset is defined as an asset held for continuing use in the business, and any asset that does not meet this description must be classified as a current asset. UITF 4 'Presentation of Long-Term Debtors in Current Assets' confirms that in most cases, disclosure in the notes to the accounts will be sufficient. However, where an amount included in debtors and due after more than one year is so material that failure to disclose it on the balance sheet could cause readers to misinterpret the accounts, UITF 4 requires the disclosure to be given on the face of the balance sheet. It quotes the following examples of items that will usually be due after more than one year and which might be material to the accounts:

—   a significant pension fund surplus included in pre-payments (and therefore in the calculation of net current assets or liabilities) which may not actually be recovered for a number of years – however, this should only be an issue where SSAP 24 has been adopted, as FRS 17 requires a different presentation of a defined benefit asset for accounting periods beginning on or after 1 January 2005 (see 12.27 above);

—   amounts due under finance leases (in the accounts of a lessor);

—   deferred consideration in respect of the sale of a fixed asset or an investment.

Presentation on the balance sheet

25.39   Where an item due after more than one year is so material that it needs to be shown on the face of the balance sheet, it must nevertheless still be shown under current assets. UITF 4 does not provide an example of a suitable presentation, but the following will usually meet the requirements of both the Act and the Abstract.

Example 25.6 – Where disclosure of amounts due after more than one year is required on the face of the balance sheet

Extract from balance sheet.

	£	20X2 £	£	20X1 £
Current assets:				
Stocks		133		157
Debtors:				
Due within 1 year	126		143	
Due after more than 1 year	75		50	
	—		—	
		201		193
Cash at bank and in hand		34		27
		—		—
		368		377

Additional detail on the amounts due after more than one year would need to be given in the notes to the accounts. More information could be shown on the face of the balance sheet if preferred.

Deciding on the form of presentation

25.40 The key points to remember when deciding on the form of presentation to use in this situation are:

— the balance sheet format prescribed by CA 1985 must be preserved (assuming that the company is preparing Companies Act accounts);

— the total for debtors (i.e. amounts due within and after one year) must still appear on the face of the balance sheet;

— the total for debtors must be shown within current assets.

LIKELY FUTURE DEVELOPMENTS

ASB Discussion Paper – 'Leases: Implementation of a New Approach'

25.41 The ASB Discussion Paper 'Leases: Implementation of a New Approach' was issued in December 1999. This document represents a Position Paper developed by the G4+1 group of accounting standard setters and reflects an agreed international approach to the accounting treatment of leases in financial reporting. In particular it proposes removing the sometimes arbitrary distinction between operating and finance leases and applying the same accounting treatment to all leases. The proposals would affect both lessee and lessor accounting. Brief details of the contents of the Discussion Paper are given in Chapter 21.

However, the current version of the ASB's Technical Plan, published in June 2005, indicates that new UK accounting standards in respect of tangible fixed assets, which will converge UK accounting with international requirements and will include a new standard on leases, are not planned to come into effect until accounting periods beginning on or after 1 January 2008. No further Exposure Drafts on this subject are expected to be issued in the near future.

Chapter 26 Financial Instruments

CLASSIFICATION OF CAPITAL INSTRUMENTS UNDER FRS 4

Definition of debenture

26.1 The CA 1985 definition of a debenture is very broad. The Act does not specify the precise terms and conditions that identify a debenture, but simply states that it includes stocks, bonds and any other securities, regardless of whether they include a charge over the assets of the company. A debenture loan is usually considered to be a loan involving formal acknowledgement of the amount borrowed and of the fact that interest is payable at regular intervals on the sum borrowed. Therefore, any loan that is the subject of a formal loan agreement will normally be a debenture loan. Bank loans will normally meet this interpretation of a debenture loan. However, bank loans should always be shown within creditors under the heading 'bank loans and overdrafts' rather than as debenture loans.

Definition of capital instruments under FRS 4

26.2 For accounting periods beginning before 1 January 2005, FRS 4 'Capital Instruments' requires capital instruments to be included in the accounts of an individual company as either liabilities or shareholders' funds. No other form of disclosure is permitted. The definition of capital instruments given in FRS 4 encompasses all types of shares and debt instruments, including options and warrants to obtain those instruments. Shares must always be included within shareholders' funds. The standard identifies two types of other capital instrument:

— those that include an obligation on the issuer to transfer economic benefits; and

— those that do not include an obligation to transfer economic benefits.

Capital instruments in the first category should be accounted for as liabilities (and will therefore be included in creditors on the balance sheet). However, capital instruments in the second category (e.g. warrants) should be included in shareholders' funds. Capital instruments that are required by FRS 4 to be accounted for as liabilities are covered by the general description of 'debt' for the purposes of the standard.

The requirements of FRS 4 on the classification, presentation and disclosure of capital instruments are superseded by FRS 25 'Financial Instruments: Disclosure and Presentation' for all entities for accounting periods beginning on or after 1 January 2005 (see 26.21 to 26.41 below). Certain other aspects of FRS 4 (those on accounting for costs associated with financial instruments that are classified as liabilities) continue in force for entities that are not required to adopt FRS 26 'Financial Instruments: Measurement' (see 26.42 to 26.59 below).

The transfer of economic benefits

26.3   An obligation to transfer economic benefits will usually involve an obligation to:

—   make cash payments to the holder of the capital instrument – these might take the form of regular interest payments or might involve a payment at the time of redemption of the instrument; or

—   transfer other assets to the holder of the capital instrument.

A contingent obligation to transfer economic benefits will also be sufficient to classify the instrument as a liability; for instance, an instrument that gives the holder the option to require a cash payment or the issue of shares will be classified as a liability for accounting purposes, because the issuer may be required to make a cash payment under the terms of the instrument. However, the following contingent obligations should not be taken into account when classifying capital instruments:

—   those that would arise only if the issuer became insolvent – taking account of these obligations would not be consistent with the preparation of accounts on a going concern basis; and

—   those that would only apply if covenants in respect of the loan were breached – provided that the issuer is expected to be able to meet the requirements set out in the covenants, these obligations should not be taken into consideration.

Shareholders' funds or liabilities?

26.4   UITF Abstract 33 'Obligations in Capital Instruments' sets out detailed requirements on accounting for more complex capital instruments and in particular those which include an obligation that may be settled either by the transfer of economic benefits or by issuing equity shares, at the discretion of the issuer. The Abstract notes specifically that it does not deal with capital instruments issued as part of the contingent purchase consideration for a business combination. The general rule is that a capital instrument should be reported within shareholders' funds only if it is a share, or if it does not contain an obligation to transfer economic benefits. All other capital instruments should be treated as liabilities, even if the obligation to transfer economic benefits does not go beyond that normally contained in a share. An obligation to transfer economic benefits should be ignored only if it would not be considered in accordance with the going concern concept (i.e. if the obligation would only arise on the insolvency of the issuer). A capital instrument other than a share should also be treated as a liability if it includes an obligation to issue another capital instrument and that instrument includes an obligation to transfer economic benefits.

UITF Abstract 33 is superseded by FRS 25 'Financial Instruments: Disclosure and Presentation' for accounting periods beginning on or after 1 January 2005 (see 26.21 to 26.41 below).

Options at the discretion of the issuer

26.5   If a capital instrument other than a share includes an obligation that can be settled either by the transfer of economic benefits or by issuing equity shares, at the discretion of the issuer, it should be treated as a liability if the number of equity shares that would need to be issued to settle the obligation will vary with changes in the fair value of the shares, so that the total fair value of the shares issued will always be equal to the amount of the obligation. An obligation to issue shares can be expressed either as an obligation to issue a specified number of shares, or as an obligation to issue shares to the value of a specified amount or an amount determined by reference to the value of another item. In the first instance, both the issuer and the holder of the capital instrument are exposed to fluctuations in the price of the shares and the instrument therefore has the essential attributes of shareholders' funds. In the second case, the issuer still has the exposure but the holder does not, so the instrument no longer has the attributes of shareholders' funds and it is therefore required by UITF Abstract 33 to be treated as a liability.

Options without commercial substance

26.6   In line with the requirements of FRS 5 'Reporting the Substance of Transactions' (see Chapter 4), greater weight should be attached to those aspects of the arrangement that are more likely to have a practical commercial effect. Options that have no genuine commercial substance should therefore be ignored in the assessment of whether the reporting entity has an obligation to transfer economic benefits. Therefore:

—   if there is no genuine commercial possibility that the option to issue shares will be exercised, the capital instrument should be treated as giving rise to an obligation to transfer economic benefits and should be reported as a liability;

— if there is no genuine commercial possibility that the option to transfer economic benefits will be exercised, the capital instrument should be treated as giving rise to an obligation that can only be settled by issuing equity shares and should therefore be reported as part of shareholders' funds.

Power to issue appropriate number of shares

26.7   Where the classification of the instrument takes into account the reporting entity's option to settle the obligation by issuing shares, consideration must also be given to whether the entity has the unconditional right and ability to issue the number of shares needed to make full settlement of the obligation. Company law generally prohibits a company from issuing shares unless the allotment is authorised by the company in general meeting or by the company's articles of association. If, at the balance sheet date, the company does not have authority to issue sufficient shares to meet the obligation in full on the settlement date, UITF Abstract 33 requires the option to issue shares to be ignored, even though there is no actual requirement for the issuer to settle the obligation at the balance sheet date. In these circumstances, the instrument must always be accounted for as a liability. Where there is uncertainty over the number of shares that will need to be issued to settle the obligation, the Abstract requires the assessment to be based on the maximum number of shares that may need to be issued.

Shares issued by a subsidiary

26.8   Additional considerations apply under UITF Abstract 33 where shares issued by a subsidiary company create an obligation for the group as a whole to transfer economic benefits.

ACCOUNTING TREATMENT UNDER FRS 4

Initial recording of debt

26.9   At the time of issue, FRS 4 'Capital Instruments' requires a debt instrument to be recorded in the accounts at the net issue proceeds. The net issue proceeds are defined as the fair value of the consideration received, less any costs that meet the stringent definition of issue costs. Net issue proceeds and issue costs in respect of debt are considered in more detail in Chapter 14.

Finance costs

26.10   Finance costs relating to the instrument must be allocated over the term of the debt at a constant rate on the carrying amount. This is considered in more detail in Chapter 14, which includes practical examples of the calculation and allocation of finance costs and consideration of the impact of options. Finance costs include any premiums payable on redemption, as well as accrued interest in respect of the debt instrument, and the accounting treatment required by FRS 4 ensures that provision for a redemption premium is made over the term of the instrument. UITF 11 'Capital Instruments: Issuer Call Options' clarifies the accounting treatment required under FRS 4 where the issuer of an instrument (but not the investor) has an option to redeem the instrument early, usually on payment of a premium. Under the Abstract, a premium payable on the exercise of an issuer option should not be treated as part of the finance cost of the instrument. However the requirements of the Abstract do not apply where:

— the option is artificial in that the issuer will be commercially obliged to exercise it; or

— the effective rate of interest increases after the date on which the option is exercisable – in this case the exercise price is deemed to compensate the investor for forgoing the increased interest.

The requirements of UITF Abstract 11 are considered in more detail in Chapter 14.

Carrying value of debt

26.11   Although the initial carrying value of the debt is the amount of the net issue proceeds, in subsequent accounting periods, this figure must be increased by the finance costs charged to the profit and loss account in that period, and reduced by any payments made in respect of the debt (e.g. interest payments made during the period). Example 3 in Chapter 14 illustrates this process. The accounting treatment required by FRS 4 ensures that the total amount payable on redemption of the debt is built up on a consistent basis over the life of the instrument.

Accrued finance costs

26.12   Where finance costs have accrued in one accounting period and will be paid in cash in the following accounting period (e.g. interest due but not actually paid at the end of the accounting period), FRS 4 permits the accrued costs to be disclosed as accruals in the accounts rather than being included in the carrying value of the debt. However, any such accrued costs should be taken into account when calculating finance costs or any gain or loss arising on early redemption of the debt.

More complex debt instruments

26.13   FRS 4 includes a separate section of Application Notes which consider how the requirements of the standard should be applied to specific types of capital instrument. The items covered in this guidance include:

— capital contribution;

— convertible capital bonds;

—   convertible debt with a premium put option;

—   convertible debt with enhanced interest;

—   debt issued with warrants;

—   deep discount bonds;

—   index linked loans;

—   limited recourse debt;

—   perpetual debt;

—   repackaged perpetual debt;

—   stepped interest bonds;

—   subordinated debt.

The guidance includes worked examples to illustrate how the requirements of FRS 4 should be applied in practice to these more complex instruments. They are also useful as a point of reference on how to deal with individual features that may be attached to other debt instruments.

The Application Notes and worked examples are withdrawn for accounting periods beginning on or after 1 January 2005 as most of FRS 4 is superseded by FRS 25 'Financial Instruments: Disclosure and Presentation' from this date (see 26.21 to 26.41 below).

ACCOUNTS DISCLOSURES UNDER FRS 4

General disclosure requirements

26.14   Both CA 1985 and FRS 4 require specific disclosures in respect of debenture loans or debt instruments. A number of these overlap, but certain disclosures are required only by the Act or only by the accounting standard. Taking the requirements of the Act and FRS 4 together, the following details must be disclosed in respect of this category of borrowing:

—   the total amount outstanding at the end of the accounting period, which is due for payment within one year (including any amounts payable on demand);

—   the total amount outstanding at the end of the accounting period which is due for payment after more than one year, analysed as follows:

    —   the amount falling due for payment in more than one year but not more than two years after the balance sheet date,

    —   the amount falling due for payment in more than two years but not more than five years after the balance sheet date,

    —   the amount falling due for payment in more than five years;

—   where any loans are wholly or partly payable after more than five years, the accounts must also show:

> — the aggregate amounts payable or repayable by instalments,
>
> — the aggregate amounts which are payable or repayable otherwise than by instalments,
>
> — details of payment or repayment terms,
>
> — details of interest rates;

— the aggregate amount of secured borrowings and an indication of the nature of the security given.

The original wording of FRS 4 was updated by paragraph 77 of FRS 13 'Derivatives and Other Financial Instruments: Disclosures' to change the disclosure of amounts due exactly five years after the balance sheet date. Previously such amounts would have been shown in the final band, which covered amounts due after five years or more. The revised wording may also affect the disclosure of amounts due exactly two years after the balance sheet date, depending on how the original wording ('amounts due between one and two years' and 'amounts due between two and five years') was interpreted.

Maturity of debt

26.15 CA 1985 does not provide any detailed guidance on assessing the maturity of debt. FRS 4 requires the maturity date to be assessed on the basis of the earliest date on which the lender can demand repayment. However, if the same lender has granted other facilities to the borrower before the balance sheet date, these may also be taken into account. For instance, if a loan is due for repayment shortly after the balance sheet date, but the lender has formally agreed, before the balance sheet date, to advance another loan of the same amount for a period of (say) three years, the loan can be disclosed as falling due between two and five years after the balance sheet date, rather than within the next 12 months. For this treatment to be available, all of the following conditions must be met:

— the debt and the facility must be available under a single agreement or course of dealing with the same lender (or group of lenders);

— the finance costs of the new debt must not be significantly higher than those of the existing debt;

— the obligations of the lender must be firm (i.e. the lender should not be able to withdraw from providing the new funds, except in circumstances which can be shown to be remote);

— there must be an expectation that the lender will be able to fulfil its obligations in respect of the new facility.

Where the maturity of debt has been assessed in this way, the accounts must disclose the amounts of debt involved, analysed by the earliest date on which the lender could demand repayment if the facilities were not available.

For accounting periods beginning on or after 1 January 2005, new requirements on the presentation of liabilities which have been the subject of a refinancing agreement have been incorporated into FRS 25 'Financial Instruments: Disclosure and Presentation', together with additional guidance on:

(i)   the impact and disclosure of defaults and similar breaches of loan agreements; and

(ii)   the disclosure of refinancing arrangements that are put into place after the balance sheet date but before the date on which the financial statements are authorised for issue.

Further details are given at 26.35 below.

Example disclosures

26.17   The disclosure requirements will usually be met by providing the required analysis as a footnote to the creditors note and supplementing this with the other details in narrative form.

Example 26.1 – Disclosure in respect of debenture loans or debt instruments

	20X2	20X1
	£000	£000
Creditors: amounts due within one year		
Debenture loans	125	50
Bank loans and overdrafts	45	37
Trade creditors	98	85
Accruals and deferred income	14	17
	282	189
Creditors: amounts due after more than one year		
Debenture loans	225	223

None of the debenture loans are repayable by instalment. The amounts due after more than one year are repayable as follows:

In two to five years	100	100
After more than five years	125	123
	225	223

The debenture loan of £125,000 (20X1: £123,000) is repayable in 20X9, at a premium of £10,000, which is being provided for as part of the finance cost of the loan. The loan bears interest at a fixed rate of 7% per annum and is secured on the company's freehold property.

The other debenture loans are unsecured.

Convertible debt

26.17 Convertible debt is debt that can be converted into shares at some point in the future. Conversion may be at the option of the holder or of the issuer, or both. For accounting periods beginning before 1 January 2005, FRS 4 requires convertible debt to be accounted for on the basis that conversion will not take place. Within the headings for creditors, CA 1985 requires any convertible debentures to be shown separately from debentures that are not convertible. FRS 4 also requires convertible debt to be shown separately from other liabilities, and requires this detail to be given on the face of the balance sheet if it is material. If the detail is not considered material, and the analysis is therefore given in the notes to the accounts, the balance sheet heading must state that convertible debt is included. Disclosure might therefore be made in the following ways:

Example 26.2 – Disclosure of convertible debt on the face of the balance sheet

Extract of balance sheet:

		20X2		*20X1*
		£000		*£000*
Net current assets		761		699
Creditors: amounts falling due after more than one year:				
Convertible debt	75		75	
Other creditors	120		118	
		(195)		(193)
Provisions for liabilities and charges		(65)		(58)
		501		448

Example 26.3 – Disclosure of convertible debt in a note

Extract of balance sheet:

	20X2	20X1
	£000	£000
Net current assets	761	699
Creditors: amounts falling due after more than one year (including convertible debt)	(195)	(193)
Provisions for liabilities and charges	(65)	(58)
	501	448

In this case, a note to the accounts would need to give the required analysis between convertible and non-convertible debt.

FRS 4 also requires the following details to be disclosed in the accounts:

— the dates of redemption;

— the amount payable on redemption;

— the number and class of shares into which the debt may be converted;

— the dates at, or periods within, which the conversion may take place;

— whether conversion is at the option of the issuer (i.e. the company) or the holder of the debt.

These details will usually be given as narrative footnotes to the main disclosures.

Example 26.4 – Convertible debt – additional disclosures in a narrative footnote

Creditors: amounts falling due after more than one year:

	20X2	20X1
	£000	£000
Convertible debt	75	75
Other debenture loans	120	118
	195	193

None of the above amounts are repayable by instalments. The amounts are payable as follows:

	20X2	20X1
Between two and five years	75	75
After more than five years	120	118
	195	193

The convertible debt is convertible into 'B' ordinary shares of £10 each on 30 June 20X5, at the option of the company, on the basis of one share for each £100 of debt. If the debt is not converted into shares it will be repaid at par on 30 June 20X5.

The debenture loan of £120,000 (20X1: £118,000) is repayable in 20X9, at a premium of £6,000, which is being provided for as part of the finance cost of the loan. The loan bears interest at a fixed rate of 7% per annum and is secured on the company's freehold property.

If the debt is subsequently converted into shares, the amount recognised as shareholders' funds at the time of conversion will be the amount shown as the liability in respect of the debt at the date of conversion. No gain or loss should be recognised at the time of conversion. This is considered in more detail in Chapter 14, which includes a practical example.

For accounting periods beginning on or after 1 January 2005, FRS 4 is superseded FRS 25 'Financial Instruments: Disclosure and Presentation' which includes new requirements on accounting for convertible debt (see 26.21 to 26.41 below).

Additional disclosures under FRS 4

26.18   FRS 4 requires further disclosures in two situations that should arise only rarely in practice:

—   where the legal nature of any instrument that has been accounted for as debt is different from that normally associated with debt, brief details should be given in the accounts;

—   where the amount shown in the accounts is significantly different to the amount actually payable, or the claim that would arise on a winding up, details of the amounts payable or claimable should be given – this information may be given in summary form for all relevant instruments (i.e. individual details are not required).

Where necessary, these disclosures will usually be given as short narrative footnotes to the main disclosures. Also, if the brief summaries required by paragraphs 62 or 63 of the standard cannot provide adequate information for the commercial effect of the instrument to be understood, this fact should be stated and details should be given of where the relevant information can be obtained. However, the principal features of the instrument should always be disclosed.

Issue of debentures during the year

26.19   Where new debentures have been issued during the year, CA 1985 requires the following information to be given in the accounts:

—   the class of debentures issued; and

—   for each class of debentures issued, the amount issued and the consideration received by the company.

Debentures held by nominee or trustee

26.20   If any of the company's debentures are held by a nominee of, or trustee for, the company, CA 1985 requires the accounts to show:

— the nominal value of the debentures; and

— the amount at which they are stated in the company's accounting records.

CLASSIFICATION OF FINANCIAL INSTRUMENTS UNDER FRS 25

Effective date of FRS 25

26.21   The presentation requirements of FRS 25 'Financial Instruments: Disclosure and Presentation' supersede those in FRS 4 'Capital Instruments' for all entities (other than those adopting the FRSSE) for accounting periods beginning on or after 1 January 2005. The standard applies to all types of financial instruments, apart from a small number of items that are specifically excluded. The standard cannot be adopted early because some requirements hinge on company law changes that also come into effect on 1 January 2005.

The disclosure requirements of FRS 25 are considered at 26.39 below.

New rules on classification

26.22   FRS 25 requires each financial instrument, or its component parts, to be classified on initial recognition as a financial asset, a financial liability or an equity instrument, based on the substance of the contractual arrangements and the definitions set out in the standard. A financial instrument is defined as any contract that gives rise to a financial asset of one entity and a financial liability or equity instrument of another entity. An equity instrument is any contract that evidences a residual interest in the assets of an entity after deducting all of its liabilities, and a financial liability is any liability that is:

(i)   a contractual obligation to deliver cash or another financial asset to another entity, or to exchange financial assets or financial liabilities with another entity under conditions that are potentially unfavourable to the entity; or

(ii)   a contract that will or may be settled in the entity's own equity instruments and is:

- a non-derivative for which the entity is or may be obliged to deliver a variable number of the entity's own equity instruments; or

- a derivative that will or may be settled other than by the exchange of a fixed amount of cash or another financial asset for a fixed number of the entity's own equity instruments.

A derivative is as defined in FRS 26 (see 26.44 below). The classification of the instrument also determines the accounting treatment of any related interest, dividends, gains and losses. The detailed requirements of the standard in respect of financial assets and equity are considered in Chapters 22 and 32 respectively. Most of the complex issues arising from the standard relate to the distinction between equity and financial liabilities.

Financial liability or equity?

26.23   The standard specifies that, in applying the above definitions, a financial instrument will be an equity instrument if, and only if:

(i)   it includes no contractual obligation to deliver cash or another financial instrument to another entity, or to exchange financial assets or financial liabilities with another entity under conditions that are potentially unfavourable to the issuer; and

(ii)   where the instrument will or may be settled in the issuer's own equity instruments, it is:

- a non-derivative that includes no contractual obligation for the issuer to deliver a variable number of its own equity instruments; or

- a derivative that will be settled only by the issuer exchanging a fixed amount of cash or another financial asset for a fixed number of its own equity instruments.

The guidance also states that a contractual obligation, including one arising from a derivative financial instrument, that will or may result in the future delivery or receipt of the issuer's own equity instruments, but which does not meet the two conditions set out above, is not an equity instrument.

A critical distinguishing feature between financial liabilities and equity is, therefore, the existence of a contractual obligation of the issuer to deliver cash or another financial asset to the holder of the instrument, or to exchange financial assets and financial liabilities with the holder on terms that could be unfavourable to the issuer. A holder of an equity instrument may be entitled to receive dividends or other distributions, but will not be in a position to require the issuer to deliver cash or another financial asset.

New treatment of certain shares

26.24   The classification requirements of FRS 25 will mean that certain shares that have previously been accounted for as share capital will in future be treated as financial liabilities and any dividends payable in respect of them will be accounted for as interest payments in the profit and loss account. CA 1985 has been amended for accounting periods beginning on or after 1 January 2005 to introduce the concept of 'substance over form' into company law and thus enable this treatment to be applied. For instance, a preference share will be a financial liability rather than an equity instrument if it:

(i)   provides for mandatory redemption by the issuer for a fixed or determinable amount at a fixed or determinable future date; or

(ii)   gives the holder the right to require the issuer to redeem it at or after a particular date for a fixed or determinable amount.

There is no change to the legal form of such shares but for accounting purposes, they must be shown as financial liabilities in the accounts rather than as part of the company's share capital, consistent with the actual substance of the arrangements.

Other examples of financial liabilities

26.25   The guidance in the standard gives the following as other examples of financial instruments that will constitute financial liabilities rather than equity:

(i)   a 'puttable financial instrument' (i.e. one that gives the holder the right to put it back to the issuer for cash or another financial asset), even if the instrument gives the holder a right to a residual interest in the assets of the issuer;

(ii)   any financial instrument under which the issuer does not have an unconditional right to avoid delivering cash or another financial assets to settle a contractual obligation;

(iii)   a financial instrument which establishes an obligation for the issuer to deliver cash or another financial instrument indirectly through its terms and conditions rather than through a contractual obligation – for instance:

●   where the issuer can avoid a transfer of cash or another financial asset only by settling a non-financial obligation included in the instrument; or

●   where the issuer must deliver either cash or another financial asset, or its own shares with a value determined to exceed substantially the value of the cash or financial asset – the value of the share alternative means that in practice the issuer will not take this option.

Contract settlement in equity

26.26   The fact that a contract may result in the delivery or receipt of own equity does not necessarily mean that the contract will be classified as an equity instrument. A key issue here is whether the contract requires the issue of a fixed or variable number of equity instruments and whether the amount of the related obligation is a fixed or variable. For instance, a contract that requires an entity to deliver as many own equity instruments as are equal to a specified value will be a financial liability rather than equity, even though the entity must settle the obligation in equity. This is on the basis that the number of equity instruments required to settle the obligation will vary, depending on the market price at the time, and so the contract does not evidence a residual interest in the entity's assets after deducting all of its liabilities. A contract that requires the entity to deliver a fixed amount of its own equity instruments in exchange for a variable amount of cash or another financial asset will also be a financial liability. By contrast, a contract that requires the entity to deliver a fixed number of its own equity instruments in exchange for a fixed amount of cash or another financial asset is an equity instrument. A share option that gives the holder the right to buy a fixed number of shares at a fixed price, or for a fixed principal sum (such as the amount of a bond) comes into this category.

Purchase of own equity instruments

26.27   Where a contract includes an obligation for an entity to purchase its own equity instruments for cash or another financial asset, this gives rise to a financial liability for the present value of the redemption amount, even if the contract is an equity instrument. When the financial liability is initially recognised, the standard requires the fair value of the obligation (ie the present value of the redemption amount) to be reclassified from equity. This accounting treatment applies even if the entity's obligation is conditional on the counterparty exercising a right to redeem. If the contract subsequently expires without being fulfilled, the carrying amount of the financial liability should be reclassified as equity.

Contingent settlement provisions

26.28   The settlement arrangements in a financial instrument may sometimes depend on the occurrence or non-occurrence of uncertain future events that are outside the control of both the issuer and the holder – for instance, changes in an index or interest rate, or the future revenues, net income or debt-equity ratio of the issuer. The guidance in the standard notes that, as the issuer will not have an unconditional right to avoid delivering cash or another financial asset in these circumstances, such an instrument will be a financial liability unless:

(i)   the element of the contingent settlement provision that would result in the instrument being classified as a financial liability is not genuine; or

(ii)   the issuer can only be required to settle the obligation in cash or another financial asset in the event of the liquidation of the issuer.

Settlement options

26.29   When a derivative financial instrument gives one party a choice over how it is settled (eg the issuer or the holder can choose settlement net in cash or by exchanging shares for cash) it is a financial asset or a financial liability unless all of the settlement alternatives would result in it being an equity instrument.

Compound financial instruments

26.30   The issuer of a non-derivative financial instrument must evaluate the terms of the instrument to determine whether it includes both a liability and an equity component. If so, the components should be classified separately as financial liabilities, financial assets or equity instruments and accounted for accordingly. For instance, a bond that is convertible into a fixed number of ordinary shares of the entity will be a compound financial instrument as it represents both a financial liability for the issuer (in terms of the obligation to deliver cash or another financial instrument. Under FRS 25, an entity that issues a compound financial instruments must account separately for

(i)   any components that create a financial liability of the issuer; and

(ii) any components that grant an option to the holder of the instrument to convert it into an equity instruments of the issuer.

The guidance notes that the economic effect of issuing a bond or similar instrument that is convertible into a fixed number of ordinary shares is the same as issuing a debt instrument with an early settlement provision and warrants to purchase ordinary shares, and in effect requires this situation to be reflected in the balance sheet presentation. As an equity instrument represents a residual interest in the assets of an entity, after all its liabilities have been deducted, the equity element of a compound instrument should be calculated as the residual amount after determining the fair value of the liability component and deducting this from the fair value of the instrument as a whole. The fair value of the liability component should be determined by measuring the fair value of a similar liability that does not have an equity component. The classification of the liability and equity elements should not be revised, even if there is a change in the likelihood of the conversion option being exercised. The guidance in the standard emphasises that the issuer's contractual obligation to make future payments remains outstanding until it is settled through conversion, maturity or some other transaction.

Transactions costs for compound instruments

26.31   Transaction costs relating to the issue of a compound financial instrument should be allocated to the liability and equity components of the instrument in proportion to the allocation of the related proceeds. Any transaction costs that relate jointly to more than one transaction (the standard gives the example of the costs of a concurrent offering of shares and a stock exchange listing of other shares) should be allocated between the transactions on a basis that is both rational and consistent with similar transactions.

Members' shares in co-operative entities

26.32   UITF Abstract 39 'Members' shares in co-operative entities and similar instruments' is based on an equivalent interpretation by the International Financial Reporting Interpretations Committee (IFRIC) and considers the application of the principles in FRS 25 to shares in co-operative entities and similar instruments issued by other entities. It summarises in particular the factors that determine whether such instruments should be classified as equity or financial liabilities when they include specific redemption terms. The key points from the consensus are that:

(i) the contractual right of the holder of the financial instrument to request redemption does not in itself result in the instrument being classified as a financial liability

(ii) in classifying the instrument for accounting purposes, the entity must consider all of the terms and conditions that apply, including relevant local laws and regulations and the entity's governing document as at the date of the classification;

(iii) members' shares that would be classified as equity if the members did not have a right to request redemption should be classified as equity if:

- the entity has an unconditional right to refuse redemption; or

- local law or regulations, or the entity's governing document, impose an unconditional prohibition on redemption.

(iv) a prohibition that is conditional on issues such as liquidity constraints being met, or not being met, does not result in the instrument being classified as equity;

(v) where an unconditional prohibition is partial, in that it prohibits redemption only if this would cause the number of members' shares or amount of paid-in capital to fall below a specified level:

- members' shares in excess of the prohibition should be classified as financial liabilities unless the entity has an unconditional right to refuse redemption; and

- a change in the number of shares or amount of paid-in capital specified in the prohibition will result in a transfer between equity and financial liabilities – in this situation, the Abstract requires separate disclosure of the amount, timing and reason for the transfer .

Measurement of redemption liability

26.33 On initial recognition, the Abstract requires the financial liability for redemption to be measured at fair value. In the case of members' shares with a redemption feature, this should be no less than the maximum amount payable under the redemption provisions of its governing charter or applicable local law, discounted from the first date that the amount could be required to be paid.

Practical examples

26.34 The practical application of the issues covered in the consensus is highlighted in seven useful examples, which the document notes are considered integral to the Abstract. The examples cover situations where:

(i)   the entity has a unconditional right to refuse redemption under its governing document but, in practice, has never done so;

(ii) the entity's governing document states that redemption is at the sole discretion of the entity but approval of a redemption request is automatic unless making the payment would violate local regulations on liquidity or reserves;

(iii) the entity's governing document imposes a maximum limit on cumulative redemptions, which is subsequently increased to a higher figure;

(iv) the entity is prevented by local law from reducing its paid-in capital below a specified level;

(v)   the entity is prevented by local law from reducing its paid-in capital below a specified level and must also meet local liquidity requirements;

(vi) redemption is prohibited, except to the extent of proceeds received from the issue of additional members' shares to new or existing members in the preceding three years; and

(vii) the entity is a co-operative bank and local law specifies a minimum level of total outstanding liabilities that must be in the form of members' shares, but the effect is that, if all of the entity's outstanding liabilities are in the form of members' shares, it is able to redeem them all.

Maturity of liabilities

26.35   FRS 25 includes the following guidance on the presentation of liabilities:

(i)   financial liabilities should be regarded as due to be settled within twelve months of the balance sheet date, and should be classified as current, even if the original term was for a period of more than twelve months and an agreement to refinance, or to reschedule payments, on a long-term basis is completed after the balance sheet date but before the financial statements are authorised for issue;

(ii) if an entity has the discretion under an existing loan facility to refinance or roll over an obligation for at least twelve months after the balance sheet, and expects to do so, the obligation should be classified as non-current even if it would otherwise be due within a shorter period;

(iii) where an undertaking under a long-term finance agreement is breached before the balance sheet date with the effect that the liability become payable on demand:

- the liability should be classified as current, even if the lender agrees after the balance sheet date and before the date on which the financial statements are authorised for issue not to demand repayment as a result of the breach;

- the liability should be classified as non-current if the lender agrees by the balance sheet date to provide a period of grace ending at least twelve months after the balance sheet date within which the entity can rectify the breach and during which the lender will not demand repayment; and

(iv)   for loans classified as current liabilities, the following should be disclosed as non-adjusting events under FRS 21 'Events After the Balance Sheet Date' if they occur between the balance sheet date and the date on which the financial statements are authorised for issue:

- refinancing on a long-term basis;

- rectification of a breach of a long-term loan agreement;

- receipt from the lender of a period of grace ending at least twelve months after the balance sheet date to rectify a breach of a long-term loan agreement.

Offsetting of financial assets and financial liabilities

26.36   A financial asset and a financial liability should be offset so that the net amounted is presented in the balance sheet when, and only when, the entity:

(i)   currently has a legally enforceable right to set off the recognised amounts; and

(ii)   intends either to settle on a net basis, or to realise the asset and settle the liability simultaneously.

In all other cases, financial assets and liabilities should continue to be presented separately in the accounts. The rules on offsetting are considered in more detail in Chapter 4.

Transitional arrangements for comparatives

26.37   FRS 25 includes special transitional arrangements in respect of the restatement of comparative information. Where an entity adopts:

(i)   the presentation requirements of the standard for an accounting period beginning before 1 January 2006; or

(ii)   the disclosure requirements of the standard for an accounting periods beginning before 1 January 2007

it need not restate comparative information to comply with those requirements. Instead, the preceding year's figures can continue to be presented on the basis of the entity's previous accounting policies for financial instruments and the accounts should disclose:

(i)   the fact that this approach has been taken;

(ii)   the accounting policies adopted for the comparative information; and

(iii) the nature of the adjustments that would be needed to make the comparative information comply with FRS 25 – the standard does not require the adjustments to be quantified, but it does require any adjustment between the closing balance sheet for the comparative period (ie prepared on the basis of the previous accounting policies) and the opening balance for the current period (ie prepared on the basis of the FRS 25 requirements) to be treated as arising from a change in accounting policy, with the disclosures required by FRS 18 'Accounting policies' (see Chapter 6).

Transitional arrangements for compound financial instruments

26.38 If the liability component of a compound financial instrument is no longer outstanding at the date of transition to the standard (this is defined as the beginning of the earliest period for which comparative information is presented in compliance with the standard), the entity need not separate the liability and equity components of the instrument when the standard is first applied.

ACCOUNTS DISCLOSURES UNDER FRS 25

Objective and scope

26.39 The detailed disclosure requirements set out in FRS 25 are intended to provide information to help users of the accounts understand the significance of financial instruments to the entity's financial position, performance and cash flows, and also the amount, timing and certainty of future cash flows relating to the instruments. The disclosures therefore focus on market risk, credit risk, liquidity risk and cash flow interest rate risk. The standard does not prescribe the format, location or level of detail of the required disclosures, although guidance is provided on the issues to be taken into account in making judgements on these.

The disclosure requirements of FRS 25, together with the requirements of FRS 23 'The Effects of Changes in Foreign Exchange Rates', FRS 24 'Financial Reporting in Hyperinflationary Economies' and FRS 26 'Financial Instruments: Measurement', form a package of new UK accounting standards that apply to listed companies for accounting periods beginning on or after 1 January 2005, and to other entities for accounting periods beginning on or after 1 January 2006 if they choose to adopt fair value accounting (although adoption from 1 January 2005 is also acceptable in this case). Entities who are not required to adopt FRS 26 are nevertheless encouraged to comply with the disclosure requirements of FRS 25 where appropriate.

Categories of risk

26.40 The guidance in the standard identifies the following specific categories of risk that can impact on the value of financial instruments:

(i) **Market risk**: This includes currency risk (i.e. the risk that the value of a financial instrument will fluctuate as a result of changes in foreign exchange rates), fair value interest rate risk (i.e. the risk that the value of a financial instrument will fluctuate as a result of changes in market interest rates), and price risk (i.e. the risk that the value of a financial instrument will fluctuate as a result of changes in market prices).

(ii) **Credit risk**: This is the risk that one party to a financial instrument will fail to meet its obligation and so give rise to a financial loss for the other party.

(iii) **Liquidity risk**: This is the risk that an entity will encounter difficulty in raising sufficient funds to meet its commitments in respect of financial instruments – it includes the risk of being unable to sell a financial asset quickly at its fair value.

(iv) **Cash flow interest rate risk**: This is the risk that the future cash flows from a financial instrument will fluctuate as a result of changes in market interest rates.

Minimum disclosures

26.41 The minimum disclosure requirements in respect of financial liabilities include:

(i) an explanation of the entity's financial risk management objectives and policies;

(ii) information on the extent and nature of the financial instruments, including significant terms and conditions that may affect the amount, timing and certainty of future cash flows;

(iii) the accounting policies adopted, including the criteria for recognition and the basis of measurement adopted – details to be disclosed might include the accounting treatment adopted in respect of:

- costs of issuance or acquisition;

- premiums and discounts; and

- changes in the estimated amount of determinable future cash flows associated with a monetary financial instrument;

- restructured financial liabilities;

(iv) information about the entity's exposure to interest rate risk, including contractual repricing or maturity dates, and effective interest rates;

(v) information about the entity's exposure to credit risk, including its maximum exposure to credit risk at the balance sheet date, without taking account of the fair value of any collateral, in the event of other parties failing to perform their obligations under financial instruments and any significant concentrations of credit risk;

(vi) the fair value of each class of financial liabilities in a way that allows this to be compared with the corresponding carrying amount in the balance sheet;

(vii) the methods and significant assumptions applied in determining fair value for each significant class of financial liabilities, and in particular whether fair values have been determined directly by reference to published price quotations in an active market or estimated using a valuation technique – additional details are required where the valuation technique used is based on assumptions that are not supported by market prices or rates;

(viii) the total change in fair value recognised in the profit and loss account for the period that was estimated using a valuation technique;

(ix) if the entity has issued an instrument that contains both a liability and en equity component and the instrument has multiple embedded derivative features whose values are interdependent (eg a callable convertible debt instrument), the existence of those features and the effective interest rate on the liability component (excluding any derivatives that are accounted for separately);

(x) the carrying amount of financial liabilities classified as held for trading;

(xi) the carrying amount of financial liabilities that were designated on initial recognition as financial liabilities at fair value through profit or loss;

(xii) where a financial liability has been designated as at fair value through profit or loss:

- the amount of the change in its fair value that is not attributable to changes in a benchmark interest rate, such as LIBOR; and

- the difference between its carrying amount and the amount the entity would be contractually required to pay at maturity to the holder of the obligation;

(xiii) for any defaults or breaches in the period in respect of loans payable at the balance sheet date, and any other breaches of loan agreements which permit the lender to demand repayment (unless the breach has been remedied, or the loan renegotiated, before the balance sheet date):

- details of the default or breach;

- the amount recognised at the balance sheet date in respect of the relevant loan; and

- whether the default has been remedied or the loan renegotiated before the date on which the financial statements were authorised for issue;

(xiv) detailed information in respect of any instruments that create a potentially significant exposure to risk, either individually or as a class; and

(xv) the basis for including in the profit and loss account realised and unrealised gains and losses, interest, and other items of income or expense associated with financial liabilities, including where appropriate the basis on which income and expenses are recognised in respect of instruments held for hedging purposes – where relevant, the standard specifically requires disclosure of the reason for presenting income and expenses on a net basis when the corresponding financial assets and financial liabilities have not been offset on the balance sheet, unless the effect is not significant.

Additional disclosure requirements apply where hedge accounting has been adopted (see 26.58 below).

ACCOUNTING FOR FINANCIAL INSTRUMENTS AT FAIR VALUE

The fair value accounting rules

26.42   The 4th and 7th EC Company Law Directives, which form the basis of the CA 1985 requirements on individual and consolidated accounts, have been amended by the EU Fair Value Directive to allow certain assets and liabilities to be included in the balance sheet at fair value, and changes in that fair value to be reflected in the profit and loss account. Fair value accounting has been introduced in the UK as option rather than as a mandatory requirement, and it can be adopted in both individual and consolidated accounts, including those prepared by small or specialised companies, for accounting periods beginning on or after 1 January 2005. Paragraphs 34A to 34 F of Schedule 4 to CA 1985 set out detailed provisions on the adoption of fair value accounting and paragraphs 45A to 45D deal with the additional disclosures that must be given in the accounts when fair value accounting has been adopted. The fair value accounting rules are considered in more detail in Chapter 1.

Under the new legislation, certain financial instruments (including derivatives) may be included in the accounts at fair value provided that this can be determined reliably on the following basis:

(i)   if a reliable market for the instrument can be readily identified, fair value should be determined by reference to its market value;

(ii)   if no such market can be readily identified for the financial instrument as a whole, but can be identified for its components or for similar instruments, fair value should be determined by reference to the market value of the components or of a similar instrument; and

(ii)   if neither (i) nor (ii) applies, fair value can be determined by using generally accepted valuation models and techniques, provided that these ensure a reasonable approximation of the market value of the financial instrument.

However, financial instruments which constitute liabilities are only included in the scope of the fair value accounting rules if they are held as part of a trading portfolio or if they are derivatives. FRS 25 'Financial instruments: Disclosure and Presentation' and FRS 26 'Financial Instruments: Measurement' (together with FRS 23 'The

Effects of Changes in Foreign Exchange Rates' and FRS 24 'Financial Reporting in Hyperinflationary Economies' where relevant) set out the detailed UK framework for the adoption of fair value accounting.

Scope of FRS 26

20.43   FRS 26 'Financial Instruments: Measurement' includes detailed requirements on:

(i)   initial measurement of financial assets and financial liabilities;

(ii)   subsequent measurement of financial assets and financial liabilities;

(iii)   recognising gains and losses on financial assets and liabilities;

(iv)   accounting for impairment and uncollectibility in respect of financial assets; and

(v)   hedge accounting.

These requirements apply to all types of financial instruments, apart from certain items that are specifically excluded in the standard – these include:

(i)   rights and obligations under leases;

(iii)   employers' rights and obligations under employee benefit plans;

(iv)   rights and obligations under most insurance contracts, although certain derivatives embedded in an insurance contract do come within the scope of the standard; and

(v)   certain contracts in respect of business combinations.

FRS 26 applies to listed companies for accounting periods beginning on or after 1 January 2005, and to other entities for accounting periods beginning on or after 1 January 2006 but only if they choose to adopt fair value accounting (in which case adoption from 1 January 2005 is also acceptable). However, the ASB published an Exposure Draft 'Amendment to FRS 26 – Financial Instruments: Measurement' in April 2005 and this proposes extending the scope of the standard and also introducing into UK accounting the recognition and derecognition requirements of the underlying international accounting standard. Further details are given at 26.61 below.

The standard is complex, and comprehensive implementation guidance together with illustrative examples are set out in the Appendices. However, many unlisted companies will be unaffected by the standard at present and so only an outline of the key requirements is given here.

Derivatives

26.44   A derivative is defined as a financial instrument or other contract within the scope of the standard with all three of the following characteristics:

(i)   its value changes in response to the change in a specified interest rate, financial instrument price, commodity price, foreign exchange rate, index of prices or rates, credit rating or credit index, or other variable, provided that, in the case of a non-financial variable, it is not specific to a party to the contract;

(ii)   it requires no initial net investment, or an initial net investment that is smaller than would be required for other types of contract with a similar response to changes in market factors; and

(iii) it is settled at a future date.

There are detailed requirements on when an embedded derivative should be separated from the host contract and accounted for separately under the standard.

Categories of financial instrument

26.45   The standard identifies the following four categories of financial instrument:

(i)   financial assets or financial liabilities at fair value through profit or loss;

(ii)   held-to-maturity investments;

(iii) loans and receivables; and

(iv)   available-for-sale financial assets.

A financial asset or financial liability at fair value through profit or loss is a financial asset or financial liability that meets one of the following conditions:

(i)   it is classified as held for trading – in other words it is:

- acquired or incurred principally for the purpose of selling or repurchasing in the near future;

- part of a portfolio of identified financial instruments that are managed together and for which there is evidence of a recent actual pattern of short-term profit-taking; or

- a derivative (other than a designated and effective hedging instrument); or

(ii)   it is designated by the entity on initial recognition as at fair value through profit or loss – however such a designation cannot be applied to investments in equity instruments that do not have a quoted market price in an active market and whose fair value cannot be measured reliably.

Held-to-maturity investments are non-derivative financial assets with fixed or determinable payments and fixed maturity that the entity has the positive intention and ability to hold to maturity, other than those:

(i)   designated by the entity on initial recognition as at fair value through profit or loss;

(ii)   designated by the entity as available for sale; and

(iii)   that meet the definition of loans and receivables.

An asset cannot be classified as held to maturity if more than an insignificant amount of the investment has been sold or reclassified before maturity in the current or two preceding financial years. Significance is to be assessed in relation to the total of held-to-maturity investments, and the following sales and reclassifications do not need to be taken into account:

(i)   those that are so close to maturity or to the asset's call date that changes in the market rate of interest would not have a significant impact on the asset's fair value;

(ii)   those that occur after the entity has collected substantially all of the asset's original principal through scheduled payments or prepayments; and

(iii)   those that are attributable to an isolated event that is beyond the entity' control, non-recurring and could not reasonably have been anticipated.

Loans and receivables are non-derivative financial assets with fixed or determinable payments that are not quoted in an active market, other than:

(i)   those that the entity intends to sell immediately or in the near future and which should therefore be classified as held for trading;

(ii)   those designated on initial recognition as at fair value through profit or loss;

(iii)   those designated on initial recognition as available for sale; or

(iv)   those for which the holder may not recover substantially all of its initial investment other than as a result of credit deterioration – these should be classified as available for sale.

Also, an interest in a pool of assets that are not loans and receivable (eg a mutual fund) cannot be a loan or receivable.

Available-for-sale financial assets are non-derivative financial assets that are designated as available for sale or not classified under one of the previous three headings.

Initial measurement

26.46   The standard requires a financial liability to be measured at fair value on initial recognition. In the case of a financial liability not at fair value through the profit and loss account, this value should be increased by any transaction costs that are directly attributable to the acquisition or issue of the financial liability.

Subsequent measurement

26.47   After initial recognition, all financial liabilities should be measured at amortised cost using the effective interest method, except for:

(i)   financial liabilities at fair value through profit or loss (including derivatives) which should be measured at fair value – the only exception is a derivative that is linked to, and which must be settled by, delivery of an unquoted equity instrument whose fair value cannot be measured reliably, which should be included at cost;

(ii)   financial liabilities that arise when a transfer of a financial asset does not qualify for derecognition.

Separate measurement requirements apply under the standard to financial liabilities that are designated as hedged items (see 26.51 to 26.59 below).

Reclassification of financial instruments

26.48   There are certain restrictions and requirements on the reclassification of financial instruments after their initial recognition, when intentions or circumstances change. In particular:

(i)   a financial instrument cannot be reclassified into or out of the fair value through profit or loss category while it is held or issued;

(ii)   if it is no longer appropriate to classify an investment as held to maturity (e.g. because intentions have changed, or because significant amounts have been disposed of without the conditions outlined in 26.45 above being met) it should be reclassified as available for sale and remeasured at fair value, with any difference between that value and its carrying amount recognised in the statement of total recognised gains and losses unless it represents an impairment loss or a foreign exchange gain or loss;

(iii)   if a reliable measure becomes available for a financial asset or financial liability and the instrument is required under the standard to be measured at fair value if a reliable measure is available, the asset or liability should be remeasured at fair value with the gain or loss recognised in accordance with the normal requirements of the standard.

The standard also considers the situation where a reliable measure of fair value ceases to be available (which is expected to be rare in practice), intentions change or, in the case of held-to-maturity investments, the two year period referred to in 26.45 above has passed, and it therefore becomes appropriate to carry a financial asset or financial liability at cost or amortised cost rather than fair value.

Accounting for gains and losses

26.49   Gains and losses on financial assets and financial liabilities that are not part of a hedging relationship should be recognised as follows:

(i)   those on financial assets and liabilities classified as at fair value through profit and loss should be recognised in the profit and loss account;

(ii)   those on available-for-sale financial assets should be recognised in the statement of total recognised gains and losses (unless they are impairment losses) until the asset is derecognised, when the cumulative gain or loss recognised in that statement should be recognised in profit or loss – however:

- interest calculated using the effective interest rate should be recognised in profit or loss; and

- dividends on available-for-sale equity instruments should be recognised in profit and loss when the entity's right to receive the dividend has been established;

(iii) those on financial assets and liabilities carried at amortised cost should be recognised in the profit and loss account when the liability is derecognised or impaired, or through the amortisation process.

The accounting treatment of gains and losses on financial instruments is considered in more detail in Chapter 14. Different treatments apply in respect of hedged items (see 26.50 to 26.59 below)

Transitional arrangements

26.50   The standard generally requires retrospective application of its requirements, unless the restating of the information for earlier periods would be impracticable, in which case that fact and the extent to which restatement has taken place must be disclosed. Also, an entity that first adopts FRS 26 for an accounting period beginning before 1 January 2007 need not restate comparative information to comply with the new requirements. Instead, the preceding year's figures can continue to be presented on the basis of the entity's previous accounting policies for financial instruments and the accounts should disclose:

(i)   the fact that this approach has been taken;

(ii)   the accounting policies adopted for the comparative information; and

(iii) the nature of the adjustments that would be needed to make the comparative information comply with FRS 26 – the standard does not require the adjustments to be quantified, but it does require any adjustment between the closing balance sheet for the comparative period (ie prepared on the basis of the previous accounting policies) and the opening balance for the current period (ie prepared on the basis of the FRS 26 requirements) to be treated as arising from a change in accounting policy, with the disclosures required by FRS 18 'Accounting policies' (see Chapter 6).

Also, on first application of the standard, an entity is permitted to designate a previously recognised financial asset or financial liability as a financial asset or financial liability at fair value through profit or loss or available for sale, even though the standard normally requires such a designation to be made on initial recognition. The standard specifies how the cumulative changes in fair value should be accounted for in these circumstances. There is also detailed transitional guidance on accounting for hedges on first application of the standard, particularly where transactions that have previously been designated as hedges or hedged items no longer qualify under the new requirements.

HEDGE ACCOUNTING

Scope of FRS 26

26.51   The standard sets out detailed requirements on the designation of hedging instruments and the accounting treatment to be applied to gains and losses arising on a hedged item and the hedging instrument where a designated hedging relationship exists between the two. The detailed coverage includes:

(i)   which financial instruments qualify as hedging instruments;

(ii)   which items qualify as hedged items;

(iii)   the designation of hedging instruments and hedged items;

(iv)   types of hedging relationships (ie fair value hedge, cash flow hedge and hedge of a net investment in a foreign operation);

(v)   the conditions that must be met for hedge accounting to be applied; and

(vi)   the hedge accounting treatment to be applied to each type of hedge.

Hedging instruments and hedged items

26.52   A hedging instrument is a designated derivative whose fair value or cash flows are expected to offset changes in the fair value or cash flows of a designated hedged item. In the case of a hedge against the risk of changes in foreign currency exchange rates, a non-derivative financial asset or liability may also be designated as a hedging instrument.

A hedged item is an asset, liability, firm commitment, highly probable forecast transaction or net investment in a foreign operation that both exposes the entity to risk of changes in fair value or future cash flows and is designated as being hedged.

Hedge effectiveness is defined as the degree to which changes in the fair value or cash flows of a hedged item that are attributable to a hedged risk are offset by changes in the fair value or cash flows of the hedging instrument.

Categories of hedging relationships

26.53   FRS 26 identifies three categories of hedging relationships:

(i)   **Fair value hedge**: This is a hedge of the exposure to changes in the fair value of a recognised assets or liability or an unrecognised firm commitment (or an identified portion of such an asset, liability or commitment) that is attributable to a particular risk and could affect profit or loss.

(ii)   **Cash flow hedge:** This is a hedge of the exposure to variations in cash flows that is attributable to a particular risk associated with a recognised asset or liability (eg future interest payments on variable rate debt), or with a highly probable forecast transaction, and which could affect profit or loss.

(iii)   **Hedge of a net investment in a foreign operation.**

When hedge accounting can be applied

26.54   A hedging relationship will qualify for hedge accounting only if all of the following conditions are met:

(i)   at the inception of the hedge, the hedging relationship is formally designated and documented, together with the entity's risk management objective and strategy for undertaking the hedge – the documentation must identify the hedged item or transaction, the hedging instrument and how the effectiveness of the hedge will be assessed;

(ii)   the hedge is expected to be highly effective, consistent with the document risk management strategy for that hedging relationship;

(iii)   for cash flow hedges, where a forecast transaction is the subject of the hedge it must be highly probable and present an exposure that could affect profit or loss;

(iv)   the effectiveness of the hedge can be measured reliably; and

(v)   the hedge is assessed on an ongoing basis and proves to be highly effective throughout the financial periods for which the hedge was designated.

Accounting for fair value hedges

26.55   A fair value hedge that meets the above conditions should be accounted for as follows:

(i)   in the case of a derivative hedging instrument, the gain or loss on remeasuring the instrument at fair value should be recognised in profit or loss;

(ii)   in the case of a non-derivative hedging instrument, the foreign currency component of the carrying amount measured in accordance with FRS 23 should be recognised in profit or loss; and

(iii)   the gain or loss on the hedged item attributable to the hedged risk should be recognised in profit or loss and adjusted on the carrying amount of that item, even if it is otherwise recognised at cost.

The requirement to recognise the gain or loss on the hedged item in profit or loss applies to an available-for-sale financial asset in the same way as to any other item. If only certain risks attributable to a hedged item are hedged, recognised changes in fair value that do not relate to the hedged risk should be recognised in accordance with the normal requirements of FRS 26 (see 26.49 above).

The standard allows separate presentation of the gain or loss on a hedged item within assets or liabilities (subject to certain conditions) in the case of a fair value hedge of the interest rate exposure of a portion of a portfolio of financial assets or financial liabilities, but not in any other case.

Adjustments to the carrying amount of a hedged item should be amortised to profit and loss, with amortisation beginning no later than when the hedged item ceases to be adjusted for changes in its fair value attributable to the risk being hedged and being based on a recalculated effective interest rate at the date that amortisation begins. In the case of a fair value hedge of the interest rate exposure of a portion of a portfolio of financial assets or financial liabilities where the gain or loss is presented separately,as described above, a straight line method of amortisation may be used if the use of a recalculated effective interest rate is not practical. The adjustment should be fully amortised by maturity of the financial instrument or, in the case of a portfolio hedge of interest rate risk, by expiry of the relevant repricing period.

The standard requires hedge accounting to be discontinued prospectively if:

(i)   the hedging instrument expires or is sold, terminated or exercised – replacement or rollover into another hedging instrument is not regarded as expiry or termination if it is part of the entity's documented hedging strategy;

(ii)   the hedge no longer meets the criteria for hedge accounting; or

(iii)   the entity revokes the designation.

Accounting for cash flow hedges

26.56   A cash flow hedge that meets the conditions for hedge accounting should be accounted for as follows:

(i)   the portion of the gain or loss on the hedging instrument that is determined to be an effective hedge should be recognised in the statement of total recognised gains and loses; and

(ii)   any ineffective portion of the gain or loss should be recognised in profit or loss.

The standard includes detailed additional requirements on accounting for hedges of forecast transactions and in particular when gains and losses previously recognised directly in reserves should be recognised in profit or loss.

The standard requires hedge accounting to be discontinued prospectively if:

(i)   the hedging instrument expires or is sold, terminated or exercised – replacement or rollover into another hedging instrument is not regarded as expiry or termination if it is part of the entity's documented hedging strategy;

(ii)   the hedge no longer meets the criteria for hedge accounting;

(iii)   a forecast transaction is no longer expected to occur; or

(iv)   the entity revokes the designation.

In each case, the standard specifies how the cumulative gains or loss already recognised directly in reserves should be accounted for.

Accounting for hedges of a net investment in a foreign operation

26.57   Hedges of a net investment in a foreign operation (including a hedge of a monetary item accounted for as part of the net investment under FRS 23 – see Chapter 50) should be accounted for as follows:

(i)   the portion of the gain or loss on the hedging instrument that is determined to be an effective hedge should be recognised in the statement of total recognised gains and loses; and

(ii)   any ineffective portion of the gain or loss should be recognised in profit or loss.

The cumulative gain or loss recognised directly in reserves should be recognised in profit or loss on disposal of the foreign operation.

Disclosures in respect of hedging activities

26.58   Where hedge accounting is adopted, FRS 25 requires the entity to describe the policy for hedging each main type of forecast transaction and to give the following disclosures separately for designated fair value hedges, cash flow hedges and hedges of a net investment in a foreign operation:

(i)   a description of the hedge;

(ii)   a description of the financial instruments designated as hedging instruments and their fair values at the balance sheet date;

(iii)   the nature of the risks being hedged;

(iv)   in the case of cash flow hedges:

- the periods in which the cash flows are expected to occur;

- when they are expected to enter into the determination of profit or loss; and

- a description of any forecast transaction for which hedge accounting has previously been used but which is no longer expected to occur; and

Also, where a gain or loss on a hedging instrument in a cash flow hedge has been recognised directly in equity through the statement of total recognised gains and losses, the accounts must disclose:

(i)   the amount recognised during the period;

(ii)   the amount removed from equity and included in profit or loss for the period; and

(iii) the amount removed from equity during the period and included in the initial measurement of the acquisition cost or other carrying amount of a non-financial asset or non-financial liability in a hedged highly probable forecast transaction.

Transitional arrangements

26.59 The standard generally requires retrospective application of its require-ments, unless the restating of the information for earlier periods would be imprac-ticable, in which case that fact and the extent to which restatement has taken place must be disclosed. Also, an entity that first adopts FRS 26 for an accounting period beginning before 1 January 2007 need not restate comparative information to comply with the new requirements. Further details are given at 26.50 above. There is also detailed transitional guidance on accounting for hedges on first application of the standard, particularly where transactions previously designated as hedges or hedged items no longer qualify under the new requirements.

LIKELY FUTURE DEVELOPMENTS

FRED 33 'Financial Instruments: Disclosures'

26.60 The ASB published FRED 33 'Financial Instruments: Disclosures' in July 2004. This sets out the draft text of a proposed new international accounting standard combining the requirements currently set out in IAS 32 'Financial Instru-ments: Disclosure and Presentation' and IAS 30 'Disclosures in the Financial Statements of Banks and Similar Financial Institutions' and also proposing certain new disclosures. The standard will apply to all UK entities, other than those adopting the FRSSE, and will supersede the disclosure requirements currently set out in FRS 25 'Financial Instruments: Disclosure and Presentation' and those that continue to apply to a small number of entitites under FRS 13 'Derivatives and Other Financial Instruments: Disclosure'. The draft sets out the detailed minimum disclosures that are considered necessary to enable users to evaluate:

(i) the significance of financial instruments to the entity's financial position and performance;

(ii) the nature and extent of risks arising from the financial instruments to which it was exposed during the period and at the period end; and

(iii) the entity's capital.

The disclosure requirements are slightly wider than the title of the document might imply. In particular, they include a number of new disclosures in respect of capital that will apply in all cases and not just where an entity makes significant use of financial instruments. Further information on these proposals is given in Chap-ter 32. The other disclosure requirements are intended to enable users of the accounts to assess the significance of financial instruments to the financial position and financial performance of the reporting entity. Given the wide variety of financial instruments available these days, the draft sets out minimum disclosure requirements, with the implication that these may need to be expanded on, depending on the particular circumstances of the business. The minimum disclosures include:

(i)   an analysis of balance sheet carrying values by specified class of financial instrument, and additional information where fair value accounting has been applied to financial assets and liabilities;

(ii)   detailed disclosures on any financial assets that have been pledged as collateral;

(iii)   details of any defaults during the period in respect of principal, interest, sinking fund or redemption provisions on outstanding loans, or other breaches of loan agreements;

(iv)   net gains or losses on financial instruments, analysed into specified categories, and details of how these amounts are determined;

(v)   all significant accounting policies in respect of financial instruments;

(vi)   detailed disclosures in respect of any hedging transactions; and

(vii)   disclosures to enable users to compare the fair values of financial assets and liabilities with their balance sheet carrying values.

The draft also proposes the disclosure of detailed information (both qualitative and quantitative) to enable users to assess the risks to which the entity is exposed as a result of the financial instruments that it holds, and the policies and procedures used to manage these. In particular, minimum disclosure requirements are proposed in respect of various aspects of credit risk, liquidity risk and market risk. The requirements of the proposed new standard will not be straightforward to deal with, and both the identification and the presentation of the relevant information are likely to need careful thought.

The June 2005 version of the ASB's Technical Plan indicates that a new standard based on FRED 33 is expected to be effective for accounting periods beginning on or after 1 January 2007.

Proposed amendments to FRS 26

26.61   In April 2005, the ASB issued an Exposure Draft 'Amendment to FRS 26 – Financial Instruments: Measurement' which proposes extending the scope of the standard and introducing into UK accounting the recognition and derecognition requirements of the underlying international accounting standard. Currently, the standard applies only to listed entities and to any other entities that choose to adopt fair value accounting (see 26.43 above), but the ASB has always made clear its intention to extend the requirements to other entities in due course. This would also mean that all entities (other than those adopting the FRSSE) are brought within the scope of the detailed disclosure requirements in respect of financial instruments (currently set out in FRS 25 'Financial Instruments: Disclosure and Presentation') and, where appropriate, of FRS 23 'The Effects of Changes in Foreign Exchange Rates' and FRS 24 'Financial Reporting in Hyperinflationary Economies'. The ASB is currently proposing that the extension in scope should apply for accounting periods beginning on or after 1 January 2007, or possibly 1 January 2008 if more preparation time is felt to be needed.

The second element of the Exposure Draft introduces the recognition and derecognition requirements of IAS 39 into UK accounting practice. At present, FRS 26 deals only with measurement issues, mainly because the ASB had concerns over a proposed new approach to derecognition that was being considered by the IASB when the Exposure Draft that led to FRS 26 was originally published. However, the IASB subsequently decided to clarify and improve its existing approach to derecognition rather than to proceed with the new model, and the ASB has therefore concluded that it is now appropriate to adopt the recognition and derecognition requirements of IAS 39 in the UK. These would supersede the derecognition principles in FRS 5 'Reporting the Substance of Transactions' for transactions in financial assets and financial liabilities, but the FRS 5 requirements would remain in force for non-financial items. The related IAS disclosure requirements in respect of recognition and derecognition would also be added to UK accounting standards.

The ASB proposes that the recognition and derecognition requirements should apply for accounting periods beginning on or after 1 January 2007, with earlier adoption permitted. However, if the measurement aspects of FRS 26 are deferred to a later date for entities not currently within the scope of the standard, the recognition and derecognition requirements would be similarly deferred. Certain transitional provisions will be included to prevent entities having to restate all earlier transactions on the new basis.

Chapter 27

Bank Loans and Overdrafts

BANK LOANS

Analysis of bank loans

27.1   For disclosure purposes, bank loans must be separated into amounts that are repayable by instalment over a period of time and those that are repayable in one sum at the end of the term of the loan. Where a bank loan is repayable in instalments, the amount outstanding at the balance sheet date must be analysed into:

—   the amounts falling due within the next year;

—   the amounts falling due after more than one year.

The amounts due to be paid within the next year will be included under creditors due within one year, and the balance will be included in creditors due after more than one year. If the company has loans where any of the instalments fall due for payment more than five years after the balance sheet date (described in CA 1985 Sch 4 para 48(1) as the 'period of five years, beginning with the day next following the end of the financial year'), the accounts must show separately the aggregate amount due in respect of those loans. Where loans are not repayable in instalments, the Act requires separate disclosure of the aggregate amount repayable after five years. The following example illustrates these disclosure requirements.

Example 27.1 – Disclosure of bank loans, including those payable in instalments

At 31 December 20X2, D Ltd has the following bank loans:

Loan A	A remaining balance of £125,000 which is payable in quarterly instalments of £25,000 on 31 March, 30 June, 30 September and 31 December each year.
Loan B	A loan of £300,000 which is payable as follows:
	— on 30 June 20X4: £100,000
	— on 30 June 20X6: £100,000
	— on 30 June 20X8:£100,000
Loan C	A loan of £175,000 repayable in full on 31 December 20X8

The company also has a bank overdraft of £54,679 at 31 December 20X2 which is repayable to the bank on demand. The analysis of the loans and overdraft at 31 December 20X2 is therefore:

	Due within on year £	*Due after one year* £
Bank overdraft	54,679	—
Loan A	100,000	25,000
Loan B	—	300,000
Loan C	—	175,000
	154,679	500,000

The accounts will therefore show £154,679 under creditors due within one year and £500,000 under creditors due after more than one year, along with the following additional details.

Amounts repayable by instalment:	
Loan not wholly repayable within five years	300,000
Amounts not repayable by instalment:	
Loan repayable after more than five years	175,000

Repayment date of loans

27.2   In assessing whether loans are repayable within, or after more than one year or, within, or after more than, five years, a loan (or an instalment) is to be taken as falling due for repayment or payment on the earliest date on which the lender could require repayment or payment, if he exercised all the options and rights available to him.

For accounting periods beginning on or after 1 January 2005, FRS 25 'Financial Instruments: Disclosure and Presentation' sets out detailed guidance on assessing the maturity of financial liabilities and in particular on dealing with any breaches of covenants or similar requirements. Further details are given in Chapter 26.

Payment terms and interest rates

27.3   CA 1985 also requires disclosure of the payment or repayment terms and interest rates for each bank loan that is wholly or partly repayable after five years. Details should be disclosed individually for each loan, unless this would result in disclosures of excessive length, in which case a general indication of payment terms and interest rates can be given instead.

Example 27.2 – Disclosure of payment/repayment terms and interest rates

Using the details from Example 27.1, details will need to be given for Loan B and Loan C as both of these involve some repayment after more than five years. No additional disclosures are required in the case of Loan A as this is wholly repayable within 15 months.

Amounts repayable by
instalment:
Loan not wholly repayable   300,000
within five years

The loan is repayable in three instalments of £100,000 which fall due in June 20X4, 20X6 and 20X8 respectively. Interest is charged on this loan at 2% above base rate.

Amounts not repayable by
instalment:
Loan wholly repayable within   175,000
five years

The loan is repayable in full on 31 December 20X8. Interest is charged on this loan at a fixed rate of 6%.

Secured loans and overdrafts

27.4   Where any bank loan or overdraft is secured, CA 1985 requires disclosure of the fact that security has been given and an indication of the nature of that security. In this case, the disclosures apply to all bank loans and overdrafts, not just those that are wholly or partly repayable after more than five years.

Example 27.3 – Disclosure where security has been given

Using the details from Example 27.1 (and assuming Loan A is unsecured):

Amounts repayable by
instalment:
Loan not wholly repayable   300,000
within five years

The loan is repayable in three instalments of £100,000 which fall due in June 20X4, 20X6 and 20X8 respectively. Interest is charged on this loan at 2% above base rate. The loan is secured by a fixed charge on the company's freehold property.

Amounts not repayable by
instalment:
Loan repayable after more   175,000
than five years

The loan is repayable in full on 31 December 20X8. Interest is charged on this loan at a fixed rate of 6%. The loan is secured by a fixed charge on the company's leasehold property.

The company's bank overdraft is secured by a fixed and floating charge over the company's assets. The amount outstanding at 31 December 20X2 was £54,679 (20X1: £70,142).

BANK OVERDRAFTS

Source of the figure for bank overdrafts

27.5   The amount shown as cash at bank or bank overdrafts in the accounts is traditionally the balance shown in the company's accounting records at the end of the financial year. In most cases, this will not be the same as the balance shown on the bank statements. The reconciliation of the balance shown in the cash records with that shown on the bank statements is a standard internal control that should be carried out on a regular basis and which will identify any amounts included in the cash records which have not been processed by the bank at the financial reporting date (ie unpresented cheques and uncleared lodgements). By including the balance shown in the accounting records, debtors and creditors are stated on the assumption that all outstanding lodgements and cheque payments will be accepted by the bank. Debtors are therefore reduced by the amount of cash received but not yet processed and creditors are reduced by the amount of cheques issued but not yet presented. This treatment of payments is justified as, once the cheques have been issued, the company is no longer in a position to control the funds that will be absorbed when the cheques are cleared.

Strictly, the position is not quite the same where the cheques have been prepared but not actually issued to creditors at the balance sheet date. In this case, the company could be considered to retain control over the funds (ie it can decide whether or not to send out the cheques). If the value of cheques drawn but not despatched at the balance sheet date is material, it will usually be appropriate to add this total back to the bank balance and reinstate the creditors.

Use of bank statement balance

27.6   Some companies choose to include the balance shown on the bank statements as the bank overdraft or cash at bank, at the year-end. The accounts are therefore presented on the basis that cash payments and receipts are not recognised until they have been accepted and processed by the bank. Adjustments will need to be made to reflect the unprocessed items in the accounts, usually by reinstating the relevant debtors and creditors. An alternative approach is to include a separate sub-heading within creditors (or debtors where appropriate) for uncleared banking items, usually with an analysis showing how this figure is made up.

Example 27.4Alternative disclosure of uncleared banking items

	20X2 £000	20X1 £000
Creditors due within one year:		
Bank overdraft	20	10
Uncleared banking items	54	29
Trade creditors	212	207
Accruals and deferred income	56	49
	342	295
Uncleared banking items comprise:		
Cheques issued but not presented	67	34
Lodgements awaiting clearance by the bank	(13)	(5)
	54	29

Even if the uncleared items are not shown as a separate sub-heading, the amounts involved are usually disclosed. As the use of the bank statement figure is not the normal method of presentation, the accounting policies should explain the method that has been adopted. The treatment should also be applied consistently from year to year and, where there is more than one bank account, all accounts should be treated in the same way. If there is a change in the method of presentation, the figures for the previous year will need to be restated and the change in policy explained (see Chapter 5).

Repayment date

27.7 In the case of bank overdrafts, the bank will usually retain the right to request immediate repayment. Where an overdraft is technically repayable on demand, it should be shown as being due within one year. This approach should normally be adopted irrespective of the date of the next formal review of the overdraft facility (which may be more than 12 months after the balance sheet date).

Combined disclosure with loans due within one year

27.8 There is no requirement to make separate disclosure in respect of bank overdrafts. The amount outstanding at the balance sheet date should therefore be aggregated with the amount of any other bank loans due within one year of that date (see Example 27.1).

Window dressing

27.9 SSAP 17 'Accounting for Post Balance Sheet Events' requires disclosure in the accounts of the reversal or maturity after the balance sheet date of any transactions entered into before the end of the accounting period, where the primary substance of the transaction was to alter the company's balance sheet. These requirements cover changes to the balance sheet commonly known as 'window dressing', many of which have an impact on the figures shown for bank balances or overdrafts in the accounts.

For accounting periods beginning on or after 1 January 2005, SSAP 17 is superseded by FRS 21 'Events After the Balance Sheet Date' which does not make any specific reference to window dressing or the separate disclosure of artificial transactions that are reversed after the year-end.

The requirements of both SSAP 17 and FRS 21 are considered in more detail in Chapter 34.

Secured overdrafts

27.10 Where any bank loan or overdraft is secured, CA 1985 requires disclosure of the fact that security has been given and an indication of the nature of that security (see 27.4 above).

OFFSETTING OF BANK BALANCES

General prohibition on offsetting

27.11 Under paragraph 29 of FRS 5 'Reporting the Substance of Transactions':

(i) assets and liabilities should not be offset;

(ii) debit and credit balances should only be aggregated into a single net item where they do not constitute separate assets and liabilities.

This reinforces the general prohibition in CA 1985 on the offsetting of assets and liabilities.

For accounting periods beginning before 1 January 2005, FRS 5 sets out the specific conditions that must be met if debit and credit balances are to be aggregated into a single net item. For accounting periods beginning on or after 1 January 2005, the offset of financial assets and financial liabilities is covered by FRS 25 'Financial Instruments: Disclosure and Presentation' and FRS 5 is amended to emphasise this.

Accounting periods beginning before 1 January 2005

27.12 For accounting periods beginning before 1 January 2005, FRS 5 requires credit and debit balances to be aggregated into a single net item where, and only where, all of the following conditions are met:

(i)   the amounts owed to and by the reporting entity are determinable monetary amounts, which are denominated either in the same currency or in freely convertible currencies (a freely convertible currency is defined as one for which quoted market rates are available and for which there is an active market, so that the amount to be offset could be exchanged without a significant effect on the exchange rate);

(ii) the reporting entity has the ability to insist on a net settlement of the outstanding balances; and

(iii) the reporting entity's ability to insist on a net settlement of the balances is assured beyond all doubt.

If all of these conditions are met, the balances are not regarded as separate assets and liabilities they should therefore be offset for accounting purposes.

Net settlement assured beyond all doubt

27.13   In order to meet the condition that net settlement is assured beyond all doubt, FRS 5 emphasises that there must be no possibility that the reporting entity could be required to transfer economic benefits to another party without being able to enforce its own access to economic benefits. In other words, there must be no possibility that the company will have to make payment of the creditor balance in its accounting records without first being able to recover payment of the debtor balance. Confirmation on this point should include consideration of the maturity dates of both the debit and the credit balance, and also the potential impact of the insolvency of the other party. The maturity date of the debit balance must be no later than the maturity date of the credit balance, so that the company is entitled to receive payment in respect of the debtor before, or at the same time as, it must pay the amount that it owes to the other party. If the company has the ability to accelerate maturity of the debt or to defer maturity of the liability, and thus achieve the same result, this condition can usually be regarded as satisfied. The company's ability to insist on a net settlement of the amounts due must be assured beyond any doubt and in particular must be capable of surviving the insolvency of the other party. Legal advice will usually need to be taken to confirm this point.

Contingent right to net settlement

27.14   Where the company's right to insist on a net settlement of the amounts due is contingent on any other matter or event, it should only be taken into account if the company would be able to enforce net settlement in all situations where the other party defaults on payment.

Members of a group

27.15   The same principles apply in the case of a group of companies, where different companies within the group may have amounts due to or from a particular third party. If all the conditions are met, offset of the relevant credit and debit balances in the group accounts is required under the standard. However, where different legal entities are involved in the various transactions (and both the group and the third party could have more than one legal entity involved) it is less likely that all of the conditions set out in FRS 5 will be properly satisfied.

Accounting periods beginning on or after 1 January 2005

27.16   Although the basic requirement of paragraph 29 of FRS 5 remains in force, the detailed guidance in that standard on the offset of financial assets and liabilities is superseded by FRS 25 'Financial Instruments: Disclosure and Presentation' for accounting periods beginning on or after 1 January 2005. Under this standard, offset is required when, and only when:

(i)   the entity has a legally enforceable right to set off the asset and the liability; and

(ii)   the entity intends either to settle on a net basis or to realise the asset and settle the liability simultaneously.

A net presentation should therefore only be adopted in the accounts if this reflects the future cash flows that are expected to arise from the settlement of the separate financial instruments. In all other cases, the instruments should be recognised separately.

Legally enforceable right of set-off

27.17   A legal right of set-off can arise by contract or other agreement and will usually be a direct arrangement between a debtor and a creditor. However, the guidance in the standard notes that, in exceptional circumstances, a debtor may have a legal right to apply an amount due from a third party against the amount due to a creditor, and this may create an enforceable right of set-off it there is a clear agreement between all the parties involved. The legal jurisdiction in which any arrangement is made, and the laws applicable to the various parties, will need to be carefully reviewed to establish whether a legally enforceable right of set-off has been created.

Settlement intention

27.18   The guidance emphasises that the existence of a legally enforceable right of set-off is not sufficient to justify the adoption of a net presentation in the accounts, because that right will not affect the future cash flows of the entity unless it is actually exercised. Equally, an intention by one party, or by both parties, to settle on a net basis without a legally enforceable right to do so cannot justify a net presentation. In this situation, the rights and obligations associated with the underlying financial instruments would remain unaltered and adopting a net presentation would therefore not give an true reflection of the arrangement. Where an entity has a right of set-off but does not intend to enforce this, or to realise the asset and settle the liability simultaneously, and this affects the entity's exposure to credit risk and liquidity risk, additional disclosures may need to be given in the accounts. The detailed disclosure requirements of the standard apply for accounting periods beginning on or after 1 January 2005 in the case of listed companies, and from the period in which FRS 26 'Financial Instruments: Measurement' is applied in other cases. For practical purposes, this will generally be if and when the entity chooses to adopt fair value accounting.

Simultaneous settlement

27.19   The guidance notes that simultaneous settlement of the asset and the liability may occur through the operation of a clearing house in an organised financial market or a face-to-face exchange. The critical point is that there should be no exposure to credit or liquidity risk as a result of the transactions. If the entity is exposed to such risks, even relatively briefly, settlement is not regarded as simultaneous. For instance, where two instruments are to be settled by the receipt and payment of separate amounts, the entity will usually be exposed (however briefly) either to credit risk in respect of the full amount of the asset, or liquidity risk in for the full amount of the liability. The standard consequently requires this to be reflected in the separate presentation of the financial asset and the financial liability. The exposure to risk can only be avoided if the transactions occur at the same moment.

Situations where offsetting is inappropriate

27.20   The guidance notes specifically that offsetting will not usually be appropriate in the following situations:

(i)   where several different financial instruments are used to emulate the features of a single financial instrument;

(ii)   where financial assets and liabilities arise from financial instruments with the same primary risk exposure but involve different counterparts;

(iii)   where financial or other assets are pledged as collateral for non-recourse financial liabilities;

(iv)   where financial assets are set aside in trust by a debtor for the purpose of discharging an obligation without the creditor actually accepting those assets in settlement;

(v)   where obligations are expected to be recovered from a third party under an insurance claim.

This is on the basis that the two conditions required for offsetting will not generally be met in the above circumstances.

Master netting arrangements

27.21   A master netting arrangement is described in the standard as one where an entity undertakes a number of financial instrument transactions with a single counterparty and enters into an agreement that provides for a single net settlement of all the instruments covered by the agreement in the event of a default on, or termination of, any one contract. A key point is that such an agreement only creates a legally enforceable right of set-off in the event of a default or other circumstances not expected to arise in the normal course of business. The guidance therefore concludes that such an arrangement does not provide the basis for offsetting in the accounts, unless both of the criteria specified in 12.6.11 are also satisfied. However, the effect of the arrangement on the entity's exposure to credit risk will usually need to be disclosed.

Chapter 28   Leasing and Hire Purchase Liabilities

CALCULATION OF LIABILITIES UNDER FINANCE LEASES

Initial recording of liability

28.1   Under SSAP 21 'Accounting for Leases and Hire Purchase Contracts', leases that are classified as finance leases should be recorded in the lessee's balance sheet as an asset and as an obligation to pay future rentals to the lessor. The distinction between leases and hire purchase contracts and the classification of individual leasing agreements as finance leases or operating leases is considered in Chapter 21. At the inception of a finance lease (which is defined in SSAP 21 as the earlier of the date when the asset is brought into use or the date from which rental payments accrue), the amount recorded as an asset and the obligation recorded to the lessor will be the same. Strictly this should be the present value of the minimum lease payments. The minimum lease payments are defined in SSAP 21 as:

> 'the minimum payments over the remaining part of the lease term (excluding charges for services and taxes to be paid by the lessor) and, in the case of the lessee, any residual amounts guaranteed by him or by a party related to him.'

They should include any initial payment made by the lessee under the agreement. An example of the calculation of the present value of minimum lease payments is given in Chapter 14. However, SSAP 21 emphasises that, for practical purposes, the fair value of the asset at the inception of the lease will usually be an acceptable figure to use when initially recording the asset and the related obligation to the lessor.

Analysis of rental payments

28.2   The rental payments made by a lessee under a finance lease will consist of two elements:

— partial repayment of the amount due to the lessor; and

— finance charges in respect of the amount effectively 'borrowed' from the lessor to finance the purchase of the asset.

The rental payments must be analysed between these two elements for accounting purposes:

— the finance charges will be charged to the profit and loss account, as part of 'interest payable and similar charges';

— the amount representing the repayment of 'borrowings' will reduce the balance due to the lessor.

The calculation of finance charges and the allocation of the charge over the term of the lease is considered in Chapter 14.

Reduction of liability to lessor

28.3   Once the finance charge has been calculated and allocated over the term of the lease, the annual repayment of the effective 'borrowings' under the lease can be calculated.

Example 28.1 – Calculation of the annual repayment of the effective borrowings

G Ltd leases an asset under a finance lease with a primary term of four years, with the option to continue to lease for as long thereafter as the company wishes on payment of a nominal rental. The rental payments during the primary term of the lease are £3,000 per annum, payable in arrears. The cash purchase price of the asset at the inception of the lease was £9,500.

The asset (and the related liability) will therefore be recorded at £9,500. Actual payments during the primary term of the lease will amount to £12,000 (ie £3,000 p.a. for four years). The total finance charge is therefore £2,500 (ie £12,000 – £9,500).

Allocation of the finance charge on an annual basis using the actuarial method, with a rate of charge of 10.05% gives the following result.

Year	Opening capital sum	Rental payment	Finance charge (10.05%)	Closing capital sum
	£	£	£	£
1	9,500	(3,000)	955	7,455
2	7,455	(3,000)	749	5,204
3	5,204	(3,000)	523	2,727
4	2,727	(3,000)	273	—
		12,000	2,500	

The analysis of rental payments between capital repayments and finance charges will therefore be:

Year	Capital repayment	Finance charge	Total rental
	£	£	£
1	2,045	955	3,000
2	2,251	749	3,000
3	2,477	523	3,000
4	2,727	273	3,000
	9,500	2,500	12,000

The liability under the lease will therefore be recorded in G Ltd's accounting records as follows:

	£
Initial liability at the inception of the lease	9,500
Repayment of capital in Year 1	(2,045)
Creditor at the end of Year 1	7,455
Repayment of capital in Year 2	(2,251)
Creditor at the end of Year 2	5,204
Repayment of capital in Year 3	(2,477)
Creditor at the end of Year 3	2,727
Repayment of capital in Year 4	(2,727)
Balance at the end of Year 4	—

Accounting policies

28.4   The accounting policies adopted for finance leases and operating leases should also be disclosed in the accounts. This is considered in more detail in Chapter 20.

SEPARATE DISCLOSURE OF LEASING OBLIGATIONS

Additional sub-heading within creditors

28.5   CA 1985 makes no specific reference to leasing and hire purchase liabilities. However, it does permit items to be shown in greater detail than is required by the formats and also allows additional items to be included, provided that they are not already shown elsewhere in the standard formats. Therefore, where a company has liabilities under a finance lease or hire purchase agreement, an additional sub-heading will usually be introduced within creditors to meet the disclosure requirements of SSAP 21. The standard requires obligations in respect of finance leases and hire purchase agreements to be shown separately from other obligations, either on the face of the balance sheet or in the notes to the accounts. As leasing commitments are similar in nature to borrowings, the additional sub-heading is usually included between bank loans and overdrafts and trade creditors.

Example 28.2 – Separate disclosure of leasing obligations

Creditors due within one year:	*20X2*	*20X1*
	£	£
Debenture loans	125	125
Bank loans and overdrafts	95	84
Obligations under finance leases and hire purchase contracts	30	42
Trade creditors	112	115
Corporation tax	22	15
Other creditors	45	39
Accruals and deferred income	31	35
	460	455

A similar analysis would need to be given for creditors due after more than one year. In the accounts of a lessor, SSAP 21 requires separate disclosure of amounts receivable under finance leases and amounts receivable under hire purchase contracts. No distinction is made in the case of lessees, and only the aggregate amount due in respect of finance leases and similar hire purchase contracts needs to be disclosed.

Alternative disclosure

28.6   The requirements of SSAP 21 can be met by including leasing and hire purchase liabilities under one of the other headings in the format (eg other creditors) and then providing separate details as a footnote to the analysis.

Example 28.3 – Alternative disclosure using a footnote

Creditors due within one year:	*20X2*	*20X1*
	£	£
Debenture loans	125	125
Bank loans and overdrafts	95	84
Trade creditors	112	115
Corporation tax	22	15
Other creditors	75	81
Accruals and deferred income	31	35
	460	455
Other creditors includes the following amounts in respect of obligations under finance leases and hire purchase contracts	30	42
	—	—

However, where leasing and hire purchase obligations are material, disclosure as a separate sub-heading will usually be more appropriate.

Security in respect of leasing obligations

28.7   CA 1985 requires details of any secured items under creditors, along with an indication of the nature of the security given. Liabilities under finance leases and hire purchase agreements will usually be secured on the related assets. The following note will usually be sufficient, as details of the assets will be shown separately within fixed assets.

Example 28.4 – Disclosure of security

Obligations under finance leases and hire purchase agreements are secured on the related assets.

This note could be cross-referenced to the fixed assets note to indicate where details of the related assets can be found.

Disclosure of future commitments

28.8   Where a company has entered into a finance lease or hire purchase agreement at the balance sheet date, but inception has not yet taken place, SSAP 21 requires disclosure of the company's commitment under the agreement. Inception of the lease is defined in the standard as the earlier of the date when the asset is brought into use or the date from which rental payments accrue. The disclosure of commitments generally is considered in Chapter 33.

ANALYSIS OF LEASING LIABILITIES

Requirements under CA 1985

28.9   CA 1985 requires separate disclosure of creditors due after more than one year and also additional disclosure in respect of liabilities that are wholly or partly repayable after five years. As most leasing and hire purchase agreements will involve payment by instalments, the accounts will need to show the aggregate liability under those finance leases or hire purchase agreements where one (or more) of the instalments fall due more than five years after the balance sheet date.

Requirements under SSAP 21

28.10   SSAP 21 requires the following analysis of leasing and hire purchase liabilities:
  (i)   amounts payable in the next year;
  (ii)   amounts payable in the second to fifth years (inclusive) from the balance sheet date;
  (iii)   the aggregate amounts payable after five years.

The disclosures required under the standard are therefore more extensive and apply to all leasing and similar liabilities, not just those that are wholly or partly payable after more than five years. Using the details in Example 28.1, the following disclosures would be given at the end of Year 1.

Example 28.5 – Disclosures at the end of Year 1

	20X2 (ie Year 1 of lease) £	20X1 £
Creditors due within one year:		
Bank loans and overdrafts	9,786	7,899
Obligations under leasing and hire purchase contracts	2,251	—
Trade creditors	22,114	20,198
Accruals and deferred income	5,677	6,713
	39,828	34,810
Creditors due after more than one year:		
Bank loans	10,000	10,000
Obligations under leasing and hire purchase contracts	5,204	—
	15,204	10,000
Obligations under finance leases and hire purchase contracts:		
Amounts payable within two to five years	5,204	—

The requirement under SSAP 21 to disclose the amount payable within one year is already covered by the requirement under CA 1985 to separate creditors due within one year from those due after more than one year.

Disclosure using gross obligations

28.11   As an alternative under SSAP 21, the lessee may analyse the gross obligations under finance leases and hire purchase agreements and show future finance charges as a deduction from the total.

Example 28.6 – Alternative disclosure at the end of Year 1

Using the details in Example 28.1, the disclosure under this approach would be:

	20X2 (ie Year 1of lease) £	20X1 £
Obligations under finance leases and hire purchase contracts:		
Gross amounts payable within one year	3,000	—
Gross amounts payable within two to five years	6,000	—
	9,000	—
Less: Finance changes allocated to future periods	(1,545)	—
Net obligations	7,455	—

Details of finance charges

28.12　　Where any of the payments in respect of finance leases or hire purchase agreements fall due after more than five years, CA 1985 requires disclosure of the payment terms and finance charges. Although the information is strictly required for each individual liability, the Act does permit a general indication to be given if the disclosures would otherwise be excessive, and this approach will usually be adopted for any disclosures required in respect of finance leases and hire purchase agreements.

Example 28.7 – Disclosure of payment terms and finance charges

	20X2 £	20X1 £
Obligations under finance leases and hire purchase contracts:		
Amounts payable within two to five years	23,750	22,456
Amounts payable after five years	5,675	6,005
	29,425	28,461

Obligations under those finance leases and hire purchase agreements where instalments fall due after more than five years are payable in quarterly instalments and bear finance charges at rates ranging from 8.6% to 10.05% per annum. The aggregate amount due in respect of these leases and agreements at 31 March 20X2 was £24,570 (20X1: £22,961).

LIKELY FUTURE DEVELOPMENTS

ASB Discussion Paper 'Leases: Implementation of a New Approach'

28.13   The ASB Discussion Paper 'Leases: Implementation of a New Approach' was issued in December 1999. This document represents a Position Paper developed by the G4+1 group of accounting standard-setters and reflects an agreed international approach to the treatment of leases in financial reporting. In particular it proposes removing the sometimes arbitrary distinction between operating and finance leases and applying the same accounting treatment to all leases. The proposals would affect both lessee and lessor accounting. Brief details of the contents of the Discussion Paper are given in Chapter 21.

However, the current version of the ASB's Technical Plan, published in June 2005, indicates that new UK accounting standards in respect of tangible fixed assets, which will converge UK accounting with international requirements and will include a new standard on leases, are not planned to come into effect until accounting periods beginning on or after 1 January 2008. No further Exposure Drafts on this subject are expected to be issued in the near future.

Chapter 29

Other Creditors, Accruals and Deferred Income

PAYMENTS RECEIVED ON ACCOUNT

Items to be included

29.1   The sub-heading for payments on account within the CA 1985 balance sheet formats is intended to be used for any payments received in advance from customers (e.g. where payment, or part payment, is requested along with the order), which are not treated as deductions from stocks (e.g. as in the case of progress payments on long-term contracts). The company will usually be liable to refund such amounts if the order is not fulfilled and such sums are therefore required to be shown separately within creditors. For accounting periods beginning on or after 1 January 2005, the balance sheet formats set out in CA 1985 are only relevant where the company prepares Companies Act accounts (as opposed to IAS accounts).

Payments on account in respect of long-term contracts

29.2   In practice, the sub-heading is most likely to be used by companies involved in long-term contracts. Under the requirements of SSAP 9 'Stocks and Long-Term Contracts', where the total payments received on account in respect of a contract exceed:

—   the amounts matched with turnover; and

—   the amounts off-set against long-term contract balances,

the excess must be shown separately within creditors as payments on account. This is considered in more detail in Chapter 24 along with practical examples of accounting for long-term contracts.

TRADE CREDITORS

Purchase ledger balances

29.3   Trade creditors will normally comprise the aggregate of the outstanding balances shown on the company's purchase ledger at the end of the accounting period. There is no guidance in CA 1985 on how to classify receipts of goods and services around the year-end date which are not invoiced until after the year-end. These amounts must clearly be included in purchases, and the liability recognised, for consistency (ie on the basis that the goods will be included in stocks if they were received before the balance sheet date). In many cases, the purchase ledger will be held open for a short period after the year-end to allow invoices in respect of such goods and services to be processed. In this case, they will form part of the year-end purchase ledger and will automatically be included in trade creditors for accounts purposes. This approach requires careful separation of invoices relating to the old and the new financial years to ensure that the cut off between the two accounting periods is accurate.

Adjustment for unprocessed items

29.4   Where invoices relating to items received before the financial year-end are not included within purchase ledger balances, an adjustment will need to be made to recognise the company's liability. Unprocessed items should normally be shown as part of trade creditors, particularly where they relate to cost of sales items. However, if the amounts involved are not material, they are sometimes included under one of the other headings (e.g. accruals and deferred income). As with other aspects of the accounts, the important point is for the figures to be presented on a consistent basis year by year. Even where the purchase ledger has been held open for a period, an adjustment may still be required in order to capture invoices received after the close-down of the ledger but which relate to the previous accounting period.

Credit notes due

29.5   Where credit notes have been issued by suppliers after the year-end in respect of invoices included in the year-end balances, or where it is certain that such credit notes will be issued (e.g. because a price reduction has been formally agreed with the supplier), it will usually be appropriate to adjust for these, so that the balance for trade creditors represents the amount that the company will actually pay in respect of the goods and services received during the year. If the goods are in stock at the balance sheet date, the price reduction should also be reflected in the stock valuation.

Settlement discounts

29.6   Similarly, some of the company's suppliers may offer settlement discounts for early payment of the invoice. The availability of settlement discounts will therefore mean that the full amount of the invoices received from suppliers may not be paid in cash. Settlement discounts are normally only given for prompt payment (e.g. payment within 7 or 14 days of the invoice date) and in most cases, there will be little difficulty in establishing the amount of discount actually taken by the company in respect of balances which were outstanding at the end of the accounting period. For accounts purposes, year-end trade creditors should be reduced by the amount of discount actually taken by the company in respect of those balances (i.e. the accounts should reflect the benefit of the discount taken on purchases made during the year).

Debit balances

29.7   If the company's accounting procedures operate efficiently, debit balances should not arise on the purchase ledger. Any small debit balances that arise from time to time can usually be ignored on the grounds that they are immaterial, but if a material debit balance arises on a purchase ledger account (e.g. as a result of the company making a duplicate payment by mistake), the debit balance should normally be transferred from creditors to debtors. However, the recoverability of the amount included in debtors as a result of the transfer will need to be carefully assessed.

TAXATION, SOCIAL SECURITY AND OTHER CREDITORS

Disclosure under CA 1985

29.8   The balance sheet formats include a sub-heading for other creditors including taxation and social security, but within this heading, the Act requires separate disclosure of the aggregate amounts relating to taxation and social security. Amounts included in respect of taxation might comprise:

—   corporation tax payable;

—   VAT payable to Customs and Excise;

—   PAYE deducted from wages and salaries, not yet paid over to the Inland Revenue;

—   excise duties payable (depending on the nature of the company's business).

Social security balances will normally comprise national insurance contributions not yet paid over to the Collector of Taxes. These will include both the employer's contributions and the employees' contributions deducted from gross wages and salaries. However, NI contributions due on potential share option gains (see Chapter 11) should normally be treated as a provision rather than as creditors, because the NI due cannot be established with certainty until the option has been exercised. Once exercise has taken place, and the NI consequently becomes payable, any amounts not paid over at the balance sheet date should be included in creditors.

For accounting periods beginning on or after 1 January 2005, the balance sheet formats set out in CA 1985 are only relevant where the company prepares Companies Act accounts (as opposed to IAS accounts).

Corporation tax payable

29.9   Although CA 1985 only requires disclosure of the aggregate amount for taxation and social security, Accounting standards previously required the amount due in respect of corporation tax to be shown separately. FRS 16 'Current Tax' includes detailed disclosure requirements in respect of the profit and loss account and statement of total recognised gains and losses, but makes no specific reference to disclosure of current tax in the balance sheet. However, separate disclosure of the amount due in respect of corporation tax can be helpful in enabling a user of the accounts to understand the movements in respect of taxation during the year (e.g. it should be possible to reconcile the opening tax liability with the closing tax liability by adjusting for taxation charged during the year and the payments and receipts shown in the cashflow statement for the year). The accounting treatment of current tax in the profit and loss account and statement of total recognised gains and losses is considered in more detail in Chapter 15.

Other creditors

29.10   There is no guidance in CA 1985 on what should be included under 'other creditors'. Basically, it covers items not disclosable elsewhere and might include liabilities such as:

—   proposed dividends, but only in accounts for periods beginning before 1 January 2005 – for accounting periods beginning on or after this date, FRS 21 'Events after the Balance Sheet Date' prohibits the recognition of a proposed dividend as a liability and the previous company law requirements on proposed dividends have been amended accordingly (see Chapter 16);

—   sundry loans (eg a loan from a director);

—   quantity rebates due to customers (i.e. rebates based on the quantity purchased over a specific period of time, rather than relating to an individual purchase or liability).

As with so many issues, the most important point is to adopt a consistent basis of disclosure year by year (e.g. in the allocation of items between other creditors and accruals and deferred income).

Example disclosure

29.11   The following example illustrates the disclosure points discussed in 29.8–29.10 above.

Example 29.1 – Taxation and social security and other creditors

Creditors due within one year:

		20X2 £		20X1 £
Bank loans and overdrafts		125		137
Obligations under finance leases		87		70
Trade creditors		359		344
Other creditors including taxation and social security:				
Corporation tax payable	63		54	
Other taxes and social security	38		34	
	101		88	
Other creditors	36		32	
		137		120
Accruals and deferred income		44		39
		752		710

ACCRUALS AND DEFERRED INCOME

Disclosure under CA 1985

29.12   The balance sheet formats set out in CA 1985 require separate disclosure of the amount included in the accounts in respect of accruals and deferred income but offer two alternative methods of presentation:

—   as a separate sub-heading within creditors (with separate disclosure of the amounts due within and after more than one year);

—   as a main heading on the balance sheet after current assets.

Each company must choose which position to use and should then use this method of presentation consistently year by year. In practice, many companies include accruals and deferred income within creditors, but the alternative treatment is also in fairly common use.

For accounting periods beginning on or after 1 January 2005, the balance sheet formats set out in CA 1985 are only relevant where the company prepares Companies Act accounts (as opposed to IAS accounts).

Items normally included

29.13   There is no guidance in CA 1985 on the items that should be included in accruals and deferred income. FRS 12 'Provisions, Contingent Liabilities and Contingent Assets' describes accruals as liabilities to pay for goods and services that have been received or supplied (including services provided by employees), but which have not yet been paid, invoiced or formally agreed with the supplier. The guidance in the standard emphasises that it may sometimes be necessary to estimate the amount or timing of accruals, but the degree of uncertainty in this case will usually be considerably lower than in the case of a provision. It also notes that accruals are often reported as part of trade and other creditors in the accounts (see 29.3–29.4 above). As with many accounts disclosures, the important point is that a consistent approach should be adopted year by year on which items are included under this heading, and in particular the allocation of items between other creditors and accruals and deferred income.

Accruals

29.14   Accruals will generally comprise the accrued element of general overhead expenses such as:

—   heat, light and power costs (eg electricity charges);
—   telephone charges;
—   legal and professional fees;
—   interest payable and similar finance charges.

This is to ensure that the full charge for the year in respect of these costs is reflected in the profit and loss account. The individual amounts involved will not usually be significant.

Deferred income

29.15   The amounts included under deferred income will vary depending on the nature of the company's activities. Examples of items which might be included under this heading are:

—   the amount of grants received which has been deferred to future years;
—   sundry deposits received from customers (i.e. which will become part of sales income in the following year);
—   rental income received in advance (e.g. where the tenant makes rental payments quarterly in advance);
—   rental income from operating leases in the accounts of a lessor (i.e. where the timing of the actual payments is not in line with the accounting requirement under SSAP 21 'Leases and Hire Purchase Contracts' for income to be recognised on a straight-line basis over the period of the lease);

— sundry income received in advance of the related costs being incurred (i.e. where the costs will arise in the following, or a subsequent, financial period).

Disclosure of amounts due after more than one year

29.16 For each item included within creditors, CA 1985 requires separate disclosure of the amount falling due after more than one year. Where accruals and deferred income is shown as a sub-heading within creditors, the amount due after more than one year must therefore be disclosed in the notes to the accounts. In practice, items included under accruals will generally be due within one year. However, certain items included under deferred income may be recognised over a period of more than one year (e.g. grants in respect of fixed assets), in which case the amount included within creditors should be analysed accordingly. There is no specific requirement in the Act for amounts due after more than one year to be shown separately where accruals and deferred income is shown as a main heading on the balance sheet. However, disclosure may sometimes be necessary for the accounts to show a true and fair view (e.g. where a material item within accruals and deferred income is due after more than one year).

ACCOUNTING FOR GOVERNMENT GRANTS

Type of grants covered by SSAP 4

29.17 Although SSAP 4 'Accounting for Government Grants' may at first sight appear to cover a relatively narrow category of grants, the definitions within the standard are broad and government is defined as including 'government and inter-governmental agencies and similar bodies, whether local, national or international'. The explanatory note to SSAP 4 also emphasises that 'government' includes:

— national government;

— all of the various tiers of local and regional government of any country;

— government agencies;

— non-departmental public bodies (ie quangos);

— the Commission of the European Community;

— other EC bodies;

— international bodies and agencies.

Grants from any of these bodies are therefore covered by the accounting requirements of SSAP 4.

What are government grants?

29.18   Government grants are defined as 'assistance by government in the form of cash or transfers of assets to an enterprise in return for past or future compliance with certain conditions relating to the operating activities of the enterprise'. The explanatory note to SSAP 4 also states that the requirements of SSAP 4 should be seen as indicative of best practice for accounting for grants and similar assistance from other sources.

General rules on recognition of grants

29.19   Grants should not be recognised for accounts purposes until:
—   all conditions for receipt of the grant have been satisfied;
—   there is reasonable assurance that the grant will be received.

This is consistent with the need for prudence and also with the requirement under the CA 1985 that only realised profits should be included in the profit and loss account. However, the requirements of SSAP 4 do not mean that grants must be received in cash (or other assets) before they can be recognised in the accounts. In many cases, the grant-making body will confirm that an application has been accepted and will then require claims to be made at specified intervals or after specific costs have been incurred. It is usually acceptable to include any amounts claimed but not yet received in debtors, and account for the grant claimed in accordance with SSAP 4 (i.e. by matching it with the related expenditure), provided it is clear that:
—   the application for grant has been accepted;
—   any conditions attaching to the grant have been met;
—   a claim has been submitted;
—   any costs in respect of the amount claimed have actually been incurred; and
—   there is no reason to believe that the submitted claim will not be accepted.

Example 29.2 – Recognition of grants

A Ltd has applied for a grant of £75,000 in respect of the installation of a new equipment costing £250,000 and has received confirmation that the application has been accepted. Claims can be submitted quarterly, based on the relevant proportion of costs incurred. Work on the new plant commenced on 1 July 20X2. A Ltd's financial year end is 30 September.

Costs in the period 1 July – 30 September 20X2 amounted to £54,000 and A Ltd claimed £16,200 of the grant in October 20X2 (i.e. 54/250 x 75); the amount claimed was received in December 20X2.

£16,200 should therefore be recorded in debtors as a grant receivable at 30 September 20X2 and also included in deferred income. Whether any of this income is recognised in the profit and loss account for the year to 30 September 20X2 will depend on whether any of the related costs are charged to the profit and loss account in the same period.

Accruals concept

29.20 FRS 18 'Accounting Policies' requires financial statements (other than cash flow information) to be prepared on the accruals basis of accounting, which it defines as requiring the non-cash effects of transactions and events to be reflected, as far as is possible, in the financial statements for the accounting period in which they occur and not in the period in which any related cash is received or paid. The standard makes a clear link with the definitions of assets and liabilities set out in FRS 5 'Reporting the Substance of Transactions' (and also in the Statement of Principles), and notes that the use of those definitions to determine which items should be recognised as assets and liabilities in the balance sheet is consistent with the accruals concept. SSAP 4 requires government grants to be matched with the expenditure towards which they are intended to contribute and, if there is no persuasive evidence otherwise, requires a grant to be presumed to contribute towards the expenditure that forms the basis of the grant payment.

Grants in respect of fixed assets

29.21 Grants in respect of fixed assets are relatively straightforward to account for, in that it will be clear that the grant relates to a specific item or items. The standard offers two alternative treatments for accounting for grants in respect of fixed assets:

— record the asset at cost and record the grant as deferred income – the grant is then released to the profit and loss account over the expected useful economic life of the asset (i.e. at the same rate as the cost of the asset is depreciated); or

— deduct the amount of the grant from the cost of the asset, so that only the net amount is depreciated over the expected useful economic life of the asset.

In the case of a company, the second treatment is not acceptable under CA 1985 Sch 4 paras 17–26, which require fixed assets to be recorded at purchase price or production cost, and also Sch 4 para 5, which prohibits the off-setting of assets and liabilities and income and expenditure. Companies must therefore treat a grant in respect of a fixed asset as deferred income and release it to the profit and loss account in line with the depreciation charged on the related asset. Other entities may follow the alternative treatment under SSAP 4 if they wish.

Example 29.3 – Accounting for fixed asset grants in corporate and non-corporate entities

B Ltd receives a grant of £14,000 in respect of a fixed asset costing £70,000. The expected useful economic life of the asset is seven years. Depreciation is charged on a straight-line basis.

The asset should be recorded at a cost of £70,000.

Depreciation will be charged at £10,000 each year for seven years.

The grant of £14,000 should be included in deferred income and should be released to the profit and loss account at £2,000 each year for seven years.

If B is not a company, it may be acceptable to record the asset at £56,000 (ie £70,000 – £14,000) and charge depreciation at £8,000 each year for seven years.

Grants in respect of non-depreciated assets

29.22   In exceptional circumstances, an asset may not need to be depreciated (eg because it has a finite useful economic life, or because it has a residual value close to its book value and depreciation would therefore be immaterial). These issues are considered in detail in Chapter 13. If a grant is received in respect of an asset that is not depreciated, the grant will not be recognised in the profit and loss account (unless the asset is disposed of) because there will be no expenditure in the profit and loss account with which to match the grant. If deferred income includes a material amount that is not being released to the profit and loss account for this reason, it will usually be advisable to explain this in the notes to the accounts, and possibly to show that element of deferred income separately from other grants.

Revenue-related grants

29.23   It can be more difficult to establish the appropriate accounting treatment for grants that relate to revenue costs (as opposed to fixed assets). The over-riding principle remains that the grant should be recognised in the profit and loss account at the same time as the related expenditure. Where the grant relates to a specific cost (or costs), the matching of the income with the related expenditure should be straightforward. The difficulties arise where grants are less specific in nature and relate (for instance) to the creation of jobs or to assistance with a broader scale project, or where there are both capital and revenue aspects (eg the purchase of new plant, coupled with the creation of new jobs). A suitable method of allocating the grant therefore needs to be found.

Relating the grant to expenditure

29.24   The first step will usually be to consider whether the grant can be linked to any specific items of expenditure. For instance, it may be that instalments of the grant can only be claimed when certain costs have been incurred. In this case, it will usually be appropriate to link the grant with those items of expenditure for matching purposes.

Relating the grant to an event

29.25   Alternatively, the grant may be linked to the achievement of an objective that is not wholly financial in nature (e.g. the creation of a specific number of new jobs, and the maintenance of those jobs for a specified period). In this case, it will usually be necessary to establish the costs associated with achieving the objective and match the grant with these. Where one of the conditions of the grant is that the new jobs are maintained for a period of (say) at least three years, the costs of providing the jobs over that period will need to be taken into account. However, this does not necessarily mean that the grant must be released evenly over such a period. The costs of creating the jobs may well be higher than the costs of maintaining them (e.g. as the result of initial training programmes and other start-up costs). This may justify releasing a higher proportion of the grant in the early years to match the higher costs.

Relating the grant to other expenditure

29.26   A grant should normally be presumed to relate to the expenditure that forms the basis of the grant. Where there is persuasive evidence that the grant should be related to other expenditure, SSAP 4 allows a different approach and recognises that this will usually be more appropriate in such circumstances. Evidence linking the grant with other expenditure might be included in:

—   the original application for the grant;

—   correspondence between the applicant and the grant-making body.

The notes to SSAP 4 quote an example of a grant being made to assist with a project, where instalments are paid once expenditure has been incurred on a specific item of equipment, but where it is clear from the underlying paperwork that the grant is intended to contribute to other related revenue costs, such as the costs of training staff to use the new equipment.

Grants to reimburse previous expenditure

29.27   Occasionally grants may be paid to reimburse an entity for expenditure that has already been incurred. Where the related expenditure has already been charged to the profit and loss account, the grant should be credited to the profit and loss account in full when it becomes receivable (i.e. when it is clear that the application has been accepted and that payment will be made).

Grants to finance general activities or to provide compensation

29.28   Certain grants may be very unspecific in nature (e.g. to support the general activities of an entity over a certain period) or may be paid to provide some element of compensation for losses incurred or to be incurred over a specified period (e.g. subsidy payments). These grants should be recognised in the profit and loss account over the period in respect of which they are paid. If the grants are not linked to a specific period, they should usually be accounted for in the period during which they become receivable.

Grants in forms other than cash

29.29   A grant may occasionally take the form of a transfer of non-monetary assets, although this is relatively rare in practice. Where such a transfer does arise, SSAP 4 requires the grant to be recorded as the fair value of the assets transferred. Fair value is usually taken to be the price at which the asset could be exchanged in an arm's length transaction.

Repayment of grants

29.30   Certain grants, or part of them, may become repayable if conditions laid down by the grant-making body are subsequently breached by the entity which has received the grant or on the occurrence of other events (e.g. in the case of grants in respect of fixed assets, part of the grant may become repayable if the asset is sold within (say) four years). Provision for repayment of a grant should only be made where it is probable that repayment will be necessary. In most cases, no such provision will be required. However, a review should be carried out at the end of each financial year to establish whether any repayment is likely to be required and whether provision should therefore be made for this. In some cases where provision for repayment is not required, it may nevertheless be necessary to disclose a contingent liability, unless the possibility of repayment being required is remote. The requirements of CA 1985 and of FRS 12 'Provisions, Contingent Liabilities and Contingent Assets' are considered in more detail in Chapter 33.

Tax treatment of grants

29.31   Grants received from government and other sources may be treated in different ways for tax purposes. Some may be completely free of tax whilst others may be taxed in full at the time when they are received. The tax treatment of a grant should not affect the accounting treatment under SSAP 4. In particular, a grant should not be credited to the profit and loss account in full in the year of receipt simply on the basis that it is taxable in that year. Where the tax treatment of the grant differs from the accounting treatment (eg the grant is taxable in full on receipt but it is credited to the profit and loss account over a number of years under SSAP 4), material timing differences should be accounted for in accordance with FRS 19 'Deferred Tax'. Deferred tax is considered in detail in Chapter 31.

Accounts disclosure

29.32   SSAP 4 requires the following disclosures in the accounts:

—   the accounting policy for government grants;

—   the effects of grants on the results for the period and/or the financial position of the entity (if material);

—   where the results are materially affected by the receipt of government assistance in other forms, the nature of the assistance and, where practicable, an estimate of the financial effect.

Accounting policy

29.33   The disclosure of the accounting policy should make clear the method (or methods) that have been adopted in accounting for government grants. The period or periods over which grants are being credited to the profit and loss account should be disclosed, although it is recognised that, where the grants are numerous and varied, detailed disclosure will not be practicable. In this case a broad indication of the future periods in which grants already received will be recognised will usually be sufficient. Wording along the following lines will usually be appropriate to cover a straightforward case.

Example 29.4 – Disclosure of accounting policy

Government grants in respect of fixed assets are treated as deferred income and credited to the profit and loss account over the expected useful economic life of the relevant assets. Grants received to date relate primarily to plant and machinery and are therefore being credited to the profit and loss account over periods of seven to ten years.

Grants relating to revenue costs are credited to the profit and loss account in line with the relevant costs. Grants to be matched with expected future costs are carried forward as deferred income. Grants carried forward in this way at 31 December 20X2 are expected to be credited to the profit and loss account in 20X3.

Effect of grants on the results and financial position

29.34   If the inclusion of grants has a material effect on the results and financial position of the recipient, or will have a material effect in future years, the effect must be disclosed in the accounts. Disclosure of the amount credited to the profit and loss account during the year in respect of grants will usually meet the requirement to disclose the effect on the results for the year. Where necessary, this information will usually be given in the note to the accounts setting out details of individual amounts charged or credited in arriving at the operating profit or loss for the year. The disclosure of a material effect on the financial position and on the accounts for future years can usually be met by disclosing the amount carried forward as deferred income in respect of grants. Using this in conjunction with the disclosure in the accounting policy of the future periods that are expected to benefit from the grants carried forward, a reader should be able to evaluate the effect on future years of the grants already received. Where the figures are particularly significant, it may be appropriate to analyse the balance for deferred grants into its major components (e.g. grants for buildings, grants for plant and machinery, grants in respect of revenue items). Where a capital grant is treated as a deduction from the cost of the asset rather than as deferred income (see 29.21 above) and the amount involved is significant, further details will usually need to be given in the notes to the accounts in order to meet this disclosure requirement.

Other forms of assistance

29.35 Where the results are materially affected by the receipt of government assistance in other forms, the nature of the assistance and, where practicable, an estimate of the financial effect should be disclosed in the accounts. This is intended to cover assistance such as:

—   consultancy and advisory services;

—   subsidised loans; and

—   credit guarantees.

A brief narrative explanation of the assistance received during the year will usually be sufficient.

RETENTION OF TITLE

Recommended accounts disclosures

29.36 Companies may sometimes supply goods that are subject to reservation of title (i.e. the supplier retains title to the goods until the related invoice is paid by the customer). The purpose of this is to attempt to provide the supplier with a degree of protection if the customer proves to be unable to meet the liability. An Accounting Recommendation issued by the Institute of Chartered Accountants in England and Wales in 1976 (but still in issue) recommends that the following disclosures are included in the accounts:

—   where the accounts are materially affected by the accounting treatment adopted in respect of purchases that are subject to retention of title, the treatment adopted should be disclosed in the accounting policies;

—   where material amounts outstanding at the balance sheet date (i.e. amounts included within creditors) are subject to retention of title clauses, this fact and, where practicable, the amount involved should be disclosed in the notes to the accounts.

Practical difficulties

29.37 The statement recognises that it will not always be practicable to quantify the amount of creditors which are subject to retention of title clauses. This will depend on the number of purchases entered into by the company which are usually covered by such clauses. For instance, if a company has purchased a major piece of equipment which is subject to reservation of title and the payment is outstanding at the balance sheet date, this should be relatively straightforward to identify and disclose. If, on the other hand, the company frequently trades with a variety of raw material suppliers, many of whom supply goods subject to retention of title, it may be a much more time-consuming exercise to quantify the total outstanding at the balance sheet date which is subject to retention of title. In some cases it may also be unclear whether the clause is legally enforceable. The statement therefore suggests that where quantification is not practicable, the notes to the accounts should explain the position and give an indication of the extent to which creditors are protected in this way.

Application in practice

29.38 In practice, few companies include such disclosures in their accounts. Provided that it is evident that the company is a going concern, the existence of retention of title clauses should have little impact. However, where there are doubts over the company's ability to continue trading and going concern is therefore an issue, additional attention will usually need to be paid to retention of title clauses and the disclosures should normally be included in the accounts where appropriate. The disclosure can usually be covered by a short statement beneath the analysis of creditors.

Example 29.5 – Where retention of title disclosures are appropriate

Trade creditors includes £45,690 in respect of goods which have been supplied subject to retention of title.

Chapter 30 Provisions for Liabilities

IDENTIFYING PROVISIONS

Definition of provision

30.1 CA 1985 defines provisions for liabilities as:

'any amount retained as reasonably necessary for the purpose of providing for any liability or loss which is either likely to be incurred, or certain to be incurred but uncertain as to amount or as to the date on which it will arise.'

The format heading for these items was originally 'Provisions for liabilities and charges' but all references to charges were removed by the *Companies Act 1985 (International Accounting Standards and Other Accounting Amendments) Regulations 2004* (SI 2004/2947) for accounting periods beginning on or after 1 January 2005.

FRS 12 'Provisions, Contingent Liabilities and Contingent Assets' defines a provision as a liability that is of uncertain timing or amount, and defines liabilities as the obligations of an entity to transfer economic benefits as a result of past transactions or events. The standard expands on these definitions by requiring a provision to be recognised when:

— an entity has a present obligation (legal or constructive) as a result of a past event;

— it is probable that a transfer of economic benefits will be required to settle the obligation; and

— a reliable estimate can be made of the amount of the obligation (cases where this is not possible are expected to be rare).

These requirements are considered in more detail in 30.6–30.16 below.

Distinction between creditors and provisions

30.2   A key distinction between creditors (including accruals) and provisions is that a creditor will usually represent a legal or contractual obligation to pay a known sum to another party at a given time, whilst a provision will be the best estimate of a known or expected liability that has not yet crystallised and where there is some uncertainty about either the timing or the amount of the payment that will eventually be required. FRS 12 makes the point that:

— trade creditors are liabilities to pay for goods and services that have been received or supplied, and that have been invoiced or formally agreed with the supplier; and

— accruals are liabilities to pay for goods and services that have been received or supplied (including services provided by employees), but which have not yet been paid, invoiced or formally agreed with the supplier.

The guidance emphasises that it may sometimes be necessary to estimate the amount or timing of accruals, but the degree of uncertainty in this case will usually be considerably lower than in the case of a provision.

Other types of provision

30.3   The term 'provision' is sometimes used in other contexts as well, such as provisions for depreciation and impairment in asset values, and provisions for bad and doubtful debts. Strictly, these are adjustments to the carrying value of the related assets rather than provisions as such. It is therefore more appropriate to treat them as a reduction of the asset values than to record them separately as provisions. FRS 12 notes specifically that they are not covered by its requirements.

Distinction between provisions and contingent liabilities

30.4   The guidance also considers the distinction between provisions and contingent liabilities. Provisions are recognised as liabilities because they represent a present obligation where it is probable that a transfer of economic benefits will be required to settle the obligation. Contingent liabilities are either:

— possible obligations – ie it is not yet certain that the entity has an obligation that will require a transfer of economic benefits; or

— present obligations which are not recognised as provisions because:

  — it is not probable that a transfer of economic benefits will be required; or

  — a sufficiently reliable estimate cannot be made of the amount involved (this is expected to be rare in practice).

Accounting for contingent liabilities under FRS 12 is considered in more detail in Chapter 33.

Items commonly treated as provisions for liabilities

30.5 Within the heading 'provisions for liabilities', the balance sheet formats require separate disclosure of provisions in respect of pension commitments (and similar obligations) and taxation, but group together any remaining provisions under the subheading 'other', although the Act does require individual details to be given for any material items. FRS 12 now requires separate disclosure for each class of provision. The identification of a class for this purpose is considered in more detail in 30.44. The following are examples of some of the categories that may be included within the provisions heading:

— product warranties;

— product claims (e.g. where a general fault has been identified);

— reorganisation or restructuring programmes;

— dilapidation or restoration (e.g. the costs of restoring land after mining or quarrying);

— environmental issues (e.g. provisions for clean-up costs).

Separate requirements on pensions apply under FRS 17 'Retirement Benefits' for accounting periods beginning on or after 1 January 2005 (see 30.49–30.53 below).

RECOGNISING PROVISIONS

Scope of FRS 12

30.6 FRS 12 'Provisions, Contingent Liabilities and Contingent Assets' covers the recognition and measurement of all provisions other than those:

— resulting from financial instruments carried at fair value;

— resulting from executory contracts, except where the contract is onerous;

— arising in insurance entities from contracts with policy holders;

— covered by another SSAP or FRS.

The guidance notes that any financial instruments (including guarantees) not carried at fair value and any provisions, contingent liabilities and contingent assets of insurance entities other than those relating to contracts with policy holders are included within the scope of the standard. Executory contracts are defined as those under which neither party has performed any of its obligations or both parties have partially performed their obligations to an equal extent. The issue of onerous contracts is considered in 30.12 below. Current SSAPs and FRSs that deal more specifically with certain types of provisions, contingent liabilities and contingent assets include:

— SSAP 9 'Stocks and long-term contracts';

— SSAP 21 'Accounting for leases and hire purchase contracts';

— FRS 17 'Retirement Benefits'; and

— FRS 19 'Deferred Tax'.

Recognition criteria

30.7   FRS 12 requires a provision to be recognised when:

— an entity has a present obligation (legal or constructive) as a result of a past event;

— it is probable that a transfer of economic benefits will be required to settle the obligation; and

— a reliable estimate can be made of the amount of the obligation (situations where this cannot be done are expected to be very rare in practice).

If these three conditions are not met, no provision should be recognised.

Present obligation

30.8   In most cases it will be clear whether or not a past event has given rise to a present obligation. Where the situation is not clear (the guidance in FRS 12 uses as an example a lawsuit where there is a dispute over whether certain events occurred or whether they have resulted in an obligation), the standard requires the entity to consider all the available evidence, including expert opinions where appropriate, and to recognise a provision if it is more likely than not that a present obligation exists at the balance sheet date. Conversely, if it is more likely that no present obligation exists at the balance sheet date, no provision should be recognised. In this case, it will usually be necessary to disclose a contingent liability (unless the transfer of economic benefits is remote). In its Information Sheet No 35, issued in February 2000, the UITF emphasises that no liability will generally arise at the balance sheet date where a regulated industry is required to reduce its prices in future years as a result of the profit levels achieved in the current year. The only exception to this is where the entity has a binding obligation at the balance sheet date to repay amounts to customers, rather than simply to adjust prices for future years.

Obligating events

30.9   The standard defines an obligating event as 'an event that creates a legal or constructive obligation that results in an entity having no realistic alternative to settling that obligation'. A legal obligation is one that derives from a contract (through either explicit or implicit terms), legislation or otherwise through the operation of the law. A constructive obligation arises where an entity creates a valid expectation on the part of other parties that it accepts and will discharge certain responsibilities. The obligation might arise from an established pattern of past practice, published policies or a specific statement by the entity. For instance, an entity with a widely published policy on environmental issues, and a history of honouring its commitment to clean up any contamination that it causes, will usually have a constructive obligation to clean up any future contamination.

The issue of obligating events is also raised in a draft Abstract published by the UITF in November 2004 in its Information Sheet No 69. 'Liabilities Arising from Participating in a Specific Market – Waste Electrical and Electronic Equipment' sets out proposed guidance on the recognition of liabilities arising from an EU Directive which makes the producers of waste electrical and electronic equipment responsible for financing certain waste management costs, including the costs of collection, treatment, recovery and recycling. The draft Abstract is based on a draft Interpretation issued by IFRIC, given that the relevant parts of FRS 12 are based on the equivalent international accounting standard (IAS 37). The consensus is that, if an entity has an obligation to contribute to waste management costs based on its market share in a measurement period, participation in the relevant market is an obligating event and therefore gives rise to a liability for which provision should be made.

Future operating costs

30.10   The guidance emphasises that financial statements deal with the position of the entity at the end of the reporting period and that no provision should be made for costs that need to be incurred to enable it to continue to operate in the future. Only liabilities that exist at the balance sheet date should be recognised in the accounts. For instance, a factory that is required by law to fit smoke filters by 30 June 2005 will not have a liability to do so at 31 December 2004 (unless it has arranged for the work to be completed by that date). No provision for the cost of fitting the filters should therefore be recognised in the accounts at 31 December 2004. If the filters are still not fitted by 31 December 2005, there is still no obligation to be recognised in the accounts in respect of the fitting of the filters. However, in this case it may be necessary to make provision for any fines for non-compliance payable under the legislation.

Future operating losses

30.11   The standard also specifically prohibits the recognition of a provision for future operating losses, on the basis that such losses do not meet the recognition criteria for provisions. However, where future operating losses are anticipated, any related fixed assets may need to be reviewed for impairment in accordance with the requirements of FRS 11 'Impairment of Fixed Assets and Goodwill'.

Onerous contracts

30.12   An onerous contract is defined as 'a contract in which the unavoidable costs of meeting the obligation under it exceed the economic benefits expected to be received under it'. A common example is a continuing lease on a property that the entity has vacated. The standard requires the present obligation under an onerous contract to be recognised and measured as a provision. The unavoidable costs are the lower of the cost of fulfilling the contract (i.e. in the above example, the cost of continuing to lease the property) and the cost of any penalties or compensation that would be due on a failure to fulfil it. In other words, the unavoidable costs represent the least net cost of exiting from the contract. Before setting up a separate provision for an onerous contract, the entity should carry out an impairment review of any assets dedicated to the contract and account for any impairment losses in accordance with FRS 11 'Impairment of Fixed Assets and Goodwill' (see Chapter 21).

Identity of third parties

30.13   Although a legal or constructive obligation will always involve a third party (ie the party to whom the obligation is owed), it is not necessary for the purposes of FRS 12 to know the identity of the third party. However, the guidance emphasises that a board or management decision does not give rise to an obligation at the balance sheet date unless the decision has been communicated to those affected in a way that raises a valid expectation that the entity will discharge its responsibilities. This point is considered further in 30.33 and 30.34 in the context of restructuring provisions.

Future events that create an obligation

30.14   Although an event may not immediately give rise to an obligation, future events or changes in circumstances may do so and may therefore require a provision to be recognised at a later stage. For instance, a company may have no obligation to rectify environmental damage at the time that it is caused, but this situation could be changed by:

—   the introduction of legislation that requires the entity to rectify the damage previously caused; or

—   a public statement in which the entity accepts responsibility for rectifying the damage previously caused.

Each of these would give rise to an obligation. A provision would therefore need to be recognised in the accounts in the year in which the event that creates the obligation takes place. In the case of new legislation, the guidance notes that an obligation will only arise when the legislation is virtually certain to be enacted as drafted and emphasises that, in many cases, this will not happen until the law is actually enacted.

Probable transfer of economic benefits

30.15   Under the guidance in FRS 12, a transfer of economic benefits, or any other event, is regarded as being probable if the probability that it will occur is greater than the probability that it will not. The degree of probability decides whether an obligation gives rise to a provision or to a contingent liability. Where there are a number of similar obligations (for instance, where an entity has given product warranties) the probability that a transfer of economic benefits will be required should be considered for the class of obligations as a whole.

Reliable estimate

30.16   Some degree of estimation is often required in accounting matters, and the inherent uncertainty surrounding provisions means that estimates are more likely to be needed here than in the case of certain other balance sheet items. FRS 12 requires a reliable estimate to be made of the amount of an obligation before a provision can be recognised, but the guidance notes that situations where this is not possible are expected to be extremely rare. Difficulty in calculating the amount should therefore not be used as a reason for not making provision. Even in some of the most difficult cases, it will usually be possible to determine a range of possible outcomes and assess the likelihood of each arising. The guidance notes that this will usually result in an estimate that is sufficiently reliable for the purposes of recognising a provision. If it is genuinely impossible to make a reliable estimate of the amount required, the obligation will be disclosable as a contingent liability. Calculating the best estimate is considered in more detail in 30.20–30.23 below.

Subsequent changes to provisions

30.17   The standard requires all provisions to be reviewed at each balance sheet date and adjusted to reflect the current best estimate of the liability. If it is no longer probable that a transfer of economic benefits will be required, the recognition criteria are no longer met and the provision should be reversed. Where a provision has been discounted, the amount carried in the balance sheet will change each year as the discount unwinds. This is considered in more detail in 30.24 below. The standard also only allows a provision to be used for the purpose for which it was originally established. This is consistent with the general prohibition on off-setting in accounts.

Recognition of an asset

30.18   In most cases, the setting up of a provision should be charged directly to the profit and loss account in the year in which the provision is recognised, and subsequent movements (eg adjustments to the current best estimate at each balance sheet date) will also be dealt with in the profit and loss account. The only exception is where the entity incurs the obligation in order to gain access to future economic benefits which will arise over more than one accounting period. For instance, a quarrying business will usually incur an obligation to restore the site of a quarry once activities have ceased there – it is prepared to incur this obligation in order to gain access to the materials that it wants to quarry. In these circumstances, an asset (representing the access to future economic benefits gained by incurring the obligation) should be recognised at the same time as the provision.

Further examples

30.19   Appendix III to FRS 12 sets out some useful examples in the form of case studies illustrating how the recognition rules might be applied in practice. These cover:

— warranties;

— contaminated land – legal obligation and constructive obligation;

— offshore oilfield – decommissioning costs;

— refunds policy in a retail outlet;

— closure of a division;

— legal requirement to fit smoke filters;

— staff retraining;

— an onerous contract (lease on vacant premises);

— a single guarantee;

— a court case;

— repairs and maintenance (involving major refits or refurbishment at specified intervals);

— self-insurance.

MEASURING PROVISIONS

Calculating the best estimate

30.20   FRS 12 requires the amount recognised as a provision to be the best estimate of expenditure required to settle the obligation at the balance sheet date. This is described as the amount that the entity would rationally pay to achieve settlement at the balance sheet date or to transfer the obligation to a third party at that time. The guidance notes that in many cases it would be prohibitively expensive, or indeed impossible, to actually settle or transfer the obligation at the balance sheet date, but this approach gives the best estimate of the liability at that date. Establishing the best estimate of an obligation will often involve a degree of judgement by those who are familiar with the business and the actual issues under consideration. Other sources of evidence might include past experience of similar issues and, in some cases, reports from independent experts. Post balance sheet events may also help to provide evidence of the position at the balance sheet date.

Dealing with uncertainty

30.21 FRS 12 requires uncertainty to be taken into account in establishing provisions. The approach to dealing with uncertainty will depend on the circumstances of each case. In the case of a single obligation, the most likely outcome may provide the best estimate of the liability, but it may sometimes be necessary to consider a variety of possible outcomes and to adjust the calculations to reflect this. Where the provision relates to a large population of items, the obligation will usually be estimated by identifying the various possible outcomes and their probabilities and weighting the possible outcomes accordingly. The guidance in FRS 12 gives the following example:

Example 30.1 – Dealing with uncertainty

An entity sells goods with a warranty under which defects that become apparent in the six months after purchase are repaired free of charge. The entity has projected the following total repair costs:

If minor defects are detected in all products	£1 million
If major defects are detected in all products	£4 million

Past experience and future expectations indicate the following probabilities:

75% of goods sold will have no defects

20% of goods sold will have minor defects

5% of goods sold will have major defects

The provision for expected repair costs is therefore calculated as:

	£
20% x £1 million	200,000
5% x £4 million	200,000
	£400,000

In practice, the most difficult aspect of these calculations will usually be identifying the probability of the various outcomes. This may be easier if there is a past history on which to base the assessments, but can be extremely difficult in the case of a new business or new product lines. It may also occasionally be necessary to consider the potential impact of the repair not being carried out successfully, with the result that further work is needed.

Adopting a cautious approach

30.22 FRS 12 also requires risk to be taken into account in reaching the best estimate of a liability. The guidance emphasises that caution is needed in dealing with any items involving judgement, to ensure that profits and assets are not overstated and expenses and liabilities are not understated. However, it also states unequivocally that uncertainty should not be used to justify excessive provisions or a deliberate overstatement of liabilities. Care should be taken not to double count risk and uncertainty. Where the provision is discounted, risk may also be taken into account in the discount rate, and care is also needed here to ensure that the risk adjustment is not in effect duplicated (i.e. by being taken into account in both the estimate of the liability and in the discounting process).

Impact of taxation

30.23   Provisions should always be measured before tax and any tax effects should be accounted for in accordance with FRS 19 'Deferred Tax' (see Chapter 31).

Discounting provisions

30.24   Where the effect is material, FRS 12 requires the amount of a provision to be discounted to arrive at the present value of the obligation at the balance sheet date. This reflects the fact that cash outflows that arise soon after the balance sheet date are more onerous than those that arise at a later date. A pre-tax discount rate should normally be used, reflecting the current market assessment of the time value of money and the risks specific to the liability. It may also be acceptable to use a risk-free discount rate, provided that the cash flows have been appropriately adjusted for risk. As noted above, the guidance emphasises that the same risk should not be duplicated by being taken into account in both the cash flow estimates and the discount rate. It is also important to consider the basis of the cash flows used to estimate the liability. If these are expressed in current prices, a real discount rate will need to be used, but if the cash flows already reflect expected changes in prices, a nominal discount rate should be used to avoid duplicating the effects of inflation.

Unwinding the discount

30.25   Where a provision is discounted, some of the discount will unwind each year, reflecting the fact that the obligation is closer than at the end of the previous reporting period. FRS 12 requires the effect of this unwinding to be shown as other finance costs adjacent to interest in the profit and loss account.

Taking account of future events

30.26   In some cases, the best estimate of the liability may be affected by anticipated future changes, such as:

—   advances in technology;

—   reduced costs as a result of the increased experience in applying existing technology; or

— reduced costs as a result of applying existing technology to larger operations than previously.

For instance, one or more of these changes might enable the cost of carrying out clean-up or restoration work to be reduced. The standard allows such changes to be taken into account in the calculations if there is sufficient objective evidence that they will happen, but emphasises that the development of completely new technology should not be anticipated without appropriate evidence.

Expected disposal of assets

30.27 When measuring provisions under FRS 12, no account should be taken of gains that the entity expects to realise on the disposal of assets, even if the disposal is closely linked to the event that triggers recognition of the provision. This changes the requirements previously set out in FRS 3 'Reporting Financial Performance' in relation to provisions on the sale or termination of an operation (see 30.36–30.42 below).

Expected reimbursement of costs

30.28 In some cases, the entity may expect to receive reimbursement for some or all of the costs that give rise to a provision. For instance, some or all of the liability may be covered by insurance arrangements or indemnity clauses in a contract. Under FRS 12, the reimbursement should only be recognised when it is virtually certain that it will be received if the entity settles the obligation that gives rise to the provision. Where it is appropriate to recognise the reimbursement, it should be treated as a separate asset and not as a reduction of the provision. In no circumstances should the reimbursement that is recognised exceed the provision. In this context, reimbursement includes a situation where the third party meets some of the entity's liability directly. Although the provision and the reimbursement must be treated separately on the balance sheet, the standard permits a net disclosure in the profit and loss account.

Reimbursement that reduces liability

30.29 In most cases where reimbursement applies, the entity will remain liable for the settlement of the full amount of the liability. In exceptional cases, where the entity is not liable for the full amount (i.e. if the third party fails to pay, the entity has no liability to meet that element of the costs), the provision should reflect only the entity's actual liability. Contingent liability disclosures may be needed if the entity has joint and several liability with other parties.

PROVISIONS FOR RESTRUCTURING

Definition of restructuring

30.30   As provisions for costs of restructuring have been a particular problem area in the past, FRS 12 includes a separate section on how the recognition and measurement rules apply in this case. Restructuring is defined as 'a programme that is planned and controlled by management, and materially changes either the scope of a business undertaken by the entity, or the manner in which that business is conducted'. The guidance notes that the following events may fall within the definition of restructuring:

—   the sale or termination of a line of business;

—   the closure of business locations in a country or region;

—   the relocation of business activities from one country or region to another;

—   changes in the management structure, for instance by eliminating a layer of management; and

—   fundamental reorganisations that have a material effect on the nature and focus of the entity's operations.

Where a restructuring meets the definition of a discontinued operation, the disclosure requirements of FRS 3 'Reporting Financial Performance' will also apply (see Chapter 9).

When a constructive obligation arises

30.31   A constructive obligation to restructure only arises when the entity:

—   has a detailed formal plan for the restructuring, identifying as a minimum:

—   the business or part of the business concerned;

—   the principal locations affected;

—   the location, function and approximate number of employees who will be compensated for terminating their services;

—   the expenditures that will be undertaken; and

—   when the plan will be implemented;

AND

—   has raised a valid expectation in those affected that it will carry out the restructuring, either by starting to implement that plan, or by announcing its main features to those affected by it.

The guidance in FRS 12 notes that evidence of implementation of the plan might include dismantling plant, selling assets or making a public announcement of the main features of the plan.

Public announcement of the plan

30.32   Public announcement of the plan will only create a constructive obligation to proceed with the restructuring if:

—   the announcement is sufficiently detailed to raise a valid expectation amongst suppliers, customers and employees (or their representatives) that the restructuring will be carried out as stated;

—   implementation is planned to begin as soon as possible; and

—   the restructuring is planned to be completed in a timescale that makes significant changes to the plan unlikely.

The guidance notes that a significant delay in implementation, or an abnormally long timescale for the restructuring, will indicate that the entity is not committed to the plan because it will have adequate opportunity to make changes should it so wish.

Management decisions

30.33   The guidance makes it clear that a management or board decision before the balance sheet date will not give rise to an obligation at that date unless the entity has already:

(i)   started to implement the plan; or

(ii)   announced the main features of the plan as explained in 30.31 and 30.32 above.

These actions must have been taken before the balance sheet date in order to create a constructive obligation at that date. If the management or board decision was taken before the balance sheet date but implementation begins or an announcement is made after that date, disclosure may be needed under the requirements of SSAP 17 'Accounting for Post Balance Sheet Events' (or, for accounting periods beginning on or after 1 January 2005, FRS 21 'Events After the Balance Sheet Date')(see Chapter 34) but no provision will be recognised in the accounts under FRS 12. However, the guidance notes that, in some cases, board membership may include representatives of interests other than management (e.g. employees) and in these circumstances a board decision might give rise to a constructive obligation, because the decision will have been communicated to these representatives.

For accounting periods beginning on or after 1 January 2005, the guidance in FRS 12 is amended to require specific disclosure under FRS 21 'Events After the Balance Sheet Date' when:

(i)   implementation or announcement of a restructuring plan takes place after the balance sheet date but before the date on which the financial statements are authorised for issue; and

(ii)   the restructuring is material and non-disclosure could influence the economic decisions of users taken on the basis of the financial statements.

Management decision confirming earlier events

30.34   In some cases, a management decision before the balance sheet date may provide formal confirmation of events that took place before that date. For instance, termination payments for employees may have been the subject of negotiations with their representative bodies for some time previously. In this case formal approval of the arrangements by management, and communication of this decision to the other parties, will give rise to a constructive obligation, provided that the other conditions set out in FRS 12 are met.

Costs to be included

30.35   Where a provision needs to be recognised for restructuring, only direct expenditures arising from the restructuring should be included – these are defined as costs that are both necessarily entailed by the restructuring and not associated with the ongoing activities of the entity. In particular, the provision should not include the costs of retraining or relocating staff, marketing activities, investment in new systems and distribution networks, future operating losses or expected gains on the disposal of assets.

PROVISIONS ON THE SALE OR TERMINATION OF AN OPERATION

Consequences of a decision to sell or terminate

30.36   Requirements on the recognition and measurement of provisions arising on the sale or termination of an operation are set out in FRS 3 'Reporting Financial Performance' rather than FRS 12. However, some small amendments to FRS 3 have been made to achieve consistency with the more extensive requirements now set out in FRS 12 'Provisions, Contingent Liabilities and Contingent Assets'. Where the decision has been taken to sell or terminate an operation, FRS 3 requires any provisions made as a result of this decision to reflect the obligations that have actually been incurred and that are not expected to be covered by the future profits of the operation (ie up to the time of sale or termination). The requirements apply regardless of whether the sale or termination is classed as a discontinued operation under FRS 3.

Entity to be demonstrably committed to the sale or termination

30.37   For an obligation to have been incurred, the standard requires the entity to be demonstrably committed to the sale or termination. If this degree of commitment does not exist, provision cannot be justified as there is no obligation to incur the related costs, even though there may be an intention to do so. The introduction of this requirement represented a significant change to general accounting practice. Prior to this, provisions were usually made on the basis of when the decision to pursue a particular course of action was taken by the board. This was justified on the basis that provision for the related costs was in accordance with the need for accounts to be prepared on a prudent basis. However, concern developed over the extensive use of provisioning and the fact that this could both distort profit trends and also result in certain costs being 'lost' within substantial provisions. The ASB has therefore moved clearly towards accounting on the basis of commitments rather than decisions, as is further evidenced by the detailed requirements now set out in FRS 12.

Evidence of demonstrable commitment

30.38   In order for an entity to be demonstrably committed to a sale or termination, FRS 3 requires:

— in the case of a sale, a binding sale agreement; and

— in the case of a termination, a detailed formal plan from which the entity cannot realistically withdraw.

The only additional guidance on these points given in FRS 3 is that the evidence might include:

— the public announcement of specific plans;

— the commencement of implementation; or

— other circumstances effectively obliging the entity to complete the sale or termination.

FRS 12 now reinforces the point that, in the case of the sale of an operation, no obligation arises until a binding sale agreement is in place and also provides further guidance on evidence of implementation and when public announcements will create a constructive obligation to proceed. These are considered above in the context of provisions for restructuring costs. Where the sale is part of a restructuring programme, a constructive obligation for the other parts may arise before a binding sale agreement is in place for the part of the business to be sold.

Commitment at the balance sheet date or subsequently?

30.39   FRS 3 does not make clear whether the demonstrable commitment to the sale or termination must exist at the balance sheet date. For instance, it does not consider the position where a management decision is taken before the balance sheet date, and implementation or announcement takes place after the balance sheet date but before the date of approval of the accounts. FRS 12 has now clarified that the obligation to proceed must exist at the balance sheet date for a provision to be recognised. Implementation or announcement after the balance sheet date but before the date of approval of the accounts may require disclosure as a post balance sheet event but will not justify provision in the accounts.

Costs included in the provision

30.40   Where a provision can justifiably be made, it should only include:

—   the direct costs of the sale or termination; and

—   any operating losses of the operation up to the date of sale or termination.

In each case, FRS 3 also requires any aggregate future profit from the activities of the operation (ie the profit that will be recognised in the profit and loss account up to the date of sale or termination) to be taken into account in calculating the provision. FRS 3 originally required profits on the disposal of assets to be taken into account as well, but this requirement has now been withdrawn to achieve consistency with FRS 12. The requirement in FRS 3 for operating losses to be taken into account appears to conflict with the prohibition in FRS 12 on making provision for future operating losses. However, this aspect of FRS 3 was not amended by FRS 12 and the requirement to adopt this approach in the case of a provision for the sale or termination of an operation still stands. It could be argued that FRS 3 is the more specific standard in these circumstances and that its requirements therefore override those in FRS 12.

Impairment of assets

30.41   Where an entity takes the decision to sell or terminate an operation, this may reflect the fact that the assets relating to that operation have become impaired. In this case, the carrying value of the assets in the entity's balances should be written down. The fact that the entity is not demonstrably committed to the sale or termination of the operation at the balance sheet date (and that provision for any direct costs or operating losses is therefore not permitted under FRS 3) does not remove the need for the carrying value of the operation's assets to be reviewed and written down where necessary.

Disclosure in the accounts

30.42   FRS 3 also requires specific disclosures to be given in the accounts when provision is made for the sale or termination of an operation. These affect both the current and subsequent years and are considered in detail in 30.47–30.48 below.

ACCOUNTS DISCLOSURE

Principal disclosure requirements

30.43   Within the heading 'provisions for liabilities', the CA 1985 balance sheet formats require separate disclosure of provisions in respect of pension commitments (and similar obligations) and taxation, but group together any remaining provisions under the sub-heading 'other', although the Act does require individual details to be given for any material items. For accounting periods beginning on or after 1 January 2005, these requirements are only relevant where the company prepares Companies Act accounts. However, FRS 12 requires separate disclosure of the following for each class of provision (see 30.44 below):

— opening and closing balances, additional provisions made in the period, amounts used and amounts reversed;

— where relevant, the increase in the discounted amount arising from the passage of time, and the effect of any change in the discount rate;

— a brief description of the nature of the obligation and the expected timing of any resulting transfers of economic benefits;

— an indication of the uncertainties over the amount or timing of those transfers, including where necessary disclosure of the main assumptions made concerning future events; and

— the amount of any expected reimbursement and the amount of any asset that has been recognised for that reimbursement.

Comparative information is not required for the first two items. The principal disclosure requirements are usually dealt with in a summary movements table in the notes to the accounts. The number of columns required will depend on how many separate items need to be disclosed. The following layout will usually be suitable:

Example 30.2 – Summary of movements

	Warranties	*Pensions*	*Deferred taxation*	*Other*	*Total*
	£000	£000	£000	£000	£000
Balance at 1 January 20X2	56	34	66	9	165
Utilised during the year	(7)	—	(14)	—	(21)
Reversed during the year	(3)	(3)			
Charge for the year in the profit and loss account	15	4	—	—	19
Balance at 31 December 20X2	61	38	52	9	160

Appendix IV to FRS 12 gives illustrative examples of suitable narrative disclosures in the case of warranties and decommissioning costs.

What constitutes a class of provision

30.44   The guidance notes that in identifying a class of provision, it will be necessary to consider whether the nature of individual items is sufficiently similar for a single statement to meet the narrative disclosure requirements of FRS 12 set out in 30.43 above. For instance, it suggests that it might be appropriate to treat warranty provisions for different products as a single class of provision, but to separate out amounts that arise under normal warranty arrangements and any that arise from legal proceedings.

Provisions linked with contingent liabilities

30.45   Where a provision and a contingent liability arise from the same set of circumstances, the disclosures should be made in a way that clarifies and explains the link between them. For instance, an entity may have joint and several liability with other parties and this may result in a provision being recognised for its own obligation, with separate disclosure of the contingent liability representing the obligation that is expected to be met by the other parties. The disclosures for the provision and the contingent liability should make clear that these obligations arise from the same transaction or arrangement.

Restriction of the disclosures

30.46   Some of the disclosures may be restricted if full disclosure would seriously prejudice the entity's position in a dispute relating to the subject of the provision, although this situation is expected to arise only very rarely. In this case, the general nature of the dispute should be disclosed along with an explanation of why the detailed disclosures have not been given. Appendix IV to FRS 12 gives an illustrative example of how this might be dealt with. The exemption does not apply if disclosure is required by law.

Sale or termination of an operation

30.47   Any provisions for costs and operating losses, and any write-down in asset values, relating to the sale or termination of an operation should be included in the results of continuing operations, unless the sale or termination meets the definition of a discontinued operation under FRS 3 (see Chapter 9). Separate disclosure will usually be required under paragraph 20 of FRS 3.

Utilisation of provisions in subsequent year

30.48   If the sale or termination does not qualify as a discontinued operation in the current year, but does so in the following year, any provisions carried forward should be offset against the results of the discontinued operation in the accounts for that year. This should be done by including the results of the operation under the appropriate statutory heading and then showing the utilisation of the provision by disclosing the amounts relating to the operating loss and the loss on sale or termination on the face of the profit and loss account, immediately below the relevant headings:

Example 30.3 – Showing the utilisation of provisions

	Continuing operations	Acquisitions	Discontinued operations	Total 20X2	Total 20X1
	£000	£000	£000	£000	£000
Turnover	5,672	784	591	7,047	6,434
Cost of sales	(3,982)	(660)	(503)	(5,145)	(4,876)
	1,690	124	88	1,902	1,558
Distribution costs	(978)	(58)	(61)	(1,097)	(994)
Administrative expenses	(531)	(21)	(39)	(591)	(476)
	181	45	(12)	214	88
Other operating income	53	20	—	73	42
Operating profit/(loss)	234	65	(12)	287	130
Utilisation of provision made in earlier years	—	—	10	10	—
	234	65	(2)	297	130
Loss on termination of operations	—	—	(10)	(10)	—
Utilisation of provision made in earlier years	—	—	7	7	—
	234	65	(5)	294	130

If the sale or termination does not qualify as a discontinued operation in the following year, the utilisation of any material provisions made in the previous year should still be disclosed in the accounts. This is now a requirement of FRS 12 as well as FRS 3.

PENSION AND SIMILAR COMMITMENTS

Nature of pension and similar commitments

30.49   FRS 17 'Retirement Benefits' defines retirement benefits as: 'All forms of consideration given by an employer in exchange for services rendered by employees that are payable after the completion of employment.' The standard therefore covers all retirement benefits that an employer is committed to making, regardless of whether the commitment is statutory, contractual or implicit. Each of the following would therefore come within the scope of the standard:

—   a commitment to provide pension and other retirement benefits (e.g. medical care) set out in the employee's contract of employment;

—   a commitment arising from custom and practice over a period of time (i.e. where the employer has traditionally made retirement arrangements for employees, even though it has no contractual obligation to do so); or

—   a commitment arising when an employer makes *ex gratia* or discretionary payments on a case by case basis.

Commitments arising outside the UK are also covered. The requirements of FRS 17 are considered in more detail in Chapter 12.

Unfunded schemes

30.50   Where an employer operates an unfunded scheme (ie benefits are simply paid as they fall due and no payments are made to fund benefits earned during the period), FRS 17 still requires a liability to be recognised in the financial statements as the benefits are earned by the employees, rather than as the actual payments become due.

Balance sheet presentation

30.51   FRS 17 requires a defined benefit asset or liability, net of any related deferred tax balance, to be shown separately on the face of the balance sheet as follows:

—   in a balance sheet prepared under Format 1, CA 1985 Sch 4, after item J (Accruals and deferred income) but before item K (Capital and reserves);

—   in a balance sheet prepared under Format 2, CA 1985 Sch 4, an asset should be shown after item D (Prepayments and accrued income) in the 'Assets' section and a liability should be shown after item D (Accruals and deferred income) in the 'Liabilities' section.

Under this standard, therefore, pension commitments are shown as a separate item on the balance sheet rather than within provisions for liabilities and charges. An example is given in Chapter 12.

Disclosure requirements

30.52   FRS 17 sets out detailed disclosure requirements in respect of both defined contribution and defined benefit retirement schemes. These are explained in Chapter 11. CA 1985 requires separate disclosure of any provisions included in the balance sheet in respect of pension commitments – this will be more than covered by the requirements of FRS 17. The Act also requires separate disclosure of any provisions in respect of pensions payable to past directors. This can usually be dealt with in a narrative footnote to the main pension disclosures:

Example 30.4 – Pensions payable to former directors

Included in the above provision for pensions is £........ (20X1 £....) in respect of pensions payable to former directors.

However, in the case of a defined benefit asset or liability recognised as a separate item in the balance sheet in accordance with FRS 17, it may not be possible to identify the amounts relating to former directors – in these circumstances, it would be advisable to explain this fact in a brief note.

Pension commitments not provided for

30.53   The disclosure requirements in respect of any pensions commitments that have not been provided for are covered in Chapter 33.

Chapter 31   Deferred Taxation

THE NATURE OF DEFERRED TAX

Differences between taxable profit and accounting profit

31.1   The profit or loss for the year shown in a company's accounts can often be very different to the taxable profit or loss that forms the basis of the tax charge for the year. As a result, the tax payable in respect of a particular accounting period may have little relationship with the accounting profit or loss shown for that period. Differences arise mainly for the following reasons:

—   certain categories of income recognised in the accounts may be tax-free;

—   certain categories of expenditure shown in the accounts may be disallowable for tax purposes;

—   occasionally, tax allowances or charges may arise with no corresponding income or expenditure in the profit and loss account; and

—   certain items of income or expenditure may be recognised in the accounts in one period, but be chargeable to, or allowable for, tax in a different period.

Some of these are classified as permanent differences because they will never become taxable or allowable for tax (or, in the case of the third category above, there will never be corresponding income or expenditure for accounting purposes). Others are classified as timing differences because the tax effect will arise in an earlier or later accounting period than the accounting effect.

Permanent difference

31.2   Permanent differences are defined in FRS 19 'Deferred Tax' as:

'Differences between an entity's taxable profits and its results as stated in the financial statements that arise because certain types of income and expenditure are non-taxable or disallowable, or because certain tax charges or allowances have no corresponding amount in the financial statements.'

Permanent differences include items such as:

— most expenditure on entertaining;

— tax-free government grants;

— interest on tax repayments.

Permanent differences result in the tax charge or credit for the accounting period being more or less than tax at the standard rate on the profit or loss shown in the accounts.

Example 31.1 – Effect of permanent differences

A Ltd's profit before tax is £42,000. The profit and loss account includes the following items:

	£
Tax-free grant received	10,500
Entertaining expenses	3,200
The rate of tax is 20%	
A Ltd's taxable profits will be:	
Profit before tax per accounts	42,000
Less: Tax-free grant	(10,500)
Add back: Disallowable expenditure	3,200
	34,700

The tax charge will therefore be £34,700 x 20% = £6,940 rather than tax at the standard rate on the profit shown in the accounts (i.e. £42,000 x 20% = £8,400).

Timing differences

31.3   Timing differences are defined in FRS 19 as:

'Differences between an entity's taxable profits and its results as stated in the financial statements that arise from the inclusion of gains and losses in tax assessments in periods different from those in which they are recognised in financial statements. Timing differences originate in one period and are capable of reversal in one or more subsequent periods.

Examples of timing differences include:

— tax deductions for the cost of a fixed asset (e.g. capital allowances) which are received before or after the cost of the asset is recognised in the profit and loss account (e.g. in the form of depreciation);

— pension liabilities which are accrued in financial statements in accordance with FRS 17 'Retirement Benefits' but which are only allowable for tax purposes when paid or contributed at a later date;

— interest charges or development costs which are capitalised in the balance sheet but are treated as revenue expenditure for tax purposes and are therefore allowed at the time that they are incurred;

— the gain recognised in the financial statements when an asset is revalued for accounting purposes, but which only becomes chargeable to tax if and when the asset is sold;

— general bad debt provisions made for accounting purposes, but which do not become allowable for tax purposes until they have been identified with specific debts.

Some timing differences will be short-term and will reverse in the next accounting period, whereas others may take a substantial time to reverse (e.g. timing differences relating to pensions).

Deferred tax

31.4   Deferred tax is defined in FRS 19 as:

'Estimated future tax consequences of transactions and events recognised in the financial statements of the current and previous periods.'

The recognition of deferred tax in financial statements is therefore an attempt to eliminate the effect of timing differences between the accounting and taxable profits at each balance sheet date, by reflecting in the accounts the tax effects of those timing differences that have arisen up to that date and which will reverse at some point in the future.

METHODS OF PROVIDING FOR DEFERRED TAX

Three alternatives

31.5   There are three methods of providing for deferred tax in financial statements:

— flow-through (or 'nil provision');

— full provision; and

— partial provision

Each of these is considered briefly below.

Flow-through method

31.6   As the alternative name for this method suggests, no provision is made for deferred tax. Under this method, therefore, the accounts reflect only the tax liability arising on the taxable profit (or loss) for the period. The main advantage of the flow-through method is that it is straightforward to apply. The main disadvantages are that it can result in large fluctuations in the tax charge year by year and that it does not match tax reliefs and charges with the related costs and income in the accounts.

Full provision

31.7   Under this method, the tax effects of all gains and losses recorded in the accounts are provided for in full. As with the flow-through method, full provision is relatively straightforward to apply and can be based on reasonably precise information. The main disadvantage is that it can result in large liabilities being included in the balance sheet, some of which will only arise far into the future, and which even then may be dependent on some future event or transaction before they actually crystallise.

Partial provision

31.8   Under this method, provision is made in the accounts for those tax liabilities that are actually expected to arise as a result of the reversal of timing differences. Liabilities that are not expected to crystallise are not provided for in the accounts. In effect, this method recognises that, if the company maintains a similar level of activity and investment, it will often have a hard core of timing differences that, for all practical purposes, will not reverse. The advantage of this method is that the accounts reflect only those liabilities that are expected to arise. However, one of the main disadvantages of partial provision is that it can involve complex calculations and a high degree of subjectivity, particularly as provision is effectively made on the basis of financial projections and capital expenditure plans covering a number of years in the future.

The UK position

31.9   For many years, the UK accounting treatment for deferred tax was based on SSAP 15 'Accounting for Deferred Tax' (issued in 1978) which required the partial provision method to be used. The ASB reconsidered this accounting treatment in the light of developments in international accounting practice and concluded that:

—   SSAP 15 was developed in the context of a very generous corporation tax system operating at that time, which enabled many companies to postpone indefinitely some or all of their deferred tax;

— the recognition rules of SSAP were very subjective and the need to anticipate future events was inconsistent with the principles underlying other aspects of financial reporting;

— the partial provision method was not appropriate for dealing with long-term deferred assets, such as those associated with provisions for retirement benefits – an amendment had already been made to SSAP 15 to allow these assets to be accounted for on a full provision basis;

— there were considerable variations in the way in which SSAP 15 was applied in practice, which had a detrimental effect on the comparability of financial statements; and

— the partial provision method was increasingly being rejected by standard-setters in other countries.

FRS 19 'Deferred Tax' was therefore published in December 2000 to supersede SSAP 15 for accounting periods ending on or after 23 January 2002. FRS 19 requires deferred tax to be accounted for on a full provision basis, subject to some specific exceptions set out in the standard.

Methods of computing deferred tax

31.10 There are two methods of computing deferred tax:

(i) the deferral method; and

(ii) the liability method.

Under the deferral method, the provision for deferred tax is calculated at the rates of taxation in force when the differences arise and no adjustments are made if rates subsequently change. When the timing differences reverse, the tax effect is again calculated at the rate in force when the differences originally arose. Under this method, therefore, the provision for deferred tax does not necessarily reflect the amount that is expected to be paid. Under the liability method, deferred tax is provided for at the rate that is expected to apply when the timing differences reverse. Therefore, the provision reflects the amount of tax that is expected to be paid. FRS 19 requires the use of the liability method, as did its predecessor standard SSAP 15. Changes in tax rates are not often known in advance and therefore, in practice, the current rate of tax will normally be used to calculate deferred tax. If a change of rate is announced in advance, the new rate should be used to calculate the provision. In addition, under the liability method it will usually be appropriate to provide for deferred tax at the small company rate if this is expected to apply at the time that the timing differences reverse. If tax rates subsequently change, the deferred tax provided in previous years will need to be revised to reflect the fact that timing differences reversing in subsequent years will do so at the new rate. The effect of a change in tax rates should be included as part of the tax charge for the period in which the change is reflected in the accounts, and should be separately disclosed.

RECOGNITION OF DEFERRED TAX UNDER FRS 19

General requirement

31.11   Under FRS 19, deferred tax should be recognised in respect of all timing differences that have originated but have not reversed at the balance sheet date, except in the situations described below. Deferred tax should not be recognised on permanent differences.

Capital allowances

31.12   Deferred tax should be recognised when allowances for the cost of a fixed asset are received before or after the cost of the asset is recognised in the profit and loss account. If capital allowances are received on an asset that is not depreciated and has not otherwise been written down to a carrying value less than cost (for instance, to reflect an impairment), the timing difference will be equivalent to the amount of capital allowances received. Most capital allowances are repayable in the form of a balancing charge if the related asset is sold for more than its tax written-down value, but in some cases (e.g. industrial buildings) the allowances are only repayable if the asset is sold within a specified period. If that period has elapsed and the asset has not been sold, any deferred tax that has been recognised on the excess of the allowances over the related depreciation should be reversed as there is no longer a timing difference to be accounted for (in other words, the difference between the allowances and the related depreciation has become a permanent difference).

Non-monetary assets

31.13   Deferred tax should be recognised on timing differences that arise when a non-monetary asset is continuously revalued to fair value, and changes in fair value are recognised in the profit and loss account – for instance, where investments are 'marked to market'. Most gains and losses on these assets will be subject to current tax when they arise and will therefore not give rise to any deferred tax. Deferred tax will only be an issue if the gains and losses are taxed when they are actually realised rather than when they are recognised for accounts purposes. Deferred tax should not be recognised on timing differences arising when other non-monetary assets are revalued unless the entity has, by the balance sheet date:

—   entered into a binding agreement to sell the revalued asset; and

—   recognised the gain or loss that is expected to arise on the sale.

Even where these conditions are met, deferred tax may not need to be recognised if it is likely that a resulting gain will be rolled over. The guidance in the standard emphasises that the fact that assets such as stocks have been purchased with a view to resale does not mean that the entity has entered into a binding agreement to sell those assets.

Roll-over of taxable gain

31.14   Deferred tax should not be recognised on timing differences arising when non-monetary assets are revalued or sold if, on the basis of all available evidence, it is more likely than not that the taxable gain will be rolled over and will only be charged to tax if and when the asset(s) into which the gain has been rolled over are sold, or are deemed to have been sold for tax purposes. Where holdover relief applies, the taxation of the gain is only postponed for a finite period, and the conclusion on whether the gain is more likely than not to be rolled over will need to take into account all the evidence available at the time (including any provided by events since the balance sheet date) and to be continually reassessed. Any adjustment to recognise or release a deferred tax provision is a change in estimate – it should therefore be charged or credited as part of the tax charge for the period (in the profit and loss account or statement of total recognised gains and losses, as appropriate) and not accounted as a prior period adjustment.

Unremitted earnings

31.15   Tax that could be payable (after allowing for any double taxation relief) on the future remittance of past earnings of a subsidiary, associate or joint venture should be provided for only to the extent that, at the balance sheet date:

—   dividends have been accrued as receivable; or

—   the subsidiary, associate or joint venture has entered into a binding agreement to distribute the past earnings in the future – this situation is expected to be rare in practice.

Deferred tax assets

31.16   Deferred tax assets should be recognised to the extent that they are regarded as recoverable – that is, to the extent that, on the basis of all available evidence, it is more likely than not that there will be suitable taxable profits from which the future reversal of the underlying timing differences can be deducted. Where the entity also has deferred tax liabilities, it can be assumed that these will give rise to future taxable profits and, if these constitute suitable profits, the deferred tax asset can be regarded as recoverable. Where there are no deferred tax liabilities, or the liabilities are insufficient to cover the deferred tax assets or unsuitable for this purpose, the likelihood of other suitable taxable profits being available will need to be assessed. Under FRS 19, suitable taxable profits are those:

— generated in the same taxable entity (or in another entity whose profits are available through group relief) and assessed by the same tax authority;

— generated in the period in which the deferred tax is expected to reverse, or in a period to which a tax loss arising from the reversal of a deferred tax asset may be carried back or forward; and

— of a type from which the reversal of the timing difference may be deducted under normal tax rules.

Factors to be taken into account

31.17 The assessment of whether a deferred tax asset is recoverable can take account of actions that the entity might take to generate suitable taxable profits (e.g. by deferring claims for capital allowances or changing from tax-free to taxable investments). The guidance in FRS 19 also notes that:

— historical information about the entity's financial performance and position may provide the most objective evidence;

— the existence of unrelieved tax losses at the balance sheet date provides strong evidence that there may not be suitable taxable profits in future against which the losses and other deferred tax assets can be recovered, unless there is other persuasive and reliable evidence to the contrary (for instance, where the losses result from an identifiable and non-recurring cause and the entity has otherwise been consistently profitable over a long period); and

— in the case of an unrelieved capital loss, there is only likely to be persuasive and reliable evidence of suitable taxable gains against which the loss can be relieved if plans are in place to sell assets which will generate a chargeable gain that has not already been recognised as a deferred tax liability, and the unrelieved loss will be offset against this gain.

If existing tax losses are likely to take some time to be relieved, the recoverability of the deferred tax asset is likely to be relatively uncertain and recognition may therefore not be appropriate.

Subsequent adjustments to a deferred tax asset

31.18 The amount recognised as a deferred tax asset may need to be adjusted in subsequent years as a result of changes in circumstances which affect the extent to which the asset is regarded as recoverable — for instance, an improved trading position or the acquisition of a new subsidiary. These adjustments are changes in estimates and should therefore be reflected in the results for the period in which the changes take place — they should not be accounted for as prior period adjustments.

MEASUREMENT OF DEFERRED TAX UNDER FRS 19

General requirement

31.19   Deferred tax should be measured at the average tax rates that are expected to apply in the periods in which the timing differences are expected to reverse, based on tax rates and laws that have been enacted, or substantively enacted, by the balance sheet date. A tax rate is regarded as substantively enacted if it is included in a Bill that has been passed by the House of Commons and is awaiting only passage through the House of Lords and Royal Assent, or in a resolution having statutory effect that has been passed under the Provisional Collection of Taxes Act 1968 (this is rarely used in practice).

Average tax rates

31.20   The guidance in the standard emphasises that the requirement to measure deferred tax at the average rates expected to apply should not be read as a requirement to average the rates applying to individual types of taxable profits, or to taxable profits arising in different jurisdictions. The rate used should reflect the nature of the individual timing differences and the tax jurisdiction in which they are expected to arise. Average rates will usually only need to be calculated if the enacted tax rates are graduated (i.e. different rates apply to different levels of taxable income).

Discounting

31.21   Deferred tax assets and liabilities may be discounted to reflect the time value of money, but there is no requirement to do so. The decision on whether to discount or not is a matter of accounting policy. Where an entity considers it appropriate to adopt a policy of discounting, all deferred tax balances measured by reference to undiscounted cash flows, and for which the impact of discounting is material, should be discounted. The standard includes guidance on factors that are likely to be relevant to the consideration of whether a policy of discounting is appropriate – these include:

— how material the impact of discounting would be to the overall results and financial position of the entity;

— whether the benefits outweigh the cost of collating the information and carrying out the calculations; and

— whether discounting is an established industry practice, and comparability would therefore be enhanced by the entity also adopting this policy.

Certain timing differences, in particular those arising in respect of provisions for pension liabilities and investments in finance leases in the accounts of a lessor, will have already been measured by reference to discounted cash flows. Related deferred tax provisions should therefore not be discounted further, and they should be disclosed in the accounts as undiscounted deferred tax balances. Discounting may be appropriate in the case of deferred tax balances arising from accelerated capital allowances, revaluation gains and losses and unrelieved tax losses carried forward.

Discounting method

31.22   Where deferred tax balances are discounted, the discount period(s) should be the number of years between the balance sheet date and the date(s) on which it is estimated that the underlying timing differences will reverse. Assumptions made when estimating reversal dates should be consistent with those made elsewhere in the financial statements – for instance, assumptions on depreciation charges and residual values should be consistent with those adopted in accounting for tangible fixed assets in the financial statements. The remaining tax effects of transactions already reflected in the financial statements should be taken into account, but no account should be taken of

— other timing differences expected to arise on future transactions; or

— the potential impact of expected future tax losses.

In the case of fixed assets, therefore, the calculations should take account of future capital allowances and depreciation on assets already held at the balance sheet date, but should ignore any capital allowances and depreciation on assets that the entity expects to purchase in future years. The guidance in FRS 19 notes that it may be possible to use approximations or averages to simplify the calculations without introducing material errors. There may be uncertainty over both the amount of tax payable and the timing of the payment, and estimates and judgements may therefore need to be made. Illustrative examples of the discounting calculations are given in paragraph 49 of, and Appendix I to, the standard.

Discount rates

31.23   The discount rates used should be the post-tax yields to maturity that could be obtained at the balance sheet date on government bonds with similar maturity dates and in similar currencies to those of the deferred tax assets or liabilities. Details of yields to maturity can be obtained from published sources, and the post-tax figure is calculated by deducting tax at the rate at which it would be paid by an entity holding the bond, once again based on enacted or substantively enacted tax rates and legislation (see 31.19 above). In theory a different discount rate should be established for each year in which a timing difference is expected to reverse and, where different tax jurisdictions are involved, for each tax jurisdiction. However, the guidance in FRS 19 notes that it may be possible to use approximations or averages to simplify the calculations without introducing material errors. An illustrative example of the calculations is given in Appendix I to the standard.

PRESENTATION OF DEFERRED TAX IN FINANCIAL STATEMENTS

Performance statements

31.24   Deferred tax should be recognised in the profit and loss account for the period, except to the extent that it is attributable to a gain or loss that is or has been recognised directly in the statement of total recognised gains and losses. In this case, the attributable deferred tax should also be recognised directly in the statement of total recognised gains and losses. The guidance in FRS 19 notes that, in exceptional circumstances, it may be difficult to determine the amount of deferred tax relating to gains and losses recognised in the statement of total gains and losses, in which case a reasonable pro-rata or other more appropriate allocation of the deferred tax charge or credit may be used. All deferred tax recognised in the profit and loss account should be included in tax on profit or loss on ordinary activities. The presentation of both current and deferred tax in performance statements is considered in more detail in Chapter 15.

Balance sheet

31.25   With the exception of deferred tax relating to a defined benefit asset or liability recognised under FRS 17 'Retirement Benefits' (see Chapter 12):

— net deferred tax liabilities should be classified as provisions for liabilities and charges; and

— net deferred tax assets should be classified as debtors (using a separate sub-heading where material).

Deferred tax assets and liabilities should be shown separately on the face of the balance sheet where the amounts are so material in the context of total net current assets or net assets that readers may misinterpret the financial statements if separate disclosure is not given.

Offset of debit and credit balances

31.26   Deferred tax debit and credit balances should be offset within these balance sheet headings only to the extent that they:

— relate to taxes levied by the same authority; and

— arise in the same taxable entity or in a group of taxable entities where the tax losses of one entity can reduce the taxable profits of another.

A company will therefore usually be able to offset deferred tax balances and this may also be possible where the companies in a group come within the same tax jurisdiction.

DISCLOSURE OF DEFERRED TAX

Performance statements

31.27   The following disclosures should be given in the notes to the financial statements:

— the amount of deferred tax charged or credited within tax on ordinary activities in the profit and loss account, showing separately, where material, amounts relating to:

  — the origination and reversal of timing differences;

  — changes in tax rates and laws;

  — adjustments to deferred tax assets arising in previous periods; and

  — where relevant, changes in the amount of discount deducted in arriving at the deferred tax balance;

— the amount of deferred tax charged or credited in the statement of total recognised gains and losses or the period, with a similar analysis of material components.

Disclosure of both current and deferred tax in the performance statements is considered in more detail in Chapter 15.

Balance sheet

31.28   CA 1985 requires the amount provided in respect of deferred tax to be shown separately from any other provisions for taxation and a detailed analysis of movements in the year, as for all provisions. Under FRS 19, the notes to the balance sheet must disclose:

— the total deferred tax balance (before discounting, where relevant) showing separately the amount recognised for each significant type of timing difference;

— where relevant, the impact of discounting on, and the discounted amount of, the deferred tax balance;

— the movements between opening and closing deferred tax balances, showing separately:

  — the amount charged or credited in the profit and loss account;

  — the amount charged or credited directly in the statement of total recognised gains and losses; and

  — movements arising from the acquisition or disposal of businesses.

Deferred tax assets

31.29   Where an entity has recognised deferred tax assets, the notes to the accounts should explain the amount and the nature of the evidence supporting this treatment if:

— recoverability is dependent on future taxable profits in excess of those arising from the reversal of deferred tax liabilities; and

— the reporting entity has suffered a loss in either the current or the previous period in the tax jurisdiction to which the deferred tax asset relates.

The guidance in the standard notes that the disclosure should set out the specific circumstances that make it reasonable to forecast the existence of suitable taxable profits against which the deferred tax assets can be recovered.

Other circumstances

31.30   The notes to the accounts should also disclose the circumstances that affect the current and total tax charges and credits for the current period or may affect the current and total tax charges or credits in future periods. This disclosure should include the following:

— a reconciliation of the current tax charge or credit on ordinary activities for the period to the current tax charge that would result from applying a relevant standard rate of tax to the profit on ordinary activities before tax – either the monetary amounts or the rates may be reconciled and the basis on which the standard rate has been determined should be disclosed (an example of this disclosure is given in Chapter 15);

— if assets have been revalued without deferred tax being recognised, or if their market value is disclosed in a note, an estimate of the amount of deferred tax that would become payable (or recoverable) if the assets were sold at those values, the circumstances in which tax would be payable (or recoverable) and an indication of the amount that may become payable (or recoverable) in the foreseeable future;

— if the entity has sold (or entered into a binding agreement to sell) an asset but has not recognised deferred tax on a taxable gain because it expects this to be rolled over, the conditions that will have to be met to obtain the rollover relief and an estimate of the tax that would become payable if those conditions were not met;

— if a deferred tax asset has not been recognised on the grounds that there is insufficient evidence of recoverability, the amount that has not been recognised and the circumstances in which the asset would be recovered;

— the nature of any other deferred tax not recognised, the circumstances in which the tax would become payable or recoverable and an indication of the amount that may become payable or recoverable in the foreseeable future.

Accounting policy

31.31   It will also usually be appropriate to disclose the accounting policy adopted for deferred tax. In line with the guidance in FRS 18 'Accounting Policies' this disclosure may be relatively brief if the policy adopted is in line with the detailed requirements set out in FRS 19.

Chapter 32

Share Capital and Reserves

AUTHORISED, ALLOTTED AND CALLED UP SHARE CAPITAL

CA 1985 disclosure requirements

32.1   The company's authorised share capital must be stated in the accounts and the standard balance sheet formats set out in CA 1985 require separate disclosure of the company's called up share capital and share premium account. Both headings are given Roman numerals and must therefore be shown on the face of the balance sheet. The notes to the balance sheet formats requires separate disclosure of:

(i)   the company's allotted share capital; and

(ii)   the amount of called up share capital that has been paid.

This information is usually given in the notes to the accounts, but may be given on the face of the balance sheet. The amount of called up share capital not paid also requires disclosure under the formats, either as a separate balance sheet heading or as a sub-heading within debtors. In many cases, all the capital that has been allotted will also have been called up and will be fully paid, in which case the required disclosures can be given as follows:

Example 32.1 – Where capital has been allotted, called up and fully paid

	20X2	20X1
	£	£
Authorised:		
5,000 ordinary shares of £1 each	5,000	5,000
Allotted, called up and fully paid:		
3,200 ordinary shares of £1 each	3,200	3,200

The disclosure is usually given in the notes to the accounts. The authorised share capital can be disclosed on the face of the balance sheet instead, but care is needed in the presentation to make it clear that the figure for authorised share capital is not included in the balance sheet totals.

Disclosure where shares are not fully paid

32.2   If the allotted shares have not been fully paid, separate disclosure is required of the amount paid.

Example 32.2 – Where shares have not been fully paid

A Ltd has an authorised share capital of 5,000 ordinary shares of £1, of which 3,200 have been allotted. The following calls have been made in respect of these shares:

— 1 July 20X2 – 50p per share

— 1 December 20X2 – 30p per share

At 31 December 20X2, A Ltd's accounting date, holders of 500 shares had not yet paid the second call of 30p per share. The accounts will therefore disclose:

	£
Authorised: 5,000 ordinary shares of £1 each	5,000
Allotted and called up:	
3,200 ordinary shares of £1 each	3,200

At 31 December 20X2, £3,050 had been paid in respect of the shares allotted and called up at that date.

The balance sheet will show share capital of £3,200 and the unpaid balance of £150 (ie 500 shares at 30p per share) will be included within debtors or as a separate heading on the face of the balance sheet.

Different classes of share

32.3   Where a company has allotted shares of more than one class, both CA 1985 and FRS 4 'Capital Instruments' require details to be disclosed for every class of shares in issue. FRS 4 also requires the same details in respect of any class of shares which is not yet in issue but which may be issued as a result of the conversion of debt or warrants that are issued.

For accounting periods beginning on or after 1 January 2005, FRS 4 is superseded by FRS 25 'Financial Instruments: Disclosure and Presentation' which does not impose the same level of detailed disclosure in respect of share capital as its predecessor.

Shares can be issued in many different forms. Some of the more common types of shares are as follows.

— *Ordinary shares* – these usually give the shareholder the residual rights in the company (ie rights which have not been granted to other classes of share-holder) and often carry the main voting powers of the company.

— *Preference shares* – these give the shareholder some preferential right (eg a right to receive a fixed cumulative dividend, or a right to receive a proportion of capital in a winding up) and they often carry limited voting rights, but there is no reason why the voting rights attached to preference shares should not be as great as, or even greater than, those attached to ordinary shares. Equally, in some cases preference shares will not carry any voting rights.

— *Redeemable shares* – these are shares that may be redeemed at some point in the future, either at a specified time or at the option of the shareholder, or of the company, or of both. Both ordinary and preference shares can be redeem-able.

The features of each type of share can be combined in various ways. The type of shares that an individual company can issue will usually be governed by its articles of association.

For accounting periods beginning on or after 1 January 2005, FRS 25 requires all financial instruments (or their component parts) to be classified on initial recognition as financial assets, financial liabilities or equity, depending on the substance of the contractual arrangements and the definitions set out in the standard. This will result in certain shares being classified for accounting purposes as financial liabilities rather than as share capital, even though their designation and legal status as a share will be unchanged. For instance, a preference share with the following features will meet the definition of a financial liability rather than equity:

(i) mandatory redemption by the issuer for a fixed or determinable amount at a fixed or determinable future date; or

(ii) a right for the holder to require redemption by the issuer on or after a particular date for a fixed or determinable amount.

The specific features of each share must therefore be carefully assessed in determining the appropriate accounting treatment. The classification of financial instruments is considered in more detail in Chapter 26.

Accounts disclosure by class of share

32.4   For accounting periods beginning before 1 January 2005, and taking the requirements of the CA 1985 and of FRS 4 together, the following details must be disclosed for each class of share:

— the number of shares allotted;

— the aggregate nominal value of the shares allotted;

— rights to dividends;

— dates of redemption and amounts payable on redemption;

— priority and amounts receivable on a winding up;

— voting rights;

— any additional information necessary to clarify why the shares have been classified as equity or non-equity;

— where rights vary depending on circumstances, an explanation of both the circumstances and the variations.

The FRS 4 disclosure requirements do not apply in the case of equity shares with all of the following features:

— no rights to dividends other than those recommended by the directors;

— no redemption rights;

— an unlimited right to share in the surplus remaining on a winding up after all other liabilities and participation rights have been satisfied; and

— one vote per share.

However, the number of shares allotted and the aggregate nominal value must be given for all shares to comply with the disclosure requirements of the Act. If the brief summaries required by FRS 4, cannot provide adequate information for the commercial effect of the instrument to be understood, this fact should be stated and details should be given of where the relevant information can be obtained. The principal features of each instrument should always be disclosed.

Example disclosure

32.5   In the case of a company which only has one class of ordinary shares in issue, the disclosure in Example 32.1 would meet the requirements of CA 1985. In a more complex case, disclosure along the following lines will usually meet the requirements of both FRS 4 and the Act.

Example 32.3 – Disclosures relating to different classes of share

	20X2 £	20X1 £
Authorised:		
2,000 'A' ordinary shares of £1 each	2,000	2,000
2,000 'B' ordinary shares of 50p each	1,000	1,000
2,000 6% cumulative preference shares of £1 each	2,000	2,000
	5,000	5,000
Allotted, called up and fully paid:		
1,000 'A' ordinary shares of £1 each	1,000	1,000
1,000 6% cumulative preference shares of £1 each	1,000	1,000
	2,000	2,000

The 'A' ordinary shares are not redeemable and carry no rights to dividends other than those recommended by the directors. These shares rank last for payment in a winding up but carry an unlimited right to share in any remaining assets after all other liabilities and participation rights have been satisfied.

The preference shares are non-voting and carry the right to a 6% cumulative dividend. They are redeemable at par on or after 1 January 20X8 at the option of the company. In a winding up, the preference shares rank ahead of the ordinary shares and are repayable at par.

If the holders of the convertible debt exercise their conversion rights they will be issued with 'B' ordinary shares. These shares are non-voting and carry the right to an annual cumulative dividend of 5p per share. In a winding up, the 'B' ordinary shares rank after the preference shares but ahead of the 'A' ordinary shares and are repayable at par.

Although details of the 'A' ordinary shares are not strictly required under FRS 4, it can be helpful to give this information for completeness, especially where it helps to clarify some of the rights attaching to the other shares.

Disclosure of share issue during the year

32.6   Where shares have been allotted during the year, CA 1985 requires disclosure of the following information:

—   the class of shares allotted;

—   for each class of shares:

         —   the number allotted,

         —   the aggregate nominal value of the shares allotted,

—   the consideration received by the company.

This detail will usually be given in the notes to the accounts. In most cases a narrative footnote to the share capital note will suffice, but a table could be used if there were a number of share issues during the period.

Example 32.4 – Issue of shares

	20X2 £	20X1 £
Authorised:		
2,000 'A' ordinary shares of £1 each	2,000	2,000
2,000 'B' ordinary shares of 50p each	1,000	1,000
2,000 6% cumulative preference shares of £1 each	2,000	2,000
	5,000	5,000
Allotted, called up and fully paid:		
1,000 'A' ordinary shares of £1 each	1,000	1,000
1,000 (20X1: 500) 6% cumulative preference shares of £1 each	1,000	500
	2,000	1,500

500 6% preference shares of £1 each were issued on 31 March 20X2, at a cash price of £6.50 per share.

The share premium account would show a premium of £2,750 on shares issued during the period (ie 500 shares at a premium of £5.50 each):

	£
Balance at 1 January 20X2	1,500
Premium on shares issued during the year	2,750
Balance at 31 December 20X2	4,250

Share awards to employees

32.7   UITF Abstract 17 'Employee Share Schemes' considers the accounting treatment of shares awarded to employees through annual bonuses or long-term incentive schemes, and requires the cost of share awards to employees to be charged to the profit and loss account over the period to which the employee's performance relates. Where new shares are issued under an employee share scheme, the amount accrued should be included within shareholders' funds in the balance sheet. The credit entry for the charge to the profit and loss account each year should be reported in the reconciliation of movements in shareholders' funds, not in the statement of total recognised gains and losses. This reflects the fact that the amount recognised represents proceeds from the issue of an equity instrument. When the shares are issued, the total amount accrued should be allocated between share capital and reserves. The requirements of Abstract 17 are considered in more detail in Chapter 11, together with the requirements of UITF Abstract 30 'Date of Award to Employees of Shares and Right to Shares'.

The ASB published FRS 20 'Share-based payment' in April 2004. This is effective for accounting periods beginning on or after 1 January 2005 in the case of listed companies, and for accounting periods beginning on or after 1 January 2006 for all other entities (other than entities which adopt the FRSSE and which are therefore exempt from the new standard). The new standard supersedes UITF Abstract 17, which is withdrawn from the relevant effective date of FRS 20. The requirements of FRS 20 are also considered in Chapter 11.

SHARE PREMIUM ACCOUNT

Creation of share premium account

32.8 Where a company issues shares at a premium, for cash or otherwise, CA 1985 requires a sum equal to the aggregate amount or value of the premiums on the shares to be transferred to the share premium account. Relief from this requirement ('merger relief') is granted in limited cases, provided that specific conditions set out in ss 131–132 of the Act are met.

Use of the share premium account

32.9 The share premium account may be applied as follows:

— in paying up unissued shares to be allotted to members as fully paid bonus shares;

— in writing off the company's preliminary expenses;

— in writing off the expenses of any issue of shares or debentures;

— in writing off any commission paid, or discount allowed, on any issue of shares or debentures;

— in providing for the premium payable on redemption of debentures of the company.

Apart from this, the share premium account must be treated as if it were paid up share capital (i.e. it can only be reduced under the specific conditions laid down in the Act for a reduction of capital). Under certain circumstances, a private company may be able to use the share premium account to purchase or redeem its own shares.

Transfers to and from share premium account

32.10   The share premium account is treated as a reserve for disclosure purposes. Therefore, where any amount is transferred to or from the share premium account, CA 1985 requires disclosure of the amounts transferred, and the source or application of those amounts, together with the balance on the share premium account at the beginning and end of the year. Comparative figures are not required for these disclosures. Example 32.12 below includes disclosure of movements on the share premium account.

EQUITY AND NON-EQUITY SHARES

Definition of equity share capital under CA 1985

32.11   CA 1985 defines equity share capital as 'issued share capital, excluding any part of that capital which, neither as respects dividends nor as respects capital, carries any right to participate beyond a specified amount in a distribution'. Therefore, in order to qualify as an equity share under the Act, a share must carry the right to participate, without restriction to a set amount, in:

—   dividends; or

—   a return of capital; or

—   both dividends and a return of capital.

For instance, a preference share which carries the right to a fixed cumulative dividend and the right to a fixed proportion of capital on a winding up will not be an equity share under the Act. However, a preference share which carries the right to a fixed cumulative dividend but also carries the right to participate beyond a set amount in a winding up will usually meet the definition of an equity share set out in the Act.

Non-equity and equity shares under FRS 4

32.12   FRS 4 defines non-equity shares as shares which have any of the following characteristics:

—   any rights to receive payments, in respect of dividends, redemption or otherwise, are for a limited amount that is not calculated by reference to the company's assets, profits or the dividends on any class of equity share;

—   any rights to participate in a surplus in a winding up are limited to a specific amount that is not calculated by reference to the company's assets or profits, and this limitation had a commercial effect in practice at the time that the shares were issued or, if later, at the time that the limitation was introduced;

—   the shares are redeemable either according to their terms or because the holder, or any party other than the issuer, can require their redemption.

This definition is widely drawn and in effect ensures that any share which carries a limited right to a dividend, or a limited right to any payment on redemption, will be classed as a non-equity share. This applies irrespective of any other rights that might be attached to the shares. Any other share is an equity share. FRS 4 acknowledges that, in rare circumstances, this definition could result in a share being classified as a non-equity share for the purposes of FRS 4, whilst meeting the definition of an equity share under the Act. In this situation, the accounts would need to disclose sufficient information to explain the position.

Definition of equity under FRS 25

32.13   For accounting periods beginning on or after 1 January 2005, FRS 4 is superseded by FRS 25 'Financial Instruments: Disclosure and Presentation'. Under the new standard, the distinction becomes one between equity and financial liabilities and rather than equity and non-equity. FRS 25 defines equity as any contract that evidences a residual interest in the assets of an entity after deducting all of its liabilities, and a financial liability as any liability that is:

(i)   a contractual obligation to deliver cash or another financial asset to another entity, or to exchange financial assets or financial liabilities with another entity under conditions that are potentially unfavourable to the reporting entity; or

(ii)   a contract that will or may be settled in the entity's own equity instruments and is:

- a non-derivative for which the entity is or may be obliged to deliver a variable number of the entity's own equity instruments; or

- a derivative that will or may be settled other than by the exchange of a fixed amount of cash or another financial asset for a fixed number of the entity's own equity instruments.

The standard also specifies that, in applying the above definitions, a financial instrument is an equity instrument if, and only if:

(i)   it includes no contractual obligation to deliver cash or another financial instrument to another entity, or to exchange financial assets or financial liabilities with another entity under conditions that are potentially unfavourable to the issuer; and

(ii)   where the instrument will or may be settled in the issuer's own equity instruments, it is:

- a non-derivative that includes no contractual obligation for the issuer to deliver a variable number of its own equity instruments; or

- a derivative that will be settled only by the issuer exchanging a fixed amount of cash or another financial asset for a fixed number of its own equity instruments.

As a result of these changes, certain shares that have previously been accounted for as share capital will in future be treated as financial liabilities and any dividends payable in respect of them will be accounted for as interest payments in the profit and loss account. CA 1985 has also been amended from the same date to introduce the concept of 'substance over form' into company law and thus enable this treatment to be applied (see Chapter 5).

Disclosure of equity and non-equity shares

32.14   FRS 4 requires total shareholders' funds to be shown on the face of the balance sheet and to be analysed between equity and non-equity interests. Where the impact of this analysis is material, it should be given on the face of the balance sheet. In other cases, the details may be given in the notes to the accounts, but where this treatment is adopted, the caption on the balance sheet must state that non-equity interests are included. The individual components of shareholders' funds (e.g. share capital, revaluation reserve, profit and loss account etc.) do not have to be analysed.

Example 32.5 – Disclosure of equity and non-equity shares

Using the details from Example 32.3, the 'A' ordinary shares are equity shares, and the 'B' ordinary shares and the preference shares are non-equity shares (because their right to receive a dividend is limited and is not based on assets, profits or equity dividends). The information might therefore be presented on the balance sheet as follows.

		20X2		20X1
	£	£	£	£
Capital and reserves:				
Called up share capital		2,000		2,000
Revaluation reserve		125		140
Profit and loss account		1,860		1,443
Shareholders' funds:				
Equity	2,985		2,583	
Non-equity	1,000		1,000	
		3,985		3,583

The alternative presentation would be:

	20X2	20X1
	£	£
Capital and reserves:		
Called up share capital	2,000	2,000
Revaluation reserve	125	140
Profit and loss account	1,860	1,443
Shareholders' funds (including non-equity interests)	3,985	3,583

There would also be a cross-reference to a note to the accounts providing the required analysis of shareholders' funds between equity and non-equity interests.

Amounts attributable to non-equity interests

32.15   The amount attributable to non-equity interests will be the net proceeds of the issue(s), plus finance costs to date, less any dividends or other payments made to date. The amount attributable to equity interests is the balancing figure. Example 32.5 assumes that the finance cost of the non-equity shares is equivalent to the dividends paid, but this will not always be the case. The accounting treatment of finance costs and dividends in respect of non-equity shares under FRS 4 is covered in Chapter 16.

Analysis of non-equity shareholders' funds

32.16   FRS 4 requires non-equity shareholders' funds to be analysed further into the amount relating to each class of non-equity shares and each series of warrants for non-equity shares (see 32.21–32.26 below). This detail will usually be given in the notes to the accounts.

Debt or equity?

32.17   For accounting periods beginning before 1 January 2005, UITF Abstract 33 'Obligations in Capital Instruments' considers how the principles set out in FRS 4 and FRS 5 'Reporting the Substance of Transactions' should be applied in the context of complex capital instruments that have characteristics of both debt and equity, and how various types of capital instrument issued as a means of raising finance should be reported in the balance sheet (ie whether they should be shown as liabilities or shareholders' funds or, in the case of consolidated financial statements, as minority interests). The Abstract notes specifically that it does not deal with capital instruments issued as part of the contingent purchase consideration for a business combination. The general rule is that a capital instrument should be reported within shareholders' funds only if it is a share, or if it does not contain an obligation to transfer economic benefits. All other capital instruments should be treated as liabilities, even if the obligation to transfer economic benefits does not go beyond that normally contained in a share. The requirements of Abstract 33 are considered in more detail in Chapter 26.

UITF Abstract 33 is superseded by FRS 25 'Financial Instruments: Disclosure and Presentation for accounting periods beginning on or after 1 January 2005. The requirements of FRS 25 on the classification of financial instruments are covered in Chapter 26.

REDEEMABLE SHARES

General disclosure requirement

32.18   Where shares are redeemable, CA 1985 requires the following disclosures in the accounts:

—   the earliest date on which the company can redeem the shares;

—   the latest date on which the company can redeem the shares;

—   whether the shares must be redeemed in any event, or whether they are liable to be redeemed at the option of the company or of the shareholder;

—   whether any premium is payable on redemption and, if so, the premium that is payable.

These overlap with some of the detailed disclosures required by FRS 4. The other disclosures required by FRS 4 also continue to apply. Example 32.3 shows the required disclosures in the case of preference shares that are redeemable at par. The following wordings might be suitable for shares redeemable at a premium. The precise wording will obviously vary depending on the underlying nature of the shares.

Example 32.6 – Shares redeemable at a premium (I)

The preference shares are non-voting and carry the right to a 5% cumulative dividend. They are redeemable on 1 January 20X9 at a premium of 4%. In a winding up, the preference shares rank ahead of the ordinary shares and are repayable at par.

Example 32.7 – Shares redeemable at a premium (II)

The 'B' ordinary shares carry one vote per share. They are redeemable between 1 January 20X4 and 31 December 20X4, at the option of either the company or the shareholder, at a premium of 4%. In a winding up, the 'B' ordinary shares rank ahead of the 'A' ordinary shares and are repayable at par.

For accounting periods beginning on or after 1 January 2005, the accounting treatment of many redeemable shares will be altered by the requirements of FRS 25 'Financial Instruments: Disclosure and Presentation'. However, as the instruments will still be shares for legal purposes, the disclosure requirements of the Act will continue to apply. Companies with complex capital structures will need to give careful through to the location and layout of the required information in the notes to the accounts to minimise any confusion that may otherwise be caused for readers.

Accounting for finance costs and dividends

32.19 The accounting treatment of finance costs and dividends in respect of redeemable shares is considered in Chapter 16.

Accounting for redemption

32.20 When the shares are redeemed, shareholders' funds should be reduced by the value of the consideration given. This will usually be the amount recorded in shareholders' funds in respect of the shares. Example 16.8 in Chapter 16 illustrates how this balance is built up over the life of the shares.

For accounting periods beginning on or after 1 January 2005, most redeemable shares will be accounted for as financial liabilities rather than as share capital, in which case there will be no impact on shareholders' funds at the time of redemption.

CONVERTIBLE INSTRUMENTS, SHARE OPTIONS AND SIMILAR RIGHTS

Convertible debt

32.21 For accounting periods beginning before 1 January 2005, where a company has issued debt that is convertible into shares, FRS 4 requires it to be reported within liabilities and the finance cost to be calculated on the assumption that the debt will not be converted. The disclosure of convertible debt is considered in Chapter 26 and the accounting treatment of the finance costs is considered in Chapter 14.

For accounting periods beginning on or after 1 January 2005, FRS 25 introduces a new requirement for an entity that issues a compound financial instruments to account separately for

(i) any components that create a financial liability of the issuer; and

(ii) any components that grant an option to the holder of the instrument to convert it into an equity instruments of the issuer.

The guidance notes that the economic effect of issuing a bond or similar instrument that is convertible into a fixed number of ordinary shares is the same as issuing a debt instrument with an early settlement provision and warrants to purchase ordinary shares, and in effect requires this situation to be reflected in the balance sheet presentation. As an equity instrument represents a residual interest in the assets of an entity, after all its liabilities have been deducted, the equity element of a compound instrument should be calculated as the residual amount after determining the fair value of the liability component and deducting this from the fair value of the instrument as a whole. The fair value of the liability component should be determined by measuring the fair value of a similar liability that does not have an equity component.

Warrants

32.22   A warrant is defined in FRS 4 as 'an instrument that requires the issuer to issue shares (whether contingently or not) and contains no obligation for the issuer to transfer economic benefits'. A warrant is therefore similar to a share option, but warrants will often be transferable, whilst options will usually be specific to an individual. Warrants issued to employees under employee share schemes are not covered by FRS 4. However, the standard is superseded by FRS 25 for accounting periods beginning on or after 1 January 2005. Under FRS 4, where a company issues warrants, any proceeds relating to the warrants should be credited directly to a warrant reserves within shareholders' funds in the year of issue and should be reported in the reconciliation of movements in shareholders' funds. The amount credited to the warrant reserve should not be adjusted subsequently to reflect any changes in the value of the instruments. A similar treatment will generally be required for accounting periods beginning on or after 1 January 2005, provided that the warrant relates to the purchase of equity shares, as defined in FRS 25. The balance on the warrant reserve must be analysed into warrants relating to equity shares and warrants relating to non-equity shares, for inclusion in the disclosure of equity and non-equity shareholders' funds under FRS 4 (see 32.11–32.17 above). This disclosure requirement is not relevant for accounting periods beginning on or after 1 January 2005.

Composite transactions

32.23   Instruments that are issued at the same time as part of a composite transaction should be considered together under FRS 4 and accounted for as a single instrument unless they can be transferred, cancelled or redeemed independently of each other.

Example 32.8 – A composite transaction?

C Ltd issues a debt instrument and a warrant on 1 January 20X2.

(a)   At the date of issue, the fair value of the debt instrument is £1,800 and the fair value of the warrant is £200.

As a fair value can be attributed to the warrant, it must be capable of being separately transferred and redeemed and should therefore be treated as a separate instrument. £200 will therefore be credited to a warrant reserve, which will be non-distributable and will form part of shareholders' funds. The proceeds of £200 will also be reported in the reconciliation of movements in shareholders' funds.

(b) The warrant cannot be separately transferred or redeemed and the fair value of the debt instrument and the warrant together at the date of issue is £2,000.

As the warrant cannot be separately transferred or redeemed, the debt and warrant should be accounted for as one instrument. In effect, the instrument is debt that is convertible into shares and should be accounted for as a liability in the accounts of the issuer. No value will be attributed to the warrant (i.e. no warrant reserve will be created in this instance).

For accounting periods beginning on or after 1 January 2005, FRS 25 requires the component parts of all compound financial instruments to be separately identified and accounted for as financial liabilities or as equity, depending on the substance of each individual component (see 32.21 above).

Exercise of warrant

32.24   When a warrant is exercised (i.e. the related shares are issued), FRS 4 requires any amount previously recognised in the accounts in respect of the warrant to be included in the net proceeds of the shares issued (eg for the purpose of calculating finance costs). However, there have been different interpretations of whether this requires the warrant reserve to be transferred to share capital (and, where appropriate, the share premium account) or whether it should remain as a warrant reserve within shareholders' funds. FRS 4 is superseded by FRS 25 for accounting periods beginning on or after 1 January 2005.

Lapse of warrant

32.25   If a warrant lapses because it has not been exercised within the specified time, any amount previously recorded on the warrant reserve becomes distributable and should be transferred from the warrant reserve to the profit and loss account as a reserves movement. It will also be reported as a gain in the statement of total recognised gains and losses for the year. If the warrant related to non-equity shares, the reserve will in effect be transferred from non-equity shareholders' funds to equity shareholders' funds.

For accounting periods beginning on or after 1 January 2005, the distinction between equity and non-equity shares is no longer relevant. Under FRS 25, the required distinction is between equity and financial liabilities and only warrants relating to the purchase of equity will be accounted for within shareholders' funds.

Disclosure requirements

32.26   The disclosures required by CA 1985 where a company has granted options or similar rights to subscribe for shares are set out in 32.27 below. These disclosure requirements apply in respect of any instrument which is convertible into shares at some point in the future. Where warrants are convertible into a class of shares that is not yet in issue, the same details must be given in respect of these shares as are required under FRS 4 for each class of shares already in issue (see 32.4 above). No similar disclosure requirements apply under FRS 25, although companies may continue to provide this information on the basis that it will be helpful to shareholders.

Share options and similar rights

32.27   Where a company has granted options to subscribe for shares, or any other similar rights to require the allotment of shares, CA 1985 requires the accounts to show:

—   the number, description and amount of shares involved;

—   the period during which the option or right is exercisable;

—   the price to be paid for the shares allotted.

This information is usually given as part of the note on share capital. Depending on the complexity of the information to be disclosed, it may be given in a narrative note or in table form.

Example 32.9 – Option disclosure: narrative note

The company has granted options in respect of 1,500 ordinary shares of £1 each which are exercisable between 1 January 20X5 and 31 December 20X5 at £2.50 per share.

Example 32.10 – Option disclosure: table form

The company has granted options in respect of 1,500 ordinary shares of £1 each which are exercisable as follows.

Number of shares	Exercise dates	Exercise price
500	1 January 20X4 to 31 December 20X4	£2.00
500	1 January 20X5 to 31 December 20X5	£2.50
500	1 January 20X6 to 31 December 20X6	£2.50
1,500		

Specific accounting and disclosure requirements apply where share options are granted to employees – these are considered in Chapter 11. Additional disclosures are also required where options or other rights to subscribe for shares are granted to directors – these are considered in more detail in Chapter 37.

TRANSACTIONS IN OWN SHARES

Holding of own shares

32.28   The situations in which CA 1985 permits a company to hold its own shares are very limited. With effect from 1 December 2003, an amendment to the legislation allows certain listed companies to purchase their own shares and hold them in treasury, subject to specific conditions. There are also limited circumstances in which a subsidiary company may hold shares in its holding company. UITF Abstract 37 'Purchases and Sales of Own Shares' requires any consideration paid for own shares to be deducted from shareholders' funds. The amount deducted must be shown separately and the number and nominal value of the shares held must be disclosed. It is therefore no longer acceptable to treat such shares as assets, even though the balance sheet formats provide headings for own shares held within both fixed and current assets. The same treatment applies in group accounts in respect of any shares in the holding company held by a subsidiary.

UITF Abstract 37 is withdrawn for accounting periods beginning on or after 1 January 2005, and replaced by similar accounting requirements under FRS 25 'Financial Instruments: Disclosure and Presentation'.

Shares held by an ESOP trust

32.29   Under the requirements of UITF Abstract 38 'Accounting for ESOP Trusts', a company which operates an Employee Share Ownership Plan (ESOP) may need to include in its own accounts shares in the company that are held by the ESOP trust. The previous Abstract on accounting for ESOP trusts required such shares to be shown as assets in the company's balance sheet, but the accounting treatment has been revised in line with the requirements now set out in UITF Abstract 37 'Purchases and Sales of Own Shares'. Consequently, where a company is required to account for an ESOP trust in accordance with UITF Abstract 38, the consideration for any shares held by the trust should be deducted from shareholders' funds, with separate disclosure of the amount deducted. The number and nominal value of the shares should also be disclosed.

EXPECTED FUTURE CHANGES IN RESPECT OF SHARE CAPITAL

FRED 33 'Financial Instruments: Disclosures'

32.30   The ASB published FRED 33 'Financial Instruments: Disclosures' in July 2004. This sets out the draft text of a proposed new international accounting standard which the ASB plans to introduce in the UK for accounting periods beginning on or after 1 January 2007 (the implementation date proposed for the new international standard), although earlier adoption will be permitted. The standard will apply to all UK entities, other than those adopting the FRSSE, and will supersede the disclosure requirements currently set out in FRS 25 'Financial Instruments: Disclosure and Presentation'.

The proposed disclosure requirements are slightly wider than the title of the document might imply. In particular, they include a number of new disclosures in respect of capital that will apply in all cases and not just where an entity makes significant use of financial instruments. These include:

(i)   qualitative information about the entity's objectives, policies and processes for managing capital;

(ii)   a description of what it regards as capital and any capital targets set by management;

(iii) any changes in the above two areas from the previous year;

(iv)   whether the entity has complied with the capital targets set by management and with any externally imposed capital requirements; and

(v)   if it has not complied with such targets or requirements, the consequences of the non-compliance.

The other proposed disclosure requirements are intended to enable users of the accounts to assess the significance of financial instruments to the financial position and financial performance of the reporting entity, the risks that it faces as a result, and how these risks are being managed. Given the wide variety of financial instruments available these days, the draft sets out minimum disclosure requirements, with the implication that these may need to be expanded on, depending on the particular circumstances of the business. Further detail on these proposals is given in Chapter 26.

REVALUATION RESERVE

Use of the alternative accounting rules

32.31   Wherever a company makes use of the alternative accounting rules (see Chapter 1), the surplus or deficit arising on revaluation of the asset to market value or current cost must be transferred to the revaluation reserve. The only widespread use of the alternative accounting rules at present is to allow land and buildings to be included in the accounts at valuation rather than historical cost. Most revaluation reserves therefore arise when land and buildings are revalued for accounts purposes. Consequently, the examples in the following sections discuss the issues in the context of the revaluation of tangible fixed assets. Chapter 21 includes a practical example showing the accounting entries where a fixed asset is revalued for accounting purposes and gives examples of the detailed disclosures that are required both in the year of valuation and in subsequent years. In accordance with the normal rules under CA 1985, when a number of assets are revalued, each item must be considered individually and surpluses and deficits should generally not be off-set against each other.

Surplus or deficit on initial revaluation

32.32   Where the initial revaluation of a fixed asset gives rise to a surplus, the accounting in the year of valuation is reasonably straightforward and the surplus results in a credit balance on the revaluation reserve. Details of the accounting entries and a practical example are given in Chapter 21. In the past considerable confusion arose over accounting for deficits arising on the first revaluation of a fixed asset. CA 1985 is clear that any provision for a permanent diminution in the value of a fixed asset must be charged to the profit and loss account. If the initial revaluation of an asset gives rise to a deficit when compared to the cost or book value of the asset, and the diminution in value is considered to be permanent, the deficit must therefore be charged to the profit and loss account. However, the Act is less clear on the treatment of diminutions in value that are not considered to be permanent and a particular problem under these provisions for many years was the distinction between permanent and temporary diminutions in value. FRS 11 'Impairment of Fixed Assets and Goodwill' has attempted to overcome these difficulties by setting out new rules on when and how assets should be reviewed for impairment and on the recognition of impairment losses in the accounts.

Debit balance on revaluation reserve

32.33   Prior to the issue of FRS 11, where an initial revaluation of a fixed asset gave rise to a diminution in value when compared to the cost or book value of the asset, but this diminution was considered to be temporary, it was possible to argue that the deficit was only being recognised in the accounts because the alternative accounting rules were being applied. Under these rules, all adjustments relating to the revaluation of assets, both surpluses and deficits, should be transferred to the revaluation reserve. If the only revaluation adjustment was a deficit, this resulted in a debit balance on the revaluation reserve. Nothing in CA 1985 appears to prevent a debit balance being shown on the revaluation reserve. However, in accounting terms, the need to adopt a prudent approach would normally required such a debit balance to be written off against the profit and loss account.

Impact of FRS 11

32.34   FRS 11 'Impairment of Fixed Assets and Goodwill' requires fixed assets and goodwill to be reviewed for impairment if events or changes in circumstances indicate that the carrying amount of the asset or goodwill may not be recoverable. To the extent that the carrying amount exceeds the recoverable amount, the fixed asset or goodwill is impaired and should be written down. The general rule is that an impairment loss (i.e. the difference between the carrying amount of a fixed asset or goodwill and its recoverable amount) should be recognised in the profit and loss account of the period, although different requirements apply in the case of assets that have previously been revalued (see 32.35 below). An impairment loss arising on an asset that has not previously been revalued must therefore always be charged to the profit and loss account, regardless of whether the diminution in value is considered to be temporary or permanent.

Impairment of previously revalued assets

32.35   In the case of assets that have previously been revalued, an impairment loss caused by a clear consumption of economic benefits should be recognised in the profit and loss account. Appendix II to FRS 11 notes that this is consistent with the requirement under CA 1985 for all permanent diminutions in value to be charged to the profit and loss account. Other impairment losses on revalued assets (for instance, those relating to general reductions in property prices) should be recognised in the statement of total recognised gains and losses until the carrying amount of the asset reaches its depreciated historical cost, and any further reduction below this amount should be recognised in the profit and loss account. The impairment of a revalued asset in this case will therefore be treated as a reduction of the revaluation reserve until the full amount of any previous surplus relating to the asset has been reversed. The requirements of FRS 11 on the measurement and recognition of impairment losses, and the reversal of impairment losses, are considered in more detail in Chapter 20.

Movements on the revaluation reserve

32.36   Once the revaluation reserve has been created, any of the following movements might arise in subsequent years:

—   adjustments for subsequent changes in the value of assets that have already been revalued;

—   surpluses on the initial revaluation of further assets;

—   transfers to the profit and loss account reserve in respect of the additional depreciation charged on the revalued assets under the requirements of FRS 15 'Tangible Fixed Assets';

—   transfers to the profit and loss account reserve in respect of revaluation surpluses that have become realised when the relevant asset is disposed of; and

—   transfers in respect of taxation relating to revalued assets.

Transfer in respect of depreciation on revalued assets

32.37   FRS 15 'Tangible Fixed Assets' requires the depreciation charge for the year to be based on the carrying value of assets rather than on their historical cost. However, the additional depreciation on the revalued element of the asset may be debited to the revaluation reserve and credited to the profit and loss account reserve each year as a movement on reserves, to reflect the fact that only depreciation on the original cost of an asset is regarded as a realised loss for distribution purposes under the Act. This issue is considered in more detail in Chapter 13.

Transfer on disposal of a revalued asset

32.38   When an asset that has been revalued is disposed of, any remaining balance in the revaluation reserve relating to that asset should be transferred to the profit and loss account reserve as a reserves movement. This reflects the fact that the revaluation surplus has been realised as a result of the disposal of the asset, and ensures compliance with the requirement under the Act that amounts no longer necessary for the valuation method used should be removed from the revaluation reserve. This is considered in more detail in Chapter 13, along with a practical example.

Accounts disclosure

32.39   The balance sheet formats set out in CA 1985 require separate disclosure of the amount carried forward on the revaluation reserve at the balance sheet date. The heading for the revaluation reserve is given a Roman numeral and it must therefore be shown on the face of the balance sheet. Under other provisions in the Act, the reserve need not be called a revaluation reserve in the accounts, but in practice it is preferable for companies to continue to use this description. CA 1985 also requires disclosure of all movements on the revaluation reserve during the year. This can be given as part of a single note setting out movements on all reserves (see Example 32.12) or can be given in a separate note covering only the revaluation reserve.

Example 32.11 – Separate note covering only the revaluation reserve

	£000
Balance at 1 January 20X2	145
Write-down of previously revalued asset	(15)
Transfer to profit and loss account reserve in respect of depreciation charged on revalued assets	(12)
Transfer to profit and loss account reserve in respect of revalued assets sold during the year	(20)
Balance at 31 December 20X2	98

Tax implications of revaluations

32.40   CA 1985 also requires disclosure of the treatment for tax purposes of any amounts credited or debited to the revaluation reserve. This means that the tax implications of any revaluations must be explained. FRS 19 'Deferred Tax' also includes accounting and disclosure requirements on the tax implications of asset revaluations. These are considered in Chapter 31. Compliance with the requirements of FRS 19 will usually be sufficient to ensure compliance with the Act.

Use of the revaluation reserve

32.41   CA 1985 permits the revaluation reserve to be used to pay up unissued shares in the company which are to be allotted to members of the company as fully or partly paid shares. It does not permit the revaluation reserve to be used for any other purpose. In particular, the revaluation reserve cannot be used to write off goodwill. This was clarified by the *Companies Act 1989*, which inserted paragraph 34(3B) into CA 1985 Sch 4. Prior to this, it was not clear that goodwill could not be written off against the revaluation reserve, and companies which made such a write-off in accounting periods beginning before 23 December 1989 were not required to reinstate the amount written off as a result of the clarification. Certain companies may therefore still show revaluation reserves which have been reduced by goodwill, but this treatment should not be adopted in any other cases.

OTHER RESERVES

Analysis of other reserves

32.42   The balance sheet formats require the following analysis of other reserves:
—   capital redemption reserve;
—   reserve for own shares;
—   reserves provided for by the articles of association;
—   other reserves.

The total must be shown separately on the face of the balance sheet, but the analysis may be given in the notes to the accounts. The sub-headings for 'reserve for own shares' and 'reserves provided for by the articles of association' are rarely used in practice. A capital redemption reserve will usually need to be created where a company purchases or redeems its own shares out of distributable profits. A transfer from distributable profits to the capital redemption reserve will normally be required to ensure that the appropriate level of capital is maintained. The capital redemption reserve is non-distributable, but it may be used in paying up unissued shares of the company to be allotted to members of the company as fully paid bonus shares. The sub-heading 'other reserves' – as its name suggests – covers any items not dealt with under any of the specific reserves headings. Generally, there will be little to disclose under this sub-heading, but if material amounts are classified as other reserves it will usually be appropriate to give a brief description of them in the accounts. In particular, a company that adopts the fair value accounting rules for accounting periods beginning on or after 1 January 2005 may need to establish a fair value reserve (see 32.44 below), although most changes in fair value will be dealt with through the profit and loss account.

Profit and loss account reserve

32.43   The profit and loss account reserve is the accumulation of retained profits and losses reported in the profit and loss account. The reserve must be shown separately on the face of the balance sheet. In some circumstances it may be appropriate to transfer amounts to the profit and loss account reserve from other reserves, and vice versa. The following examples are considered elsewhere in this book:

— transfers between the revaluation reserve and the profit and loss account reserve in respect of depreciation on revalued assets (Chapter 13).

— transfers between the profit and loss account and share premium account in respect of issue costs (Chapter 14 and Chapter 16).

Chapter 7 also considers a specific situation where exchange gains and losses in respect of foreign currency borrowings and foreign currency investments may be taken directly to the profit and loss account reserve (ie without passing through the profit and loss account).

Fair value reserve

32.44 For accounting periods beginning on or after 1 January 2005, company law is amended by the *Companies Act 1985 (International Accounting Standards and Other Accounting Amendments) Regulations 2004* (SI 2004/2947) to allow fair value accounting to be applied to certain assets and liabilities. In effect, the new provisions allow certain investments to be marked to market and also facilitate the use of hedge accounting in specific circumstances. The fair value accounting rules are considered in more detail in Chapter 1.

A change in the fair value of a financial instrument or other asset accounted for under the fair value accounting rules should normally be included in the profit and loss account. However, in the following two cases, the legislation requires the change to be debited or credited to a separate fair value reserve:

(i) where a financial instrument is a hedging instrument accounted for under a hedge accounting system that allows some or all of the change in value not to be shown in the profit and loss account; and

(ii) where the change in value relates to an exchange difference arising on a monetary item that forms part of a company's net investment in a foreign entity.

A change in value may also be debited or credited to the fair value reserve where the financial instrument in question is an available for sale financial asset and is not a derivative. The fair value reserve should be adjusted where any of the amounts included in it are no longer required for the purposes of fair value accounting (for instance, where the related item has been disposed of).

Where fair value accounting has been adopted and there have been movements on the fair value reserve in the year, the notes to the accounts must include a table giving the same analysis of movements as for other reserves (see 32.45 below). The treatment for tax purposes of any amounts debited or credited to the fair value reserve should also be explained. Other disclosures required by the fair value accounting provisions are summarised in Chapter 1.

Disclosure of movements on reserves

32.45   Where any amount is transferred to or from any reserve during the year, CA 1985 requires disclosure of the following:

— the amount of the reserve at the beginning of the year;

— any amounts transferred to or from the reserve during the year;

— the source and application (respectively) of the amounts transferred; and

— the amount of the reserve at the end of the year.

This disclosure requirement is usually dealt with by presenting a movements table for reserves in the notes to the accounts. Depending on the level of detail requiring disclosure, it may be possible to combine the disclosures for all reserves including the share premium account and revaluation reserve, in one note.

Example 32.12 – Disclosure for all reserves in one note

	Share premium	Revaluation reserve	Other reserves	Profit and loss account
	£000	£000	£000	£000
Balance at 1 January 20X2	35	—	4	65
Premium on shares issued during the year	10	—	—	—
Surplus on revaluation of property during the year	—	55	—	—
Retained profit for the year	—	—	—	40
Balance at 31 December 20X2	45	55	4	105

Comparative figures are not required for movements on reserves.

OTHER DISCLOSURE REQUIREMENTS

Disclosure of non-distributable reserves

32.46   There is no requirement under CA 1985 to distinguish between distributable and non-distributable reserves in the accounts (or between realised and unrealised reserves). However, if a substantial element of reserves is non-distributable it is usually advisable to disclose this fact in a narrative footnote to the reserves table.

Example 32.13 – Disclosure where substantial element of reserves is non-distributable

Of the total reserves shown above, £100,000 is not available for distribution.

A brief outline of the issues relating to distributable and non-distributable reserves is given in Chapter 16.

Dividend arrears

32.47   Where a company has issued shares carrying a fixed cumulative dividend, and these dividends are in arrears (ie because there are insufficient distributable reserves to pay the dividends), CA 1985 requires the accounts to disclose:

— the amount of the arrears; and

— the period for which the dividends are in arrears (if more than one class of shares is affected, details must be given for each class of share affected).

The disclosure will usually be covered in a narrative note, which will normally form part of the reserves note, but could be included elsewhere in the accounts (e.g. in the share capital note, which provides details of each class of shares in issue).

Example 32.14 – Disclosure of dividend arrears

No dividends have been paid in respect of the 5% cumulative preference shares since 20X1; total dividend arrears at 31 December 20X3 amount to £9,000.

The accounting treatment of fixed cumulative dividends under the requirements of FRS 4 'Capital Instruments' and FRS 25 'Financial Instruments: Disclosure and Presentation' is considered in Chapter 16.

Chapter 33　Commitments and Contingencies

CONTINGENT LIABILITIES

Definition of contingent liability

33.1　FRS 12 'Provisions, Contingent Liabilities and Contingent Assets' defines a contingent liability as:

— a possible obligation that arises from past events and whose existence will be confirmed only by the occurrence of one or more uncertain future events not wholly within the entity's control; or

— a present obligation that arises from past events but is not recognised because:

— it is not probable that a transfer of economic benefits will be required to settle the obligation; or

— the amount of the obligation cannot be measured with sufficient reliability.

Distinction between provisions and contingent liabilities

33.2　FRS 12 also considers the distinction between provisions and contingent liabilities. A provision is defined as a liability that is of uncertain timing or amount, and liabilities are defined as the obligations of an entity to transfer economic benefits as a result of past events. The standard requires a provision to be recognised when:

— an entity has a present obligation (legal or constructive) as a result of a past event;

— it is probable that a transfer of economic benefits will be required to settle the obligation; and

— a reliable estimate can be made of the amount of the obligation (situations where this is not possible are expected to be rare in practice).

The principal distinctions between provisions and contingent liabilities are, therefore:

— whether the obligation is present or possible at the balance sheet date; and

— in the case of a present obligation, the likelihood of a transfer of economic benefits being required to settle the obligation (ie whether such a transfer is probable or not).

These issues are considered in more detail in Chapter 29.

Items commonly identified as contingent liabilities

33.3 A wide variety of items might come into the category of contingent liabilities, depending on the circumstances in each case. Some of the more common ones include:

— outstanding claims and litigation;

— performance bonds;

— guarantees;

— forward foreign exchange contracts;

— warranties and indemnities;

— deferred consideration (eg in respect of an acquisition).

Accounting treatment

33.4 Under FRS 12, a contingent liability should not be recognised in the accounts, but should be disclosed unless the possibility of a transfer of economic benefits is remote. For instance, a situation where the possibility of the transfer of economic benefits is remote might arise where an entity assigns a lease to another tenant and signs an authorised guarantee agreement in respect of the performance of the assignee. The entity would continue to have a liability to the landlord if the assignee defaults on the lease, but if there is no evidence to suggest that the assignee is unlikely to meet the rental payments, the possibility of the liability crystallising will usually be sufficiently remote to justify non-disclosure.

Regular review

33.5 The guidance in FRS 12 emphasises the need for contingent liabilities to be assessed continually to determine whether a transfer of economic benefits has become probable. If such a transfer becomes probable in respect of an item previously disclosed as a contingent liability, a provision should be recognised in the accounts of the period in which the change in probability occurs (assuming that all of the recognition criteria are met).

Joint and several liability

33.6   Where an entity has joint and several liability with other entities for a present obligation at the balance sheet date, the liability will usually need to be considered in two parts. Where it is probable that a transfer of economic benefits will be required for the entity to settle its part of the obligation and a reliable estimate of this can be made (ie the recognition criteria set out in FRS 12 are met), the entity should recognise a provision for its own part of the obligation. The obligation that is expected to be met by the other parties will normally be treated as a contingent liability. A different approach will be required if it is apparent that one or more of the other entities may not be able to meet their part of the obligation. In this case there will usually be a higher degree of probability that the entity will need to make an additional transfer of economic benefits and this may therefore need to be recognised as a provision in the accounts.

Detailed disclosures

33.7   CA 1985 requires the following details to be given in respect of any contingent liability that is not provided for in the accounts:
— the amount (or estimated amount) of the liability;
— its legal nature;
— whether any valuable security has been provided by the company and, if so, what.

For accounting periods beginning on or after 1 January 2005, these disclosure requirements only apply where the company prepares Companies Act accounts.

For each class of contingent liability, FRS 12 requires the accounts to give a brief description of the nature of the liability at the balance sheet date and, where practicable, the following additional information:
— an estimate of the financial effect, measured in accordance with the criteria set out in paragraphs 36 to 55 of FRS 12 (ie those applying to the measurement of provisions – see Chapter 30);
— an indication of the uncertainties relating to the amount or timing of any outflow; and
— the possibility of any reimbursement.

In determining a class of liability for these purposes, the guidance notes that it will be necessary to consider whether the nature of the items is sufficiently similar for a single statement about them to meet the disclosure requirements set out in the first two categories above. If any of the required information is not disclosed because it is not practicable to do so, this fact must be stated.

Provisions linked with contingent liabilities

33.8 Where a provision and a contingent liability arise from the same set of circumstances, the disclosures should be made in a way that clarifies and explains the link between them. For instance, an entity may have joint and several liability with other parties and this may result in a provision being recognised for its own obligation, with separate disclosure of the contingent liability representing the obligation that is expected to be met by the other parties. The disclosures for the provision and the contingent liability should make clear that these obligations arise from the same transaction or arrangement.

Restriction of the disclosures

33.9 Some of the disclosures may be restricted if full disclosure would seriously prejudice the entity's position in a dispute relating to the subject of the provision, although this situation is expected to arise only very rarely. In this case, the general nature of the dispute should be disclosed along with an explanation of why the detailed disclosures have not been given. Appendix IV to FRS 12 gives an illustrative example of how this might be dealt with in the context of a provision – the same approach would be appropriate in the case of a contingent liability. The exemption does not apply if disclosure is required by law.

Example disclosure

33.10 Standard disclosure cannot be provided, as the details will inevitably vary depending on the precise circumstances of each case, but the information is often disclosed along the following lines:

Example 33.1 – Contingent liability disclosure

The company is the defendant in proceedings which began in June 20X2 as a result of a claim by a customer that the company was negligent in the performance of contract work carried out in 20X1. The customer is claiming damages of £100,000. This claim is being vigourously defended and the directors are confident that the company will be successful in its defence of the claim. Full provision has been made in the accounts for legal costs of £15,000 incurred to date in defending the claim. It is not practicable at this stage to quantify any additional costs that may be incurred.

CONTINGENT ASSETS

Definition of contingent asset

33.11 FRS 12 defines a contingent asset as 'a possible asset that arises from past events and whose existence will be confirmed only by the occurrence of one or more uncertain future events not wholly within the entity's control.' Contingent assets usually result from unexpected or unplanned events, and the guidance in the standard quotes as an example a claim that is being pursued through the legal system, where the outcome is uncertain.

Accounting treatment

33.12 Under FRS 12, an entity should not recognise a contingent asset in the accounts. To do so would mean recognising a profit that might not actually be realised. However, the guidance notes that, where realisation of the profit is virtually certain, the related asset is no longer contingent (ie it does not meet the definition in 33.11 above) and it should therefore be recognised in the accounts. A contingent asset should only be disclosed in the accounts where an inflow of economic benefits is probable. This is to prevent the accounts giving a misleading impression of the likelihood of future profits arising from contingent assets.

Regular review

33.13 As with contingent liabilities, the standard requires contingent assets to be assessed continually. Where an inflow of economic benefits becomes virtually certain, the asset and the related profit should be recognised in the accounts in the year in which the change in circumstances takes place. If an inflow of economic benefits becomes probable, the contingent asset should be disclosed in the accounts. Under the guidance in paragraph 23 of FRS 12, a transfer of economic benefits, or any other event, is regarded as being probable if the probability that it will occur is greater than the probability that it will not.

Detailed disclosures

33.14 Where an inflow of economic benefits is probable, the accounts should disclose a brief description of the contingent asset at the balance sheet date and, where practicable, an estimate of the financial effect, measured using the principles set out in paragraphs 36 to 55 of FRS 12 (ie those applying to the measurement of provisions – see Chapter 30). In drafting these disclosures, care should be taken to avoid giving a misleading indication of the likelihood of future profits arising from a contingent asset.

Restriction of the disclosures

33.15 Some of the disclosures may be restricted if full disclosure would seriously prejudice the entity's position in a dispute relating to the subject of the provision, although this situation is expected to arise only very rarely. In this case, the general nature of the dispute should be disclosed along with an explanation of why the detailed disclosures have not been given. The exemption does not apply if disclosure is required by law. If any of the required disclosures are not given because it is not practicable to do so, the standard requires this fact to be stated in the accounts.

GUARANTEES

Disclosure under CA 1985

33.16 CA 1985 also requires disclosure of any other financial commitments which have not been provided for in the accounts and which are relevant to an assessment of the company's state of affairs. Where any disclosable commitments are undertaken on behalf of any parent, fellow subsidiary or subsidiary undertaking, these commitments must be shown separately (see 33.19 below). For accounting periods beginning on or after 1 January 2005, these disclosure requirements only apply where the company prepares Companies Act accounts.

Disclosure of amount outstanding and maximum liability

33.17 A commitment or contingent liability that frequently requires disclosure, especially in the accounts of companies which are members of a group, is the existence of guarantees in respect of borrowings taken out by other members of the group. Where the company has given a guarantee in respect of a loan to another company, the amount outstanding at the end of the year should be disclosed as part of the contingent liability note. In the case of a guarantee relating to an overdraft facility, the maximum amount covered by the guarantee should be stated as well as the amount outstanding at the balance sheet date. The same principle would apply to a guarantee of a loan where the amount could vary (eg where the guarantee covers a facility up to a specified level, but the full amount has not been drawn down at the balance sheet date).

Example 33.2 – Disclosure of a loan/overdraft guarantee

The company has guaranteed an unsecured bank loan of £25,000 to a fellow subsidiary. This loan is repayable in full in June 20X4.

The company has also guaranteed the bank overdraft of its parent company; the maximum amount available under this facility is £100,000 and the amount outstanding at the balance sheet date was £45,678 (20X1: £51,332). No security has been provided by the company.

Aggregate disclosure

33.18 Where the company has guaranteed the overdrafts of more than one company within the group, the aggregate amount outstanding on these accounts at the end of the year should be disclosed, along with the maximum potential liability. Where the bank accounts of some of these companies are in credit at the end of the year, the precise terms of the agreement will need to be reviewed to establish whether the company's liability is for the aggregate amount of the overdrafts outstanding at the balance sheet date or for the net amount outstanding (ie the aggregate of all the relevant accounts, regardless of whether they are in credit or overdraft). The amount (or amounts) disclosed in the contingent liabilities note should reflect the company's actual liability under the guarantee arrangements.

Separate disclosure of group items

33.19   CA 1985 requires financial commitments and contingencies undertaken on behalf of other group companies to be shown separately from other commitments and contingencies. Group items must be analysed into two categories:

—   those involving any parent undertaking or any fellow subsidiary undertaking (ie any member of a wider group of which the company is a part); and

—   those involving any subsidiary undertaking (ie any member of a group headed by the company).

Once again, these disclosure requirements are set out in Sch 4 to CA 1985 and so, for accounting periods beginning on or after 1 January 2005, only apply where the company prepares Companies Act accounts.

Charge on the company's assets

33.20   If a guarantee or any other financial commitment involves a charge over the company's assets, details of the security given must also be disclosed under the requirements of CA 1985.

Example 33.3 – Where a charge over the company's assets is included

The company has guaranteed an unsecured bank loan of £25,000 to a fellow subsidiary; this loan is repayable in full in June 20X4.

The company has also guaranteed the bank overdraft of its parent company; the maximum amount available under this facility is £100,000 and the amount outstanding at the balance sheet date was £45,678 (20X1: £51,332). The amount outstanding at any time (up to a maximum of £100,000) is secured on the company's freehold property.

CAPITAL COMMITMENTS

Disclosure under CA 1985

33.21   CA 1985 requires separate disclosure of commitments in respect of capital expenditure contracts entered into by the balance sheet date. The disclosure relates only to contracts for which no provision has been made in the accounts (for instance because work has not been started before the balance sheet date). The disclosures can be given in either table or narrative form.

Example 33.4 – Tabular disclosure; capital commitments

The following capital expenditure has been authorised but has not been provided for in the accounts.

	20X2	*20X1*
	£	£
Capital expenditure contracted for	345	114

Example 33.5 – Narrative form: capital commitments

At 30 September 20X2, the company had contracted for capital expenditure amounting to £345,000 (20X1: £114,000) which is not provided for in these accounts.

As with the other CA 1985 disclosure requirements discussed in this chapter, the requirement to show capital commitments is set out in Sch 4 to CA 1985 and so, for accounting periods beginning on or after 1 January 2005, only applies where the company prepares Companies Act accounts.

No capital commitments

33.22   Where there are no capital commitments at the balance sheet date, there is no formal requirement to state this fact, but it is good practice to do so.

Example 33.6 – Where there are no capital commitments

The company had no unprovided commitments in respect of capital expenditure contracted for at either 30 September 20X2 or 30 September 20X1.

PENSION COMMITMENTS

Disclosure of amounts not provided

33.23   Both the Act and FRS 17 'Retirement Benefits' (or, for accounting periods beginning before 1 January 2005, its predecessor standard, SSAP 24 'Accounting for Pension Costs') require disclosure of the amounts provided in respect of pension commitments. These requirements are considered in detail in Chapter 11 and Chapter 30. In addition, CA 1985 requires separate disclosure of any pension commitments that have not been provided for in the accounts, with separate details of any amounts relating to pensions payable to past directors. Whilst FRS 17 (or, where appropriate, SSAP 24) does not specifically refer to this, it does require extensive disclosures on the funding and valuation of pension schemes, as well as requiring appropriate provision to be made in the accounts for all pension obligations, whether contractual or implied. Compliance with the accounting and disclosure requirements of the accounting standard will usually ensure that all the requirements of the Act in respect of pensions commitments are adequately met.

LEASING COMMITMENTS

Lessee commitments under finance leases

33.24   Where a company has entered into a finance lease or hire purchase agreement at the balance sheet date, but inception has not yet taken place, SSAP 21 'Accounting for Leases and Hire Purchase Contracts' requires disclosure of the company's commitment under the agreement. Inception of a lease is defined in SSAP 21 as the earlier of the date when the asset is brought into use or the date from which rental payments accrue.

Example 33.7 – Agreement entered into, but inception has not taken place

At the balance sheet date, the company had entered into commitments amounting to £35,000 (20X1: £46,000) in respect of a finance lease, the inception of which took place after the balance sheet date.

Further detail on accounting for finance leases under SSAP 21 can be found in Chapter 21.

Lessee commitments under operating leases

33.25   SSAP 21 also requires disclosure of the payments that the lessee is committed to make during the next year in respect of operating leases. Separate details must be given for leases of land and buildings and other leases. The leases must be analysed into those which expire:

—   within the next year;

—   in years two to five (inclusive); and

—   more than five years after the balance sheet date.

The requirement for this analysis sometimes gives rise to confusion. The figure to be disclosed is the total amount payable during the next year in respect of operating leases, analysed into the above categories. The accounts are not required to show the amount payable in one year, in two to five years and after more than five years (ie the disclosure requirement in respect of operating lease commitments should not be confused with the requirement – also in SSAP 21 – for leasing and hire purchase creditors to be analysed into amounts payable within one year, in two to five years and after five years).

Example

33.26   In most cases, the clearest method of disclosure will be to set out the required information in table form.

Example 33.8 – Tabular disclosure for operating lease commitments

The following amounts are payable in the next twelve months under non-cancellable operating leases:

	20X2 *Land and buildings* £	*20X2* *Other* £	*20X1* *Land buildings* £	*20X1* *Other* £
Operating leases which expire:				
Within one year	—	10	—	12
In two to five years (inclusive)	34	20	30	15
Over five years	76	—	76	—
	110	30	106	27

However, if there is only a small amount of detail to disclose, a narrative note may suffice.

Example 33.9 – Narrative disclosure for operating lease commitments

In the next twelve months, the company is committed to paying £51,500 (20X1: £47,800) under a non-cancellable operating lease in respect of land and buildings. This lease expires after more than five years. The company has no other operating lease commitments.

Chapter 34 Events After the Balance Sheet Date and Other Disclosures

ADJUSTING EVENTS

Definition of post balance sheet events

34.1   For accounting periods beginning before 1 January 2005, SSAP 17 'Accounting for Post Balance Sheet Events' defines post balance sheet events as 'those events, both favourable and unfavourable, which occur between the balance sheet date and the date on which the financial statements are approved by the board of directors'. Events which arise after the date of approval of the accounts are not covered by SSAP 17, although it is noted that the directors may need to consider publishing relevant information in respect of material events in this category.

SSAP 17 is superseded by FRS 21 'Events After the Balance Sheet Date' for accounting periods beginning on or after 1 January 2005. FRS 21 cannot be adopted early as one of the main requirements (the accounting treatment of proposed dividends) hinges on company law changes that also come into effect from 1 January 2005. The other aspects of FRS 21 are generally in line with the requirements of SSAP 17, but with some subtle changes in terminology. For instance, FRS 21 sets out a similar definition of events after the balance sheet date, but refers to the date on which the financial statements are authorised for issue rather than the date of approval by the directors.

Definition of adjusting events

34.2   SSAP 17 defines adjusting events as 'post balance sheet events which provide additional evidence of conditions existing at the balance sheet date. They include events which because of statutory or conventional requirements are reflected in financial statements'. As adjusting events provide additional evidence of the situation at the balance sheet date, and it is this situation that must form the basis for the accounts, the effect of an adjusting event should be reflected in the accounts if it is material.

For accounting periods beginning on or after 1 January 2005, FRS 21 defines adjusting events more simply as 'those that provide evidence of conditions that existed at the balance sheet date'.

In particular, it should be noted that the wording of the SSAP 17 definition of adjusting events in effect permitted a parent company to recognise as an asset a dividend declared after the balance sheet date by a subsidiary or associate if it related to a period before that date and was therefore reflected in the accounts of the subsidiary or associate as a proposed dividend. Under FRS 21, the subsidiary or associate will not be able to recognise a proposed dividend as a liability and so the parent will no longer be allowed to recognise it as an asset.

Examples of adjusting events

34.3   The appendix to SSAP 17 lists a number of events that would normally need to be classified as adjusting events, and that would therefore usually result in adjustments being made to the accounts. The examples include:

— the subsequent finalisation of the purchase price of a fixed asset purchased before the year-end – the agreed price should be used as the purchase price of the asset;

— the finalisation of the selling price for an asset sold before the year-end – the agreed price should be used for the sales proceeds of the asset;

— a property valuation that provides evidence of an impairment in value at the balance sheet date – the carrying amount of the property at the balance sheet date should be written down to its recoverable amount;

— the receipt of a copy of the accounts or other information in respect of an unlisted company that provides evidence of an impairment in the value of a long-term investment – the investment should be written down to its recoverable amount;

— the receipt of sales proceeds after the end of the year which indicates that the net realisable value of certain stocks at the balance sheet date is lower than cost – the value of the stocks would therefore need to be reduced to net realisable value;

— the insolvency of a debtor – in this case, provision will usually need to be made against the balance outstanding at the end of the year;

— the receipt of a sum due in respect of an insurance claim which was under negotiation at the balance sheet date – the agreed amount should therefore be reflected in debtors at the balance sheet date.

FRS 21 includes a number of similar examples, together with the following additional items:

(i)   the settlement after the balance sheet date of a court case that confirms that the entity had a present obligation at the balance sheet date;

(ii)   the determination after the balance sheet date of the amount of profit-sharing or bonus payments, provided that the entity had a present legal or constructive obligation at the balance sheet date to mke such payments as the result of an event before that date; and

(iii)   the discovery of fraud or errors that show that the financial statements are incorrect.

Events which impact on the use of the going concern concept

34.4   Certain events which occur after the balance sheet date may indicate the need to reconsider whether it is still appropriate to prepare accounts on the going concern basis (see Chapter 1). Such events will usually be rare, but might include:

—   a serious deterioration in operating results and financial position;

—   the loss of business with a major customer (ie business on which the company is dependent for its future viability);

—   an adverse judgement in respect of major litigation which puts into question the company's ability to continue trading.

If, as a result of such an event, it is no longer considered appropriate to prepare accounts on a going concern basis, the event will usually need to be treated as an adjusting event (ie the basis of the accounts will need to be adjusted). For accounting periods beginning on or after 1 January 2005, FRS 21 is more specific that financial statements should not be prepared on a going concern basis if management decides after the balance sheet date to liquidate the entity or to cease trading, or concludes that it has no realistic alternative but to do so.

NON-ADJUSTING EVENTS

Definition of non-adjusting events

34.5   For accounting periods beginning before 1 January 2005, SSAP 17 defines non-adjusting events as 'post balance sheet events which concern conditions which did not exist at the balance sheet date'. As the accounts must be based on conditions in existence at the balance sheet date, it would usually be inappropriate to adjust the accounts for such events. However, where such an event is material, details should be disclosed in the accounts to ensure that they are not misleading. For accounting periods beginning on or after 1 January 2005, similar requirements apply under FRS 21, which defines non-adjusting events as those that are indicative of conditions that arose after the balance sheet date.

Examples of non-adjusting events

34.6 The appendix to SSAP 17 lists a number of events that would normally be classified as non-adjusting events, and that would therefore usually require disclosure in the accounts (if the effect is material) but which would not normally result in adjustments to the figures shown in the accounts. The examples include:

— the issue of shares or debentures;

— the purchase of a major fixed asset;

— the disposal of a major fixed asset;

— the loss of stock (or other assets) as a result of a fire or flood;

— the commencement of new trading activities or a major extension of the existing activities;

— the closure of a significant trading activity;

— a decline in the value of a property or investment, where it can be clearly demonstrated that the reduction in value took place after the year-end;

— significant changes in foreign exchange rates;

— increases in pensions benefits.

FRS 21 sets out a similar list of examples, which includes the following additional items:

(i) a major business combination after the balance sheet date;

(ii) announcing a plan to discontinue an operation;

(iii) announcing, or commencing the implementation of, a major restructuring;

(iv) changes in tax rates or tax laws announced after the balance sheet date, which have a significant impact or current and/or deferred tax liabilities;

(v) entering into significant commitments or contingent liabilities (eg by issuing significant guarantees);

(vi) commencing major litigation arising solely from events after the balance sheet date.

Window dressing

34.7 SSAP 17 also requires disclosure of the reversal or maturity after the year-end of a transaction entered into before the balance sheet date, where the main substance of the transaction was to alter the appearance of the balance sheet. This disclosure covers adjustments to the balance sheet that are commonly referred to as 'window dressing'. Such transactions will usually (but not always) involve the movement of cash, the aim usually being to show a bank balance that is higher than normal or a bank overdraft that is lower than normal, or to remove a loan from the balance sheet. The transaction may be as simple as delaying a purchase ledger payment run that is normally made at the end of the month and making the payments at the beginning of the following month (ie in the new accounting year) instead. Creditors at the year-end will therefore be higher than is usually the case, but the bank position will be improved (eg it might become a bank balance rather than a bank overdraft). Other arrangements might be more complex, for instance a company may be able to arrange:

— to repay a loan immediately prior to the balance sheet date, and then take out a similar loan with the same lender a few days later – the balance sheet will therefore show lower borrowings than is normally the case;

— for a loan to become unsecured immediately prior to the balance sheet date, and then grant security again a few days into the new accounting year – the accounts would show unsecured borrowings at the balance sheet date, even though, in practice, the lender has security over some of the company's assets.

Where any transaction along these lines has a material impact on the accounts, details should be disclosed under SSAP 17.

FRS 21 makes no specific reference to window dressing or the separate disclosure of artificial transactions that are reversed after the year-end.

DISCLOSURE OF POST BALANCE SHEET EVENTS

Details to be disclosed

34.8 CA 1985 requires the directors' report to include particulars of any important events affecting the company (and, where relevant, its subsidiaries) which have occurred since the end of the financial year. The Act does not specify the details that should be disclosed in respect of a post balance sheet event, requiring only 'particulars' to be given. For accounting periods beginning before 1 January 2005, SSAP 17 requires disclosure of:

— the nature of the event; and

— an estimate of the financial effect.

Where it is not practicable to estimate the financial effect, this fact must be stated. The tax implications of the financial effect must also be explained separately where necessary to enable a user of the accounts to understand the financial position shown in the accounts. The details are usually disclosed in a separate note to the accounts.

Example 34.1 – Possible wording for a post balance sheet event disclosure I

On 10 October 20X2 the company disposed of a freehold property which is included in the accounts at 30 June 20X2 at a value of £134,750. This transaction gave rise to a profit on disposal of £25,400.

Example 34.2 – Possible wording for a post balance sheet event disclosure II

On 13 December 20X2 the company issued 5,000 £1 ordinary shares at £3.50 per share.

For accounting periods beginning on or after 1 January 2005, similar disclosures are required under FRS 21. The new standard also clarifies that other disclosures in the accounts (for instance, details of contingent liabilities) should be updated for any new information that arises after the balance sheet date, even though the figures in the accounts are unchanged.

Distinctions between accounting standards and CA 1985

34.9   There are two major distinctions between accounting standards and CA 1985 in respect of the disclosure of post balance sheet events:

—   SSAP 17 and FRS 21 require details of non-adjusting post balance sheet events to be disclosed in the accounts, whilst the Act requires disclosure in the directors' report; and

—   SSAP 17 and FRS 21 do not require disclosure of adjusting events as these will have been reflected in the accounts – as the Act does not distinguish between adjusting and non-adjusting events, the directors' report may need to give brief details of any major adjusting events and explain how these have been dealt with in the accounts although, in practice, such events will not usually be sufficiently material to warrant this treatment.

Location of the disclosures

34.10   To avoid an unnecessary duplication of information, it will usually be acceptable to give the detailed disclosures in either the notes to the accounts or the directors' report only (preferably in the notes to the accounts, although there is no firm rule on this) and include a cross- reference in the other location to show where the details can be found. Disclosure in the directors' report alone will not be sufficient to meet the requirements of SSAP 17 or FRS 21. If details of a post balance sheet event are disclosed separately in both the directors' report and the notes to the accounts it is important that the information given in each location is consistent.

DATE OF APPROVAL OF ACCOUNTS

Importance of date of approval of accounts

34.11   Events after the balance sheet date are defined as events which occur between the date of balance sheet and the date on which the accounts are approved by the directors or otherwise authoirsed for issue. Any adjusting events which occur during this period must be reflected in the accounts and details of any significant non-adjusting events must be disclosed in the notes to the accounts. Events arising after the date of approval or authorisation of the accounts are not covered by the requirements of either SSAP 17 or FRS 21.

For accounting periods beginning before 1 January 2005, the key date under SSAP 17 is the date on which the accounts are formally approved by the directors. For accounting periods beginning on or after 1 January 2005, FRS 21 refers to the date on which the financial statements are authorised for issue rather than the date of approval. The supplementary guidance material in the standard notes that, in some cases, there may be a formal requirement for an entity to submit its financial statements to its shareholders for approval after they have been issued. In these circumstances, the financial statements should be regarded as authorised for issue on the date of issue and not on the date of approval by the shareholders. The guidance also considers a situation where the financial statements must be passed to a non-executive supervisory board for final approval and notes that such financial statements should be regarded as having been authorised for issue when management authorises them for issue to the supervisory board rather than the date on which that board confirms its approval.

Finalisation process

34.12   Individual companies will adopt different procedures for finalising their statutory accounts, but formal approval by the directors will always be required at some stage and this will normally be given at a board meeting. In some cases this will be the meeting at which the final accounts are discussed in detail, in other cases it may be a meeting at which final accounts are approved, having been discussed in detail at a draft stage (ie earlier in the finalisation process). Where changes are needed to the accounts after consideration by the board, formal approval will usually need to be given at a later stage (ie when the final version of the accounts is available).

Disclosure of the date of approval of the accounts

34.13   As the date on which the accounts were approved or authorised is so significant, both SSAP 17 and FRS 21 require this date to be disclosed in the accounts. This can be done in one of two ways. The date of approval or authorisation of the accounts can be shown on the face of the balance sheet, linked with the signature of the director (or directors).

Example 34.3 – Date of approval on the face of the balance sheet

These accounts were [approved]/[authorised for issue] by the board of directors on 12 December 20X2 and signed on its behalf by:

....

AJ Jones, Director

Alternatively, the date of approval or authorisation of the accounts can be disclosed in a separate note to the accounts.

Example 34.4 – Date of approval in a note

The accounts were [approved]/[authorised for issue] by the board of directors on 12 December 20X2.

Both methods of disclosure are in common use.

FRS 21 specifically requires the disclosure to state who authorised the accounts for issue and, where relevant, to include a statement that the entity's owners or others have the power to amend the financial statements after issue.

DISCLOSURES IN RESPECT OF PARENT UNDERTAKINGS

Disclosures required by CA 1985

34.14   In the case of a subsidiary company, the Act requires details to be disclosed in the accounts in respect of:

—   the parent company of the smallest group for which group accounts are prepared and which include the company;

—   the parent company of the largest group for which group accounts are prepared and which include the company.

The following details must be given in the company's accounts in respect of each of the above:

—   the name of the parent undertaking;

—   if it is incorporated outside Great Britain, the country in which it is incorporated;

—   if it is unincorporated, the address of its principal place of business;

—   if the relevant group accounts are available to the public, the address from which copies can be obtained.

In most cases, this disclosure will be straightforward and will usually be given in a separate note to the accounts.

Example 34.5 – Disclosure of details on parent company

The company's immediate parent company is G Ltd. The group accounts of G Ltd can be obtained from [Address]. The ultimate parent undertaking is X AG, a company incorporated in Germany. The group accounts of X AG can be obtained from [Address].

Ultimate parent company/controlling party

34.15   CA 1985 also requires disclosure of the name of the company's ultimate parent company, if this is different (for instance, where the ultimate parent company does not prepare group accounts) and the country in which it is incorporated, if this is outside Great Britain and if the information is known to the directors. FRS 8 'Related Party Disclosures' requires disclosure of the controlling party and ultimate controlling party (if different). In many cases, these will be the same as the parent and ultimate parent. The disclosure requirements of FRS 8 are considered in Chapter 17.

SEGMENTAL REPORTING OF NET ASSETS

Analysis of net assets

34.16 The segmental reporting of net assets is one of the additional disclosures required by SSAP 25 'Segmental Reporting'. It is not required by CA 1985 and therefore only applies to public and larger private companies (see Chapter 18 for precise details of the scope of SSAP 25). Normally only operating assets and liabilities that are non-interest bearing will need to be analysed. However, the segmental analysis of net assets should be consistent with the analysis of results. In certain circumstances the standard requires interest to be included in the analysis of results, and in these cases the analysis of net assets should include the corresponding interest bearing assets and liabilities. The approach to segmental analysis is considered in more detail in Chapter 18.

Apportionment of operating assets and liabilities

34.17 Where some of the operating assets and liabilities relate jointly to more than one segment, they should be allocated between the relevant segments on a reasonable basis.

Link with balance sheet

34.18 The total of the amounts disclosed in the segmental analysis of net assets should agree with the total shown in the balance sheet. If it does not, a reconciliation of the two amounts should also be provided.

Comparative information

34.19 SSAP 25 requires comparative information to be provided for all segmental disclosures.

OTHER BALANCE SHEET DISCLOSURES

Financial assistance for the purchase of own shares

34.20 Where any item in the balance sheet includes outstanding loans made under CA 1985 s 153(4)(b), (bb) or (c) or s 155 (all of which deal with financial assistance for the purchase of own shares), the aggregate amount of the loans must be disclosed for each balance sheet item affected.

Dormant companies acting as agents

34.21 The Companies Act 1985 (Audit Exemption) (Amendment) Regulations 2000 introduced a new disclosure requirement for dormant companies which act as agent for another party. Where the directors take advantage of the exemption from audit conferred by CA 1985 s 249AA and the company has acted as agent for another party during the year, the accounts are required to disclose this fact. CA 1985 Schs 4, 8 and 8A were all amended to incorporate this disclosure requirement. The disclosure must therefore also be given in abbreviated accounts where the company chooses to prepare these for filing purposes.

Chapter 35   Cash Flow Statement

REQUIREMENT TO PREPARE A CASH FLOW STATEMENT

Nature of the statement

35.1   There is no specific requirement in company law for accounts to include a cash flow statement. However, the general requirement for accounts to comply with applicable accounting standards means that the requirements of FRS 1 'Cash Flow Statements' are effectively brought within the law. The cash flow statement is a primary statement within the accounts, along with the profit and loss account, balance sheet and statement of total recognised gains and losses. Although FRS 1 'Cash Flow Statements' does not prescribe the positioning of the cash flow statement it is usually presented as a separate page of the accounts, immediately after the profit and loss account and balance sheet.

Prescribed structure

35.2   The inclusion of a cash flow statement in the accounts ensures that an entity reports its cash generation and absorption during the period and provides users of the accounts with information to help them assess the liquidity, solvency and financial adaptability of the business. The use of standard headings and a prescribed structure for the statement is intended to highlight the key components of cash flow during the period and aid comparison between businesses. The accounting standard sets out the required structure for the cash flow statement and the minimum level of disclosure.

Exemption for small companies

35.3   Companies which meet the CA 1985 criteria for a small company (see Chapter 8) are exempt from the requirement to include a cash flow statement in their accounts. In line with the other CA 1985 provisions for small companies, the exemption is not available to the following, even if they meet the size criteria:

— public companies;

— banking companies, insurance companies and other entities with permission under Part 4 of FSMA 2000 to carry on one or more regulated activities; and

— members of a group containing any of the above entities.

Unincorporated entities which meet the small company size criteria set out in CA 1985 are also exempt from the requirement to include a cash flow statement in their accounts. Despite the exemption in FRS 1, the Financial Reporting Standards for Smaller Entities (FRSSE) encourages the inclusion of a cash flow statement in the accounts of a small company, although it does not formally require this (see 8.32).

Exemption for subsidiary undertakings

35.4   The original FRS 1 included an exemption for wholly-owned subsidiaries, subject to stringent requirements set out in the standard. When the standard was revised in 1996, the exemption was widened and the conditions simplified. A subsidiary undertaking is now exempt from the requirement to include a cash flow statement in its accounts provided that:

— 90% or more of the voting rights in the subsidiary are controlled within the group; and

— consolidated financial statements including the subsidiary are publicly available.

Exemption for specialised businesses

35.5   Certain specialised businesses, such as mutual assurance companies, pension funds and open-ended investment funds (subject to certain conditions) are also exempt from the requirements of FRS 1.

Statement on availability of exemption

35.6   Where a company is exempt from the requirement to include a cash flow statement in its annual accounts, there is no requirement in the standard for this fact to be disclosed. However, it is best practice to include a brief note explaining the position. This is usually included in the note on accounting policies.

Example 35.1 – Exemption statement: small company

The company is exempt from the requirement to prepare a cash flow statement under FRS 1 as it meets the qualifying conditions for a small company set out in CA 1985 ss 246, 247.

Example 35.2 – Exemption statement: subsidiary undertaking

The company is exempt from the requirement to prepare a cash flow statement under FRS 1 as it is a subsidiary undertaking and 90% or more of its voting rights are controlled within the group. The company is included in the consolidated financial statements of ABC Limited.

No cash flow transactions

35.7   Most companies with no cash flow transactions will be entitled to one of the exemptions set out in the standard (i.e. as a small company or as a subsidiary undertaking where 90% or more of the voting rights are controlled within the group). If this is not the case, the requirement to present a cash flow statement still stands and should be covered by an explanatory note:

Example 35.3 – No cash flow transactions

There were no transactions giving rise to a cash flow in either the current year or the previous year. A cash flow statement is therefore not included in these accounts.

STRUCTURE OF A CASH FLOW STATEMENT

Definitions

35.8   The standard sets out definitions of cash flow, cash, overdraft, liquid resources, and net debt for the purposes of FRS 1. A clear understanding of these definitions is important to ensure the correct treatment of items in the cash flow statement, especially where more complex financial arrangements (e.g. multi-option facilities) are involved.

— *Cash flow:* Cash flow is defined as an increase or decrease in an amount of cash.

— *Cash:* Cash is defined as cash in hand and deposits repayable on demand with any qualifying financial institution, less overdrafts from any qualifying financial institution repayable on demand. A qualifying financial institution is defined as an entity that as part of its business receives deposits or other repayable funds and grants credit for its own account.

— *Deposits:* The definition of cash goes on to clarify that deposits should be regarded as repayable on demand if:

  — they can be withdrawn at any time without notice and without penalty; or

  — if a maturity or period of notice of not more than 24 hours or one working day has been agreed.

  Deposits must be genuinely repayable on demand in order to fall within this definition. Deposit accounts that require a period of notice of more than 24 hours or one working day before withdrawal is possible will constitute investments rather than cash, and will usually be treated as liquid resources in the cash flow statement. The standard emphasises that no investments, however liquid or close to maturity, can be treated as cash. In the case of deposits which have a fixed maturity date but which may be redeemed early if required, and which may therefore appear to be repayable on demand, it will usually be necessary to review the detailed terms of the arrangement. If penalties of any sort are incurred as a result of early redemption, the balance will not meet the FRS 1 definition of a deposit.

— *Foreign currency:* The definition also clarifies that cash includes cash in hand and any relevant deposits denominated in foreign currencies.

— *Overdraft:* An overdraft is defined as a borrowing facility repayable on demand that is used by drawing on a current account with a qualifying financial institution.

— *Liquid resources:* Liquid resources are current asset investments held as readily disposable stores of value. The definition goes on to define a readily disposable investment as one that can be disposed of by the reporting entity without curtailing or disrupting its business and which is:

—   readily convertible into known amounts of cash at or close to its carrying amount; or

—   traded in an active market (which is defined in the standard as 'a market of sufficient depth to absorb the investment held without a significant effect on the price.

Depending on the circumstances, items such as short-term deposits, loan stock, equity investments and government securities might all be classed as liquid resources.

The standard requires each entity to explain in the accounts which items it treats as liquid resources in the cash flow statement, and also any changes in its policy. FRS 4 'Capital instruments' includes an explanatory section on the maturity of debt (see 26.16), which may be helpful in assessing the maturity date of more complex financial arrangements and thus in establishing the appropriate treatment of these transactions within the cash flow statement. For accounting periods beginning on or after 1 January 2005, most of FRS 4 is superseded by FRS 25 'Financial Instruments: Disclosure and Presentation' which includes updated guidance on the maturity of debt and the related presentation of liabilities (see Chapter 26).

Standard headings

35.9   The cash flow statement should show inflows and outflows of cash, analysed under the following standard headings:

—   operating activities;

—   dividends from joint ventures and associates;

— returns on investments and servicing of finance;

— taxation;

— capital expenditure and financial investment;

— acquisitions and disposals;

— equity dividends paid;

— management of liquid resources; and

— financing.

The first seven headings must be shown in the order set out above. Cash flows relating to the management of liquid resources and financing can be combined under one heading provided that:

— the cash flows relating to the management of liquid resources and financing are shown separately; and

— separate sub-totals for each are given in the cash flow statement.

Analysis of each heading

35.10   Only the total for each heading needs to be given on the face of the cash flow statement. The standard specifies which items should be included under each heading and a more detailed analysis of the individual categories of cash inflows and outflows within each heading should be given in the notes to the cash flow statement. The analysis of each heading may be given in more detail than is suggested in the standard and any items not specifically covered in the standard should be included under the most appropriate heading.

Reporting of cash inflows and outflows

35.11   The standard requires the cash flow statement to cover all the cash inflows and outflows of the reporting entity. Conversely, transactions which do not result in a flow of cash (for instance, the inception of a finance lease) should not be reported in the cash flow statement but may nevertheless require disclosure in the notes. The classification of cash flows in the statement should reflect the underlying substance of the transaction that gives rise to the cash flow.

Gross or net disclosure?

35.12   Cash inflows and outflows should normally be shown gross, except in the case of cash flows relating to operating activities. Certain cash flows relating to the management of liquid resources or financing may be netted against each other where:

— they relate in substance to a single financing transaction; or

— they arise from rollover or reissue facilities.

Continuing and discontinued operations

35.13   Where the profit and loss account includes an analysis between continuing, discontinued and acquired operations in accordance with the requirements of FRS 3 'Reporting Financial Performance' (see Chapter 9), it will usually be appropriate for the cash flow in respect of operating activities to be analysed in a similar way. However, this analysis is not a specific requirement of either FRS 1 or FRS 3, although FRS 1 encourages the disclosure where appropriate. Some of the illustrative examples in FRS 1 show the separate presentation of cash flows relating to continuing and discontinued operations.

Exceptional items and cash flows

35.14   Cash flows relating to exceptional items should be shown under the appropriate standard heading, but where necessary additional information should be given in a note to enable a reader of the accounts to understand the cash effect of any exceptional items. The disclosure should also explain the relationship between the cash flows and the exceptional item shown in the profit and loss account or related notes. The same principal applies in the case of extraordinary items, but in practice these are now very rare under the requirements of FRS 3 'Reporting Financial Performance'. If an exceptional cash flow arises during the year but there is no related exceptional item requiring disclosure in the profit and loss account or related notes, sufficient detail should be given to explain the nature and cause of the exceptional cash flow.

Totals

35.15   Provided that the prescribed order of headings is followed, totals and sub-totals can be drawn at any point in the cash flow statement. All of the examples given in FRS 1 show the increase or decrease in cash as the residual value on the cash flow statement, but sub-totals are drawn at various points within the statement.

Reconciliations

35.16   The following reconciliations with profit and loss account and balance sheet figures must be given in the notes to the accounts:

—   operating profit (which will usually be profit before interest) must be reconciled with the net cash flow from operating activities; and

—   the movement in cash during the period must be reconciled with the movement in net debt, and changes in net debt during the period should be analysed in sufficient detail to allow the components of net debt to be identified in the opening and closing balance sheets.

These reconciliations are considered in more detail in 35.35–35.40 below. The reconciliations can be presented adjoining the cash flow statement or in the notes to the accounts. However, the reconciliations are not part of the cash flow statement and, where one or both of the reconciliations are presented alongside the statement, the standard requires each reconciliation to be clearly headed and separated from the cash flow statement itself.

Need to present comparatives

35.17 Comparative figures are required for each item within the cash flow statement and the related notes, except for the note analysing changes in the balances making up net debt and certain disclosures required in group accounts. Headings will also be needed for any items which appeared in the previous year's statement but which do not feature in the current year. If there are no cash flows in the current year, but cash flows arose in the previous year, a full cash flow statement will be required to present the information for the previous year. If there are no cash flows in either the current year or the previous year, the requirements of FRS 1 can be met by a narrative note as explained in 35.7 above.

Material non-cash transactions

35.18 Material transactions during the year which have no cash flow effect should be disclosed in a note to the cash flow statement if this is necessary to enable a reader of the accounts to understand the underlying transaction. For instance, this might include:

— the issue of shares as part of the purchase consideration in an acquisition;

— the inception of a significant finance lease (SSAP 21 'Accounting for leases and hire purchase contracts' requires a finance lease to be accounted for by recording a 'loan' from the lessor and the purchase of the asset, but these aspects of the transaction do not give rise to an actual cash flow – the only cash flows for the lessee are the rental payments under the lease); and

— a major asset exchange.

Illustrative examples

35.19 The standard includes four illustrative examples of cash flow statements and the related reconciliations, covering the following entities:

— an individual company;

— a group;

— a bank; and

— an insurance company.

The example for an individual company illustrates the presentation of both reconciliations adjoining the cash flow statement. The example for a group presents the reconciliation of net cash flow to movement in net debt adjoining the cash flow statement, but gives the reconciliation of operating profit to operating cash flow in the notes. Appendix III to the FRSSE includes an example of a cash flow statement for a small company (see also 8.32).

NET CASH FLOW FROM OPERATING ACTIVITIES

Alternative disclosure methods

35.20   Cash flows from operating activities are the cash effects of all the transactions that arise from or relate to the company's operating and trading activities. The results of these activities will be included within operating profit in the profit and loss account. The standard permits operating cash flows to be shown on the direct or the indirect method. The direct method shows the following cash receipts and cash payments relating to operating activities:

—   receipts from customers;

—   payments to suppliers;

—   payments to and on behalf of employees; and

—   other cash payments

resulting in an aggregate net cash flow from operating activities. Very few companies choose to present operating cash flow information in this way, probably because of the increased work and analysis required to obtain the relevant details. The reconciliation of operating profit to operating cash flow must still be given. The indirect method is by far the most common presentation, beginning with operating profit and adjusting for non-cash charges and credits to the profit and loss account, to arrive at the net cash flow from operating activities.

Provisions

35.21   The standard emphasises that operating item cash flows which relate to provisions should be included in operating cash flow, even if the provision was not originally charged against operating profit. For example, the costs of a fundamental restructuring are required by paragraph 20 of FRS 3 'Reporting Financial Performance' to be charged in the profit and loss account below operating profit – when the payments are subsequently made, the cash outflows in respect of operating items (e.g. redundancy payments) will need to be reported within cash flow from operating activities, even though the related redundancy costs were not charged against operating profit.

VAT and similar taxes

35.22   In most cases, cash flows will be shown net of VAT in the cash flow statement. The net movement in the amount payable to or receivable from Customs and Excise in respect of VAT should normally be included as part of the cash flow from operating activities, unless another classification is more appropriate (this is likely to be rare in practice). If the VAT is irrecoverable, cash flows should be shown gross (i.e. including the related VAT). If this is impractical for any reason (and it is difficult to think of a situation where this would be the case), the irrecoverable VAT should be included under the most appropriate standard heading. Other sales taxes should be treated in the same way as VAT.

RETURNS ON INVESTMENTS AND SERVICING OF FINANCE

Items to be included

35.23 Returns on investments are cash receipts resulting from the ownership of investments. Servicing of finance represents payments to providers of finance, including non-equity shareholders and minority interests, but excludes the repayment of capital and other items required by the standard to be included under other headings. The most common items in this category are:

— interest paid (including any withholding tax deducted);

— dividends paid on non-equity shares;

— dividends paid to minority interests;

— cash flows in respect of other finance costs;

— interest received (including any related tax recovered); and

— dividends received (net of any tax credits), other than those received from equity-accounted entities (see 35.29 below).

Interest paid

35.24 The standard specifically requires all interest paid to be reported in this section of the cash flow statement, even if some of it has been capitalised for accounting purposes. The interest element of any payments under finance leases should be included and, if material, may need to be shown separately. Where relevant, interest paid should be shown gross (i.e. it should include the amount of any tax deducted and paid over to the relevant tax authority). The figure required is the interest actually paid during the year. The charge in the profit and loss account will therefore need to be adjusted for any interest prepaid or accrued (i.e. included in debtors or creditors) at the end of the current and previous year.

Dividends paid

35.25 Only dividends paid to non-equity shareholders and to minority interests should be included in this section of the cash flow statement. Dividends paid to equity shareholders were previously included here as well, but the standard now requires them to be shown under a separate heading. The figure for dividends paid should exclude any tax credit.

For accounting periods beginning on or after 1 January 2005, the definitions of equity and non-equity dividends are updated in line with the requirements of FRS 25 'Financial Instruments: Disclosure and Presentation'. Consequently, dividends relating to financial instruments that are classified as liabilities should be accounted for as non-equity dividends, and dividends relating to financial instruments that are classified as equity should be accounted for as equity dividends.

Adjustments should be made for any proposed dividends included within creditors at the end of the current or previous year, to arrive at the amount actually paid in the year. However, for accounting periods beginning on or after 1 January 2005, FRS 21 'Events After the Balance Sheet Date' prohibits the recognition of proposed dividends as liabilities at the balance sheet date, and associated changes are made to the Companies Act 1985. In future, therefore, no such adjustment should be necessary when preparing a cash flow statement.

Other finance costs

35.26 Cash flows relating to other finance costs of debt and non-equity shares should also be included under this heading. For instance, this might include items such as issue costs and redemption premiums relating to debt and non-equity shares.

Interest received

35.27 Interest received should include any related withholding tax. Once again, adjustment should be made for any amounts receivable or prepaid at the end of the current and previous year, to arrive at the figure for interest actually received during the year.

Dividends received

35.28 Dividends received should be shown net of any related tax credits. Scrip dividends do not have any cash flow effect and should therefore not be included as dividends received in the cash flow statement. Adjustment should be made for any amounts receivable at the end of the current or previous year, to arrive at the amount actually received during the year.

OTHER SECTIONS OF THE STATEMENT

Joint ventures and associates

35.29 Where a company holds an investment in an associate or joint venture, only actual cash flows between the investing company and the associate or joint venture should be included in the cash flow statement. The most common item will usually be dividends paid by the associate or joint venture and the original requirements of FRS 1 on the disclosure of these items were updated by FRS 9 'Associates and Joint

Ventures'. Dividends from associates and joint ventures must now be shown as a separate item in the cash flow statement between operating activities and returns on investment and the servicing of finance. Any other cash flows between the investing company and the associate or joint venture (e.g. advances or repayment of loans) should be shown under the appropriate cash flow heading.

Taxation

35.30   This section of cash flow statement covers cash paid to and received from the relevant tax authorities in respect of the company's revenue and capital profits. It specifically *excludes*:

—   any payments and receipts relating to VAT or other sales taxes (these are discussed in 35.22 above); and

—   payments to the tax authorities in respect of income tax deducted from wages and salaries paid to employees – the gross cost of wages and salaries (i.e. before deduction of tax) is included within operating profit and operating cash flow.

The following items should be included:

—   payments in respect of corporation tax and capital gains, including purchases of certificates of tax deposit;

—   receipts from the Inland Revenue in the form of rebates or returns of overpayments, again relating to corporation tax and capital gains; and

—   in the case of group companies, any payments or receipts in respect of group relief.

Where relevant, it may be appropriate to show separately the amounts relating to UK and overseas taxation, although this is not a specific requirement under the standard.

Capital expenditure and financial investment

35.31   This section of the cash flow statement deals with cash flows relating to the acquisition or disposal of:

—   any fixed assets held by the company, other than those required by the standard to be included under the heading 'Acquisitions and disposals'; and

—   any current asset investments held by the company, other than those classified as liquid resources.

If there are no cash flows relating to investments, the heading can be shortened to 'Capital expenditure'. The following items will usually appear in this category:

—   cash paid to acquire property, plant or equipment;

—   cash received from the sale or disposal of property, plant or equipment;

— loans made by the company to other entities;

— cash received in repayment of loans made by the company to other entities;

— cash paid by the company to acquire debt instruments of other entities (other than payments forming part of an acquisition or disposal, or relating to a movement in liquid resources);

— cash received by the company from the sale of debt instruments of other entities (other than receipts forming part of an acquisition or disposal, or relating to a movement in liquid resources); and

— cash flows relating to any development costs that have been capitalised.

The amounts included should represent cash actually paid or received during the period – any amounts accrued in respect of fixed asset or investment purchases and any amounts included in debtors in respect of fixed assets and investments sold should therefore be excluded from the amounts shown in the cash flow statement. Adjustments will also need to be made to the figure for fixed asset additions during the year, as shown in the accounts, to exclude any assets acquired under finance leases or similar hire purchase arrangements. The capital element of any finance lease payments is dealt with under 'Financing' (see 35.33 below). Cash flows relating to the acquisition or disposal of:

— any trade or business; or

— an investment in any entity that is, or, as a result of the transaction, becomes, or ceases to be, a subsidiary, associate or joint venture of the reporting entity

— should be shown within the 'Acquisitions and Disposals' section of the cash flow statement.

Equity dividends paid

35.32   The amount actually paid during the year to equity shareholders in the form of dividends is now required to be shown under a separate heading in the cash flow statement. This figure should exclude any related tax credit. For accounting periods beginning on or after 1 January 2005, the definitions of equity and non-equity dividends are updated in line with the requirements of FRS 25 'Financial Instruments: Disclosure and Presentation'. Only dividends in respect of financial instruments that are classified as equity under the new standard should be accounted for as equity dividends.

Management of liquid resources

35.33   As explained in 35.8 above, each entity is required to explain what it treats as liquid resources and also any changes in its policy. Cash flows relating to liquid resources will usually include:

— payments into short-term deposits (other than those that meet the definition of cash);

— withdrawals from short-term deposits (other than those that meet the definition of cash);

— receipts from the disposal or redemption of any investments classified as liquid resources; and

— payments to acquire any investments classified as liquid resources.

Cash flows relating to the management of liquid resources can be shown under a single heading with the disclosures required under 'Financing' provided that separate sub-totals for each are given.

Financing

35.34 Financing cash flows comprise:

— receipts of principal from external providers of finance; and

— payments to external providers of finance in respect of the repayment of principal amounts of finance.

External providers of finance include shareholders. The most common items to appear here will be:

— cash received on the issue of shares or any other equity instruments;

— cash received on the issue of debentures;

— cash received on taking out loans and other long-term or short-term borrowings (other than overdrafts);

— the repayment of the amounts borrowed (other than overdrafts);

— expenses or commissions on the issue of equity shares;

— payments to acquire or redeem the company's own shares; and

— the capital element of payments under finance leases.

In the case of shares, only the proceeds of shares issued for cash should be included in the cash flow statement. Shares issued as consideration for the purchase of another business have no cash flow effect and therefore do not appear in the cash flow statement. They may, however, require disclosure as a material non-cash transaction (see 35.18 above). Only issue costs relating to equity shares will be included in this section of the cash flow statement. Issue costs relating to non-equity shares and debt instruments will normally be accounted for as finance costs under the requirements of FRS 4 'Capital Instruments'. They will therefore be shown in the cash flow statement under the heading 'Returns on investments and servicing of finance'. For accounting periods beginning on or after 1 January 2005, FRS 4 is generally superseded by FRS 25 'Financial Instruments: Disclosure and Presentation', although certain aspects of the earlier standard (principally those on the presentation and disclosure of finance costs in respect of debt) remain in place for entities that are not required to adopt FRS 26 'Financial Instruments: Measurement'. FRS 25 amends certain definitions in FRS 1 and removes the references to FRS 4 but does not change the basic accounting requirements.

RECONCILIATION OF OPERATING PROFIT TO NET CASH FLOW FROM OPERATING ACTIVITIES

Items to be shown

35.35   Regardless of whether the direct or indirect method is used, the notes to the accounts should include a reconciliation of operating profit to net cash flow from operating activities. The reconciliation should show separately the movements in stocks, debtors and creditors relating to operating activities, and any other differences between operating cash flows and profits.

Debtors and creditors

35.36   When calculating the amounts to be included for debtors and creditors it is important to exclude items within these figures that do not relate to operating activities, as these will be dealt with elsewhere in the cash flow statement. The most common items are:

—   interest accruals and prepayments;

—   accruals for expenditure on fixed assets;

—   anticipated proceeds from the sale of fixed assets, included within debtors; and

—   corporation tax payable or recoverable.

Debtors and creditors for the current and previous year therefore require careful analysis to ensure that all non-operating items are identified and excluded.

Other common reconciling items

35.37   In addition to movements in stocks, debtors and creditors, the more common reconciling items are likely to be:

—   depreciation charges;

—   profits or losses on the sale of fixed assets; and

—   certain foreign exchange items (as discussed in 35.41 below).

The aim is to adjust for all items charged or credited to the profit and loss account that have not resulted in a cash flow.

RECONCILIATION OF NET CASH FLOW TO MOVEMENT IN NET DEBT

Purpose of the reconciliation

35.38   The accounts should include a reconciliation of the movement in cash during the period with the movement in net debt. This can be presented in the notes or adjoining the cash flow statement, provided that it is clearly headed and separated from the statement itself. The main purpose of the reconciliation is to provide additional information to assist in the assessment of the entity's liquidity, solvency and financial adaptability.

Definition of net debt

35.39   Net debt is defined in the standard as:

— the borrowings of the reporting entity, which comprise:

—   debt as defined in paragraph 6 of FRS 4 'Capital Instruments' (or, for accounting periods beginning on or after 1 January 2005, capital instruments classified as liabilities in accordance with FRS 25 'Financial Instruments: Disclosure and Presentation' (see Chapter 26));

—   related derivatives; and

—   obligations under finance leases,

less

— cash and liquid resources.

If cash and liquid resources exceed borrowings, the reconciliation should refer to 'net funds' rather than 'net debt'.

Analysis of changes in net debt

35.40   The notes to the accounts should also provide an analysis of the changes in net debt during the year. Changes arising from the following should be shown separately where they are material:

— the cash flows of the entity;

— the acquisition or disposal of subsidiary undertakings;

— other non-cash changes; and

— the recognition of changes in market value and movements in exchange rates.

Sufficient detail must be given to enable a user of the accounts to identify the individual components of net debt in the opening and closing balance sheets. Possible formats for these disclosures are illustrated in the examples in FRS 1 and in the Appendix to this chapter.

FOREIGN CURRENCY TRANSLATION

Exchange differences

35.41   The treatment of foreign exchange translation differences will depend on the nature and status of the underlying transaction and where the differences have been charged or credited in the accounts. Exchange gains and losses relating to transactions settled during the period should be reflected in the cash flow statement. Exchange gains and losses relating to transactions that are unsettled at the balance sheet date should not be reflected in the cash flow statement because they will not have had a cash flow effect during the year in question. In most cases, exchange differences will be charged or credited in arriving at operating profit. If any of these exchange differences relate to non-operating items they will therefore need to be eliminated from operating cash flow and will appear as reconciling items in the reconciliation of operating profit with operating cash flow. Conversely, if exchange differences have been dealt with elsewhere in the profit and loss account, an adjustment will need to be made to bring those differences which relate to operating activities into operating cash flow. This will also be shown in the reconciliation of operating profit with operating cash flow.

Settled transactions relating to operating activities

35.42   Exchange differences that relate to operating transactions which have been settled during the period should be included in operating cash flow. If the differences have been charged or credited in arriving at operating profit, no further adjustment will be required. If the differences have not been included in operating profit, they will need to be included in the reconciliation of operating profit to operating cash flow as explained in 35.41 above.

Unsettled transactions relating to operating activities

35.43   Exchange differences that relate to operating activities but which are still outstanding at the end of the period should be excluded from operating cash flow. If these exchange differences have been charged or credited in arriving at operating profit, the unrealised element will automatically be eliminated from operating cash flow by the trade debtors and trade creditors adjustments which form part of the reconciliation between operating profit and operating cash flow. If these exchange differences have not been included in operating profit, they will need to be brought into the reconciliation of operating profit to operating cash flow (as explained in 35.41 above) so that they effectively cancel out with the trade debtors and creditors adjustments.

Interest on foreign currency borrowings

35.44   Exchange gains and losses in respect of foreign currency borrowings may be included as part of the interest charge in the profit and loss account. In calculating interest paid during the year, the normal adjustments for interest accrued or prepaid should automatically eliminate the effect of any unrealised exchange gains and losses in respect of interest. However, a separate adjustment will be needed to remove any unrealised exchange gains or losses relating to the loan itself.

Liquid resources, financing items and cash

35.45   Exchange differences that arise on the translation of liquid resources, financing items or cash should be excluded from the cash flow statement. They should be shown as movements during the year in the note reconciling the opening and closing balances of the individual components of net debt.

Hedging transactions

35.46   Cash flows that arise from hedging transactions should be reported in the same section of the cash flow statement as the transaction that is being hedged.

APPENDIX

Worked example of a cash flow statement

A1 The profit and loss account of A Ltd for the year ended 31 March 20X2

		20X2
		£
Turnover		565,750
Cost of sales		(432,500)
Gross profit		133,250
Distribution costs		(46,700)
Administrative expenses		(37,250)
Operating profit		49,300
Interest receivable		5,600
Interest payable		(13,400)
Profit on ordinary activities before tax		41,500
Taxation		(9,400)
Profit after tax for the financial year		32,100
Dividends paid and proposed:		
Equity	10,000	
Non-equity	2,000	(12,000)
Retained profit for the financial year		20,100

A2 The balance sheets of A Ltd at 31 March 20X2 and 20X1

		31 March 20X2		31 March 20X1
		£		£
Fixed assets:				
Tangible assets		130,600		110,700
Investments		36,000		10,000
		166,000		120,700
Current assets:				
Stocks	99,500		79,300	
Debtors	65,850		59,200	
Short-term deposits	3,000		1,750	
Cash at bank	7,300		3,450	
	175,650		143,700	

Creditors: due within 1 year	(164,600)		(134,250)
	11,050		9,450
	177,650		130,150
Creditors: due after more than 1 year	(85,000)		(65,000)
Provisions for liabilities and charges	(12,000)		(10,000)
Net assets	80,650		55,150
Called up share capital	29,000		25,000
Share premium account	6,000		4,600
Profit and loss account	45,650		25,550
	80,650		55,150

The following details are also relevant.

A3 Tangible fixed assets

Movements in tangible fixed assets during the year were as follows:

	£
Cost:	
Balance at 1 April 20X1	179,900
Additions in 20X1/20X2	39,300
Disposals in 20X1/20X2	(13,000)
Balance at 31 March 200X2	206,200
Depreciation:	
Balance at 1 April 20X1	69,200
Charge for 20X1/20X2	15,400
Applicable to disposals	(9,000)
Balance at 31 March 20X2	75,600
Net book value 31 March 20X2	130,600
Net book value 31 March 20X1	110,700

Additions includes an asset held under a finance lease, which was acquired at a cost of £15,350 (see A8 below).

Details of the fixed asset disposal are as follows:

	£
Cost of asset	13,000
Depreciation to date of sale	(9,000)
Net book value at date of sale	4,000
Sales proceeds	7,000
Profit on disposal	3,000

A4 Investments

On 1 September 20X1, A Ltd acquired a 15% shareholding in B Ltd at a cost of £26,000 which was paid in cash.

A5 Debtors

Debtors is made up as follows:

	20X2	20X1
	£	£
Trade debtors	54,700	51,150
Accrued interest receivable	2,250	1,700
Pre-payments	8,900	6,350
	65,850	59,200

A6 Short term deposits

	£
Movements during the year are as follows:	
Balance on deposit at 1 April 20X1	1,750
Additional amounts placed on deposit	5,500
Amounts withdrawn from deposit	(4,250)
Balance on deposit at 31 March 20X2	3,000

A7 Creditors due within one year

Creditors due within one year is made up as follows:

	20X2	*20X1*
	£	*£*
Bank overdraft	20,500	18,700
Obligations under finance leases	9,950	7,200
Trade creditors	70,300	69,550
Corporation tax	8,900	8,430
Accruals:		
Interest payable		2,150
Fixed assets		20,200
Other		25,600
Proposed dividend (equity shares)	7,000	5,000
	164,600	134,250

A8 Creditors due after more than one year

Creditors due after more than one year is made up as follows:

	20X2	*20X1*
	£	*£*
Bank loans	69,400	53,900
Obligations under finance leases	15,600	11,100
	85,000	65,000

The movement on bank loans during the year was as follows:

	£
Loans taken at 1 April 1996	53,900
New loan taken out 1996/97	15,500
Loans at 31 March 1997	69,400

Movements on finance leases during the year were as follows:

	Due within 1 year	*Due after 1 year*	*Total*
	£	*£*	*£*
Balance at 1 April 20X1	7,200	11,100	18,300
Repayments during 20X1/20X2	(8,100)	—	(8,100)
New lease of fixed asset	3,350	12,000	15,350
Transfer between categories	7,500	(7,500)	—
	9,950	15,600	25,550

A9 Provisions for liabilities and charges

Provisions for liabilities and charges is made up as follows:

	20X2 £	20X1 £
Deferred taxation	5,000	3,500
Pensions	7,000	6,500
	12,000	10,000

Movements during the year were as follows:

	Deferred tax £	Pensions £
Balance at 1 April 20X1	3,500	6,500
Charged to the profit and loss account for 20X1/20X2	1,500	500
Balance at 31 March 20X2	5,000	7,000

A10 Called up share capital and share premium

Called up share capital is made up as follows:

	20X2 £	20X1 £
At 31 March 1997:		
29,000 £1 ordinary shares	29,000	
At 31 March 1996:		
25,000 £1 ordinary shares		25,000

4,000 £1 ordinary shares were issued on 1 January 20X2 at a premium of 35p per share. The movement on the share premium account was therefore:

	£
Balance at 1 April 20X1	4,600
4,000 shares at a premium of 35p per share	1,400
Balance at 31 March 20X2	6,000

CASH FLOW STATEMENT – WORKING SHEET

Balance sheet	20X2	20X1	Movement	Operating profit	Ret on inv/ serv of fin	Taxation	Cap exp & fin'l invest	Equity dividends	Liquid resources	Financing	Cash	Total
Tangible fixed assets	130,600	110,700	19,900	15,400			(39,600)					0
							7,000					0
Investments	36,000	10,000	26,000	(3,000)			(26,000)					0
Stocks	99,500	79,300	20,200	(20,200)								0
Trade debtors	54,700	51,150	3,550	(3,550)								0
Accrued interest	2,250	1,700	550		(550)							0
Pre-payments	8,900	6,350	2,550	(2,550)								0
Short-term deposits	3,000	1,750	1,250						(1,250)			0
Cash at bank	7,300	3,450	3,850								(3,850)	0
Bank overdraft	(20,500)	(18,700)	(1,800)								1,800	0
Finance leases	(25,550)	(18,300)	(7,250)				15,350			(8,100)		0
Trade creditors	(70,300)	(69,550)	(750)	750								0
Corporation tax	(8,900)	(8,430)	(470)			470						0
Accrued interest	(2,150)	(1,970)	(180)		180							0
Fixed asset accruals	(20,200)	0	(20,200)				20,200					0
Other accruals	(25,600)	(23,400)	(2,200)	2,200								0
Proposed equity dividend	(7,000)	(5,000)	(2,000)					2,000				0
Bank loans	(69,400)	(53,900)	(15,500)							15,500		0
Deferred tax	(5,000)	(3,500)	(1,500)			1,500						0
Pension provisions	(7,000)	(6,500)	(500)	500								0
Share capital	(29,000)	(25,000)	(4,000)							4,000		0
Share premium	(6,000)	(4,600)	(1,400)							1,400		0
Profit and loss	(46,650)	(25,550)	(20,100)									(20,100)
Carried forward	0	0	0	(10,450)	(370)	1,970	(22,750)	2,000	(1,250)	12,800	(2,050)	(20,100)

Profit and loss account

	20X2	20X1	Movement	Operating profit	Ret on inv/ serv of fin	Taxation	Cap exp & fin'l invest	Equity dividends	Liquid resources	Financing	Cash	Total
Brought forward	0	0	0	(10,450)	(370)	1,970	(22,750)	2,000	(1,250)	12,800	(2,050)	(20,100)
Profit and loss account:												
Operating profit		49,300		49,300								49,300
Interest receivable		5,600			5,600							5,600
Interest payable		(13,400)			(13,400)							(13,400)
Taxation		(9,400)				(9,400)						(9,400)
Dividends:												
Equity		(10,000)						(10,000)				(10,000)
Non-equity		(2,000)			(2,000)							(2,000)
	20,100			38,850	(10,170)	(7,430)	(22,750)	(8,000)	(1,250)	12,800	(2,050)	0

Cash flow statement for the year ended 31 March 20X2

	£
Net cash inflow from operating activities (Note 1)	38,850
Returns on investment and servicing of finance (Note 2)	(10,170)
Taxation (Note 2)	(7,430)
Capital expenditure and financial investment (Note 2)	(22,750)
Equity dividends paid	(8,000)
	(9,500)
Management of liquid resources (Note 2)	(1,250)
Financing (Note 2)	12,800
Increase in cash during the period	2,050

Reconciliation of net cash flow to movement in net debt (note 3)

	£	£
Increase in cash during the period	2,050	
Cash inflow from new bank loan	(15,500)	
Cash outflow in respect of finance leases	8,100	
Cash outflow from increase liquid resources	1,250	
Change in net debt resulting from cash flows		(4,100)
New finance lease		(15,350)
Movement in net debt during the period		(19,450)
Net debt at 1 April 20X1		(85,700)
Net debt at 31 March 20X2		(105,150)

Notes to the cash flow statement

1 Reconciliation of operating profit to net cash flow

	£
Operating profit	49,300
Depreciation charge	15,400
Profit on sale of fixed assets	(3,000)
Increase in stocks	(20,200)
Increase in debtors (a)	(6,100)
Increase in creditors (b)	2,950
Increase in provisions	500
Net cash flow from operating activities	38,850

(a)   Trade debtors £3,550 + pre-payments £2,550

(b)   Trade creditors £750 + 'other' accruals £2,200

2 Gross cash flows

	£	£
Returns on investments and servicing of finance:		
Interest received	5,050	
Interest paid	(13,220)	
Non-equity dividends paid	(2,000)	
		(10,170)
Taxation:		
Corporation tax paid		(7,430)
Management of liquid resources*:		
Amounts placed on deposit	(5,500)	
Amounts withdrawn from deposit	4,250	
		(1,250)
Financing:		
Issue of ordinary share capital	5,400	
New long-term bank loan	15,500	
Repayment of capital element of finance leases	(8,100)	
		12,800

* The company classifies amounts held on short term deposit as liquid resources.

3 Analysis of changes in net debt

	1 April 20X1 £	Cash flows £	Other changes £	31 March 20X2 £
Cash at bank	3,450	3,850	—	7,300
Bank overdraft	(18,700)	(1,800)	—	(20,500)
	(15,250)	2,050	—	(13,200)
Debt due after 1 year	(53,900)	(15,500)	—	(69,400)
Finance leases	(18,300)	8,100	(15,350)	(25,550)
Short-term deposits	1,750	1,250	—	3,000
Total	(85,700)	(4,100)	(15,350)	(105,150)

4 Major non-cash transactions

During the year the company entered into a finance lease arrangement in respect of an asset with a capital value of £15,350 at the inception of the lease.

Additional working notes

B1 Interest received

	£
Accrued interest at 31 March 20X1 (see A5)	1,700
Interest receivable per profit and loss account	5,600
Accrued interest at 31 March 20X2 (see A5)	(2,250)
Interest actually received in 20X1/20X2	5,050

B2 Interest paid

	£
Accrued interest at 31 March 20X1 (see A7)	1,970
Interest receivable per profit and loss account	13,400
Accrued interest at 31 March 20X2 (see A7)	(2,150)
Interest actually received in 20X1/20X2	13,220

B3 Dividends paid

	Equity £	Non-equity £
Proposed dividend at 31 March 20X1 (see A7)	5,000	—
Dividends per profit and loss account	10,000	2,000
Proposed dividend at 31 March 20X2 (see A7)	(7,000)	—
Dividends actually paid in 20X1/20X2	8,000	2,000

B4 Corporation tax

	£	£
Tax payable at 31 March 20X1 (see A7)		8,430
Charge in profit and loss account	9,400	
Less: element relating to deferred tax (see A9)	(1,500)	
		7,900
Tax payable at 31 March 20X2 (see A7)		(8,900)
Tax actually paid in 20X1/20X2		7,430

B5 *Purchase of tangible fixed assets*

Fixed asset accruals at 31 March 20X1 (see A7)	—
Additions in 20X1/20X2 per fixed asset table (see A3)	39,300
Less: asset acquired under finance lease (see A3 and A8)	(15,350)
Fixed asset accruals at 31 March 20X2 (see A7)	(20,200)
Payments in 20X1/20X2 in respect of fixed asset purchases	3,750

Chapter 36   Other statements

STATEMENT OF TOTAL RECOGNISED GAINS AND LOSSES

Nature and purpose of the statement

36.1   Although CA 1985 requires movements on individual reserves to be disclosed each year, there is no specific requirement in company law for accounts to include a statement of total gains and losses recognised during the year. However, the general requirement for accounts to comply with applicable accounting standards means that the requirement in FRS 3 'Reporting Financial Performance' for such a statement to be presented in the accounts is effectively brought within the law. Although the major part of a company's performance is reflected in the profit and loss account, certain gains and losses are currently permitted or required to be taken directly to reserves. The most common item in this category is an unrealised gain arising on the revaluation of a fixed asset which must be taken directly to the revaluation reserve. The main purpose of the statement of total recognised gains and losses is to draw together all the gains and losses recognised in the accounts and show the total effect of these items on shareholders' funds. The statement is an additional primary statement and must be presented with the same prominence as the other primary statements (ie the profit and loss account, balance sheet and cash flow statement). It is usually presented on a separate page, alongside the profit and loss account, balance sheet and cash flow statement.

Requirement to prepare

36.2   A statement of total gains and losses must be given in every set of accounts intended to show a true and fair view of an entity's financial position and profit or loss (or income and expenditure) for the year. There is no exemption from this requirement for smaller companies. Where there are no recognised gains and losses, in either the current year or the previous year, other than those recorded in the profit and loss account, the standard requires a statement to this effect to be given immediately below the profit and loss account.

Example 36.1 – Where there are no recognised gains or losses

There were no recognised gains and losses in either the current year or the previous year, other than the profit for the year as shown in the profit and loss account.

This statement is not required if the Financial Statement for Smaller Entities (FRSSE) has been adopted (see Chapter 8).

Main items

36.3   The main items featuring in the statement will usually be:

—   profit or loss for the financial year;

—   gains and losses on the revaluation of fixed assets during the year;

—   certain impairment losses arising on fixed assets and goodwill;

—   unrealised translation differences on foreign currency net investments; and

—   tax relating to any items recognised directly in the statement of total recognised gains and losses.

Profit for the financial year

36.4   The statement will include the profit or loss for the financial year, as shown in the profit and loss account. For accounting periods beginning before 1 January 2005, this is the figure before dividends.

Gains and losses

36.5   The same gains and losses should not be recognised twice in the accounts. For instance, a surplus on the revaluation of a fixed asset, which is recognised in the accounts at the time of the revaluation, should not be recognised a second time when the asset is sold. Any profit or loss on disposal is therefore measured by reference to the revalued amount and not to original cost. Gains and losses are interpreted in line with the definitions in the ASB's 'Statement of Principles': gains are increases in ownership interest, other than those relating to contributions from owners and losses are decreases in ownership interest, other than those relating to distributions to owners'. The statement of total recognised gains and losses should therefore exclude any amounts arising from transactions with shareholders (e.g. the proceeds of share issues and dividends payable to shareholders). These are dealt with separately in the reconciliation of movements in shareholders' funds (see 36.16 below).

Goodwill

36.6   Goodwill adjustments should only be recorded as recognised gains and losses when they are reflected in the profit and loss account. This will happen where:

— goodwill is amortised over its useful economic life;

— an impairment loss is recognised in respect of the goodwill; or

— the reporting entity closes or disposes of a previously acquired business, in which case the profit or loss on closure or disposal will include any goodwill not yet amortised through the profit and loss account.

Where goodwill is accounted for in accordance with FRS 10 'Goodwill and Intangible Assets', amortisation is charged to the profit and loss account over the useful economic life of the goodwill. The goodwill is therefore treated as a recognised loss as it is amortised through the profit and loss account. The predecessor accounting standard to FRS 10 (SSAP 22 'Accounting for Goodwill') allowed two alternative accounting treatments for purchased goodwill: capitalisation and amortisation, or immediate write-off against reserves. The preferred treatment on implementing FRS 10 is for goodwill that has previously been eliminated against reserves to be reinstated to the extent that it would not have been fully written down under the requirements of the new standard. However, the ASB accepted that this would not always be practicable and included certain transitional arrangements in FRS 10, which allow the option of not reinstating the goodwill. Where a company does not reinstate goodwill and subsequently closes or disposes of a business that was previously acquired, the profit or loss on closure or disposal should include the full amount of the related goodwill, on the basis that it has not yet been amortised through the profit and loss account. The goodwill will therefore be recognised in the year of closure or disposal. The impact on reserves of goodwill that is not reinstated on implementing FRS 10 is considered in more detail in Chapter 20.

Gains and losses on revalued fixed assets

36.7   FRS 15 'Tangible Fixed Assets' requires certain gains and losses arising on the revaluation of tangible fixed assets to be recognised in the statement of total recognised gains and losses rather than in the profit and loss account. Further details of these requirements are given in Chapter 21.

Impairment of fixed assets and goodwill

36.8   FRS 11 'Impairment of Fixed Assets and Goodwill' requires certain impairment losses in respect of previously revalued assets to be recognised in the statement of total recognised gains and losses. A similar treatment applies to the reversal of such an impairment loss, provided that recognition of the reversal is permitted by the standard. The requirements of FRS 11 are considered in detail in Chapter 21.

Taxation

36.9   FRS 16 'Current Tax' requires current tax to be recognised in the profit and loss account for the period, except to the extent that it is attributable to a gain or loss that is, or has been, recognised directly in the statement of total recognised gains and losses, in which case the tax attributable should also be recognised directly in that statement. Any tax expense (or income) for the period shown in the statement of total recognised gains and losses should be analysed into:

—   UK tax; and

—   foreign tax.

Each of these should be analysed to distinguish tax estimated for the current period from any adjustments recognised in respect of prior periods. Similarly, FRS 19 'Deferred Tax' requires deferred tax to be recognised in the profit and loss account for the period, except to the extent that it is attributable to a gain or loss that is or has been recognised directly in the statement of total recognised gains and losses. In this case, the attributable deferred tax should also be recognised directly in the statement of total recognised gains and losses. The amount of deferred tax recognised directly in the statement of total recognised gains and losses should be disclosed, showing separately material amounts such as:

—   the origination and reversal of timing differences;

—   changes in tax rates and laws;

—   adjustments to deferred tax assets arising in previous periods; and

—   where relevant, changes in the amount of discount deducted in arriving at the deferred tax balance.

The requirements of FRS 16 and FRS 19, including the calculation the tax attributable to an item recognised in the statement of total recognised gains and losses, are considered in more detail in Chapter 15 and Chapter 29.

Share issue costs

36.10   The treatment of share issue costs is dealt with in FRS 4 'Capital Instruments' rather than FRS 3. For accounting periods beginning on or after 1 January 2005, FRS 4 is generally superseded by FRS 25 'Financial Instruments: Disclosure and Presentation', although similar requirements on the presentation and disclosure of transactions with shareholders apply under the new standard. On the face of it, share issue costs may appear to be a recognised loss in the year of the share issue. However, share issue costs relate directly to a transaction with share-holders and should therefore be reflected in the reconciliation of movements in shareholders' funds rather than the statement of total recognised gains and losses. This is done by including the net proceeds of the share issue (ie after deduction of the issue costs) in the reconciliation of movements in shareholders' funds.

Amounts attributable to different classes of shareholder

36.11   Where there are different classes of shareholder and the accounts recognise a material movement between the amounts attributable to each class which has no effect on total shareholders' funds, this movement will not be reflected as a gain or loss in the statement of total recognised gains and losses. FRS 3 suggests that an explanatory footnote to the statement may be appropriate in these circumstances. This situation is likely to be rare in practice.

Worked example

36.12   The following is an example of how the statement might be presented.

Example 36.2 – Statement of total recognised gains and losses

	20X2	20X1
	£	£
Profit for the financial year	32	61
Unrealised surplus on revaluation of properties (a)	—	8
Currency translation differences on foreign currency net investments (b)	7	(6)
Total gains and losses recognised since the last annual accounts	39	63

(a) This figure will represent the amount credited to the revaluation reserve in respect of revaluations undertaken during the year.

(b) This figure will represent the unrealised gain or loss arising during the year on the translation of foreign currency net investments to Sterling at the appropriate exchange rate at the end of each year.

Comparative figures

36.13   Comparative figures should be given for each item in the statement of total recognised gains and losses. Headings will also be needed for any items which appeared in the previous year's statement but which do not feature in the current year movements.

Prior period adjustments

36.14   Where a prior period adjustment is required in the accounts, the gains and losses for the previous period will need to be adjusted where appropriate. The total effect of the adjustments should also be noted at the end of the statement of total recognised gains and losses for the current year. This is because the adjustments represent gains and losses recognised in the current period even though they relate to previous periods.

Example 36.3 – Where there is a prior period adjustment

Using details from Example 36.2	20X2	20X1
	£	£
Profit for the financial year	32	61
Unrealised surplus on revaluation of properties	—	8
Currency translation differences on foreign currency net investments	7	(6)
Total recognised gains and losses relating to the year	39	63
Prior period adjustment (as explained in note 1)	(13)	
Total gains and losses recognised since the last annual accounts	26	

Full details of the prior period adjustment will need to be given elsewhere in the accounts.

Likely future developments

36.15   The ASB published FRED 22 'Revision of FRS 3: Reporting Financial Performance' in December 2000. The exposure draft puts forward some significant changes to current reporting and disclosure requirements, and reflects an agreed international approach to reporting financial performance. Under the proposals, the profit and loss account and statement of total recognised gains and losses would be replaced with a single performance statement showing all gains and losses recognised during the reporting period and relating to that period. The proposed performance statement is divided into three sections:

—   operating;

—   financing and treasury; and

—   other gains and losses.

Most gains and losses will be shown in the operating section, but items that are currently required to be shown in the statement of total recognised gains and losses will generally be reported in the other sections of the financial performance statement. FRED 22 is considered in more detail in Chapter 9.

RECONCILIATION OF MOVEMENTS IN SHAREHOLDERS' FUNDS

Changes in shareholders' funds

36.16   Although CA 1985 requires movements on share capital and individual reserves to be disclosed each year, there is no specific requirement in company law for accounts to include a reconciliation of the overall movements in shareholders' funds during the year. However, the general requirement for accounts to comply with applicable accounting standards means that the requirement in FRS 3 'Reporting Financial Performance' for such a reconciliation to be presented in the accounts is effectively brought within the law. A company's profit and loss account and statement of total recognised gains and losses summarise its performance during the year. However, there may be other changes in shareholders' funds which, because of their nature, are not required to be shown in these two statements but which might nevertheless be important in helping an accounts user understand changes in the company's financial position. The main purpose of the reconciliation of movements in shareholders' funds is to summarise and draw attention to these other changes. The note effectively pulls together the company's performance, as reflected in the profit and loss account and statement of total recognised gains and losses, and any other changes in shareholders' funds during the year. The reconciliation must be given whenever there have been movements in shareholders' funds during the year, although it is not required in accounts prepared under the FRSSE (see Chapter 8).

Presentation

36.17   The reconciliation is not one of the primary statements in the accounts, but it is intrinsically linked with the primary statements, in particular the profit and loss account and statement of total recognised gains and losses. It is therefore often presented alongside the primary statements. Alternatively it can be given within the notes to the accounts, usually alongside the notes on share capital and reserves. The standard emphasises that where the note is presented with the primary statements, it must be shown separately from the statement of total recognised gains and losses (ie the movements cannot be summarised into one statement).

Negative statement

36.18   Where there are no movements in shareholders' funds in either the current year or the previous year (for instance, because the company is dormant), there is no requirement in the standard for this fact to be disclosed in the accounts. However, a statement on the following lines is generally helpful to a user of the accounts.

Example 36.4 – Where there are no movements in the year

There were no movements in shareholders' funds in either the current year or the previous year. Consequently a reconciliation of movements in shareholders' funds is not presented as part of these accounts.

Reconciling items

36.19   The main items featuring in the reconciliation will be:

— the profit or loss for the financial year;

— other gains and losses recognised during the year; and

— other changes in shareholders' funds during the year.

The reconciliation will include the profit or loss for the financial year, as shown in the profit and loss account. For accounting periods beginning before 1 January 2005, this is the figure before dividends. Other gains and losses recognised during the year will be disclosed in detail in the statement of total recognised gains and losses. They therefore need only be shown in summarised form in the reconciliation of movements in shareholders' funds. It may be helpful to show separately in the reconciliation any particularly large items that arise only occasionally (e.g. a significant transfer to or from revaluation reserve on revaluation of a company's properties), but there is no requirement in the standard for this to be done.

Other changes in shareholders' funds

36.20   Apart from the profit for the financial year and other gains and losses shown in detail in the statement of total recognised gains and losses, the most common items to feature in the reconciliation will be transactions with shareholders, for example:

— new share capital issued during the year;

— transaction costs (net of any related tax benefit) relating to the issue of an equity instrument; and

— dividends.

FRS 4 'Capital Instruments' specifically requires share issue costs to be reflected in the reconciliation of movements in shareholders' funds rather than in the statement of total recognised gains and losses. For accounting periods beginning on or after 1 January 2005, most of FRS 4 is superseded by the presentation requirements of FRS 25 'Financial Instruments: Disclosure and Presentation'. FRS 25 specifically requires dividends on any shares that are classified as equity instruments under the standard to be accounted for directly in the reconciliation of shareholders' funds, and also requires any transaction costs relating to the issue of an equity instrument, or to the equity component of a compound instrument, to be accounted for as a deduction from equity, net of any related income tax benefit. This does not include transaction costs that are directly attributable to the acquisition of a business, which should be accounted for in accordance with FRS 6 'Acquisitions and Mergers'. The standard also requires any transaction costs accounted for as deduction from equity to be disclosed separately. This disclosure forms part of the presentation requirements of the standard and so applies in all cases for accounting periods beginning on or after 1 January 2005.

Shares issued under employee share schemes

36.21   UITF Abstract 17 considers the accounting treatment of shares awarded to employees through annual bonuses or long-term incentive schemes, and requires the cost of share awards to employees to be charged to the profit and loss account over the period to which the employee's performance relates. Where new shares are issued under an employee share scheme, the credit entry for the charge to the profit and loss account should be reported in the reconciliation of movements in shareholders' funds, not in the statement of total recognised gains and losses. This reflects the fact that the amount recognised represents proceeds from the issue of an equity instrument. The requirements of Abstract 17 are considered in more detail in Chapter 11.

Worked example

36.22   The following is an example of how the reconciliation might be presented.

Example 36.5 – Reconciliation of movements in shareholders' funds (I)

	20X2	20X1
	£	£
Profit for the financial year	32	61
Dividends	(10)	(15)
	22	46
Other recognised gains and losses (net) (a)	3	2
New equity share capital subscribed (b)	10	—
Net addition to shareholders funds	35	48
Opening shareholders funds	375	327
Closing shareholders funds	410	375

(a) This figure will represent the net effect of all gains and losses, other than the profit for the financial year, shown individually in the statement of total recognised gains and losses.

(b) This figure will represent the net proceeds of equity shares issued during the year, including any amount credited to the share premium account and after deducting any share issue costs.

Example 36.5 follows the presentation used in the illustrative example in FRS 3. However, it is equally acceptable to present the information in the following way.

Example 36.6 – Reconciliation of movements in shareholders' funds (II)

	20X2	20X1
	£	£
Opening shareholders funds	375	327
Profit for the financial year	32	61
Dividends	(10)	(15)
Other recognised gains and losses (net)	3	2
New equity share capital subscribed	10	—
Closing shareholders funds	410	375

Comparative figures

36.23   Comparative figures should be given for each item in the reconciliation of movements in shareholders' funds. Headings will also be needed for any items which appeared in the previous year's reconciliation but which do not feature in the current year movements.

Prior period adjustments

36.24   Where a prior period adjustment is required, the opening balance for shareholders' funds for the previous year will need to be adjusted for the cumulative effect of the prior period adjustment up to that date and other comparative figures within the reconciliation may need to be restated. The illustrative example in FRS 3 suggests that the adjustment to the opening balance could be dealt with in narrative form within the note.

Example 36.7– Prior period adjustment (I)

Extract from Example 36.6

	20X2	20X1
	£	£
		(restated)
Net addition to shareholders funds	35	48
Opening shareholders funds (originally 340,000 for 20X1, before prior period adjustment of 13,000)	375	327
Closing shareholders funds	410	375

Alternatively, this could be shown in columnar form.

Example 36.7 – Prior period adjustment (II)

Extract from Example 36.6

	20X2		20X1
	£	£	£
			(restated)
Net addition to shareholders funds	35		48
Opening shareholders funds:			
As previously reported		340	
Prior period adjustment		(13)	
	375		327
Closing shareholders funds	410		375

Full details of the prior period adjustment will need to be given elsewhere in the accounts.

Likely future developments

36.25 The ASB published FRED 22 'Revision of FRS 3: Reporting Financial Performance' in December 2000. The exposure draft puts forward some significant changes to current reporting and disclosure requirements, and reflects an agreed international approach to reporting financial performance. Under the proposals, the profit and loss account, and statement of total recognised gains and losses would be replaced with a single performance statement showing all gains and losses recognised during the reporting period and relating to that period. The proposed changes include the following two points:

— dividends will not be reported in the performance statement as they represent transactions with owners rather than elements of financial performance (although the exposure draft does propose that they should be shown as a memorandum item at the foot of the statement) – this represented a conflict with company law when FRED 22 was published, because CA 1985 required dividends to be reported in the profit and loss account, but the law has been amended for accounting periods beginning on or after 1 January 2005 by the *Companies Act 1985 (International Accounting Standards and Other Accounting Amendments) Regulations 2004* (SI 2004/2947) to enable companies to comply with the similar presentation requirements of FRS 25 'Financial Instruments: Disclosure and Presentation'; and

— a reconciliation of ownership interests must be given as a primary statement – this brings together the performance for the period and all other changes in ownership interests, including dividends paid and new capital contributed, and is very similar to the reconciliation of shareholders' funds currently required by FRS 3.

FRED 22 is considered in more detail in Chapter 9.

NOTE OF HISTORICAL COST PROFITS AND LOSSES

Nature and purpose of the note

36.26   There is no specific requirement in company law for a set of accounts to include a note of historical cost profits and losses. However, the general requirement for accounts to comply with applicable accounting standards means that the requirement in FRS 3 'Reporting Financial Performance' for a note of historical cost profits and losses is effectively brought within the law. FRS 3 explains that the note of historical cost profits and losses is intended to be a memorandum item which has two main purposes:

— to aid comparison between companies who are carrying assets at revalued amounts and those who are showing all assets at historical cost; and

— to enable users of the accounts to identify the profit or loss on disposal of assets on the basis of historical cost.

FRS 3 requires the note to be given whenever there is a material difference between the results shown in the profit and loss account and the results that would have been shown if historical cost accounting had been adopted throughout the accounts, although it is not required in accounts prepared under the FRSSE (see Chapter 7). The note must be given immediately below the profit and loss account or immediately below the statement of total recognised gains and losses.

Detailed disclosures

36.27   The standard requires the note to reconcile the reported profit or loss on ordinary activities before taxation to the equivalent amount under historical cost accounting, and to show the retained profit or loss for the year on the historical cost basis. In practice, the most common reconciling items will be:

— the realisation during the year of revaluation gains or losses reflected in the accounts in previous years (ie where assets revalued in previous years have been disposed of during the current year); and

— the difference between depreciation charged in the year on revalued assets and the depreciation that would have been charged if the assets had been included at historical cost.

The standard identifies two particular accounting treatments that are not to be regarded as departures from historical cost accounting for the purpose of the note on historical cost profits and losses:

— adjustments made to reflect the impact of hyper-inflation on foreign operations (dealt with in UITF 9 'Accounting for Operations in Hyper-Inflationary Economies');

— the marking of investments to market where this is established industry practice (eg in the accounts of market makers and investment dealers).

Including fixed assets at valuation

36.28 CA 1985 and accounting practice allow (but do not require) companies to include fixed assets in their accounts at valuation rather than historical cost (see Chapter 1 and Chapter 20). The result is that some companies make no use of valuations whilst others may show certain assets at valuation and others at cost. The requirement for companies who have made use of valuations in their accounts to make separate disclosure of what their results would have been if they had included all assets at historical cost is intended to make direct comparisons between companies easier.

Profits and losses on disposal of assets

36.29 Paragraph 21 of FRS 3 'Reporting Financial Performance' requires profits and losses on the disposal of assets to be accounted for:

— in the period in which the disposal occurs; and

— as the difference between net sales proceeds and the carrying value of the asset.

This means that, where an asset has been revalued for accounts purposes, any profit or loss on disposal must be based on the revalued figure rather than on historical cost. Prior to FRS 3, some companies chose to calculate the profit or loss on disposal as the difference between sales proceeds and historical cost (rather than the valuation figure) by crediting any remaining balance on the revaluation reserve to the profit and loss account. Under FRS 3, any remaining balance on the revaluation reserve, relating to the asset that has been disposed of, is transferred to the profit and loss account reserve as a reserves movement. The amount transferred between reserves in this way also appears within the note of historical cost profits and losses as it is an item that arises from the use of valuation rather than historical cost in accounting for fixed assets. In historical cost terms, this amount represents an additional gain on disposal of the asset. This gain has been recognised in the accounts in previous years (by including the asset at valuation) but is only realised when the asset is disposed of. If the relevant historical cost figures are unavailable or cannot be obtained without unreasonable expense or undue delay, FRS 3 permits the use of the earliest available values in place of actual historical cost.

Negative statement

36.30 Where there is no material difference between the actual results and the results that would have been shown on the historical cost basis, there is no requirement in the standard for this fact to be disclosed in the accounts. However, a statement on the following lines is generally helpful to a user of the accounts.

Example 36.8 – Where there is no material difference

There is no material difference between the results as disclosed in the profit and loss account and the results that would have been shown on an unmodified historical cost basis.

Where such a statement is given, it should be positioned immediately below the profit and loss account or immediately below the statement of total recognised gains and losses (ie in the same place as the note would have been given under FRS 3).

Worked example

36.31   The following is an example of how the note might be presented:

Example 36.9 – Note of historical cost profits and losses

Profit and loss account for the year ended 31 December 20X2

	20X2	20X1
	'000	'000
Turnover	820	715
Cost of sales	(727)	(595)
Gross profit	93	120
Distribution costs	(21)	(16)
Administration expenses	(20)	(18)
Operating profit	52	86
Interest payable	(7)	(6)
Profit on ordinary activities before taxation	45	80
Tax on profit on ordinary activities	(13)	(19)
Profit for the financial year	32	61

Note of historical cost profits and losses

Reported profit on ordinary activities before taxation (a)	45	80
Realisation of property revaluation gains recognised in previous years (b)	14	9
Difference between historical cost depreciation charge and actual depreciation charge based on revalued amounts (c)	5	4
Historical cost profit on ordinary activities before taxation	64	93
Historical cost profit for the financial year (d)	51	74

(a)   Profit on ordinary activities before taxation as shown in the profit and loss account.

(b)   This figure represents the balance transferred from the revaluation reserve to the profit and loss account reserve in respect of assets disposed of during the year – details have not been given for the purpose of this illustration.

(c)   This needs to be calculated separately – details have not been given for the purpose of this illustration. The example assumes that assets have increased in value as a result of the revaluation; the depreciation charge on the historical cost basis will therefore be lower than the actual charge and this reconciling item increases the profit for the year as a result.

(d) Calculated as:

Historical cost profit as shown at the end of the reconciliation	64	93
Less:		
Taxation (per profit and loss account)	(13)	(19)
	51	74

Comparative figures

36.32   Comparative figures should be given for each item in the note on historical cost profit and losses.

Prior period adjustments

36.33   Where a prior period adjustment is required, the figures in the previous note of historical cost profits and losses will need to be restated where appropriate.

Likely future developments

36.34   The ASB published FRED 22 'Revision of FRS: Reporting Financial Performance' in December 2000. The exposure draft puts forward some significant changes to current reporting and disclosure requirements, and reflects an agreed international approach to reporting financial performance. Under the proposals, the note of historical cost profits and losses currently required by FRS 3 becomes an optional disclosure. FRED 22 is considered in more detail in Chapter 9.

Chapter 37   Directors' Loans And
Other Transactions

LOANS AND RELATED ARRANGEMENTS

General prohibition on loans to directors

37.1   Section 330(2) of CA 1985 generally prohibits any company from:

(i)   making a loan to a director of the company;

(ii)   making a loan to a director of the company's holding company;

(iii)   guaranteeing a loan to a director of the company or to a director of the company's holding company;

(iv)   providing any security in connection with a loan to a director of the company or to a director of the company's holding company.

The main purpose of these provisions of the Act is to provide a safeguard against the directors abusing their position of authority within the company and effectively using the company's assets for their own interests. They are drawn sufficiently widely to ensure that the prohibition on the making of loans to directors extends to any guarantees or security that might be given by a company in connection with a loan to a director, irrespective of who makes the actual loan, and also to any indirect arrangements which the company might otherwise use to circumvent the prohibitions set out in the Act. Reference should also be made to the company's memorandum and articles of association, as these may include even wider restrictions than the Act. Special rules also apply in the case of banks and money-lending companies. These are set out in section 338 of CA 1985 but are not discussed here.

Definition of loan

37.2   The Act does not provide a definition of a loan, but in a case under the Companies Act 1948, the judge held that a dictionary definition of a loan should apply and that a loan was therefore 'a sum of money lent for a time to be returned in money or money's worth'. (*Champagne Perrier-Jouet SA v HH Finch* [1982] 3 All ER 713). This is usually taken to apply equally to the provisions of the *Companies Act 1985*. The following would normally be classed as loans and would therefore be prohibited by the Act for all companies:

(i)   a loan for the purchase of a house;

(ii)   a bridging loan;

(iii)   a loan for improvements to a house;

(iv)   a season ticket loan, if the director receives the money from the company and buys the ticket himself.

Definition of director

37.3   Under section 741(1) of CA 1985, the term 'director' includes any person occupying the position of director, by whatever name called. An individual's title within the organisation is therefore not particularly important. What matters is the role that he fulfils in practice and the responsibilities that he takes. For instance, an individual who attends board meetings, takes part in the decisions reached and votes on proposals put forward at the meeting, would usually be regarded as fulfilling the role of a director, even if he is not given the title of director. Conversely, someone may be given the title of director simply to denote a status level within the organisation, but without being given the role and responsibilities usually associated with the office of company director.

Shadow directors

37.4   The provisions of the Act on loans to directors apply equally to shadow directors. A shadow director is a person in accordance with whose directions or instructions the directors are accustomed to act. This might include, for instance, a significant shareholder who plays a major part in directing the operations of the company, but who is not technically a director.

The Act specifically provides that where the directors follow advice given by a person in a professional capacity, he/she is not to be treated as a shadow director simply on this basis. This would include professional advice given by a lawyer or an accountant. However, this does not mean that such an individual could never be classed as a shadow director. If he/she also provided other advice to the directors or was otherwise involved in managing or directing a company, they might nevertheless be regarded as a shadow director for the purposes of the Act.

Alternate directors

37.5   A company's articles of association may provide for the appointment of an alternate director to act in the absence of the full director who appoints him. The provisions of the Act relating to loans to directors are likely to apply equally to alternate directors who have acted as directors during the year. However, legal advice should be sought where alternate directors have entered into loans and similar transactions with the company.

Exception for small loans

37.6   Under section 334 of CA 1985, a company is not prohibited from making a loan to a director of the company, or to a director of the company's holding company, if the aggregate of the relevant amounts does not exceed £5,000. Section 339 of CA 1985 defines the relevant amounts that have to be aggregated when applying the exceptions set out in sections 334 as well as those in sections 335 and 337 (see 37.7 below). The relevant amounts are:

(i)   the value of the proposed transaction;

(ii)   the amount outstanding under any other transaction made under the same exception;

(iii) the value of any arrangement under section 330(6) or (7) of CA 1985 which was made under the same exception – these subsections cover the assignment to a company, or assumption by it, of rights, obligations or liabilities under a transaction which would have contravened section 330 if it had been entered into by the company.

In the case of existing transactions and arrangements, the items to be included are:

(i)   in the case of a proposed transaction for a director, transactions and arrangements made for the same director, or for any person connected with him;

(ii)   in the case of a proposed transaction for a person connected with a director, transactions and arrangements made for that director, or for any person connected with him.

Therefore, the items to be aggregated in each case are those relating to transactions and arrangements that have been entered into under the same exception and for the same director (including, where relevant, his connected persons).

Value and amount outstanding

37.7   Section 340 of CA 1985 sets out how the value of each type of transaction is determined. In the case of a loan, its value is the amount of the loan principal. In the case of an arrangement under section 330(6) or (7), its value is the value of the underlying transaction, less any amount by which the liabilities have been reduced. The amount outstanding under any transaction is the original value of the transaction, less any amount by which it has been reduced.

Groups of companies

37.8   When assessing the relevant amounts in the case of a company that is a member of a group, the following transactions and arrangements must be taken into account:

(i)   in the case of a transaction with a director of the company:

- transactions and arrangements entered into by the company; and

- transactions and arrangements entered into by any of the company's subsidiaries;

(ii)   in the case of transactions with a director of the company's holding company:

- transactions and arrangements entered into by the holding company; and

- transactions and arrangements entered into by any of the holding company's subsidiaries.

Example 37.1 – Relevant amounts in a group context

Mr Smith is a director of Company A, but is not a director of either of its subsidiaries, Company B and Company C.

Mr Brown is a director of Company B but is not a director of either Company A or Company C.

Scenario 1

Company B wishes to make a loan of £2,500 to Mr Brown. To establish whether it may do so, it must take into account any existing transactions and arrangements between itself and Mr Brown. However any transactions between:

- Mr Brown and Company A
- Mr Brown and Company C

are disregarded, as these companies are not subsidiaries of Company B.

Scenario 2

Company A wishes to make a loan of £2,500 to Mr Smith. To establish whether it may do so, it must take into account any existing transactions and arrangements between itself and Mr Smith and also between:

- Mr Smith and Company B
- Mr Smith and Company C

as these companies are subsidiaries of Company A.

Scenario 3

Company B wishes to make a loan of £2,500 to Mr Smith. To establish whether it may do so, it must take into account any existing transactions and arrangements between itself and Mr Smith and also between:

- Mr Smith and Company A
- Mr Smith and Company C.

The proposed loan is to a director of Company B's holding company and transactions with the holding company (i.e. Company A) and any of its subsidiaries must therefore also be considered.

Loan from a holding company to a director of a subsidiary

37.9   As noted in 37.1 above, a company is generally prohibited from making a loan to one of its own directors or to a director of its holding company. The Act does not, however, prohibit a holding company from making a loan to a director of one of its subsidiary companies, provided that the director is not also a director of the holding company. However, the subsidiary company is not permitted to guarantee or secure the loan in any way.

Example 37.2 – Loan to director of subsidiary

The following example uses the details from Example 37.1.

Company A is generally prohibited from making, guaranteeing or securing a loan to Mr Smith.

Company B is generally prohibited from making, guaranteeing or securing a loan to Mr Smith or to Mr Brown.

Company A is not prohibited from making, guaranteeing or securing a loan to Mr Brown.

OTHER TRANSACTIONS

Additional prohibitions for relevant companies

37.10   In the case of relevant companies, the general prohibition on loans to directors extends to other transactions and arrangements. Broadly, it is extended to cover quasi-loans and credit transactions involving directors, and loans and quasi-loans and credit transactions involving any person connected with a director of the company or with a director of the company's holding company. A relevant company is therefore also prohibited from:

(i)   making a quasi-loan to a director of the company or to a director of the company's holding company;

(ii)   making a loan or a quasi-loan to a person connected with a director of the company or with a director of the company's holding company;

(iii)   guaranteeing a loan or quasi-loan to:
- a director of the company,
- a director of the company's holding company,
- a person connected with a director of the company,
- a person connected with a director of the company's holding company;

(iv)   providing any security in connection with a loan or quasi-loan to:
- a director of the company,
- a director of the company's holding company,

- • a person connected with a director of the company,
- • a person connected with a director of the company's holding company;

(v) entering into a credit transaction as creditor for:
- • a director of the company,
- • a director of the company's holding company,
- • a person connected with a director of the company,
- • a person connected with a director of the company's holding company;

(vi) guaranteeing a credit transaction made by any other person for:
- • a director of the company,
- • a director of the company's holding company,
- • a person connected with a director of the company,
- • a person connected with a director of the company's holding company;

(vii) providing any security in connection with a credit transaction made by any other person for:
- • a director of the company,
- • a director of the company's holding company,
- • a person connected with a director of the company,
- • a person connected with a director of the company's holding company.

Definition of relevant company

37.11   A relevant company is defined in CA 1985 as:

(i)   a public company;

(ii)   a subsidiary of a public company;

(iii)   a subsidiary of a company which has another subsidiary which is a public company; or

(iv)   the holding company of a subsidiary which is a public company.

Therefore, a relevant company is essentially any member of a group which includes a public company. Any other company is a non-relevant company.

Permitted transactions for non-relevant companies

37.12   Only relevant companies are affected by the prohibition on quasi-loans and credit transactions, and the extension of the general prohibition on loans and similar transactions to those involving connected persons. Non-relevant companies are therefore permitted to:

(i)   make, guarantee or secure quasi-loans to a director of the company or of the company's holding company;

(ii)   enter into, guarantee or secure credit transactions for a director of the company or of the company's holding company;

(iii)   make, guarantee or secure loans and quasi-loans to a person connected with a director of the company or with a director of the company's holding company;

(iv)   enter into, guarantee or secure credit transactions for a person connected with a director of the company or with a director of the company's holding company.

However, when considering whether to enter into such a transaction, directors must remember that they still have an overriding fiduciary duty to act in the best interests of the company.

Individuals connected with a director

37.13   For the purposes of this part of the Act, only the following members of a director's close family are regarded as connected persons:

(i)   his spouse;

(ii)   a child or children under the age of 18 (including both legitimate and illegitimate children);

(iii)   a step-child or step-children under the age of 18.

In subsequent sections of this Chapter, these individuals are referred to as the director's immediate family. Other members of the close family (e.g. parents, brothers, sisters) and children over the age of 18 are not considered to be connected persons under the Act. However, a person who is a director of the same company in his own right is not treated as a connected person of another director, even if he meets the criteria set out above.

Body corporate connected with a director

37.14   Under section 740 of CA 1985, a body corporate includes a company incorporated in Great Britain or elsewhere. For simplicity, the term 'company' is usually used in the following sections of this Chapter, although in most cases, the Act uses the term 'body corporate'. If a director is associated with a body corporate, the body corporate is deemed to be a person connected with the director for the purposes of this part of the Act. A director is associated with a body corporate if, and only if, the director and his connected persons:

(i)   are interested in at least 20% of the nominal value of the equity share capital;

(ii)   are entitled to exercise more than 20% of the voting power at a general meeting of the body; or

(iii)   control the exercise of more than 20% of the voting power at a general meeting of the body.

The rules set out in Part I of Schedule 13 to the CA 1985 determine whether or not someone holds an interest in shares. The definition is broad and covers 'any kind of interest whatsoever'.

Interests in share capital

37.15   An interest in share capital may arise as a result of:

(i)   a direct holding of shares;

(ii)   an indirect holding of shares (e.g. where the shares are held by another company); or

(iii)   a combination of direct and indirect holdings.

In the case of an indirect holding of shares, a person is treated as being interested in the shares if a company is interested in those shares and either:

(i)   the company or its directors are accustomed to act in accordance with the person's directions or instructions; or

(ii)   the person is entitled to exercise, or control the exercise of, more than 50% of the voting power at a general meeting of the company.

The inclusion of indirect holdings in the calculations is effectively restricted by this part of the Act, in that indirect holdings that do not come within these criteria are disregarded. However, where the criteria set out in paragraph 4 of Schedule 13 to CA 1985 are met, the full amount of the indirect shareholding is included in the calculations.

Control of voting power

37.16   When assessing whether a director and his connected persons control more than 20% of the voting power of a company, shares held by another company are included in the calculation if the director in question controls that company. A director is considered to control a company (i.e. the 'second company') if:

(i)   the director and his connected persons have an interest in the share capital of the second company; and

(ii)   the interests of:

  •   the director and his connected persons; and

  •   the other directors of the second company,

  taken together amount to more than 50% of the second company's share capital; or

(iii)   the director and his connected persons, together with the other directors of the second company, are entitled to exercise, or control the exercise of, more than 50% of the voting power at a general meeting of the second company.

If a director controls the second company in this way, he is deemed to control all of the shares held by the second company in the first company (i.e. the company of which he is a director).

Company as a connected person

37.17　For the purpose of section 346(4) and (5) of CA 1985 only, which determine whether a director is associated with a body corporate:

(i)　another company with which the director is associated is not treated as being connected with him unless it is also connected with him by virtue of it being:

- a trustee of a trust, and the director or his immediate family are among the beneficiaries; or

- a partner of the director or his immediate family;

(ii)　a trustee of a trust, where the beneficiaries include (or might include) a company with which the director is associated, is not treated as connected with a director simply as a result of this connection (although it may be connected if it meets other conditions as well).

Other persons connected with a director

37.18　The following are also to be treated as persons connected with a director:

(i)　the trustee of any trust, where the beneficiaries include:

- the director,

- his spouse,

- his child (as defined above),

- a body corporate with which he is associated (as defined above);

(ii)　the trustee of a trust whose terms confer on the trustees a power that may be exercised for the benefit of those noted in (i) above (a person acting as trustee under an employee share scheme or a pension scheme is specifically excluded);

(iii)　a partner of the director or of any person connected with the director;

(iv)　a Scottish firm in which:

- the director is a partner: or

- any person connected with the director is a partner; and

(v)　a Scottish firm which has as a partner another Scottish firm in which the director, or a person connected with him, is a partner.

Complex rules

37.19　The above rules are very complex and it is easy to see that the calculations can become very complicated where a director and his immediate family hold shares in several companies, especially if there are also shareholdings between the companies. The following examples illustrate some of the rules in practice.

Example 37.3 – Who is a connected person (I)

X Ltd and Y Ltd each have equity share capital of 100 ordinary shares of £1. Mr Brown holds 45% of the shares in X Ltd and 15% of the shares in Y Ltd. X Ltd holds 60% of the shares in Y Ltd. The other shares in X Ltd and Y Ltd are held by unconnected third parties. Mr Brown is not a director of either company and has no direct involvement with either company. Mr Brown is a director of W Ltd.

The shareholding structure can therefore be summarised as follows.

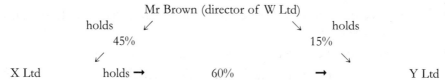

(i) Mr Brown is associated with X Ltd because he holds more than 20% of the equity share capital.

(ii) Mr Brown also appears to have an effective shareholding in Y Ltd of 42%.

His own shareholding	15%
45% x X Ltd's holding of 60% =	27%
	42%

However, under paragraph 4 of Schedule 13, Mr Brown is only treated as being interested in the shares held by X Ltd if:

(i) he is entitled to exercise, or control the exercise of more than 50% of the voting power in X Ltd; or

(ii) X Ltd or its directors act in accordance with Mr Brown's instructions.

As neither of these apply, X Ltd's shareholding in Y Ltd is disregarded. Mr Brown is therefore not associated with Y Ltd.

Therefore:

(i) any transactions between W Ltd and X Ltd will be transactions with a person connected with a director;

(ii) transactions between W Ltd and Y Ltd can be disregarded.

Example 37.4 – Who is a connected person (II)

X Ltd and Y Ltd each have equity share capital of 100 ordinary shares of £1. Mr Brown holds 60% of the shares of X Ltd and 12% of the shares of Y Ltd. X Ltd holds 10% of the shares in Y Ltd. The other shares in X Ltd and Y Ltd are held by unconnected third parties. Mr Brown is not a director of either company and has no direct involvement with either company. Mr Brown is a director of W Ltd. The shareholding structure can therefore be summarised as follows.

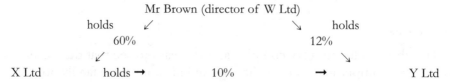

(i) Mr Brown is associated with X Ltd because he holds more than 20% of the equity share capital. He also exercises more than 50% of the voting power.

(ii) Mr Brown appears to have an effective shareholding in Y Ltd of 18%.

His own shareholding	12%
60% x X Ltds holding of 10% =	6%
	18%

However, Mr Brown is entitled to exercise more than 50% of the voting power in X Ltd. As a result he is treated as being interested in the whole of X Ltd's shareholding in Y Ltd. This gives him an effective shareholding of 22% in Y Ltd (i.e. his own shareholding of 12% plus X Ltd's shareholding of 10%). Mr Brown is therefore also associated with Y Ltd.

Therefore:

(i) any transactions between W Ltd and X Ltd will be transactions with a person connected with a director;

(ii) transactions between W Ltd and Y Ltd will be transactions with a person connected with a director.

Example 37.5 – Who is a connected person (III)

The share capital of M Ltd is as follows: 100 Ordinary 'A' shares of £1, which carry 10 votes each and 600 Ordinary 'B' shares of £1, which carry 1 vote each. Mr Black owns 90% of the 'A' shares in M Ltd. Mrs Black owns 5% of the 'B' shares in M Ltd. Unconnected third parties hold the remaining 'A' and 'B' shares. S Ltd has share capital of 100 ordinary shares of £1; M Ltd holds 23% of the shares in S Ltd. Mr Black is not a director of either company and has no direct involvement with either company. Mr Black is a director of T Ltd.

(i) Mr Black's interest in the equity share capital of M Ltd is:

Shares held by Mr Black – 90 A shares	90
Shares held by Mrs Black – 30 B shares	30
(i.e. 5% x 600 shares)	
	120

This represents only 17.1% of the total equity share capital of £700. However, in terms of voting power, Mr Black holds:

90 shares at 10 votes per share	900
30 shares at 1 vote per share	30
	930

The total voting power is 1,000 + 600 = 1,600. Mr Black therefore holds 58.1% of the voting power in M Ltd. Mr Black is therefore associated with M Ltd.

(ii) M Ltd holds 23% of the share capital (and also the voting power) in S Ltd. Mr Black is interested in shares in M Ltd and he and his connected persons control more than 50% of the voting power. Mr Black is therefore considered to control M Ltd. As a result, he is also considered to control all of the shares that M Ltd holds in S Ltd (i.e. 23%). Mr Black is therefore also associated with S Ltd.

Therefore:

(i) any transactions between T Ltd and M Ltd will be transactions with a person connected with a director;

(ii) transactions between T Ltd and S Ltd will be transactions with a person connected with a director.

Inter-group loans

37.20   Under section 333 of CA 1985, where a relevant company is a member of a group, it is not prohibited from making, guaranteeing or securing a loan to another member of the group simply because a director of one group company is associated with another group company. A member of a group of companies may therefore make a loan to another member of the same group even if the receiving company is connected with a director of the lending company under the rules in the *Companies Act 1985*.

Quasi-loans

37.21   A quasi-loan is a transaction between two parties (the creditor and the borrower) where the creditor:

(i)   pays otherwise than in pursuance of an agreement, or agrees to pay, a sum on behalf of the borrower; or

(ii)   reimburses otherwise than in pursuance of an agreement, or agrees to reimburse, expenditure incurred by the borrower;

and the transaction takes place:

(i)   on terms that the borrower will reimburse the creditor; or

(ii)   on terms that a person will reimburse the creditor on the borrower's behalf; or

(iii)   in circumstances giving rise to a liability on the borrower to reimburse the creditor; or

(iv)   in circumstances giving rise to a liability on another person to reimburse the creditor on behalf of the borrower.

The following are examples of quasi-loans.

(i)   The purchase of any goods or services through the company, where the company becomes liable to pay the supplier and is subsequently reimbursed by the director. The liability arises at the time that the goods are delivered or the services are provided, not when the invoice is received.

(ii)   Personal use of a company credit card by the director, where the company settles the liability and the director subsequently reimburses the company. The director effectively commits the company when he signs the credit slip, and the quasi-loan arises at this point rather than when the bill is received from the credit card company.

(iii)   A season ticket loan, if the company buys the ticket on behalf of the director and the director makes subsequent repayments, either in cash or by deduction from his salary.

(iv)   Any personal costs paid by the company and subsequently reimbursed by the director (e.g. the cost of travel arrangements for his wife if she accompanies him on a business trip).

Special rules on quasi-loans apply in the case of banks and money-lending companies. These are set out in section 338 of CA 1985 but are not discussed here.

Exception for short-term quasi-loans

37.22   A relevant company is not prohibited from making a quasi-loan to a director, or to a director of the company's holding company, if:

(i)   the director, or a person on his behalf, is required by the terms of the quasi-loan to reimburse the expenditure within two months of when it is incurred; and

(ii)   the aggregate of:

- the amount of that quasi-loan, and
- the amount outstanding under each relevant quasi-loan,

is not more than £5,000 – in effect, a director must not have more than £5,000 outstanding in quasi-loans at any one time for this exception to apply.

For this purpose, a relevant quasi-loan is a quasi-loan made to the same director:

(i)   by the company or its subsidiary; or

(ii)   in the case of a quasi-loan to a director of the company's holding company, by the company, its subsidiary or any other subsidiary of the holding company.

The exception relates only to quasi-loans made by a relevant company to a director of the company or of the company's holding company. It does not extend to any guarantee or security connected with a quasi-loan to a director or any quasi-loan to a person connected with a director. Therefore, any guarantee and security in respect of a quasi-loan and all quasi-loans to connected persons are prohibited.

Value of a quasi-loan

37.23   The value of a quasi-loan is the maximum amount which the recipient of the quasi-loan is liable to reimburse to the creditor. The amount outstanding under a quasi-loan is its original value, less any amount by which it has been reduced.

Inter-group quasi-loans

37.24   Where a relevant company is a member of a group, it is not prohibited from making, guaranteeing or securing a quasi-loan to another member of the group simply because a director of one group company is associated with another group company.

Credit transactions

37.25   A credit transaction is a transaction under which one party (the creditor):

(i)   supplies goods under a hire purchase agreement or a conditional sale agreement;

(ii)   sells land under a hire purchase agreement or a conditional sale agreement;

(iii)   leases or hires goods in return for periodical payments;

(iv)   leases or hires land in return for periodical payments;

(v)   otherwise supplies goods or services on the understanding that payment is to be deferred;

(vi)   otherwise disposes of land on the understanding that payment is to be deferred.

A credit transaction is therefore a transaction where full payment is deferred in some way rather than taking place when the transaction is completed. Most transactions in the ordinary course of business will be credit transactions, as settlement is often due after a period of 30 days.

Exception for minor credit transactions

37.26   However, a relevant company is not prohibited from entering into a credit transaction for a director or a connected person, or guaranteeing or securing such a transaction, if the aggregate of the relevant amounts is not more than £10,000.

Value of a credit transaction

37.27   The value of a credit transaction is the price that could reasonably be expected to be obtained for the respective goods, services or land if they had been supplied in the ordinary course of business and on the same terms (apart from price) as they are supplied in the transaction under consideration, in other words, the price that would normally be obtained in an arm's length transaction. The amount outstanding under a credit transaction is its original value, less any amount by which it has been reduced.

Business transactions

37.28   A relevant company is not prohibited from entering into a credit transaction for a director or a connected person, or guaranteeing or securing such a transaction, if:

(i)   the company enters the transaction in the ordinary course of business; and

(ii)   the value and terms of the transaction are not more favourable than those which the company could reasonably be expected to offer to a person of similar financial standing who was not connected with the company.

There is no financial limit on the transactions that may be entered into under this exception.

Funding of directors' expenditure

37.29   Section 330 of CA 1985 does not prohibit a company from providing a director with funds to meet expenses incurred, or to be incurred, by him to enable him to carry out his duties as a director of the company, provided that:

(i)   the director's actions have the prior approval of the company at a general meeting at which the following are disclosed:

- the purpose of the expenditure,

- the amount of the funds provided by the company,

- the extent of the company's liability under any connected transaction; or

(ii)   the actions are carried out on the condition that, if the approval of the company is not given at the next general meeting, the director will repay the loan and discharge any liability under the transaction within six months from the end of the meeting; and

(ii)   in the case of a relevant company, the aggregate of the relevant amounts does not exceed £20,000 (there is no limit in the case of a non-relevant company).

It should be noted that this exception applies only to funds provided to the company's own directors. Funds provided to a director of the company's holding company are not covered.

This exception appears to permit a certain level and type of loan, quasi-loan and credit transactions, and related guarantee or security arrangements, in both relevant and non-relevant companies, provided that the specific requirements of the Act are followed. For instance, it is possible that a relevant company may be permitted to make a bridging loan of up to £20,000 to a director, if the director is moving house to enable him to carry out his duties more effectively and thus to benefit the company, provided that all the other conditions in section 337 are met. However, it would be advisable to take appropriate legal advice before making such a loan.

Directors' business expenditure

37.30   It is usually accepted that sums advanced to directors to cover expenses genuinely incurred on the company's business are not caught by section 330 of CA 1985. This is mainly because the director has no liability to reimburse the company in these circumstances. A company may therefore make available to a director advances and floats (in the form of sterling, foreign currency, traveller's cheques etc.) for genuine business expenditure, provided that the amounts advanced are not excessive when compared with the level of expenditure incurred and that it is clearly intended that the expenses incurred will be borne by the company. The use of a company credit card to settle genuine business expenditure should also not give rise to problems. Difficulties only arise when such cards are used by a director to meet his own personal expenditure.

Transactions between a subsidiary and its holding company

37.31   The following transactions between a subsidiary and its holding company are specifically excepted from the prohibitions set out in section 330 of the Act :

(i)   a company making a loan or quasi-loan to its holding company;

(ii)   a company giving a guarantee or providing security in respect of a loan or quasi-loan made by any person to its holding company;

(iii)   a company entering into a credit transaction for its holding company;

(iv)   a company guaranteeing or providing security for a credit transaction made by another company for its holding company.

Other prohibited transactions and arrangements

37.32   The provisions of CA 1985 are specifically extended to cover any indirect arrangement under which a company might otherwise be able to avoid the prohibitions set out in the Act.

Assignment or assumption of rights

37.33   Section 330(6) of CA 1985 prohibits a company from arranging:

(i)   an assignment to the company of any rights, obligations or liabilities under a transaction that would have contravened the Act if it had been entered into by the company;

(ii)   the assumption by the company of any rights, obligations or liabilities under a transaction that would have contravened the Act if it had been entered into by the company.

For instance, this would prevent a company from arranging for a bank to make a loan to a director, with the agreement that the company takes over the loan at a later date and makes the repayments.

Indirect arrangements

37.34   In a similar vein, section 330(7) of CA 1985 prevents a company from becoming involved in any arrangement under which:

(i) another person enters a transaction which would have contravened the Act if it had been entered into by the company; and

(ii) the other person obtains, or is to obtain, as part of the arrangement, any benefit from:

- the company,
- the company's holding company,
- a subsidiary of the company,
- a subsidiary of the company's holding company.

For instance, this would probably prohibit:

(i) a transaction where a company arranges to make a deposit with a bank, in return for which the bank makes a loan of a similar amount to a director;

(ii) an arrangement where one company makes loans to the directors of another company in return for a reciprocal arrangement for its own directors to receive loans from the other company.

Value of transactions and arrangements

37.35   Under section 340 of CA 1985, the value of an arrangement covered by section 330(6) and (7) is the value of the underlying transaction less any amount by which the related liabilities have been reduced. The value of a guarantee or security is the amount guaranteed or secured. The value of other transactions or arrangements is the price that could reasonably be expected to be obtained for the respective goods, services or land if they had been supplied in the ordinary course of business and on the same terms (apart from price) as they are supplied in the transaction under consideration – in other words, the price that would normally be obtained in an arm's length transaction. If the value of any transaction or arrangement covered by section 330 cannot be expressed as a specific sum of money, for whatever reason, its value is deemed to exceed £100,000.

DISCLOSURE OF LOANS AND SIMILAR TRANSACTIONS WITH DIRECTORS

General disclosure requirement

37.36   There is a general requirement under CA 1985 for details of all loans and similar transactions with directors to be disclosed in the notes to the accounts, regardless of whether the transaction is permitted or prohibited under the Act. The requirement to disclose is set out in section 232 of the Act and the detailed disclosure requirements are covered in Part II of Schedule 6 to the Act.

Individuals covered and details to be disclosed

37.37   The disclosure must cover all transactions involving anyone who was:

(i)   a director of the company at any time during the financial year;

(ii)   a director of the company's holding company at any time during the financial year;

(iii) a person connected with such a director.

The required details (see 37.40 below) must be given for:

(i)   each individual transaction or arrangement of the kind described in section 330 of CA 1985 entered into by the company or its subsidiary; and

(ii)   any agreement by the company or its subsidiary to enter into such a transaction or arrangement involving these individuals.

In the case of non-relevant companies, therefore, quasi-loans and credit transactions with directors, and loans and similar transactions with connected persons, are still disclosable under the Act, even though the company is permitted to enter into such transactions. This is emphasised in paragraph 19(a) of Schedule 6 to CA 1985.

Transactions prior to appointment as director

37.38   The fact that a transaction may have taken place before an individual became a director of the company will not exempt it from disclosure, if there was an amount outstanding under that transaction during the year in which he was appointed. For example, if an employee receives a loan from the company at the beginning of the year and subsequently becomes a director of the company half way through the year, details of the loan will be disclosable in the accounts for that year, even if repayment is made before the end of the year. Similar considerations apply when individuals become connected persons.

Transactions with a subsidiary company

37.39   The disclosure requirements also apply irrespective of whether or not the company that entered into the transaction or arrangement was a subsidiary at the time that it did so.

Example 37.6 – Disclosure where company becomes a subsidiary

Mr Jones is a director of Company A but not of Company B, which is totally independent of Company A. Company B makes a loan of £25,000 to Mr Jones on 1 June 1996. The loan is still outstanding on 1 October 1996 when Company B becomes a subsidiary of Company A. The loan therefore becomes disclosable in the accounts of both companies:

(i) in the accounts of Company B as a loan made by the company to a director of its holding company;

(ii) in the accounts of Company A as a loan made to a director of the company by a subsidiary.

Disclosure is required even though Company B was not a subsidiary of Company A at the time the loan was actually made.

Details required for all loans and similar transactions

37.40   The following details must generally be given for each individual loan, quasi-loan, credit transaction or related arrangement:

(i)   a statement that the transaction or arrangement was made or existed during the year;

(ii)   the name of the director involved, or the name of the connected person involved and the name of the director with whom he is connected; and

(iii)   the principal terms of the transaction, arrangement or agreement.

The expression 'principal terms' is not defined in the Act, but it is usually considered to include:

(i)   the arrangements for repayment of any money advanced (e.g. whether the sum is repayable on an agreed date or in instalments over an agreed period);

(ii)   the rate of interest charged on the amount outstanding;

(iii)   any guarantees or security given in respect of the loan or transaction.

Other disclosures may be appropriate, depending on the actual terms of the transactions or arrangement.

Additional details in respect of loans

37.41   In the case of a loan, or an arrangement or agreement relating to a loan, the following information must be given:

(i)   the amount of the liability in respect of principal and interest at the beginning of the year and at the end of the year;

(ii)   the maximum amount of the liability in respect of principal and interest during the year;

(iii)   the amount of any interest due which has not been paid;

(iv)   the amount of any provision arising from the failure, or expected failure, of the borrower to:

- repay all or part of the loan; or
- pay all or part of the interest.

Comprehensive details are therefore required for each loan, including the maximum amount of any loan that existed during the year, even if there was no outstanding balance on the loan at either the beginning or the end of the year (i.e. the loan was both taken out and repaid in full during the year).

Additional details in respect of guarantees and securities

37.42   In the case of a guarantee or security, or an arrangement relating to a guarantee or security, the following information must be given:

(i)   the amount of the company's liability under the guarantee or security at the beginning of the year and at the end of the year;

(ii)   the maximum amount for which the company may become liable;

(iii)   any amount paid and any liability incurred by the company, or by its subsidiary, in fulfilling the guarantee or discharging the security, including any loss incurred as a result of the guarantee or security being enforced.

Additional details in respect of quasi-loans and credit transactions

37.43   In the case of a quasi-loan or credit transaction, or an arrangement or agreement relating to a quasi-loan or credit transaction, the following information must be given:

(i)   the value of the transaction or arrangement; or

(ii)   the value of the transaction or arrangement to which the agreement relates.

The disclosures in respect of quasi-loans and credit transactions are therefore much more limited than those for loans, guarantees and securities, but the original value of the quasi-loan or credit transaction remains disclosable each year until the amount is settled in full. It will therefore need to be given in the year in which the director makes the full, or final, repayment or reimbursement. In the case of quasi-loans and credit transactions, the amounts outstanding at the beginning and end of the year do not have to be disclosed, although companies may give this information voluntarily and will probably wish to do so if the year-end balance is significantly lower than the value of the transaction (i.e. if the director has repaid or reimbursed some or all of the amount originally owed).

General exemptions from disclosure

37.44   The disclosure requirements set out above do not apply to the following:

(i)   a transaction, agreement or arrangement between two companies, where a director of one company (or of its subsidiary or holding company) is interested only because he is a director of the second company – this exempts many inter-group transactions that would otherwise have been disclosable;

(ii)   contracts of service (but not contracts for services) between the company and its own directors or a director of its holding company, or between a director of the company and a subsidiary;

(iii)   a transaction which was not entered into during the year and did not exist at any time during the year – this means that previous transactions (i.e. those that were entered into and settled in earlier years) do not continue to be disclosable after they have been settled.

There is also no requirement to give comparative figures for the disclosures.

De minimis limit for credit transactions

37.45 Credit transactions and related guarantees, securities and arrangements are not disclosable if the aggregate of the values of each transaction or arrangement for that director and his connected persons, after allowing for any reduction of the liabilities, does not exceed £5,000. Therefore, if an individual director, together with any connected person, does not have more than £5,000 outstanding in respect of credit transactions, the details do not have to be disclosed.

However, there is no de minimis disclosure exemption in respect of loans and quasi-loans, and related guarantees, securities and arrangements, to directors and connected persons.

Loans and quasi-loans between group companies

37.46 The disclosure requirements of paragraph 22(c)–(f) of Schedule 6 to CA 1985 do not apply where a company makes a loan or quasi-loan, or a related arrangement, to or for another company and:

(i) the lending company is a wholly-owned subsidiary of the recipient company; or

(ii) the recipient company is a wholly-owned subsidiary of the lending company; or

(iii) the lending company and the recipient company are both wholly- owned subsidiaries of the same holding company; and

(iv) the details would otherwise only be disclosable in the accounts of the lending company because one of its directors was associated with the recipient company during the relevant period.

The disclosures required by paragraph 22(2)(a) and (b) and 22(1) still have to be given:

(i) the fact that the transaction or arrangement was made or existed during the year;

(ii) the name of the director and, where relevant, connected person involved;

(iii) the principal terms.

It should also be noted that credit transactions between group companies are not included in the exemption and so remain fully disclosable.

Directors' duty to disclose

37.47 Under section 317 of CA 1985, a director has a duty to disclose to the other directors any interest that he has in a contract, arrangement or agreement with the company. Loans, quasi-loans and credit transactions are specifically included in this duty to disclose.

Company procedures

37.48 It is important that companies establish procedures to identify disclosable, and potentially illegal, transactions as they arise. Directors must also understand the rules set out in CA 1985 so that they are able to recognise potentially illegal and disclosable transactions. Company procedures might include detailed guidance in the form of a directors' code of conduct to ensure that disclosable transactions are kept to a minimum. For instance, clear rules on the way in which company credit cards are to be used and how any purchases through the company should be dealt with, may help to ensure that disclosable transactions do not arise (e.g. if purchases through the company are paid for by the director when the order is raised, the transaction should not come within the definition of a quasi-loan). Some companies also find it useful to develop a standard form for completion each year requiring every director:

(i) to give formal confirmation that he has not been involved in any illegal or disclosable transactions or arrangements with the company; or

(ii) to provide the relevant information.

Such a form could include a summary of the requirements of the Act to remind the director of the importance of these matters.

Audit requirements

37.49 As part of the annual audit, the auditors will need to review the disclosures in the accounts and consider whether they comply with the requirements of the Act. Under section 237(4) of CA 1985, if the disclosure requirements of Schedule 6 have not been complied with, the auditors must include the relevant details in their audit report, so far as they are reasonably able to do so. The Act does not set out any requirement for the accounts to disclose whether a particular transaction or arrangement between a director and the company is legal or not and there is similarly no requirement for the auditors to express an opinion on the legality of any items disclosed in their audit report as a result of section 237(4). They are simply required to make good any deficiencies in the disclosures required by Schedule 6.

Loans to officers of the company

37.50 A company must also disclose in its annual accounts details of loans and similar transactions involving other officers of the company. Once again, there are separate rules in respect of banks and money-lending companies, which are not considered here. There are, however, no prohibitions on making loans to officers of the company (provided that they are not directors). The detailed disclosure requirements are set out in Part III of Schedule 6. All definitions are the same as those for loans to and similar transactions with directors.

Definition of officer

37.51   The Act does not provide very much guidance on who is to be regarded as an officer of a company. The definition of an officer in section 744 simply states that it 'includes a director, manager or secretary'. The usual interpretation is that all senior managers should be treated as officers. For some purposes of CA 1985, the auditor is regarded as an officer of the company and this probably applies in respect of loans to officers. However, professional and ethical standards would usually prevent an auditor from entering into such transactions with the company.

Items covered by the disclosure requirements

37.52   The disclosures cover the following to officers:

(i)   loans;

(ii)   quasi-loans;

(iii)   credit transactions.

In each case, guarantees and securities, arrangements of the kind described in section 330(6) and (7), and agreements to enter into any of these transactions, are covered by the disclosure requirements. The transactions to be disclosed are those entered into by the company or by its subsidiary for persons who were officers of the company at any time during the year. Transactions involving directors and shadow directors are specifically excluded as they are subject to separate disclosure requirements. For each of the categories set out above, the accounts must show:

(i)   the aggregate amounts outstanding at the end of the year in respect of transactions and arrangements with officers; and

(ii)   the number of officers involved.

Details do not have to be disclosed individually for each officer, and there is no requirement for comparative figures to be given.

De minimis limit

37.53   If an officer is involved in relevant transactions and arrangements but the aggregate amount outstanding at the end of the year for that officer does not exceed £2,500, no disclosure is required. The total of loans, quasi-loans, credit transactions and related arrangements involving that individual must therefore be no more than £2,500 for the exemption to apply.

Audit requirements

37.54   As with loans and transactions involving directors, if the disclosure requirements of Schedule 6 in respect of officers have not been complied with, the
auditors must include the relevant details in their audit report, so far as they are
reasonably able to do so.

DISCLOSURE OF OTHER TRANSACTIONS WITH DIRECTORS

Legal requirements on disclosure

37.55   In addition to the specific disclosure requirements in respect of loans and
quasi-loans to, and credit transactions with, directors, the Act generally requires
detailed disclosure of any other transaction or arrangement in which a director had
a material interest, either directly or indirectly. The details must be disclosed in the
notes to the accounts and must include:

(i)   a statement that the transaction or arrangement was made or existed during
the year;

(ii)   the name of the person involved and, where that person is a connected
person, the name of the director with whom he is connected;

(iii)   the name of the director who has a material interest and the nature of that
interest;

(iv)   the value of the transaction or arrangement; and

(v)   the principal terms of the transaction or arrangement.

The above details must be given individually for each relevant transaction during the
year, but comparative figures do not have to be given. The transactions covered by
these disclosure requirements are those entered into by the company or by its
subsidiary for:

(i)   any person who was a director of the company, or a director of the
company's holding company, at any time during the financial year; and

(ii)   any person who was connected with a director of the company or with a
director of the company's holding company.

Purpose of the disclosures

37.56   The main purpose of the disclosure requirements is to ensure that shareholders and other interested parties are able to identify whether any of the
company's directors are gaining a particular personal benefit or advantage from their
relationship with the company. The disclosures also draw to the attention of the
shareholders and other users of the accounts the possibility that the results and
financial state of affairs of the company may have been affected by material
transactions between the company and the directors.

Material interest

37.57   Only those transactions in which a director has a material interest are disclosable and one of the most difficult aspects of this part of the legislation over the years has been the interpretation of what constitutes a material interest. For the purpose of the disclosure requirements, a director is treated as being interested in any transaction between:

(i)   the company and the director;

(ii)   the company's holding company and the director;

(iii) the company and a person connected with the director;

(iv)   the company's holding company and a person connected with the director.

However, the Act does not go on to define or provide any guidance on what constitutes a material interest.

Disclosure under FRS 8

37.58   Under the requirements of FRS 8 'Related Party Disclosures', the accounts must disclose information on transactions between the reporting entity and any related parties. Directors and shadow directors of the reporting entity (as defined in the Act) are specifically included in the definition of related parties in paragraph 2.5(b) of the standard. Members of a director's close family (which is defined as 'family members, or members of the same household, who may be expected to influence or be influenced by the individual in their dealings with the reporting entity') are also presumed to be related parties for the purposes of FRS 8. The detailed disclosure requirements of FRS 8 are summarised at 37.66 below and are considered in more detail in Chapter 18.

Director's duty to disclose

37.59   Under section 317, a director has a duty to disclose to the other directors any interest that he has in a contract, arrangement or agreement with the company. The disclosure should be made at a meeting of the directors. Where appropriate it can take the form of a general disclosure that he is:

(i)   a member of a specified company or firm and should be regarded as interested in any contract with that company or firm after the date of disclosure; or

(ii)   connected with a specified individual and should be regarded as interested in any contract with that individual after the date of disclosure.

In companies where there is only one director disclosure must still be made. Disclosure should be in writing if no one else is present but may be given verbally if another person (e.g. the company secretary) is present at the meeting. Shadow directors have a similar duty to disclose, but in this case the disclosure must be given in writing. The company's memorandum and articles of association may include additional provisions on contracts and transactions in which directors have an interest.

Board's opinion on materiality

37.60   The Act does provide that an interest is not material for disclosure purposes if the board of directors of the company are of the opinion that it is not material. It is generally accepted that the board must act in good faith in reaching this decision, although the Act makes no specific statement on this. In this context, the board is defined as 'the directors of the company preparing the accounts, or a majority of those directors, but excluding in either case the director whose interest it is'. Therefore, the director involved in the transaction may not take part in the board's decision on whether or not the transaction is material for disclosure purposes. The Act does not mention recording such a decision, but in practice it should be formally minuted. If the board have not specifically considered whether a particular transaction is material, it should not be presumed that the transaction is not material for disclosure purposes.

Interpretation of 'material'

37.61   Two approaches to the interpretation of 'material' have developed over the years, usually described as:

(i)   the relevant view; and

(ii)   the substantive view.

Under the relevant view, 'material' is interpreted as being relevant to those for whom the information is provided (i.e. the shareholders and other users of the accounts). In other words, if knowledge of a particular transaction might influence the decisions taken by the shareholders or users of the accounts, or be of specific interest to them, then it should be considered material for disclosure purposes. Under the substantive view, 'material' is interpreted as relating to the extent of the director's interest in the transaction. If his interest is substantial, then the transaction is material. This approach has also been known as the 'Mars bar' approach, in that the example commonly used to illustrate the substantive view is where a director purchases and eats a bar of chocolate in the company canteen, although the transaction itself is small, the director's interest in it is substantial and therefore the transaction is material (and potentially disclosable).

Over the years, there have been differing views on which of these should be the preferred approach. One of the major problems with the substantive view is that a small interest in a major contract could be considered insubstantial and therefore not material (e.g. a commission of 1% payable to a director on a company contract worth £1 million), whereas many people would consider that this is precisely the sort of arrangement shareholders would probably want to know about. The balance has tended, therefore, to favour the relevant view.

FRS 8 approach to materiality

37.62   The ASB has also adopted the relevant view in FRS 8 'Related Party Disclosures' but nevertheless preserves some element of the substantive view in respect of transactions involving directors:

'Transactions are material when their disclosure might reasonably be expected to influence decisions made by users of general purpose financial statements. The materiality of related party transactions is to be judged, not only in terms of their significance to the reporting entity, but also in relation to the other related party when that party is:

(a)   a director, key manager or other individual in a position to influence, or accountable for stewardship of, the reporting entity; or

(b)   a member of the close family of any individual mentioned above; or

(c)   an entity controlled by any individual mentioned in (a) or (b) above.'

Further consideration of FRS 8 can be found in Chapter 18.

Legal advice

37.63   This remains a difficult area and if there is any doubt over whether a transaction involving a director, or a person connected with him, is a transaction in which the director has a material interest, legal advice should be taken.

Value and amount outstanding

37.64   The value of a transaction or arrangement is the price that could reasonably be expected to be obtained for the respective goods, services or land if they had been supplied in the ordinary course of business and on the same terms (apart from price) as they are supplied in the transaction under consideration – in other words, the price that would normally be obtained in an arm's length transaction. If the value of any transaction or arrangement cannot be expressed as a specific sum of money, for whatever reason, its value is deemed to exceed £100,000. The amount outstanding under a transaction is the original value of the transaction, less any amount by which it has been reduced.

Principal terms

37.65   The expression 'principal terms' is not defined in the Act, but it is usually considered to include:

(i) any guarantees or security given in respect of the transaction;

(ii) the arrangements for repayment of any money advanced (e.g. whether the sum is repayable on an agreed date or in instalments over an agreed period);

(iii) the rate of interest charged on any amount outstanding.

Other disclosures may be appropriate, depending on the actual terms of the transactions or arrangement (e.g. the rate of commission earned by the director in respect of a contract involving the company).

FRS 8 disclosure requirements

37.66   FRS 8 'Related Party Disclosures' specifies that the details disclosed in respect of transactions with related parties should include the following, some of which (in the case of transactions with directors) duplicate the specific disclosures required by the Act:

(i) the names of the transacting parties;

(ii) a description of the relationship between the related parties;

(iii) a description of the transaction;

(iv) the amounts involved;

(v) any other elements of the transaction necessary for an understanding of the financial statements;

(vi) the amounts due to or from the related parties at the balance sheet date and any provisions for doubtful debts due from related parties at that date;

(vii) any amounts written off during the period in respect of debts due to or from related parties.

FRS 8 does permit some aggregation of similar transactions with the same related party. However, in the case of directors, individual disclosure of each relevant transaction is required under the Act.

Audit requirements

37.67   As part of the annual audit, the auditors will review the disclosures in the accounts and consider whether they comply with the requirements of the Act and FRS 8. Under section 237(4) of CA 1985, if the disclosure requirements of Schedule 6 have not been complied with, the auditors must include the relevant details in their audit report, so far as they are reasonably able to do so.

Exceptions to the general disclosure requirement

37.68   A transaction between two companies does not need to be disclosed under the provisions of the Act if the director's interest in the contract only arises from the fact that he is a director of both of the companies involved in the transaction, and a contract of service does not need to be disclosed under these provisions if it is between the company and:

(i)   one of the company's directors; or

(ii)   a director of the company's holding company; or

(iii)   a director of any of the company's subsidiaries.

However, this exception does not cover a contract 'for' services between a director and the company. There is also no requirement to disclose a transaction or arrangement which was not entered into during the year and did not exist at any time during the year. This means that previous transactions (i.e. those that were entered into and settled in earlier years) do not continue to be disclosable after they have been settled.

Inter-group transactions in the ordinary course of business

37.69   Two amendments were introduced to the original legislation to try and avoid the need for excessive disclosure in the accounts of companies within the same group which regularly enter into transactions with each other. However, the drafting of the second amendment in particular is confusing and it is not entirely clear, therefore, that this provision does actually fulfil its objective. Firstly, a transaction or arrangement does not require disclosure under the provisions of the Act if:

(i)   companies which are members of the same group enter into a transaction or arrangement in the ordinary course of business; and

(ii)   the terms of the transaction are not less favourable to those companies than they would normally have been if a director had not had a material interest in the transaction or arrangement.

Therefore, any transaction between group companies which is at arm's length should not require disclosure under the provisions of the Act on transactions in which a director has a material interest. Secondly, a transaction or arrangement does not require disclosure where:

(i)   the company is a member of a group; and

(ii)   either the company is a wholly-owned subsidiary, or no member of the group (other than the company or its subsidiary) was a party to the transaction or arrangement; and

(iii)   the director in question was associated with the company at some time during the financial year; and

(iv)   the material interest of the director would not have arisen if he had not been associated with the company during the financial year.

The main difficulties in understanding this paragraph relate to the fact that it seems to suggest that the underlying disclosure requirement arises from the fact that the director is associated with the reporting company. In fact it arises from his association with the other entity (i.e. the one with which the reporting company is entering a transaction). The stated intention of this provision is to exempt from disclosure any transaction between group companies which would otherwise be disclosable because a director has a material interest in the transaction, except in the case of a transaction involving a company where there are minority interests (when disclosure would continue to be required).

De minimis exception

37.70   Disclosure is not required where the value of:

(i)   each transaction or arrangement between the director and the company (or a subsidiary) during the year in which the director had a material interest (either directly or indirectly); and

(ii)   the amount outstanding in respect of each such transaction or arrangement made in earlier years

did not at any time during the financial year exceed, in aggregate, £1,000 or, if more, did not exceed the lower of £5,000, or 1% of the company's net assets at the end of the financial year. For the purposes of this paragraph, a company's net assets are the aggregate of its assets, less the aggregate of its liabilities, including any provisions for liabilities.

Chapter 38   Directors' Report

REQUIREMENT TO PREPARE A DIRECTORS' REPORT

Company law requirements

38.1   Under CA 1985 s 234, the directors of a company are required to prepare a report for each financial year and to file this with the registrar. The report must be approved by the board of directors and signed on behalf of the board by a director or by the company secretary. The name of the signatory must also be clearly stated on the report. This is usually done by typing the relevant name under the actual signature. The copy filed with the registrar must include a manuscript signature. There are penalties for failure to comply with these requirements. A small company is permitted to prepare and file a modified directors' report – this is considered in more detail in Chapter 8.

For accounting periods beginning on or after 1 April 2005, a new section 234 is inserted into CA 1985 by the *Companies Act 1985 (Operating and Financial Review and Directors' Report etc.) Regulations 2005* (SI 2005/1011). This changes some of the detailed content of the annual directors' report and also creates new reporting responsibilities for auditors in relation to the report. The sections below summarise the requirements that apply for accounting periods beginning on or after 1 April 2005, with the most recent changes highlighted where appropriate.

Detailed contents of the report

38.2   The detailed contents of the report are set out partly in section 234 and 234ZZA of CA 1985 and partly in Schedule 7 to that Act. Schedule 7 is also updated by the *Companies Act 1985 (Operating and Financial Review and Directors' Report etc.) Regulations 2005*. Under the new section 234, the report must include:

(i)   a business review; and

(ii)   if the company's accounts have been audited, a statement by the directors on the disclosure of information to the auditors.

For accounting periods beginning before 1 April 2005, the legislation required the report to include a fair review of the development of the business during the year and its position at the year end, but did not specify the content of the review in the same level of detail as under the new provisions.

If the company is a parent company, the directors' report must be a consolidated report, covering the parent company and the subsidiary undertakings that have been consolidated into the group accounts. In this case the legislation allows greater emphasis to be given to matters that are significant to the group as a whole. A quoted company that is required to prepare a statutory Operating and Financial Review (OFR) need not repeat relevant information that is given in the OFR, even if it would otherwise need to be disclosed in the directors' report. The preparation of a statutory OFR is considered in Chapter 39.

In addition to the business review, the directors' report must include:

—   the amount recommended by the directors to be paid as dividend;

—   the principal activities of the company (and any subsidiaries) during the course of the year and any significant changes in activities;

—   an indication of likely future developments in the business;

—   an indication of any activities in the field of research and development;

—   an indication of the existence of any branches of the company outside the UK;

—   particulars of any important events affecting the company (and any subsidiaries) which have occurred since the end of the financial year;

—   details of any substantial difference between the market values and the balance sheet values of interests in land held by the company or its subsidiaries;

—   the names of all those who were directors of the company at any time during the year;

—   the interests (ie the number or amount) held by each director (or a member of his immediate family) in the shares or debentures of the company or of any other body corporate in the same group – the details to be given are:

        —   all interests held at the end of the financial year;

        —   for each director with interests at the end of the year, his interests at the beginning of the year or at the time of his appointment if this took place during the year;

— the number or amount of any rights to subscribe for shares or debentures in the company or another body corporate in the same group which were granted to or exercised by each director (or a member of his immediate family) during the year;

— where the company has made any donation to a registered party or to any other EU political organisation or incurred any EU political expenditure and the aggregate of all such donations and expenditure exceeded £200, the directors' report must include:

— the name of each registered party or other political organisation to whom a donation was made;

— the total amount donated to each party or organisation during the financial year; and

— the total amount of any other EU political expenditure during the financial year;

(wholly-owned subsidiaries of a company incorporated in Great Britain are exempt from this disclosure requirement);

— if the company has made any contribution to a non-EU political party, the directors' report must state the amount of the contribution or, where relevant, the total amount of the contributions made during the financial year (wholly-owned subsidiaries of a company incorporated in Great Britain are exempt from this disclosure requirement);

— if the company has given more than £200 for charitable purposes, the directors' report must state the amount given during the financial year for each charitable purpose (wholly-owned subsidiaries of a company incorporated in Great Britain are exempt from this disclosure requirement);

— where the average number of employees exceeds 250, a statement on the company's policy on employment, training, career development and promotion of disabled persons;

— where the average number of employees exceeds 250, a statement on the action taken during the year to introduce, maintain or develop arrangements to:

— provide employees with relevant information;

— consult employees or their representatives on a regular basis;

— encourage employee involvement in the company's performance; and

— achieve a common awareness among employees of financial and economic factors affecting the company's performance;

— in the case of a company that was at any time during the year a public company or a member of a group headed by a public company, and did not qualify as small or medium-sized in relation to that year, details of the company's policy and practice on payment of creditors.

— for accounting periods beginning on or after 1 January 2005, unless the information is not material for an assessment of the company's (or group's) assets, liabilities, financial position and results, an indication of:

  — the entity's financial risk management objectives and policies, including the policy for hedging if hedge accounting is used; and

  — the entity's exposure to price risk, credit risk, liquidity risk and cash flow risk.

— for reports approved on or after 6 April 2005, if the company has provided a qualifying third party indemnity for the benefit of a director of the company or of an associated company during the year, or if such a provision is in force at the time of approval of the report, a statement of that fact.

Additional disclosures in respect of shares

38.3   Where shares in the company have been:

— purchased by the company;

— acquired by the company by forfeiture or surrender in lieu of forfeiture;

— acquired by the company otherwise than for valuable consideration under CA 1985 s 143(3);

— acquired by another person with financial assistance from the company, and the company has a beneficial interest in the shares;

— acquired by a nominee of the company without direct or indirect financial assistance from the company, and the company has a beneficial interest in the shares; and

— made subject to lien or charge taken by the company under CA 1985 s 150 or Companies Consolidation (Consequential Provisions) Act 1985 s 6(3),

the following disclosures must be given in the directors' report for that year:

— the number and nominal value of shares purchased, the aggregate amount of consideration paid and the reasons for the purchase;

— the number and nominal value of shares acquired or charged during the year in the way explained above;

— the maximum number and nominal value of shares held by the company or the other person during the year, having been acquired or charged in the way explained above;

— the number and nominal value of shares disposed of by the company or by the other person, or cancelled by the company during the year, having been acquired or charged as explained above;

— where shares have been disposed of as set out above, the amount or value of the consideration;

— in each of these cases, the percentage of the called-up share capital represented by the shares in question; and

— where shares have been charged, the amount of the charge in each case.

Consistency with accounts

38.4 A number of the disclosures in the directors' report relate to information that also has to be given within the accounts. Care must be taken to ensure that details disclosed in the report are consistent with any related information given in the accounts. The following sections in this chapter include consideration of the areas where problems are most likely to arise.

For accounting periods beginning on or after 1 April 2005, the auditors' report must include an opinion on whether the information in the directors' report is consistent with the related financial statements. The Auditing Practices Board (APB) is in the process of developing guidance for auditors on this new reporting responsibility. For accounting periods beginning before 1 April 2005, the auditors were expected to review the directors' report for consistency with the accounts but were only required to report on any unresolved inconsistencies.

BUSINESS REVIEW

Accounting periods before 1 April 2005

38.5 For accounting periods beginning before 1 April 2005, CA 1985 requires the directors' report to include a fair review of the development of the business during the year, and the position at the year end, although companies that qualify as small are exempt from this requirement. The legislation does not specify a format or indicate what should be covered in the review. Directors are, therefore, free to decide how to present their review. The main purpose of this section of the report is to provide additional information to explain the details shown in the profit and loss account and balance sheet and help the reader to understand the results for the year and the year end position. This section of the report should normally include a brief review of the results for the year and should identify any significant features or changes during the year that need to be drawn to the attention of the members. It is impossible to give a standard list of items to include in the review as the contents must inevitably vary year by year and business by business. The impact of certain events will also be different, depending on the circumstances of the company. However, the types of issue that might require explanation include:

(i) significant changes in income or expenditure compared with the previous year;

(ii) significant changes in balance sheet headings compared with the previous year

(iii) any major restructuring or reorganisation that has taken place during the year;

(iv) significant changes in employee levels during the year;

(v) major changes in economic or market conditions during the year;

(vi) major changes in the company's products or services during the year; and

(vii) the impact of foreign currency exchange gains or losses.

The legislation requires the review to be 'fair', and the wording and tone of the commentary should be consistent with the result shown in the profit and loss account. For instance, it will usually be inappropriate to present a very positive statement about the success of the business in the year if the profit and loss account shows reduced turnover and a loss for the year. The report should also be balanced and cover both good and bad aspects of the year. Some or all of the information may be set out in a separate section of the annual accounts (for instance, in a Chairman's statement or a separate operating and financial review statement). This is acceptable, provided that the directors' report includes a cross-reference to show where the additional detailed information is presented.

Changes from 1 April 2005

38.6 For accounting periods beginning on or after 1 April 2005, the requirement for the directors' report to include a business review becomes more prescriptive. The new legislation requires the directors' report to include a balanced and comprehensive review of the business and details of the principal risks and uncertainties that it faces. The review must include:

(i) explanations of amounts included in the financial statements for the year;

(ii) analysis using key financial performance indicators; and

(iii) where appropriate, analysis using other key performance indicators (KPIs), particularly on environmental and employee issues.

Where a parent company prepares group accounts, the review should cover the company and the subsidiary undertakings included in the consolidation.

Section 246(4) of CA 1985 has been amended to maintain the existing position for small companies, whereby they are exempt from including a business review in the directors' report, and also to exempt medium-sized companies from the requirement to disclose non-financial KPIs, although they are still expected to provide relevant financial indicators. Companies within the size criteria which do not generally qualify for SME exemptions because they are part of an ineligible group are also granted the same directors' report exemptions as other smaller companies from 1 April 2005, although they continue to be ineligible for other accounts exemptions.

RS 1 'Operating and Financial Review'

38.7 Whilst the ASB's Reporting Standard 1 (RS 1) 'Operating and Financial Review' is designed primarily for quoted companies preparing a statutory OFR, it may nevertheless provide useful guidance for other companies on issues that may need to be discussed in the business review section of the directors' report, including the particular strengths and weaknesses of the business, the uncertainties that underlie it and the key risks that it faces. In particular, RS 1 includes detailed guidance on the use of KPIs in business reviews. Further information on RS 1 can be found in Chapter 39.

For accounting periods beginning before 1 April 2005, similar guidance was set out in the ASB's non-mandatory Statement 'Operating and Financial Review'. Whilst this was also directed primarily at listed and larger entities, and did not cover KPIs in detail, it did include guidance on describing the business, its objectives and its strategy in order to put the directors' discussion of performance and financial position into context and an encouragement for directors to:

(i) recognise that business objectives and performance may encompass both financial and non-financial measures (eg corporate social responsibility);

(ii) explain the strengths and resources of the business, especially any which are not reflected in the balance sheet, together with action taken to enhance future performance; and

(iii) highlight the accounting policies which are key to understanding the entity's performance and financial position, focusing in particular on any policies to which the results are particularly sensitive.

PROPOSED DIVIDEND

Consistency with accounts

38.8 The directors' report must disclose the amount that the directors recommend to be paid as the dividend for the year. For accounting periods beginning before 1 January 2005, this figure will also appear on the face of the profit and loss account or should be disclosed in an analysis of the profit and loss account dividends figure in the notes to the accounts. For accounting periods beginning on or after 1 January 2005, proposed dividends will not be reflected in the accounts but details are required to be shown in the notes to the accounts (see Chapter 16). The details given in the directors' report must therefore be consistent with those shown in the accounts, regardless of whether the amounts are actually reflected in the profit and loss account and balance sheet or are simply disclosed in the notes to the accounts.

Normal practice on disclosure

38.9 In practice, the details given in the directors' report usually cover both the interim dividend (if any) paid during the course of the year and the proposed final dividend, making up the total dividend for the year. Details are usually given for both the dividend per share and total amount payable.

Example 38.1

An interim dividend of ... p per share amounting to £... was paid on [date]. The directors propose a final dividend of ... p per share amounting to £..., making a total dividend for the year of ... p per share.

PRINCIPAL ACTIVITIES

Statement on activities

38.10   CA 1985 requires a statement on the principal activities of the company and any subsidiaries during the year, and also on any changes in activities that have taken place during the year. The wording of the Act suggests that information on subsidiaries is required even if the company is exempt from the requirement to prepare group accounts.

Consistency with accounts

38.11   The principal activities identified in the directors' report disclosures should normally be consistent with any segmental information given in the accounts under CA 1985 or under SSAP 25 'Segmental Reporting' (see Chapter 18). Similarly, any changes in principal activities during the year disclosed in the directors' report should normally be consistent with the disclosures on continuing, acquired and discontinued operations, as required by FRS 3 'Reporting Financial Performance' (see Chapter 9). It is, however, possible that the sale or cessation of part of the business may need to be disclosed as a change in activities in the directors' report, even though it does not meet the FRS 3 criteria for a discontinued operation.

LIKELY FUTURE DEVELOPMENTS

Form and contents

38.12   CA 1985 requires the directors to give an indication of the likely future developments of the company and, where relevant, any subsidiaries. Once again, information on subsidiaries appears to be required even if the company does not have to prepare group accounts. As with the business review, the Act provides no detailed guidance on the form that this statement should take or the type of issue that should be covered and directors are therefore free to decide how best to present the information. UITF Abstract 21 'Accounting Issues Arising from the Proposed Introduction of the Euro' recommends that, where the potential impact of the introduction of the euro is likely to be significant to the reporting entity, additional information should be disclosed in the annual report and accounts. This should include an indication of the total costs likely to be incurred. The disclosures may be given in the directors' report, an operating and financial review or any other statement published as part of the annual report. Smaller entities who adopt the Financial Reporting Standard for Smaller Entities (FRSSE) are exempt from the detailed requirements of Abstract 21 but they are nevertheless encouraged to consider the potential issues and make disclosures where appropriate.

Guidance on wording

38.13 It is usually advisable to keep the statement fairly general in nature. The wording of the statement is a particular problem area for listed companies and those quoted on similar markets as they need to ensure that comments made by the directors cannot later be deemed to constitute a profit forecast. Whilst this is not such a problem for private companies, it is still advisable to refer only to general issues such as:

— expected economic and trading conditions in the next period;

— broad indication of expected level of activity in the next period compared with the current year;

— broad indication of management plans to deal with any expected problem areas.

It is also advisable to keep the statement relatively brief. In September 2003, the Institute of Chartered Accountants in England & Wales (ICAEW) published 'Prospective Financial Information: Guidance for UK Directors'. This is intended to encourage the publication of high quality PFI and sets out the broad principles that directors should follow, the legal and regulatory background, and detailed guidance on the preparation of specific forms of PFI. Whilst most PFI will be published in order to comply with listing and other regulatory requirements, the guidance includes a separate section on voluntary PFI, which includes relevant disclosures in a directors' report or Operating and Financial Review (OFR) on expected future developments within the business. The guidance draws heavily on the principles and supporting guidance set out in the ASB's 'Statement of principles for financial reporting'. In particular, it notes that, in order to be useful, PFI should be:

(i) understandable;

(ii) relevant;

(iii) reliable; and

(iv) comparable.

Because of the focus on the future, uncertainty will always be a key issue and disclosure of uncertainties and the related assumptions, sensitivities and alternative outcomes is therefore important. In terms of reliability, the guidance emphasises that the information should be a faithful representation of the company's strategies and plans. For PFI to be comparable, it should be capable of subsequent validation by comparison with the actual outcome in the form of published historical financial information. The document also emphasises the need to distinguish between targets and PFI and to ensure that the wording of any disclosures makes this distinction clear to users.

The ASB's Reporting Standard 1 (RS 1) 'Operating and Financial Review' (see 39.14 below) also considers the provision of prospective information in an OFR and notes that directors may want to include a statement that, even though it is provided in good faith, forward-looking information should be treated with caution in view of the surrounding uncertainties.

RESEARCH AND DEVELOPMENT

Nature of disclosures

38.14   CA 1985 requires the directors to give an indication of activities (if any) in the field of research and development. The disclosure should cover both the company and any subsidiaries, regardless of whether group accounts are prepared. The disclosures required in the directors' report should not be confused with the separate accounts disclosures under SSAP 13 'Research and Development' (see Chapter 19). The accounting standard requires the disclosure of the accounting policy adopted in respect of research and development costs, expenditure during the year and movements on any deferred development costs. The directors' report should not repeat this information, but should discuss the commercial aspects of the company's research and development activity rather than the accounting treatment adopted.

Consistency with accounts

38.15   However, it is clear that any discussion on research and development should be consistent with the accounts. On a basic level, if research and development costs are disclosed in the accounts, a discussion of the general activities would be expected in the directors' report. Similarly, if research and development activities are discussed in the directors' report, it will usually be appropriate for an accounting policy on research and development expenditure to be included in the accounts.

Form and content

38.16   CA 1985 does not give any guidance on the information to be included and the level of disclosure will clearly vary depending on the extent of the company's activities and also on how central research and development is to its overall business. For instance, more extensive disclosures would usually be expected from a pharmaceutical company than from a construction company. The discussion might include:

—   broad indication of the level and nature of research and development activity;

— explanation of any changes in the level or nature of activity during the year;

— brief comment on any specific projects undertaken during the year;

— brief comment on any particular area of expertise;

— indication of any major contacts or joint projects with other research bodies.

Research and development activities in certain fields can be particularly sensitive areas and companies will often be reluctant to make too much detail available to competitors. As CA 1985 does not specify any minimum level of disclosure, a broad indication of the work being undertaken in the field of research and development should be sufficient to meet the disclosure requirement.

POST BALANCE SHEET EVENTS

Interaction with accounting standards

38.17 The directors are required to give particulars of any important events affecting the company or its subsidiaries which have occurred since the end of the financial year. FRS 21 'Events After the Balance Sheet Date' (which is effective for accounting periods beginning on or after 1 January 2005) identifies two categories of post balance sheet event:

— adjusting events, which, if material, require an adjustment to be made to the figures in the accounts; and

— non-adjusting events, which do not require an adjustment to be made to the accounts, but which, if material, require disclosure in the notes to the accounts.

For accounting periods beginning before 1 January 2005, similar requirements were set out in SSAP 17 'Accounting for Post Balance Sheet Events'. Consequently, there appears to be some duplication with the requirement under CA 1985 for information on material post balance sheet events to be given in the directors' report. The distinction between adjusting and non-adjusting events is discussed in more detail in Chapter 34.

Disclosure of adjusting events

38.18 Neither FRS 21 nor SSAP 17 requires disclosure of adjusting events as these will have been reflected in the accounts, although disclosure as an exceptional item may be necessary if the effect on the accounts is sufficiently material. As CA 1985 does not distinguish between adjusting and non-adjusting events, the directors' report may need to give brief details of any major adjusting events and explain how these have been dealt with in the accounts. In practice, this situation is likely to be rare as most adjusting events arise from additional evidence on the value of assets and liabilities as at the year-end date and they will not usually be sufficiently material to warrant separate disclosure in the directors' report.

Disclosure of non-adjusting events

38.19   There is a major distinction between the accounting standards and CA 1985, in that both FRS 21 and SSAP 17 requires details of non-adjusting events to be disclosed in the accounts. Disclosure in the directors' report alone is not sufficient to comply with the relevant accounting standard. To avoid the unnecessary duplication of information it is acceptable to give the detailed disclosures in one location only (preferably the notes to the accounts) and include a cross-reference in the other location to show where the details can be found. If details of a post balance sheet event are disclosed separately in both the directors' report and the notes to the accounts it is important that the information given in each location is consistent.

FIXED ASSETS

Market value of land and buildings

38.20   The directors' report must include details of any material difference between the book value and the market value of any interest in land held by the company (or, where relevant, the group). Disclosure of a substantial difference between the market value and the book value of land and buildings is required if, in the opinion of the directors, the difference is of such significance that it should be drawn to the attention of the members or debenture-holders. In practice, it is advisable to disclose any material difference that arises. CA 1985 requires the difference to be stated 'with such degree of precision as is practicable'. In practice, the disclosure will often be based on a recent professional valuation of the property, although there is no formal requirement for this. Where an entity chooses to adopt a policy of valuation for some of its fixed assets, FRS 15 'Tangible Fixed Assets' now requires the valuations to be kept up to date and any significant valuation gains or losses should therefore be incorporated into the accounts, unless the transitional rules have been adopted (see Chapter 21).

Need for additional explanation

38.21   If land and buildings are included in the accounts at depreciated historical cost and the market value of the properties is significantly higher than book value, no further comment will usually be needed as there is no requirement at present for fixed assets to be included in the accounts at valuation. However, if market value is significantly lower than book value, but the directors have decided that no write-down is necessary, some additional comment will usually be required to explain why this approach is justified.

DIRECTORS AND THEIR INTERESTS

Names of directors

38.22 The requirement under CA 1985 is for the directors' report to give the names of all those who were directors of the company at any time during the year. It is usual to indicate the dates of any resignations, retirements and appointments that have taken place during the year.

Example 38.2

The following directors have held office during the year:

— A D Evans

— C B Jones (resigned 3 September 20X2)

— E L Wright (appointed 16 September 20X2)

— J T Smith

It is also usual to give details of any appointments, resignations or retirements between the year-end date and the date on which the accounts and directors' report are approved and signed, although this is not a requirement. These changes should also be noted in the following year's report as they will actually take place in the year covered by that report.

Directors' share interests

38.23 The disclosure requirements on directors' share interests are extremely complex and only the more common problem areas are considered here. In more unusual situations, reference should be made to company law publications to establish whether a particular item constitutes a disclosable interest. In certain cases, specific legal advice may be needed as the wording or meaning of CA 1985 is not always clear and opinions and interpretations may vary. The details may be given either in the directors' report or in the notes to the accounts, but most commonly they are set out in the directors' report. If the details are given in the notes to the accounts, it is helpful to include a cross-reference in the directors' report. The required information must be given for each individual director and must cover all those who were directors at the end of the year. For the purpose of these disclosure requirements, the term 'director' includes shadow directors. A shadow director is defined in CA 1985 as a person in accordance with whose directions or instructions the directors of the company are accustomed to act. However, a person will not be deemed to be a shadow director where the directors act only on advice given by him/her in a professional capacity.

Definition of 'interest'

38.24 An 'interest' in shares or debentures for the purpose of these disclosures is given the very broad definition set out in CA 1985 Sch 13 para 1, which also applies for the purposes of the duty of directors to disclose shareholdings to the company. In general terms, any interest, of any kind whatsoever, in shares and debentures constitutes a notifiable and therefore a disclosable interest for the purposes of CA 1985.

Interests at the end of the year

38.25   For each person who was a director at the end of the financial year, the directors' report or accounts must state:

— whether, at the year-end date, he/she was interested in the shares or debentures of the company; and

— whether, at the year-end date, he/she was interested in the shares or debentures of another body corporate in the same group.

The wording of the legislation requires a negative statement to be given for any individuals who were directors at the end of the financial year but did not hold interests in shares or debentures of the company, or any other company in the group. Disclosable interests are those recorded in the register of directors' interests under the requirements of CA 1985 and include interests held by a director's immediate family. In this context, a body corporate in the same group as the company means a holding company, a subsidiary company or a fellow subsidiary company. However, under the Companies (Disclosure of Directors' Interests) (Exceptions) Regulations 1985, SI 1985/802, where a company is wholly-owned by a body corporate incorporated outside Great Britain, interests in the shares or debentures of that body corporate, or any other body corporate incorporated outside Great Britain, are not notifiable or disclosable.

Interests at the beginning of the year

38.26   For each director who had disclosable interests at the end of the year, the following details must also be given:

— the name of the company (or companies) in which he/she had an interest at the end of the year;

— the number of shares in each company held at the end of the year;

— the amount of debentures of each company held at the end of the year;

— if he/she was also a director at the beginning of the year, the same details for any interests held at that time; and

— if he/she was appointed as a director during the year, the same details for any interests held at the date of appointment.

If a director is appointed on more than one occasion during a financial year, the disclosable interest is that at the time of his/her first appointment. The wording of the legislation means that there is no requirement to disclose interests held at the beginning of the year (or at the date of appointment) by a director who did not have disclosable interests at the end of the year. However, this information is often given voluntarily for completeness.

Interests held by director's immediate family

38.27   The disclosure requirements specifically cover interests in shares and debentures held by the director's immediate family. For disclosure purposes, these are deemed to be interests held by the director. In this context 'immediate family' means the director's spouse, infant children and infant step-children (ie those under the age of 18). It therefore does not include the director's parents, brothers, sisters or children over the age of 18. If any members of a director's immediate family are also directors of the company, their interests are separately disclosable and are therefore not treated as interests of the director.

Change of holding company during the year

38.28   The disclosures can be particularly complicated where there is a change of holding company during the year and the directors of a subsidiary company have disclosable interests in the shares of one or both of the holding companies. The details that need to be disclosed under CA 1985 are:

—   interests in the new holding company at the end of the year for all those who are directors at the end of the year; and

—   for the directors who have disclosable interests in the new holding company at the end of the year, the interests that they held in the former holding company at the beginning of the year or at the date of their appointment if this took place during the year.

It may be appropriate to disclose additional information to clarify the interests in different companies and any movements in those interests, but this is not strictly a requirement of CA 1985. The normal disclosure requirements apply in respect of any interests held by the directors in the shares or debentures of the subsidiary company itself. The same approach would apply to any disclosable interests in the shares or debentures of other group companies if these also change as a result of the change in holding company.

Beneficial and non-beneficial interests

38.29   It is common practice to show separately the beneficial and non-beneficial interests held by the directors, but this is not a requirement of CA 1985. However, a listed company is required by the UK Listing Rules to give this disclosure.

Options to subscribe for shares or debentures

38.30   The directors' report or notes to the accounts must also disclose details of directors' rights to subscribe for shares in or debentures of the company or any other company in the group. Rights to subscribe are notifiable interests for the purpose of the register of directors' shareholdings. As with interests in shares and debentures, options held by the director's immediate family must also be included. The following details must be given individually for each person who was a director at the end of the financial year:

— whether during the year he/she was granted any rights to subscribe for shares in or debentures of the company or any other company in the group; and

— whether during the year he exercised any rights to subscribe for shares in and debentures of the company or any other company in the group.

For each director who had disclosable interests in options at the end of the year, the following details must be given:

— the name of the company (or companies) in which he/she was granted or exercised a right to subscribe;

— the number of shares in each company in respect of which he/she was granted or exercised a right to subscribe; and

— the amount of debentures of each company in respect of which he/she was granted or exercised a right to subscribe.

The wording of the legislation requires a negative statement to be given for any directors at the end of the financial year who did not hold rights to subscribe for shares in or debentures of the company, or any other company in the group. The disclosure requirements on directors' remuneration also include certain details of options (see Chapter 17).

Cumulative details of options held

38.31   The disclosure requirements in respect of options relate solely to options granted and exercised during the year. There is no specific requirement to disclose details of total options held. There is an argument that options are covered by the broad definition of an 'interest' in shares and debentures but the wording of CA 1985 is very confusing on this point. Options to subscribe for shares and debentures may also be disclosable under the provisions of CA 1985 on arrangements in which a director has a material interest. If so, details of unexercised options granted to date would need to be disclosed in addition to options granted and exercised during the year. For accounting periods ending on or after 31 December 2002, quoted companies are also required by law to include detailed information on options held, granted to and exercised by directors in their annual directors' remuneration report (see Chapter 17).

Directors of wholly-owned subsidiaries

38.32   Where a director of a wholly-owned subsidiary is also a director of its holding company, and his interests in the shares and debentures of companies within the group (including options) will be disclosed in the directors' report of the holding company, the information is not required to be given in the directors' report of the subsidiary. In this case, it is usual to explain the situation in the directors' report of the subsidiary company.

Example 38.3

A D Evans is also a director of ... Ltd, the company's ultimate holding company, and his interests in the shares and debentures of group companies are disclosed in the directors' report of that company.

POLITICAL DONATIONS AND EXPENDITURE

Political Parties, Elections and Referendums Act 2000

38.33   Significant changes to the rules on political donations were introduced by the *Political Parties, Elections and Referendums Act 2000*, which came into effect on 16 February 2001. The new legislation is complex and wide-ranging. In the context of political donations by companies it inserts a new Part XA into CA 1985 and also amends Sch 7 paras 3–5. The new legislation broadly requires:

—   prior shareholder approval for political expenditure within the EU and for aggregate donations to EU political organisations of more than £5,000 by a company and its subsidiaries in any twelve-month period beginning with the company's 'relevant date' (see 38.34);

—   disclosure of the individual recipients, and the amounts given, where the aggregate amount of political expenditure and political donations in the EU by a company or group exceeds £200; and

—   disclosure of the aggregate amount paid or donated to non-EU political parties by a company or group (in this case there is no *de minimis* amount).

Where a payment or donation is to be made by a subsidiary, prior approval must also be obtained from the shareholders of the holding company. This is to prevent a company circumventing the approval provisions by making payments through a subsidiary. Wholly-owned subsidiaries of UK parent companies are exempt from the disclosure requirements, on the basis that the details will be given in the parent company's accounts. If the new approval requirements are not followed the directors will be personally liable to make good the amount paid or donated and to pay damages for any loss suffered by the company. In the case of non-compliance by a subsidiary, the directors of the holding company will also be personally liable.

The DTI White Paper *Company Law Reform* published in March 2005 includes proposals to increase the £200 disclosure threshold for political donations to £2,000.

Relevant date

38.34 A company's relevant date is the earlier of:

— the date of its AGM, if one is held within 12 months of 16 February 2001; or

— 16 February 2002.

Shareholder approval must be in place for any payments or donations made after the relevant date and the new disclosures must be given in the directors' report for financial years starting on or after the first anniversary of the relevant date.

Definition of EU political expenditure

38.35 The legislation defines EU political expenditure as any expenditure incurred by the company in respect of:

— the preparation, publication or dissemination of any advertising or other promotional or publicity material, of whatever nature and however published or otherwise disseminated, that at the time of publication or dissemination can reasonably be regarded as intended to affect public support for any EU political organisation;

— any activities that can reasonably be regarded as intended to affect public support for any EU political organisation; and

— any activities which can reasonably be regarded as intended to influence voters in any national or regional referendum held under the law of any EU member state.

An EU political organisation is any party registered under Political Parties, Elections and Referendums Act 2000 Pt II, any other political party participating in any elections to public office in an EU member state other than the UK, or any independent candidates at any such elections.

Definition of donations

38.36 A donation to a registered party is given a very broad definition in the legislation, covering:

— any gift of money or other property;

— any sponsorship provided;

— any subscription or fee paid for affiliation to, or membership of, the party;

— any money spent (otherwise than by or on behalf of the party) in paying for any expenses incurred directly or indirectly by the party;

— any money lent to the party, other than on commercial terms; and

— the provision of any property, services or facilities to the party (including the services of any persons) other than on commercial terms.

A subscription for membership of an EU trade association is specifically excluded from the definition of a donation. However, payments made to finance any particular activity of the association are not considered to be subscriptions.

Gifts

38.37   A gift is defined as including:

— any money or other property transferred to the party in a transaction or arrangement where the monetary value of any consideration provided by or on behalf of the party is less than the value of the money or the market value of the property transferred;

— anything that is given or transferred indirectly through a third person; and

— a bequest.

Also, anything given or transferred to any officer, member, trustee or agent of a registered party in his capacity as such (i.e. not for his own use or benefit) is to be treated as if it had been given or transferred to the party. The value of a gift is its market value or, where appropriate, the difference between its market value and the total monetary value of any consideration provided by or on behalf of the party.

Sponsorship

38.38   Sponsorship is provided to a registered party if any money or other property is transferred to the party, or to any person for the benefit of the party, and the purpose (or one of the purposes) is or can reasonably be assumed to be:

— to meet, or help the party to meet, any defined expenses incurred or to be incurred by or on behalf of the party; or

— to secure to any extent that such expenses are not incurred.

Defined expenses are those connected with:

— any conference, meeting or event organised by or on behalf of the party;

— the preparation, production or dissemination of any publication by or on behalf of the party; or

— any study or research organised by or on behalf of the party.

The following are specifically excluded from the definition of sponsorship in the legislation:

— payment of any charge for admission to a conference, meeting or event;

— payment of the purchase price of any publication (or similar charge for access to it); and

— payment for the inclusion of an advertisement in any publication, provided that this is made at the appropriate commercial rate.

The value of any sponsorship provided is the value of the money provided or, where relevant, the market value of the property transferred. The monetary value of any benefit conferred on the person providing the sponsorship is to be disregarded. Where the sponsorship provides the party with an enduring benefit that lasts for two or more financial periods of the donor company, the amount to be disclosed in the directors' report is the amount accruing to the period covered by the report – the total value donated will therefore need to be apportioned between the reporting periods covered.

Loans, services and facilities provided

38.39   The value of a donation provided in the form of a loan or of other services and facilities is the difference between:

—   the total monetary value of the consideration that would have had to be provided by or on behalf of the party if the loan, services or facilities had been provided on commercial terms; and

—   the total monetary value of any consideration actually provided by or on behalf of the party.

In determining whether a transaction has been undertaken on commercial terms, the legislation requires the assessment to take into account the total value, in monetary terms, of any consideration provided by or on behalf of the party in respect of the transaction.

Contributions to non-EU political parties

38.40   The legislation requires disclosure of the total amount contributed to non-EU political parties – there is no *de minimis* amount in this case. A non-EU political party is any political party whose activities are carried on wholly outside the member states of the EU. The legislation defines a contribution as:

—   any gift of money to the organisation, whether made directly or indirectly;

—   any subscription or other fee paid for affiliation or membership of the organisation; and

—   any money spent (other than by or on behalf of the organisation) in paying any expenses incurred directly or indirectly by the organisation.

CHARITABLE DONATIONS

Donations for charitable purposes

38.41   The directors' report must disclose the total amount given for charitable purposes by the company (and, where relevant, the group) during the financial year, unless the total given is £200 or less. Where amounts have been given for more than one charitable purpose during the year, the amount given for each purpose must be shown. The same threshold applies to both companies and groups. Wholly-owned subsidiaries of a company incorporated in Great Britain are exempt from the disclosure on the basis that the information will be shown in the directors' report of the parent company. The legislation states that the expression 'charitable purposes' means purposes that are exclusively charitable. In this case, therefore, sponsorship payments will not usually be covered by the disclosure requirements as there will usually be an element of advertising or marketing connected with them, and there will consequently be a fairly evident commercial element to the transaction. Similarly, any payments to a charity that are of a direct commercial nature (e.g. payments for services provided by the charity) will not be disclosable. Money given for charitable purposes to a person who was ordinarily resident outside the UK at the time that the gift was made, is also specifically excluded from the disclosure requirements by the legislation.

The DTI White Paper *Company Law Reform* published in March 2005 includes proposals to increase the £200 disclosure threshold for charitable donations to £2,000.

Payments via a charitable trust

38.42 Some companies make payments to a company trust, which then has discretion to make donations to individual charities. In this case the amount paid to the trust will usually be disclosable, together with brief details of its objectives.

EMPLOYEE DISCLOSURES

Scope of the disclosure requirements

38.43 The disclosure requirements on disabled persons and employee involvement apply only to companies where the average number of employees in each week of the financial year exceeds 250. Other companies are free to give the information voluntarily if they wish. CA 1985 is very specific on how the average number of employees should be calculated in order to establish whether the disclosure requirements apply. The figure must be calculated by:

— ascertaining the number of people employed by the company under contracts of service in each week of the financial year, regardless of whether they were employed for the full week or only for part of it;

— adding up the numbers ascertained in this way for each week of the financial year; and

— dividing the resultant total by the number of weeks in the financial year.

People employed to work wholly or mainly outside the UK should be excluded from the calculation.

Disabled persons

38.44   The directors' report must include a statement on the company's policy during the financial year for:

—   giving full and fair consideration to applications for employment made by disabled persons, having regard to their particular aptitudes and abilities;

—   continuing the employment of, and arranging appropriate training for, any employees who have become disabled during the period when they were employed by the company;

—   the training, career development and promotion of disabled persons employed by the company.

The information is usually given in a short narrative statement on the issues specifically required to be covered by CA 1985. The note might usefully include discussion of the following:

—   contacts with local organisations for disabled persons;

—   specific actions to encourage applications from disabled persons;

—   adaptations to buildings to allow easier access for disabled persons; and

—   training programmes offered to disabled persons and whether these are identical to those offered to other employees.

The DTI White Paper *Company Law Reform* published in March 2005 proposes removing the requirement to disclose the company's policy on the employment of disabled persons in the directors' report on the basis that it has now been overtaken by substantive requirements under the *Disability Discrimination Act*.

Employee involvement

38.45   The directors' report must include a statement on the action taken during the year to introduce, maintain and develop arrangements for:

—   providing employees with information on matters of concern to them as employees;

—   consulting employees or their representatives on a regular basis so that their views can be taken into account in making decisions likely to affect their interests;

—   encouraging the involvement of employees in the company's performance;

—   achieving a common awareness on the part of all employees of the financial and economic factors affecting the performance of the company.

The information is usually given in a narrative statement, which often includes discussion of the following:

—   use of internal seminars and training programmes to provide appropriate information to employees;

— use of in-house newsletters and information bulletins;

— relationship with recognised trade unions and other employee groups or bodies;

— arrangements for regular meetings between employee representatives and management;

— details of employee share schemes;

— details of profit-related pay schemes; and

— action to promote equal opportunities.

The DTI White Paper *Company Law Reform* published in March 2005 proposes removing the requirement to disclose information on employee involvement in the directors' report on the basis that it has now been overtaken by more substantive requirements under the European Works Council Directive and the Information and Consultation Directive.

PAYMENT OF CREDITORS

Scope of the disclosure requirements

38.46 Disclosures on the company's policy and practice on the payment of creditors are only required in the accounts of a company that:

— is a public company at any time during the year; or

— was at any time during the year a member of a group headed by a public company, and did not qualify as small or medium-sized in relation to that year.

Detailed disclosures

38.47 A company that comes within this definition must disclose in its directors' report:

— whether it is the company's policy to follow any code or standard on payment practice for some or all of its suppliers and, if so:

    — the name of the code or standard; and

    — details of the place where information about and copies of the code or standard can be obtained;

— whether it is the company's policy:

    — to settle terms of payment with some or all of its suppliers when agreeing the terms of each transaction;

    — to make those suppliers aware of the terms of payment; and

    — to abide by those terms of payment;

— where the company's policy in respect of some or all of its suppliers differs from either of the above, its actual policy on payment of those suppliers must be stated;

    — if the company has different policies for different suppliers (or classes of suppliers), the suppliers (or classes of suppliers) to which the different policies apply; and

    — the number of days' purchases outstanding at the end of the period, which should be calculated by dividing the amount owed to trade creditors at the end of the period by the average daily amount invoiced to the company by its suppliers during the accounting period.

Suppliers are defined as any person whose claim on the reporting company in respect of goods and services supplied would be included under 'trade creditors' within 'Creditors: amounts falling due within one year' in a balance sheet drawn up in accordance with balance sheet Format 1 under CA 1985 Sch 4 (see Chapter 18).

STATEMENT OF DIRECTORS' RESPONSIBILITIES

Requirement to include a statement

38.48   Statement of Auditing Standards 600 (SAS 600) 'Auditors' Reports on Financial Statements' requires auditors to refer in their report to a description of the responsibilities of the directors in respect of the accounts and to distinguish the responsibilities of the auditors from those of the directors. The statement must therefore be given whenever the accounts are subject to audit. It is preferable for the directors to make their own statement of their responsibilities and it is usual practice for this to be set out on a separate page of the accounts, immediately preceding the audit report. However, it is also acceptable to include the statement within the directors' report. If a statement of the directors' responsibilities is not given in the accounts or directors' report, or if the statement given is not adequate, the auditors are required to include an appropriate description of the directors' responsibilities in their audit report.

For accounting periods beginning on or after 15 December 2004, SAS 600 is replaced by ISA 700 'The Auditor's Report on Financial Statements', but similar disclosure requirements continue to apply. ISA 700 was introduced in the UK as a transitional measure and the standard is expected to be revised during the course of 2005.

Matters to be covered

38.49   The following matters should be covered in the statement:

— the company law requirement for directors to prepare annual accounts giving a true and fair view of the profit or loss for the year and of the state of affairs at the end of the year;

— in preparing those accounts, the requirement for the directors to:

— select suitable accounting policies;

— apply those accounting policies on a consistent basis;

— make judgments and estimates that are prudent and reasonable;

— state whether applicable accounting standards have been followed, subject to any material departures disclosed and explained in the accounts; and

— prepare the accounts on a going concern basis unless it is not appropriate to presume that the company will continue in business;

— the requirement for the directors to:

— keep proper accounting records;

— safeguard the assets of the company; and

— take reasonable steps to prevent and detect fraud and other irregularities.

Small and medium-sized companies are not required to state whether their accounts have been prepared in accordance with applicable accounting standards. SAS 600 therefore recognises that it would be inappropriate for a comment on this to be included in the directors' responsibilities statement for small and medium-sized companies. The statement on applicable accounting standards is therefore only required where the company does not qualify as small or medium-sized under CA 1985.

Draft Bulletin 2005/4 'Auditors' Reports on Financial Statements' published by the Auditing Practices Board (APB) in May 2005 also suggests that an additional paragraph should be included at the end of the statement of directors' responsibilities where the company's financial statements are published on a website. Further details are given at 38.50 below.

Example wording

38.50 SAS 600 suggests the following wording for the statement in the case of a company.

Example 38.4 – Statement of directors' responsibilities

Company law requires the directors to prepare financial statements for each financial year which give a true and fair view of the state of affairs of the company and of the profit and loss of the company for that period. In preparing those financial statements, the directors are required to:

— select suitable accounting policies and then apply them consistently;

— make judgments and estimates that are reasonable and prudent;

— state whether applicable accounting standards have been followed, subject to any material departures disclosed and explained in the financial statements*; and

— prepare the financial statements on the going concern basis unless it is inappropriate to presume that the company will continue in business.

The directors are responsible for keeping proper accounting records which disclose with reasonable accuracy at any time the financial position of the company and to enable them to ensure that the financial statements comply with CA 1985. They are also responsible for safeguarding the assets of the company and hence for taking reasonable steps for the prevention and detection of fraud and other irregularities.

* Not required for companies that qualify as small or medium-sized under CA 1985.

Draft Bulletin 2005/4 'Auditors' Reports on Financial Statements' published by the Auditing Practices Board (APB) in May 2005 sets out revised illustrative examples of auditors' reports on the accounts of companies incorporated in Great Britain and Northern Ireland which reflect the requirement for EU listed companies to prepare group accounts in accordance with international financial reporting standards (IFRSs) for accounting periods beginning on or after 1 January 2005, together with other recent changes. The draft also includes an updated example of a statement of directors' responsibilities for a non-publicly traded company which prepares accounts in accordance with UK accounting practice. This includes the following new opening paragraph:

'The directors are responsible for preparing the annual report and financial statements in accordance with applicable law and United Kingdom Generally Accepted Accounting Practice.'

The draft also suggests that the following additional paragraph should be included at the end of the statement where the company's financial statements are published on a website:

'The directors are responsible for the maintenance and integrity of the company website. Legislation in the United Kingdom governing the preparation and dissemination of financial statements may differ from legislation in other jurisdictions.'

The draft Bulletin notes that, where financial statements are prepared under EU-adopted interntional accounting standards, directors may need to take legal advice on what to include in their statement of responsibilities.

Audit exemption

38.51 In the case of a small company which is eligible for audit exemption under the provisions of CA 1985, a different statement of responsibilities is required from the directors. In this case, the legislation requires the directors to state that:

—   for the year in question, the company is entitled to the exemption under CA 1985 s 249A(1) or (2);

—   no notice has been deposited under CA 1985 s 249B(2) requiring an audit for that year;

—   they acknowledge their responsibilities for:

    —   ensuring that the company maintains accounting records which comply with CA 1985 s 221; and

    —   preparing accounts which give a true and fair view of the state of affairs of the company at the end of the financial year and of the profit or loss for that year in accordance with CA 1985 s 226, and which comply with the relevant accounting requirements of CA 1985.

This statement must be positioned above the director's signature on the balance sheet. Where the company also prepares shorter form accounts, the statement is usually combined with the directors' formal statement on those accounts (see Chapter 8).

Specialised businesses and unincorporated entities

38.52   SAS 600 and ISA 700 apply to all audit reports. The wording of the statement of directors' responsibilities may need to be amended to reflect the specific requirements applying to specialised businesses (e.g. banks, insurance companies). In the case of unincorporated entities (e.g. charities, pension funds) the responsibilities of the directors, managers or trustees may not be so clearly defined and may vary quite considerably between apparently similar entities. Care must be taken to ensure that the statement properly reflects the responsibilities actually in place under the relevant constitution or trust deed.

FINANCIAL RISK

Disclosures required from 1 January 2005

38.53   For accounting periods beginning on or after 1 January 2005, there is a new company law requirement for the directors' report to include information on the company's use of financial instruments, unless it is not material for an assessment of the company's (or group's) assets, liabilities, financial position and results. There is a specific exemption from the disclosure requirement for companies that qualify as small and choose to take advantage of the option to prepare a modified directors' report. For all other companies, the directors' report should include an indication of:

(i)   the entity's financial risk management objectives and policies, including the policy for hedging if hedge accounting is used; and

(ii)   the entity's exposure to price risk, credit risk, liquidity risk and cash flow risk.

Practice has still to develop in dealing with these new disclosure requirements. In the meantime, directors may find it helpful to refer to guidance set out in FRS 25 'Financial Instruments: Disclosure and Presentation', FRED 33 'Financial Instruments: Disclosure' and the ASB's Reporting Standard 1 (RS1) 'Operating and Financial Review'. Whilst these documents deal primarily with details to be given by listed and other larger entities at present, they are aimed at providing information that is helpful to users of annual accounts and report, and so provide a useful source of information for directors preparing the new disclosures for the annual directors' report.

Use of financial instruments

38.54   FRS 25 'Financial Instruments: Disclosure and Presentation' and FRED 33 'Financial Instruments: Disclosure' include detailed guidance material on narrative disclosures on the risks that a business faces and the risk management techniques that it employs. FRS 25 suggests that a description of financial risk management objectives and policies might include:

(i)   the extent to which financial instruments are used;

(ii)   the associated risks and the business purposes served; and

(iii)   management's policies for controlling the identified risks, including:

- the hedging of risk exposures;

- the avoidance of undue concentrations of risk; and

- requirements for collateral to mitigate credit risk.

Interest rate risk

38.55   In the case of interest rate risk, the guidance in FRS 25 and FRED 33 suggests that a company should provide information on:

(i)   which financial assets and liabilities are exposed to interest rate risk;

(ii)   the length of time for which interest rates are fixed;

(iii)   known, or expected, maturity or repricing dates; and

(iv)   the nature and extent of any exposure to interest rate risk as a result of a transaction in which no financial asset or liability is recognised on the balance sheet.

Credit risk

38.56   In the case of credit risk, the guidance in FRS 25 and FRED 33 suggests that a company should provide information on:

(i)   the amount that best represents its maximum credit risk exposure at the balance sheet date

(ii)   details of any related collateral; and

(iii)   any significant concentrations of credit risk.

Cash flow and liquidity

38.57   The ASB's Reporting Standard 1 (RS1) 'Operating and Financial Review' (see 38.14 below) includes guidance on reporting on liquidity and cash flow. The suggested disclosures in respect of liquidity include:

(i)   a commentary on the level of borrowings at the balance sheet date;

(ii)   the seasonality of borrowing requirements and the peak level of borrowings during the period under review;

(iii)   the maturity profile of both borrowings and any undrawn but committed borrowing facilities;

(iv)   the funding requirements for any investment commitments;

(v)   internal sources of liquidity and any significant restrictions on the ability to transfer funds within the group;

(vi)   details of any known or expected breaches of covenants with lenders and the measures taken or proposed to remedy the situation; and

(vii)   details of any other covenants or negotiations with lenders that could restrict the use of credit facilities.

Suggested disclosures in respect of cash flow include the main sources of cash inflows and outflows, any special factors that have influenced cash flow in the period and any factors that may have a significant impact on cash flow in the future.

DISCLOSURE OF INFORMATION TO AUDITORS

Changes to auditors' rights to information

38.58   The *Companies (Audit, Investigations and Community Enterprise) Act 2004* amends section 389A of CA 1985 to give every company officer and employee, any person accountable for the company's books, accounts or vouchers, and any subsidiary incorporated in Great Britain (together with its officers, employees or auditors) a statutory duty to respond to enquiries by the company's auditors. The duty also extends to former officers and employees who were in post at the time to which the auditors' enquiries relate. In the case of overseas subsidiaries, the auditors of a parent company can require that parent to obtain any information or explanations considered necessary for the audit. Individuals will commit an offence if they fail to respond, or to delay responding, to the auditors' enquiries, or if they knowingly or recklessly make an oral or written statement to the auditors that is misleading, false or deceptive in any material respect.

Requirement for formal statement by directors

38.59   The same legislation also introduces a new section 234(ZA) into CA 1985. Under this section, wherever a company's accounts are subject to audit the directors' report must include a formal statement, as at the date on which the report is approved, that:

(i)   so far as each director is aware, there is no relevant audit information of which the company's auditors are unaware; and

(ii)   each director has taken all the steps that he/she ought to have taken as a director to make themselves aware of any relevant audit information and to establish that the company's auditors are aware of that information.

In essence, this means that the directors must be able to confirm each year that no director has withheld information which he/she knows, or ought to know, would be relevant to the audit. The duty of the directors is therefore extended so that, as well as responding to enquiries by the auditors, they must also volunteer any additional information that could be relevant to the audit. As with similar company law provisions, what a director ought to do or know is determined on the basis of the knowledge, skill and experience that would reasonably be expected of a person carrying out the same functions as the director in relation to the company, and also the specific knowledge, skill and experience that each individual director has. In terms of the steps that directors are expected to take, the legislation requires each director to have made appropriate enquiries of his/her fellow directors and of the company's auditors, and to have taken any other steps required by the general duty to exercise due care, skill and diligence in the carrying out the role of director. The new provisions come into effect on 6 April 2005, but the disclosure does not have to be given in a directors' report relating to a financial year beginning before 1 April 2005 or ending before 6 April 2005.

Chapter 39

Operating and Financial Review

THE STATUTORY OPERATING AND FINANCIAL REVIEW

Development of OFR reporting

39.1   The ASB issued a non-mandatory Statement 'Operating and Financial Review' in July 1993 to provide a framework for the discussion within the annual report of the main factors underlying a company's financial performance and financial position, its particular strengths and weaknesses, the uncertainties that underlie it and the structure of its financing. At this stage, company law required the preparation of an annual directors' report including a fair review of the development of the business during the year and its financial position at the year-end and likely future developments, but did not provide any detailed guidance on the issues to be covered. In publishing its guidance, the ASB hoped to further encourage the development of best practice in OFR reporting. A revised version of the ASB Statement was published in January 2003 and provided a broader framework for the discussion of business performance than its 1993 predecessor. It set out the principles that directors should follow when preparing an Operating and Financial Review (OFR) together with detailed guidance on their practical application. The guidance was intended primarily for listed companies and other larger organisations, but the principles were nevertheless relevant to all entities. The Statement is superseded by Reporting Standard 1 (RS 1) 'Operating and Financial Review' for accounting periods beginning on or after 1 April 2005 (see 39.13 below).

Introduction of statutory OFRs

39.2   A major review of UK company was undertaken between 1998 and 2001. The final report published by the Company Law Review Steering Group in July

2001 set out the conclusions drawn from the review and the Group's recommendations for change, based on the issues covered in the various consultation documents issued as part of the review. One of the recommendations was that larger companies at least should be required by statute to publish an Operating and Financial Review (OFR). The DTI issued draft regulations on this in May 2004 and the original intention was to make these effective for accounting periods beginning on or after 1 January 2005. However, a number of concerns were raised during the consultation process and the Government announced in November 2004 that implementation would be deferred to accounting periods beginning on or after 1 April 2005 to allow appropriate changes to be made. The Foreword to the DTI consultation document and draft regulations emphasised the higher expectations of companies in the modern economy and the need for high-quality engagement with shareholders. The OFR is intended to provide shareholders with the full and accurate information that they need and also to provide a discipline on management to encourage them to analyse and report effectively on the company's performance and prospects. Although voluntary OFR reporting has been regarded as best practice for some time, the DTI noted that a significant number of large companies were currently falling short of the ASB recommendations. The *Companies Act 1985 (Operating and Financial Review and Directors' Report etc.) Regulations 2005* (SI 2005 No 1011), which introduce the new requirements, came into effect on 22 March 2005 and generally apply for accounting periods beginning on or after 1 April 2005.

Requirement to prepare an OFR

39.3   The statutory requirement for company directors to prepare an OFR for each financial year is set out in a new section 234AA of the Companies Act 1985 and applies only to quoted companies. In this context, a quoted company is defined as a company whose equity share capital is:

(i)   included in the Official List of the London Stock Exchange;

(ii)   officially listed in an EEA State; or

(iii) admitted to dealing on the New York Stock Exchange or the Nasdaq exchange.

If the company is a parent company preparing group accounts, the OFR must be a consolidated review covering the company and the subsidiary undertakings that are included in the consolidated accounts. However, the legislation specifies that, where appropriate, a group OFR can give greater emphasis to matters that are significant to the group as a whole rather than to the individual entities included in the consolidation. It is an offence for a director of a quoted company to knowingly or recklessly fail to comply with the provisions on the preparation of an OFR or to fail to take all reasonable steps to secure compliance.

Approval, signature and issue of the OFR

39.4   A new section 234AB of the Companies Act 1985 requires the OFR to be formally approved by the board of directors and signed on behalf of the board by a director or by the company secretary. The name of the signing individual must be stated in every copy of the review that is laid before the company in general meeting or otherwise issued, published or circulated. A copy of the review must also be delivered to the Registrar of Companies with the annual accounts, directors' report and directors' remuneration report, and this copy must be signed in manuscript by the relevant individual. The requirements on issuing the OFR to shareholders and other entitled persons are the same as those that apply to the company's financial statements and other annual reports.

Objective of a statutory OFR

39.5   Detailed requirements on the objective and content of a statutory OFR are set out in a new Schedule 7ZA to the Companies Act 1985. The review must provide a balanced and comprehensive analysis, consistent with the size and complexity of the business, of:

(i)   the performance and development of the business during the year;

(ii)   the position of the company (or group) at the end of the year;

(iii) the main trends and factors underlying performance and development during the year; and

(iv)   the main trends and factors likely to affect the company's (or group's) future performance, development and position.

The review should be targeted at the needs of the company's shareholders, with the objective of enabling them to assess the strategies that the company has adopted and the potential for the company to succeed, although the information provided will invariably be of interest to a much wider group of stakeholders.

Required contents

39.6   The legislation specifies that the OFR must include:

(i)   a statement of the company's (or group's) business, objectives and strategies;

(ii)   a description of the resources that are available to the company (or group);

(iii) a description of the principal risks and uncertainties facing the company (or group); and

(iv)   a description of the company's (or group's) capital structure, treasury policies and objectives, and liquidity.

The legislation also specifies that, to the extent necessary to achieve compliance with the general requirements on the objective and contents of an OFR, the review must include appropriate information and analysis in respect of:

(i)   environmental matters, including the impact of the company's (or group's) business on the environment;

(ii)   the company's (or group's) employees;

(iii) social and community issues;

(iv)   those with whom the company (or group) has contractual or other arrangements which are essential to the business; and

(v)   information on receipts from, and returns to, members of the company in respect of the shares held by them.

If any of these issues are not discussed in the OFR, the directors must state which items have been excluded. For items (i) to (iii) above, the discussion should include details of the company's (or group's) policies in each area and the extent to which these have been successfully implemented. The review should also include relevant references to, and additional explanations of, the figures that appear in the financial statements of the company or the group.

Key performance indicators

39.7   The legislation also requires the review to include analysis using financial and appropriate non-financial key performance indicators (KPIs), particularly in relation to environmental and employee issues. In this context, KPIs are defined as 'factors by reference to which the development, performance or position of the business of the company can be measured effectively' (CA 1985, Sch 7ZA, para 6(2)). The disclosure of KPIs is considered in more detail at 39.19 below.

Disclosure exemption

39.8   Section 234AA provides that nothing in Schedule 7ZA to the Companies Act 1985 requires disclosure about impending developments or matters in the course of negotiation if, in the opinion of the directors, disclosure would be seriously prejudicial to the interests of the company or group. The ASB considers this issue in Appendix C to Reporting Standard 1 (see 39.13 below) which summarises the background to the development of the standard. The ASB advocates a stringent approach and draws a parallel with the provision in the UK Listing Rules for a company to seek authorisation for non-disclosure in certain circumstances, noting that such requests are rare and that omission is only permitted if investors are unlikely to be misled. The ASB suggests that a similar, high-level test should be applied in respect of OFR reporting.

Compliance with reporting standards

39.9   The Government is keen to avoid a mechanical approach to compliance with the new statutory OFR requirement and so has asked the ASB to develop new standards on OFR reporting and these have been given the same statutory authority as accounting standards. Further details are given at 39.13 below. The review must state whether it has been prepared in accordance with these standards and give details of, and reasons for, any departures from them. Under the legislation, compliance with the reporting standards will be presumed to constitute compliance with the statutory OFR reporting requirement, unless the contrary can be proved.

The DTI has also issued more detailed guidance for directors on the issues that should be considered when deciding what to include in the OFR. The guidance was issued whilst the Regulations were still in draft form and is now expected to be updated to reflect the final legislative requirements. Further details of the current version of the guidance are given at 39.20 below.

Audit requirements

39.10   Section 235 of the Companies Act 1985 is amended to require the auditors of a quoted company to state in their audit report:

(i)   whether, in their opinion, the information given in the OFR is consistent with the company's (or group's) financial statements for that year; and

(ii)   whether any matters have come to their attention during the course of their work as auditors which, in their opinion, are inconsistent with information given in the OFR.

Guidance on the form and content of auditors' reports is currently set out in Auditing Standards and related Bulletins issued by the Auditing Practices Board (APB). Following the adoption of International Standards on Auditing (ISAs) in the UK and Ireland for accounting periods beginning on or after 15 December 2004, and recent updates to the underlying international requirements, the APB is expected to issue new examples of auditors' reports during the course of 2005 and these should reflect the above additional reporting requirements in respect of quoted companies. The APB is also in the process of developing more detailed guidance on the auditors' new responsibilities in relation to the OFR and the additional work that auditors will need to carry out as a result.

Defective OFRs

39.11   Section 245 of the Companies Act 1985 is amended to provide for the voluntary revision of a defective OFR in the same way as for defective accounts, directors' reports and directors' remuneration reports. These changes apply for accounting periods beginning on or after 1 April 2005. Sections 245A, 245B, 245C and 245F are also amended to bring OFRs within the scope of the legislative provisions on compulsory revision of defective accounts and reports, and within the remit of the Financial Reporting Review Panel (FRRP), which will in future be able to review OFRs on a proactive basis as well as where potentially defective documents are drawn to its attention. However, these provisions do not take effect until accounting periods beginning on or after 1 April 2006, so companies will have a period of twelve months to get to grips with the new reporting requirements before their OFRs become subject to detailed external scrutiny.

The OFR and summary financial statements

39.12   For some years, listed companies have been able to issue a summary financial statement to shareholders in place of the full accounts, subject to certain conditions, for accounting periods beginning on or after 1 January 2005 this facility is being extended to all companies whose accounts are subject to audit (see Chapter 43). The DTI is in the process of revising the regulations on the preparation of summary financial statements, and a consultation document incorporating a draft of the proposed new Regulations was published in March 2005. These remove the requirement for a summary financial statement to include a summarised directors' report, but give companies the option to include material from a directors' report or OFR in the summary financial statement. The *Companies Act 1985 (Operating and Financial Review and Directors' Report etc.) Regulations 2005* (SI 2005 No 1011) amend section 251 of the Companies Act 1985 to specify that, where a quoted company sends a summary financial statement to shareholders and does not send with that statement a full copy of its OFR for the year, it must publish the full OFR on a website throughout the period beginning at least 21 days before the date of the meeting at which the company's accounts and reports are to be laid and ending with the conclusion of the meeting. Similar provisions are also included in the proposed new Regulations.

OFR REPORTING STANDARDS

Legal provisions

39.13   The Government is keen to avoid a mechanical approach to compliance with the statutory OFR requirement and bland, 'boiler-plate' reporting. The ASB has therefore been asked to develop new standards on OFR reporting and these have been given the same statutory authority as accounting standards.

RS 1 'Operating and Financial Review'

39.14   The ASB published Reporting Standard 1 (RS 1) on the subject of the statutory OFR in May 2005, with the content based heavily on its previous non-mandatory Statement 'Operating and Financial Review' (see 39.1 above). The standard has two main sections – one setting out the principles that directors should apply when preparing an OFR and the other providing a disclosure framework. In each case, certain elements of the text are set out in bold, but the ASB explains that this is merely to highlight the main aspects and that all paragraphs should be treated as having equal authority. The standard is supplemented by separate 'Implementation Guidance' which gives illustrative examples of how some of the disclosures might be dealt with.

The ASB emphasises that it is for directors to decide how best to use the disclosure framework set out in the standard to structure the OFR. The document illustrates the topics and issues that may need to be covered, but neither this part of the standard nor the related 'Implementation Guidance' is intended to be exhaustive and other matters may need to be considered, depending on the particular circumstances of the reporting entity.

Scope and effective date of RS 1

39.15   RS 1 is effective for accounting periods beginning on or after 1 April 2005 and applies to all quoted companies and to any other entity that purports to prepare an OFR. The ASB clarifies in an Appendix that, for entities other than quoted companies, the standard will only apply if the review is described as an OFR. All entities that come within the scope of the standard must give details of, and reasons for, any departures from its requirements.

Presentation of OFR analysis

39.16   The standard emphasises that the OFR analysis should be presented through the eyes of the directors and should focus on issues of concern to members, although the information provided will doubtless also be of interest to other stakeholders. The report should have a forward-looking orientation, as the aim is to help shareholders understand and assess the company's strategies and the potential for these to succeed. In particular, it should cover:

(i)   the development and performance of the business during the year;

(ii)   the position of the business at the end of the year;

(iii)   the main trends and factors underlying the above; and

(iv)   the main trends and factors likely to affect the business's future development, performance and financial position and its progress towards the achievement of long-term business objectives.

The issues discussed should be those that have affected performance in the period and those that are expected to affect the future performance and financial position of the business. The discussion should include comments on the impact of any significant events that arise after the balance sheet date and on any predictive comments made in previous statements that have not been borne out by events.

The standard also notes that directors may want to include a statement that, even though it is provided in good faith, forward-looking information should be treated with caution in view of the surrounding uncertainties. This is to help address concerns over the absence of any 'safe harbour' provisions in the new legislation on OFR reporting.

Other key principles

39.17   In addition to the above, the other key principles are that the OFR should:

(i)   both complement and supplement the details provided in the financial statements;

(ii)   be written in a clear and readily understandable style;

(iii)   be comprehensive and understandable;

(iv)   be balanced and neutral, dealing even-handedly with both positive and negative issues; and

(v)   be comparable over successive periods and, if appropriate, with other entities in the same industry or sector.

The OFR should provide additional explanations of amounts shown in the financial statements and explain the conditions and events that have shaped the financial information presented in those statements. Where relevant, the directors should explain the source of information provided and the extent to which it is objectively supportable, to enable shareholders assess its reliability. As under the previous guidance, any adjustment of information from the financial statements should be highlighted and a reconciliation of the figures provided.

However, the standard also emphasises that the objective of the OFR is quality rather than quantity of content, and that the inclusion of too much information can obscure the significant issues and so fail to promote understanding.

Detailed disclosures

39.18   There is a particular emphasis on the disclosure of the key performance indicators, both financial and non-financial, that the directors consider to be the most effective in managing the business and measuring delivery of the company's strategies (see 39.19 below). As under the previous guidance, the directors should also discuss:

(i)   the resources available to the business, especially any that are not reflected in the balance sheet, and how these are managed – depending on the nature of the business, this might include:

- corporate reputation;
- brand strength;
- employees;
- natural resources;

- research and development activities;
- intellectual capital;
- licences, patents, trademarks and copyright;

(ii) the risks and uncertainties facing the business, and how these are managed;

(iii) significant relationships likely to influence performance and business value;

(iv) the company's capital structure, cash flows, liquidity and treasury policies – this might include:

- the balance between equity and debt;
- the maturity profile of debt;
- types of capital instrument used;
- interest rate and currency profiles;
- how treasury activities are controlled;
- short and longer term funding plans;
- any special factors affecting cash flows during the period;
- the seasonality of borrowing requirements and the maturity profile of any committed but undrawn borrowing facilities;
- any covenants with lenders which could restrict the use of credit facilities, and any existing or expected negotiations on the operation of these covenants;
- where a covenant has been breached, or is expected to be breached, the measures taken or proposed to remedy the situation;
- any restrictions on the use of internal sources of liquidity;

(v) any receipts from, and returns to, shareholders.

The discussion should include a description of the business and the external environment in which it operates, including its major markets and competitive position and the significant features of the regulatory, economic and social environment that influences the business. The OFR should also explain the longer-term objectives of the business, including where relevant objectives in non-financial areas, and the directors' strategies for achieving these.

Key performance indicators

39.19 One of the most significant issues for directors is likely to be which key performance indicators (KPIs) to use in the OFR. The number and type of KPIs disclosed should reflect what the directors consider to be critical in the management of the business. However, the ASB recognises that directors may need additional guidance in this area, in the early years of OFR reporting at least, given the wide range of measures currently available. The Implementation Guidance sets out examples of KPIs that might be used and the issues that the directors need to consider in each case. For instance, possible KPIs might include:

(a)   return on capital employed;

(b)   market share;

(c)   average revenue per customer/user;

(d)   sales per square foot;

(e)   environmental spillage;

(f) CO_2 emissions;

(g)   employee morale;

(h)   employee health and safety.

The standard does specify the information that should be disclosed for each KPI shown in the OFR, in order to help members understand and evaluate the details provided. The required disclosures here include:

(i)   the definition, purpose and calculation method used;

(ii)   the source of underlying data and, where relevant, an explanation of any assumptions made;

(iii)   quantification of, or commentary on, future targets; and

(iv)   where available, the corresponding amount for the previous year.

Any changes to key performance indicators, or to the calculation methods used, from the previous year should also be disclosed and any significant changes in the underlying accounting policies adopted in the financial statements should be explained.

DTI GUIDANCE FOR DIRECTORS

Development of guidance for directors

39.20   In December 2002, the DTI established a separate working group to develop broad principles and practical guidance for directors on how to establish whether an item is sufficiently material to be included in the OFR. The Operating and Financial Review Working Group on Materiality published a consultation paper setting out its initial proposals in June 2003. The final version of the guidance 'The Operating and Financial Review: Practical Guidance for Directors' was issued in May 2004, in conjunction with the DTI consultation document and draft Regulations on the statutory OFR. An updated version of the guidance is expected to be published now that the Regulations have been finalised. The new guidance does not have legal status, nor does it cover the form and content of the OFR which are dealt with in new reporting standards developed by the ASB (see 39.13 above).

Scope of OFR reporting

39.21   Although the DTI guidance is clearly aimed at the directors of quoted companies, the document notes that a successful company is one whose directors look at long-term as well as short-term issues and take account of all the factors that affect the company's relationships with others. It therefore considers that OFR reporting is likely to become an established feature of corporate reporting even for businesses that are not required by law to produce such a statement. The new Regulations set out a framework for OFR reporting and identify a number of key issues that should always be covered, but for the most part it will be down to the directors of each company to decide what should be included in the OFR each year.

Assessing materiality

39.22   Part I of the guidance therefore covers the need for directors to understand the objectives of the OFR and to:

(i)   take a broad view, which includes exploring and understanding the agendas of all the stakeholders that are likely to influence the company's performance, either directly or indirectly;

(ii)   act collectively in making good faith, honest judgements on what should and need not be reported and on how the information is presented;

(iii) identify any areas where access to additional skills and knowledge is required (e.g. environmental, social and community issues); and

(iv)   achieve an appropriate balance between historic review and the trends and factors most likely to affect future performance.

Whether an individual item is disclosed or not will depend not only on its nature and size but also on the effect that it may have in the particular circumstances of the business and on how it may be viewed in conjunction with other information about the company or group. For each area, the guidance explains the underlying principles and then illustrates them with practical examples of issues that may arise in a specific type of business and the sort of disclosure that the directors might make in these circumstances.

Process for OFR reporting

39.23   Part II of the guidance highlights the importance of establishing a sound process to provide evidence that the directors have taken their OFR reporting responsibilities seriously. In particular, the process should be properly planned, recorded and communicated and should have a clear timetable which allows for appropriate consultation, both within the organisation and externally where necessary. The guidance also recommends a major internal review of the process every three to five years, linked to the company's strategic planning cycle. The process should conclude with a formal sign-off by the board as a whole, not only on the inclusion or exclusion of individual items, but also that the information given provides a thorough and balanced picture, and that nothing of significance has been overlooked. It was originally suggested that the auditors would be required to review and report on the process followed by the directors, but this has not been included in the final Regulations.

Chapter 40   Corporate Governance Disclosures

BACKGROUND TO UK CORPORATE GOVERNANCE REPORTING

The Cadbury Code of Best Practice

40.1   The corporate governance debate in the UK began in earnest in May 1991 with the establishment of the Cadbury Committee. Following a series of high profile corporate disasters, including the Maxwell affair and the BCCI collapse, it was felt that steps needed to be taken to improve confidence in financial reporting. In particular, there was a perceived need for a more rigourous and structured approach to internal control, a strengthening of accounting standards and an improvement of the position of external auditors in dealing with boards of directors. Following a detailed review of the current position, the Cadbury Committee, under the chairmanship of Sir Adrian Cadbury, published its final report in December 1992. At the heart of this report was the 'Cadbury Code of Best Practice' and, following an amendment to the UK Listing Rules, listed companies were required to state whether they had complied with this Code and to give reasons for any non-compliance.

The Cadbury Report and resultant Code was based on the premise that company directors should have the freedom to develop their companies, but that they should do so within an effective framework of accountability. The recommendations therefore focused primarily on the structure of the board, its control and reporting functions, and the role of the external auditors, and drew on principles that were already being widely followed. Although the recommendations were aimed mainly at listed companies, the Committee's objective was to raise the overall standards of corporate governance and the general level of public confidence in financial reporting. All entities were therefore encouraged to follow the new recommendations.

Openness, integrity and accountability

40.2   Corporate governance was defined in the 'Cadbury Report' as 'the system by which companies are directed and controlled'. Shareholders are responsible for appointing both the directors and the external auditors, and need to be satisfied that an appropriate governance structure is in place within the entity. The board of directors is responsible for setting the company's aims and objective, providing the leadership to put these into effect, supervising the management of the business and reporting to shareholders on its stewardship. The financial aspects of corporate governance are identified as the way in which the board sets financial policy and oversees its implementation (including the use of financial controls) and the process of reporting to the shareholders on the activities and development of the company.

The 'Cadbury Code of Best Practice' was based on the principles of openness, integrity and accountability. Openness was described as the basis for the confidence that must exist between a business and those who have a stake in its success – an open approach to the disclosure of information contributes to the efficient working of the market economy, prompts boards to take effective action and allows shareholders and other interested parties to scrutinise companies more closely. Integrity was described as straightforward dealing and completeness – financial reporting should be honest and should present a balanced view of the company's affairs. Accountability was described as being achieved through the quality of information provided by the board to the shareholders and by the willingness of the shareholders to exercise their responsibilities as owners of the business.

Greenbury Code of Best Practice

40.3   Following concerns over the substantial salary increases and share options being awarded to directors, the Greenbury Committee was established to develop a voluntary code of best practice in respect of directors' remuneration and in particular to encourage the adoption of appropriate structures and procedures for the setting of remuneration and other rewards to directors, and to create a significantly more rigourous disclosure regime. The intention was to ensure that shareholders were provided with all the necessary information to assess the performance of individual companies and their directors. The Committee's final report, published in July 1995 emphasised three principles in respect of directors' remuneration:

(i) **Accountability**: Directors are accountable to the shareholders for their stewardship and for the performance of the company, and responsibility for determining executive remuneration should be delegated to a disinterested body (the remuneration committee).

(ii) **Transparency**: Corporate policy on executive remuneration should be reported on annually to shareholders and details of individual directors' packages should be set out in the annual report and accounts.

(iiI) **Performance**: Executive rewards should be linked to the performance of both the company and the individual, and the interests of directors should be aligned with those of shareholders.

Following the publication of the 'Greenbury Report', amendments were made to the UK Listing Rules to require:

(i) the disclosure of individual directors' remuneration;

(ii) the preparation of an annual remuneration committee report;

(iii) an annual statement on compliance with certain best practice provisions in respect of remuneration committees; and

(iv) an annual statement that full consideration had been given to further best practice provisions relating to remuneration policy, service contracts and any payments for compensation for loss of office.

The Combined Code

40.4 The next Committee on corporate governance was chaired by Sir Ronald Hampel and was set up to review progress with the implementation of the Cadbury and Greenbury recommendations rather than in response to any identified need for specific reform. The Committee's final report was published in January 1998 and established a set of broad 'Principles of Corporate Governance' covering directors, their remuneration, shareholders, accountability and audit, many of which drew on elements of the earlier best practice codes.

The Committee continued to advocate a flexible approach to compliance and urged shareholders to take note of the reasons given by companies for variations from best practice.

A major element of the final report was the proposed consolidation of the existing codes and the new principles into one consolidated code of best practice. The first 'Combined Code' was subsequently published in June 1998 and the UK Listing Rules were amended to require companies to give certain disclosures on compliance with the new Code for accounting periods ending on or after 31 December 1998.

As part of the post-Enron review, the UK Government commissioned Derek Higgs to lead a short independent review of the role and effectiveness of non-executive directors in the UK. The 'Higgs Report' was published in January

2003 and set out recommendations to increase rigour and transparency in the appointment process for non-executive directors and to widen the spread of experience in UK boardrooms. The Report also set out the draft of a revised Combined Code, incorporating these recommendations.

Another small working group was appointed by the FRC, under the chairmanship of Sir Robert Smith, to develop further the initial guidance on audit committees included in the Combined Code. The resulting report 'Audit Committees: Combined Code Guidance' (commonly referred to as the 'Smith Report') was published in January 2003, at the same time as the 'Higgs Report'. This report noted that audit committees had a particular role, acting independently from the executive, in ensuring that the interests of shareholders in relation to financial reporting and internal control were properly protected. The 'Smith Report' included the draft of a revised section of the 'Combined Code' on audit committees, together with supplementary guidance intended to assist boards in establishing and operating an audit committee and also to assist directors who serve as members of an audit committee.

A new 'Combined Code' was eventually published in July 2003 and applies for accounting periods beginning on or after 1 November 2003. The document notes that departure from the detailed Code provisions may be justified in particular circumstances, but it is still expected that listed companies will comply with them most of the time. Some specific relaxations are permitted for companies below the FTSE 350 although they are still encouraged to consider full compliance.

Ongoing monitoring and review

40.5   The FRC announced in June 2004 that it intends to keep the 'Combined Code' under regular review, to ensure that it is working effectively and to identify any amendments that may be needed. The first formal review is expected to take place in the second half of 2005, although initial discussions with companies and investors began in the second half of 2004. In January 2005, the FRC announced that its initial informal assessment of the impact of the revised 'Combined Code' had concluded that encouraging progress had been made. In particular, the FRC found that:

(i)   both investors and companies thought that the corporate governance climate had improved over the last 12 months;

(ii)   investors reported an increased dialogue with companies and greater involvement by company chairmen on corporate governance issues;

(iii)   a number of companies had already commented in their 2004 annual reports on their position in relation to the revised 'Combined Code';

(iv)   issues such as performance evaluation and professional development are being taken more seriously.

However, the FRC also acknowledged that companies need more time to plan and implement some of the new provisions, such as those relating to the number of independent non-executive directors and the balance of skills and experience within the board.

REPORTING ON COMPLIANCE WITH THE COMBINED CODE

Requirement for compliance statement

40.6 For accounting periods ending on or after 31 December 1998, Chapter 12.43A of the UK Listing Rules requires a listed company to include in its accounts:

(i)   a narrative statement of how it has applied the principles set out in the 'Combined Code', with explanations to enable the shareholders to evaluate how the principles have been applied; and

(ii) a statement on whether or not it has complied throughout the accounting period with the best practice provisions set out in the 'Combined Code', with details of, and the reasons for, any areas or periods of non-compliance.

In addition, provision C.1.2. of the 'Combined Code' requires the directors to report that the business is a going concern, with supporting assumptions or qualifications as appropriate, and provision C.2.1 requires the directors to report to shareholders that they have reviewed the effectiveness of the company's system of internal control at least once a year. The going concern reporting requirement is considered in more detail at 40.15 to 40.35 below and the internal control reporting requirement is considered at 40.36 to 40.49 below. Other specific disclosures are required by certain sections of the Code and these are summarised in Schedule C to the new Code for ease of reference.

The preamble to the 'Combined Code' emphasises that neither the form nor the content of the compliance statement has been prescribed. The Committee intends that directors should have a free hand in explaining their corporate governance policies in the light of the principles set out in the 'Combined Code', including any special circumstances that may have led the directors to take a particular approach.

A checklist of the reporting requirements under the Combined Code is given in the Appendix to this chapter.

The role of the auditors

40.7 Where the UK Listing Authority requires the directors to include a statement on compliance with the 'Combined Code' and a statement on going concern, the UK Listing Rules also stipulate that these statements must be reviewed by the auditors. In the case of the compliance statement, the auditors are only required to review compliance with the following provisions:

(i) C.1.1 – The directors should explain in the annual accounts their responsibility for preparing the accounts and there should be a statement by the auditors about their reporting responsibilities.

(ii) C.2.1 – The board should, at least annually, conduct a review of the effectiveness of the group's system of internal controls and should report to the shareholders that they have done so. The review should cover all material controls, including financial, operational and compliance controls and risk management systems.

(iii) C.3.1 – The board should establish an audit committee of at least three, or in the case of smaller companies two, members who should all be independent non-executive directors. The board should satisfy itself that at least one member of the audit committee has recent and relevant financial experience.

(iv) C.3.2 – The main role and responsibilities of the audit committee should be set out in written terms of reference and should include the specific matters set out in Code Provision C.3.2.

(v) C.3.3 – The terms of reference of the audit committee, including its role and the authority delegated to it by the board, should be made available. A separate section of the annual report should describe the work of the committee in discharging those responsibilities.

(vi) C.3.4 – The audit committee should review arrangements by which staff of the company may, in confidence, raise concerns about possible improprieties in matters of financial reporting or other matters. The audit committee's objective should be to ensure that arrangements are in place for a proportionate and independent investigation of such matters and for appropriate follow-up action.

(vii) C.3.5 – The audit committee should monitor and review the effectiveness of the internal audit activities. Where there is no internal audit function, the audit committee should consider annually whether there is a need for an internal audit function and make a recommendation to the board, and the reasons for the absence of such a function should be explained in the relevant section of the annual report.

(viii) C.3.6 – The audit committee should have primary responsibility for making a recommendation on the appointment, reappointment and removal of the external auditors. If the board does not accept the audit committee's recommendation, it should include in the annual report, and in any papers recommending appointment or reappointment, a statement from the audit committee explaining the recommendation and should set out reasons why the board has taken a different position.

(ix) C.3.7 – The annual report should explain to shareholders how, if the auditor provides non-audit services, auditor objectivity and independence have been safeguarded.

Form of auditors' report

40.8   When corporate governance reporting was first introduced in the UK, the guidance issued by the Auditing Practices Board (APB) required auditors to issue a formal report to the directors on the results of their review and recommended strongly that their report was published in the company's annual report. This guidance was withdrawn for accounting periods ending on or after 31 December 1998, on the grounds that the scope of the review now required by the UK Listing Rules is very narrow when compared with the totality of the 'Combined Code', in that auditors are only required to review compliance with nine of the detailed Code provisions and are not required to review the directors' statement on how they have applied the Principles set out in the 'Combined Code'. Consequently the APB decided that it was no longer appropriate for auditors' reports on compliance statements to be published in the annual report. Instead, the auditors' review of the company's compliance with the 'Combined Code' is explained in an expanded description of the auditors' responsibilities within the audit report. For accounting periods beginning on or after 1 November 2003, example wording is set out in APB Bulletin 2004/3 'The Combined Code on Corporate Governance: Requirements of auditors under the Listing Rules of the Financial Services Authority'.

In May 2005, the APB published a draft Bulletin 2005/4 'Auditors' Reports on Financial Statements' setting out revised illustrative examples of auditors' reports on the accounts of companies incorporated in Great Britain and Northern Ireland. The proposed changes reflect the following recent developments:

- the requirement for EU listed companies to prepare group accounts in accordance with international financial reporting standards (IFRSs) for accounting periods beginning on or after 1 January 2005;

- the option for most other companies to adopt IFRSs from the same date;

- recent changes to the requirements of the Companies Act 1985; and

- the adoption in the UK of International Standards on Auditing (ISAs) for accounting periods beginning on or after 15 December 2004.

At this stage, the Bulletin has been issued in draft form in order to provide interim guidance on the various complex issues that arise from these changes.

One of the potential difficulties arises from the fact that a parent company preparing IFRS group accounts may prepare its own individual accounts in accordance with IFRSs or in accordance with UK GAAP. The illustrative example reports therefore cater for both situations. The draft guidance notes that, where such a parent company prepares its own accounts in accordance with UK GAAP, it may choose to present these in a separate section of the annual report. In these circumstances, the APB proposes that a separate auditors' report should be provided on each set of accounts. Where this approach is adopted, it is also suggested that the auditors' opinion in respect of the company's corporate governance disclosures is given in the report on the group financial statements, but the opinion on the directors' remuneration report is given in the report on the parent company's financial statements. There are further complications where advantage is taken of the exemption in section 230 of the *Companies Act 1985* from publication of the parent company's own profit and loss account and certain related information.

Structure of the Combined Code

40.9   The Combined Code was originally divided into two sections, the first setting out the principles of good governance under the key headings and the second giving the best practice provisions for each of those principles. The latest version of the Code has been restructured, so that the main principles, supporting principles and best practice provisions are set out together for each of the following headings:

(i)   Section 1: COMPANIES

    A.   Directors

    B.   Remuneration

    C.   Accountability and Audit

    D.   Relations with Shareholders

(ii)   Section 2: INSTITUTIONAL SHAREHOLDERS

    E.   Institutional Shareholders

The main principles in each section are summarised below, but reference should also be made to the supporting principles and the detailed best practice provisions for each section when considering the directors' reporting requirements in respect of compliance with the Code.

Directors

40.10   Section A of the 'Combined Code' sets out the following main principles in respect of directors:

(i)   **The board**: Every company should be headed by an effective board, which is collectively responsible for the success of the company.

(ii)   **Chairman and chief executive**: There should be a clear division of responsibilities at the head of the company between the running of the board and the executive responsibility for the running of the company's business. No one individual should have unfettered powers of decision.

(iii) **Board balance and independence**: The board should include a balance of executive and non-executive directors (and in particular independent non-executive directors) such that no individual or small group of individuals can dominate the board's decision taking.

(iv) **Appointments to the board**: There should be a formal, rigourous and transparent procedure for the appointment of new directors to the board

(v) **Information and professional development**: The board should be supplied in a timely manner with information in a form and of a quality appropriate to enable it to discharge its duties. All directors should receive induction on joining the board and should regularly update and refresh their skills and knowledge.

(vi) **Performance evaluation**: The board should undertake a formal and rigourous annual evaluation of its own performance and that of its committees and individual directors.

(vii) **Re-election**: all directors should be submitted to re-election at regular intervals, subject to continued satisfactory performance. The board should ensure planned and progressive refreshing of the board.

The supporting principles explain that the board should set the company's strategic aims, ensure the availability of appropriate financial and human resources and review management performance. The board is also responsible for setting the company's values and standards and ensuring that obligations to shareholders are understood and met. All directors must take decisions objectively in the interests of the company. The role of the non-executive directors is also explained in detail in the supporting principles. The supporting principles in respect of appointments to the board note that appointments should be made on merit and against objective criteria, and that care should be taken to ensure that appointees have enough time available for the role, especially if they are to act as chairman of one of the main board committees. The board is also required to satisfy itself that appropriate succession plans are in place for both the board and senior management to ensure a continuing balance of skills and experience.

Directors' remuneration

40.11   Section B of the 'Combined Code' sets out the following main principles in respect of remuneration:

(i) **Level and make-up of remuneration**: Levels of remuneration should be sufficient to to attract, retain and motivate directors of the quality needed to run the company successfully, but companies should avoid paying more than is necessary for this purpose. A significant proportion of executive directors' remuneration should be structured to link rewards to corporate and individual performance.

(ii)   **Procedure**: There should be a formal and transparent procedure for developing policy on executive remuneration and for fixing the remuneration packages of individual directors. No director should be involved in setting his/her own remuneration.

The supporting principles note that the remuneration committee should judge where to position the company relative to other companies, but should use such comparisons with caution in view of the risk of increasing remuneration levels without a corresponding improvement in performance. They should also be sensitive to pay and employment conditions elsewhere in the group, especially when determining annual salary increases. The best practice guidance deals separately and in detail with remuneration policy, and service contracts and compensation

Accountability and Audit

40.12   Section C of the 'Combined Code' identifies three main principles on accountability and audit:

(i)   **Financial reporting**: The board should present a balanced and understandable assessment of the company's position and prospects.

(ii)   **Internal control**: The board should maintain a sound system of internal control to safeguard the shareholders' investment and the company's assets;

(iii) **Audit committee and auditors**: The board should establish formal and transparent arrangements for considering how they should apply the financial reporting and internal control principles mentioned above, and for maintaining an appropriate relationship with the company's auditors.

The supporting principles clarify that the board's responsibility to present balanced and understandable information extends to interim reports, other price-sensitive reports and reports to regulators. The best practice provisions cover the recommendations that the directors should:

(i)   explain their responsibility for preparing the accounts;

(ii)   report that the business is a going concern, with supporting assumptions or qualifications as necessary; and

(iii) review the effectiveness of the system of internal control annually at least and report to shareholders that they have done so.

Relations with shareholders

40.13   Section D of the 'Combined Code' includes the following main principles in respect of the company's relations with its shareholders:

(i) **Dialogue with institutional shareholders**: There should be a dialogue with shareholders based on the mutual understanding of objectives. The board as a whole is responsible for ensuring that this dialogue takes place.

(ii) **Constructive use of the AGM**: The board should use the AGM to communicate with private investors and encourage their participation.

The supporting principles note that, whilst recognising most shareholder contact will be with the chief executive and finance director, the chairman and where appropriate other directors (including the senior independent director) should maintain sufficient contact with shareholders to understand their issues and concerns, using whichever methods are most practical and efficient. In its preliminary, informal assessment of the impact of the revised Combined Code, carried out in preparation for a more detailed review later in 2005, the FRC specifically noted that investors are now reporting improved dialogue with companies and greater involvement by company chairmen on corporate governance issues. Also, the recent company law review has resulted in a number of proposals designed to improve the quality of shareholder input at the AGM and in particular to give shareholders adequate opportunity to raise matters of concern.

Institutional shareholders

40.14 Section E of the 'Combined Code' includes the following main principles in respect of institutional shareholders:

(i) **Dialogue with companies**: Institutional shareholders should enter into a dialogue with companies based on the mutual understanding of objectives.

(ii) **Evaluation of governance disclosures**: When evaluating governance arrangements, particularly those relating to board structure and composition, institutional shareholders should give due weight to all relevant factors drawn to their attention.

(iii) **Shareholder voting**: Institutional shareholders have a responsibility to make considered use of their votes.

The supporting principles encourage institutional shareholders to apply the principles set out in the guidance published by the Institutional Shareholders' Committee and to carry out their evaluation of corporate governance disclosures with common sense in order to promote partnership and trust, based on mutual understanding. In particular, the recommendations emphasise that governance should not be evaluated in a mechanistic way and departures from the Combined Code should not automatically be treated as breaches.

REPORTING ON GOING CONCERN

Reporting under the Combined Code

40.15   The 'Combined Code' recommends that the directors should report in the annual report and accounts that the business is a going concern, with supporting assumptions or qualifications as necessary. This disclosure was originally recommended by the 'Cadbury Code of Best Practice', but the disclosure requirement under that Code did not become fully until additional guidance was issued to directors in the document 'Going concern and financial reporting – guidance for directors of listed companies', published in November 1994. In the case of listed companies, the inclusion of a statement on going concern is now a direct requirement of the UK Listing Rules and the statement must also be reviewed by the auditors.

The guidance set out in 'Going concern and financial reporting – guidance for directors of listed companies' was developed by a Joint Working Group (JWG) and sets out the governance principles that directors should adopt in relation to going concern. The guidance is addressed primarily to listed companies, but it was hoped that the clarification of the concept of going concern would be of general benefit to all entities, and would assist directors in discharging their obligations under CA 1985 (see Chapter 1). The document has three main objectives:

(i)   to explain the significance of going concern in relation to financial statements;

(ii)   to describe the procedures that an explicit statement on going concern may entail; and

(iii)   to recommend appropriate disclosures.

Definition of going concern

40.16   FRS 18 'Accounting Policies' describes the going concern basis as the hypothesis that the entity is to continue in operational existence for the foreseeable future and notes that this basis will usually provide the most relevant information to users of the accounts. The standard therefore requires directors to assess, when preparing accounts, whether there are any significant doubts about the entity's ability to continue as a going concern and requires the financial statements to be prepared on a going concern basis unless:

(i)   the entity is being liquidated or has ceased trading;

(ii)   the directors intend to liquidate the entity or to cease trading; or

(iii)   the directors have no realistic alternative but to liquidate the entity or cease trading.

As originally drafted, FRS 18 stated that, in these circumstances, the accounts may, if appropriate, be prepared on a different basis. For accounting periods beginning on or after 1 January 2005, the requirements of FRS 18 are made more stringent by amendments introduced in FRS 21 'Events After the Balance Sheet Date'. Under the new requirements, accounts should not be prepared on a going concern basis in any of the above circumstances. Also under FRS 21, management decisions in the period between the balance sheet date and the date on which the financial statements are authorised for issue must be taken into account in making the assessment.

The JWG guidance emphasises that it will not usually be appropriate to adopt the going concern basis for the accounts if there is any intention or need to:

(i)   enter into a scheme of arrangement with the company's creditors;

(ii) make an application for an administration order; or

(iii) put the company into administrative receivership or liquidation.

However, the restructuring of a business, even on a major scale, is a relatively common practice these days and will not usually result in the going concern basis being an inappropriate basis for the preparation of the accounts.

Foreseeable future

40.17   Neither accounting standards nor CA 1985 explain the term 'foreseeable future' and the Joint Working Group guidance emphasises that it is not appropriate to set a minimum period to which the directors should pay particular attention when considering the issue of going concern. However, the guidance does make the following points:

(i)   any consideration involving the foreseeable future involves making judgements about future events which are inherently uncertain;

(ii) in general terms, the degree of uncertainty increases significantly, the further into the future the consideration is taken;

(iii) the judgement is valid only at the point in time at which it is made; and

(iv) in assessing going concern, the directors should take into account all the information of which they are aware at the time the judgement is made, and their statement on going concern should be made on the basis of the information that is known to them at the date on which they approve the financial statements.

Although no minimum review period is specified, the guidance does note that where the period considered by the directors has been limited, for example, to a period of less than one year from the date of approval of the financial statements, the directors should consider whether additional disclosure should be made to explain the assumptions underlying the adoption of the going concern basis. In these circumstances, FRS 18 'Accounting Policies' (which is mandatory for accounting periods ending on or after 22 June 2001) also requires disclosure in the accounts of the fact that the directors' going concern assessment has been limited to a period of less than twelve months from the date of approval of the accounts. Under the UK and Ireland version of ISA 570 'Going concern', which applies for accounting periods beginning on or after 15 December 2004, the auditors must ask the directors to extend the period of their review to twelve months from the balance sheet date if it has covered a shorter period. Where the directors identify factors which cast doubt on the presumption that the company will continue in operational existence for the foreseeable future, it will usually be appropriate to make additional disclosure in the annual report and accounts. Once again, FRS 18 requires specific disclosures to be given where such circumstances arise in accounting periods ending on or after 22 June 2001.

Procedures to be carried out

40.18   In order to be able to make the required statement on going concern each year, the directors will need to:

(i)   give formal consideration to going concern each year;

(ii)   consider whether there are any factors which cast doubt on the entity's ability to continue in operational existence for the foreseeable future, and whether the going concern basis is appropriate for the financial statements;

(iii)   consider whether additional disclosure is necessary in the annual report and accounts; and

(iv)   make a statement on going concern in the annual report and accounts.

It is not acceptable for directors to simply assume that the business can be treated as a going concern without carrying out any procedures to confirm this. However, many of the recommended procedures will already be carried out by directors and senior management for other purposes, such as the development of strategic plans, the preparation of budgets and forecasts, and risk management. All that may be necessary in these circumstances is to summarise the procedures already carried out, and the issues arising from them, and for the directors to consider whether any additional procedures need to be undertaken to cover any aspects that have not already been adequately dealt with. In practice, much of the work will be done prior to the approval of the accounts. However, since the directors are required to make their assessment on the basis of the information known to them on the date on which the accounts are approved, they will need to update their review to take account of any changes in circumstances that have arisen since the detailed procedures were carried out.

Factors to consider

40.19   Many different factors will be relevant to a consideration of whether a company or group is a going concern, and these will vary according to the nature of the business under review. Some factors will be within the control of the directors, others may be external and, therefore, outside their direct control. Similar factors will need to be taken into account in preparing budgets and forecasts so the directors should have a good understanding of the most significant issues for their company. Further guidance on going concern issues is given in Chapter 1.

The JWG guidance sets out examples of major areas that directors will usually need to consider in order to identify whether they are, or could become, significant in relation to going concern – the list is not intended to be exhaustive but rather to indicate the types of procedures that should be undertaken in considering going concern. The areas identified in the guidance are:

   (i)   forecasts and budgets;

   (ii)   borrowing requirements;

   (iii)   liability management;

   (iv)   contingent liabilities;

   (v)   products and markets;

   (vi)   financial risk management; and

   (vii)   financial adaptability.

An appendix to the document sets out detailed procedures that may be followed. However, the guidance emphasises that these should not be regarded as checklists, partly because not all of the procedures will be relevant in every case, and also because procedures which are not listed may be appropriate in certain circumstances. Each of the main areas is considered briefly below.

Forecasts and budgets

40.20   Budgets and cash flows forecasts should be prepared for at least the period to the next balance sheet date. Alternatively, they may be prepared on a rolling basis covering a twelve-month period. Subsequent periods will usually be covered by medium or long-term plans, giving a general indication of how the business is expected to perform. Budgets and forecasts will usually be supported by a detailed summary of the underlying assumptions and the directors will usually need to confirm that these are reasonable. Directors may also wish to carry out sensitivity analyses on the figures, particularly where the timing of cash receipts may be uncertain or the level of activity may vary significantly. Other factors that may need to be considered include:

   (i)   whether the budgets and forecasts need to be updated for changes in the assumptions or actual results to date;

(ii)   the interaction between assumptions;

(iii)   whether the budgets and forecasts provide adequately for rising costs;

(iv)   whether the budgets and forecasts take appropriate account of seasonal fluctuations; and

(v)   the accuracy of budgets and forecasts in previous years – it may be appropriate to document and analyse significant variances and consider whether these are likely to arise again in the current year.

Borrowing requirements

40.21   The facilities available to the company should be reviewed and compared in detail to cash flow forecasts for at least the period to the next balance sheet date. It will often be appropriate to carry out sensitivity analyses on the critical assumptions when making this comparison, to identify whether facilities would be adequate in a worst case scenario, or whether covenants would be likely to be breached in these circumstances. The directors should seek to ensure that there are no anticipated shortfalls in facilities against requirements, no arrears of interest and no other breaches of covenants. There may be mitigating factors which would enable the directors to cope with any potential problems, for instance where they have scope to alter the amount or timing of significant cash flows. Any potential deficits, arrears or breaches that cannot be covered should be discussed with the company's bankers at an early stage to determine any action that needs to be taken and to prevent problems crystallising if possible. The onus is on the directors to be satisfied that appropriate and committed financing arrangements are in place.

Liability management

40.22   The directors should ensure that the company's financial plans indicate appropriate matching of cash outflows with cash inflows. It is particularly important to ensure that cash outflows should include all known liabilities, such as loan repayments, payments of tax and VAT, and any commitments which may be off-balance sheet (for instance, certain leasing commitments, or forward exchange contracts). It may also be appropriate to consider whether the company is particularly dependent on individual suppliers, and the impact that a failure in supply might have on the company's ability to meet its cash outflows.

Contingent liabilities

40.23   The directors should review the company's exposure to contingent liabilities, including:

(i)   liabilities experienced in the past and which might recur, such as legal proceedings, guarantees and warranties, and product liability claims not covered by insurance; and

(ii) new contingencies that may arise in the future, such as environmental clean-up costs or future decommissioning costs.

Products and markets

40.24 The directors should consider the size and strength of the market, the company's market share, and whether the market may change as a result of economic, political or other factors. In more complex businesses, this will usually need to be done by major product line. Depending on the nature of the business, this review may also need to take into account technical research and development, to confirm that this is adequate and can be maintained at an appropriate level for the foreseeable future. Other factors that may need to be considered include:

(i) product quality and expected life;

(ii) the adequacy of the company's marketing strategy;

(iii) the adequacy of the company's costing system, and in particular whether costs are updated on a regular basis;

(iv) the customer mix, and in particular whether the business is dependent on a small number of significant customers – if so, the risk of losing one or more of them and the likelihood of finding alternative sales markets may also need to be assessed; and

(v) the level of dependence on inter-group trading and the financial implications of this.

Financial risk management

40.25 Directors should identify which financial risks are most significant for their company and their current approach to managing these. For instance, financial risks might include exposure to fixed price contracts or to significant fluctuations in foreign currency exchange rates. Sensitivity analyses may need to be performed if assumptions on factors such as interest rates and foreign currency are particularly critical to the cash flow forecasts.

Financial adaptability

40.26 Financial adaptability is the ability of the company to take effective action to alter the amounts and timings of cash flows to respond to unexpected needs or opportunities. Financial adaptability can help to mitigate any of the factors discussed above in relation to going concern. Consideration of financial adaptability might include reviewing:

(i) the ability to dispose of assets or postpone the replacement of assets, or to finance assets from other sources (e.g. leasing rather than outright purchase);

(ii)   the potential for obtaining new sources of finance;

(iii)   the possibility of extending or renewing loans, or restructuring debt; and

(iv)   the possibility of raising additional share capital.

Other factors

40.27   The Joint Working Group identifies a number of other factors that may need to be taken into account in particular circumstances, including:

   (i)   recurring operating losses or fluctuating profits and losses;

  (ii)   the impact of dividend arrears;

 (iii)   non-compliance with statutory capital requirements;

  (iv)   the impact of labour difficulties;

   (v)   the potential impact of the loss of key management and staff, and the likelihood of finding suitable replacements quickly;

  (vi)   the potential impact of the loss of a key patent or franchise;

 (vii)   the impact of long-overdue debtors, or high stock levels;

(viii)   the impact of potential losses on long-term contracts; and

  (ix)   the potential impact of the company's fixed asset replacement policy (e.g. if funds are not available to replace assets regularly, there is the potential for increased maintenance costs, higher levels of down-time or quality control problems).

Overall assessment and conclusion

40.28   Once they have carried out all the individual procedures that they consider appropriate, the directors should determine the likely outcome by considering the range of potential outcomes and the probability of their occurrence and taking into account the implications of any interaction between the various factors. In practice, this will usually be evidenced by the board:

   (i)   considering a paper summarising the going concern position of the company;

  (ii)   discussing the implications of the issues; and

 (iii)   reaching a formal conclusion on going concern.

If the directors become aware of any factors that cast doubt on the ability of the entity to continue in operational existence for the foreseeable future, they will need to carry out additional detailed investigations to determine the extent of the problem, and to decide how the company can best respond to it. They will also usually need to make additional disclosure in the annual report and accounts.

Content of disclosure

40.29 Having carried out appropriate procedures, the directors should be able to reach one of three possible conclusions:

(i) that there is a reasonable expectation that the company will continue in operational existence for the foreseeable future, and the going concern basis is therefore appropriate for the financial statements;

(ii) that there are factors that cast doubt on the ability of the company to continue in operational existence for the foreseeable future, but the directors consider that it is still appropriate to use the going concern basis in preparing the financial statements; or

(iii) that it is unlikely that the company will continue in operational existence for the foreseeable future and it is therefore not appropriate to use the going concern basis in preparing the financial statements.

The JWG guidance sets out recommendations on disclosure in each of these circumstances.

Going concern presumption appropriate

40.30 Where the directors conclude that there are no indications to suggest that the company will be unable to continue in operational existence for the foreseeable future, and that the going concern is presumption is, therefore, an appropriate basis for the preparation of the accounts, the JWG guidance suggests the following basic disclosure:

> 'After making enquiries, the directors have a reasonable expectation that the company has adequate resources to continue in operational existence for the foreseeable future. For this reason, they continue to adopt the going concern basis in preparing the accounts.'

The implication of this recommendation is that details of the 'supporting assumptions or qualifications as necessary' specifically required by the 'Combined Code' only need to be given where there are some doubts or uncertainties over the continuation of the business. A number of companies have gone beyond the basic disclosure suggested in the guidance, and given details of the steps that the directors have taken in reaching their conclusions, along the following lines:

> 'The directors have reviewed the company's budget for 20XX and outline plans for the following two years. After taking into account the cash flow implications of the plans, including proposed capital expenditure and reorganisation costs, and after comparing these to the company's committed borrowing facilities, the directors are satisfied that it is appropriate to prepare the accounts on a going concern basis.'

Going concern basis used despite certain doubts

40.31   If there are some doubts or uncertainties over the appropriateness of the going concern basis for the accounts, the directors should explain the circumstances by giving details of:

(i)   the factors that give rise to the problems (including any external factors that are beyond their control); and

(ii)   the action being taken to deal with the problem.

The guidance sets out the following example of a situation where the company has breached loan covenants and is in the process of renegotiating borrowing facilities as a result:

> 'The company is in breach of certain loan covenants at its balance sheet date and so the company's bankers could recall their loans at any time. The directors continue to be involved in negotiations with the company's bankers and as yet no demands for repayments have been received. The negotiations are at an early stage and, although the directors are optimistic about the outcome, it is as yet too early to make predictions with any certainty. In the light of the actions described ... the directors consider it appropriate to adopt the going concern basis in preparing the accounts.'

In this situation, the loan will usually need to be shown as a current rather than a long-term liability, on the basis that it has become repayable on demand and the renegotiated facility is not in place at the balance sheet date. This is not a going concern adjustment, but a reflection of the entity's financial position at the balance sheet date. Further details of the requirements of accounting standards on this issue are given at 1.22, 26.15 and 26.35 above.

Going concern basis not appropriate

40.32   Where the directors conclude that the company is unlikely to continue in operational existence for the foreseeable future, they will need to prepare the accounts on an alternative basis such as a break-up basis. This situation is expected to arise only rarely in practice, but in these circumstances the directors will have to state that, in their opinion, the company is no longer a going concern. The directors will usually need to take legal advice on the wording of such a statement. The fact that the company is not considered to be a going concern does not necessarily mean that it is insolvent, but the directors will need to give appropriate consideration to this and in particular to the wrongful trading provisions of insolvency law.

Location of the directors' statement

40.33   The Joint Working Group guidance suggests that the directors' statement on going concern should be given in the Operating and Financial Review, as the considerable amount of discussion and analysis given in this will usually help to put the going concern statement into context. In practice, many companies present the going concern statement as part of a separate section of the annual report and accounts dealing with corporate governance issues rather than as part of the Operating and Financial Review. The accounts themselves may also need to refer to the use of the going concern basis in the note on accounting policies, especially if there are doubts or uncertainties over the going concern presumption. In these circumstances it will usually be necessary to cross-reference the directors' statement to the details given in the accounts.

Application of the guidance to Groups

40.34   In the case of a group, the JWG guidance notes that the directors of the parent company should make a going concern statement in relation to both the parent company and the group as a whole. However, the statement in respect of the group should not be taken as implying that each of the individual companies within the group is considered to be a going concern.

Interim reporting

40.35   Going concern will not usually be considered in the same level of detail in the context of an interim report as in the case of the annual report and accounts. However, the guidance states that at the time that the interim report is approved, the directors should review their previous work on going concern and see whether any of the significant factors identified at that time have changed in the intervening period to such an extent as to affect the appropriateness of the going concern presumption. More information on the preparation of interim reports is given in Chapter 41.

REPORTING ON INTERNAL CONTROL

Reporting under the Combined Code

40.36   Principle C.2 of the revised 'Combined Code' deals with internal control as follows:

> 'The board should maintain a sound system of internal control to safeguard the shareholders' investment and the company's assets.'

Provision C.2.1 states that:

> 'Directors should, at least annually, conduct a review of the effectiveness of the group's system of internal control and should report to shareholders that they have done so. The review should cover all material controls, including financial, operational and compliance controls and risk management.'

The 'Combined Code' therefore requires the directors' statement to cover all aspects of internal control, rather than just internal financial control, and emphasises that directors must review the effectiveness of the system of internal control on an annual basis. However, there is no formal requirement for directors to report on the effectiveness of the system of control – they are only required to report that they have carried out an appropriate review.

Turnbull Guidance

40.37   Guidance on reviewing internal control and reporting under the 'Combined Code' was developed by a working party of the Institute of Chartered Accountants in England and Wales chaired by Nigel Turnbull. Their final report 'Internal Control – Guidance for Directors on the Combined Code' (usually referred to as the 'Turnbull Guidance') was published in September 1999 and clarifies what is expected of the board of a listed company in terms of:

(i)   applying Principle C.2 of the Combined Code (maintaining a sound system of internal control to safeguard the shareholders' investment and the company's assets); and

(ii)   determining the extent of their compliance with the best practice guidance set out in provision C.2.1 of Part 2 of the Combined Code (review of the effectiveness of the system of internal control).

It also deals with the annual consideration of whether an internal audit function should be established, if the company does not already have one. The Turnbull Guidance is now attached as an Appendix to the revised Combined Code issued in July 2003.

The objective of the Internal Control Working Party was to develop guidance that:

(i)   can be tailored to the circumstances of an individual company;

(ii)   identifies sound business practice, by linking internal control with risk management and placing emphasis on the key controls that a company should maintain;

(iii)   provides meaningful high level information and avoids extensive disclosure that does not add to a user's understanding; and

(iv)   will remain relevant and be capable of evolving with the business environment.

This approach is in line with the preamble to the 'Combined Code', which emphasises that it is not the intention to prescribe the form or content of the various reporting statements required by the Code, but rather that companies should be free to explain their governance policies in the light of the principles set out in the Code and in the context of any special circumstances specific to the company.

In December 2004, the FRC issued a consultation document on proposals to review the current effectiveness of the Turnbull Guidance and establish whether it requires updating for developments in the intervening period and whether companies should be disclosing additional information to shareholders in respect of internal control issues. In a press release on 16 June 2005, the FRC announced that the review group had concluded that the guidance had helped to improve internal control in UK listed companies and that only limited changes were required to bring it up to date. In particular:

(i) the guidance should continue to cover all internal controls, and not be restricted to those over financial reporting;

(ii) it should be updated to reflect changes in the Combined Code and Listing Rules since 1999 and the proposed statement of directors' duties in the draft Company Law Reform Bill;

(iii) boards should review their application of the guidance on a continuing basis;

(iv) boards should not be required to make a statement in the annual report and accounts on the effectiveness of the company's internal control system, but they should confirm that necessary action has been or is being taken to remedy any significant failings or weaknesses identified from the reviews of the effectiveness of the internal control system;

(v) boards should look on the internal control statement in the annual report and accounts as an opportunity to explain to shareholders how they manage risk; and

(vi) there should be no extension of the external auditors' responsibilities in relation to the company's internal control statement.

The review also concluded that there should be no need for companies that are already applying the guidance to develop additional processes in order to comply with the requirement to identify principal risks in the Operating and Financial Review (OFR), but companies should be encouraged to ensure that the OFR and the internal control statement are complementary. A revised draft of the guidance is expected to be published for further consultation in mid-2005, with a view to the updated guidance applying for accounting periods beginning on or after 1 January 2006.

Internal control and SEC reporting

40.38   Also in December 2004, the FRC issued an additional guide for companies registered with the US Securities and Exchange Commission (SEC) on how the Turnbull Guidance should be used in complying with the new US requirement for companies to report on internal controls over financial reporting. UK companies need to comply with this SEC reporting requirement for financial periods ending on or after 15 July 2005. The SEC has accepted that the Turnbull Guidance provides a suitable framework for companies to evaluate internal control in this area. The guide can be downloaded from the FRC website at http://www.frc.org.uk/corporate.

Importance of internal control and risk management

40.39   The Turnbull Guidance notes that a sound system of internal control plays a key role in the management of risks that could have a significant impact on the fulfilment of business objectives and helps to safeguard both the company's assets and the shareholders' investment. Significant business risks (e.g. operational, financial and compliance risks) must be identified and assessed on an ongoing basis. Suggested areas for the board to consider include whether the company has clear objectives, whether these have been communicated to employees in a way that provides direction on risk assessment and control issues, and whether objectives and related business plans include measurable performance indicators and targets. Financial controls are an important element of internal control, as they help to:

(i)   avoid exposure to avoidable financial risk;

(ii)   ensure the reliability of financial information for both internal and external use; and

(iii)   safeguard assets, including the prevention and detection of fraud.

The risks that any entity faces will inevitably change as the business develops and the environment in which it operates evolves. Companies must, therefore, regularly review and evaluate the risks to which they are exposed. The aim will usually be to manage and control business risk rather than to attempt to eliminate it completely.

The guidance is based on the principle that companies will adopt a risk-based approach to the establishment of a system of internal control and to the regular review of its effectiveness. The intention is that the review of the effectiveness of the internal control system should be part of the normal process of managing the business rather than a specific exercise carried out only in order to comply with the recommendations of the Combined Code.

Application to groups

40.40   The guidance notes specifically that, where reference is made to a 'company' this should be taken where relevant to refer to the group as a whole. The directors of the parent company are therefore responsible for the reviewing the effectiveness of internal control from the perspective of the group as a whole and for reporting to shareholders on this.

Where the board's statement on internal control does not cover any joint ventures or associates of the group, this fact should be disclosed.

Responsibility for maintaining a system of internal control

40.41 The detailed work involved in establishing, operating and managing a system of internal control should be carried out by individuals with the necessary skills, technical knowledge, objectivity and understanding of the business, its objectives, the industries and markets in which it operates and the risks that it faces. This detailed work will usually be delegated by the board to management and all employees will have some responsibility for internal control as part of their accountability for achieving objectives. However, the board as a whole retains ultimate responsibility for the company's system of internal control. It must therefore set appropriate policies on internal control and satisfy itself on a regular basis that the system is functioning effectively and that it is effective in managing the risks that the business faces.

A system of internal control can never provide absolute protection against business failure, material errors, fraud or breaches of law and regulation, but it should be able to provide reasonable assurance against them. The guidance notes that, in determining policies on internal control and assessing what constitutes a sound system of internal control in the particular circumstances of the company, the board should consider:

(i) the nature and extent of the risks that the company faces;

(ii) the extent and categories of risk that it regards as acceptable for the company to bear;

(iii) the likelihood of the risks crystallising;

(iv) the company's ability to reduce the incidence and impact on the business of risks that do crystallise; and

(v) the costs and benefits of operating relevant controls.

The limitations on any system of internal control will include human fallibility, management override of controls and the risk of unforeseen events and circumstances arising.

Definition of internal control

40.42 An internal control system is defined as encompassing the policies, processes, tasks, behaviours and other aspects of the company that, taken together:

(i) facilitate its effective and efficient operation by enabling it to respond appropriately to significant risks (business, operational, financial and compliance);

(ii) help to ensure the quality of internal and external reporting; and

(iii) help to ensure compliance with applicable laws and regulations.

This will include safeguarding assets from loss, fraud or inappropriate use, identifying and managing liabilities and maintaining proper records and processes that generate information that is timely, relevant and reliable.

Elements of a sound system of internal control

40.43   A system of internal control should reflect the company's control environment and organisational structure and includes:

(i)   control activities;

(ii)   information and communication processes; and

(iii)   processes for monitoring the continuing effectiveness of the system.

The system of internal control should be embedded in the company's operations and form part of its culture. It must also be capable of responding promptly to new risks as the business evolves and should include procedures for reporting immediately to management when significant control weaknesses or failures are identified. Information provided to management and the board might include regular reports on progress against the company's business objectives (e.g. agreed performance indicators) together with information on issues such as customer satisfaction and employee attitudes.

Control environment

40.44   A company's control environment is usually considered to include issues such as:

(i)   a commitment by directors, management and employees to competence, integrity and a climate of trust (e.g. leadership by example, development of an appropriate culture within the business);

(ii)   the communication to all managers and employees of agreed standards of behaviour and control consciousness, which support the business objectives and risk management and internal control systems (e.g. written codes of conduct, formal disciplinary procedures, formal process of performance appraisal);

(iii)   clear organisational structures, which help to ensure that authority, responsibility and accountability are clearly defined and that decisions and action are taken by the appropriate people;

(iv)   clear communication to employees of what is expected of them and their freedom to act (e.g. in relation to customer relations, service levels, health and safety issues, environmental matters, financial and other reporting issues);

(v)   allocation of sufficient time and resources to risk management and internal control;

(vi)   the provision of relevant training on risk and control issues, so that management and employees develop the necessary knowledge, skills and tools to support achievement of the company's objectives and the effective management of risk.

Reviewing the effectiveness of internal control

40.45   The board may delegate to the audit committee (or other board committees) certain aspects of the review of the effectiveness of the system of internal control (e.g. the aspects that are particularly relevant to their activities), but the board as a whole should form its own view on the adequacy of the review after due and careful enquiry. In other words, it will not be sufficient for the audit committee alone to review the effectiveness of the system of internal control. The audit committee should report formally to the board, who should then take a collective decision on the adequacy of the review.

The precise role of the audit committee will vary between companies and will depend on factors such as the size, style and composition of the board and the nature of the principal risks that the business faces. The audit committee will usually consider financial controls, but may also be asked by the board to act as the focal point for reviews of the wider aspects of internal control. These issues should be considered by the board when the terms of reference for the audit committee are established and reviewed.

The process of the review

40.46   The guidance notes that there should be a defined process for the board's review of the effectiveness of the company's system of internal control, to provide adequate support for the statement in the annual report. The board should take account of all the information available to it up to the date on which the annual report is approved and signed.

The board should not rely solely on the monitoring processes that form part of the business operations, but should receive and review regular reports on internal control, and also carry out a specific annual assessment to support the statement in the annual report to ensure that all significant aspects of internal control have been covered. The guidance suggests the following approach:

(i)   there should be an agreed procedure for the board (or relevant committee) to receive and review regular reports on internal control from management or others qualified to prepare them (e.g. internal audit) – these reports should provide a balanced assessment of the areas covered identifying the significant risks and the effectiveness of the internal control system in managing those risks;

(ii)   the board (or relevant committee) should:

- consider the key risks and assess how they have been identified, evaluated and managed;

- assess the effectiveness of the internal control system in managing those risks, taking into account the impact of any weaknesses or control failings that have been reported;

- consider whether appropriate and prompt action is being taken to remedy weaknesses or failings;

- consider whether the findings indicate a need for more extensive monitoring of the internal control system;

(iii)   the board should carry out a specific annual assessment to support the statement in the annual report, covering:

- changes since the last review in the nature and extent of significant risks;

- the company's ability to respond effectively to change (both internal and external);

- the scope and quality of the ongoing monitoring of the system of internal control, including where appropriate the internal audit function;

- the extent and frequency of reporting to the board (or relevant committee) of the results of the monitoring process, enabling it to build up a cumulative assessment of the state of internal control and the effectiveness with which risk is managed;

- the incidence of major control weaknesses or failings identified during the period and the extent to which they have resulted in unforeseen outcomes or contingencies that have had, could have had, or may in future have, a material impact on results; and

- the effectiveness of the year-end financial reporting process.

Where significant control weaknesses or failings are identified, the board should determine how these arose and should reassess the effectiveness of management's ongoing processes for designing, operating and monitoring the system of internal control.

The annual statement on internal control

40.47   The board's annual statement on internal control should provide users of the annual report and accounts with meaningful, high-level information. Particular care should be taken to ensure that the statement does not give a misleading impression. As a minimum, the board should disclose where applicable:

(i)   that there is an ongoing process for identifying, evaluating and managing key risks:

(ii)   that this process has been in place for the year under review and up to the date of approval of the annual report and accounts; and

(iii)   that this process accords with the relevant guidance on internal control, and that it is regularly reviewed by the board.

It should also summarise the process that the board has applied in reviewing the effectiveness of the system of internal control, including where relevant the role of the audit committee or other committees. The guidance notes that, in addition, the board may wish to provide additional information to help users of the accounts to understand the company's risk management processes and the system of internal control.

If the board is unable to make any of these disclosures, this fact should be stated and the board should explain what action is being taken to rectify the situation.

The statement should also include an acknowledgement that the board is responsible for the company's system of internal control and for reviewing its effectiveness, together with an explanation that such a system can only provide reasonable and not absolute assurance against material misstatement or loss. Where relevant, listed companies will also need to disclose the fact that they have failed to conduct a review of the effectiveness of the internal control system, or that they have not reviewed the need for an internal audit function (if they do not already have one).

The guidance suggests additional disclosures where weaknesses in internal control have resulted in significant problems which have been disclosed in the annual accounts. In this situation, the board should describe the processes that it has applied to deal with the internal control aspects of the problems.

Review of the need for an internal audit function

40.48   Provision C.3.5 of the revised 'Combined Code' requires the audit committees of companies which do not have an internal audit function to review annually the need to establish one. The guidance suggests that the review should take into account:

(i)   whether the board has other means of obtaining sufficient and objective assurance on the effectiveness of the company's system of internal control;

(ii)   whether there are any trends or current factors in the company's internal environment, markets or other aspects of its external environment that have increased, or are expected to increase, the risks faced by the company – for example:

(iii)   changes in organisational structure, reporting processes or information systems;

(iv)   changes in key risks as a result of changes in products or services, entry into new markets, or changes in regulatory requirements;

(v)   adverse trends apparent from the monitoring of internal control systems; or

(vi)   increased incidence of unexpected or unacceptable results.

Where there is an internal audit function, the guidance suggests that the board should review its remit, authority, resources and scope of work, also on an annual basis.

Role of the external auditors

40.49   Where directors are required under the UK Listing Rules to include in the annual report and accounts a statement on compliance with the 'Combined Code' and a statement on going concern, these statements must be reviewed by the auditors. In the case of the compliance statement, the review is only required to cover certain aspects of the Code's requirements, but these specifically include the directors' statement on internal control (see 40.7 above)

APPENDIX

Checklist of Combined Code Reporting Requirements

A listed company must include the following disclosures in its annual report and accounts:

- A narrative statement of how it has applied the principles set out in the 'Combined Code', with explanations to enable the shareholders to evaluate how the principles have been applied;

- A statement on whether or not it has complied throughout the accounting period with the best practice provisions set out in the 'Combined Code', with details of, and the reasons for, any areas or periods of non-compliance.

- A statement on how the board operates, including a high level statement on which types of decision are taken by the board and which are delegated to management [A.1.1]

- The names of the chairman, deputy chairman (where relevant), chief executive and senior independent director [A.1.2]

- The names of chairmen and members of the main board committees (ie audit, nomination and remuneration) [A.1.2]

- The number of meetings of the board and its main committees, and details of individual attendance by directors [A.1.2]

- The names of the non-executive directors whom the board considers to be independent [A.3.1]

- The reasons for considering a director to be independent if there are relationships or circumstances that might be deemed to affect this [A.3.1]

- The other significant commitments of the chairman and any changes to them during the year [A.4.3.]

- A description of the work of the nomination committee, in a separate section of the report, including:

    - the process used in respect of board appointments;

    - an explanation if neither external consultancy nor open advertising has been used in the appointment of a chairman or non-executive director [A.4.6]

- How performance evaluation of the board, its committees and the individual directors has been conducted [A.6.1]

- A description of the work of the remuneration committee as required by the Directors' Remuneration Report Regulations 2002

- Where an executive director serves as a non-executive elsewhere, whether or not the director will retain the relevant earnings and, if so, what the remuneration is [B.1.4]

- An explanation of the directors' responsibilities for preparing the accounts and a statement on the reporting responsibilities of the auditors [C.1.1]

- A statement from the directors that the business is a going concern, with supporting assumptions or qualifications as necessary [C.1.2]

- A report that the board has conducted a review of the effectiveness of the company's (or group's) system of internal control [C.2.1]

- A description of the work of the audit committee, in a separate section of the report [C.3.3]

- Where relevant, the reasons for the absence of an internal audit function [C.3.5]

- Where relevant, a statement from the audit committee explaining its recommendation on the appointment, reappointment or removal of the external auditor and the reasons why the board has taken a different position [C.3.6] (NB this should also be included in the papers sent out to shareholders on the appointment or reappointment of an external auditor)

- If the external auditor provides non-audit services, an explanation of how auditor independence and objectivity is safeguarded [C.3.7]

In addition, the following information is required to be made publicly available (eg by inclusion on the company's website or by making it available on request):

- The terms of reference of the nomination committee [A.4.1.]

- The terms of reference of the remuneration committee [B.2.1]

- The terms of reference of the audit committee [C.3.3]

- Where remuneration consultants are appointed, a statement on whether they have any other connection with the company [B.2.1]

The Combined Code also requires the following information to be made available:

- The terms and conditions of appointment of non-executive directors should be made available for inspection by any person at the company's registered office during normal business hours, for 15 minutes prior to the AGM and during the AGM [A.4.4]

- The papers sent out to shareholders in respect of a resolution to elect or re-elect a director should include:

  - sufficient biographical details and any other relevant information to enable shareholders to make an informed decision [A.7.1]

  - why the board considers that an individual should be elected as a non-executive director [A.7.2]

  - in the case of re-election, confirmation from the chairman that, following formal performance evaluation, the individual continues to make an effective contribution and to demonstrate commitment to the role, including time for board and committee meetings and any other duties [A.7.2]

Chapter 41   Interim Reports

PREPARATION OF AN INTERIM REPORT

Requirement to prepare an interim statement

41.1   The UK Listing Authority's Listing Rules require listed companies to issue an interim statement each year, giving details of their results for the first half of the financial year. An interim statement must be notified to the Authority within 90 days of the half-year reporting date and the minimum contents required under the Listing Rules are now broadly in line with the recommended contents set out in the ASB's non-mandatory Statement 'Interim reports'. Companies may issue information on a more regular basis if they wish (eg quarterly). Where this approach is adopted, the reports for the first and third quarters tend to be less detailed than those produced for the half-year. However, innovative high growth companies who take advantage of the provisions of Chapter 25 of the Listing Rules when seeking admission to listing are already required to publish a quarterly report on their activities and the UK Listing Authority is currently considering whether quarterly reporting should be introduced for all listed companies. Unlisted companies are free to issue interim statements on a voluntary basis if they wish, although few choose to do so.

The value of interim reports

41.2   For listed companies, interim reports form an important part of the process of communicating with shareholders and with the financial market as a whole, enabling readers to monitor the progress and development of the business and assess the impact of recent events on its financial performance and financial position. The reaction of the financial markets to information given in interim reports can be significant and many companies provide more than the minimum details required by the UK Listing Authority to prevent misunderstandings and misinterpretations, and also to safeguard against the accidental disclosure of price-sensitive information. However, despite the significance of these interim reports, there was no detailed guidance on their preparation until the Accounting Standards Board (ASB) issued its Statement in September 1997.

Timing and distribution of interim reports

41.3   Interim reports are issued to all shareholders. The ASB Statement recommends that the interim report should be issued within 60 days of the period-end. However, the UK Listing Authority allows a slightly longer period for issue, requiring listed companies to issue their interim statement within 90 days of the period-end. The Companies Act 1985 now clarifies that references to sending accounts and reports to those entitled to receive them include:

(i)   sending copies by electronic communication to the address notified to the company for that purpose by the person entitled to receive the documents; or

(ii)   where the company and the person entitled to receive the accounts so agree, publishing the documents on a website, notifying the person in the manner agreed that they have been published in this way and providing him/her with both the address of the website and details of where and how the documents may be accessed on the website.

There is no reason why interim reports should not be distributed in a similar manner to those shareholders who have notified an appropriate e-mail address to the company and confirmed that they are happy to receive company information in one of these ways.

Review by the auditors

41.4   There is currently no formal requirement for auditors to review or report on interim reports before they are published. However, the Cadbury Report recommended that auditors should be required to review interim statements prior to their release, although it did not comment on publication of an auditors' report following such a review. Auditing Practices Board (APB) Bulletin 1999/4 'Review of Interim Financial Information' sets out guidance for auditors on the procedures to be undertaken when reviewing interim statements. The Bulletin also included examples of reports to be issued by the auditors following such a review, but these have been superseded by updated guidance in APB Bulletin 2001/2 'Revisions to the Wording of Auditors' Reports on Financial Statements and the Interim Review Report'. Because the recommended review work is limited in scope, and does not constitute an audit, the auditors will normally report in terms of 'negative assurance' – in other words, they will report that they are not aware of any material modification that should be made to the information presented in the interim report.

Where interim information is reviewed in accordance with the APB guidance, the Listing Rules require the auditors' review report to be published as part of the company's interim report, and the ASB Statement 'Interim Reports' also recommends disclosure of the extent to which the information given in the interim report has been audited or reviewed. APB Bulletin 1999/4 notes that the directors, or the audit committee acting on behalf of the board, may ask the auditors to carry out specific agreed procedures as an alternative to the review set out in the APB guidance. However, if the scope of the work carried out by the auditors is less than that set out in the APB guidance, the Bulletin recommends that the directors describe the financial information in the interim report as 'neither audited nor reviewed'.

CONTENTS OF AN INTERIM REPORT

The ASB Statement 'Interim Reports'

41.5   The ASB published its Statement 'Interim Reports' in September 1997 in response to certain issues raised in the Cadbury Report. The objective of the Statement is to improve the timeliness, quality, relevance and consistency of information published in the form of interim reports. The Statement is non-mandatory but it sets out best practice for companies that are required to publish an interim report, and all listed companies are encouraged to follow its recommendations. Many companies were already providing much of the information recommended in the ASB Statement, but it is helpful to have formal guidance on the contents of an interim report, and in particular on the principles to be followed in dealing with some of the potentially difficult issues that can arise. The principles set out in the guidance are equally relevant to reports produced on a more regular basis.

For accounting periods beginning on or after 1 January 2005, interim reports come within the remit of the Financial Reporting Review Panel (FRRP) and so may be subject to external scrutiny for compliance with accounting standards and other requirements (see 1.12 above). In 2005, the FRRP is expected to pay particular attention to the interim reports of companies who are required to adopt international accounting standards (see 1.3 above and 41.8 below).

Recommended contents of an interim report

41.6   The recommended contents for an interim report are as follows.

(i)   A balanced narrative commentary on the main factors influencing performance during the period and the financial position at the period end (see 41.15 to 41.17 below).

(ii)   A summarised profit and loss account, showing:

- turnover;

- operating profit or loss;
- net interest payable/receivable;
- profit or loss on ordinary activities before tax;
- tax on profit or loss on ordinary activities;
- profit or loss on ordinary activities after tax;
- minority interests;
- profit or loss for the period; and
- dividends paid and proposed.

(iii) A statement of total recognised gains and losses.

(iv) A summarised balance sheet, showing:
- fixed assets;
- current assets:
- stocks;
- debtors;
- cash at bank and in hand; and
- other;
- creditors: amounts falling due within one year;
- net current assets/liabilities;
- total assets less current liabilities;
- creditors: amounts falling due after more than one year;
- provisions for liabilities and charges;
- capital and reserves; and
- minority interests.

(v) A summarised cash flow statement, showing:
- net cash inflow/outflow from operating activities;
- returns on investments and servicing of finance;
- taxation;
- capital expenditure and financial investment;
- acquisitions and disposals;
- equity dividends paid;
- management of liquid resources;
- financing; and
- increase/decrease in cash.

A reconciliation of movements in shareholders' funds only needs to be included where there are additional movements to be explained (i.e. movements other than those shown in the statement of total recognised gains and losses).

The Listing Rules have been updated since the ASB Statement was prepared and now impose contents requirements that are broadly similar to the above.

Other disclosures

41.7   The ASB Statement recommends the following additional disclosures:

(i)   where relevant, amounts relating to associates and joint ventures should be shown separately in the summarised profit and loss account;

(ii)   turnover and operating profit in respect of any acquisitions or discontinued operations should be shown separately on the face of the summarised profit and loss account – for this purpose, operations are to be regarded as discontinued if the sale or termination was completed in the interim period, or by the earlier of the date of approval of the interim report or three months after the end of the interim period;

(iii)   segmental analyses of turnover and profit or loss before interest should be given, using the same business and geographical classifications as in the annual accounts;

(iv)   any exceptional items occurring in the interim period, including items required to be shown separately in the profit and loss account under FRS 3 'Reporting financial performance' (i.e. profits and losses on the sale or termination of an operation, costs of a fundamental reorganisation or restructuring, and profits and losses on the disposal of fixed assets);

(v)   reconciliations of operating profit to operating cashflow and the movement of cash to the movement in net debt; and

(vi)   the following information:

- the period covered by the interim report;
- the date on which the interim report was formally approved by the board of directors; and
- the extent to which the information in the interim report has been audited or reviewed (see 41.4 above).

The results of operations that are in the process of discontinuing, or which are expected to be classified as discontinued in the accounts for the full financial year, may be shown separately in the notes to the interim report.

Accounting policies

41.8   Interim reports should be prepared using the company's normal accounting policies and should include a statement that the policies are the same as those disclosed in the last published accounts, or explain any differences. Where it is known that a change in accounting policy is to be made in the accounts for the full financial year, the interim report should normally be prepared on the basis of the new policy, all relevant comparative figures should be restated and the cumulative effect on opening reserves should be disclosed. If the interim figures are not presented on the basis of the new accounting policy, the estimated financial effect of the change in policy should be disclosed. Any other prior period adjustments (for instance, due to the correction of fundamental errors) should be reflected in the interim report in the same way as changes in accounting policy. For accounting periods beginning on or after 1 January 2005, listed companies are required by the EU IAS Regulation to prepare group accounts in accordance with international accounting standards (IASs) rather than UK accounting standards and will also need to rework comparative figures for 2004 on the same basis. As a result, interim statements for periods ending on or after 30 June 2005, and the comparative information in those statements, will also have to be presented on the basis of IASs.

Earnings per share

41.9   Basic earnings per share should be calculated from the interim results and disclosed in the interim report in the same way as in the full annual accounts. If the company adopts a policy of disclosing additional calculations of earnings per share in its annual accounts, the same details should be given in the interim report.

Basis of presentation of financial information

41.10   One particular issue that arises in the case of an interim report is whether the interim period is treated as part of an annual reporting cycle or as a discrete accounting period, distinct from the annual cycle. The ASB Statement recommends that the latter method is used so that the measurement and recognition of income and expenditure is consistent with the annual accounts. Specific guidance is given in the Statement on accounting for items such as bonuses, profit-sharing arrangements and volume discounts that will normally only be calculated at the end of the financial year. The treatment depends on whether there is an obligation at the end of the interim period to transfer economic benefits as a result of past events. For instance, if a profit-related bonus is to be paid at the end of the year, it will be appropriate to recognise a proportion of this in the interim period, based on the profit earned to date, if past practice shows that the company has a constructive obligation to make the payment. A genuinely discretionary bonus paid at the end of the year would not be recognised in the interim figures. However, the Statement also notes that it will sometimes be necessary to look at the expected income or expense for the full year in order to calculate the amount to be recognised in the interim period.

Taxation

41.11   The most obvious example of a situation where the expected income or expense for the full year must be considered when presenting information in a interim report is taxation, and considerable guidance is given on this in the ASB Statement. The likely effective tax rate for the full year should be calculated, expressed as a percentage of the expected results for the full year, and this percentage should be applied to the interim profit or loss to calculate the interim tax charge. More detailed calculations may be needed where different tax jurisdictions are involved or where different tax rates apply to material categories of income.

Other presentation issues

41.12   Other points to note in relation to the presentation of financial information in interim reports are:

(i)   the results of foreign group entities should be translated in line with the company's usual accounting policy;

(ii)   asset revaluations will not usually be required for interim report purposes, although certain disclosures are recommended; and

(iii)   materiality should be assessed in relation to the interim period rather than the expected results and financial position at the end of the financial year.

FRS 23 'The Effects of Changes in Foreign Exchange Rates' amends the wording of the ASB Statement to clarify that the actual closing and average rates for the interim period should be used to translate the results of foreign operations, and that changes in exchange rates in the remainder of the financial period should not be anticipated. Similarly, all exchange differences should be recognised in the interim period in accordance with the requirements of FRS 23 and should not be deferred on the basis that they are expected to reverse later in the period. In the case of listed companies, FRS 23 is effective for accounting periods beginning on or after 1 January 2005.

Comparative figures

41.13   Comparative figures for the summarised profit and loss account, statement of total recognised gains and losses and summarised cash flow statement should cover the corresponding interim period in the previous year and also the last full financial year. This is to help provide a meaningful view of the company's performance to date, especially where the business is seasonal. In the case of the balance sheet, the critical comparative figures are those for the last full financial year, although those for the corresponding interim period may also be given.

Statutory disclosure

41.14   Where an interim report contains information for a full financial year of the company or information as at the company's normal financial year-end (for instance, comparative profit and loss account information for the previous financial year, and comparative balance sheet information as at the end of the last financial year), the interim report will constitute 'non-statutory accounts' under section 240 of the *Companies Act* 1985 and must therefore include the formal statements required by that section. All interim reports should therefore state

(i)   that they are not the company's statutory accounts;

(ii)   whether statutory accounts for any financial year covered by the non-statutory accounts have been delivered to the Registrar;

(iii)   whether the auditors have reported on the statutory accounts for any financial year covered by the non-statutory accounts;

(iv)   whether any auditors' report was qualified or contained a statement under section 237(2) or (3) of the *Companies Act* 1985 on inadequate records or returns, accounts not in agreement with the records or returns, or failure of the auditors to obtain all necessary information and explanations; and

(v)   for accounting periods beginning on or after 1 January 2005, whether the auditors' report included a reference to any matters of emphasis, without qualification of the report.

MANAGEMENT COMMENTARY

Focus of the report

41.15   Because the interim report is intended to update shareholders and other interested parties on the company's performance since the latest annual accounts, the management commentary should focus on recent events, activities and circumstances. It should, therefore, discuss the financial information shown in the interim profit and loss account, statement of total recognised gains and losses, balance sheet and cash flow statement in the context of events since the previous financial year end. It is important that the review does not concentrate solely on performance in the period, as shown in the profit and loss account, but also considers related issues such as working capital, liquidity and net debt. Significant trends and events mentioned in the commentary should be supported by the figures shown in the primary statements or by additional disclosures in the notes. Additional information should be given where this is necessary for an understanding of the significant items in the primary statement (for instance, additional information about company borrowings may need to be given if this is a significant issue).

Balanced view

41.16   The ASB Statement recommends that the management commentary on the interim figures explains the reasons for significant movements in key indicators and gives a balanced view of the perceived trends within the business, so that readers of the report can understand the main factors influencing the company's performance during the period under review and its position at the end of that period. The report should, therefore, discuss both positive and negative aspects of the interim period. Where the business is seasonal, it will be particularly important to provide sufficient information for readers to understand the interim results in the context of the full financial year. The commentary should also draw attention to any events and changes occurring during the interim period that are likely to have a significant impact in the second part of the year, even though they may not have affected the company's performance in the period under review. Where relevant it should also cover significant changes in fixed assets and investments, capital structure, financing, commitments and contingencies. The Listing Rules also specify that the interim statement should include any significant information to enable investors to make an informed assessment of the trend of the company's (or group's) activities and profit or loss.

Additional guidance

41.17 The management commentary included in an interim report is not intended to be as detailed as an Operating and Financial Review presented as part of the annual report. However, the guidance in the ASB's Reporting Standard 1 (RS 1) 'Operating and Financial Review' (see Chapter 39) may be useful in helping to identify the key issues that should be considered for discussion in an interim report.

Chapter 42   Preliminary Announcements

PREPARATION OF A PRELIMINARY ANNOUNCEMENT

Requirement to prepare a preliminary announcement

42.1 The UK Listing Authority's Listing Rules require listed companies to notify the Authority of their preliminary statement of annual results and dividends immediately after it has been approved by the board and within 120 days of the accounting period at the latest (although an extension of this deadline may be granted in exceptional circumstances). The minimum contents of the preliminary announcement specified in the Listing Rules are now broadly into line with the recommended contents set out in the ASB's non-mandatory Statement 'Preliminary Announcements'. In many ways, interim reports and preliminary announcements are very similar in nature. Both communicate new information on the company's performance and financial position and, in each case, the reaction of the financial markets to the information given can be significant. In particular, the preliminary announcement represents the first formal communication of the company's performance for the full financial year and enables the market to assess how the results compare with expectations. There was little formal guidance on the form and content of a preliminary announcement until the ASB issued its Statement in July 1998. The contents of the Statement are similar to the related guidance on interim reports and are considered to represent best practice, so all listed companies are encouraged to follow the ASB's recommendations.

Timing of preliminary announcement

42.2 The ASB Statement encourages companies to issue their preliminary announcement within 60 days of the financial year-end, and to issue the full report and accounts (and, where relevant, the summary financial statement) as soon as practicable thereafter, although it acknowledges that individual circumstances may make it impracticable for some companies to achieve the 60 day target. However, the UK Listing Authority allows a considerably longer period, specifying that the preliminary announcement must be issued within 120 days of the end of the accounting period.

Auditors' agreement to issue of the preliminary announcement

42.3   It is important that the information released in the preliminary announcement is reliable and the UK Listing Authority therefore requires the directors to obtain agreement from the auditors before the preliminary announcement is approved for issue. Auditing Practices Board (APB) Bulletin 2004/1 'The Auditors' Association with Preliminary Announcements' recommends that the role of the auditors in relation to the preliminary announcement is set out in writing (usually by including an appropriate paragraph in the audit engagement letter, and that the auditors issue a formal letter to the directors to signify their agreement to the publication of the preliminary announcement.

In February 2003 the APB wrote to the auditors of all listed companies expressing concern over the possibility that shareholders were being misled by the way in which certain pro-forma financial information is included in some preliminary announcements, and providing guidance on additional issues that should be considered before they give their formal consent to publication (see 42.15 to 42.16 below). This guidance has been incorporated in APB Bulletin 2004/1. It is also a requirement that, if the audit report is likely to be qualified, the preliminary announcement should include details of the nature of the qualification.

Procedures to help ensure reliability

42.4   The ASB Statement gives detailed consideration to the timing of the preliminary announcement and the need for the figures to be reliable. It recommends that:

(i)   the audit of the draft financial statements should be substantially complete at the date of the announcement;

(ii)   all the figures in the preliminary announcement should agree with the draft financial statements on which the audit is substantially complete; and

(iii)   any non-financial information or commentary included in the preliminary announcement should be consistent with the draft financial statements and with the figures given in the preliminary announcement.

Companies are encouraged to make their preliminary announcement as soon as the main figures have been agreed by the auditors, rather than waiting for the audit to be fully completed. This recognises that, in practice, it will often take time to finalise the detailed notes and other reports included in the published accounts but this will not affect the reliability of the key figures. APB Bulletin 2004/1 provides guidance on when the audit should be regarded as being at a sufficiently advanced stage to allow release of the preliminary announcement. To prevent any misunderstanding, the Statement recommends that preliminary announcements should state that the audit report on the full financial statements has yet to be signed if that is the case.

Distribution of preliminary announcement

42.5 Interim reports are issued to all shareholders, but preliminary announcements tend to be issued only to financial analysts and institutional shareholders. The ASB Statement emphasises that, in principle, all shareholders should be treated equally and suggests that companies should be encouraged to make better use of technology (for instance, by making preliminary announcements available on the internet) and that all shareholders should be given the option of receiving a copy of the preliminary announcement as soon as it is issued (for instance, by establishing a pre-registration scheme or publishing an address or telephone number from which copies can be obtained).

CONTENTS OF A PRELIMINARY ANNOUNCEMENT

The ASB Statement 'Preliminary announcements'

42.6 The ASB issued its Statement Preliminary announcements in July 1998, several months after publication of the related guidance on interim reports. The objective of the Statement is to improve the timeliness, quality, relevance and consistency of information published in preliminary announcements. Many companies already provided much of the information recommended in the ASB Statement, but it is helpful to have formal guidance on the contents of a preliminary announcement and on the principles to be followed in preparing and issuing the document.

Recommended contents of a preliminary announcement

42.7 Initially, the only required contents of a preliminary announcement under the Listing Rules were profit and loss account information and any significant information to enable investors to assess the results being announced. However, in practice many companies provided more than this to improve communication with the financial markets, prevent misunderstandings and misinterpretations and safeguard against the accidental disclosure of price-sensitive information. The Listing Rules now specify that the preliminary announcement must include, as a minimum, a profit and loss account, balance sheet and cash flow statement, together with any significant information to enable the company's results and financial position to be properly assessed. This brings the requirements broadly into line with the ASB Statement, which recommends the following contents for a preliminary announcement:

(i)   A balanced narrative commentary on the main factors influencing performance during the period and the financial position at the period end (see 42.14 below).

(ii)   A summarised profit and loss account, showing:

   * turnover;

   * operating profit or loss;

   * net interest payable/receivable;

   * profit or loss on ordinary activities before tax;

   * tax on profit or loss on ordinary activities;

   * profit or loss on ordinary activities after tax;

   * minority interests;

   * profit or loss for the period; and

   * dividends paid and proposed.

(iii)   A statement of total recognised gains and losses, where material gains and losses, other than the profit or loss for the period, are recognised in the period.

(iv)   A summarised balance sheet, showing:

   * fixed assets;

   * current assets:

   * stocks;

   * debtors;

   * cash at bank and in hand; and

   * other current assets;

   * creditors: amounts falling due within one year;

   * net current assets/liabilities;

   * total assets less current liabilities;

   * creditors: amounts falling due after more than one year;

   * provisions for liabilities and charges;

   * capital and reserves; and

   * minority interests.

(v)   A summarised cash flow statement, showing:

   * net cash inflow/outflow from operating activities;

   * dividends received from joint ventures and associates;

- returns on investments and servicing of finance;
- taxation;
- capital expenditure and financial investment;
- acquisitions and disposals;
- equity dividends paid;
- management of liquid resources;
- financing; and
- increase/decrease in cash.

(vi) A reconciliation of movements in shareholders' funds only needs to be included in the preliminary announcement where there are additional movements to be explained (i.e. movements other than those shown in the statement of total recognised gains and losses).

Other disclosures

42.8 The ASB Statement also recommends the following additional disclosures:

(i) where significant, amounts relating to associates and joint ventures should be shown separately in the summarised profit and loss account;

(ii) turnover and operating profit in respect of any acquisitions or discontinued operations should be shown separately on the face of the summarised profit and loss account in accordance with the requirements of FRS 3 'Reporting financial performance';

(iii) where significant, the segmental analyses of turnover and profit or loss before interest to be given in the full report and accounts should also be disclosed in the preliminary announcement;

(iv) sufficient information should be given for readers to understand any significant changes in the effective tax rate from the previous year – in some cases, the tax charge may need to be analysed into its main components;

(v) any exceptional items should be disclosed, either on the face of the profit and loss account or in the notes, in accordance with FRS 3 and an adequate description should be given;

(vi) reconciliations of operating profit to operating cashflow and the movement of cash to the movement in net debt should be given; and

(vii) the preliminary announcement should state the period covered and the date on which it was formally approved by the board of directors.

APB Bulletin 2004/1 also notes that, where the auditors' report is likely to include an explanatory paragraph dealing with a fundamental uncertainty, the auditors should not agree to the release of the preliminary announcement unless it includes an explanation by the directors of the issues relating to that uncertainty.

Accounting policies

42.9   The accounting policies used in preparing the preliminary announcements should be consistent with those in the full accounts, and the preliminary announcement should include a statement that the policies are the same as those disclosed in the last published accounts, or explain any differences. If there has been a change in accounting policy, the preliminary announcement should be prepared on the new accounting policy, all relevant comparative figures should be restated on the basis of the new policy and the cumulative effect on opening reserves should be disclosed at the foot of the statement of total recognised gains and losses. If any other prior period adjustments are necessary (for instance, due to the correction of fundamental errors) these should be reflected in the preliminary announcement in the same way as changes in accounting policy.

Earnings per share

42.10   Basic and diluted earnings per share should be calculated and disclosed in the preliminary announcement in the same way as in the full annual accounts. If the company adopts a policy of disclosing additional calculations of earnings per share in its annual accounts, the same details should be given in the preliminary announcement.

Comparative figures

42.11   Comparative figures for the summarised profit and loss account, statement of total recognised gains and losses, summarised balance sheet and summarised cash flow statement should cover the last full financial year. The ASB Statement also recommends that the preliminary announcement should set out financial information for the second half of the year, together with comparatives for the equivalent period in the previous year, to support the management commentary and facilitate an understanding of current performance.

Statutory disclosure

42.12   A preliminary announcement contains information for the current and previous financial years of the company and also information as at the company's current and previous financial year-end. It therefore constitutes 'non-statutory accounts' under section 240 of the CA 1985 and so must include the statements required by that section. the formal statements required by that section. All preliminary statements should therefore state

(i)   that they are not the company's statutory accounts;

(ii)   whether statutory accounts for any financial year covered by the non-statutory accounts have been delivered to the Registrar;

(iii)   whether the auditors have reported on the statutory accounts for any financial year covered by the non-statutory accounts;

(iv)   whether any auditors' report was qualified or contained a statement under section 237(2) or (3) of the CA 1985 on inadequate records or returns, accounts not in agreement with the records or returns, or failure of the auditors to obtain all necessary information and explanations; and

(v)   for accounting periods beginning on or after 1 January 2005, whether the auditors' report included a reference to any matters of emphasis, without qualification of the report.

As figures for two full financial years will be included in a preliminary announcement, the above statements must be made in respect of both the current year and the previous year.

MANAGEMENT COMMENTARY

Focus of the report

42.13   The aim of the management commentary in the preliminary announcement is to enable shareholders and other interested parties to understand the main factors that have influenced the company's performance during the financial year and its financial position at the year end. As well as commenting on the year as a whole, the ASB Statement recommends that management discuss and explain in particular the salient features of the second half of the year (i.e. the period not covered by the interim report). These represent new information for shareholders, but are often subsumed into the details of the full year without specific comment. It is also important that the review does not concentrate solely on performance in the period, as shown in the profit and loss account, but also considers related issues such as working capital, liquidity and net debt. Significant trends and events mentioned in the commentary should be supported by the figures shown in the primary statements or by additional disclosures in the notes. Additional information should be given where this is necessary for an understanding of the significant items in the primary statement (for instance, additional information about company borrowings may need to be given if this is a significant issue). The information provided should be succinct, consistent with the details to be given in the full report and accounts, and comparable with reports previously published.

Balanced view

42.14   The report should discuss both positive and negative aspects of the financial year and should include adequate information on any seasonal activity, so that the impact of this can be fully appreciated. The commentary should also draw attention to any events and changes occurring during the current financial year that are likely to have a significant impact in the following year, even though they may not have affected the company's performance in the period under review. Where relevant it should also cover significant changes in fixed assets and investments, capital structure, financing, commitments and contingencies (including any off balance sheet financial instruments), and also post balance sheet events, foreign exchange movements and the impact of revised actuarial valuations on pension costs.

Additional guidance

42.15   The management commentary included in a preliminary announcement is not intended to be as detailed as an operating and financial review presented as part of the annual accounts and reports. However, the guidance in the ASB's Reporting Standard 1 (RS 1) 'Operating and Financial Review' (see Chapter 39) may be useful in helping to identify the key issues that should be considered for discussion in an interim report.

INCLUSION OF PRO-FORMA INFORMATION

Guidance for companies

42.16   Companies sometimes include in preliminary announcements and financial reports information that has been prepared on a basis other than generally accepted accounting practice. This is usually described as pro-forma information and is shown for illustrative purposes only. However, there is concern that shareholders may sometimes be misled by the inclusion of such information, particularly where it is given a high degree of prominence in the announcement or report. In the January 2003 edition of its 'List!' newsletter, the UK Listing Authority drew attention to the need for companies to give careful consideration to the way in which pro-forma information is presented, and referred them to a statement issued in 2002 by the International Organisation for Securities Commissions (IOSCO). The IOSCO statement highlights in particular the need for pro-forma information to be presented consistently, adequately defined and used in a way that does not obscure the financial results drawn up on the basis of generally accepted accounting practice. The statement is available from the IOSCO website at http://www.iosco.org/news/

APB guidance for auditors

42.17   In February 2003, the APB wrote to the auditors of all listed companies expressing concern over the possibility that shareholders were being misled by the way in which certain pro-forma financial information is included in preliminary announcements, and recommending that they consider the following additional issues before giving their formal consent to publication of a preliminary announcement:

(i)   whether appropriate prominence has been given to the statutory information;

(ii)   whether any pro-forma information includes a clear statement on why it has been prepared ;

(iii) whether any pro-form information is reconciled to the related statutory information; and

(iv)   whether any pro-forma information is misleading in the form or context in which it is presented.

This guidance has now been incorporated in APB Bulletin 2004/1. If the auditors are not satisfied on any of these issues, they may need to withhold their consent to the publication of the announcement.

Chapter 43   Summary Financial Statements

PROCESS FOR ISSUING SUMMARY FINANCIAL STATEMENTS

Background

43.1   The *Companies Act 1989* introduced legislation permitting listed companies to issue a summary financial statement to their shareholders rather than the full annual report and accounts, although all shareholders retain the right to receive the full document if they so wish. The introduction of the legislation coincided with the significant increase in the number of individual shareholders as a result of the privatisation programme of the Government at that time. When the introduction of summary financial statements was first proposed, the idea was generally greeted with enthusiasm, but in practice only a comparatively small number of companies opted to produce them for their shareholders. Certain changes to the legislation were introduced in 1995 to simplify the process for issuing summary financial statements as it was felt that the administrative problems sometimes caused might be discouraging their use.

For accounting periods beginning on or after 1 January 2005, the *Companies Act 1985 (International Accounting Standards and Other Accounting Amendments) Regulations 2004* (SI 2004/2947) amend the relevant sections of the Companies Act 1985 to extend the option to prepare summary financial statements to all companies. The same Regulations also amend section 245 of the *Companies Act 1985* to allow for the voluntary revision of a summary financial statement. A DTI consultation on the operation of the new requirements was published in March 2005.

Detailed requirements

43.2   The basic provisions on the issue of summary financial statements are set out in section 251 of the *Companies Act 1985* and these are currently supplemented by the detailed requirements of the *Companies (Summary Financial Statement) Regulations 1995* (SI 1995/2092) which prescribe the form and content of summary financial statements and the conditions under which they can be issued. In March 2005, the DTI issued a consultation document on proposed amendments to the regulations to reflect the extension of the summary financial statement provisions to a much wider range of companies and to recognise the fact that listed companies ·must prepare group accounts in accordance with international accounting standards (IASs) for accounting periods beginning on or after 1 January 2005.

Legal position

43.3   Under the present Regulations, a company is not permitted to issue a summary financial statement if it is prohibited from doing so by its Memorandum or Articles of Association. If the Memorandum or Articles of Association require copies of the full accounts and reports to be sent to entitled persons, this will effectively prohibit the company from issuing a summary financial statement, unless its constitutional documents are amended. Where the company has issued debentures, and the instrument constituting or governing the debentures prohibits the issue of a summary financial statement, or requires copies of the full accounts and reports to be sent to entitled persons, the company cannot issue a summary financial statement to the debenture holders, but should be able to issue such a document to other individuals entitled to receive copies of the accounts, provided that it is allowed to do so by its Memorandum or Articles of Association.

The right of entitled persons to receive full accounts

43.4   Entitled persons are defined in section 251(1) of the *Companies Act 1985* and are basically members of the company, holders of the company's debentures and any other person who is entitled to receive notice of general meetings of the company. Every entitled person retains the right to receive full accounts in respect of any financial year. A company cannot issue a summary financial statement to any entitled person in place of the full annual accounts and reports without first ascertaining that the individual does not wish to receive the full documents. This must be based on:

(i)   a relevant notification in writing given to the company by the entitled person; or

(ii)   failure by the entitled person to respond to an opportunity given to him/her to elect to receive copies of the full accounts and reports.

Consultation with entitled persons

43.5   A company may send or give each entitled person notice that, in future, he/she will be sent a summary financial statement for each financial year in place of copies of the full accounts and reports, unless the company is notified in writing of his/her wish to receive the full documents. The notice must:

(i) state that the summary financial statement for a financial year will contain a summary of the company (or group) profit and loss account, balance sheet and directors' report for that year;

(ii) include a prominent statement to the effect that a summary financial statement will not contain sufficient information to allow as full an understanding of the results and state of affairs of the company (or group) as would be provided by the full accounts and reports, and that members and debenture holders have the right to obtain a copy of the full accounts and reports free of charge;

(iii) state that the summary financial statement will contain a statement by the auditors on whether:

- the summary financial statement is consistent with the full accounts and reports for the relevant financial year;

- the summary financial statement complies with the requirements of section 251 of CA 1985 and the related Regulations; and

- their report on the accounts was qualified.

The notice must be accompanied by a prepaid reply card (or form) enabling each entitled person to notify his/her wish to receive the full accounts for each financial year by marking a box and returning the card. The company can state in the notice that the reply card must be returned by a specified date, which must be at least 21 days after the date of the notice and not less than 28 days before the first date on which copies of the full accounts and reports for the next financial year are sent out under section 238(1) of the *Companies Act 1985*. The company is generally not required to pay the postage on the reply card if the contact address of the entitled person is not within in EEA State. There is also no requirement to send a reply paid card to entitled persons in subsequent years, even though they each retain the right to request a copy of the full accounts and reports.

Alternative method of consultation

43.6 As an alternative, a company can send each entitled person a copy of the full accounts and reports and also a summary financial statement for that financial year, and at the same time notice that in future he/she will be sent a summary financial statement for each financial year in place of copies of the full accounts and reports, unless the company is notified in writing of his/her wish to receive the full documents. The notice must be accompanied by a prepaid reply card (or form) enabling each entitled person to notify his/her wish to receive the full accounts for each financial year by marking a box and returning the card. The company is generally not required to pay the postage on the reply card if the contact address of the entitled person is not within in an EEA State.

Revision of summary financial statements

43.7   For accounting periods beginning on or after 1 January 2005, section 245 of CA 1985 has been amended to provide specifically for the voluntary revision of a summary financial statement, even if the underlying accounts do not require adjustment. The DTI is in the process of developing new regulations on the preparation of summary financial statements to cater for the fact that all companies will in future have the option of issuing a summary financial statement (see 43.1 above) and also to allow for the adoption of international accounting standards. Draft Regulations were issued by the DTI in March 2005 (see 43.12 below) and these include a revised framework for the revision of summary financial statements. This is based closely on the requirements that are already in place for the revision of accounts and directors' reports and the DTI hopes that the new provisions will remove any uncertainty for companies over how they should proceed when published reports need to be revised.

FORM AND CONTENT OF SUMMARY FINANCIAL STATEMENTS

Requirements of the Regulations

43.8   Section 251(3) of the *Companies Act 1985* requires the summary financial statement to be derived from the company's annual accounts and directors' report. The related Regulations currently set out the following minimum contents of a summary financial statement:

(i)   a summary of the directors' report, which must include:

- a fair review of the development of the business;
- any important post balance sheet events;
- likely future developments in the business;
- the names of all those who were directors during the year; and
- the amount recommended to be paid as dividend, if this is not disclosed in the summary profit and loss account;

(ii)   a summary profit and loss account, which must include, in the following order:

- turnover;
- income from shares in group undertakings and participating interests;
- other interest receivable and similar income, and interest payable and similar charges;
- profit or loss on ordinary activities before taxation;
- tax on profit or loss on ordinary activities;
- profit or loss on ordinary activities after tax;
- extraordinary income and charges after tax;

- profit or loss for the financial year; and
- the aggregate of dividends paid and, if not disclosed in the summary directors' report, dividends proposed.

(iii) either the whole of the directors' remuneration report or, as a minimum:

- the aggregate information on directors' remuneration required by paragraph 1(1) of Schedule 6 to CA 1985;
- the statement of the company's policy on directors' remuneration for future years; and
- the performance graph summarising shareholder return;

(iv) a summary balance sheet showing a single amount for each of the headings which are assigned letters in the standard balance sheet format used by the company (as set out in paragraph 8 of Schedule 4 to the Companies Act 1985) – the details must be given in the order set out in the format, and under headings that the directors consider appropriate.

Comparative figures must be shown for each item in the summary financial statement and, where the company is required to prepare group accounts, consolidated figures must be presented. Separate details are set out in the Regulations for banking companies and groups and insurance companies and groups. In practice, many companies who prepare summary financial statements provide more than the minimum information – for instance, summarised cash flow information and details on corporate governance issues are often included.

For accounting periods beginning on or after 1 April 2005, the *Companies Act 1985 (Operating and Financial Review and Directors' Report etc.) Regulations 2005* (SI 2005/1011) amend s 251 of CA 1985 to:

(i) remove references to the directors' report – in future, there will no longer be a requirement to include information from this report in a summary financial statement;

(ii) require a summary financial statement to state whether it contains additional information derived from the directors' report or OFR and, if so, to state that it does not contain the full text of that report or review;

(iii) require a listed company that does not send out a full copy of its OFR with the summary financial statement to publish the full OFR on a website throughout the period beginning at least 21 days before the date of the meeting at which the accounts and reports are to be laid and ending with the conclusion of the meeting – in this case, the summary financial statement must include the website address and details of how the OFR can be accessed;

(iv) require a summary financial statement to state how entitled persons can obtain full copies of the accounts and reports from which the summary statement is derived (this is currently included in the Regulations); and

(v)   update the disclosure requirements in respect of the auditors' report to cover their opinion on consistency between the accounts and directors' report and, where relevant, between the accounts and the OFR.

Other statements and disclosures

43.9   The summary financial statement must be signed by a director on behalf of the board, and the name of the signing director must be stated. The document must also include a clear statement that it is only a summary of the information given in the company's annual accounts and directors' report. The Regulations currently require a summary financial statement to include a formal statement, in a prominent position, that the summary does not contain sufficient information to allow as full an understanding of the results and state of affairs of the company (or group) as would be provided by the full annual accounts and reports, and that members and debenture holders requiring more information have the right to obtain a copy of the last full accounts and reports free of charge, together with clear information on:

(i)   how members and debenture holders can obtain these copies; and

(ii)   how they can elect in writing to receive full accounts and reports for future years in place of the summary financial statement.

Implications of wider publication

43.10   A summary financial statement does not meet the definition of statutory accounts set out in section 240(5) of CA 1985. However, by virtue of section 251(7), the requirement to include certain statements in non-statutory accounts does not apply in respect of a summary financial statement provided that it is only issued to persons entitled to receive it. Where a summary financial statement is made more generally available for public inspection (for instance, by publication on a company website) it will constitute non-statutory accounts and should therefore include the statement required by section 240(3) of the *Companies Act 1985* as well as the details set out above. In these circumstances, a summary financial statement must therefore state:

(i)   that it is not the company's statutory accounts;

(ii)   whether statutory accounts for any financial year covered by the non-statutory accounts have been delivered to the Registrar;

(iii)   whether the auditors have reported on the statutory accounts for any financial year covered by the non-statutory accounts;

(iv)   whether any auditors' report was qualified or contained a statement under section 237(2) or (3) of CA 1985 on inadequate records or returns, accounts not in agreement with the records or returns, or failure of the auditors to obtain all necessary information and explanations; and

(v)   for accounting periods beginning on or after 1 January 2005, whether the auditors' report included a reference to any matters of emphasis, without qualification of the report.

As figures for two full financial years will be included the document, the above statements must be made in respect of both the current year and the previous year.

Audit requirements

43.11   A summary financial statement must include a report from the auditors on whether the summarised financial information is consistent with the full accounts and reports, and on whether it complies with the relevant Regulations. Guidance on the procedures that auditors are required to carry out in order to provide such a report is set out in Bulletin 1999/6: 'The Auditors' Statement on the Summary Financial Statement' issued by the Auditing Practices Board in December 1999. This guidance emphasises that:

(i)   the scope of the auditors' work covers only the summary financial statement and not any additional information that may be included in the summarised annual report (e.g. a Chairman's statement or business review), although the auditors' will need to read any additional information that is presented to confirm that it is consistent with the summary financial statement;

(ii)   the scope of the auditors' work and the respective responsibilities of the directors and the auditors should be set out in a formal engagement letter.

The example auditors' statement on summary financial statements set out in Bulletin 1999/6 has been superseded by subsequent pronouncements and the latest version can be found in APB Bulletin 2002/2 'The United Kingdom Directors' Remuneration Report Regulations 2002'.

In July 2005 the APB published an Exposure Draft of a UK and Ireland ISA 800 'The Independent Auditor's Report on Summary Audited Financial Statements' seeking views on whether this should be adopted for future reporting on summary financial statements or whether an updated version of Bulletin 1999/6 would be more appropriate. For comparison purposes, the document includes an example of an auditor's statement based on the present Bulletin 1999/6, updated for recent legislative changes, and an example auditor's report based on the proposals in the draft ISA.

PROPOSALS FOR CHANGE

DTI consultation

43.12   A DTI document 'A Consultation on Extending the Use of Summary Financial Statements and Other Minor Changes' published in March 2005 sets out proposals to amend certain items of secondary legislation in line with recent changes to the *Companies Act 1985* (CA 1985) and to make a number of additional amendments to the main legislation. The appendices to the consultation document include the draft text of the *Companies (Summary Financial Statement)(Amendment) Regulations* 2005. The intention is for these new Regulations to be laid before Parliament in the summer or early autumn of 2005 and for them to come into force on 1 October 2005.

Impact of recent legislative changes

43.13   The *Companies Act 1985* has recently been amended to give all companies the option of issuing a summary financial statement to shareholders and other entitled persons in place of the full accounts, subject to certain conditions. As explained at 43.8 above, the requirements on the detailed content of summary financial statements are currently based on the standard profit and loss account and balance sheet formats set out in the *Companies Act 1985*. However, listed groups who must now adopt IASs, and any other companies who choose to prepare their accounts on this basis, will no longer have to follow the standard accounts formats set out in the Act. Changes are therefore proposed to the current Regulations to reflect this, as well as to cater for the wider range of companies who will in future have the option of preparing summary financial statements. The Regulations as amended for the latest proposals will:

(i)   specify that a company can only take advantage of the option to issue a summary financial statement if its full accounts have been audited;

(ii)   include a new Schedule on the form and content of a summary financial statement where the underlying accounts have been prepared in accordance with IASs; and

(iii)   remove the requirement for a summary financial statement to include a summarised directors' report, but give companies the option to include material from a directors' report or Operating and Financial Review (OFR) in the statement.

Also, a listed company that does not issue its full OFR with the summary financial statement will in future have to publish the full OFR on a website and refer to this in the summary financial statement. This is consistent with the new OFR regulations that are intended to come into effect for accounting periods beginning on or after 1 April 2005 (see 39.12 above).

Audit requirement

43.14   The auditors will continue to be required to express an opinion on the proper preparation of the summary financial statement and on its consistency with the full accounts that have been subject to audit.

ADVANTAGES AND DISADVANTAGES OF SUMMARY FINANCIAL STATEMENTS

The purpose of summary financial statements

43.15   The provisions allowing listed companies to prepare and issue summary financial statements were introduced to recognise the fact that the needs of shareholders and other users of the accounts can vary quite significantly. The disclosures required by accounting standards and company law are becoming increasingly complex, and whilst the information now required may be highly relevant to technically sophisticated users of accounts, it is evident that many private shareholders are confused by the volume of detail given in a full set of accounts. In some cases the level of detailed disclosures can actually obscure the key information that private shareholders require from the accounts. The main objectives of summary financial statements are to remove many of the more complex disclosures and concentrate on the key issues that are of relevance to individual shareholders, and to enable companies to present this key information in a user-friendly manner, for instance by making appropriate use of charts and graphs.

The company view

43.16   A working party established by the Institute of Chartered Accountants in England and Wales (ICAEW) reported in 1996 on the results of:

(i)   research amongst companies on why they decided to produce, or not to produce, a summary financial statement; and

(ii)   research amongst shareholders on the relative merits to them of full accounts and a summary financial statement.

The report 'Summary Financial Statements – The Way Forward' included short commentaries by three companies on their experiences of preparing summary financial statements and summarised the results of various surveys into why companies choose to prepare, or not to prepare, summary financial statements. The main reasons given for not making use of summary financial statements were:

(i)   potentially higher production costs, especially in the first year, and no significant cost savings anticipated in subsequent years;

(ii)   the additional administrative burden; and

(iii)   that the preparation of a summary financial statement runs counter to the present philosophy of providing fuller information to shareholders.

The main advantages reported by companies who had issued summary financial statements were better communication with shareholders and actual cost savings. It is particularly interesting to note that, whilst the majority of companies who decided to prepare summary financial statements did so primarily to improve communication with their shareholders, nearly all of them found that the exercise also achieved some cost savings. It may be that companies not currently using summary financial statements are being unnecessarily pessimistic in their assessment of the costs and the additional administrative effort required. It should also be noted that most of the research referred to in the report was undertaken before the changes to simplify the consultation process with shareholders and this may already have helped to alleviate some of the concerns over costs and administration.

The shareholder view

43.17   The report also summarised the results of a survey to assess the reactions of shareholders to summary financial statements. This indicated a high degree of enthusiasm for summary financial statements amongst shareholders, with a significant majority of respondents indicating that they did read the document and, in some cases, retain it for a period of time. The key conclusions from the research were:

(i)   the summarised results, Chairman's statement and overall business review were the most widely read parts of the document;

(ii)   other financial information, the report by the auditors and any additional details (for instance on corporate governance issues) were generally not widely read by shareholders; and

(iii)   there was a clear preference for a short document rather than a longer one.

Overall, the research indicated that shareholders were more likely to read some or all of the summary financial statement than to open and read the full accounts, and that a summarised document is consequently helpful in improving communication with shareholders. Where a summary financial statement was made available, a very high proportion of shareholders (in the order of 90%) opted to receive the summary rather than the full annual report and accounts. A further point highlighted by the research was that very few companies had carried out any direct consultation with shareholders to try and identify their specific needs and ensure that these were being satisfied, despite the fact that the research amongst companies had indicated that shareholder pressure would encourage them to consider preparing a summary financial statement.

Alternative methods of preparation

43.18   There are essentially two approaches to the preparation of a summary financial statement:

(i)   the production of two completely separate and free-standing documents – the summary financial statement and the full annual report and accounts; and

(ii)   the production of a summary financial statement and a supplementary document containing additional information – in this case, the summary financial statement and the supplementary document together constitute the full annual report and accounts.

The second approach is by far the more common in practice. Failure to consider this method of preparation may be one of the factors that explains why companies not preparing summary financial statements quote potentially higher costs (or no anticipated cost savings) as one of the reasons against using them, whilst those preparing summary financial statements have achieved actual cost savings. A potential disadvantage of the second approach is that analysts and other technically-minded users of the accounts may find it irritating to have to refer to two documents. However, this can usually be overcome by careful planning of the contents of each part of the document and clear cross-referencing.

Usual contents of summary financial statements

43.19   There is a broad consensus amongst companies who do prepare summary financial statements on the basic contents of the document. These invariably go beyond the minimum contents laid down in the current Regulations and usually comprise:

   (i)   financial highlights;
  (ii)   Chairman's statement;
 (iii)   an operational review of the business, which often makes extensive use of colour, photographs and other illustrations;
 (iv)   the summarised profit and loss account and balance sheet;
  (v)   summarised cash flow information;
 (vi)   information on directors' remuneration; and
(vii)   financial calendar;

Corporate governance issues are also usually referred to in the summary financial statement, but the level of detail varies. Some companies give the full disclosures in the summary financial statement, but others give only brief details and cross-reference these to the full disclosures in the supplementary document. Despite the preference for short documents highlighted in the shareholder research, summary financial statements these days are often substantial documents, with many being between 20 and 40 pages in length.

Chapter 44

Requirement For Group Accounts

FORM AND CONTENT OF GROUP ACCOUNTS

Requirement to prepare group accounts

44.1   Section 227 of CA 1985 sets out the requirement for the directors of any company that is a parent company to prepare group accounts, as well as individual accounts for the company. Certain small and medium-sized groups are exempt from the requirement to prepare group accounts, as are certain parent companies who are part of a larger group. These exemptions are considered in more detail at 44.10 below.

For accounting periods beginning before 1 January 2005, group accounts must be consolidated accounts and must comply with the detailed provisions of Schedule 4A to CA 1985. For accounting periods beginning on or after 1 January 2005, group accounts may be prepared in accordance with a new section 227A (which essentially maintains the existing provisions on the form and content of group accounts), in which case they are designated as 'Companies Act group accounts' or may be prepared in accordance with IASs, in which case they are designated as 'IAS group accounts'. Listed companies are required by an EU Regulation to prepare group accounts in accordance with IASs, but other companies (other than those with charitable status) have the option of preparing either Companies Act or IAS group accounts. Charitable companies must continue to prepare Companies Act group accounts, on the basis that IASs have been developed with profit-making entities in mind and are therefore not appropriate for the charity sector at present. Special rules apply in the case of banking, insurance and investment companies which are not considered here.

This Chapter summarises the requirements that apply to the preparation of Companies Act group accounts.

Requirements of FRS 2

44.2   FRS 2 'Accounting for Subsidiary Undertakings' applies to all parent undertakings that prepare consolidated accounts that are required to show a true and fair view, irrespective of whether they report under CA 1985. FRS 2 requires a parent undertaking to prepare consolidated accounts for its group, unless one of the exemptions set out in the standard applies. These exemptions are considered in more detail at 44.10 below and the requirements of FRS 2 in respect of the process of consolidation are considered in Chapter 47.

True and fair view

44.3   The consolidated accounts are required to show a true and fair view of the state of affairs of the group at the balance sheet date and of its profit or loss for the financial year ending on that date, so far as concerns the members of the parent company. The true and fair view is considered in more detail in Chapter 3. Where compliance with the provisions of Schedule 4A, and with other accounting requirements of the Act, is not sufficient for the accounts to give a true and fair view, the necessary additional information must be given in the group accounts or in the related notes. If, in special circumstances, compliance with the provisions of the Act is inconsistent with the requirement for the group accounts to show a true and fair view, the directors must depart from the requirements of the Act to the extent necessary to show a true and fair view and the group accounts must disclose:

(i)   particulars of the departure;

(ii)   the reasons for the departure; and

(iii)   the effect of the departure.

The issues considered in Chapter 3 in respect of these disclosures, and the use of the true and fair override generally, apply to group accounts in the same way as to individual company accounts.

Standard formats

44.4   Paragraph 1(1) of Schedule 4A requires group accounts to comply, as far as is practicable, with the requirements of Schedule 4 as if the undertakings included in the consolidation were a single company. Group accounts must therefore follow one of the standard formats for the profit and loss account and balance sheet set out in Schedule 4 but these formats are modified to:

(i)   include a profit and loss account heading for minority interests and also separate disclosure of any extraordinary items relating to minority interests;

(ii)   include a balance sheet heading for minority interests – there are two alternative locations for this heading in Format 1 (i.e. only one should be used);

(iii)   analyse the profit and loss accounts heading for income from participating interests into:

- income from associated undertakings; and
- income from other participating interests;

(iv)   analyse the balance sheet heading for participating interests into:

- interests in associated undertakings; and
- other participating interests.

Amended versions of the formats for both the profit and loss account and balance sheet are included in the appendices to this chapter. The rules in respect of the standard formats apply to group accounts in the same way as to the accounts of individual companies. These rules are explained in Chapter 9 and Chapter 19. For the purpose of the rules on adapting or combining headings:

(i)   the profit and loss accounts headings in respect of minority interests are to be treated as if they had been assigned an Arabic number; and

(ii)   the balance sheet heading for minority interests is to be treated as if it had been assigned a letter.

The requirements of Schedule 4A in respect of consolidation adjustments, consistency of accounting, acquisitions and mergers, and goodwill are considered in Chapters 47 to 49.

Additional profit and loss accounts items

44.5   In addition to the headings in the standard formats, the group profit and loss account, in the same way as an individual company's profit and loss account, must show the profit or loss on ordinary activities before taxation and the notes to the accounts must show:

(i)   amounts set aside or withdrawn from reserves;

(ii)   the aggregate of dividends paid in the year, other than those for which a liability existed at the previous balance sheet date;

(iii)   the aggregate amount of dividends that the company is liable to pay at the balance sheet date; and

(iv)   the aggregate amount of dividends proposed before the date of approval of the accounts and not included in the above disclosures.

However, in the case of dividends, only amounts paid and proposed by the parent company should be disclosed in the notes to the group accounts. The above requirements were introduced for accounting periods beginning on or after 1 January 2005 by the *Companies Act (International Accounting Standards and Other Accounting Amendments) Regulations 2004* (SI 2004.2947). For accounting periods beginning before 1 January 2005, parent company dividends paid and proposed by were required to be shown in the group profit and loss account, with proposed dividends shown separately, either on the face of the group profit and loss account, or in the notes to the accounts.

Additional disclosures under FRS 3

44.6   FRS 3 'Reporting Financial Performance' introduced a number of new accounts disclosures that generally apply to group accounts in the same way as to the accounts of an individual company. These include:

(i)   separate disclosure of the sub-total for operating profit on the face of the profit and loss account;

(ii)   analysis of certain profit and loss account items into continuing, acquired and discontinued operations;

(iii)   inclusion of a statement of total recognised gains and losses;

(iv)   inclusion of a reconciliation of movements in shareholders' funds;

(v)   inclusion of a note of historical cost profits and losses.

These are covered in more detail the following chapters:

(i)   profit and loss account analysis and disclosures – Chapter 9

(ii)   calculation of profits and losses on the disposal of fixed assets – Chapter 13

(iii)   statement of total recognised gains and losses, reconciliation of movements in shareholders' funds and note of historical cost profits and losses – Chapter 36

FRS 3 does not state whether a separate statement of total recognised gains and losses should be given for the parent company alone. As the emphasis in group accounts is on the performance of the group as a whole, and the separate profit and loss account of the parent company does not have to be published, it is usually considered unnecessary to include a separate statement of total recognised gains and losses for the parent company.

A reconciliation of movements in shareholders' funds for the group as a whole should be included in the group accounts. Once again, FRS 3 makes no mention of whether a separate reconciliation should be included for the parent company. The reconciliation of movements in shareholders' funds draws together the financial effect of all the changes that have taken place during the year and summarises the net movements in shareholders' funds as shown on the balance sheet. As the parent company balance sheet is presented as part of the group accounts, there is some logic in including a separate reconciliation for the parent company alone. However, there is no requirement to do so and in practice many companies only present the reconciliation for the group as a whole.

The note of historical cost profits and losses should also be given for the group as a whole. This note provides additional information in respect of the profit or loss for the year. As the profit and loss account for the parent company is not included, it is generally accepted that the note only needs to be given for the group, although FRS 3 is not specific on this point.

Disclosures in respect of directors

44.7   Disclosures in respect of directors in the group accounts (e.g. directors' remuneration, loans to directors, transactions with directors) are only required in respect of directors of the parent company, but should include amounts paid by or received from subsidiary undertakings and remuneration relating to services as a director of a subsidiary. The detailed requirements are considered in Chapter 17 and Chapter 37.

Auditors' remuneration

44.8   Paragraph 1(1) of Schedule 4A emphasises that the figure disclosed for auditors' remuneration in the group accounts should be the aggregate for all the undertakings included in the consolidation. The disclosure requirements in respect of audit fees and fees for non-audit services are considered in more detail in Chapter 18.

Directors' Report and Operating and Financial Review (OFR)

44.9   In general, the directors' report must cover details for the parent and all of its subsidiary undertakings. Therefore, items such as the review of the development of the business, details of activities in the field of research and development, changes in fixed assets, post balance sheet events etc. must cover the group as a whole. However, details in respect of directors relate only to those who are (or were) directors of the parent company. The detailed requirements of CA 1985 in respect of the directors' report are considered in Chapter 38.

Similarly, the statutory Operating and Financial Review (OFR) that quoted companies are required to prepare for accounting periods beginning on or after 1 April 2005 must be a consolidated review covering the company and the subsidiary undertakings that are included in the consolidated accounts. However, the legislation specifies that, where appropriate, a group OFR can give greater emphasis to matters that are significant to the group as a whole rather than to the individual entities included in the consolidation. The requirements of CA 1985 in respect of the statutory OFR are considered in Chapter 39.

EXEMPTIONS FROM THE PREPARATION OF GROUP ACCOUNTS

Small companies and groups

44.10   CA 1985 sets out specific criteria to define a small company and a small group. These criteria and the rules on qualification as a small company or group are considered in detail in Chapter 8. Two exemptions in respect of group accounts are granted to small companies and groups:

(i)   a parent company is not required to prepare consolidated group accounts for a financial year in which the group which it heads:

- qualifies as a small group; and

- is not an ineligible group;

(ii)   a small company that prepares shorter form accounts under the special provisions of the Act, and which is preparing group accounts for the same year, may also prepare the group accounts in accordance with Schedule 8, subject to a small number of exceptions in respect of the disclosure of investments.

There is no provision in the Act for a small parent company to file abbreviated group accounts. The provisions of the Act relating to small companies and groups, and the specific rules relating to shorter form accounts, are considered in more detail in Chapter 8. The disclosures required by FRS 2, paragraph 22 will need to be given where a small group takes advantage of the exemption in (i) above (see 44.18 below).

Medium-sized companies and groups

44.11   The Act sets out specific criteria to define a medium-sized company and a medium-sized group. These criteria and the rules on qualification as a medium-sized company or group are considered in detail in Chapter 8. A parent company is not required to prepare consolidated group accounts for a financial year in which the group which it heads:

(i)   qualifies as a medium-sized group; and

(ii)   is not an ineligible group.

The disclosures required by FRS 2, paragraph 22 will need to be given where a medium-sized group takes advantage of this exemption (see 44.18 below).

Parent company which is part of a larger group

44.12   A parent company is generally exempt from the requirement to prepare consolidated accounts for the group if:

(i)   it is itself a subsidiary undertaking and its immediate parent undertaking is established under the law of an EEA State; and

(ii)   it is either a wholly-owned subsidiary of that parent undertaking, or the parent undertaking holds more than 50% of the shares in the company and notice requesting the preparation of group accounts has not been served on the company by shareholders holding in aggregate more than half of the remaining shares in the company, or 5% of the total shares in the company; and

(iii)   all of the specific conditions laid down in the Act are complied with.

For accounting periods beginning on or after 1 January 2005, a new section 228A is introduced by the *Companies Act (International Accounting Standards and Other Accounting Amendments) Regulations 2004* (SI 2004/2947) and this extends the exemption to a parent company that is a subsidiary undertaking of a parent not established under the law of an EEA State. The same conditions on shareholding levels and the right of minority shareholders to require the preparation of group accounts apply as under the existing provisions for intermediate parents within an EEA group. The other conditions are also broadly similar, although with various wording changes to reflect the fact that the company's parent undertaking is not established in an EEA State.

Ineligible companies

44.13   The exemption does not apply to any company whose securities are listed on a stock exchange in any EEA State. In this context, the expression 'securities' is given the broad definition set out in section 228(6) of CA 1985 and includes:

(i)   shares and stock;

(ii)   debenture stock, loan stock, bonds, certificates of deposit, warrants and other instruments acknowledging indebtedness;

(iii)   warrants or other instruments that entitle the holder to subscribe for securities in (i) and (ii);

(iv)   certificates or other instruments that confer rights in respect of securities.

Wholly-owned subsidiary

44.14   A wholly-owned subsidiary is defined in section 736(2) of CA 1985 as a company that has no members other than:

(i)   the holding company; and

(ii)   any other wholly-owned subsidiaries of the holding company; or

(iii)   persons acting on behalf of the holding company or its wholly-owned subsidiaries.

Under section 228(4) of CA 1985, any shares held by the directors in order to comply with a share qualification requirement can be disregarded in this case (i.e.

such holdings will not prevent an intermediate parent company meeting the definition of 'wholly-owned' in this context). However, the definition effectively covers all types of shares, not just ordinary shares. For instance, where a company has preference shares which are held by other unrelated shareholders, it will not meet the definition of a wholly-owned subsidiary, even though all of the ordinary shares may be held by the holding company.

Majority-owned subsidiary

44.15   In assessing whether the parent holds more than 50% of the shares in a company, the following shares should be attributed to the parent:

(i)   shares held by, or on behalf of, the parent; and

(ii)   shares held by, or on behalf of, any wholly-owned subsidiary of the parent.

However, the provision in section 228(4) of CA 1985 in respect of directors' share qualifications does not apply in this case. Therefore, in order for a company to be more than 50% owned, the appropriate number of shares must be held by the parent and its wholly-owned subsidiaries, or by persons acting on their behalf.

Shareholders requesting the preparation of consolidated accounts

44.16   The preparation of consolidated accounts for the group can be requested by shareholders holding in aggregate:

(i)   more than half of the remaining shares in the company; or

(ii)   5% of the total shares in the company.

Example 44.1 – When consolidated accounts can be requested

A Ltd has a share capital of 1,000 ordinary shares of £1 and is the parent company of B Ltd and C Ltd.

700 of the shares in A Ltd are held by D Ltd which is incorporated in the UK. Provided the other conditions in the Act are satisfied, A Ltd will not need to prepare consolidated accounts unless these are requested by shareholders holding:

(i) more than half of the remaining shares = 300 x 50% = 150 shares, or

(ii) 5% of the total shares = 5% x 1,000 = 50 shares.

In this case therefore, shareholders holding in aggregate 50 shares or more could request preparation of consolidated accounts.

If D Ltd held 920 of the shares in A Ltd, the calculations would be as follows:

* more than half of the remaining shares = 80 x 50% = 40 shares

* 5% of the total shares = 5% x 1,000 = 50 shares.

In this case therefore, shareholders holding in aggregate more than 40 shares could request preparation of consolidated accounts.

Conditions for exemption to apply

44.17   The Companies Act 1985 sets out the following conditions, all of which must be met for the exemption to apply:

(i)   the company must be included in consolidated accounts for a larger group, drawn up to the same date, or to a date earlier in the financial year, by a parent undertaking – this need not be the immediate parent of the company for which exemption is to be claimed, and there is no requirement for the immediate parent to be wholly-owned by the parent preparing the consolidated accounts;

(ii)   in the case of an EEC parent, the consolidated accounts and annual report must be drawn up and audited in accordance with the law of the member state and with the EC Seventh Company Law Directive or, for accounting periods beginning on or after 1 January 2005, in accordance with international accounting standards;

(iii)   in the case of a non-EEC parent, the consolidated accounts and annual report must be drawn up in accordance with the EC Seventh Company Law Directive, or in an equivalent manner, and the accounts must be audited by one or more persons authorised to do so under the law under which the parent preparing them is established;

(iv)   the company must disclose in its individual accounts:

-    the fact that it is exempt from the requirement to prepare and file consolidated accounts for the group;

-    the name of the parent undertaking preparing consolidated accounts, and its country of incorporation if this is outside Great Britain – if this parent is unincorporated, the address of its principal place of business must be given;

(v)   the company must deliver to the registrar copies of:

-    the consolidated accounts;

-    the parent's annual report; and

-    the report of the auditors,

within the period allowed for filing its own individual accounts and, if the documents are not in English, a certified translation must be attached (i.e. both the original version and the translation must be filed) – however, the special provisions of section 710B of CA 1985 apply in respect of documents in Welsh filed by companies registered in Wales.

Exemptions under FRS 2

44.18   FRS 2 'Accounting for Subsidiaries' sets out similar requirements to CA 1985 on exemption from the preparation of group accounts for small and medium-sized companies and groups and intermediate parent companies within a larger group. Where a parent company takes advantage of one of these exemptions, the standard requires the accounts to include a note disclosing:

(i)   the fact that the accounts present information about the parent as an individual undertaking and not about the group; and

(ii)   the grounds on which the parent is exempt from preparing consolidated group accounts.

These disclosures are required in addition to those set out in the Act for a parent company that does not prepare consolidated group accounts (see 45.11).

EXCLUSION OF SUBSIDIARIES FROM THE CONSOLIDATION

Legal provisions on exclusion

44.19   In general, CA 1985 requires the accounts of the parent company and all of its subsidiary undertakings to be included in the consolidation. However, a subsidiary undertaking may be excluded from the consolidation if:

(i)   its inclusion is not material for the purpose of the true and fair view – however, two or more subsidiary undertakings may only be excluded if they are not material when taken together;

(ii)   severe long-term restrictions substantially hinder the exercise of the parent's rights over the assets and management of the undertaking;

(iii)   the necessary information cannot be obtained without disproportionate expense or undue delay;

(iv)   the interest is held exclusively with a view to resale.

Rights and interests are to be interpreted in accordance with section 258 and Schedule 10A (see Chapter 45). For accounting periods beginning before 1 January 2005, the exclusion in (iv) above applied only if the entity had not previously been included in the consolidation, and FRS 2 'Accounting for Subsidiary Undertakings' continues to impose this as an additional requirement (see 44.20 below.)

Where all the subsidiary undertakings in a group are eligible for exclusion from the consolidation, the parent company is not required to prepare consolidated accounts for the group.

Exclusions under FRS 2

44.20   FRS 2 'Accounting for Subsidiaries' requires subsidiary undertakings to be excluded from the consolidation in the following circumstances:

(i)   where severe long-term restrictions substantially hinder the exercise of the parent's rights over the assets or management of the undertaking; or

(ii)   where the interest is held exclusively with a view to resale and the subsidiary has not previously been included in the consolidation of the accounts of the parent and its subsidiary undertakings.

In particular, it should be noted that FRS 2 requires exclusion from the consolidation in these circumstances, whereas the Act permits it, and in the case of an investment held exclusively with a view to resale, the standard is more restrictive, in that exclusion applies only where the entity has not previously been consolidated in group accounts prepared by the parent. Also, under FRS 2 a subsidiary undertaking cannot be excluded from the consolidation on the grounds that the necessary information cannot be obtained without disproportionate expense or undue delay, and the standard makes no reference to materiality, as the requirements of accounting standards do not have to be applied to immaterial items (see 1.7 above).

The standard also specifies the accounting treatment that should be adopted for any subsidiaries that have been excluded from the consolidation (see 44.22 and 44.28 below).

Severe restrictions hindering parent's rights

44.21   The rights of the parent in this case are the specific rights without which the company would not be the parent of the other undertaking under the requirements of the Act. FRS 2 emphasises that, in many cases, restrictions will be best dealt with by additional disclosure in the accounts rather than excluding a subsidiary from the consolidation. Exclusion is only justified where the effect of the restrictions is that the parent no longer controls the subsidiary. FRS 2 defines 'control' as the ability to direct the operating and financial policies of the entity, with a view to gaining economic benefit. It is the practical effect of the restrictions that is important, rather than the way in which they are imposed, and the threat of restrictions will not in itself be sufficient to justify exclusion. The standard quotes as an example of restrictions in practice a situation where a subsidiary is subject to a UK insolvency procedure, which results in control passing to an administrator, administrative receiver or liquidator. However, it also notes that a company voluntary arrangement will not necessarily lead to a loss of control by the parent.

Accounting treatment

44.22   Where exclusion on the grounds of severe long-term restrictions is justified, FRS 2 requires the subsidiary to be treated as a fixed asset investment. If the restrictions are in force from the date of acquisition, the investment should be carried at cost; if the restrictions come into effect at a later date, the investment should be carried in the accounts at a fixed amount calculated using the equity method of accounting at the date when the restrictions begin. The equity method of accounting is considered in Chapter 46.

While restrictions are in force

44.23   Whilst the restrictions are in force, no further accruals should be made for the profits or losses of the subsidiary, unless the parent retains significant influence over it. In this case the entity should be accounted for as an associate using the equity method of accounting. The definition of significant influence and the accounting treatment of associates are considered in Chapter 46.

Regular review of carrying value

44.24   The carrying value of the investment should be reviewed each year and, where appropriate, provisions should be made for any impairment in value. Any balances between the entity and other members of the group will need to be similarly reviewed and written down where necessary. If more than one subsidiary is subject to restrictions, the amounts relating to each one should be considered individually.

Lifting of the restrictions

44.25   If the restrictions are subsequently lifted, the amount of profit or loss that has not been recognised during the period of the restrictions should be reflected in the consolidated profit and loss account for the period during which the parent resumes control and should be separately disclosed. It will usually be appropriate to show this as a single entry in the profit and loss account. Consolidation of individual items of income and expenditure in these circumstances could be misleading. Any write-back of amounts charged for impairment during the period of the restrictions should also be separately disclosed. The results of the subsidiary will then be consolidated under the normal rules from the date on which the restrictions are lifted.

Interest held exclusively with a view to subsequent resale

44.26   The Act permits a subsidiary undertaking to be excluded from the consolidation if the interest is held exclusively with a view to resale. FRS 2 requires the subsidiary to be excluded in these circumstances, but only if it has never formed part of the continuing activities of the group, and has not previously been included in consolidated accounts drawn up by the parent. For instance, the conditions might be met where an undertaking has recently been acquired as part of a larger acquisition but where the parent has no intention that it should be part of the future activities of the new group. The fact that the interest must be held exclusively with a view to resale will mean that an undertaking that has previously been part of the group but which has now been identified as being available for sale, and for which a purchaser is being sought, will not meet the conditions set out in the standard, although it would qualify for exclusion under the Act (as amended – see 44.19

above). Such an undertaking must continue to be fully consolidated up to the actual date of disposal, even though it may be available for sale at the end of the parent's accounting period.

Definition under FRS 2

44.27 FRS 2 defines an interest held exclusively with a view to subsequent resale as:

(i) an interest for which a purchaser has been identified or is being sought, and which is reasonably expected to be disposed of within approximately one year of its date of acquisition; or

(ii) an interest that was acquired as a result of enforcement of a security, unless the interest has become part of the continuing activities of the group or the holder acts as if it intends the interest to become so.

To meet the first part of this definition, there will have to be an immediate intention to sell and the expectation that this can be achieved within one year. The explanation section of FRS 2 emphasises that a sale that is not actually completed within one year may nevertheless meet the conditions if, at the date of approval of the accounts, the terms of a sale have been agreed and the disposal process is substantially complete. The implication, therefore, is that if negotiations are still in progress at this point, the conditions set out in FRS 2 will not have been met and the entity will therefore have to be consolidated.

Example 44.2 – Subsequent resale: accounting treatment

E Ltd acquires F Ltd and it subsidiaries G Ltd and H Ltd on 2 February 1996. It intends to retain F Ltd and G Ltd as part of the group but immediately seeks a purchaser for H Ltd.

E Ltd makes up its accounts to 31 December; the accounts for the year to 31 December 1996 are approved on 14 April 1997.

(i) If at 14 April 1997, the sale of H Ltd has been agreed and the disposal is substantially complete, it can be excluded from the consolidation, even though the sale was not completed within one year of acquisition.

(ii) If at 14 April 1997, the sale of H Ltd is still under negotiation, its exclusion from the consolidation will generally not be permitted under the conditions laid down in FRS 2.

Accounting treatment

44.28 Where a subsidiary is excluded from the consolidation on the grounds that the interest is held exclusively with a view to subsequent resale, FRS 2 requires it to be accounted for as a current asset investment. It should therefore be included in the consolidated balance sheet at the lower of cost and net realisable value.

Dissimilar activities

44.29   For accounting periods beginning before 1 January 2005, both CA 1985 and FRS 2 required a subsidiary undertaking to be excluded from the consolidation where its activities were so different from those of other undertakings included in the consolidation that to include them would be incompatible with the requirement for the accounts to give a true and fair view. However, involvement in different industrial, commercial or service activities, working with different products, or providing different services was generally not sufficient to justify exclusion on these grounds. Section 229(4), which set out this exclusion requirement, was removed by the *Companies Act (International Accounting Standards and Other Accounting Amendments) Regulations 2004* (SI 2004/2947) and FRS 2 was amended accordingly.

If, in exceptional circumstances, exclusion from the consolidation was considered necessary on these grounds, both CA 1985 and FRS 2 required the excluded subsidiary undertaking to be accounted for in the group accounts using the equity method of accounting. FRS 2 also required:

(i)   the accounts of the excluded subsidiary to be attached to the group accounts; or

(ii)   if it did not account for more than 20% of any one or more of group operating profit, group turnover or group net assets (including amounts relating to any subsidiaries excluded from the consolidation), summarised information to be given as an alternative.

If more than one subsidiary was excluded on the grounds of dissimilar activities, subsidiaries with similar operations could be taken together in assessing whether the 20% limits had been reached.

Exclusion of quasi-subsidiaries from the consolidation

44.30   FRS 5 'Reporting the Substance of Transactions' requires the assets, liabilities, profits, losses and cash flows of quasi-subsidiaries to be included in the consolidation in the same way as entities that meet the legal definition of a subsidiary. The requirements set out in FRS 2 should be followed in respect of the quasi-subsidiary, except that a quasi-subsidiary should only be excluded from the consolidation if the interest is held exclusively with a view to resale. Exclusion on other grounds is not considered relevant as:

(i)   an immaterial quasi-subsidiary will not come within the scope of FRS 5;

(ii)   the existence of severe long-term restrictions will inevitably mean that the level of control necessary to meet the definition of a quasi-subsidiary will not exist; and

(iii)   for accounting periods beginning before 1 January 2005, the fact that the activities of the quasi-subsidiary differ from those of the rest of the group may need to be disclosed, but will not justify its exclusion from the consolidation.

Quasi-subsidiaries are considered in more detail in Chapter 45.

Disclosure requirements

44.31 Both CA 1985 and FRS 2 require disclosure of the names of any subsidiary undertakings that have been excluded from the consolidation, and the reason for exclusion in each case. In addition, FRS 2 requires the following details to be given for any subsidiary that is excluded from the consolidation:

(i) details of balances between the excluded subsidiary and other members of the group;

(ii) the nature and extent of transactions between the excluded subsidiary and other members of the group;

(iii) if the subsidiary is not accounted for under the equity method of accounting, the amounts included in the accounts for:

- dividends received and receivable from the excluded subsidiary; and

- any write-down of the investment in the subsidiary or of amounts due from the subsidiary;

(iv) in the case of a subsidiary excluded on the grounds of dissimilar activities, the financial statements of the undertaking (or summarised information in certain circumstances, as explained in 44.29 above) – however, exclusion on these grounds is not required or permitted for accounting periods beginning on or after 1 January 2005.

Individual information should generally be given for each excluded subsidiary. However, the details may be presented for a sub-unit of excluded subsidiaries if this is considered more appropriate, provided that the subsidiaries have been excluded from the consolidation for the same reason. Individual disclosures must be given for any subsidiary (including its own sub-group where relevant) that accounts for more than 20% of any one or more of:

(i) group operating profit;

(ii) group turnover;

(iii) group net assets.

The group figures should include the relevant amounts for all subsidiaries excluded from the consolidation.

Likely future developments

44.32 The ASB published FRED 32 'Disposal of non-current assets and presentation of discontinued operations' in July 2003 as part of its project to achieve convergence between UK and international accounting standards. If implemented, the proposals in FRED 32 will remove the exemption from consolidation for subsidiaries acquired and held exclusively with a view to resale. This is on the basis that all assets held for sale should be treated in the same way. The IASB has therefore agreed that:

(i)   all subsidiaries should be consolidated; and

(ii)   all assets and disposal groups that meet the criteria for classification as assets held for sale should be treated in the same way and disclosed separately in the balance sheet.

ACCOUNTING DATES OF SUBSIDIARIES

Requirement for consistency with parent company

44.33   There is a strong emphasis in both CA 1985 and FRS 2 'Accounting for Subsidiaries' on the need for subsidiaries to have the same accounting date as their parent. Section 223(5) of CA 1985 requires the directors of a parent company to ensure that the financial year of each subsidiary undertaking coincides with that of the parent unless, in their opinion, there are good reasons against this. FRS 2 requires the accounts of all subsidiary undertakings included in the consolidation to be for the same accounting period and made up to the same accounting date as the accounts of the parent, wherever this is practicable.

Different accounting dates

44.34   Where the accounting date of a subsidiary is different to that of the parent, the Act provides an option between:

(i)   using the latest accounts of the subsidiary, provided that these are for a period ending not more than three months before the end of the parent's financial year; or

(ii)   using interim accounts for the subsidiary, prepared as at the end of the parent's financial year.

FRS 2 takes a more stringent approach where the accounting date of a subsidiary differs from that of its parent and the emphasis is very much on the preparation of interim accounts for the subsidiary for use in the consolidation. The latest statutory accounts of the subsidiary can only be used if the preparation of interim accounts is not practicable, and even then there are two further requirements:

(i)   the latest accounts can only be used if they are for a period ending not more than three months before the parent's accounting date (which is consistent with the Act); and

(ii)   adjustments must be made for any changes in the intervening period which have a material effect on the group accounts.

Where a subsidiary undertaking is included in the consolidation on the basis of accounts prepared to a different accounting date or for a different accounting period, FRS 2 also requires the accounts to disclose:

(i)   the name of the subsidiary undertaking;

(ii)   the relevant accounting date or accounting period used;

(iii) the reason for using a different accounting date or accounting period for this subsidiary undertaking.

Change of subsidiary's accounting date

44.35   An interesting issue arises where a subsidiary changes its accounting date (e.g. to bring this into line with the accounting date of the parent) and extends its accounting period in order to do so. If the subsidiary has previously been included in the consolidation on the basis of interim accounts, there should be little difficulty in calculating the figures to be consolidated in the year of the change, although some apportionment of the profit and loss account will be needed to ensure that no items of income and expenditure are double-counted.

Example 44.3 – Subsidiary brings its accountancy date in line with that of the parent: interim accounts previously used

A Ltd is a subsidiary of B Ltd and makes up its accounts to 31 October. B Ltd's accounting date is 31 December.

In 20X2, A Ltd changes its accounting date to 31 December to bring it into line with the accounting date of its parent. It therefore prepares accounts for a fourteen month period from 1 November 20X1 to 31 December 20X2.

A Ltd was included in the 20X1 group accounts of B Ltd on the basis of interim accounts made up to 31 December 20X1. Therefore in preparing the 20X2 group accounts, profit and loss account transactions for the period 1 November 20X1 to 31 December 20X1 will need to be eliminated from A Ltd's 20X2 accounts, as these transactions will already have been included in the 20X1 group accounts.

However, if the subsidiary was previously included in the group accounts on the basis of its latest statutory accounts, adjusted for any material changes, the calculations are less straightforward. The requirement under FRS 2 for the accounting period of the subsidiary to be the same as that of the parent will usually mean that it will be inappropriate to consolidate accounts covering a period of more than twelve months, unless the effect is not material. The most appropriate treatment will usually be as follows.

(i)   Allocate the results of the subsidiary for the extended period into the results for the last twelve months and the results for previous months. It may be possible to base this allocation on detailed information (e.g. reliable management accounts). If not, care will be needed to ensure that the effects of any seasonal and similar variations are properly accounted for (i.e. a straight apportionment over the period will not necessarily be the most appropriate allocation).

(ii)   Consolidate the results of the subsidiary for the last twelve months into the group accounts for the current year.

(iii) Restate the figures for previous years, so that the accounts reflect the position that would have been shown if the subsidiary had always been included in the group accounts on the basis of accounts made up to the parent's accounting date.

Where adjustments were made in previous years to reflect material changes between the subsidiary's accounting date and that of the parent, these will also need to be taken into account.

Example 44.4 – Subsidiary brings its accounting date in line with that of the parent: statutory accounts

A Ltd is a subsidiary of B Ltd and makes up its accounts to 31 October. B Ltd's accounting date is 31 December.

In 20X2, A Ltd changes its accounting date to 31 December to bring it into line with the accounting date of its parent. It therefore prepares accounts for a 14-month period from 1 November 20X1 to 31 December 20X2.

A Ltd was included in the 20X1 group accounts of B Ltd on the basis of its statutory accounts for the year ended 31 October 20X1. No adjustments were considered necessary for changes in the intervening 2 months.

The group accounts of B Ltd for the year ended 31 December 20X2 should be prepared as follows:

 (i)   the group profit and loss account for 20X2 should include the results of A Ltd for the period 1 January 20X2 to 31 December 20X2;

 (ii) the 20X1 group profit and loss account will need to be restated:

   ● to include the results of A Ltd for the period 1 November 20X1 to 31 December 20X1; and

   ● to exclude the results of A Ltd for the period 1 November 20X0 to 31 December 20X0

   so that it reflects the results of A Ltd for the calendar year 20X1;

(iii) the opening reserves at 1 January 20X1 will need to be adjusted to include the results of A Ltd for the period 1 November 20X0 to 31 December 20X0 (which were previously included in the 20X1 group accounts but have now been excluded);

(iv) the comparative figures in the balance sheet will also need to be restated to reflect these adjustments.

The end result of these adjustments is that both the 20X1 and 20X2 figures in the group accounts of B Ltd include the results of A Ltd for the same accounting period (i.e. the calendar year) and to the same accounting date (i.e. 31 December) as its parent.

PARENT COMPANY PROFIT AND LOSS ACCOUNT

Exemption from publication

44.36   Where a parent company is required by the Act to prepare group accounts, it need not publish its own profit and loss account. The results of the parent company will, of course, continue to be included in the consolidated profit and loss account. A strict interpretation of section 230(3) would suggest that a parent company that is not required to prepare group accounts under the Act (e.g. because it is a member of a larger group) but chooses to do so will not be entitled to this exemption. The exemption is only available if:

(i)   the notes to the parent company balance sheet show the company's profit or loss for the financial year; and

(ii)   the accounts disclose the fact that the exemption is available and has been applied.

The profit or loss for the financial year is the profit or loss before dividends and other appropriations (i.e. the last item on the standard profit and loss account format). The two required disclosures can usually be combined in a single note to the accounts.

Example 44.5 – Note on parent's profit and loss account

As permitted by section 230(3) of the *Companies Act 1985*, the profit and loss account of the parent company is not presented in these accounts. The parent company's profit for the financial year was £13,566 (20X1: £12,450).

Requirement to prepare a profit and loss account

44.37   The exemption in section 230(3) relates only to the publication of the parent company's profit and loss account in the group accounts. The company must still prepare a full profit and loss account (which will in any case be required for consolidation purposes) in the standard format required by the Act and following the accounting requirements of the Act. This profit and loss account must be formally approved by the board of directors. It will usually be appropriate to deal with this at the same time as the group accounts and parent company balance sheet are formally approved.

However, although the parent company must continue to prepare a profit and loss account in the standard format, it need not comply with the additional disclosure requirements set out in paragraphs 52 to 57 of Schedule 4. These paragraphs normally require disclosure of the following:

(i)   an analysis of interest and similar charges;

(ii)   particulars of the tax charge;

(iii)   analyses of turnover;

(iv) details of extraordinary items;

(v) details of exceptional items;

(vi) any amounts relating to a preceding financial year.

Although these items do not need to be shown in the parent company's own profit and loss account, they must still be identified for inclusion in the appropriate disclosures in the group accounts.

APPENDIX

Standard Formats For Group Accounts

The headings inserted by Schedule 4A are shown in bold

Consolidated profit and loss account: Format 1

1. Turnover.
2. Cost of sales.
3. Gross profit or loss.
4. Distribution costs.
5. Administrative expenses.
6. Other operating income.
7. Income from shares in group undertakings.
8. **Income from interests in associated undertakings.**
9. **Income from other participating interests.**
10. Income from other fixed asset investments.
11. Other interest receivable and similar income.
12. Amounts written off investments.
13. Interest payable and similar charges.
14. Tax on profit or loss on ordinary activities.
15. Profit or loss on ordinary activities after taxation.
16. **Minority interests.**
17. Extraordinary income.
18. Extraordinary charges.
19. Extraordinary profit or loss.
20. Tax on extraordinary profit or loss.
21. **Minority interests (i.e. in extraordinary items).**
22. Other taxes not shown under the above items.
23. Profit or loss for the financial year.

The following items must also be shown:

(i) Under the *Companies Act 1985*, the profit or loss on ordinary activities before taxation;

(ii) Under FRS 3 'Reporting Financial Performance', operating profit.

Consolidated profit and loss account: Format 2

1. Turnover.

2.   Change in stocks of finished goods and work in progress.

3.   Own work capitalised.

4.   Other operating income.

5.   (a)   Raw materials and consumables,

       (b)   Other external charges.

6.   Staff costs:

       (a)   wages and salaries,

       (b)   social security costs,

       (c)   other pension costs.

7.   (a)   Depreciation and other amounts written off tangible and intangible fixed assets.

       (b)   Exceptional amounts written off current assets.

8.   Other operating charges.

9.   Income from shares in group undertakings.

10.   Income from interests in associated undertakings.

11.   Income from other participating interests.

12.   Income from other fixed asset investments.

13.   Other interest receivable and similar income.

14.   Amounts written off investments.

15.   Interest payable and similar charges.

16.   Tax on profit or loss on ordinary activities.

17.   Profit or loss on ordinary activities after taxation.

18.   Minority interests.

19.   Extraordinary income.

20.   Extraordinary charges.

21.   Extraordinary profit or loss.

22.   Tax on extraordinary profit or loss.

23.   Minority interests (i.e. in extraordinary items).

24.   Other taxes not shown under the above items.

25.   Profit or loss for the financial year.

The following items must also be shown:

 (i)   Under the Companies Act 1985, the profit or loss on ordinary activities before taxation;

 (ii)   Under FRS 3 'Reporting Financial Performance', operating profit.

Consolidated profit and loss account: Format 3

A.   Charges

1.   Cost of sales.

2.   Distribution costs.

3.   Administrative expenses.

4.   Amounts written off investments.

5.   Interest payable and similar charges.

6.   Tax on profit or loss on ordinary activities.

7.   Profit or loss on ordinary activities after taxation.

8.   Minority interests.

9.   Extraordinary charges.

10.   Tax on extraordinary profit or loss.

11.   Minority interests (i.e. in extraordinary charges).

12.   Other taxes not shown under the above items.

13.   Profit or loss for the financial year.

B.   Income

1.   Turnover.

2.   Other operating income.

3.   Income from shares in group undertakings.

4.   Income from interests in associated undertakings.

5.   Income from other participating interests.

6.   Income from other fixed asset investments.

7.   Other interest receivable and similar income.

8.   Profit or loss on ordinary activities after taxation.

9.   Minority interests.

10.   Extraordinary income.

11.   Minority interests (i.e. in extraordinary income).

12.   Profit or loss for the financial year.

The following items must also be shown:

(i)   Under the Companies Act 1985, the profit or loss on ordinary activities before   taxation;

(ii)   Under FRS 3 'Reporting Financial Performance', operating profit.

Consolidated profit and loss account: Format 4

A.   Charges

1.   Reduction in stocks of finished goods and work in progress.

2.   (a)   Raw materials and consumables,

      (b)   Other external charges.

3.   Staff costs:

      (a)   wages and salaries,

      (b)   social security costs,

      (c)   other pension costs.

4.   (a)   Depreciation and other amounts written off tangible and intangible fixed assets.

      (b)   Exceptional amounts written off current assets.

5.   Other operating charges.

6.   Amounts written off investments.

7.   Interest payable and similar charges.

8.   Tax on profit or loss on ordinary activities.

9.   Profit or loss on ordinary activities after taxation.

10.   Minority interests.

11.   Extraordinary charges.

12.   Tax on extraordinary profit or loss.

13.   Minority interests (i.e. in extraordinary charges).

14.   Other taxes not shown under the above items.

15.   Profit or loss for the financial year.

B.   Income

1.   Turnover.

2.   Increase in stocks of finished goods and work in progress.

3.   Own work capitalised.

4.   Other operating income.

5.   Income from shares in group undertakings.

6.   Income from interests in associated undertakings.

7.   Income from other participating interests.

8.   Income from other fixed asset investments.

9.   Other interest receivable and similar income.

10.   Profit or loss on ordinary activities after taxation.

11.   Minority interests.

12. Extraordinary income.

13. Minority interests (i.e. in extraordinary income).

14. Profit or loss for the financial year.

The following items must also be shown:

(i) Under the Companies Act 1985, the profit or loss on ordinary activities before taxation;

(ii) Under FRS 3 'Reporting Financial Performance', operating profit.

Consolidated balance sheet: Format 1

A.(*) **Called up share capital not paid**

B. **Fixed assets**

I. Intangible assets.

    1. Development costs.

    2. Concessions, patents, licences, trade marks and similar rights and assets.

    3. Goodwill.

    4. Payments on account.

II. Tangible assets.

    1. Land and buildings.

    2. Plant and machinery.

    3. Fixtures, fittings, tools and equipment.

    4. Payments on account and assets in course of construction.

III. Investments.

    1. Shares in group undertakings.

    2. Loans to group undertakings.

3. Interests in associated undertakings.

4. Other participating interests.

5. Loans to undertakings in which the company has a participating interest.

6. Other investments other than loans.

7. Other loans.

8. Own shares.

C. **Current assets**

I. Stocks.

    1. Raw materials and consumables.

    2.   Work in progress.

    3.   Finished goods and goods for resale.

    4.   Payments on account.

II.   Debtors.

    1.   Trade debtors.

    2.   Amounts owed by group undertakings.

    3.   Amounts owed by undertakings in which the company has a participating interest.

    4.   Other debtors.

(*)5. Called up share capital not paid.

(*)6. Prepayments and accrued income.

III.   Investments.

    1.   Shares in group undertakings.

    2.   Own shares.

    3.   Other investments.

IV.   Cash at bank and in hand.

D.(*) Prepayments and accrued income

E.   Creditors: amounts falling due within one year

1.   Debenture loans.

2.   Bank loans and overdrafts.

3.   Payments received on account.

4.   Trade creditors.

5.   Bills of exchange payable.

6.   Amounts owed to group undertakings.

7.   Amounts owed to undertakings in which the company has a participating interest.

8.   Other creditors including taxation and social security.

(*)9. Accruals and deferred income.

F.   Net current assets (liabilities)

G.   Total assets less current liabilities

H.   Creditors: amounts falling due after more than one year

1.   Debenture loans.

2.   Bank loans and overdrafts.

3. Payments received on account.

4. Trade creditors.

5. Bills of exchange payable.

6. Amounts owed to group undertakings.

7. Amounts owed to undertakings in which the company has a participating interest.

8. Other creditors including taxation and social security.

(*)9. Accruals and deferred income.

I.   Provisions for liabilities

1. Pensions and similar obligations.

2. Taxation, including deferred taxation.

3. Other provisions.

J.(*)   Accruals and deferred income

K.(*)   Minority interests

L.   Capital and reserves

I.   Share capital.

II.   Share premium account.

III.   Revaluation reserve.

IV.   Other reserves.

    1.   Capital redemption reserve.

    2.   Reserve for own shares.

    3.   Reserves provided for by the articles of association.

    4.   Other reserves.

V.   Profit and loss account.

M.(*)   Minority interests

(*) = alternative positions

Consolidated balance sheet: Format 2

ASSETS

A.(*)   Called up share capital not paid

B.   Fixed assets

I.   Intangible assets.

1.   Development costs.

2.   Concessions, patents, licences, trade marks and similar rights and assets.

3.   Goodwill.

4.   Payments on account.

II.   Tangible assets.

1.   Land and buildings.

2.   Plant and machinery.

3.   Fixtures, fittings, tools and equipment.

4.   Payments on account and assets in course of construction.

III.   Investments.

1.   Shares in group undertakings.

2.   Loans to group undertakings.

3.   Interests in associated undertakings.

4.   Other participating interests.

5.   Loans to undertakings in which the company has a participating interest.

6.   Other investments other than loans.

7.   Other loans.

8.   Own shares.

C.   **Current assets**

I.   Stocks.

1.   Raw materials and consumables.

2.   Work in progress.

3.   Finished goods and goods for resale.

4.   Payments on account.

II.   Debtors.

1.   Trade debtors.

2.   Amounts owed by group undertakings.

3.   Amounts owed by undertakings in which the company has a participating interest.

4.   Other debtors.

(*)5.   Called up share capital not paid.

(*)6.   Prepayments and accrued income.

III.   Investments.

      1.   Shares in group undertakings.

      2.   Own shares.

      3.   Other investments.

IV.   Cash at bank and in hand.

D.(*) Prepayments and accrued income

LIABILITIES

A.   Capital and reserves

I.   Share capital.

II.   Share premium account.

III.   Revaluation reserve.

IV.   Other reserves.

      1.   Capital redemption reserve.

      2.   Reserve for own shares.

      3.   Reserves provided for by the articles of association.

      4.   Other reserves.

V.   Profit and loss account.

B.   Minority interests

C.   Provisions for liabilities

1.   Pensions and similar obligations.

2.   Taxation, including deferred taxation.

3.   Other provisions.

D.   Creditors

1.   Debenture loans.

2.   Bank loans and overdrafts.

3.   Payments received on account.

4.   Trade creditors.

5.   Bills of exchange payable.

6.   Amounts owed to group undertakings.

7.   Amounts owed to undertakings in which the company has a participating interest.

8.   Other creditors including taxation and social security.

(*)9.   Accruals and deferred income.

E.(*) Accruals and deferred income

(*) = alternative positions

Chapter 45   Subsidiaries

IDENTIFICATION OF SUBSIDIARIES

Legal definition of parent undertaking and subsidiary undertaking

45.1   Under section 258 of CA 1985, an undertaking is the parent undertaking of another undertaking if:

  (i)   it holds a majority of the voting rights; or

 (ii)   it is a member of the undertaking and has the right to appoint or remove a majority of the board of directors; or

(iii)   it has the right to exercise dominant influence over the undertaking as a result of:

- provisions contained in the undertaking's memorandum or articles; or

- a control contract; or

(iv)   it is a member of the undertaking and controls alone, through an agreement with other shareholders or members, a majority of the voting rights; or

 (v)   it has the power to exercise, or actually exercises, dominant influence or control over it, or both undertakings are managed on a unified basis.

These definitions apply for most accounting purposes under the Act, including related disclosure requirements, such as directors' remuneration. For accounting periods beginning before 1 January 2005, an undertaking was only a subsidiary under definition (v) above if the parent had a participating interest in it and actually exercised dominant influence over it or the two undertakings were managed on a unified basis. The changes were introduced by the *Companies Act (International Accounting Standards and Other Accounting Amendments) Regulations 2004* (SI 2004/2947).

Where a subsidiary undertaking has its own subsidiary undertaking, this is also regarded as a subsidiary undertaking of the parent undertaking for the purposes of section 258.

Definition of subsidiary undertaking under FRS 2

45.2 FRS 2 'Accounting for Subsidiary Undertakings' essentially repeats the definitions of a subsidiary undertaking as set out in CA 1985, but incorporates some of the interpretation of voting rights from Schedule 10A to the Act into the definitions. Under the standard, an undertaking is a parent undertaking of another undertaking (a subsidiary undertaking) if:

(i)   it holds a majority of voting rights;

(ii)   it is a member of the undertaking and has the right to appoint or remove directors holding a majority of voting rights at meetings of the board on all, or substantially all, matters;

(iii)   it has the right to exercise dominant influence over the undertaking:

- through provisions in the undertaking's memorandum or articles; or

- through a control contract which must be in writing, of a kind authorised by the undertaking's memorandum or articles, and permitted by the law under which the undertaking is established;

(iv)   it is a member of the undertaking and controls alone, through an agreement with other shareholders or members, a majority of voting rights;

(v)   it has the power to exercise, or actually exercises a dominant influence or control over the undertaking, or it and the undertaking are managed on a unified basis.

The standard was also updated with effect from 1 January 2005 to reflect the changes to definition (v) above made by the *Companies Act (International Accounting Standards and Other Accounting Amendments) Regulations 2004* (see 1.1 above). For accounting periods beginning before this date, the standard also required the parent to have a participating interest in the other entity and to actually exercise a dominant influence over it.

Definition of holding company and subsidiary

45.3 Section 736(1) of CA 1985 also includes separate definitions of 'holding company' and 'subsidiary' which apply for most general purposes other than accounting issues (e.g. loans to and transactions with directors). A company is a subsidiary of another company (which is described as the holding company) if the latter:

(i)   holds a majority of the voting rights; or

(ii)   is a member and has the right to appoint or remove a majority of the board of directors; or

(iii)   is a member and controls alone, through an agreement with other shareholders or members, a majority of the voting rights.

Where the Act refers to a 'subsidiary undertaking', the definitions set out in 45.1 above apply. These definitions are broader than those in section 736 and encompass non-corporate entities as well as companies. Where the Act refers to a 'subsidiary' the narrower definitions set out above apply. These definitions relate specifically to companies and also exclude the broader definitions in section 258 covering dominant influence and unified management. If a subsidiary company has its own subsidiary company, this is also regarded as a subsidiary of the holding company for the purposes of section 736. A company is a wholly-owned subsidiary if it has no members other than:

(i)   the holding company; and

(ii)   any other wholly-owned subsidiaries of the holding company; or

(iii)   persons acting on behalf of the holding company or its wholly- owned subsidiaries.

Dominant influence

45.4   The terms 'actually exercises a dominant influence' and 'managed on a unified basis' are not explained in CA 1985, although Schedule 10A does state that:

> 'an undertaking shall not be regarded as having the right to exercise a dominant influence over another undertaking unless it has a right to give directions with respect to the operating and financial policies of that other undertaking which its directors are obliged to comply with whether or not they are for the benefit of that other undertaking.'

FRS 2 defines dominant influence as 'Influence that can be exercised to achieve the operating and financial policies desired by the holder of the influence, notwithstanding the rights or influence of any other party'. The standard goes on to explain that:'The right to exercise dominant influence means that the holder has a right to give directions with respect to the operating and financial policies of another undertaking with which its directors are obliged to comply, whether or not they are for the benefit of that undertaking'.

It also states that:

> 'The actual exercise of dominant influence is the exercise of an influence that achieves the result that the operating and financial policies of the undertaking influenced are set in accordance with the wishes of the holder of the influence and for the holder's benefit, whether or not those wishes are explicit. The

actual exercise of dominant influence is identified by its effect in practice rather than by the way in which it is exercised.'

For accounting periods beginning on or after 1 January 2005, the standard includes a further definition of the power to exercise dominant influence as 'a power that, if exercised, would give rise to the actual exercise of dominant influence' (as defined above).

An interesting issue arises here, because company directors in the UK have a legal duty to act in the best interests of the company. The definitions of dominant influence in both the Act and FRS 2 refer to the fact that for such influence to exist, the directors of the 'subsidiary' must be obliged to comply with the directions of the other party, even though this may not be in the best interests of their company. Therefore, the existence of dominant influence as defined in the Act and FRS 2 might result in the directors breaching their fiduciary duty.

Actual exercise of dominant influence

45.5   FRS 2 emphasises that the actual exercise of dominant influence should be identified by its practical effect (i.e. the end result rather than the mechanism used to achieve it) and that the assessment should take account of all the available information, including both formal and informal agreements between the parties. Dominant influence may be exercised in a variety of ways; for instance it might include:

(i)   the parent setting out in detail the operating and financial policies of the subsidiary; or

(ii)   the parent outlining the overall results that should be achieved, but then only intervening on critical issues.

Each case must therefore be considered on its own merits. FRS 2 also emphasises that once evidence of dominant influence has been established, it should be assumed to continue, unless there is new evidence to the contrary. An assessment will therefore need to be made each year to establish whether the situation has changed.

Managed on a unified basis

45.6   Under FRS 2, two or more undertakings should only be considered to be managed on a unified basis if the whole of the operations are fully integrated and the undertakings are managed as a single unit. This definition will rarely be met in practice. In particular, the standard emphasises that a situation where two or more undertakings are subject to common management, or where one undertaking manages another, will not in itself meet the conditions set out in FRS 2.

Control and control contracts

45.7   FRS 2 defines control as 'The ability of an undertaking to direct the financial and operating policies of another undertaking with a view to gaining economic benefits from its activities'. A control contract is defined in paragraph 4(2) of Schedule 10A to CA 1985 as a contract in writing which is:

(i)   of a kind authorised by the memorandum or articles of the undertaking; and

(ii)   permitted by the law under which the undertaking is established.

Participating interest

45.8   For accounting periods beginning before 1 January 2005, a participating interest was defined in both CA 1985 and FRS 2 as:

'An interest held by an undertaking in the shares of another undertaking which it holds on a long-term basis for the purpose of securing a contribution to its activities by the exercise of control or influence arising from or relating to that interest'.

A holding of 20% or more was presumed to be a participating interest unless it could be shown that this was not the case, and an interest included options and any other interests that were convertible into shares, or into an interest in shares. No minimum holding was laid down in the Act, and it was therefore possible that a holding of less than 20% could still qualify as a participating interest if the other conditions set out in section 260 (1) of CA 1985 were fulfilled. The Act also included the following provisions in respect of participating interests:

(i)   an interest held on behalf of an undertaking was to be treated as being held by it;

(ii)   any interests held by a subsidiary undertaking were to be attributed to the parent undertaking; and

(iii) the reference in section 260(1) to the purposes and activities of an undertaking included the purposes and activities of a parent, subsidiary or fellow subsidiary undertaking.

The last two provisions applied only for the purposes of the definition of a subsidiary undertaking under section 258. However, the definition of a participating interest is no longer relevant in the context of subsidiaries (see 45.1 above).

Definition of 'member'

45.9   For the purposes of section 258 of CA 1985, an undertaking is to be treated as a member of another undertaking if:

(i)   any of its subsidiary undertakings is a member; or

(ii)   any of the shares are held by a person acting on its behalf or on behalf of any of its subsidiary undertakings.

Quasi-subsidiaries

45.10   FRS 5 'Reporting the Substance of Transactions' recognises that assets and liabilities are sometimes held by an undertaking that is effectively controlled by the reporting entity, but which does not meet the definition of a subsidiary undertaking under the Act or FRS 2. Such an entity is referred to in FRS 5 as a 'quasi-subsidiary'. Accounting for quasi-subsidiaries is considered in more detail at 45.19 below.

Disclosures in respect of subsidiaries

45.11   Schedule 5 to CA 1985 sets out the detailed disclosures in respect of subsidiary undertakings that must be given in the accounts of a parent undertaking. The requirements differ, depending on whether or not the parent is required to prepare group accounts and certain exemptions are also granted by section 231 of CA 1985. In addition to the disclosures required by the Act, FRS 2 requires the following details to be given where group accounts are prepared:

(i)   for each subsidiary whose results or financial position principally affects the figures shown in the consolidated accounts:

- the proportion of voting rights held by the parent and its subsidiary undertakings; and

- an indication of the nature of the business; and

(ii)   in the case of an undertaking which is only a subsidiary because the parent has the power to exercise, or actually exercises, dominant influence or control over it, the basis of the parent's dominant influence or control.

GENERAL INTERPRETATION OF 'RIGHTS'

Rights exercisable only in certain circumstances

45.12   Schedule 10A explains how expressions used to define parent and subsidiary undertakings in section 258 should be interpreted, and section 736A sets out similar details in respect of the definitions of subsidiary and holding company in section 736 of the Act. Rights that can only be exercised in certain circumstances should only be taken into account when:

(i)   those circumstances actually arise, and for as long as they continue to apply; or

(ii)   those circumstances are within the control of the person holding the rights.

For instance, preference shareholders who are entitled to a fixed cumulative dividend might be given additional rights that apply only when the dividend is in arrears. If the dividend was actually in arrears, these additional rights would have to be taken into account when assessing whether a parent/subsidiary relationship existed. If the dividend was not in arrears, the additional rights would be ignored. Rights that are normally available, but which are temporarily incapable of exercise for some reason, should continue to be taken into account.

Rights held by trustees and nominees

45.13 Rights that are held by a person in a fiduciary capacity are not to be treated as being held by him. . For instance, this would cover a situation where shares are held by a trustee. Rights held by one person as nominee for another person are to be treated as being held by that other person. Rights are treated as held by a nominee for another person if they can only be exercised on his instruction or with his consent or agreement. However, paragraph 9(2) of Schedule 10A and paragraph 8 of section 736A specifically state that this is not to be construed as requiring rights held by a parent undertaking to be treated as held by any of its subsidiary undertakings. Any rights held by a parent undertaking (or holding company) as nominee for a subsidiary are therefore to be treated as being held by the parent.

Rights held by way of security

45.14 Rights attached to shares held as security, are to be treated as being held by the person providing the security if:

(i)   the rights can only be exercised in accordance with his instructions;

(ii) the shares are held in connection with the granting of a loan as part of normal business activities, and the rights can only be exercised in his interests.

In both cases, any right to exercise in order to preserve the value of the security or to realise the security is specifically excluded. If these conditions are not satisfied, the rights will normally be treated as being held by the person who holds them as security, although this may depend on whether any other provisions of Schedule 10A or section 736A also come into effect.

Shares held by a group undertaking

45.15 In the case of shares held by an undertaking, rights are treated as being exercisable in accordance with its instructions or interests if they are exercisable in accordance with the instructions or interests of any undertaking within the same group (i.e. a parent, subsidiary or fellow subsidiary undertaking in the case of section 258, or a holding company, subsidiary or fellow subsidiary in the case of section 736). Once again, any rights held by a parent undertaking (or holding company) cannot be treated as being held by a subsidiary. Any rights held by a parent on behalf of a subsidiary must therefore be treated as being held by the parent.

Rights attributed to a parent undertaking or holding company

45.16 A parent undertaking is to be treated as holding any rights that are held by any of its subsidiary undertakings. Similarly, a holding company is to be treated as holding any rights that are held by any of its subsidiary companies.

Voting rights

45.17 Voting rights are the rights given to shareholders in respect of their shares, or to members (in a company which does not have a share capital) to vote at general meetings of the undertaking (or company) on all, or substantially all, matters. Non-voting shares, or shares which only carry the right to vote on certain limited matters, should therefore not be taken into account when assessing whether or not one undertaking holds a majority of the voting rights in another undertaking. It should be noted that the Act effectively makes a distinction between rights that always apply, but that are limited in nature, and rights that only apply in certain circumstances. Since section 258 covers all undertakings, not just companies, Schedule 10A allows for a situation where the entity does not hold general meetings at which decisions are made on the basis of voting rights. In this case, the expression 'holding a majority of the voting rights' is to be interpreted as having the right, under the constitution of the undertaking, to:

(i) direct the overall policy of the undertaking; or

(ii) alter the terms of its constitution.

As section 736 relates specifically to companies, no provision for this is required in section 736A.

Any voting rights held by the undertaking itself must be disregarded in the calculations.

Example 45.1 – Disregard of certain voting rights

Company A has an issued share capital of 1,000 ordinary shares of £1. Each share carries one vote at general meetings of the company.

Company B is a subsidiary of Company A.

Company A's shares are held as follows:

Company X	450
Company B	150
Mr R	100
Mr S	100
Mr T	200
	1,000

The shares held by B must be treated as being held by A, because A is B's parent. In assessing whether A is a subsidiary of X, the shares held by B must therefore be disregarded. The total voting rights in A are therefore deemed to be 850 (i.e. 1,000 − 150). X's voting rights represent more than 50% of this total and A is therefore a subsidiary of X.

Right to appoint and remove directors

45.18 The right to appoint or remove a majority of the board of directors is to be interpreted as the right to appoint or remove directors holding a majority of voting rights at board meetings on all, or substantially all, matters. The key issue, therefore, is the extent of the voting rights held by the directors appointed, rather than the actual number of directors appointed. An undertaking or company is treated as having the right to appoint a director if:

(i) a person's appointment to that directorship follows necessarily from his appointment as a director of the undertaking (or company); or

(ii) the directorship is held by the undertaking (or company) itself.

A right to appoint or remove a director which can only be exercised with the consent or concurrence of another person should be disregarded, unless no other person can appoint or remove a director to or from that directorship.

Example 45.2 – Right to appoint director only with consent

Company X has the right to appoint a director to the board of Company Y, but cannot do so without the consent of Company A. All three companies are completely independent of each other.

The right to appoint the director would normally be attributed to Company A rather than to Company X, as X is in effect acting as a nominee for A. The right would only be treated as being held by Company X if it could not be attributed to any other person.

ACCOUNTING FOR QUASI-SUBSIDIARIES

Impact of FRS 5

45.19 Before the implementation of FRS 5 'Reporting the Substance of Transactions', many schemes to keep finance off the balance sheet involved the use of specially created 'vehicles' which failed to meet the definition of a subsidiary and which were therefore excluded from the group accounts. The broader definition of a subsidiary undertaking introduced in the *Companies Act 1989* and FRS 2 'Accounting for Subsidiary Undertakings' went a long way towards encompassing these entities, and therefore ensuring that their assets and liabilities were included in the group accounts. The requirements of FRS 5 in respect of quasi-subsidiaries are designed to cover any remaining 'vehicles' which are still not caught by the new definitions of a subsidiary undertaking. For accounting periods beginning on or after 1 January 2005, the changes to the definition of a subsidiary made by the *Companies Act (International Accounting Standards and Other Accounting Amendments)*

Regulations 2004 (see 45.1 above) are likely to mean that some entities that were previously included in consolidated accounts as quasi-subsidiaries will in future be accounted for as subsidiaries.

Definition of quasi-subsidiary

45.20 FRS 5 defines a quasi-subsidiary as:

'a company, trust, partnership or other vehicle that, though not fulfilling the definition of a subsidiary, is directly or indirectly controlled by the reporting entity and gives rise to benefits for that entity that are in substance no different from those that would arise were the vehicle a subsidiary'.

Control is separately defined as 'the ability to direct the financial and operating policies of that entity, with a view to gaining economic benefit from its activities'. This is consistent with the definition of control in FRS 2 (see 45.7 above).

Benefits and risks

45.21 FRS 5 places great emphasis on the assessment of benefits and risks when considering the substance of transactions (see Chapter 4). The decision on whether an entity meets the definition of a quasi-subsidiary under FRS 5 must therefore take into account:

(i)   who gains the benefit from the entity's net assets;

(ii)   who bears the inherent risks relating to the net assets; and

(iii)   who directs the operating and financial policies of the entity.

Risk is identified in FRS 5 as including the potential to gain as well as the possible exposure to loss. A key question, therefore, is who will benefit if the entity is more successful than anticipated as well as who may lose if it fails to achieve what is expected. The ability to prevent others from gaining access to the benefits or directing the entity's policies are equally relevant in this assessment.

Inclusion in group accounts

45.22 An entity that meets the definition of a quasi-subsidiary should normally be included in the group accounts in exactly the same way as any other subsidiary. Its profits and losses, cash flows and balance sheet items will therefore be consolidated on the same basis as those for other subsidiaries. The process of consolidation is considered in more detail in Chapter 47.

Exclusion from consolidation

45.23 Both the Act and FRS 2 require or permit subsidiaries to be excluded from the consolidation in certain circumstances. In the case of a quasi-subsidiary these exclusions are generally not available. The only situation where a quasi-subsidiary should be excluded from the consolidation is where:

(i)   it is held exclusively with a view to resale; and

(ii) it has not previously been included in the reporting entity's consolidated accounts.

Exclusion from the consolidation on these grounds is likely to be rare in practice.

Reporting entity that does not prepare group accounts

45.24   If the reporting entity does not have other subsidiaries and therefore does not prepare group accounts, FRS 5 requires it to consolidate its own accounts with those of the quasi-subsidiary and to include these consolidated statements in its own accounts. The consolidated accounts must be given the same prominence as the entity's own financial statements. This is to ensure that the consolidated statements are not 'hidden', for instance by printing them in a smaller typeface at the end of the accounts.

Linked presentation

45.25   In exceptional circumstances, FRS 5 requires the quasi-subsidiary to be included in the consolidated accounts using a linked presentation. This form of presentation is considered in more detail Chapter 4 and Chapter 25. This accounting treatment should only be adopted where the quasi-subsidiary holds a single item, or a single portfolio of similar items, and the effect of the arrangement is that this item is 'ring-fenced' from the point of view of the group. The standard sets out stringent conditions that must be met to achieve 'ring-fencing'.

Additional disclosures in the accounts

45.26   Where a quasi-subsidiary is included in the consolidated accounts, the notes to the accounts should disclose:

(i)   the fact that the quasi-subsidiary is included;

(ii) summary financial statements for the quasi-subsidiary, showing each main heading in the profit and loss account, balance sheet, cash flow statement and statement of total recognised gains and losses, for which there is a material item, and also giving comparative figures.

Where more than one quasi-subsidiary is included, details should normally be given individually for each entity, but a combined summary may be given for quasi-subsidiaries that are similar in nature.

Chapter 46

Associates And Joint Ventures

IDENTIFICATION OF ASSOCIATES

Introduction

46.1 Over the years, it has become increasingly common for companies and groups to carry out part of their operations through entities that are not subsidiaries, but over which the investor nevertheless has a significant degree of influence. SSAP 1 'Accounting for Associated Companies' was developed to introduce a standard accounting treatment for such entities and the principles originally set out in that standard have now been developed further in FRS 9 'Associates and Joint Ventures' which supersedes SSAP 1 for all entities. Smaller entities which adopt the Financial Reporting Standard for Smaller Entities (FRSSE) are only required to comply with FRS 9 if they prepare group accounts.

Treatment of associates and joint ventures in group accounts

46.2 From the outset it has been generally accepted that, whilst it would be inappropriate to require consolidation of the results of these entities in the group accounts, it was equally unacceptable to treat them in the same way as ordinary investments by simply including dividends received in the group profit and loss account. FRS 9 therefore requires the results of associated entities to be accounted for under the equity method of accounting. Under this accounting treatment, the investing group's share of the associated entity's profits and losses is included in the group profit and loss account and its share of the underlying net assets of the entity is reflected in the consolidated balance sheet. The mechanics of the equity method of accounting are considered in more detail at 46.15 below.

FRS 9 deals mainly with the accounting treatment of joint ventures and associates in the context of group accounts, but there are also separate requirements on the treatment to be adopted by an investing company in its individual accounts. Additional disclosures are required where the company does not prepare group accounts, unless it is exempt from preparing group accounts, or would be exempt if it had subsidiaries. Exemption from the preparation of group accounts is considered in Chapter 44, but it essentially applies to wholly-owned subsidiaries whose results and assets are included in groups accounts which are delivered to the registrar and to certain small and medium-sized groups. The accounting treatment and disclosures required under FRS 9 where the investor is not required to prepare consolidated accounts are considered in Chapter 22.

Definition of associate

46.3   FRS 9 defines an associate as an entity other than a subsidiary in which the investor has a participating interest and over whose operating and financial policies the investor exercises a significant influence. The emphasis in FRS 9 is very much on the actual relationship in practice between investor and investee. The definition in the standard is consistent with the definition of an associated undertaking paragraph 20(1) of Schedule 4A to CA 1985. The term 'undertaking' in the legislation is broad and encompasses entities such as partnerships and unincorporated associations as well as companies.

The guidance in FRS 9 emphasises that the classification of an entity as an associate should not change according to whether it is profitable or loss-making, or has net assets or net liabilities. Similarly, once an investment has been classified and accounted for as an associate, its status will not change simply because the investor intends to dispose of the investment.

Participating interest

46.4   A participating interest is defined in CA 1985 as:

> 'an interest held by an undertaking in the shares of another undertaking which it holds on a long-term basis for the purpose of securing a contribution to its activities by the exercise of control or influence arising from or related to that interest.'

The expression 'shares' includes an interest which is convertible into shares and an option to acquire shares or to acquire an interest in shares, regardless of whether the shares are issued or unissued at the time. A participating interest is defined in FRS 9 as an interest in the shares of another entity, held on a long-term basis, for the purpose of securing a contribution to the investor's activities by the exercise of control or influence arising from or relating to that interest. The following points are made in the standard:

(i) the reference to shares includes:

- allotted shares in an entity with share capital;

- rights to share in the capital of an entity with capital but no share capital;

- in the case of entity without capital, interests conferring any right to share in profits, imposing a liability to contribute to losses or giving an obligation to contribute to debts or expenses in a winding up;

(ii) an interest in shares includes an interest that is convertible into an interest in shares, or an option to acquire shares;

(iii) the investor's interest must be beneficial and the expected benefits must be linked to the exercise of its significant influence over the operating and financial policies of the investee; and

(iv) the benefits may be obtained in various ways (e.g. dividends, fees based on performance etc.).

For accounting periods beginning on or after 1 January 2005, the *Companies Act 1985 (International Accounting Standards and Other Accounting Amendments) Regulations 2005* (SI 2005/2947) remove the requirement for a parent to have a participating interest in an entity that it controls in order for it to be classed as a subsidiary (see 45.1 above). The DTI consultation document on these changes noted that it would seem sensible to align the definitions of subsidiary and associate in this respect, so that an entity was deemed to be an associate if the investor could exercise significant influence over it, irrespective of the existence of a participating interest. Views were specifically invited on this point but no firm proposals have been put forward as yet to implement such a change.

Long-term factors

46.5 For an investment to qualify as an associate, the interest must be held on a long-term basis and the conclusion should therefore be based on long-term factors. An interest held on a long-term basis is defined as an interest held other than exclusively with a view to subsequent resale (which is defined as in FRS 2 – see 44.27 above). The guidance notes that once an entity has been classified as an associate, temporary or minor changes in the relationship between the investor and investee should not change its status for accounting purposes.

Shareholding of 20% or more

46.6 Under CA 1985, a holding of 20% or more of the shares of another undertaking is presumed to be a participating interest, unless it can be demonstrated that this is not the case. In this case, interests which are convertible into shares, and options to acquire shares or interests, do not have to be taken into account. The standard refers to this provision in CA 1985 and emphasises that the presumption will be rebutted if the interest is not long-term or is not beneficial.

Exercise of significant influence

46.7   A key distinction between a subsidiary and an associate is the degree of influence that the investing company is able to exercise over the operating and financial policies of the investee:

(i)   under the Act and FRS 2 'Accounting for Subsidiary Undertakings', an entity is a subsidiary if the investor has the power to exercise, or actually exercises, dominant influence over it;

(ii)   under the Act and FRS 9 'Associates and Joint Ventures', an entity is an associate if the investor has a participating interest in it and exercises significant influence over it.

A key distinction, therefore, is the difference between dominant influence and significant influence.

Dominant influence under FRS 2

46.8   FRS 2 defines dominant influence as 'influence that can be exercised to achieve the operating and financial policies desired by the holder of the influence, notwithstanding the rights or influence of any other party'. The standard goes on to explain that:

> 'The right to exercise dominant influence means that the holder has a right to give directions with respect to the operating and financial policies of another undertaking with which its directors are obliged to comply, whether or not they are for the benefit of that undertaking'.

It also states that:

> 'The actual exercise of dominant influence is the exercise of an influence that achieves the result that the operating and financial policies of the undertaking influenced are set in accordance with the wishes of the holder of the influence and for the holder's benefit, whether or not those wishes are explicit. The actual exercise of dominant influence is identified by its effect in practice rather than by the way in which it is exercised.'

Dominant influence is considered in more detail in Chapter 45.

Significant influence under FRS 9

46.9   For a participating interest to qualify as an associate under FRS 9, the investor must exercise significant influence over the operating and financial policies of the investee. In order to meet this condition, the investor must be both actively involved and influential in the direction of the investee through participation in policy decisions on issues relevant to the investor. The guidance notes that this includes decisions on strategic issues and gives the following examples:

(i)   the expansion or contraction of the business;

(ii)   participation in other entities;

(iii)   changes in products, markets and activities;

(iv)   determination of the balance between dividends and reinvestment.

In effect, the investor will use the associate as a medium through which to conduct part of its business, although this does mean that the associate must necessarily be involved in the same field of activity as the investor. The fact that the investor's interest must be long-term should mean that the investor will not necessarily look only for high dividends, but will also support a degree of reinvestment by the investee.

Development of policies of the investee

46.10   The guidance notes that, over time, an associate will usually implement policies that are consistent with those of the investor and avoid implementing policies that conflict with those of the investor. If the investee is able to continually pursue policies that are contrary to the strategy of the investor, this will usually indicate that the investor does not exercise significant influence.

Board participation

46.11   An investor will usually exercise its influence over the associate by being actively involved on the board of directors (or any equivalent body), but this is not a requirement. A different arrangement may still allow the investor to be actively involved in policy-setting decisions. The guidance emphasises that it is the practical, day-to-day relationship between the investor and investee that will decide whether or not significant influence is exercised, not any formal structure that may be put in place.

Future changes

46.12   Once the relationship between investor and associate has been established and the investor has been treated as exercising significant influence, that relationship should be regarded as continuing, until an event or transaction changes the circumstances and removes the investor's ability to exercise the appropriate degree of influence.

Interest of 20% or more in voting rights

46.13   Where the investor's interest in another entity represents 20% or more of the equity voting rights this suggests, but does not necessarily ensure, that the investor will be able to exercise significant influence over the investee. CA 1985 states that such an investor is presumed to exercise significant influence over the operating and financial policies of the other undertaking, unless it can be demonstrated that this is not the case. Rights include those held by the investor and by any of its subsidiary undertakings. However, any rights held by other associates of the investor should be excluded. More guidance on the interpretation of voting rights is given in Chapter 45.

Where an investor holds more than 20% of the voting rights in another entity, his ability to exercise significant influence over the operating and financial policies may depend on the distribution of the remaining voting rights. For instance:

(i)   if the remaining voting rights are widely held so that there are no other significant holdings, the investor will usually be in a position to exercise significant influence;

(ii)   if the remaining voting rights are held by (say) two other investors, each of whom holds 40%, the investor with 20% of the voting rights is unlikely to be in a position to exercise significant influence.

Interest of less than 20% in voting rights

46.14   Conversely, where an investor's interest in another entity represents less than 20% of the equity voting rights, this will usually suggest that the investing company is not able to exercise significant influence over the entity. It may, however, be possible to demonstrate that the investor still has the appropriate level of influence without holding a substantial basis of voting power. In most cases, this would require a formal statement from the investee, acknowledging that the investor is able to exercise such influence.

THE EQUITY METHOD OF ACCOUNTING

Definition in FRS 9

46.15   CA 1985 requires associated undertakings to be included in group accounts using the equity method of accounting unless the amounts involved are not material, but does not provide any detailed guidance on this accounting treatment This is set out instead in FRS 9 which defines the equity method of accounting as:

'A method of accounting that brings an investment into its investor's financial statements initially at its cost, identifying any goodwill arising. The carrying amount of the investment is adjusted in each period by the investor's share of the results of its investee less any amortisation or write-off for goodwill, the investor's share of any relevant gains or losses, and any other changes in the investee's net assets including distributions to its owners, for example by dividend. The investor's share of its investee's results is recognised in its profit and loss account. The investor's cash flow statement includes the cash flows between the investor and its investee, for example relating to dividends and loans.'

Investor's share of associates' operating results

46.16   FRS 9 requires the investor's share of its associates' operating results to be included in the consolidated profit and loss account as a separate item immediately after group operating result (but after the investor's share of the results of any joint ventures). The Act also specifies where this item should be shown and describes it as 'Income from interests in associated undertakings'.

Example 46.1 – Investor's share of associates' operating results

A Ltd has a share capital of 1,000 ordinary shares of £1; each share carries one vote.

B Ltd holds 240 shares in A Ltd and is represented on the board of A Ltd and accounts for A Ltd as an associate in its group accounts.

Both companies have an accounting date of 30 September.

A Ltd's profit and loss account for the year to 30 September 20X4 is as follows:

	£000
Turnover	446
Cost of sales	254
Gross profit	192
Distribution costs	(86)
Administrative expenses	(52)
Operating profit	54
Interest payable	(12)
Profit on ordinary activities before taxation	42
Taxation	(11)
Profit on ordinary activities after taxation for the financial year	31
Dividends paid and proposed	(20)
Retained profit for the year	11

B Ltd's consolidated profit and loss account for the year ended 30 September 20X4 will include £13,000 in respect of A Ltd's operating profit (i.e. 24% of A Ltd's operating of £54,000).

The first part of B Ltd's consolidated profit and loss account will be presented as follows:

		£000
Group turnover		3,290
Cost of sales		2,455
Gross profit		835
Administrative expenses		(574)
		£000
Group operating profit		261
Share of operating profit in:		
Joint venture	35	
Associate	13	
		48
		309

Amortisation or write-down of goodwill

46.17   FRS 9 also requires any amortisation or write-down of goodwill relating to associates to be charged at this point in the consolidated profit and loss accounts and to be disclosed separately.

Investor's share of items shown below operating profit

46.18   FRS 3 'Reporting Financial Performance' requires certain items to be disclosed separately below operating profit but before interest (i.e. profits and losses on the sale or termination of an operation, costs of a fundamental reorganisation or restructuring and profits or losses on the disposal of fixed assets). If the associate's accounts include any of these items, the investor's share of them should be shown separately from any similar amounts relating to the group in the consolidated profit and loss account.

Investor's share of interest

46.19   Any interest payable or receivable by associates should also be shown separately from that for the group in the consolidated profit and loss account:

Example 46.2 – Separate disclosure of associate's interest payable

Using the details set out in Example 46.1, B Ltd's consolidated profit and loss accounts must also show B Ltd's share of A Ltd's interest payable (i.e. 24% of £12,000 = £2,880):

		£000
Group operating profit		261
Share of operating profit in:		
Joint venture	35	
Associate	13	
	48	
		309
Interest payable:		
Group	75	
Associate	3	
		(78)
Profit on ordinary activities before taxation		231

Investor's share of taxation

46.20   At and below the level of profit on ordinary activities before taxation, the standard requires the relevant amounts for associates to be included with those for the group, but for items such as taxation requires the amount relating to associates to be disclosed in the accounts. This may be done in the notes rather than on the face of the profit and loss account.

Example 46.3 – Disclosure of associate's taxation

Using the details from Example 46.1 above, the tax charge in B Ltd's consolidated profit and loss account will include £2,640 (i.e. £11,000 x24%) in respect of the associate and the tax note will be analysed to show tax relating to the group (i.e. parent and subsidiaries), joint venture and associate.

Investor's share of extraordinary items

46.21   Extraordinary items are now very rare under the stringent requirements of FRS 3 'Reporting Financial Performance'. If the accounts of an associate include an extraordinary item, the investor's share should be included as an extraordinary item in its consolidated profit and loss account only if it would still meet the criteria for an extraordinary item in the context of the group. If it does not meet these criteria, it should be included in the profit or loss on ordinary activities for the year.

Dividends and retained profit or loss for the year

46.22   The group's share of any dividends paid by the associates should cancel with the dividends received shown in the consolidated accounts of the investor and its subsidiaries. Neither the payment nor the receipt should appear in the group profit and loss account.

The investor's share of the retained profits or losses of associates for the year (i.e. after dividends) should be shown separately in the group accounts. This figure will form part of the increase in the value of the investment during the year. The group share of the dividend paid by the associate during the year effectively represents the conversion into cash of part of the investment, and must therefore be excluded from the balance sheet value of the interest in the associate.

Additional disclosure of turnover and operating profit

46.23   Where it is helpful to give an indication of the size of the business as a whole, FRS 9 permits the disclosure of a total combining the investor's share of the turnover of associates with that for the group as a memorandum item in the consolidated profit and loss account. This figure must be clearly distinguished from group turnover in the profit and loss account. Under no circumstances should the turnover of associates be aggregated with that of the group (i.e. the parent and its subsidiaries) in the consolidated profit and loss account.

Any segmental analysis of turnover and operating profit given in the accounts must also clearly distinguish the group figures (i.e. the parent and its subsidiaries) from those relating to associates.

Statement of total recognised gains and losses

46.24   The consolidated statement of total recognised gains and losses should include the investor's share of gains and losses relating to associates. If the amounts involved are material, they should be shown separately under each heading within the statement. This disclosure can be given in the statement itself or in the notes to the accounts.

Balance sheet presentation

46.25   When an interest in an associate is acquired:

(i)   the underlying assets and liabilities of the associate should be identified using the accounting policies of the investor;

(ii)   fair values should be attributed to those underlying assets and liabilities (excluding any goodwill that is shown in the accounts of the associate);

(iii)   the investor's share of those fair values should be compared with the consideration paid by the investor and any difference between these two amounts will represent goodwill on the acquisition.

The consideration paid and any goodwill arising on the acquisition should be calculated in the same way as on the acquisition of a subsidiary. Goodwill relating to associates should be accounted for in accordance with the Act and with the requirements of FRS 10 'Goodwill and Intangible Assets' (for accounting periods ending on or after 23 December 1998). The carrying amount within fixed asset investments in the consolidated balance sheet will therefore comprise:

(i)   the investing group's share of the net assets of the associate; and

(ii)   goodwill arising on acquisition of the interest in the associate, less any amounts amortised or written off.

These amounts should be disclosed separately.

The value recorded for the associate will increase or decrease each year to reflect:

(i)   the share of profits and losses of the associate (as shown in the group profit and loss account) and the share of any other gains and losses (as shown in the statement of total recognised gains and losses), less any dividends paid by the associate, and

(ii)   any write down in the value of goodwill.

In effect, the investor's share in the associate's net assets will be made up of:

(i)   the investing group's share of the net assets of the associate (excluding any goodwill) based on the fair values of those net assets at the time of acquisition;

(ii)   the retained profits or losses of the associate since acquisition (i.e. after the appropriation of dividends); and

(iii)   the investor's share of any goodwill in the balance sheet of the associate, to the extent that this has not been amortised or written off.

Cash flow statement

46.26   Only actual cash flows between associates and the group should be included in the consolidated cash flow statement. Dividends received from associates should be shown as a separate item between operating activities and returns on investments and the servicing of finance. Any other cash flows between associates and the group (e.g. repayment of loans) should be included under the appropriate cash flow heading.

Elimination of profits and losses on transactions with associates

46.27   Where the carrying amount of assets in the accounts of either the investor or its associates includes profits or losses resulting from transactions between the investor and its associates, the investor's share of the profit or loss should be eliminated from the consolidated accounts. Any impairment of those or similar assets should also be taken into account. The elimination of profits and losses on transactions between group entities is considered in more detail in Chapter 47. It should be noted that balances between the group (i.e. the parent and its subsidiaries) and its associates are not eliminated. Unsettled trading transactions will therefore continue to be shown as current assets or as current liabilities in the consolidated balance sheet.

Consistency of accounting policies

46.28   The accounting policies of the investor should be applied in calculating the amounts to be included for associates in the consolidated accounts under the equity method. Consistency of accounting in a group context is considered in more detail in Chapter 47.

Limited access to information

46.29   In applying the equity method of accounting, the standard requires similar principles to be applied as in the case of subsidiaries (e.g. consistency of accounting policies, elimination of certain profits and losses). However, the investor's access to information about an associate may be much more restricted than in the case of a subsidiary, where the investor has control rather than just significant influence. The standard allows estimates to be used where access to the relevant information is limited, but also emphasises that where access is severely restricted, the investor's relationship with the investee may need to be reassessed to establish whether the investor's influence is genuinely significant.

Aggregation of group interest

46.30   Where the investor is a group, the share of the associate to be included in the consolidated accounts is the aggregate of the holdings of the parent and its subsidiaries. Any holdings by the group's joint ventures or other associates should be ignored.

Associate with subsidiaries

46.31   Where an associate also has subsidiary undertakings, the Act requires the investing group's accounts to include the consolidated results and net assets of the associate and its subsidiary undertakings. Where the associate also has joint ventures or associates of its own, FRS 9 emphasises that the results and net assets to be included in the investor's consolidated accounts under the equity method are those reported in the consolidated accounts of the associate (i.e. including its share of the results and net assets of joint ventures and associates) after allowing for any adjustment to bring into effect the accounting policies of the investor.

Impact of options, convertibles and non-equity shares

46.32   In certain circumstances, the conditions attached to options, convertibles and non-equity shares held by the investor in an associate are such that the investor should take them into account when reflecting the results and net assets of the investee in consolidated accounts under the equity method. In this case, the costs of exercising the options or converting the convertibles and any future payments in relation to the non-equity shares should also be taken into account.

Impairment of goodwill attributable to an associate

46.33   Where there has been an impairment of any goodwill attributable to an associate, the goodwill should be written down, and the amount of any write-down during the year should be separately disclosed in the accounts. Accounting for goodwill in the context of group accounts is considered in more detail in Chapter 48.

Treatment of losses and net liabilities

46.34   Changes in the carrying value of each associate should continue to be accounted for even if the equity method results in net liabilities, except where there is sufficient evidence that an event has irrevocably changed the relationship between the investor and investee so that it is no longer a joint venture or associate. Where an associate has a deficiency of net assets, it will usually have to be supported by its shareholders if it is to continue in operation and in these circumstances, it will usually be appropriate to reflect the investing group's share of the deficiency in the group accounts. The net liability recorded in these circumstances should be shown as a provision or liability. The explanatory material in FRS 9 suggests that evidence of an irrevocable change in relationship will include a public statement by the investor that it is withdrawing from its investee, together with a demonstrable commitment to this or evidence that responsibility for the operating and financial policies of the investee has been transferred (e.g. to its creditors).

Additional liabilities in the case of unincorporated associates

46.35   If the associate is unincorporated, additional liabilities could arise in excess of the investor's share of the associate's net assets (or net liabilities) – for instance in a situation of joint and several liability. Particular care needs to be taken in these circumstances to ensure that all of the investor's liabilities in respect of the associate are properly reflected in the consolidated accounts. Consideration should therefore be given to whether an additional provision needs to be made in the group accounts, or whether a contingent liability needs to be disclosed.

ACCOUNTING FOR JOINT VENTURES

Definition of joint venture

46.36   A joint venture is an entity in which the investor has a long-term interest and which is jointly controlled by the participants under a contractual arrangement. In effect, CA 1985 defines a joint venture as an undertaking managed jointly with one or more undertakings that are not included in the consolidation. The FRS 9 definition of joint control incorporates two key elements:

(i)   none of the participants alone can control the entity but all together can do so; and

(ii)   decisions on financial and operating policy essential to the activities, economic performance and financial position of the entity require the consent of each participant.

The explanatory material in the standard makes the following points in respect of joint control:

(i)   the participants in the venture exercise joint control for their mutual benefit and each participant conducts its part of the arrangement with a view to its own benefit;

(ii)   each venturer should play an active part in setting the operating and financial policies of the joint venture, at a strategic level at least.

The contractual arrangement may give one participant overall responsibility for the management of the joint venture, but this should not preclude a situation of joint control. If the arrangement provides for all the participants to be involved in reaching a collective agreement on the policies to be followed and gives them the power to ensure that the agreed policies are followed, this will usually constitute joint control.

Right of veto

46.37   An important aspect of the FRS 9 definition of joint control is that each venturer is in effect able to veto decisions on operating and financial policy. Without this veto, the venture would be subject to majority rule rather than joint control. The standard emphasises that there is no need for this aspect to be set out in a formal agreement – it is the way that the venture operates in practice that establishes whether or not it meets the definition of a joint venture.

Long-term factors

46.38   Another significant feature of a joint venture is that the interest is held on a long-term basis. An interest held on a long-term basis is defined as an interest held other than exclusively with a view to subsequent resale (which is defined as in FRS 2 – see 44.27 above). The conclusion on whether or not an entity qualifies as a joint venture should be based on long-term factors, and the guidance notes that once an entity has been classified as a joint venture, temporary or minor changes in the relationship between the investor and investee should not change its status as a joint venture for accounting purposes.

The guidance in FRS 9 also emphasises that the classification of an entity as a joint venture should not change according to whether it is profitable or loss-making, or has net assets or net liabilities. Similarly, once an investment has been classified and accounted for as a joint venture, its status will not change simply because the investor intends to dispose of the investment.

Joint venture where an investor does not share control

46.39   It is possible for an investor to have an interest in an entity that is a joint venture without sharing control. In these circumstances, the entity will not be a joint venture as far as that investor is concerned and the interest should be accounted for simply as an investment. If the other investors share control of the entity, it will be a joint venture for them and they will account for it as such.

Joint venture that qualifies as a subsidiary of a participant

46.40   A joint venture is sometimes set up so that one investor holds a majority of voting rights and is therefore technically the 'parent'. However, the contractual arrangements with the other investors will usually create severe long-term restrictions that hinder the exercise of the parent's rights (see 44.21 above). The venture will therefore be excluded from the 'parent's' consolidated accounts under FRS 2 'Accounting for Subsidiary Undertakings' and should be accounted for under FRS 9 instead.

Structure with the form but not the substance of a joint venture

46.41   It is also possible to set up a structure that appears to be a joint venture, but where the participants are simply using the structure as a means of carrying out their own business. In these circumstances, FRS 9 requires each participant to account for its own share of the assets, liabilities and cash flows within the structure rather than treating it as a joint venture (see 46.67 to 46.71 below).

Gross equity method of accounting

46.42 Joint ventures should be included in consolidated accounts using the gross equity method of accounting. This is broadly the same as the equity method of accounting described above in relation to associates, but with two additional disclosures:

(i) the investor's share of the turnover of joint ventures should be shown in the consolidated profit and loss account – but not as part of the turnover of the group (i.e. the parent and its subsidiaries);

(ii) the investor's share of the gross assets and liabilities underlying the net equity amount included for joint ventures should be shown in the consolidated balance sheet.

Care is needed in the presentation of these figures to ensure that they are not confused with those for the group, or appear to be included as part of the totals for the group. All of the requirements and the guidance on the equity method of accounting set out at 46.15 to 46.35 apply to joint ventures in exactly the same way as to associates.

CA 1985 allows a joint venture that is not a body corporate or a subsidiary undertaking of the parent company to be included in the group accounts using proportional consolidation, but this treatment is not permitted by FRS 9.

Supplemental disclosure in certain circumstances

46.43 Where an entity conducts a major part of its business through joint ventures, it may be necessary to give more detailed information about those joint ventures in the accounts. Where supplemental information is given about joint ventures in either the profit and loss account or balance sheet, the details must be clearly separated from the amounts for the group and must not be shown as part of the totals for the group. This requirement does not apply in the case of items shown below profit before tax in the consolidated profit and loss account, where amounts for joint ventures, associates and the group should be aggregated with separate disclosure in the notes where necessary.

Columnar presentation

46.44 The standard notes that a columnar presentation of the figures is one option for presenting additional information about joint ventures so that it is clearly separated from the equivalent figures for the group. An appendix to the standard gives an example of this presentation.

CHANGES IN SHAREHOLDINGS AND STATUS

Date of becoming or ceasing to be an associate or joint venture

46.45   Under FRS 9 an entity becomes an associate on the date on which the investor begins to fulfil the two essential elements of the definition of an associate:

(i)   the holding of a participating interest: and

(ii)   the exercise of significant influence.

An entity ceases to be an associate on the date on which the investor ceases to fulfil either of these elements.

An entity becomes a joint venture on the date on which the investor begins to control the entity jointly with other venturers. An entity ceases to be a joint venture on the date on which the investor ceases to have joint control.

Profit or loss on disposal of a joint venture or associate

46.46   When the investor disposes of an interest in an associate or joint venture, the profit or loss on disposal should be calculated after taking account of any related goodwill not already written off through the profit and loss account or attributed to prior amortisation or impairment on applying the transitional arrangements of FRS 10 'Goodwill and Intangible Assets'. This aspect is considered in more detail in Chapter 48. Specific requirements apply under UITF Abstract 32 where an entity exchanges a business or other non-monetary assets for equity in a subsidiary, joint venture or associate.

Acquisition or disposal in stages

46.47   When an interest in an associate or joint venture is acquired or disposed of in stages, the same procedures should be followed as for subsidiaries under paragraphs 50 to 52 of FRS 2 'Accounting for Subsidiary Undertakings'. This is considered in more detail in Chapter 49.

Transition from joint venture or associate to investment

46.48   If an entity ceases to be an associate or joint venture, but the investor retains an interest in it, the initial carrying amount of the investment should be based on the percentage of the final carrying amount of the associate retained by the investor (including any goodwill) at the date on which the entity ceases to be an associate. This initial carrying value should then be reviewed and, if necessary, written down to its recoverable amount. The entity's profits or losses up to the date that it ceases to be an associate or joint venture should therefore be included in the consolidated profit and loss account and reflected in the carrying value of the investment at that date. However, an appropriate adjustment to the carrying value will need to be made if the entity subsequently pays a dividend out of profits earned during the period when it was an associate or joint venture.

The carrying value of the investment will need to be reviewed each year in the same way as any other investment, and provision should be made for any impairment in value.

Existing investment that becomes an associate

46.49 An existing investment in the accounts of the investor may become an associate, for instance, if:

(i) the group acquires additional shares, which take the group shareholding over 20%; or

(ii) the group acquires significant influence which it did not previously have (e.g. by appointing a director to the board).

In the first case, the total consideration paid by the investor will be the cost of the original investment, plus the cost of the additional shares acquired by the group, and this total should be compared with the appropriate share of the fair value of the underlying net assets of the associate at the date that it becomes an associate (i.e. the date on which the group shareholding reaches the 20% threshold). In the second case, the total consideration paid by the investor is the cost of the original investment, and this should be compared with the appropriate share of the fair value of the underlying net assets of the associate at the date that it becomes an associate (i.e. the date on which the group acquires significant influence). In both cases the difference between these two amounts will represent goodwill on the acquisition.

Subsidiary that becomes an associate

46.50 If a parent undertaking disposes of part of its interest in a subsidiary but retains an investment of more than 20% (i.e. it still has a participating interest) and also retains significant influence over the entity, the undertaking that was formerly a subsidiary will become an associate. The normal accounting treatment would be as follows (assuming that the disposal takes place part way through the parent's financial year):

(i) the results of the subsidiary should be consolidated up to the date that it ceased to be a subsidiary;

(ii) a profit or loss on disposal should be calculated by comparing the disposal proceeds with the group's share of the net assets of the subsidiary at the date of disposal and adjusting for any goodwill relating to the subsidiary;

(iii) the results of the associate should be included in the group accounts from the date that the former subsidiary became an associate;

(iv)   the investment in the associate should be shown in the group balance sheet at the cost of the investment (i.e. the original total cost less the cost of the investment disposed of), plus the appropriate share of the associate's retained profit or loss since acquisition of the original interest, less any goodwill written off.

Example 46.4 – Subsidiary that becomes an associate

C Ltd owns 100% of the ordinary share capital of D Ltd, which it acquired some years ago at a cost of £50,000. No goodwill arose at the time of acquisition (i.e. the fair value of D Ltd's net assets at the date of acquisition was also £50,000). The accounting date of both companies is 31 December.

On 1 July 20X4, C Ltd sold 70% of its shareholding in D Ltd for £65,000. It retained the remaining 30% and continues to be represented on the board of D Ltd. D Ltd is therefore to be accounted for as an associate from 1 July 20X4.

The summarised results of D Ltd for the year to 31 December 20X4 were as follows:

	£000
Turnover	975
Cost of sales	765
	210
Other operating expenses	(140)
Operating profit	70
Interest payable	(40)
Profit on ordinary activities before tax	30
Taxation	(10)
Retained profit	20

D Ltd has no other gains and losses.

The net assets of D Ltd at 1 July 20X4 were £80,000 (i.e. including the retained profit for the first half of 20X4). The profit for 20X4 has accrued evenly throughout the year.

C Ltd's individual accounts will show a profit on disposal of £30,000 (i.e. the cost of the investment of £50,000 x 70% = £35,000 compared with disposal proceeds of £65,000).

The group accounts of C Ltd will include:

(i)   the results of D Ltd for the 6 months from 1 January 20X4 to 30 June 20X4, which will be consolidated under the normal rules for a subsidiary;

(ii)   a profit on disposal of £9,000 (i.e. the share of net assets at the date of disposal of £80,000 x 70% = £56,000 compared with disposal proceeds of £65,000);

(iii)   operating profit of an associate of £10,500 (i.e. D Ltd's operating profit from 1 July to 31 December – i.e. £70,000 x 6/12 x 30%), interest payable relating to an associate of £6,000 and tax relating to an associate of £1,500 (all calculated in the same way);

(iv)   the investment in D Ltd as an associate valued at £27,000 made up as follows:

- 30% of the fair value of the net assets at the original date of acquisition (i.e. £50,000 x 30% = £15,000),

- 30% of the retained profits of D Ltd from the original date of acquisition to 1 July 20X4 – in this case, post-acquisition retained profits are calculated as the net asset value at 1 July 20X4 less the fair value of the original net assets (i.e. £80,000 – £50,000 = £30,000) and 30% of £30,000 = £9,000),
- 30% of the retained profit for the period 1 July to 31 December 20X4 which is the £3,000 reflected in the group profit and loss account (i.e. £10,500 – £6,000–£1,500 = £3,000).

The total value is therefore £27,000 (i.e. £15,000 + £9,000 + £3,000).

Exchange transactions

46.51   Separate considerations apply under UITF Abstract 32 where an entity exchanges an existing business or other non-monetary assets for equity in a subsidiary, joint venture or associate. The detailed requirements of the Abstract are considered in more detail in Chapter 49.

ACCOUNTING DATE OF ASSOCIATES AND JOINT VENTURES

Amounts to be consolidated

46.52   The amounts to be included in the consolidated accounts should be based on financial statements for the associate or joint venture prepared to the accounting date of the investor. If this is not practicable, accounts for a period ending not more that three months before the accounting date of the investor may be used.

Potential release of price-sensitive information

46.53   Particular care is needed where the associate or joint venture is subject to regulations on the dissemination of information, to ensure that only published financial information is disclosed in the investor's accounts. If the use of accounts made up to the investor's accounting date, or to a date three months before this, would result in the release of restricted price-sensitive information, a date not more than six months before the accounting date of the investor may be used. The explanatory material in the FRS 9 emphasises the need for investors who find themselves in this situation to pay adequate attention to planning how to satisfy any regulations affecting the associate or joint venture whilst still fulfilling the requirements of the standard.

Changes in the intervening period

46.54   Where the accounts of the associate or joint venture are made up to an earlier date than those of the investor, changes between the two accounting dates should be adjusted for if they materially affect the view given by the investor's financial statements.

Use of management accounts

46.55   The accounts of an associate or joint venture need not necessarily be statutory accounts, although this will be preferable in most cases. In certain circumstances it may be acceptable to use management accounts, provided that these are prepared on the same basis as statutory accounts and there is adequate evidence of their reliability.

ACCOUNTS DISCLOSURES

Requirements under CA 1985

46.56   Where any undertaking included in the consolidation has an interest in an associated undertaking, CA 1985 requires the following details must be given in the accounts:

(i)   the name of the associated undertaking;

(ii)   if the associated undertaking is incorporated outside Great Britain, its country of incorporation;

(iii)   if it is unincorporated, the address of its principal place of business;

(iv)   details of:

- each class of share held in the associated undertaking, and

- the proportion of the nominal value of the shares in that class that the holding represents.

In each case, the details in (iv) above should be shown separately for shares held by the parent company and shares held by other members of the group.

The Act also specifies the disclosures to be in respect of any unincorporated joint venture that is included in the consolidated accounts by proportional consolidation but, as noted at 46.36 above, this accounting treatment is not permitted by FRS 9.

The Act also requires detailed disclosures to be given in respect of significant shareholdings in other undertakings. These are considered in more detail in Chapter 22. The exemptions from disclosure granted by section 231 of CA 1985 apply where appropriate.

Principal associates and joint ventures

46.57   FRS 9 requires the following disclosures in respect of each principal associate and joint venture:

(i)   its name;

(ii)   the proportion of the issued shares in each class held by the investing company or group, together with an indication of any special rights or constraints attaching to them;

(iii)   the accounting period or date of the financial statements used, if these differ from those of the investing company or group; and

(iv)   an indication of the nature of its business.

In the case of an unincorporated joint venture, the Act also requires disclosure of the factors on which joint management is based.

Notes on contingent liabilities and commitments

46.58   Where the notes to the accounts of an associate or joint venture include matters that are material to understanding the effect of the investment on the investor, or if the notes would have included such matters if the investor's accounting policies had been followed, details should also be disclosed in the investor's accounts. These disclosures should include in particular:

(i)   the investor's share in contingent liabilities incurred jointly with other venturers or investors; and

(ii)   the investor's share of the capital commitments of joint ventures or associates.

Significant restrictions on ability to distribute reserves

46.59   Where the ability of an associate or joint venture to distribute its reserves is significantly restricted as a result of statutory, contractual or exchange control requirements, the extent of the restriction should be indicated in the accounts of the investor. This does not apply to reserves that are shown as non-distributable in the accounts of the associate or joint venture.

Amounts owed to or by associates or joint ventures

46.60   Any amounts owed to or by associates or joint ventures should be analysed into:

(i)   amounts relating to loans; and

(ii)   amounts relating to trading balances.

Significant associates and joint ventures

46.61   Additional disclosures are required when certain thresholds in respect of:

(i)   gross assets;

(ii)   gross liabilities;

(iii)   turnover; and

(iv)   operating results (on a three-year average)

are exceeded. The thresholds are applied by comparing the relevant figures for the investor (excluding any amounts included for associates and joint ventures under the equity method of accounting), with the investor's share of the equivalent figures for joint ventures in aggregate and for individual joint ventures.

Associates where an aggregate threshold of 15% is exceeded

46.62   Where the share relating to associates exceeds 15% of the group threshold, the accounts should disclose the investor's share (in aggregate) of the following for associates:

(i)   turnover (unless this is already shown as a memorandum item);

(ii)   fixed assets;

(iii)   current assets;

(iv)   liabilities due within one year; and

(v)   liabilities due after more than one year.

Joint ventures where an aggregate threshold of 15% is exceeded

46.63   Where the share relating to joint ventures exceeds 15% of the relevant figure for the investor, the accounts should disclose the investor's share (in aggregate) of the following for joint ventures:

(i)   fixed assets;

(ii)   current assets;

(iii)   liabilities due within one year; and

(iv)   liabilities due after more than one year.

Disclosures where a individual threshold of 25% is exceeded

46.64   Where the investor's share in any individual associate or joint venture exceeds 25% of the group threshold, the accounts should disclose the name of the associate or joint venture and the investor's share of the following:

(i)   turnover;

(ii)   profit before tax;

(iii)   taxation;

(iv)   profit after tax;

(v)   fixed assets;

(vi)   current assets;

(vii)   liabilities due within one year; and

(viii) liabilities due after more than one year.

Further analysis should be given where this is necessary for an understanding of the nature of the total amounts involved. However, where an individual associate or joint venture accounts for nearly all of the amounts included for that class of investment, only the aggregate amounts need to be given, provided that this is explained and the name of the individual associate or joint venture is disclosed.

Segmental disclosure under SSAP 25

46.65   Where associated undertakings account for at least 20% of the total results or 20% of the total net assets of the reporting entity, SSAP 25 'Segmental Reporting' requires segmental disclosure of the aggregate amounts of:

(i)   the entity's share of the results of associated undertakings before taxation, minority interests and extraordinary items; and

(ii)   the entity's share of the net assets of associated undertakings (as included in the accounts under FRS 9).

However, the information need not be disclosed if it is unobtainable or if publication would be prejudicial to the business of the associate. In this case, the notes to the accounts must state the reason for non-disclosure and give a brief description of the omitted business or

Why an investment has not been treated as an associate

46.66   Where one of the following presumptions has been rebutted:

(i)   that a holding of 20% or more of the shares in another entity constitutes a participating interest; or

(ii)   that an investor holding 20% or more of the voting rights in another entity exercises significant influence over the operating and financial policies of that entity,

the notes to the accounts should explain the reasons why the investment has not been treated as an associate.

JOINT ARRANGEMENTS THAT ARE NOT ENTITIES

Definition of an entity

46.67   In the course of their activities, businesses enter into a variety of agreements with other entities, but these agreements do not always result in formation of another wholly separate entity. FRS 9 defines an entity as:

'A body corporate, partnership or unincorporated association carrying on a trade or business with or without a view to profit. The reference to carrying on a trade or business means a trade or business of its own and not just a part of the trades or businesses of entities that have interests in it.'

The explanatory material in FRS 9 considers some of the factors to be taken into account when deciding whether or not an arrangement results in a separate trade or business. The following features will usually indicate that the joint arrangement has a separate trade or business:

(i)   it has some independence in following its own commercial strategy (i.e. in buying and selling); and

(ii)   it has access to the market in its own right for its main inputs and outputs or, if it buys from or sells to the participants, it does so on terms that are generally the same as those available in the market.

The following features will usually indicate that the joint arrangement does not have a separate trade or business:

(i)   the participants benefit from the products or services by taking them in kind rather than by receiving a share of trading results (this does not necessarily preclude receiving the benefit of a product in cash); or

(ii)   each participant's share of the output or result is determined by its supply of key inputs to the joint activity that produces the output or result.

Definition of joint arrangement that is not an entity

46.68   FRS 9 defines a joint arrangement that is not an entity as follows:

'A contractual arrangement under which the participants engage in joint activities that do not create an entity because it would not be carrying on a trade or business of its own. A contractual arrangement where all significant matters of operating and financial policy are predetermined does not create an entity because the policies are those of its participants, not of a separate entity.'

In practice, joint activities that are not entities are likely to involve some element of cost-sharing or risk-sharing in carrying out a process that forms part of the business activities of the participants. The standard gives the following examples:

(i)   a joint marketing or distribution network;

(ii)   a shared production facility.

Joint arrangement to carry out a single project

46.69   The standard also emphasises that carrying on a trade or activity implies some continuity and repetition in the activity of buying and selling. Where a joint arrangement is set up to carry out one specific project, there is no continuing activity and the arrangement therefore will not usually constitute a separate trade or business. For instance, it is relatively common in the construction industry for two or more entities to collaborate on a single project without any ongoing arrangement between them once the project has been completed. In the past, this type of collaboration has often been referred to as a joint venture, but it will not constitute a joint venture under FRS 9.

Accounting treatment under FRS 9

46.70   Under the FRS 9 definition, a joint venture must be an entity. Consequently, where two or more parties set up a joint arrangement that is not an entity, this will not constitute a joint venture under the standard, even though the various parties to the agreement may have a long-term interest and may have joint control under the terms of the agreement. The standard therefore sets out separate requirements on accounting for joint arrangements that are not entities, under which the participants are required to account for their own share of the assets, liabilities and cash flows of the joint arrangement. These should be measured according to the terms of the overall agreement that sets up the joint arrangement. The same treatment applies in both individual and consolidated accounts.

Changes in the nature of the arrangement

46.71   The standard notes that the nature of a joint arrangement may change over time. For example, an initial agreement to establish and operate a pipeline to provide a service for the participants (i.e. a joint arrangement) may subsequently develop into a pipeline business providing services to third parties as well (i.e. a joint venture). In these circumstances, the accounting treatment should be amended in the year of the change to reflect the new nature the joint activities.

Chapter 47   Consolidation

THE CONSOLIDATION PROCESS

Line by line aggregation

47.1　Accounting standards have for some time required group accounts to be prepared in the form of consolidated accounts, but prior to CA 1985, companies legislation allowed them to be prepared in other forms (e.g. by attaching the accounts of the subsidiary to those of the parent). Consolidated accounts are now the only acceptable form of Companies Act group accounts, under both the Act and FRS 2 'Accounting for Subsidiary Undertakings'. FRS 2 defines consolidation as:

> 'The process of adjusting and combining financial information from the individual financial statements of a parent undertaking and its subsidiary undertaking to prepare consolidated financial statements that present financial information for the group as a single economic entity'.

The consolidation process essentially involves aggregating the detailed figures shown in the accounts of the parent and its subsidiary undertakings on a line by line basis, to calculate the totals for the group. Various adjustments must then be made where necessary:

(i)　to achieve consistent accounting policies;

(ii)　to eliminate intra-group balances and transactions;

(iii)　to eliminate certain intra-group profits and losses;

(iv)　to eliminate both the parent company's investment in its subsidiary undertakings and the share capital and pre-acquisition reserves of the subsidiaries from the consolidated balance sheet;

(v)   to calculate, and where appropriate write off or amortise, any goodwill arising on consolidation;

(vi)   to account for the amounts attributable to minority interests.

Full consolidation

47.2   Both the Act and FRS 2 require full consolidation of the financial information relating to subsidiary undertakings. For instance, where a parent company holds (say) 70% of the shares in a subsidiary, with the balance held by an outside shareholder (i.e. a minority interest), all of the subsidiary's income and expenditure, and assets and liabilities, should be included in the consolidation and the 30% attributable to the outside shareholder should then be accounted for as a minority interest. It is not permissible to just consolidate 70% of the results and net assets of the subsidiary.

CA 1985 specifically notes that the requirement for full consolidation is subject to:

(i)   adjustments required or authorised by other provisions in Schedule 4A to the Act; or

(ii)   appropriate adjustments in accordance with generally accepted accounting principles or practice.

Use of group consolidation packages

47.3   Rather than using the financial statements of subsidiaries for the detailed consolidation process, some groups find it more convenient to develop standard consolidation packages for the subsidiaries to complete. This can help to ensure that information is presented on a consistent basis for inclusion in the group accounts and that all the necessary information is obtained. The disadvantage of this approach is that it will often involve some duplication of effort for the subsidiaries as they will still have to prepare statutory accounts. In straightforward cases, it should be possible to use the statutory accounts (or a draft of them), along with a separate package covering the additional information that will be needed at group level in order to complete the consolidation process. For instance, this might include:

(i)   details of intra-group balances and transactions;

(ii)   details of assets which include intra-group profits and losses;

(iii) details of any fixed asset transfers between group entities;

(iv)   details of any payments by the subsidiary to directors of the parent company, and details of any transactions or arrangements between the subsidiary and these directors (these details will usually be disclosable in the group accounts).

Accounting date of subsidiary undertakings

47.4 Both CA 1985 and FRS 2 require the accounts of subsidiary undertakings to be made up to the same date as those of the parent wherever this is practicable. Accounts made up to a different date may be used in certain circumstances, but FRS 2 requires adjustments to be made for any material changes in the intervening period. In this case, the subsidiary's figures can either be adjusted before they are consolidated, or the adjustments can be processed as part of the consolidation exercise. The detailed rules on the accounting date of subsidiary undertakings are considered in Chapter 45.

Overseas subsidiary undertakings

47.5 Where the accounts of an overseas subsidiary undertaking are prepared in a foreign currency, they will need to be translated into sterling before they can be included in the consolidation. The translation of accounts for consolidation purposes is considered in more detail in Chapter 50.

Disclosure of accounting principles in respect of consolidation

47.6 The key accounting principles adopted in the consolidation process should be disclosed as part of the accounting policies in the group accounts. The disclosure will normally cover:

(i)   the treatment adopted in respect of acquisitions and mergers;

(ii) the specific treatment adopted for subsidiary undertakings acquired or disposed of during the year;

(iii) the accounting policy for consolidation goodwill;

(iv) the accounting policy for the translation of accounts prepared in a foreign currency;

(v)   the accounting treatment of associates and joint ventures.

Uniform accounting policies

47.7 Both the Companies Act 1985 and FRS 2 require uniform accounting policies to be used throughout the group in valuing assets and liabilities and accounting for items of income and expenditure.

Where the parent company and all of its subsidiaries are based in the UK there will usually be little difficulty in ensuring that consistent accounting policies are adopted, particularly as many of these will be laid down in accounting standards, which all UK companies are required to follow (see Chapter 1). Occasional differences may arise where accounting standards permit alternative treatments, but these are very much the exception.

Most variations in accounting policy arise in the case of overseas subsidiaries, where local legislation and accounting rules may permit or require different accounting policies to be used. For instance, there may be a different approach to accounting for fixed assets, particularly as regards depreciation, or certain countries may allow stocks to be valued on a LIFO basis, which is generally not acceptable in the UK

Where the accounting rules followed by the parent in its individual accounts differ from those used in the group accounts, CA 1985 requires both the differences and the reasons for them to be disclosed in a note to the accounts.

Consolidation adjustments

47.8   Where group entities have prepared their accounts on the basis of different accounting policies, adjustments will need to be made as part of the consolidation process to bring the accounting treatment into line with that adopted elsewhere in the group and, where relevant, into line with generally accepted accounting practice in the UK. The adjustments can either be calculated by the subsidiary and processed at group level, or both calculated and processed at group level on the basis of additional information provided by the subsidiary. For instance, if an overseas entity has valued stock on the LIFO basis, it could either:

(i)   be requested to provide a separate valuation of stock using FIFO or an acceptable alternative, depending on the valuation methods used elsewhere in the group; or

(ii)   be requested to provide sufficient additional information in respect of year-end stocks to enable the adjustment to be calculated at group level.

As well as processing the adjustments at the end of the current year, any equivalent adjustments made at the end of the previous accounting period will also need to be taken into account.

Use of different accounting policies

47.9   In exceptional circumstances, the directors are permitted to depart from the normal rules and include items in the group accounts on the basis of different accounting policies. Both the Act and the standard envisage that this should be very rare in practice. The Act requires the following disclosures to be given and this is reinforced by FRS 2:

(i)   particulars of the departure;

(ii)   the reasons for the departure; and

(iii)   the effect of the departure.

FRS 18 'Accounting Policies' also states unequivocally that, where companies' legislation expresses disclosure requirements in these terms in relation to a departure from a specific statutory requirement, the details given must include disclosures equivalent to those required under the accounting standard whenever the true and fair override is applied. These disclosure requirements are considered in more detail in Chapter 3.

Disclosure of accounting policies

47.10 The accounting policies adopted by the group should be disclosed in the group accounts, along with details of any material departures from applicable accounting standards. The general requirements in respect of these disclosures (which apply to groups in exactly the same way as to individual companies) are considered in Chapter 5.

Restrictions on distributions

47.11 Where the ability of a subsidiary undertaking to distribute profits is significantly restricted by statutory, contractual or exchange control regulations, with the result that the parent's access to those reserves is seriously limited, FRS 2 requires the nature and extent of the restrictions to be disclosed in the group accounts.

ELIMINATION OF GROUP BALANCES AND TRANSACTIONS

Amounts due to and from group companies

47.12 Material amounts due to or from entities included within the consolidation should be eliminated from the group accounts. It is good practice for groups to have procedures for agreeing balances between group entities on a regular basis, and especially at the end of the financial year. This should ensure that the accounts of the creditor show the same figure as the accounts of the debtor. In these circumstances, the elimination of the balances on consolidation should be a straightforward matter.

Differences between balances

47.13 Any differences between group balances should be properly investigated and appropriate adjustments made in the accounts of the individual subsidiaries to reflect any outstanding transactions. For instance the balances may not immediately agree as a result of:

(i) cash in transit;

(ii) invoices raised by one entity but not yet received or processed by the recipient; or

(iii) credit notes due but not yet issued.

All of these issues should generally be taken into account in establishing year-end debtors and creditors for accounts purposes. In the case of overseas entities, exchange differences may also have an impact.

Off-setting of group balances

47.14   Where financial information for consolidation purposes is collected by means of a group consolidation package, amounts due to and from group entities are sometimes recorded under a single heading to make elimination of the balances easier. However, this is only permissible for consolidation purposes. In the statutory accounts of the individual subsidiaries, each balance with another group entity should be shown within debtors or creditors, as appropriate, to comply with the general prohibition on the off-setting of assets and liabilities.

Elimination of group transactions

47.15   Material transactions between group entities should also be eliminated from the consolidated profit and loss account, to ensure that individual items of income and expenditure are not overstated from the point of view of the group as a whole. This is consistent with the requirement that the accounts should reflect the results of the group as if it was a single entity.

Example 47.1 – Elimination of group transactions

Subsidiary A has bought goods from subsidiary B during the year at a total cost of £120,000 and then used them in its own production process.

On consolidation, the detailed profit and loss accounts of A and B will be aggregated. The transactions totalling £120,000 between A and B should then be eliminated from both turnover (i.e. the sales to A recorded in the accounts of B) and cost of sales (i.e. the purchases from B recorded in the accounts of A). In the group accounts, turnover and cost of sales will therefore both be reduced by £120,000.

This adjustment is only for the purposes of the group accounts and the individual accounts of A and B will therefore be unaffected. B will continue to show the sales to A as turnover and A will continue to show the purchases from B within cost of sales.

FRS 1 'Cash Flow Statements' similarly requires cash flows between group entities to be eliminated from the group cash flow statement.

Transfers of fixed assets

47.16   Where any items in fixed assets have been transferred between entities within the group, these transfers should be excluded from additions and from disposals in the group accounts, although they will continue to be shown as movements during the year in the individual accounts of the subsidiaries involved. Particular care is required if an asset has not been transferred at book value. In this case, any profit or loss relating to the transfer will also need to be eliminated from the consolidated profit and loss account, so that the asset continues to be shown at its original cost to the group, rather than at the higher or lower value at which it might be shown in the accounts of the recipient after the transfer. However, if the asset has been transferred at a loss, its carrying value may need to be reviewed and should be written down in the group accounts if necessary.

The elimination of intra-group profits and losses

47.17 Where one group entity has sold goods to another, and those items are included in the assets that will be shown on the consolidated balance sheet, any profit or loss included in the value of the goods should be eliminated on consolidation if the effect is material. This treatment is required by the Act and FRS 2. The most common examples of this situation are:

(i) goods sold to a fellow subsidiary, which are held in stock by the recipient at the end of the accounting period (e.g. goods supplied by a fellow subsidiary which the recipient will use in its own production process in due course); and

(ii) goods sold to a fellow subsidiary, which are included in the fixed assets of the recipient (e.g. an item of plant manufactured by a fellow subsidiary).

Where the selling company has made a profit on the transaction, this must be eliminated from the group accounts, so that the asset is reduced to its cost to the group.

Example 47.2 – Elimination of intra-group profit

Subsidiary C constructs an item of plant for subsidiary D and sells it to D for £350,000 which includes a profit of £75,000.

C will therefore record:

	£
Turnover	350,000
Cost of sales	(275,000)
Profit	75,000

D will record the plant in fixed assets at £350,000.

In the group accounts:

(i) the transaction between C and D must be eliminated from the accounts, and

(ii) the profit of £75,000 must be eliminated from the accounts.

Therefore:

(iii) turnover in the consolidated profit and loss account will be reduced by £350,000,

(iv) cost of sales in the consolidated profit and loss account will be reduced by £275,000,

(v) the value of the plant held by D will be reduced by £75,000 to £275,000 (i.e. the cost to C, which is the cost to the group).

In effect, the consolidated accounts will show that the group constructed its own fixed asset at a cost of £275,000.

Other related adjustments

47.18   Where the consolidation adjustment affects an item such as a fixed asset, other related adjustments may need to be made in the group accounts. For example, the depreciation charge for the year will also be affected (i.e. because depreciation will need to be based on a different figure for 'cost'). There will also be a continuing impact each year over the life of the asset or until the asset is disposed of outside the group. Keeping track of such adjustments can be a complex issue over the years.

Full elimination of profit or loss

47.19   Where a subsidiary is not wholly-owned by the parent, CA 1985 permits the profit or loss on such intra-group transactions to be eliminated on a proportional basis. However, this approach is not allowed by FRS 2, which requires the full profit or loss to be eliminated and the adjustment to be allocated between the group and the minority interest. The allocation should be based on the relevant shareholdings in the entity that recorded the profit.

Example 47.3 – Profit elimination where there is a minority interest

Subsidiary E has sold goods to subsidiary F for £78,000 on which it made a profit of £12,000. All of these goods are included in F's stocks at the end of the financial year.

E is 70% owned by the parent and F is 80% owned by the parent.

E's accounts therefore include:

	£
Turnover	78,000
Cost of sales	(66,000)
Profit	12,000

and F's accounts show stock valued at £78,000.

In the group accounts, the transaction between E and F must be eliminated, as must the full amount of the profit of £12,000.

Therefore:

- turnover in the consolidated accounts will be reduced by £78,000;
- cost of sales in the consolidated accounts will be reduced by £66,000;
- the value of stock in the consolidated accounts will be reduced by £12,000 to £66,000 (i.e. the cost to the group).

The reduction of profit by £12,000 will be apportioned between the group and the minority interest, based on the shareholdings in E (i.e. the entity that recorded the profit). The group element will therefore be £8,400 (i.e. £12,000 x 70%) and the minority interest element will be £3,600 (i.e. £12,000 x 30%).

The fact that only 80% of the stocks held by F at the year end relate to the group (i.e. because F is only 80% owned by the parent) will be accounted for as part of the minority interest adjustment in the balance sheet.

Impact only where assets are still held at year end

47.20   The need to eliminate intra-group profits and losses in this way only arises where the items involved are included as assets in the consolidated balance sheet. For instance, in Example 70.3 above, if F had already used half of the goods purchased from E during the year, so that only £39,000 was included in stocks at the end of the year, the profit elimination would be reduced to £6,000 and the stocks would be valued at £33,000 (i.e. £39,000 – £6,000) in the consolidated balance sheet.

Subsidiaries excluded from the consolidation

47.21   Where a subsidiary has been excluded from the consolidation on the grounds of different activities, profits or losses on transactions between the subsidiary and other members of the group should continue to be eliminated. Exclusion from the consolidation on these grounds is no longer permitted for accounting periods beginning on or after 1 January 2005 (see 44.29 above). Elimination will not usually be necessary when subsidiaries are excluded for other reasons, unless the subsidiary is included in the group accounts using the equity method of accounting.

ACCOUNTING FOR MINORITY INTERESTS

Shares held outside the group

47.22   Where the parent (or the parent together with its other subsidiary undertakings) holds all of the shares in a subsidiary, there will be no minority interest in that subsidiary. All of the profits or losses relating to the subsidiary and all of its net assets are therefore attributable to the group. Where some of the shares are held outside the immediate group, the fact that some of the profits or losses and some of the net assets of the subsidiary belong in effect to another shareholder must be reflected in the consolidated profit and loss account and the consolidated balance sheet. Schedule 4A to CA 1985 specifies where these items are to be shown, as explained in Chapter 44.

Consolidated profit and loss account

47.23   The Act and FRS 2 require the profit and loss account to show separately the element of the consolidated profit or loss on ordinary activities and any extraordinary profits or losses relating to the minority interest. As extraordinary items are extremely rare under the stringent requirements of FRS 3 'Reporting Financial Performance', the disclosure relating to extraordinary profits and losses is not considered further here.

The requirement under CA 1985 and FRS 2 for full consolidation means that the statutory headings in the consolidated profit and loss account must include the full amount of each item of income and expenditure relating to the subsidiary. If the subsidiary has achieved a net profit for the year, the share attributable to the minority interest must be deducted from the consolidated profit for the year. If the subsidiary has made a loss, the element to be borne by the minority interest will be added back to the consolidated profit for the year.

Example 47.4 – Profit or loss on ordinary activities

A Ltd is the parent company of B Ltd and holds 75% of its share capital. The results of the two companies for the year ended 30 June 20X2 are as follows.

	A Ltd	B Ltd
Turnover	'000	'000
Cost of sales	455	210
	310	150
	145	60
Other operating expenses	(90)	(30)
Operating profit	55	30
Interest receivable	10	
Interest payable	(25)	(15)
Profit on ordinary activities before tax	40	15
Taxation	(10)	(3)
Profit for the financial year	30	12

The companies do not trade with each other, but B Ltd has paid interest of £10,000 to A Ltd during the year. The interest paid and received between the two companies must therefore be eliminated on consolidation.

The consolidated profit and loss account for the year will therefore show.

	A Ltd '000	B Ltd '000	Group '000
Turnover	455	210	665
Cost of sales	310	150	460
	145	60	205
Other operating expenses	(90)	(30)	(120)
Operating profit	55	30	85
Interest receivable	10		
Interest payable	(25)	(15)	(30)
Profit on ordinary activities before tax	40	15	55
Taxation	(10)	(3)	(13)
Profit on ordinary activities after tax	30	12	42

However, as A Ltd only holds 75% of B Ltd, an adjustment must be made to the consolidated profit and loss account to reflect the amount of B Ltd's profit for the year that is attributable to the other shareholder (i.e. £12,000 x 25% = £3,000). The group profit and loss account shown above will therefore need to include the following additional headings:

	Group '000
Profit on ordinary activities after tax	42
Minority interest	(3)
Profit for the financial year attributable to the group	39

Impact of dividend paid by subsidiary

47.24   The group profit and loss account should only reflect dividends paid by the parent company to its own shareholders. If a subsidiary has paid a dividend during the year, any element paid to the parent company should automatically cancel out on consolidation (i.e. because the parent should have accounted for a dividend receivable in its own accounts). However, an adjustment will need to be made for any element of the dividend that has been paid to the minority interest.

Example 47.5 – Dividend paid to a minority interest

C Ltd is the parent of D Ltd and holds 70% of its share capital. There are no transactions between the two companies. Their results for the year to 30 September 20X3 are as follows.

	C Ltd	D Ltd
	'000	'000
Operating profit	500	270
Income from shares in group companies	70	–
Interest payable	(120)	(75)
Profit on ordinary activities before tax	450	195
Taxation	(135)	(45)
Profit on ordinary activities after tax	315	150
Dividend paid	(150)	(100)
Retained profit for the year	165	50

£70,000 of the dividend paid by D Ltd will cancel with the dividend received shown in the accounts of C Ltd. The balance of £30,000 relating to the minority interest must be removed from the consolidated profit and loss account and will be dealt with in the movements on the balance for minority interests in the balance sheet. The group profit and loss account will therefore be as follows.

	C Ltd	D Ltd	Group
	'000	'000	'000
Operating profit	500	270	770
Income from shares in group companies	70		
Interest payable	(120)	(75)	(195)
Profit on ordinary activities before tax	450	195	575
Taxation	(135)	(45)	(180)
Profit on ordinary activities after tax	315	150	395
Minority interests (150 x 30%)			(45)
Profit for the financial year attributable to the group			350
Dividend paid	(150)	(100)	(150)
Retained profit for the year	165	50	200

The retained profit for the group therefore represents £165,000 in respect of the parent company and £35,000 (i.e. £50,000 x 70%) in respect of the subsidiary.

The group cash flow statement should show dividends paid to minority interests as a separate item under returns on investments and servicing of finance.

Analysis of profit and loss account adjustment

47.25   For accounting periods beginning before 1 January 2005, FRS 4 'Capital Instruments' requires the aggregate figure for minority interests in the consolidated profit and loss account to be analysed between equity and non-equity shares. This disclosure should be given on the face of the profit and loss account. However, FRS

4 is generally superseded by FRS 25 'Financial Instruments: Disclosure and Presentation' for accounting periods beginning on or after 1 January 2005. The definition and accounting treatment of equity and other shares under both FRS 4 and FRS 25 is considered in Chapter 32.

Consolidated balance sheet

47.26   The consolidated balance sheet must show as a separate item the net assets of the subsidiary attributable to the minority interest. There are two alternative locations for this heading on the consolidated balance sheet, as explained in Chapter 44. The amount attributable to the minority interest of the subsidiary will be the appropriate proportion of the share capital and reserves of the subsidiary undertaking.

Example 47.6 – Calculating the minority interest

Using the details from Example 47.5 above, the balance sheets of C Ltd and D Ltd at the beginning of the year (i.e. 1 October 20X2) are as follows.

	C Ltd	D Ltd
	£	£
Share capital	10,000	1,000
Profit and loss account	60,000	15,000
Revaluation reserve	12,000	5,000
	82,000	21,000

The balance sheets at the end of the year (i.e. 30 September 20X3) are:

	C Ltd	D Ltd
	£	£
Share capital	10,000	1,000
Profit and loss account	225,000	65,000
Revaluation reserve	12,000	5,000
	247,000	71,000

The minority interest in D Ltd at 1 October 20X2 is as follows:

	£
Share capital 1,000 x 30%	300
Profit and loss account 15,000 x 30%	4,500
Revaluation reserve 5,000 x 30%	1,500
	6,300

The minority interest at 30 September 20X2 is:

	£
Share capital 1,000 x 30%	300
Profit and loss account 65,000 x 30%	19,500
Revaluation reserve 5,000 x 30%	1,500
	21,300

The movement in the year can be proved as follows:

	£
Opening balance relating to minority interest	6,300
Profit for the year attributable to minority interest (see Example 47.5)	45,000
Dividend paid to minority interest (see Example 47.5)	(30,000)
Closing balance relating to minority interest	21,300

Proposed dividends

47.27   For accounting periods beginning on or after 1 January 2005, FRS 21 'Events After the Balance Sheet Date' prohibits the recognition of proposed dividends as a liability (see Chapter 34). For accounting periods beginning before 1 January 2005, where the subsidiary has provided for a proposed dividend, the principles set out in 47.26 still apply. In these circumstances, the subsidiary's accounts will show a creditor for the total dividend payable and the parent company's accounts should show a debtor for the element of the dividend that is receivable by the parent. After eliminating the intra-group element, the remaining balance will represent the element of the dividend that is payable to the minority interest. This can remain within creditors, but should not be described as a dividend payable in the analysis of group creditors – only amounts payable by the parent company should be included under this heading. The most usual heading for this item would normally be 'other creditors'.

Minority interest in net liabilities

47.28   Where a subsidiary has incurred losses, the amount attributable to the minority interest may become an interest in net liabilities rather than an interest in net assets. Under FRS 2, the minority interest should continue to be calculated and disclosed as shown above, even though it will appear as a negative figure in the consolidated balance sheet. However, the group may need to make provision for any obligation that it has (either formal or implied) to provide finance for the subsidiary which may not be recoverable in respect of the accumulated loss attributable to the minority interest. Such provisions should be set directly against the amounts for minority interests shown in the consolidated profit and loss account and consolidated balance sheet.

Significant minority interest

47.29   Under the definitions of a subsidiary undertaking in both the Act and FRS 2, it is possible for an undertaking to be classed as a subsidiary even though the parent company has only a small (or even no) interest in the shares of the undertaking. For instance, if the parent holds 20% of the shares and exercises dominant influence over the entity, it will meet the definition of a subsidiary and will therefore need to be consolidated. In this situation, there will be a 'minority' interest of 80% in the subsidiary. The normal consolidation rules continue to apply and the amounts attributable to the minority interest should be shown in the consolidated profit and loss accounts and consolidated balance sheet as described above. However, additional detail may need to be given in the notes to the accounts to explain the situation.

Analysis of minority interests

47.30   For accounting periods beginning before 1 January 2005, FRS 4 'Capital Instruments' requires the figure for minority interests shown in the consolidated balance sheet to be analysed between equity and non-equity interests. The detailed disclosure may be given in the notes but the balance sheet heading must indicate that non-equity items are included where relevant. However, FRS 4 is generally super-seded by FRS 25 'Financial Instruments: Disclosure and Presentation' for accounting periods beginning on or after 1 January 2005. The definition and accounting treatment of equity and other shares under both FRS 4 and FRS 25 is considered in Chapter 32.

Shares that create a liability for the group as a whole

47.31   For accounting periods beginning before 1 January 2005, UITF Abstract 33 'Obligations in Capital Instruments' clarifies how various types of capital instru-ment issued as a means of raising finance should be reported in the balance sheet (i.e. whether they should be shown as liabilities or shareholders' funds or, in the case of consolidated financial statements, as minority interests). The Abstract notes specifically that it does not deal with capital instruments issued as part of the contingent purchase consideration for a business combination. The general rule is that a capital instrument should be reported within shareholders' funds only if it is a share, or if it does not contain an obligation to transfer economic benefits. All other capital instruments should be treated as liabilities, even if the obligation to transfer economic benefits does not go beyond that normally contained in a share.

However, the Abstract gives specific consideration to shares issued by a subsidiary company which create an obligation for the group as a whole to transfer economic benefits. The Abstract requires this issue to be considered in the context of the obligations that usually arise from shares. Where the effect on the group as a whole is that the group has an obligation to transfer economic benefits that does not go beyond the obligation to transfer economic benefits that would normally attach to shares of that type, the shares should not be treated as a liability. If the obligation goes beyond that normally attaching to shares, the shares should be treated as a liability in the group accounts rather than as minority interests. The Abstract gives the following examples of obligations that go beyond those normally attaching to shares:

(i) an obligation to pay dividends or amounts in respect of redemption even if there are insufficient profits available;

(ii) a guarantee given by the group in respect of the obligation normally attaching to the shares – whether this is sufficient to require the shares to be treated as a liability rather than as minority interests will depend on the extent to which, and the manner in which, the guarantee has been subordinated to other liabilities (i.e. the greater the degree of subordination, the less likely it is that the guarantee will impose obligations that require the shares to be treated as a liability).

The assessment should take into account all guarantees and any other surrounding arrangements to the transaction.

For accounting periods beginning on or after 1 January 2005, the Abstract is superseded by FRS 25 'Financial Instruments: Disclosure and Presentation'.

Chapter 48 Consolidation Goodwill

CALCULATING GOODWILL

The nature of goodwill

48.1   Goodwill is a means of recognising that the value of a business as a whole will often be more or less than the aggregate values of its individual parts. FRS 10 'Goodwill and intangible assets' defines purchased goodwill as 'the difference between the cost of an acquired entity and the aggregate of the fair values of that entity's identifiable assets and liabilities.' Identifiable assets and liabilities are defined as 'the assets and liabilities of an entity that are capable of being disposed of or settled separately, without disposing of a business of the entity'. Positive goodwill arises where the cost of acquisition exceeds the aggregate fair values of the identifiable assets and liabilities of the business acquired – in other words, where the value of the business as a whole is considered to be more than the aggregate of the values of its component parts and the purchaser is therefore prepared to pay more than the value of individual assets and liabilities that make up the business. Negative goodwill arises in the converse situation – where the value of the business is considered to be less than the value of the component parts and the aggregate fair values of the identifiable assets and liabilities are therefore more than the cost of acquisition. Negative goodwill is expected to arise only rarely.

Recognition of goodwill

48.2   Neither CA 1985 nor FRS 10 permit internally generated goodwill to be recognised on the balance sheet. Goodwill is therefore only recognised for accounting purposes when the business to which it relates is purchased by another party. When a company buys an unincorporated business (in the form of a trade and the related assets) the purchased goodwill relating to the acquisition will be reflected in the company's own balance sheet. This is because the assets and liabilities acquired will also be recorded in the company's own accounts. When a company buys a business by acquiring shares in another company, the goodwill will only be recorded when the accounts of the parent and its subsidiary are consolidated to form group accounts. In this case the assets and liabilities of the acquired company will continue to be recorded separately from those of the parent (i.e. in the separate accounts of the subsidiary). The accounting requirements of FRS 10 apply in all cases where goodwill arises, regardless of whether the goodwill is recorded in the accounts of the acquiring company or arises only on consolidation. Under FRS 10:

(i) positive purchased goodwill should be capitalised and classified as an asset on the balance sheet;

(ii) any negative goodwill that arises on an acquisition should be recognised in the accounts and shown separately on the face of the balance sheet immediately below the goodwill heading; and

(iii) a sub-total of the net amount of positive and negative goodwill should also be shown.

Purchased goodwill arising on a single transaction should not be divided into positive and negative components.

Acquisition or merger accounting

48.3   Consolidation goodwill only arises when an acquisition is accounted for using the acquisition method of accounting. FRS 6 'Mergers and acquisitions' sets out stringent conditions that must be met for a transaction to be classified as a merger and accounted for under the merger accounting rules. In practice, therefore, most acquisitions will be accounted for using acquisition accounting and will give rise to consolidation goodwill. The requirements of FRS 6 are considered in more detail in Chapter 49 of this manual.

The value of purchased goodwill

48.4   CA 1985 and FRS 10 set out specific (and similar) rules on the calculation of goodwill. When a business is acquired, the value of the purchased goodwill is established by comparing the fair values of the various assets and liabilities at the time of acquisition with the fair value of the consideration given by the purchaser (which will usually be in the form of cash or shares). Any excess of the consideration over the fair values of the net assets represents the value of the purchased goodwill.

Example 48.1 – Calculating goodwill at the time of acquisition

On 1 July 20X3 A Ltd acquires 100% of the share capital of B Ltd for £128,000 which is paid in cash.

The capital and reserves of B Ltd at 1 July 20X3 are as follows:

	£
Share capital	10,000
Profit and loss account reserve	60,000
Revaluation reserve	15,000
	85,000

A review of the fair value of B Ltd's net assets at 1 July 20X3 shows that the value of B Ltd's property exceeds its book value by £30,000. Other assets and liabilities are unchanged.

Goodwill is therefore calculated as follows.

	£
Capital and reserves of B Ltd at 1 July 20X3	85,000
Fair value adjustment	30,000
Fair value of the net assets acquired	115,000
Fair value of the purchase consideration	128,000
Goodwill	13,000

Detailed guidance on establishing fair values for the assets and liabilities acquired, and for the purchase consideration, is set out in FRS 7 'Fair Values in Acquisition Accounting'. The requirements of FRS 7 are considered in Chapter 49.

FRS 23 'The Effects of Changes in Foreign Exchange Rates' was published in December 2004, but can only be adopted by entities that have also adopted FRS 26 'Financial Instruments: Measurement'. FRS 26 applies to listed companies for accounting periods beginning on or after 1 January 2005, and to other entities for accounting periods beginning on or after 1 January 2006 if they choose to adopt fair value accounting. Where FRS 23 applies, any goodwill arising on the acquisition of a foreign operation, and any fair value adjustments to the carrying values of assets and liabilities at the time of acquisition, should be treated as assets and liabilities of the foreign operation. Consequently, they should be expressed in the functional currency of the foreign operation and translated at the closing rate in accordance with the normal requirements of FRS 23. These are considered in more detail in Chapter 50.

Partly-owned subsidiaries

48.5   If the parent acquires only part of the share capital of the subsidiary, the value of the net assets acquired must be apportioned accordingly.

Example 48.2 – Where the parent acquires only part of the share capital

The details are as for Example 48.1 above except that A Ltd acquires 80% of the share capital of B Ltd for £128,000.

Goodwill in this case will be:

	£
Capital and reserves of B Ltd at 1 July 20X3	85,000
Fair value adjustment	30,000
Fair value of total net assets	115,000
Fair value of net assets acquired 115,000 x 80%	92,000
Fair value of the purchase consideration	128,000
Goodwill	36,000

FRS 2 'Accounting for Subsidiary Undertakings' emphasises that goodwill should only be recognised in respect of the interest acquired by the parent and its subsidiaries. No goodwill should be attributed to the minority interest.

Separable intangible assets

48.6   Where material intangible assets are acquired as part of a business (e.g. patents, licences, trade marks etc.) and their value can be measured reliably at the time of the acquisition, they should be recorded separately as intangible fixed assets in the consolidated accounts. This treatment should be adopted in the group accounts even though the intangible assets may not be shown in the balance sheet of the entity being acquired (for instance because they were internally generated and did not have a readily ascertainable market value). In this case, a consolidation adjustment will need to be made each year to bring the assets onto the group balance sheet. An intangible asset acquired as part of a business should normally be capitalised at its fair value at the date of acquisition, but where the asset does not have a readily ascertainable market value, the fair value should be limited to an amount that does not create or increase any negative goodwill relating to the acquisition. This is considered in more detail in Chapter 49. If the value of an intangible asset cannot be measured reliably at the time of the acquisition it should be subsumed within the amount attributed to goodwill.

Once recorded in the consolidated balance sheet, intangible assets should be accounted for in accordance with FRS 10, as described in Chapter 20.

Negative goodwill

48.7   The standard emphasises that, where an acquisition appears to give rise to negative goodwill, the fair values of the assets acquired should be tested for impairment and the fair values of the liabilities acquired should be reviewed carefully to confirm that they have not been understated and that no items have been overlooked. As explained in 48.6 above, FRS 10 requires the fair values of certain intangible assets to be limited to an amount that does not create or increase any negative goodwill arising on the acquisition.

ACCOUNTING FOR CONSOLIDATION GOODWILL

Creation of goodwill in the group accounts

48.8 When the accounts of the parent are consolidated with those of its subsidiary to form the group accounts, the share capital and pre-acquisition reserves of the subsidiary and the investment shown in the parent company's accounts must be eliminated and will be replaced with the goodwill arising on consolidation. These adjustments will need to be processed each time consolidated accounts are prepared.

Example 48.3 – Creation of goodwill in the group accounts

A Ltd has acquired 100% of the share capital of B Ltd, as described in Example 48.1, on 1 July 20X3.

A Ltd and B Ltd make up their accounts to 30 June each year. The balance sheets of the two companies at 30 June 20X4 are as follows.

	£	*A Ltd* £	£	*B Ltd* £
Share capital		45,000		10,000
Profit and loss account:				
Opening balance	174,000		60,000	
Profit for 20X3/X4	30,000		20,000	
		204,000		80,000
Revaluation reserve		–		15,000
		249,000		105,000
Investment in subsidiary		128,000		
Tangible fixed assets		71,000		53,000
Other net assets		50,000		52,000
		249,000		105,000

B Ltd has therefore not incorporated the property valuation at 1 July 20X3 into its own accounts.

The adjustments on consolidation will be as follows.

(i)   To incorporate the property uplift of £30,000:

	£	£
Dr Fixed assets	30,000	
Cr Revaluation reserve		30,000

(ii)   To eliminate the share capital of B Ltd and its pre-acquisition reserves – in effect, these reserves will include the £30,000 uplift in the value of the property processed above, as the increase in value took place before acquisition.

(iii)   To eliminate A Ltd's investment in B Ltd.

(iv)   To record the goodwill arising on consolidation in the group accounts:

	£	£
Dr Share capital	10,000	
Dr Profit and loss reserve	60,000	
Dr Revaluation reserve (15 + 30)	45,000	
Dr Consolidation goodwill	13,000	
Cr Investment in subsidiary		128,000
	128,000	128,000

These adjustments are illustrated below.

	A Ltd	B Ltd	A + B		Adjustments	Group
	£	£	£		£	£
Share capital	45	10	55	(ii)	(10)	45
Profit and loss	204	80	284	(ii)	(60)	224
Revaluation reserve	–	15	15	(i)	30	
				(ii)	(45)	
	249	105	354		(85)	269
Investment	128		128	(iii)	(128)	
Consolidation goodwill				(iv)	13	13
Tangible fixed assets	71	53	124	(i)	30	154
Other net assets	50	52	102			102
	249	105	354		(85)	269

The balance on the profit and loss account reserve in the consolidated balance sheet represents:

	£
Profit and loss account of A Ltd	204
Profit recorded by B Ltd in 20X3/X4 (i.e. from the date of acquisition by A Ltd 1 July 20X3)	20
	224

Minority interests

48.9   Where the parent holds less than 100% of the shares in the subsidiary, the minority interest must be shown separately in the consolidated balance sheet. Accounting for minority interests is covered in more detail in Chapter 47, but the example below illustrates how the relevant consolidation adjustments would be processed in the situation set out in Example 48.2.

Example 48.4 – Creation of goodwill in consolidated accounts where there is a minority interest

A Ltd has acquired 80% of the share capital of B Ltd, as described in Example 48.2, on 1 July 20X3.

A Ltd and B Ltd make up their accounts to 30 June each year. The balance sheets of the two companies at 30 June 20X4 are as follows.

		A Ltd	B Ltd
		£	*£*
Share capital		45,000	10,000
Profit and loss account:			
Opening balance	174,000		60,000
Profit for 1995/96	30,000		20,000
		204,000	80,000
Revaluation reserve		–	15,000
		249,000	105,000
Investment in subsidiary		128,000	
Tangible fixed assets		71,000	53,000
Other net assets		50,000	52,000
		249,000	105,000

B Ltd has therefore not incorporated the property valuation at 1 July 20X3 into its own accounts.

In this case the adjustments on consolidation will be as follows.

(i) To incorporate the property uplift of £30,000:

	£	*£*
Dr Fixed assets	30,000	
Cr Revaluation reserve		30,000

(ii) To eliminate the share capital and pre-acquisition reserves of B Ltd.

(iii) To eliminate A Ltd's investment in B Ltd.

(iv) To record the goodwill arising on consolidation in the group accounts.

(v) To record the minority interest in the group accounts:

Dr Share capital	10,000	
Dr Profit and loss reserve	60,000	
Dr Revaluation reserve (15 + 30)	45,000	
Dr Consolidation goodwill	36,000	
Dr Profit and loss account 20X3/X4		
see below	4,000	
Cr Investment in subsidiary		128,000
Cr Minority interest see below		27,000
	155,000	155,000

The minority interest is made up as follows.

	£
Share capital of B Ltd 20% x 10,000	2,000
Profit and loss account of B Ltd at 1 July 20X3 20% x 60,000	12,000
Revaluation reserve of B Ltd at 1 July 20X3 20% x 15,000	3,000
Fair value adjustment at 1 July 20X3 20% x 30,000	6,000
Minority interest at date of acquisition	23,000
Profit for 20X3/X4 20% x 14,000	4,000
	27,000

The consolidation adjustments are illustrated below.

	A Ltd	B Ltd	A + B		Adjustments		Group
	£	£	£		£		£
Share capital	45	10	55	(ii)	(10)		45
Profit and loss	204	80	284	(ii)	(60)		220
				(v)	(4)		
Revaluation reserve	–	15	15	(i)	30		
				(ii)	(45)		
	249	105	354		(89)		265
Minority interest				(v)	27		27
	249	105	354		(62)		292
Investment	128		128	(iii)	(128)		–
Consolidation goodwill				(iv)	36		36
Tangible fixed assets	71	53	124	(i)	30		154
Other net assets	50	52	102				102
	249	105	354		(62)		292

In this case, the balance on the profit and loss account reserve in the consolidated balance sheet represents:

	£
Profit and loss account of A Ltd	204
Group share of B Ltd's profit for 20X3/X4 (i.e. from the date of acquisition by A Ltd 1 July 20X3):	
80% x 20,000	16
	220

Amortisation

48.10   Once the consolidation adjustments described above have been processed, the purchased goodwill that has been created in the group accounts must be accounted for in accordance with the Act and FRS 10. Under FRS 10:

(i)   where purchased goodwill is regarded as having a limited useful economic life, it should be amortised on a systematic basis over that life;

(ii) where purchased goodwill is considered to have an indefinite useful economic life, it should not be amortised.

No residual value should be attributed to purchased goodwill. CA 1985 requires goodwill to be amortised systematically over a finite period, and a group following the requirements of FRS 10 in respect of goodwill that is considered to have indefinite life will therefore need to adopt the true and fair override and make appropriate disclosures in the accounts. Amortisation charged in the year will need to be disclosed as required by the standard profit and loss account formats.

Determining the useful economic life of goodwill

48.11   FRS 10 defines the useful economic life of purchased goodwill as 'the period over which the value of the underlying business acquired is expected to exceed the values of its identifiable net assets.' The standard also notes that, if purchased goodwill includes intangible assets that have not been recognised separately because their values cannot be measured reliably, the useful economic lives of the intangible assets will need to be taken into account when assessing the useful economic life of the goodwill. There is a rebuttable presumption that the useful economic life of goodwill should be no more than 20 years, and this presumption can only be rebutted if:

(i)   the durability of the acquired business can be demonstrated and justifies a life of more than 20 years; and

(ii) the goodwill is capable of continued measurement so that annual impairment reviews can be carried out.

Need to establish useful economic life

48.12   The guidance in the standard emphasises that it is inappropriate to assume that the premium of an acquired business over its net asset value can be maintained indefinitely. In practice, purchased goodwill will usually be replaced by internally generated goodwill over time and, because internally generated goodwill should not be recognised for accounting purposes, it is important that the write-off period for the purchased goodwill is sufficiently short to allow it to be eliminated from the accounts before it is fully replaced with internally generated goodwill. The standard notes that the useful economic life of goodwill will often be uncertain, but this does not justify an assumption that it has a life of 20 years, or that its life is indefinite. Conversely, uncertainty should not be used to justify the adoption of an unrealistically short life. A prudent but realistic estimate of the useful economic life must be made in each case where goodwill arises.

Durability and continued measurement

48.13   The guidance in the standard emphasises that the durability of a business will vary depending on various factors, including:

(i)   the nature of the business;

(ii)   the stability of the industry in which it operates;

(iii)   the typical lifespan of the products to which the goodwill relates;

(iv)   the extent to which the acquisition overcomes market entry barriers that will continue to exist; and

(v)   the expected impact of competition in future years.

In practice, these are factors that will also need to be considered when determining the useful economic life of goodwill. The standard also notes that the goodwill will not be capable of continued measurement where the cost of carrying out the measurement is unjustifiably high – for instance, where the acquired business is merged with an existing business to such an extent that the acquired goodwill cannot be separately identified and reviewed in future years.

Method of amortisation

48.14   The standard requires amortisation to be charged on a systematic basis over the useful economic life of the goodwill, using a method that reflects the expected pattern of depletion. A straight-line method should be used unless another method can be shown to be more appropriate. The guidance notes that an amortisation method that is less conservative than the straight-line method is unlikely to be justifiable. In particular, interest rate methods, such as the 'reverse sum of digits' or the annuity method, are not appropriate methods of amortising goodwill.

Review of economic life

48.15   The useful economic life of purchased goodwill should be reviewed at the end of each accounting period and revised where necessary. Where the useful economic life is adjusted, the carrying value of the goodwill should be amortised over its revised remaining useful economic life. This applies equally where the presumption of a 20-year life has previously been rebutted. If the revision extends the life of the goodwill to a period of more than 20 years from the date of its acquisition, the additional requirements of FRS 10 on annual impairment reviews automatically come into effect.

UITF Abstract 27 'Revision to estimates of the useful economic life of goodwill and intangible assets' considers the accounting treatment to be adopted where an entity has previously rebutted the presumption that the useful economic life of goodwill or an intangible asset is limited to a period of 20 years or less, but is now unable to rebut this presumption (or no longer wishes to do so). The UITF consensus is that a decision not to rebut the presumption is not a change of accounting policy, but a change in the way in which useful economic life is estimated. The requirement under FRS 10 for the carrying value of an asset to be amortised over its revised remaining useful economic life therefore applies equally where the presumption of a 20-year life has previously been rebutted.

Requirement for impairment reviews

48.16 Goodwill that is amortised over a period of 20 years or less should be reviewed for impairment at the end of the first full financial year following acquisition and in other periods if events or changes in circumstances indicate that its carrying value may not be fully recoverable. Goodwill that is amortised over a period of more than 20 years, or is not amortised, should be reviewed for impairment at the end of each accounting period.

Procedures for impairment reviews

48.17 Impairment is defined in FRS 10 as 'a reduction in the recoverable amount of a fixed asset or goodwill below its carrying value.' Recoverable amount is defined as the higher of:

(i)   net realisable value – which is the amount at which an asset could be disposed of, less any direct selling costs; or

(ii)   value in use – which is the present value of the future cash flows obtainable as a result of an asset's continued use, including those resulting from its ultimate disposal.

Impairment reviews should generally be carried out in accordance with the requirements of FRS 11. However, the first year impairment review for goodwill amortised over 20 years or less may be carried out by comparing post-acquisition performance in the first year with pre-acquisition forecasts used to support the purchase price, and only carrying out a full impairment review if this exercise indicates that post-acquisition performance has failed to meet expectations, or if other factors indicate that the carrying value of the goodwill may not be fully recoverable.

Impact of impairment losses

48.18 Impairment losses should be accounted for in accordance with FRS 11. If an impairment loss needs to be recognised, the revised carrying value of the goodwill should be amortised over the current estimate of its remaining useful economic life. The guidance in FRS 10 emphasises that:

(i)   the recognition of an impairment loss must be justified by reference to expected future cash flows, in the same way as the absence of an impairment loss; and

(ii)   the fact that the value of the goodwill may not be capable of continued measurement in future does not necessarily justify writing off the entire balance at the time of the first year impairment review.

Where the implementation of FRS 10 results in the recognition of an impairment loss relating to goodwill previously capitalised, the loss should be charged in the profit and loss account of the period.

Where the review indicates that the value of consolidation goodwill has been impaired, the parent company should also review the carrying value of the related investment in its own individual balance sheet, and write this down where appropriate.

Where the implementation of FRS 10 results in the recognition of an impairment loss relating to goodwill previously capitalised, the loss should be charged in the profit and loss account of the period.

Restoration of impairment losses

48.19   The reversal of an impairment loss in respect of goodwill can only be recognised when:

(i)   the original impairment loss was caused by an external event; and

(ii)   subsequent external events clearly and demonstrably reverse the effects of that event in a way that was not foreseen when the original impairment calculations were carried out.

The guidance in the standard emphasises that most reversals will be the result of the internal generation of goodwill and should therefore not be recognised in the accounts. Where a reversal is recognised, it should be treated as arising in the current year.

Accounting for negative goodwill

48.20   Negative goodwill up to the fair values of the non-monetary assets acquired should be recognised in the profit and loss account in the period in which those assets are recovered (i.e. through depreciation or on sale of the assets). Any negative goodwill in excess of the fair values of the non-monetary assets acquired should be recognised in the profit and loss account in the periods expected to benefit. An FRRP case reported in 2002 concluded that, where the particular circumstances of the transaction made this method of accounting for negative goodwill inappropriate, the true and fair view needed to be invoked in order to credit the negative goodwill arising to reserves (see 49.49 to 49.51 below).

Transitional arrangements on implementing FRS 10

48.21   The predecessor UK accounting standard to FRS 10 was SSAP 22 'Accounting for Goodwill' and this allowed two alternative accounting treatments for purchased goodwill: capitalisation and amortisation, or immediate write-off against reserves. FRS 10 notes that any changes in accounting policy necessary to implement its requirements should be applied retrospectively. The preferred treatment, therefore, is for goodwill that has previously been eliminated against reserves to be reinstated to the extent that it would not have been fully written down under the requirements of the new standard. However, the ASB accepted that this would not always be practicable and included certain transitional arrangements in FRS 10 that allow goodwill not to be reinstated, subject to certain conditions.

Goodwill reinstated in implementing FRS 10

48.22   Where goodwill previously eliminated against reserves is reinstated on implementing FRS 10:

(i)   any impairment attributed to prior periods must be determined on the basis of reviews performed in accordance with FRS 11;

(ii)   the notes to the accounts should disclose:

- the original cost of the goodwill;
- the amount attributed to prior period amortisation; and
- the amount attributed to prior period impairment;

(iii)   intangible assets subsumed within the goodwill need not be identified separately.

The reinstatement of the goodwill will therefore give rise to a prior period adjustment.

Goodwill not reinstated on implementing FRS 10

48.23   Where goodwill that was previously eliminated against reserves is not reinstated on the implementation of FRS 10, the following treatment should be adopted:

(i)   the accounting policy followed in respect of that goodwill should be disclosed;

(ii)   the cumulative amounts of positive goodwill eliminated against reserves and negative goodwill added to reserves, net of any goodwill attributable to businesses disposed of before the balance sheet date, should be shown, except that:

- amounts relating to overseas business need not be given if it would be prejudicial to the business and official agreement has been obtained; and

- disclosure need not be made for acquisitions before 23 December 1989 if the information is unavailable or cannot be obtained without unreasonable expense or undue delay.

the exclusion of these amounts, and the reasons for it, should be explained;

(iii) the eliminated goodwill should be offset against the profit and loss account or another suitable reserve – it should not be shown as a debit balance on a goodwill write-off reserve, nor should the amount by which the profit and loss account or other reserve has been reduced be shown separately on the face of the balance sheet; and

(iv) in the reporting period in which the related business is disposed of or closed, the profit or loss on disposal or closure should include any attributable goodwill not already written off in the profit and loss account, and this should be separately disclosed as a component of the profit or loss (if it is not practicable to ascertain the goodwill attributable to a business acquired before 1 January 1989 this fact, and the reasons, should be disclosed).

Accounting for goodwill on disposals

48.24   Whilst SSAP 22 was still in force, specific requirements on accounting for goodwill on disposal were introduced by UITF Abstract 3 'Treatment of Goodwill on Disposal of a Business'. Under FRS 10, goodwill is amortised through the profit and loss account and the profit or loss on disposal of a previously acquired business will automatically include any goodwill not yet amortised because it will be calculated by comparing sales proceeds with the carrying value of the asset (i.e. including any unamortised goodwill). UITF Abstract 3 was therefore withdrawn when FRS 10 was issued. However, where goodwill written off against reserves in accordance with SSAP 22 is not reinstated under the transitional arrangements, the requirements of UITF Abstract 3 effectively still apply and are encompassed in paragraph 71(c) of FRS 10:

(i) the calculation of the profit or loss on disposal or closure must include any purchased goodwill that has not previously been amortised through the profit and loss account; and

(ii) the accounts must show separately, as part of the profit or loss on disposal or closure, the amount of goodwill included in the calculation.

Where purchased goodwill in respect of a previous acquisition has been written off against reserves, the full amount of the goodwill will therefore need to be included in the calculation of the profit or loss on disposal.

Example 48.5 – Calculation of goodwill on disposal under the transitional arrangements

C Ltd acquired 100% of the share capital of D Ltd some years ago at a cost of £100,000. The fair value of the net assets of D Ltd at the time of acquisition was £77,000 and the goodwill of £23,000 arising on consolidation was immediately written off to reserves.

On 1 September 20X4, C Ltd sells its entire shareholding in D Ltd for £91,000. The carrying value of the net assets of D Ltd in the group accounts at 1 September 20X4 was £80,000.

In the group accounts, the result of the disposal will be recorded as follows:

	£
Carrying value of D Ltd at 1 September 20X4	80,000
Goodwill written off to reserves on acquisition	23,000
	103,000
Less: Disposal proceeds	(91,000)
Loss on disposal	(12,000)

Where goodwill previously written off is not reinstated on implementing FRS 10, the group will need to retain detailed records of the goodwill relating to each previous acquisition (whether of a subsidiary or an associate – the requirements apply in both cases) so that the necessary calculations can be carried out if any of the entities are subsequently disposed of or closed. Where it is impractical or impossible to establish the goodwill attributable to an acquisition made before 1 January 1989, this fact should be stated in the accounts in the year of disposal or closure, and the reasons given.

Potential future changes

48.25 In December 2002, the ASB published a consultation paper on the International Accounting Standards Board's (IASB's) proposals on accounting for business combinations, impairment and intangible assets. The proposals completed Phase I of the IASB's business combinations project. The key changes for the UK would be that merger accounting would be prohibited and goodwill arising on an acquisition would not be subject to amortisation but would be reviewed periodically for impairment. However, in its preface to the consultation paper, the ASB highlighted reservations over the following issues:

(i) the proposal to use acquisition accounting for all business combinations, with rules for identifying an acquirer even when an acquirer does not exist;

(ii) the proposal that goodwill should never be amortised but should be carried subject to an impairment test;

(iii) the fact that the impairment tests proposed by the IASB are less rigourous than present UK practice in identifying impairments, particularly of acquired goodwill;

(iv) the likelihood that under the proposals, more intangible assets than at present will be recognised when they are acquired either individually or in a combination – the validity or usefulness of separate recognition and measurement for some of these is considered to be questionable; and

(v)   the lack of symmetry under the proposals in the treatments of intangible assets and goodwill, which could give rise to problems, given the lack of clarity of the borderline between the two.

However, the ASB concluded that it would be more appropriate to defer detailed consultation on UK implementation of the proposals until the material for Phase II of the project was also available. The IASB has subsequently completed Phase II and exposure drafts setting out new international accounting proposals are due to be published in the second quarter of 2005. The ASB has indicated that it intends to issue similar UK exposure drafts at the same time, with a view to new UK standards coming into effect from the same date as the equivalent international versions.

ACCOUNTS DISCLOSURES IN RESPECT OF GOODWILL

Disclosures required by the Act

48.26   Most of the detailed disclosure requirements in respect of goodwill are set out in FRS 10. However the Act also requires the following specific disclosures in the accounts:

(i)   where goodwill is amortised over a period, the period of write-off and the reasons for choosing it must be disclosed;

(ii)   movements during the year on the goodwill account must be disclosed; and

(iii)   the accounts must disclose the cumulative amount of goodwill relating to acquisitions which has been written off, except where the write-off has been charged to the consolidated profit and loss account in either the current year or in previous years – this figure should be shown net of any goodwill relating to subsidiary undertakings or businesses disposed of prior to the balance sheet date (i.e. the amount of goodwill written off directly against reserves in respect of group entities still held at the end of the year must be shown in the accounts).

Detailed disclosures under FRS 10

48.27   FRS 10 requires the following detailed disclosures, which effectively encompass those set out in the Act:

(i)   separately for positive goodwill and negative goodwill:

●   the cost at the beginning and end of the period;

●   the cumulative provision for amortisation or impairment at the beginning and end of the period;

●   a reconciliation of movements, showing additions, disposals, transfers, amortisation, impairment losses, reversals of past impairment losses and negative goodwill written back in the period; and

- the net carrying amount at the balance sheet date;

(ii) the profit or loss on each material disposal of a previously acquired business or business segment;

(iii) the methods and periods of amortisation and the reasons for choosing those periods;

(iv) where an amortisation period is shortened or extended after a review of remaining useful economic lives, the reasons and the effect if material (i.e. in the year of change only);

(v) where the amortisation method has been changed, the reasons and the effect if material (i.e. in the year of change only);

(vi) where the amortisation period is more than 20 years from the date of acquisition, or where no amortisation is charged, the grounds for rebutting the 20 year presumption, including specific factors contributing to the durability of the acquired business (see below);

(vii) where goodwill is not amortised, the true and fair override disclosures (which should incorporate the explanation of the specific factors contributing to the durability of the acquired business);

(viii) the period(s) in which any negative goodwill is being written back in the profit and loss account; and

(ix) where negative goodwill exceeds the fair values of the non-monetary assets acquired, an explanation of the amount and source of the excess and of the period(s) in which it is being written back.

In May 2004, the Financial Reporting Review Panel (FRRP) issued a press release noting that it had identified a number of cases where inadequate disclosure had been made in the notes to the accounts on the amortisation of intangible assets and goodwill. In a number of the cases investigated by the FRRP, directors had argued that the factors supporting the durability of the relevant assets were already well known and understood and that further comment in the accounts was unnecessary. The FRRP did not accept these arguments and concluded that there were no grounds for failing to give the detailed disclosures required by FRS 10. The relevant details should therefore be given in all cases.

Accounting policy

48.28   Wording along the following lines will usually be suitable for disclosure of the accounting policy in respect of consolidation goodwill:

Example 48.6 – Accounting policy for consolidation goodwill

Basis of preparation of group accounts

The group accounts consolidate the financial statements of the company and its subsidiary undertakings made up to 30 June 20X4. The profits and losses of subsidiary undertakings are consolidated from the date of acquisition and, where relevant, up to the date of disposal. Purchased goodwill arising on consolidation represents the difference between the aggregate of the fair values of the identifiable assets and liabilities acquired and the fair value of the consideration given. This goodwill is capitalised and amortised through the profit and loss account on a straight-line basis over its useful economic life.

Impact of goodwill on distributable reserves

48.29   It is important to recognise that the issue of whether a particular reserve is distributable or not is only significant in relation to an individual company, even if the company has subsidiaries and prepares group accounts. This is because it is the company, rather than the group, that pays dividends to its shareholders. The distinction between distributable and non-distributable reserves in the context of a group is therefore not as significant as in the case of an individual company and there is no requirement to disclose this analysis in the accounts. However, some groups choose to give this information to illustrate how much of the group reserves would be distributable by the parent to its shareholders if the subsidiaries were to pay out the full amount of their distributable reserves in dividends.

The issue of distributable reserves and realised profits and losses is considered briefly in Chapter 16. These are highly complex areas and only an outline of the main issues is given. The potential impact of goodwill on distributable reserves is not an issue where goodwill is accounted for in accordance with FRS 10 'Goodwill and Intangible Assets'. However, where a company follows the transitional arrangements in FRS 10 and does not reinstate goodwill previously eliminated directly against reserves, the impact of this write-off on distributable reserves may still need to be considered as explained in Chapter 20.

Chapter 49   Acquisitions, Disposals And Mergers

ACQUISITION AND MERGER ACCOUNTING

Prevalence of acquisition accounting

49.1   CA 1985 requires all acquisitions of subsidiary undertakings to be accounted for by the acquisition method of accounting, unless the specific conditions for a merger are met, in which case merger accounting may be used. The Act also requires the notes to the accounts to disclose the name of any undertaking acquired during the year (or the name of the parent undertaking if a group is acquired) and whether the acquisition has been accounted for by the acquisition or merger method of accounting.

In practice, the requirements of accounting standards must also be taken into account. FRS 6 'Acquisitions and Mergers' sets out stringent additional conditions that must be met for a transaction to be classified as a merger and accounted for under the merger accounting rules. Most acquisitions are therefore accounted for using acquisition accounting. It is also likely that merger accounting will be prohibited under both international accounting standards and UK accounting standards in the relatively near future (see 48.25 above).

In addition to the disclosures required under CA 1985, FRS 6 also requires the date of each merger or acquisition to be disclosed.

Acquisition accounting

49.2   The legislation sets out the following provisions in respect of the acquisition method of accounting:

(i) the identifiable assets and liabilities of the undertaking acquired must be included in the consolidated balance sheet at their fair values at the date of acquisition – identifiable assets and liabilities are defined as those that are capable of being disposed of or discharged separately, without disposing of the business of the undertaking;

(ii) the income and expenditure of the undertaking acquired must only be included in the group accounts from the date of acquisition;

(iii) the interest acquired in the adjusted capital and reserves of the undertaking must be off-set against the acquisition cost, and any resulting difference must be treated as goodwill (if positive) or as a negative consolidation difference (if negative).

The mechanics of the acquisition method of accounting are considered in more detail in Chapter 47 and the treatment of consolidation goodwill is considered in Chapter 48.

Company law conditions for the use of merger accounting

49.3 Under CA 1985, all of the following conditions must be met for an acquisition to be accounted for as a merger:

(i) at least 90% of the nominal value of the relevant shares in the undertaking acquired must be held by or on behalf of the parent and its subsidiary undertakings – 'relevant shares' are defined as shares carrying unrestricted rights to participate both in distributions and in the assets of the undertaking on liquidation;

(ii) this holding must be attained by an arrangement which provides for the issue of equity shares by the parent undertaking or one or more of its subsidiary undertakings;

(iii) the fair value of any consideration other than the issue of equity shares under this arrangement must not exceed 10% of the nominal value of the shares issued; and

(iv) the adoption of merger accounting must accord with generally accepted accounting principles or practice – in effect this means that merger accounting will only be permitted where the conditions set out in FRS 6 'Acquisitions and Mergers' are also met (see 49.65 below).

FRS 6 definitions of merger and acquisition

49.4 A merger is defined in FRS 6 'Acquisitions and Mergers' as:

'A business combination that results in the creation of a new reporting entity formed from the combining parties, in which the shareholders of the combining entities come together in a partnership for the mutual sharing of the risks and benefits of the combined entity, and in which no party to the combination in substance obtains control over any other, or is otherwise seen to be dominant, whether by virtue of the proportion of its shareholders' rights in the combined entity, the influence of its directors or otherwise'.

An acquisition is defined as a business combination that is not a merger. The standard sets out five criteria, all of which must be met for the combination to qualify as a merger. These are considered in more detail at 49.65 below. A transaction that meets the conditions in FRS 6 must be currently accounted for as a merger (ie merger accounting is not optional under the standard). Where a new parent company is established to hold the shares of each of the parties to a combination, the appropriate accounting treatment (i.e. acquisition or merger) depends on the substance of the combination of the entities other than the new parent.

FRS 6 also permits group reconstructions to be accounted for as mergers even if they do not meet the criteria for a merger, provided that:

(i)   the use of merger accounting is permitted under CA 1985;

(ii)   the ultimate shareholders remain the same and the relative rights of each shareholder are unchanged; and

(iii)   no minority's interest in the net assets of the group is changed as a result of the reconstruction.

Merger method of accounting

49.5   The Act sets out the following provisions in respect of the merger method of accounting:

(i)   the assets and liabilities of the undertaking acquired must be included in the group accounts at the figures shown in the accounts of that undertaking, subject to any adjustments authorised or required by Schedule 4A to CA 1985;

(ii)   the income and expenditure of the undertaking acquired must be included in the group for the entire financial year, including any period before acquisition;

(iii)   the corresponding figures in the group accounts must be stated as if the undertaking acquired had been included for the whole of that year as well;

(iv)   the nominal value of the issued share capital held by the parent and its subsidiary undertakings in the undertaking acquired must be off-set against the aggregate of:

•   the appropriate amount in respect of the qualifying shares issued by the parent and its subsidiary undertakings in consideration for shares in the undertaking acquired, and

- the fair value of any other consideration for shares in the undertaking, determined at the date when those shares were acquired

and any resulting difference must be shown as an adjustment to consolidated reserves.

The appropriate amount in respect of qualifying shares is defined as follows:

(i)   in the case of shares to which section 131 (merger relief) applies, the nominal value: and

(ii)   in the case of shares to which section 132 (relief in respect of group constructions) applies, the nominal value together with any minimum premium value within the meaning of that section.

FRS 6 sets out the following points in respect of merger accounting:

(i)   the carrying values of assets and liabilities of the entities are not required to be adjusted to fair values on consolidation, but appropriate adjustments should be made to achieve uniform accounting policies;

(ii)   the results and cash flows of the entities should be included in the financial statements of the combined entity from the beginning of the financial year in which combination takes place; corresponding figures for the profit and loss account and balance sheet should be restated on the same basis;

(iii) any difference between the nominal value of the shares issued, together with the fair value of any other consideration, and the nominal value of the shares received in exchange should be shown as a movement on the consolidated reserves and in the reconciliation of movements in shareholders' funds;

(iv)   any existing share premium account or capital redemption reserve in the accounts of the new subsidiary should be brought into the consolidated accounts as a movement on reserves and shown in the reconciliation of movements in shareholders' funds;

(v)   merger expenses should be charged to the profit and loss account as reorganisation or restructuring expenses under FRS 3 'Reporting Financial Performance.

Disclosure of impact on group accounts

49.6   Where an acquisition has a significant effect on the group accounts, CA 1985 requires the following additional details to be given

(i)   the composition and fair value of the consideration given by the parent and its subsidiary undertakings;

(ii)   where acquisition accounting has been used:

- a table setting out the book values immediately prior to acquisition, and the fair values, of each class of assets and liabilities acquired, and

- the amount of goodwill or negative consolidation difference, and
- an explanation of any significant adjustments;

(iii) where merger accounting has been used:

- an explanation of any significant adjustments made to the assets and liabilities acquired, and
- a statement of any adjustment to the consolidated reserves (including the restatement of opening consolidated reserves).

In the case of the acquisition of a group, the figures should be stated after the normal consolidation adjustments required under the Act.

The disclosures in respect of acquisitions required by FRS 6 are summarised in the Appendix to this Chapter. Different requirements apply, depending on whether the transaction has been accounted for as an acquisition or as a merger.

Accounts disclosures in respect of disposals

49.7 Similarly, where the disposal of an undertaking or group during the year has a significant effect on the group accounts, the Act requires the notes to the accounts to disclose the name of the undertaking disposed of (or the name of the parent undertaking if it is a group) and the extent to which the profit or loss in the group accounts is attributable to that undertaking (or group). FRS 2 requires the following disclosures to be given in addition to the details required by CA 1985:

(i) the name of any material undertaking that has ceased to be a subsidiary in the period;

(ii) any ownership interest retained by the group;

(iii) if an undertaking has ceased to be a subsidiary other than by the disposal of all or part of the interest held by the group (e.g. through a loss of control), an explanation of the circumstances.

Exemptions from disclosure

49.8 The disclosures normally required in respect of acquisitions and disposals need not be given for an undertaking that:

(i) is established under the law of a country outside the United Kingdom; or

(ii) carries on business outside the United Kingdom

if, in the opinion of the directors, the disclosure would be seriously prejudicial to the business of that undertaking, or to the business of the parent or any of its subsidiary undertakings, and if the Secretary of State agrees that the information need not be disclosed.

DATE OF ACQUISITION OR DISPOSAL

Significance of date of acquisition or disposal

49.9   The date of acquisition or disposal of a subsidiary is a critical point under the acquisition method of accounting. This is because, under acquisition accounting, the results and cash flows of a subsidiary must be included in the group accounts from the date of its acquisition and up to the date of its disposal.

Date of acquisition

49.10   FRS 2 'Accounting for Subsidiary Undertakings' defines the date of acquisition as the date on which control passes to the new parent. Control is defined in the standard as the ability to direct the operating and financial policies of the undertaking. Control will usually pass when an offer becomes unconditional and is accepted. In the case of private companies, this will usually happen when a binding contract comes into effect. In most cases this will also be the date on which the entity becomes a subsidiary under the definitions in section 258 of CA 1985 (see 45.1 above) The Explanatory Note to FRS 2 emphasises that the date on which control passes is a matter of fact and cannot be backdated or otherwise altered.

Date on which consideration passes

49.11   In many cases, the date on which the purchase consideration is paid will be the same as the date on which control passes to the new parent. However, FRS 2 emphasises that the date on which payment is made is not conclusive evidence of the date on which control transfers. This is because the arrangements could specifically require payment to be made on a different date, with compensation included for any delay or acceleration in the passing of control. The arrangements may also provide for the consideration to be paid in instalments.

Date of disposal

49.12   Under FRS 2, an entity ceases to be a subsidiary on the date that the former parent relinquishes control over it. In the case of a straightforward sale, this will usually be when a binding contract comes into effect. FRS 2 refers to the date on which an entity ceases to be a subsidiary rather than the date of disposal, and emphasises that the same rules and considerations apply in any situation where an entity ceases to be a subsidiary. For instance, this might be as a result of a straightforward disposal, a deemed disposal or some other event (e.g. closure of the subsidiary).

Deemed disposals

49.13   In many cases, an entity will cease to be a subsidiary because the group has reduced the proportion of the interest that it holds in the entity. In a straightforward disposal, the reduction will usually involve the sale of all or part of the shares held by the group. A deemed disposal arises when the group's interest is reduced without the sale of shares. For instance, this may occur when:

(i)   the group does not take up a rights issue or scrip dividend and other shareholders in the entity do, thus increasing the proportion of shares held by the latter;

(ii)   another party exercises options or warrants, thus changing the ratio of shareholdings;

(iii)   the subsidiary issues shares to parties outside the group.

As some of the definitions of a subsidiary also rest on the ability of the parent to control or influence the entity, changes in these factors could also result in the entity ceasing to be a subsidiary.

Gain or loss on disposal

49.14   The gain or loss on the disposal of a subsidiary is to be calculated by comparing the carrying amount of the net assets attributable to the group at the date of disposal (i.e. after taking account of the results of the subsidiary up to that date) with:

(i)   any disposal proceeds; and

(ii)   any remaining carrying value attributable to the group interest after the disposal.

The net asset value must include any related goodwill that has not already been written off through the profit and loss account, or treated as prior period amortisation or impairment at the time that FRS 10 'Goodwill and Intangible Assets' was first implemented. Where goodwill is being amortised, this will include the amount of goodwill that has not yet been charged to the profit and loss account. It will also any include goodwill that was previously written off against reserves under SSAP 22 'Accounting for Goodwill' and which has not been reinstated because the company has followed the transitional arrangements set out in FRS 10. An example of the calculation of gains and losses on disposal is given in Chapter 48.

The standard emphasises that these calculations should be carried out in the case of a deemed disposal as well as in the case of a straightforward sale of shares.

FRS 23 'The Effects of Changes in Foreign Exchange Rates' was published in December 2004, but can only be adopted by entities that have also adopted FRS 26 'Financial Instruments: Measurement'. FRS 26 applies to listed companies for accounting periods beginning on or after 1 January 2005, and to other entities for accounting periods beginning on or after 1 January 2006 if they choose to adopt fair value accounting. Where a foreign operation is disposed of and FRS 23 applies, the cumulative amount of the exchange differences recognised through the statement of total recognised gains and losses in relation to that operation must be recognised in the profit and loss account when the gain or loss on disposal is recognised. The standard includes the following additional guidance:

(i)   in the case of a partial disposal, only the proportionate share of the related accumulated exchange differences should be included in the gain or loss;

(ii)   the payment of a dividend is part of a disposal only when it constitutes a return of the investment (e.g. when it is paid out of pre-acquisition profits); and

(iii) a write-down of the carrying amount of a foreign operation does not constitute a partial disposal and so no part of the accumulated exchange differences should be recognised in the profit and loss account at the time of the write-down.

The requirements of FRS 23 are considered in more detail in Chapter 50.

MEASURING FAIR VALUES OF ASSETS AND LIABILITIES

Principles of recognition and measurement

49.15   Where an acquisition is accounted for by the acquisition method of accounting, the assets and liabilities of the new subsidiary must be brought into the consolidated balance sheet at fair value at the date of acquisition. FRS 7 'Fair Values in Acquisition Accounting' sets out the principles that should be followed in measuring the fair values of the identifiable assets and liabilities of the acquired entity. Only assets and liabilities that existed at the date of acquisition should be included in the valuation. The standard emphasises that the following do not affect fair values at the date of acquisition and should be treated as post-acquisition items:

(i)   changes resulting from the acquirer's intentions or future actions;

(ii)   impairment or other changes resulting from events after the acquisition;

(iii) provisions or accruals for future operating losses, or for reorganisation and integration costs that are expected to be incurred as a result of the acquisition.

Subject to the detailed requirements set out in FRS 7, fair values should be determined in accordance with the acquirer's accounting policies for similar assets and liabilities.

The approach adopted to the measurement of the fair values of the assets and liabilities can have a significant impact on the results reported in the post-acquisition profit and loss account of the group. This is because the fair values attributed to the net assets of the new subsidiary have a direct impact on the calculation of goodwill in respect of the acquisition. The accounting treatment of consolidation goodwill is considered in Chapter 48.

A FRRP case reported in July 2001 highlights the importance of giving careful consideration to the wording of disclosures made in the financial statements, so that they demonstrate compliance with the appropriate standard as well as explaining the treatment adopted. The FRRP carried out a review of the accounts of Avesco Plc for the year ended 31 March 2000, during which the company acquired an investment in an associate. The financial statements stated that the cost of the investment had been determined by the book value of the equipment transferred, together with associated acquisition costs, whereas FRS 9 'Associates and Joint Ventures' requires the acquisition cost and related goodwill to be determined by reference to fair values, established in accordance with FRS 7 'Fair Values in Acquisition Accounting'. The directors confirmed to the FRRP that, in their view, the book value of the assets approximated their fair value and that, having considered both the fixed assets and the revenue stream transferred, they were satisfied that none of the assets was impaired. The directors agreed to include a note in the 2001 accounts to clarify that the net book value of the assets transferred approximated their fair value.

Where FRS 23 applies (see 49.14 above), any goodwill arising on the acquisition of a foreign operation, and any fair value adjustments to the carrying values of assets and liabilities at the time of acquisition, should be treated as assets and liabilities of the foreign operation. Consequently, they should be expressed in the functional currency of the foreign operation and translated at the closing rate in accordance with the normal requirements of FRS 23. These are considered in more detail in Chapter 50.

Prohibition on provisions for future loss and reorganisation costs

49.16 Prior to FRS 7, it had become relatively common for groups to establish significant provisions for future operating losses, or for the costs of reorganising operations, resulting from the acquisition and to treat these as part of the fair value adjustment on acquisition. The effect of this was to increase the goodwill relating to the acquisition and either avoid charging the costs to the profit and loss account (where goodwill was written off directly against reserves) or spread the charge to the profit and loss account over the useful economic life of the goodwill. Under FRS 7 provisions for these costs cannot be established as part of the acquisition unless it can be demonstrated that the acquired entity was already committed to the costs at the date of acquisition (i.e. they represent identifiable liabilities of the acquired entity at that date).

Provisions raised during the negotiation period

49.17   The Explanatory Note to FRS 7 emphasises that particular care is required where provisions are raised by the acquired entity during the period of negotiation with the acquirer. A liability should only be recognised in the fair value exercise if the acquired entity is demonstrably committed to the expenditure, irrespective of whether the acquisition proceeds. In addition, if there is evidence that the acquirer is able to influence the decisions of the acquired entity during this period, this may indicate that control has already passed to the acquirer and that the date of acquisition is therefore earlier than had been thought.

Identifiable assets and liabilities

49.18   The identifiable assets and liabilities of the acquired entity may include items that were not previously recognised in the accounts of the entity. For instance:

(i)   pension fund surpluses or deficits;

(ii)   contingent assets and liabilities that crystallise as the result of the acquisition;

(iii)   liabilities under onerous contracts.

These should be recognised in the fair value exercise to the extent that they represent rights to future economic benefits or obligations to transfer economic benefits, as defined in the ASB's 'Statement of Principles for Financial Reporting' (see Chapter 2), and that they were in existence before the acquisition took place. If assets and liabilities which exist at the date of acquisition are not included in the fair value exercise, the reported post-acquisition results of the group could be distorted by recognising them in future years. UITF Abstract 22 'The Acquisition of a Lloyd's Business' specifically requires profit commissions receivable by Lloyd's managing agents and similar businesses to be included for all periods prior to acquisition, even though those periods may not yet have been closed.

Business closures

49.19   In cases where the acquired entity has taken the decision to close part of the business before the acquisition, FRS 7 refers specifically to the principles set out in FRS 3 'Reporting Financial Performance'. Under this standard, provision for closure costs can only be justified if the entity is demonstrably committed to the sale or termination. These requirements of FRS 3 are considered in Chapter 30.

Fair value

49.20   Fair value is defined in FRS 7 as the amount for which an asset or liability could be exchanged in an arm's length transaction between informed and willing parties. The appropriate method of establishing fair value will vary depending on the nature of the asset or liability.

Market price

49.21 Where similar assets are bought and sold on a readily accessible market, market price will usually represent fair value. Market price may be a quoted price, or may be estimated on the basis of valuation or discounting techniques. It is important that market value is only used where it is appropriate in the circumstances. For instance, it may be possible to obtain a market price for an item of plant, but this will not usually be an appropriate value to use if the entity would not purchase second-hand equipment.

Recoverable amount

49.22 The fair value attributed to an asset should not exceed the amount that the business expects to recover from the asset, either by disposing of the asset or by using it in its normal activities. The recoverable amount is defined as the greater of:

(i)   the net realisable value; and

(ii)   the value in use (i.e. the present value of the future cash flows obtainable from the asset's continued use, including the ultimate disposal proceeds).

The future intentions of the acquirer in respect of the asset should not be taken into account as these do not affect the value of the asset at the date of acquisition. In the case of an impaired asset (which is described in FRS 7 as an asset where the replacement cost is not fully recoverable due to lack of profitability, under-utilisation or obsolescence) the fair value will be the estimated recoverable amount. The effect of any impairment arising after the acquisition should be ignored for valuation purposes.

Tangible fixed assets

49.23 The fair value of certain tangible fixed assets (e.g. investments and properties for which there is a ready market) will usually be based on market values. Most other tangible fixed assets (e.g. specialised properties and plant and equipment) will usually be valued on the basis of depreciated replacement cost. In this case, the valuation should normally be based on the estimated assets lives and residual values used by the acquirer for similar assets, to avoid any future distortion of the group profit and loss account.

Intangible fixed assets

49.24 The fair value of an intangible asset should be based on its replacement cost, which will usually be its estimated market value. However, intangible assets should only be valued if they meet the other requirements of FRS 7 (i.e. if they are identifiable assets that are capable of being disposed of separately). Also, under the requirements of FRS 10 'Goodwill and Intangible Assets', where an intangible asset does not have a readily ascertainable market value, its fair value should be restricted to an amount that does not create or increase any negative goodwill arising in respect of the acquisition.

The last point was emphasised in July 2002 in the published results of an FRRP enquiry into the report and accounts of Equator Group Plc for the year ended 31 December 1999. The matter at issue was the accounting treatment adopted for the purchase of Equator Films Limited in June 1999 and the subsequent accounting for the principal assets acquired. Film libraries with a book value of £1,090,000 were revalued individually at open market value at the date of acquisition to a total of £13,158,000, giving rise to negative goodwill of £1,830,000. Under the company's accounting policy, the film libraries were not to be amortised but impairment reviews were to be carried out at least annually and any permanent decreases in value were to be charged to the profit and loss account. FRS 10 'Goodwill and Intangible Assets' requires intangible assets acquired as part of the acquisition of a business to be capitalised separately from goodwill if their value can be measured reliably. They should initially be recorded at fair value, but this should be limited to an amount that does not create or increase negative goodwill arising on the acquisition unless the assets have readily ascertainable market values. The Panel took the view that:

(i)   although the rights attaching to each film were similar, the films themselves were unique and could not, therefore, belong to a homogenous population of assets that was equivalent in all respects; and

(ii)   the market in which film libraries are bought and sold is not an 'active market'.

The Panel therefore concluded that the films did not have a readily ascertainable market value, as defined in FRS 10. The revaluation of the films to fair value at the date of purchase of the business should consequently have been limited to an amount that did not give rise to negative goodwill.

The FRRP raised a further issue in respect of the useful economic lives of the film libraries. The directors accepted the Panel's views and in their preliminary announcement for the year ended 31 December 2001 corrected both matters by way of prior year adjustment.

Stocks and work-in-progress

49.25   The fair value of most stock items will be the lower of replacement cost and net realisable value. The only exception is stocks that the acquired entity trades on a market as both buyer and seller, which should be valued at current market value. Replacement cost is the cost at which the acquired entity would have replaced the stocks. The value should therefore take account of its normal purchasing process and the prices that it is able to obtain. For instance, in the case of a manufacturer, the replacement cost of finished stocks will be the current cost of manufacturing the goods, not the cost of purchasing them from another source. If, in the case of long-term maturing stocks, there is no suitable market from which to assess replacement cost, the fair value may be estimated using the historical cost of bringing the stocks to their present location and condition and including an appropriate amount of interest to reflect the cost of holding the stocks. The guidance in FRS 19 'Deferred Tax' emphasises that no deferred tax should be recognised on any adjustment to reflect the fair value of stocks.

Any material write-down of stocks to net realisable value must be justified by the circumstances of the acquired entity at the date of acquisition. If exceptional profits appear to be made on these items in subsequent years, the fair values must be re-examined and, if necessary, adjusted, with a corresponding adjustment to good-will. However, if the exceptional profit is due to post-acquisition events rather than an understatement of fair values at the date of acquisition, it will need to be separately disclosed in accordance with paragraph 30 of FRS 6.

Long-term contracts

49.26   Where long-term contracts are accounted for in accordance with SSAP 9 'Stocks and Long-term Contracts', no adjustments to book values should be required, other than:

(i)   normal adjustments resulting from the assessment of the outcome of the contract;

(ii)   any adjustments to bring accounting policies into line with those of the acquirer.

Quoted investments

49.27   In the case of quoted investments, market values may need to be adjusted to eliminate the effects of any short-term fluctuations in price or to reflect the fact that a large holding may have a reduced value because of the difficulties of disposal, or an increased value because it represents substantial voting rights.

Monetary assets and liabilities

49.28   The fair value of most monetary assets and liabilities (e.g. debtors, prepay-ments, creditors and accruals) will be the amount that is expected to be received or paid on settlement or redemption, and this will usually be the same as book value. However, in the case of certain long-term monetary assets and liabilities, fair value may be significantly different to book value. For instance:

(i)   if the acquired entity has material long-term borrowings at fixed interest rates that do not reflect current borrowing rates, the fair value may be greater or lower than book value depending on whether interest rates have increased or decreased;

(ii)   if the acquired entity has a material long-term debtor and there is no interest charge to provide compensation for the long settlement period, the fair value of the debtor will differ from the book value.

Therefore, FRS 7 requires monetary items to be recognised at fair value where this is materially different to book value. In these cases, fair value will usually be calculated by considering the current terms for a similar monetary asset or liability, or by discounting the total amount to be paid or received to its present value. The difference between book value and fair value represents a discount or premium on acquisition, which will be reflected in the interest charge or credit in the group profit and loss account over the term of the relevant monetary asset or liability. Different considerations apply in the case of quoted debt instruments.

Contingencies

49.29   The fair value attributed to a contingent asset or contingent liability at the date of acquisition should reflect the best estimate of the likely outcome.

Pensions and other post-retirement benefits

49.30   Fair values should also be attributed to:

(i)   a deficiency in a funded scheme;

(ii)   accrued obligations in respect of an unfunded scheme;

(iii)   a surplus in a funded scheme, to the extent that this can be recovered through reduced contributions or through refunds from the scheme.

This will ensure that these items are recognised as liabilities or assets of the new group. The effect of any changes in pension or similar arrangements that take place after the acquisition should be reflected in the post-acquisition profit and loss account. For instance, this might include the costs of improving benefits in order to bring the arrangements for employees of the acquired entity into line with those for employees elsewhere in the group. FRS 17 'Retirement Benefits' also notes that:

(i)   an increase in the recoverable amount of a surplus as a result of an increase in the active membership of the scheme due to the acquisition of another business should be accounted for as a post-acquisition operating gain and not as an adjustment to the purchase consideration and related goodwill;

(ii)   the method of arriving at the fair value of a deficit or surplus may be different under FRS 17 from that previously used on acquisition, but any such difference should be treated as a change in assumptions (i.e. an actuarial gain or loss), and goodwill arising on the acquisition should therefore not be restated.

Deferred taxation

49.31   Adjustments to the fair values of assets and liabilities are accounted for in the same way as they would be if they were timing differences arising in the entity's own accounts. For instance, where a building has been valued at market value, the tax payable on the sale of the building at that value should be provided for only if, before the acquisition, the entity had entered into a binding agreement to sell the asset and the resultant gain could not be rolled over. Where the acquisition results in previously unrecognised deferred tax assets (e.g. unrelieved tax losses) becoming recoverable, the assets should be recognised in the accounts as follows:

(i)   deferred tax assets of the acquired entity should be recognised in the fair value exercise on the basis that they are contingent assets that have crystallised as a result of the acquisition;

(ii)   deferred tax assets of the acquirer or other entities within the acquiring group should be recognised as a credit to the tax charge in the post-acquisition period – they are not assets of the acquired entity and should therefore not be recognised as part of the fair value exercise.

Business sold or held exclusively with a view to resale

49.32   Where the acquired entity includes a subsidiary or separate business operation that is sold, or expected to be sold, as a single unit within approximately one year of the acquisition, the investment in that part of the business should be accounted for as a single asset. A fair value should therefore be attributed to the unit as a whole rather than to its individual assets and liabilities. The assets, liabilities, results and activities of the unit should be clearly distinguishable (physically, operationally and for financial reporting purposes) from the rest of the entity. In practice, the net realised value of the unit will usually provide the best indication of its fair value at the date of acquisition. If the unit is not sold before the first accounts following the acquisition are approved, its fair value should be based on the estimated net sales proceeds, provided that:

(i)   a purchaser has been identified or is being sought; and

(ii)   the disposal is reasonably expected to take place within approximately one year of the acquisition.

The estimate should be adjusted to reflect the actual sales proceeds once these are known. The fair value of the unit should be included as a separate item within current assets.

If the unit is not sold within one year, it should be consolidated under the normal rules, with fair values attributed to the individual assets and liabilities as at the date of acquisition. An appropriate adjustment should be made to goodwill where necessary.

Adjustments in subsequent years

49.33   The preference is for fair values to be established for inclusion in the first group accounts following the acquisition (i.e. the accounts for the year in which the acquisition takes place). However, FRS 7 recognises that this may not always be practicable and therefore permits the use of estimated values where necessary in the first accounts. These estimates should be adjusted to actual fair values in the accounts for the first full financial year after the acquisition, with a corresponding adjustment to goodwill. For instance, this may allow more accurate fair values to be established in the case of contingent assets and liabilities. If further adjustments prove necessary in subsequent years, they should be reflected in the profit and loss account of the year in which they are identified. In other words, goodwill should not be adjusted after the first full financial year after acquisition. However, where the later adjustments relate to the correction of fundamental errors, they should be accounted for as prior period adjustments in accordance with FRS 3 'Reporting Financial Performance'.

Acquisition of a Lloyd's Business

49.34   UITF Abstract 22 'The Acquisition of a Lloyd's Business' considers the recognition of assets and liabilities under the requirements of FRS 7 'Fair Values in Acquisition Accounting' when a business such as a Lloyd's managing agent is acquired. The principal issue is whether profit commissions receivable in respect of years that are not yet closed should be included as assets. The consensus is that the identifiable assets and liabilities to be recognised on acquisition should include all profit commissions receivable in respect of periods before the acquisition, even if those periods are not yet closed. Such profit commissions should be recognised at their fair value, based on the best estimate of the likely outcome. The Abstract also concludes that the acquisition of other businesses with analogous circumstances should be accounted for in the same way. Provisional valuations should be amended where necessary in the next financial statements, with a corresponding adjustment to goodwill (see 49.33 above).

Potential future changes

49.35   The ASB published FRED 32 'Disposal of non-current assets and presentation of discontinued operations' in July 2003 as part of its project to achieve convergence between UK and international accounting standards. The Exposure Draft proposes a new classification of assets held for sale (which applies to individual non-current assets and also to a disposal group) and requires separate disclosure on the balance sheet of non-current assets and, in the case of disposal groups, liabilities held for sale. If implemented, the proposals in FRED 32 will require newly acquired assets that meet the criteria for assets held for sale (e.g. surplus assets acquired as part of a business combination) to be recognised at fair value less disposal costs rather than at fair value as required under current UK accounting practice. The ASB has indicated that a new UK accounting standard based on FRED 32 could be introduced for accounting periods beginning on or after 1 January 2007.

FAIR VALUE OF ACQUISITION COSTS

Cost of acquisition

49.36　　The cost of acquisition is defined in FRS 7 'Fair Values in Acquisition Accounting' as:

(i)　　the amount of cash paid;

(ii)　　the fair value of any other purchase consideration; and

(iii)　　the expenses of the acquisition.

The expenses of the acquisition are defined as fees and similar costs incurred directly in making the acquisition, other than the issue costs of shares, which are required by FRS 4 'Capital Instruments' (or, for accounting periods beginning on or after 1 January 2005, FRS 25 'Financial Instruments: Disclosure and Presentation') to be accounted for as a reduction of the proceeds of the share issue.

Purchase consideration

49.37　　The purchase consideration in respect of the acquisition may comprise one of, or a mixture of, the following:

(i)　　cash;

(ii)　　other monetary items (e.g. the assumption of liabilities by the acquirer);

(iii)　　capital instruments issued by the acquirer; and

(iv)　　non-monetary assets (e.g. shares in other entities).

The fair value of each component of the consideration must be established separately and these values totalled to determine the fair value of the purchase consideration as a whole.

Cash and other monetary items

49.38　　The fair value of cash and other monetary items will usually be the actual amount paid or received in respect of the item in question. If the settlement of cash consideration is deferred, the fair value should be obtained by discounting the expected payments to their present value. The discount rate will be the rate at which the acquirer could obtain similar borrowings, taking into account factors such as the credit standing of the acquirer and any security given.

Capital instruments and non-monetary items

49.39   The fair value of unquoted shares and other capital instruments issued by the acquirer will need to be estimated, taking into account:

(i)   the value of any similar quoted securities;

(ii)   the present value of the future cash flows of the instrument;

(iii)   any cash alternative;

(iv)   the value of any underlying security into which there is an option to convert.

Different considerations apply in the case of quoted shares and capital instruments. Market price will usually provide the most reliable measure of fair value in this case.

The fair value of any non-monetary items included in the purchase consideration should be determined on the basis of market price, an independent valuation, estimated realisable value or other similar evidence.

Contingent consideration

49.40   The acquisition agreement may provide for some of the consideration to be paid at a future date, and to depend on factors such as the performance of the acquired entity over a specified period of time. In these circumstances, the cost of the acquisition should include a reasonable estimate of the amounts expected to be paid. The estimates should then be revised as more information becomes available over time.

Contingent consideration in the form of shares

49.41   Where contingent consideration is payable in the form of shares, there is no obligation on the acquirer to transfer economic benefits and it would therefore be inappropriate to recognise a liability. For accounting periods beginning before 1 January 2005, the amount recognised in respect of this element of the consideration should be included as a separate caption within shareholders' funds (for instance 'Shares to be issued'), representing shares to be issued at a future date and will need to be analysed into equity and non-equity interests in line with the requirements of FRS 4 'Capital Instruments'. When the shares are eventually issued, the amount already recognised will be transferred to called up share capital and the share premium account as appropriate. For accounting periods beginning on or after 1 January 2005, FRS 4 is generally superseded by FRS 25 'Financial Instruments: Disclosure and Presentation' and the requirements of this standard on the recognition of equity and financial liabilities will need to be taken into account in future (see Chapter 26). The guidance in FRS 7 is updated to require the amount attributed to any contingent consideration that is to be satisfied by the issue of shares to be allocated between equity and financial liabilities in accordance with FRS 25.

Contingent consideration in the form of either cash or shares

49.42 Where the acquirer has the option of issuing shares or paying cash in respect of the contingent consideration, there is once again no obligation to transfer economic benefits and the contingent consideration should therefore be accounted for on the basis that it will be paid in the form of shares until the final decision is made. In this case it may be more appropriate to use the caption 'Potential shares to be issued'. If it is decided to make the payment in cash rather than shares, the amount originally recognised within shareholders' funds will be transferred to creditors until payment is actually made. If the shares are issued the transfers will be to called up share capital and the share premium account as appropriate.

Vendor option to require payment in either cash or shares

49.43 However, where the vendor is able to require payment of the contingent consideration in either cash or shares, the acquirer does have an obligation to transfer economic benefits and the contingent consideration should therefore be recognised as a liability until the cash is paid or shares are issued.

Acquisition expenses

49.44 Direct expenses relating to the acquisition should be treated as part of the acquisition cost. These will normally comprise professional fees paid to merchant banks, accountants, legal advisers, valuers and other consultants. The costs should not include any allocation of internal costs or other expenses (for instance, management remuneration) that would have been incurred irrespective of whether the acquisition took place or not. For accounting periods beginning before 1 January 2005, costs that meet the definition of issue costs under FRS 4 'Capital Instruments' should also be excluded from acquisition costs, as FRS 4 requires issue costs to be accounted for as a deduction from the proceeds of the issue. For accounting periods beginning on or after 1 January 2005, a similar treatment is required by FRS 25 'Financial Instruments: Disclosure and Presentation'. In 1999, the UITF was asked to consider whether costs such as arrangement fees for bridging finance facilities, participation fees and the costs of researching alternative financing arrangements for a takeover could properly be treated as acquisition costs. In its information Sheet No 35, issued in February 2000, the UITF emphasises that such costs do not meet the FRS 4 definition of issue costs and are not incremental costs incurred directly in making the acquisition. They should therefore be written off immediately and should not be included as part of the cost of the acquisition.

PIECEMEAL ACQUISITIONS AND DISPOSALS

Accounting for an acquisition in stages

49.45 The investment in a subsidiary undertaking may not be acquired in a single transaction. Shares may be acquired in stages, until the level of the group's interest and, where appropriate, its ability to control or influence the entity, results in the entity meeting the definition of a subsidiary undertaking under CA 1985 and FRS 2 'Accounting for Subsidiary Undertakings'.

Both the Act and FRS 2 require the assets and liabilities of the entity to be brought into the consolidation at their fair values on the date that the entity becomes a subsidiary undertaking. This means that any changes in the net asset value of the subsidiary between the date when the group first acquired an interest in it and the date it actually becomes a subsidiary are included in the calculation of goodwill. This represents a practical approach and avoids the need for a complex assessment of fair values at a variety of dates. However, where this approach would not give a true and fair view, the standard requires a different treatment.

Associate that becomes a subsidiary

49.46 Where the group has an investment in an associate which has been accounted for under the equity method of accounting in accordance with FRS 9 'Associates and Joint Ventures', the group's share of the post-acquisition reserves of the associate will have been recognised in the group accounts. If the group increases its interest in the associate so that it becomes a subsidiary, the accounting treatment normally required by CA 1985 and FRS 2 for piecemeal acquisitions would result in those post-acquisition reserves being reclassified as goodwill (which in most cases would be negative goodwill). In this case, therefore, FRS 2 requires the goodwill on each element of the acquisition to be calculated separately, by comparing the fair value of the acquisition cost with the fair value of the underlying assets and liabilities at each acquisition date. This approach requires the use of the true and fair override under CA 1985, and the specific disclosures required by section 227A(6) of CA 1985 and by FRS 18 'Accounting Policies' will need to be given. These are considered in more detail in Chapter 3. In this case the disclosures will include the difference between goodwill calculated as explained above, and goodwill calculated under the treatment normally required by the Act.

Previous investment written down

49.47 A similar situation arises where a group has written down an investment (for instance, to reflect an impairment in value) and the investment subsequently becomes a subsidiary undertaking. If the treatment normally required was adopted in this case, the write-down would in effect be reversed and replaced by goodwill. FRS 2 therefore requires the approach described in 49.46 above to be adopted in this case as well. Once again, the true and fair override disclosures will be required.

Increasing the interest in an existing subsidiary

49.48 If a group increases its interest in an entity that is already a subsidiary undertaking, the assets and liabilities of the subsidiary must be revalued to fair values at the date on which the interest is increased, so that the goodwill relating to the increased investment can be based on those values. However, if there is no material difference between fair values and the values currently included in the consolidation in respect of the subsidiary, this adjustment need not be made.

FRRP case on acquisition of minority interest

49.49 In February 2002, the Financial Reporting Review Panel (FRRP) published its findings following a review of the report and accounts of Liberty International PLC for the period ended 31 December 2000. The single matter at issue was the company's accounting treatment of its acquisition, in November 2000, of the minority interest of shares in a 75% owned subsidiary, Capital Shopping Centres PLC (CSC), a property company specialising in the ownership, management and development of prime regional shopping centres. The Panel accepted the accounting treatment adopted by the company but only on the basis that there were 'special circumstances' attaching to the acquisition which justified the use of the true and fair override under the CA 1985. The directors made certain restatements of the comparative figures in the accounts for the year ended 31 December 2001 and gave the following additional disclosures in response to the Panel's view:

(i) presented a revised fair value table, in which property assets were brought in at a fair value, which was £193.2 million higher than previously reported;

(ii) as a consequence, recognised negative goodwill of £193.2 million which did not arise in the figures previously reported, and then credited it to reserves; and

(iii) restated certain notes to the accounts to include the disclosures required when the true and fair override is invoked.

The restatement involved no change to the profit and loss account, the balance sheet (other than the reclassification of group reserves), distributable profits, earnings or net assets per share, or cash flows.

Acquisition and accounting treatment

49.50 The acquisition was a share for share exchange, with a small cash inducement designed to bring the market value of the consideration to a modest premium over the market value of each CSC share acquired. Paragraph 51 of FRS 2 'Accounting for Subsidiary Undertakings' specifies the treatment that is to be adopted where a group increases its interest in an undertaking that is already its subsidiary undertaking. The identifiable assets and liabilities of the subsidiary undertaking should be revalued to fair value and goodwill arising on the increase in interest should be calculated by reference to those fair values and accounted for in accordance with FRS 10 'Goodwill and Intangible Assets'.

The directors had a range of concerns about goodwill arising from the acquisition of a minority interest in a company that holds, manages and develops investment properties. They concluded that the 'negative consolidation difference' arose from a fundamental disparity between the basis of valuation adopted for the consideration and that for the net assets acquired. They considered that most of the difference represented potential capital gains tax and purchaser's costs of property acquisition, both of which were considered to be reflected in the acquired company's discounted share price. However, neither liability could be recognised as part of the fair value process and, consistent with UK GAAP, the company did not have a policy of recognising purchaser's costs or contingent capital gains tax on assets that were not due for sale. In the circumstances, the directors considered it more appropriate to treat the fair value of net assets acquired as equating to the fair value of the consideration.

A note to the 2000 accounts gave details of the transaction and included a fair value table as required by FRS 6 and Schedule 4A to CA 1985. The note showed a fair value for net assets at the date of acquisition of £395.6 million, after a net credit adjustment of £197.3 million, £193.2 million of which was taken against investment properties. The net fair value of £395.6 million was the same amount as the fair value of the shares and cash given as consideration for the minority interest. Hence, no goodwill, either positive or negative, was deemed to have arisen from the transaction.

FRRP enquiries and consensus

49.51   The FRRP queried the substance of the £193.2 million 'fair value' credit adjustment against the investment properties. At 31 December 2000, the value of the investment properties was brought back up to market value through the usual annual revaluation process, required by SSAP 19, which included a reversal of the £193.2 million downwards adjustment. Had the fair value table retained the carrying value of the properties as the fair value of the net assets acquired, negative goodwill of £193.2 million would have arisen which, under FRS 10, would have been classified as a negative amount under purchased goodwill in the balance sheet. This negative goodwill, up to the value of the non-monetary assets acquired, would fall to be recognised in the profit and loss account in the periods in which the non-monetary assets were recovered through depreciation or sale. In the meantime, it would reduce the net assets of the group for accounting purposes.

The Panel considered that paragraph 51 of FRS 2 should be applied to the transaction. However, it agreed that to account for the goodwill in accordance with paragraph 49 of FRS 10 would not be compliant with the requirement to give a true and fair view. Having considered the issue very carefully, the Panel came to the view that, in accordance with CA 1985, the directors should override the requirements of FRS 10 with respect to the negative goodwill arising from this transaction for the following reasons:

(i)   as investment properties are exempt from the need to depreciate under FRS 15, the company was not able to recover the property values through depreciation, as envisaged by FRS 10;

(ii) the property assets of CSC, being shopping centres, were not easily replaceable – the directors had no intention of selling them, either in the long or short term and CSC was therefore not likely to recover the property values through disposal, the alternative method envisaged by the standard;

(iii) the balance described as negative goodwill reflected a fundamental difference in the valuation bases of the consideration and the identifiable net assets acquired, including the fact that certain contingent liabilities were reflected in the share price but could not be recognised in the fair value process – it was not appropriate to carry this balance on the balance sheet indefinitely; and

(iv) the net assets of CSC before the acquisition represented some 90% of the net assets of the group and the effect of the acquisition ought not, economically, to result in an apparent reduction of group net assets, which would be the result of recognising negative goodwill in accordance with paragraph 49 of FRS 10 – there was a slight change in the relative proportional interests of the shareholders of CSC in the group assets before and after the transaction but, in substance, the acquisition was similar to that of a group reorganisation because the interest of the former minority in the group net assets was not substantially altered by the transfer, and the same overall body of shareholders continued both before and after the transaction (this argument was dependent on the transaction being a share deal rather than a purchase for cash or cash equivalent).

The Panel therefore accepted that a true and fair view would be shown in the circumstances of this acquisition if the negative goodwill arising on consolidation were transferred to reserves.

Reducing the interest in an existing subsidiary

49.52   If a group reduces its interest in a subsidiary undertaking, the entity may cease to be a subsidiary or it may still meet the definition of a subsidiary despite the reduction in the interest held by the group. The profit or loss on the disposal of the interest must always be reported in the group accounts, even where the entity continues to be a subsidiary. The situation where a subsidiary undertaking becomes an associate is considered in Chapter 46.

EXCHANGE TRANSACTIONS

Exchange of business for equity

49.53   It is becoming increasingly common for entities to exchange an existing business for equity in another business – for instance, this might happen where two separate entities form a joint venture that combines part of their existing businesses. In other words, each entity sells part of its existing business for a share in the new joint venture formed by the combining businesses. In October 2001, the UITF issued Abstract 31 'Exchanges of businesses or other non-monetary assets for an interest in a subsidiary, joint venture or associate' which sets out guidance on how such exchanges should be accounted for and considered in particular:

(i)   whether such transactions should be accounted for at fair value at the date of the transaction or at previous book values; and

(ii)   how any gains or loss arising on the transaction should be accounted for.

Analysis of the transaction

49.54   The UITF has concluded that such transactions should be analysed in terms of net changes in ownership interests. Any part of the original business that the entity still owns, either directly or indirectly through its new shareholding, is treated as being owned throughout the transaction and should therefore remain at book value, but the share of net assets that the entity acquires through the new shareholding should be accounted for at fair value. Goodwill is recognised in respect of the newly acquired interest and a gain or loss is recognised in respect of the part of the original business that the reporting entity no longer owns, either directly or indirectly. The consideration for the new interest will include the part of the business or non-monetary assets that the entity no longer owns – in some cases, the consideration may also include cash or monetary assets. The Abstract notes that where it is difficult to value the consideration given, the best estimate may be arrived at by valuing what has been acquired.

Element of the business owned throughout

49.55   To the extent that an entity retains an interest in the business or non-monetary assets forming part of the exchange, the retained interest and any related goodwill should be included in the accounts at their pre-transaction carrying amount. This approach also applies when the interest is held indirectly after the transaction – for instance, through a subsidiary, joint venture or associate.

Share of net assets acquired

49.56   The entity's share of net assets acquired as a result of the new interest that it holds after the transaction should be accounted for at fair value as at the date of the transaction, and any difference between the fair value of the net assets acquired and the fair value of the consideration given should be accounted for as goodwill.

Recognition of gain or loss on disposal

49.57   The fair value of the consideration received by the entity should be compared with the total of:

(i) the book value of the business or non-monetary assets that it has relinquished in the transaction (including any related goodwill); and

(ii) any cash given up.

Where the fair value of the consideration received exceeds this total, the entity should recognise a gain on disposal. Any gain that is unrealised should be included in the statement of total recognised gains and losses. Where the fair value of the consideration received by the entity is less than this total, the entity should recognise a loss. Where a loss arises, all relevant assets should be reviewed for impairment and any impairment identified should be accounted for in accordance with FRS 11 'Impairment of Fixed Assets and Goodwill'. Any remaining loss should be recognised in the profit and loss account. Where an impairment is identified, it will usually be necessary to review any similar assets for impairment.

Artificial transactions

49.58 No gain or loss should be recognised if the transaction is artificial or has no substance – for instance, where an exchange purports to give rise to a recognisable gain but the assets exchanged would be unlikely otherwise to be saleable. This situation is expected to be rare in practice – where it does arise, the circumstances should be explained in the notes to the accounts.

ACQUISITIONS AND DISPOSALS IN A CASH FLOW STATEMENT

Amounts included in the cash flow statement on acquisition

49.59 When a group acquires a subsidiary undertaking, the only amount to be included in the cash flow statement will be the amount of cash paid as consideration and the amount of any cash or overdrafts transferred (i.e. within the net assets of the new subsidiary). The revised FRS 1 requires any cash or overdrafts transferred to be shown separately within the heading 'Acquisitions and disposals' in the cash flow statement.

Share issues

49.60 If shares are issued for cash and the cash is then used to acquire the subsidiary, the cash flow statement should reflect the cash received in respect of the share issue and the cash paid in respect of the acquisition. However, where the purchase consideration is settled by the issue of shares, no entry will appear in the cash flow statement, other than the effect of any cash or overdrafts acquired as part of the net assets of the subsidiary. The share issue will, however, be shown in the note to the cash flow statement showing the effect of the acquisition.

Example 49.1 – Cash flow effect of acquisitions

In 20X3 A Ltd acquired:

(i) 100% of the share capital of B Ltd for £50,000 paid in cash. B Ltd's net assets at the date of acquisition included cash of £5,000.

(ii) 100% of the share capital of C Ltd for £40,000 which was settled by the issue of 4,000 ordinary shares in A Ltd. C Ltd's net assets at the date of acquisition included a bank overdraft of £13,000.

In addition A Ltd issued a further 2,000 ordinary shares for £20,000.

The group cash flow for 20X3 will show:

Under Acquisitions and disposals:	
Purchase of subsidiary undertaking	(50,000)
Net overdrafts acquired with subsidiary undertakings	(8,000)*
Under Financing:	
Issue of shares	20,000
* Made up as follows:	
Overdraft of C Ltd	(13,000)
Cash of B Ltd	5,000

The 4,000 shares issued in respect of the acquisition of C Ltd do not have any cash flow effect. Therefore, neither the share issue nor the purchase of C Ltd appears in the cash flow statement.

Amounts included in the cash flow statement in respect of disposals

49.61   The entries in the cash flow statement in the case of a disposal are similar to those included in the case of an acquisition. The cash flow statement will therefore include any cash received as part of the consideration and any cash or overdrafts transferred (i.e. as part of the net assets of the subsidiary). If the consideration is settled in the form of shares, only the amount of cash or overdrafts transferred as part of the net assets of the subsidiary will appear in the cash flow statement.

Cash flows of subsidiary undertakings acquired and disposed of

49.62   Where a subsidiary joins or leaves the group during the year, the group cash flow statement should include the following cash flows of the subsidiary:

(i)   in the case of a subsidiary that has joined the group, from the date of acquisition;

(ii)   in the case of a subsidiary that has left the group, up to the date on which it ceased to be a subsidiary.

The profits or losses and cash flows of the subsidiary are therefore recorded in the group profit and loss account and the group cash flow statement on a consistent basis.

Material effect on standard heading in cash flow statement

49.63   Where the amounts reported under the standard headings in the cash flow statement are materially affected by the cash flows of a subsidiary that has been acquired or disposed of, the effect should be disclosed in a note to the cash flow statement, as far as is practicable. The analysis of changes in net debt should also show separately any material changes resulting from the acquisition or disposal of subsidiary undertakings.

Example 49.2 – Note when acquisition/disposal has material effect on the cash flow statement

The subsidiary undertakings acquired during the year contributed £350,000 to the group's net operating cash flows, paid £104,000 in respect of net returns on investments and servicing of finance and £125,000 in respect of taxation, and utilised £121,000 for investing activities.

Disclosure is only required in the period during which the acquisition or disposal takes place.

Effects of acquisition or disposal

49.64   FRS 1 'Cash Flow Statements' requires the effect of acquisitions and disposals to be shown in a note to the cash flow statement.

Example 49.3 – Note on effect of acquisitions

Using the details from Example 49.1, the fair values of the net assets of B Ltd and C Ltd at the date of acquisition were as follows.

	B Ltd	C Ltd	Total
	'000	'000	'000
Tangible fixed assets	55	48	103
Stocks	35	59	94
Debtors	46	53	99
Cash at bank	5	–	5
Bank overdraft	–	(13)	(13)
Finance leases	(30)	(40)	(70)
Creditors	(42)	(75)	(117)
Deferred tax	(32)		(32)
	37	32	69
Cost:			
Cash	50	–	50
Shares	–	40	40
Goodwill	13	8	21

The note to the group cash flow statement in 20X3 will therefore show the following.

Acquisition of subsidiary undertakings

Net assets acquired:	'000
Tangible fixed assets	103
Stocks	94
Debtors	99
Cash at bank	5
Bank overdraft	(13)
Finance leases	(70)
Creditors	(117)
Deferred tax	(32)
	69
Goodwill	21
	90
Satisfied by:	
Cash	50
Shares issued	40
	90

Details of any disposals during the year should be set out in a similar note.

Example 49.4 – Note on the effect of a disposal

Sale of subsidiary undertakings

Net assets disposed of:	'000
Fixed assets	63
Stocks	98
Debtors	40
Bank overdraft	(30)
Creditors	(105)
	66
Profit on disposal	14
	80
Satisfied by:	
Cash	80

MERGER TRANSACTIONS

Criteria for a merger

49.65   FRS 6 'Acquisitions and Mergers' sets out five criteria, all of which must be met for an acquisition to be classified as a merger:

(i)   no party to the combination is portrayed as either acquirer or acquired;

(ii)   all parties to the combination participate in:

- establishing the management structure of the combined entity, and

- selecting the management personnel,

and such decisions are based on a consensus between the parties rather than the exercise of voting rights;

(iii)   the relative sizes of the combining entities are not so disparate that one party dominates the combined entity by virtue of its relative size;

(iv)   under the terms of the combination:

- the consideration received by the equity shareholders of each party to the combination, in relation to their equity holding, comprises primarily equity shares in the combined entity, and

- any non-equity consideration, or equity shares with substantially reduced voting or distribution rights, represents an immaterial proportion of the fair value of the consideration received by the equity shareholders of that party.

(acquisitions of equity shares by one entity in another of the combining entities within the two years before the combination must also be taken into account); and

(v)   no equity shareholders of the combining entities retain any material interest in the future performance of only part of the combined entity.

Each of these conditions is examined in more detail below. The standard also requires any convertible share or loan stock to be treated as equity if it is converted into equity as a result of the business combination. .

The objective of the standard is that merger accounting should only be used for business combinations that genuinely represent an equal partnership between two or more entities. The criteria are therefore stringent, and few business combinations are likely to meet them in practice. Where a business combination does meet the criteria, merger accounting must be used (i.e. merger accounting is a requirement, not an option, in these circumstances). The specific requirements set out in CA 1985 in respect of a merger must also be met (see 49.– above). Special arrangements apply in the case of group reconstructions.

Portrayal of business combination

49.66   No party to the business combination must be portrayed as being the dominant party or being dominated by another party to the combination. This will depend on the actual circumstances of each case, but the following factors may need to be taken into account:

(i)   the form of the combination;

(ii)   the future plans for the combined entity, including any proposals for closures or disposals, and which party these relate to;

(iii)   the proposed corporate image of the combined entity (for instance, its name and logo, and the location of its headquarters).

Management structure

49.67   All parties to the combination must be involved in establishing the management structure of the combined entity and must reach a genuine consensus on the appointment of individuals to the agreed management posts. This does not prevent the new management team coming primarily from one of the entities, provided that there is genuine agreement between the parties on the appointments. It is important to consider who will actually be involved in the key decisions on operating and financial policy and how the decision-making process will work in practice.

Relative size of the parties

49.68   Where one party to the combination is substantially larger than any other party, it must be assumed that the larger party can and will dominate the combined entity. In such circumstances, the combination cannot be classified as a merger. A party should be presumed to dominate if it is more than 50% larger than each of the other parties to the combination in terms of ownership interest (i.e. in terms of the proportion of the equity of the combined entity that is attributable to the shareholders of each combining party), unless it can be clearly demonstrated that this is not the case. For instance, voting or share agreements may mean that a large party to the combination does not in fact have the degree of influence indicated by its size. Where relevant, the accounts should explain why the presumption has been rebutted.

Non-equity consideration

49.69   This criterion considers the extent to which equity shareholders of the combining parties receive consideration in a form other than equity of the combined entity. Non-equity consideration includes items such as cash, preference shares, loan stock and other assets. The definition of equity shares in FRS 6 is narrower than that in CA 1985 and is consistent with the definition in FRS 4 'Capital Instruments' for accounting periods beginning before 1 January 2005, and with that in FRS 25 'Financial Instruments: Disclosure and Presentation' for accounting periods beginning on or after that date. All arrangements in conjunction with the combination must be taken into account, along with relevant share acquisitions in the previous two years, and the equity shareholders of the combining parties must receive no more than an immaterial proportion of the fair value of the consideration in a form other than equity. For instance, where the combination includes a specific arrangement for them to exchange or redeem the equity shares they receive, they will be deemed to have disposed of their original shares for cash and the combination will therefore not be a merger. However, a privately arranged sale should not cause problems in this respect. The issue of shares with substantially reduced rights will also usually prevent the combination from being classified as a merger.

Retention of partial interest only

49.70   The concept of a merger under FRS 6 is that there is genuine sharing of the risks and rewards relating to the new entity. Therefore, if the ability of one party to share in the risks or rewards of the combined entity is restricted or preferred in some way (for instance, by being dependent on the performance of only one section of the combined business), the combination cannot be regarded as a genuine merger.

Merger accounting

49.71   The principle of merger accounting is that the accounts of the combined entity are prepared as if the parties had always operated as a combined entity. The accounts of the combining parties are therefore aggregated (subject to adjustments to achieve consistent accounting policies) and, in particular, all the reserves of the combining parties are included as reserves in the accounts of the combined entity, regardless of whether they arose before or after the actual merger took place. The profit and loss account and cash flow statement of the group include the results and cash flows of the combined entities for the whole of the financial year and all comparative figures must be restated so that they are presented on the same basis as the figures for the current year.

Elimination of investment in subsidiary

49.72   As part of the acquisition, one company (the parent) will have acquired the shares of another entity (the subsidiary) and will have issued shares in exchange, possibly with a small element of other consideration as well. The parent's accounts will therefore show an investment in the subsidiary, which must be eliminated when the accounts are combined. The investment will usually be shown at the nominal value of the shares issued, plus the fair value of any other consideration, and this amount must be set against the share capital of the subsidiary when the accounts of the two entities are combined. The difference between the investment recorded in the accounts of the parent and the nominal value of the shares acquired should be shown as a movement on the consolidated reserves. However, it does not constitute goodwill and should not be recorded as such.

Share premium or capital redemption reserve of the subsidiary

49.73 As in the case of acquisition accounting, only the share capital of the parent is shown as share capital in the consolidated balance sheet of the combined entities. If the subsidiary's balance sheet includes a share premium account or capital redemption reserve, this must be transferred into the consolidated balance sheet as a movement on reserves, and will usually be disclosed as a capital reserve within 'other reserves'.

Merger relief

49.74 The provisions of CA 1985 in relating to merger relief operate completely independently of the provisions on merger accounting and the related requirements of FRS 6. It is therefore possible for a parent company to take advantage of the provisions on merger relief, but to account for the subsidiary acquired in the transaction using the acquisition method of accounting. Separate considerations apply in the case of group reconstructions, which are covered by section 132 of CA 1985.

Acquisition of 90% holding in another company

49.75 The provisions on merger relief are set out in section 131 of CA 1985. This section applies where a company (the acquiring company):

(i) has obtained a holding of at least 90% of the equity share capital of another company under an arrangement; and

(ii) the arrangement requires the acquiring company to allot equity shares; and

(iii) the consideration for the shares allotted by the acquiring company is:

- the issue or transfer of equity shares in the other company to the acquiring company, or

- the cancellation of any such shares not already held by the acquiring company.

Where these conditions are met, any premium on the shares issued by the acquiring company is not transferred to the share premium account, as would normally be required by section 130 of CA 1985. The definition of equity share capital under the Act is considered in Chapter 32. Merger relief continues to be available where the arrangement also provides for additional consideration in a different form (for instance, cash or other capital instruments) provided that the conditions are met. However, where the equity share capital of the other company is divided into different classes of shares, the 90% holding must be obtained for each class of those equity shares before the relief is available.

Any shares in the company being acquired that are held by the holding company, subsidiaries or fellow subsidiaries (as defined by section 736(1) of CA 1985 – see 45.3 above) of the acquiring company, or by any of their nominees, are to be treated as being held by the acquiring company.

Accounting treatment of premium where merger relief applies

49.76 There are two possible treatments in the accounts of the parent company where merger relief applies:

(i) the parent company can record only the nominal value of the shares issued – in this case, the investment in the subsidiary (or the relevant part of it) will also be recorded at this amount, plus the fair value of any additional consideration; or

(ii) the parent company can record the investment at fair value and record the related premium on the shares issued in a separate reserve, usually described as a 'merger reserve' – this should be shown within 'other reserves' on the balance sheet.)

If the investment is recorded at nominal value, and acquisition accounting is adopted for the group accounts, a consolidation adjustment will be required to create the merger reserve and the appropriate amount of goodwill in the group balance sheet when the net assets of the subsidiary are brought in at fair value at the date of acquisition. If the investment is recorded at fair value in the parent company's accounts, the normal consolidation process will suffice.

Acquisition of non-equity shares

49.77 If the same arrangement also provides for the acquiring company to issue shares (in this case either equity or non-equity), for which the consideration will be the issue, transfer or similar cancellation of non-equity shares in the other company, merger relief will also be available in respect of this share issue. It should be noted that the effect of sections 131(1) and 131 (3) of CA 1985 is that merger relief is not available in respect of any non-equity shares issued by the acquiring company in return for equity shares in the other company. The position can be summarised as follows:

Acquiring company issues	Other company issues, transfers or cancels	Merger relief available
Equity shares	Equity shares	Yes
AND		
(i) Equity shares	Non-equity shares	Yes
(ii) Non-equity shares	Non-equity shares	Yes
(iii) Non-equity shares	Equity shares	No

The extension of the relief to shares issued by the acquiring company in return for non-equity shares in the other company only applies if the merger conditions have already been met in respect of equity shares under the arrangement, as explained in 49.65 above.

Piecemeal acquisitions

49.78   Merger relief is only available in respect of the shares that are issued under the arrangement that brings the shareholding to or above the 90% threshold, but prior holdings should be taken into account in assessing whether the 90% threshold has been reached. Consequently, there is no requirement for the whole of the 90% holding to be achieved under a single arrangement for merger relief to be available. For instance, where the acquiring company and its subsidiaries already hold (say) 75% of the shares in the other undertaking, and the company acquires a further 15% under an appropriate arrangement, merger relief will be available, but only in respect of the shares that are issued by the company to acquire the final 15% shareholding.

APPENDIX

A – Disclosures in the case of a combination accounted for as an acquisition

In addition to the disclosures required in respect of all business combinations, FRS 6 requires the following specific details to be given when the combination is accounted for as an acquisition. The relevant information should be given:

(i) individually for each material acquisition; and

(ii) in aggregate for other acquisitions.

The detailed disclosures are as follows.

(i) The composition and fair value of the consideration given by the acquiring company and its subsidiary undertakings, including:

- the nature of any deferred consideration, and

- in the case of contingent consideration, the range of possible outcomes and principal factors that affect the outcome.

(ii) A table showing for each class of assets and liabilities of the acquired entity:

- the book values recorded in the entity's accounting records immediately prior to acquisition (i.e. before any fair value adjustments);

- the fair value adjustments, analysed into:

    - revaluations,

    - adjustments to achieve consistency of accounting policies,

    - any other significant adjustments (with reasons for the adjustment); and

- the fair values at the date of acquisition.

It should also include a statement of the goodwill arising on the acquisition.

(iii) Where liabilities in the above table include:

- provisions for reorganisation and restructuring costs, and

- any related asset write-downs

made by the acquired company in the twelve months up to the date of acquisition, these amounts should be identified separately.

(iv) Where the fair values of assets and liabilities, or the purchase consideration, can only be determined on a provisional basis at the end of the accounting period during which the acquisition took place, this fact should be stated and the reasons given – any subsequent material adjustment to the provisional figures, and the corresponding adjustment to goodwill, must be disclosed and explained.

(v) The post-acquisition results of the acquired entity should be disclosed in accordance with FRS 3 'Reporting Financial Performance'. Where the acquisition has a material impact on a business segment, this should be disclosed and explained. If it is not possible to determine the post-acquisition results of an operation to the end of the accounting period, an indication should be given of the contribution of the entity to the turnover and operating profit of continuing operations, or an explanation of why this is not possible.

(vi) Any exceptional profit or loss in the periods following the acquisition, determined using the fair values recognised on acquisition, should be disclosed in accordance with FRS 3 'Reporting Financial Performance' and identified as relating to the acquisition. For instance, this might include items such as:

- abnormal margins on the disposal of acquired stocks;

- the release of provisions in respect of long-term contracts that have become profitable;

- the realisation of contingent assets or liabilities at amounts that are materially different from the fair values attributed at the date of acquisition.

(vii) The profit or loss account, or note to the accounts, for the periods following the acquisition should show separately any costs incurred in that period relating to the reorganisation, restructuring and integration of the acquisition; these are:

- costs that would not have been incurred if the acquisition had not taken place, and

- costs that relate to a project identified and controlled by management as part of a reorganisation or integration programme set up at the time of acquisition or as a direct consequence of an immediate post-acquisition review.

(viii) Movements on provisions or accruals for costs related to an acquisition should be disclosed and analysed between:

- amounts used for the specific purpose for which they were created, and

- amounts released unused.

(ix) The cash flow statement should include the disclosures required by FRS 1 'Cash Flow Statements' in respect of acquisitions.

Material acquisitions

In the case of material acquisitions only, the profit after tax and minority interests of the acquired entity should be given for:

(i) the period from the beginning of the acquired entity's financial year to the date of acquisition, and the date on which this period began should be disclosed,

(ii)   the previous financial year.

Substantial acquisitions

Additional disclosures are required in respect of substantial acquisitions which are defined as combinations where:

(i)   the net assets or operating profit of the acquired entity exceed 15% of those of the acquiring entity; or

(ii)   the fair value of the consideration given exceeds 15% of the net assets of the acquiring company

and in any other exceptional cases where the acquisition is so significant that additional information is necessary for a true and fair view. Net assets and profits are defined as those shown in the accounts for the last financial year before the date of the acquisition, and net assets should be augmented by any purchased goodwill that has been eliminated against reserves as a matter of accounting policy and not charged through the profit and loss account.

Separate criteria apply in the case of listed companies under paragraph 37 of FRS 6 and UITF Abstract 15 'Disclosure of Substantial Acquisitions'.

The additional disclosures required in respect of substantial acquisitions are:

(i)   a summarised profit and loss account and statement of total recognised gains and losses for the acquired entity for the period from the beginning of its financial year (and this date should be disclosed) to the date of acquisition – as a minimum, the summarised profit and loss account should show:

- turnover,
- operating profit,
- exceptional items falling within FRS 3, paragraph 20,
- profit before taxation,
- taxation and minority interests,
- extraordinary items;

(ii)   the profit after taxation and minority interests for the acquired entity's previous financial year.

These details should be given on the basis of the accounting policies adopted by the acquired entity prior to the acquisition.

B – Disclosures in the case of a combination accounted for as a merger

In addition to the disclosures required in respect of all business combinations, FRS 6 requires the following specific details to be given when a combination is accounted for as a merger:

(i) an analysis of the principal components of the current year's profit and loss account and statement of total recognised gains and losses into:

- amounts relating to each combining party up to the date of the merger,

- amounts relating to the merged entity for the period after the date of the merger,

which, in the case of the profit and loss account, should show as a minimum the analysis of:

- turnover,

- operating profit,

- exceptional items,

- profit before taxation,

- taxation,

- minority interests,

- extraordinary items,

with the first three items analysed further into continuing, discontinued and acquired operations in accordance with FRS 3 'Reporting Financial Performance';

(ii) a similar analysis of the principal components of the previous year's profit and loss account and statement of total recognised gains and losses between the combining parties;

(iii) the composition and fair value of the consideration given by the issuer and its subsidiary undertakings;

(iv) the aggregate book value of the net assets of each combining party as at the date of the merger;

(v) the nature and amount of any significant accounting adjustments made to the assets of any combining party to achieve consistency of accounting policies;

(vi) an explanation of any other significant adjustments to the net assets of any combining party as a result of the merger;

(vii) a statement of the adjustments to consolidated reserves resulting from the merger.

However, where revaluation gains and losses have been recognised as a result of a revaluation of assets at the end of the accounting period, it is not necessary to obtain additional valuations as at the date of the merger simply to allow these gains and losses to be apportioned between the pre-merger and post-merger periods. Group reconstructions under FRS 6, paragraph 13 are exempt from the above disclosure requirements but should continue to give the disclosures required by the Act in respect of merger accounting.

Chapter 50   Accounting For Foreign Operations

BACKGROUND TO ACCOUNTING FOR FOREIGN OPERATIONS

Current UK accounting requirements

50.1 For many companies, the requirements of SSAP 20 'Foreign Currency Translation' currently apply to the translation of the accounts of:

(i) a foreign enterprise – this is defined in the standard as a subsidiary, associated company or branch whose operations are based in a country other than that of the investing company or whose assets and liabilities are denominated mainly in a foreign currency; and

(ii) a foreign branch – this is defined in the standard as either a legally constituted enterprise overseas or a group of assets and liabilities which are accounted for in foreign currencies .

A company is defined as 'any enterprise which comes within the scope of accounting standards'. Therefore, although the requirements of the standard are considered mainly in the context of a foreign subsidiary undertaking, the basic principles set out in the standard apply equally to the translation of the results and net assets of associates and other foreign entities. SSAP 20 also deals with the translation of business transactions in other currencies entered into by an individual company. This aspect of the standard is considered in Chapter 7.

In December 2004, the ASB published a package of new UK accounting standards (based on equivalent international accounting standards) that apply to listed companies for accounting periods beginning on or after 1 January 2005, and to other entities for accounting periods beginning on or after 1 January 2006 but only if they choose to adopt fair value accounting (see Chapter 1). The package of new standards comprises:

(i)   FRS 23 'The Effects of Changes in Foreign Prices';

(ii)   FRS 24 'Financial Reporting in Hyperinflationary Economies';

(iii)   the disclosure requirements of FRS 25 'Financial Instruments: Disclosure and Presentation' (note that the presentation requirements of this standard apply to all entities for accounting periods beginning on or after 1 January 2005); and

(iv)   FRS 26 'Financial Instruments: Measurement'.

The ASB has already issued proposals to extend the scope of FRS 26 and this will in turn widen the scope of FRS 23 and FRS 24 (see 26.61 above).

The new standards cannot be adopted early because many of their requirements hinge on company law changes that also come into effect on 1 January 2005. Unlisted entities who are required to adopt the package from 1 January 2006 can voluntarily apply the new standards from 1 January 2005 if they wish, provided that they apply all of the standards in the package – it is not acceptable to adopt some of the standards but not the others. For entities that are required to adopt the package, FRS 23 supersedes SSAP 20 and FRS 24 supersedes UITF Abstract 9 'Accounting for Operations in Hyperinflationary Economies'. Entities that have not adopted FRS 26 are not permitted to adopt FRS 23 or FRS 24 and so the requirements of SSAP 20 (and UITF Abstract 9, where relevant) remain in force in these cases.

The sections below deal primarily with the accounting issues that arise from SSAP 20, on the basis that most UK entities are likely to continue to apply this standard for the immediate future at least, but significant changes under new standards are also highlighted where relevant.

Requirement for translation

50.2   A group may carry out part of its operations through a foreign enterprise or a foreign branch, which maintains its accounting records in the local currency and therefore prepares its annual accounts in that currency. For group accounts purposes, the parent company will need to translate the accounts of the foreign enterprise into its own currency so that the details can be included in the consolidation. SSAP 20 defines translation as 'the process whereby financial data denominated in one currency are expressed in terms of another currency'. It emphasises that translation applies both to individual transactions (which are considered in Chapter 7) and also to a full set of accounts.

Local currency

50.3   Local currency is defined in SSAP 20 as 'the currency of the primary economic environment in which [the entity] operates and generates net cash flow'.

For UK accounting purposes, therefore, foreign currency translation usually refers to the conversion of amounts denominated in other currencies into sterling.

FRS 23 takes a different approach and includes separate definitions of foreign currency, functional currency and presentation currency. These definitions are considered in more detail at 7.6 above. The standard requires each entity to determine its functional currency and measure its results in that currency, but then allows the entity to report its results in any presentation currency that it chooses.

Relationship between the investor and the foreign entity

50.4   SSAP 20 requires the method of translation to reflect the nature of the financial and operational relationship that exists between the investing company and the foreign entity and distinguishes between two translation methods:

(i)   the closing rate/net investment method – which is the method that should be used in most cases;

(ii)   the temporal method – which should be used in certain specified circumstances.

The treatment to be adopted in the case of a foreign branch will depend on the structure of the business and the relationship between the branch and the investing company. If the branch effectively operates as a separate business unit, with its own local finance, it should be accounted for using the closing rate/net investment method. If the branch is in effect an extension of the investing company's own trade (i.e. the cash flows of the branch impact directly on the cash flows of the investing company) the foreign branch should be accounted for using the temporal method.

FRS 23 does not refer to the two translation methods identified in SSAP 20, but the requirement under the new standard for the reporting entity to identify and use its functional currency should mean that the effect of FRS 23 will be the same in situations where the SSAP 20 requires use of the temporal method.

Consistency of accounting

50.5   The general requirement for consistency of accounting applies in respect of the methods used to translate the accounts of foreign entities. Therefore:

(i)   once the decision has been taken on the appropriate translation method to use (i.e. the closing rate/net investment or temporal), this method should be adopted consistently year by year;

(ii)   once the decision has been taken on which exchange rate to use to translate the profit and loss account (i.e. closing rate or average rate), this should also be applied consistently from year to year.

However, if the financial and operational relationships between the investing company and the foreign entity change, it will usually be necessary to reassess whether the accounting treatment adopted is still appropriate and to change the translation method used where necessary. A company may also be able to justify changing from using the closing rate to using the average rate for translation of the profit and loss account on the basis that this gives a fairer presentation of the results of the foreign entity. It will usually be more difficult to justify changing from an average rate to the closing rate, especially in view of the prevalence of the use of average rates in practice. Such changes will constitute a change in accounting policy and the disclosures required by FRS 18 'Accounting Policies' will therefore need to be given in the accounts. These are explained in Chapter 6.

Translating cash flows

50.6   FRS 1 'Cash Flow Statements' requires the cash flows of a foreign entity to be translated for inclusion in the group cash flow statement using the same basis as is used to translate the results of the entity for inclusion in the consolidated profit and loss account. The same basis should also be used in presenting movements in stock, debtors and creditors in the reconciliation of operating profit to operating cash flow. If inter-group cash flows can be separately identified, the actual exchange rate (or an approximation to this) may be used to ensure that group cash flows cancel out on consolidation. If the actual rate is not used for inter-group cash flows, any exchange differences that arise should be included in the reconciliation of net cash flow to net debt. The main issues arising from foreign currency translation in the context of a cash flow statement are considered in Chapter 35.

USE OF THE TEMPORAL METHOD

When the temporal method should be applied

50.7   The temporal method should only be used where the foreign entity is in effect an extension of the trade of the investing company, with the result that the foreign entity is more dependent on the economic environment of the investing company's currency than on that of the local currency. This situation arises only rarely in the UK. Most foreign enterprises within UK groups operate as separate businesses and should therefore be accounted for under the closing rate/net investment method.

SSAP 20 emphasises that all of the available evidence should be taken into account when assessing whether the relationship between the investing company and the foreign operation justifies use of the temporal method. The following factors may be relevant:

(i)   the extent to which cash flows in the foreign entity have a direct impact on those of the investing company;

(ii)   the extent to which the operations of the foreign entity are directly dependent on the investing company;

(iii)   the currency in which most trading transactions are denominated;

(iv)   the main currency to which the foreign entity is exposed in its financing.

The standard includes the following examples of situations where the use of the temporal method may be appropriate:

(i)   where the foreign entity acts as a selling agent, receiving goods from the investing company and remitting the sales proceeds back to the company;

(ii)   where the foreign entity produces raw materials, or manufactures parts or sub-assemblies, which are then transferred to the investing company for use in its own production.

As noted at 50.4 above, FRS 23 no longer makes a specific distinction between translation methods, but the effect of the new standard should be the same in situations where SSAP 20 requires use of the temporal method.

Applying the temporal method

50.8   Where the temporal method is used, the transactions entered into by the foreign entity are reflected in the consolidated accounts as if they had been entered into directly by the investing company. The requirements of SSAP 20 on the translation of individual transactions and balances therefore apply. These requirements are considered in detail in Chapter 7. UITF Abstract 21 concludes that no special treatment is required under the temporal method on the introduction of the euro.

USE OF THE CLOSING RATE/NET INVESTMENT METHOD

When the closing rate/net investment method should be applied

50.9   More commonly, the investing company will have invested in the net worth of the foreign entity, rather than in its underlying assets and liabilities, and will retain this investment until the foreign entity is closed or sold. In this case, the foreign entity will need to draw up accounts in its local currency and these will be translated for inclusion in the consolidated accounts of the group. Depending on the nature of the relationship between the investing company and the foreign entity, inclusion in the group accounts may involve full consolidation of the results and net assets (e.g. in the case of a subsidiary undertaking) or may be by adopting the equity method of accounting (e.g. in the case of an associate). In either case, the initial step will be to translate the results and net assets of the foreign entity.

Translation of the balance sheet

50.10   Individual assets and liabilities shown in the balance sheet of the foreign entity should be translated using the rate of exchange at the balance sheet date (i.e. the closing rate). An exchange rate is defined in SSAP 20 as 'a rate at which two currencies may be exchanged for each other at a particular point in time'. The closing rate is defined as 'the exchange rate for spot transactions ruling at the balance sheet date'. The closing rate is also defined in more detail as the average of buying and selling rates at the close of business on the day for which the rate is to be ascertained. Therefore, if the balance sheet date is 31 March, the closing rate will be the average of the buying and selling rate at the close of business on 31 March. If there is no trading on the balance sheet date, the equivalent rate on the last previous trading day is usually used as the best approximation.

FRS 23 also requires the balance sheet to be translated at the closing rate, which it defines as the spot exchange rate at the balance sheet date.

Different accounting dates

50.11   Wherever possible, group entities should make up their accounts to the same accounting date as the parent company, although different accounting dates may be used in certain circumstances and under specific conditions. If a foreign subsidiary or associate makes up its accounts to a different accounting date, the closing rate will be the exchange rate at the end of the foreign entity's accounting period. However, if exchange rates move significantly between this date and the accounting date of the parent, additional disclosure, or even adjustment of the accounts, may be necessary under the requirements of SSAP 17 'Accounting for Post Balance Sheet Events', FRS 2 'Accounting for Subsidiary Undertakings' or FRS 9 'Associates and Joint Ventures' (or, for accounting periods beginning on or after 1 January 2005, FRS 21 'Events after the Balance Sheet Date').

The same approach is required under FRS 23.

Long-term financing

50.12   SSAP 20 notes that, in many cases, a company will invest in a foreign entity by purchasing shares in the entity. However, the standard recognises that investments may also be made by means of long-term loans or deferred inter-group trading balances. Where, for all practical purposes, such financing is intended to be as permanent as an equity investment, the loans and inter-company balances can be treated as part of the net investment in the foreign entity. The long-term nature of the financing will usually need to be formally evidenced in some way for this treatment to be acceptable.

FRS 23 also notes that a reporting entity may have a monetary item receivable from, or payable to, a foreign operation for which settlement is neither planned nor likely to occur in the foreseeable future and which is in substance part of the entity's net investment in the operation. It should therefore be be treated as part of the net investment rather than as a monetary item. However, trading balances between the entities should not be regarded as part of the net investment.

Translation of the profit and loss account

50.13   SSAP 20 allows two options for translation of the individual items shown in the profit and loss account. Translation may be at either:

(i)   the closing rate (i.e. the rate used for balance sheet purposes); or

(ii)   an average rate for the accounting period.

The majority of companies currently use an average rate for translation of the profit and loss account. Once a decision has been taken on which of the two rates to use, this rate should be used consistently year by year.

There is no definitive guidance on how to calculate the average rate for an accounting period. The most appropriate method of calculation will often depend on the nature of the entity's activities and the detailed accounting procedures and records maintained. In very straightforward cases, a simple average may suffice, but care needs to be taken to ensure that factors such as seasonal trading and any significant variations in the rate at certain points during the year are properly considered and accounted for. In most cases, some form of weighting will be necessary. As a minimum, the average will usually be calculated on a monthly basis (e.g. using the average of the rates ruling at the beginning (or end) of each month during the accounting period). In some cases, it may be necessary to take weekly or even daily rates, depending on the stability of the exchange rate during the accounting period and the regularity of the volume of transactions throughout the year.

FRS 23 requires income and expenses for each income statement to be translated at the exchange rate ruling at the date of the transaction, but for practical purposes allows the use of an average rate unless rates have fluctuated significantly over the period. Use of the closing rate to translate the profit and loss account is therefore no longer permitted under this standard.

Translation of the cash flow statement

50.14   FRS 1 'Cash Flow Statements' requires the cash flow statement of a foreign entity to be translated at the same rate as is used for the entity's profit and loss account. The cash flow statement should therefore be prepared initially in the local currency and then translated using either:

(i)   the closing rate; or

(ii)   the average rate, if this has been calculated and used to translate the profit and loss account.

As noted at 50.13 above, where FRS 23 has been adopted, the option of using the closing rate to translate the profit and loss account and cash flow statement will no longer be available.

Accounting for exchange differences

50.15   Two exchange differences will usually arise when the results of a foreign entity are translated for consolidation purposes:

(i)   the exchange difference arising from the use of different closing rates at the current balance sheet date and the previous balance sheet date; and

(ii)   if the profit and loss account is translated using the average rate, the difference between translation of the results at this rate for profit and loss account purposes and at the closing rate for balance sheet purposes – if the profit and loss account is translated at the closing rate, this difference will not arise.

Under SSAP 20, all exchange differences arising on the translation of foreign entities for consolidation purposes should be taken directly to reserves. The amount dealt with in reserves should be shown separately as part of the movement on reserves and will also appear in the statement of total recognised gains and losses. UITF Abstract 21 'Accounting Issues Arising from the Introduction of the Euro' considers the impact of the irrevocable locking of the national currencies of the participating Member States on cumulative translation differences recognised in accounting periods prior to the introduction of the euro. The Abstract emphasises that paragraph 56 of FRS 3 'Reporting financial performance' states clearly that the same gains and losses should not be recognised twice. As exchange differences arising on the translation of the financial statements of foreign entities in earlier years will have been reported in the statement of total recognised gains and losses for those years, the Abstract concludes that there is no question of reporting the cumulative differences in the profit and loss account when they become permanent on the introduction of the euro. They should therefore remain in reserves.

FRS 23 also requires all exchange differences arising on the translation of foreign operations to be recognised initially in the statement of total recognised gains and losses in the consolidated accounts. On disposal of the foreign operation, the cumulative amount of exchange differences recognised in respect of that entity should then be recognised in profit or loss. However, the standard also specifies that exchange differences arising on a monetary item that forms part of the entity's net investment in a foreign operation should be recognised in the profit and loss account in the separate accounts of the reporting entity or the foreign operation as follows:

(i)   if the item is denominated in the functional currency of the reporting entity, an exchange difference should be recognised in the profit and loss account of the foreign operation;

(ii) if the item is denominated in the functional currency of the foreign operation, an exchange difference should be recognised in the individual profit and loss account of the reporting entity.

On consolidation, such exchange differences should be recognised initially in the statement of total recognised gains and losses and then in the profit and loss account on the disposal of the net investment. However, where such a monetary item is denominated in a currency that is not the functional currency of either entity, any exchange differences that arise on translation into the functional currencies of these entities should not be recognised through the statement of total recognised gains and losses in the consolidated accounts but should remain recognised in the profit and loss account.

Goodwill

50.16 SSAP 20 makes no specific reference to goodwill, but FRS 23 requires any goodwill arising on the acquisition of a foreign operation and any fair value adjustments to the carrying amounts of assets and liabilities arising on that acquisition to be treated as assets and liabilities of the foreign operation. They should therefore be expressed in the functional currency of the foreign operation and translated at the closing rate in the same way as other assets and liabilities.

FOREIGN EQUITY INVESTMENTS

Financing arrangements for foreign equity investments

50.17 Where a group has taken out foreign currency borrowings to finance or hedge against a foreign equity investment, any increase or decrease in the liability in respect of the borrowings will usually be matched by a corresponding decrease or increase in the carrying value of the underlying net assets of the foreign entity. In certain circumstances, therefore, exchange gains or losses on foreign currency borrowings which would otherwise be charged to the group profit and loss account, may be off-set against the exchange differences that arise on retranslation of the net investment. However, if both the investment and the loan show a gain for the year, the gain on the loan must be credited in full to the profit and loss account. Similarly, if both show a loss for the year, the loss on the loan must be charged in full to the profit and loss account.

In cases where the gain or loss on retranslation of the borrowings is taxable (e.g. where a matching election is not made for tax purposes), UITF Abstract 19 requires any tax charges or credits that are directly and solely attributable to the exchange differences to be similarly taken to reserves and reported in the statement of total recognised gains and losses.

The approach to this situation under FRS 23 is summarised at 50.15 above.

Conditions

50.18   Under SSAP 20, the following conditions must be met for this treatment to be adopted:

(i)   the relationship between the investing company and the foreign entity must justify the use of the closing rate/net investment method;

(ii)   in any accounting period, exchange gains and losses arising on the borrowings may only be off-set to the extent of the exchange gains and losses arising on the net investment in foreign entities (i.e. any gain or loss on borrowings that is in excess of the corresponding loss or gain on the net investment will have to be charged or credited to the profit and loss account);

(iii)   the foreign currency borrowings in respect of which gains and losses are off-set should not exceed, in aggregate, the total amount of cash that the net investments are expected to be able to generate, from profits or otherwise;

(iv)   if a company chooses to adopt this treatment, it must be applied consistently from year to year; where relevant, this would include the year in which the investment is sold.

There is no specific requirement for the investment and the borrowings to be in the same currency, or for the investment and borrowings to be held by the same entity within the group. Under UITF Abstract 19, the restriction in (ii) above must be applied after taking into account any tax charges or credits that are directly and solely attributable to the borrowings, and the comparison in (iii) above should also be considered in after-tax terms.

Disclosure of adoption

50.19   The fact that this treatment has been adopted should be disclosed in the accounting policy on foreign currency translation. UITF Abstract 19 specifically requires disclosure of the amount of tax charges or credits taken directly to reserves and reported in the statement of total recognised gains and losses, in addition to the gross amount of the exchange differences.

Other parent company investments

50.20   Under SSAP 20, a similar treatment may be adopted by an individual company in respect of equity investments. This is explained in Chapter 7. Where a parent company has adopted this treatment in its own accounts, and the equity investment does not qualify as either a subsidiary undertaking or an associate, the off-set treatment may be adopted in the consolidated accounts as well as in the parent's own accounts.

ACCOUNTS DISCLOSURES

Detailed disclosures

50.21   SSAP 20 requires the following information to be given in the notes to the accounts:

(i)   the methods used for translating the financial statements of foreign enterprises;

(ii)   the treatment adopted for exchange differences arising on the translation of those accounts;

(iii)   the net amount of exchange gains and losses on foreign currency borrowings less foreign currency deposits, showing separately:

- the amount off-set in reserves (i.e. as explained at 50.16 above), with separate disclosure of any tax charges or credits; and

- the amount credited or charged to the profit and loss account;

(iv)   the net movement on reserves relating to exchange differences.

Compliance with the disclosure requirements of SSAP 20 will usually satisfy the disclosure requirement in respect of foreign currency translation in CA 1985.

Where relevant, the disclosures will also need to cover the methods used to translate foreign currency transactions (e.g. between a UK group entity and an unrelated foreign entity) and to account for any resulting exchange differences. These disclosures are considered in Chapter 7.

FRS 23 requires disclosure of:

(i)   the amount of exchange differences recognised in the profit and loss account;

(ii)   the net exchange differences recognised in the statement of total recognised gains and losses, together with a reconciliation of such amounts at the beginning and end of the period; and

(iii)   where there is a change in the functional currency of the reporting entity or of a significant foreign operation, a statement of that fact and the reasons for the change.

Other disclosures required by FRS 23 are summarised in Chapter 7.

Accounting policy

50.22   The first two of the SSAP 20 disclosure requirements described in 50.21 above will usually be covered in an accounting policy note on the translation of the accounts of foreign entities. The wording of the policy will clearly depend on the circumstances of the company, but the wording along the following lines will usually be suitable.

Example 50.1 – Accounting policy on translation of foreign entities

The assets and liabilities of overseas subsidiary undertakings and associates are translated at the rate of exchange ruling at the balance sheet date, and their results are translated at an appropriate average rate of exchange for the accounting period. All exchange differences are dealt with through reserves.

Where a company chooses to adopt the alternative treatment in respect of foreign borrowings and equity investments, this will also need to be explained in the accounting policy note.

Example 50.2 – Accounting policy note on use of alternative treatment for foreign borrowings and equity investments

Where equity investments in overseas subsidiary undertakings are financed by foreign currency borrowings, gains and losses on translation of the borrowings are taken directly to reserves and are off-set against the corresponding gains and losses arising on translation of the underlying net assets. Any gains and losses on translation of the borrowings which are in excess of the related losses or gains on translation of the underlying net assets are included in the profit and loss account.

Reserves note

50.23   The remaining disclosure requirements in respect of the translation of foreign group entities will be dealt with in the reserves note. Gains and losses taken directly to reserves will also be included in the statement of total recognised gains and losses for the group.

DEALING WITH HYPERINFLATIONARY ECONOMIES

The effects of hyperinflation

50.24   The Explanatory Note to SSAP 20 includes the comment that:

> 'Where a foreign enterprise operates in a country in which a very high rate of inflation exists it may not be possible to present fairly in historical cost accounts the financial position of a foreign enterprise simply by the translation process. In such circumstances the local currency financial statements should be adjusted where possible to reflect current price levels before the translation process is undertaken.'

UITF Abstract 9 'Accounting for Operations in Hyper-inflationary Economies' was issued in June 1993 to provide additional guidance on this point. The Abstract is superseded by FRS 24 'Financial Reporting in Hyperinflationary Economies' for entities that are required to adopt FRS 26 (see 50.1 above) but continues to apply in all other cases.

The need for adjustment

50.25 If a group entity operates in a hyper-inflationary environment and adjustments are not made to its accounts before translation under SSAP 20, the impact of the hyper-inflation will result in:

(i) the results shown in the profit and loss account being overstated; and

(ii) a corresponding overstatement of the debit to reserves in respect of exchange differences.

The Abstract requires adjustments to be made wherever the effects of hyper-inflation will distort the true and fair view shown by the group accounts. In particular, adjustments should be made when a material group entity operates in an economy where the cumulative inflation rate over three years is approaching, or in excess of, 100%.

Method of adjustment

50.26 The Abstract offers two options for eliminating the distortions:

(i) adjust the local currency accounts of the foreign entity to reflect current price levels and then translate the adjusted figures for inclusion in the consolidation; or

(ii) use a relatively stable currency as the measurement currency for the foreign entity (described in Abstract 9 as 'the functional currency') – in this case, transactions are remeasured into the functional currency using the temporal method, and the accounts are then translated under the normal rules for inclusion in the consolidation.

In the rare situation where neither of these methods are considered appropriate, the reasons should be explained and an alternative method should be used to eliminate the distortions.

In any case where material group operations are carried out in hyper-inflationary economies, the accounting policy adopted for eliminating the distortions should be explained in the accounts.

Under FRS 23, the result of an entity whose functional currency is that of a hyperinflationary economy must be restated in accordance with FRS 24 before being translated for consolidation purposes. FRS 24 requires the financial statements of such an entity to be stated in terms of the measuring unit current at the balance sheet date. Corresponding figures for the previous period and any information in respect of earlier periods must also be stated in terms of the measuring unit current at the end of the reporting period. The gain or loss on the net monetary position should be included in the profit and loss account. Restatement under FRS 24 is considered in more detail at 7.39 above. Once restated, all amounts should be translated at the closing rate at the date of the most recent balance sheet date.

However, Comparative amounts should be those that were presented as current year amounts in the financial statements for the previous year, without adjustment for subsequent changes in price levels of exchange rates. The standard also requires certain additional disclosures to be given in the accounts. When an economy ceases to be hyperinflationary, so that restatement in accordance with FRS 24 is no longer necessary, the amounts restated to the price level at the date that restatement ceases should be treated as the historical costs for translation purposes.

Index